YEARBOOK OF LABOUR STATISTICS
Country profiles

ANNUAIRE DES STATISTIQUES DU TRAVAIL
Profils des pays

ANUARIO DE ESTADISTICAS DEL TRABAJO
Perfiles de los países

CREF

2008

YEARBOOK OF LABOUR STATISTICS
Country profiles

ANNUAIRE DES STATISTIQUES DU TRAVAIL
Profils des pays

ANUARIO DE ESTADISTICAS DEL TRABAJO
Perfiles de los países

INTERNATIONAL LABOUR OFFICE   GENEVA
BUREAU INTERNATIONAL DU TRAVAIL   GENÈVE
OFICINA INTERNACIONAL DEL TRABAJO   GINEBRA

Copyright © International Labour Organization 2008

Copyright © Organisation internationale du Travail 2008

Copyright © Organización Internacional del Trabajo 2008

ISBN 978-92-2-021217-2

ISSN 0084-3857

GSG
REF
HD
4826
.I63

ILO publications can be obtained through major booksellers or ILO local offices in many countries, or direct from ILO Publications, International Labour Office, CH-1211 Geneva 22, Switzerland. A catalogue or list of new publications will be sent free of charge from the above address.

Les publications du BIT peuvent être obtenues dans les principales librairies ou les bureaux locaux du BIT dans de nombreux pays, ou sur demande adressée directement à Publications du BIT, Bureau international du Travail, CH-1211 Genève 22, Suisse, lequel enverra également sur demande un catalogue ou une liste des nouvelles publications.

Las publicaciones de la OIT pueden obtenerse en las principales librerías o en oficinas locales de la OIT en muchos países o pidiéndolas a: Publicaciones de la OIT, Oficina Internacional del Trabajo, CH-1211 Ginebra 22, Suiza, que también puede enviar a quienes lo soliciten un catálogo o una lista de nuevas publicaciones.

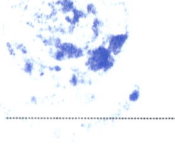

Printed by the International Labour Office, Geneva, Switzerland.

Imprimé par le Bureau international du Travail, Genève, Suisse.

Impreso por la Oficina Internacional del Trabajo, Ginebra, Suiza.

Contents

IX	Alphabetic index of countries, areas and territories
XV	Preface
XXI	Signs and symbols used in the tables

1   **Country profiles**

Selected countries, areas and territories are not shown in this publication if no statistics are available.

The country profiles appear in alphabetic order using the country name in the language used in official correspondence between the country in question and the ILO. Separate alphabetically ordered indexes in English, French and Spanish (using the country name in the language of the index) show the page location of each country profile. These indexes are located immediately after the Contents.

An index of country profiles in English is shown on page IX.

413   **Supplement**

Global and regional estimates of labour market indicators

415	Labour force participation rates
416	Employment rates
417	Sectoral shares in employment
418	Other selected labour market indicators
427	Global and regional estimates of consumer price inflation

431   **Appendix**

433   Explanatory notes

Classifications used in the *Yearbook*

467	International Standard Industrial Classification of All Economic Activities (ISIC – Rev 2, 1968)
473	International Standard Industrial Classification of All Economic Actiivities (ISIC – Rev 3)
478	International Classification by Status in Employment (ICSE – 1958 and 1993)
484	International Standard Classification of Occupations (ISCO – 1968)
490	International Standard Classification of Occupations (ISCO – 1988)
496	International Standard Classification of Education (ISCED – 76)
499	International Standard Classification of Education (ISCED – 97)
503	References
507	Master table

Table des matières

XI	**Index alphabétique des pays, zones et territoires**
XVII	**Préface**
XXI	**Signes et symboles utilisés dans les tableaux**

1	**Profils des pays**

Les pays, zones ou territoires pour lesquels aucune statistique n'est disponible ne figurent pas dans cette publication.
L'ordre de présentation des profils des pays suit l'ordre alphabétique en utilisant le nom du pays dans la langue utilisée dans la correspondance officielle entre ce pays et le BIT. Des index alphabétiques en français, anglais et espagnol sont également présentés, où le nom du pays figure dans la langue de chaque index, avec une indication du numéro de page de chaque profil. Ces index figurent immédiatement après la table des matières.

Un index des profils des pays en français figure page XI.

413	**Supplément**
	Estimations mondiales et régionales des indicateurs du marché du travail
419	Taux d'activité
420	Taux de chômage
421	Taux de répartition sectorielle de l'emploi
422	Sélection des autres indicateurs du marché du travail
428	Estimations mondiales et régionales de l'inflation des prix à la consommation

431	**Annexe**
443	Notes explicatives
	Classifications utilisées dans l'*Annuaire*
469	Classification internationale type, par industrie, de toutes les branches d'activité économique (CITI-Rév. 2, 1968)
474	Classification internationale type, par industrie, de toutes les branches d'activité économique (CITI-Rév. 3)
480	Classification internationale d'après la situation dans la profession (CISP-1993)
486	Classification internationale type des professions (CITP-1968)
492	Classification internationale type des professions (CITP-88)
497	Classification internationale type de l'éducation (CITE-76)
500	Classification internationale type de l'éducation (CITE-97)
503	Références
507	Tableau principal

Indice general

XIII	**Indice alfabético de países, áreas y territorios**
XIX	**Prefacio**
XXI	**Símbolos y signos utilizados en los cuadros**

1 **Perfiles de los países**

Los países, áreas y territorios para los cuales no se dispone de estadísticas no figuran en esta publicación.

El orden de presentación de los perfiles de los países sigue el orden alfabético utilizando la denominación del país en el idioma de trabajo utilizado en la correspondencia oficial entre el país y la OIT. También se presentan por separado índices alfabéticos en español, francés e inglés en los cuales la denominación del país figura en el idioma de cada índice, con una indicación del número de página de cada perfil. Estos índices figuran inmediatamente después del índice general.

Un índice de los perfiles de los países en español figura en la página XIII.

413 **Suplemento**

Estimaciones mundiales y regionales de los indicadores del mercado de trabajo

423	Tasa de participación de la fuerza de trabajo
424	Tasa de desempleo
425	Tasa de repartición sectorial en el empleo
426	Otros indicadores del mercado laboral
429	Estimaciones mundiales y regionales de la inflación en los precios al consumidor

431 **Apéndice**

455 Notas explicativas

Clasificaciones empleadas en el *Anuario*

471	Clasificación Industrial Internacional Uniforme de Todas las Actividades Económicas (CIIU-Rev. 2, 1968)
476	Clasificación Industrial Internacional Uniforme de Todas las Actividades Económicas (CIIU-Rev. 3)
482	Clasificación Internacional de la Situación en el Empleo (CISE-1993)
488	Clasificación Internacional Uniforme de Ocupaciones (CIUO-1968)
494	Clasificación Internacional Uniforme de Ocupaciones (CIUO-88)
498	Clasificación Internacional Normalizada de la Educación (CINE-76)
501	Clasificación Internacional Normalizada de la Educación (CINE-97)
503	Referencias
507	Cuadro maestro

Alphabetic index of countries, areas and territories

Afghanistan	1	Costa Rica	81	Isle of Man	173
Albania	2	Côte d'Ivoire	83	Israel	175
Algeria	4	Croatia	84	Italy	177
American Samoa	6	Cuba	86	Jamaica	180
Andorra	8	Cyprus	88	Japan	182
Angola	9	Czech Republic	90	Jersey	184
Anguilla	10	Denmark	92	Jordan	186
Antigua and Barbuda	12	Djibouti	94	Kazakhstan	187
Argentina	14	Dominica	95	Kenya	189
Armenia	17	Dominican Republic	303	Kiribati	190
Aruba	19	Ecuador	97	Korea, Dem. People's Rep. of	(a)
Australia	21	Egypt	99	Korea, Republic of	191
Austria	23	El Salvador	101	Kosovo (Serbia)	193
Azerbaijan	25	Equatorial Guinea	143	Kuwait	194
Bahamas	27	Eritrea	103	Kyrgyzstan	196
Bahrain	29	Estonia	107	Lao People's Dem. Rep.	306
Bangladesh	31	Ethiopia	109	Latvia	198
Barbados	33	Faeroe Islands	111	Lebanon	202
Belarus	35	Falkland Islands (Malvinas)	112	Lesotho	200
Belgium	37	Fiji	113	Liberia	203
Belize	39	Finland	115	Libyan Arab Jamahiriya	204
Benin	41	France	117	Liechtenstein	205
Bermuda	42	French Guiana	150	Lithuania	206
Bhutan	44	French Polynesia	295	Luxembourg	208
Bolivia	45	Gabon	119	Macau, China	211
Bosnia and Herzegovina	48	Gambia	121	Macedonia, The former Yugoslav Rep. of	213
Botswana	49	Georgia	123	Madagascar	215
Brazil	51	Germany	125	Malawi	217
Brunei Darussalam	53	Ghana	127	Malaysia	219
Bulgaria	55	Gibraltar	129	Maldives	221
Burkina Faso	57	Greece	131	Mali	223
Burundi	59	Greenland	133	Malta	225
Cambodia	61	Grenada	134	Marshall Islands	229
Cameroon	63	Guadeloupe	136	Martinique	231
Canada	65	Guam	138	Mauritania	233
Cape Verde	67	Guatemala	140	Mauritius	234
Cayman Islands	68	Guernsey	142	Mexico	237
Central African Republic	305	Guinea	145	Moldova, Republic of	239
Chad	367	Guinea-Bissau	147	Monaco	241
Channel Islands	(a)	Guyana	148	Mongolia	242
Chile	70	Haiti	152	Montenegro	244
China	72	Honduras	154	Montserrat	246
Colombia	74	Hong Kong, China	156	Morocco	227
Comoros	76	Hungary	159	Mozambique	247
Congo	77	Iceland	161	Myanmar	248
Congo, Democratic Republic of	78	India	163		
Cook Islands	79				

IX

Namibia	250	Saint Kitts and Nevis	317	Thailand	369
Nauru	(a)	Saint Lucia	318	Timor-Leste	(a)
Nepal	253	Saint Pierre and Miquelon	322	Togo	371
Netherlands	255	Saint Vincent and the Grenadines	320	Tokelau	(a)
Netherlands Antilles	258	Samoa	323	Tonga	372
New Caledonia	275	San Marino	324	Trinidad and Tobago	374
New Zealand	260	Sao Tome and Principe	326	Tunisia	376
Nicaragua	263	Saudi Arabia	327	Turkey	378
Niger	265	Senegal	329	Turkmenistan	381
Nigeria	267	Serbia	331	Turks and Caicos Islands	382
Niue	269	Seychelles	333	Tuvalu	383
Norfolk Island	270	Sierra Leone	335	Uganda	384
Northern Mariana Islands	271	Singapore	337	Ukraine	386
Norway	272	Slovakia	339	United Arab Emirates	388
Oman	277	Slovenia	341	United Kingdom	390
Pakistan	279	Solomon Islands	343	United States	392
Palau	281	Somalia	(a)	Uruguay	394
Panama	282	South Africa	344	Uzbekistan	396
Papua New Guinea	284	Spain	104	Vanuatu	397
Paraguay	286	Sri Lanka	346	Venezuela, Bolivarian Rep. of	398
Peru	288	Sudan	349	Viet Nam	400
Philippines	291	Suriname	352	Virgin Islands (British)	402
Poland	293	Swaziland	354	Virgin Islands (US)	403
Portugal	297	Sweden	356	Wallis and Futuna Islands	(a)
Puerto Rico	299	Switzerland	350	West Bank and Gaza Strip	404
Qatar	301	Syrian Arab Republic	358	Western Sahara	(a)
Réunion	307	Taiwan, China	360	Yemen, Republic of	406
Romania	309	Tajikistan	362	Zambia	408
Russian Federation	311	Tanzania (Tanganyika)	364	Zimbabwe	410
Rwanda	313	Tanzania (Zanzibar)	366		
Saint Helena	315	Tanzania, United Republic of	(a)	(a) Statistics not available.	

Index alphabétique des pays, zones et territoires

Afghanistan	1	Corée, République de	191	Iles Féroé	111
Afrique du Sud	344	Costa Rica	81	Iles Mariannes du Nord	271
Albanie	2	Côte d'Ivoire	83	Iles Marshall	229
Algérie	4	Croatie	84	Iles Salomon	343
Allemagne	125	Cuba	86	Iles Turques et Caïques	382
Andorre	8	Danemark	92	Iles Vierges (américaines)	403
Angola	9	Djibouti	94	Iles Vierges (britanniques)	402
Anguilla	10	Dominique	95	Iles Wallis et Futuna	(a)
Antigua-et-Barbuda	12	Egypte	99	Inde	163
Antilles néerlandaises	258	El Salvador	101	Indonésie	165
Arabie saoudite	327	Emirats arabes unis	388	Iran, Rép. islamique d'	167
Argentine	14	Equateur	97	Iraq	169
Arménie	17	Erythrée	103	Irlande	171
Aruba	19	Espagne	104	Islande	161
Australie	21	Estonie	107	Israël	175
Autriche	23	Etats-Unis	392	Italie	177
Azerbaïdjan	25	Ethiopie	109	Jamahiriya arabe libyenne	204
Bahamas	27	Fidji	113	Jamaïque	180
Bahreïn	29	Finlande	115	Japon	182
Bangladesh	31	France	117	Jersey	184
Barbade	33	Gabon	119	Jordanie	186
Bélarus	35	Gambie	121	Kazakhstan	187
Belgique	37	Géorgie	123	Kenya	189
Belize	39	Ghana	127	Kirghizistan	196
Bénin	41	Gibraltar	129	Kiribati	190
Bermudes	42	Grèce	131	Kosovo (Serbie)	193
Bhoutan	44	Grenade	134	Koweït	194
Bolivie	45	Groenland	133	Lesotho	200
Bosnie-Herzégovine	48	Guadeloupe	136	Lettonie	198
Botswana	49	Guam	138	Liban	202
Brésil	51	Guatemala	140	Libéria	203
Brunéi Darussalam	53	Guernesey	142	Liechtenstein	205
Bulgarie	55	Guinée	145	Lituanie	206
Burkina Faso	57	Guinée équatoriale	143	Luxembourg	208
Burundi	59	Guinée-Bissau	147	Macao, Chine	211
Cambodge	61	Guyana	148	Macédoine, Ex-Rép. yougoslave de	213
Cameroun	63	Guyane française	150	Madagascar	215
Canada	65	Haïti	152	Malaisie	219
Cap-Vert	67	Honduras	154	Malawi	217
Chili	70	Hong-kong, Chine	156	Maldives	221
Chine	72	Hongrie	159	Mali	223
Chypre	88	Ile de Man	173	Malte	225
Colombie	74	Ile Norfolk	270	Maroc	227
Comores	76	Iles Anglo-Normandes	(a)	Martinique	231
Congo	77	Iles Caïmanes	68		
Congo, Rép. dém. du	78	Iles Cook	79		
Corée, Rép. pop. dém. de	(a)	Iles Falkland (Malvinas)	112		

XI

Maurice	234	Porto Rico	299	Soudan	349
Mauritanie	233	Portugal	297	Sri Lanka	346
Mexique	237	Qatar	301	Suède	356
Moldavie, République de	239	République arabe syrienne	358	Suisse	350
Monaco	241	République centrafricaine	305	Suriname	352
Mongolie	242	République dém. pop. lao	306	Swaziland	354
Monténégro	244	République dominicaine	303	Tadjikistan	362
Montserrat	246	République tchèque	90	Taïwan, Chine	360
Mozambique	247	Réunion	307	Tanzanie (Tanganyika)	364
Myanmar	248	Rive occidentale et Bande de Gaza	404	Tanzanie (Zanzibar)	366
Namibie	250			Tanzanie, République-Unie de	(a)
Nauru	(a)	Roumanie	309	Tchad	367
Népal	253	Royaume-Uni	390	Thaïlande	369
Nicaragua	263	Russie, Fédération de	311	Timor-Leste	(a)
Niger	265	Rwanda	313	Togo	371
Nigéria	267	Sahara occidental	(a)	Tokélaou	(a)
Nioué	269	Sainte-Hélène	315	Tonga	372
Norvège	272	Sainte-Lucie	318	Trinité-et-Tobago	374
Nouvelle-Calédonie	275	Saint-Kitts-et-Nevis	317	Tunisie	376
Nouvelle-Zélande	260	Saint-Marin	324	Turkménistan	381
Oman	277	Saint-Pierre-et-Miquelon	322	Turquie	378
Ouganda	384	Saint-Vincent-et-Grenadines	320	Tuvalu	383
Ouzbékistan	396	Samoa	323	Ukraine	386
Pakistan	279	Samoa américaines	6	Uruguay	394
Palaos	281	Sao Tomé-et-Principe	326	Vanuatu	397
Panama	282	Sénégal	329	Venezuela, Rép. bolivarienne du	398
Papouasie-Nouvelle-Guinée	284	Serbie	331	Viet Nam	400
Paraguay	286	Seychelles	333	Yémen, République du	406
Pays-Bas	255	Sierra Leone	335	Zambie	408
Pérou	288	Singapour	337	Zimbabwe	410
Philippines	291	Slovaquie	339		
Pologne	293	Slovénie	341		
Polynésie française	295	Somalie	(a)		

(a) Données non disponibles.

Indice alfabético de países, áreas y territorios

Afganistán	1	Corea, República de	191	Iraq	169
Albania	2	Costa Rica	81	Irlanda	171
Alemania	125	Côte d'Ivoire	83	Isla de Man	173
Andorra	8	Croacia	84	Isla Norfolk	270
Angola	9	Cuba	86	Islandia	161
Anguila	10	Dinamarca	92	Islas Caimán	68
Antigua y Barbuda	12	Djibouti	94	Islas Cook	79
Antillas Neerlandesas	258	Dominica	95	Islas del Canal	(a)
Arabia Saudita	327	Ecuador	97	Islas Feroé	111
Argelia	4	Egipto	99	Islas Malvinas (Falkland)	112
Argentina	14	El Salvador	101	Islas Marianas del Norte	271
Armenia	17	Emiratos Arabes Unidos	388	Islas Marshall	229
Aruba	19	Eritrea	103	Islas Salomón	343
Australia	21	Eslovaquia	339	Islas Turcos y Caicos	382
Austria	23	Eslovenia	341	Islas Vírgenes (Británicas)	402
Azerbaiyán	25	España	104	Islas Vírgenes (EE.UU.)	403
Bahamas	27	Estados Unidos	392	Islas Wallis y Futuna	(a)
Bahrein	29	Estonia	107	Israel	175
Bangladesh	31	Etiopía	109	Italia	177
Barbados	33	Fiji	113	Jamahiriya Arabe Libia	204
Belarús	35	Filipinas	291	Jamaica	180
Bélgica	37	Finlandia	115	Japón	182
Belice	39	Francia	117	Jersey	184
Benin	41	Gabón	119	Jordania	186
Bermudas	42	Gambia	121	Kazajstán	187
Bhután	44	Georgia	123	Kenya	189
Bolivia	45	Ghana	127	Kirguistán	196
Bosnia y Herzegovina	48	Gibraltar	129	Kiribati	190
Botswana	49	Granada	134	Kosovo (Serbia)	193
Brasil	51	Grecia	131	Kuwait	194
Brunei Darussalam	53	Groenlandia	133	Lesotho	200
Bulgaria	55	Guadalupe	136	Letonia	198
Burkina Faso	57	Guam	138	Líbano	202
Burundi	59	Guatemala	140	Liberia	203
Cabo Verde	67	Guayana Francesa	150	Liechtenstein	205
Camboya	61	Guernesey	142	Lituania	206
Camerún	63	Guinea	145	Luxemburgo	208
Canadá	65	Guinea Ecuatorial	143	Macao, China	211
Chad	367	Guinea-Bissau	147	Macedonia, Ex Rep. Yugoslava de	213
Chile	70	Guyana	148	Madagascar	215
China	72	Haití	152	Malasia	219
Chipre	88	Honduras	154	Malawi	217
Colombia	74	Hong Kong, China	156	Maldivas	221
Comoras	76	Hungría	159	Malí	223
Congo	77	India	163	Malta	225
Congo, Rep. Dem. del	78	Indonesia	165	Marruecos	227
Corea, Rep. Pop. Dem. de	(a)	Irán, Rep. Islámica del	167		

XIII

Martinica	231	Puerto Rico	299	Suecia	356
Mauricio	234	Qatar	301	Suiza	350
Mauritania	233	Reino Unido	390	Suriname	352
México	237	República Arabe Siria	358	Swazilandia	354
Moldova, República de	239	República Centroafricana	305	Tailandia	369
Mónaco	241	República Checa	90	Taiwan, China	360
Mongolia	242	República Dem. Pop. Lao	306	Tajikistán	362
Montenegro	244	República Dominicana	303	Tanzanía (Tangañika)	364
Montserrat	246	Reunión	307	Tanzanía (Zanzibar)	366
Mozambique	247	Ribera occidental y Faja de Gaza	404	Tanzanía, República Unida de	(a)
Myanmar	248	Rumania	309	Timor-Leste	(a)
Namibia	250	Rusia, Federación de	311	Togo	371
Nauru	(a)	Rwanda	313	Tokelau	(a)
Nepal	253	Sahara occidental	(a)	Tonga	372
Nicaragua	263	Saint Kitts y Nevis	317	Trinidad y Tabago	374
Níger	265	Samoa	323	Túnez	376
Nigeria	267	Samoa Americana	6	Turkmenistán	381
Niue	269	San Marino	324	Turquía	378
Noruega	272	San Pedro y Miquelón	322	Tuvalu	383
Nueva Caledonia	275	San Vicente y las Granadinas	320	Ucrania	386
Nueva Zelandia	260	Santa Elena	315	Uganda	384
Omán	277	Santa Lucía	318	Uruguay	394
Países Bajos	255	Santo Tomé y Príncipe	326	Uzbekistán	396
Pakistán	279	Senegal	329	Vanuatu	397
Palau	281	Serbia	331	Venezuela, Rep. Bolivariana de	398
Panamá	282	Seychelles	333	Viet Nam	400
Papua Nueva Guinea	284	Sierra Leona	335	Yemen, República del	406
Paraguay	286	Singapur	337	Zambia	408
Perú	288	Somalia	(a)	Zimbabwe	410
Polinesia Francesa	295	Sri Lanka	346		
Polonia	293	Sudáfrica	344		
Portugal	297	Sudán	349	(a) No se dispone de estadísticas.	

Preface

The *Yearbook of Labour Statistics: Country Profiles* is a publication of the International Labour Office, prepared by the Bureau of Statistics. It shows the latest available disaggregated statistics for each country, presenting the principal labour statistics for over 200 countries, areas or territories.

The publication also includes a supplement showing global and regional estimates of economically active population, employment, unemployment and consumer prices. These estimates have been produced by the ILO's Employment Trends Unit or, in the case of consumer price indices, by the Federal Reserve Bank of Cleveland in collaboration with the ILO.

The statistics are shown in the country profile for the year with the most recent set of disaggregated data. To the extent possible, in order to present a complete and comparable picture of the labour market, preference is given to statistics from the same source and year for all components for each classification, provided the year is not more than three years prior to that for the most recent disaggregated data for any component. It is therefore possible that the data presented in this publication for a particular component may be older than that available in the Yearbook of Labour Statistics: Time Series and in the ILO's on-line statistical database LABORSTA for that component. Countries may provide the ILO with statistics from more than one source. In this publication, statistics are shown only from the most comprehensive source or the source considered to provide the best quality statistics (for example, from labour force surveys for statistics on economically active population, employment and unemployment, and from establishment surveys for statistics on paid employment, wages and hours of work).

For more recent totals, more detailed statistics, statistics on additional variables or from alternative sources, and full descriptions of sources, please see the Yearbook CD-ROM or visit the ILO's on-line statistical database LABORSTA at http://laborsta.ilo.org/.

Not all countries are in a position to provide the ILO with the statistics for every table in the country profile section. For some, figures may not be available until several years after the reference year, or not available at all. The data published in this publication are those available in the ILO at the end of September 2008.

The figures in the country profiles have been drawn mainly from information sent to the ILO by national statistical services, or taken from official publications. In some cases (including all statistics on employment classified by age), statistics have been derived by the ILO by subtracting or adding the statistics provided by countries for other components. The activity rates and the unemployment rates by age group, shown in table 2, have also been calculated by the ILO from the relevant statistics by age group provided by the countries. The statistics have not been adjusted by the ILO to conform with the international recommendations on labour statistics. Nevertheless, reporting agencies were requested to supply information conforming as closely as possible to the international standards.

Statistics are generally presented for totals and women only. Statistics for men may be derived from these statistics. In some tables, separate data by sex are also shown.

Arrangement of material

For each country, area or territory, the statistics are grouped into five main tables comprising statistics on (i) the economically active population, employment, unemployment classified by age group, branch of economic activity (industry), occupation, education level and status in employment; (ii) population, activity rate and unemployment rate by broad age groups; (iii) paid employment, hours of work and wages by branch of economic activity (industry); (iv) occupational injuries, strikes and lockouts by branch of economic activity (industry); and (v) consumer price indices.

The coverage of the series in terms of groups of workers or types of data is shown on the first line of the table, where relevant. Additional information concerning the coverage may be shown as endnotes for each country. More general explanatory notes briefly indicating the main characteristics of the different types of data published are shown in an Appendix.

Base period of indices

For the series of consumer price indices, a uniform base (2000=100) has been adopted in the *Yearbook* in accordance with the practice followed by the statistical services of the United Nations and the specialized agencies. If data are available only for periods after 2000, the indices are shown usually with the first calendar year for which the figures are available as the base period. When a series has been interrupted and replaced by a new series, the latter is linked to the former if the two series are sufficiently comparable; otherwise it is published on a new base. The break in continuity is indicated by an explanatory footnote where appropriate.

Classifications used in the *Yearbook*

Data are published wherever possible according to the latest versions of the international standard classifications that are in use: the *International Standard Industrial Classification of all Economic Activities (ISIC) Revision 3*; the *International Standard Classification of Occupations (ISCO-88)*; the *International Classification of Status in Employment (ISCE-93)* and the *International Standard Classification of Education (ISCED-97)*, respectively. If statistics are not available according to the latest classifications, the former classifications continue to be used. The classifications are given in the Appendix. It should be noted that the latest version of ISIC, Revision 4, is not yet in use in countries.

If the data being presented for different topics relate to different versions of a classification, then the table block is generally repeated with different group titles. However, age classifications are generally amended to show alternative groupings without repeating the table block.

The latest versions of international classifications differ in general structure from previous versions, so that direct comparisons are not always possible. For this reason, the ILO Bureau of Statistics has not attempted to convert data from one version to another.

Language of presentation

The text used within each country profile is in one language only – in English, French or Spanish when the national language of the country, or the language commonly used in it, is one of the three languages; in other cases, the language is that working language used in official correspondence between the country in question and the ILO.

A master set of tables appears at the end of the publication showing table titles, column headings, other terms used in tables and names of statistical sources in trilingual form. Textual group titles relating to consumer price indices also appear in these master tables. Group titles from international classifications are not shown in the master tables but may be seen in the Appendix of Classifications.

End notes are shown trilingually for each country.

Order of country presentation

The Country Profiles appear in alphabetic order using the country name in English, French or Spanish as described above. Separate alphabetically ordered indexes in English, French and Spanish (using the country name in the language of the index) show the page location of each country profile. These indexes are located immediately after the Contents.

Acknowledgement

The International Labour Office wishes to express its gratitude to the national statistical services for their valuable collaboration in providing the statistics shown in this *Yearbook*.

Other regular statistical publications

Yearbook of Labour Statistics: Time Series (published annually): This publication presents the principal labour statistics for over 190 countries, areas and territories and for the last ten years. It contains 31 tables corresponding to nine major substantive chapters on the following: Economically active population; Employment; Unemployment; Hours of work; Wages; Labour cost; Consumer prices; Occupational injuries; and Strikes and lockouts.

Bulletin of Labour Statistics (published 6-monthly): Monthly, quarterly, half-yearly and annual data on employment, unemployment, hours of work, wages and consumer price indices for the last four years are published in the *Bulletin of Labour Statistics*. The *Bulletin* also features articles of professional interest to labour statisticians.

Occupational Wages and Hours of Work and Retail Food Prices, Statistics from the ILO October Inquiry (published annually): This publication presents data on occupational wages and hours of work and retail food prices collected by the ILO each year through its October Inquiry.

CD-ROMs containing longer time series are available annually for the *Yearbook of Labour Statistics and for the Occupational Wages and Hours of Work and Retail Food Prices, Statistics from the ILO October Inquiry*.

Methodology

Information on the scope of the statistics, their definitions and the methods used by the national statistical services in establishing the data published in this *Yearbook*, in the *Yearbook of Labour Statistics: Time Series* and in the *Bulletin of Labour Statistics* is given in the series *Sources and Methods: Labour Statistics* (formerly *Statistical Sources and Methods*).

Ten volumes have been issued: *1 - Consumer price indices; 2 - Employment, wages, hours of work and labour cost (establishment surveys); 3 - Economically active population, employment, unemployment and hours of work (household surveys); 4 - Employment, unemployment, wages and hours of work (administrative records and related sources); 5 - Total and economically active population, employment and unemployment (population censuses); 6 - Household income and expenditure surveys; 7 - Strikes and lockouts; 8 - Occupational injuries; 9 - Transition countries; and 10 - Estimates and projections of the economically active population 1950-2010.* These publications, which complement the brief explanations given in the tables, should enable a better understanding of the data and facilitate their international comparison.

A list of ILO documents dealing with the methodology recommended for the compilation of labour statistics is given in the Appendix (see "References").

For viewing and downloading a more complete set of statistics:
http://laborsta.ilo.org

Please visit the Bureau of Statistics' web site:
http://www.ilo.org/stat/

For further information, please contact:
Bureau of Statistics
International Labour Office
CH-1211 Geneva 22
Switzerland

Fax: + 41 22 799 6957
Tel.:   + 41 22 799 8631
E-mail: STAT@ilo.org

Préface

L'*Annuaire des statistiques du travail: Profils des pays* est une publication du Bureau international du Travail, préparée par le Bureau de statistique. Il propose les statistiques détaillées les plus récentes sous forme de profil pour chaque pays et présente les principales statistiques du travail pour quelque 200 pays, zones ou territoires.

La publication inclut aussi un supplément dans lequel figurent des estimations globales et régionales de la population active, de l'emploi, du chômage et des indices des prix à la consommation. Ces estimations ont été produites par l'Unité des tendances de l'emploi du BIT ou, dans le cas des indices des prix à la consommation, par la Banque fédérale de Réserve de Cleveland en coopération avec le BIT.

Les statistiques sont présentées dans le profil du pays pour l'année présentant l'ensemble le plus récent de données désagrégées. Dans la mesure du possible, afin de présenter une image exhaustive et comparable du marché du travail, la préférence a été donnée aux statistiques dérivées de la même source et disponibles pour la même année pour toutes les composantes de chaque classification, à condition que l'année ne soit pas antérieure de plus de trois ans à celle qui fournit les données désagrégées les plus récentes pour l'une ou l'autre des composantes. Il est donc possible que les données présentées dans cette publication pour une composante quelconque soient antérieures à celles présentées dans l'*Annuaire des statistiques du travail: Séries chronologiques* et à celles qui sont disponibles dans la base de données en ligne LABORSTA pour cette même composante. Il est également possible que des pays fournissent au BIT des statistiques dérivées de plusieurs sources. Dans cette publication, seules sont présentées les statistiques dérivées de la source la plus complète, ou de la source qui est considérée comme fournissant des données de la meilleure qualité (par exemple, les enquêtes auprès de la main-d'œuvre pour les statistiques de la population active, de l'emploi et du chômage, et les enquêtes auprès des établissements pour les données sur l'emploi rémunéré, les salaires et la durée du travail).

Pour obtenir des informations sur les totaux les plus récents, des statistiques plus détaillées, des données sur des variables supplémentaires ou dérivées d'autres sources, ainsi que les descriptions détaillées des sources, consulter le CD-ROM de l'*Annuaire* ou la base de données en ligne LABORSTA sur le site: http://laborsta.ilo.org.

Tous les pays ne sont pas en mesure de fournir au BIT des statistiques qui couvrent la totalité des tableaux de la section «Profils». Pour quelques-uns, les données ne seront peut-être disponibles que plusieurs années après l'année de référence ou pas disponibles du tout. Les données publiées dans cette édition de l'*Annuaire* sont celles disponibles au BIT fin septembre 2008.

Les données présentées dans les profils proviennent principalement d'informations communiquées au Bureau par les services statistiques nationaux ou de publications officielles. Dans certains cas (y compris toutes les statistiques sur l'emploi par groupe d'âge), les données ont été obtenues par le BIT par soustraction ou en additionnant celles fournies par les pays pour d'autres composantes. Les taux d'activité et les taux de chômage par groupe d'âge du tableau 2 ont aussi été calculés par le BIT d'après les groupes d'âge appropriés fournis par les pays. Ces données n'ont pas été ajustées par le Bureau pour leur assurer une parfaite conformité avec les recommandations internationales en matière de statistiques du travail. Il faut noter cependant que les services statistiques nationaux ont été invités à fournir des renseignements aussi conformes que possible aux normes internationales existantes.

Les statistiques sont généralement présentées pour les totaux et les femmes. Les données concernant les hommes peuvent en être déduites. Dans quelques tableaux figurent des données séparées par sexe.

Disposition des sujets traités

Pour chaque pays, zone ou territoire, les statistiques sont groupées en cinq tableaux principaux incluant des données sur (i) la population active, l'emploi, le chômage, classés par groupe d'âge, branche d'activité économique (industrie), profession, niveau d'instruction, et situation dans la profession; (ii) population, taux d'activité et taux de chômage par grands groupes d'âge; (iii) emploi rémunéré, durée du travail et salaires par branche d'activité économique (industrie); (iv) lésions professionnelles, grèves et lock-out par branche d'activité économique; et (v) indices des prix à la consommation.

Dans la mesure du possible, la portée des statistiques en termes de groupes de travailleurs et de types de données apparaît sur la première ligne du tableau. Des informations supplémentaires concernant la portée peuvent être signalées en notes de fin de document pour chaque pays. Des notes explicatives plus générales indiquant brièvement les caractéristiques principales des divers types de données publiées sont disponibles dans l'Annexe.

Période de base des indices

Pour les séries des indices des prix à la consommation, une base uniforme (100 en 2000) a été adoptée dans l'*Annuaire*, conformément à la pratique suivie par les services statistiques des Nations Unies et des institutions spécialisées. Lorsque des données ne sont disponibles que pour des périodes postérieures à 2000, les indices sont généralement présentés avec, pour période de base, la première année civile pour laquelle des chiffres sont disponibles. Lorsqu'une série est interrompue et remplacée par une nouvelle série, cette dernière est enchaînée à la précédente dans la mesure où ces deux séries sont suffisamment comparables, ou publiée sur une nouvelle base dans le cas contraire; cette discontinuité dans l'homogénéité des séries est indiquée par un trait vertical séparant les deux séries et par une note explicative de bas de page.

Classifications utilisées dans l'*Annuaire*

Dans la mesure du possible, les données sont publiées selon les versions les plus récentes des classifications internationales types qui sont utilisées: la *Classification internationale type, par industrie, de toutes les branches d'activité économique (CITI), révision 3*; la *Classification internationale type des professions (CITP-88)*; la *Classification interna-*

tionale d'après la situation dans la profession (CISP-93) et la *Classification internationale type de l'éducation (CITE-97)*. Si les statistiques ne sont pas disponibles selon les dernières classifications, on continue d'utiliser les anciennes classifications. Les diverses classifications sont présentées dans l'Annexe. Il faudrait noter que la dernière version de la CITI, révision 4, n'est pas encore utilisée par les pays.

Si les données présentées pour divers sujets sont classées selon des versions différentes d'une même classification, le tableau est généralement répété avec des codes de ligne différents. Cependant les classifications par groupe d'âge sont en principe modifiées de façon à présenter des regroupements alternatifs, sans répéter le tableau.

La structure générale des classifications révisées diffère de celle des versions précédentes, de sorte que les comparaisons directes ne sont pas toujours possibles. C'est pourquoi le Bureau de statistique du BIT a renoncé à convertir les données d'une version à l'autre.

Langue de présentation

Une seule langue est utilisée pour chaque profil: l'anglais, le français ou l'espagnol, quand la langue nationale de ce pays, ou celle qui y est communément utilisée, est l'une de ces trois langues. Dans les autres cas, la langue est la langue de travail utilisée dans la correspondance officielle entre ce pays et le BIT.

Un jeu principal de tableaux figure à la fin de la publication, qui présente les titres des tableaux, les en-têtes de colonnes, les autres termes utilisés dans les tableaux et les noms des sources nationales dans les trois langues. Les titres des groupes des indices des prix à la consommation figurent également dans ces tableaux. Par contre, les titres des groupes des classifications internationales ne figurent pas dans ce tableau principal, mais sont fournis dans l'Annexe des Classifications.

Pour chaque pays, les notes de fin de document sont également disponibles dans les trois langues.

Ordre de présentation des pays

L'ordre de présentation des profils des pays suit l'ordre alphabétique en utilisant le nom du pays dans la langue utilisée comme indiqué ci-dessus. Des index alphabétiques en français, anglais et espagnol sont également présentés, où le nom du pays figure dans la langue de chaque index, avec une indication du numéro de page de chaque profil. Ces index figurent immédiatement après la table des matières.

Remerciements

Le Bureau international du Travail tient à exprimer sa gratitude aux services statistiques nationaux pour leur précieuse collaboration dans la transmission des données présentées dans cet *Annuaire*.

Autres publications statistiques régulières

Annuaire des statistiques du travail: Séries chronologiques (publication annuelle): Cette publication présente les principales statistiques du travail pour quelques 190 pays, zones ou territoires pour les 10 dernières années. Il contient 31 tableaux correspondant aux neuf grands chapitres suivants: Population active; Emploi; Chômage; Durée du travail; Salaires; Coût de la main-d'œuvre; Prix à la consommation; Lésions professionnelles; Grèves et lock-out.

Bulletin des statistiques du travail (publié semestriellement): cette publication présente les données mensuelles, trimestrielles, semestrielles et annuelles sur l'emploi, le chômage, les heures de travail, les salaires et les indices des prix à la consommation pour les quatre dernières années. Le *Bulletin* propose également des articles professionnels dédiés aux statisticiens du travail.

Salaires et durée du travail par profession et prix de détail de produits alimentaires, Statistiques de l'enquête d'octobre du BIT (publiée annuellement): cette publication présente les données sur les salaires et la durée du travail par profession et sur des prix au détail des produits alimentaires collectés par le BIT chaque année au travers de l'Enquête d'octobre.

Des CD-ROM, qui contiennent les séries chronologiques plus complètes, sont disponibles chaque année pour l'*Annuaire des statistiques du travail* et pour les *Salaires et durée du travail par profession et prix de détail de produits alimentaires, statistiques de l'enquête d'octobre du BIT*.

Méthodologie

Des renseignements sur la portée des statistiques, leur définition et les méthodes utilisées par les services statistiques nationaux lors de l'établissement des données publiées dans cet annuaire, l'*Annuaire des statistiques du travail: Séries chronologiques*, et dans le *Bulletin des statistiques du travail* sont présentés dans une série de publications intitulée *Sources et méthodes: statistiques du travail* (précédemment *Sources et méthodes statistiques*).

Dix volumes sont disponibles, à savoir: 1. *Indices des prix à la consommation*; 2. *Emploi, salaires, durée du travail et coût de la main-d'œuvre (enquêtes auprès des établissements)*; 3. *Population active, emploi, chômage et durée du travail (enquêtes auprès des ménages)*; 4. *Emploi, chômage, salaires et durée du travail (documents administratifs et sources assimilées)*; 5. *Population totale et population active, emploi et chômage (recensements de population)*; 6. *Enquêtes sur le revenu et les dépenses des ménages*; 7. *Grèves et lock-out*; 8. *Lésions professionnelles*; 9. *Pays en transition* et 10. *Evaluations et projections de la population active 1950-2010*. Ces publications complètent les renseignements succincts qui figurent dans les notes explicatives aux tableaux et devraient permettre une bonne compréhension des statistiques et une meilleure comparaison sur le plan international.

Une liste des documents du BIT traitant des méthodes statistiques recommandées pour l'établissement des statistiques du travail est fournie dans l'annexe du présent *Annuaire* (voir «Références»).

Pour visualiser et télécharger les données:
http://laborsta.ilo.org

Pour visualiser le site Web du Bureau de statistique:
http://www.ilo.org/stat/

Pour tout renseignement complémentaire, s'adresser à:
Bureau de statistique
Bureau international du Travail
CH-1211 Genève 22
Suisse

Fax: + 41 22 799 6957
Tél.: + 41 22 799 8631
Courriel: STAT@ilo.org

Prefacio

El *Anuario de Estadísticas del Trabajo: Perfiles de los países* es una publicación de la Oficina Internacional del Trabajo, preparada por la Oficina de Estadística. En esta edición figuran las estadísticas detalladas más recientes en forma de perfil para cada país y se presentan las principales estadísticas del trabajo para unos 200 países, áreas y territorios.

La publicación incluye también un suplemento en el que figuran estimaciones globales de la población activa, el empleo, el desempleo y los índices de los precios al consumidor. Estas estimaciones fueron producidas por la Unidad de Tendencias del Empleo de la OIT y, en el caso de los índices de precios al consumidor, por el Banco de la Reserva Federal de Cleveland en colaboración con la OIT

Las estadísticas que figuran en el perfil del país abarcan el año que presenta el conjunto más reciente de datos desagregados. En la medida de lo posible, con el fin de presentar una imagen exhaustiva y comparable del mercado de trabajo, se dio preferencia a las estadísticas derivadas de una misma fuente y disponibles para el mismo año para todos los componentes de cada clasificación, a condición de que este año no fuera más de tres años anterior para el cual se dispone de datos desagregados más recientes para cualquier componente. Así pues, es posible que los datos de cualquier componente presentados en esta publicación sean anteriores a los datos que figuran en el *Anuario de estadísticas del trabajo: Series cronológicas* y a los que figuran en la base de datos en línea LABORSTA. También sucede que los países suministran a la OIT estadísticas derivadas de fuentes diferentes. En esta publicación sólo figuran las estadísticas derivadas de la fuente más completa, o de la fuente que se considera proporciona datos de mejor calidad (como, por ejemplo, las encuestas de la fuerza de trabajo para las estadísticas de la población activa, el empleo y el desempleo, y las encuestas de establecimientos para las estadísticas sobre el empleo remunerado, las horas de trabajo y los salarios).

Para obtener información sobre los totales más recientes, estadísticas más detalladas, datos sobre variables suplementarias, o derivadas de otras fuentes, así como las descripciones metodológicas de las fuentes, se recomienda consultar el CD-ROM del *Anuario* o la base de datos en línea LABORSTA en el sitio: http://laborsta.ilo.org.

No todos los países proporcionan estadísticas que abarcan todos los cuadros de la sección «Perfiles». Para algunos, las cifras están disponibles varios años después del año al que se refieren o no están disponibles en absoluto. Los datos que se publican en esta edición del *Anuario* son aquellos que estaban disponibles en la OIT a finales de septiembre de 2008.

Las cifras que figuran en los perfiles provienen, en su mayor parte, de las informaciones que los servicios estadísticos nacionales envían a la Oficina, o de publicaciones oficiales de cada país. En algunos casos (incluidas todas las estadísticas sobre el empleo por grupo de edad) las estadísticas fueron calculadas por la OIT restando o sumando las estadísticas proporcionadas por los países para otros componentes. Las tasas de actividad y las tasas de desempleo por grupo de edad presentadas en el cuadro 2 han sido también calculadas por la OIT según los grupos de edad apropiados proporcionados por los países. La OIT no efectúa ningún ajuste de acuerdo con las recomendaciones internacionales en materia de estadísticas del trabajo. Sin embargo, siempre se pide a los servicios estadísticos que suministren datos conformes, en lo posible, con las normas internacionales existentes.

En general, se presentan estadísticas de los totales y para las mujeres. De éstos se pueden deducir los datos para los hombres. En algunos cuadros figuran datos separados por sexo.

Disposición de los temas tratados

Para cada país, zona o territorio los temas se hallan agrupados en cinco cuadros principales, que abarcan i) la población activa, el empleo y el desempleo, clasificados por grupo de edad, rama de actividad económica, ocupación, nivel de educación, y situación en el empleo; ii) población, tasa de actividad y tasa de desempleo por grandes grupos de edad; iii) empleo remunerado, horas de trabajo y salarios por actividad económica; iv) lesiones profesionales, huelgas y cierres patronales por actividad económica; y v) índices de los precios al consumidor.

El alcance de las series, en cuanto a los grupos de trabajadores abarcados y a los tipos de datos, figura en la primera línea del cuadro. Otras informaciones pertinentes sobre el alcance pueden indicarse en notas de pie de documento para cada país. Notas explicativas más generales indicando brevemente las características principales de los diversos tipos de datos publicados se encuentran en el Apéndice.

Período base de los índices

Para las series sobre los índices de precios al consumidor el *Anuario* ha adoptado una base uniforme (2000 = 100), de conformidad con la práctica seguida por los servicios estadísticos de las Naciones Unidas y las instituciones especializadas. Cuando sólo se dispone de datos para períodos posteriores a 2000, los índices se presentan generalmente tomando como período base el primer año civil para el cual se dispone de cifras. Si una serie queda interrumpida y se sustituye por otra nueva, esta última serie se enlaza con la anterior cuando existe suficiente comparabilidad entre las series; en caso contrario, se publica sobre una nueva base. Esta discontinuidad en las series se indica con una raya vertical entre las dos series y una nota explicativa al pie de la página.

Clasificaciones utilizadas en el *Anuario*

Los datos se ajustan en lo posible a las últimas versiones de las clasificaciones internacionales que son utilizadas: la *Clasificación Internacional Industrial Uniforme de Todas las Actividades Económicas (CIIU), Revisión 3*; la *Clasificación Internacional Uniforme de Ocupaciones (CIUO-88)*; la *Clasificación Internacional de la Situación en el Empleo*

(CISE-93) y la *Clasificación Internacional Normalizada de la Educación (CINE-97)*. Si no se dispone de datos de acuerdo con las últimas clasificaciones, se utilizan las versiones anteriores. Las diversas clasificaciones figuran en el Apéndice. Se debería notar que la última versión de la CIIU, Revisión 4, no es todavía utilizada por los países.

Si los datos presentados para los diversos temas se clasifican según diferentes versiones de una misma clasificación, se repite el cuadro con diferentes códigos de línea. Sin embargo, en principio, las clasificaciones por grupo de edad se ajustan con el fin de presentar agrupaciones alternativas sin repetir el cuadro.

Como la estructura general de las clasificaciones revisadas difiere de las versiones anteriores, no siempre es posible compararlas directamente. Por tal motivo la Oficina de Estadística de la OIT no ha tratado de convertir los datos de una versión en otra.

Idioma de presentación

Se utiliza sólo un idioma para cada perfil: español, francés o inglés, cuando el idioma nacional o de uso general es una de estas tres lenguas. En otros casos, la lengua corresponde al idioma de trabajo utilizado en la correspondencia oficial entre el país y la OIT.

Un cuadro maestro figura al fin de la publicación, que presenta los títulos de los cuadros, los membretes de las columnas, otros términos utilizados en los cuadros y las denominaciones de las fuentes nacionales, en tres lenguas. En estos cuadros también figuran los títulos de los grupos de índices de precios al consumidor en las tres lenguas. Sin embargo, los títulos de los grupos de las clasificaciones internacionales no figuran en este cuadro maestro, sino en el Apéndice.

Metodología

Informaciones sobre el ámbito de las estadísticas, sus definiciones y los métodos utilizados por los servicios nacionales de estadística para producir los datos que se publican en este *Anuario*, en el *Anuario de Estadísticas del Trabajo: Series cronológicas* y en el *Boletín de Estadísticas del Trabajo* figuran en la serie de publicaciones titulada *Fuentes y Métodos: Estadísticas del Trabajo* (anteriormente *Fuentes y métodos estadísticos*).

Se han publicado diez volúmenes: 1 – *Indices de los precios al consumidor*; 2 – *Empleo, salarios, horas de trabajo y costo de la mano de obra (encuestas de establecimientos)*; 3 – *Población económicamente activa, empleo, desempleo y horas de trabajo (encuestas de hogares)*; 4 – *Empleo, desempleo, salarios y horas de trabajo (registros administrativos y fuentes relacionadas)*; 5 – *Población total y población económicamente activa, empleo y desempleo (censos de población)*; 6 – *Encuestas sobre los ingresos y gastos de los hogares*; 7 – *Huelgas y cierres patronales*; 8 – *Lesiones profesionales*; 9 – *Países en transición*, y 10 – *Evaluaciones y proyecciones de la población económicamente activa 1950-2010*. Estas publicaciones complementan las breves indicaciones dadas en las notas explicativas de los cuadros y permiten comprender mejor las estadísticas y facilitar su comparación internacional.

En el Apéndice figura una lista de documentos de la Oficina Internacional del Trabajo que tratan de los métodos estadísticos recomendados para compilar estadísticas del trabajo (véase «Referencias»).

Para cada país, las notas de pie de documento también figuran en los tres idiomas.

Orden de presentación de los países

El orden de presentación de los perfiles de los países sigue el orden geográfico y alfabético, utilizando la denominación del país en el idioma de trabajo como indicado más arriba. También se presentan por separado índices alfabéticos en español, francés e inglés, en los cuales la denominación del país figura en el idioma de cada índice, con una indicación del número de página de publicación de cada perfil. Estos índices figuran inmediatamente después del índice general.

Agradecimiento

La Oficina Internacional del Trabajo desea expresar su gratitud a los servicios estadísticos de los diferentes países por su preciosa colaboración en el suministro de los datos presentados en este *Anuario*.

Otras publicaciones estadísticas regulares

Anuario de Estadísticas del Trabajo: Series Cronológicas (publicación anual): Esta publicación presenta las principales estadísticas del trabajo para unos 190 países, áreas y territorios para los diez últimos años. Contiene 31 cuadros correspondientes a los nueve temas principales siguientes: Población económicamente activa; Empleo; Desempleo; Horas de trabajo; Salarios; Costos de la mano de obra; Precios al consumidor; Lesiones profesionales, y Huelgas y cierres patronales.

Boletín de Estadísticas del Trabajo (publicado 2 veces por año): contiene datos mensuales, trimestrales, semestrales y datos anuales sobre el empleo, el desempleo, las horas de trabajo, los salarios y el índice de los precios al consumidor durante los cuatro últimos años. *El Boletín* también publica artículos de interés profesional en estadístas del trabajo.

Salarios y Horas de Trabajo por Ocupación y Precios al por menor de artículos alimenticios, Estadísticas de la Encuesta de octubre de la OIT (publicados anualmente): esta publicación presenta datos sobre salarios y horas de trabajo por ocupación y los precios de artículos alimenticios al detalle reunidos por la OIT cada año a través de la Encuesta de octubre.

Los CD-ROM que contienen series cronológicas más completas están disponibles anualmente para el *Anuario de Estadísticas de Trabajo* y para los *Salarios y Horas de Trabajo por Ocupación y Precios al por menor de artículos alimenticios, Estadísticas de la Encuesta de octubre de la OIT*.

Para visualizar y obtener datos:
http://laborsta.ilo.org

El sitio Web de la Oficina de Estadística:
http://www.ilo.org/stat/

Para más información, diríjase a:
Oficina de Estadística
Oficina Internacional del Trabajo
CH-1211 Ginebra 22
Suiza

Fax: + 41 22 799 6957
Tel: + 41 22 799 8631
Correo electrónico: STAT@ilo.org

Signs and symbols used in the tables

.	Not available
-	Insignificant, less than half the unit used or sampling variability too high
0	Nil
Ø	Mean of the observations
★	Statistics have been derived by addition or substraction of components
	Decimal figures are separated by a point

Signes et symboles utilisés dans les tableaux

.	Pas disponible
-	Négligeable, inférieur à la moitié de l'unité retenue, ou variabilité d'échantillonnage trop grande
0	Nul
Ø	Moyenne des observations
★	Les statistiques ont été obtenues par addition ou soustraction des composantes
	Un point sépare les unités des décimales

Signos y símbolos utilizados en los cuadros

.	No disponible
-	Insignificante, inferior a la mitad de la unidad utilizada, o con variabilidad muestral demasiado grande
0	Nulo
Ø	Promedio de observaciones
★	Las estadísticas has sido obtenidas por la adición o la sustracción de los componentes
	Un punto separa las unidades de los decimales

Country profiles

Profils des pays

Perfiles de los países

Afghanistan

1. Economically active population, Employment and Unemployment ('000)

Age group	Economically active population Total	Women (%)	Employment Total	Women (%)	Unemployment Total	Women (%)
	2005[1] Labour force survey		2005[1] Labour force survey		2005[1] Labour force survey	
Total	4 296.3	47.0	3 932.5	46.5	363.8	52.5

2. Population ('000), Activity rate and Unemployment rate

Age group	Population			Activity rate			Unemployment rate 2005[1] Labour force survey		
	Total	Men	Women	Total	Men	Women	Total	Men	Women
Total	.	.	.	.	.	.	8.5	7.6	9.5

3. Paid employment ('000), Hours of work (weekly) and Wages

Statistics not available.

4. Occupational injuries and Strikes and Lockouts

Statistics not available.

5. Consumer price indices (base period: 2000=100)

Statistics not available for the period 2002-2007.

[1] Persons aged 15 years and over.   [1] Personnes âgées de 15 ans et plus.   [1] Personas de 15 años y más.

Albania

1. Economically active population, Employment and Unemployment ('000)

	Economically active population		Employment		Unemployment	
	Total	Women (%)	Total	Women (%)	Total	Women (%)
Age group	2002 [1] Labour force survey		2001 ★ Population census		2006 [1 2] Employment office records	
Total	1 318.1	43.7	1 041.8	37.6	149.8	.
15-19	128.2	52.1	124.5	43.8	11.3	.
20-24	126.2	49.3	79.0	54.8	.	.
20-34	.	.	.	.	60.1	.
25-29	123.7	52.2	97.1	41.1	.	.
30-34	158.5	46.6	128.1	35.0	.	.
35+	.	.	.	.	78.4	.
35-39	178.7	44.4	143.4	32.4	.	.
40-44	182.1	45.0	145.9	31.2	.	.
45-49	153.4	39.5	135.3	39.0	.	.
50-54	105.9	39.5	.	.	.	.
55-59	67.5	27.4	.	.	.	.
60-64	46.0	31.8	.	.	.	.
65+	48.1	24.4	.	.	.	.
Economic activity (ISIC-Rev.3)			2006 Official estimates			
Total	.	.	935	.	.	.
A-B	.	.	542	.	.	.
C Mining and Quarrying	.	.	5	.	.	.
D Manufacturing	.	.	58	.	.	.
E Electricity, Gas and Water Supply	.	.	10	.	.	.
F Construction	.	.	53	.	.	.
G Wholesale and Retail Trade; Repair of Motor Vehicles ...	.	.	68	.	.	.
H Hotels and Restaurants	.	.	16	.	.	.
I Transport, Storage and Communications	.	.	19	.	.	.
J-L, O-Q	.	.	90	.	.	.
M Education	.	.	48	.	.	.
N Health and Social Work	.	.	25	.	.	.
Education level (ISCED-97)	2002 [1] Labour force survey		2001 ★ Population census		2006 [1 2] Employment office records	
Total	1 318.1	.	1 041.8	.	149.8	.
X No schooling	27.2	.	19.1	.	.	.
1 Primary education or first stage of basic education	134.7	.	91.6	.	81.3	.
2 Lower secondary or second stage of basic education	657.7	.	503.3	.	.	.
2-3	.	.	.	.	65.1	.
3 Upper secondary education	393.9	.	330.7	.	.	.
5A First stage of tertiary education - theoretically based	104.7	.	.	.	.	.
5A, 6	.	.	.	.	3.4	.

2. Population ('000), Activity rate and Unemployment rate

	Population 2002 Labour force survey			Activity rate 2002 Labour force survey			Unemployment rate 2001 [1 3] Population census		
Age group	Total	Men	Women	Total	Men	Women	Total	Men	Women
Total	3 112.0	1 520.5	1 591.5	42.4	48.8	36.2	22.7	18.8	28.4
15+	2 211.2	1 042.9	1 168.3	59.6	71.2	49.3	22.7	18.8	28.4
15-24	507.1	224.6	282.5	50.2	55.8	45.7	35.5	41.6	27.1
25-54	1 162.9	555.2	607.8	77.6	90.1	66.1	.	.	.
55+	541.2	263.2	278.0	29.8	44.3	16.1	.	.	.

3. Paid employment ('000), Hours of work (weekly) and Wages

Economic activity (ISIC-Rev.3)	Paid employment 2005 Labour-related establishment census			Hours of work 2004 [4] Industrial/commercial survey Hours actually worked / Wage earners			Wages 2006 Labour-related establishment census Earnings per month / Employees / Lek		
	Total	Men	Women	Total	Men	Women	Total	Men	Women
Total	120.419	.	.	.	.	.	.	.	.
B	0.195	.	.	.	.	.	.	.	.
C	5.652	.	.	.	.	.	.	.	.
C-D	.	.	.	139.8	.	.	.	.	.
D	37.613	.	.	.	.	.	19 750	.	.
E	13.775	.	.	.	.	.	24 167	.	.
F	19.828	.	.	.	.	.	19 167	.	.
G	15.014	.	.	.	.	.	20 667	.	.
H	.	.	.	.	.	.	17 250 [5]	.	.
H, J-Q	16.516	.	.	.	.	.	.	.	.
I	11.826	.	.	.	.	.	31 333	.	.
K	.	.	.	.	.	.	24 417	.	.
O-P	.	.	.	.	.	.	18 250	.	.

Share of women in wage employment in the non-agricultural sector (2003 - Labour-related establishment survey): .%

4. Occupational injuries and Strikes and Lockouts

Statistics not available.

Albania

5. Consumer price indices (base period: 2000=100)

	2002	2003	2004	2005	2006	2007
General indices	108.4	110.8	114.0	116.7	119.5	123.0
Food index, including non-alcoholic beverages	110.2	115.0	114.9	114.3	115.6	119.0
Electricity, gas and other fuel indices	119.5	124.9	158.9	198.7	210.0	224.9
Clothing indices, including footwear	89.7	85.8	83.8	81.7	83.2	78.7
Rent indices	131.5	130.9	136.9	142.2	149.7	154.7
General index, excluding housing	108.6	112.0	114.8	117.1	119.2	.

[1] Persons aged 15 years and over. [2] Dec. [3] April. [4] Per month. [5] Incl. division 74 of tabulation category K and divisions 90, 93 of tabulation category O.

[1] Personnes âgées de 15 ans et plus. [2] Déc. [3] Avril. [4] Par mois. [5] Y compris la division 74 de la catégorie de classement K et les divisions 90, 93 de la catégorie de classement O.

[1] Personas de 15 años y más. [2] Dic. [3] Abril. [4] Por mes. [5] Incl. la división 74 de la categoría de tabulación K y las divisiones 90, 93 de la categoría de tabulación O.

Algérie

1. Population active, Emploi et Chômage ('000)

	Population active Total	Femmes (%)	Emploi Total	Femmes (%)	Chômage Total	Femmes (%)
Groupe d'âge	2006 [1,2] Enquête sur la main-d'oeuvre		2006 ★ Enquête sur la main-d'oeuvre		2006 [1,2] Enquête sur la main-d'oeuvre	
Total	10 109.6	.	8 868.8	.	1 240.8	.
15-19	635.8	.	469.4	.	166.4	.
20-24	1 571.7	.	1 201.7	.	370.0	.
25-29	1 693.9	.	1 360.4	.	333.5	.
30-34	1 475.6	.	1 305.2	.	170.4	.
35-39	1 344.2	.	1 253.1	.	91.1	.
40-44	1 254.0	.	1 205.1	.	48.9	.
45-49	853.8	.	825.3	.	28.4	.
50-54	648.3	.	622.8	.	25.5	.
55+	632.4	.	625.8	.	6.6	.
Activité économique (CITI-Rév.3)	2004 ★ Enquête sur la main-d'oeuvre		2004 [1,2] Enquête sur la main-d'oeuvre		2004 [1,2] Enquête sur la main-d'oeuvre	
Total	9 469.9	17.5	7 798.4	17.4	1 671.5	18.0
A Agriculture, chasse et sylviculture	1 666.3	17.8	1 585.2	18.7	81.1	0.4
B Pêche	33.0	20.9	31.0	22.3	2.0	.
C Activités extractives	146.2	6.8	135.1	6.8	11.1	7.0
D Activités de fabrication	894.9	41.2	846.7	42.2	48.2	22.7
E Production et distribution d'électricité, de gaz et d'eau	84.9	5.8	79.1	5.7	5.8	7.3
F Construction	1 090.3	1.2	967.6	1.1	122.7	1.3
G Commerce de gros et de détail; réparation de véhicules ...	1 269.6	3.6	1 174.4	3.9	95.2	0.9
H Hôtels et restaurants	192.7	6.0	164.8	6.2	27.9	4.9
I Transports, entreposage et communications	463.4	3.6	435.9	3.7	27.5	2.4
J Intermédiation financière	72.5	33.6	68.8	33.1	3.7	42.6
K Immobilier, locations et activités de services aux entreprises	78.8	24.1	72.4	22.7	6.4	40.4
L Administration publique et défense; sécurité sociale obligatoire	1 137.2	10.4	1 104.1	10.3	33.1	11.8
M Education	661.7	42.3	634.0	41.3	27.7	66.9
N Santé et action sociale	240.3	43.3	235.5	42.6	4.8	77.2
O Autres activités de services collectifs, sociaux et personnels	.	.	.	.	15.1	30.1
P Ménages privés employant du personnel domestique	39.4	44.6	34.9	45.0	4.5	41.9
Q Organisations et organismes extraterritoriaux	4.3	25.6	3.9	28.2	0.4	.
X Ne pouvant être classés selon l'activité économique	21.0	17.1	16.2	19.8	4.8	8.2
Chômeurs n'ayant jamais travaillé	.	.	.	.	1 149.4	21.5
Profession (CITP-88)	2004 ★ Enquête sur la main-d'oeuvre		2004 [1,2] Enquête sur la main-d'oeuvre		2004 [1,2] Enquête sur la main-d'oeuvre	
Total	9 469.9	17.5	7 798.4	17.4	1 671.5	18.0
1 Membres de l'exécutif et des corps législatifs, cadres ...	544.5	4.2	459.9	4.9	84.6	0.4
2 Professions intellectuelles et scientifiques	333.8	30.8	322.7	31.6	11.1	7.0
3 Professions intermédiaires	755.2	36.1	707.0	37.0	48.2	22.7
4 Employés de type administratif	358.3	36.5	352.5	37.0	5.8	7.3
5 Personnel des services et vendeurs de magasin et de marché	1 476.5	6.2	1 353.8	6.7	122.7	1.3
6 Agriculteurs et ouvriers qualifiés de l'agriculture	1 394.4	16.6	1 299.1	17.7	95.3	0.9
7 Artisans et ouvriers des métiers de type artisanal	1 282.5	26.3	1 255.0	26.8	27.5	2.4
8 Conducteurs d'installations et de machines ...	502.0	2.5	494.9	1.9	7.1	43.6
9 Ouvriers et employés non qualifiés	1 521.3	13.6	1 432.7	12.1	88.6	37.9
0 Forces armées	151.9	3.1	120.7	2.5	31.2	5.7
Chômeurs n'ayant jamais travaillé	.	.	.	.	1 149.4	21.5
Niveau d'instruction (CITE-97)					2004 [1,2] Enquête sur la main-d'oeuvre	
Total	.	.	.	.	1 671.5	18.0
X Non scolarisé	.	.	.	.	84.2	11.6
0 Education préprimaire	.	.	.	.	21.0	13.2
1 Enseignement primaire ou premier cycle de l'éducation ...	.	.	.	.	297.3	6.8
2 Premier cycle de l'enseignement secondaire ou deuxième ...	.	.	.	.	694.0	11.2
3 Enseignement secondaire (deuxième cycle)	.	.	.	.	384.7	23.8
5A Premier cycle de l'enseignement supérieur - théorie [3]	.	.	.	.	190.3	52.2
Situation dans la profession (CISP-1993)			2004 [1,2] Enquête sur la main-d'oeuvre			
Total	.	.	7 798.4	17.4	.	.
1 Salariés	.	.	4 660.6	14.5	.	.
2 Employeurs	.	.	387.8	4.5	.	.
3 Personnes travaillant pour leur propre compte	.	.	2 084.0	23.0	.	.
5 Travailleurs familiaux collaborant à l'entreprise familiale	.	.	639.6	28.9	.	.
6 Inclassables d'après la situation	.	.	26.5	13.6	.	.

2. Population ('000), Taux d'activité et Taux de chômage

	Population 1996 [4] Enquête sur la main-d'oeuvre			Taux d'activité 1996 [4] Enquête sur la main-d'oeuvre			Taux de chômage 2006 [1,2] Enquête sur la main-d'oeuvre		
Groupe d'âge	Total	Hommes	Femmes	Total	Hommes	Femmes	Total	Hommes	Femmes
Total	28 866.0	14 632.0	14 234.0	27.4	47.0	7.2	12.3	11.8	14.4
15+	17 594.0	8 873.0	8 721.0	44.9	77.5	11.8	12.3	.	.
15-24	6 083.0	3 108.0	2 975.0	40.7	65.0	15.3	24.3	.	.
25-54	9 120.0	4 613.0	4 507.0	54.0	95.2	11.8	9.6	.	.
55+	2 391.0	1 152.0	1 239.0	21.0	40.0	3.4	1.0	.	.

Algérie

3. Emploi rémunéré ('000), Durée du travail (hebdomadaire) et Salaires

Activité économique (CITI-Rév.3)	Emploi rémunéré Total	Hommes	Femmes	Durée du travail Total	Hommes	Femmes	Salaires 1998 Fichiers administratifs et sources connexes Gains par mois / Salariés / Dinar Total	Hommes	Femmes
L	.	.	.	.	.	.	11 400	.	.
M	.	.	.	.	.	.	12 732	.	.

4. Lésions professionnelles et Grèves et lock-out

Activité économique (CITI-Rév.3)	Taux de lésions mortelles 2004 Fichiers des assurances Pour 100 000 travailleurs assurés Lésions indemnisées Total	Hommes	Femmes	Taux de lésions non mortelles 2004 Fichiers des assurances Pour 100 000 travailleurs assurés Lésions indemnisées Total	Hommes	Femmes	Grèves et lock-out 2004 [5] Fichiers des relations du travail Grèves et lock-out	Travailleurs impliqués	Journées non effectuées
Total	17.6	.	.	1 002.7	.	.	.	56 861	628 838
A-B	.	.	.	.	.	.	1	330	37
C	.	.	.	.	.	.	0	0	0
D	.	.	.	.	.	.	8	14 148	18 282
E	.	.	.	.	.	.	0 [6]	0 [6]	0 [6]
F	.	.	.	.	.	.	11	1 796	30 485
G	.	.	.	.	.	.	0	0	0
H	.	.	.	.	.	.	0	0	0
I	.	.	.	.	.	.	2	3 298	4 904
J-K	.	.	.	.	.	.	0	0	0
L	.	.	.	.	.	.	5	2 330	564 397
M	.	.	.	.	.	.	5	26 674	6 618
N	.	.	.	.	.	.	1	4 950	1 500
Q	.	.	.	.	.	.	1	3 285	568
X	.	.	.	.	.	.	1	50	2 047

5. Indices des prix à la consommation (période de base: 2000=100)

	2002	2003	2004	2005	2006	2007
Indices généraux	105.8	109.5	114.5	116.7	118.8	123.5
Indices de l'alimentation, y compris les boissons non alcoolisées	106.2	111.0	116.4	116.6	119.3	126.7
Indices de l'habillement, y compris les chaussures	107.4	109.3	111.9	113.5	113.7	114.2
Indices du loyer [7]	102.0	104.8	107.1	121.6	125.9	126.1

[1] Persons aged 15 years and over. [2] Sep. [3] Levels 5A-5B. [4] First quarter. [5] Strikes only. [6] Incl. sanitary services. [7] Incl. water, electricity, gas and other fuels.

[1] Personnes âgées de 15 ans et plus. [2] Sept. [3] Niveaux 5A-5B. [4] Premier trimestre. [5] Grèves seulement. [6] Y compris les services sanitaires. [7] Y compris l'eau, l'électricité, le gaz et autres combustibles.

[1] Personas de 15 años y más. [2] Sept. [3] Niveles 5A-5B [4] Primer trimestre. [5] Huelgas solamente. [6] Incl. los servicios de saneamiento. [7] Incl. el agua, la electricidad, el gas y otros combustibles.

American Samoa

1. Economically active population, Employment and Unemployment ('000)

	Economically active population		Employment		Unemployment	
Age group	Total	Women (%)	Total	Women (%)	Total	Women (%)
	2000 [1 2] Population census		1990 ★ Population census		1990 [1 2] Population census	
Total			13.5	41.3	0.7	38.6
16+	18.0	38.9	.	.	.	.
16-19			0.4	44.7	0.1	49.3
20-24			1.9	45.2	0.2	44.7
25-29			2.3	45.4	0.1	34.5
30-34			2.3	41.0	0.1	34.9
35-39			1.8	43.1	0.0	40.9
40-44			1.5	38.9	0.0	26.2
45-49			1.1	35.5	0.0	32.3
50-54			0.9	35.5	0.0	15.6
55-59			0.5	32.8	0.0	30.0
60-64			0.4	40.2	0.0	60.0
65-69			0.2	41.9	0.0	.
70-74			0.1	32.1	0.0	100.0
75+			0.1	39.4	0.0	100.0

Economic activity (ISIC-Rev.2)	1980 [1 2] Population census		1990 [1 2] Population census	
Total	8.3	39.3	13.5	41.3
1 Agriculture, Hunting, Forestry and Fishing	.	.	0.3	5.5
1-2	0.1	9.3	.	.
2 Mining and Quarrying	.	.	0.0	25.0
3 Manufacturing	1.9	47.6	4.6	53.1
4 Electricity, Gas and Water	.	.	0.2	10.9
4,7	0.7	18.2	.	.
5 Construction	0.6	5.1	1.2	7.0
6 Wholesale and Retail Trade and Restaurants and Hotels	0.9	47.4	2.1	48.1
7 Transport, Storage and Communication	.	.	0.8	16.9
8 Financing, Insurance, Real Estate and Business Services	0.2	51.9	0.3	50.3
9 Community, Social and Personal Services	3.6	42.8	2.3	5.8
0 Activities not Adequately Defined	0.0	50.0	1.7	94.8

Occupation (ISCO-1968)	1980 [1 2] Population census	
Total	8.3	39.3
0/1 Professional, technical and related workers	1.4	46.8
2 Administrative and managerial workers	0.8	20.7
3 Clerical and related workers	1.1	61.9
4 Sales workers	0.5	60.6
5 Service workers	1.0	40.5
6 Agriculture, animal husbandry and forestry workers ...	0.2	26.0
7/8/9 Production and related workers, transport equipment ...	3.1	30.1

Status in employment (ICSE-1993)	1990 [1 2] Population census	
Total			13.5	41.3
1 Employees			13.1	41.7
2 Employers			0.3	21.9
3 Own-account workers			-	.
4 Members of producers' cooperatives			.	.
5 Contributing family workers			0.0	67.9
6 Not classifiable by status			-	.

2. Population ('000), Activity rate and Unemployment rate

	Population			Activity rate			Unemployment rate		
Age group	2000 [2 3] Population census			2000 [2 3] Population census			1990 [1 2] Population census		
	Total	Men	Women	Total	Men	Women	Total	Men	Women
Total							5.1	5.3	4.8
15+	34.0	17.0	17.0	52.9	58.8	41.2	5.1	.	.
15-24							12.0	11.8	12.1
25-54							3.8	4.3	3.1
55+							1.5	.	.

3. Paid employment ('000), Hours of work (weekly) and Wages

Statistics not available.

4. Occupational injuries and Strikes and Lockouts

Statistics not available.

American Samoa

5. Consumer price indices (base period: 2000=100)

	2002	2003	2004	2005	2006	2007
General indices [4]	103.4	108.4	116.1	122.1	125.7	.
Food index, including non-alcoholic beverages	103.1	109.7	123.5	130.4	132.2	.
Clothing indices, including footwear	100.2	100.6	101.0	101.0	100.6	.
Rent indices	101.2	107.8	107.5	116.2	121.2	.

[1] Persons aged 16 years and over. [2] April. [3] "De jure" population. [4] Excl. "Rent".

[1] Personnes âgées de 16 ans et plus. [2] Avril. [3] Population "de jure". [4] Non compris le groupe "Loyer".

[1] Personas de 16 años y más. [2] Abril. [3] Población "de jure". [4] Excl. el grupo "Alquiler".

Andorre

1. Population active, Emploi et Chômage ('000)

Données non disponibles.

2. Population ('000), Taux d'activité et Taux de chômage

Groupe d'âge	Population 2007 [1,2] Recensement de la population			Taux d'activité			Taux de chômage		
	Total	Hommes	Femmes	Total	Hommes	Femmes	Total	Hommes	Femmes
Total	83.1	43.5	39.6	.	.	.	.	.	.
15+	71.0	37.1	33.9	.	.	.	.	.	.
15-24	8.7	4.5	4.2	.	.	.	.	.	.
25-54	43.9	23.1	20.8	.	.	.	.	.	.
55+	18.4	9.5	8.8	.	.	.	.	.	.

3. Emploi rémunéré ('000), Durée du travail (hebdomadaire) et Salaires

Activité économique (CITI-Rév.3)	Emploi rémunéré 2007 Fichiers des assurances			Durée du travail			Salaires 2007 Fichiers administratifs et sources connexes Gains par mois / Salariés / Euro		
	Total	Hommes	Femmes	Total	Hommes	Femmes	Total	Hommes	Femmes
Total	43.240	23.088	20.147	.	.	.	1 810.7	2 098.4	1 480.9
A-B	.	.	.	.	.	.	1 299.9	1 388.6	1 149.0
C-Q	.	.	.	.	.	.	1 812.4	2 101.3	1 481.8
A	0.147	0.093	0.054	.	.	.	1 299.6	1 388.6	1 149.0
D	1.730	1.140	0.590	.	.	.	1 902.5	2 108.9	1 503.1
E	0.159	0.122	0.037	.	.	.	3 054.2	3 324.1	2 166.8
F	6.682	6.099	0.583	.	.	.	1 904.8	1 952.4	1 407.2
G	11.316	5.468	5.848	.	.	.	1 596.1	1 864.8	1 345.0
H	5.523	2.519	3.005	.	.	.	1 410.2	1 579.7	1 269.2
I	1.300	0.852	0.447	.	.	.	1 940.5	2 129.0	1 581.8
J	1.609	0.865	0.744	.	.	.	4 057.2	5 288.7	2 621.3
K	4.215	2.085	2.130	.	.	.	1 734.0	2 106.9	1 369.3
L	4.452	2.049	2.403	.	.	.	2 208.9	2 483.1	1 975.5
M	0.670	0.161	0.509	.	.	.	1 904.8	2 241.7	1 798.6
N	1.431	0.300	1.130	.	.	.	1 964.0	2 774.2	1 748.8
O	2.441	1.186	1.254	.	.	.	1 557.8	1 865.4	1 290.3
P	1.334	0.116	1.218	.	.	.	1 087.8	1 473.9	1 050.9
Q	0.009	0.004	0.005	.	.	.	1 616.5	1 529.3	1 738.6
X	0.217	0.028	0.189	.	.	.	1 075.3	1 461.5	1 018.2

Pourcentage de salariées dans le secteur non agricole qui sont femmes (2007 - Fichiers des assurances): **46.4%**

4. Lésions professionnelles et Grèves et lock-out

Données non disponibles.

5. Indices des prix à la consommation (période de base: 2000=100)

[3,2]	2002	2003	2004	2005	2006	2007
Indices généraux	104.5	107.5	111.1	114.6	118.2	122.8
Indices de l'alimentation, y compris les boissons non alcoolisées [4]	106.2	109.9	111.9	113.1	116.2	119.8
Indices de l'électricité, gaz et autres combustibles	103.7	105.8	122.6	138.1	135.1	156.0
Indices de l'habillement, y compris les chaussures	106.3	107.8	109.0	111.0	112.7	114.7
Indices du loyer [5]	103.4	106.9	111.2	115.4	122.8	130.2

[1] Incl. the armed forces. [2] Dec. [3] Index base 2001=100. [4] Incl. beverages and tobacco. [5] Incl. water and gas.

[1] Y compris les forces armées. [2] Déc. [3] Indice base 2001=100. [4] Y compris les boissons et le tabac. [5] Y compris l'eau et le gaz.

[1] Incl. las fuerzas armadas. [2] Dic. [3] Indice base 2001=100. [4] Incl. las bebidas y el tabaco. [5] Incl. el agua y el gas.

Angola

1. Population active, Emploi et Chômage ('000)

	Population active		Emploi		Chômage	
	Total	Femmes (%)	Total	Femmes (%)	Total	Femmes (%)
Groupe d'âge			1996 Estimations officielles		1996 [1] Fichiers des bureaux de placement	
Total	.	.	475.214	23.5	18.999	18.3
Activité économique (CITI-Rév.2)			1992 [2] Enquête sur la main-d'oeuvre			
Total	.	.	497.21	.	.	.
1 Agriculture, chasse, sylviculture et pêche	.	.	25.15	.	.	.
2 Industries extractives	.	.	14.54	.	.	.
3 Industries manufacturières	.	.	60.99	.	.	.
4 Electricité, gaz et eau	.	.	4.48	.	.	.
5 Bâtiment et travaux publics	.	.	22.32	.	.	.
6 Commerce de gros et de détail; restaurants et hôtels	.	.	144.33	.	.	.
7 Transports, entrepôts et communications	.	.	42.22	.	.	.
8 Banques, assurances, affaires immobilières et services ...	.	.	11.90	.	.	.
9 Services fournis à la collectivité, services sociaux ...	.	.	132.88	.	.	.
0 Activités mal désignées	.	.	38.41	.	.	.

2. Population ('000), Taux d'activité et Taux de chômage

Données non disponibles.

3. Emploi rémunéré ('000), Durée du travail (hebdomadaire) et Salaires

Activité économique (CITI-Rév.2)	Emploi rémunéré 1986 Estimations officielles			Durée du travail			Salaires		
	Total	Hommes	Femmes	Total	Hommes	Femmes	Total	Hommes	Femmes
Total	367.626	294.194	73.432	.	.	.	.	.	.
2-9	.	235.006	57.165	.	.	.	.	.	.
1	75.455	.	.	.	.	.	.	.	.
3	66.096	.	.	.	.	.	.	.	.
5	21.608	.	.	.	.	.	.	.	.
6	31.931	.	.	.	.	.	.	.	.
7	27.370	.	.	.	.	.	.	.	.
8	1.604	.	.	.	.	.	.	.	.
9	135.153	.	.	.	.	.	.	.	.
0	8.409	.	.	.	.	.	.	.	.

4. Lésions professionnelles et Grèves et lock-out

Données non disponibles.

5. Indices des prix à la consommation (période de base: 2000=100)

Luanda	2002	2003	2004	2005	2006	2007
Indices généraux	527.6	1 045.8	1 501.2	1 846.0	2 091.6	2 347.7
Indices de l'alimentation, y compris les boissons non alcoolisées	508.6	1 062.4	1 587.5	1 957.0	2 292.4	2 617.7

[1] Persons aged 14 years and over. [2] Luanda.   [1] Personnes âgées de 14 ans et plus. [2] Luanda.   [1] Personas de 14 años y más. [2] Luanda.

Anguilla

1. Economically active population, Employment and Unemployment ('000)

	Economically active population		Employment		Unemployment	
	Total	Women (%)	Total	Women (%)	Total	Women (%)
Age group	2001 [1 2 3] Population census		2001 ★ Population census		2001 [2 3] Population census	
Total	6.049	46.8	5.643	46.6	0.406	48.8
15-19	0.434	47.5	0.344	45.1	0.090	56.7
20-24	0.684	48.4	0.625	46.9	0.059	64.4
25-29	0.790	47.5	0.748	47.5	0.042	47.6
30-34	0.901	48.5	0.854	48.1	0.047	55.3
35-39	0.941	49.0	0.899	49.3	0.042	42.9
40-44	0.782	49.2	0.745	49.7	0.037	40.5
45-49	0.607	44.3	0.583	44.8	0.024	33.3
50-54	0.372	45.2	0.358	44.7	0.014	57.1
55-59	0.214	39.3	0.199	40.2	0.015	26.7
60+	0.324	34.6	0.297	37.4	0.027	3.7

Economic activity (ISIC-Rev.3)
2001 [1 2 3] Population census

	Total	Women (%)
Total	5.644	46.6
A Agriculture, Hunting and Forestry	0.058	24.1
B Fishing	0.105	4.8
C Mining and Quarrying	0.020	10.0
D Manufacturing	0.135	37.0
E Electricity, Gas and Water Supply	0.081	22.2
F Construction	0.829	3.3
G Wholesale and Retail Trade; Repair of Motor Vehicles ...	0.558	53.6
H Hotels and Restaurants	1.588	60.3
I Transport, Storage and Communications	0.381	26.8
J Financial Intermediation	0.200	70.0
K Real Estate, Renting and Business Activities	0.233	48.9
L Public Administration and Defence; Compulsory Social ...	0.662	53.5
M Education	0.242	78.9
N Health and Social Work	0.139	76.3
O Other Community, Social and Personal Service Activities	0.164	48.2
P Households with Employed Persons	0.164	77.4
X Not classifiable by economic activity	0.086	51.2

Occupation (ISCO-88)
2001 [1 2 3] Population census

	Total	Women (%)
Total	5.644	46.6
1 Legislators, senior officials and managers	0.369	52.0
2 Professionals	0.551	57.4
3 Technicians and associate professionals	0.569	42.4
4 Clerks	0.842	77.0
5 Service workers and shop and market sales workers	1.314	68.6
6 Skilled agricultural and fishery workers	0.270	9.3
7 Craft and related trade workers	0.801	6.5
8 Plant and machine operators and assemblers	0.233	4.7
9 Elementary occupations	0.605	32.7
X Not classifiable by occupation	0.090	48.9

Education level (ISCED-97)

	2001 [1 2 3] Population census		2001 ★ Population census		2001 [2 3] Population census	
	Total	Women (%)	Total	Women (%)	Total	Women (%)
Total	6.049	46.8	5.648	46.6	0.401	49.4
X No schooling [4]	0.063	38.1	0.054	37.0	0.009	44.4
1 Primary education or first stage of basic education	1.720	36.6	1.614	36.7	0.106	35.8
2 Lower secondary or second stage of basic education	0.770	43.5	0.688	44.2	0.082	37.8
3 Upper secondary education	2.314	52.5	2.153	51.7	0.161	62.7
4 Post-secondary non-tertiary education	0.401	54.4	0.386	54.4	0.015	53.3
5A First stage of tertiary education - theoretically based	0.711	52.3	0.683	52.6	0.028	46.4
? Level not stated	0.070	48.6	0.070	48.6	-	.

Status in employment (ICSE-1993)
2001 [1 2 3] Population census

	Total	Women (%)
Total	5.644	46.6
1 Employees	3.644	47.7
2 Employers	0.958	59.5
3 Own-account workers	0.101	35.6
4 Members of producers' cooperatives	0.013	53.8
5 Contributing family workers	0.337	28.2
6 Not classifiable by status	0.591	30.8

2. Population ('000), Activity rate and Unemployment rate

	Population 2001 [1 3 5] Population census			Activity rate 2001 [1 3 5] Population census			Unemployment rate 2001 [2 3] Population census		
Age group	Total	Men	Women	Total	Men	Women	Total	Men	Women
Total	11.430	5.628	5.802	52.9	57.2	48.7	6.7	6.5	7.0
15+	8.228	4.038	4.190	73.5	79.8	67.5	6.6	6.5	6.7
15-24	1.756	0.852	0.904	63.7	68.2	59.4	13.3	10.3	16.6
25-54	4.975	2.470	2.505	88.3	93.0	83.6	4.7	4.8	4.5
55+	1.497	0.716	0.781	35.9	47.8	25.1	7.8	10.8	2.6

Anguilla

3. Paid employment ('000), Hours of work (weekly) and Wages

Economic activity (ISIC-Rev.3)	Paid employment			Hours of work			Wages 2000 Labour-related establishment survey Earnings per month / Employees / EC dollar		
	Total	Men	Women	Total	Men	Women	Total	Men	Women
D	.	.	.	.	.	.	1 494.73	.	.
E	.	.	.	.	.	.	1 988.27	.	.
F	.	.	.	.	.	.	3 025.00	.	.
G	.	.	.	.	.	.	2 901.17	.	.
H	.	.	.	.	.	.	2 721.76	.	.
I	.	.	.	.	.	.	1 363.98	.	.
J	.	.	.	.	.	.	2 833.05	.	.
K	.	.	.	.	.	.	2 942.60	.	.
L-N	.	.	.	.	.	.	3 263.94	.	.
O	.	.	.	.	.	.	1 301.93	.	.

4. Occupational injuries and Strikes and Lockouts

Economic activity (ISIC-Rev.2)	Rates of fatal injuries			Rates of non-fatal injuries			Strikes and lockouts 1997 Special data collection		
	Total	Men	Women	Total	Men	Women	Strikes and lockouts	Workers involved	Days not worked
Total	.	.	.	.	.	.	0	0	0

5. Consumer price indices (base period: 2000=100)

[6]	2002	2003	2004	2005	2006	2007
General indices	100.5	103.8	108.3	113.5	122.7	129.1
Food index, including non-alcoholic beverages	100.5	98.0	102.1	105.4	112.4	119.4
Electricity, gas and other fuel indices	94.2	100.8	105.0	119.8	135.2	134.4
Clothing indices, including footwear	114.1	112.3	125.1	158.1	146.0	143.4
Rent indices	100.4	85.5	83.3	89.1	98.4	103.3

[1] Excl. armed forces. [2] Persons aged 15 years and over. [3] May. [4] Levels X-0. [5] "De jure" population. [6] Index base 2001=100.

[1] Non compris les forces armées. [2] Personnes âgées de 15 ans et plus. [3] Mai. [4] Niveaux X-0. [5] Population "de jure". [6] Indice base 2001=100.

[1] Excl. las fuerzas armadas. [2] Personas de 15 años y más. [3] Mayo. [4] Niveles X-0. [5] Población "de jure". [6] Indice base 2001=100.

Antigua and Barbuda

1. Economically active population, Employment and Unemployment ('000)

	Economically active population		Employment		Unemployment	
	Total	Women (%)	Total	Women (%)	Total	Women (%)
Age group	2001 [1][2] Population census		2001 ★ Population census		2001 [1][2] Population census	
Total	39.552	50.0	36.223	49.8	3.329	52.3
15-19	1.418	43.0	0.950	40.8	0.468	47.4
20-24	4.896	48.9	4.111	47.8	0.785	54.1
25-29	5.699	51.1	5.221	50.5	0.478	57.9
30-34	6.239	52.6	5.796	51.9	0.443	61.4
35-39	5.948	51.4	5.572	51.1	0.376	55.1
40-44	4.959	52.3	4.690	52.2	0.269	53.9
45-49	3.677	50.7	3.474	51.2	0.203	42.9
50-54	2.735	48.3	2.602	48.9	0.133	36.1
55-59	1.812	48.4	1.724	49.1	0.088	35.2
60-64	1.028	42.2	0.981	42.7	0.047	31.9
65-69	0.577	39.9	0.551	41.0	0.026	15.4
70-74	0.342	38.3	0.335	38.8	0.007	14.3
75-79	0.134	37.3	0.132	37.1	0.002	50.0
80+	0.068	23.5	0.065	24.6	0.003	.

Economic activity (ISIC-Rev.3)			2001 [1][2] Population census			
Total	.	.	36.233	49.8	.	.
A Agriculture, Hunting and Forestry	.	.	0.691	28.8	.	.
B Fishing	.	.	0.255	0.8	.	.
C Mining and Quarrying	.	.	0.106	17.9	.	.
D Manufacturing	.	.	1.541	39.9	.	.
E Electricity, Gas and Water Supply	.	.	0.513	18.3	.	.
F Construction	.	.	3.122	3.9	.	.
G Wholesale and Retail Trade; Repair of Motor Vehicles ...	.	.	4.846	53.1	.	.
H Hotels and Restaurants	.	.	5.081	59.7	.	.
I Transport, Storage and Communications	.	.	2.808	35.0	.	.
J Financial Intermediation	.	.	1.049	69.6	.	.
K Real Estate, Renting and Business Activities	.	.	1.460	45.0	.	.
L Public Administration and Defence; Compulsory Social ...	.	.	4.376	51.9	.	.
M Education	.	.	1.711	77.0	.	.
N Health and Social Work	.	.	1.716	82.5	.	.
O Other Community, Social and Personal Service Activities	.	.	2.686	56.3	.	.
P Households with Employed Persons	.	.	1.304	81.7	.	.
Q Extra-Territorial Organizations and Bodies	.	.	0.503	39.0	.	.
X Not classifiable by economic activity	.	.	2.467	50.2	.	.

Occupation (ISCO-88)			2001 [1][2] Population census			
Total	.	.	36.232	49.8	.	.
1 Legislators, senior officials and managers	.	.	1.589	45.1	.	.
2 Professionals	.	.	2.110	55.2	.	.
3 Technicians and associate professionals	.	.	3.794	54.3	.	.
4 Clerks	.	.	5.066	81.0	.	.
5 Service workers and shop and market sales workers	.	.	7.254	63.5	.	.
6 Skilled agricultural and fishery workers	.	.	0.520	19.4	.	.
7 Craft and related trade workers	.	.	5.453	9.4	.	.
8 Plant and machine operators and assemblers	.	.	1.764	6.3	.	.
9 Elementary occupations	.	.	6.311	55.1	.	.
0 Armed forces	.	.	2.372	50.7	.	.

2. Population ('000), Activity rate and Unemployment rate

	Population			Activity rate			Unemployment rate		
Age group	2001 [2] Population census			2001 [2] Population census			2001 [1][2] Population census		
	Total	Men	Women	Total	Men	Women	Total	Men	Women
Total	76.9	36.1	40.8	51.4	54.7	48.5	8.4	8.0	8.8
15+	55.1	25.3	29.8	71.8	78.2	66.2	8.4	8.0	.
15-24	12.4	5.9	6.5	51.0	56.2	46.3	19.8	18.3	21.6
25-54	33.2	15.1	18.1	88.2	94.1	83.2	6.5	6.1	6.9
55+	9.5	4.2	5.3	41.5	52.4	32.8	4.4	5.4	.

3. Paid employment ('000), Hours of work (weekly) and Wages

Statistics not available.

Antigua and Barbuda

4. Occupational injuries and Strikes and Lockouts

Economic activity (ISIC-Rev.2)	Rates of fatal injuries			Rates of non-fatal injuries			Strikes and lockouts 1996 Labour relations records		
	Total	Men	Women	Total	Men	Women	Strikes and lockouts	Workers involved	Days not worked[3]
Total	.	.	.	.	.	.	2	332	46
1	.	.	.	.	.	.	0	0	0
2	.	.	.	.	.	.	0	0	0
3	.	.	.	.	.	.	0	0	0
4	.	.	.	.	.	.	0	0	0
5	.	.	.	.	.	.	0	0	0
6	.	.	.	.	.	.	0	0	0
7	.	.	.	.	.	.	0	0	0
8	.	.	.	.	.	.	1	32	8
9	.	.	.	.	.	.	1	300	38
0	.	.	.	.	.	.	0	0	0

5. Consumer price indices (base period: 2000=100)

Statistics not available for the period 2002-2007.

[1] Persons aged 15 years and over. [2] May. [3] Computed on the basis of an eight-hour working day.

[1] Personnes âgées de 15 ans et plus. [2] Mai. [3] Calculées sur la base de journées de travail de huit heures.

[1] Personas de 15 años y más. [2] Mayo. [3] Calculados en base a días de trabajo de ocho horas.

Argentina

1. Población económicamente activa, Empleo y Desempleo ('000)

	Población económicamente activa		Empleo		Desempleo	
	Total	Mujeres (%)	Total	Mujeres (%)	Total	Mujeres (%)
Grupo de edad	2006 [1,2,3]		2006 ★		2006 [1,2,3]	
	Encuesta de la fuerza de trabajo		Encuesta de la fuerza de trabajo		Encuesta de la fuerza de trabajo	
Total	11 089.7	43.4	10 040.5	42.4	1 049.2	53.4
10-14	38.2	29.9	33.7	31.6	4.5	16.6
15-19	584.4	41.9	404.1	36.4	180.2	54.3
20-24	1 381.7	43.1	1 102.2	40.6	279.6	53.0
25-29	1 558.9	45.0	1 420.2	44.0	138.7	54.8
30-34	1 459.4	42.3	1 363.7	41.2	95.7	58.7
35-39	1 220.4	45.0	1 151.7	43.7	68.7	66.2
40-44	1 120.4	46.7	1 063.3	45.7	57.1	66.2
45-49	1 016.6	44.3	957.4	43.9	59.3	51.7
50-54	936.2	44.1	882.7	43.7	53.5	50.0
55-59	808.8	42.2	759.1	42.6	49.6	36.8
60-64	528.2	39.1	490.2	38.6	37.9	44.5
65-69	256.9	38.0	237.5	39.2	19.5	23.2
70-74	116.8	38.2	114.3	38.6	2.5	20.0
75+	62.9	27.8	60.5	28.2	2.4	18.3
Actividad económica (CIIU-Rev.3)	2006 [1,2,3]		2006 [1,2,3]		2006 [1,2,3]	
	Encuesta de la fuerza de trabajo		Encuesta de la fuerza de trabajo		Encuesta de la fuerza de trabajo	
Total	11 089.7	43.4	10 040.5	42.4	1 049.2	53.4
A Agricultura, ganadería, caza y silvicultura	79.7	19.7	72.9	18.7	6.8	30.7
B Pesca	9.8	8.4	9.0	9.1	0.8	.
C Explotación de minas y canteras	41.4	15.3	39.8	14.3	1.6	39.7
D Industrias manufactureras	1 523.5	31.4	1 410.7	29.9	112.8	49.5
E Suministro de electricidad, gas y agua	45.3	13.2	44.1	13.6	1.2	.
F Construcción	1 026.1	3.6	884.7	3.4	141.5	4.7
G Comercio al por mayor y al por menor; reparación ...	2 166.7	38.3	2 018.6	37.4	148.1	51.1
H Hoteles y restaurantes	427.1	45.1	380.8	43.8	46.2	55.9
I Transporte, almacenamiento y comunicaciones	695.8	15.1	644.0	13.4	51.8	35.7
J Intermediación financiera	203.0	50.3	189.4	49.4	13.6	63.8
K Actividades inmobiliarias, empresariales y de alquiler	886.1	35.2	809.8	34.8	76.3	39.4
L Administración pública y defensa; planes de seguridad ...	775.3	42.4	768.7	42.2	6.5	65.6
M Enseñanza	821.9	77.0	806.8	77.0	15.1	80.5
N Servicios sociales y de salud	607.8	72.4	590.2	72.3	17.6	75.5
O Otras actividades de servicios comunitarios ...	592.4	43.6	546.7	42.0	45.7	63.0
P Hogares privados con servicio doméstico	918.8	97.6	797.0	97.7	121.8	97.0
Q Organizaciones y órganos extraterritoriales	2.2	7.5	2.2	7.5	-	.
X No pueden clasificarse según la actividad económica	266.8	64.0	25.0	44.6	107.9	76.2
Desempleados sin empleo anterior	.	.	.	.	134.0	57.8
Ocupación (CIUO-88)	2006 [1,2,3]		2006 [1,2,3]		2006 [1,2,3]	
	Encuesta de la fuerza de trabajo		Encuesta de la fuerza de trabajo		Encuesta de la fuerza de trabajo	
Total	11 089.7	43.4	10 040.5	42.4	1 037.9	53.4
1 Miembros del poder ejecutivo y de los cuerpos legislativos ...	19.0	23.1	19.0	23.1	-	.
2 Profesionales científicos e intelectuales	412.8	52.5	399.9	52.8	12.9	43.7
3 Técnicos y profesionales de nivel medio	1 412.2	54.7	1 359.5	54.6	52.7	58.7
4 Empleados de oficina	1 234.7	56.4	1 154.9	55.8	79.8	65.5
5 Trabajadores de los servicios y vendedores de comercios ...	2 140.0	48.5	1 946.4	47.2	193.7	60.9
6 Agricultores y trabajadores calificados agropecuarios ...	30.8	16.4	28.8	16.9	1.9	9.0
7 Oficiales, operarios y artesanos de artes mecánicas ...	1 621.6	13.3	1 465.1	12.7	156.5	19.0
8 Operadores de instalaciones y máquinas y montadores	909.3	19.3	859.9	18.6	49.4	30.1
9 Trabajadores no calificados	2 196.3	56.6	1 945.7	56.4	250.6	57.9
0 Fuerzas armadas	78.4	26.9	77.9	27.0	0.5	.
X No pueden clasificarse según la ocupación	1 034.7	41.3	783.4	33.6	105.9	75.9
Desempleados sin empleo anterior	.	.	.	.	134.0	57.8
Nivel de educación (CINE-97)	2006 [1,2,3]		2006 ★		2006 [1,2,3]	
	Encuesta de la fuerza de trabajo		Encuesta de la fuerza de trabajo		Encuesta de la fuerza de trabajo	
Total	11 089.7	43.4	10 040.5	42.4	1 049.2	53.4
X Sin escolaridad	71.4	43.7	66.1	41.4	5.3	72.3
0 Enseñanza preescolar	11.9	43.8	11.1	43.5	0.9	47.7
1 Enseñanza primaria o primer ciclo de la educación básica	687.0	36.4	618.1	36.5	68.9	34.9
2 Primer ciclo de enseñanza secundaria o segundo ciclo de ...	3 230.7	35.7	2 908.0	34.7	322.7	44.9
3 Segundo ciclo de enseñanza secundaria	3 729.6	42.3	3 291.2	40.2	438.5	58.3
5A Primer ciclo de la educación terciaria - teóricos [4]	1 107.6	63.5	1 028.6	63.0	79.0	70.7
6 Segundo ciclo de la enseñanza terciaria	2 168.3	49.1	2 041.0	48.6	127.3	57.3
? Nivel desconocido	83.1	34.6	76.4	34.0	6.7	42.0
Situación en el empleo (CISE-1993)	2006 [1,2,3]		2006 [1,2,3]		2006 ★	
	Encuesta de la fuerza de trabajo		Encuesta de la fuerza de trabajo		Encuesta de la fuerza de trabajo	
Total	11 089.7	43.4	10 040.5	42.4	1 049.2	53.4
1 Asalariados	8 275.1	45.6	7 608.3	44.8	666.8	54.0
2 Empleadores	416.9	25.8	414.3	25.8	2.6	12.3
3 Trabajadores por cuenta propia	2 044.8	34.6	1 905.9	35.0	138.9	29.1
5 Trabajadores familiares auxiliares	114.0	62.2	112.0	61.9	2.0	77.5
6 Inclasificables según la situación	238.8	66.1	-	.	238.8	66.1

Argentina

2. Población ('000), Tasa de actividad y Tasa de desempleo

Grupo de edad	Población 2006 [1,3,5] Encuesta de la fuerza de trabajo			Tasa de actividad 2006 [1,3,5] Encuesta de la fuerza de trabajo			Tasa de desempleo 2006 [1,2,3] Encuesta de la fuerza de trabajo		
	Total	Hombres	Mujeres	Total	Hombres	Mujeres	Total	Hombres	Mujeres
Total	24 007.4	11 388.5	12 618.9	46.2	55.1	38.1	9.5	7.8	11.7
15+	17 973.3	8 306.7	9 666.6	61.5	75.2	49.7	9.5	7.8	11.7
15-24	4 281.7	2 096.1	2 185.6	45.9	53.7	38.4	23.4	19.0	29.3
25-54	9 117.4	4 279.2	4 838.1	80.2	94.8	67.3	6.5	4.9	8.4
55+	4 574.2	1 931.4	2 642.8	38.8	55.2	26.8	6.3	6.7	5.7

3. Empleo remunerado ('000), Horas de trabajo (por semana) y Salarios

Actividad económica (CIIU-Rev.3)	Empleo remunerado 2006 [1,2,3] Encuesta de la fuerza de trabajo			Horas de trabajo 2005 [2,3,6] Encuesta de la fuerza de trabajo Horas efectivamente trabajadas / Asalariados			Salarios 2006 [7,8] Encuesta industrial/comercial Ganancias por hora / Obreros / Peso		
	Total	Hombres	Mujeres	Total	Hombres	Mujeres	Total	Hombres	Mujeres
Total	7 608.3	4 197.2	3 411.0	40.8	46.6	33.6	.	.	.
C-Q	.	.	.	40.9	46.7	33.7	.	.	.
A	46.7	35.7	11.0	.	.	.	.	.	.
B	8.3	7.5	0.8	.	.	.	.	.	.
C	38.9	33.3	5.6	55.1	57.2	48.8	.	.	.
D	1 106.5	807.6	298.9	45.3	47.7	38.8	9.72	.	.
E	43.5	37.5	5.9	44.1	44.6	39.2	.	.	.
F	548.2	521.3	27.0	44.2	44.3	39.4	.	.	.
G	1 114.5	728.4	386.0	45.3	48.4	38.9	.	.	.
H	283.0	162.8	120.2	43.7	46.8	40.0	.	.	.
I	516.6	443.0	73.5	52.3	54.4	41.8	.	.	.
J	176.7	86.4	90.3	42.5	43.8	40.8	.	.	.
K	505.6	310.8	194.8	42.3	46.6	35.9	.	.	.
L	768.7	444.4	324.3	41.8	45.2	36.9	.	.	.
M	743.1	170.5	572.6	30.1	35.1	28.4	.	.	.
N	488.9	127.8	361.0	37.5	46.6	34.3	.	.	.
O	405.8	249.3	156.5	38.5	42.2	33.6	.	.	.
P	789.3	17.0	772.4	27.2	27.9	27.2	.	.	.
Q	2.2	2.0	0.2	55.8	71.0	31.7	.	.	.
X	21.8	11.9	9.9	.	.	.	.	.	.

Proporción de mujeres entre los empleados remunerados en el sector no agrícola [1,2,3] (2006 - Encuesta de la fuerza de trabajo): **45.0%**

4. Lesiones profesionales y Huelgas y cierres patronales

Actividad económica (CIIU-Rev.2)	Tasas de lesiones mortales 2006 [9] Registros de seguros Por 100 000 trabajadores asegurados Lesiones declaradas			Tasas de lesiones no mortales 2006 [9] Registros de seguros Por 100 000 trabajadores asegurados Lesiones declaradas			Huelgas y cierres patronales		
	Total	Hombres	Mujeres	Total	Hombres	Mujeres	Huelgas y cierres patronales	Trabajadores implicados	Días no trabajados
Total	149.1	.	.	81	.	.	.	.	.
1	351.7	.	.	116	.	.	.	.	.
2	238.5	.	.	73	.	.	.	.	.
3	175.7	.	.	123	.	.	.	.	.
4	162.3	.	.	59	.	.	.	.	.
5	415.9	.	.	193	.	.	.	.	.
6	106.3	.	.	81	.	.	.	.	.
7	316.7	.	.	87	.	.	.	.	.
8	113.1	.	.	63	.	.	.	.	.
9	68.9	.	.	48	.	.	.	.	.

Actividad económica (CIIU-Rev.3)	Tasas de lesiones mortales			Tasas de lesiones no mortales			Huelgas y cierres patronales 2007 Registros administrativos y fuentes relacionadas		
	Total	Hombres	Mujeres	Total	Hombres	Mujeres	Huelgas y cierres patronales [10]	Trabajadores implicados [10]	Días no trabajados [11]
Total	.	.	.	.	.	.	843	1 119 272	8 215 064
A	.	.	.	.	.	.	4	816	4 638
B	.	.	.	.	.	.	0	0	0
C	.	.	.	.	.	.	28	16 013	164 743
D	.	.	.	.	.	.	71	39 656	210 344
E	.	.	.	.	.	.	27	4 635	17 551
F	.	.	.	.	.	.	17	56 931	13 554
G	.	.	.	.	.	.	16	13 869	28 433
H	.	.	.	.	.	.	2	6 533	13 132
I	.	.	.	.	.	.	108	29 302	295 668
J	.	.	.	.	.	.	16	24 762	161 111
K	.	.	.	.	.	.	5	2 443	2 761
L	.	.	.	.	.	.	295	237 124	1 671 141
M	.	.	.	.	.	.	128	563 084	4 108 827
N	.	.	.	.	.	.	147	116 289	1 475 355
O	.	.	.	.	.	.	25	7 815	47 546

Argentina

5. Índices de precios al consumidor (periodo de base: 2000=100)

Buenos Aires [12]	2002	2003	2004	2005	2006	2007
Índices generales	124.5	141.3	147.5	161.7	179.4	195.2
Índices de la alimentación incluyendo las bebidas no alcohólicas	132.0	157.3	165.1	183.3	205.5	228.5
Índices de la electricidad, gas y otros combustibles	103.1	112.9	113.8	118.6	115.9	.
Índices del vestido, incl. calzado	129.6	157.6	168.2	187.2	215.6	.
Índices del aquiler	98.1	96.2	96.9	106.2	124.9	.
Índices generales, excluyendo la vivienda	127.1	145.0	151.4	165.6	183.6	.

[1] 31 Urban agglomerations. [2] Persons aged 10 years and over. [3] Second semester. [4] Levels 5A-5B. [5] "De jure" population. [6] 28 urban agglomerations. [7] Local units with 10 or more workers. [8] Production and related workers. [9] Year ending in June of the year indicated. [10] Work stoppages beginning in the year indicated. [11] Computed on the basis of an eight-hour working day. [12] Metropolitan areas.

[1] 31 agglomérations urbaines. [2] Personnes âgées de 10 ans et plus. [3] Second semestre. [4] Niveaux 5A-5B. [5] Population "de jure". [6] 28 agglomérations urbaines. [7] Unités locales occupant 10 ouvriers et plus. [8] Ouvriers à la production et assimilés. [9] Année se terminant en juin de l'année indiquée. [10] Arrêts du travail commençant pendant l'année indiquée. [11] Calculées sur la base de journées de travail de huit heures. [12] Régions métropolitaines.

[1] 31 aglomerados úrbanos. [2] Personas de 10 años y más. [3] Segundo semestre. [4] Niveles 5A-5B [5] Población "de jure". [6] 28 aglomerados úrbanos. [7] Unidades locales con 10 y más obreros. [8] Obreros manufactureros y trabajadores asimilados. [9] Año que se termina en junio del año indicado. [10] Interrupciones del trabajo que empiezan en el año indicado. [11] Calculados en base a días de trabajo de ocho horas. [12] Areas metropolitanas.

Armenia

1. Economically active population, Employment and Unemployment ('000)

	Economically active population		Employment		Unemployment	
	Total	Women (%)	Total	Women (%)	Total	Women (%)
Age group	2001 [1,2] Population census		2007 [3] Official estimates		2007 [4,5] Employment office records	
Total	1 591.0	47.2	1 085.3	45.7	75.1	.
15-19	127.0	41.7	.	.	.	.
16-19	.	.	.	.	0.3	.
20-24	194.0	44.3	.	.	5.0	.
25-29	179.0	45.8	.	.	10.2	.
30-34	170.0	48.2	.	.	9.8	.
35-39	207.0	49.8	.	.	.	.
35-45	.	.	.	.	22.7	.
40-44	236.0	49.6	.	.	.	.
45-49	178.0	50.6	.	.	18.6	.
50+	.	.	.	.	8.5	.
50-54	123.0	49.6	.	.	.	.
55-59	53.0	45.3	.	.	.	.
60-64	63.0	39.7	.	.	.	.
65+	61.5	45.6	.	.	.	.
Economic activity (ISIC-Rev.3)			2006 [3] Official estimates			
Total	.	.	1 092.4	45.7	.	.
A Agriculture, Hunting and Forestry	.	.	504.3	45.6	.	.
B Fishing	.	.	0.2	.	.	.
C Mining and Quarrying	.	.	7.6	17.1	.	.
D Manufacturing	.	.	110.5	35.5	.	.
E Electricity, Gas and Water Supply	.	.	22.8	18.0	.	.
F Construction	.	.	29.7	8.8	.	.
G Wholesale and Retail Trade; Repair of Motor Vehicles ...	.	.	105.9	35.8	.	.
H Hotels and Restaurants	.	.	7.7	50.6	.	.
I Transport, Storage and Communications	.	.	48.6	31.3	.	.
J Financial Intermediation	.	.	6.6	53.0	.	.
K Real Estate, Renting and Business Activities	.	.	23.3	40.8	.	.
L Public Administration and Defence; Compulsory Social ...	.	.	34.9	44.1	.	.
M Education	.	.	100.8	76.3	.	.
N Health and Social Work	.	.	48.8	76.6	.	.
O Other Community, Social and Personal Service Activities	.	.	40.8	55.1	.	.
Occupation (ISCO-88)			2001 [1,2] Population census			
Total	.	.	1 020.8	44.0	.	.
1 Legislators, senior officials and managers	.	.	43.9	23.9	.	.
2 Professionals	.	.	124.4	64.3	.	.
3 Technicians and associate professionals	.	.	78.2	66.9	.	.
4 Clerks	.	.	21.6	72.8	.	.
5 Service workers and shop and market sales workers	.	.	67.2	34.9	.	.
6 Skilled agricultural and fishery workers	.	.	333.9	49.4	.	.
7 Craft and related trade workers	.	.	49.7	25.9	.	.
8 Plant and machine operators and assemblers	.	.	29.5	4.5	.	.
9 Elementary occupations	.	.	41.5	41.8	.	.
0 Armed forces	.	.	50.9	3.2	.	.
X Not classifiable by occupation	.	.	180.1	38.3	.	.
Education level (ISCED-97)					2007 [4,5] Employment office records	
Total	.	.	.	.	75.1	.
1-2	.	.	.	.	3.9	.
3-4	.	.	.	.	62.3	.
5-6	.	.	.	.	8.9	.
Status in employment (ICSE-1993)			2007 [3] Official estimates			
Total	.	.	1 085.3	.	.	.
1 Employees	.	.	539.3	.	.	.
3 Own-account workers	.	.	546.0	.	.	.

2. Population ('000), Activity rate and Unemployment rate

	Population 2006 [6] Official estimates			Activity rate 2001 [2,6] Population census			Unemployment rate 2007 [4] Official estimates		
Age group	Total	Men	Women	Total	Men	Women	Total	Men	Women
Total	3 221.1	1 555.8	1 665.3	.	.	.	7.1	3.8	10.8
15+	2 571.4	1 214.0	1 357.4	65.4	73.9	58.0	.	.	.
15-24	627.6	316.9	310.7	55.2	63.0	47.6	.	.	.
25-54	1 381.7	661.7	720.0	83.2	89.7	77.4	.	.	.
55+	562.1	235.4	326.7	33.0	44.6	24.8	.	.	.

Armenia

3. Paid employment ('000), Hours of work (weekly) and Wages

Economic activity (ISIC-Rev.3)	Paid employment 2006 [3] Official estimates			Hours of work 2006 [7] Labour force survey Hours actually worked / Total employment			Wages 2007 Labour-related establishment survey Earnings per month / Employees / Dram		
	Total	Men	Women	Total	Men	Women	Total	Men	Women
Total	533.5	.	.	.	47.1	43.0	77 776	.	.
A-B	.	.	.	34.6	35.4	33.6	57 799	.	.
C-Q	.	.	.	.	50.8	46.6	77 939	.	.
A	3.2	.	.	34.3	34.9	33.7	58 001	.	.
B	0.1	.	.	40.9	42.6	30.5	44 057	.	.
C	7.6	.	.	49.9	49.9	49.8	167 791	.	.
D	106.2	.	.	47.3	47.6	45.2	77 294	.	.
E	22.8	.	.	49.4	49.4	46.4	109 604	.	.
F	29.6	.	.	56.4	57.5	54.2	102 549	.	.
G	61.4	.	.	59.1	62.9	53.2	54 697	.	.
H	6.9	.	.	50.4	48.9	59.1	69 191	.	.
I	44.9	.	.	39.6	40.6	38.8	90 716	.	.
J	6.2	.	.	52.9	55.8	50.4	231 098	.	.
K	21.5	.	.	44.0	45.2	42.1	103 885	.	.
L	34.9	.	.	41.6	43.3	41.3	99 631	.	.
M	100.8	.	.	48.2	44.1	48.8	55 381	.	.
N	48.5	.	.	50.1	55.1	43.5	45 125	.	.
O	38.9	.	.	40.6	25.3	50.8	50 932	.	.
P	.	.	.	48.7	35.5	57.5	.	.	.
Q	.	.	.	39.1	42.0	37.2	.	.	.

4. Occupational injuries and Strikes and Lockouts

Statistics not available.

5. Consumer price indices (base period: 2000=100)

	2002	2003	2004	2005	2006	2007
General indices	104.2	109.2	116.3	117.0	121.1	126.5
Food index, including non-alcoholic beverages	107.0	114.4	125.8	126.8	132.0	140.9
Electricity, gas and other fuel indices	99.9	102.1	103.8	106.0	107.6	106.3
Clothing indices, including footwear	101.3	102.8	101.8	99.7	102.1	105.8
Rent indices	100.6	100.7	116.6	132.8	147.2	156.4
General index, excluding housing	104.3	109.2	116.2	116.9	120.8	126.2

[1] Persons aged 15 years and over. [2] Oct. [3] Excl. armed forces. [4] Persons aged 16 to 63 years. [5] Dec. [6] "De jure" population. [7] Employed persons and at work.

[1] Personnes âgées de 15 ans et plus. [2] Oct. [3] Non compris les forces armées. [4] Personnes âgées de 16 à 63 ans. [5] Déc. [6] Population "de jure". [7] Personnes pourvues d'un emploi et au travail

[1] Personas de 15 años y más. [2] Oct. [3] Excl. las fuerzas armadas. [4] Personas de 16 a 63 años de edad. [5] Dic. [6] Población "de jure". [7] Personas con empleo y trabajando.

Aruba

1. Economically active population, Employment and Unemployment ('000)

	Economically active population		Employment		Unemployment	
	Total	Women (%)	Total	Women (%)	Total	Women (%)
Age group	1991 [1,2] Population census		1997 [3] Labour force survey		1997 [3] Labour force survey	
Total	31.110	42.5	41.501	43.4	3.339	49.3
14-14	0.009	22.2	.	.	.	.
15-19	0.925	46.7	.	.	0.422	61.4
20-24	3.354	46.2	.	.	0.603	53.4
25-29	4.881	46.1	.	.	0.431	42.5
30-34	5.641	44.8	.	.	0.534	55.1
35-39	4.939	44.8	.	.	0.420	37.1
40-44	3.954	41.9	.	.	0.443	40.4
45-49	2.933	39.3	.	.	0.226	58.8
50-54	2.144	36.0	.	.	0.145	51.0
55-59	1.310	29.5	.	.	0.059	44.1
60-64	0.525	25.7	.	.	.	.
60-69	.	.	.	.	0.056	35.7
65+	0.405	24.0	.	.	.	.
?	0.090	52.2	.	.	.	.

Economic activity (ISIC-Rev.3)	1997 ★ Labour force survey		1997 [3] Labour force survey		1997 [3] Labour force survey	
Total	44.840	.	41.501	43.4	3.339	.
A Agriculture, Hunting and Forestry	0.212	.	0.196	25.0	0.016	.
B Fishing	-	.	-	.	-	.
C Mining and Quarrying	-	.	-	.	-	.
D Manufacturing	2.749	.	2.585	18.9	0.164	.
E Electricity, Gas and Water Supply	0.809	.	0.776	8.1	0.033	.
F Construction	3.803	.	3.409	5.9	0.394	.
G Wholesale and Retail Trade; Repair of Motor Vehicles ...	7.747	.	7.238	50.7	0.509	.
H Hotels and Restaurants	7.544	.	7.019	47.9	0.525	.
I Transport, Storage and Communications	3.457	.	3.375	31.0	0.082	.
J Financial Intermediation	1.540	.	1.507	65.1	0.033	.
K Real Estate, Renting and Business Activities	3.452	.	3.222	42.5	0.230	.
L Public Administration and Defence; Compulsory Social ...	4.420	.	4.338	37.7	0.082	.
M Education	1.347	.	1.298	63.6	0.049	.
N Health and Social Work	2.127	.	2.061	79.4	0.066	.
O Other Community, Social and Personal Service Activities	3.278	.	3.032	44.5	0.246	.
P Households with Employed Persons	1.384	.	1.302	96.2	0.082	.
Q Extra-Territorial Organizations and Bodies	0.043	.	0.010	100.0	0.033	.
X Not classifiable by economic activity	0.927	.	0.133	58.6	0.794	.

Occupation (ISCO-88)	1997 ★ Labour force survey		1997 [3] Labour force survey		1997 [3] Labour force survey	
Total	44.840	.	41.501	43.4	3.339	.
1 Legislators, senior officials and managers	4.235	.	4.087	33.4	0.148	.
2 Professionals	2.800	.	2.310	34.2	0.490	.
3 Technicians and associate professionals	4.517	.	4.402	45.4	0.115	.
4 Clerks	9.427	.	8.852	64.8	0.575	.
5 Service workers and shop and market sales workers	9.223	.	8.550	52.6	0.673	.
6 Skilled agricultural and fishery workers	0.307	.	0.291	15.5	0.016	.
7 Craft and related trade workers	4.822	.	4.280	7.0	0.542	.
8 Plant and machine operators and assemblers	2.262	.	2.213	5.2	0.049	.
9 Elementary occupations	6.650	.	6.272	50.3	0.378	.
0 Armed forces	.	.	0.212	.	.	.
X Not classifiable by occupation	0.385	.	0.032	50.0	0.353	.

Education level (ISCED-76)					1997 [3] Labour force survey	
Total	.	.	.	.	3.339	.
X-1	.	.	.	.	1.703	.
2 Second level, first stage	.	.	.	.	1.277	.
3 Second level, second stage	.	.	.	.	0.164	.
5 Third level, first stage, leading to an award not equivalent ...	.	.	.	.	0.049	.
6 Third level, first stage, leading to a first university degree ...	.	.	.	.	0.082	.
7 Third level, second stage	.	.	.	.	0.016	.
9 Education not definable by level	.	.	.	.	0.048	.

Status in employment (ICSE-1993)	1991 [1,2] Population census		1997 [3] Labour force survey			
Total	31.110	42.5	41.501	43.4	.	.
1 Employees	26.879	43.9	40.160	.	.	.
2 Employers	1.107	26.0	1.075	.	.	.
3 Own-account workers	1.058	19.8	.	.	.	.
5 Contributing family workers	0.090	80.0	0.220	.	.	.
6 Not classifiable by status	0.085	34.1	0.046	.	.	.

2. Population ('000), Activity rate and Unemployment rate

	Population			Activity rate			Unemployment rate		
Age group	1991 [2] Population census			1991 [2] Population census			1991 [1,2] Population census		
	Total	Men	Women	Total	Men	Women	Total	Men	Women
Total	.	.	.	.	.	.	6.1	5.9	6.3
15+	50.283	24.310	25.973	61.7	73.4	50.7	.	.	.
15-24	8.913	4.557	4.356	48.0	50.4	45.5	.	.	.
25-54	31.470	15.278	16.192	77.8	91.1	65.3	.	.	.
55+	9.900	4.475	5.425	22.6	36.2	11.4	.	.	.

Aruba

3. Paid employment ('000), Hours of work (weekly) and Wages

Statistics not available.

4. Occupational injuries and Strikes and Lockouts

Economic activity (ISIC-Rev.3)	Rates of fatal injuries			Rates of non-fatal injuries			Strikes and lockouts 2007 Administrative records and related sources		
	Total	Men	Women	Total	Men	Women	Strikes and lockouts	Workers involved [4]	Days not worked [5]
Total	.	.	.	.	.	.	3	222	52
D	.	.	.	.	.	.	0	.	0
E	.	.	.	.	.	.	0	0	0
F	.	.	.	.	.	.	0	0	0
G	.	.	.	.	.	.	1	15	42
H	.	.	.	.	.	.	0	0	0
I	.	.	.	.	.	.	0	0	0
J	.	.	.	.	.	.	0	0	0
K	.	.	.	.	.	.	1	7	4
N	.	.	.	.	.	.	1	200	6
X	.	.	.	.	.	.	0	0	0

5. Consumer price indices (base period: 2000=100)

	2002	2003	2004	2005	2006	2007
General indices	106.3	110.2	113.0	116.8	121.0	128.3
Food index, including non-alcoholic beverages	106.7	110.1	114.4			

[1] Persons aged 14 years and over. [2] Oct. [3] Persons aged 15 years and over. [4] Excl. workers indirectly involved. [5] Computed on the basis of an eight-hour working day.

[1] Personnes âgées de 14 ans et plus. [2] Oct. [3] Personnes âgées de 15 ans et plus. [4] Non compris les travailleurs indirectement impliqués. [5] Calculées sur la base de journées de travail de huit heures.

[1] Personas de 14 años y más. [2] Oct. [3] Personas de 15 años y más. [4] Excl. los trabajadores indirectamente implicados. [5] Calculados en base a días de trabajo de ocho horas.

Australia

1. Economically active population, Employment and Unemployment ('000)

	Economically active population		Employment		Unemployment	
	Total	Women (%)	Total	Women (%)	Total	Women (%)
Age group	2007 [1,2,3] Labour force survey		2007 ★ Labour force survey		2007 [2,3] Labour force survey	
Total	10 927.6	45.1	10 444.0	44.9	483.6	49.8
15-19	834.6	50.1	715.8	50.2	118.8	49.7
20-24	1 199.0	47.0	1 123.7	47.1	75.3	45.6
25-29	1 187.2	44.5	1 134.6	44.4	52.6	46.8
30-34	1 174.8	43.2	1 129.6	42.8	45.2	54.0
35-39	1 269.4	44.4	1 228.2	44.1	41.2	51.2
40-44	1 259.3	46.1	1 216.9	45.6	42.4	59.9
45-49	1 290.2	47.1	1 255.0	46.8	35.2	59.1
50-54	1 098.3	46.6	1 065.5	46.6	32.8	46.3
55-59	877.1	43.8	852.8	43.9	24.3	42.8
60-64	492.1	38.5	478.7	38.6	13.4	34.3
65-69	166.3	32.8	164.2	32.7	2.1	38.1
70+	79.3	28.4	78.9	28.5	0.4	.

Economic activity (ISIC-Rev.3)	2007 [1,2,3] Labour force survey		2007 [1,2,3] Labour force survey		2007 [2,3] Labour force survey	
Total	10 927.6	45.1	10 444.1	44.9	483.5	49.5
A Agriculture, Hunting and Forestry	357.9	31.5	345.2	31.4	12.7	34.6
B Fishing	12.4	15.4	11.6	16.4	0.9	11.1
C Mining and Quarrying	103.6	11.6	102.0	11.7	1.5	6.7
D Manufacturing	1 114.5	25.7	1 077.5	25.8	37.1	25.3
E Electricity, Gas and Water Supply	87.5	20.6	86.1	20.4	1.4	35.7
F Construction	971.5	11.7	944.0	11.7	27.4	9.9
G Wholesale and Retail Trade; Repair of Motor Vehicles ...	2 049.1	48.2	1 982.4	48.1	66.7	50.7
H Hotels and Restaurants	542.5	56.1	516.5	55.8	26.0	62.7
I Transport, Storage and Communications	695.8	26.7	679.1	26.6	16.7	30.5
J Financial Intermediation	409.1	51.6	401.5	51.5	7.6	56.6
K Real Estate, Renting and Business Activities	1 309.9	44.8	1 278.6	44.7	31.3	50.2
L Public Administration and Defence; Compulsory Social ...	617.1	47.1	608.0	47.1	9.1	48.4
M Education	751.6	67.4	740.7	67.5	11.0	60.0
N Health and Social Work	1 111.4	79.2	1 091.8	79.2	19.6	78.1
O Other Community, Social and Personal Service Activities	559.6	55.5	544.7	55.4	14.9	59.1
P Households with Employed Persons	2.0	75.8	1.8	77.8	0.1	100.0
Q Extra-Territorial Organizations and Bodies	1.3	57.4	1.0	60.0	0.2	100.0
X Not classifiable by economic activity	32.6	31.3	31.8	31.4	91.7	59.2
Unemployed seeking their first job	.	.	.	.	107.5	53.3

Occupation (ISCO-88)	2007 [1,2,3] Labour force survey		2007 [1,2,3] Labour force survey		2007 [2,3] Labour force survey	
Total	10 927.6	45.1	10 444.4	44.9	483.6	49.5
1 Legislators, senior officials and managers	1 357.7	37.1	1 334.5	37.1	23.2	42.2
2 Professionals	2 004.1	53.1	1 977.3	53.0	26.9	60.2
3 Technicians and associate professionals	1 424.0	61.7	1 403.3	61.6	20.6	64.6
4 Clerks	1 377.1	66.8	1 334.4	67.0	42.8	63.1
5 Service workers and shop and market sales workers	1 464.4	66.1	1 406.5	66.1	58.0	65.9
6 Skilled agricultural and fishery workers	294.5	21.5	287.3	21.6	7.2	16.7
7 Craft and related trade workers	1 269.4	5.2	1 233.4	5.2	36.0	7.5
8 Plant and machine operators and assemblers	804.6	8.8	777.3	8.6	27.5	12.7
9 Elementary occupations	649.7	39.7	609.4	39.8	40.3	38.5
X Not classifiable by occupation	83.6	34.9	81.0	35.4	93.6	58.3
Unemployed seeking their first job	.	.	.	.	107.5	53.3

Education level (ISCED-97)	2007 [1,3,4] Labour force survey		2007 ★ Labour force survey		2007 [3,4] Labour force survey	
Total	10 580.1	45.4	10 121.0	45.2	459.1	49.2
1 Primary education or first stage of basic education [5]	608.4	39.9	542.8	39.1	65.6	46.3
2 Lower secondary or second stage of basic education	2 385.0	49.3	2 230.3	49.3	154.7	49.1
3 Upper secondary education	3 810.2	37.9	3 661.6	37.5	148.6	46.6
4 Post-secondary non-tertiary education	319.4	54.9	311.3	55.3	8.1	38.3
5A First stage of tertiary education - theoretically based [6]	2 480.8	50.2	2 428.5	50.1	52.3	55.8
5B First stage of tertiary education - practically oriented	976.2	53.2	946.4	53.0	29.8	60.1

Status in employment (ICSE-1993)			2007 [1,2,3] Labour force survey			
Total	.	.	10 444.1	44.9	.	.
1 Employees	.	.	9 185.9	46.5	.	.
2 Employers	.	.	284.0	34.2	.	.
3 Own-account workers	.	.	945.3	32.7	.	.
5 Contributing family workers	.	.	28.8	58.0	.	.

2. Population ('000), Activity rate and Unemployment rate

	Population 2007 [1,7] Labour force survey			Activity rate 2007 [1,7] Labour force survey			Unemployment rate 2007 [2,3] Labour force survey		
Age group	Total	Men	Women	Total	Men	Women	Total	Men	Women
Total	21 017.2	10 451.7	10 565.5	52.0	57.4	46.7	4.4	4.1	4.8
15+	16 943.6	8 361.1	8 582.5	64.5	71.7	57.5	4.4	4.1	.
15-24	2 931.8	1 499.1	1 432.6	69.4	70.2	68.5	9.5	9.7	9.5
25-54	8 919.8	4 446.1	4 473.6	81.6	89.5	73.8	3.4	3.0	4.0
55+	5 092.1	2 415.8	2 676.3	31.7	39.9	24.3	2.5	2.6	.

Australia

3. Paid employment ('000), Hours of work (weekly) and Wages

Economic activity (ISIC-Rev.3)	Paid employment 2007 [1,2,3] Labour force survey Total	Men	Women	Hours of work 2007 [3,8] Labour force survey Hours actually worked / Employees Total	Men	Women	Wages 2006 [4,9] Labour-related establishment survey Earnings per hour / Employees / Dollar Total	Men	Women
Total	9 186.1	4 915.5	4 270.6	34.6	39.0	29.2	.	.	.
A-B	.	.	.	41.6	47.1	29.2	.	.	.
C-Q	.	.	.	.	.	.	25.65	27.10	23.29
A	169.7	119.1	50.7	41.7	47.4	29.3	.	.	.
B	8.3	7.1	1.2	36.7	38.7	26.5	.	.	.
C	100.5	88.8	11.8	43.5	44.3	37.9	34.98	35.84	27.09
D	1 007.0	751.6	255.1	37.9	39.9	32.3	25.36	26.11	23.45
E	84.5	67.2	17.4	38.7	39.6	34.9	31.57	33.17	26.93
F	676.5	592.7	83.8	38.7	40.4	25.4	24.33	24.89	20.88
G	1 789.5	911.7	877.8	31.8	36.9	26.3	22.55	22.84	20.56
H	476.8	209.4	267.3	31.3	36.1	27.4	19.22	19.16	19.16
I	599.3	432.7	166.6	38.4	40.8	31.7	26.80	28.53	23.23
J	383.3	181.5	201.9	36.1	40.4	32.1	29.48	34.52	25.11
K	1 084.8	595.3	489.6	35.5	39.6	30.5	26.77	29.42	24.17
L	604.5	319.0	285.5	34.2	36.7	31.5	29.51	31.04	27.84
M	715.4	229.8	485.5	33.1	35.6	31.4	29.30	31.03	28.23
N	1 031.5	206.2	825.4	30.0	35.6	28.5	24.42	29.44	23.25
O	422.4	182.1	240.3	30.8	34.8	27.6	24.68	25.80	23.29
P	1.8	0.5	1.4	23.9	28.6	22.4	.	.	.
Q	1.0	0.5	0.6	35.8	37.0	34.9	.	.	.
X	29.5	20.7	8.8	41.4	44.3	35.0	.	.	.

Share of women in wage employment in the non-agricultural sector [1,2,3] (2007 - Labour force survey): **46.9%**

4. Occupational injuries and Strikes and Lockouts

Economic activity (ISIC-Rev.3)	Rates of fatal injuries 2006 [10] Insurance records Per 100,000 employees Compensated injuries Total	Men	Women	Rates of non-fatal injuries 2006 [10] Insurance records Per 100,000 employees Compensated injuries Total	Men	Women	Strikes and lockouts 2007 [11,12] Special data collection Strikes and lockouts	Workers involved	Days not worked
Total	2	4	0	1 070	1 412	680	135	36 000	49 700
A-B	12	16	2	2 100	2 350	1 460	.	600	300
C	10	12	0	1 460	1 660	330	5	700	3 500
D	3	4	0	1 080	1 420	100	48	5 500	15 000
E	6	8	0	490	580	160	3	700	300
F	5	5	0	1 840	2 050	340	29	4 700	6 800
G	1	1	0	810	1 090	570	.	.	.
G-H	.	.	.	.	.	.	3	100	700
H	1	2	0	1 050	1 230	930	.	.	.
I	7	9	1	1 560	1 910	660	22	2 100	1 900
J	0	0	0	210	110	280	.	.	.
J-K	.	.	.	.	.	.	3	0	300
K	2	3	1	650	860	400	.	.	.
L	1	1	0	660	850	460	.	200	200
M	0	1	0	570	660	530	6	17 300	17 100
N	.	.	.	.	.	.	10 [13]	3 800 [13]	3 300 [13]
N-O	1	2	0	1 050	1 300	940	.	.	.
O	.	.	.	.	.	.	8	400	300
X	.	.	.	.	.	.	0	.	.

5. Consumer price indices (base period: 2000=100)

	2002	2003	2004	2005	2006	2007
General indices	107.6	110.5	113.1	116.1	120.2	123.1
Food index, including non-alcoholic beverages	110.4	114.4	117.1	120.0	129.2	132.3
Electricity, gas and other fuel indices [14]	110.0	116.0	119.7	124.2	129.4	135.4
Clothing indices, including footwear	103.6	103.5	102.4	100.7	98.9	99.8
Rent indices	105.7	107.7	110.4	112.9	116.5	122.9
General index, excluding housing	107.4	109.9	112.1	114.7	118.8	121.1

[1] Excl. armed forces. [2] Feb., May, Aug. and Nov. [3] Persons aged 15 years and over. [4] May. [5] Levels 0-1. [6] Levels 5A and 6. [7] "De jure" population. [8] Civilian labour force employed. [9] Full-time adult non-managerial employees. [10] Financial year ending in year indicated; excl. Victoria and Australian Capital Territory. [11] Excl. work stoppages in which less than 10 workdays not worked. [12] Figures rounded to nearest 100. [13] Incl. community services. [14] Incl. water and sewerage.

Austria

1. Economically active population, Employment and Unemployment ('000)

	Economically active population		Employment		Unemployment	
	Total	Women (%)	Total	Women (%)	Total	Women (%)
Age group	2007 [1,2] Labour force survey		2007 ★ Labour force survey		2007 [2] Labour force survey	
Total	4 213.5	45.5	4 027.9	45.2	185.6	51.6
15-19	219.4	44.8	194.8	44.0	24.6	51.6
20-24	382.6	48.2	355.0	48.2	27.6	47.5
25-29	450.7	45.9	426.4	45.6	24.3	50.6
30-34	478.5	45.3	458.9	44.9	19.6	55.6
35-39	600.9	46.4	578.2	45.8	22.7	62.6
40-44	641.6	46.6	620.5	46.4	21.1	53.6
45-49	567.3	46.4	547.7	46.2	19.6	52.0
50-54	440.3	47.0	425.4	47.0	14.9	45.0
55-59	282.5	39.5	272.8	39.4	9.7	42.3
60+	149.8	33.2	148.3	33.2	1.5	26.7
Economic activity (ISIC-Rev.3)	2007 [1,2] Labour force survey		2007 [1,2] Labour force survey		2007 [2] Labour force survey	
Total	4 213.5	45.5	4 027.9	45.2	185.6	51.6
A Agriculture, Hunting and Forestry	233.3	46.5	230.7	46.5	2.6	50.0
B Fishing	0.6	45.9	0.6	50.0	.	.
C Mining and Quarrying	9.0	15.0	8.8	14.8	0.1	100.0
D Manufacturing	756.5	26.1	730.5	25.7	26.0	38.1
E Electricity, Gas and Water Supply	30.4	19.7	30.1	19.9	0.3	.
F Construction	345.9	12.2	329.1	12.2	16.8	11.3
G Wholesale and Retail Trade; Repair of Motor Vehicles ...	677.9	53.0	645.6	52.7	32.3	57.3
H Hotels and Restaurants	275.9	64.1	258.6	64.3	17.2	61.6
I Transport, Storage and Communications	251.8	27.5	243.2	27.4	8.6	31.4
J Financial Intermediation	137.6	49.4	135.1	48.9	2.5	68.0
K Real Estate, Renting and Business Activities	380.4	49.1	363.3	48.5	17.1	60.2
L Public Administration and Defence; Compulsory Social ...	280.6	43.7	275.4	43.6	5.1	51.0
M Education	215.2	71.6	211.6	71.5	3.5	80.0
N Health and Social Work	354.9	76.6	347.3	76.5	7.6	77.6
O Other Community, Social and Personal Service Activities	212.3	56.0	202.9	55.7	9.4	60.6
P Households with Employed Persons	9.0	94.0	8.8	93.2	0.3	100.0
Q Extra-Territorial Organizations and Bodies	6.3	45.1	6.3	46.0	-	.
X Not classifiable by economic activity	36.2	59.8	.	.	7.4	71.6
Unemployed seeking their first job	.	.	.	.	28.7	56.8
Occupation (ISCO-88)	2007 [1,2] Labour force survey		2007 [1,2] Labour force survey		2007 [2] Labour force survey	
Total	4 213.5	45.5	4 027.9	45.2	185.6	51.6
1 Legislators, senior officials and managers	291.7	26.8	286.7	26.7	5.0	30.0
2 Professionals	406.5	45.1	399.0	44.9	7.4	54.1
3 Technicians and associate professionals	816.3	49.3	796.5	49.3	19.8	49.5
4 Clerks	533.0	69.1	512.1	69.0	20.9	72.2
5 Service workers and shop and market sales workers	582.4	71.0	554.5	71.0	27.9	69.9
6 Skilled agricultural and fishery workers	213.3	47.4	211.2	47.3	2.1	57.1
7 Craft and related trade workers	573.4	7.3	552.4	7.2	21.0	10.5
8 Plant and machine operators and assemblers	259.2	13.5	250.4	13.5	8.9	15.7
9 Elementary occupations	489.7	55.1	453.6	55.2	36.1	54.0
0 Armed forces	11.9	2.8	11.5	2.6	0.4	.
X Not classifiable by occupation	36.2	59.8	.	.	7.4	71.6
Unemployed seeking their first job	.	.	.	.	28.7	56.8
Education level (ISCED-97)	2007 [1,2] Labour force survey		2007 ★ Labour force survey		2007 [2] Labour force survey	
Total	4 213.5	45.5	4 027.9	45.2	185.6	51.6
0 Pre-primary education [3]	795.5	54.0	725.1	54.1	70.4	53.7
3 Upper secondary education	2 206.5	42.4	2 121.9	42.2	84.6	48.5
4 Post-secondary non-tertiary education	440.1	53.8	428.0	53.6	12.1	60.3
5A First stage of tertiary education - theoretically based [4]	446.5	42.2	433.3	41.9	13.2	53.8
5B First stage of tertiary education - practically oriented	297.3	37.0	292.0	36.8	5.3	49.1
Status in employment (ICSE-1993)	2007 [1,2] Labour force survey		2007 [1,2] Labour force survey		2007 ★ Labour force survey	
Total	4 213.5	45.5	4 027.9	45.2	185.6	51.6
1 Employees	3 629.4	46.5	3 450.2	46.3	179.2	52.0
2 Employers	209.4	25.7	207.6	25.5	1.8	51.7
3 Own-account workers	277.9	42.7	273.8	42.8	4.1	35.8
5 Contributing family workers	96.4	55.2	96.3	55.1	0.1	127.3
6 Not classifiable by status	0.3	58.8	.	.	.	.

2. Population ('000), Activity rate and Unemployment rate

	Population			Activity rate			Unemployment rate		
Age group	2007 [1,5] Labour force survey			2007 [1,5] Labour force survey			2007 [2] Labour force survey		
	Total	Men	Women	Total	Men	Women	Total	Men	Women
Total	8 190.7	3 984.8	4 206.0	51.4	57.7	45.5	4.4	3.9	5.0
15+	6 905.1	3 325.9	3 579.1	61.0	69.1	53.5	4.4	3.9	5.0
15-24	990.2	491.7	498.5	60.8	65.0	56.7	8.7	8.3	9.1
25-54	3 638.2	1 823.3	1 814.9	87.4	93.7	81.1	3.8	3.3	4.5
55+	2 276.7	1 011.0	1 265.7	19.0	26.8	12.7	2.6	2.5	2.8

Austria

3. Paid employment ('000), Hours of work (weekly) and Wages

Economic activity (ISIC-Rev.3)	Paid employment 2007 [1,2] Labour force survey			Hours of work 2007 Labour force survey Hours actually worked / Employees			Wages 2007 [6] Industrial/commercial survey Earnings per hour / Employees / Euro		
	Total	Men	Women	Total	Men	Women	Total	Men	Women
Total	3 450.2	1 853.9	1 596.2	34.6	38.6	29.5	.	.	.
A-B	.	.	.	36.0	38.8	31.9	.	.	.
C-Q	.	.	.	34.0	38.1	28.8	.	.	.
A	38.2	22.4	15.8	36.0	38.7	31.9	.	.	.
B	0.2	0.2	0.0	43.4	44.2	40.0	.	.	.
C	8.5	7.3	1.1	37.0	37.9	32.2	.	.	.
C-D	.	.	.	.	.	.	15.25	.	.
C-F	.	.	.	.	.	.	15.05	.	.
D	688.7	510.2	178.5	35.6	37.4	30.1	.	.	.
E	29.5	23.6	5.9	34.3	35.3	30.4	20.40	.	.
F	297.9	259.7	38.2	36.1	37.2	27.7	13.69	.	.
G	576.0	258.4	317.7	33.2	38.4	28.4	.	.	.
H	202.1	62.4	139.7	37.4	43.6	33.9	.	.	.
I	227.2	163.9	63.4	37.6	40.0	31.0	.	.	.
J	129.0	63.3	65.7	33.6	38.2	28.6	.	.	.
K	283.5	129.6	154.0	33.1	38.7	27.0	.	.	.
L	275.4	155.3	120.1	34.6	38.7	29.1	.	.	.
M	203.4	57.3	146.1	27.9	32.7	26.0	.	.	.
N	313.2	66.0	247.1	30.5	37.6	28.3	.	.	.
O	163.3	70.3	93.0	32.0	37.1	27.9	.	.	.
P	7.5	0.5	7.0	20.1	26.0	19.7	.	.	.
Q	6.3	3.5	2.9	37.0	41.2	31.9	.	.	.

Share of women in wage employment in the non-agricultural sector [1,2] (2007 - Labour force survey): **46.3%**

4. Occupational injuries and Strikes and Lockouts

Economic activity (ISIC-Rev.3)	Rates of fatal injuries 2006 Insurance records Per 100,000 workers insured Reported injuries			Rates of non-fatal injuries 2006 Insurance records Per 100,000 workers insured Reported injuries			Strikes and lockouts 2006 Records of employers'/workers' organizations		
	Total	Men	Women	Total	Men	Women	Strikes and lockouts	Workers involved [7]	Days not worked [8]
Total	3.9	6.8	0.4	3 925	5 611	1 855	0	0	0
A	26.0	41.1	0.0	5 811	7 858	2 286	.	.	.
B	0.0	0.0	0.0	3 077	4 348	0	.	.	.
C	7.9	9.1	0.0	3 004	3 397	417	.	.	.
D	2.8	3.1	2.4	4 908	5 988	2 642	.	.	.
E	4.0	4.9	0.0	3 308	3 925	392	.	.	.
F	17.1	19.1	3.3	9 570	10 829	927	.	.	.
G	1.8	3.2	0.4	3 135	4 206	2 136	.	.	.
H	0.0	0.0	0.0	2 125	2 756	1 713	.	.	.
I	11.8	16.9	0.0	4 522	5 754	1 644	.	.	.
J	0.9	1.8	0.0	463	400	527	.	.	.
K	2.1	4.1	0.0	3 152	4 878	1 298	.	.	.
L	1.3	3.7	0.0	1 569	3 055	720	.	.	.
M	0.0	0.0	0.0	2 665	2 092	2 944	.	.	.
N	0.0	0.0	0.0	4 323	5 113	4 086	.	.	.
O	3.4	8.8	0.0	2 830	5 345	1 274	.	.	.
P	0.0	0.0	0.0	1 504	2 821	1 364	.	.	.
Q	0.0	0.0	0.0	767	1 046	500	.	.	.

5. Consumer price indices (base period: 2000=100)

	2002	2003	2004	2005	2006	2007
General indices	104.5	105.9	108.1	110.6	112.3	114.7
Food index, including non-alcoholic beverages	105.2	107.3	109.5	111.0	112.5 [9]	117.1
Electricity, gas and other fuel indices	98.0	99.0	105.3	115.1	122.4	127.2
Clothing indices, including footwear	102.7	103.9	104.4	104.3	104.0	106.2
Rent indices [10]	104.6	109.1	113.0	116.8	119.4	121.7
General index, excluding housing	104.5	105.8	107.9	110.4	111.9	114.4

[1] Excl. conscripts on compulsory military service. [2] Persons aged 15 years and over. [3] Levels 0-2. [4] Levels 5A and 6. [5] "De jure" population. [6] Per hour paid. [7] Excl. workers indirectly involved. [8] Computed on the basis of an eight-hour working day. [9] Series replacing former series; prior to 2006: incl. alcoholic beverages. [10] Housing.

[1] Non compris conscrits ceux du contingent. [2] Personnes âgées de 15 ans et plus. [3] Niveaux 0-2. [4] Niveaux 5A et 6. [5] Population "de jure". [6] Par heure rémunérée. [7] Non compris les travailleurs indirectement impliqués. [8] Calculées sur la base de journées de travail de huit heures. [9] Série remplaçant la précédente; avant 2006: y compris les boissons alcoolisées. [10] Logement.

[1] Excl. los conscriptos del servicio obligatorio. [2] Personas de 15 años y más. [3] Niveles 0-2. [4] Niveles 5A y 6. [5] Población "de jure". [6] Por hora pagada. [7] Excl. los trabajadores indirectamente implicados. [8] Calculados en base a días de trabajo de ocho horas. [9] Serie base que substituye a la anterior; antes d 2006: incl. las bebidas alcohólicas. [10] Vivienda.

Azerbaijan

1. Economically active population, Employment and Unemployment ('000)

	Economically active population		Employment		Unemployment	
	Total	Women (%)	Total	Women (%)	Total	Women (%)
Age group	2007 [1,2] Labour force survey		2007 ★ Labour force survey		2007 [2] Labour force survey	
Total	4 295.1	49.0	4 014.0	49.7	281.1	39.6
15-19	138.9	61.3	117.1	67.3	21.8	29.4
20-24	507.8	51.3	438.8	52.6	69.0	43.0
25-29	560.4	50.2	508.3	50.3	52.1	48.8
30-34	541.4	51.0	505.9	51.5	35.5	43.1
35-39	576.6	54.4	542.0	54.4	34.6	53.8
40-44	660.5	51.1	638.1	52.0	22.4	25.0
45-49	635.4	47.3	617.2	47.7	18.2	33.0
50-54	414.9	42.0	396.4	43.0	18.5	22.2
55-59	190.4	30.9	182.4	32.3	8.0	.
60-64	36.0	24.7	35.1	25.4	0.9	.
65+	32.8	25.9	32.8	25.9	-	.
Economic activity (ISIC-Rev.3)			2007 [1,2] Labour force survey			
Total	.	.	4 014.0	49.7	.	.
A Agriculture, Hunting and Forestry	.	.	1 543.0	54.1	.	.
B Fishing	.	.	4.4	61.4	.	.
C Mining and Quarrying	.	.	44.1	11.8	.	.
D Manufacturing	.	.	194.0	27.0	.	.
E Electricity, Gas and Water Supply	.	.	40.0	15.3	.	.
F Construction	.	.	228.7	5.2	.	.
G Wholesale and Retail Trade; Repair of Motor Vehicles ...	.	.	659.5	71.7	.	.
H Hotels and Restaurants	.	.	27.1	21.0	.	.
I Transport, Storage and Communications	.	.	203.5	12.3	.	.
J Financial Intermediation	.	.	17.8	47.2	.	.
K Real Estate, Renting and Business Activities	.	.	129.7	58.1	.	.
L Public Administration and Defence; Compulsory Social ...	.	.	275.5	39.2	.	.
M Education	.	.	334.3	64.0	.	.
N Health and Social Work	.	.	180.7	71.5	.	.
O Other Community, Social and Personal Service Activities	.	.	131.1	32.8	.	.
P Households with Employed Persons	.	.	-	.	.	.
Q Extra-Territorial Organizations and Bodies	.	.	0.7	.	.	.
Occupation (ISCO-88)			2007 [1,2] Labour force survey		2007 [2,3] Employment office records	
Total	.	.	4 014.0	49.7	50.6	50.0
1 Legislators, senior officials and managers	.	.	52.0	5.2	1.3	30.8
2 Professionals	.	.	667.1	54.2	7.1	52.1
3 Technicians and associate professionals	.	.	216.3	47.7	9.1	56.0
4 Clerks	.	.	89.1	43.8	6.0	51.7
5 Service workers and shop and market sales workers	.	.	284.9	29.6	6.3	58.7
6 Skilled agricultural and fishery workers	.	.	756.7	33.5	4.5	46.7
7 Craft and related trade workers	.	.	300.3	9.7	5.1	56.9
8 Plant and machine operators and assemblers	.	.	215.8	12.9	3.4	41.2
9 Elementary occupations	.	.	1 425.2	76.6	4.9	59.2
0 Armed forces	.	.	6.7	.	2.9	.
Education level (ISCED-97)	2007 [1,2] Labour force survey		2007 ★ Labour force survey		2007 [2] Labour force survey	
Total	4 295.1	49.0	4 014.0	49.7	281.1	39.6
1 Primary education or first stage of basic education	11.0	48.2	9.5	50.5	1.5	33.3
2 Lower secondary or second stage of basic education	145.0	58.8	128.8	62.4	16.2	29.6
3 Upper secondary education	2 607.9	49.6	2 420.3	50.4	187.6	38.5
4 Post-secondary non-tertiary education	573.8	54.2	539.7	54.1	34.1	55.1
5A First stage of tertiary education - theoretically based	957.4	42.9	915.6	43.3	41.8	35.6
Status in employment (ICSE-1993)			2007 [1,2] Labour force survey			
Total	.	.	4 014.0	49.7	.	.
1 Employees	.	.	1 677.2	38.9	.	.
2 Employers	.	.	202.7	13.0	.	.
3 Own-account workers	.	.	2 134.1	61.6	.	.
4 Members of producers' cooperatives	.	.	-	.	.	.
5 Contributing family workers	.	.	-	.	.	.

2. Population ('000), Activity rate and Unemployment rate

	Population 2007 [1,4] Labour force survey			Activity rate 2007 [1,4] Labour force survey			Unemployment rate 2007 [2] Labour force survey		
Age group	Total	Men	Women	Total	Men	Women	Total	Men	Women
Total	8 629.9	4 258.1	4 371.8	49.8	51.4	48.1	6.5	7.8	5.3
15+	6 630.0	3 197.4	3 432.6	64.8	68.5	61.3	.	.	.
15-24	1 797.4	919.8	877.6	36.0	32.7	39.4	14.0	18.2	10.4
25-54	3 778.8	1 813.4	1 965.4	89.7	94.1	85.6	5.3	6.2	4.5
55+	1 053.8	464.2	589.6	24.6	39.4	12.9	.	.	.

Azerbaijan

3. Paid employment ('000), Hours of work (weekly) and Wages

Economic activity (ISIC-Rev.3)	Paid employment 2007 [5] Labour-related establishment survey			Hours of work 2007 [6] Labour-related establishment census Hours actually worked / Employees			Wages 2007 Labour-related establishment census Earnings per month / Employees / Manat		
	Total	Men	Women	Total	Men	Women	Total	Men	Women
Total	1 376.0	774.2	601.8	152.9	165.8	97.5	215.8	277.1	140.0
A-B	.	.	.	149.8	141.9	200.2	86.7	82.3	116.1
C-Q	.	.	.	.	.	.	219.6	284.8	140.5
A	45.0	36.3	8.7	.	57.5	82.4	86.8	82.2	117.8
B	0.8	0.6	0.2	.	99.7	92.7	.	66.8	62.1
C	41.2	35.3	5.9	149.2	153.9	121.6	845.5	872.6	689.4
D	110.8	78.0	32.8	142.3	158.7	96.1	190.5	212.7	128.1
E	44.6	36.1	8.5	160.3	168.6	124.8	210.0	220.8	163.5
F	69.0	63.3	5.7	138.5	145.9	71.9	381.4	401.2	197.8
G	268.5	182.4	86.1	160.2	164.7	151.8	173.7	177.9	164.0
H	14.9	10.1	4.8	170.2	172.8	169.0	212.3	216.0	211.2
I	90.3	68.1	22.2	157.3	172.4	114.0	250.4	274.1	181.3
J	16.2	10.7	5.6	158.7	175.9	107.2	709.1	831.0	479.3
K	66.7	42.6	24.0	153.1	184.6	62.3	504.7	675.3	205.7
L	51.9	37.5	14.4	162.5	171.8	138.8	210.6	223.4	180.4
M	338.9	102.8	236.1	145.6	158.0	129.8	145.4	185.7	129.8
N	136.3	35.7	100.6	147.1	160.0	125.6	94.7	146.0	80.4
O	80.9	34.7	46.2	154.9	168.0	118.3	140.0	189.4	106.5

Share of women in wage employment in the non-agricultural sector [1,2] (2007 - Labour force survey): **39.2%**

4. Occupational injuries and Strikes and Lockouts

Economic activity (ISIC-Rev.2)	Rates of fatal injuries			Rates of non-fatal injuries			Strikes and lockouts 1990 Source unknown		
	Total	Men	Women	Total	Men	Women	Strikes and lockouts	Workers involved	Days not worked
Total	.	.	.	.	.	.	230	340 786	1 075 162
3	.	.	.	.	.	.	160	112 696	809 165
5	.	.	.	.	.	.	15	39 435	158 621
7	.	.	.	.	.	.	42	134 261	89 546
0	.	.	.	.	.	.	13	54 394	17 830

Economic activity (ISIC-Rev.3)	Rates of fatal injuries 2007 Labour inspectorate records Per 1,000 employees Reported injuries			Rates of non-fatal injuries 2007 Labour inspectorate records Per 1,000 employees Reported injuries			Strikes and lockouts		
	Total	Men	Women	Total	Men	Women	Strikes and lockouts	Workers involved	Days not worked
Total	0.13	0.24	0.00	0.20	0.37	0.02	.	.	.
A	0.18	0.25	0.00	0.27	0.38	0.00	.	.	.
C	0.68	0.16	0.00	0.68	0.62	1.05	.	.	.
D	0.32	0.46	0.00	0.83	1.14	0.13	.	.	.
E	0.57	0.71	0.00	0.07	0.09	0.00	.	.	.
F	1.46	1.65	0.00	2.20	2.45	0.00	.	.	.
G	0.43	0.56	0.00	0.32	0.42	0.00	.	.	.
H	0.00	0.00	0.00	0.00	0.00	0.00	.	.	.
I	0.03	0.04	0.00	0.10	0.13	0.00	.	.	.
J	0.00	0.00	0.00	0.00	0.00	0.00	.	.	.
K	0.05	0.10	0.00	0.05	0.10	0.00	.	.	.
L	0.04	0.10	0.00	0.08	0.16	0.02	.	.	.
M	0.00	0.01	0.00	0.00	0.00	0.00	.	.	.
N	0.00	0.00	0.00	0.13	0.31	0.00	.	.	.
O	0.08	0.10	0.06	0.08	0.00	0.06	.	.	.

5. Consumer price indices (base period: 2000=100)

	2002	2003	2004	2005	2006	2007
General indices	104.4	106.7	113.9	124.8	135.2	157.7
Food index, including non-alcoholic beverages [7]	106.5	109.9	120.9	134.1	150.2	174.6
Electricity, gas and other fuel indices	99.9	99.9	109.6	191.1	217.6	434.4
Clothing indices, including footwear	105.2	107.6	110.0	111.9	117.0	160.4

[1] Excl. armed forces and conscripts. [2] Men aged 15 to 61 years; women aged 15 to 56 years. [3] Dec. [4] "De facto" population. [5] Beginning 2004: Number of employees in the payroll at the end of the year. [6] Per month. [7] Incl. tobacco.

[1] Non compris les forces armées et les conscrits. [2] Hommes âgés de 15 à 61 ans; femmes âgées de 15 à 56 ans. [3] Déc. [4] Population "de facto". [5] A partir de 2004: Nombre d'employés dans le registre du personnel à la fin de l'an. [6] Par mois. [7] Y compris le tabac.

[1] Excl. las fuerzas armadas y los conscriptos. [2] Hombres de 15 a 61 años; mujeres de 15 a 56 años. [3] Dic. [4] Población "de facto". [5] A partir de 2004: Empleados en la nómina al final del año. [6] Por mes. [7] Incl. el tabaco.

Bahamas

1. Economically active population, Employment and Unemployment ('000)

	Economically active population		Employment		Unemployment	
	Total	Women (%)	Total	Women (%)	Total	Women (%)
Age group	2007 [1,2,3] Labour force survey		2007 ★ Labour force survey		2007 [2,3] Labour force survey	
Total	186.105	48.4	171.490	47.7	14.615	55.9
15-19	9.620	45.8	7.015	41.2	2.605	58.2
20-24	22.150	43.9	18.750	43.6	3.400	45.6
25-34	46.875	50.2	43.545	49.6	3.330	58.7
35-44	51.570	49.9	48.775	49.6	2.795	55.8
45-54	34.550	50.8	32.885	49.9	1.665	68.8
55-64	15.935	44.7	15.150	44.3	0.785	52.9
65+	4.430	36.1	4.430	36.1	-	.
?	0.975	36.4	0.940	37.8	0.035	.

Economic activity (ISIC-Rev.2)					2007 [2,3] Labour force survey	
Total	.	.	.	.	14.613	55.9
1 Agriculture, Hunting, Forestry and Fishing	.	.	.	.	0.369	.
2 Mining and Quarrying	.	.	.	.	0.030	.
3 Manufacturing	.	.	.	.	0.621	26.6
4 Electricity, Gas and Water	.	.	.	.	0.151	19.2
5 Construction	.	.	.	.	2.269	5.1
6 Wholesale and Retail Trade and Restaurants and Hotels	.	.	.	.	5.311	72.6
7 Transport, Storage and Communication	.	.	.	.	0.386	37.3
8 Financing, Insurance, Real Estate and Business Services	.	.	.	.	1.087	71.7
9 Community, Social and Personal Services	.	.	.	.	1.900	69.1
0 Activities not Adequately Defined	.	.	.	.	0.090	31.1
Unemployed seeking their first job	.	.	.	.	2.399	72.6

Economic activity (ISIC-Rev.3)			2007 [1,2,3] Labour force survey			
Total	.	.	171.490	47.7	.	.
A-B	.	.	3.940	5.1	.	.
C,E	.	.	2.965	21.4	.	.
D Manufacturing	.	.	6.420	36.9	.	.
F Construction	.	.	21.340	6.6	.	.
G Wholesale and Retail Trade; Repair of Motor Vehicles ...	.	.	24.885	48.4	.	.
H Hotels and Restaurants	.	.	27.410	57.9	.	.
I Transport, Storage and Communications	.	.	13.275	29.8	.	.
J-K	.	.	20.175	60.5	.	.
L-P	.	.	50.690	65.1	.	.
X Not classifiable by economic activity	.	.	0.390	37.2	.	.

Occupation (ISCO-88)	2007 ★ Labour force survey		2007 [1,2,3] Labour force survey		2007 [2,3] Labour force survey	
Total	186.105	48.4	171.490	47.7	14.615	55.9
1 Legislators, senior officials and managers	17.096	43.5	16.685	43.2	0.411	54.3
2-3	34.140	63.2	33.200	63.3	0.940	57.8
4 Clerks	23.075	84.6	21.490	83.8	1.585	96.1
5 Service workers and shop and market sales workers	36.259	58.3	33.265	56.7	2.994	76.0
6 Skilled agricultural and fishery workers	3.664	1.6	3.475	1.7	0.189	.
7-8	36.764	9.5	34.390	9.9	2.374	3.7
9 Elementary occupations	31.743	46.2	28.110	45.9	3.633	48.1
X Not classifiable by occupation	0.965	45.4	0.875	46.9	0.090	31.1
Unemployed seeking their first job	.	.	.	.	2.399	72.6

Education level (ISCED-97)	2006 [2,4] Labour force survey		2006 ★ Labour force survey		2006 [2,4] Labour force survey	
Total	181.890	48.9	168.060	48.5	13.830	53.9
X No schooling	4.755	32.5	3.920	29.8	0.835	44.9
1 Primary education or first stage of basic education	16.040	38.9	14.545	37.7	1.495	50.5
2 Lower secondary or second stage of basic education [5]	114.635	47.6	104.465	47.0	10.170	53.9
5A First stage of tertiary education - theoretically based [6]	46.315	57.3	44.985	57.1	1.330	63.5
? Level not stated	0.145	20.7	0.145	20.7	-	.

Status in employment (ICSE-1993)	1990 [2,4] Population census					
Total	114.415	46.7	.	.	.	.
1 Employees	97.321	48.5	.	.	.	.
2 Employers	5.525	22.9	.	.	.	.
3 Own-account workers	7.741	36.6	.	.	.	.
5 Contributing family workers	0.388	64.9	.	.	.	.
6 Not classifiable by status	3.440	54.4	.	.	.	.

2. Population ('000), Activity rate and Unemployment rate

	Population			Activity rate			Unemployment rate		
Age group	1998 [1,3] Labour force survey			1998 [1,3] Labour force survey			2007 [2,3] Labour force survey		
	Total	Men	Women	Total	Men	Women	Total	Men	Women
Total	328.5	159.8	168.7	47.6	49.6	45.8	7.9	6.7	9.1
15+	221.4	105.8	115.6	69.8	74.1	65.9	.	.	.
15-24	55.7	27.9	27.8	54.8	57.1	52.6	18.9	16.7	21.7
25-54	131.3	63.3	68.0	84.0	86.4	81.8	5.9	4.7	7.0
55+	34.4	14.6	19.8	39.6	53.2	29.7	.	.	.

Bahamas

3. Paid employment ('000), Hours of work (weekly) and Wages

Economic activity (ISIC-Rev.3)	Paid employment Total	Men	Women	Hours of work 1994 Labour force survey Hours actually worked / Employees Total	Men	Women	Wages Total	Men	Women
A	.	.	.	35.0	35.5	33.0	.	.	.
B	.	.	.	39.9	40.5	.	.	.	.
C	.	.	.	45.0	45.0	.	.	.	.
D	.	.	.	40.7	42.5	38.8	.	.	.
E	.	.	.	40.6	40.1	42.6	.	.	.
F	.	.	.	39.8	39.9	37.6	.	.	.
G	.	.	.	40.1	40.6	39.6	.	.	.
H	.	.	.	40.5	40.9	40.1	.	.	.
I	.	.	.	41.6	41.9	41.0	.	.	.
J	.	.	.	41.7	43.9	40.8	.	.	.
K	.	.	.	39.9	39.9	39.9	.	.	.
L	.	.	.	41.1	41.5	40.5	.	.	.
M	.	.	.	37.4	37.6	37.3	.	.	.
N	.	.	.	40.1	41.5	39.8	.	.	.
O	.	.	.	41.3	42.4	40.2	.	.	.
P	.	.	.	35.8	37.1	35.4	.	.	.
Q	.	.	.	36.5	38.6	32.9	.	.	.

4. Occupational injuries and Strikes and Lockouts

Economic activity (ISIC-Rev.2)	Rates of fatal injuries Total	Men	Women	Rates of non-fatal injuries Total	Men	Women	Strikes and lockouts 1992 Labour relations records Strikes and lockouts	Workers involved	Days not worked
Total	.	.	.	.	.	.	0	0	0

5. Consumer price indices (base period: 2000=100)

New Providence	2002	2003	2004	2005	2006	2007
General indices	104.2	107.4	108.6	110.8	112.8	115.6
Food index, including non-alcoholic beverages	104.1	104.7	107.8	111.2	116.4	120.5
Clothing indices, including footwear	101.0	101.0	101.3	99.0	100.2	.
Rent indices [7]	100.3	101.0	101.7	103.7	105.4	.

[1] Excl. armed forces. [2] Persons aged 15 years and over. [3] April. [4] May. [5] Levels 2-3. [6] Levels 5-6. [7] Incl. "Fuel and light" and certain household equipment.

[1] Non compris les forces armées. [2] Personnes âgées de 15 ans et plus. [3] Avril. [4] Mai. [5] Niveaux 2-3. [6] Niveaux 5-6. [7] Y compris le groupe "Combustible et éclairage" et certains biens d'équipement de ménage.

[1] Excl. las fuerzas armadas. [2] Personas de 15 años y más. [3] Abril. [4] Mayo. [5] Niveles 2-3. [6] Niveles 5-6. [7] Incl. "Combustible y luz" y ciertos enseres domésticos.

Bahrain

1. Economically active population, Employment and Unemployment ('000)

	Economically active population		Employment		Unemployment	
	Total	Women (%)	Total	Women (%)	Total	Women (%)
Age group	2001 [1 2] Population census		2001 ★ Population census		2007 [1 2] Employment office records	
Total	308.341	21.7	291.376	20.5	9.536	87.0
15-19	6.533	21.3	3.868	15.9	0.162	45.7
20-24	39.028	30.4	32.537	27.8	1.931	75.5
25-29	56.333	25.2	52.658	23.6	.	.
25-34	.	.	.	.	5.003	93.0
30-34	58.450	24.1	56.555	23.3	.	.
35-39	50.648	22.0	49.579	21.5	.	.
35-49	.	.	.	.	2.277	92.8
40-44	42.476	17.8	41.899	17.7	.	.
45-49	28.510	14.8	28.200	14.7	.	.
50+	26.365	9.0	26.082	9.1	0.163	56.4
Economic activity (ISIC-Rev.3)			2001 [1 3] Population census			
Total	.	.	291.378	20.5	.	.
A Agriculture, Hunting and Forestry	.	.	2.269	3.3	.	.
B Fishing	.	.	2.214	1.7	.	.
C Mining and Quarrying	.	.	2.780	7.1	.	.
D Manufacturing	.	.	49.979	14.5	.	.
E Electricity, Gas and Water Supply	.	.	2.515	3.7	.	.
F Construction	.	.	26.416	1.7	.	.
G Wholesale and Retail Trade; Repair of Motor Vehicles ...	.	.	34.477	9.7	.	.
H Hotels and Restaurants	.	.	13.093	14.5	.	.
I Transport, Storage and Communications	.	.	13.769	15.6	.	.
J Financial Intermediation	.	.	6.475	28.9	.	.
K Real Estate, Renting and Business Activities	.	.	16.213	9.6	.	.
L Public Administration and Defence; Compulsory Social ...	.	.	52.388	8.1	.	.
M Education	.	.	13.557	57.7	.	.
N Health and Social Work	.	.	7.572	58.0	.	.
O Other Community, Social and Personal Service Activities	.	.	10.544	16.8	.	.
P Households with Employed Persons	.	.	29.583	74.1	.	.
Q Extra-Territorial Organizations and Bodies	.	.	2.107	23.5	.	.
X Not classifiable by economic activity	.	.	5.427	5.1	.	.
Occupation (ISCO-88)			2001 [1 3] Population census			
Total	.	.	291.378	20.5	.	.
1 Legislators, senior officials and managers	.	.	20.741	12.3	.	.
2 Professionals	.	.	26.008	25.1	.	.
3 Technicians and associate professionals	.	.	20.624	43.9	.	.
4 Clerks	.	.	30.512	26.6	.	.
5 Service workers and shop and market sales workers	.	.	84.763	32.3	.	.
6 Skilled agricultural and fishery workers	.	.	6.898	0.2	.	.
7 Craft and related trade workers	.	.	23.732	24.4	.	.
8 Plant and machine operators and assemblers	.	.	73.502	0.1	.	.
X Not classifiable by occupation	.	.	4.598	7.5	.	.
Education level (ISCED-76)	1991 [1 4] Population census				2007 [1 2] Employment office records	
Total	226.448	17.5	.	.	9.536	87.0
X No schooling	21.545	11.1	.	.	0.128	81.3
0 Education preceding the first level	.	.	.	.	0.441	79.4
1 First level	76.437	11.1	.	.	0.366	69.7
2 Second level, first stage	33.139	11.1	.	.	1.801	86.7
3 Second level, second stage	56.482	22.7	.	.	3.703	87.6
5 Third level, first stage, leading to an award not equivalent ...	12.840	36.0	.	.	1.000	87.0
6 Third level, first stage, leading to a first university degree ...	18.223	31.4	.	.	2.009	93.3
7 Third level, second stage	6.851	23.7	.	.	0.011	45.5
9 Education not definable by level	.	.	.	.	0.077	44.2
? Level not stated	0.931	30.8	.	.	-	.

2. Population ('000), Activity rate and Unemployment rate

Age group	Population 2006 [2] Official estimates			Activity rate 2001 [2] Population census			Unemployment rate 2001 Population census		
	Total	Men	Women	Total	Men	Women	Total	Men	Women
Total	742.6	427.2	315.4	47.4	64.6	24.1	5.5	4.1	10.5
15+	539.7	323.6	216.4	65.7	86.0	35.5	5.5	4.1	10.5
15-24	125.9	67.2	58.7	41.5	55.2	25.9	20.1	17.2	27.1
25-54	370.3	233.0	137.3	.	.	.	.	.	.
55+	43.4	23.4	20.4	.	.	.	.	.	.

Bahrain

3. Paid employment ('000), Hours of work (weekly) and Wages

Economic activity (ISIC-Rev.2)	Paid employment 2007 [5,6] Insurance records			Hours of work			Wages 2007 [5,6] Insurance records Earnings per month / Employees / Dinar		
	Total	Men	Women	Total	Men	Women	Total	Men	Women
Total	332.616	300.461	32.155	.	.	.	213	205	287
2-9	.	.	.	.	.	.	215	207	287
1	4.484	4.431	0.053	.	.	.	72	70	232
2	0.012	0.010	0.002	.	.	.	117	95	225
3	64.128	58.442	5.686	.	.	.	225	230	177
4	1.372	1.301	0.071	.	.	.	403	404	392
5	101.983	98.723	3.326	.	.	.	108	105	188
6	81.010	72.621	8.389	.	.	.	151	144	213
7	13.818	11.087	2.731	.	.	.	520	549	402
8	16.846	13.205	3.641	.	.	.	915	979	681
9	48.654	40.445	8.209	.	.	.	196	183	262
0	0.309	0.196	0.113	.	.	.	540	653	343

4. Occupational injuries and Strikes and Lockouts

Economic activity (ISIC-Rev.2)	Rates of fatal injuries 2007 Insurance records Per 100,000 workers employed Reported injuries			Rates of non-fatal injuries 2007 Insurance records Per 100,000 workers employed Reported injuries			Strikes and lockouts		
	Total	Men	Women	Total	Men	Women	Strikes and lockouts	Workers involved	Days not worked
Total	7.0	.	.	296.0	.	.	.	.	.
1	0.0	.	.	156.0	.	.	.	.	.
2	0.0	.	.	0.0	.	.	.	.	.
3	8.0	.	.	513.0	.	.	.	.	.
4	0.0	.	.	146.0	.	.	.	.	.
5	9.0	.	.	418.0	.	.	.	.	.
6	7.0	.	.	112.0	.	.	.	.	.
7	7.0	.	.	353.0	.	.	.	.	.
8	0.0	.	.	160.0	.	.	.	.	.
9	2.0	.	.	120.0	.	.	.	.	.

5. Consumer price indices (base period: 2000=100)

	2002	2003	2004	2005	2006	2007
General indices	98.3	100.0	102.3	104.9	107.1	.
Food index, including non-alcoholic beverages	97.6	96.2	98.3	101.3	103.3	.
Electricity, gas and other fuel indices [7]	72.6	72.4	72.5	72.4	72.5	.
Clothing indices, including footwear	101.9	102.4	103.8	103.2	102.5	.
Rent indices	104.5	109.7	117.0	124.7	129.6	.

[1] Persons aged 15 years and over. [2] Jan. [3] April. [4] Nov. [5] Private sector. [6] Establishments with 10 or more persons employed. [7] Incl. water.

[1] Personnes âgées de 15 ans et plus. [2] Janv. [3] Avril. [4] Nov. [5] Secteur privé. [6] Etablissements occupant 10 personnes et plus. [7] Y compris l'eau.

[1] Personas de 15 años y más. [2] Enero. [3] Abril. [4] Nov. [5] Sector privado. [6] Establecimientos con 10 y más trabajadores. [7] Incl. el agua.

Bangladesh

1. Economically active population, Employment and Unemployment ('000)

Age group	Economically active population Total	Women (%)	Employment Total	Women (%)	Unemployment Total	Women (%)
	2005 [1,2,3] Labour force survey		2005 ★ Labour force survey		2005 [2,3] Labour force survey	
Total	49 461	24.5	47 357	23.8	2 104	40.6
15-19	4 764	14.3	4 351	12.3	413	35.4
20-24	6 353	29.1	5 736	28.8	617	32.1
25-29	6 633	31.0	6 225	30.6	408	36.0
30-34	6 108	28.8	5 929	28.1	179	51.4
35-39	6 506	26.8	6 355	26.2	151	53.0
40-44	5 311	24.3	5 238	23.7	73	65.8
45-49	4 694	21.0	4 625	20.5	69	60.9
50-54	3 307	20.7	3 255	20.2	52	50.0
55-59	2 228	20.1	2 184	19.3	44	56.8
60-64	1 626	18.1	1 594	17.3	32	59.4
65+	1 931	17.7	1 865	16.7	66	45.5

Economic activity (ISIC-Rev.3)
2005 [2,3] Labour force survey

	Total	Women (%)
Total	47 357	23.8
A Agriculture, Hunting and Forestry	21 672	34.6
B Fishing	1 095	16.3
C Mining and Quarrying	51	13.7
D Manufacturing	5 224	24.8
E Electricity, Gas and Water Supply	76	3.9
F Construction	1 524	6.8
G Wholesale and Retail Trade; Repair of Motor Vehicles ...	7 108	5.7
H Hotels and Restaurants	712	7.2
I Transport, Storage and Communications	3 976	1.7
J Financial Intermediation	507	22.7
K Real Estate, Renting and Business Activities	239	4.6
L Public Administration and Defence; Compulsory Social ...	882	11.8
M Education	1 306	26.3
N Health and Social Work	362	33.7
O Other Community, Social and Personal Service Activities	2 622	36.9

Occupation (ISCO-1968)
2005 [2,3] Labour force survey

	Total	Women (%)
Total	47 357	23.8
0/1 Professional, technical and related workers	2 231	22.1
2 Administrative and managerial workers	223	9.9
3 Clerical and related workers	1 015	14.2
4 Sales workers	2 757	31.4
5 Service workers	6 710	3.5
6 Agriculture, animal husbandry and forestry workers ...	22 926	33.6
7/8/9 Production and related workers, transport equipment ...	11 429	15.8
X Not classifiable by occupation	64	1.6

Education level (ISCED-97)
2005 [2,3] Labour force survey

	Total	Women (%)
Total	2 104	40.6
X No schooling	559	55.1
1 Primary education or first stage of basic education	375	44.4
2A	316	40.1
2C	4	19.4
3 Upper secondary education	251	35.3
4 Post-secondary non-tertiary education	262	27.1
5A First stage of tertiary education - theoretically based	8	46.3
5B First stage of tertiary education - practically oriented	285	26.4
6 Second stage of tertiary education	41	30.0
? Level not stated	2	48.3

Status in employment (ICSE-1993)
2005 [2,3] Labour force survey

	Total	Women (%)
Total	47 357	23.8
1 Employees	6 567	20.1
2 Employers	130	10.0
3-4	29 975	9.9
5 Contributing family workers	10 268	66.0
6 Not classifiable by status	417	44.8

2. Population ('000), Activity rate and Unemployment rate

Age group	Population 2005 [1,2] Labour force survey Total	Men	Women	Activity rate 2005 [1,2] Labour force survey Total	Men	Women	Unemployment rate 2005 [2,3] Labour force survey Total	Men	Women
Total	137 299	70 040	67 259	36.0	53.3	18.0	4.3	3.4	7.0
15+	84 587	43 007	41 580	58.5	86.8	29.2	4.3	3.4	7.0
15-24	23 415	12 096	11 319	47.5	71.0	22.3	9.3	8.0	13.6
25-54	49 732	24 690	25 042	65.5	97.4	34.0	2.9	2.1	5.1
55+	11 440	6 221	5 219	50.6	75.6	20.8	2.5	1.4	6.8

Bangladesh

3. Paid employment ('000), Hours of work (weekly) and Wages

Economic activity (ISIC-Rev.3)	Paid employment 2005 [2,3] Labour force survey			Hours of work 2006 Labour force survey Hours actually worked / Total employment			Wages 1996 [4] Industrial/commercial census Wage rates per day / Skilled / Taka		
	Total	Men	Women	Total	Men	Women	Total	Men	Women
Total	17 114	.	.	46.0	52.0	26.0	.	.	.
A	5 452	.	.	.	.	.	.	.	.
B	138	.	.	.	.	.	.	.	.
C	33	.	.	56.0	57.0	47.0	.	.	.
D	3 687	.	.	54.0	56.0	49.0	61.90	.	.
E	60	.	.	52.0	51.0	68.0	.	.	.
F	1 194	.	.	50.0	51.0	36.0	.	.	.
G	894	.	.	55.0	56.0	35.0	.	.	.
H	175	.	.	60.0	61.0	44.0	.	.	.
I	1 131	.	.	57.0	57.0	53.0	.	.	.
J	461	.	.	46.0	47.0	43.0	.	.	.
K	109	.	.	50.0	51.0	45.0	.	.	.
L	807	.	.	48.0	49.0	43.0	.	.	.
M	1 214	.	.	48.0	49.0	44.0	.	.	.
N	248	.	.	49.0	52.0	45.0	.	.	.
O	1 507	.	.	49.0	53.0	41.0	.	.	.

4. Occupational injuries and Strikes and Lockouts

Economic activity (ISIC-Rev.2)	Rates of fatal injuries 2000 Labour inspectorate records Per 100,000 production and related workers			Rates of non-fatal injuries 2000 Labour inspectorate records Per 100,000 production and related workers			Strikes and lockouts 2000 Labour relations records		
	Total	Men	Women	Total	Men	Women	Strikes and lockouts	Workers involved	Days not worked
Total	.	.	.	.	.	.	4	1 698	2 284
1	.	.	.	.	.	.	0	0	0
2	.	.	.	.	.	.	0	0	0
3	5.2	.	.	134	.	.	0	0	0
4	.	.	.	.	.	.	4	1 698	2 284
5	.	.	.	.	.	.	0	0	0
6	.	.	.	.	.	.	0	0	0
7	.	.	.	.	.	.	0	0	0
8	.	.	.	.	.	.	0	0	0
9	.	.	.	.	.	.	0	0	0

5. Consumer price indices (base period: 2000=100)

[5]	2002	2003	2004	2005	2006	2007
General indices	105.4	111.5	118.4	126.7	135.3	147.6
Food index, including non-alcoholic beverages	103.4	110.1	118.3	127.8	137.5	151.9

[1] Excl. armed forces. [2] Year ending in June of the year indicated. [3] Persons aged 15 years and over. [4] Managerial, administrative, technical, and production workers. [5] Government officials.

[1] Non compris les forces armées. [2] Année se terminant en juin de l'année indiquée. [3] Personnes âgées de 15 ans et plus. [4] Directeurs, cadres administratifs supérieurs, personnel technique et travailleurs à la production. [5] Fonctionnaires.

[1] Excl. las fuerzas armadas. [2] Año que se termina en junio del año indicado. [3] Personas de 15 años y más. [4] Directores, funcionarios públicos superiores, técnicos y trabajadores participando en el proceso de producción. [5] Funcionarios.

Barbados

1. Economically active population, Employment and Unemployment ('000)

	Economically active population		Employment		Unemployment	
	Total	Women (%)	Total	Women (%)	Total	Women (%)
Age group	2003 [1,2] Labour force survey		2003 ★ Labour force survey		2003 [2] Labour force survey	
Total	145.5	48.7	129.5	47.9	16.0	55.6
15-19	5.3	43.4	3.3	42.4	2.0	45.0
20-24	15.3	46.4	11.9	44.5	3.4	52.9
25-29	16.9	48.5	14.3	47.6	2.6	53.8
30-34	18.7	50.8	16.7	50.3	2.0	55.0
35-39	20.2	51.5	18.4	50.0	1.8	66.7
40-44	20.4	52.5	19.1	51.3	1.3	69.2
45-49	17.8	47.8	16.8	47.6	1.0	50.0
50-54	14.6	48.6	13.8	48.6	0.8	50.0
55-59	9.6	45.8	8.8	43.2	0.8	75.0
60-64	4.4	40.9	4.2	40.5	0.2	50.0
65+	2.3	39.1	2.2	40.9	0.1	.

Economic activity (ISIC-Rev.2)			2003 [1,2] Labour force survey		2003 [2] Labour force survey	
Total	.	.	129.5	47.9	16.0	55.6
1 Agriculture, Hunting, Forestry and Fishing	.	.	5.9	37.3	0.5	20.0
3 Manufacturing	.	.	7.9	48.1	0.9	66.7
4 Electricity, Gas and Water	.	.	2.6	46.2	0.2	50.0
5 Construction [3]	.	.	12.3	4.9	2.7	7.4
6 Wholesale and Retail Trade and Restaurants and Hotels [4]	.	.	19.6	56.6	2.9	72.4
7 Transport, Storage and Communication	.	.	4.8	29.2	0.3	33.3
8 Financing, Insurance, Real Estate and Business Services	.	.	9.0	65.6	0.6	83.3
9 Community, Social and Personal Services	.	.	53.1	52.5	4.3	65.1
0 Activities not Adequately Defined [5]	.	.	14.0	55.0	1.9	73.7
Unemployed seeking their first job					1.3	61.5

Occupation (ISCO-88)			2003 [1,2] Labour force survey		2003 [2] Labour force survey	
Total	.	.	129.5	47.9	16.0	55.6
1 Legislators, senior officials and managers	.	.	9.8	44.9	0.2	50.0
2 Professionals	.	.	14.2	62.0	0.5	80.0
3 Technicians and associate professionals	.	.	10.5	39.0	0.9	44.4
4 Clerks	.	.	15.2	79.6	1.5	86.7
5 Service workers and shop and market sales workers	.	.	24.8	66.1	3.9	82.1
6 Skilled agricultural and fishery workers	.	.	3.8	18.4	0.5	.
7 Craft and related trade workers	.	.	17.4	10.3	1.9	10.5
8 Plant and machine operators and assemblers	.	.	8.0	21.3	0.7	28.6
9 Elementary occupations	.	.	25.4	47.2	4.3	46.5
X Not classifiable by occupation	.	.	0.4	50.0	0.4	50.0
Unemployed seeking their first job					1.3	61.5

Education level (ISCED-97)	2003 [1,2] Labour force survey		2003 ★ Labour force survey		2003 [2] Labour force survey	
Total	145.5	48.7	129.5	47.9	16.0	55.6
X No schooling	0.7	42.9	0.6	50.0	0.1	.
1 Primary education or first stage of basic education	21.4	42.5	19.3	42.0	2.1	47.6
2 Lower secondary or second stage of basic education [6]	87.3	48.9	75.8	47.8	11.5	56.5
4 Post-secondary non-tertiary education	7.8	28.2	7.0	25.7	0.8	50.0
5A First stage of tertiary education - theoretically based	26.8 [7]	60.1	25.4	59.4	1.4	71.4
? Level not stated	1.5	33.3	1.3	30.8	0.2	50.0

Status in employment (ICSE-1993)			2004 [1,2] Labour force survey			
Total	.	.	132.0	48.3	.	.
1 Employees	.	.	111.4	51.3	.	.
2 Employers	.	.	1.6	18.8	.	.
3 Own-account workers	.	.	18.4	33.7	.	.
5 Contributing family workers	.	.	0.1	100.0	.	.
6 Not classifiable by status	.	.	0.5	20.0	.	.

2. Population ('000), Activity rate and Unemployment rate

	Population			Activity rate			Unemployment rate		
Age group	2004 [1] Labour force survey			2004 [1] Labour force survey			2003 [2] Labour force survey		
	Total	Men	Women	Total	Men	Women	Total	Men	Women
Total	.	.	.	.	.	.	11.0	9.6	12.6
15+	210.4	99.6	110.9	69.6	75.4	64.4	11.0	.	.
15-24	35.9	18.0	18.0	57.4	62.8	51.7	26.2	24.1	28.7
25-54	118.6	57.1	61.5	90.8	94.9	87.0	8.7	7.4	10.1
55+	55.9	24.5	31.4	32.4	39.2	27.4	6.7	.	.

Barbados

3. Paid employment ('000), Hours of work (weekly) and Wages

Economic activity (ISIC-Rev.2)	Paid employment			Hours of work			Wages 1991 Labour-related establishment census Earnings per week / Wage earners / Dollar		
	Total	Men	Women	Total	Men	Women	Total	Men	Women
1	.	.	.	.	.	.	234.00	.	.
2	.	.	.	.	.	.	296.58	.	.
3	.	.	.	.	.	.	255.71	.	.
4	.	.	.	.	.	.	312.82	.	.
5	.	.	.	.	.	.	268.52	.	.
6	.	.	.	.	.	.	252.30	.	.
7	.	.	.	.	.	.	284.56	.	.
8	.	.	.	.	.	.	241.00	.	.
9	.	.	.	.	.	.	284.65	.	.

4. Occupational injuries and Strikes and Lockouts

Economic activity (ISIC-Rev.3)	Rates of fatal injuries 1995 Labour inspectorate records Per 100,000 workers insured Reported injuries			Rates of non-fatal injuries			Strikes and lockouts 2002 Special data collection		
	Total	Men	Women	Total	Men	Women	Strikes and lockouts	Workers involved	Days not worked[8]
Total	0	.	.	.	.	.	5	577	1 911
A	.	.	.	.	.	.	0	0	0
B	.	.	.	.	.	.	0	0	0
C	.	.	.	.	.	.	0	0	0
D	.	.	.	.	.	.	1	110	90
E	.	.	.	.	.	.	1	60	390
F	.	.	.	.	.	.	0	0	0
G	.	.	.	.	.	.	0	0	0
H	.	.	.	.	.	.	0	0	0
I	.	.	.	.	.	.	0	0	0
J	.	.	.	.	.	.	0	0	0
K	.	.	.	.	.	.	0	0	0
L	.	.	.	.	.	.	0	0	0
M	.	.	.	.	.	.	0	0	0
N	.	.	.	.	.	.	0	0	0
O	.	.	.	.	.	.	3	407	1 431
X	.	.	.	.	.	.	0	0	0

5. Consumer price indices (base period: 2000=100)

	2002	2003	2004	2005	2006	2007
General indices	103.0	104.6	106.1	112.5	120.8	125.7
Food index, including non-alcoholic beverages	107.1	110.1	115.0	123.1	132.8	142.2
Electricity, gas and other fuel indices [9]	100.0	103.8	98.8	106.3	122.7	118.8
Clothing indices, including footwear [9]	100.0	97.0	97.3	96.6	88.9	88.3
Rent indices [9][10]	100.0	99.6	99.3	109.6	120.3	125.4

[1] Excl. armed forces. [2] Persons aged 15 years and over. [3] Incl. quarrying. [4] Wholesale and retail trade. [5] Tourism. [6] Levels 2-3. [7] Levels 5A, 5B and 6. [8] Computed on the basis of an eight-hour working day. [9] Index base 2002=100. [10] Housing.

[1] Non compris les forces armées. [2] Personnes âgées de 15 ans et plus. [3] Y compris les carrières. [4] Commerce de gros et de détail. [5] Tourisme. [6] Niveaux 2-3. [7] Niveaux 5A, 5B et 6. [8] Calculées sur la base de journées de travail de huit heures. [9] Indice base 2002=100. [10] Logement.

[1] Excl. las fuerzas armadas. [2] Personas de 15 años y más. [3] Incl. las canteras. [4] Comercio al por mayor y por menor. [5] Turismo. [6] Niveles 2-3. [7] Niveles 5A, 5B y 6. [8] Calculados en base a días de trabajo de ocho horas. [9] Indice base 2002=100. [10] Vivienda.

Belarus

1. Economically active population, Employment and Unemployment ('000)

	Economically active population		Employment		Unemployment	
	Total	Women (%)	Total	Women (%)	Total	Women (%)
Age group	1999 [1,2] Population census		2007 Labour-related establishment survey		2007 [3,4] Employment office records	
Total	4 742.9	48.6	4 445.3	52.8	44.1	65.5
15-19	147.3	40.2	.	.	.	.
16-19	.	.	.	.	4.0	70.0
20-24	524.0	46.1	.	.	7.8	69.2
25-29	587.3	48.3	.	.	5.7	70.2
30-34	622.3	49.6	.	.	5.1	66.7
35-39	757.0	50.4	.	.	4.7	63.8
40-44	734.2	51.7	.	.	4.7	63.8
45-49	608.0	52.5	.	.	5.1	66.7
50-54	408.9	51.7	.	.	5.5	70.9
55+	353.9	33.8	.	.	1.5	.

Economic activity (ISIC-Rev.2)			1994 Labour-related establishment survey			
Total	.	.	4 700.9	.	.	.
1 Agriculture, Hunting, Forestry and Fishing	.	.	995.7	.	.	.
2 Mining and Quarrying	.	.	27.2	.	.	.
3 Manufacturing	.	.	1 245.6	.	.	.
4 Electricity, Gas and Water	.	.	38.7	.	.	.
5 Construction	.	.	328.9	.	.	.
6 Wholesale and Retail Trade and Restaurants and Hotels	.	.	422.3	.	.	.
7 Transport, Storage and Communication	.	.	318.0	.	.	.
8 Financing, Insurance, Real Estate and Business Services	.	.	40.9	.	.	.
9 Community, Social and Personal Services	.	.	1 099.7	.	.	.
0 Activities not Adequately Defined	.	.	183.9	.	.	.

Education level (ISCED-76)					2007 [3,4] Employment office records	
Total	.	.	.	.	44.1	65.5
X-2	.	.	.	.	4.4	63.6
3 Second level, second stage	.	.	.	.	17.2	70.9
5 Third level, first stage, leading to an award not equivalent ...	.	.	.	.	17.4	63.8
6-7	.	.	.	.	5.1	54.9

2. Population ('000), Activity rate and Unemployment rate

	Population			Activity rate			Unemployment rate		
Age group	2007 [5,6] Official estimates			1999 [2] Population census			2007 [3,4] Employment office records		
	Total	Men	Women	Total	Men	Women	Total	Men	Women
Total	9 689.8	4 521.4	5 168.4	47.2	51.7	43.3	1.0	0.7	1.2
15+	8 268.1	3 790.7	4 477.4	58.7	65.7	52.7	.	.	.
15-24	1 552.4	792.8	759.6	44.7	48.4	40.9	.	.	.
25-54	4 356.7	2 125.3	2 231.4	88.3	88.9	87.6	.	.	.
55+	2 359.0	872.6	1 486.4	14.9	26.4	8.1	.	.	.

3. Paid employment ('000), Hours of work (weekly) and Wages

Economic activity (ISIC-Rev.3)	Paid employment 2006 Labour-related establishment survey			Hours of work 2007 [7] Labour-related establishment census Hours actually worked / Employees			Wages 2007 [3] Labour-related establishment census Earnings per month / Employees / Rouble		
	Total	Men	Women	Total	Men	Women	Total	Men	Women
Total	3 999.0	.	.	158	.	.	785	887	695
A-B	.	.	.	176	.	.	485	500	462
C-Q	.	.	.	155	.	.	831	969	720

Share of women in wage employment in the non-agricultural sector (2001 - Labour-related establishment survey): **56.0%**

4. Occupational injuries and Strikes and Lockouts

Economic activity (ISIC-Rev.3)	Rates of fatal injuries 2007 Labour-related establishment census Per 100,000 workers employed Reported injuries			Rates of non-fatal injuries 2007 Labour-related establishment census Per 100,000 workers employed Reported injuries			Strikes and lockouts 2004 Records of employers'/workers' organizations		
	Total	Men	Women	Total	Men	Women	Strikes and lockouts	Workers involved	Days not worked
Total	5.4	10.6	0.6	84	128	43	0	0	0

5. Consumer price indices (base period: 2000=100)

	2002	2003	2004	2005	2006	2007
General indices	229.8	295.0	348.3	384.3	411.2	445.9
Food index, including non-alcoholic beverages	217.9	267.6	320.1	358.2	380.1	417.4
Electricity, gas and other fuel indices	624.9	1 374.1	1 623.2	1 645.6	1 810.1	1 999.3
Clothing indices, including footwear	178.1	201.2	214.1	218.8	223.0	227.5
Rent indices	977.8	1 348.8	2 236.4	3 201.6	4 097.7	4 313.3

Belarus

[1] Persons aged 15 years and over. [2] Feb. [3] Dec. [4] Men aged 16 to 59 years; women aged 16 to 54 years. [5] "De jure" population. [6] Excl. armed forces. [7] Per month.

[1] Personnes âgées de 15 ans et plus. [2] Fév. [3] Déc. [4] Hommes âgés de 16 à 59 ans; femmes âgées de 16 à 54 ans. [5] Population "de jure". [6] Non compris les forces armées. [7] Par mois.

[1] Personas de 15 años y más. [2] Feb. [3] Dic. [4] Hombres de 16 a 59 años; mujeres de 16 a 54 años. [5] Población "de jure". [6] Excl. las fuerzas armadas. [7] Por mes.

Belgique

1. Population active, Emploi et Chômage ('000)

	Population active		Emploi		Chômage	
	Total	Femmes (%)	Total	Femmes (%)	Total	Femmes (%)
Groupe d'âge	2006 [1][2] Enquête sur la main-d'oeuvre		2006 ★ Enquête sur la main-d'oeuvre		2006 [2] Enquête sur la main-d'oeuvre	
Total	4 647.202	44.4	4 264.002	43.9	383.200	50.2
15-19	60.521	37.8	43.092	35.7	17.429	42.9
20-24	381.507	46.6	308.268	45.4	73.239	51.6
25-29	589.137	47.5	529.461	47.1	59.676	51.6
30-34	624.717	46.7	574.411	46.2	50.306	52.3
35-39	673.843	45.6	625.331	45.1	48.512	51.7
40-44	706.353	45.3	661.399	44.9	44.954	50.8
45-49	646.604	44.0	609.837	43.9	36.767	46.5
50-54	528.126	41.6	495.336	41.1	32.790	49.3
55-59	318.275	38.4	302.447	38.0	15.828	44.9
60-64	86.806	32.0	83.347	31.7	3.459	39.8
65+	31.311	34.0	31.072	33.9	0.239	43.9
Activité économique (CITI-Rév.3)	2006 [1][2] Enquête sur la main-d'oeuvre		2006 [1][2] Enquête sur la main-d'oeuvre		2006 [2] Enquête sur la main-d'oeuvre	
Total	4 647.202	44.4	4 262.800	43.9	383.200	50.2
A Agriculture, chasse et sylviculture	85.689	29.1	82.900	29.0	2.766	36.7
B Pêche	0.484	0.0	0.400	.	0.091	.
C Activités extractives	10.066	15.0	9.400	14.9	0.662	17.2
D Activités de fabrication	764.794	24.9	715.200	24.0	49.554	37.5
E Production et distribution d'électricité, de gaz et d'eau	36.321	19.8	35.100	19.9	1.180	13.2
F Construction	311.269	7.2	292.900	7.3	18.413	6.3
G Commerce de gros et de détail; réparation de véhicules ...	604.732	47.8	559.400	47.5	45.291	51.3
H Hôtels et restaurants	161.150	49.4	140.100	48.8	21.098	53.6
I Transports, entreposage et communications	338.558	24.2	320.000	24.0	18.604	26.4
J Intermédiation financière	160.508	47.5	155.600	47.0	4.940	60.9
K Immobilier, locations et activités de services aux entreprises	430.413	44.2	404.400	43.7	25.987	51.3
L Administration publique et défense; sécurité sociale obligatoire	438.711	46.7	422.100	46.7	16.619	46.8
M Education	389.789	68.2	375.600	68.0	14.221	74.2
N Santé et action sociale	548.420	76.8	528.900	76.9	19.499	75.4
O Autres activités de services collectifs, sociaux et personnels	186.970	54.9	172.000	54.7	14.955	57.5
P Ménages privés employant du personnel domestique	25.259	87.7	23.700	88.2	1.533	80.2
Q Organisations et organismes extraterritoriaux	25.671	44.8	24.800	43.5	0.906	79.2
X Ne pouvant être classés selon l'activité économique	128.401	56.7	.	.	45.936	56.4
Chômeurs n'ayant jamais travaillé	.	.	.	.	80.946	56.7
Profession (CITP-88)	2006 [1][2] Enquête sur la main-d'oeuvre		2006 [1][2] Enquête sur la main-d'oeuvre		2006 [2] Enquête sur la main-d'oeuvre	
Total	4 647.202	44.4	4 264.000	43.9	383.200	50.2
1 Membres de l'exécutif et des corps législatifs, cadres ...	500.316	31.7	487.600	31.5	12.694	38.3
2 Professions intellectuelles et scientifiques	922.588	55.2	898.700	55.0	23.883	59.7
3 Professions intermédiaires	528.079	38.8	505.100	38.4	22.931	46.8
4 Employés de type administratif	674.645	64.3	639.000	64.2	35.619	65.4
5 Personnel des services et vendeurs de magasin et de marché	508.952	66.7	460.300	66.8	48.663	65.9
6 Agriculteurs et ouvriers qualifiés de l'agriculture ...	91.207	26.5	86.800	26.3	4.439	29.2
7 Artisans et ouvriers des métiers de type artisanal	460.520	7.3	427.300	7.1	33.163	10.5
8 Conducteurs d'installations et de machines ...	346.258	16.2	318.100	14.7	28.148	32.6
9 Ouvriers et employés non qualifiés	440.558	51.3	394.900	51.9	45.628	45.9
0 Forces armées	33.536	6.0	33.000	6.1	0.490	13.3
X Ne pouvant être classés selon la profession	140.543	55.3	13.000	43.1	46.595	56.1
Chômeurs n'ayant jamais travaillé	.	.	.	.	80.946	56.7
Niveau d'instruction (CITE-97)	2006 [1][2] Enquête sur la main-d'oeuvre		2006 ★ Enquête sur la main-d'oeuvre		2006 [2] Enquête sur la main-d'oeuvre	
Total	4 647.202	44.4	4 264.002	43.9	383.200	50.2
0 Education préprimaire [3]	1 167.371	37.9	1 097.766	37.4	69.605	45.1
2 Premier cycle de l'enseignement secondaire ou deuxième ...	1 236.185	41.3	1 144.330	41.0	91.855	44.8
3 Enseignement secondaire (deuxième cycle)	472.929	45.6	332.205	42.6	140.724	52.9
4 Enseignement postsecondaire qui n'est pas du supérieur	92.852	53.5	87.347	53.0	5.505	61.3
5A Premier cycle de l'enseignement supérieur - théorie	926.056	59.0	892.937	59.5	33.119	47.2
5B Premier cycle de l'enseignement supérieur - pratique	724.853	40.1	683.364	38.8	41.489	62.4
6 Deuxième cycle de l'enseignement supérieur	26.854	32.6	25.952	32.1	0.902	47.0
? Niveau inconnu	0.102	100.0	.	.	.	.
Situation dans la profession (CISP-1993)	2006 [1][2] Enquête sur la main-d'oeuvre		2006 [1][2] Enquête sur la main-d'oeuvre		2006 ★ Enquête sur la main-d'oeuvre	
Total	4 647.202	44.4	4 262.900	43.9	384.302	50.2
1 Salariés	3 971.676	46.0	3 620.300	45.6	351.376	50.4
2 Employeurs	201.964	22.9	199.300	22.7	2.664	37.0
3 Personnes travaillant pour leur propre compte	389.293	32.0	377.900	31.9	11.393	33.0
5 Travailleurs familiaux collaborant à l'entreprise familiale	65.968	84.1	65.400	84.3	0.568	67.1
6 Inclassables d'après la situation	18.301	57.8	.	.	.	.

Belgique

2. Population ('000), Taux d'activité et Taux de chômage

Groupe d'âge	Population 2006[1] Enquête sur la main-d'oeuvre			Taux d'activité 2006[1] Enquête sur la main-d'oeuvre			Taux de chômage 2006[2] Enquête sur la main-d'oeuvre		
	Total	Hommes	Femmes	Total	Hommes	Femmes	Total	Hommes	Femmes
Total	.	.	.	.	.	.	8.3	7.5	9.4
15+	8 749.4	4 243.8	4 505.5	53.1	60.9	45.8	8.2	7.4	9.3
15-24	1 274.0	645.4	628.6	34.7	37.4	31.9	20.5	18.8	22.6
25-54	4 460.9	2 248.4	2 212.5	84.5	91.9	77.0	7.2	6.5	8.1
55+	3 014.4	1 350.0	1 664.4	14.5	20.4	9.6	4.5	4.0	5.4

3. Emploi rémunéré ('000), Durée du travail (hebdomadaire) et Salaires

Activité économique (CITI-Rév.3)	Emploi rémunéré 2006[1,2] Enquête sur la main-d'oeuvre			Durée du travail 2006[4,5] Enquête auprès des établissements, relative au travail Heures rémunérées / Salariés			Salaires 2006[4,5] Enquête auprès des établissements, relative au travail Gains par heure / Salariés / Euro		
	Total	Hommes	Femmes	Total	Hommes	Femmes	Total	Hommes	Femmes
Total	3 619.9	1 969.4	1 650.5	.	.	.	.	.	.
A	19.4	15.0	4.4	.	.	.	.	.	.
B	0.3	0.3	-	.	.	.	.	.	.
C	9.2	7.8	1.4	36.56	36.41	37.78	16	16	17
D	667.2	506.6	160.7	36.42	36.63	35.42	16	17	15
E	34.3	27.4	6.9	37.42	37.59	36.81	21	22	16
F	224.7	210.1	14.6	35.92	35.84	37.51	14	14	14
G	417.2	205.9	211.3	36.28	36.57	35.64	16	16	14
H	85.9	41.5	44.4	33.00	34.08	31.47	12	13	11
I	298.0	225.4	72.6	37.34	37.44	36.97	16	16	15
J	140.6	70.8	69.8	36.03	36.29	35.58	22	24	19
K	298.3	152.7	145.6	36.12	36.42	35.48	18	19	16
L	420.3	224.1	196.2	.	.	.	.	.	.
M	371.4	118.0	253.4	27.58	36.62	26.52	15	16	15
N	457.2	87.7	369.5	36.22	36.86	36.02	15	16	15
O	128.4	60.0	68.4	36.22	36.35	35.26	16	17	14
P	23.1	2.5	20.6	.	.	.	.	.	.
Q	24.4	13.7	10.7	.	.	.	.	.	.

Pourcentage de salariées dans le secteur non agricole qui sont femmes [1,2] (2006 - Enquête sur la main-d'oeuvre): **45.7%**

4. Lésions professionnelles et Grèves et lock-out

Activité économique (CITI-Rév.3)	Taux de lésions mortelles 2004[6] Fichiers des assurances Pour 100 000 salariés Lésions indemnisées			Taux de lésions non mortelles 2004[6] Fichiers des assurances Pour 100 000 salariés Lésions indemnisées			Grèves et lock-out 2005 Collecte spéciale de données		
	Total	Hommes	Femmes	Total	Hommes	Femmes	Grèves et lock-out	Travailleurs impliqués	Journées non effectuées
Total	4.4	7.2	0.4	3 797	5 177	1 851	.	.	669 982
A	3.8	5.4	0.0	4 260	5 170	2 129	.	.	175
B	0.0	0.0	0.0	2 414	1 732	11 429	.	.	0
C	0.0	0.0	0.0	13 331	14 443	1 099	.	.	2 762
D	4.4	5.8	0.0	5 063	5 865	2 450	.	.	334 862
E	7.1	8.9	0.0	1 419	1 627	599	.	.	4 629
F	14.9	15.8	0.0	7 778	8 171	1 363	.	.	28 089
G	1.5	2.5	0.5	3 310	4 623	1 889	.	.	38 755
H	0.9	1.8	0.0	2 393	2 582	2 220	.	.	3 916
I	22.2	28.1	3.1	7 235	8 581	2 809	.	.	112 403
J	0.0	0.0	0.0	403	386	421	.	.	12 333
K	2.1	3.9	0.0	1 911	2 616	1 070	.	.	22 498
L	5.8	16.0	0.0	1 987	3 815	936	.	.	14 211
M	72.7	211.9	0.0	52 582	64 195	46 512	.	.	18 429
N	0.3	0.0	0.4	2 184	3 348	1 874	.	.	69 842
O	1.0	2.2	0.0	2 577	3 212	2 065	.	.	7 044
P	38.2	0.0	53.0	5 840	7 104	5 350	.	.	2
Q	0.0	0.0	0.0	40 909	38 095	43 478	.	.	25
X	.	.	.	.	.	.	.	.	5

5. Indices des prix à la consommation (période de base: 2000=100)

	2002	2003	2004	2005	2006	2007
Indices généraux	104.2	105.8	108.0	111.0	113.0	115.1
Indices de l'alimentation, y compris les boissons non alcoolisées	106.5	108.7	110.4	112.5	115.0	119.1
Indices de l'électricité, gaz et autres combustibles	99.5	98.8	103.5	112.9	123.0	.
Indices de l'habillement, y compris les chaussures	102.1	103.2	104.0	104.3	106.5	.
Indices du loyer	104.5	106.8	108.8	111.0	114.9	.
Indices généraux, non compris le logement	104.3	106.0	108.1	110.6	111.9	.

[1] Incl. professional army. [2] Persons aged 15 years and over. [3] Levels 0-1. [4] Full-time employees only. [5] Oct. [6] Private sector.

[1] Y compris les militaires de carrière. [2] Personnes âgées de 15 ans et plus. [3] Niveaux 0-1. [4] Salariés à plein temps seulement. [5] Oct. [6] Secteur privé.

[1] Incl. los militares profesionales. [2] Personas de 15 años y más. [3] Niveles 0-1. [4] Asalariados a tiempo completo solamente. [5] Oct. [6] Sector privado.

Belize

1. Economically active population, Employment and Unemployment ('000)

	Economically active population		Employment		Unemployment	
	Total	Women (%)	Total	Women (%)	Total	Women (%)
Age group	2005 [1 2 3] Labour force survey		2005 ★ Labour force survey		2005 [2 3] Labour force survey	
Total	110.786	36.7	98.589	34.2	12.197	57.2
10-14	0.634	20.0	0.507	15.6	0.127	37.8
15-19	11.429	35.6	8.521	29.4	2.908	53.9
20-24	17.195	39.6	14.525	36.1	2.670	58.6
25-29	14.918	41.5	13.525	39.2	1.393	64.6
30-34	14.352	41.0	13.238	38.1	1.114	74.6
35-39	13.187	40.1	12.143	37.4	1.044	71.1
40-44	11.698	37.2	10.913	35.6	0.785	59.0
45-49	9.932	34.5	9.194	33.2	0.738	50.7
50-54	6.591	31.1	6.004	30.2	0.587	39.5
55-59	3.961	26.4	3.584	24.4	0.377	44.6
60-64	3.017	23.8	2.756	23.3	0.261	29.1
65-69	1.737	16.8	1.611	18.1	0.126	0.0
70-74	0.947	19.9	0.916	18.6	0.031	58.1
75+	0.937	17.0	0.902	17.6	0.035	0.0
?	0.251	40.2	.	.	.	.

Economic activity (ISIC-Rev.3)			2005 [1 2 3] Labour force survey			
Total	.	.	98.589	34.2	.	.
A Agriculture, Hunting and Forestry	.	.	17.458	4.5	.	.
B Fishing	.	.	1.792	18.4	.	.
C Mining and Quarrying	.	.	0.211	7.1	.	.
D Manufacturing	.	.	9.575	33.0	.	.
E Electricity, Gas and Water Supply	.	.	0.934	16.4	.	.
F Construction	.	.	6.884	2.3	.	.
G Wholesale and Retail Trade; Repair of Motor Vehicles ...	.	.	16.928	39.0	.	.
H Hotels and Restaurants	.	.	8.740	62.8	.	.
I Transport, Storage and Communications	.	.	6.365	14.6	.	.
J Financial Intermediation	.	.	1.594	60.4	.	.
K Real Estate, Renting and Business Activities	.	.	2.114	27.7	.	.
L Public Administration and Defence; Compulsory Social ...	.	.	6.771	32.3	.	.
M Education	.	.	6.170	65.8	.	.
N Health and Social Work	.	.	2.682	75.0	.	.
O Other Community, Social and Personal Service Activities	.	.	3.853	43.1	.	.
P Households with Employed Persons	.	.	5.818	74.2	.	.
Q Extra-Territorial Organizations and Bodies	.	.	0.554	45.7	.	.
X Not classifiable by economic activity	.	.	0.146	39.7	.	.

Occupation (ISCO-88)			2005 [1 2 3] Labour force survey			
Total	.	.	98.589	34.2	.	.
1 Legislators, senior officials and managers	.	.	8.737	41.3	.	.
2 Professionals	.	.	4.358	47.2	.	.
3 Technicians and associate professionals	.	.	7.024	51.3	.	.
4 Clerks	.	.	7.043	68.2	.	.
5 Service workers and shop and market sales workers	.	.	16.530	56.3	.	.
6 Skilled agricultural and fishery workers	.	.	10.552	3.1	.	.
7 Craft and related trade workers	.	.	13.484	15.6	.	.
8 Plant and machine operators and assemblers	.	.	7.231	9.0	.	.
9 Elementary occupations	.	.	23.183	31.1	.	.
0 Armed forces	.	.	0.102	14.7	.	.
X Not classifiable by occupation	.	.	0.345	9.0	.	.

Education level (ISCED-76)	2005 [1 2 3] Labour force survey		2005 ★ Labour force survey		2005 [2 3] Labour force survey	
Total	110.786	36.7	98.589	34.2	12.197	57.2
X No schooling	6.551	38.4	6.002	36.4	0.549	59.6
0 Education preceding the first level	23.783	27.6	21.401	24.3	2.382	57.6
1 First level	38.229	33.2	33.079	30.2	5.150	52.7
2 Second level, first stage	8.621	41.2	7.339	37.6	1.282	61.7
3 Second level, second stage	18.096	45.4	15.971	43.1	2.125	63.0
5 Third level, first stage, leading to an award not equivalent ...	9.016	50.9	8.512	49.9	0.504	68.8
6 Third level, first stage, leading to a first university degree ...	2.900	50.3	2.799	50.1	0.101	56.4
7 Third level, second stage	1.775	42.0	1.728	42.1	0.047	38.3
9 Education not definable by level	1.814	18.7	1.757	18.3	0.057	31.6

Status in employment (ICSE-1993)			2005 [1 2 3] Labour force survey			
Total	.	.	98.589	34.2	.	.
1 Employees	.	.	68.314	36.5	.	.
2 Employers	.	.	6.956	21.7	.	.
3 Own-account workers	.	.	19.341	30.0	.	.
5 Contributing family workers	.	.	3.871	37.5	.	.
6 Not classifiable by status	.	.	0.104	28.8	.	.

Belize

2. Population ('000), Activity rate and Unemployment rate

Age group	Population 2005 [1,3] Labour force survey			Activity rate 2005 [1,3] Labour force survey			Unemployment rate 2005 [2,3] Labour force survey		
	Total	Men	Women	Total	Men	Women	Total	Men	Women
Total	289.875	143.327	146.548	38.2	48.9	27.8	11.0	7.4	17.2
15+	179.287	87.911	91.374	61.3	79.0	44.3	11.0	7.4	17.1
15-24	57.882	28.885	28.996	49.5	61.5	37.5	19.5	13.8	28.8
25-54	95.481	45.385	50.096	74.0	95.8	54.3	8.0	4.9	13.0
55+	25.924	13.641	12.282	40.9	60.1	19.5	7.8	6.9	10.9

3. Paid employment ('000), Hours of work (weekly) and Wages

Statistics not available.

4. Occupational injuries and Strikes and Lockouts

Statistics not available.

5. Consumer price indices (base period: 2000=100)

	2002	2003	2004	2005	2006	2007
General indices	103.4	106.1	109.3	113.1	118.2	120.9
Food index, including non-alcoholic beverages [4]	101.6	104.2	106.9	111.8	116.6	122.7
Electricity, gas and other fuel indices	103.5	111.6	122.7	132.1	.	.
Clothing indices, including footwear	95.6	96.3	96.7	96.7	98.1	98.9
Rent indices [5]	101.0	104.7	110.1	114.7	120.3	121.9

[1] Incl. the armed forces. [2] Persons aged 14 years and over. [3] April. [4] Incl. tobacco. [5] Incl. water, electricity, gas and other fuels.

[1] Y compris les forces armées. [2] Personnes âgées de 14 ans et plus. [3] Avril. [4] Y compris le tabac. [5] Y compris l'eau, l'électricité, le gaz et autres combustibles.

[1] Incl. las fuerzas armadas. [2] Personas de 14 años y más. [3] Abril. [4] Incl. el tabaco. [5] Incl. el agua, la electricidad, el gas y otros combustibles

Bénin

1. Population active, Emploi et Chômage ('000)

Groupe d'âge	Population active Total	Femmes (%)	Emploi Total	Femmes (%)	Chômage Total	Femmes (%)
	2002 [1] Recensement de la population		2002 ★ Recensement de la population		2002 [1] Recensement de la population	
Total	3 065.980	49.8	3 045.514	49.9	20.466	33.5
0-14	482.785	52.8	480.023	52.8	2.762	49.4
15-19	325.483	53.0	323.331	53.1	2.152	41.2
20-24	381.977	54.9	378.308	55.1	3.669	39.4
25-29	419.276	51.6	415.250	51.8	4.026	32.0
30-34	341.331	47.2	338.781	47.4	2.550	25.7
35-39	283.714	47.5	282.005	47.6	1.709	25.3
40-44	220.891	46.4	219.643	46.5	1.248	21.3
45-49	163.961	45.6	163.042	45.7	0.919	18.9
50-54	136.685	45.0	136.089	45.2	0.596	15.6
55-59	71.342	44.5	71.046	44.6	0.296	18.2
60-64	85.927	47.0	85.733	47.1	0.194	24.2
65-69	43.383	47.2	43.277	47.2	0.106	30.2
70-74	45.728	43.4	45.634	43.4	0.094	42.6
75+	63.497	40.2	63.352	40.1	0.145	47.6

Activité économique (CITI-Rév.2)	1992 [2][3] Recensement de la population					
Total	2 085.4	42.6	.	.	.	.
1 Agriculture, chasse, sylviculture et pêche	1 147.7	32.0	.	.	.	.
2 Industries extractives	0.7	7.9	.	.	.	.
3 Industries manufacturières	160.4	41.9	.	.	.	.
4 Electricité, gaz et eau	1.2	2.0	.	.	.	.
5 Bâtiment et travaux publics	51.7	1.3	.	.	.	.
6 Commerce de gros et de détail; restaurants et hôtels	432.5	91.5	.	.	.	.
7 Transports, entrepôts et communications	52.8	1.2	.	.	.	.
8 Banques, assurances, affaires immobilières et services ...	3.1	12.9	.	.	.	.
9 Services fournis à la collectivité, services sociaux ...	164.5	23.4	.	.	.	.
0 Activités mal désignées	38.5	33.6	.	.	.	.

Situation dans la profession (CISP-58)	1992 [2][3] Recensement de la population					
Total	2 085.4	42.6	.	.	.	.
1 Employeurs et personnes travaillant à leur propre compte	1 217.5	46.6	.	.	.	.
2 Salariés	111.0	20.9	.	.	.	.
3 Travailleurs familiaux non rémunérés	636.4	39.9	.	.	.	.
4 Inclassables d'après la situation	120.5	37.1	.	.	.	.

2. Population ('000), Taux d'activité et Taux de chômage

Groupe d'âge	Population 2002 [1][4] Recensement de la population			Taux d'activité 2002 [1][4] Recensement de la population			Taux de chômage 2002 [1] Recensement de la population		
	Total	Hommes	Femmes	Total	Hommes	Femmes	Total	Hommes	Femmes
Total	5 345.9	2 563.7	2 782.2	57.4	60.1	54.8	0.7	0.9	0.4
15+	3 600.2	1 662.3	1 937.9	71.8	78.9	65.6	0.7	0.9	0.4
15-24	1 217.2	565.5	651.7	58.1	57.5	58.7	0.8	1.1	0.6
25-54	1 915.3	880.1	1 035.2	81.8	92.6	72.5	0.7	1.0	0.4
55+	467.7	216.7	251.0	66.3	79.4	55.0	0.3	0.3	0.2

3. Emploi rémunéré ('000), Durée du travail (hebdomadaire) et Salaires

Données non disponibles.

4. Lésions professionnelles et Grèves et lock-out

Données non disponibles.

5. Indices des prix à la consommation (période de base: 2000=100)

Cotonou	2002	2003	2004	2005	2006	2007
Indices généraux	106.5	108.1	109.0	114.9	119.2	120.8
Indices de l'alimentation, y compris les boissons non alcoolisées [5]	108.0	105.5	104.7	114.4	113.8	112.6
Indices de l'habillement, y compris les chaussures	101.4	101.9	101.2	101.4	103.1	102.0
Indices du loyer [6]	107.4	112.9	114.6	123.3	131.9	131.4

[1] Feb. [2] Persons aged 10 years and over. [3] March. [4] "De jure" population. [5] Incl. alcoholic beverages and tobacco. [6] Incl. water, electricity, gas and other fuels.

[1] Fév. [2] Personnes âgées de 10 ans et plus. [3] Mars. [4] Population "de jure". [5] Y compris les boissons alcoolisées et le tabac. [6] Y compris l'eau, l'électricité, le gaz et autres combustibles.

[1] Feb. [2] Personas de 10 años y más. [3] Marzo. [4] Población "de jure". [5] Incl. las bebidas alcohólicas y el tabaco. [6] Incl. el agua, la electricidad, el gas y otros combustibles.

Bermuda

1. Economically active population, Employment and Unemployment ('000)

	Economically active population		Employment		Unemployment	
	Total	Women (%)	Total	Women (%)	Total	Women (%)
Age group	2000 [1,2] Population census		2000 ★ Population census		2000 [1,2] Population census	
Total	36.878	48.5	35.877	48.7	1.001	40.7
15-19	1.124	51.3	0.952	54.3	0.172	34.9
20-24	2.286	50.6	2.092	51.6	0.194	39.7
25-29	4.101	49.6	3.973	49.7	0.128	46.9
30-34	4.926	47.5	4.845	47.5	0.081	49.4
35-39	5.598	47.8	5.486	47.8	0.112	44.6
40-44	5.094	49.7	4.999	49.9	0.095	40.0
45-49	4.257	49.1	4.189	49.3	0.068	38.2
50-54	3.607	49.2	3.539	49.4	0.068	38.2
55-59	2.526	47.6	2.482	47.8	0.044	34.1
60-64	1.762	46.8	1.739	47.0	0.023	34.8
65-69	0.918	41.1	0.907	40.9	0.011	54.5
70-74	0.444	42.1	0.440	42.3	0.004	25.0
75+	0.235	43.8	0.234	44.0	0.001	.

Economic activity (ISIC-Rev.3)			2000 [1,2] Population census			
Total	.	.	36.878	48.5	.	.
A Agriculture, Hunting and Forestry	.	.	0.420	9.8	.	.
B Fishing	.	.	0.082	1.2	.	.
C Mining and Quarrying	.	.	0.071	1.4	.	.
D Manufacturing	.	.	1.176	33.5	.	.
E Electricity, Gas and Water Supply	.	.	0.425	19.8	.	.
F Construction	.	.	3.792	4.7	.	.
G Wholesale and Retail Trade; Repair of Motor Vehicles ...	.	.	4.773	50.2	.	.
H Hotels and Restaurants	.	.	4.297	44.3	.	.
I Transport, Storage and Communications	.	.	2.843	35.1	.	.
J Financial Intermediation	.	.	2.791	70.8	.	.
K Real Estate, Renting and Business Activities	.	.	3.652	52.8	.	.
L Public Administration and Defence; Compulsory Social ...	.	.	2.510	45.7	.	.
M Education	.	.	1.691	77.9	.	.
N Health and Social Work	.	.	2.335	80.3	.	.
O Other Community, Social and Personal Service Activities	.	.	1.762	54.2	.	.
P Households with Employed Persons	.	.	0.963	85.2	.	.
Q Extra-Territorial Organizations and Bodies	.	.	0.037	51.4	.	.
X Not classifiable by economic activity	.	.	3.258	56.4	.	.

Occupation (ISCO-1968)	1991 [2,3] Population census		2005 [4,5] Labour-related establishment census			
Total	33.120	47.9	38.947	48.0	.	.
0/1 Professional, technical and related workers	5.440	53.4	7.877	55.6	.	.
2 Administrative and managerial workers	4.460	36.9	5.631	44.2	.	.
3 Clerical and related workers	6.774	85.4	7.290	84.5	.	.
4 Sales workers	1.959	66.1	2.315	62.3	.	.
5 Service workers	6.485	53.8	7.417	48.0	.	.
6 Agriculture, animal husbandry and forestry workers ...	0.738	2.0	0.949	4.7	.	.
7/8/9 Production and related workers, transport equipment ...	7.003	8.7	7.468	8.2	.	.
X Not classifiable by occupation	0.261	46.7	.	.	.	.

Education level (ISCED-97)	2000 [1,2] Population census		2000 ★ Population census		2000 [1,2] Population census	
Total	36.878	48.5	35.877	48.7	1.001	40.7
X No schooling	0.064	34.4	0.064	34.4	-	.
1 Primary education or first stage of basic education	1.663	37.2	1.620	37.1	0.043	39.5
2 Lower secondary or second stage of basic education	1.369	35.1	1.319	35.4	0.050	28.0
3 Upper secondary education	12.412	45.2	11.888	45.6	0.524	36.3
4 Post-secondary non-tertiary education	10.606	54.1	10.409	54.3	0.197	44.7
5A First stage of tertiary education - theoretically based	10.576	50.3	10.397	50.3	0.179	53.1
6 Second stage of tertiary education	0.082	47.6	0.077	48.1	0.005	40.0
? Level not stated	0.106	37.7	0.103	37.9	0.003	33.3

Status in employment (ICSE-1993)	2000 [1,2] Population census					
Total	37.9	48.3				
1 Employees	33.0	50.7				
2 Employers	1.5	25.4				
3 Own-account workers	2.1	31.2				
5 Contributing family workers	0.1	55.9				
6 Not classifiable by status	1.1	41.2				

2. Population ('000), Activity rate and Unemployment rate

	Population			Activity rate			Unemployment rate		
Age group	2000 [2] Population census			2000 [2] Population census			2000 [1,2] Population census		
	Total	Men	Women	Total	Men	Women	Total	Men	Women
Total	62.1	29.8	32.3	59.4	63.8	55.4	3.0	3.0	2.0
15+	50.2	23.9	26.3	73.4	79.5	67.9	2.7	3.1	.
15-24	6.8	3.3	3.4	50.4	50.3	50.5	10.7	13.7	7.9
25-54	30.8	15.1	15.8	89.4	93.9	85.1	2.0	2.2	1.8
55+	12.6	5.5	7.1	46.7	57.9	38.0	1.4	1.7	.

Bermuda

3. Paid employment ('000), Hours of work (weekly) and Wages

Economic activity (ISIC-Rev.3)	Paid employment 2006 [4,5] Labour-related establishment census			Hours of work 2006 [6] Labour-related establishment census Hours actually worked / Employees			Wages 2006 [6] Labour-related establishment census Earnings per month / Employees / Dollar		
	Total	Men	Women	Total	Men [6]	Women [6]	Total	Men	Women
Total	39.686	20.730	18.956	34.1	36.9	31.1	4 222	4 365	4 062
A-B	.	.	.	36.6	37.1	31.2	.	.	.
C-Q	.	.	.	.	.	.	4 235	4 390	4 063
A	0.569	0.520	0.049	39.4	40.0	33.1	3 181	3 154	3 600
B	0.118	0.111	0.007	22.8	23.1	18.1	4 500	4 500	.
C	0.005	0.005	-	28.8	28.8	.	.	.	.
D	0.965	0.684	0.281	35.6	36.9	32.4	3 692	3 792	3 490
E	0.372	0.295	0.077	31.8	35.3	18.4	4 793	4 813	4 647
F	3.653	3.453	0.200	39.4	39.9	31.8	4 392	4 409	4 016
G	4.775	2.485	2.290	33.9	36.5	31.2	3 166	3 696	2 719
H	4.901	2.821	2.080	37.6	41.2	32.8	2 787	2 942	2 573
I	2.829	1.869	0.960	36.0	37.6	32.7	3 990	4 279	3 668
J	2.902	0.844	2.058	42.3	42.0	42.4	4 625	6 555	4 257
K	4.609	2.213	2.396	33.1	35.6	30.8	4 553	5 093	4 340
L	4.069	1.972	2.097	25.7	31.8	20.0	4 640	4 545	4 794
M	0.884	0.211	0.673	20.7	20.0	20.9	6 132	6 322	6 056
N	2.337	0.515	1.822	32.8	34.7	32.2	4 144	4 269	4 116
O	1.504	0.667	0.837	28.9	29.9	28.2	3 281	3 577	2 989
P	0.678	0.102	0.576	29.5	33.1	28.9	2 500	2 625	2 464
Q	4.516	1.963	2.553	33.9	35.0	33.1	6 862	10 645	5 812
X	-	-	-	.	.	.	.	.	.

Share of women in wage employment in the non-agricultural sector [4,5] (2006 - Labour-related establishment census): **48.5%**

4. Occupational injuries and Strikes and Lockouts

Economic activity (ISIC-Rev.2)	Rates of fatal injuries 1995 Labour inspectorate records Per 1,000 workers employed Reported injuries			Rates of non-fatal injuries			Strikes and lockouts		
	Total	Men	Women	Total	Men	Women	Strikes and lockouts	Workers involved	Days not worked
Total	0.029	.	.	.	.	.	.	.	.
1	0.000	.	.	.	.	.	.	.	.
3	0.000	.	.	.	.	.	.	.	.
4	0.000	.	.	.	.	.	.	.	.
5	0.614	.	.	.	.	.	.	.	.
6	0.000	.	.	.	.	.	.	.	.
7	0.000	.	.	.	.	.	.	.	.
8	0.000	.	.	.	.	.	.	.	.
9	0.000	.	.	.	.	.	.	.	.

Economic activity (ISIC-Rev.3)	Rates of fatal injuries			Rates of non-fatal injuries			Strikes and lockouts 1997 [7] Labour relations records		
	Total	Men	Women	Total	Men	Women	Strikes and lockouts	Workers involved [8]	Days not worked
Total	.	.	.	.	.	.	3	520	790
D	.	.	.	.	.	.	1	250	250
H	.	.	.	.	.	.	2	270	540

5. Consumer price indices (base period: 2000=100)

	2002	2003	2004	2005	2006	2007
General indices	105.3	108.6	112.5	116.0	119.5	124.1
Food index, including non-alcoholic beverages	103.5	105.6	108.2	111.4	113.6	117.6
Electricity, gas and other fuel indices	98.0	102.7	104.6	110.5	120.7	127.4
Clothing indices, including footwear	101.9	103.8	105.8	108.0	111.4	111.6
Rent indices	104.1	106.0	108.4	111.4	116.2	118.7
General index, excluding housing [9]	.	.	.	.	100.0	104.0

[1] Persons aged 15 years and over. [2] May. [3] Persons aged 16 years and over. [4] Aug. [5] Excl. unpaid family workers. [6] Last week of Aug. of each year. [7] Strikes only. [8] Excl. workers indirectly involved. [9] Index base: 2006=100.

Bhutan

1. Economically active population, Employment and Unemployment ('000)

	Economically active population		Employment		Unemployment	
	Total	Women (%)	Total	Women (%)	Total	Women (%)
Age group	2005 [1,2] Population census		2005 ★ Population census		2005 [1,2] Population census	
Total	256.895	36.6	249.030	36.5	7.865	39.4
15-19	23.793	50.2	22.343	50.3	1.450	49.0
20-24	45.779	34.7	42.921	34.0	2.858	45.2
25-29	41.770	34.4	40.609	34.4	1.161	34.2
30-34	31.505	34.0	30.945	34.0	0.560	31.1
35-39	28.956	34.3	28.476	34.4	0.480	32.1
40-44	22.227	36.0	21.879	36.1	0.348	27.9
45-49	20.251	36.3	19.886	36.4	0.365	29.6
50-54	15.371	37.1	15.090	37.4	0.281	24.9
55-59	10.509	37.6	10.333	37.8	0.176	26.1
60-64	7.695	37.8	7.598	37.9	0.097	30.9
65+	9.039	36.4	8.950	36.5	0.089	22.5

Economic activity (ISIC-Rev.3)			2005 [1,2] Population census			
Total	.	.	249.030	36.4	.	.
A Agriculture, Hunting and Forestry	.	.	108.617	52.6	.	.
B Fishing	.	.	-	.	.	.
C Mining and Quarrying	.	.	2.839	21.8	.	.
D Manufacturing	.	.	4.882	33.3	.	.
E Electricity, Gas and Water Supply	.	.	4.116	9.7	.	.
F Construction	.	.	30.887	8.4	.	.
G Wholesale and Retail Trade; Repair of Motor Vehicles ...	.	.	6.747	48.5	.	.
H Hotels and Restaurants	.	.	4.017	46.6	.	.
I Transport, Storage and Communications	.	.	8.057	8.0	.	.
J Financial Intermediation	.	.	2.287	30.0	.	.
L Public Administration and Defence; Compulsory Social ...	.	.	17.494	8.5	.	.
M Education	.	.	7.832	36.2	.	.
N Health and Social Work	.	.	2.521	33.9	.	.
O-X	.	.	48.734	34.9	.	.

Status in employment (ICSE-1993)			2005 [1,2] Population census			
Total	.	.	249.030	36.4	.	.
1 Employees	.	.	98.357	16.6	.	.
2 Employers	.	.	3.260	19.4	.	.
3 Own-account workers	.	.	49.552	43.7	.	.
4 Members of producers' cooperatives	.	.	-	.	.	.
5 Contributing family workers	.	.	80.610	58.2	.	.
6 Not classifiable by status	.	.	17.251	31.8	.	.

2. Population ('000), Activity rate and Unemployment rate

Age group	Population 2005 [2,3] Population census			Activity rate 2005 [2,3] Population census			Unemployment rate 2005 [1,2] Population census		
	Total	Men	Women	Total	Men	Women	Total	Men	Women
Total	.	.	.	.	.	.	3.1	2.9	3.3
15+	425.023	227.831	197.192	60.4	71.5	47.7	3.1	2.9	3.3
15-24	145.810	77.758	68.052	47.7	53.7	40.9	6.2	5.5	7.2
25-54	218.502	118.414	100.088	73.3	87.8	56.0	2.0	2.1	1.8
55+	60.711	31.659	29.052	44.9	54.0	34.9	1.3	1.6	0.9

3. Paid employment ('000), Hours of work (weekly) and Wages

Statistics not available.

4. Occupational injuries and Strikes and Lockouts

Statistics not available.

5. Consumer price indices (base period: 2000=100)

	2002	2003	2004	2005	2006	2007
General indices	106.0	107.6	110.9	116.8	122.6	129.0
Food index, including non-alcoholic beverages	103.6	104.5	102.9	108.8	114.2	123.5
Clothing indices, including footwear [4]	.	.	100.0	104.2	110.6	120.1
Rent indices [4,5]	.	.	100.0	109.4	114.4	117.4

[1] Persons aged 15 years and over. [2] May. [3] "De facto" population. [4] Index base: 2004=100. [5] Incl. water, electricity, gas and other fuels.

[1] Personnes âgées de 15 ans et plus. [2] Mai. [3] Population "de facto". [4] Base de l'indice: 2004=100. [5] Y compris l'eau, l'électricité, le gaz et autres combustibles.

[1] Personas de 15 años y más. [2] Mayo. [3] Población "de facto". [4] Base del indice: 2004=100. [5] Incl. el agua, la electricidad, el gas y otros combustibles.

Bolivia

1. Población económicamente activa, Empleo y Desempleo ('000)

	Población económicamente activa		Empleo		Desempleo	
	Total	Mujeres (%)	Total	Mujeres (%)	Total	Mujeres (%)

Grupo de edad
2000 [1,2,3] — Encuesta de la fuerza de trabajo (PEA y Empleo); 2000 [2,3] — Encuesta de la fuerza de trabajo (Desempleo)

Grupo de edad	Total PEA	Mujeres (%)	Empleo Total	Mujeres (%)	Desempleo Total	Mujeres (%)
Total	3 823.94	44.6	.	.	168.62	54.1
10-14	248.24	46.0	.	.	7.83	23.1
15-19	370.51	47.8	.	.	30.75	51.4
20-24	463.81	42.5	.	.	40.53	57.2
25-29	458.50	45.1	.	.	26.00	54.8
30-34	404.74	43.2	.	.	13.40	52.2
35-39	422.77	44.7	.	.	18.35	67.4
40-44	387.72	44.0	.	.	7.68	66.4
45-49	343.35	48.4	.	.	9.13	66.4
50-54	223.50	42.3	.	.	4.56	63.6
55-59	179.03	43.8	.	.	5.36	20.1
60-64	118.44	42.5	.	.	2.40	10.8
65+	203.33	42.7	.	.	1.55	46.5

Actividad económica (CIIU-Rev.3)
2000 [1,2,3] — Encuesta de la fuerza de trabajo (Empleo); 1995 [2,3] — Encuesta de la fuerza de trabajo (Desempleo)

Actividad	Empleo Total	Mujeres (%)	Desempleo Total	Mujeres (%)
Total	2 091.18	44.2	47.47	48.7
A Agricultura, ganadería, caza y silvicultura	102.65	30.2	0.78	33.2
B Pesca	-	.	.	.
C Explotación de minas y canteras	35.33	14.9	1.12	22.6
D Industrias manufactureras	320.10	36.3	9.40	48.0
E Suministro de electricidad, gas y agua	15.86	8.6	0.45	25.5
F Construcción	218.86	3.8	5.23	2.5
G Comercio al por mayor y al por menor; reparación ...	536.07	61.0	7.76	59.0
H Hoteles y restaurantes	124.44	75.9	2.62	77.3
I Transporte, almacenamiento y comunicaciones	144.33	9.3	2.30	.
J Intermediación financiera	19.97	32.2	0.58	29.5
K Actividades inmobiliarias, empresariales y de alquiler	95.83	25.5	1.82	45.7
L Administración pública y defensa; planes de seguridad ...	72.65	24.9	3.09	36.9
M Enseñanza	132.79	57.4	1.40	49.3
N Servicios sociales y de salud	48.80	56.7	1.18	60.7
O Otras actividades de servicios comunitarios ...	98.78	52.2	1.89	54.9
P Hogares privados con servicio doméstico	126.79	95.9	3.63	100.0
Q Organizaciones y órganos extraterritoriales	2.77	64.6	0.20	100.0
X No pueden clasificarse según la actividad económica	-	.	4.04	70.2
Desempleados sin empleo anterior	.	.	14.11	55.4

Ocupación (CIUO-88)
2000 [1,2,3] — Encuesta de la fuerza de trabajo (Empleo); 1995 [2,3] — Encuesta de la fuerza de trabajo (Desempleo)

Ocupación	Empleo Total	Mujeres (%)	Desempleo Total	Mujeres (%)
Total	2 091.18	44.2	47.47	48.7
1 Miembros del poder ejecutivo y de los cuerpos legislativos ...	43.42	35.8	1.58	22.9
2 Profesionales científicos e intelectuales	200.38	48.6	0.83	10.6
3 Técnicos y profesionales de nivel medio	114.06	23.7	5.26	42.6
4 Empleados de oficina	111.33	56.6	4.56	68.3
5 Trabajadores de los servicios y vendedores de comercios ...	511.07	70.2	7.29	81.4
6 Agricultores y trabajadores calificados agropecuarios ...	77.69	28.0	0.70	37.1
7 Oficiales, operarios y artesanos de artes mecánicas ...	541.48	18.4	10.59	24.0
8 Operadores de instalaciones y máquinas y montadores	155.59	1.8	3.11	6.7
9 Trabajadores no calificados	335.30	71.3	9.52	58.2
0 Fuerzas armadas	5.68	.	.	.
X No pueden clasificarse según la ocupación	.	.	4.04	70.2
Desempleados sin empleo anterior	.	.	14.11	55.4

Nivel de educación (CINE-76)
2000 [1,2,3] — Encuesta de la fuerza de trabajo

Nivel	Total	Mujeres (%)
Total	3 823.94	44.6
X Sin escolaridad	448.86	68.4
0 Enseñanza anterior al primer grado	4.22	57.3
1 Enseñanza de primer grado	1 898.68	43.8
2 Enseñanza de segundo grado, ciclo inferior [4]	927.44	36.3
5 Enseñanza de tercer grado que no permite obtener un ...	335.68	46.5
6 Enseñanza de tercer grado que permite obtener un primer ...	185.39	35.9
7 Enseñanza de tercer grado que permite obtener un título ...	21.60	27.5
? Nivel desconocido	2.08	.

Situación en el empleo (CISE-1993)
2000 [1,2,3] — Encuesta de la fuerza de trabajo

Situación	Empleo Total	Mujeres (%)
Total	2 091.18	44.2
1 Asalariados	1 040.73	38.5
2 Empleadores	62.35	23.4
3 Trabajadores por cuenta propia	821.61	49.5
4 Miembros de cooperativas de productores	8.29	6.8
5 Trabajadores familiares auxiliares	163.02	63.0

Bolivia

2. Población ('000), Tasa de actividad y Tasa de desempleo

Grupo de edad	Población 2000 [1,2] Encuesta de la fuerza de trabajo			Tasa de actividad 2000 [1,2] Encuesta de la fuerza de trabajo			Tasa de desempleo 2000 [2,3] Encuesta de la fuerza de trabajo		
	Total	Hombres	Mujeres	Total	Hombres	Mujeres	Total	Hombres	Mujeres
Total	8 280.2	4 064.0	4 216.2	46.2	52.1	40.5	7.5	6.2	9.0
15+	5 082.8	2 413.1	2 669.7	70.3	82.2	59.6	4.5	3.6	5.6
15-24	1 616.9	765.6	851.3	51.6	60.1	43.9	8.5	7.0	10.4
25-54	2 682.0	1 284.0	1 398.1	83.5	96.5	71.7	3.5	2.5	4.8
55+	783.9	363.5	420.4	63.9	78.5	51.3	1.9	2.5	1.0

3. Empleo remunerado ('000), Horas de trabajo (por semana) y Salarios

Actividad económica (CIIU-Rev.2)	Empleo remunerado			Horas de trabajo 1996 [5,6] Encuesta de la fuerza de trabajo Horas pagadas / Asalariados			Salarios		
	Total	Hombres	Mujeres	Total	Hombres	Mujeres	Total	Hombres	Mujeres
2	.	.	.	.	44.21	.	.	.	.
3	.	.	.	44.67	44.69	44.53	.	.	.
4	.	.	.	40.00	40.00	40.00	.	.	.
5	.	.	.	.	46.82	.	.	.	.
6	.	.	.	44.10	44.35	43.74	.	.	.
7	.	.	.	42.02	42.03	42.00	.	.	.
8	.	.	.	40.42	40.38	40.46	.	.	.
9	.	.	.	37.40	39.45	35.54	.	.	.

Actividad económica (CIIU-Rev.3)	Empleo remunerado			Horas de trabajo			Salarios 2007 Registros administrativos y fuentes relacionadas Tasas de salarios por mes / Asalariados / Boliviano		
	Total	Hombres	Mujeres	Total	Hombres	Mujeres	Total	Hombres	Mujeres
E	.	.	.	.	.	.	5 018	5 006	5 111
F	.	.	.	.	.	.	1 749	1 728	2 186
G	.	.	.	.	.	.	1 970	2 037	1 819
H [7]	.	.	.	.	.	.	1 628	1 578	1 722
I [8]	.	.	.	.	.	.	2 682	2 798	2 300
J	.	.	.	.	.	.	4 227	4 919	3 346
K	.	.	.	.	.	.	2 666	2 757	2 468
N	.	.	.	.	.	.	1 588	2 112	1 351

4. Lesiones profesionales y Huelgas y cierres patronales

Actividad económica (CIIU-Rev.2)	Tasas de lesiones mortales 1998 Registros de seguros Por 100 000 trabajadores asegurados Lesiones indemnizadas			Tasas de lesiones no mortales			Huelgas y cierres patronales		
	Total	Hombres	Mujeres	Total	Hombres	Mujeres	Huelgas y cierres patronales	Trabajadores implicados	Días no trabajados
Total	6.6	.	.	.	.	.	.	.	.
1	0.0	.	.	.	.	.	.	.	.
2	88.7	.	.	.	.	.	.	.	.
3	6.5	.	.	.	.	.	.	.	.
4	0.0	.	.	.	.	.	.	.	.
5	11.0	.	.	.	.	.	.	.	.
6	0.0	.	.	.	.	.	.	.	.
7	0.0	.	.	.	.	.	.	.	.
8	21.9	.	.	.	.	.	.	.	.
9	4.0	.	.	.	.	.	.	.	.

Actividad económica (CIIU-Rev.3)	Tasas de lesiones mortales			Tasas de lesiones no mortales			Huelgas y cierres patronales 1999 Registros de relaciones laborales		
	Total	Hombres	Mujeres	Total	Hombres	Mujeres	Huelgas y cierres patronales	Trabajadores implicados	Días no trabajados
Total	.	.	.	.	.	.	174	.	.
A-B	.	.	.	.	.	.	1	.	.
C	.	.	.	.	.	.	3	.	.
D	.	.	.	.	.	.	7	.	.
E	.	.	.	.	.	.	1	.	.
F	.	.	.	.	.	.	1	.	.
G	.	.	.	.	.	.	0	.	.
I	.	.	.	.	.	.	13	.	.
J	.	.	.	.	.	.	0	.	.
L	.	.	.	.	.	.	43	.	.
M	.	.	.	.	.	.	43	.	.
N	.	.	.	.	.	.	28	.	.
X	.	.	.	.	.	.	34	.	.

Bolivia

5. Índices de precios al consumidor (periodo de base: 2000=100)

[9]	2002	2003	2004	2005	2006	2007
Índices generales	102.5	105.9	110.6	116.6	121.6	132.2
Índices de la alimentación incluyendo las bebidas no alcohólicas	99.7	103.2	109.3	115.7	122.2	138.9
Índices de la electricidad, gas y otros combustibles	108.9	114.2	118.8	123.0	124.1	125.5
Índices del vestido, incl. calzado	105.9	109.0	111.4	114.7	119.1	125.1
Índices del aquiler	101.1	109.0	111.0	112.3	112.7	113.1

[1] Excl. conscripts. [2] Urban areas, Nov. [3] Persons aged 10 years and over. [4] Levels 2-3. [5] Excl. overtime. [6] Sep. [7] Excl. restaurants. [8] Excl. communications. [9] Urban areas.

[1] Non compris les conscrits. [2] Régions urbaines, nov. [3] Personnes âgées de 10 ans et plus. [4] Niveaux 2-3. [5] Non compris les heures supplémentaires. [6] Sept. [7] Excl. restaurants. [8] Non compris les communications. [9] Régions urbaines.

[1] Excl. los conscriptos. [2] Areas urbanas, nov. [3] Personas de 10 años y más. [4] Niveles 2-3. [5] Excl. las horas extraordinarias. [6] Sept. [7] Excl. restaurantes. [8] Excl. las comunicaciones. [9] Areas urbanas.

Bosnia and Herzegovina

1. Economically active population, Employment and Unemployment ('000)

	Economically active population		Employment		Unemployment	
	Total	Women (%)	Total	Women (%)	Total	Women (%)
Age group		2007[1]		2007 ★		2007[1]
		Labour force survey		Labour force survey		Labour force survey
Total	1 196	36.5	849	34.4	347	41.5
15-24	162	37.7	67	34.3	95	40.0
25-49	774	37.7	564	35.3	210	44.3
50-64	231	32.0	190	32.6	41	29.3
65+	29	34.5	.	.	.	.
Education level (ISCED-76)		2007[1]		2007 ★		2007[1]
		Labour force survey		Labour force survey		Labour force survey
Total	1 196	36.5	849	34.4	347	41.5
X No schooling[2]	290	39.0	200	37.0	90	43.3
2 Second level, first stage	774	33.9	532	30.8	242	40.5
3 Second level, second stage[3]	132	46.2	118	45.8	14	50.0
Status in employment (ICSE-1993)				2007[1]		
				Labour force survey		
Total	.	.	850	34.4	.	.
1 Employees	.	.	620	34.7	.	.
2,3	.	.	192	27.1	.	.
5 Contributing family workers	.	.	37	70.3	.	.

2. Population ('000), Activity rate and Unemployment rate

	Population			Activity rate			Unemployment rate		
Age group	2007			2007			2007[1]		
	Labour force survey			Labour force survey			Labour force survey		
	Total	Men	Women	Total	Men	Women	Total	Men	Women
Total	3 315	1 613	1 703	36.1	47.1	25.6	29.0	26.7	32.9
15+	2 725	1 317	1 408	43.9	57.8	31.0	28.9	26.5	32.7
15-24	485	248	236	33.4	40.7	25.8	58.6	55.4	62.3

3. Paid employment ('000), Hours of work (weekly) and Wages

Economic activity (ISIC-Rev.3)	Paid employment			Hours of work			Wages		
							2006[4]		
							Administrative records and related sources		
							Earnings per month / Employees / Marka		
	Total	Men	Women	Total	Men	Women	Total	Men	Women
Total	.	.	.	.	.	.	887.07	.	.
A	.	.	.	.	.	.	820.17	.	.
B	.	.	.	.	.	.	589.38	.	.
C	.	.	.	.	.	.	771.23	.	.
D	.	.	.	.	.	.	672.78	.	.
E	.	.	.	.	.	.	1 521.90	.	.
F	.	.	.	.	.	.	642.15	.	.
G	.	.	.	.	.	.	747.69	.	.
H	.	.	.	.	.	.	639.08	.	.
I	.	.	.	.	.	.	1 128.25	.	.
J	.	.	.	.	.	.	1 696.40	.	.
K	.	.	.	.	.	.	896.57	.	.
L	.	.	.	.	.	.	1 169.47	.	.
M	.	.	.	.	.	.	901.82	.	.
N	.	.	.	.	.	.	1 009.06	.	.
O	.	.	.	.	.	.	916.90	.	.

4. Occupational injuries and Strikes and Lockouts

Statistics not available.

5. Consumer price indices (base period: 2000=100)

Statistics not available for the period 2002-2007.

---

[1] Persons aged 15 years and over. [2] Levels X-1. [3] Levels 3-7. [4] Data refer to the Federation of Bosnia and Herzegovina.

[1] Personnes âgées de 15 ans et plus. [2] Niveaux X-1. [3] Niveaux 3-7. [4] Les données se réfèrent à la Fédération de Bosnie-Herzégovine.

[1] Personas de 15 años y más. [2] Niveles X-1. [3] Niveles 3-7. [4] Los datos se refieren a la Federación de Bosnia y Herzegovina.

Botswana

1. Economically active population, Employment and Unemployment ('000)

	Economically active population		Employment		Unemployment	
	Total	Women (%)	Total	Women (%)	Total	Women (%)
Age group	2001 [1][2][3] Population census		2001 ★ Population census		2006 [2] Labour force survey	
Total	589.782	44.0	480.264	42.0	114.422	55.5
12-14	2.488	25.0	1.736	18.7	0.218	78.9
15-19	35.804	45.0	18.417	37.6	10.749	51.4
20-24	105.053	48.2	66.575	43.6	36.784	55.9
25-29	111.471	45.9	89.265	43.3	24.836	56.4
30-34	87.555	45.1	76.420	43.8	13.308	64.3
35-39	70.946	45.4	63.488	45.0	9.670	57.6
40-44	53.999	44.2	49.364	44.2	7.023	57.8
45-49	42.105	41.7	39.013	42.0	5.194	52.1
50-54	27.232	37.6	25.579	38.0	3.341	36.5
55-59	17.712	36.1	16.718	36.5	1.517	40.0
60+	32.257	34.0	30.969	34.1	1.782	31.6
?	3.160	7.0	2.730	7.2	.	.

Economic activity (ISIC-Rev.3)			2003 [1][2] Labour force survey		1996 [2] Labour force survey	
Total	.	.	462.366	46.9	94.528	51.9
A-B	.	.	98.102	28.6	21.911	45.1
C Mining and Quarrying	.	.	13.764	18.1	1.876	5.7
D Manufacturing	.	.	44.557	58.9	5.386	62.9
E Electricity, Gas and Water Supply	.	.	4.412	20.9	0.355	3.7
F Construction	.	.	41.917	14.8	15.248	26.1
G Wholesale and Retail Trade; Repair of Motor Vehicles ...	.	.	61.658	66.1	7.895	66.6
H Hotels and Restaurants	.	.	14.744	74.2	2.166	85.9
I Transport, Storage and Communications	.	.	12.599	25.1	1.302	15.0
J Financial Intermediation	.	.	4.930	68.8	0.547	62.7
K Real Estate, Renting and Business Activities	.	.	14.340	35.7	1.559	26.9
L Public Administration and Defence; Compulsory Social ...	.	.	67.232	46.1	4.252	40.1
M Education	.	.	38.703	63.3	2.762	70.9
N Health and Social Work	.	.	13.964	68.1	0.542	75.8
O Other Community, Social and Personal Service Activities	.	.	9.556	57.7	0.790	70.9
P Households with Employed Persons	.	.	21.621	89.0	5.860	93.7
Q Extra-Territorial Organizations and Bodies	.	.	0.223	.	.	.
Q-X	.	.	.	.	1.231	50.3
X Not classifiable by economic activity	.	.	0.043	.	.	.
Unemployed seeking their first job	.	.	.	.	20.837	61.8

Occupation (ISCO-88)			2003 [1][2] Labour force survey		1996 [2] Labour force survey	
Total	.	.	462.366	46.9	94.520	51.9
1 Legislators, senior officials and managers	.	.	12.803	33.0	0.234	13.7
2 Professionals	.	.	23.534	41.4	0.262	94.3
3 Technicians and associate professionals	.	.	33.000	58.3	2.949	61.5
4 Clerks	.	.	33.544	77.1	3.467	67.4
5 Service workers and shop and market sales workers	.	.	55.724	60.0	8.515	68.5
6 Skilled agricultural and fishery workers	.	.	59.779	34.0	19.183	49.3
7 Craft and related trade workers	.	.	70.303	38.4	10.640	27.9
8 Plant and machine operators and assemblers	.	.	27.097	6.2	1.984	5.0
9 Elementary occupations	.	.	144.103	52.4	25.066	50.3
X Not classifiable by occupation	.	.	2.479	.	1.395	54.6
Unemployed seeking their first job	.	.	.	.	20.837	61.8

Education level (ISCED-97)					2003 [2] Labour force survey	
Total	.	.	.	.	144.460	53.7
X No schooling	.	.	.	.	10.504	25.7
1 Primary education or first stage of basic education	.	.	.	.	32.467	48.1
2 Lower secondary or second stage of basic education	.	.	.	.	62.096	57.8
3 Upper secondary education	.	.	.	.	39.393	59.4

Status in employment (ICSE-1993)			2003 [1][2] Labour force survey			
Total	.	.	462.4	46.9		
1 Employees	.	.	338.6	46.1		
2 Employers	.	.	12.5	39.5		
2,3	.	.	56.3	64.7		
3 Own-account workers	.	.	43.8	71.9		
5 Contributing family workers	.	.	10.4	46.5		
6 Not classifiable by status	.	.	57.1	34.2		

2. Population ('000), Activity rate and Unemployment rate

	Population			Activity rate			Unemployment rate		
Age group	2001 [1][3] Population census			2001 [1][3] Population census			2001 [2][3] Population census		
	Total	Men	Women	Total	Men	Women	Total	Men	Women
Total	1 680.863	813.625	867.238	35.1	40.6	29.9	19.6	16.4	23.9
15+	1 061.300	501.247	560.053	55.0	65.0	46.2	18.5	15.7	22.1
15-24	374.319	179.800	194.519	37.6	41.2	34.3	39.7	33.9	46.1
25-54	541.817	257.963	283.854	72.6	84.8	61.5	12.8	11.1	14.8
55+	145.164	63.484	81.680	34.4	51.4	21.3	4.6	4.8	4.1

Botswana

3. Paid employment ('000), Hours of work (weekly) and Wages

Economic activity (ISIC-Rev.3)	Paid employment 2004 [1,4] Labour-related establishment survey			Hours of work 1995 [5] Labour force survey Hours actually worked / Employees			Wages 2006 [4] Labour-related establishment survey Earnings per month / Employees / Pula		
	Total	Men	Women	Total	Men	Women	Total	Men	Women
Total	297.4	180.1	117.3	.	.	.	.	.	.
A-B	5.8	3.7	2.1	.	.	.	.	.	.
A	.	.	.	.	.	.	1 010	1 081	912
C	9.3	8.4	1.0	43.2	43.8	41.3	6 936	6 435	6 930
D	34.7	17.4	17.3	42.7	45.2	40.4	1 590	2 053	1 134
E	2.6	2.1	0.5	38.6	38.5	40.8	7 777	7 881	7 358
F	27.5	23.5	3.9	38.9	42.2	31.7	2 698	2 818	2 037
G	41.7	23.1	18.5	52.2	52.4	52.0	2 065	2 452	1 625
H	11.6	4.3	7.3	54.7	60.0	52.9	1 208	1 711	988
I	12.3	9.2	3.1	50.7	53.2	43.3	3 842	3 717	4 142
J	4.4	1.6	2.8	40.6	42.0	39.6	9 191	11 799	7 448
K	16.6	12.0	4.5	51.5	55.1	40.4	.	.	.
70	.	.	.	.	.	.	4 179	4 349	3 728
L	118.4	69.2	49.2	37.3	38.7	35.0	.	.	.
M	8.3	4.0	4.3	34.7	39.4	31.9	4 179	6 652	4 560
N	1.9	0.6	1.3	38.5	40.9	37.8	4 154	5 079	3 793
O	2.4	1.0	1.4	39.1	41.8	35.2	1 966	2 282	1 735
P	.	.	.	51.0	43.3	51.9	.	.	.
Q	.	.	.	41.3	41.1	42.1	.	.	.

Share of women in wage employment in the non-agricultural sector [1,4] (2004 - Labour-related establishment survey): **39.5%**

4. Occupational injuries and Strikes and Lockouts

Economic activity (ISIC-Rev.3)	Rates of fatal injuries 1990 [6] Labour inspectorate records Per 100,000 workers insured Reported injuries			Rates of non-fatal injuries 1990 [6] Labour inspectorate records Per 100,000 workers insured Reported injuries			Strikes and lockouts 2000 [7] Labour relations records		
	Total	Men	Women	Total	Men	Women	Strikes and lockouts	Workers involved [8]	Days not worked
Total	11	.	.	440	.	.	14	1 443	27 794
A	.	.	.	.	.	.	0	0	0
B	.	.	.	.	.	.	0	0	0
C	.	.	.	.	.	.	0	0	0
D	.	.	.	.	.	.	6	505	16 692
E	.	.	.	.	.	.	0	0	0
F	.	.	.	.	.	.	5	685	9 679
G	.	.	.	.	.	.	0	0	0
H	.	.	.	.	.	.	0	0	0
I	.	.	.	.	.	.	0	0	0
J	.	.	.	.	.	.	0	0	0
K	.	.	.	.	.	.	0	0	0
L	.	.	.	.	.	.	0	0	0
M	.	.	.	.	.	.	0	0	0
N	.	.	.	.	.	.	0	0	0
O	.	.	.	.	.	.	3	253	1 423

5. Consumer price indices (base period: 2000=100)

	2002	2003	2004	2005	2006	2007
General indices	115.1	125.8	134.4	146.1	163.0	174.5
Food index, including non-alcoholic beverages	112.2	125.0	130.9	137.9	155.2	172.7
Electricity, gas and other fuel indices	115.1	118.0	125.2	147.1	.	254.5
Clothing indices, including footwear	107.8	112.4	114.8	116.9	118.1	120.0
Rent indices [9,10]	125.0	138.0	153.9	163.9	100.0[11]	104.7

[1] Excl. armed forces. [2] Persons aged 12 years and over. [3] Aug. [4] Sep. [5] On the main job. [6] Per 100,000 manual workers. [7] Strikes only. [8] Excl. workers indirectly involved. [9] Index base: 2006=100. [10] Incl. water, electricity, gas and other fuels. [11] Series (base 2006=100) replacing former series.

[1] Non compris les forces armées. [2] Personnes âgées de 12 ans et plus. [3] Août. [4] Sept. [5] Emploi principal. [6] Pour 100 000 travailleurs manuels. [7] Grèves seulement. [8] Non compris les travailleurs indirectement impliqués. [9] Base de l'indice: 2006=100. [10] Y compris l'eau, l'électricité, le gaz et autres combustibles. [11] Série (base 2006=100) remplaçant la précédente.

[1] Excl. las fuerzas armadas. [2] Personas de 12 años y más. [3] Agosto. [4] Sept. [5] Empleo principal. [6] Por 100 000 trabajadores manuales. [7] Huelgas solamente. [8] Excl. los trabajadores indirectamente implicados. [9] Base del indice: 2006=100. [10] Incl. el agua, la electricidad, el gas y otros combustibles. [11] Serie (base 2006=100) que substituye a la anterior.

Brasil

1. Población económicamente activa, Empleo y Desempleo ('000)

	Población económicamente activa		Empleo		Desempleo	
	Total	Mujeres (%)	Total	Mujeres (%)	Total	Mujeres (%)
Grupo de edad	2006 [1 2 3] Encuesta de la fuerza de trabajo		2006 ★ Encuesta de la fuerza de trabajo		2006 [2 3] Encuesta de la fuerza de trabajo	
Total	97 528	43.7	89 318	42.5	8 210	57.2
10-14	1 909	35.6	1 724	34.5	185	45.4
15-19	8 791	42.0	6 821	38.6	1 970	53.8
20-24	13 392	43.7	11 423	41.4	1 969	57.6
25-29	13 096	44.6	11 851	42.8	1 245	61.9
30-34	11 788	45.4	10 972	44.0	816	63.7
35-39	11 319	45.7	10 714	44.6	605	65.3
40-44	10 813	45.5	10 314	44.7	499	62.3
45-49	8 623	45.9	8 237	45.4	386	54.7
50-54	7 084	42.9	6 836	42.8	248	46.0
55-59	4 686	40.9	4 529	40.9	157	40.1
60-64	2 807	38.4	2 725	38.7	82	26.8
65-69	1 627	35.5	1 600	35.6	27	33.3
70-74	890	34.5	875	34.6	15	26.7
75+	704	33.1	699	33.2	5	20.0

Actividad económica (CIIU-Rev.3)

2006 [2 3] Encuesta de la fuerza de trabajo

	Total	Mujeres (%)
Total	89 318	42.5
A Agricultura, ganadería, caza y silvicultura	16 864	33.4
B Pesca	400	13.5
C Explotación de minas y canteras	343	8.2
D Industrias manufactureras	12 497	37.3
E Suministro de electricidad, gas y agua	396	17.9
F Construcción	5 837	2.9
G Comercio al por mayor y al por menor; reparación ...	15 748	38.8
H Hoteles y restaurantes	3 395	51.6
I Transporte, almacenamiento y comunicaciones	4 064	13.0
J Intermediación financiera	1 071	49.6
K Actividades inmobiliarias, empresariales y de alquiler	5 431	34.8
L Administración pública y defensa; planes de seguridad ...	4 452	37.8
M Enseñanza	4 856	78.3
N Servicios sociales y de salud	3 162	76.0
O Otras actividades de servicios comunitarios ...	3 800	59.1
P Hogares privados con servicio doméstico	6 782	93.2
Q Organizaciones y órganos extraterritoriales	4	50.0
X No pueden clasificarse según la actividad económica	218	8.3

Ocupación (CIUO-88)

2006 [2 3] Encuesta de la fuerza de trabajo

	Total	Mujeres (%)
Total	89 318	42.5
1 Miembros del poder ejecutivo y de los cuerpos legislativos ...	4 741	35.2
2 Profesionales científicos e intelectuales	5 846	58.8
3 Técnicos y profesionales de nivel medio	6 572	46.9
4 Empleados de oficina	7 228	59.1
5 Trabajadores de los servicios y vendedores de comercios ...	12 992	57.1
6 Agricultores y trabajadores calificados agropecuarios ...	16 848	33.7
7 Oficiales, operarios y artesanos de artes mecánicas ...	10 201	12.5
8 Operadores de instalaciones y máquinas y montadores	8 380	27.1
9 Trabajadores no calificados	15 839	55.5
0 Fuerzas armadas	665	5.1
X No pueden clasificarse según la ocupación	6	50.0

Nivel de educación (CINE-97)

	Población económicamente activa		Empleo		Desempleo	
	2006 [2 3] Encuesta de la fuerza de trabajo		2006 ★ Encuesta de la fuerza de trabajo		2006 [2 3] Encuesta de la fuerza de trabajo	
	Total	Mujeres (%)	Total	Mujeres (%)	Total	Mujeres (%)
Total	97 528	43.7	89 318	42.5	8 210	57.2
X Sin escolaridad	8 102	36.0	7 771	35.6	331	45.3
0 Enseñanza preescolar	10 764	36.9	10 204	36.2	560	48.9
1 Enseñanza primaria o primer ciclo de la educación básica	24 899	39.5	22 881	38.4	2 018	51.7
2 Primer ciclo de enseñanza secundaria o segundo ciclo de ...	16 942	42.8	14 723	40.7	2 219	57.1
3 Segundo ciclo de enseñanza secundaria [4]	28 171	49.3	25 414	47.8	2 757	63.1
5A Primer ciclo de la educación terciaria - teóricos [5]	8 428	55.2	8 130	54.7	298	69.5
? Nivel desconocido	222	49.5	195	47.2	27	66.7

Situación en el empleo (CISE-1993)

2006 [2 3] Encuesta de la fuerza de trabajo

	Total	Mujeres (%)
Total	89 318	42.5
1 Asalariados	56 838	44.0
2 Empleadores	3 977	26.4
3 Trabajadores por cuenta propia	18 924	32.3
5 Trabajadores familiares auxiliares	5 402	56.7
6 Inclasificables según la situación	4 177	63.9

Brasil

2. Población ('000), Tasa de actividad y Tasa de desempleo

Grupo de edad	Población 2006 [1,3,6] Encuesta de la fuerza de trabajo			Tasa de actividad 2006 [1,3,6] Encuesta de la fuerza de trabajo			Tasa de desempleo 2006 [2,3] Encuesta de la fuerza de trabajo		
	Total	Hombres	Mujeres	Total	Hombres	Mujeres	Total	Hombres	Mujeres
Total	187 228	91 196	96 031	52.1	60.2	44.4	8.4	6.4	11.0
15+	138 582	66 310	72 271	69.0	81.0	58.0	8.4	6.4	11.0
15-24	34 710	17 289	17 420	63.9	73.1	54.8	17.8	13.8	23.0
25-54	77 189	37 017	40 171	81.3	93.1	70.4	6.1	4.3	8.2
55+	26 683	12 004	14 680	40.2	55.0	28.0	2.7	2.8	2.4

3. Empleo remunerado ('000), Horas de trabajo (por semana) y Salarios

Actividad económica (CIIU-Rev.3)	Empleo remunerado 2004 [3,7] Encuesta de la fuerza de trabajo			Horas de trabajo 2006 [8,9] Encuesta de la fuerza de trabajo Horas efectivamente trabajadas / Empleo total			Salarios 2002 [10] Informes administrativos Ganancias por mes / Asalariados / Real		
	Total	Hombres	Mujeres	Total	Hombres	Mujeres	Total	Hombres	Mujeres
Total	53 172	30 012	23 161	41.4	43.8	38.4	885.39	952.64	783.69
A-B	.	.	.	44.1	44.6	39.9	409.22	415.89	362.68
C-Q	.	.	.	41.2	43.7	38.4	905.83	986.79	789.22
A	4 825	4 260	564	44.0	44.5	39.9	409.26	415.65	364.04
B	67	66	1	48.2	48.4	35.5	407.43	430.43	318.03
C	269	250	19	45.2	45.5	41.4	1 517.46	1 527.57	1 396.64
D	8 862	6 270	2 592	43.9	44.4	42.7	901.85	1 009.75	618.61
E	351	298	53	41.4	42.0	38.8	2 300.30	2 335.29	2 114.28
F	2 690	2 595	95	43.9	44.0	40.4	637.16	629.96	733.45
G	8 046	5 083	2 962	45.0	45.7	43.8	564.55	608.03	493.88
H	1 635	788	847	44.7	45.5	44.0	420.78	453.31	386.29
I	2 560	2 168	392	46.4	47.5	41.0	924.31 [11]	928.07 [11]	905.16 [11]
J	927	469	459	39.0	39.8	38.3	2 195.92	2 527.30	1 824.07
K	3 499	2 195	1 304	41.6	43.0	39.2	788.11	857.73	651.59
L	4 196	2 632	1 564	38.8	40.5	35.9	1 161.02	1 393.33	989.15
M	4 336	927	3 409	32.6	35.0	31.9	1 161.80	1 422.09	1 001.18
N	2 379	533	1 846	39.0	39.5	38.9	793.29	1 041.77	708.25
O	2 013	1 014	999	39.8	40.8	38.9	733.40	810.53	651.29
P	6 472	432	6 040	36.9	42.7	36.5	292.05	348.25	253.44
Q	4	2	2	35.5	41.3	32.5	2 214.33	2 255.21	2 170.22
X	41	29	12	42.2	43.9	38.0	.	.	.

Proporción de mujeres entre los empleados remunerados en el sector no agrícola [3,7] (2004 - Encuesta de la fuerza de trabajo): **46.8%**

4. Lesiones profesionales y Huelgas y cierres patronales

Actividad económica (CIIU-Rev.3)	Tasas de lesiones mortales 2000 Registros de seguros Por 100 000 asalariados Lesiones indemnizadas			Tasas de lesiones no mortales 2000 Registros de seguros Por 100 000 asalariados Lesiones indemnizadas			Huelgas y cierres patronales 2004 [12] Registros de organizaciones de empleadores/trabajadores		
	Total	Hombres	Mujeres	Total	Hombres	Mujeres	Huelgas y cierres patronales	Trabajadores implicados	Días no trabajados
Total	11.5	.	.	1 491	.	.	304	1 289 332	150 183 670
A	14.3	.	.	1 768	.	.	.	.	.
B	0.0	.	.	0	.	.	.	.	.
C	29.2	.	.	2 055	.	.	.	.	.
D	11.6	.	.	2 460	.	.	.	.	.
E	18.6	.	.	2 069	.	.	.	.	.
F	26.4	.	.	2 037	.	.	.	.	.
G	11.1	.	.	881	.	.	.	.	.
H	6.1	.	.	856	.	.	.	.	.
I	30.4	.	.	1 521	.	.	.	.	.
J	3.7	.	.	899	.	.	.	.	.
K	9.9	.	.	1 101	.	.	.	.	.
L	4.2	.	.	620	.	.	.	.	.
M	1.6	.	.	432	.	.	.	.	.
N	3.1	.	.	1 948	.	.	.	.	.
O	7.5	.	.	1 326	.	.	.	.	.
P	29.3	.	.	1 231	.	.	.	.	.
Q	0.0	.	.	677	.	.	.	.	.

5. Índices de precios al consumidor (periodo de base: 2000=100)

	2002	2003	2004	2005	2006	2007
Índices generales	115.9	132.9	141.7	151.4	157.8	163.5
Índices de la alimentación incluyendo las bebidas no alcohólicas [13]	117.0	140.8	146.5	151.0	151.0	.
Índices del vestido, incl. calzado	112.5	124.1	135.2	147.3	156.1	.
Índices del aquiler	120.6	136.8	148.6	158.3	165.7	.

[1] Included armed forces and conscripts. [2] Persons aged 10 years and over. [3] Sep. [4] Levels 3-4. [5] Levels 5-6. [6] "De jure" population. [7] Employees of 10 years and over. [8] Excl. the rural population of Rondonia, Acre, Amazonas, Pará and Amapá. [9] Major activity. [10] Dec. [11] Services. [12] Strikes only. [13] Incl. alcoholic beverages.

[1] Y compris les forces armées et les conscrits. [2] Personnes âgées de 10 ans et plus. [3] Sept. [4] Niveaux 3-4. [5] Niveaux 5-6. [6] Population "de jure". [7] Salariés de 10 ans et plus. [8] Non compris la population rurale de Rondonia, Acre, Amazonas, Pará et Amapá. [9] Activité principale. [10] Déc. [11] Services. [12] Grèves seulement. [13] Y compris les boissons alcoolisées.

[1] Incluye las fuezas armadas y los conscriptos. [2] Personas de 10 años y más. [3] Sept. [4] Niveles 3-4. [5] Niveles 5-6. [6] Población "de jure". [7] Asalariados de 10 años y más. [8] Excl. la población rural de Rondonia, Acre, Amazonas, Pará y Amapá. [9] Actividad principal. [10] Dic. [11] Servicios. [12] Huelgas solamente. [13] Incl. las bebidas alcohólicas.

Brunei Darussalam

1. Economically active population, Employment and Unemployment ('000)

	Economically active population		Employment		Unemployment	
	Total	Women (%)	Total	Women (%)	Total	Women (%)
Age group	2001 [1,2] Population census		2001 [1,2] Population census		2003 Employment office records	
Total	157.594	41.3	146.254	41.3	7.075	56.7
15-19	5.745	45.1	.	.	.	.
20-24	24.087	47.3	.	.	.	.
25-29	30.761	44.1	.	.	.	.
30-34	29.236	44.2	.	.	.	.
35-39	23.791	41.0	.	.	.	.
40-44	19.441	36.2	.	.	.	.
45-49	13.047	34.8	.	.	.	.
50-54	7.348	32.3	.	.	.	.
55-59	2.048	22.4	.	.	.	.
60-64	1.389	20.4	.	.	.	.
65-69	0.423	18.2	.	.	.	.
70+	0.278	8.3	.	.	.	.

Economic activity (ISIC-Rev.3)			2001 [1,2] Population census			
Total	.	.	146.254	41.3	.	.
A Agriculture, Hunting and Forestry	.	.	1.518	12.1	.	.
B Fishing	.	.	0.476	5.5	.	.
C Mining and Quarrying	.	.	3.954	19.6	.	.
D Manufacturing	.	.	12.455	37.5	.	.
E Electricity, Gas and Water Supply	.	.	2.639	15.8	.	.
F Construction	.	.	12.301	7.6	.	.
G Wholesale and Retail Trade; Repair of Motor Vehicles ...	.	.	12.931	34.3	.	.
H Hotels and Restaurants	.	.	7.107	46.6	.	.
I Transport, Storage and Communications	.	.	4.803	29.2	.	.
J-K	.	.	8.190	38.3	.	.
L-P	.	.	79.880	51.5	.	.

Occupation (ISCO-88)			2001 [1,2] Population census		2003 Employment office records	
Total	.	.	146.254	41.3	7.075	56.7
1 Legislators, senior officials and managers	.	.	5.097	25.7	.	.
2 Professionals	.	.	10.689	37.1	.	.
3 Technicians and associate professionals	.	.	18.570	47.9	.	.
4 Clerks	.	.	16.161	65.9	2.270	70.0
5 Service workers and shop and market sales workers	.	.	27.461	28.6	2.129	73.5
6 Skilled agricultural and fishery workers	.	.	1.275	15.0	0.023	30.4
7 Craft and related trade workers	.	.	20.945	23.3	0.264	19.3
8 Plant and machine operators and assemblers	.	.	7.186	5.6	0.330	.
9 Elementary occupations	.	.	38.580	57.5	0.913	20.9
X Not classifiable by occupation	.	.	0.290	25.5	1.146	53.4

Education level (ISCED-76)					2003 Employment office records	
Total	.	.	.	.	7.075	56.7
X No schooling	.	.	.	.	0.333	79.6
1 First level	.	.	.	.	2.912	47.2
2 Second level, first stage	.	.	.	.	3.047	63.2
3 Second level, second stage	.	.	.	.	0.299	47.8
5 Third level, first stage, leading to an award not equivalent ...	.	.	.	.	0.198	66.7
6 Third level, first stage, leading to a first university degree ...	.	.	.	.	0.286	61.2

Status in employment (ICSE-1993)			1991 [1,2] Population census			
Total	.	.	106.746	32.2	.	.
1 Employees	.	.	101.337	32.6	.	.
2 Employers	.	.	1.018	15.3	.	.
3 Own-account workers	.	.	3.902	24.8	.	.
4 Members of producers' cooperatives	.	.	-	.	.	.
5 Contributing family workers	.	.	0.489	44.4	.	.
6 Not classifiable by status	.	.	-	.	.	.

2. Population ('000), Activity rate and Unemployment rate

	Population			Activity rate			Unemployment rate		
Age group	2001 [2] Population census			2001 [2] Population census			1983 Employment office records		
	Total	Men	Women	Total	Men	Women	Total	Men	Women
Total	332.8	169.0	163.9	47.3	54.8	39.7	6.0	2.0	22.3
15+	231.9	116.7	115.3	67.9	79.3	56.4	.	.	.
15-24	60.6	29.4	31.2	49.3	53.9	44.9	.	.	.
25-54	150.9	77.0	73.9	81.9	95.3	67.9	.	.	.
55+	20.4	10.2	10.2	20.3	32.2	8.3	.	.	.

Brunei Darussalam

3. Paid employment ('000), Hours of work (weekly) and Wages

Economic activity (ISIC-Rev.2)	Paid employment 2003[3] Labour-related establishment census			Hours of work			Wages		
	Total	Men	Women	Total	Men	Women	Total	Men	Women
Total	104.820	73.649	31.171	.	.	.	.	.	.
1	4.196	3.501	0.695	.	.	.	.	.	.
2	4.866	4.084	0.782	.	.	.	.	.	.
3	19.215	10.186	9.029	.	.	.	.	.	.
5	28.315	26.529	1.786	.	.	.	.	.	.
6	25.519	14.500	11.019	.	.	.	.	.	.
7	5.174	3.908	1.266	.	.	.	.	.	.
8	6.854	4.170	2.684	.	.	.	.	.	.
9	10.681	6.771	3.910	.	.	.	.	.	.

4. Occupational injuries and Strikes and Lockouts

Economic activity (ISIC-Rev.2)	Rates of fatal injuries 1986 Source unknown Per 1,000 workers employed Compensated injuries			Rates of non-fatal injuries			Strikes and lockouts		
	Total	Men	Women	Total	Men	Women	Strikes and lockouts	Workers involved	Days not worked
Total	0.167	.	.	.	.	.	.	.	.
1	0.000	.	.	.	.	.	.	.	.
2	0.000	.	.	.	.	.	.	.	.
3	0.000	.	.	.	.	.	.	.	.
4	0.000	.	.	.	.	.	.	.	.
5	0.540	.	.	.	.	.	.	.	.
6	0.000	.	.	.	.	.	.	.	.
7	0.000	.	.	.	.	.	.	.	.
8	0.000	.	.	.	.	.	.	.	.
9	0.000	.	.	.	.	.	.	.	.
0	0.000	.	.	.	.	.	.	.	.

5. Consumer price indices (base period: 2000=100)

	2002	2003	2004	2005	2006	2007
General indices	98.3	98.6	99.5	100.5	100.7	101.0
Food index, including non-alcoholic beverages	100.8	100.0	101.7	102.2	102.5	104.7
Clothing indices, including footwear	97.4	94.6	92.7	91.2	89.8	89.1
Rent indices [4]	98.9	98.1	97.4	97.6	96.5	95.7

[1] Persons aged 15 years and over. [2] Aug. [3] Private sector. [4] Incl. "Fuel and light" and expenditure on maintenance and repairs of dwelling.

[1] Personnes âgées de 15 ans et plus. [2] Août. [3] Secteur privé. [4] Y compris le groupe "Combustible et éclairage" et les dépenses pour l'entretien et la réparation du logement.

[1] Personas de 15 años y más. [2] Agosto. [3] Sector privado. [4] Incl. el grupo "Combustible y alumbrado" y los gastos de conservación y reparación de la vivienda.

Bulgaria

1. Economically active population, Employment and Unemployment ('000)

	Economically active population		Employment		Unemployment	
	Total	Women (%)	Total	Women (%)	Total	Women (%)
Age group	2007 [1,2] Labour force survey		2007 ★ Labour force survey		2007 [2] Labour force survey	
Total	3 492.8	47.0	3 252.6	46.8	240.2	49.8
15-19	40.6	43.6	27.9	44.4	12.7	41.7
20-24	253.7	44.1	221.9	43.5	31.8	48.1
25-29	345.6	42.6	319.6	42.6	26.0	42.3
30-34	437.4	46.7	411.1	46.6	26.3	48.7
35-39	505.1	48.8	473.5	48.6	31.6	51.3
40-44	501.1	48.5	475.0	48.3	26.1	52.5
45-49	540.5	49.5	509.2	49.0	31.3	57.5
50-54	379.6	51.7	356.6	51.4	23.0	55.2
55-59	327.1	49.3	304.5	49.2	22.6	51.3
60-64	117.0	27.4	109.3	26.7	7.7	36.4
65-74	40.9	29.3	39.8	29.6	1.1	18.2
75+	4.1	26.8	.	.	.	.

Economic activity (ISIC-Rev.3)	2007 [1,2] Labour force survey		2007 [1,2] Labour force survey		2007 [2] Labour force survey	
Total	3 492.8	47.0	3 252.6	46.8	240.2	49.8
A-B	264.8	36.0	245.4	35.2	19.4	46.4
C Mining and Quarrying	36.8	19.3	35.5	19.2	1.3	23.1
D Manufacturing	799.7	51.1	766.5	50.8	33.2	58.1
E Electricity, Gas and Water Supply	62.1	22.1	60.4	22.0	1.7	23.5
F Construction	307.0	8.3	292.3	8.3	14.6	8.2
G Wholesale and Retail Trade; Repair of Motor Vehicles ...	537.6	52.8	519.2	52.5	18.5	59.5
H Hotels and Restaurants	174.1	64.6	163.0	64.6	11.1	64.0
I Transport, Storage and Communications	228.7	25.2	220.0	25.0	8.7	31.0
J Financial Intermediation	44.1	71.4	43.7	71.4	0.3	100.0
K Real Estate, Renting and Business Activities	167.2	41.4	163.2	41.5	4.1	36.6
L Public Administration and Defence; Compulsory Social ...	248.0	40.8	238.9	40.5	9.0	48.9
M Education	225.1	81.1	217.5	81.1	7.6	82.9
N Health and Social Work	166.9	77.5	161.7	77.3	5.2	84.6
O Other Community, Social and Personal Service Activities	134.8	55.3	.	.	.	.
O-Q	.	.	125.3	56.6	17.5	56.0
P Households with Employed Persons	6.8	79.4	.	.	.	.
Q Extra-Territorial Organizations and Bodies	1.1	72.7	.	.	.	.
X Not classifiable by economic activity	88.1	47.3	-	-	34.9	50.7
Unemployed seeking their first job	.	.	.	.	53.2	45.1

Occupation (ISCO-88)	2007 [1,2] Labour force survey		2007 [1,2] Labour force survey		2007 [2] Labour force survey	
Total	3 492.8	47.0	3 252.6	46.8	240.2	49.8
1 Legislators, senior officials and managers	216.9	31.4	214.7	31.4	2.2	36.4
2 Professionals	406.1	66.0	400.0	65.9	6.1	68.9
3 Technicians and associate professionals	320.6	55.1	310.8	55.2	9.7	51.5
4 Clerks	234.4	75.1	225.1	75.0	9.2	79.3
5 Service workers and shop and market sales workers	552.4	61.6	526.7	61.3	25.7	68.5
6 Skilled agricultural and fishery workers	161.1	43.3	156.1	42.9	5.1	56.9
7 Craft and related trade workers	534.6	26.4	512.6	26.2	22.0	31.4
8 Plant and machine operators and assemblers	481.9	30.9	462.1	30.8	19.8	34.8
9 Elementary occupations	466.4	44.4	414.7	43.6	51.7	50.7
X Not classifiable by occupation	118.5	37.5	29.7	9.1	35.5	49.9
Unemployed seeking their first job	.	.	.	.	53.2	45.1

Education level (ISCED-97)	2007 [1,2] Labour force survey		2007 ★ Labour force survey		2007 [2] Labour force survey	
Total	3 492.8	47.0	3 252.6	46.8	240.2	49.8
1 Primary education or first stage of basic education	76.2	44.6	51.9	43.7	24.3	46.5
2 Lower secondary or second stage of basic education	495.7	42.7	419.7	40.9	76.0	52.4
3 Upper secondary education	2 071.4	43.2	1 952.1	43.0	119.3	46.9
5A First stage of tertiary education - theoretically based [3]	704.7	56.3	687.7	56.2	17.0	58.2
5B First stage of tertiary education - practically oriented	144.8	71.8	141.2	71.8	3.6	72.2

Status in employment (ICSE-1993)	2007 [1,2] Labour force survey		2007 [1,2] Labour force survey		2007 ★ Labour force survey	
Total	3 492.8	47.0	3 252.6	46.8	240.2	49.8
1 Employees	2 996.0	48.5	2 848.9	48.4	147.1	51.5
2 Employers	132.4	27.1	131.8	27.1	0.6	33.3
3 Own-account workers	237.5	35.2	234.0	35.1	3.5	37.1
5 Contributing family workers	38.3	65.8	37.9	66.0	0.4	50.0
6 Not classifiable by status	88.6	47.5	.	.	88.6	47.5

2. Population ('000), Activity rate and Unemployment rate

	Population 2007 [1,4] Labour force survey			Activity rate 2007 [1,4] Labour force survey			Unemployment rate 2007 [2] Labour force survey		
Age group	Total	Men	Women	Total	Men	Women	Total	Men	Women
Total	7 672.8	3 714.4	3 958.4	45.5	49.9	41.4	6.9	6.5	7.3
15+	6 641.1	3 184.4	3 456.6	52.6	58.2	47.5	6.9	6.5	7.3
15-24	1 018.6	519.0	499.5	28.9	31.7	25.9	15.1	14.5	15.9
25-54	3 207.4	1 605.4	1 602.0	84.5	87.5	81.4	6.1	5.7	6.5
55+	2 415.1	1 060.0	1 355.1	20.3	26.7	15.2	.	.	.

Bulgaria

3. Paid employment ('000), Hours of work (weekly) and Wages

Economic activity (ISIC-Rev.3)	Paid employment 2007 Labour-related establishment survey			Hours of work 2006 [5] Labour-related establishment census Hours actually worked / Employees			Wages 2007 [6,7] Labour-related establishment census Earnings per month / Employees / Leva		
	Total	Men	Women	Total	Men	Women	Total	Men	Women
Total	2 342.8	.	.	34	.	.	431	.	.
A-B	.	.	.	35	.	.	.	.	.
C-Q	.	.	.	34	.	.	435	.	.
A	64.7	.	.	35	.	.	305	.	.
B	0.5	.	.	35	.	.	212	.	.
C	28.2	.	.	31	.	.	738	.	.
D	628.5	.	.	34	.	.	388	.	.
E	53.4	.	.	33	.	.	739	.	.
F	183.1	.	.	35	.	.	362	.	.
G	373.2	.	.	35	.	.	351	.	.
H	101.8	.	.	35	.	.	291	.	.
I	167.0	.	.	34	.	.	550	.	.
J	43.2	.	.	34	.	.	1 000	.	.
K	154.9	.	.	34	.	.	426	.	.
L	133.3	.	.	34	.	.	637	.	.
M	185.4	.	.	31	.	.	432	.	.
N	126.6	.	.	32	.	.	457	.	.
O	99.0	.	.	33	.	.	347	.	.

Share of women in wage employment in the non-agricultural sector (2006 - Labour-related establishment survey): **51.4%**

4. Occupational injuries and Strikes and Lockouts

Economic activity (ISIC-Rev.3)	Rates of fatal injuries 2006 Administrative reports Per 100,000 workers insured Reported injuries			Rates of non-fatal injuries 2006 Administrative reports Per 100,000 workers insured Reported injuries			Strikes and lockouts		
	Total	Men	Women	Total	Men	Women	Strikes and lockouts	Workers involved	Days not worked
Total	7.2	12.1	2.2	167	228	105	.	.	.
A	10.4	13.6	4.3	144	163	109	.	.	.
B	0.0	0.0	0.0	0	0	0	.	.	.
C	25.8	27.1	20.0	1 054	1 215	341	.	.	.
D	6.1	9.1	3.2	245	352	139	.	.	.
E	11.5	15.5	0.0	352	338	393	.	.	.
F	19.1	22.4	0.0	214	242	53	.	.	.
G	7.8	13.4	2.6	66	103	31	.	.	.
H	0.0	0.0	0.0	68	86	57	.	.	.
I	13.0	17.8	3.8	282	297	253	.	.	.
J	4.8	13.6	0.0	91	102	86	.	.	.
K	3.1	5.1	0.9	87	105	68	.	.	.
L	3.4	3.9	3.1	126	128	126	.	.	.
M	3.3	12.5	0.0	79	53	88	.	.	.
N	0.8	0.0	1.1	143	141	144	.	.	.
O	8.3	15.5	2.2	112	165	66	.	.	.
Q	0.0	0.0	0.0	0	0	0	.	.	.

5. Consumer price indices (base period: 2000=100)

	2002	2003	2004	2005	2006	2007
General indices	113.6	116.3	123.4	129.6	139.0	150.7
Food index, including non-alcoholic beverages	106.5	105.4	112.5	117.0	123.4	140.0
Electricity, gas and other fuel indices	117.7	131.0	142.8	154.1	162.0	170.2
Clothing indices, including footwear	100.1	97.9	98.3	99.2	102.6	109.8
Rent indices	121.8	121.4	124.7	132.3	139.5	144.8
General index, excluding housing	113.6	116.3	123.4	129.6	139.1	150.8

[1] Excl. conscripts. [2] Persons aged 15 years and over. [3] Levels 5A and 6. [4] "De jure" population. [5] Official estimates. [6] Employees under labour contract. [7] Provisional data.

[1] Non compris les conscrits. [2] Personnes âgées de 15 ans et plus. [3] Niveaux 5A et 6. [4] Population "de jure". [5] Estimations officielles. [6] Salariés sous contrat de travail. [7] Données provisoires.

[1] Excl. los conscriptos. [2] Personas de 15 años y más. [3] Niveles 5A y 6. [4] Población "de jure". [5] Estimaciones oficiales. [6] Asalariados bajo contrato de trabajo. [7] Datos provisionales.

Burkina Faso

1. Population active, Emploi et Chômage ('000)

	Population active		Emploi		Chômage	
	Total	Femmes (%)	Total	Femmes (%)	Total	Femmes (%)
Groupe d'âge	1991 [1,2] Enquête sur la main-d'oeuvre				2000 [3] Fichiers des bureaux de placement	
Total	4 679.8	49.4	.	.	6.6	18.7
10-14	762.9	47.2	.	.	.	.
10-19	.	.	.	.	0.2	14.0
15-19	673.1	43.1	.	.	.	.
20-24	508.1	46.1	.	.	2.3	20.3
25-29	484.5	54.3	.	.	.	.
25-44	.	.	.	.	3.9	18.8
30-34	404.6	56.2	.	.	.	.
35-39	356.2	54.6	.	.	.	.
40-44	315.0	54.9	.	.	.	.
45-49	255.1	51.0	.	.	.	.
45-54	.	.	.	.	0.2	1.3
50-54	221.3	44.4	.	.	.	.
55-59	229.3	53.2	.	.	.	.
60+	374.7	42.9	.	.	.	.
?	95.0	62.3	.	.	.	.
Activité économique (CITI-Rév.2)	1991 [1,2] Enquête sur la main-d'oeuvre					
Total	4 679.2	48.7	.	.	.	.
1 Agriculture, chasse, sylviculture et pêche	4 293.8	49.6	.	.	.	.
2 Industries extractives	2.6	11.7	.	.	.	.
3 Industries manufacturières	51.7	47.8	.	.	.	.
4 Electricité, gaz et eau	3.8	21.0	.	.	.	.
5 Bâtiment et travaux publics	11.0	0.3	.	.	.	.
6 Commerce de gros et de détail; restaurants et hôtels	120.3	60.0	.	.	.	.
7 Transports, entrepôts et communications	15.0	2.8	.	.	.	.
8 Banques, assurances, affaires immobilières et services ...	2.1	20.5	.	.	.	.
9 Services fournis à la collectivité, services sociaux ...	111.6	24.6	.	.	.	.
0 Activités mal désignées	17.5	52.1	.	.	.	.
Profession (CITP-1968)	1985 [1,4] Recensement de la population				2000 [3] Fichiers des bureaux de placement	
Total	4 067.0	48.9	.	.	6.6	18.7
0/1 Personnel des professions scientifiques, techniques ...	27.4	25.8	.	.	.	.
0/1-2					1.1	33.3
2 Directeurs et cadres administratifs supérieurs	0.4	13.5	.	.	.	.
3 Personnel administratif et travailleurs assimilés	12.6	32.4	.	.	0.0	41.7
4 Personnel commercial et vendeurs	111.9	66.0	.	.	2.8	28.0
5 Travailleurs spécialisés dans les services	37.9	22.1	.	.	0.1	31.3
6 Agriculteurs, éleveurs, forestiers, pêcheurs et chasseurs	3 712.2	49.8	.	.	0.0	13.3
7/8/9 Ouvriers et manoeuvres non agricoles et conducteurs ...	98.6	34.8	.	.	2.6	1.9
X Ne pouvant être classés selon la profession	8.1	33.6	.	.	-	.
AF Forces armées	15.1	1.0	.	.	.	.
Niveau d'instruction (CITE-76)					2000 [3] Fichiers des bureaux de placement	
Total	.	.	.	.	6.6	18.7
X Non scolarisé	.	.	.	.	1.9	1.5
1-2	.	.	.	.	3.1	22.8
3 Second degré, deuxième cycle	.	.	.	.	1.3	31.4
6-7	.	.	.	.	0.4	27.7
? Niveau inconnu	.	.	.	.	0.0	6.3
Situation dans la profession (CISP-1993)	1996 [1,4] Recensement de la population					
Total	4 975.6	48.5	.	.	.	.
1 Salariés	155.3	19.3	.	.	.	.
2 Employeurs	17.8	29.0	.	.	.	.
3 Personnes travaillant pour leur propre compte	1 671.0	22.0	.	.	.	.
4 Membres de coopératives de producteurs	27.2	14.0	.	.	.	.
5 Travailleurs familiaux collaborant à l'entreprise familiale	3 090.3	64.7	.	.	.	.
6 Inclassables d'après la situation	14.0	37.2	.	.	.	.

2. Population ('000), Taux d'activité et Taux de chômage

	Population			Taux d'activité			Taux de chômage		
Groupe d'âge	1991 [2] Enquête sur la main-d'oeuvre			1991 [2] Enquête sur la main-d'oeuvre					
	Total	Hommes	Femmes	Total	Hommes	Femmes	Total	Hommes	Femmes
Total	9 190.8	4 492.2	4 698.6	50.9	52.7	49.2	.	.	.
15+	4 553.9	2 168.2	2 385.6	83.9	88.9	79.4	.	.	.
15-24	1 494.9	787.8	707.2	79.0	83.4	74.1	.	.	.
25-54	2 257.9	969.2	1 288.7	90.2	98.0	84.3	.	.	.
55+	801.1	411.3	389.8	75.4	78.1	72.6	.	.	.

3. Emploi rémunéré ('000), Durée du travail (hebdomadaire) et Salaires

Données non disponibles.

Burkina Faso

4. Lésions professionnelles et Grèves et lock-out

Activité économique (CITI-Rév.2)	Taux de lésions mortelles 2000 Fichiers des assurances Pour 100 000 travailleurs assurés Lésions déclarées			Taux de lésions non mortelles 2000 Fichiers des assurances Pour 100 000 travailleurs assurés Lésions déclarées			Grèves et lock-out 1991 Source inconnue		
	Total	Hommes	Femmes	Total	Hommes	Femmes	Grèves et lock-out	Travailleurs impliqués	Journées non effectuées
Total	4.4	.	.	1 895	.	.	3	321	1 692
1	0.0	.	.	245	.	.	0	0	0
2	0.0	.	.	556	.	.	0	0	0
3	35.9	.	.	24 169	.	.	1	126	882
4	0.0	.	.	3 751	.	.	0	0	0
5	0.0	.	.	741	.	.	1	60	540
6	0.0	.	.	582	.	.	0	0	0
7	6.7	.	.	874	.	.	0	0	0
8	0.0	.	.	269	.	.	0	0	0
9	7.2	.	.	401	.	.	1	135	270
0	.	.	.	.	.	.	0	0	0

5. Indices des prix à la consommation (période de base: 2000=100)

Ouagadougou	2002	2003	2004	2005	2006	2007
Indices généraux	107.3	109.5	109.0	116.0	118.8	118.5
Indices de l'alimentation, y compris les boissons non alcoolisées	112.2	110.3	104.9	120.2	120.0	117.9
Indices de l'habillement, y compris les chaussures	100.8	111.0	110.3	110.2	112.7	115.1
Indices du loyer [5]	104.9	110.0	111.0	111.3	116.4	114.8

[1] Persons aged 10 years and over. [2] July. [3] Four employment offices. [4] Dec. [5] Incl. water, electricity, gas and other fuels.

[1] Personnes âgées de 10 ans et plus. [2] Juillet. [3] Quatre bureaux de placement. [4] Déc. [5] Y compris l'eau, l'électricité, le gaz et autres combustibles.

[1] Personas de 10 años y más. [2] Julio. [3] Cuatro oficinas de colocación. [4] Dic. [5] Incl. el agua, la electricidad, el gas y otros combustibles.

Burundi

1. Population active, Emploi et Chômage ('000)

Groupe d'âge	Population active Total	Population active Femmes (%)	Emploi Total	Emploi Femmes (%)	Chômage Total	Chômage Femmes (%)
	1990 [1,2] Recensement de la population		1990 ★ Recensement de la population		1990 [1,2] Recensement de la population	
Total	2 779.8	52.6	2 765.9	52.7	13.8	30.5
10-14	226.4	53.4	224.7	53.5	1.7	45.0
15-19	361.0	53.6	358.7	53.7	2.4	33.6
20-24	396.2	53.5	393.6	53.6	2.7	30.1
25-29	395.8	52.0	393.7	52.1	2.1	30.0
30-34	354.4	51.1	352.9	51.2	1.5	24.1
35-39	261.2	50.3	260.2	50.5	1.0	22.5
40-44	179.1	52.7	178.5	52.8	0.7	23.4
45-49	136.7	53.2	136.2	53.3	0.5	23.2
50-54	130.4	55.7	130.0	55.8	0.4	21.7
55-59	91.1	52.6	90.8	52.7	0.3	16.8
60-64	86.6	56.4	86.4	56.5	0.2	28.9
65+	158.9	51.2	158.4	51.2	0.5	39.8
?	2.0	36.9	2.0	36.9	0.0	37.0

Activité économique (CITI-Rév.2)	1990 [1,2] Recensement de la population				1990 [3] Fichiers des bureaux de placement	
Total	2 765.9	52.7	.	.	14.5	.
1 Agriculture, chasse, sylviculture et pêche	2 574.4	55.2	.	.	1.9	.
2 Industries extractives	1.2	3.3	.	.	0.2	.
3 Industries manufacturières	33.9	28.8	.	.	3.4	.
4 Electricité, gaz et eau	1.9	3.9	.	.	0.3	.
5 Bâtiment et travaux publics	19.7	1.5	.	.	3.4	.
6 Commerce de gros et de détail; restaurants et hôtels	25.8	23.8	.	.	1.3	.
7 Transports, entrepôts et communications	8.5	3.7	.	.	1.5	.
8 Banques, assurances, affaires immobilières et services ...	2.0	30.8	.	.	1.1	.
9 Services fournis à la collectivité, services sociaux ...	85.2	19.1	.	.	1.5	.
0 Activités mal désignées	13.3	34.8	.	.	-	.

Profession (CITP-1968)	1990 [1,2] Recensement de la population					
Total	2 765.9	52.7	.	.	.	.
0/1 Personnel des professions scientifiques, techniques ...	27.3	30.4	.	.	.	.
2 Directeurs et cadres administratifs supérieurs	2.9	13.4	.	.	.	.
3 Personnel administratif et travailleurs assimilés	10.5	36.2	.	.	.	.
4-5	20.6	19.9	.	.	.	.
6 Agriculteurs, éleveurs, forestiers, pêcheurs et chasseurs	2 567.8	55.3	.	.	.	.
7/8/9 Ouvriers et manoeuvres non agricoles et conducteurs ...	123.8	14.2	.	.	.	.
X Ne pouvant être classés selon la profession	13.0	34.5	.	.	.	.

Situation dans la profession (CISP-58)	1990 [1,2] Recensement de la population					
Total	2 765.9	52.7	.	.	.	.
1 Employeurs et personnes travaillant à leur propre compte	1 748.0	53.1	.	.	.	.
2 Salariés	140.8	14.3	.	.	.	.
3 Travailleurs familiaux non rémunérés	841.0	59.8	.	.	.	.
4 Inclassables d'après la situation	36.2	21.4	.	.	.	.

2. Population ('000), Taux d'activité et Taux de chômage

Groupe d'âge	Population 1990 [2] Recensement de la population			Taux d'activité 1990 [2] Recensement de la population			Taux de chômage 1990 [1,2] Recensement de la population		
	Total	Hommes	Femmes	Total	Hommes	Femmes	Total	Hommes	Femmes
Total	.	.	.	.	.	.	0.5	0.7	0.3
15+	2 824.9	1 343.8	1 481.2	90.3	90.1	90.6	0.5	0.7	0.3
15-24	927.6	447.6	480.0	81.6	78.7	84.4	0.7	1.0	0.4
25-54	1 498.9	712.4	786.5	97.2	98.2	96.4	0.4	0.7	0.2
55+	398.4	183.8	214.7	84.5	86.3	82.9	0.3	0.4	0.2

3. Emploi rémunéré ('000), Durée du travail (hebdomadaire) et Salaires

Données non disponibles.

Burundi

4. Lésions professionnelles et Grèves et lock-out

Activité économique (CITI-Rév.2)	Taux de lésions mortelles 1987 Pour 100 000 travailleurs exposés au risque Lésions déclarées			Taux de lésions non mortelles			Grèves et lock-out 2001 Fichiers administratifs et sources connexes		
	Total	Hommes	Femmes	Total	Hommes	Femmes	Grèves et lock-out	Travailleurs impliqués	Journées non effectuées
Total	30.1	.	.	.	.	.	4	5 420	54 200
1	54.3	.	.	.	.	.	.	.	.
2	0.0	.	.	.	.	.	.	.	.
3	0.0	.	.	.	.	.	.	.	.
4	139.9	.	.	.	.	.	.	.	.
5	23.4	.	.	.	.	.	.	.	.
6	0.0	.	.	.	.	.	.	.	.
7	32.2	.	.	.	.	.	.	.	.
8	0.0	.	.	.	.	.	.	.	.
9	38.4	.	.	.	.	.	.	.	.
0	0.0	.	.	.	.	.	.	.	.

5. Indices des prix à la consommation (période de base: 2000=100)

Bujumbura	2002	2003	2004	2005	2006	2007
Indices généraux	106.7	118.1	127.9	144.8	148.6	161.0
Indices de l'alimentation, y compris les boissons non alcoolisées	95.5	107.5	119.0	139.4	139.5	151.6
Indices de l'habillement, y compris les chaussures	90.8	105.2	117.8	126.7	125.9	119.1
Indices du loyer [4]	136.9	142.3	148.7	163.2	176.6	195.5

[1] Persons aged 10 years and over. [2] Aug. [3] Bujumbura. [4] Incl. "Fuel and light" and certain household equipment.

[1] Personnes âgées de 10 ans et plus. [2] Août. [3] Bujumbura. [4] Y compris le groupe "Combustible et éclairage" et certains biens d'équipement de ménage.

[1] Personas de 10 años y más. [2] Agosto. [3] Bujumbura. [4] Incl. "Combustible y luz" y ciertos enseres domésticos.

Cambodia

1. Economically active population, Employment and Unemployment ('000)

	Economically active population		Employment		Unemployment	
	Total	Women (%)	Total	Women (%)	Total	Women (%)
Age group	2004 [1,2] Labour force survey		2004 [1,2] Labour force survey		2001 [1,2] Labour force survey	
Total	7 557.576	49.4	6 560.630	51.9	115.841	61.3
10-14	874.591	48.0	.	.	11.597	62.1
15-19	1 241.165	48.9	.	.	40.258	52.9
20-24	1 206.606	48.2	.	.	21.855	51.4
25-29	708.957	48.1	.	.	11.303	51.4
30-34	753.053	48.3	.	.	8.023	66.9
35-39	714.039	49.2	.	.	9.347	87.3
40-44	624.712	50.2	.	.	2.726	74.0
45-49	461.556	54.0	.	.	5.029	83.1
50-54	362.654	55.4	.	.	1.947	100.0
55-59	249.361	51.7	.	.	2.396	100.0
60+	360.882	49.0	.	.	1.361	100.0

Economic activity (ISIC-Rev.3)
2004 [1,2] Labour force survey

	Total	Women (%)	Total	Women (%)	Total	Women (%)
Total	.	.	6 560.630	.	.	.
A Agriculture, Hunting and Forestry	.	.	2 577.622	.	.	.
B Fishing	.	.	31.473	.	.	.
C Mining and Quarrying	.	.	3.946	.	.	.
D Manufacturing	.	.	218.313	.	.	.
E Electricity, Gas and Water Supply	.	.	0.232	.	.	.
F Construction	.	.	8.900	.	.	.
G Wholesale and Retail Trade; Repair of Motor Vehicles ...	.	.	404.832	.	.	.
H Hotels and Restaurants	.	.	25.105	.	.	.
I Transport, Storage and Communications	.	.	5.166	.	.	.
J Financial Intermediation	.	.	3.039	.	.	.
K Real Estate, Renting and Business Activities	.	.	4.766	.	.	.
L Public Administration and Defence; Compulsory Social ...	.	.	17.466	.	.	.
M Education	.	.	33.130	.	.	.
N Health and Social Work	.	.	11.886	.	.	.
O Other Community, Social and Personal Service Activities	.	.	42.733	.	.	.
P Households with Employed Persons	.	.	14.525	.	.	.
Q Extra-Territorial Organizations and Bodies	.	.	2.972	.	.	.

Occupation (ISCO-88)
2004 [1,2] Labour force survey

	Total
Total	6 560.630
1 Legislators, senior officials and managers	17.962
2 Professionals	6.380
3 Technicians and associate professionals	140.708
4 Clerks	49.721
5 Service workers and shop and market sales workers	440.541
6 Skilled agricultural and fishery workers	4 619.951
7 Craft and related trade workers	363.502
8 Plant and machine operators and assemblers	81.343
9 Elementary occupations	356.100
0 Armed forces	29.506

Status in employment (ICSE-1993)
2004 [1,2] Labour force survey

	Total
Total	6 560.630
1 Employees	846.873
2 Employers	14.601
3 Own-account workers	2 687.398
5 Contributing family workers	2 998.067
6 Not classifiable by status	10.913

2. Population ('000), Activity rate and Unemployment rate

	Population 2004 [2] Labour force survey			Activity rate 2004 [2] Labour force survey			Unemployment rate 2004 [1,2] Labour force survey		
Age group	Total	Men	Women	Total	Men	Women	Total	Men	Women
Total							7.1	7.6	6.7
15+	8 310.2	3 921.1	4 389.1	80.4	85.9	75.5	.	.	.
15-24	3 148.6	1 593.1	1 555.5	77.7	79.1	76.4	.	.	.
25-54	4 133.1	1 898.7	2 234.4	87.7	95.1	81.4	.	.	.
55+	1 028.4	429.3	599.1	59.3	70.9	51.0	.	.	.

Cambodia

3. Paid employment ('000), Hours of work (weekly) and Wages

Economic activity (ISIC-Rev.3)	Paid employment			Hours of work			Wages 2001 [3] Administrative reports Wage rates per month / Employees / Riel		
	Total	Men	Women	Total	Men	Women	Total	Men	Women
D	.	.	.	.	.	.	243 000	.	.
E	.	.	.	.	.	.	283 500	.	.
F	.	.	.	.	.	.	324 000	.	.
G	.	.	.	.	.	.	270 000	.	.
H	.	.	.	.	.	.	200 000	.	.
I	.	.	.	.	.	.	270 000	.	.
J	.	.	.	.	.	.	486 000	.	.
K	.	.	.	.	.	.	229 500	.	.
M	.	.	.	.	.	.	297 000	.	.
N	.	.	.	.	.	.	189 000	.	.
O	.	.	.	.	.	.	270 000	.	.

4. Occupational injuries and Strikes and Lockouts

Economic activity (ISIC-Rev.3)	Rates of fatal injuries			Rates of non-fatal injuries			Strikes and lockouts 2001 Labour inspectorate records		
	Total	Men	Women	Total	Men	Women	Strikes and lockouts	Workers involved [4]	Days not worked
Total	.	.	.	.	.	.	95	38 558	60 358
A	.	.	.	.	.	.	0	0	0
B	.	.	.	.	.	.	0	0	0
C	.	.	.	.	.	.	0	0	0
D	.	.	.	.	.	.	95	38 558	60 358
E	.	.	.	.	.	.	0	0	0
F	.	.	.	.	.	.	0	0	0
G	.	.	.	.	.	.	0	0	0
H	.	.	.	.	.	.	0	0	0
I	.	.	.	.	.	.	0	0	0
J	.	.	.	.	.	.	0	0	0
K	.	.	.	.	.	.	0	0	0
L	.	.	.	.	.	.	0	0	0
M	.	.	.	.	.	.	0	0	0
N	.	.	.	.	.	.	0	0	0
O	.	.	.	.	.	.	0	0	0

5. Consumer price indices (base period: 2000=100)

Phnom Penh	2002	2003	2004	2005	2006	2007
General indices	102.7	103.9	107.9	114.1	119.5	126.5
Food index, including non-alcoholic beverages [5]	99.7	101.2	107.6	116.6	124.2	136.6
Electricity, gas and other fuel indices [6]	102.5	103.0	.	.	.	.
Clothing indices, including footwear [6]	92.9	91.7	90.9	94.3	98.0	101.1
General index, excluding housing [6]	101.2	102.7	107.7	115.4	122.5	131.9

[1] Persons aged 10 years and over. [2] Nov. [3] Private sector. [4] Excl. workers indirectly involved. [5] Incl. tobacco. [6] Index base 2001=100.

[1] Personnes âgées de 10 ans et plus. [2] Nov. [3] Secteur privé. [4] Non compris les travailleurs indirectement impliqués. [5] Y compris le tabac. [6] Indice base 2001=100.

[1] Personas de 10 años y más. [2] Nov. [3] Sector privado. [4] Excl. los trabajadores indirectamente implicados. [5] Incl. el tabaco. [6] Indice base 2001=100.

Cameroun

1. Population active, Emploi et Chômage ('000)

Groupe d'âge	Population active Total	Population active Femmes (%)	Emploi Total	Emploi Femmes (%)	Chômage Total	Chômage Femmes (%)
	1985 [1,2] Estimations officielles		2001 [3] Enquête auprès des ménages		2001 [3] Enquête auprès des ménages	
Total	3 917.6	38.5	5 806.0	49.2	468.0	43.8
0-14	248.8	43.4	.	.	.	.
15-19	396.8	43.7	.	.	.	.
20-24	480.4	38.0	.	.	.	.
25-29	478.4	37.3	.	.	.	.
30-49	1 564.0	38.6	.	.	.	.
50-69	651.3	35.8	.	.	.	.
70-74	49.3	30.1	.	.	.	.
75+	48.8	27.9	.	.	.	.

Activité économique (CITI-Rév.2)	1985 [1,2] Estimations officielles		1986 Estimations officielles		1986 [3,4,5] Fichiers des bureaux de placement	
Total	3 917.635	38.5	3 813.251	.	7.173	.
1 Agriculture, chasse, sylviculture et pêche	2 900.871	45.7	2 931.250	.	0.018	.
2 Industries extractives	1.793	5.6	1.906	.	0.003	.
3 Industries manufacturières	174.498	21.1	183.036	.	0.482	.
4 Electricité, gaz et eau	3.522	4.2	3.813	.	0.074	.
5 Bâtiment et travaux publics	66.684	1.5	71.689	.	0.777	.
6 Commerce de gros et de détail; restaurants et hôtels	154.014	25.2	163.969	.	0.037	.
7 Transports, entrepôts et communications	51.688	2.0	53.385	.	0.441	.
8 Banques, assurances, affaires immobilières et services ...	8.009	7.0	7.626	.	.	.
9 Services fournis à la collectivité, services sociaux ...	292.922	12.9	308.873	.	0.834	.
0 Activités mal désignées	35.959	48.5	87.704	.	4.507 [6]	.

Profession (CITP-1968)	1982 [1,2] Estimations officielles				1981 [3,4,5] Fichiers des bureaux de placement	
Total	3 543.000	37.5	.	.	4.748	.
0/1 Personnel des professions scientifiques, techniques ...	85.000	14.0	.	.	0.411	.
2 Directeurs et cadres administratifs supérieurs	3.500	5.7	.	.	0.039	.
3 Personnel administratif et travailleurs assimilés	67.300	14.4	.	.	0.145	.
4 Personnel commercial et vendeurs	113.400	27.8	.	.	0.043	.
5 Travailleurs spécialisés dans les services	70.900	15.7	.	.	2.420	.
6 Agriculteurs, éleveurs, forestiers, pêcheurs et chasseurs	2 607.600	45.2	.	.	0.137	.
7/8/9 Ouvriers et manoeuvres non agricoles et conducteurs ...	400.400	8.2	.	.	0.436	.
X Ne pouvant être classés selon la profession	33.630	36.1	.	.	0.662	.
Chômeurs n'ayant jamais travaillé	.	.	.	.	0.455	.

Situation dans la profession (CISP-58)	1982 [1,2] Estimations officielles					
Total	3 543.0	37.5	.	.	.	.
1 Employeurs et personnes travaillant à leur propre compte	2 134.1	36.5	.	.	.	.
2 Salariés	518.7	9.0	.	.	.	.
3 Travailleurs familiaux non rémunérés	638.4	68.1	.	.	.	.
4 Inclassables d'après la situation	251.7	27.0	.	.	.	.

Situation dans la profession (CISP-1993)			2001 [3] Enquête auprès des ménages			
Total	.	.	5 806.0	49.2	.	.
1 Salariés	.	.	1 112.0	22.2	.	.
2 Employeurs	.	.	94.0	34.0	.	.
3 Personnes travaillant pour leur propre compte	.	.	3 351.0	51.6	.	.
5 Travailleurs familiaux collaborant à l'entreprise familiale	.	.	1 055.0	73.5	.	.
6 Inclassables d'après la situation	.	.	193.6	36.2	.	.

2. Population ('000), Taux d'activité et Taux de chômage

Groupe d'âge	Population 1985 [2] Estimations officielles			Taux d'activité 1985 [2] Estimations officielles			Taux de chômage 2001 [3] Enquête auprès des ménages		
	Total	Hommes	Femmes	Total	Hommes	Femmes	Total	Hommes	Femmes
Total	10 166.5	5 081.3	5 085.2	38.5	47.4	29.6	7.5	8.2	6.7
15+	5 607.2	2 792.7	2 814.5	65.4	81.3	49.7	.	.	.
15-24	1 824.1	917.1	907.0	48.1	56.9	39.2	.	.	.

3. Emploi rémunéré ('000), Durée du travail (hebdomadaire) et Salaires

Données non disponibles.

Cameroun

4. Lésions professionnelles et Grèves et lock-out

Activité économique (CITI-Rév.2)	Taux de lésions mortelles			Taux de lésions non mortelles			Grèves et lock-out 1986 Source inconnue		
	Total	Hommes	Femmes	Total	Hommes	Femmes	Grèves et lock-out	Travailleurs impliqués	Journées non effectuées
Total	.	.	.	.	.	.	11	.	.
1	.	.	.	.	.	.	6	46	.
2	.	.	.	.	.	.	0	0	.
3	.	.	.	.	.	.	0	0	.
4	.	.	.	.	.	.	0	0	.
5	.	.	.	.	.	.	5	.	.
6	.	.	.	.	.	.	0	0	.
7	.	.	.	.	.	.	0	0	.
8	.	.	.	.	.	.	0	0	.
9	.	.	.	.	.	.	0	0	.

5. Indices des prix à la consommation (période de base: 2000=100)

	2002	2003	2004	2005	2006	2007
Indices généraux	107.4	108.1	108.4	110.5	116.2	117.2
Indices de l'alimentation, y compris les boissons non alcoolisées	112.1	111.4	109.2	110.3	117.9	119.1
Indices de l'électricité, gaz et autres combustibles [7]	102.5	108.7	111.4	113.5	119.3	120.4
Indices de l'habillement, y compris les chaussures	100.1	100.6	100.5	101.8	100.4	100.3

[1] Persons aged 12 years and over. [2] June. [3] Persons aged 15 years and over. [4] Douala, Yaoundé, Nkongsamba and Garoua. [5] May. [6] Incl. persons seeking their first job. [7] Incl. "rent" and household items.

[1] Personnes âgées de 12 ans et plus. [2] Juin. [3] Personnes âgées de 15 ans et plus. [4] Douala, Yaoundé, Nkongsamba et Garoua. [5] Mai. [6] Y compris les personnes en quête de leur premier emploi. [7] Y compris le groupe "loyer" et les articles de ménage.

[1] Personas de 12 años y más. [2] Junio. [3] Personas de 15 años y más. [4] Duala, Yaundé, Nkongsamba y Garoua. [5] Mayo. [6] Incl. las personas en busca de su primer empleo. [7] Incl. el grupo "alquiler" y artículos domésticos.

Canada

1. Economically active population, Employment and Unemployment ('000)

	Economically active population		Employment		Unemployment	
	Total	Women (%)	Total	Women (%)	Total	Women (%)
Age group	2007 [1,2,3] Labour force survey		2007 ★ Labour force survey		2007 [2,3] Labour force survey	
Total	17 945.8	47.1	16 866.4	47.3	1 079.4	44.1
15-19	1 177.8	50.1	994.6	51.4	183.2	42.5
20-24	1 737.3	47.7	1 586.4	48.2	150.9	42.6
25-29	1 904.7	47.3	1 792.6	47.7	112.1	41.3
30-34	1 914.7	46.7	1 819.3	46.8	95.4	43.3
35-39	1 974.0	47.4	1 871.6	47.4	102.4	48.5
40-44	2 299.4	47.3	2 183.7	47.3	115.7	47.3
45-49	2 267.7	48.3	2 163.9	48.4	103.8	46.9
50-54	2 049.3	47.7	1 960.0	47.9	89.3	43.4
55-59	1 468.0	45.9	1 394.1	46.0	73.9	44.1
60-64	786.5	43.6	746.8	43.7	39.7	42.6
65+	366.4	34.7	353.4	34.7	13.0	33.1
Economic activity (ISIC-Rev.3)	2007 [1,2,3] Labour force survey		2007 [1,2,3] Labour force survey		2007 [2,3] Labour force survey	
Total	17 945.8	47.1	16 866.4	47.3	1 079.4	44.1
A Agriculture, Hunting and Forestry	418.9	28.6	393.1	28.5	25.8	29.5
B Fishing	35.4	18.4	28.8	17.4	6.6	22.7
C Mining and Quarrying	265.0	19.2	254.7	19.4	10.3	14.6
D Manufacturing	2 247.9	29.4	2 116.0	29.1	131.8	34.6
E Electricity, Gas and Water Supply	140.1	28.2	138.0	28.3	2.0	20.0
F Construction	1 217.4	11.7	1 133.5	12.1	83.9	7.4
G Wholesale and Retail Trade; Repair of Motor Vehicles ...	3 073.3	46.5	2 947.4	46.5	125.8	45.9
H Hotels and Restaurants	1 149.4	59.1	1 069.4	59.4	79.9	54.9
I Transport, Storage and Communications	1 097.0	28.9	1 061.0	28.9	36.0	26.7
J Financial Intermediation	773.1	63.7	760.2	63.7	12.9	65.9
K Real Estate, Renting and Business Activities	2 243.0	44.0	2 142.7	44.1	100.4	42.9
L Public Administration and Defence; Compulsory Social ...	882.5	50.1	862.1	50.2	20.4	48.5
M Education	1 227.3	65.2	1 183.2	65.0	44.1	69.6
N Health and Social Work	1 877.8	82.6	1 846.1	82.5	31.6	84.2
O Other Community, Social and Personal Service Activities	910.3	56.8	868.3	57.0	42.0	51.7
P Households with Employed Persons	63.6	95.3	59.5	95.3	4.1	95.1
Q Extra-Territorial Organizations and Bodies	2.5	.	2.5	.	-	.
X Not classifiable by economic activity	321.5	48.9	.	.	321.5	48.9
Occupation (ISCO-88)	2007 [1,2,3] Labour force survey		2007 [1,2,3] Labour force survey		2007 [2,3] Labour force survey	
Total	17 945.8	47.1	16 866.4	47.3	1 079.4	44.1
1 Legislators, senior officials and managers	1 559.0	37.1	1 533.2	36.9	25.9	45.2
2 Professionals	2 994.4	52.2	2 930.8	52.2	63.6	49.7
3 Technicians and associate professionals	2 639.9	60.9	2 562.8	61.0	77.2	57.9
4 Clerks	2 380.5	76.5	2 278.5	76.7	101.9	71.7
5 Service workers and shop and market sales workers	2 587.7	63.1	2 458.1	63.3	129.6	60.0
6 Skilled agricultural and fishery workers	409.8	24.9	386.0	24.8	23.8	27.3
7 Craft and related trade workers	1 813.4	8.4	1 717.8	8.3	95.6	8.7
8 Plant and machine operators and assemblers	1 674.8	19.1	1 572.7	18.9	102.2	23.3
9 Elementary occupations	1 532.2	33.3	1 395.9	33.7	136.4	29.8
0 Armed forces	4.2	7.1	3.7	5.4	.	.
X Not classifiable by occupation	321.5	48.9	.	.	321.5	48.9
Education level (ISCED-97)	2007 [1,2,3] Labour force survey		2007 ★ Labour force survey		2007 [2,3] Labour force survey	
Total	17 945.8	47.1	16 866.4	47.3	1 079.4	44.1
0 Pre-primary education	492.6 [4]	36.8	431.2	36.3	61.4	40.1
2 Lower secondary or second stage of basic education	1 986.2	41.1	1 748.2	41.2	238.0	40.1
3 Upper secondary education	5 146.2	47.1	4 819.0	47.3	327.2	43.9
4 Post-secondary non-tertiary education	2 036.1	32.9	1 919.6	32.9	116.5	31.4
5A First stage of tertiary education - theoretically based [5]	4 111.9	49.3	3 961.0	49.3	150.9	50.1
5B First stage of tertiary education - practically oriented	4 172.9	56.0	3 987.5	56.1	185.4	53.7
Status in employment (ICSE-1993)	2007 [1,2,3] Labour force survey		2007 [1,2,3] Labour force survey		2007 ★ Labour force survey	
Total	17 945.8	47.1	16 866.4	47.3	1 079.4	44.1
1 Employees	14 989.3	49.2	14 251.4	49.6	737.9	42.3
2 Employers	858.2	26.5	855.5	26.5	2.7	22.2
3 Own-account workers	1 751.1	38.4	1 734.2	38.5	16.9	33.7
4 Members of producers' cooperatives	25.7	68.9	25.3	69.6	.	.
5 Contributing family workers	321.5	48.9	.	.	296.2	47.1

2. Population ('000), Activity rate and Unemployment rate

	Population			Activity rate			Unemployment rate		
Age group	2007 [1,6] Labour force survey			2007 [1,6] Labour force survey			2007 [2,3] Labour force survey		
	Total	Men	Women	Total	Men	Women	Total	Men	Women
Total	.	.	.	.	.	.	6.0	6.4	5.6
15+	26 553.4	13 065.5	13 487.9	67.6	72.7	62.7	6.0	6.4	5.6
15-24	4 353.5	2 220.9	2 132.5	67.0	67.4	66.5	11.5	12.8	10.0
25-54	14 328.7	7 155.4	7 173.3	86.6	91.1	82.1	5.0	5.2	4.7
55+	7 871.2	3 689.2	4 182.1	33.3	40.0	27.3	4.8	4.9	4.7

Canada

3. Paid employment ('000), Hours of work (weekly) and Wages

Economic activity (ISIC-Rev.3)	Paid employment 2007 [1,2,3] Labour force survey Total	Men	Women	Hours of work 2007 [7,8] Labour-related establishment survey Hours paid for / Wage earners Total	Men	Women	Wages 2007 [9] Labour-related establishment survey Earnings per week / Employees / Dollar Total	Men	Women
Total	14 251.4	7 185.8	7 065.6	31.2	.	.	770.82	.	.
A	169.0	115.9	53.1	38.7 [9]	.	.	975.97	.	.
B	13.3	10.7	2.6	.	.	.	.	.	.
C	233.2	187.9	45.3	39.6	.	.	1 409.12	.	.
D	2 010.5	1 423.0	587.5	38.5	.	.	936.04	.	.
E	137.9	98.8	39.1	39.6	.	.	1 126.58	.	.
F	780.5	678.0	102.5	38.9	.	.	935.81	.	.
G	2 539.9	1 296.8	1 243.0	28.2	.	.	619.25	.	.
H	970.4	378.4	592.0	24.2	.	.	324.34	.	.
I	915.9	624.7	291.2	36.0	.	.	847.17	.	.
J	686.7	224.4	462.3	28.8	.	.	990.85	.	.
K	1 493.3	794.4	698.9	30.9	.	.	805.58	.	.
L	862.0	429.6	432.4	34.5	.	.	969.04	.	.
M	1 129.9	391.5	738.4	29.7	.	.	833.20	.	.
N	1 620.9	248.4	1 372.4	28.7	.	.	703.04	.	.
O	652.4	280.3	372.2	25.4	.	.	545.82	.	.
P	33.3	1.5	31.7	.	.	.	.	.	.
Q	2.5	-	-	.	.	.	.	.	.

Share of women in wage employment in the non-agricultural sector [1,2,3] (2007 - Labour force survey): **49.8%**

4. Occupational injuries and Strikes and Lockouts

Economic activity (ISIC-Rev.3)	Rates of fatal injuries 2006 Insurance records Per 100,000 employees Compensated injuries Total	Men	Women	Rates of non-fatal injuries 2006 Insurance records Per 100,000 employees Compensated injuries Total	Men	Women	Strikes and lockouts 2007 [10] Labour relations records Strikes and lockouts	Workers involved [11]	Days not worked
Total	5.9	10.7	0.6	1 998	2 505	1 416	207	66 885	1 808 392
A	9.9	13.4	0.9	1 500	1 632	1 154	0	0	0
B	19.7	23.2	0.0	2 423	2 521	1 870	0	0	0
C	31.6	39.0	2.1	1 394	1 676	207	6	1 425	45 580
D	9.4	12.8	1.0	3 492	3 949	2 317	49	12 332	712 695
E	19.7	25.9	0.0	1 666	1 991	624	3	187	3 120
F	19.1	21.3	1.7	3 134	3 396	991	16	16 329	222 282
G	2.5	4.2	0.4	1 910	2 391	1 335	10	752	18 820
H	0.7	1.0	0.5	1 872	1 857	1 864	9	445	15 330
I	11.9	16.7	0.8	2 536	3 054	1 336	27	12 008	221 822
J	0.0	0.0	0.0	83	47	105	2	176	10 670
K	1.3	2.2	0.3	552	701	365	5	286	2 558
L	9.7	18.8	0.2	2 651	3 569	1 682	10	7 006	287 480
M	1.1	2.4	0.4	745	889	663	18	9 494	138 801
N	1.0	2.6	0.6	2 350	2 313	2 350	32	3 169	49 984
O	3.0	6.1	0.9	1 639	2 418	1 090	20	3 276	79 250
P	0.0	0.0	0.0	279	310	276	.	.	.
Q	0.0	0.0	0.0	788	652	0	.	.	.
X	.	.	.	.	.	.	0	0	0

5. Consumer price indices (base period: 2000=100)

	2002	2003	2004	2005	2006	2007
General indices	104.8	107.8	109.8	112.2	114.4	116.9
Food index, including non-alcoholic beverages	107.2	109.1	111.3	114.1	116.8	119.9
Electricity, gas and other fuel indices [12]	106.0	115.5	119.2	127.0	133.4	134.2
Clothing indices, including footwear	99.7	97.9	97.7	97.3	95.5	95.4
Rent indices	103.6	105.1	106.3	107.1	108.2	109.8
General index, excluding housing [13,14,15]	104.9	107.5	109.3	100.0	112.9	114.8

[1] Excl. full-time members of the armed forces. [2] Excl. residents of the Territories and indigenous persons living on reserves. [3] Persons aged 15 years and over. [4] Levels 0-1. [5] Levels 5A and 6. [6] "De facto" population. [7] Employees paid by the hour. [8] Incl. overtime. [9] Excl. agriculture and hunting. [10] Strikes lasting at least half a day with more than 10 days lost. [11] Excl. workers indirectly involved. [12] Incl. water. [13] Excl. also expenditure on insurance, maintenance and repairs. [14] Excl. Water, Electricity, Gas and Other Fuels. [15] Excl. also property taxes, mortgage interest and replacement costs.

[1] Non compris les membres à temps complet des forces armées. [2] Non compris les habitants des "Territoires" et les populations indigènes vivant dans les réserves. [3] Personnes âgées de 15 ans et plus. [4] Niveaux 0-1. [5] Niveaux 5A et 6. [6] Population "de facto". [7] Salariés rémunérés à l'heure. [8] Y compris les heures supplémentaires. [9] Non compris l'agriculture et la chasse. [10] Grèves d'une durée d'une demi-journée au moins et dans lesquelles 10 jours de travail sont perdus. [11] Non compris les travailleurs indirectement impliqués. [12] Y compris l'eau. [13] Non compris aussi les dépenses pour l'assurance, l'entretien et la réparation. [14] Non compris l'eau, l'électricité, le gaz et autres combustibles. [15] Non compris aussi les impôts sur la propriété, intérêts hypothécaires et coûts de remplacement.

[1] Excl. los miembros a tiempo completo de las fuerzas armadas. [2] Excl. a los habitantes de los "Territorios" y a las poblaciones indígenas que viven en reservas. [3] Personas de 15 años y más. [4] Niveles 0-1. [5] Niveles 5A y 6. [6] Población "de facto". [7] Asalariados remunerados por hora. [8] Incl. las horas extraordinarias. [9] Excl. agricultura y caza. [10] Huelgas con duración de media jornada laboral por lo menos y con más de 10 días perdidos. [11] Excl. los trabajadores indirectamente implicados. [12] Incl. el agua. [13] Excl. también los gastos de seguridad, conservación y reparación. [14] Excl. el agua, la electricidad, el gas y otros combustibles. [15] Excl. también los impuestos de propiedad, interés por hipoteca y costo de reemplazo.

Cap-Vert

1. Population active, Emploi et Chômage ('000)

	Population active		Emploi		Chômage	
	Total	Femmes (%)	Total	Femmes (%)	Total	Femmes (%)
Groupe d'âge	1990 [1,2] Recensement de la population		2000 [1] Recensement de la population		1995 Fichiers des bureaux de placement	
Total	120.565	37.1	141.815	45.8	0.640	.
10-14	6.112	38.2	.	.	.	.
15-19	19.390	37.8	.	.	.	.
20-24	23.014	38.0	.	.	.	.
25-29	19.161	37.3	.	.	.	.
30-34	13.477	40.9	.	.	.	.
35-39	8.837	44.6	.	.	.	.
40-44	4.328	41.1	.	.	.	.
45-49	4.237	40.4	.	.	.	.
50-54	5.844	36.9	.	.	.	.
55-59	5.248	30.1	.	.	.	.
60-64	4.602	25.8	.	.	.	.
65-69	2.346	22.4	.	.	.	.
70-74	1.676	22.1	.	.	.	.
75+	2.293	20.4	.	.	.	.

Situation dans la profession (CISP-1993)			2000 [1] Recensement de la population			
Total	.	.	141.815	45.8		
1 Salariés	.	.	55.102	38.9		
2 Employeurs	.	.	3.579	29.6		
3 Personnes travaillant pour leur propre compte	.	.	41.555	45.7		
5 Travailleurs familiaux collaborant à l'entreprise familiale	.	.	14.613	65.8		
6 Inclassables d'après la situation	.	.	26.966	51.3		

2. Population ('000), Taux d'activité et Taux de chômage

	Population			Taux d'activité			Taux de chômage		
Groupe d'âge	1990 [2] Recensement de la population			1990 [2] Recensement de la population			1990 [1,2] Recensement de la population		
	Total	Hommes	Femmes	Total	Hommes	Femmes	Total	Hommes	Femmes
Total	341.5	161.5	180.0	35.3	46.9	24.9	25.8	26.0	25.3
15+	188.0	84.6	103.3	60.9	85.1	41.1	.	.	.
15-24	66.8	33.1	33.7	63.5	79.5	47.8	.	.	.
25-54	82.8	35.2	47.6	67.5	95.6	46.7	.	.	.
55+	38.4	16.3	22.0	42.1	73.8	18.7	.	.	.

3. Emploi rémunéré ('000), Durée du travail (hebdomadaire) et Salaires

Données non disponibles.

4. Lésions professionnelles et Grèves et lock-out

Activité économique (CITI-Rév.2)	Taux de lésions mortelles			Taux de lésions non mortelles			Grèves et lock-out 1997 [3] Fichiers des relations du travail		
	Total	Hommes	Femmes	Total	Hommes	Femmes	Grèves et lock-out	Travailleurs impliqués	Journées non effectuées
Total	.	.	.	.	.	.	17	.	.
5	.	.	.	.	.	.	3	.	.
6	.	.	.	.	.	.	5	.	.
8	.	.	.	.	.	.	1	.	.
9	.	.	.	.	.	.	1	.	.
0	.	.	.	.	.	.	7	.	.

5. Indices des prix à la consommation (période de base: 2000=100)

	2002	2003	2004	2005	2006	2007
Indices généraux	105.4	106.5	104.5	104.9	110.6	115.5
Indices de l'alimentation, y compris les boissons non alcoolisées [4]	.	100.0	96.5	96.4	102.7	107.9
Indices de l'habillement, y compris les chaussures [4]	.	100.0	94.2	86.9	82.0	85.4
Indices du loyer [4,5]	.	100.0	103.5	114.0	127.8	139.9

[1] Persons aged 10 years and over. [2] June. [3] Strikes only. [4] Index base 2003=100. [5] Incl. water, electricity, gas and other fuels.

[1] Personnes âgées de 10 ans et plus. [2] Juin. [3] Grèves seulement. [4] Indice base 2003=100. [5] Y compris l'eau, l'électricité, le gaz et autres combustibles.

[1] Personas de 10 años y más. [2] Junio. [3] Huelgas solamente. [4] Indice base 2003=100. [5] Incl. el agua, la electricidad, el gas y otros combustibles.

Cayman Islands

1. Economically active population, Employment and Unemployment ('000)

Age group	Economically active population Total	Women (%)	Employment Total	Women (%)	Unemployment Total	Women (%)
	2007 [1 2 3] Labour force survey		2007 ★ Labour force survey		2007 [2 3] Labour force survey	
Total	36.476	48.0	35.081	47.8	1.395	52.5
15-19	0.658	58.8	0.506	60.1	0.152	54.6
20-24	2.280	55.7	2.105	55.4	0.175	59.4
25-34	10.359	47.5	10.006	47.3	0.353	52.4
35-44	11.718	46.6	11.379	46.4	0.339	54.9
45-54	7.276	50.9	7.063	50.4	0.213	67.1
55-64	3.209	42.4	3.094	42.9	0.115	28.7
65+	0.960	40.7	0.912	42.9	0.048	.

Economic activity (ISIC-Rev.3)

2007 [1 2 3] Labour force survey

	Total	Women (%)
Total	35.081	47.8
A-B	0.639	7.4
C,E	0.550	27.5
D Manufacturing	0.658	21.3
F Construction	5.646	7.4
G Wholesale and Retail Trade; Repair of Motor Vehicles ...	3.619	50.7
H Hotels and Restaurants	3.499	54.6
I Transport, Storage and Communications	2.004	50.1
J Financial Intermediation	3.332	64.1
K Real Estate, Renting and Business Activities	4.200	50.4
L Public Administration and Defence; Compulsory Social ...	2.509	39.2
M-N	2.833	75.4
O Other Community, Social and Personal Service Activities	2.008	42.7
P Households with Employed Persons	2.786	93.9
Q Extra-Territorial Organizations and Bodies	0.018	100.0
X Not classifiable by economic activity	0.780	51.8

Occupation (ISCO-88)

2007 [1 2 3] Labour force survey

	Total	Women (%)
Total	35.081	47.8
1 Legislators, senior officials and managers	4.605	46.0
2-3	8.839	51.5
4 Clerks	4.647	78.0
5 Service workers and shop and market sales workers	4.452	55.6
6 Skilled agricultural and fishery workers	0.711	2.7
7 Craft and related trade workers	5.057	5.1
8 Plant and machine operators and assemblers	1.568	10.6
9 Elementary occupations	4.625	70.2
X Not classifiable by occupation	0.576	55.0

Education level (ISCED-97)

2007 [1 2 3] Labour force survey

	Total	Women (%)
Total	36.476	48.0
0 Pre-primary education	0.349	29.8
1 Primary education or first stage of basic education	1.188	47.9
2 Lower secondary or second stage of basic education	6.216	48.0
3 Upper secondary education	11.412	46.0
4 Post-secondary non-tertiary education	3.076	46.3
5A First stage of tertiary education - theoretically based [4]	7.212	48.0
5B First stage of tertiary education - practically oriented	5.483	51.9
? Level not stated	1.537	56.4

Status in employment (ICSE-1993)

2007 [1 2 3] Labour force survey

	Total	Women (%)
Total	35.081	47.8
1 Employees	32.227	49.3
2 Employers	1.309	33.5
3 Own-account workers	1.363	26.0
6 Not classifiable by status	0.181	44.8

2. Population ('000), Activity rate and Unemployment rate

Age group	Population 2007 [1 3] Labour force survey Total	Men	Women	Activity rate 2007 [1 3] Labour force survey Total	Men	Women	Unemployment rate 2007 [2 3] Labour force survey Total	Men	Women
Total	53.886	26.773	27.113	67.7	70.8	64.6	3.8	3.5	4.2
15+	44.465	22.362	22.104	82.0	84.8	79.1	3.8	3.5	.
15-24	5.382	2.569	2.814	54.6	49.9	58.9	11.1	10.9	11.3
25-54	31.132	15.769	15.363	94.3	96.8	91.7	3.1	2.6	3.6
55+	7.951	4.024	3.927	52.4	60.1	44.6	3.9	5.4	.

3. Paid employment ('000), Hours of work (weekly) and Wages

Statistics not available.

Cayman Islands

4. Occupational injuries and Strikes and Lockouts

Statistics not available.

5. Consumer price indices (base period: 2000=100)

	2002	2003	2004	2005	2006	2007
General indices	103.6	104.2	108.8	116.8	117.7	121.4
Food index, including non-alcoholic beverages	105.7	109.1	113.9	117.0	120.1	126.6
Clothing indices, including footwear	98.1	97.0	92.8	90.7	95.2	99.4
Rent indices	100.8	97.7	105.0	127.8	120.8	119.4

[1] Excl. armed forces and conscripts. [2] Persons aged 15 years and over. [3] Oct. [4] Levels 5A and 6.

[1] Non compris les forces armées et les conscrits. [2] Personnes âgées de 15 ans et plus. [3] Oct. [4] Niveaux 5A et 6.

[1] Excl. las fuerzas armadas y los conscriptos. [2] Personas de 15 años y más. [3] Oct. [4] Niveles 5A y 6.

Chile

1. Población económicamente activa, Empleo y Desempleo ('000)

	Población económicamente activa		Empleo		Desempleo	
	Total	Mujeres (%)	Total	Mujeres (%)	Total	Mujeres (%)
Grupo de edad	2007 [1,2] Encuesta de la fuerza de trabajo		2007 ★ Encuesta de la fuerza de trabajo		2007 [1,2] Encuesta de la fuerza de trabajo	
Total	7 078.1	36.9	6 567.4	36.2	510.7	45.2
15-19	236.9	33.2	180.5	29.5	56.4	44.9
20-24	726.4	39.2	602.5	37.7	123.9	46.3
25-29	795.4	40.7	710.7	39.9	84.7	47.8
30-34	830.7	39.0	775.7	38.1	55.0	51.1
35-39	861.7	37.2	814.2	36.8	47.5	45.1
40-44	944.3	38.1	901.6	37.9	42.7	41.9
45-49	845.1	37.5	812.6	37.1	32.5	48.0
50-54	734.3	36.9	701.4	36.6	32.9	41.6
55-59	486.5	32.5	464.6	32.3	21.9	37.4
60-64	333.8	28.2	324.8	28.7	9.0	12.2
65-69	162.8	26.9	159.1	27.2	3.7	13.5
70+	120.3	27.4	120.2	27.3	0.1	100.0
Actividad económica (CIIU-Rev.2)	2007 ★ Encuesta de la fuerza de trabajo		2007 [1,2] Encuesta de la fuerza de trabajo		2007 [1,2] Encuesta de la fuerza de trabajo	
Total	7 076.8	36.9	6 566.1	36.2	510.7	45.2
1 Agricultura, caza, silvicultura y pesca	835.4	17.0	808.3	16.5	27.1	31.7
2 Explotación de minas y canteras	98.9	4.6	93.0	4.0	5.9	13.6
3 Industrias manufactureras	917.3	27.0	857.0	26.4	60.3	36.7
4 Electricidad, gas y agua	43.7	14.2	40.1	14.0	3.6	16.7
5 Construcción	602.3	4.5	545.0	4.4	57.3	4.9
6 Comercio al por mayor y al por menor y restaurantes y ...	1 377.0	50.0	1 285.0	50.0	92.0	50.9
7 Transportes, almacenamiento y comunicaciones	577.0	16.6	538.6	15.7	38.4	29.2
8 Establecimientos financieros, seguros, bienes inmuebles ...	671.1	40.2	618.4	38.7	52.7	57.9
9 Servicios comunales, sociales y personales	1 861.5	57.7	1 780.2	57.2	81.3	68.1
0 Actividades no bien especificadas	-	.	-	.	.	.
Desempleados sin empleo anterior	.	.	.	.	91.5	56.7
Ocupación (CIUO-1968)	2007 ★ Encuesta de la fuerza de trabajo		2007 [1,2] Encuesta de la fuerza de trabajo		2007 [1,2] Encuesta de la fuerza de trabajo	
Total	7 076.9	36.9	6 566.1	36.2	510.8	45.1
0/1 Profesionales, técnicos y trabajadores asimilados	767.0	50.2	738.0	50.1	29.0	53.8
2 Directores y funcionarios públicos superiores	269.3	23.4	265.3	23.2	4.0	35.0
3 Personal administrativo y trabajadores asimilados	1 076.1	51.3	992.0	50.6	84.1	59.7
4 Comerciantes y vendedores	861.6	55.3	812.0	55.3	49.6	55.6
5 Trabajadores de los servicios	1 012.4	65.7	933.7	65.9	78.7	62.5
6 Trabajadores agrícolas y forestales, pescadores y cazadores	836.6	16.3	810.0	15.9	26.6	29.3
7/8/9 Obreros no agrícolas, conductores de máquinas y ...	2 107.4	13.0	1 961.1	12.6	146.3	18.4
X No pueden clasificarse según la ocupación	55.1	8.0	54.1	7.9	1.0	10.0
Desempleados sin empleo anterior	.	.	.	.	91.5	56.7
Nivel de educación (CINE-76)	2007 [1,2] Encuesta de la fuerza de trabajo		2007 ★ Encuesta de la fuerza de trabajo		2007 [1,2] Encuesta de la fuerza de trabajo	
Total	7 076.9	36.9	6 566.1	36.2	510.8	45.1
X Sin escolaridad	65.2	24.8	64.3	24.5	0.9	44.4
0 Enseñanza anterior al primer grado	1.5	14.5	1.5	.	.	.
1 Enseñanza de primer grado [3]	1 727.6	30.5	1 641.0	30.0	86.6	38.8
3 Enseñanza de segundo grado, ciclo superior	3 477.2	36.4	3 181.2	35.7	296.0	43.5
5 Enseñanza de tercer grado que no permite obtener un ...	609.3	47.9	552.3	47.0	57.0	57.2
6 Enseñanza de tercer grado que permite obtener un primer ... [4]	1 174.3	42.8	1 104.7	42.3	69.6	50.6
9 Enseñanza que no puede definirse por grados	21.7	28.5	21.1	29.3	0.6	.
Situación en el empleo (CISE-1993)	2006 [1,2] Encuesta de la fuerza de trabajo		2006 [1,2] Encuesta de la fuerza de trabajo		2006 ★ Encuesta de la fuerza de trabajo	
Total	6 821.0	35.9	6 411.0	35.6	410.0	41.0
1 Asalariados	4 866.4	37.1	4 556.8	36.9	309.6	40.5
2 Empleadores	190.1	20.9	187.8	20.9	2.3	20.7
3 Trabajadores por cuenta propia	1 574.5	31.8	1 544.4	31.8	30.1	28.1
5 Trabajadores familiares auxiliares	122.3	56.1	122.1	56.1	0.2	44.2
6 Inclasificables según la situación	67.6	53.3	.	.	.	.

2. Población ('000), Tasa de actividad y Tasa de desempleo

	Población 2007 [2,5] Encuesta de la fuerza de trabajo			Tasa de actividad 2007 [2,5] Encuesta de la fuerza de trabajo			Tasa de desempleo 2007 [1,2] Encuesta de la fuerza de trabajo		
Grupo de edad	Total	Hombres	Mujeres	Total	Hombres	Mujeres	Total	Hombres	Mujeres
Total	16 660	8 247	8 413	42.5	54.2	31.0	7.2	6.3	8.8
15+	12 720	6 241	6 479	55.6	71.6	40.3	7.2	.	8.8
15-24	2 880	1 489	1 391	33.4	40.3	26.1	18.7	16.2	22.8
25-54	6 718	3 300	3 418	74.6	93.8	56.1	5.9	5.1	7.2
55+	3 122	1 452	1 670	35.3	53.3	19.7	3.1	.	3.0

Chile

3. Empleo remunerado ('000), Horas de trabajo (por semana) y Salarios

Actividad económica (CIIU-Rev.2)	Empleo remunerado 2007 [1,2] Encuesta de la fuerza de trabajo			Horas de trabajo 2007 [1,6] Encuesta de la fuerza de trabajo Horas efectivamente trabajadas / Empleo total			Salarios		
	Total	Hombres	Mujeres	Total	Hombres	Mujeres	Total	Hombres	Mujeres
Total	4 460.8	2 959.8	1 501.0	41.7	43.3	39.1	.	.	.
2-9	.	.	.	41.6	43.2	39.1	.	.	.
1	490.3	399.8	90.5	42.2	42.7	39.8	.	.	.
2	86.0	82.4	3.6	45.3	45.3	44.7	.	.	.
3	661.6	510.5	151.1	41.7	43.4	36.8	.	.	.
4	39.0	33.4	5.6	43.2	43.8	39.4	.	.	.
5	431.5	408.1	23.3	43.1	43.1	42.3	.	.	.
6	753.0	397.6	355.4	42.9	45.1	40.6	.	.	.
7	380.9	309.5	71.3	45.2	46.1	40.4	.	.	.
8	508.3	301.6	206.7	42.1	43.0	40.7	.	.	.
9	1 110.2	516.8	593.4	38.8	39.8	38.1	.	.	.

Actividad económica (CIIU-Rev.3)	Empleo remunerado			Horas de trabajo			Salarios 2006 [7,8] Encuesta de establecimientos relacionada con el trabajo Ganancias por mes / Asalariados / Peso		
	Total	Hombres	Mujeres	Total	Hombres	Mujeres	Total	Hombres	Mujeres
C-Q	.	.	.	.	.	.	295 257	.	.
D	.	.	.	.	.	.	300 948	.	.
E	.	.	.	.	.	.	626 603	.	.
F	.	.	.	.	.	.	269 536	.	.
G	.	.	.	.	.	.	258 354	.	.
H	.	.	.	.	.	.	187 058	.	.
I	.	.	.	.	.	.	296 486	.	.
J	.	.	.	.	.	.	592 288	.	.
K	.	.	.	.	.	.	240 041	.	.
L	.	.	.	.	.	.	452 831	.	.
M	.	.	.	.	.	.	383 675	.	.
N	.	.	.	.	.	.	308 164	.	.
O	.	.	.	.	.	.	294 318	.	.

4. Lesiones profesionales y Huelgas y cierres patronales

Actividad económica (CIIU-Rev.2)	Tasas de lesiones mortales 2004 [9] Registros de seguros Por 100 000 trabajadores asegurados Lesiones declaradas			Tasas de lesiones no mortales 2004 [9] Registros de seguros Por 100 000 trabajadores asegurados Lesiones declaradas			Huelgas y cierres patronales 2006 [10] Registros de relaciones laborales		
	Total	Hombres	Mujeres	Total	Hombres	Mujeres	Huelgas y cierres patronales	Trabajadores implicados [11]	Días no trabajados
Total	9	.	.	7 318	.	.	134	15 602	195 344
1	.	.	.	.	.	.	8	829	5 270
2	.	.	.	.	.	.	3	2 137	52 269
3	.	.	.	.	.	.	44	4 568	49 051
4	.	.	.	.	.	.	1	42	672
5	.	.	.	.	.	.	6	875	11 418
6	.	.	.	.	.	.	20	1 823	28 191
7	.	.	.	.	.	.	13	1 418	13 947
8	.	.	.	.	.	.	8	997	14 081
9	.	.	.	.	.	.	31	2 913	20 445
0	.	.	.	.	.	.	0	0	0

5. Índices de precios al consumidor (periodo de base: 2000=100)

Santiago	2002	2003	2004	2005	2006	2007
Índices generales	106.1	109.1	110.3	113.6	117.5	122.7
Índices de la alimentación incluyendo las bebidas no alcohólicas	102.9	105.8	104.4	107.4	110.6	120.5
Índices del vestido, incl. calzado	90.6	86.2	84.0	83.0	82.4	81.2
Índices del aquiler [12]	109.6	115.0	118.4	122.1	127.5	135.7

[1] Persons aged 15 years and over. [2] Fourth quarter. [3] Levels 1-2. [4] Levels 6-7. [5] "De facto" population. [6] Excl. armed forces. [7] Incl. family allowances and the value of payments in kind. [8] April. [9] Incl. commuting accidents. [10] Strikes only. [11] Excl. workers indirectly involved. [12] Incl. "Fuel and light" and certain household equipment.

[1] Personnes âgées de 15 ans et plus. [2] Quatrième trimestre. [3] Niveaux 1-2. [4] Niveaux 6-7. [5] Population "de facto". [6] Non compris les forces armées. [7] Y compris les allocations familiales et la valeur des paiements en nature. [8] Avril. [9] Y compris les accidents de trajet. [10] Grèves seulement. [11] Non compris les travailleurs indirectement impliqués. [12] Y compris le groupe "Combustible et éclairage" et certains biens d'équipement de ménage.

[1] Personas de 15 años y más. [2] Cuarto trimestre. [3] Niveles 1-2. [4] Niveles 6-7. [5] Población "de facto". [6] Excl. las fuerzas armadas. [7] Incl. las asignaciones familiares y el valor de los pagos en especie. [8] Abril. [9] Incl. accidentes del trayecto. [10] Huelgas solamente. [11] Excl. los trabajadores indirectamente implicados. [12] Incl. "Combustible y luz" y ciertos enseres domésticos.

China

1. Economically active population, Employment and Unemployment ('000)

	Economically active population		Employment		Unemployment	
	Total	Women (%)	Total	Women (%)	Total	Women (%)
Age group		1990 [1,2] *Population census*		2007 [3,4,5] *Official estimates*		2007 [1,5,6] *Official estimates*
Total	647 245	45.0	769 900	.	8 300	.
15-19	77 894	51.3	.	.	.	.
15-24	.	.	.	.	3 010	58.2
20-24	114 634	48.1	.	.	.	.
25-29	98 459	46.8	.	.	.	.
30-34	79 641	45.9	.	.	.	.
35-39	82 103	46.4	.	.	.	.
40-44	59 689	44.9	.	.	.	.
45-49	44 106	42.7	.	.	.	.
50-54	35 829	37.2	.	.	.	.
55-59	27 204	32.9	.	.	.	.
60-64	15 548	28.9	.	.	.	.
65+	12 136	22.7	.	.	.	.

Economic activity (ISIC-Rev.2)			2002 [3,4,5] *Official estimates*			
Total	.	.	737 400	.	.	.
1 Agriculture, Hunting, Forestry and Fishing	.	.	324 870	.	.	.
2 Mining and Quarrying	.	.	5 580	.	.	.
3 Manufacturing	.	.	83 070	.	.	.
4 Electricity, Gas and Water	.	.	2 900	.	.	.
5 Construction	.	.	38 930	.	.	.
6 Wholesale and Retail Trade and Restaurants and Hotels	.	.	49 690	.	.	.
7 Transport, Storage and Communication	.	.	20 840	.	.	.
8 Financing, Insurance, Real Estate and Business Services [7]	.	.	4 580	.	.	.
9 Community, Social and Personal Services	.	.	43 900	.	.	.
0 Activities not Adequately Defined	.	.	163 040	.	.	.

Occupation (ISCO-1968)	1990 [1,2] *Population census*					
Total	650 444	44.8	.	.	.	.
0/1 Professional, technical and related workers	34 394	45.3	.	.	.	.
2 Administrative and managerial workers	11 328	11.5	.	.	.	.
3 Clerical and related workers	11 276	25.7	.	.	.	.
4 Sales workers	19 472	46.7	.	.	.	.
5 Service workers	15 512	51.6	.	.	.	.
6 Agriculture, animal husbandry and forestry workers ...	456 820	47.9	.	.	.	.
7/8/9 Production and related workers, transport equipment ...	98 125	35.7	.	.	.	.
X Not classifiable by occupation	318	42.5	.	.	.	.
AF Armed forces	3 199	3.2	.	.	.	.

Occupation (ISCO-88)			2005 *Official estimates*			
Total	.	.	668 749	45.3	.	.
1 Legislators, senior officials and managers	.	.	11 157	16.8	.	.
2-3	.	.	38 142	51.7	.	.
4 Clerks	.	.	20 710	30.3	.	.
5 Service workers and shop and market sales workers	.	.	61 370	50.0	.	.
6 Skilled agricultural and fishery workers	.	.	431 077	48.5	.	.
7-9	.	.	105 850	33.4	.	.

2. Population ('000), Activity rate and Unemployment rate

	Population			Activity rate			Unemployment rate		
Age group		1990 [2] *Population census*			1990 [2] *Population census*			1994 [1,5,6] *Official estimates*	
	Total	Men	Women	Total	Men	Women	Total	Men	Women
Total	.	.	.	.	.	.	2.8	.	.
15+	817 509	418 957	398 552	79.2	85.0	73.0	.	.	.
15-24	245 920	125 884	120 036	78.3	77.4	79.2	1.0	0.8	1.1
25-54	432 910	225 090	207 820	92.4	97.8	86.5	.	.	.
55+	138 679	67 983	70 696	39.6	56.9	22.9	.	.	.

China

3. Paid employment ('000), Hours of work (weekly) and Wages

Economic activity (ISIC-Rev.3)	Paid employment 2007 [5,8] Labour-related establishment survey			Hours of work 1998 [9,10] Labour-related establishment survey Hours actually worked / Wage earners			Wages 2007 [8] Labour-related establishment survey Earnings per month / Employees / Yuan		
	Total	Men	Women	Total	Men	Women	Total	Men	Women
Total	114 270	.	.	.	.	.	2 077.67	.	.
A-B	3 855	.	.	.	.	.	923.80	.	.
C	5 238 [11]	.	.	.	.	.	2 364.75 [12]	.	.
D	33 584	.	.	162.9	.	.	1 740.33	.	.
E	2 977	.	.	.	.	.	2 817.42	.	.
F	9 616	.	.	138.1	.	.	1 565.42	.	.
G-H	4 794 [13]	.	.	.	.	.	1 740.67 [13]	.	.
I	5 835 [14]	.	.	.	.	.	2 369.50	.	.
J	3 111	.	.	.	.	.	4 119.58	.	.
K	1 513 [7]	.	.	.	.	.	2 202.08	.	.
L	12 601	.	.	.	.	.	2 347.58 [15]	.	.
M	14 836 [16]	.	.	.	.	.	2 180.17 [16]	.	.
N	-	.	.	.	.	.	.	.	.
X	-	.	.	.	.	.	.	.	.

4. Occupational injuries and Strikes and Lockouts

Statistics not available.

5. Consumer price indices (base period: 2000=100)

	2002	2003	2004	2005	2006	2007
General indices	99.9	101.1	105.0	106.9	108.5	113.7
Food index, including non-alcoholic beverages	99.4	102.8	113.0	116.2	118.9	133.5
Clothing indices, including footwear	97.6	96.8	95.4	93.7	93.2	92.6

[1] Persons aged 15 years and over. [2] July. [3] Whole national economy. [4] Excl. armed forces and reemployed retired persons. [5] Dec. [6] Unemployed in urban areas. [7] Excl. business services. [8] State-owned units, urban collective-owned units and other ownership units. [9] Per month. [10] 4 cities; state-owned enterprises. [11] Excl. quarrying. [12] Mining only. [13] Incl. catering. [14] Excl. communications, incl. post. [15] State organs, social organizations. [16] Incl. cultural, art, radio and television activities.

[1] Personnes âgées de 15 ans et plus. [2] Juillet. [3] Ensemble de l'économie nationale. [4] Non compris les forces armées et les retraités réemployés. [5] Déc. [6] Chômeurs dans les régions urbaines. [7] Non compris les services aux entreprises. [8] Unités d'Etat, unités collectives urbaines et autres. [9] Par mois. [10] 4 villes; entreprises d'Etat. [11] Non compris les carrières. [12] Mines seulement. [13] Y compris la restauration. [14] Non compris les communications, y compris la poste. [15] Organes d'Etat, organisations sociales. [16] Y compris les activités culturelles, artistiques, radiophoniques et télévisuelles.

[1] Personas de 15 años y más. [2] Julio. [3] Toda la economía nacional. [4] Excl. las fuerzas armadas y los jubilados que trabajan. [5] Dic. [6] Desempleados en áreas urbanas. [7] Excl. servicios para las empresas. [8] Unidades estatales, unidades colectivas y otras. [9] Por mes. [10] 4 ciudades; empresas estatales. [11] Excl. las canteras. [12] Minas solamente. [13] Incl. la restauración. [14] Excl. las comunicaciones, incl. el correo. [15] Organos estatales, organizaciones sociales. [16] Incl. actividades culturales, artísticas, radiofónicas y televisuales.

Colombia

1. Población económicamente activa, Empleo y Desempleo ('000)

	Población económicamente activa		Empleo		Desempleo	
	Total	Mujeres (%)	Total	Mujeres (%)	Total	Mujeres (%)
Grupo de edad	2007 [1,2,3]		2007 ★		2007 [2,3]	
	Encuesta de la fuerza de trabajo		Encuesta de la fuerza de trabajo		Encuesta de la fuerza de trabajo	
Total	20 365.2	42.3	18 151.6	40.9	2 213.6	53.8
0-11	11.0	13.9	10.9	14.0	0.1	.
12-17	680.7	31.0	560.8	27.7	119.9	46.6
18-24	3 247.2	44.3	2 540.1	41.0	707.1	56.4
25-55	14 100.6	43.9	12 841.1	42.7	1 259.5	55.8
56+	2 325.8	33.4	2 198.9	33.8	126.9	26.8
Actividad económica (CIIU-Rev.3)	2007 ★		2007 [1,2,3]		2007 [2,3]	
	Encuesta de la fuerza de trabajo		Encuesta de la fuerza de trabajo		Encuesta de la fuerza de trabajo	
Total	20 365.2	42.3	18 151.6	40.9	2 213.6	53.8
A Agricultura, ganadería, caza y silvicultura	3 513.3	14.4	3 341.9	14.2	171.4	18.8
C Explotación de minas y canteras	115.4	9.9	108.3	9.9	7.1	9.9
D Industrias manufactureras	2 674.7	45.6	2 444.5	44.5	230.2	56.6
E Suministro de electricidad, gas y agua	100.3	19.2	88.7	16.8	11.6	37.9
F Construcción	1 077.9	4.3	916.9	4.1	161.0	5.3
G-H	5 050.5	49.2	4 563.1	47.9	487.4	61.2
I Transporte, almacenamiento y comunicaciones	1 619.4	20.7	1 491.8	20.2	127.6	26.5
J Intermediación financiera	262.5	55.0	237.6	53.9	24.9	66.3
K Actividades inmobiliarias, empresariales y de alquiler	1 172.6	46.5	1 064.0	45.6	108.6	55.8
L-Q	4 330.0	70.2	3 885.6	69.4	444.4	77.6
X No pueden clasificarse según la actividad económica	17.0	31.2	9.3	20.4	7.7	44.2
Desempleados sin empleo anterior	.	.	.	.	431.7	59.8
Ocupación (CIUO-1968)	2000 ★		2000 [1,4]		2000 [4]	
	Encuesta de la fuerza de trabajo		Encuesta de la fuerza de trabajo		Encuesta de la fuerza de trabajo	
Total	7 435.7	47.6	5 909.7	45.2	1 526.0	56.7
0/1 Profesionales, técnicos y trabajadores asimilados	915.4	49.6	745.8	49.5	169.6	50.0
2 Directores y funcionarios públicos superiores	173.9	38.5	151.2	38.2	22.7	40.5
3 Personal administrativo y trabajadores asimilados	1 000.7	58.8	678.9	57.9	321.8	60.5
4 Comerciantes y vendedores	1 526.8	50.7	1 205.3	44.1	321.5	75.2
5 Trabajadores de los servicios	1 600.5	72.9	1 296.0	71.7	304.5	78.4
6 Trabajadores agrícolas y forestales, pescadores y cazadores	73.6	16.4	68.7	15.7	4.9	26.5
7/8/9 Obreros no agrícolas, conductores de máquinas y ...	2 080.8	22.5	1 705.2	22.0	375.6	25.0
X No pueden clasificarse según la ocupación	63.9	11.1	58.5	9.9	5.4	24.1
Nivel de educación (CINE-76)	1998 [5,6]				2007 [2,3]	
	Estimaciones oficiales				Encuesta de la fuerza de trabajo	
Total	6 653.2	45.1	.	.	1 781.8	52.4
X Sin escolaridad	108.1	45.6	.	.	50.0	20.4
1 Enseñanza de primer grado	1 601.8	42.4	.	.	416.6	45.7
2 Enseñanza de segundo grado, ciclo inferior [7]	3 244.6	45.7	.	.	947.9	54.4
5 Enseñanza de tercer grado que no permite obtener un ... [8]	1 672.0	46.5	.	.	366.4	59.2
? Nivel desconocido	26.8	45.7	.	.	0.9	.
Situación en el empleo (CISE-1993)			2007 [1,2,3]			
			Encuesta de la fuerza de trabajo			
Total	.	.	18 151.6	40.9	.	.
1 Asalariados	.	.	9 848.8	42.3	.	.
2 Empleadores	.	.	835.6	27.2	.	.
3 Trabajadores por cuenta propia	.	.	6 637.3	38.7	.	.
5 Trabajadores familiares auxiliares	.	.	793.2	56.9	.	.
6 Inclasificables según la situación	.	.	36.7	30.8	.	.

2. Población ('000), Tasa de actividad y Tasa de desempleo

	Población 2007 [1,3]			Tasa de actividad 2007 [1,3]			Tasa de desempleo 2007 [2,3]		
Grupo de edad	Encuesta de la fuerza de trabajo			Encuesta de la fuerza de trabajo			Encuesta de la fuerza de trabajo		
	Total	Hombres	Mujeres	Total	Hombres	Mujeres	Total	Hombres	Mujeres
Total	46 067.3	21 987.7	24 079.6	44.2	53.4	35.8	10.9	8.7	13.8
15+	35 093.3	16 437.2	18 656.0	58.0	71.4	46.2	10.9	8.7	13.8
15-24	10 778.6	5 260.7	5 517.9	36.4	43.3	29.9	21.1	16.3	27.5
25-54	17 893.6	8 324.5	9 569.0	78.8	95.1	64.6	8.9	7.0	11.4
55+	6 421.1	2 851.9	3 569.1	36.2	54.3	21.8	5.5	6.0	4.4

Colombia

3. Empleo remunerado ('000), Horas de trabajo (por semana) y Salarios

Actividad económica (CIIU-Rev.3)	Empleo remunerado 2007 [1 2 3] Encuesta de la fuerza de trabajo			Horas de trabajo 2007 [1 2 3] Encuesta de la fuerza de trabajo Horas efectivamente trabajadas / Asalariados			Salarios 2007 [1 2 9] Encuesta de la fuerza de trabajo Ganancias por mes / Asalariados / Peso		
	Total	Hombres	Mujeres	Total	Hombres	Mujeres	Total	Hombres	Mujeres
Total	9 848.8	5 681.0	4 167.8	46.0	48.5	45.7	657 756	899 250	608 984
C-Q	.	.	.	47.0	49.2	43.5	885 833	992 440	842 561
A	1 678.8	1 469.7	209.1	42.5	44.1	33.2	323 267	321 007	338 950
C	81.9	74.9	7.0	49.9	50.1	48.1	1 060 428	993 928	1 493 385
D	1 441.1	907.6	533.6	45.1	49.2	40.0	694 244	847 898	505 713
E	85.4	71.0	14.4	49.1	49.6	46.4	1 264 793	1 362 844	894 490
F	486.2	457.6	28.6	46.7	46.8	43.2	545 936	526 053	1 038 930
G	1 842.6	976.3	866.3	48.1	51.8	44.1	539 798	647 511	419 708
I	601.9	436.7	165.2	54.0	55.9	46.9	653 935	672 639	583 934
J	210.2	91.0	119.2	44.6	45.4	43.9	1 264 278	1 389 348	1 164 655
K	558.0	317.8	240.2	43.9	48.2	38.8	1 049 838	1 338 518	702 165
O	2 859.8	876.2	1 983.6	42.0	45.7	40.4	899 250	1 153 220	780 068
X	2.8	2.2	0.6	41.7	39.2	51.7	629 403	690 402	419 787

Proporción de mujeres entre los empleados remunerados en el sector no agrícola [1 2 3] (2007 - Encuesta de la fuerza de trabajo): **48.5%**

4. Lesiones profesionales y Huelgas y cierres patronales

Actividad económica (CIIU-Rev.2)	Tasas de lesiones mortales			Tasas de lesiones no mortales			Huelgas y cierres patronales 1995 [10] Registros de relaciones laborales		
	Total	Hombres	Mujeres	Total	Hombres	Mujeres	Huelgas y cierres patronales	Trabajadores implicados	Días no trabajados
2	.	.	.	.	.	.	3	.	.
3	.	.	.	.	.	.	6	128	.

Actividad económica (CIIU-Rev.3)	Tasas de lesiones mortales 1995 Registros de seguros Por 100 000 trabajadores asegurados Lesiones declaradas			Tasas de lesiones no mortales			Huelgas y cierres patronales		
	Total	Hombres	Mujeres	Total	Hombres	Mujeres	Huelgas y cierres patronales	Trabajadores implicados	Días no trabajados
Total	7.7	.	.	.	.	.	.	.	.
A	8.4	.	.	.	.	.	.	.	.
B	0.0	.	.	.	.	.	.	.	.
C	32.8	.	.	.	.	.	.	.	.
D	3.5	.	.	.	.	.	.	.	.
E	18.9	.	.	.	.	.	.	.	.
F	23.7	.	.	.	.	.	.	.	.
G	4.2	.	.	.	.	.	.	.	.
H,O	4.7	.	.	.	.	.	.	.	.
I	23.3	.	.	.	.	.	.	.	.
J	1.5	.	.	.	.	.	.	.	.
K	4.5	.	.	.	.	.	.	.	.
L	34.6	.	.	.	.	.	.	.	.
N	9.4	.	.	.	.	.	.	.	.
P	0.0	.	.	.	.	.	.	.	.

5. Índices de precios al consumidor (periodo de base: 2000=100)

[11]	2002	2003	2004	2005	2006	2007
Índices generales	116.5	125.0	132.5	139.6	145.2	153.4
Índices de la alimentación incluyendo las bebidas no alcohólicas	118.4	127.2	134.6	143.1	150.5	162.5
Índices del vestido, incl. calzado	105.8	107.2	108.9	109.6	109.7	111.4
Índices del aquiler [12]	105.1	108.3	112.7	117.0	121.1	.
Índices generales, excluyendo la vivienda	118.2	127.0	123.4	.	.	.

[1] Excl. armed forces. [2] Persons aged 10 years and over. [3] Third quarter. [4] 7 main cities; Sep. of each year; Persons aged 12 years and over. [5] 7 main cities. [6] Sep. [7] Levels 2-3. [8] Levels 5-7. [9] Fourth quarter. [10] Incl. "paros" (public service and illegal stoppages). [11] Low income group. [12] Incl. "Fuel and light" and certain household equipment.

[1] Non compris les forces armées. [2] Personnes âgées de 10 ans et plus. [3] Troisième trimestre. [4] 7 villes principales; sept. de chaque année; Personnes âgées de 12ans et plus. [5] 7 villes principales. [6] Sept. [7] Niveaux 2-3. [8] Niveaux 5-7. [9] Quatrième trimestre. [10] Y compris "paros" (arrêts de travail illégaux et des services publics). [11] Familles à revenu modique. [12] Y compris le groupe "Combustible et éclairage" et certains biens d'équipement de ménage.

[1] Excl. las fuerzas armadas. [2] Personas de 10 años y más. [3] Tercer trimestre. [4] 7 ciudades principales; sept. de cada año; Personas de 12 años y más. [5] 7 ciudades principales. [6] Sept. [7] Niveles 2-3. [8] Niveles 5-7. [9] Cuarto trimestre. [10] Incl. paros (suspensiones de los servicios públicos y huelgas ilegales). [11] Familias de ingresos módicos. [12] Incl. "Combustible y luz" y ciertos enseres domésticos.

Comores

1. Population active, Emploi et Chômage ('000)

	Population active Total	Population active Femmes (%)	Emploi Total	Emploi Femmes (%)	Chômage Total	Chômage Femmes (%)
Groupe d'âge	1980 [1,2] Recensement de la population				1991 [1,3] Recensement de la population	
Total	99.463	26.4	.	.	25.245	25.8
10-14	4.820	33.8	.	.	.	.
15-19	10.336	34.4	.	.	.	.
20-24	11.963	29.8	.	.	.	.
25-29	12.093	27.5	.	.	.	.
30-34	11.391	25.3	.	.	.	.
35-39	9.451	25.3	.	.	.	.
40-44	10.112	24.0	.	.	.	.
45-49	6.091	21.6	.	.	.	.
50-54	7.016	24.9	.	.	.	.
55-59	3.273	20.6	.	.	.	.
60-64	5.082	22.3	.	.	.	.
65-69	2.006	19.0	.	.	.	.
70-74	2.830	21.2	.	.	.	.
75+	2.499	21.4	.	.	.	.
?	0.500	14.2	.	.	.	.
Activité économique (CITI-Rév.2)	1980 [1,2] Recensement de la population					
Total	99.5	26.4	.	.	.	.
1 Agriculture, chasse, sylviculture et pêche	53.1	27.8	.	.	.	.
2 Industries extractives	0.1	4.8	.	.	.	.
3 Industries manufacturières	3.9	35.6	.	.	.	.
4 Electricité, gaz et eau	0.1	1.6	.	.	.	.
5 Bâtiment et travaux publics	3.3	0.8	.	.	.	.
6 Commerce de gros et de détail; restaurants et hôtels	1.9	23.3	.	.	.	.
7 Transports, entrepôts et communications	2.1	1.7	.	.	.	.
8 Banques, assurances, affaires immobilières et services ...	0.2	7.6	.	.	.	.
9 Services fournis à la collectivité, services sociaux ...	7.1	12.4	.	.	.	.
0 Activités mal désignées	27.7	31.3	.	.	.	.
Profession (CITP-1968)	1980 [1,2] Recensement de la population					
Total	99.5	26.4	.	.	.	.
0/1 Personnel des professions scientifiques, techniques ...	3.0	22.3	.	.	.	.
2 Directeurs et cadres administratifs supérieurs	0.2	.	.	.	.	.
3 Personnel administratif et travailleurs assimilés	1.5	17.7	.	.	.	.
4 Personnel commercial et vendeurs	1.8	23.5	.	.	.	.
5 Travailleurs spécialisés dans les services	2.5	5.5	.	.	.	.
6 Agriculteurs, éleveurs, forestiers, pêcheurs et chasseurs	49.7	27.8	.	.	.	.
7/8/9 Ouvriers et manoeuvres non agricoles et conducteurs ...	10.4	12.5	.	.	.	.
X Ne pouvant être classés selon la profession	30.4	31.6	.	.	.	.
Situation dans la profession (CISP-58)	1980 [1,2] Recensement de la population					
Total	99.5	26.4	.	.	.	.
1 Employeurs et personnes travaillant à leur propre compte	47.3	25.1	.	.	.	.
2 Salariés	25.5	24.1	.	.	.	.
4 Inclassables d'après la situation	26.7	30.9	.	.	.	.

2. Population ('000), Taux d'activité et Taux de chômage

Groupe d'âge	Population 1980 [2] Recensement de la population Total	Hommes	Femmes	Taux d'activité 1980 [2] Recensement de la population Total	Hommes	Femmes	Taux de chômage 1991 [1,3] Recensement de la population Total	Hommes	Femmes
Total	335.2	167.1	168.1	29.7	43.8	15.6	20.0	21.3	16.9
15+	175.8	85.2	90.6	53.5	81.7	27.1	.	.	.
15-24	56.6	26.7	29.9	39.4	56.8	23.8	.	.	.
25-54	91.2	44.1	47.1	61.6	95.3	29.9	.	.	.
55+	28.0	14.4	13.6	56.0	85.9	24.4	.	.	.

3. Emploi rémunéré ('000), Durée du travail (hebdomadaire) et Salaires

Données non disponibles.

4. Lésions professionnelles et Grèves et lock-out

Données non disponibles.

5. Indices des prix à la consommation (période de base: 2000=100)

Données non disponibles pour la période de 2002 à 2007.

---

[1] Persons aged 12 years and over. [2] Sep. [3] November. [1] Personnes âgées de 12 ans et plus. [2] Sept. [3] Novembre. [1] Personas de 12 años y más. [2] Sept. [3] Noviembre.

Congo

1. Population active, Emploi et Chômage ('000)

Groupe d'âge	Population active Total	Population active Femmes (%)	Emploi Total	Emploi Femmes (%)	Chômage Total	Chômage Femmes (%)
		1984 [1,2] Recensement de la population				
Total	625.3	44.5	.	.	.	.
10-14	9.5	60.3	.	.	.	.
15-19	38.4	50.3	.	.	.	.
20-24	71.9	40.3	.	.	.	.
25-29	91.6	39.2	.	.	.	.
30-34	77.6	40.6	.	.	.	.
35-39	67.2	41.9	.	.	.	.
40-44	56.1	42.0	.	.	.	.
45-49	56.7	44.9	.	.	.	.
50-54	46.5	49.1	.	.	.	.
55-59	36.3	53.0	.	.	.	.
60-64	29.2	53.8	.	.	.	.
65+	39.7	49.0	.	.	.	.
?	4.6	50.2	.	.	.	.

2. Population ('000), Taux d'activité et Taux de chômage

Groupe d'âge	Population Total	Population Hommes	Population Femmes	Taux d'activité Total	Taux d'activité Hommes	Taux d'activité Femmes	Taux de chômage Total	Taux de chômage Hommes	Taux de chômage Femmes
	1984 [2] Recensement de la population			1984 [2] Recensement de la population					
15+	1 037.8	490.4	547.4	58.9	69.6	49.3	.	.	.
15-24	377.7	181.7	196.1	29.2	34.2	24.6	.	.	.
25-54	512.3	243.5	268.8	77.2	93.7	62.3	.	.	.
55+	147.7	65.2	82.5	71.2	78.0	65.8	.	.	.

3. Emploi rémunéré ('000), Durée du travail (hebdomadaire) et Salaires

Activité économique (CITI-Rév.3)	Emploi rémunéré Total	Emploi rémunéré Hommes	Emploi rémunéré Femmes	Durée du travail Total	Durée du travail Hommes	Durée du travail Femmes	Salaires Total	Salaires Hommes	Salaires Femmes
	1999 Enquête auprès des établissements, relative au travail								
Total	68.7	.	.	.	.	.	.	.	.
A	2.0	.	.	.	.	.	.	.	.
B	0.1	.	.	.	.	.	.	.	.
C	0.1	.	.	.	.	.	.	.	.
D	0.5	.	.	.	.	.	.	.	.
E	-	.	.	.	.	.	.	.	.
F	1.0	.	.	.	.	.	.	.	.
G	0.4	.	.	.	.	.	.	.	.
H	0.4	.	.	.	.	.	.	.	.
I	0.0	.	.	.	.	.	.	.	.
K	0.7	.	.	.	.	.	.	.	.
L	63.1	.	.	.	.	.	.	.	.
N	0.3	.	.	.	.	.	.	.	.
O	-	.	.	.	.	.	.	.	.
X	0.2	.	.	.	.	.	.	.	.

4. Lésions professionnelles et Grèves et lock-out

Données non disponibles.

5. Indices des prix à la consommation (période de base: 2000=100)

Brazzaville, Afric.	2002	2003	2004	2005	2006	2007
Indices généraux	104.4	103.8	106.4	109.6	116.8	119.9
Indices de l'alimentation, y compris les boissons non alcoolisées	102.9	96.9	90.8	95.6	105.3	.
Indices de l'électricité, gaz et autres combustibles [3]	114.0	106.8	110.3	112.5	127.4	.
Indices de l'habillement, y compris les chaussures	106.3	95.5	106.7	106.6	101.8	.
Indices du loyer	113.1	115.0	118.9	121.5	124.9	.

[1] Persons aged 10 years and over. [2] Dec. [3] Incl. water. [1] Personnes âgées de 10 ans et plus. [2] Déc. [3] Y compris l'eau. [1] Personas de 10 años y más. [2] Dic. [3] Incl. el agua.

Congo, Rép. dém. du

1. Population active, Emploi et Chômage ('000)

	Population active		Emploi		Chômage	
Groupe d'âge	Total	Femmes (%)	Total	Femmes (%)	Total	Femmes (%)
	2000 [1] Estimations officielles					
Total	1 024.2	.	.	.	.	.

2. Population ('000), Taux d'activité et Taux de chômage

Groupe d'âge	Population 2000 Estimations officielles			Taux d'activité 2000 Estimations officielles			Taux de chômage		
	Total	Hommes	Femmes	Total	Hommes	Femmes	Total	Hommes	Femmes
Total	3 170.1	.	.	32.3	.	.	.	.	.

3. Emploi rémunéré ('000), Durée du travail (hebdomadaire) et Salaires

Données non disponibles.

4. Lésions professionnelles et Grèves et lock-out

Données non disponibles.

5. Indices des prix à la consommation (période de base: 2000=100)

Données non disponibles pour la période de 2002 à 2007.

[1] Persons aged 15 years and over.   [1] Personnes âgées de 15 ans et plus.   [1] Personas de 15 años y más.

Cook Islands

1. Economically active population, Employment and Unemployment ('000)

	Economically active population		Employment		Unemployment	
	Total	Women (%)	Total	Women (%)	Total	Women (%)
Age group	2001 [1] Population census		1991 ★ Population census		1991 [1,2] Population census	
Total	.	.	6.607	35.3	0.515	46.2
15-19	0.622	40.8	0.671	33.7	0.193	48.2
20-24	0.855	48.4	1.178	39.9	0.130	50.0
25-29	0.877	49.9	0.985	35.7	0.069	50.7
30-34	0.967	46.1	0.790	38.0	0.045	37.8
35-39	0.957	42.2	0.621	39.8	0.017	35.3
40-44	0.758	42.9	0.602	34.7	0.019	57.9
45-49	0.586	42.2	0.546	39.0	0.019	31.6
50-54	0.504	36.7	0.505	33.3	0.010	20.0
55-59	0.369	42.3	0.369	27.1	0.012	25.0
60-64	0.189	41.3	0.184	17.9	0.001	.
65+	0.136	27.9	0.156	10.3	-	.
Economic activity (ISIC-Rev.2)	1996 [1,2] Population census					
Total	6.0	38.8	.	.	.	.
1 Agriculture, Hunting, Forestry and Fishing	0.6	14.3	.	.	.	.
2 Mining and Quarrying	0.3	40.0	.	.	.	.
4 Electricity, Gas and Water	0.1	10.8	.	.	.	.
5 Construction	0.2	3.8	.	.	.	.
6 Wholesale and Retail Trade and Restaurants and Hotels	1.5	57.1	.	.	.	.
7 Transport, Storage and Communication	0.5	27.2	.	.	.	.
8 Financing, Insurance, Real Estate and Business Services	0.3	49.6	.	.	.	.
9 Community, Social and Personal Services	1.9	44.7	.	.	.	.
Occupation (ISCO-88)			2001 [1,2] Population census			
Total	.	.	5.928	42.9	.	.
1 Legislators, senior officials and managers	.	.	0.817	36.1	.	.
2 Professionals	.	.	0.783	58.5	.	.
3 Technicians and associate professionals	.	.	0.372	34.1	.	.
4 Clerks	.	.	0.720	76.1	.	.
5 Service workers and shop and market sales workers	.	.	1.056	63.3	.	.
6 Skilled agricultural and fishery workers	.	.	0.301	11.6	.	.
7 Craft and related trade workers	.	.	0.608	7.7	.	.
8 Plant and machine operators and assemblers	.	.	0.271	14.4	.	.
9 Elementary occupations	.	.	1.000	32.5	.	.
Status in employment (ICSE-58)	1991 [1,2] Population census					
Total	7.1	36.1	.	.	.	.
1 Employers and own-account workers	0.7	32.4	.	.	.	.
2 Employees	5.5	36.5	.	.	.	.
3 Unpaid family workers	0.5	26.1	.	.	.	.
4 Not classifiable by status	0.5	46.2	.	.	.	.

2. Population ('000), Activity rate and Unemployment rate

	Population 2001 Population census			Activity rate 2001 Population census			Unemployment rate 1991 [1,2] Population census		
Age group	Total	Men	Women	Total	Men	Women	Total	Men	Women
Total	15.0	7.7	7.3	.	.	.	7.2	6.1	9.3
15+	9.9	5.0	4.9	69.0	76.4	61.4	.	.	.
15-24	2.3	1.2	1.1	63.3	68.4	58.1	14.9	12.5	18.5
25-54	5.5	2.8	2.7	85.2	93.8	76.2	4.2	3.8	4.9
55+	2.1	1.1	1.0	33.1	39.7	26.4	.	.	.

3. Paid employment ('000), Hours of work (weekly) and Wages

Economic activity (ISIC-Rev.3)	Paid employment 1993 [3] Labour-related establishment survey			Hours of work			Wages		
	Total	Men	Women	Total	Men	Women	Total	Men	Women
Total	6.406	4.069	2.337	.	.	.	.	.	.
A-B	0.457	0.395	0.062	.	.	.	.	.	.
C	0.016	0.016	-	.	.	.	.	.	.
D	0.290	0.174	0.116	.	.	.	.	.	.
E	0.254	0.229	0.025	.	.	.	.	.	.
F	0.215	0.209	0.006	.	.	.	.	.	.
G-H	1.338	0.535	0.803	.	.	.	.	.	.
I	0.770	0.612	0.158	.	.	.	.	.	.
J-K	0.231	0.097	0.134	.	.	.	.	.	.
L-Q	2.835	1.802	1.033	.	.	.	.	.	.

Share of women in wage employment in the non-agricultural sector [3] (1993 - Labour-related establishment survey): **38.2%**

Cook Islands

4. Occupational injuries and Strikes and Lockouts

Statistics not available.

5. Consumer price indices (base period: 2000=100)

Rarotonga	2002	2003	2004	2005	2006	2007
General indices	112.4	114.6	115.6	118.5	122.4	125.4
Food index, including non-alcoholic beverages [4]	116.9	119.9	120.9	122.3	125.2	125.4
Electricity, gas and other fuel indices	111.3	111.6	113.5	128.2	151.1	171.9
Clothing indices, including footwear	113.3	112.2	115.1	115.9	115.8	104.1
Rent indices [5]	117.4	122.4	124.5	130.5	147.7	159.4

[1] Persons aged 15 years and over. [2] Dec. [3] Sep. [4] Excl. beverages. [5] Housing; incl. water.

[1] Personnes âgées de 15 ans et plus. [2] Déc. [3] Sept. [4] Non compris les boissons. [5] Logement; y compris l'eau.

[1] Personas de 15 años y más. [2] Dic. [3] Sept. [4] Excl. las bebidas. [5] Vivienda; incl. el agua.

Costa Rica

1. Población económicamente activa, Empleo y Desempleo ('000)

	Población económicamente activa		Empleo		Desempleo	
	Total	Mujeres (%)	Total	Mujeres (%)	Total	Mujeres (%)
Grupo de edad	2007 [1 2]		2007 ★		2007 [1 2]	
	Encuesta de la fuerza de trabajo		Encuesta de la fuerza de trabajo		Encuesta de la fuerza de trabajo	
Total	2 018.4	37.4	1 925.6	36.5	92.8	55.5
12-14	11.3	14.2	9.9	14.1	1.4	14.3
15-19	153.8	32.1	128.5	29.3	25.3	45.8
20-24	310.4	40.8	285.9	39.2	24.5	59.2
25-29	263.8	42.5	251.4	41.5	12.4	62.9
30-34	240.4	38.0	232.9	37.0	7.5	69.3
35-39	240.0	40.7	235.4	40.3	4.6	58.7
40-44	226.0	38.2	221.2	37.8	4.8	56.3
45-49	196.9	38.3	192.1	37.6	4.8	66.7
50-54	167.3	34.4	163.1	33.8	4.2	59.5
55-59	98.2	30.9	96.2	31.0	2.0	25.0
60-64	58.1	27.0	56.9	26.9	1.2	33.3
65-69	25.5	23.5	25.4	23.6	0.1	.
70-74	12.2	18.9	12.1	19.0	0.1	.
75+	11.6	11.2	11.5	10.4	0.1	100.0
?	2.8	35.7	.	.	.	.
Actividad económica (CIIU-Rev.3)	2007 [1 2]		2007 [1 2]		2007 [1 2]	
	Encuesta de la fuerza de trabajo		Encuesta de la fuerza de trabajo		Encuesta de la fuerza de trabajo	
Total	2 018.4	37.4	1 925.7	36.5	92.8	55.5
A Agricultura, ganadería, caza y silvicultura	254.3	15.1	244.8	14.3	9.6	35.4
B Pesca	10.0	8.9	9.8	9.2	0.2	.
C Explotación de minas y canteras	2.6	12.1	2.6	11.5	-	.
D Industrias manufactureras	262.0	33.2	251.6	32.2	10.4	58.7
E Suministro de electricidad, gas y agua	21.6	21.9	21.1	20.9	0.5	60.0
F Construcción	157.0	3.3	151.8	3.5	5.2	.
G Comercio al por mayor y al por menor; reparación ...	381.2	36.1	366.5	35.3	14.6	58.2
H Hoteles y restaurantes	114.8	60.2	108.3	59.1	6.6	77.3
I Transporte, almacenamiento y comunicaciones	129.9	13.9	125.7	13.4	4.2	26.2
J Intermediación financiera	50.0	48.1	49.5	47.9	0.5	80.0
K Actividades inmobiliarias, empresariales y de alquiler	126.0	30.9	121.6	30.7	4.4	38.6
L Administración pública y defensa; planes de seguridad ...	89.9	38.4	88.7	38.4	1.2	41.7
M Enseñanza	113.8	69.4	110.7	69.0	3.0	83.3
N Servicios sociales y de salud	64.9	64.1	64.0	63.6	0.9	100.0
O Otras actividades de servicios comunitarios ...	76.5	51.8	72.7	50.6	3.8	76.3
P Hogares privados con servicio doméstico	135.0	89.4	128.6	89.0	6.4	96.9
Q Organizaciones y órganos extraterritoriales	1.3	41.0	1.1	36.4	0.2	100.0
X No pueden clasificarse según la actividad económica	27.6	51.4	6.6	39.4	0.4	50.0
Desempleados sin empleo anterior	.	.	.	.	20.6	55.8
Ocupación (CIUO-88)	2007 [1 2]		2007 [1 2]		2007 [1 2]	
	Encuesta de la fuerza de trabajo		Encuesta de la fuerza de trabajo		Encuesta de la fuerza de trabajo	
Total	2 018.4	37.4	1 925.7	36.5	92.8	55.5
1 Miembros del poder ejecutivo y de los cuerpos legislativos ...	65.3	27.1	65.2	27.0	0.1	100.0
2 Profesionales científicos e intelectuales	193.4	53.2	190.6	52.8	2.9	75.9
3 Técnicos y profesionales de nivel medio	232.7	34.7	228.4	34.4	4.3	51.2
4 Empleados de oficina	174.8	58.1	162.4	57.1	12.4	70.2
5 Trabajadores de los servicios y vendedores de comercios ...	300.0	55.5	282.4	54.1	17.6	76.7
6 Agricultores y trabajadores calificados agropecuarios ...	81.8	9.6	81.2	9.6	0.6	.
7 Oficiales, operarios y artesanos de artes mecánicas ...	224.2	13.6	219.6	13.5	4.6	17.4
8 Operadores de instalaciones y máquinas y montadores	175.0	14.4	169.3	13.5	5.8	41.4
9 Trabajadores no calificados	545.0	38.4	521.3	38.2	23.7	42.2
X No pueden clasificarse según la ocupación	26.2	48.3	5.2	23.1	0.4	.
Desempleados sin empleo anterior	.	.	.	.	20.6	55.8
Nivel de educación (CINE-97)	2007 [1 2]		2007 ★		2007 [1 2]	
	Encuesta de la fuerza de trabajo		Encuesta de la fuerza de trabajo		Encuesta de la fuerza de trabajo	
Total	2 018.4	37.4	1 925.6	36.5	92.8	55.5
X Sin escolaridad	47.4	24.5	46.3	24.5	1.1	27.3
1 Enseñanza primaria o primer ciclo de la educación básica	795.6	30.2	757.1	29.0	38.5	55.1
2 Primer ciclo de enseñanza secundaria o segundo ciclo de ...	348.8	35.8	326.8	34.7	22.0	51.4
3 Segundo ciclo de enseñanza secundaria	374.4	43.0	353.9	42.3	20.5	56.1
4 Enseñanza postsecundaria, no terciaria	107.5	44.3	102.7	43.7	4.8	56.3
5A Primer ciclo de la educación terciaria - teóricos	149.5	49.6	146.1	48.9	3.4	79.4
5B Primer ciclo de la educación terciaria - práctica	144.4	51.9	141.9	51.5	2.5	72.0
6 Segundo ciclo de la enseñanza terciaria	45.0	40.1	45.0	40.1	-	.
? Nivel desconocido	6.0	30.5	6.0	30.5	-	.
Situación en el empleo (CISE-1993)	2007 [1 2]		2007 [1 2]		2007 ★	
	Encuesta de la fuerza de trabajo		Encuesta de la fuerza de trabajo		Encuesta de la fuerza de trabajo	
Total	2 018.4	37.4	1 925.7	36.5	92.7	55.5
1 Asalariados	1 474.1	38.9	1 406.6	38.0	67.5	56.9
2 Empleadores	139.6	20.4	139.2	20.3	0.4	66.3
3 Trabajadores por cuenta propia	349.1	34.8	344.8	34.9	4.3	32.5
5 Trabajadores familiares auxiliares	35.1	55.3	35.1	55.3	.	.
6 Inclasificables según la situación	20.6	55.8	.	.	.	.

Costa Rica

2. Población ('000), Tasa de actividad y Tasa de desempleo

Grupo de edad	Población 2007 [2,3] Encuesta de la fuerza de trabajo			Tasa de actividad 2007 [2,3] Encuesta de la fuerza de trabajo			Tasa de desempleo 2007 [1,2] Encuesta de la fuerza de trabajo		
	Total	Hombres	Mujeres	Total	Hombres	Mujeres	Total	Hombres	Mujeres
Total	4 443.1	2 195.7	2 247.4	45.4	57.6	33.6	4.6	3.3	6.8
15+	3 262.8	1 573.2	1 689.7	61.4	79.6	44.5	4.6	.	.
15-24	902.8	451.5	451.3	51.4	63.9	39.0	10.7	8.2	14.8
25-54	1 776.1	850.0	926.1	75.1	95.8	56.2	2.9	1.7	4.6
55+	583.9	271.7	312.3	35.2	55.2	17.8	1.7	.	.

3. Empleo remunerado ('000), Horas de trabajo (por semana) y Salarios

Actividad económica (CIIU-Rev.3)	Empleo remunerado 2007 [1,2] Encuesta de la fuerza de trabajo			Horas de trabajo 2007 [4] Encuesta de la fuerza de trabajo Horas usualmente trabajadas / Empleo total			Salarios 2007 [4] Encuesta de la fuerza de trabajo Ganancias por hora / Asalariados / Colón		
	Total	Hombres	Mujeres	Total	Hombres	Mujeres	Total	Hombres	Mujeres
Total	1 406.6	871.4	535.2	46.5	49.9	40.5	1 221.6	1 236.5	1 197.4
A-B	.	.	.	45.3	46.2	40.3	686.5	690.1	666.9
C-Q	.	.	.	46.6	50.7	40.5	1 294.6	1 344.3	1 124.1
A	157.6	133.0	24.6	44.9	45.6	40.3	683.8	687.6	663.5
B	6.4	5.9	0.5	57.2	59.1	39.6	753.0	746.3	833.3
C	2.2	1.9	0.3	58.6	57.8	64.3	869.7	898.4	700.9
D	192.3	137.5	54.7	47.6	51.0	40.4	1 210.2	1 325.5	923.4
E	21.1	16.7	4.4	51.0	52.7	44.4	1 894.9	1 658.9	2 721.6
F	110.4	106.3	4.1	52.2	52.7	38.7	870.0	857.5	1 208.7
G	216.5	143.4	73.0	47.4	51.0	40.8	1 037.7	1 092.8	930.8
H	82.7	34.3	48.4	49.0	52.4	46.6	920.6	1 059.8	821.6
I	80.1	65.2	14.9	53.2	54.3	46.0	1 327.6	1 303.9	1 428.4
J	48.5	25.1	23.4	47.3	47.8	46.7	2 346.1	2 500.6	2 183.1
K	84.4	57.2	27.2	46.9	50.2	39.4	1 462.4	1 460.7	1 465.7
L	88.7	54.6	34.1	47.8	50.1	44.2	1 959.8	1 940.5	1 990.8
M	106.1	32.4	73.7	40.9	41.9	40.4	1 912.3	2 215.9	1 777.3
N	59.6	21.0	38.6	47.7	50.1	46.3	1 742.1	1 889.4	1 662.5
O	42.7	23.6	19.1	38.2	43.1	33.4	1 230.3	1 309.6	1 129.3
P	100.6	9.5	91.1	34.6	37.0	34.2	606.0	718.9	594.4
Q	1.1	0.8	0.4	53.2	54.4	48.0	3 276.3	3 850.4	766.7
X	5.6	3.1	2.6	46.2	48.4	41.0	1 214.9	1 384.0	960.7

Proporción de mujeres entre los empleados remunerados en el sector no agrícola [1,2] (2007 - Encuesta de la fuerza de trabajo): **41.0%**

4. Lesiones profesionales y Huelgas y cierres patronales

Actividad económica (CIIU-Rev.2)	Tasas de lesiones mortales 2005 Registros de seguros Por 100 000 trabajadores asegurados Lesiones indemnizadas			Tasas de lesiones no mortales 2005 Registros de seguros Por 100 000 trabajadores asegurados Lesiones indemnizadas			Huelgas y cierres patronales 1997 Registros de relaciones laborales		
	Total	Hombres	Mujeres	Total	Hombres	Mujeres	Huelgas y cierres patronales	Trabajadores implicados	Días no trabajados
Total	6.4	.	.	11 802	.	.	9	17 003	254 782
9	.	.	.	.	.	.	5	15 262	239 832

5. Índices de precios al consumidor (periodo de base: 2000=100)

[5]	2002	2003	2004	2005	2006	2007
Índices generales	121.5	132.9	149.3	169.9	189.4	207.1
Índices de la alimentación incluyendo las bebidas no alcohólicas [6]	121.8	133.3	151.6	176.5	.	.
Índices de la electricidad, gas y otros combustibles	146.3	160.1	198.0	239.1	.	.
Índices del vestido, incl. calzado	108.6	113.1	118.1	124.8	.	.
Índices del aquiler	116.9	123.5	129.1	136.3	.	.
Índices generales, excluyendo la vivienda	120.2	132.1	147.7	168.5	.	.

[1] Persons aged 12 years and over. [2] July. [3] "De jure" population. [4] Main occupation; July. [5] Central area. [6] Incl. tobacco.

[1] Personnes âgées de 12 ans et plus. [2] Juillet. [3] Population "de jure". [4] Occupation principale; juillet. [5] Région centrale. [6] Y compris le tabac.

[1] Personas de 12 años y más. [2] Julio. [3] Población "de jure". [4] Ocupación principal, julio. [5] Región central. [6] Incl. el tabaco.

Côte d'Ivoire

1. Population active, Emploi et Chômage ('000)

	Population active		Emploi		Chômage	
	Total	Femmes (%)	Total	Femmes (%)	Total	Femmes (%)
Groupe d'âge	1998 [1][2] Recensement de la population				1998 [3][4] Fichiers des bureaux de placement	
Total	6 248.1	37.1	.	.	163.6	28.9
0-14	534.5	45.4	.	.	.	.
15-19	756.6	43.2	.	.	.	.
20-24	928.6	37.2	.	.	.	.
25-29	892.6	35.5	.	.	.	.
30-34	783.6	35.6	.	.	.	.
35-39	634.7	35.5	.	.	.	.
40-44	499.3	35.0	.	.	.	.
45-49	369.3	33.5	.	.	.	.
50-54	275.9	35.5	.	.	.	.
55-59	196.8	34.8	.	.	.	.
60-64	155.7	34.5	.	.	.	.
65+	220.6	29.7	.	.	.	.
Profession (CITP-1968)	1988 [1][2] Recensement de la population					
Total	3 780.5	33.5	.	.	.	.
0/1 Personnel des professions scientifiques, techniques ...	130.6	17.2	.	.	.	.
2 Directeurs et cadres administratifs supérieurs	15.3	10.4	.	.	.	.
3 Personnel administratif et travailleurs assimilés	100.7	29.8	.	.	.	.
4 Personnel commercial et vendeurs	500.5	59.2	.	.	.	.
5 Travailleurs spécialisés dans les services	146.1	35.9	.	.	.	.
6 Agriculteurs, éleveurs, forestiers, pêcheurs et chasseurs	2 480.0	33.4	.	.	.	.
7/8/9 Ouvriers et manoeuvres non agricoles et conducteurs ...	391.0	8.3	.	.	.	.
X Ne pouvant être classés selon la profession	16.4	25.5	.	.	.	.
Situation dans la profession (CISP-58)	1988 [1][2] Recensement de la population					
Total	3 780.5	33.5	.	.	.	.
1 Employeurs et personnes travaillant à leur propre compte	1 975.4	28.7	.	.	.	.
2 Salariés	620.5	15.2	.	.	.	.
3 Travailleurs familiaux non rémunérés	1 175.3	51.3	.	.	.	.
4 Inclassables d'après la situation	9.4	40.6	.	.	.	.

2. Population ('000), Taux d'activité et Taux de chômage

	Population			Taux d'activité			Taux de chômage		
Groupe d'âge	1998 [2] Recensement de la population			1998 [2] Recensement de la population			1998 [3][4] Fichiers des bureaux de placement		
	Total	Hommes	Femmes	Total	Hommes	Femmes	Total	Hommes	Femmes
Total	15 366.7	7 844.6	7 522.0	40.7	50.1	30.9	2.6	17.1	28.9
15+	8 767.2	4 461.6	4 305.5	65.2	81.5	48.3	.	.	.
15-24	3 267.7	1 619.1	1 648.6	51.6	62.5	40.8	.	.	.
25-54	4 623.8	2 381.1	2 242.6	74.7	94.0	54.3	.	.	.
55+	875.7	461.4	414.3	65.4	83.5	45.4	.	.	.

3. Emploi rémunéré ('000), Durée du travail (hebdomadaire) et Salaires

Données non disponibles.

4. Lésions professionnelles et Grèves et lock-out

Données non disponibles.

5. Indices des prix à la consommation (période de base: 2000=100)

Abidjan, Afric.	2002	2003	2004	2005	2006	2007
Indices généraux	107.6	111.1	112.7	117.1	119.9	122.2
Indices de l'alimentation, y compris les boissons non alcoolisées [5]	111.6	116.1	111.6	114.3	117.5	123.8
Indices de l'électricité, gaz et autres combustibles [6]	100.0	113.1	110.7	113.6	114.0	.
Indices de l'habillement, y compris les chaussures	100.9	99.9	100.2	101.9	101.4	100.9
Indices du loyer [7]	107.4	114.4	116.3	126.1	128.3	127.7
Indices généraux, non compris le logement [6]	100.0	105.6	103.4	105.8	106.8	.

[1] Persons aged 6 years and over. [2] March. [3] Persons aged 14 to 55 years. [4] 31st Dec. of each year. [5] Incl. alcoholic beverages and tobacco. [6] Index base 2002=100. [7] Incl. water, electricity, gas and other fuels.

[1] Personnes âgées de 6 ans et plus. [2] Mars. [3] Personnes âgées de 14 à 55 ans. [4] 31 déc. de chaque année. [5] Y compris les boissons alcoolisées et le tabac. [6] Indice base 2002=100. [7] Y compris l'eau, l'électricité, le gaz et autres combustibles.

[1] Personas de 6 años y más. [2] Marzo. [3] Personas de 14 a 55 años. [4] 31 dic. de cada año. [5] Incl. las bebidas alcohólicas y el tabaco. [6] Indice base 2002=100. [7] Incl. el agua, la electricidad, el gas y otros combustibles.

Croatia

1. Economically active population, Employment and Unemployment ('000)

	Economically active population		Employment		Unemployment	
	Total	Women (%)	Total	Women (%)	Total	Women (%)
Age group	2007 [1,2] Labour force survey		2007 ★ Labour force survey		2007 [2] Labour force survey	
Total	1 785.4	45.2	1 614.4	44.4	171.0	52.3
15-19	36.4	43.4	22.0	39.1	14.4 [3]	50.0
20-24	147.2	40.4	117.6	38.4	29.6 [3]	48.0
25-29	187.9	45.4	163.7	44.3	24.2 [3]	52.9
30-34	184.2	45.7	167.0	44.4	17.2 [3]	58.1
35-39	211.2	51.1	194.1	50.1	17.1 [3]	63.2
40-44	245.3	49.0	227.1	47.9	18.2 [3]	62.1
45-49	265.2	48.0	247.2	47.1	18.0 [3]	60.6
50-54	246.5	43.4	228.5	43.1	18.0 [3]	47.8
55-59	156.0	34.7	146.0	34.0	10.0 [3]	46.0
60+	68.1	66.4	63.8	70.4	4.3 [3]	7.0
Economic activity (ISIC-Rev.3)	2007 [1,2] Labour force survey		2007 [1,2] Labour force survey		2007 [2] Labour force survey	
Total	1 785.4	45.2	1 614.4	44.4	171.0	52.3
A Agriculture, Hunting and Forestry	212.9	49.1	206.0	49.5	6.9 [3]	36.2
C Mining and Quarrying	10.7	9.3	10.5 [3]	.	.	.
D Manufacturing	347.7	38.6	312.2	36.4	35.4 [3]	58.2
E Electricity, Gas and Water Supply	29.1	24.7	28.6 [3]	24.1	.	.
F Construction	155.9	7.4	142.4	7.7	13.5 [3]	5.2
G Wholesale and Retail Trade; Repair of Motor Vehicles ...	252.3	55.1	230.0	53.9	22.3 [3]	67.3
H Hotels and Restaurants	112.0	52.4	95.3	51.4	16.7 [3]	58.1
I Transport, Storage and Communications	122.5	21.9	114.8	21.8	7.6 [3]	22.4
J Financial Intermediation	37.4	67.6	36.4 [3]	67.9	3.0 [3]	50.0
K Real Estate, Renting and Business Activities	87.6	47.7	83.8	48.0	4.0 [3]	50.0
L Public Administration and Defence; Compulsory Social ...	96.2	43.6	93.7	43.6	3.0 [3]	66.7
M Education	91.5	74.0	88.9	73.9	2.0 [3]	50.0
N Health and Social Work	92.6	77.6	90.6	77.4	1.0 [3]	0.0
O Other Community, Social and Personal Service Activities	76.1	52.4	71.1	52.2	5.0 [3]	80.0
P Households with Employed Persons	6.3	92.1	5.1 [3]	92.2	1.3 [3]	61.5
Unemployed seeking their first job	.	.	.	.	49.3 [3]	56.6
Occupation (ISCO-88)	2007 ★ Labour force survey		2007 [1,2] Labour force survey		2007 [2] Labour force survey	
Total	1 785.4	45.2	1 614.4	44.4	171.0	52.3
1 Legislators, senior officials and managers	84.6	21.3	81.6	20.8	3.0 [3]	33.3
2 Professionals	153.3	54.1	149.8	55.0	3.5 [3]	14.3
3 Technicians and associate professionals	246.4	48.1	235.2	48.0	11.2 [3]	50.9
4 Clerks	207.4	70.6	196.2	70.4	11.2 [3]	73.2
5 Service workers and shop and market sales workers	268.1	61.4	237.1	60.5	31.0 [3]	68.4
6 Skilled agricultural and fishery workers	184.8	51.7	183.8	52.0	1.0 [3]	.
7 Craft and related trade workers	242.7	8.2	225.6	7.6	17.1 [3]	15.2
8 Plant and machine operators and assemblers	186.3	25.9	167.8	23.4	18.5 [3]	49.2
9 Elementary occupations	149.6	55.6	125.9	56.3	23.7 [3]	51.9
0 Armed forces	12.9	3.9	11.4 [3]	.	1.5 [3]	33.3
Unemployed seeking their first job	.	.	.	.	49.3 [3]	56.6
Education level (ISCED-97)	2007 [1,2] Labour force survey		2007 ★ Labour force survey		2007 [2] Labour force survey	
Total	1 785.4	45.2	1 614.4	44.4	171.0	52.3
1 Primary education or first stage of basic education	134.4 [4]	24.1	130.3	23.3	4.1 [3]	48.8
2 Lower secondary or second stage of basic education	269.5	50.1	238.7	49.6	30.8 [3]	53.6
3 Upper secondary education	1 130.9	41.7	1 015.0	40.6	115.9	51.3
5A First stage of tertiary education - theoretically based	196.6	52.3	185.6	51.8	11.0 [3]	61.8
5B First stage of tertiary education - practically oriented	127.4	49.5	118.2	49.4	9.2 [3]	50.0
Status in employment (ICSE-1993)			2007 [1,2] Labour force survey			
Total	.	.	1 614.4	44.4	.	.
1 Employees	.	.	1 266.2	45.2	.	.
2 Employers	.	.	87.0	24.4	.	.
3 Own-account workers	.	.	224.7	43.1	.	.
5 Contributing family workers	.	.	36.6	73.0	.	.

2. Population ('000), Activity rate and Unemployment rate

	Population 2007 [1,5] Labour force survey			Activity rate 2007 [1,5] Labour force survey			Unemployment rate 2007 [2] Labour force survey		
Age group	Total	Men	Women	Total	Men	Women	Total	Men	Women
Total	4 225.2	2 000.5	2 224.7	42.3	48.9	36.3	9.6	8.3	11.1
15+	3 657.4	1 714.9	1 942.5	47.8	57.1	41.5	9.8	8.3	11.2
15-24	531.7	277.3	254.4	34.5	39.1	29.6	24.0	20.8	28.5
25-54	1 657.5	819.7	837.8	80.9	86.4	75.4	8.4	6.8	10.2
55+	1 468.2	617.9	850.3	15.3	26.2	11.7	6.4	6.4	4.9

Croatia

3. Paid employment ('000), Hours of work (weekly) and Wages

Economic activity (ISIC-Rev.3)	Paid employment 2007 Labour-related establishment survey			Hours of work 2007 [1,2] Labour force survey Hours actually worked / Employees			Wages 2006 [5] Labour-related establishment survey Earnings per month / Employees / Kuna		
	Total	Men	Women	Total	Men	Women	Total	Men	Women
Total	1 377.9	745.2	632.6	41.2	41.7	40.3	6 575	6 909	6 149
A-B	.	.	.	41.1	.	.	5 525	5 711	4 957
C-Q	.	.	.	41.1	41.7	40.2	6 600	6 948	6 165
A	29.3	20.7	8.6	.	.	.	5 571	5 764	4 994
B	3.0	2.4	0.6	.	.	.	4 620	4 765	3 982
C	8.7	7.3	1.4	.	.	.	7 405	7 372	7 572
D	289.2	179.3	109.9	41.0	41.2	40.8	5 833	6 377	4 874
E	26.9	21.4	5.5	.	.	.	7 150	7 216	6 883
F	125.5	110.5	15.0	43.1	43.4	.	5 412	5 346	5 923
G	245.2	116.1	129.2	40.8	41.5	40.4	5 686	6 290	5 057
H	76.2	31.6	44.5	42.4	.	.	5 583	6 108	5 135
I	90.4	64.4	26.0	42.2	42.9	.	7 475	7 580	7 206
J	35.7	10.4	25.3	.	.	.	10 359	12 788	9 327
K	98.1	54.1	44.0	40.3	.	.	7 335	7 662	6 842
L	104.8	59.2	45.6	40.3	40.8	39.6	7 437	7 925	6 759
M	97.4	23.8	73.6	38.8	.	38.7	6 681	7 730	6 326
N	85.1	17.8	67.3	40.6	.	40.4	7 680	9 614	7 102
O	52.0	24.7	27.4	40.8	.	.	6 577	7 130	6 340
P	8.8	0.5	8.3	.	.	.	.	.	.
X	1.4	0.9	0.6	.	.	.	.	.	.

Share of women in wage employment in the non-agricultural sector [1,2] (2007 - Labour force survey): **45.5%**

4. Occupational injuries and Strikes and Lockouts

Economic activity (ISIC-Rev.3)	Rates of fatal injuries 2007 [7] Insurance records Per 100,000 workers employed Compensated injuries			Rates of non-fatal injuries 2007 Insurance records Per 100,000 workers employed Compensated injuries			Strikes and lockouts		
	Total	Men	Women	Total	Men	Women	Strikes and lockouts	Workers involved	Days not worked
Total	4.7	7.9	0.8	1 540	2 011	965	.	.	.
A	15.1	21.8	0.0	2 704	3 343	1 254	.	.	.
B	0.0	0.0	0.0	1 207	1 616	208	.	.	.
C	0.0	0.0	0.0	2 557	3 156	501	.	.	.
D	4.1	5.9	1.0	2 945	3 818	1 486	.	.	.
E	3.9	4.9	0.0	2 148	2 040	1 105	.	.	.
F	22.0	25.4	0.0	2 929	3 272	670	.	.	.
G	1.8	2.8	0.9	1 166	1 400	944	.	.	.
H	4.5	10.0	0.0	1 810	1 863	1 769	.	.	.
I	4.9	7.1	0.0	2 117	2 483	1 295	.	.	.
J	0.0	0.0	0.0	606	751	776	.	.	.
K	1.8	1.5	2.5	884	984	717	.	.	.
L	8.1	12.7	2.1	1 623	2 057	1 182	.	.	.
M	2.0	4.2	1.3	779	741	792	.	.	.
N	1.3	0.0	1.6	2 093	2 699	1 836	.	.	.
O	21.4	44.9	0.0	3 563	2 311	1 015	.	.	.
P	0.0	0.0	0.0	0	0	0	.	.	.
Q	0.0	0.0	0.0	143	255	0	.	.	.

5. Consumer price indices (base period: 2000=100)

	2002	2003	2004	2005	2006	2007
General indices	106.3	108.2	110.4	114.0	117.7	121.1
Food index, including non-alcoholic beverages	102.3	104.0	105.5	110.4	113.1	116.9
Electricity, gas and other fuel indices	114.0	119.1	122.1	126.9	132.5	132.5
Clothing indices, including footwear	105.5	105.6	105.0	105.6	108.0	113.6
Rent indices	106.2	107.8	111.1	115.5	146.6	161.9

[1] Excl. conscripts. [2] Persons aged 15 years and over. [3] Estimate not sufficiently reliable. [4] Levels 0-1. [5] "De jure" population. [6] Excl. employees in craft and trade. [7] Deaths occurring within one day of accident.

[1] Non compris les conscrits. [2] Personnes âgées de 15 ans et plus. [3] Estimation pas suffisamment fiable. [4] Niveaux 0-1. [5] Population "de jure". [6] Non compris les salariés dans l'artisanat et dans le commerce. [7] Décès survenant pendant le jour qui suit l'accident.

[1] Excl. los conscriptos. [2] Personas de 15 años y más. [3] Estimación no suficientemente fiable. [4] Niveles 0-1. [5] Población "de jure". [6] Excl. los asalariados en el artesanado y el comercio. [7] Fallecimientos que se producen durante el día posterior al accidente.

Cuba

1. Población económicamente activa, Empleo y Desempleo ('000)

	Población económicamente activa		Empleo		Desempleo	
	Total	Mujeres (%)	Total	Mujeres (%)	Total	Mujeres (%)
Grupo de edad	2007 [1,2]		2007 ★		2007 [1,2]	
	Encuesta de la fuerza de trabajo		Encuesta de la fuerza de trabajo		Encuesta de la fuerza de trabajo	
Total	4 956.3	38.1	4 867.7	38.0	88.6	39.8
15-19	152.6	39.6	145.8	39.8	6.8	35.3
20-29	889.6	40.4	859.5	40.6	30.1	36.9
30-39	1 417.9	39.6	1 390.1	39.5	27.8	44.6
40-59	2 317.9	37.5	2 294.0	37.5	23.9	39.3
60+	178.4	19.9	.	.	.	.
Actividad económica (CIIU-Rev.2)			2007 [1,2]			
			Encuesta de la fuerza de trabajo			
Total	.	.	4 867.7	38.0		
1 Agricultura, caza, silvicultura y pesca	.	.	912.3	17.4		
2 Explotación de minas y canteras	.	.	25.7	19.8		
3 Industrias manufactureras	.	.	523.3	30.8		
4 Electricidad, gas y agua	.	.	85.0	26.2		
5 Construcción	.	.	243.7	16.5		
6 Comercio al por mayor y al por menor y restaurantes y ...	.	.	613.6	42.3		
7 Transportes, almacenamiento y comunicaciones	.	.	289.3	25.0		
8 Establecimientos financieros, seguros, bienes inmuebles ...	.	.	111.4	54.5		
9 Servicios comunales, sociales y personales	.	.	2 063.4	52.0		
Ocupación (CIUO-1968)			2007 [1,2]			
			Encuesta de la fuerza de trabajo			
Total	.	.	4 867.7	38.0		
0/1 Profesionales, técnicos y trabajadores asimilados	.	.	1 403.5	59.9		
2 Directores y funcionarios públicos superiores	.	.	386.7	31.1		
3 Personal administrativo y trabajadores asimilados	.	.	248.7	61.2		
4-5	.	.	1 108.1	40.6		
6-7/8/9	.	.	1 720.7	16.7		
Nivel de educación (CINE-97)	2007 [1,2]		2007 ★		2007 [1,2]	
	Encuesta de la fuerza de trabajo		Encuesta de la fuerza de trabajo		Encuesta de la fuerza de trabajo	
Total	4 956.3	38.1	4 867.7	38.0	88.6	39.8
1 Enseñanza primaria o primer ciclo de la educación básica	396.7 [3]	20.8	391.0	20.6	5.7	35.1
2 Primer ciclo de enseñanza secundaria o segundo ciclo de ...	1 353.9	27.5	1 321.5	27.3	32.4	35.5
4 Enseñanza postsecundaria, no terciaria	2 476.2 [4]	43.2	2 429.8	43.2	46.4	43.1
5A Primer ciclo de la educación terciaria - teóricos [5]	729.5	49.6	725.4	49.6	4.1	43.9
Situación en el empleo (CISE-1993)			2007 [1,2]			
			Encuesta de la fuerza de trabajo			
Total	.	.	4 867.7	38.0		
1 Asalariados	.	.	4 045.9	42.8		
3 Trabajadores por cuenta propia	.	.	579.7	13.5		
4 Miembros de cooperativas de productores	.	.	242.1	17.2		

2. Población ('000), Tasa de actividad y Tasa de desempleo

	Población			Tasa de actividad			Tasa de desempleo		
Grupo de edad	2007 [1,2]			2007 [1,2]			2007 [1,2]		
	Encuesta de la fuerza de trabajo			Encuesta de la fuerza de trabajo			Encuesta de la fuerza de trabajo		
	Total	Hombres	Mujeres	Total	Hombres	Mujeres	Total	Hombres	Mujeres
Total	11 236.8	5 627.3	5 609.4	44.1	54.5	33.6	1.8	1.7	1.9
15+	9 218.4	4 589.0	4 629.4	53.8	66.9	40.8	.	.	.

3. Empleo remunerado ('000), Horas de trabajo (por semana) y Salarios

	Empleo remunerado			Horas de trabajo			Salarios		
Actividad económica (CIIU-Rev.2)	2007 [1,2]			2007			2007 [6]		
	Encuesta de la fuerza de trabajo			Registros administrativos y fuentes relacionadas			Informes administrativos Ganancias por mes / Asalariados / Peso		
				Horas efectivamente trabajadas / Asalariados					
	Total	Hombres	Mujeres	Total	Hombres	Mujeres	Total	Hombres	Mujeres
Total	4 045.9	2 314.3	1 731.6	.	.	.	.	.	.
2-9	.	.	.	41	.	.	.	.	.
1	249.1	178.2	70.9	41	.	.	420	.	.
2	27.9	22.9	5.0	47	.	.	544	.	.
3	591.4	409.1	182.3	41	.	.	433	.	.
4	71.8	53.2	18.6	41	.	.	508	.	.
5	256.8	216.8	40.0	43	.	.	497	.	.
6	639.4	368.3	271.1	41	.	.	353	.	.
7	254.7	186.7	68.0	52	.	.	418	.	.
8	105.9	49.7	56.2	45	.	.	493	.	.
9	1 848.9	829.4	1 019.5	41	.	.	398	.	.

Cuba

4. Lesiones profesionales y Huelgas y cierres patronales

Actividad económica (CIIU-Rev.3)	Tasas de lesiones mortales 2007 Registros administrativos y fuentes relacionadas Por 1 000 000 horas trabajadas Lesiones declaradas			Tasas de lesiones no mortales 2007 Registros administrativos y fuentes relacionadas Por 1 000 000 horas trabajadas Lesiones declaradas			Huelgas y cierres patronales		
	Total	Hombres	Mujeres	Total	Hombres	Mujeres	Huelgas y cierres patronales	Trabajadores implicados	Días no trabajados
Total	0.007	.	.	0.869	.	.	.	.	.

5. Índices de precios al consumidor (periodo de base: 2000=100)

	2002	2003	2004	2005	2006	2007
Índices generales	106.1	108.2	105.9	108.9	114.4	121.8
Índices de la alimentación incluyendo las bebidas no alcohólicas [7]	108.4	110.3	107.0	110.3	117.9	124.7
Índices de la electricidad, gas y otros combustibles [8]	88.6	93.1	93.8	103.9	113.9	133.8
Índices del vestido, incl. calzado	104.1	112.4	110.5	101.8	105.8	128.1

[1] Men aged 17 to 60 years; women aged 17 to 55 years. [2] Dec. [3] Levels 0-1. [4] Levels 3-4. [5] Levels 5-6. [6] State sector (civilian). [7] Incl. alcoholic beverages; excl. tobacco. [8] Incl. the materials to repair the housings.

[1] Hommes âgés de 17 à 60 ans; femmes âgées de 17 à 55 ans. [2] Déc. [3] Niveaux 0-1. [4] Niveaux 3-4. [5] Niveaux 5-6. [6] Secteur d'Etat (civils). [7] Y compris les boissons alcoolisées; non compris le tabac. [8] Y compris les matériaux pour réparer les logements.

[1] Hombres de 17 a 60 años; mujeres de 17 a 55 años. [2] Dic. [3] Niveles 0-1. [4] Niveles 3-4. [5] Niveles 5-6. [6] Sector de Estado (civil). [7] Incl. las bebidas alcohólicas; excl. el tabaco. [8] Incl. los materiales para reparar las viviendas.

Cyprus

1. Economically active population, Employment and Unemployment ('000)

	Economically active population		Employment		Unemployment	
	Total	Women (%)	Total	Women (%)	Total	Women (%)
Age group	2007 [1][2][3] Labour force survey		2007 ★ Labour force survey		2007 [2][3] Labour force survey	
Total	393.4	44.9	377.9	44.6	15.4	52.4
15-19	4.2	48.7	3.6	49.9	0.5	40.0
20-24	34.9	51.2	31.4	51.5	3.4	48.1
25-29	56.6	47.9	53.9	47.6	2.6	55.4
30-34	52.9	47.2	51.0	47.5	1.9	38.9
35-39	48.3	47.9	46.9	47.4	1.3	68.3
40-44	50.2	46.2	49.1	45.6	1.2	69.2
45-49	48.4	44.1	47.0	43.6	1.5	59.4
50-54	40.1	42.3	38.6	41.7	1.4	59.2
55-59	31.0	40.2	30.0	39.9	1.0	48.8
60-64	16.8	31.3	16.3	31.8	0.5	16.0
65+	10.1	22.2	.	.	.	.
Economic activity (ISIC-Rev.3)	2007 [1][2][3] Labour force survey		2007 [1][2][3] Labour force survey		2007 [2][3] Labour force survey	
Total	393.4	44.9	377.9	44.6	15.4	52.4
A Agriculture, Hunting and Forestry	16.4	24.7	15.9	24.6	0.5	30.0
B Fishing	0.7	21.4	0.7	21.4	-	.
C Mining and Quarrying	0.6	6.6	0.5	7.8	0.1	.
D Manufacturing	38.6	31.9	37.2	31.8	1.4	35.4
E Electricity, Gas and Water Supply	2.7	14.1	2.7	14.1	-	.
F Construction	45.8	8.8	44.7	9.0	1.2	3.2
G Wholesale and Retail Trade; Repair of Motor Vehicles ...	70.4	44.8	68.0	44.3	2.5	58.8
H Hotels and Restaurants	26.5	56.7	23.9	55.6	2.6	67.0
I Transport, Storage and Communications	23.4	40.5	22.4	40.1	1.0	49.8
J Financial Intermediation	18.8	53.4	18.8	53.5	0.0	.
K Real Estate, Renting and Business Activities	32.1	54.4	31.4	54.2	0.7	63.7
L Public Administration and Defence; Compulsory Social ...	31.5	37.7	31.2	37.1	0.3	94.2
M Education	26.8	71.8	26.4	71.6	0.4	84.2
N Health and Social Work	17.2	71.0	16.9	71.0	0.3	75.5
O Other Community, Social and Personal Service Activities	19.6	53.5	18.8	53.3	0.8	58.8
P Households with Employed Persons	15.8	98.9	15.7	98.9	0.0	100.0
Q Extra-Territorial Organizations and Bodies	3.0	24.9	2.8	24.6	0.3	27.9
X Not classifiable by economic activity	3.3	54.8	-	.	.	.
Unemployed seeking their first job	.	.	.	.	3.3	54.8
Occupation (ISCO-88)	2007 [1][2][3] Labour force survey		2007 [1][2][3] Labour force survey		2007 [2][3] Labour force survey	
Total	393.4	44.9	377.9	44.6	15.4	52.4
1 Legislators, senior officials and managers	13.7	15.2	13.4	15.4	0.2	.
2 Professionals	58.3	51.5	57.5	51.5	0.8	56.8
3 Technicians and associate professionals	45.3	43.6	44.4	43.6	0.9	43.9
4 Clerks	57.6	75.8	56.0	75.7	1.6	82.4
5 Service workers and shop and market sales workers	64.5	57.0	61.0	56.3	3.4	68.1
6 Skilled agricultural and fishery workers	11.0	18.7	10.9	18.5	0.1	60.3
7 Craft and related trade workers	55.0	3.9	53.7	3.9	1.3	4.4
8 Plant and machine operators and assemblers	21.4	10.4	20.6	10.1	0.8	17.5
9 Elementary occupations	59.2	60.0	56.3	60.4	2.9	52.3
0 Armed forces	4.2	13.5	4.2	13.6	0.0	.
X Not classifiable by occupation	3.3	54.8	-	.	.	.
Unemployed seeking their first job	.	.	.	.	3.3	54.8
Education level (ISCED-97)	2007 [1][2][3] Labour force survey		2007 ★ Labour force survey		2007 [2][3] Labour force survey	
Total	393.4	44.9	377.9	44.6	15.4	52.4
X No schooling [4]	5.2	46.9	5.1	45.9	0.1	85.2
1 Primary education or first stage of basic education	50.1	37.0	47.9	36.6	2.2	45.9
2 Lower secondary or second stage of basic education	37.3	41.9	35.5	41.4	1.8	52.1
3 Upper secondary education	151.9	39.7	145.8	39.6	6.1	41.6
4 Post-secondary non-tertiary education	9.3	75.7	8.9	75.1	0.4	90.0
5A First stage of tertiary education - theoretically based	87.1	49.5	83.9	49.0	3.3	61.9
5B First stage of tertiary education - practically oriented	50.3	57.2	48.8	56.8	1.5	73.4
6 Second stage of tertiary education	2.1	29.9	2.1	29.9	-	.
Status in employment (ICSE-1993)	2007 [1][2][3] Labour force survey		2007 [1][2][3] Labour force survey		2007 ★ Labour force survey	
Total	393.4	44.9	377.9	44.6	15.4	52.4
1 Employees	312.3	48.7	301.1	48.6	11.2	52.3
2 Employers	23.2	13.1	23.0	13.1	0.2	10.2
3 Own-account workers	47.9	31.0	47.4	30.8	0.5	44.2
5 Contributing family workers	6.6	71.0	6.5	70.6	0.2	86.5
6 Not classifiable by status	3.3	54.8	-	.	3.3	54.8

Cyprus

2. Population ('000), Activity rate and Unemployment rate

Age group	Population 2007 [1,5] Labour force survey			Activity rate 2007 [1,5] Labour force survey			Unemployment rate 2007 [2,3] Labour force survey		
	Total	Men	Women	Total	Men	Women	Total	Men	Women
Total	752.3	366.9	385.5	52.3	59.1	45.8	3.9	3.4	4.6
15+	610.9	294.5	316.4	64.4	73.6	55.8	3.9	3.4	4.6
15-24	93.7	43.7	50.1	41.7	43.9	39.7	10.2	11.0	9.4
25-54	341.8	168.1	173.7	86.7	95.0	78.7	3.4	2.7	4.1
55+	175.4	82.7	92.6	33.0	45.8	21.5	.	.	.

3. Paid employment ('000), Hours of work (weekly) and Wages

Economic activity (ISIC-Rev.3)	Paid employment 2007 [1,2,3] Labour force survey			Hours of work 2006 [6,7] Labour-related establishment survey Hours paid for / Employees			Wages 2006 [6,7,8] Labour-related establishment survey Earnings per hour / Employees / Pound		
	Total	Men	Women	Total	Men	Women	Total	Men	Women
Total	301.1	154.8	146.3	39.9	40.2	39.5	6.83	7.53	5.91
A-B	.	.	.	40.7	41.8	39.3	4.14	4.89	3.16
C-Q	.	.	.	39.9	40.2	39.5	6.86	7.55	5.94
A	4.6	3.7	0.9	40.6	41.6	39.3	4.13	4.89	3.16
B	0.4	0.2	0.2	45.8	47.0	38.0	4.87	4.99	4.08
C	0.5	0.5	0.0	43.4	43.9	38.7	7.24	7.24	7.20
D	29.8	19.3	10.5	40.4	41.0	39.4	5.01	5.68	3.70
E	2.7	2.4	0.4	39.3	39.6	38.3	8.60	9.87	7.12
F	33.4	29.4	3.9	39.2	39.2	38.4	7.19	7.17	7.46
G	49.9	25.1	24.8	40.0	40.4	39.6	4.94	6.00	3.62
H	19.4	7.7	11.7	40.8	40.8	40.8	4.68	5.55	4.00
I	18.6	9.9	8.7	40.3	41.0	39.1	8.20	9.26	6.19
J	17.8	8.2	9.6	38.3	38.5	38.2	10.73	12.33	9.43
K	24.0	9.7	14.3	40.0	40.2	39.9	8.08	10.19	6.13
L	31.2	19.6	11.6	39.9	40.0	39.8	7.86	8.25	7.27
M	23.9	6.9	17.1	38.3	38.7	38.1	10.81	11.91	10.34
N	14.0	3.5	10.5	40.9	41.9	40.5	8.39	10.98	7.52
O	12.4	6.5	6.0	39.7	40.0	39.3	6.86	7.55	5.90
P	15.7	0.2	15.5	.	.	.	.	.	.
Q	2.8	2.1	0.7	.	.	.	.	.	.

Share of women in wage employment in the non-agricultural sector [1,2,3] (2007 - Labour force survey): **49.1%**

4. Occupational injuries and Strikes and Lockouts

Economic activity (ISIC-Rev.3)	Rates of fatal injuries 2007 Labour inspectorate records Per 100,000 employees Reported injuries			Rates of non-fatal injuries 2007 [9] Labour inspectorate records Per 100,000 employees Reported injuries			Strikes and lockouts 2006 Special data collection		
	Total	Men	Women	Total	Men	Women	Strikes and lockouts	Workers involved	Days not worked
Total	5	10	0	694	1 069	297	10	25 955	26 898
A	44	54	0	966	950	1 032	0	0	0
B	0	0	0	2 326	2 326	0	0	0	0
C	195	211	0	2 335	2 532	0	0	0	0
D	7	10	0	1 742	2 335	650	1	8	40
E	0	0	0	873	1 016	0	0	0	0
F	12	14	0	1 676	1 868	230	1	25 000	25 000
G	4	8	0	549	754	342	1	150	900
H	5	13	0	1 685	2 196	1 349	1	25	25
I	11	20	0	603	888	277	3	360	360
J	0	0	0	118	86	145	0	0	0
K	0	0	0	125	195	77	0	0	0
L	3	5	0	257	337	121	3	412	573
M	0	0	0	58	58	59	0	0	0
N	0	0	0	222	201	229	0	0	0
O	0	0	0	322	480	150	0	0	0
P	0	0	0	0	0	0	.	.	.
Q	0	0	0	0	0	0	.	.	.

5. Consumer price indices (base period: 2000=100)

	2002	2003	2004	2005	2006	2007
General indices	104.8	109.2	111.7	114.5	117.4	120.2
Food index, including non-alcoholic beverages	108.9	114.4	119.0	120.9	126.7	133.7
Clothing indices, including footwear	90.0	91.1	90.4	88.5	88.2	88.4
Rent indices [10]	105.7	111.1	115.7	122.0	125.3	128.4

[1] Incl. armed forces, Excl. conscripts. [2] Government-controlled area. [3] Persons aged 15 years and over. [4] Levels X-0. [5] "De jure" population. [6] Adults. [7] Oct. [8] Incl. family allowances and the value of payments in kind. [9] Incapacity of 4 days or more. [10] Housing; incl. water.

Czech Republic

1. Economically active population, Employment and Unemployment ('000)

	Economically active population		Employment		Unemployment	
	Total	Women (%)	Total	Women (%)	Total	Women (%)
Age group	2007 [1] Labour force survey		2007 ★ Labour force survey		2007 [1] Labour force survey	
Total	5 198.3	43.6	4 922.0	43.0	276.3	55.3
15-19	46.1	37.5	33.7	36.2	12.4	41.1
20-24	381.7	41.4	348.2	41.4	33.5	42.1
25-29	648.2	40.5	614.5	39.9	33.7	51.9
30-34	763.2	40.2	723.3	38.6	39.9	67.9
35-39	651.5	44.9	620.3	43.6	31.2	69.6
40-44	661.5	47.5	632.0	46.9	29.5	58.6
45-49	606.8	48.5	579.7	48.2	27.1	56.5
50-54	678.7	49.3	642.6	48.7	36.1	60.1
55-59	518.7	40.8	490.9	40.7	27.8	42.1
60-64	175.0	29.9	170.7	30.1	4.3	23.3
65+	66.8	36.8	66.0	36.8	0.8	37.5
Economic activity (ISIC-Rev.3)	2007 [1] Labour force survey		2007 [1] Labour force survey		2007 [1] Labour force survey	
Total	5 198.3	43.6	4 922.0	43.0	276.0	55.4
A-B		.		.	9.0	55.6
A Agriculture, Hunting and Forestry	182.4	31.8	173.0	30.6	.	.
B Fishing	3.2	15.7	3.0	.	.	.
C Mining and Quarrying	59.2	10.8	54.0	11.1	5.0	.
D Manufacturing	1 474.2	37.1	1 406.0	36.2	69.0	55.1
E Electricity, Gas and Water Supply	73.8	20.0	73.0	20.5	1.0	.
F Construction	463.0	8.3	447.0	8.3	16.0	6.3
G Wholesale and Retail Trade; Repair of Motor Vehicles ...	646.4	53.8	613.0	52.9	33.0	72.7
H Hotels and Restaurants	196.8	57.1	181.0	56.4	15.0	66.7
I Transport, Storage and Communications	374.5	28.0	364.0	27.7	11.0	36.4
J Financial Intermediation	104.5	63.0	102.0	62.7	3.0	66.7
K Real Estate, Renting and Business Activities	362.5	43.6	353.0	43.3	10.0	50.0
L Public Administration and Defence; Compulsory Social ...	337.1	49.3	326.0	49.4	11.0	45.5
M Education	297.2	75.2	290.0	75.2	7.0	85.7
N Health and Social Work	348.0	80.1	338.0	80.2	10.0	80.0
O Other Community, Social and Personal Service Activities	202.0	50.5	194.0	51.0	8.0	37.5
P Households with Employed Persons	2.7	91.6	3.0	66.7	-	.
Q Extra-Territorial Organizations and Bodies	1.0	19.6	1.0	.	.	.
X Not classifiable by economic activity	69.8	59.2	1.0	.	29.0	69.0
Unemployed seeking their first job	.	.	.	.	40.0	52.5
Occupation (ISCO-88)	2007 [1] Labour force survey		2007 [1] Labour force survey		2007 [1] Labour force survey	
Total	5 198.3	43.6	4 922.0	43.0	276.0	55.4
1 Legislators, senior officials and managers	331.6	28.7	328.0	28.7	4.0	25.0
2 Professionals	549.8	51.6	544.0	51.5	6.0	50.0
3 Technicians and associate professionals	1 119.4	53.2	1 099.0	53.0	21.0	57.1
4 Clerks	359.3	75.8	344.0	75.6	15.0	80.0
5 Service workers and shop and market sales workers	618.9	67.5	578.0	66.8	41.0	78.0
6 Skilled agricultural and fishery workers	77.8	39.2	73.0	37.0	5.0	60.0
7 Craft and related trade workers	956.7	12.7	915.0	12.0	42.0	26.2
8 Plant and machine operators and assemblers	709.3	26.3	682.0	25.8	27.0	40.7
9 Elementary occupations	391.0	57.2	345.0	57.7	46.0	54.3
0 Armed forces	14.5	9.2	14.0	7.1	-	.
X Not classifiable by occupation	69.9	59.3	1.0	.	29.0	69.0
Unemployed seeking their first job	.	.	.	.	40.0	52.5
Education level (ISCED-97)	2007 [1] Labour force survey		2007 ★ Labour force survey		2007 [1] Labour force survey	
Total	5 198.3	43.6	4 922.0	43.0	276.3	55.3
1 Primary education or first stage of basic education [2]	367.1	57.0	293.5	57.5	73.6	54.9
3 Upper secondary education [3]	4 080.1	42.8	3 890.0	42.1	190.1	56.3
5A First stage of tertiary education - theoretically based [4]	750.1	41.9	737.7	41.9	12.4	42.7
Status in employment (ICSE-1993)	2007 [1] Labour force survey		2007 [1] Labour force survey		2007 ★ Labour force survey	
Total	5 198.3	43.6	4 922.0	43.0	276.3	55.2
1 Employees	4 305.5	46.3	4 111.0	45.9	194.5	54.3
2 Employers	184.9	21.4	184.0	21.2	0.9	60.8
3 Own-account workers	593.2	28.0	582.0	27.7	11.2	46.3
4 Members of producers' cooperatives	14.3	34.3	14.0	35.7	0.3	-43.4
5 Contributing family workers	30.5	76.5	30.0	76.7	0.5	67.6
6 Not classifiable by status	69.9	58.7	1.0	.	68.9	59.6

2. Population ('000), Activity rate and Unemployment rate

	Population 2007 [5] Labour force survey			Activity rate 2007 [5] Labour force survey			Unemployment rate 2007 [1] Labour force survey		
Age group	Total	Men	Women	Total	Men	Women	Total	Men	Women
Total	10 320.4	5 045.4	5 275.0	50.4	58.1	43.0	5.3	4.2	6.7
15+	8 845.1	4 287.2	4 557.8	58.8	68.3	49.8	5.3	4.2	6.7
15-24	1 340.4	687.4	653.0	31.9	36.7	26.9	10.7	10.6	10.9
25-54	4 568.1	2 320.5	2 247.6	87.8	95.0	80.3	4.9	3.5	6.7
55+	2 936.6	1 279.3	1 657.2	25.9	36.9	17.4	4.3	4.2	4.5

Czech Republic

3. Paid employment ('000), Hours of work (weekly) and Wages

Economic activity (ISIC-Rev.3)	Paid employment 2007[1] Labour force survey Total	Men	Women	Hours of work 2006[6] Labour-related establishment survey Hours actually worked / Wage earners Total	Men	Women	Wages 2006[7] Labour-related establishment survey Earnings per month / Employees / Koruna Total	Men	Women
Total	4 111	2 223	1 888	.	.	.	19 003	.	.
A-B	130	85	45	.	.	.	14 413	.	.
C-Q	.	.	.	.	.	.	19 167	.	.
A	127	83	44	.	.	.	14 393	.	.
B	3	2	0	.	.	.	16 238	.	.
C	53	47	6	39.5	.	.	23 944	.	.
D	1 295	807	489	40.5	.	.	18 112	.	.
E	69	54	14	39.7	.	.	26 026	.	.
F	279	250	30	.	.	.	18 906	.	.
G	464	191	273	.	.	.	17 690	.	.
H	147	58	89	.	.	.	10 820	.	.
I	319	224	96	.	.	.	20 591	.	.
J	77	26	51	.	.	.	39 246	.	.
K	226	123	104	.	.	.	20 930	.	.
L	322	162	160	.	.	.	22 896	.	.
M	280	69	212	.	.	.	18 275	.	.
N	312	57	255	.	.	.	18 321	.	.
O	135	71	64	.	.	.	15 927	.	.
P	2	0	2	.	.	.	.	.	.
Q	1	1	0	.	.	.	.	.	.
X	-	-	-	.	.	.	.	.	.

Share of women in wage employment in the non-agricultural sector [1] (2007 - Labour force survey): **46.3%**

4. Occupational injuries and Strikes and Lockouts

Economic activity (ISIC-Rev.3)	Rates of fatal injuries 2007 Administrative reports Per 100,000 workers insured Reported injuries Total	Men	Women	Rates of non-fatal injuries 2007 Administrative reports Per 100,000 workers insured Reported injuries Total	Men	Women	Strikes and lockouts 1996 Labour-related establishment survey Strikes and lockouts	Workers involved[8]	Days not worked[8]
Total	4.1	7.3	0.5	1 680	2 354	921	2	11 500	16 400
A	16.9	23.0	5.5	4 132	4 431	3 563	0	0	0
B	0.0	0.0	0.0	2 226	2 262	2 062	0	0	0
C	14.6	16.9	0.0	2 090	2 321	612	1	1 600	200
D	4.4	6.7	0.9	3 034	3 851	1 770	0	0	0
E	1.9	2.6	0.0	927	1 101	424	0	0	0
F	36.1	43.8	0.0	2 921	3 362	861	0	0	0
G	2.8	6.0	0.5	1 794	2 409	1 346	0	0	0
H	0.0	0.0	0.0	1 812	2 140	1 562	0	0	0
I	12.7	18.9	2.0	2 049	2 429	1 397	0	0	0
J	0.0	0.0	0.0	178	172	182	0	0	0
K	2.8	4.9	0.7	919	1 170	645	0	0	0
L	0.5	1.3	0.0	787	1 529	360	0	0	0
M	0.0	0.0	0.0	538	486	560	0	0	0
N	0.8	3.5	0.0	910	1 206	822	1	9 700	16 100
O	5.6	9.1	1.9	1 401	2 149	606	1	200	100
X	0.0	0.0	0.0	926	1 395	339	.	.	.

5. Consumer price indices (base period: 2000=100)

	2002	2003	2004	2005	2006	2007
General indices	106.6	106.6	109.7	111.7	114.6	117.9
Food index, including non-alcoholic beverages [9]	104.3	104.0	109.0	110.3	111.5	118.0
Electricity, gas and other fuel indices	122.4	120.8	123.1	131.0	146.9	151.6
Clothing indices, including footwear	96.1	91.4	87.7	83.1	78.1	77.5
Rent indices	118.4	123.6	129.8	132.5	135.7	142.5
General index, excluding housing	105.5	105.2	107.5	107.1	108.8	114.7

[1] Persons aged 15 years and over. [2] Levels 1-2. [3] Levels 3-4. [4] Levels 5-6. [5] "De jure" population. [6] Enterprises with 20 or more employees. [7] Estimates. [8] Figures rounded to nearest 100. [9] Incl. tobacco, beverages and public catering.

[1] Personnes âgées de 15 ans et plus. [2] Niveaux 1-2. [3] Niveaux 3-4. [4] Niveaux 5-6. [5] Population "de jure". [6] Entreprises occupant 20 salariés et plus. [7] Estimations. [8] Chiffres arrondis au 100 le plus proche. [9] Y compris le tabac, les boissons et la restauration.

[1] Personas de 15 años y más. [2] Niveles 1-2. [3] Niveles 3-4. [4] Niveles 5-6. [5] Población "de jure". [6] Empresas con 20 y más asalariados. [7] Estimaciones. [8] Cifras redondeadas al 100 más próximo. [9] Incl. el tabaco, las bebidas y la restauración.

Denmark

1. Economically active population, Employment and Unemployment ('000)

	Economically active population		Employment		Unemployment	
	Total	Women (%)	Total	Women (%)	Total	Women (%)
Age group	2007 [1][2] Labour force survey		2007 ★ Labour force survey		2007 [2] Labour force survey	
Total	2 893.188	47.1	2 778.649	46.9	114.539	51.9
15-19	206.214	48.5	185.244	49.1	20.970	43.3
20-24	238.232	47.1	223.071	47.0	15.161	48.8
25-29	276.512	47.5	263.687	47.2	12.825	53.9
30-34	336.801	47.4	323.887	46.9	12.914	59.3
35-39	356.077	47.5	345.009	47.3	11.068	54.7
40-44	384.993	47.2	375.232	47.1	9.761	50.2
45-49	334.780	47.8	326.802	47.6	7.978	58.5
50-54	309.893	47.9	301.978	47.7	7.915	57.8
55-59	297.157	47.6	284.630	47.2	12.527	55.3
60-64	133.110	39.2	130.690	39.4	2.420	28.3
65-66	19.420	29.4	18.420	27.6	1.000	61.8
Economic activity (ISIC-Rev.3)	2007 ★ Labour force survey		2007 [1][2] Labour force survey		2007 [2] Labour force survey	
Total	2 893.188	47.1	2 778.649	46.9	114.539	51.9
A Agriculture, Hunting and Forestry	79.660	24.5	79.660	24.5	-	.
B Fishing	.	.	.	.	-	.
C Mining and Quarrying	5.200	24.2	5.200	24.2	.	.
D Manufacturing	446.574	32.2	432.867	31.8	13.707	45.6
E Electricity, Gas and Water Supply	16.526	24.9	16.526	24.9	.	.
F Construction	197.480	9.6	192.946	9.6	4.534	10.5
G Wholesale and Retail Trade; Repair of Motor Vehicles ...	427.492	43.1	412.067	42.8	15.425	49.8
H Hotels and Restaurants	87.824	57.0	81.104	53.5	6.720	100.0
I Transport, Storage and Communications	179.267	28.9	173.134	28.8	6.133	31.3
J Financial Intermediation	85.930	50.0	85.930	50.0	.	.
K Real Estate, Renting and Business Activities	280.178	41.3	268.442	40.9	11.736	50.7
L Public Administration and Defence; Compulsory Social ...	164.222	49.2	164.222	49.2	.	.
M Education	221.170	58.8	215.177	59.0	5.993	49.9
N Health and Social Work	514.112	82.3	499.871	82.3	14.241	80.5
O Other Community, Social and Personal Service Activities	150.773	51.3	145.667	50.9	5.106	60.8
P Households with Employed Persons	3.901	93.1	3.901	93.1	.	.
Q Extra-Territorial Organizations and Bodies	1.936	100.0	1.936	100.0	.	.
X Not classifiable by economic activity	6.848	7.8	-	.	6.848	7.8
Unemployed seeking their first job	.	.	.	.	24.096	51.3
Occupation (ISCO-88)	2007 ★ Labour force survey		2007 [1][2] Labour force survey		2007 [2] Labour force survey	
Total	2 893.188	47.1	2 778.649	46.9	114.539	51.9
1 Legislators, senior officials and managers	218.018	28.6	214.385	27.9	3.633	68.2
2 Professionals	415.528	43.5	408.195	43.4	7.333	48.8
3 Technicians and associate professionals	605.803	57.3	594.160	57.2	11.643	60.3
4 Clerks	261.306	74.4	254.556	74.5	6.750	71.9
5 Service workers and shop and market sales workers	475.249	73.7	458.221	73.8	17.028	70.6
6 Skilled agricultural and fishery workers	59.902	18.9	59.902	18.9	-	.
7 Craft and related trade workers	294.824	6.5	290.562	6.6	4.262	.
8 Plant and machine operators and assemblers	188.942	19.7	183.260	19.7	5.682	20.2
9 Elementary occupations	318.983	42.8	303.064	42.9	15.919	41.8
0 Armed forces	11.480	5.8	11.480	5.8	-	.
X Not classifiable by occupation	19.057	51.7	0.864	59.6	18.193	51.4
Unemployed seeking their first job	.	.	.	.	24.096	51.3
Education level (ISCED-97)					2007 [2] Labour force survey	
Total	.	.	.	.	114.539	51.8
X-0	.	.	.	.	-	.
1 Primary education or first stage of basic education	.	.	.	.	.	.
2 Lower secondary or second stage of basic education	.	.	.	.	41.065	48.4
3 Upper secondary education	.	.	.	.	40.218	55.4
4 Post-secondary non-tertiary education	.	.	.	.	.	.
5A First stage of tertiary education - theoretically based	.	.	.	.	21.142	57.2
5B First stage of tertiary education - practically oriented	.	.	.	.	5.203	61.5
6 Second stage of tertiary education	.	.	.	.	-	.
? Level not stated	.	.	.	.	6.911	29.2
Status in employment (ICSE-1993)	2003 [3] Population census		2007 [1][2] Labour force survey			
Total	2 860.636	46.9	2 778.649	46.9	.	.
1 Employees	2 532.461	48.3	2 533.335	48.7	.	.
2 Employers	72.070	21.4	.	.	.	.
2, 3	.	.	228.949	25.1	.	.
3 Own-account workers	126.676	26.4	.	.	.	.
5 Contributing family workers	10.179	92.8	16.365	76.4	.	.
6 Not classifiable by status	.	.	-	.	.	.

Denmark

2. Population ('000), Activity rate and Unemployment rate

Age group	Population 2007 [1,4] Labour force survey			Activity rate 2007 [1,4] Labour force survey			Unemployment rate 2007 [2] Labour force survey		
	Total	Men	Women	Total	Men	Women	Total	Men	Women
Total	.	.	.	.	.	.	4.0	3.6	4.4
15+	3 706.3	1 868.8	1 837.6	78.1	81.9	74.1	4.0	3.6	4.4
15-24	622.1	318.2	303.9	71.4	73.0	69.9	8.1	8.5	7.8
25-54	2 244.6	1 132.7	1 111.9	89.1	92.6	85.5	3.1	2.6	3.7

3. Paid employment ('000), Hours of work (weekly) and Wages

Economic activity (ISIC-Rev.3)	Paid employment 2007 [1,2] Labour force survey			Hours of work 1993 [5] Labour-related establishment survey Hours actually worked / Wage earners			Wages 2006 [6,7] Labour-related establishment census Earnings per hour / Employees / Krone		
	Total	Men	Women	Total	Men	Women	Total	Men	Women
Total	2 533.335	1 300.796	1 232.539	.	.	.	.	.	.
C-Q	.	.	.	.	.	.	342.70	329.78	217.13
A	39.194	27.762	11.432	.	.	.	.	.	.
B	-	-	-	.	.	.	.	.	.
C	3.850	1.900	1.950	.	.	.	328.34	329.78	318.45
D	417.102	283.854	133.247	31.5	.	.	235.63	244.60	213.44
E	16.377	12.308	4.068	.	.	.	304.41	318.92	262.39
F	156.447	140.979	15.468	.	.	.	233.80	235.86	211.17
G	371.378	208.437	162.941	.	.	.	224.65	243.87	192.59
H	71.186	31.128	40.057	.	.	.	178.49	188.12	170.52
I	161.333	112.800	48.533	.	.	.	231.84	239.59	212.87
J	84.642	41.715	42.927	.	.	.	314.83	356.81	274.18
K	222.951	125.509	97.442	.	.	.	269.04	297.79	226.56
L	164.025	83.314	80.711	.	.	.	.	.	.
M	210.263	85.192	125.071	.	.	.	218.75	226.99	213.10
N	478.346	78.840	399.506	.	.	.	214.34	226.92	209.50
O	127.615	63.025	64.590	.	.	.	251.53	266.87	234.26
P	3.705	2.533	1.172	.	.	.	.	.	.
Q	-	-	-	.	.	.	.	.	.
X	4.921	1.500	3.421	.	.	.	.	.	.

Share of women in wage employment in the non-agricultural sector [1,2] (2007 - Labour force survey): **48.9%**

4. Occupational injuries and Strikes and Lockouts

Economic activity (ISIC-Rev.3)	Rates of fatal injuries 2001 Labour inspectorate records Per 100,000 workers employed Reported injuries			Rates of non-fatal injuries 2001 Labour inspectorate records Per 100,000 workers employed Reported injuries			Strikes and lockouts 2007 Records of employers'/workers' organizations		
	Total	Men	Women	Total	Men	Women	Strikes and lockouts	Workers involved	Days not worked [8]
Total	2	3	0	1 574	1 876	1 226	862	61 113	91 700
A	7	8	4	704	729	621	.	.	.
B	0	0	0	239	233	347	.	.	.
A-C	.	.	.	.	.	.	0	0	0
C	0	0	0	1 929	2 207	226	.	.	.
D	2	2	0	3 219	3 758	2 089	306	24 599	39 900
E	0	0	0	1 641	1 981	455	0	0	0
F	5	6	0	2 319	2 500	631	103	2 751	4 200
G	2	3	0	775	921	566	106	4 097	6 500
H	0	0	0	855	844	865	4	479	0
I	6	7	2	1 955	2 056	1 694	214	8 407	19 000
J	0	0	0	237	232	242	0	0	0
K	1	1	1	609	668	533	0	0	0
L	3	4	1	1 727	2 021	1 416	0	0	0
M	1	1	0	878	870	883	0	0	0
N	0	0	0	1 674	1 469	1 714	0	0	0
O	1	1	0	1 055	1 517	588	0	0	0
P	110	307	0	2 519	2 454	2 555	.	.	.
Q	0	0	0	0	0	0	.	.	.
X	8	15	0	4 406	6 055	2 612	129	20 780	22 100

5. Consumer price indices (base period: 2000=100)

	2002	2003	2004	2005	2006	2007
General indices	104.8	107.0	108.3	110.2	112.3	114.2
Food index, including non-alcoholic beverages	106.1	107.7	106.6	107.3	110.2	115.1
Electricity, gas and other fuel indices	105.7	107.0	108.2	115.4	121.4	121.5
Clothing indices, including footwear	100.8	101.8	101.8	101.1	99.1	97.4
Rent indices	105.3	108.2	111.2	113.9	116.1	118.6
General index, excluding housing	104.7	106.7	107.6	109.4	111.4	113.1

[1] Included armed forces and conscripts. [2] Persons aged 15 to 66 years. [3] Jan. [4] "De jure" population. [5] ISIC Rev. 2, major division 3. [6] Private sector. [7] Excl. young people aged less than 18 years and trainees. [8] Figures rounded to nearest 100.

[1] Y compris les forces armées et les conscrits. [2] Personnes âgées de 15 à 66 ans. [3] Janv. [4] Population "de jure". [5] CITI Rév. 2, branche 3. [6] Secteur privé. [7] Non compris les jeunes gens âgés de moins de 18 ans et les apprentis. [8] Chiffres arrondis au 100 le plus proche.

[1] Incluye las fuezas armadas y los conscriptos. [2] Personas de 15 a 66 años. [3] Enero. [4] Población "de jure". [5] CIIU Rev. 2, gran división 3. [6] Sector privado. [7] Excl. los jovenenes de menos de 18 años y los aprendices. [8] Cifras redondeadas al 100 más próximo.

Djibouti

1. Population active, Emploi et Chômage ('000)

	Population active		Emploi		Chômage	
	Total	Femmes (%)	Total	Femmes (%)	Total	Femmes (%)
Groupe d'âge						1982
					\multicolumn{2}{r}{Fichiers des bureaux de placement}
Total	.	.	.	.	3.046	40.5
0-19	.	.	.	.	0.341	36.7
20-24	.	.	.	.	1.367	52.5
25-44	.	.	.	.	1.305	29.1
45+	.	.	.	.	0.033	33.3
Activité économique (CNTI)						1982
					\multicolumn{2}{r}{Fichiers des bureaux de placement}
Total	.	.	.	.	3.046	40.5
2	.	.	.	.	0.078	.
4	.	.	.	.	0.039	.
5	.	.	.	.	0.740	.
6	.	.	.	.	0.315	34.6
7	.	.	.	.	0.114	15.8
8	.	.	.	.	0.420	64.3
0	.	.	.	.	1.340	62.5

2. Population ('000), Taux d'activité et Taux de chômage

Données non disponibles.

3. Emploi rémunéré ('000), Durée du travail (hebdomadaire) et Salaires

Activité économique (CITI-Rév.2)	Emploi rémunéré 1982 [1] Estimations officielles			Durée du travail			Salaires		
	Total	Hommes	Femmes	Total	Hommes	Femmes	Total	Hommes	Femmes
Total	1.803	.	.	.	.	.	.	.	.
2-9	.	1.482	0.321	.	.	.	.	.	.
2	0.089	.	.	.	.	.	.	.	.
4	0.053	.	.	.	.	.	.	.	.
5	0.510	.	.	.	.	.	.	.	.
6	0.221	.	.	.	.	.	.	.	.
7	0.076	.	.	.	.	.	.	.	.
8	0.512	.	.	.	.	.	.	.	.
0	0.342	.	.	.	.	.	.	.	.

4. Lésions professionnelles et Grèves et lock-out

Données non disponibles.

5. Indices des prix à la consommation (période de base: 2000=100)

Données non disponibles pour la période de 2002 à 2007.

---

[1] Non-agricultural activities.   [1] Activités non agricoles.   [1] Actividades no agrícolas.

Dominica

1. Economically active population, Employment and Unemployment ('000)

	Economically active population		Employment		Unemployment	
	Total	Women (%)	Total	Women (%)	Total	Women (%)
Age group	2001 [1,2] Population census		2001 ★ Population census		2001 [1,2] Population census	
Total	27.87	38.9	24.81	39.5	3.05	33.5
15-19	1.51	36.2	0.94	34.9	0.58	38.2
20-24	3.19	41.9	2.55	42.1	0.64	41.0
25-29	3.74	42.1	3.29	43.0	0.44	35.3
30-34	4.18	41.1	3.77	42.0	0.41	33.6
35-39	3.99	38.4	3.66	39.4	0.34	27.5
40-44	3.40	38.3	3.15	39.3	0.25	26.1
45-49	2.68	37.6	2.52	38.6	0.16	22.5
50-54	1.92	38.6	1.83	39.4	0.10	23.5
55-59	1.32	33.5	1.24	34.5	0.08	19.5
60-64	0.79	34.7	0.74	35.3	0.05	24.4
65+	1.15	30.8	1.12	30.9	0.02	29.2
Economic activity (ISIC-Rev.2)			2001 [1,2] Population census			
Total			24.81	39.5		
1 Agriculture, Hunting, Forestry and Fishing			5.22	15.5		
2 Mining and Quarrying			0.16	8.5		
3 Manufacturing			1.93	42.2		
4 Electricity, Gas and Water			0.41	19.0		
5 Construction			2.42	2.1		
6 Wholesale and Retail Trade and Restaurants and Hotels			5.12	59.6		
7 Transport, Storage and Communication			1.56	21.4		
8 Financing, Insurance, Real Estate and Business Services			1.14	60.0		
9 Community, Social and Personal Services			6.77	58.0		
0 Activities not Adequately Defined			0.08	53.2		
Economic activity (ISIC-Rev.3)					1997 [1] Labour force survey	
Total					7.71	54.0
A Agriculture, Hunting and Forestry					0.57	54.4
B Fishing					0.02	.
D Manufacturing					0.62	67.7
E Electricity, Gas and Water Supply					0.02	.
F Construction					1.00	2.0
G Wholesale and Retail Trade; Repair of Motor Vehicles ...					0.53	67.9
H Hotels and Restaurants					0.49	71.4
I Transport, Storage and Communications					0.25	28.0
J Financial Intermediation					0.06	33.3
K Real Estate, Renting and Business Activities					0.05	60.0
L Public Administration and Defence; Compulsory Social ...					0.33	27.3
M Education					0.12	75.0
N Health and Social Work					0.06	100.0
O Other Community, Social and Personal Service Activities					0.21	52.4
P Households with Employed Persons					0.61	96.7
X Not classifiable by economic activity					0.58	43.1
Unemployed seeking their first job					2.22	64.0
Occupation (ISCO-88)	1997 ★ Labour force survey		2001 [1,2] Population census		1997 [1] Labour force survey	
Total	33.40	45.8	24.81	39.5	7.71	54.0
1 Legislators, senior officials and managers	1.58	58.9	1.98	48.4	0.09	55.6
2 Professionals	1.19	45.4	0.92	45.5	0.09	11.1
3 Technicians and associate professionals	2.26	65.0	2.61	57.7	0.11	63.6
4 Clerks	2.08	76.4	2.38	78.4	0.20	100.0
5 Service workers and shop and market sales workers	4.62	67.7	3.40	57.0	1.14	80.7
6 Skilled agricultural and fishery workers	5.29	25.5	4.43	14.9	0.17	64.7
7 Craft and related trade workers	5.30	15.1	4.16	13.2	1.23	13.8
8 Plant and machine operators and assemblers	1.39	7.9	1.31	5.7	0.17	23.5
9 Elementary occupations	7.12	52.8	3.92	47.0	2.17	49.8
X Not classifiable by occupation	0.38	50.0	0.02	20.0	0.15	53.3
Unemployed seeking their first job					2.22	64.0
Education level (ISCED-76)					1997 [1] Labour force survey	
Total					7.72	54.0
X No schooling					0.28	57.1
0 Education preceding the first level					0.04	.
1 First level					5.67	49.4
2 Second level, first stage					1.38	73.2
3 Second level, second stage					0.14	35.7
5 Third level, first stage, leading to an award not equivalent ...					0.11	54.5
6 Third level, first stage, leading to a first university degree ...					0.05	100.0
9 Education not definable by level					0.05	80.0
Status in employment (ICSE-1993)			2001 [1,2] Population census			
Total			24.81	39.5		
1 Employees			16.95	43.8		
2 Employers			1.24	25.6		
3 Own-account workers			6.05	30.0		
5 Contributing family workers			0.38	51.5		
6 Not classifiable by status			0.20	31.3		

Dominica

2. Population ('000), Activity rate and Unemployment rate

Age group	Population 2001 [2,3] Population census			Activity rate 2001 [2,3] Population census			Unemployment rate 2001 [1,2] Population census		
	Total	Men	Women	Total	Men	Women	Total	Men	Women
Total	.	.	.	.	.	.	11.0	11.9	9.5
15+	48.30	24.26	24.04	57.7	70.2	45.1	11.0	11.9	9.5
15-24	10.90	5.58	5.32	43.2	50.5	35.4	25.8	26.0	25.6
25-54	25.91	13.49	12.43	76.8	89.2	63.4	8.5	9.8	6.4
55+	11.50	5.20	6.30	28.3	42.0	17.0	4.6	5.4	3.2

3. Paid employment ('000), Hours of work (weekly) and Wages

Statistics not available.

4. Occupational injuries and Strikes and Lockouts

Economic activity (ISIC-Rev.2)	Rates of fatal injuries			Rates of non-fatal injuries			Strikes and lockouts 1997 Labour relations records		
	Total	Men	Women	Total	Men	Women	Strikes and lockouts	Workers involved	Days not worked
Total	.	.	.	.	.	.	4	655	1 746

5. Consumer price indices (base period: 2000=100)

[4]	2002	2003	2004	2005	2006	2007
General indices	100.2	101.6	104.1	105.8	.	.
Food index, including non-alcoholic beverages	101.5	101.9	104.8	107.4	.	.
Electricity, gas and other fuel indices	103.7	115.6	124.3	140.2	.	.
Clothing indices, including footwear	99.0	98.0	98.1	98.1	.	.

[1] Persons aged 15 years and over. [2] May. [3] "De facto" population. [4] Index base 2001=100.

[1] Personnes âgées de 15 ans et plus. [2] Mai. [3] Population "de facto". [4] Indice base 2001=100.

[1] Personas de 15 años y más. [2] Mayo. [3] Población "de facto". [4] Indice base 2001=100.

Ecuador

1. Población económicamente activa, Empleo y Desempleo ('000)

	Población económicamente activa		Empleo		Desempleo	
	Total	Mujeres (%)	Total	Mujeres (%)	Total	Mujeres (%)
Grupo de edad	2006 [1,2,3] Encuesta de la fuerza de trabajo		2006 ★ Encuesta de la fuerza de trabajo		2006 [1,2,3] Encuesta de la fuerza de trabajo	
Total	4 373.4	41.5	4 031.6	40.1	341.8	58.0
10-14	92.6	32.5	80.1	34.5	12.5	19.6
15-19	343.3	35.4	274.3	32.5	69.1	47.0
20-24	563.6	41.0	484.5	37.7	79.1	61.2
25-29	556.1	42.8	509.3	40.2	46.7	70.3
30-34	470.7	42.8	440.6	41.5	30.0	62.2
35-39	470.0	47.3	446.9	46.2	23.0	67.2
40-44	512.6	45.6	491.2	44.1	21.4	81.1
45-49	415.3	41.3	394.9	40.3	20.4	60.6
50-54	365.1	41.7	348.8	41.0	16.3	56.9
55-59	228.3	37.4	217.9	37.4	10.4	38.1
60-64	147.8	39.3	142.4	38.1	5.4	73.0
65-69	98.6	33.7	95.0	34.2	3.6	21.8
70+	109.6	32.1	105.7	32.8	3.9	11.6
Actividad económica (CIIU-Rev.3)	2006 [1,2,3] Encuesta de la fuerza de trabajo		2006 [1,2,3] Encuesta de la fuerza de trabajo		2006 [1,2,3] Encuesta de la fuerza de trabajo	
Total	4 373.4	41.5	4 031.6	40.1	341.8	58.0
A Agricultura, ganadería, caza y silvicultura	293.3	21.7	285.0	21.8	8.3	18.0
B Pesca	54.4	16.1	48.9	13.8	5.5	36.8
C Explotación de minas y canteras	17.6	9.6	15.8	10.1	1.8	4.9
D Industrias manufactureras	588.1	34.4	555.5	33.7	32.6	45.8
E Suministro de electricidad, gas y agua	21.2	17.8	19.4	18.7	1.9	8.8
F Construcción	311.4	4.0	290.1	4.1	21.3	2.7
G Comercio al por mayor y al por menor; reparación ...	1 208.0	46.5	1 151.8	45.9	56.2	58.6
H Hoteles y restaurantes	239.9	62.9	225.4	62.1	14.6	75.0
I Transporte, almacenamiento y comunicaciones	308.0	14.4	292.3	13.9	15.7	23.7
J Intermediación financiera	49.6	48.8	47.9	47.5	1.6	89.3
K Actividades inmobiliarias, empresariales y de alquiler	207.2	26.9	200.7	26.9	6.5	25.1
L Administración pública y defensa; planes de seguridad ...	178.5	27.3	170.3	25.8	8.1	59.0
M Enseñanza	291.6	65.0	281.0	64.3	10.6	82.0
N Servicios sociales y de salud	123.3	65.2	116.0	63.5	7.3	91.9
O Otras actividades de servicios comunitarios ...	170.0	60.7	162.9	60.3	7.1	70.7
P Hogares privados con servicio doméstico	184.5	94.2	167.7	94.2	16.8	94.6
Q Organizaciones y órganos extraterritoriales	0.9	100.0	0.9	100.0	-	.
X No pueden clasificarse según la actividad económica	125.8	69.4	-	.	-	.
Desempleados sin empleo anterior	.	.	.	.	125.8	69.4
Ocupación (CIUO-88)	2006 [1,2,3] Encuesta de la fuerza de trabajo		2006 [1,2,3] Encuesta de la fuerza de trabajo		2006 [1,2,3] Encuesta de la fuerza de trabajo	
Total	4 373.4	41.5	4 031.6	40.1	341.8	58.0
1 Miembros del poder ejecutivo y de los cuerpos legislativos ...	125.8	27.6	121.9	27.7	3.9	24.0
2 Profesionales científicos e intelectuales	349.1	51.3	339.2	50.7	9.9	71.5
3 Técnicos y profesionales de nivel medio	285.3	48.1	268.0	47.7	17.4	53.7
4 Empleados de oficina	301.2	58.7	280.6	57.8	20.6	71.8
5 Trabajadores de los servicios y vendedores de comercios ...	1 066.5	53.9	1 012.9	53.2	53.5	67.9
6 Agricultores y trabajadores calificados agropecuarios ...	135.2	19.1	131.7	19.4	3.5	7.3
7 Oficiales, operarios y artesanos de artes mecánicas ...	636.0	19.2	603.6	19.0	32.4	22.8
8 Operadores de instalaciones y máquinas y montadores	292.3	8.1	281.9	7.7	10.3	17.9
9 Trabajadores no calificados	1 039.5	43.5	975.2	42.9	64.4	51.4
0 Fuerzas armadas	16.8	.	16.7	.	0.1	0.0
X No pueden clasificarse según la ocupación	125.8	69.4	-	.	-	.
Desempleados sin empleo anterior	.	.	.	.	125.8	69.4
Nivel de educación (CINE-97)	2006 [1,2,3] Encuesta de la fuerza de trabajo		2006 ★ Encuesta de la fuerza de trabajo		2006 [1,2,3] Encuesta de la fuerza de trabajo	
Total	4 373.4	41.5	4 031.6	40.1	341.8	58.0
X Sin escolaridad	105.0	48.7	96.9	48.1	8.1	55.5
1 Enseñanza primaria o primer ciclo de la educación básica	1 433.3	36.8	1 328.8	35.6	104.5	51.6
2 Primer ciclo de enseñanza secundaria o segundo ciclo de ... [4]	1 700.5	40.5	1 551.9	38.6	148.5	60.4
5A Primer ciclo de la educación terciaria - teóricos [5]	1 134.6	48.1	1 054.0	47.1	80.6	62.3
Situación en el empleo (CISE-1993)			2006 [1,2,3] Encuesta de la fuerza de trabajo			
Total	.	.	4 031.6	40.1	.	.
1 Asalariados	.	.	2 405.7	36.6	.	.
2 Empleadores	.	.	261.4	28.0	.	.
3 Trabajadores por cuenta propia	.	.	1 079.8	44.7	.	.
5 Trabajadores familiares auxiliares	.	.	284.7	62.8	.	.
6 Inclasificables según la situación	.	.	-	.	.	.

2. Población ('000), Tasa de actividad y Tasa de desempleo

	Población 2006 [1,3,6] Encuesta de la fuerza de trabajo			Tasa de actividad 2006 [1,3,6] Encuesta de la fuerza de trabajo			Tasa de desempleo 2006 [1,2,3] Encuesta de la fuerza de trabajo		
Grupo de edad	Total	Hombres	Mujeres	Total	Hombres	Mujeres	Total	Hombres	Mujeres
Total	8 940.1	4 391.4	4 548.7	48.9	58.3	39.9	7.8	5.6	10.9
15+	6 306.6	3 046.4	3 260.2	67.9	82.0	54.7	7.7	5.3	11.0
15-24	1 767.0	895.7	871.3	51.3	61.9	40.5	16.3	12.2	22.9
25-54	3 382.5	1 614.7	1 767.8	82.5	97.3	68.9	5.7	3.3	8.7
55+	1 157.1	536.0	621.1	50.5	69.5	34.1	4.0	3.8	4.3

Ecuador

3. Empleo remunerado ('000), Horas de trabajo (por semana) y Salarios

Actividad económica (CIIU-Rev.3)	Empleo remunerado 2006 [1,2,3] Encuesta de la fuerza de trabajo			Horas de trabajo 2006 Encuesta de la fuerza de trabajo Horas efectivamente trabajadas / Empleo total			Salarios 2004 Censo industrial/comercial Ganancias por mes / Asalariados / US dollar		
	Total	Hombres	Mujeres	Total	Hombres	Mujeres	Total	Hombres	Mujeres
Total	2 405.7	1 525.9	879.8	43	46	40	.	.	.
A	168.9	145.7	23.2	39	41	32	.	.	.
B	38.9	33.1	5.8	47	51	44	.	.	.
C	13.7	12.2	1.5	54	55	53	832.11	.	.
D	338.3	239.5	98.8	46	48	41	370.60	.	.
E	19.2	15.6	3.6	44	44	43	.	.	.
F	218.1	209.5	8.5	42	42	36	.	.	.
G	404.6	269.1	135.5	43	45	41	423.63	.	.
H	91.4	41.0	50.4	44	48	42	257.22	.	.
I	169.7	138.1	31.6	50	51	44	.	.	.
J	45.7	24.1	21.7	44	45	43	604.80	.	.
K	127.2	92.7	34.5	47	51	38	215.18	.	.
L	170.3	126.4	43.9	46	48	43	.	.	.
M	267.8	96.3	171.5	38	40	36	.	.	.
N	92.8	32.5	60.3	43	46	41	334.39	.	.
O	70.4	40.4	30.0	33	41	28	384.02	.	.
P	167.7	9.7	158.0	43	45	43	.	.	.
Q	0.9	-	0.9	44	.	44	.	.	.

Proporción de mujeres entre los empleados remunerados en el sector no agrícola [1,2,3] (2006 - Encuesta de la fuerza de trabajo): **38.7%**

4. Lesiones profesionales y Huelgas y cierres patronales

Actividad económica (CIIU-Rev.3)	Tasas de lesiones mortales 1994 Registros de seguros Por 1 000 trabajadores asegurados Lesiones indemnizadas			Tasas de lesiones no mortales			Huelgas y cierres patronales 2007 Registros de relaciones laborales		
	Total	Hombres	Mujeres	Total	Hombres	Mujeres	Huelgas y cierres patronales	Trabajadores implicados	Días no trabajados
Total	0.168	.	.	.	.	.	8	1 525	68 439
A	.	.	.	.	.	.	0	0	0
B	.	.	.	.	.	.	0	0	0
C	.	.	.	.	.	.	0	0	0
D	.	.	.	.	.	.	3	211	28 846
E	.	.	.	.	.	.	2	518	8 232
F	.	.	.	.	.	.	1	111	23 643
G	.	.	.	.	.	.	0	0	0
H	.	.	.	.	.	.	0	0	0
I	.	.	.	.	.	.	0	0	0
J	.	.	.	.	.	.	0	0	0
K	.	.	.	.	.	.	0	0	0
L	.	.	.	.	.	.	2	685	7 718
M	.	.	.	.	.	.	0	0	0
N	.	.	.	.	.	.	0	0	0
O	.	.	.	.	.	.	0	0	0

5. Índices de precios al consumidor (periodo de base: 2000=100)

	2002	2003	2004	2005	2006	2007
Índices generales	154.9	167.1	171.7	175.5	181.2	185.4
Índices de la alimentación incluyendo las bebidas no alcohólicas	142.5	146.0	147.7	100.0 [7]	106.0	109.5
Índices de la electricidad, gas y otros combustibles	203.9	.	.	100.0 [8]	100.1	100.2
Índices del vestido, incl. calzado	132.5	124.6	115.9	100.0 [8]	100.6	101.5
Índices del aquiler	198.1	.	.	100.0 [8]	108.2	114.5

[1] Urban areas. [2] Persons aged 10 years and over. [3] Nov. [4] Levels 2-3. [5] Levels 5A-5B. [6] "De jure" population. [7] Series (base 2005=100) replacing former series; prior to 2005 incl. alcoholic beverages and tobacco. [8] Series (base 2005=100) replacing former series.

[1] Régions urbaines. [2] Personnes âgées de 10 ans et plus. [3] Nov. [4] Niveaux 2-3. [5] Niveaux 5A-5B. [6] Population "de jure". [7] Série (base 2005=100) remplaçant la précédente; avant 2005 y compris les boissons alcoolisées et le tabac. [8] Série (base 2005=100) remplaçant la précédente.

[1] Areas urbanas. [2] Personas de 10 años y más. [3] Nov. [4] Niveles 2-3. [5] Niveles 5A-5B [6] Población "de jure". [7] Serie (base 2005=100) que substituye a la anterior; antes de 2005 incl. las bebidas alcohólicas y el tabaco. [8] Serie (base 2005=100) que substituye a la anterior.

Egypt

1. Economically active population, Employment and Unemployment ('000)

	Economically active population		Employment		Unemployment	
	Total	Women (%)	Total	Women (%)	Total	Women (%)
Age group	2006 [1,2] Labour force survey		2006 ★ Labour force survey		2006 [2,3] Labour force survey	
Total	23 352.3	22.0	20 917.8	18.7	2 434.5	50.4
15-19	1 787.5	24.8	1 281.8	14.4	505.7	51.2
20-24	3 678.5	27.9	2 551.6	18.6	1 126.9	48.9
25-29	3 341.0	24.6	2 784.2	19.4	556.8	50.6
30-39	5 377.8	22.4	5 164.1	20.9	213.7	60.4
40-49	5 073.1	22.1	5 047.6	22.1	25.5	22.0
50-59	3 125.1	14.8	3 119.1	14.8	6.0	3.3
60-64	495.3	6.1	495.3	6.1	-	.
65+	327.6	4.2	.	.	.	.

Economic activity (ISIC-Rev.3)			2006 [1,2,3] Labour force survey		2006 [2,3] Labour force survey	
Total			20 443.6	19.0	2 434.5	50.4
A Agriculture, Hunting and Forestry	.	.	6 208.9	27.0	18.9	3.2
B Fishing	.	.	161.8	0.8	-	.
C Mining and Quarrying	.	.	53.3	7.1	0.2	.
D Manufacturing	.	.	2 380.8	8.1	31.0	26.8
E Electricity, Gas and Water Supply	.	.	250.4	8.5	0.5	.
F Construction	.	.	1 822.9	0.9	34.9	2.6
G Wholesale and Retail Trade; Repair of Motor Vehicles ...	.	.	2 171.9	9.5	50.5	15.4
H Hotels and Restaurants	.	.	411.4	4.1	12.3	.
I Transport, Storage and Communications	.	.	1 357.3	4.2	14.7	7.5
J Financial Intermediation	.	.	175.0	23.6	0.5	100.0
K Real Estate, Renting and Business Activities	.	.	431.8	13.2	10.7	29.0
L Public Administration and Defence; Compulsory Social ...	.	.	1 901.7	22.4	3.4	47.1
M Education	.	.	1 969.9	42.1	13.6	64.7
N Health and Social Work	.	.	545.5	52.1	3.7	86.5
O Other Community, Social and Personal Service Activities	.	.	507.5	6.9	3.2	6.3
P Households with Employed Persons	.	.	45.0	23.8	0.2	.
Q Extra-Territorial Organizations and Bodies	.	.	2.5	16.0	0.2	.
X Not classifiable by economic activity	.	.	46.2	12.1	35.0	23.7
Unemployed seeking their first job	.	.	.	.	2 201.2	53.7

Occupation (ISCO-88)			2006 [1,2,3] Labour force survey		2006 [2,3] Labour force survey	
Total			20 443.6	19.0	2 435.0	50.4
1 Legislators, senior officials and managers	.	.	1 593.9	10.8	3.5	5.7
2 Professionals	.	.	2 688.2	32.1	23.4	44.0
3 Technicians and associate professionals	.	.	1 790.9	32.4	13.2	50.8
4 Clerks	.	.	694.4	31.1	8.2	34.1
5 Service workers and shop and market sales workers	.	.	2 053.6	8.9	56.9	14.9
6 Skilled agricultural and fishery workers	.	.	6 217.5	26.7	18.8	3.2
7 Craft and related trade workers	.	.	3 104.7	2.4	51.8	8.7
8 Plant and machine operators and assemblers	.	.	1 523.1	4.3	20.3	12.8
9 Elementary occupations	.	.	742.9	8.4	8.9	2.2
X Not classifiable by occupation	.	.	34.4	20.3	28.3	27.9
Unemployed seeking their first job	.	.	.	.	2 201.0	53.7

Status in employment (ICSE-1993)			2006 [1,2,3] Labour force survey			
Total			20 444.0	19.0	.	.
1 Employees	.	.	12 635.0	16.5	.	.
2 Employers	.	.	2 736.1	4.0	.	.
3 Own-account workers	.	.	2 388.1	17.7	.	.
5 Contributing family workers	.	.	2 684.2	47.2	.	.

2. Population ('000), Activity rate and Unemployment rate

	Population			Activity rate			Unemployment rate		
Age group	2006 [1] Labour force survey			2006 [1] Labour force survey			2006 [2,3] Labour force survey		
	Total	Men	Women	Total	Men	Women	Total	Men	Women
Total	72 010.4	36 827.7	35 182.7	32.4	49.4	14.6	10.6	6.8	24.0
15+	49 405.5	25 155.0	24 250.9	47.0	71.9	21.1	.	.	.
15-24	16 189.8	8 651.1	7 539.1	33.8	46.2	19.5	29.9	20.6	55.2

Egypt

3. Paid employment ('000), Hours of work (weekly) and Wages

Economic activity (ISIC-Rev.3)	Paid employment 2006 [1,2,3] Labour force survey			Hours of work 2006 [4,5] Labour-related establishment census Hours paid for / Wage earners			Wages 2006 [4,5] Labour-related establishment census Earnings per week / Wage earners / Pound		
	Total	Men	Women	Total	Men	Women	Total	Men	Women
Total	12 635.0	10 550.0	2 085.1	55	55	57	229	236	188
A-B	.	.	.	57	57	59	142	141	160
C-Q	.	.	.	55	55	57	229	236	188
A	1 507.1	1 424.4	82.7	58	58	59	143	142	167
B	60.4	60.0	0.4	50	50	.	131	236	128
C	51.8	48.0	3.8	50	50	.	535	534	592
D	1 929.7	1 778.9	150.8	56	56	58	203	210	159
E	249.1	227.9	21.2	52	52	55	339	334	387
F	1 367.6	1 353.8	13.8	51	51	57	244	242	274
G	883.2	801.6	81.6	55	54	55	241	248	204
H	321.4	309.7	11.7	57	57	57	149	148	168
I	965.8	912.5	53.3	56	55	59	286	279	367
J	174.5	133.2	41.3	51	51	47	359	356	368
K	261.7	214.4	47.3	55	55	54	227	225	242
L	1 898.7	1 473.1	425.6	.	.	.	.	.	.
M	1 961.2	1 133.7	827.5	51	53	52	98	104	94
N	526.5	246.3	280.2	54	54	54	130	170	96
O	401.9	370.7	31.2	54	54	53	133	136	118
P	39.5	30.4	9.1	.	.	.	.	.	.
Q	2.5	2.1	0.4	.	.	.	.	.	.
X	32.7	29.5	3.2	.	.	.	.	.	.

Share of women in wage employment in the non-agricultural sector [1,2,3] (2006 - Labour force survey): **18.1%**

4. Occupational injuries and Strikes and Lockouts

Economic activity (ISIC-Rev.3)	Rates of fatal injuries 2003 [6,7] Labour inspectorate records Per 100,000 employees Reported injuries			Rates of non-fatal injuries 2003 [6] Labour inspectorate records Per 100,000 employees Reported injuries			Strikes and lockouts 2003 Labour relations records		
	Total	Men	Women	Total	Men	Women	Strikes and lockouts	Workers involved [8]	Days not worked
Total	7	.	.	1 580	.	.	4	1 046	19 969
A	6	.	.	159	.	.	0	0	0
B	0	.	.	0	.	.	0	0	0
C	13	.	.	1 145	.	.	0	0	0
D	7	.	.	2 633	.	.	3	863	19 420
E	12	.	.	516	.	.	0	0	0
F	9	.	.	2 672	.	.	0	0	0
G	0	.	.	506	.	.	0	0	0
H	0	.	.	11	.	.	0	0	0
I	2	.	.	5	.	.	1	183	549
J	2	.	.	334	.	.	0	0	0
K	5	.	.	866	.	.	0	0	0
L	0	.	.	447	.	.	0	0	0
M	9	.	.	1 962	.	.	0	0	0
N	2	.	.	23	.	.	0	0	0
O	0	.	.	169	.	.	0	0	0

5. Consumer price indices (base period: 2000=100)

	2002	2003	2004	2005	2006	2007
General indices	105.0	109.5	127.4	133.7	143.9	157.6
Food index, including non-alcoholic beverages	105.3	112.3	100.0 [9]	105.0	115.7	130.6
Electricity, gas and other fuel indices	100.6	100.6	.	.	.	.
Clothing indices, including footwear	104.3	105.9	100.0 [10]	105.0	106.8	.
Rent indices [11]	100.7	102.2	100.0 [10]	104.5	108.4	.

[1] Excl. armed forces. [2] Persons aged 15 to 64 years. [3] May and Nov. [4] Establishments with 10 or more persons employed. [5] Oct. [6] Establishments with 50 or more persons employed. [7] Deaths occurring within six months of accident. [8] Excl. workers indirectly involved. [9] Series (base 2004=100) replacing former series; prior to 2004: incl. tobacco. [10] Series (base 2004=100) replacing former series. [11] Incl. water, electricity, gas and other fuels.

[1] Non compris les forces armées. [2] Personnes âgées de 15 à 64 ans. [3] Mai et nov. [4] Etablissements occupant 10 personnes et plus. [5] Oct. [6] Etablissements occupant 50 personnes et plus. [7] Les décès survenant pendant les six mois qui suivent l'accident. [8] Non compris les travailleurs indirectement impliqués. [9] Série (base 2004=100) remplaçant la précédente; avant 2004: y compris le tabac. [10] Série (base 2004=100) remplaçant la précédente. [11] Y compris l'eau, l'électricité, le gaz et autres combustibles.

[1] Excl. las fuerzas armadas. [2] Personas de 15 a 64 años. [3] Mayo y nov. [4] Establecimientos con 10 y más trabajadores. [5] Oct. [6] Establecimientos con 50 y más trabajadores. [7] Los fallecimientos que se produzcan durante los seis meses que siguen el accidente. [8] Excl. los trabajadores indirectamente implicados. [9] Serie base (2004=100) que substituye a la anterior: antes de 2004: incl. el tabaco. [10] Serie (base 2004=100) que substituye a la anterior. [11] Incl. el agua, la electricidad, el gas y otros combustibles.

El Salvador

1. Población económicamente activa, Empleo y Desempleo ('000)

	Población económicamente activa		Empleo		Desempleo	
	Total	Mujeres (%)	Total	Mujeres (%)	Total	Mujeres (%)
Grupo de edad	2006 [1,2]		2006 ★		2006 [1,2]	
	Encuesta de la fuerza de trabajo		Encuesta de la fuerza de trabajo		Encuesta de la fuerza de trabajo	
Total	2 874.6	41.4	2 685.9	42.6	188.7	24.6
10-14	93.9	27.2	86.0	28.2	7.9	16.6
15-19	258.7	32.2	223.3	32.8	35.3	28.2
20-24	381.2	39.6	337.3	40.6	43.9	31.8
25-29	400.9	42.3	377.0	42.7	23.9	34.8
30-34	354.3	46.0	335.3	47.4	19.1	21.0
35-39	329.0	50.3	317.2	51.1	11.8	30.6
40-44	276.1	47.6	266.6	48.6	9.5	18.3
45-49	216.8	42.9	209.3	43.7	7.5	19.9
50-54	198.0	41.7	188.6	43.0	9.4	15.5
55-59	135.4	35.9	128.4	37.6	7.0	4.4
60-64	88.9	33.5	84.7	35.0	4.2	2.7
65-69	65.6	33.7	61.8	35.8	3.8	0.0
70+	75.9	32.9	70.3	35.3	5.6	2.2
Actividad económica (CIIU-Rev.3)			2006 [1,2]		2006 [1,2]	
			Encuesta de la fuerza de trabajo		Encuesta de la fuerza de trabajo	
Total	.	.	2 685.9	42.6	188.7	24.6
A Agricultura, ganadería, caza y silvicultura	.	.	491.6	10.8	63.5	10.3
B Pesca	.	.	14.9	10.5	0.8	.
C Explotación de minas y canteras	.	.	2.2	0.0	.	.
D Industrias manufactureras	.	.	423.4	49.7	19.8	27.2
E Suministro de electricidad, gas y agua	.	.	10.3	13.1	0.3	20.7
F Construcción	.	.	181.3	3.2	27.8	0.5
G-H	.	.	803.1	60.9	23.7	50.6
I Transporte, almacenamiento y comunicaciones	.	.	120.4	7.8	6.3	4.8
J-K	.	.	114.9	36.0	6.3	20.2
L Administración pública y defensa; planes de seguridad ...	.	.	105.9	27.3	3.5	31.0
M Enseñanza	.	.	93.8	64.6	1.3	56.2
N-O	.	.	189.5	63.5	3.9	58.9
P Hogares privados con servicio doméstico	.	.	134.5	90.4	5.2	78.9
X No pueden clasificarse según la actividad económica	.	.	.	.	-	-
Desempleados sin empleo anterior	.	.	.	.	26.5	47.4
Ocupación (CIUO-88)			2006 [1,2]		2006 [1,2]	
			Encuesta de la fuerza de trabajo		Encuesta de la fuerza de trabajo	
Total	.	.	2 685.9	42.6	188.7	24.6
1 Miembros del poder ejecutivo y de los cuerpos legislativos ...	.	.	44.1	28.8	1.5	58.5
2 Profesionales científicos e intelectuales	.	.	84.9	47.3	8.5	20.2
3 Técnicos y profesionales de nivel medio	.	.	205.1	48.1	7.1	50.1
4 Empleados de oficina	.	.	125.7	61.9	14.1	65.8
5 Trabajadores de los servicios y vendedores de comercios ...	.	.	511.8	68.8	26.5	3.5
6 Agricultores y trabajadores calificados agropecuarios ...	.	.	175.0	5.6	23.7	4.4
7 Oficiales, operarios y artesanos de artes mecánicas ...	.	.	421.4	37.4	11.3	19.0
8 Operadores de instalaciones y máquinas y montadores	.	.	207.4	30.7	68.4	19.7
9 Trabajadores no calificados	.	.	904.6	36.6	26.5	47.4
0 Fuerzas armadas	.	.	5.7	.	1.1	72.8
Desempleados sin empleo anterior	.	.	.	.	-	.
Nivel de educación (CINE-76)	1996 [1,2]		1996 ★		1996 [1,2]	
	Encuesta de la fuerza de trabajo		Encuesta de la fuerza de trabajo		Encuesta de la fuerza de trabajo	
Total	2 227.4	37.0	2 056.5	37.5	171.0	31.3
X Sin escolaridad	424.7	34.3	397.5	35.3	27.1	19.6
1 Enseñanza de primer grado [3]	935.8	35.2	839.3	36.2	96.4	26.7
3 Enseñanza de segundo grado, ciclo superior	336.1	33.8	300.9	32.6	35.2	43.8
5 Enseñanza de tercer grado que no permite obtener un ... [4]	530.8	44.4	518.7	44.1	12.1	57.2
Situación en el empleo (CISE-1993)			2006 [1,2]			
			Encuesta de la fuerza de trabajo			
Total	.	.	2 685.9	42.6	.	.
1 Asalariados	.	.	1 469.0	33.1	.	.
2 Empleadores	.	.	115.7	27.3	.	.
3 Trabajadores por cuenta propia	.	.	705.6	55.3	.	.
4 Miembros de cooperativas de productores	.	.	0.5	6.4	.	.
5 Trabajadores familiares auxiliares	.	.	248.4	45.6	.	.
6 Inclasificables según la situación	.	.	146.6	83.0	.	.

2. Población ('000), Tasa de actividad y Tasa de desempleo

	Población			Tasa de actividad			Tasa de desempleo		
Grupo de edad	2006 [2]			2006 [2]			2006 [1,2]		
	Encuesta de la fuerza de trabajo			Encuesta de la fuerza de trabajo			Encuesta de la fuerza de trabajo		
	Total	Hombres	Mujeres	Total	Hombres	Mujeres	Total	Hombres	Mujeres
Total	6 980.3	3 288.4	3 691.9	41.2	51.2	32.2	6.6	8.5	3.9
15+	4 611.2	2 070.5	2 540.6	60.3	78.1	45.8	6.5	8.4	3.9
15-24	1 345.8	639.9	705.9	47.5	63.4	33.2	12.4	13.6	10.2
25-54	2 383.8	1 033.6	1 350.2	74.5	93.9	59.6	4.6	6.2	2.6
55+	881.6	397.0	484.6	41.5	60.6	25.9	5.6	8.3	0.4

El Salvador

3. Empleo remunerado ('000), Horas de trabajo (por semana) y Salarios

Actividad económica (CIIU-Rev.3)	Empleo remunerado 2006 [1,2] Encuesta de la fuerza de trabajo			Horas de trabajo 2007 [5] Encuesta de establecimientos relacionada con el trabajo Horas efectivamente trabajadas / Obreros			Salarios 2007 [5] Encuesta de establecimientos relacionada con el trabajo / Obreros / US dollar		
	Total	Hombres	Mujeres	Total	Hombres	Mujeres	Total	Hombres	Mujeres
Total	2 437.4	1 407.2	1 030.2	.	.	.	.	.	.
A-B	.	.	.	44.0	44.0	44.0	.	.	.
A	385.5	347.4	38.1	.	.	.	.	.	.
B	13.4	12.3	1.2	.	.	.	.	.	.
C	2.2	2.2	-	.	.	.	.	.	.
D	389.6	203.5	186.2	48.0	50.0	47.0	1.28	1.30	1.11
E	10.3	9.0	1.4	.	.	.	.	.	.
F	179.6	174.0	5.6	.	.	.	.	.	.
G-H	700.5	283.3	417.2	46.0	46.0	46.0	1.29	1.36	1.18
I	119.5	110.5	9.1	.	.	.	.	.	.
J-K	114.3	73.4	40.9	.	.	.	.	.	.
L	105.9	76.9	28.9	.	.	.	.	.	.
M	93.8	33.2	60.7	.	.	.	.	.	.
N-O	188.2	68.7	119.5	.	.	.	.	.	.
P	134.4	12.9	121.5	.	.	.	.	.	.
Q	-	-	-	.	.	.	.	.	.
X	-	-	-	.	.	.	.	.	.

Proporción de mujeres entre los empleados remunerados en el sector no agrícola [1,2] (2006 - Encuesta de la fuerza de trabajo): **48.6%**

4. Lesiones profesionales y Huelgas y cierres patronales

Actividad económica (CIIU-Rev.2)	Tasas de lesiones mortales 2003 [8,7] Registros de seguros Por 100 000 trabajadores asegurados Lesiones indemnizadas			Tasas de lesiones no mortales 2003 [6,7,8] Registros de seguros Por 100 000 trabajadores asegurados Lesiones indemnizadas			Huelgas y cierres patronales		
	Total	Hombres	Mujeres	Total	Hombres	Mujeres	Huelgas y cierres patronales	Trabajadores implicados	Días no trabajados
Total	35.1	66.4	1.8	3 607	5 586	1 487	.	.	.
1	.	.	.	1 435			.	.	.
2	.	.	.	3 221			.	.	.
3	.	.	.	4 137			.	.	.
4	.	.	.	4 008			.	.	.
5	.	.	.	6 690			.	.	.
6	.	.	.	5 094			.	.	.
7	.	.	.	2 126			.	.	.
8	.	.	.	378			.	.	.
9	.	.	.	2 736			.	.	.

Actividad económica (CIIU-Rev.3)	Tasas de lesiones mortales			Tasas de lesiones no mortales			Huelgas y cierres patronales 2007 Registros de relaciones laborales		
	Total	Hombres	Mujeres	Total	Hombres	Mujeres	Huelgas y cierres patronales	Trabajadores implicados	Días no trabajados
Total	.	.	.	.	.	.	11	2 436	3 883
A	.	.	.	.	.	.	0	0	0
B	.	.	.	.	.	.	0	0	0
C	.	.	.	.	.	.	0	0	0
D	.	.	.	.	.	.	4	2 008	1 974
E	.	.	.	.	.	.	0	0	0
F	.	.	.	.	.	.	0	0	0
G	.	.	.	.	.	.	2	12	80
H	.	.	.	.	.	.	0	0	0
I	.	.	.	.	.	.	3	307	914
J	.	.	.	.	.	.	0	0	0
K	.	.	.	.	.	.	0	0	0
L	.	.	.	.	.	.	1	35	175
M	.	.	.	.	.	.	1	74	740
N	.	.	.	.	.	.	0	0	0
O	.	.	.	.	.	.	0	0	0

5. Índices de precios al consumidor (periodo de base: 2000=100)

[5]	2002	2003	2004	2005	2006	2007
Índices generales	105.7	107.9	112.7	118.0	122.8	128.4
Índices de la alimentación incluyendo las bebidas no alcohólicas	106.6	108.6	115.5	122.6	126.3	134.2
Índices de la electricidad, gas y otros combustibles	125.3	128.8	126.9	133.4	145.1	152.4
Índices del vestido, incl. calzado	93.5	92.3	91.5	98.5	99.5	100.9
Índices del aquiler	105.0	106.0	109.0	113.3	115.1	114.8

[1] Persons aged 10 years and over. [2] Dec. [3] Levels 1-2. [4] Levels 5-7. [5] Urban areas. [6] Excl. agricultural workers, own-account workers, domestic service, public employees and casual workers. [7] From 1998, including public sector. [8] Excl. cases of permanent incapacity.

[1] Personnes âgées de 10 ans et plus. [2] Déc. [3] Niveaux 1-2. [4] Niveaux 5-7. [5] Régions urbaines. [6] Non compris les travailleurs agricoles, à leur propre compte, les services domestiques, salariés publics et occasionnels. [7] A partir de 1998, y compris le secteur public. [8] Non compris les cas d'incapacité permanente.

[1] Personas de 10 años y más. [2] Dic. [3] Niveles 1-2. [4] Niveles 5-7. [5] Areas urbanas. [6] Excl. a los trabajadores: agrícolas, por cuenta propia, servicio doméstico, asalariados públicos y eventuales. [7] Desde 1998, incl. el sector público. [8] Excl. casos de incapacidad permanente.

Eritrea

1. Economically active population, Employment and Unemployment ('000)

	Economically active population		Employment		Unemployment	
	Total	Women (%)	Total	Women (%)	Total	Women (%)
Occupation (ISCO-88)			1996 [1] Labour-related establishment survey			
Total	.	.	57.80	31.6	.	.
1 Legislators, senior officials and managers	.	.	1.14	17.0	.	.
2 Professionals	.	.	0.57	22.9	.	.
3 Technicians and associate professionals	.	.	0.65	35.4	.	.
4 Clerks	.	.	4.55	47.6	.	.
5 Service workers and shop and market sales workers	.	.	15.44	43.2	.	.
6 Skilled agricultural and fishery workers	.	.	1.26	7.9	.	.
7 Craft and related trade workers	.	.	8.69	15.9	.	.
8 Plant and machine operators and assemblers	.	.	5.37	25.1	.	.
9 Elementary occupations	.	.	19.55	29.5	.	.
X Not classifiable by occupation	.	.	0.59	40.9	.	.
Status in employment (ICSE-1993)			1996 [1] Labour-related establishment survey			
Total	.	.	57.80	31.6	.	.
1 Employees	.	.	45.27	30.5	.	.
2 Employers	.	.	7.65	36.9	.	.
3 Own-account workers	.	.	3.52	39.2	.	.
5 Contributing family workers	.	.	0.91	10.1	.	.
6 Not classifiable by status	.	.	0.45	35.0	.	.

2. Population ('000), Activity rate and Unemployment rate

Statistics not available.

3. Paid employment ('000), Hours of work (weekly) and Wages

Economic activity (ISIC-Rev.3)	Paid employment 1996 [1] Labour-related establishment survey			Hours of work			Wages 1996 Labour-related establishment survey / Employees / Nakfa		
	Total	Men	Women	Total	Men	Women	Total	Men	Women
Total	45.20	31.42	13.78	.	.	.	.	.	.
A-B	2.07	1.72	0.35	.	.	.	438.59	502.44	293.87
C-Q	.	.	.	.	.	.	438.59	502.44	293.87
C	7.96	3.21	4.75	.	.	.	397.88	416.38	268.25
D	5.82	4.37	1.44	.	.	.	478.48	522.04	346.48
E-F	1.03	0.85	0.18	.	.	.	549.62	558.13	454.70
G-H	11.12	10.20	0.92	.	.	.	337.94	430.41	211.06
I-J	11.12	6.43	4.69	.	.	.	561.12	579.13	505.29
L	5.82	4.46	1.37	.	.	.	571.12	658.50	354.66
M-O	0.26	0.19	0.08	.	.	.	548.14	571.27	490.33

Share of women in wage employment in the non-agricultural sector [1] (1996 - Labour-related establishment survey): **32.3%**

4. Occupational injuries and Strikes and Lockouts

Statistics not available.

5. Consumer price indices (base period: 2000=100)

Statistics not available for the period 2002-2007.

[1] June, July, Aug.   [1] Juin, juillet, août.   [1] Junio, julio, agosto.

España

1. Población económicamente activa, Empleo y Desempleo ('000)

	Población económicamente activa		Empleo		Desempleo	
	Total	Mujeres (%)	Total	Mujeres (%)	Total	Mujeres (%)
Grupo de edad	2007 [1,2] Encuesta de la fuerza de trabajo		2007 ★ Encuesta de la fuerza de trabajo		2007 [2] Encuesta de la fuerza de trabajo	
Total	22 189.9	42.3	20 356.0	41.1	1 833.9	55.5
16-19	548.2	40.0	390.8	35.9	157.4	50.1
20-24	1 885.9	45.2	1 600.6	43.5	285.3	54.9
25-29	3 139.7	45.6	2 852.3	44.7	287.4	54.7
30-34	3 453.8	43.6	3 193.5	42.4	260.3	57.6
35-39	3 187.8	42.4	2 965.8	41.2	222.0	58.5
40-44	2 962.4	43.0	2 764.7	41.8	197.7	60.4
45-49	2 577.4	42.5	2 417.3	41.5	160.1	57.8
50-54	2 028.4	40.1	1 899.5	39.1	128.9	55.9
55-59	1 465.8	36.1	1 376.8	35.3	89.0	48.4
60-64	793.7	33.8	750.0	33.4	43.7	41.9
65-69	98.9	32.8	97.2	32.5	1.7	47.1
70-74	34.2	30.4	33.9	30.1	0.3	66.7
75+	13.6	25.8	.	.	.	.
Actividad económica (CIIU-Rev.3)	2007 ★ Encuesta de la fuerza de trabajo		2007 [1,2] Encuesta de la fuerza de trabajo		2007 [2] Encuesta de la fuerza de trabajo	
Total	22 189.9	42.3	20 356.0	41.1	1 833.9	55.5
A Agricultura, ganadería, caza y silvicultura	966.9	29.3	873.3	27.6	93.6	45.9
B Pesca	55.5	18.6	52.2	18.4	3.3	21.2
C Explotación de minas y canteras	61.1	11.0	60.1	10.8	1.0	20.0
D Industrias manufactureras	3 221.7	26.3	3 089.8	25.6	131.9	41.2
E Suministro de electricidad, gas y agua	114.6	20.3	111.9	20.0	2.7	33.3
F Construcción	2 880.7	5.6	2 697.3	5.7	183.4	4.2
G Comercio al por mayor y al por menor; reparación ...	3 306.5	49.8	3 128.6	49.0	177.9	62.7
H Hoteles y restaurantes	1 592.4	55.8	1 450.5	55.0	141.9	63.3
I Transporte, almacenamiento y comunicaciones	1 228.3	23.4	1 177.1	22.9	51.2	34.6
J Intermediación financiera	507.9	46.9	500.0	46.6	7.9	64.6
K Actividades inmobiliarias, empresariales y de alquiler	2 114.0	50.7	2 017.1	50.0	96.9	64.0
L Administración pública y defensa; planes de seguridad ...	1 288.5	40.7	1 238.4	39.9	50.1	61.7
M Enseñanza	1 142.1	65.3	1 112.3	65.1	29.8	73.5
N Servicios sociales y de salud	1 278.3	76.8	1 229.2	76.5	49.1	83.3
O Otras actividades de servicios comunitarios ...	899.9	51.7	846.2	51.4	53.7	56.2
P Hogares privados con servicio doméstico	825.1	91.6	770.0	91.8	55.1	89.3
Q Organizaciones y órganos extraterritoriales	2.2	45.5	2.1	47.6	0.1	0.0
X No pueden clasificarse según la actividad económica	.	.	.	.	506.2 [3]	65.5
Desempleados sin empleo anterior	.	.	.	.	198.1	61.3
Ocupación (CIUO-88)	2007 ★ Encuesta de la fuerza de trabajo		2007 [1,2] Encuesta de la fuerza de trabajo		2007 [2] Encuesta de la fuerza de trabajo	
Total	22 189.9	42.3	20 356.0	41.1	1 833.9	55.5
1 Miembros del poder ejecutivo y de los cuerpos legislativos ...	1 528.1	32.2	1 511.3	32.0	16.8	44.0
2 Profesionales científicos e intelectuales	2 566.3	52.9	2 516.6	52.7	49.7	62.4
3 Técnicos y profesionales de nivel medio	2 496.9	44.7	2 421.6	44.5	75.3	48.9
4 Empleados de oficina	1 980.3	65.7	1 886.2	65.4	94.1	72.7
5 Trabajadores de los servicios y vendedores de comercios ...	3 401.3	64.4	3 138.9	63.7	262.4	72.1
6 Agricultores y trabajadores calificados agropecuarios ...	518.7	22.2	503.8	22.2	14.9	22.8
7 Oficiales, operarios y artesanos de artes mecánicas ...	3 540.7	6.4	3 357.5	6.2	183.2	11.1
8 Operadores de instalaciones y máquinas y montadores	1 964.4	14.1	1 881.5	13.3	82.9	30.6
9 Trabajadores no calificados	3 399.8	54.5	3 050.5	54.7	349.3	52.5
0 Fuerzas armadas	89.3	10.0	88.3	9.9	1.0	20.0
X No pueden clasificarse según la ocupación	.	.	.	.	506.2 [3]	65.5
Desempleados sin empleo anterior	.	.	.	.	198.1	61.3
Nivel de educación (CINE-97)	2007 [1,2] Encuesta de la fuerza de trabajo		2007 ★ Encuesta de la fuerza de trabajo		2007 [2] Encuesta de la fuerza de trabajo	
Total	22 189.9	42.3	20 356.0	41.1	1 833.9	55.5
X Sin escolaridad	83.0	37.9	61.9	34.5	21.1	47.9
1 Enseñanza primaria o primer ciclo de la educación básica	3 420.1	35.3	3 057.2	33.7	362.9	48.8
2 Primer ciclo de enseñanza secundaria o segundo ciclo de ...	6 308.4	37.4	5 666.0	35.4	642.4	54.9
3 Segundo ciclo de enseñanza secundaria	5 298.1	44.6	4 867.0	43.3	431.1	58.8
4 Enseñanza postsecundaria, no terciaria	16.7	47.2	14.4	45.7	2.3	56.5
5A Primer ciclo de la educación terciaria - teóricos	4 683.2	52.8	4 444.8	52.3	238.4	62.2
5B Primer ciclo de la educación terciaria - práctica	2 228.3	40.1	2 096.8	39.1	131.5	56.4
6 Segundo ciclo de la enseñanza terciaria	152.0	36.9	147.9	36.6	4.1	48.8
Situación en el empleo (CISE-1993)			2007 [1,2] Encuesta de la fuerza de trabajo			
Total	.	.	20 356.0	41.1	.	.
1 Asalariados	.	.	16 760.1	43.2	.	.
2 Empleadores	.	.	1 117.9	24.6	.	.
3 Trabajadores por cuenta propia	.	.	2 167.4	32.1	.	.
4 Miembros de cooperativas de productores	.	.	79.5	29.6	.	.
5 Trabajadores familiares auxiliares	.	.	221.9	60.3	.	.
6 Inclasificables según la situación	.	.	9.3	33.3	.	.

España

2. Población ('000), Tasa de actividad y Tasa de desempleo

Grupo de edad	Población 2007[1] Encuesta de la fuerza de trabajo			Tasa de actividad 2007[1] Encuesta de la fuerza de trabajo			Tasa de desempleo 2007[2] Encuesta de la fuerza de trabajo		
	Total	Hombres	Mujeres	Total	Hombres	Mujeres	Total	Hombres	Mujeres
Total	44 630.1	22 061.5	22 568.5	49.7	58.0	41.6	8.3	6.4	10.9
15+	37 662.9	18 480.7	19 182.2	58.9	69.3	48.9	8.3	6.4	10.9
15-24	4 642.3	2 379.5	2 262.8	52.4	57.2	47.4	18.2	15.2	21.9
25-54	20 946.9	10 665.6	10 281.3	82.8	92.6	72.7	7.2	5.4	9.7
55+	12 073.7	5 435.5	6 638.1	19.9	28.7	12.7	.	.	.

3. Empleo remunerado ('000), Horas de trabajo (por semana) y Salarios

Actividad económica (CIIU-Rev.3)	Empleo remunerado 2007[1,2] Encuesta de la fuerza de trabajo			Horas de trabajo 2007[1,2] Encuesta de la fuerza de trabajo Horas efectivamente trabajadas / Empleo total			Salarios 2007[4] Encuesta de establecimientos relacionada con el trabajo Ganancias por hora / Asalariados / Euro		
	Total	Hombres	Mujeres	Total	Hombres	Mujeres	Total	Hombres	Mujeres
Total	16 760.1	9 521.8	7 238.3	34.7	37.5	30.8	.	.	.
A-B	.	.	.	39.6	41.6	34.5	.	.	.
C-Q	.	.	.	34.5	37.3	30.7	12.41 [5]	.	.
A	460.3	334.6	125.8	40.1	42.0	35.0	.	.	.
B	34.1	30.5	3.5	30.8	33.7	21.4	.	.	.
C	55.9	49.9	6.0	37.7	38.4	32.1	14.85	.	.
D	2 711.8	2 008.7	703.1	36.1	37.2	32.9	13.35	.	.
E	108.6	87.1	21.5	35.1	35.9	32.1	21.62	.	.
F	2 167.0	2 046.1	121.0	37.9	38.3	31.2	10.67	.	.
G	2 282.7	1 102.7	1 180.0	36.1	39.2	32.8	10.28	.	.
H	1 104.7	451.6	653.1	38.2	42.2	35.1	8.25	.	.
I	953.2	710.3	243.0	37.7	38.8	32.0	13.35	.	.
J	444.7	231.8	212.9	33.7	36.5	32.6	24.57	.	.
K	1 577.7	713.0	864.8	33.7	37.9	29.6	12.00	.	.
L	1 238.4	744.2	494.1	31.3	32.3	29.8	.	.	.
M	1 055.7	362.9	692.8	25.4	27.2	24.4	16.46	.	.
N	1 149.5	256.7	892.7	31.6	34.4	30.7	16.50	.	.
O	645.0	327.7	317.2	32.5	33.9	31.2	11.08	.	.
P	770.0	63.3	706.7	25.9	33.8	25.2	.	.	.
Q	0.8	0.7	0.1	30.2	38.3	22.5	.	.	.

Proporción de mujeres entre los empleados remunerados en el sector no agrícola [1,2] (2007 - Encuesta de la fuerza de trabajo): **43.7%**

4. Lesiones profesionales y Huelgas y cierres patronales

Actividad económica (CIIU-Rev.3)	Tasas de lesiones mortales 2007[6] Registros de seguros Por 100 000 trabajadores asegurados Lesiones declaradas			Tasas de lesiones no mortales 2007 Registros de seguros Por 100 000 trabajadores asegurados Lesiones declaradas			Huelgas y cierres patronales 2007 Registros de relaciones laborales		
	Total	Hombres	Mujeres	Total	Hombres	Mujeres	Huelgas y cierres patronales	Trabajadores implicados[7]	Días no trabajados
Total	3.8	.	.	5 815	.	.	752	497 022	1 187 654
A	3.4	.	.	2 945	.	.	5	321	2 471
B	47.8	.	.	7 834	.	.	0	0	0
C	24.5	.	.	20 193	.	.	14	1 724	2 685
D	4.2	.	.	9 719	.	.	363	102 084	290 719
E	6.5	.	.	5 680	.	.	8	1 070	8 004
F	10.3	.	.	12 736	.	.	16	90 323	320 703
G	1.4	.	.	4 664	.	.	22	1 289	8 932
H	1.2	.	.	5 376	.	.	8	279	1 087
I	12.8	.	.	6 903	.	.	94	31 077	111 085
J	1.0	.	.	524	.	.	3	1 419	1 728
K	1.2	.	.	2 588	.	.	41	19 949	81 688
L	.	.	.	.	.	.	34	29 083	82 529
L,Q	2.2	.	.	3 546	.	.	.	.	.
M	0.6	.	.	1 178	.	.	21	54 521	60 077
N	0.8	.	.	3 117	.	.	57	27 865	78 371
O	2.0	.	.	4 991	.	.	64	15 460	17 017
P	0.0	.	.	3 057	.	.	0	0	0
X	.	.	.	.	.	.	2 [8]	120 558 [8]	120 558 [8]

5. Índices de precios al consumidor (periodo de base: 2000=100)

[9]	2002	2003	2004	2005	2006	2007
Índices generales	103.5	106.7	109.9	113.6	117.6	120.9
Índices de la alimentación incluyendo las bebidas no alcohólicas	104.7	109.0	113.2	116.3	121.5	126.0
Índices de la electricidad, gas y otros combustibles	98.9	100.2	102.1	108.5	119.2	121.4
Índices del vestido, incl. calzado	105.1	109.1	111.1	112.6	144.0	145.5
Índices del aquiler	104.2	108.7	113.2	118.0	123.1	128.5
Índices generales, excluyendo la vivienda	103.5	106.6	109.9	113.5	117.5	120.7

España

[1] Excl. compulsory military service. [2] Persons aged 16 years and over. [3] Unemployed whose last job was 3 years ago and over. [4] Incl. overtime payments and irregular gratuities. [5] Excl. categories L, P and Q; before 2000, excl. categories L-Q. [6] Deaths occurring within one month of accident. [7] Excl. workers indirectly involved. [8] General strikes. [9] Index base 2001=100.

[1] Non compris les militaires du contingent. [2] Personnes âgées de 16 ans et plus. [3] Chômeurs dont le dernier travail date de 3 ans ou plus. [4] Y compris la rémunération des heures supplémentaires et les gratifications versées irrégulièrement. [5] Non compris les catégories L, P et Q; avant 2000: non compris les catégories L-Q. [6] Les décès survenant pendant le mois qui suit l'accident. [7] Non compris les travailleurs indirectement impliqués. [8] Grèves générales. [9] Indice base 2001=100.

[1] Excl. a los militares en servicio obligatorio. [2] Personas de 16 años y más. [3] Desempleados cuyo último trabajo fue hace 3 años o más. [4] Incl. los pagos por horas extraordinarias y las gratificaciones pagadas irregularmente. [5] Excl. las categorías L, P y Q; antes de 2000: excl. las categorías L-Q. [6] Los fallecimientos que se produzcan durante el mes posterior al accidente. [7] Excl. los trabajadores indirectamente implicados. [8] Huelgas generales. [9] Indice base 2001=100.

Estonia

1. Economically active population, Employment and Unemployment ('000)

	Economically active population		Employment		Unemployment	
	Total	Women (%)	Total	Women (%)	Total	Women (%)
Age group	2007 [1,2] Labour force survey		2007 ★ Labour force survey		2007 [2] Labour force survey	
Total	687.4	49.2	655.4	49.6	32.0	40.9
15-19	14.4	39.6	11.5	41.7	2.9	31.0
20-24	64.4	42.1	59.4	43.1	5.0	30.0
25-29	80.3	42.2	76.7	41.5	3.6	58.3
30-34	81.5	45.5	78.5	46.4	3.0	23.3
35-39	80.8	47.8	76.8	47.1	4.0	60.0
40-44	81.6	50.2	77.7	50.3	3.9	48.7
45-49	88.3	53.0	85.0	52.9	3.3	54.5
50-54	79.9	53.9	76.9	54.2	3.0	46.7
55-74	116.2	56.0	112.9	57.2	3.3	15.2
Economic activity (ISIC-Rev.3)	2007 [1,2] Labour force survey		2007 [1,2] Labour force survey		2007 [2] Labour force survey	
Total	687.4	49.2	655.3	49.7	32.0	40.9
A-B					2.3	43.5
A Agriculture, Hunting and Forestry	30.9	33.7	28.8	32.6	.	.
B Fishing	2.3	21.7	2.1	23.8	.	.
C Mining and Quarrying	5.6	10.7	5.5	10.9	.	.
C-F					12.7	30.7
D Manufacturing	142.4	46.3	134.8	46.1	.	.
E Electricity, Gas and Water Supply	10.3	12.6	9.5	13.7	.	.
F Construction	85.0	9.1	80.9	9.3	.	.
G Wholesale and Retail Trade; Repair of Motor Vehicles ...	91.2	59.9	88.1	59.3	.	.
G-Q					8.7	58.6
H Hotels and Restaurants	24.6	80.9	22.8	82.5	.	.
I Transport, Storage and Communications	59.9	32.7	58.4	33.0	.	.
J Financial Intermediation	9.5	73.7	9.4	73.4	.	.
K Real Estate, Renting and Business Activities	50.3	47.9	49.5	47.9	.	.
L Public Administration and Defence; Compulsory Social ...	39.6	53.8	39.2	54.1	.	.
M Education	54.8	83.8	54.5	83.7	.	.
N Health and Social Work	36.5	88.2	36.4	87.9	.	.
O Other Community, Social and Personal Service Activities	36.2	68.2	35.6	68.3	.	.
X Not classifiable by economic activity	8.3	37.3	-	.	.	.
Unemployed seeking their first job	.	.	.	.	8.3	37.3
Occupation (ISCO-88)	2007 [1,2] Labour force survey		2007 [1,2] Labour force survey		2007 [2] Labour force survey	
Total	687.4	49.2	655.3	49.7	32.0	59.1
1 Legislators, senior officials and managers	84.0	33.9	83.1	33.9	-	.
2 Professionals	95.8	69.6	95.2	69.7	.	.
3 Technicians and associate professionals	84.7	67.4	83.3	67.1	1.4	.
4 Clerks	32.0	77.8	31.5	77.1	-	.
5 Service workers and shop and market sales workers	82.0	81.2	77.8	81.9	4.1	.
6 Skilled agricultural and fishery workers	12.8	40.6	12.4	39.5	-	.
7 Craft and related trade workers	116.7	11.3	110.2	11.2	6.5	87.7
8 Plant and machine operators and assemblers	95.5	31.2	90.5	30.8	4.9	61.2
9 Elementary occupations	72.0	59.7	67.8	60.9	4.2	59.5
X Not classifiable by occupation	8.3	37.3	3.5	14.3	.	.
Unemployed seeking their first job	.	.	.	.	8.3	62.7
Education level (ISCED-97)	2007 [1,2] Labour force survey		2007 ★ Labour force survey		2007 [2] Labour force survey	
Total	687.4	49.2	655.4	49.6	32.0	40.9
1 Primary education or first stage of basic education	4.6	15.2	4.6	15.2	-	.
2 Lower secondary or second stage of basic education	67.3	34.6	59.9	35.1	7.4	31.1
3 Upper secondary education	339.5	42.4	322.1	42.5	17.4	40.2
4 Post-secondary non-tertiary education	43.9	63.8	42.8	64.3	1.1	45.5
5A First stage of tertiary education - theoretically based	158.9	60.4	156.5	60.5	2.4	54.2
5B First stage of tertiary education - practically oriented	70.3	64.4	67.4	64.5	2.9	62.1
6 Second stage of tertiary education	2.3	34.8	.	.	.	.
Status in employment (ICSE-1993)	2007 [1,2] Labour force survey		2007 [1,2] Labour force survey		2007 ★ Labour force survey	
Total	687.4	49.2	655.3	49.7	32.1	40.8
1 Employees	620.1	51.2	596.8	51.6	23.3	42.1
2 Employers	20.8	23.6	20.7	23.7	0.1	.
3 Own-account workers	36.8	32.1	36.5	31.8	0.3	66.7
5 Contributing family workers	1.4	71.4	1.4	.	.	.
6 Not classifiable by status	8.3	37.3	-	.	8.3	37.3

2. Population ('000), Activity rate and Unemployment rate

	Population			Activity rate			Unemployment rate		
Age group	2007 [1,3] Labour force survey			2007 [1,3] Labour force survey			2007 [2] Labour force survey		
	Total	Men	Women	Total	Men	Women	Total	Men	Women
Total	1 342.4	618.2	724.2	51.2	56.4	46.7	4.7	5.4	3.9
15+	1 142.4	515.4	627.0	60.2	67.7	54.0	4.7	5.4	3.9
15-24	207.3	105.8	101.6	38.0	43.6	32.3	10.0	12.1	7.3
25-54	557.7	269.8	288.0	88.3	93.3	83.5	4.2	4.2	4.3

Estonia

3. Paid employment ('000), Hours of work (weekly) and Wages

Economic activity (ISIC-Rev.3)	Paid employment 2007 [1,2] Labour force survey			Hours of work 2005 Labour-related establishment survey Hours actually worked / Employees			Wages 2007 Labour-related establishment survey Earnings per month / Employees / Kroon		
	Total	Men	Women	Total	Men	Women	Total	Men	Women
Total	596.8	288.9	307.9	34.8	.	.	11 336	.	.
A-B	.	.	.	36.3	.	.	.	.	.
C-Q	.	.	.	34.8	.	.	.	.	.
A	19.0	12.8	6.2	36.4	.	.	.	.	.
01	.	.	.	.	.	.	8 609	.	.
02	.	.	.	.	.	.	11 014	.	.
B	1.3	-	-	35.5	.	.	9 212	.	.
C	5.5	4.9	0.6	30.9	.	.	12 920	.	.
D	129.0	69.0	60.0	34.2	.	.	10 651	.	.
E	9.4	8.1	1.3	34.8	.	.	12 560	.	.
F	68.9	61.6	7.3	35.4	.	.	13 020	.	.
G	78.0	29.1	48.9	36.0	.	.	10 961	.	.
H	21.8	3.3	18.5	35.3	.	.	7 146	.	.
I	53.8	34.8	18.9	35.8	.	.	12 545	.	.
J	8.9	2.3	6.6	35.3	.	.	21 205	.	.
K	42.9	21.7	21.2	36.3	.	.	12 248	.	.
L	39.2	18.0	21.2	34.0	.	.	14 301	.	.
M	53.9	8.6	45.3	31.6	.	.	9 393	.	.
N	35.6	4.0	31.6	35.6	.	.	11 051	.	.
O	29.9	9.9	20.0	35.4	.	.	9 556	.	.

Share of women in wage employment in the non-agricultural sector [1,2] (2007 - Labour force survey): **52.3%**

4. Occupational injuries and Strikes and Lockouts

Economic activity (ISIC-Rev.3)	Rates of fatal injuries 2007 Insurance records Per 100,000 workers insured Compensated injuries			Rates of non-fatal injuries 2007 Insurance records Per 100,000 workers insured Compensated injuries			Strikes and lockouts 2005 Labour relations records		
	Total	Men	Women	Total	Men	Women	Strikes and lockouts	Workers involved	Days not worked
Total	3.2	6.4	0.0	562	757	365	0	0	0
A	6.9	10.3	0.0	639	551	819	.	.	.
B	0.0	0.0	0.0	95	125	0	.	.	.
C	18.1	20.4	0.0	964	979	.	.	.	.
D	3.0	5.5	0.0	1 106	1 402	760	.	.	.
E	0.0	0.0	0.0	221	171	538	.	.	.
F	6.2	6.8	0.0	515	550	173	.	.	.
G	4.5	11.1	0.0	420	624	280	.	.	.
H	0.0	0.0	0.0	338	425	319	.	.	.
I	3.4	5.1	0.0	485	522	409	.	.	.
J	0.0	0.0	0.0	85	120	72	.	.	.
K	2.0	3.9	0.0	394	515	262	.	.	.
L	5.1	11.1	0.0	791	1 278	377	.	.	.
M	0.0	0.0	0.0	152	227	138	.	.	.
N	0.0	0.0	0.0	264	364	250	.	.	.
O	0.0	0.0	0.0	256	513	156	.	.	.

5. Consumer price indices (base period: 2000=100)

	2002	2003	2004	2005	2006	2007
General indices	109.5	111.0	114.4	119.0	124.3	132.5
Food index, including non-alcoholic beverages	111.6	109.6	114.2	118.3	124.2	135.8
Electricity, gas and other fuel indices	128.9	133.4	138.5	150.4	163.4	185.5
Clothing indices, including footwear	108.1	109.5	109.1	111.1	114.0	118.0
Rent indices	110.4	113.6	120.0	125.8	154.1	195.3
General index, excluding housing	107.8	108.8	111.9	116.2	120.4	126.1

[1] Excl. conscripts. [2] Persons aged 15 to 74 years. [3] "De facto" population.

[1] Non compris les conscrits. [2] Personnes âgées de 15 à 74 ans. [3] Population "de facto".

[1] Excl. los conscriptos. [2] Personas de 15 a 74 años. [3] Población "de facto".

Ethiopia

1. Economically active population, Employment and Unemployment ('000)

	Economically active population		Employment		Unemployment	
	Total	Women (%)	Total	Women (%)	Total	Women (%)
Age group	2006 [1,2,3,4] Labour force survey		2006 ★ Labour force survey		2006 [2,3,4] Labour force survey	
Total	4 603.9	48.5	3 836.8	45.3	767.1	64.4
10-14	160.4	45.4	149.6	44.4	10.8	60.2
15-19	572.5	58.4	440.4	56.4	132.1	65.0
20-24	847.3	51.6	626.0	47.3	221.3	63.7
25-29	816.9	48.5	661.4	44.3	155.5	66.3
30-34	542.7	43.9	468.5	40.3	74.2	67.1
35-39	484.8	49.8	433.1	46.9	51.7	74.7
40-44	335.6	45.3	299.8	41.8	35.8	74.0
45-49	289.9	48.2	259.5	45.9	30.4	68.1
50-54	189.7	44.4	175.9	43.2	13.8	60.1
55-59	135.5	38.9	117.4	38.1	18.0	43.8
60-64	101.5	40.3	93.0	40.7	8.5	36.5
65+	127.2	32.6	112.8	34.9	14.4	13.9
Economic activity (ISIC-Rev.3)			2006 [1,2,3,4] Labour force survey			
Total	.	.	3 836.8	50.1	.	.
A-B	.	.	331.0	32.1	.	.
C Mining and Quarrying	.	.	13.4	10.6	.	.
D Manufacturing	.	.	585.6	50.4	.	.
E Electricity, Gas and Water Supply	.	.	38.6	22.2	.	.
F Construction	.	.	209.0	13.9	.	.
G Wholesale and Retail Trade; Repair of Motor Vehicles ...	.	.	872.6	48.4	.	.
H Hotels and Restaurants	.	.	369.1	80.3	.	.
I Transport, Storage and Communications	.	.	154.5	7.0	.	.
J Financial Intermediation	.	.	44.4	29.7	.	.
K Real Estate, Renting and Business Activities	.	.	56.4	31.5	.	.
L Public Administration and Defence; Compulsory Social ...	.	.	268.6	31.4	.	.
M-N	.	.	314.4	44.3	.	.
O Other Community, Social and Personal Service Activities	.	.	349.5	86.1	.	.
P Households with Employed Persons	.	.	201.7	93.3	.	.
Q Extra-Territorial Organizations and Bodies	.	.	25.1	38.0	.	.
X Not classifiable by economic activity	.	.	3.1	65.6	.	.
Occupation (ISCO-88)			2006 [1,2,3,4] Labour force survey			
Total	.	.	3 836.8	50.1	.	.
1 Legislators, senior officials and managers	.	.	94.9	15.7	.	.
2 Professionals	.	.	116.3	26.4	.	.
3 Technicians and associate professionals	.	.	263.9	36.1	.	.
4 Clerks	.	.	219.7	54.7	.	.
5 Service workers and shop and market sales workers	.	.	978.8	58.0	.	.
6 Skilled agricultural and fishery workers	.	.	241.2	31.7	.	.
7 Craft and related trade workers	.	.	846.2	50.9	.	.
8 Plant and machine operators and assemblers	.	.	166.1	10.0	.	.
9 Elementary occupations	.	.	904.4	61.9	.	.
X Not classifiable by occupation	.	.	5.3	37.9	.	.
Education level (ISCED-76)	1999 [5] Labour force survey					
Total	27 272.2	45.5	.	.	.	.
X No schooling	19 545.8	52.8	.	.	.	.
0 Education preceding the first level	1 190.9	13.1	.	.	.	.
1 First level	4 176.9	26.4	.	.	.	.
2 Second level, first stage	1 431.5	35.1	.	.	.	.
3 Second level, second stage	606.1	39.9	.	.	.	.
5 Third level, first stage, leading to an award not equivalent ... [6]	305.3	28.9	.	.	.	.
? Level not stated	15.6	18.8	.	.	.	.
Education level (ISCED-97)					2005 [3,5] Labour force survey	
Total	.	.	.	.	1 653.7	74.1
X No schooling	.	.	.	.	756.2	87.8
1 Primary education or first stage of basic education	.	.	.	.	505.2	64.4
2 Lower secondary or second stage of basic education	.	.	.	.	88.7	58.2
3 Upper secondary education	.	.	.	.	203.3	63.5
4 Post-secondary non-tertiary education	.	.	.	.	16.2	55.7
5A First stage of tertiary education - theoretically based	.	.	.	.	3.6	49.1
5B First stage of tertiary education - practically oriented	.	.	.	.	15.4	66.4
6 Second stage of tertiary education	.	.	.	.	33.7	48.2
? Level not stated	.	.	.	.	31.4	58.0
Status in employment (ICSE-1993)			2006 [1,2,3,4] Labour force survey			
Total	.	.	3 836.8	45.3	.	.
1 Employees	.	.	1 777.2	41.7	.	.
2 Employers	.	.	26.3	23.8	.	.
3 Own-account workers	.	.	1 604.3	47.0	.	.
4 Members of producers' cooperatives	.	.	11.4	25.7	.	.
5 Contributing family workers	.	.	383.9	57.4	.	.
6 Not classifiable by status	.	.	16.2	36.8	.	.

Ethiopia

2. Population ('000), Activity rate and Unemployment rate

Age group	Population 2006 [147] Labour force survey Total	Men	Women	Activity rate 2006 [147] Labour force survey Total	Men	Women	Unemployment rate 2006 [23] Labour force survey Total	Men	Women
Total	10 015.0	4 661.6	5 353.3	46.0	50.9	41.7	16.7	11.5	22.1
15+	6 639.3	3 022.6	3 616.7	66.9	75.6	59.7	17.0	11.7	22.6
15-24	2 709.4	1 198.8	1 510.6	52.4	54.1	51.1	24.9	19.5	29.4
25-54	3 178.6	1 482.3	1 696.3	83.7	95.0	73.8	13.6	8.1	19.7
55+	751.3	341.5	409.8	48.5	67.1	32.9	11.2	12.1	9.6

3. Paid employment ('000), Hours of work (weekly) and Wages

Economic activity (ISIC-Rev.3)	Paid employment 2004 [138] Labour force survey Total	Men	Women	Hours of work 2005 [9] Labour force survey Hours actually worked / Total employment Total	Men	Women	Wages Total	Men	Women
Total	1 411.0	847.4	563.6	28	34	22	.	.	.
A-B	52.5	40.5	12.0	27	32	20	.	.	.
C	5.5	4.9	0.6	34	38	26	.	.	.
D	161.2	110.6	50.6	28	41	23	.	.	.
E	27.5	20.3	7.2	45	47	39	.	.	.
F	118.1	101.2	16.9	38	39	34	.	.	.
G	105.7	72.9	32.8	33	40	29	.	.	.
H	65.5	25.5	40.2	34	52	32	.	.	.
I	82.9	73.1	9.9	51	52	39	.	.	.
J	21.2	16.2	5.0	45	47	42	.	.	.
K	17.3	8.7	8.6	45	45	45	.	.	.
L	199.7	139.2	60.5	43	47	35	.	.	.
M-N	223.2	131.2	91.7	39	40	36	.	.	.
O	101.2	68.3	32.9	45	47	41	.	.	.
P	213.8	22.4	191.4	38	41	32	.	.	.
Q	15.0	11.8	3.2	55	62	54	.	.	.
X	0.3	0.3	0.0	36	39	30	.	.	.

Share of women in wage employment in the non-agricultural sector [138] (2004 - Labour force survey): **40.6%**

4. Occupational injuries and Strikes and Lockouts

Statistics not available.

5. Consumer price indices (base period: 2000=100)

[10]	2002	2003	2004	2005	2006	2007
General indices	101.6	119.6	123.6	138.0	156.6	184.8
Food index, including non-alcoholic beverages	102.6	130.9	134.8	153.3	175.2	214.3

[1] Excl. armed forces. [2] Urban areas. [3] Persons aged 10 years and over. [4] July. [5] March. [6] Levels 5-7. [7] "De jure" population. [8] Urban areas, April. [9] Urban areas. [10] Index base 2001=100.

[1] Non compris les forces armées. [2] Régions urbaines. [3] Personnes âgées de 10 ans et plus. [4] Juillet. [5] Mars. [6] Niveaux 5-7. [7] Population "de jure". [8] Régions urbaines, avril. [9] Régions urbaines. [10] Indice base 2001=100.

[1] Excl. las fuerzas armadas. [2] Areas urbanas. [3] Personas de 10 años y más. [4] Julio. [5] Marzo. [6] Niveles 5-7. [7] Población "de jure". [8] Areas urbanas, abril. [9] Areas urbanas. [10] Indice base 2001=100.

Faeroe Islands

1. Economically active population, Employment and Unemployment ('000)

Age group	Economically active population Total	Women (%) 2005 [1,2] Labour force survey	Employment Total	Women (%) 2005 ★ Labour force survey	Unemployment Total	Women (%) 2005 [1,2] Labour force survey
Total	28.1	45.2	27.2	44.9	0.9	55.6
16-19	2.8	46.4	2.4	45.8	0.4	50.0
20-24	2.5	44.0	2.4	41.7	0.1	100.0
25-34	5.4	42.6	5.2	42.3	0.2	50.0
35-44	6.8	47.1	6.7	46.3	0.1	100.0
45-54	5.8	48.3	5.7	49.1	0.1	.
55-64	4.8	43.8	4.7	44.7	0.1	.

Economic activity (ISIC-Rev.2)			2005 [1,2] Labour force survey			
Total	.	.	27	44.4	.	.
1 Agriculture, Hunting, Forestry and Fishing	.	.	3	33.3	.	.
2-4	.	.	4	25.0	.	.
5 Construction	.	.	2	.	.	.
6 Wholesale and Retail Trade and Restaurants and Hotels	.	.	3	66.7	.	.
7 Transport, Storage and Communication	.	.	2	.	.	.
8 Financing, Insurance, Real Estate and Business Services	.	.	2	50.0	.	.
9 Community, Social and Personal Services	.	.	11	63.6	.	.
0 Activities not Adequately Defined	.	.	-	.	.	.

2. Population ('000), Activity rate and Unemployment rate

Age group	Population Total	Men	Women	Activity rate Total	Men	Women	Unemployment rate 2005 [1,2] Labour force survey Total	Men	Women
Total	.	.	.	.	.	.	3.2	2.6	3.9
15+	.	.	.	.	.	.	3.6	.	.
15-24	.	.	.	.	.	.	9.4	.	12.5
25-54	.	.	.	.	.	.	2.2	.	.

3. Paid employment ('000), Hours of work (weekly) and Wages

Statistics not available.

4. Occupational injuries and Strikes and Lockouts

Statistics not available.

5. Consumer price indices (base period: 2000=100)

	2002	2003	2004	2005	2006	2007
General indices	105.2	106.5	107.2	109.3	111.0	114.9
Food index, including non-alcoholic beverages	108.9	109.4	109.9	111.1	114.1	118.9
Electricity, gas and other fuel indices [3]	96.0	98.7	103.8	117.5	126.0	125.7
Clothing indices, including footwear [3]	101.5	100.0	96.6	93.1	91.6	92.4
Rent indices [3]	108.6	114.1	117.3	116.9	127.5	165.2

[1] Persons aged 16 years and over. [2] Sep. [3] Index base 2001=100.

[1] Personnes âgées de 16 ans et plus. [2] Sept. [3] Indice base 2001=100.

[1] Personas de 16 años y más. [2] Sept. [3] Indice base 2001=100.

Falkland Islands (Malvinas)

1. Economically active population, Employment and Unemployment ('000)

Age group	Economically active population Total	Women (%)	Employment Total	Women (%)	Unemployment Total	Women (%)
	1991 [1][2] Population census					
Total	1.132	35.2	.	.	.	.
15-19	0.063	36.5	.	.	.	.
20-24	0.116	35.3	.	.	.	.
25-29	0.140	40.0	.	.	.	.
30-34	0.153	41.8	.	.	.	.
35-39	0.157	33.8	.	.	.	.
40-44	0.128	38.3	.	.	.	.
45-49	0.115	37.4	.	.	.	.
50-54	0.102	23.5	.	.	.	.
55-59	0.076	27.6	.	.	.	.
60-64	0.051	37.3	.	.	.	.
65-69	0.019	10.5	.	.	.	.
70-74	0.009	33.3	.	.	.	.
75+	0.003	.	.	.	.	.

2. Population ('000), Activity rate and Unemployment rate

Age group	Population 1991[2] Population census Total	Men	Women	Activity rate 1991[2] Population census Total	Men	Women	Unemployment rate Total	Men	Women
Total	2.050	1.095	0.955	55.2	67.0	41.7	.	.	.
15+	1.628	0.881	0.747	69.5	83.3	.	.	.	.
15-24	0.289	0.156	0.133	61.9	73.7	48.1	.	.	.
25-54	0.968	0.521	0.447	82.1	97.1	64.7	.	.	.
55+	0.371	0.204	0.167	42.6	55.4	.	.	.	.

3. Paid employment ('000), Hours of work (weekly) and Wages

Statistics not available.

4. Occupational injuries and Strikes and Lockouts

Statistics not available.

5. Consumer price indices (base period: 2000=100)

Stanley	2002	2003	2004	2005	2006	2007
General indices	102.0	103.2	.	.	.	.

[1] Persons aged 15 years and over. [2] Nov.   [1] Personnes âgées de 15 ans et plus. [2] Nov.   [1] Personas de 15 años y más. [2] Nov.

Fiji

1. Economically active population, Employment and Unemployment ('000)

	Economically active population		Employment		Unemployment	
	Total	Women (%)	Total	Women (%)	Total	Women (%)
Age group	1996 [1] Population census		2005 [2] Labour force survey		2005 [2] Labour force survey	
Total	297.8	32.8	320.4	30.3	15.5	39.2
15-19	24.4	32.5	.	.	.	.
20-24	42.4	34.8	.	.	.	.
25-29	42.5	32.6	.	.	.	.
30-34	42.8	32.3	.	.	.	.
35-39	40.1	32.5	.	.	.	.
40-44	31.9	33.2	.	.	.	.
45-49	25.3	31.9	.	.	.	.
50-54	18.7	31.4	.	.	.	.
55-59	12.9	32.7	.	.	.	.
60-64	8.0	33.1	.	.	.	.
65-69	4.8	33.2	.	.	.	.
70-74	2.3	33.3	.	.	.	.
75+	1.7	37.2	.	.	.	.

Education level (ISCED-97)					2005 [2] Labour force survey	
Total	.	.	.	.	15.5	39.2
X No schooling	.	.	.	.	0.2	0.0
1-2	.	.	.	.	8.0	25.4
3 Upper secondary education	.	.	.	.	5.2	57.5
4 Post-secondary non-tertiary education	.	.	.	.	1.8	51.0
5-6	.	.	.	.	0.3	43.4

Status in employment (ICSE-1993)			2005 [2] Labour force survey			
Total	.	.	320.4	30.3	.	.
1 Employees	.	.	187.6	29.3	.	.
2 Employers	.	.	3.5	30.2	.	.
3 Own-account workers	.	.	78.1	24.2	.	.
5 Contributing family workers	.	.	46.9	41.3	.	.
6 Not classifiable by status	.	.	4.2	65.1	.	.

2. Population ('000), Activity rate and Unemployment rate

Age group	Population 1996 Population census			Activity rate 1996 Population census			Unemployment rate 2005 [2] Labour force survey		
	Total	Men	Women	Total	Men	Women	Total	Men	Women
Total	775.1	393.9	381.1	38.4	50.8	25.6	4.6	4.1	5.9
15+	500.9	252.7	248.2	59.4	79.2	39.4	.	.	.
15-24	150.6	77.3	73.4	44.4	57.2	30.9	.	.	.
25-54	288.2	145.6	142.6	69.8	93.4	45.7	.	.	.
55+	62.1	29.8	32.2	47.9	66.6	30.6	.	.	.

3. Paid employment ('000), Hours of work (weekly) and Wages

Economic activity (ISIC-Rev.2)	Paid employment 2003 [3] Labour-related establishment census			Hours of work			Wages 2003 [3] Labour-related establishment census Wage rates per day / Wage earners / Dollar		
	Total	Men	Women	Total	Men	Women	Total	Men	Women
Total	116.0	.	.	.	.	.	20.82	.	.
1	1.7	.	.	.	.	.	19.45	.	.
2	1.9	.	.	.	.	.	28.46	.	.
3	25.1	.	.	.	.	.	17.69	.	.
4	2.3	.	.	.	.	.	29.02 [4]	.	.
5	6.8	.	.	.	.	.	23.73	.	.
6	23.7	.	.	.	.	.	20.91 [5]	.	.
7	9.8	.	.	.	.	.	23.20	.	.
8	7.1	.	.	.	.	.	.	.	.
9	37.5	.	.	.	.	.	20.36	.	.

4. Occupational injuries and Strikes and Lockouts

Statistics not available.

5. Consumer price indices (base period: 2000=100)

	2002	2003	2004	2005	2006	2007
General indices	105.0	109.4	112.5	115.1	118.1	123.7
Food index, including non-alcoholic beverages	104.6	111.0	115.2	117.1	119.2	130.9
Electricity, gas and other fuel indices	102.5	105.3	114.0	130.2	138.8	137.6
Clothing indices, including footwear	101.9	103.1	102.0	103.0	104.5	107.5
Rent indices [6]	103.4	105.8	107.1	108.3	111.0	114.2

Fiji

[1] Persons aged 15 years and over. [2] Persons aged 15 to 55 years. [3] June. [4] Excl. gas and water. [5] Excl. restaurants and hotels. [6] Housing; incl. water.

[1] Personnes âgées de 15 ans et plus. [2] Personnes âgées de 15 à 55 ans. [3] Juin. [4] Non compris le gaz et l'eau. [5] Non compris les restaurants et hôtels. [6] Logement; y compris l'eau.

[1] Personas de 15 años y más. [2] Personas de 15 a 55 años. [3] Junio. [4] Excl. gas y agua. [5] Excl. restaurantes y hoteles. [6] Vivienda; incl. el agua.

Finland

1. Economically active population, Employment and Unemployment ('000)

	Economically active population		Employment		Unemployment	
	Total	Women (%)	Total	Women (%)	Total	Women (%)
Age group	2007 [1,2] Labour force survey		2007 ★ Labour force survey		2007 [2] Labour force survey	
Total	2 695	48.1	2 512	47.9	183	50.8
15-19	118	49.2	90	48.9	28	50.0
20-24	243	47.3	214	46.7	29	51.7
25-29	280	45.0	260	45.0	20	45.0
30-34	278	45.7	263	45.2	15	53.3
35-39	295	46.4	280	45.7	15	60.0
40-44	341	48.7	324	48.5	17	52.9
45-49	338	48.8	322	48.8	16	50.0
50-54	336	51.5	318	51.6	18	50.0
55-59	299	50.5	277	50.9	22	45.5
60-64	135	48.9	129	48.8	6	50.0
65-74	33	33.3	.	.	.	.

Economic activity (ISIC-Rev.3)	2007 [1,2] Labour force survey		2007 [1,2] Labour force survey		2007 [2] Labour force survey	
Total	2 695	48.1	2 512	47.9	183	50.8
A Agriculture, Hunting and Forestry	114	28.1	111	27.9	3	33.3
B Fishing	2	50.0	2	50.0	-	.
C Mining and Quarrying	5	.	5	20.0	-	.
D Manufacturing	461	27.8	445	27.4	16	37.5
E Electricity, Gas and Water Supply	17	23.5	16	25.0	1	.
F Construction	183	6.6	174	6.3	10	10.0
G Wholesale and Retail Trade; Repair of Motor Vehicles ...	323	49.8	311	49.5	13	46.2
H Hotels and Restaurants	89	73.0	84	73.8	5	60.0
I Transport, Storage and Communications	180	27.8	175	27.4	5	20.0
J Financial Intermediation	51	66.7	50	68.0	1	.
K Real Estate, Renting and Business Activities	322	44.4	308	44.2	14	50.0
L Public Administration and Defence; Compulsory Social ...	140	47.1	137	46.7	3	66.7
M Education	173	66.5	166	66.3	7	71.4
N Health and Social Work	391	88.2	373	88.7	18	77.8
O Other Community, Social and Personal Service Activities	153	60.8	141	61.7	12	58.3
P Households with Employed Persons	9	55.6	7	57.1	2	50.0
Q Extra-Territorial Organizations and Bodies	1	.	1	.	.	.
X Not classifiable by economic activity	80	53.8	6	33.3	5	40.0
Unemployed seeking their first job	.	.	.	.	68	55.9

Occupation (ISCO-88)	2007 [1,2] Labour force survey		2007 [1,2] Labour force survey		2007 [2] Labour force survey	
Total	2 695	48.1	2 512	47.9	183	50.8
1 Legislators, senior officials and managers	253	28.5	249	28.5	4	25.0
2 Professionals	459	50.1	449	50.1	10	50.0
3 Technicians and associate professionals	413	60.5	401	60.8	12	50.0
4 Clerks	178	79.2	169	79.3	9	77.8
5 Service workers and shop and market sales workers	410	80.5	390	80.5	20	80.0
6 Skilled agricultural and fishery workers	111	32.4	105	32.4	6	50.0
7 Craft and related trade workers	323	8.7	306	8.5	18	11.1
8 Plant and machine operators and assemblers	217	18.0	207	17.9	10	20.0
9 Elementary occupations	224	56.7	203	57.1	21	52.4
0 Armed forces	30	3.3	30	3.3	-	.
X Not classifiable by occupation	77	53.2	4	25.0	4	50.0
Unemployed seeking their first job	.	.	.	.	68	55.9

Education level (ISCED-97)	2007 [1,2] Labour force survey		2007 ★ Labour force survey		2007 [2] Labour force survey	
Total	2 695	48.1	2 512	47.9	183	50.8
0 Pre-primary education	530 [3]	41.9	465	41.3	65	46.2
3 Upper secondary education	1 227 [4]	44.9	1 143	44.4	84	51.2
5A First stage of tertiary education - theoretically based	528	51.7	513	51.3	15	66.7
5B First stage of tertiary education - practically oriented	384	62.2	366	62.6	18	55.6
6 Second stage of tertiary education	27	40.7	26	42.3	1	.

Status in employment (ICSE-1993)	2007 [1,2] Labour force survey		2007 [1,2] Labour force survey		2007 ★ Labour force survey	
Total	2 695	48.1	2 512	47.9	183	50.8
1 Employees	2 285	50.5	2 178	50.6	107	48.6
2 Employers	303	31.4	300	31.3	3	33.3
5 Contributing family workers	14	35.7	14	35.7	.	.
6 Not classifiable by status	93	43.0	20	.	73	54.8

2. Population ('000), Activity rate and Unemployment rate

	Population 2007 [1,5] Labour force survey			Activity rate 2007 [1,5] Labour force survey			Unemployment rate 2007 [2] Labour force survey		
Age group	Total	Men	Women	Total	Men	Women	Total	Men	Women
Total	5 289	2 590	2 698	51.0	54.1	48.0	6.8	6.4	7.2
15+	4 389	2 131	2 258	.	.	.	.	.	.
15-24	658	336	322	54.9	56.0	53.7	15.8	14.9	16.8
25-54	2 122	1 077	1 045	88.0	90.4	85.6	5.4	4.8	5.8
55+	1 609	718	891	.	.	.	.	.	.

Finland

3. Paid employment ('000), Hours of work (weekly) and Wages

Economic activity (ISIC-Rev.3)	Paid employment 2007 [1,2] Labour force survey Total	Men	Women	Hours of work 2007 Labour force survey Hours actually worked / Employees Total	Men	Women	Wages 2006 [6,7] Labour-related establishment survey Earnings per month / Employees / Euro Total	Men	Women
Total	2 178	1 075	1 103	35.9	37.8	33.9	.	.	.
A-B	.	.	.	36.4	37.7	33.2	.	.	.
C-Q	.	.	.	.	.	.	2 636	2 924	2 344
A	32	23	9	36.5	37.8	33.3	.	.	.
B	1	1	-	32.7	34.0	30.1	.	.	.
C	4	4	-	41.0	41.1	39.6	2 707	2 744	2 461
D	420	305	116	37.7	38.3	36.1	2 788	2 921	2 447
E	16	12	4	36.8	37.5	34.9	2 953	3 098	2 497
F	135	125	10	38.5	38.8	34.0	2 578	2 605	2 273
G	268	129	139	34.8	37.7	32.1	2 582	2 886	2 225
H	73	17	56	32.2	34.3	31.5	1 992	2 191	1 930
I	153	108	45	37.7	39.1	34.4	2 553	2 661	2 319
J	48	15	33	36.2	38.9	35.0	3 176	4 368	2 711
K	263	140	123	35.4	37.1	33.4	2 826	3 132	2 422
L	117	53	64	36.7	39.1	34.6	2 707	3 074	2 408
M	164	55	109	33.1	34.0	32.6	2 783	3 066	2 635
N	358	38	320	35.9	37.5	35.6	2 321	3 251	2 216
O	112	45	67	32.1	34.9	30.2	2 364	2 657	2 160
P	7	3	4	27.5	34.2	21.9	.	.	.
Q	1	-	-	39.5	41.7	37.2	.	.	.
X	5	3	2	33.9	35.3	32.1	.	.	.

Share of women in wage employment in the non-agricultural sector [1,2] (2007 - Labour force survey): **51.0%**

4. Occupational injuries and Strikes and Lockouts

Economic activity (ISIC-Rev.3)	Rates of fatal injuries 2006 Insurance records Per 100,000 employees Compensated injuries Total	Men	Women	Rates of non-fatal injuries 2006 [8] Insurance records Per 100,000 employees Compensated injuries Total	Men	Women	Strikes and lockouts 2007 Records of employers'/workers' organizations Strikes and lockouts	Workers involved	Days not worked
Total	2.2	4.1	0.4	2 892	4 281	1 537	91	89 729	94 579
A	3.0	4.3	0.0	3 824	3 799	3 884	0	0	0
B	0.0	0.0	0.0	4 000	4 800	2 667	0	0	0
C	0.0	0.0	0.0	3 064	3 279	600	2	74	30
D	1.7	2.3	0.0	3 912	4 695	1 923	69	26 281	27 552
E	6.0	7.9	0.0	1 837	2 276	421	0	0	0
F	7.3	7.9	0.0	8 105	8 487	2 768	2	0	0
G	0.4	0.8	0.0	2 256	3 129	1 452	6	6 365	36 802
H	0.0	0.0	0.0	2 441	3 283	2 181	0	0	0
I	8.1	11.5	0.0	4 467	5 442	2 132	5	965	978
J	0.0	0.0	0.0	290	321	277	0	0	0
K	1.6	3.0	0.0	2 218	2 941	1 382	5	90	56
L	4.4	5.6	3.3	8 106	6 786	9 271	0	0	0
M	1.2	3.6	0.0	306	489	215	.	.	.
N	0.3	0.0	0.3	499	926	445	1	52 000	0
O	0.9	0.0	1.6	1 356	1 973	931	0	0	0
P	14.3	37.0	0.0	4 286	9 111	1 256	.	.	.
Q	0.0	0.0	0.0	333	750	0	.	.	.
X	.	.	.	.	.	.	1	3 954	29 162

5. Consumer price indices (base period: 2000=100)

	2002	2003	2004	2005	2006	2007
General indices	104.2	105.1	105.3	106.2	107.9	110.6
Food index, including non-alcoholic beverages	107.4	108.1	108.9	109.2	110.7	113.0
Electricity, gas and other fuel indices	101.8	112.7	115.8	122.1	130.0	134.9
Clothing indices, including footwear	100.0	99.8	100.0	99.4	97.6	98.0
Rent indices	107.1	109.6	111.7	114.8	117.4	120.3
General index, excluding housing	104.0	104.8	104.8	105.6	106.4	108.2

[1] Included armed forces and conscripts. [2] Persons aged 15 to 74 years. [3] Levels 0-2. [4] Levels 3-4. [5] "De jure" population. [6] Full-time employees. [7] Fourth quarter. [8] Incapacity of 3 days or more.

[1] Y compris les forces armées et les conscrits. [2] Personnes âgées de 15 à 74 ans. [3] Niveaux 0-2. [4] Niveaux 3-4. [5] Population "de jure". [6] Salariés à plein temps. [7] Quatrième trimestre. [8] Incapacité de 3 jours et plus.

[1] Incluye las fuezas armadas y los conscriptos. [2] Personas de 15 a 74 años. [3] Niveles 0-2. [4] Niveles 3-4. [5] Población "de jure". [6] Asalariados a tiempo completo. [7] Cuarto trimestre. [8] Incapacidad de 3 días y más.

France

1. Population active, Emploi et Chômage ('000)

	Population active		Emploi		Chômage	
	Total	Femmes (%)	Total	Femmes (%)	Total	Femmes (%)
Groupe d'âge	2007 [1]		2007 ★		2007 [1]	
	Enquête sur la main-d'oeuvre		Enquête sur la main-d'oeuvre		Enquête sur la main-d'oeuvre	
Total	27 843.0	47.2	25 628.0	46.9	2 215.0	50.6
15-19	639.1	36.8	475.1	34.5	164.0	43.3
20-24	2 266.3	47.6	1 885.3	47.3	381.0	48.8
25-29	3 410.3	46.6	3 061.3	46.3	349.0	49.3
30-34	3 547.8	46.0	3 272.8	45.2	275.0	54.9
35-39	3 806.9	46.5	3 547.9	46.1	259.0	52.5
40-44	3 941.3	47.8	3 705.3	47.5	236.0	52.5
45-49	3 723.8	49.1	3 521.8	48.9	202.0	53.5
50-54	3 478.9	48.0	3 279.9	47.7	199.0	51.8
55-59	2 388.7	48.3	2 260.7	48.4	128.0	47.7
60-64	505.7	47.6	484.7	48.2	21.0	33.3
65+	134.0	38.7	132.0	38.5	2.0	50.0

Activité économique (CITI-Rév.3)

2007 [1] — Enquête sur la main-d'oeuvre

	Total	Femmes (%)
Total	25 628.0	46.9
A Agriculture, chasse et sylviculture	864.6	29.6
B Pêche	14.5	9.0
C Activités extractives	23.8	21.8
D Activités de fabrication	3 971.4	29.7
E Production et distribution d'électricité, de gaz et d'eau	202.5	22.2
F Construction	1 758.0	8.8
G Commerce de gros et de détail; réparation de véhicules ...	3 548.5	45.6
H Hôtels et restaurants	874.0	50.4
I Transports, entreposage et communications	1 603.1	29.0
J Intermédiation financière	829.5	59.0
K Immobilier, locations et activités de services aux entreprises	2 673.7	45.4
L Administration publique et défense; sécurité sociale obligatoire	2 584.7	51.2
M Education	1 733.7	67.8
N Santé et action sociale	3 144.5	78.8
O Autres activités de services collectifs, sociaux et personnels	1 157.4	56.4
P Ménages privés employant du personnel domestique	585.8	83.3
Q Organisations et organismes extraterritoriaux	18.3	55.2
X Ne pouvant être classés selon l'activité économique	39.9	41.9

Profession (CITP-88)

2007 [1] — Enquête sur la main-d'oeuvre

	Total	Femmes (%)
Total	25 628.0	46.9
1 Membres de l'exécutif et des corps législatifs, cadres ...	2 211.7	37.9
2 Professions intellectuelles et scientifiques	3 331.9	43.8
3 Professions intermédiaires	4 633.7	51.8
4 Employés de type administratif	3 089.9	76.4
5 Personnel des services et vendeurs de magasin et de marché	3 236.2	72.7
6 Agriculteurs et ouvriers qualifiés de l'agriculture ...	937.2	26.7
7 Artisans et ouvriers des métiers de type artisanal	3 004.5	8.0
8 Conducteurs d'installations et de machines ...	2 348.2	18.9
9 Ouvriers et employés non qualifiés	2 464.4	65.8
0 Forces armées	338.8	13.4
X Ne pouvant être classés selon la profession	31.6	12.3

Niveau d'instruction (CITE-97)

	Population active		Emploi		Chômage	
	Total	Femmes (%)	Total	Femmes (%)	Total	Femmes (%)
	2007 [1]		2007 ★		2007 [1]	
	Enquête sur la main-d'oeuvre		Enquête sur la main-d'oeuvre		Enquête sur la main-d'oeuvre	
Total	27 843.0	47.2	25 628.0	46.9	2 215.0	50.6
0 Education préprimaire	80.9	48.9	66.9	48.7	14.0	50.0
1 Enseignement primaire ou premier cycle de l'éducation ...	2 129.4	48.4	1 878.4	47.9	251.0	52.2
2 Premier cycle de l'enseignement secondaire ou deuxième ...	5 111.8	45.3	4 479.8	45.3	632.0	45.3
3 Enseignement secondaire (deuxième cycle)	12 304.9	44.6	11 430.9	44.0	874.0	52.7
4 Enseignement postsecondaire qui n'est pas du supérieur	26.7	73.0	23.7	73.8	3.0	66.7
5A Premier cycle de l'enseignement supérieur - théorie	4 560.0	50.3	4 298.0	50.0	262.0	53.8
5B Premier cycle de l'enseignement supérieur - pratique	3 469.2	54.6	3 299.2	54.7	170.0	52.4
6 Deuxième cycle de l'enseignement supérieur	160.2	36.2	151.2	35.7	9.0	44.4

Situation dans la profession (CISP-1993)

2007 [1] — Enquête sur la main-d'oeuvre

	Total	Femmes (%)
Total	25 628.0	46.9
1 Salariés	22 849.6	48.8
2 Employeurs	1 114.3	24.5
3 Personnes travaillant pour leur propre compte	1 497.6	32.3
4 Membres de coopératives de producteurs	2.2	45.5
5 Travailleurs familiaux collaborant à l'entreprise familiale	164.3	71.7

2. Population ('000), Taux d'activité et Taux de chômage

	Population			Taux d'activité			Taux de chômage		
	2007 [2]			2007 [2]			2007 [1]		
Groupe d'âge	Enquête sur la main-d'oeuvre			Enquête sur la main-d'oeuvre			Enquête sur la main-d'oeuvre		
	Total	Hommes	Femmes	Total	Hommes	Femmes	Total	Hommes	Femmes
Total	.	.	.	.	.	.	8.0	7.4	8.5
15+	49 425.5	23 752.0	25 673.4	56.3	61.9	51.2	8.0	.	8.5
15-24	7 850.0	3 965.9	3 884.1	37.0	40.1	33.8	18.8	18.0	19.6
25-54	24 829.2	12 245.0	12 584.2	88.2	94.2	82.4	6.9	6.3	7.7
55+	16 746.3	7 541.1	9 205.1	18.1	21.0	15.7	5.0	.	4.8

France

3. Emploi rémunéré ('000), Durée du travail (hebdomadaire) et Salaires

Activité économique (CITI-Rév.3)	Emploi rémunéré 2007[1] Enquête sur la main-d'oeuvre Total	Hommes	Femmes	Durée du travail 2007[3,4] Enquête sur la main-d'oeuvre Heures habituellement travaillées / Salariés Total	Hommes	Femmes	Salaires 2005[5] Fichiers administratifs et sources connexes Gains par heure / Salariés / Euro Total	Hommes	Femmes
Total	22 849.6	11 709.8	11 139.8	37.49	38.34	36.25	.	.	.
A-B	.	.	.	38.21	38.88	35.66	.	.	.
C-Q	.	.	.	37.48	38.32	36.25	.	.	.
A	316.2	218.5	97.7	37.69	38.26	35.61	.	.	.
B	10.8	10.0	0.8	51.43	52.41	39.42	.	.	.
C	23.0	17.9	5.0	41.04	40.14	44.22	16.74	16.83	16.00
C-K	.	.	.	.	.	.	16.15	17.23	14.12
D	3 756.7	2 623.1	1 133.5	37.19	37.59	36.11	16.77	17.65	14.48
E	202.0	157.1	44.9	36.01	36.17	35.22	21.19	21.78	19.14
F	1 417.1	1 289.1	128.1	37.35	37.40	36.49	14.62	14.61	14.65
G	3 027.6	1 594.4	1 433.3	37.92	39.00	36.17	14.39	16.09	12.27
H	710.6	338.9	371.7	40.88	42.62	38.69	11.32	12.03	10.50
I	1 527.7	1 068.5	459.2	38.21	39.08	35.74	14.95	15.20	14.32
J	801.0	319.9	481.1	37.71	39.80	35.99	23.55	29.67	18.72
K	2 330.6	1 218.0	1 112.6	38.26	39.19	36.85	17.54	19.38	14.99
L	2 584.2	1 260.2	1 324.0	37.79	38.59	36.77	.	.	.
M	1 710.7	544.4	1 166.3	34.20	34.81	33.85	.	.	.
M-Q	.	.	.	36.31	37.19	35.89	.	.	.
N	2 829.9	507.7	2 322.2	37.08	38.14	36.77	.	.	.
O	959.6	413.4	546.1	37.39	38.60	36.21	.	.	.
P	585.1	98.0	487.1	36.86	38.33	36.00	.	.	.
Q	17.7	8.2	9.6	38.48	38.27	38.67	.	.	.
X	39.0	22.5	16.5	36.76	37.56	34.60	.	.	.

Pourcentage de salariées dans le secteur non agricole qui sont femmes [1] (2007 - Enquête sur la main-d'oeuvre): **49.0%**

4. Lésions professionnelles et Grèves et lock-out

Activité économique (CITI-Rév.3)	Taux de lésions mortelles 2006[6] Fichiers des assurances Pour 100 000 travailleurs assurés Lésions indemnisées Total	Hommes	Femmes	Taux de lésions non mortelles 2006[6] Fichiers des assurances Pour 100 000 travailleurs assurés Lésions indemnisées Total	Hommes	Femmes	Grèves et lock-out 2006[7] Enquête auprès des établissements, relative au travail Grèves et lock-out	Travailleurs impliqués	Journées non effectuées
Total	3.0	.	.	3 940	.	.	.	.	1 414 700
D	.	.	.	.	.	.	.	.	379 600
E	.	.	.	.	.	.	.	.	243 200
F	.	.	.	.	.	.	.	.	14 000
G	.	.	.	.	.	.	.	.	24 900
H	.	.	.	.	.	.	.	.	9 000
I	.	.	.	.	.	.	.	.	614 500
J	.	.	.	.	.	.	.	.	29 800
K	.	.	.	.	.	.	.	.	56 800
M	.	.	.	.	.	.	.	.	3 300
N	.	.	.	.	.	.	.	.	22 900
O	.	.	.	.	.	.	.	.	16 700

5. Indices des prix à la consommation (période de base: 2000=100)

	2002	2003	2004	2005	2006	2007
Indices généraux	103.6	105.8	108.0	109.9	111.8	113.4
Indices de l'alimentation, y compris les boissons non alcoolisées	107.8	110.2	110.9	111.0	112.7	114.3
Indices de l'électricité, gaz et autres combustibles [8]	100.9	103.4	105.7	113.2	121.1	123.4
Indices de l'habillement, y compris les chaussures	101.5	101.1	101.4	101.6	101.8	102.5
Indices du loyer	103.2	106.2	108.8	112.7	116.6	120.3
Indices généraux, non compris le logement	101.7	105.8	107.9	109.7	111.4	.

[1] Persons aged 15 years and over. [2] "De facto" population. [3] Full-time employees. [4] Fourth quarter. [5] Incl. managerial staff and intermediary occupations. [6] Cases recognized for compensation during the year. [7] Localized strikes (the call to strike concerns only one establishment). [8] Incl. water.

[1] Personnes âgées de 15 ans et plus. [2] Population "de facto". [3] Salariés à plein temps. [4] Quatrième trimestre. [5] Y compris les cadres et les professions intermédiaires. [6] Cas reconnus pour indemnisation dans l'année. [7] Grèves localisées (le mot d'ordre de grève est interne à l'établissement). [8] Y compris l'eau.

[1] Personas de 15 años y más. [2] Población "de facto". [3] Asalariados a tiempo completo. [4] Cuarto trimestre. [5] Incl. el personal directivo y las ocupaciones intermediarias. [6] Casos recogidos para indemnización en el año. [7] Huelgas localizadas (la contraseña de huelga afecta a un establecimiento). [8] Incl. el agua.

Gabon

1. Population active, Emploi et Chômage ('000)

	Population active		Emploi		Chômage	
	Total	Femmes (%)	Total	Femmes (%)	Total	Femmes (%)
Groupe d'âge	1993 [1 2] Recensement de la population		1993 ★ Recensement de la population		1993 [1 2] Recensement de la population	
Total	375.944	44.5	308.322	45.4	67.622	40.5
10-14	3.716	58.5	2.274	64.6	1.442	49.0
15-19	19.897	53.8	11.003	57.2	8.894	49.6
20-24	46.663	45.4	28.291	45.1	18.372	45.7
25-29	57.837	40.5	43.445	39.1	14.392	44.5
30-34	56.069	38.9	47.909	38.8	8.160	39.5
35-39	44.068	38.0	39.360	38.6	4.708	33.1
40-44	34.019	37.4	30.764	38.8	3.255	24.8
45-49	27.243	41.9	24.700	44.0	2.543	21.2
50-54	24.657	47.4	22.055	50.7	2.602	19.4
55-59	20.770	55.6	19.451	57.9	1.319	21.0
60-64	15.932	59.6	15.145	61.4	0.787	24.8
65+	25.073	58.2	23.880	59.6	1.193	30.7

Activité économique (CITI-Rév.2)			1993 [1 2] Recensement de la population			
Total	.	.	308.322	45.4	.	.
1 Agriculture, chasse, sylviculture et pêche	.	.	134.167	63.7	.	.
2 Industries extractives	.	.	7.485	14.8	.	.
3 Industries manufacturières	.	.	7.952	18.0	.	.
4 Electricité, gaz et eau	.	.	12.444	5.3	.	.
5 Bâtiment et travaux publics	.	.	1.656	28.1	.	.
6 Commerce de gros et de détail; restaurants et hôtels	.	.	76.570	41.1	.	.
7 Transports, entrepôts et communications	.	.	15.775	11.7	.	.
8 Banques, assurances, affaires immobilières et services ...	.	.	1.967	46.5	.	.
9 Services fournis à la collectivité, services sociaux ...	.	.	50.306	33.3	.	.
0 Activités mal désignées	.	.	.	-	.	.

Profession (CITP-88)					1993 [1 2] Recensement de la population	
Total					67.622	40.5
1 Membres de l'exécutif et des corps législatifs, cadres ...					0.395	26.6
2 Professions intellectuelles et scientifiques					0.588	37.8
3 Professions intermédiaires					2.483	32.8
4 Employés de type administratif					7.339	15.7
5 Personnel des services et vendeurs de magasin et de marché					2.475	56.8
6 Agriculteurs et ouvriers qualifiés de l'agriculture ...					6.477	28.9
7 Artisans et ouvriers des métiers de type artisanal					7.855	3.5
8 Conducteurs d'installations et de machines ...					7.385	51.2
9 Ouvriers et employés non qualifiés					0.832	93.8
0 Forces armées					0.626	4.8
Chômeurs n'ayant jamais travaillé					31.167	47.0

Niveau d'instruction (CITE-76)					1993 [1 2] Recensement de la population	
Total					67.622	40.5
X Non scolarisé					8.440	36.5
0 Enseignement précédant le premier degré					0.184	45.1
1 Premier degré					25.541	42.0
2 Second degré, premier cycle					21.927	42.8
3 Second degré, deuxième cycle					5.956	30.1
5-7					5.574	41.6

Situation dans la profession (CISP-1993)			1993 [1 2] Recensement de la population			
Total	.	.	308.322	45.4	.	.
1 Salariés	.	.	139.445	29.3	.	.
2 Employeurs	.	.	1.853	16.0	.	.
3 Personnes travaillant pour leur propre compte	.	.	138.315	58.1	.	.
4 Membres de coopératives de producteurs	.	.	0.909	14.0	.	.
5 Travailleurs familiaux collaborant à l'entreprise familiale	.	.	10.828	68.9	.	.
6 Inclassables d'après la situation	.	.	16.972	64.6	.	.

2. Population ('000), Taux d'activité et Taux de chômage

	Population			Taux d'activité			Taux de chômage		
Groupe d'âge	1993 [2 3] Recensement de la population			1993 [2 3] Recensement de la population			1993 [1 2] Recensement de la population		
	Total	Hommes	Femmes	Total	Hommes	Femmes	Total	Hommes	Femmes
Total	716.015	350.897	365.118	52.5	59.4	45.9	18.0	19.3	16.4
15+	594.389	290.813	303.576	62.6	71.2	54.4	17.8	19.3	16.1
15-24	190.877	91.105	99.772	34.9	38.1	31.9	41.0	41.7	40.2
25-54	302.375	155.480	146.895	80.7	94.0	66.6	14.6	15.5	13.3
55+	101.137	44.228	56.909	61.1	59.1	62.6	5.3	.	2.4

3. Emploi rémunéré ('000), Durée du travail (hebdomadaire) et Salaires

Données non disponibles.

Gabon

4. Lésions professionnelles et Grèves et lock-out

Activité économique (CITI-Rév.2)	Taux de lésions mortelles 1999 Fichiers des assurances Pour 100 000 travailleurs occupés Lésions indemnisées			Taux de lésions non mortelles 1999 Fichiers des assurances Pour 100 000 travailleurs occupés Lésions indemnisées			Grèves et lock-out 2000 [4] Fichiers d'inspection du travail		
	Total	Hommes	Femmes	Total	Hommes	Femmes	Grèves et lock-out	Travailleurs impliqués	Journées non effectuées
Total	15.0	.	.	1 604	.	.	14	3 221	24 867
1	.	.	.	.	.	.	2	68	.
2	.	.	.	.	.	.	0	0	0
3	.	.	.	.	.	.	0	0	0
4	.	.	.	.	.	.	0	0	0
5	.	.	.	.	.	.	0	0	0
6	.	.	.	.	.	.	1	29	.
7	.	.	.	.	.	.	7	2 756	24 867
8	.	.	.	.	.	.	0	0	0
9	.	.	.	.	.	.	1	315	4 725
0	.	.	.	.	.	.	3	53	.

5. Indices des prix à la consommation (période de base: 2000=100)

Libreville, Afric.	2002	2003	2004	2005	2006	2007
Indices généraux	102.3	104.4	104.9	104.9	109.1	112.7
Indices de l'alimentation, y compris les boissons non alcoolisées [5]	105.2	107.1	105.1	105.5	112.2	.
Indices de l'habillement, y compris les chaussures	.	97.3	105.4	103.3	105.0	109.8
Indices du loyer [6]	.	104.3	101.7	100.0	102.5	113.1

[1] Persons aged 10 years and over. [2] July. [3] "De facto" population. [4] Computed on the basis of an eight-hour working day. [5] Incl. beverages and tobacco. [6] Incl. water, electricity, gas and other fuels.

[1] Personnes âgées de 10 ans et plus. [2] Juillet. [3] Population "de facto". [4] Calculées sur la base de journées de travail de huit heures. [5] Y compris les boissons et le tabac. [6] Y compris l'eau, l'électricité, le gaz et autres combustibles.

[1] Personas de 10 años y más. [2] Julio. [3] Población "de facto". [4] Calculados en base a días de trabajo de ocho horas. [5] Incl. las bebidas y el tabaco. [6] Incl. el agua, la electricidad, el gas y otros combustibles.

Gambia

1. Economically active population, Employment and Unemployment ('000)

	Economically active population		Employment		Unemployment	
	Total	Women (%)	Total	Women (%)	Total	Women (%)
Age group	1993 [1,2] Population census						

Age group	Total	Women (%)
Total	345.4	40.0
10-14	20.1	53.4
15-19	34.5	52.4
20-24	46.8	41.6
25-29	54.7	40.7
30-34	44.4	40.6
35-39	35.6	38.1
40-44	30.4	38.3
45-49	21.6	31.8
50-54	18.9	33.8
55-59	10.6	27.3
60-64	11.6	31.7
65+	16.3	27.8

Economic activity (ISIC-Rev.2) — 1983 [1,2] Population census

Economic activity	Total	Women (%)
Total	325.6	46.3
1 Agriculture, Hunting, Forestry and Fishing	239.9	53.7
2 Mining and Quarrying	0.1	54.5
3 Manufacturing	8.1	13.7
4 Electricity, Gas and Water	1.2	4.2
5 Construction	4.4	1.5
6 Wholesale and Retail Trade and Restaurants and Hotels	16.6	27.2
7 Transport, Storage and Communication	8.0	5.4
8-9	22.3	31.2
0 Activities not Adequately Defined	25.0	34.9

Occupation (ISCO-1968) — 1983 [1,2] Population census

Occupation	Total	Women (%)
Total	325.6	46.3
0/1 Professional, technical and related workers	8.1	26.5
2 Administrative and managerial workers	0.7	14.5
3 Clerical and related workers	6.0	27.6
4 Sales workers [3]	13.9	28.4
5 Service workers	11.0	40.6
6 Agriculture, animal husbandry and forestry workers ...	237.1	54.1
7/8/9 Production and related workers, transport equipment ...	25.3	6.2
X Not classifiable by occupation [4]	23.3	36.6

Status in employment (ICSE-58) — 1983 [1,2] Population census

Status	Total	Women (%)
Total	325.6	46.3
1 Employers and own-account workers	254.1	44.1
2 Employees	1.8	20.1
3 Unpaid family workers	46.6	63.9
4 Not classifiable by status	23.2	37.3

2. Population ('000), Activity rate and Unemployment rate

Age group	Population			Activity rate			Unemployment rate		
	1993 [2] Population census			1993 [2] Population census					
	Total	Men	Women	Total	Men	Women	Total	Men	Women
Total	1 038.1	520.0	518.2	33.3	39.9	26.6	.	.	.
15+	566.1	281.9	284.1	57.5	70.2	44.8	.	.	.
15-24	199.9	97.2	102.7	40.7	45.0	36.5	.	.	.
25-54	299.7	148.4	151.3	68.6	85.4	52.0	.	.	.
55+	66.5	36.3	30.2	57.9	75.6	36.8	.	.	.

3. Paid employment ('000), Hours of work (weekly) and Wages

Economic activity (ISIC-Rev.3)	Paid employment			Hours of work			Wages		
				1998 [5,6] Labour-related establishment census Hours actually worked / Employees			1998 [5,6] Labour-related establishment census Earnings per month / Employees / Dalasi		
	Total	Men	Women	Total	Men	Women	Total	Men	Women
Total	.	.	.	44.76	.	.	1 975.42	.	.
C-Q	.	.	.	47.40	.	.	1 769.18	.	.
D	.	.	.	53.08	.	.	969.69	.	.
F	.	.	.	58.05	.	.	1 729.32	.	.
G	.	.	.	44.74	.	.	1 224.77	.	.
H	.	.	.	48.10	.	.	2 493.17	.	.
I	.	.	.	41.37	.	.	2 065.81	.	.
J	.	.	.	39.70	.	.	2 565.79	.	.
O	.	.	.	46.76	.	.	1 335.70	.	.

Gambia

4. Occupational injuries and Strikes and Lockouts

Statistics not available.

5. Consumer price indices (base period: 2000=100)

Banjul,Kombo St. Mary	2002	2003	2004	2005	2006	2007
General indices	113.5	132.8	151.7	156.5	.	.
Food index, including non-alcoholic beverages	117.2	141.2	164.0	169.2	.	.
Electricity, gas and other fuel indices [7]	132.9	153.0	186.7	196.2	.	.
Clothing indices, including footwear [7,8]	162.1	180.4	187.9	191.2	.	.
Rent indices [7]	330.9	349.4	392.1	397.0	.	.

[1] Persons aged 10 years and over. [2] April. [3] Incl. major groups 5, 6, 7, 8 and 9. [4] Incl. unskilled, manual and general occupations. [5] Establishments with 5 or more persons employed. [6] Survey results influenced by a low response rate. [7] Index base: 1990=100. [8] Incl. household linen.

[1] Personnes âgées de 10 ans et plus. [2] Avril. [3] Y compris les grands groupes 5, 6, 7, 8 et 9. [4] Y compris les occupations non qualifiées, manuelles et générales. [5] Etablissements occupant 5 personnes et plus. [6] Résultats de l'enquête influencés par un taux de réponse faible. [7] Indices base: 1990=100. [8] Y compris le linge de maison.

[1] Personas de 10 años y más. [2] Abril. [3] Incl. los grandes grupos 5, 6, 7, 8 y 9. [4] Incl. las ocupaciones no calificadas, manuales y generales. [5] Establecimientos con 5 y más trabajadores. [6] Resultados de la encuesta condicionados por una baja tasa de respuesta. [7] Indices base: 1990=100. [8] Incl. la ropa de casa.

Georgia

1. Economically active population, Employment and Unemployment ('000)

	Economically active population		Employment		Unemployment	
	Total	Women (%)	Total	Women (%)	Total	Women (%)
Age group	2007 [1,2] Labour force survey		2007 ★ Labour force survey		2007 [2] Labour force survey	
Total	1 965.3	47.5	1 704.3	47.9	261.0	44.9
15-19	45.1	40.1	32.6	38.7	12.5	44.0
20-24	138.0	38.6	92.8	35.0	45.2	46.0
25-29	167.6	42.8	124.4	42.0	43.2	45.4
30-34	188.5	42.3	156.1	42.2	32.4	43.2
35-39	189.1	47.5	161.1	48.0	28.0	44.3
40-44	222.4	48.0	195.0	47.9	27.4	48.9
45-49	219.5	47.4	193.1	47.5	26.4	46.6
50-54	216.8	51.4	197.8	51.9	19.0	46.8
55-59	180.9	52.0	163.7	52.6	17.2	46.5
60-64	106.3	47.1	100.2	48.6	6.1	23.0
65+	291.0	53.0	287.5	53.2	3.5	34.3

Economic activity (ISIC-Rev.3)			2007 [1,2] Labour force survey				
Total			1 704.3	47.9			
A Agriculture, Hunting and Forestry			910.5	50.8			
B Fishing			-	.			
C Mining and Quarrying			4.7	8.5			
D Manufacturing			82.7	26.7			
E Electricity, Gas and Water Supply			18.2	19.2			
F Construction			71.2	6.5			
G Wholesale and Retail Trade; Repair of Motor Vehicles ...			168.8	47.7			
H Hotels and Restaurants			18.0	61.1			
I Transport, Storage and Communications			71.7	8.4			
J Financial Intermediation			17.3	53.8			
K Real Estate, Renting and Business Activities			34.7	37.8			
L Public Administration and Defence; Compulsory Social ...			64.3	26.0			
M Education			124.2	82.9			
N Health and Social Work			59.9	84.5			
O Other Community, Social and Personal Service Activities			43.9	49.4			
P Households with Employed Persons			11.1	88.3			
Q Extra-Territorial Organizations and Bodies			2.9	62.1			
X Not classifiable by economic activity			-	.			

Occupation (ISCO-88)			2007 [1,2] Labour force survey				
Total			1 704.3	47.9			
1 Legislators, senior officials and managers			60.6	34.0			
2 Professionals			218.5	63.1			
3 Technicians and associate professionals			100.1	59.1			
4 Clerks			16.1	66.5			
5 Service workers and shop and market sales workers			162.8	54.6			
6 Skilled agricultural and fishery workers			891.2	51.6			
7 Craft and related trade workers			104.2	10.8			
8 Plant and machine operators and assemblers			60.6	2.0			
9 Elementary occupations			89.8	29.7			
0 Armed forces			.	.			
X Not classifiable by occupation			-	.			

Education level (ISCED-97)	2007 [1,2] Labour force survey		2007 ★ Labour force survey		2007 [2] Labour force survey	
Total	1 965.3	47.5	1 704.3	47.9	261.0	44.9
1 Primary education or first stage of basic education	42.8	56.1	42.4	55.9	0.4	75.0
2 Lower secondary or second stage of basic education	143.3	51.1	130.4	52.5	12.9	36.4
3 Upper secondary education	760.1	43.0	677.1	43.9	83.0	35.4
4 Post-secondary non-tertiary education	426.6	52.0	372.5	51.3	54.1	56.7
5A First stage of tertiary education - theoretically based	588.6	48.6	478.1	48.9	110.5	47.1
? Level not stated	3.9	48.7	3.9	48.7	-	.

Status in employment (ICSE-1993)			2007 [1,2] Labour force survey				
Total			1 704.3				
1 Employees			625.4				
2 Employers			19.4				
3 Own-account workers			575.8				
4 Members of producers' cooperatives			.				
5 Contributing family workers			483.6				
6 Not classifiable by status			0.1				

2. Population ('000), Activity rate and Unemployment rate

	Population			Activity rate			Unemployment rate		
Age group	2005 [1,3] Labour force survey			2005 [1,3] Labour force survey			2007 [2] Labour force survey		
	Total	Men	Women	Total	Men	Women	Total	Men	Women
Total							13.3	13.9	12.6
15+	3 160.0	1 461.0	1 698.9	64.0	73.5	55.9	13.3	13.9	12.6
15-24	578.3	293.2	285.1	33.8	41.7	25.6	31.5	28.1	36.8
25-54	1 584.9	745.9	839.0	79.6	90.6	69.9	14.7	15.0	14.3
55+	996.8	421.9	574.8	56.8	65.6	50.4	4.6	5.8	3.6

Georgia

3. Paid employment ('000), Hours of work (weekly) and Wages

Economic activity (ISIC-Rev.3)	Paid employment 2007 [1,2] Labour force survey Total	Men	Women	Hours of work 1999 Labour force survey Hours actually worked / Employees Total	Men	Women	Wages 2006 Labour-related establishment census Earnings per month / Employees / Lari Total	Men	Women
Total	625.4	.	.	33.45	36.30	30.47	277.9	362.0	177.6
A-B		.	.	.	.	.	146.1	152.8	130.4
C-Q	.	.	.	38.39	41.92	34.41	279.1	364.5	177.6
A	22.2	.	.	.	.	.	148.1	155.8	130.9
B	-	.	.	.	.	.	94.4	95.5	83.3
C	4.6	.	.	28.86	30.74	27.04	352.3	367.7	287.6
D	63.0	.	.	37.88	39.20	35.01	260.5	293.7	191.8
E	17.1	.	.	39.92	41.34	33.82	398.2	422.6	320.1
F	53.9	.	.	41.55	41.86	36.69	391.0	399.2	250.4
G	73.7	.	.	44.49	44.72	44.18	246.4	303.1	181.8
H	14.4	.	.	47.68	49.35	45.35	196.5	266.7	150.6
I	40.4	.	.	43.15	44.35	39.01	391.3	421.2	301.2
J	16.7	.	.	40.62	43.38	38.44	779.0	1 356.4	449.1
K	33.3	.	.	37.84	40.21	34.90	284.2	327.4	203.3
L	62.7	.	.	43.22	45.21	38.81	448.0	482.8	354.3
M	120.6	.	.	26.16	30.94	25.07	122.1	141.8	116.5
N	57.3	.	.	35.59	39.00	34.77	143.3	219.1	125.3
O	36.6	.	.	36.83	38.49	35.20	175.6	201.4	154.6
P	6.6	.	.	36.09	34.56	37.87	.	.	.
Q	2.8	.	.	45.11	45.87	43.43	.	.	.
X	-	.	.	.	.	.	.	.	.

Share of women in wage employment in the non-agricultural sector [1,2] (2005 - Labour force survey): **48.6%**

4. Occupational injuries and Strikes and Lockouts

Statistics not available.

5. Consumer price indices (base period: 2000=100)

[4]	2002	2003	2004	2005	2006	2007
General indices	110.5	115.8	122.4	132.5	144.6	158.0
Food index, including non-alcoholic beverages [5]	114.6	122.7	132.2	149.6	167.1	183.4
Electricity, gas and other fuel indices	114.2	114.9	122.6	125.9	159.2	181.1
Clothing indices, including footwear	100.3	98.8	99.7	101.5	106.1	101.3
Rent indices [6]	110.8	114.0	116.9	131.0	131.0	185.5
General index, excluding housing	110.5	115.8	122.4	132.4	144.3	156.2

[1] Excl. armed forces. [2] Persons aged 15 years and over. [3] "De facto" population. [4] 5 cities. [5] Incl. tobacco. [6] Housing.

[1] Non compris les forces armées. [2] Personnes âgées de 15 ans et plus. [3] Population "de facto". [4] 5 villes. [5] Y compris le tabac. [6] Logement.

[1] Excl. las fuerzas armadas. [2] Personas de 15 años y más. [3] Población "de facto". [4] 5 ciudades. [5] Incl. el tabaco. [6] Vivienda.

Germany

1. Economically active population, Employment and Unemployment ('000)

	Economically active population		Employment		Unemployment	
	Total	Women (%)	Total	Women (%)	Total	Women (%)
Age group	2007 [1,2,3] Labour force survey		2007 ★ Labour force survey		2007 [2,3] Labour force survey	
Total	41 771	45.3	38 163	45.3	3 608	46.1
15-19	1 558	43.8	1 359	43.6	199	44.7
20-24	3 469	45.9	3 081	46.4	388	42.0
25-29	3 985	46.6	3 589	46.9	396	43.9
30-34	4 067	44.2	3 727	44.2	340	44.1
35-39	5 445	44.9	5 041	44.8	404	46.0
40-44	6 553	45.7	6 086	45.4	467	48.8
45-49	5 661	47.0	5 234	46.9	427	49.2
50-54	4 883	46.5	4 476	46.4	407	47.2
55-59	3 948	45.4	3 520	44.9	428	49.5
60-64	1 601	38.5	1 455	38.4	146	39.0
65+	601	38.1	601	38.1	-	.
Economic activity (ISIC-Rev.3)	2007 [1,2,3] Labour force survey		2007 [2,3] Labour force survey		2007 [2,3] Labour force survey	
Total	41 771	45.3	38 163	45.3	3 608	46.1
A Agriculture, Hunting and Forestry	983	33.6	854	32.6	129	40.3
B Fishing	6	16.7	5	20.0	1	.
C Mining and Quarrying	122	12.3	107	10.3	15	26.7
D Manufacturing	9 049	29.0	8 395	28.2	654	40.1
E Electricity, Gas and Water Supply	348	23.9	334	23.7	14	35.7
F Construction	2 928	11.6	2 527	12.0	401	9.2
G Wholesale and Retail Trade; Repair of Motor Vehicles ...	5 810	52.9	5 308	52.5	502	56.8
H Hotels and Restaurants	1 653	58.5	1 428	58.5	224	58.5
I Transport, Storage and Communications	2 320	27.8	2 148	27.7	172	28.5
J Financial Intermediation	1 347	50.9	1 303	50.7	44	56.8
K Real Estate, Renting and Business Activities	4 250	47.7	3 909	47.5	340	50.0
L Public Administration and Defence; Compulsory Social ...	3 045	44.3	2 916	44.4	129	41.1
M Education	2 348	67.1	2 237	67.1	111	66.7
N Health and Social Work	4 659	75.5	4 398	75.5	261	74.7
O Other Community, Social and Personal Service Activities	2 262	56.9	2 058	57.1	203	55.2
P Households with Employed Persons	224	92.9	206	93.2	18	94.4
Q Extra-Territorial Organizations and Bodies	32	40.6	29	41.4	.	.
X Not classifiable by economic activity	386	49.7	.	.	.	.
Unemployed seeking their first job	.	.	.	.	386	49.7
Occupation (ISCO-88)	2007 [1,2,3] Labour force survey		2007 [2,3] Labour force survey		2007 [2,3] Labour force survey	
Total	41 771	45.3	38 163	45.3	3 608	46.1
1 Legislators, senior officials and managers	2 801	38.2	2 658	37.9	15	0.0
2 Professionals	5 603	39.8	5 449	39.7	143	44.1
3 Technicians and associate professionals	8 097	57.9	7 720	57.8	154	42.2
4 Clerks	4 851	67.7	4 510	67.5	377	59.2
5 Service workers and shop and market sales workers	5 222	74.5	4 677	74.6	340	70.3
6 Skilled agricultural and fishery workers	799	32.7	713	31.1	545	73.2
7 Craft and related trade workers	6 361	10.0	5 730	9.5	87	44.8
8 Plant and machine operators and assemblers	3 049	16.3	2 747	15.4	631	14.1
9 Elementary occupations	3 798	51.7	3 227	52.8	302	24.2
0 Armed forces	258	4.3	243	4.1	571	45.4
X Not classifiable by occupation	932	44.1	488	40.0	58	41.4
Unemployed seeking their first job	.	.	.	.	386	49.7
Education level (ISCED-97)	2007 [1,2,3] Labour force survey		2007 ★ Labour force survey		2007 [2,3] Labour force survey	
Total	41 771	45.3	38 163	45.3	3 608	46.1
1 Primary education or first stage of basic education	1 076	41.5	797	41.9	279	40.5
2 Lower secondary or second stage of basic education	6 037	48.9	5 121	49.4	916	46.1
3 Upper secondary education	21 631	45.8	19 757	45.7	1 874	46.7
4 Post-secondary non-tertiary education	3 021	52.5	2 864	52.9	157	45.9
5A First stage of tertiary education - theoretically based	5 889	41.5	5 648	41.2	241	46.5
5B First stage of tertiary education - practically oriented	3 600	40.3	3 469	39.9	131	49.6
6 Second stage of tertiary education	514	29.8	504	29.6	10	40.0
Status in employment (ICSE-1993)	2007 [1,2,3] Labour force survey		2007 [2,3] Labour force survey		2007 ★ Labour force survey	
Total	41 771	45.3	38 163	45.3	3 608	46.1
1 Employees	36 672	46.6	33 607	46.7	3 065	46.4
2 Employers	4 307	30.9	4 160	30.9	147	29.3
5 Contributing family workers	405	76.8	396	77.0	9	66.7
6 Not classifiable by status	386	49.7	.	.	.	.

2. Population ('000), Activity rate and Unemployment rate

	Population 2007 [1,3,4] Labour force survey			Activity rate 2007 [1,3,4] Labour force survey			Unemployment rate 2007 [2,3] Labour force survey		
Age group	Total	Men	Women	Total	Men	Women	Total	Men	Women
Total	82 257	40 271	41 986	50.8	56.7	45.1	8.6	8.5	8.8
15+	71 194	34 597	36 599	58.7	66.0	51.7	.	.	.
15-24	9 684	5 025	4 660	51.9	54.8	48.8	11.7	12.1	11.1
25-54	35 138	17 716	17 422	87.1	93.5	80.5	8.0	7.9	8.1
55+	26 372	11 856	14 517	23.3	29.6	18.2	.	.	.

Germany

3. Paid employment ('000), Hours of work (weekly) and Wages

Economic activity (ISIC-Rev.3)	Paid employment 2007 [2,3] Labour force survey			Hours of work 2007 Labour-related establishment survey Hours paid for / Employees			Wages 2007 Labour-related establishment survey Earnings per hour / Employees / Euro		
	Total	Men	Women	Total	Men	Women	Total	Men	Women
Total	33 607	17 927	15 680	.	.	.	.	.	.
A	444	305	138	.	.	.	.	.	.
B	-	-	-	.	.	.	.	.	.
C	105	95	10	40.4	40.6	38.5	18.00	18.10	16.66
D	7 996	5 733	2 262	38.4	38.5	37.9	19.09	20.01	15.27
E	328	250	78	38.1	38.2	37.7	22.99	23.72	19.49
F	2 047	1 792	255	39.1	39.1	38.8	15.03	15.11	13.87
G	4 574	2 033	2 541	39.1	39.3	38.5	16.60	17.82	14.01
H	1 145	429	716	39.3	39.5	39.1	10.95	11.98	9.91
I	1 984	1 424	560	40.1	40.5	38.6	15.39	15.48	15.00
J	1 149	523	626	38.5	38.6	38.5	22.95	25.95	19.00
K	3 047	1 453	1 594	38.8	39.1	38.4	17.80	19.08	15.01
L	2 916	1 620	1 295	.	.	.	.	.	.
M	2 094	678	1 416	38.6	38.9	38.3	18.03	19.03	17.28
N	3 969	894	3 075	38.9	39.2	38.8	17.41	21.21	15.41
O	1 594	667	927	39.2	39.5	38.6	17.13	18.90	14.38
P	185	11	174	.	.	.	.	.	.
Q	29	17	12	.	.	.	.	.	.

Share of women in wage employment in the non-agricultural sector [2,3] (2007 - Labour force survey): **46.9%**

4. Occupational injuries and Strikes and Lockouts

Economic activity (ISIC-Rev.3)	Rates of fatal injuries 2005 [5] Insurance records Per 100,000 full-time equivalent workers Compensated injuries			Rates of non-fatal injuries 2005 [6] Insurance records Per 100,000 full-time equivalent workers Compensated injuries			Strikes and lockouts 2007 [7] Labour relations records		
	Total	Men	Women	Total	Men	Women	Strikes and lockouts	Workers involved [8]	Days not worked
Total	2.38	.	.	2 835	.	.	.	106 483 [9]	286 368 [9]
A	.	.	.	.	.	.	.	0	0
B	.	.	.	.	.	.	.	0	0
C	.	.	.	.	.	.	.	0	0
D	.	.	.	.	.	.	.	77 653	36 054
E	.	.	.	.	.	.	.	0	0
F	.	.	.	.	.	.	.	696	8 159
G	.	.	.	.	.	.	.	11 698	32 434
H	.	.	.	.	.	.	.	0	0
I	.	.	.	.	.	.	.	16 242	209 227
J	.	.	.	.	.	.	.	0	0
K	.	.	.	.	.	.	.	0	0
L	.	.	.	.	.	.	.	100 [9]	0 [9]
M	.	.	.	.	.	.	.	0	0
N	.	.	.	.	.	.	.	0	0
O	.	.	.	.	.	.	.	0	0
P	.	.	.	.	.	.	.	.	0
Q	.	.	.	.	.	.	.	0	.

5. Consumer price indices (base period: 2000=100)

	2002	2003	2004	2005	2006	2007
General indices	103.4	104.5	106.2	108.3	110.1	112.5
Food index, including non-alcoholic beverages	105.3	105.2	104.8	105.3	107.3	111.5
Electricity, gas and other fuel indices	108.0	111.8	116.1	129.8	143.4	148.6
Clothing indices, including footwear	101.5	100.7	100.0	98.1	97.2	98.8
Rent indices	102.6	103.8	104.8	105.9	107.0	108.3
General index, excluding housing	103.6	104.7	106.7	109.1	111.0	113.9

[1] Included armed forces and conscripts. [2] Persons aged 15 years and over. [3] March. [4] "De jure" population. [5] Deaths occurring within one month of accident. [6] Incapacity of 4 days or more. [7] Incl. work stoppages lasting less than one day if more than 100 workdays not worked. [8] Excl. workers indirectly involved. [9] Excl. public administration.

[1] Y compris les forces armées et les conscrits. [2] Personnes âgées de 15 ans et plus. [3] Mars. [4] Population "de jure". [5] Les décès survenant pendant le mois qui suit l'accident. [6] Incapacité de 4 jours et plus. [7] Y compris les arrêts du travail d'une durée inférieure à une journée si plus de 100 journées de travail non effectuées. [8] Non compris les travailleurs indirectement impliqués. [9] Non compris l'administration publique.

[1] Incluye las fuezas armadas y los conscriptos. [2] Personas de 15 años y más. [3] Marzo. [4] Población "de jure". [5] Los fallecimientos que se produzcan durante el mes posterior al accidente. [6] Incapacidad de 4 días y más. [7] Incl. las interrupciones del trabajo de menos de un día si no se han trabajado más de 100 días. [8] Excl. los trabajadores indirectamente implicados. [9] Excl. la administración pública.

Ghana

1. Economically active population, Employment and Unemployment ('000)

	Economically active population		Employment		Unemployment	
	Total	Women (%)	Total	Women (%)	Total	Women (%)
Age group	2000 [1,2] Population census		2000 ★ Population census		2000 [1,2] Population census	
Total	9 039.318	49.6	8 030.764	49.4	1 008.554	51.0
7-14	747.204	48.4	597.905	48.1	149.299	49.6
15-19	753.484	49.3	607.272	48.9	146.212	51.2
20-24	1 120.968	52.7	956.892	52.7	164.076	52.2
25-29	1 241.046	52.2	1 119.079	52.1	121.967	52.8
30-34	1 079.818	51.4	995.132	51.2	84.686	53.9
35-39	938.331	50.7	871.513	50.5	66.818	53.2
40-44	811.438	48.4	755.259	48.2	56.179	51.3
45-49	659.442	46.0	613.097	45.8	46.345	48.2
50-54	507.897	48.5	470.882	48.2	37.015	52.4
55-59	308.244	46.0	283.078	45.7	25.166	49.3
60-64	278.008	48.7	251.901	48.6	26.107	50.1
65-69	182.791	46.6	162.755	46.7	20.036	46.4
70-74	138.051	46.5	121.428	46.3	16.623	48.0
75+	272.596	41.0	224.571	40.6	48.025	42.7

Economic activity (ISIC-Rev.3)	2000 [1,2] Population census					
Total	9 039.3	49.6	.	.	.	.
A Agriculture, Hunting and Forestry	4 567.8	48.6	.	.	.	.
B Fishing	280.6	42.9	.	.	.	.
C Mining and Quarrying	160.6	36.6	.	.	.	.
D Manufacturing	958.4	52.4	.	.	.	.
E Electricity, Gas and Water Supply	31.3	32.6	.	.	.	.
F Construction	265.3	19.2	.	.	.	.
G Wholesale and Retail Trade; Repair of Motor Vehicles ...	1 339.5	64.6	.	.	.	.
H Hotels and Restaurants	199.2	78.0	.	.	.	.
I Transport, Storage and Communications	261.8	16.2	.	.	.	.
J Financial Intermediation	46.5	34.6	.	.	.	.
K Real Estate, Renting and Business Activities	83.8	31.3	.	.	.	.
L Public Administration and Defence; Compulsory Social ...	116.2	25.7	.	.	.	.
M Education	283.9	43.0	.	.	.	.
N Health and Social Work	71.3	49.9	.	.	.	.
O Other Community, Social and Personal Service Activities	266.2	60.7	.	.	.	.
P Households with Employed Persons	101.9	61.2	.	.	.	.
Q Extra-Territorial Organizations and Bodies	5.1	37.1	.	.	.	.

Occupation (ISCO-88)	2000 [1,2] Population census					
Total	9 039.3	49.6	.	.	.	.
1 Legislators, senior officials and managers	26.4	32.3	.	.	.	.
3 Technicians and associate professionals	673.9	39.7	.	.	.	.
4 Clerks	392.2	24.1	.	.	.	.
5 Service workers and shop and market sales workers	1 863.5	67.9	.	.	.	.
6 Skilled agricultural and fishery workers	4 508.9	48.7	.	.	.	.
8 Plant and machine operators and assemblers	1 424.3	42.6	.	.	.	.
X Not classifiable by occupation	150.1	30.5	.	.	.	.

Status in employment (ICSE-1993)	2000 [1,2] Population census					
Total	9 039.3	49.6	.	.	.	.
1 Employees	1 315.0	31.7	.	.	.	.
2 Employers	432.7	47.6	.	.	.	.
3 Own-account workers	5 969.5	53.4	.	.	.	.
5 Contributing family workers	822.8	53.7	.	.	.	.
6 Not classifiable by status	499.2	45.8	.	.	.	.

2. Population ('000), Activity rate and Unemployment rate

	Population			Activity rate			Unemployment rate		
Age group	2000 [2] Population census			2000 [2] Population census			2000 [1,2] Population census		
	Total	Men	Women	Total	Men	Women	Total	Men	Women
Total	18 912.1	9 357.4	9 554.7	47.8	48.7	46.9	11.2	10.9	11.5
15+	11 105.2	5 435.8	5 669.4	74.7	76.7	72.7	10.4	10.1	10.7
15-24	3 484.6	1 724.2	1 760.4	53.8	52.9	54.7	16.6	16.4	16.7
25-54	5 899.5	2 853.3	3 046.2	88.8	91.7	86.0	7.9	7.5	8.2
55+	1 721.1	858.3	862.9	68.5	74.7	62.4	11.5	11.3	11.7

Ghana

3. Paid employment ('000), Hours of work (weekly) and Wages

Economic activity (ISIC-Rev.2)	Paid employment 1991[3] Labour-related establishment survey			Hours of work			Wages 1991[3] Labour-related establishment census Earnings per month / Employees / Cedi		
	Total	Men	Women	Total	Men	Women	Total	Men	Women
Total	186.3	.	.	.	.	.	35 212	.	.
1	14.7	.	.	.	.	.	38 231	.	.
2	17.1	.	.	.	.	.	27 417	.	.
3	20.6	.	.	.	.	.	34 226	.	.
4	1.7	.	.	.	.	.	27 286	.	.
5	7.8	.	.	.	.	.	25 958	.	.
6	7.5	.	.	.	.	.	30 181	.	.
7	10.4	.	.	.	.	.	39 119	.	.
8	8.4	.	.	.	.	.	50 016	.	.
9	98.1	.	.	.	.	.	35 901	.	.

4. Occupational injuries and Strikes and Lockouts

Economic activity (ISIC-Rev.2)	Rates of fatal injuries			Rates of non-fatal injuries			Strikes and lockouts 1991 Labour relations records		
	Total	Men	Women	Total	Men	Women	Strikes and lockouts	Workers involved	Days not worked
Total	.	.	.	.	.	.	24	5 557	9 692

5. Consumer price indices (base period: 2000=100)

	2002	2003	2004	2005	2006	2007
General indices	151.8	193.3	217.7	250.7	278.0	331.9
Food index, including non-alcoholic beverages	145.6	181.6	211.8	244.7	267.2	300.6
Clothing indices, including footwear	164.1	193.7	207.7	220.6	233.9	275.6
Rent indices [4]	173.9	289.7	355.0	443.2	499.4	543.9

[1] Persons aged 7 years and over. [2] March. [3] Dec. [4] Incl. water, electricity, gas and other fuels.

[1] Personnes âgées de 7 ans et plus. [2] Mars. [3] Déc. [4] Y compris l'eau, l'électricité, le gaz et autres combustibles.

[1] Personas de 7 años y más. [2] Marzo. [3] Dic. [4] Incl. el agua, la electricidad, el gas y otros combustibles.

Gibraltar

1. Economically active population, Employment and Unemployment ('000)

	Economically active population		Employment		Unemployment	
	Total	Women (%)	Total	Women (%)	Total	Women (%)
Age group	1981 [1,2] Population census		2007 [3] Labour-related establishment survey		2007 [4] Employment office records	
Total	13.3	28.0	19.7	41.0	0.5	40.0
15-19	1.1	46.0	.	.	.	.
20-24	1.5	38.2	.	.	.	.
25-44	6.2	24.7	.	.	.	.
45-49	1.3	25.3	.	.	.	.
50-54	1.1	24.0	.	.	.	.
55-59	0.9	25.8	.	.	.	.
60-64	0.7	23.4	.	.	.	.
65+	0.6	23.6	.	.	.	.
Economic activity (ISIC-Rev.2)	1990 [1,3] Official estimates					
Total	14.2	34.5	.	.	.	.
3 Manufacturing	0.9	13.2	.	.	.	.
4 Electricity, Gas and Water	0.3	1.9	.	.	.	.
5 Construction	2.2	5.8	.	.	.	.
6 Wholesale and Retail Trade and Restaurants and Hotels	3.2	44.5	.	.	.	.
7 Transport, Storage and Communication	0.7	19.5	.	.	.	.
8 Financing, Insurance, Real Estate and Business Services	1.4	60.8	.	.	.	.
9 Community, Social and Personal Services	4.4	40.6	.	.	.	.
0 Activities not Adequately Defined	1.2	38.0	.	.	.	.
Economic activity (ISIC-Rev.3)			2007 [3] Labour-related establishment survey			
Total	.	.	19.7	.	.	.
D Manufacturing	.	.	0.4	.	.	.
E Electricity, Gas and Water Supply	.	.	0.3	.	.	.
F Construction	.	.	2.5	.	.	.
G Wholesale and Retail Trade; Repair of Motor Vehicles ...	.	.	2.8	.	.	.
H Hotels and Restaurants	.	.	1.1	.	.	.
I Transport, Storage and Communications	.	.	1.1	.	.	.
J Financial Intermediation	.	.	1.9	.	.	.
K Real Estate, Renting and Business Activities	.	.	2.5	.	.	.
L Public Administration and Defence; Compulsory Social ...	.	.	2.3	.	.	.
M Education	.	.	0.9	.	.	.
N Health and Social Work	.	.	1.6	.	.	.
O Other Community, Social and Personal Service Activities	.	.	2.5	.	.	.
Occupation (ISCO-1968)	1991 [1,3] Official estimates					
Total	15.1	32.8	.	.	.	.
0/1 Professional, technical and related workers	1.8	.	.	.	.	.
2 Administrative and managerial workers	1.3	.	.	.	.	.
3 Clerical and related workers	3.3	.	.	.	.	.
4 Sales workers	1.0	.	.	.	.	.
5 Service workers	2.5	.	.	.	.	.
7/8/9 Production and related workers, transport equipment ...	5.2	.	.	.	.	.
Status in employment (ICSE-1993)	1991 [1,3] Population census					
Total	12.3	35.8	.	.	.	.
1 Employees	11.1	37.1	.	.	.	.
2 Employers	0.2	24.0	.	.	.	.
3 Own-account workers	1.0	23.8	.	.	.	.
6 Not classifiable by status	0.0	100.0	.	.	.	.

2. Population ('000), Activity rate and Unemployment rate

	Population			Activity rate			Unemployment rate		
Age group	1981 [2] Population census			1981 [2] Population census					
	Total	Men	Women	Total	Men	Women	Total	Men	Women
Total	26.5	13.8	12.7	50.3	69.3	29.4	.	.	.
15+	20.8	10.9	9.9	64.0	87.9	37.6	.	.	.
15-24	3.8	2.0	1.8	69.9	78.8	60.3	.	.	.
25-54	11.2	6.5	4.7	76.1	99.1	44.5	.	.	.
55+	5.8	2.5	3.3	36.7	65.5	15.5	.	.	.

Gibraltar

3. Paid employment ('000), Hours of work (weekly) and Wages

Economic activity (ISIC-Rev.2)	Paid employment 2006 [3,5] Labour-related establishment survey			Hours of work			Wages		
	Total	Men	Women	Total	Men	Women	Total	Men	Women
Total	18.5	.	.	.	.	.	.	.	.
3	0.5	.	.	.	.	.	.	.	.
4	0.3	.	.	.	.	.	.	.	.
5	2.1	.	.	.	.	.	.	.	.
6	3.8	.	.	.	.	.	.	.	.
7	1.0	.	.	.	.	.	.	.	.
8	3.8	.	.	.	.	.	.	.	.
9	7.0	.	.	.	.	.	.	.	.

Economic activity (ISIC-Rev.3)	Paid employment			Hours of work 2007 [3,6] Labour-related establishment census Hours paid for / Employees			Wages 2007 [3,6] Labour-related establishment census Earnings per week / Wage earners / Pound		
	Total	Men	Women	Total	Men	Women	Total	Men	Women
Total	.	.	.	41.7	43.1	37.2	.	341.47	230.00
C-Q	.	.	.	41.7	43.1	37.2	.	341.47	230.00
D	.	.	.	47.2	48.3	37.1	.	437.20	267.90
E	.	.	.	52.5	52.5	.	.	650.80	.
F	.	.	.	41.9	42.1	34.8	.	353.80	280.50
G	.	.	.	38.4	39.3	37.2	.	264.80	222.20
H	.	.	.	37.8	39.2	36.0	.	228.00	184.90
I	.	.	.	46.0	46.8	35.1	.	359.90	212.40
J	.	.	.	36.9	39.1	35.4	.	853.40	307.70
K	.	.	.	41.6	43.5	36.9	.	352.10	212.40
L	.	.	.	48.6	49.3	44.5	.	457.30	354.30
M	.	.	.	49.2	56.2	46.8	.	459.00	368.40
N	.	.	.	47.1	55.3	40.4	.	461.70	318.90
O	.	.	.	45.0	48.5	35.3	.	371.80	242.40

4. Occupational injuries and Strikes and Lockouts

Statistics not available.

5. Consumer price indices (base period: 2000=100)

	2002	2003	2004	2005	2006	2007
General indices	102.5	105.2	107.6	110.9	113.8	116.9
Food index, including non-alcoholic beverages	107.1	111.3	115.1	117.4	120.4	124.4
Clothing indices, including footwear	93.5	95.9	96.8	98.1	99.8	99.6
Rent indices [7]	101.5	102.3	106.4	113.5	115.3	122.6
General index, excluding housing [8]	102.8	105.8	108.0	110.3	113.5	.

[1] Persons aged 15 years and over. [2] Nov. [3] Oct. [4] Persons aged 15 to 65 years. [5] Non-agricultural activities. [6] Excl. part-time workers and juveniles. [7] Incl. housing, water, electriciy and other fuels. [8] Excl. housing, water, electriciy and other fuels.

[1] Personnes âgées de 15 ans et plus. [2] Nov. [3] Oct. [4] Personnes âgées de 15 à 65 ans. [5] Activités non agricoles. [6] Non compris les travailleurs à temps partiel et les jeunes. [7] Y compris le logement, l'eau, l'électricité et autres combustibles. [8] Non compris le logement, l'eau, l'électricité autres combustibles.

[1] Personas de 15 años y más. [2] Nov. [3] Oct. [4] Personas de 15 a 65 años. [5] Actividades no agrícolas. [6] Excl. los trabajadores a tempo parcial y los jóvenes. [7] Incl. la vivienda, el agua, la electricidad y otros combustibles. [8] Excl. la vivienda, el agua, la electricidad y otros combustibles.

Greece

1. Economically active population, Employment and Unemployment ('000)

	Economically active population		Employment		Unemployment	
	Total	Women (%)	Total	Women (%)	Total	Women (%)
Age group	2007 [1,2,3] Labour force survey		2007 ★ Labour force survey		2007 [2,3] Labour force survey	
Total	4 917.9	40.9	4 519.9	38.9	398.0	63.8
15-19	54.6	40.2	41.0	33.3	13.6	61.0
20-24	309.0	44.9	242.5	39.4	66.5	65.1
25-29	671.9	43.5	576.1	41.1	95.8	58.0
30-34	707.9	43.0	643.9	40.7	64.0	66.3
35-39	714.1	42.5	665.1	40.1	49.0	74.7
40-44	699.8	42.7	660.1	41.4	39.7	64.5
45-49	607.6	41.1	579.0	39.6	28.6	71.0
50-54	512.2	37.9	491.2	36.7	21.0	64.8
55-59	358.0	32.6	343.4	32.0	14.6	46.6
60-64	192.4	34.4	188.4	34.5	4.0	27.5
65-69	59.1	30.2	58.2	30.1	0.9	33.3
70+	31.3	25.8	31.1	25.9	0.2	.
Economic activity (ISIC-Rev.3)	2007 [1,2,3] Labour force survey		2007 [1,2,3] Labour force survey		2007 [2,3] Labour force survey	
Total	4 917.9	40.9	4 520.0	38.9	398.0	63.8
A Agriculture, Hunting and Forestry	513.0	43.0	507.3	43.0	5.7	35.1
B Fishing	15.5	14.9	15.1	13.9	0.4	50.0
C Mining and Quarrying	19.5	9.2	18.1	7.2	1.3	38.5
D Manufacturing	599.3	29.6	558.9	27.6	40.4	56.9
E Electricity, Gas and Water Supply	41.9	21.2	40.0	21.3	1.9	21.1
F Construction	409.2	2.1	394.4	2.0	14.9	4.7
G Wholesale and Retail Trade; Repair of Motor Vehicles ...	844.9	43.1	800.6	42.1	44.2	61.3
H Hotels and Restaurants	355.0	47.1	317.9	45.4	37.1	62.0
I Transport, Storage and Communications	281.6	20.8	267.6	19.5	14.0	45.0
J Financial Intermediation	116.3	49.9	112.7	49.3	3.6	66.7
K Real Estate, Renting and Business Activities	315.0	46.4	294.8	44.8	20.2	69.8
L Public Administration and Defence; Compulsory Social ...	404.0	37.0	390.9	36.3	13.1	58.8
M Education	338.3	63.0	328.4	62.5	9.9	77.8
N Health and Social Work	250.1	65.3	240.9	64.1	9.3	95.7
O Other Community, Social and Personal Service Activities	176.4	49.4	162.4	48.6	14.0	60.0
P Households with Employed Persons	73.3	93.7	68.5	93.6	4.7	97.9
Q Extra-Territorial Organizations and Bodies	1.4	8.8	1.4	7.1	-	.
X Not classifiable by economic activity	163.2	71.6	.	.	23.3	85.4
Unemployed seeking their first job	.	.	.	.	139.9	69.3
Occupation (ISCO-88)	2007 [1,2,3] Labour force survey		2007 [1,2,3] Labour force survey		2007 [2,3] Labour force survey	
Total	4 917.9	40.9	4 520.0	38.9	398.0	63.8
1 Legislators, senior officials and managers	476.6	27.8	468.4	27.7	8.2	35.4
2 Professionals	661.8	48.9	644.4	48.4	17.4	64.9
3 Technicians and associate professionals	409.5	49.7	392.8	48.9	16.7	68.3
4 Clerks	549.7	62.3	510.3	61.0	39.4	79.9
5 Service workers and shop and market sales workers	692.8	55.5	632.4	54.6	60.4	65.2
6 Skilled agricultural and fishery workers	508.3	42.2	505.3	42.2	3.0	33.3
7 Craft and related trade workers	721.2	9.5	687.9	8.5	33.3	29.7
8 Plant and machine operators and assemblers	349.2	9.7	329.2	8.4	20.0	31.5
9 Elementary occupations	325.8	57.1	290.2	56.0	35.6	66.0
X Not classifiable by occupation	223.1	55.3	59.0	11.0	24.1	82.6
Unemployed seeking their first job	.	.	.	.	139.9	69.3
Education level (ISCED-97)	2007 [1,2,3] Labour force survey		2007 ★ Labour force survey		2007 [2,3] Labour force survey	
Total	4 917.9	40.9	4 519.9	38.9	398.0	63.8
X No schooling	18.8	46.6	17.0	45.1	1.8	61.1
1 Primary education or first stage of basic education	997.9	37.1	929.8	35.7	68.1	56.4
2 Lower secondary or second stage of basic education	561.7	31.4	513.1	28.5	48.6	61.5
3 Upper secondary education	1 623.9	39.2	1 478.9	36.8	145.0	64.6
4 Post-secondary non-tertiary education	443.2	52.9	395.4	50.7	47.8	70.9
5A First stage of tertiary education - theoretically based	838.6	47.1	786.7	46.0	51.9	62.8
5B First stage of tertiary education - practically oriented	410.3	44.8	376.4	42.6	33.9	70.2
6 Second stage of tertiary education	23.5	27.5	22.5	25.2	1.0	80.0
Status in employment (ICSE-1993)	2007 [1,2,3] Labour force survey		2007 [1,2,3] Labour force survey		2007 ★ Labour force survey	
Total	4 917.9	40.9	4 520.0	38.9	397.9	63.9
1 Employees	3 114.8	43.1	2 896.4	41.8	218.4	59.6
2 Employers	372.0	19.5	369.7	19.6	2.3	10.2
3 Own-account workers	975.4	30.0	963.4	29.8	12.0	49.5
5 Contributing family workers	292.5	64.6	290.4	64.7	2.1	46.2
6 Not classifiable by status	163.2	71.6	.	.	.	.

2. Population ('000), Activity rate and Unemployment rate

	Population 2007 [1,3,4] Labour force survey			Activity rate 2007 [1,3,4] Labour force survey			Unemployment rate 2007 [2,3] Labour force survey		
Age group	Total	Men	Women	Total	Men	Women	Total	Men	Women
Total	10 754	5 285	5 469	45.7	55.0	36.8	8.1	5.0	12.6
15+	9 207	4 490	4 717	53.4	64.7	42.7	8.1	.	.
15-24	1 172	590	583	31.0	34.4	27.6	22.0	14.1	32.1
25-54	4 773	2 404	2 369	82.0	94.5	69.3	7.6	4.6	11.8
55+	3 262	1 496	1 765	19.6	28.9	11.8	3.1	.	.

Greece

3. Paid employment ('000), Hours of work (weekly) and Wages

Economic activity (ISIC-Rev.3)	Paid employment 2007 [1,2,3] Labour force survey Total	Men	Women	Hours of work 2007 [1,2,3] Labour force survey Hours actually worked / Total employment Total	Men	Women	Wages 2002 [5] Labour-related establishment survey Earnings per month / Wage earners / Euro Total	Men	Women
Total	2 896.4	1 685.3	1 211.0	39.9	42.3	36.2	.	.	.
A-B	.	.	.	38.2	43.2	31.4	.	.	.
C-Q	.	.	.	40.1	42.1	36.9	.	.	.
A	29.4	21.3	8.1	38.0	43.0	31.4	.	.	.
B	5.0	4.0	1.0	45.8	47.1	38.0	.	.	.
C	16.5	15.6	0.9	41.8	41.8	41.6	2 155	.	.
D	408.1	288.4	119.7	42.0	43.0	39.3	1 140	.	.
E	40.0	31.6	8.5	38.9	39.1	38.1	2 672	.	.
F	263.6	258.8	4.8	41.5	41.5	40.3	1 150	.	.
G	419.6	212.6	207.0	43.4	45.4	40.6	961	.	.
H	184.3	93.3	91.1	47.0	49.3	44.3	731	.	.
I	193.1	145.5	47.7	44.6	46.4	37.4	1 494	.	.
J	100.3	48.5	51.8	38.5	39.4	37.6	1 897	.	.
K	165.8	75.7	90.2	40.2	42.3	37.7	1 076	.	.
L	390.9	249.1	141.8	37.2	38.5	35.0	.	.	.
M	302.0	110.8	191.2	23.6	24.5	23.0	.	.	.
N	198.7	62.5	136.1	37.6	39.7	36.4	.	.	.
O	114.1	63.2	50.9	39.1	39.8	38.4	.	.	.
P	63.6	3.3	60.3	38.7	40.9	38.5	.	.	.
Q	1.4	1.3	0.1	32.4	31.8	38.0	.	.	.

Share of women in wage employment in the non-agricultural sector [1,2,3] (2007 - Labour force survey): **42.0%**

4. Occupational injuries and Strikes and Lockouts

Economic activity (ISIC-Rev.2)	Rates of fatal injuries 2003 Insurance records Per 100,000 workers insured Compensated injuries Total	Men	Women	Rates of non-fatal injuries 2003 Insurance records Per 100,000 workers insured Compensated injuries Total	Men	Women	Strikes and lockouts 1998 Special data collection Strikes and lockouts	Workers involved	Days not worked [6]
Total	5.4	.	.	772	.	.	99	33 633	283 903
1	.	.	.	.	.	.	0	0	0
2	.	.	.	.	.	.	0	0	0
3	.	.	.	.	.	.	12	2 029	23 824
4	.	.	.	.	.	.	9	330	2 640
5	.	.	.	.	.	.	10	3 673	29 384
6	.	.	.	.	.	.	3	195	1 560
7	.	.	.	.	.	.	14	1 287	10 528
8	.	.	.	.	.	.	9	713	8 744
9	.	.	.	.	.	.	4	180	1 440
0	.	.	.	.	.	.	38 [7]	25 226 [7]	205 783 [7]

5. Consumer price indices (base period: 2000=100)

	2002	2003	2004	2005	2006	2007
General indices	107.1	110.9	114.1	118.2	122.0	125.5
Food index, including non-alcoholic beverages	110.7	116.2	116.8	117.5	121.9	125.9
Electricity, gas and other fuel indices	102.0	106.1	110.9	131.2	147.0	147.3
Clothing indices, including footwear	107.1	109.2	113.6	119.0	121.9	126.1
Rent indices	109.1	114.8	120.9	126.0	131.5	137.5
General index, excluding housing	107.0	110.7	113.8	117.8	121.5	124.9

[1] Excl. conscripts. [2] Persons aged 15 years and over. [3] Second quarter. [4] "De facto" population. [5] Establishments with 10 or more persons employed. [6] Computed on the basis of an average number of workhours per day. [7] General strikes.

[1] Non compris les conscrits. [2] Personnes âgées de 15 ans et plus. [3] Deuxième trimestre. [4] Population "de facto". [5] Etablissements occupant 10 personnes et plus. [6] Calculées sur la base d'une moyenne d'heures de travail par jour. [7] Grèves générales.

[1] Excl. los conscriptos. [2] Personas de 15 años y más. [3] Segundo trimestre. [4] Población "de facto". [5] Establecimientos con 10 y más trabajadores. [6] Calculados en base a un promedio de horas de trabajo por día. [7] Huelgas generales.

Greenland

1. Economically active population, Employment and Unemployment ('000)

| | Economically active population || Employment || Unemployment ||
Age group	Total	Women (%)	Total	Women (%)	Total	Women (%)
	2006 [1,2] Official estimates		2005 [1,2] Official estimates		2006 [1,2] Official estimates	
Total	27.590	48.7	24.819	49.3	2.317	38.8

2. Population ('000), Activity rate and Unemployment rate

| | Population ||| Activity rate ||| Unemployment rate 2006 [1,2] Official estimates |||
Age group	Total	Men	Women	Total	Men	Women	Total	Men	Women
Total	.	.	.	.	.	.	8.4	10.0	6.7

3. Paid employment ('000), Hours of work (weekly) and Wages

Statistics not available.

4. Occupational injuries and Strikes and Lockouts

Statistics not available.

5. Consumer price indices (base period: 2000=100)

	2002	2003	2004	2005	2006	2007
General indices	107.2	109.0	112.0	113.3	116.2	118.5
Food index, including non-alcoholic beverages	107.6	109.8	111.4	114.5	117.4	120.9
Electricity, gas and other fuel indices	111.1	110.5	110.9	117.2	137.0	142.2
Clothing indices, including footwear	103.4	104.4	104.5	106.4	105.8	103.3
Rent indices	111.0	114.5	125.4	125.7	125.6	132.2

[1] Persons aged 15 years and over. [2] Jan.   [1] Personnes âgées de 15 ans et plus. [2] Janv.   [1] Personas de 15 años y más. [2] Enero.

Grenada

1. Economically active population, Employment and Unemployment ('000)

	Economically active population		Employment		Unemployment	
	Total	Women (%)	Total	Women (%)	Total	Women (%)
Age group	1998 [1 2] Labour force survey		1998 ★ Labour force survey		1998 [2] Labour force survey	
Total	41.015	43.5	34.787	40.4	6.228	60.8
15-19	3.482	35.9	2.031	28.5	1.451	46.3
20-24	6.209	47.8	4.610	42.9	1.599	61.9
25-29	5.694	42.0	4.746	36.6	0.948	68.9
30-34	5.832	47.7	5.025	43.5	0.807	74.0
35-39	5.197	47.8	4.691	46.2	0.506	62.6
40-44	3.864	44.4	3.556	42.0	0.308	72.7
45-49	3.277	41.6	3.198	41.4	0.079	46.8
50-54	2.679	41.1	2.383	36.6	0.296	77.7
55-59	1.398	42.8	1.281	40.8	0.117	64.1
60-64	1.535	32.8	1.460	29.4	0.075	100.0
65+	1.689	36.5	1.647	37.4	0.042	0.0

Economic activity (ISIC-Rev.2)

1998 [1 2] Labour force survey

	Total	Women (%)
Total	34.789	40.4
1 Agriculture, Hunting, Forestry and Fishing	4.794	28.4
2 Mining and Quarrying	0.058	63.8
3 Manufacturing	2.579	54.3
4 Electricity, Gas and Water	0.505	0.0
5 Construction	5.163	5.4
6 Wholesale and Retail Trade and Restaurants and Hotels	8.298	51.3
7 Transport, Storage and Communication	2.043	15.5
8 Financing, Insurance, Real Estate and Business Services	1.312	58.3
9 Community, Social and Personal Services	8.716	62.3
0 Activities not Adequately Defined	1.321	15.5

Occupation (ISCO-88)

1998 [1 2] Labour force survey

	Total	Women (%)
Total	34.767	40.4
1 Legislators, senior officials and managers	2.118	49.3
2 Professionals	0.738	43.0
3 Technicians and associate professionals	3.344	54.7
4 Clerks	3.257	77.4
5 Service workers and shop and market sales workers	5.378	50.7
6 Skilled agricultural and fishery workers	3.841	23.8
7 Craft and related trade workers	7.032	16.2
8 Plant and machine operators and assemblers	2.018	9.3
9 Elementary occupations	5.342	56.3
X Not classifiable by occupation	1.699	22.0

Status in employment (ICSE-1993)

1998 [1 2] Labour force survey

	Total	Women (%)
Total	34.789	40.4
1 Employees	24.795	42.6
2 Employers	1.947	29.7
3 Own-account workers	6.005	40.4
5 Contributing family workers	0.390	62.3
6 Not classifiable by status	1.652	14.6

2. Population ('000), Activity rate and Unemployment rate

	Population 1988 Labour force survey			Activity rate 1988 Labour force survey			Unemployment rate 1998 [2] Labour force survey		
Age group	Total	Men	Women	Total	Men	Women	Total	Men	Women
Total	97.495	46.621	50.874	39.9	42.9	37.2	15.2	10.5	21.2
15+	60.910	27.828	33.082				15.2	10.6	21.8
15-24	19.098	8.840	10.258	62.6	65.7	59.9	31.5	25.4	39.4
25-54	28.218	13.428	14.790	82.2	90.3	74.8	11.1	6.6	17.4
55+	13.594	5.560	8.034				5.1	2.9	8.7

3. Paid employment ('000), Hours of work (weekly) and Wages

Statistics not available.

4. Occupational injuries and Strikes and Lockouts

Statistics not available.

5. Consumer price indices (base period: 2000=100)

	2002	2003	2004	2005	2006	2007
General indices	104.3	106.6	109.0	.	.	.
Food index, including non-alcoholic beverages	101.4	102.1	105.3	.	.	.
Electricity, gas and other fuel indices	104.2	108.3	111.8	.	.	.
Clothing indices, including footwear	101.3	100.7	99.6	.	.	.
Rent indices	102.7	104.8	106.9	.	.	.

Grenada

[1] Excl. conscripts. [2] Persons aged 15 years and over.   [1] Non compris les conscrits. [2] Personnes âgées de 15 ans et plus.   [1] Excl. los conscriptos. [2] Personas de 15 años y más.

Guadeloupe

1. Population active, Emploi et Chômage ('000)

Groupe d'âge	Population active Total	Population active Femmes (%)	Emploi Total	Emploi Femmes (%)	Chômage Total	Chômage Femmes (%)
	1999 [1][2] Recensement de la population		1999 ★ Recensement de la population		2006 [1][3] Enquête sur la main-d'oeuvre	
Total	191.4	49.1	125.8	46.4	46.2	54.9
15-19	2.1	36.8	0.5	35.6	.	.
15-24	.	.	.	.	7.6	44.4
20-24	15.7	47.1	6.1	43.5	.	.
25-29	29.0	51.1	15.6	47.6	.	.
25-49	.	.	.	.	33.8	57.5
30-34	31.4	51.5	19.4	46.5	.	.
35-39	31.8	49.5	21.4	45.8	.	.
40-44	26.3	49.2	19.2	46.7	.	.
45-49	21.8	49.9	16.6	48.3	.	.
50+	.	.	.	.	4.7	53.5
50-54	17.6	47.5	13.9	46.7	.	.
55-59	10.4	45.8	8.4	46.2	.	.
60-64	4.1	43.6	3.5	44.0	.	.
65-69	0.7	36.1	0.7	36.1	.	.
70-74	0.2	34.0	0.2	34.0	.	.
75+	0.3	38.4	0.3	38.4	.	.

Activité économique (CITI-Rév.2)			1980 Estimations officielles		1991 [4][5] Fichiers des bureaux de placement	
Total	.	.	81.400	.	34.347	59.4
1 Agriculture, chasse, sylviculture et pêche	.	.	22.100	.	1.320	23.9
2 Industries extractives	.	.	-	.	0.207	.
3 Industries manufacturières	.	.	10.600	.	1.714	48.7
4 Electricité, gaz et eau	.	.	-	.	0.473	4.2
5 Bâtiment et travaux publics	.	.	7.000	.	5.398	1.0
6 Commerce de gros et de détail; restaurants et hôtels	.	.	8.500 [6]	.	9.243	84.0
7 Transports, entrepôts et communications	.	.	3.500 [7]	.	2.043	4.7
8 Banques, assurances, affaires immobilières et services ...	.	.	2.000	.	0.169	68.0
9 Services fournis à la collectivité, services sociaux ...	.	.	28.000	.	13.719	81.4
0 Activités mal désignées	.	.	-	.	0.061	49.2

Niveau d'instruction (CITE-97)	1999 [1][2] Recensement de la population					
Total	191.4	49.1	.	.	.	.
1 Enseignement primaire ou premier cycle de l'éducation ...	33.3	42.5	.	.	.	.
2 Premier cycle de l'enseignement secondaire ou deuxième ...	85.5	46.6	.	.	.	.
3 Enseignement secondaire (deuxième cycle)	40.5	56.5	.	.	.	.
5A Premier cycle de l'enseignement supérieur - théorie [8]	32.1	53.6	.	.	.	.

2. Population ('000), Taux d'activité et Taux de chômage

Groupe d'âge	Population 1999 [2] Recensement de la population			Taux d'activité 1999 [2] Recensement de la population			Taux de chômage 1999 [1] Recensement de la population		
	Total	Hommes	Femmes	Total	Hommes	Femmes	Total	Hommes	Femmes
Total	422.2	203.1	219.1	45.3	47.9	42.9	34.2	30.7	37.9
15+	322.5	152.5	170.1	59.3	63.8	55.3	34.2	30.7	37.9
15-24	61.4	31.1	30.3	29.0	31.0	27.0	62.8	60.7	65.2
25-54	184.7	87.3	97.4	85.4	90.4	81.0	32.8	28.6	37.0
55+	76.4	34.1	42.4	20.6	25.6	16.5	16.7	17.0	16.3

3. Emploi rémunéré ('000), Durée du travail (hebdomadaire) et Salaires

Activité économique (CITI-Rév.3)	Emploi rémunéré 2005 Estimations officielles			Durée du travail			Salaires 2001 Enquête auprès des établissements, relative au travail Gains par heure / Salariés / Euro		
	Total	Hommes	Femmes	Total	Hommes	Femmes	Total	Hommes	Femmes
Total	115.105	.	.	.	.	.	10.29	10.77	9.72
A-B	2.934	.	.	.	.	.	9.10 [9]	9.10 [9]	.
D	6.983	.	.	.	.	.	.	.	.
E	1.513	.	.	.	.	.	15.02	15.56	12.19
F	6.819	.	.	.	.	.	8.35	8.38	8.04
G	16.673	.	.	.	.	.	.	.	.
50	.	.	.	.	.	.	9.02	9.16	8.46
51	.	.	.	.	.	.	9.90	10.48	8.81
52	.	.	.	.	.	.	7.82	8.58	7.24
H	6.966	.	.	.	.	.	7.52	7.88	7.20
I	7.200	.	.	.	.	.	10.44 [10]	10.93 [10]	9.38 [10]
64	.	.	.	.	.	.	13.55	14.54	12.09
J	2.440	.	.	.	.	.	13.80	16.86	11.82
K	8.340	.	.	.	.	.	10.20	10.96	9.42
73	.	.	.	.	.	.	14.10	15.27	12.18
L	17.953	.	.	.	.	.	13.17	15.22	12.21
M	15.263	.	.	.	.	.	6.36	6.46	6.28
N	12.000	.	.	.	.	.	12.90	14.35	12.10
O	4.913	.	.	.	.	.	9.10	9.71	8.71
92	.	.	.	.	.	.	10.81	12.15	9.02
P	5.107	.	.	.	.	.	5.63	6.17	5.49

Guadeloupe

4. Lésions professionnelles et Grèves et lock-out

Activité économique (CITI-Rév.2)	Taux de lésions mortelles			Taux de lésions non mortelles			Grèves et lock-out 1991 Source inconnue		
	Total	Hommes	Femmes	Total	Hommes	Femmes	Grèves et lock-out	Travailleurs impliqués	Journées non effectuées
Total	.	.	.	.	.	.	31	1 542	23 000
1	.	.	.	.	.	.	0	0	0
2	.	.	.	.	.	.	0	0	0
3	.	.	.	.	.	.	0	0	0
4	.	.	.	.	.	.	0	0	0
5	.	.	.	.	.	.	6	492	13 809
6	.	.	.	.	.	.	11	753	4 171
7	.	.	.	.	.	.	0	0	0
8	.	.	.	.	.	.	0	0	0
9	.	.	.	.	.	.	14	297	5 020
0	.	.	.	.	.	.	0	0	0

5. Indices des prix à la consommation (période de base: 2000=100)

	2002	2003	2004	2005	2006	2007
Indices généraux	105.0	107.1	108.6	112.1	114.3	115.8
Indices de l'alimentation, y compris les boissons non alcoolisées	108.0	111.7	113.1	116.1	115.7	118.1
Indices de l'électricité, gaz et autres combustibles	104.9	105.2	108.4	121.8	133.6	133.9
Indices de l'habillement, y compris les chaussures	98.1	94.4	90.8	93.5	93.0	90.9
Indices du loyer	102.3	103.4	104.6	106.5	108.3	111.1

[1] Persons aged 15 years and over. [2] March. [3] June. [4] Persons aged 16 years and over. [5] Dec. [6] Incl. financing, insurance and real estate; excl. restaurants and hotels. [7] Civilian labour force employed. [8] Levels 5-6. [9] Excl. hunting. [10] Excl. storage and communications.

[1] Personnes âgées de 15 ans et plus. [2] Mars. [3] Juin. [4] Personnes âgées de 16 ans et plus. [5] Déc. [6] Y compris les banques, les assurances et affaires immobilières; non compris les restaurants et hôtels. [7] Main-d'oeuvre civile occupée. [8] Niveaux 5-6. [9] Non compris la chasse. [10] N.c. l'entreposage et les communications.

[1] Personas de 15 años y más. [2] Marzo. [3] Junio. [4] Personas de 16 años y más. [5] Dic. [6] Incl. establecimientos financieros, seguros y bienes inmuebles; excl. restaurantes y hoteles. [7] Fuerza de trabajo civil ocupada. [8] Niveles 5-6. [9] Excl. la caza. [10] Excl. el almacenamiento y las comunicaciones.

Guam

1. Economically active population, Employment and Unemployment ('000)

	Economically active population		Employment		Unemployment	
	Total	Women (%)	Total	Women (%)	Total	Women (%)
Age group	1990 [1][2] Population census				1987 Labour force survey	
Total	66.14	37.4	.	.	1.62	41.4
16-19	4.55	39.4	.	.	0.57	40.4
20-24	11.71	34.9	.	.	0.41	39.0
25-29	11.20	38.4	.	.	.	.
25-44	.	.	.	.	0.52	46.2
30-34	9.72	38.5	.	.	.	.
35-39	8.50	38.7	.	.	.	.
40-44	6.81	39.0	.	.	.	.
45+	.	.	.	.	0.12	33.3
45-49	4.42	37.9	.	.	.	.
50-54	3.59	38.1	.	.	.	.
55-59	2.62	36.5	.	.	.	.
60-64	1.80	30.3	.	.	.	.
65-69	0.84	22.9	.	.	.	.
70-74	0.26	26.5	.	.	.	.
75+	0.13	38.0	.	.	.	.

Occupation (ISCO-1968)	1990 [1][2] Population census					
Total	66.1	37.4	.	.	.	.
0/1 Professional, technical and related workers	6.7	49.9	.	.	.	.
2 Administrative and managerial workers	6.8	41.2	.	.	.	.
3 Clerical and related workers	8.7	74.3	.	.	.	.
4 Sales workers	6.3	63.0	.	.	.	.
5 Service workers	8.3	51.8	.	.	.	.
6 Agriculture, animal husbandry and forestry workers ...	0.6	12.6	.	.	.	.
7/8/9 Production and related workers, transport equipment ...	14.8	7.4	.	.	.	.
X Not classifiable by occupation	2.0	54.0	.	.	.	.
AF Armed forces	12.0	13.5	.	.	.	.

Status in employment (ICSE-1993)	1990 [1][2] Population census					
Total	66.1	37.4	.	.	.	.
1 Employees	62.4	36.7	.	.	.	.
2 Employers	0.0	.	.	.	.	.
3 Own-account workers	1.6	41.4	.	.	.	.
5 Contributing family workers	0.1	55.1	.	.	.	.
6 Not classifiable by status	2.0	54.0	.	.	.	.

2. Population ('000), Activity rate and Unemployment rate

	Population 1990 [2] Population census			Activity rate 1990 [2] Population census			Unemployment rate 1986 [1] Labour force survey		
Age group	Total	Men	Women	Total	Men	Women	Total	Men	Women
Total	133.2	70.9	62.2	49.7	58.4	39.7	6.1	5.1	6.9
15+	91.0	49.4	41.6	72.7	83.8	59.5	6.3	5.7	7.2
15-24	24.3	13.7	10.6	66.9	75.8	55.5	16.4	16.5	16.3
25-54	53.9	29.2	24.7	82.1	93.2	69.0	.	.	.
55+	12.8	6.6	6.3	44.0	58.3	28.9	.	.	.

3. Paid employment ('000), Hours of work (weekly) and Wages

Economic activity (ISIC-Rev.2)	Paid employment 2006 [3][4] Labour-related establishment survey			Hours of work 2007 [3][4][5] Labour-related establishment survey Hours paid for / Wage earners			Wages 2007 [3][4] Labour-related establishment survey Earnings per hour / Wage earners / US dollar		
	Total	Men	Women	Total	Men	Women	Total	Men	Women
Total	43.2	24.8	18.4	36.4	.	.	11.29	.	.
1	0.3	0.2	0.0	39.3	.	.	8.32 [5]	.	.
3	1.6	1.3	0.4	41.5	.	.	14.42	.	.
5	4.1	3.8	0.3	41.3	.	.	12.66	.	.
6	14.1	7.2	6.8	.	.	.	.	.	.
61	.	.	.	36.5	.	.	9.35	.	.
62	.	.	.	31.6	.	.	9.96	.	.
7	5.0	3.0	2.0	39.3	.	.	14.80	.	.
8	2.4	0.7	1.7	38.9	.	.	12.19	.	.
9	15.8	8.5	7.3	36.1	.	.	9.85	.	.

4. Occupational injuries and Strikes and Lockouts

Statistics not available.

Guam

5. Consumer price indices (base period: 2000=100)

	2002	2003	2004	2005	2006	2007
General indices	99.4	102.0	108.1	116.3	129.8	138.6
Food index, including non-alcoholic beverages	112.6	118.9	130.1	140.8	150.0	154.6
Clothing indices, including footwear	87.4	84.2	85.8	90.3	97.1	92.6
Rent indices [6]	91.0	86.5	84.8	87.6	91.7	97.0

[1] Persons aged 16 years and over. [2] April. [3] Private sector. [4] Dec. [5] Excl. hunting, forestry and fishing. [6] Housing.

[1] Personnes âgées de 16 ans et plus. [2] Avril. [3] Secteur privé. [4] Déc. [5] Non compris la chasse, la sylviculture et la pêche. [6] Logement.

[1] Personas de 16 años y más. [2] Abril. [3] Sector privado. [4] Dic. [5] Excl. caza, silvicultura y pesca. [6] Vivienda.

Guatemala

1. Población económicamente activa, Empleo y Desempleo ('000)

	Población económicamente activa		Empleo		Desempleo	
	Total	Mujeres (%)	Total	Mujeres (%)	Total	Mujeres (%)
Grupo de edad	\multicolumn{2}{c}{2006 Encuesta de la fuerza de trabajo}	\multicolumn{2}{c}{2006 [1,2] Encuesta de la fuerza de trabajo}	\multicolumn{2}{c}{1991 [3] Encuesta de la fuerza de trabajo}
Total	5 565.2	38.1	5 390.5	38.1	24.4	51.6
0-9	74.6	28.1	.	.	.	.
10-14	458.1	31.8	.	.	2.4	83.3
15-19	744.2	35.2	.	.	7.9	54.4
20-24	752.6	39.9	.	.	5.3	58.5
25-29	650.2	40.3	.	.	2.8	39.3
30-34	575.3	42.3	.	.	2.4	62.5
35-39	497.9	42.7	.	.	1.3	30.8
40-44	429.9	41.0	.	.	0.4	.
45-49	376.2	40.8	.	.	0.9	22.2
50-54	336.5	41.1	.	.	0.6	.
55-59	234.7	33.4	.	.	0.2	.
60-64	157.3	32.4	.	.	-	.
65-69	113.6	31.0	.	.	0.2	.
70-74	78.4	28.6	.	.	.	.
75+	85.8	23.0	.	.	.	.
Actividad económica (CIIU-Rev.2)	\multicolumn{2}{c}{1994 [4,5] Censo de población}			\multicolumn{2}{c}{1991 [13] Encuesta de la fuerza de trabajo}
Total	2 462.5	19.0	.	.	23.0	48.7
1 Agricultura, caza, silvicultura y pesca	1 293.3	6.4	.	.	0.6	66.7
2 Explotación de minas y canteras	4.2	8.5	.	.	-	.
3 Industrias manufactureras	320.8	19.9	.	.	6.6	33.3
4 Electricidad, gas y agua	11.0	12.7	.	.	-	.
5 Construcción	141.9	2.2	.	.	0.9	33.3
6 Comercio al por mayor y al por menor y restaurantes y ...	233.3	40.3	.	.	3.2	65.6
7 Transportes, almacenamiento y comunicaciones	85.2	11.4	.	.	0.9	22.2
8 Establecimientos financieros, seguros, bienes inmuebles ...	73.2	37.8	.	.	1.5	40.0
9 Servicios comunales, sociales y personales	291.7	62.1	.	.	5.6	57.1
0 Actividades no bien especificadas	7.8	40.9	.	.	.	.
Desempleados sin empleo anterior	.	.	.	.	3.7	59.5
Actividad económica (CIIU-Rev.3)			\multicolumn{2}{c}{2006 [1,2] Encuesta de la fuerza de trabajo}		
Total	.	.	5 390.5	38.1	.	.
A-B	.	.	1 791.4	18.4	.	.
C Explotación de minas y canteras	.	.	7.5	2.9	.	.
D Industrias manufactureras	.	.	854.8	48.7	.	.
E Suministro de electricidad, gas y agua	.	.	12.4	10.5	.	.
F Construcción	.	.	354.9	1.6	.	.
G-H	.	.	1 226.9	57.4	.	.
I Transporte, almacenamiento y comunicaciones	.	.	160.7	8.8	.	.
J-K	.	.	176.1	26.6	.	.
L Administración pública y defensa; planes de seguridad ...	.	.	115.5	24.1	.	.
M Enseñanza	.	.	219.8	66.7	.	.
N-O	.	.	457.4	77.4	.	.
Q Organizaciones y órganos extraterritoriales	.	.	13.2	39.2	.	.
Ocupación (CIUO-1968)	\multicolumn{2}{c}{1991 ★ Encuesta de la fuerza de trabajo}	\multicolumn{2}{c}{1991 [1,2,3] Encuesta de la fuerza de trabajo}	\multicolumn{2}{c}{1991 [13] Encuesta de la fuerza de trabajo}
Total	704.4	34.5	681.4	34.0	23.0	48.7
0/1 Profesionales, técnicos y trabajadores asimilados	69.5	41.4	67.3	40.9	2.2	59.1
2 Directores y funcionarios públicos superiores	30.8	23.7	30.1	24.3	0.7	.
3 Personal administrativo y trabajadores asimilados	58.3	53.5	55.7	53.3	2.6	57.7
4 Comerciantes y vendedores	108.0	56.5	105.7	56.3	2.3	65.2
5 Trabajadores de los servicios	72.8	69.1	69.9	69.0	2.9	72.4
6 Trabajadores agrícolas y forestales, pescadores y cazadores	95.2	6.3	94.8	6.1	0.4	50.0
7/8/9 Obreros no agrícolas, conductores de máquinas y ...	266.1	21.2	257.9	20.9	8.2	29.3
Desempleados sin empleo anterior	.	.	.	.	3.7	59.5
Nivel de educación (CINE-97)	\multicolumn{2}{c}{2006 Encuesta de la fuerza de trabajo}				
Total	5 565.2	38.1	.	.	.	.
X Sin escolaridad	1 297.4	44.8	.	.	.	.
0 Enseñanza preescolar	25.0	29.7	.	.	.	.
1 Enseñanza primaria o primer ciclo de la educación básica	2 623.3	33.5	.	.	.	.
2 Primer ciclo de enseñanza secundaria o segundo ciclo de ...	583.1	34.3	.	.	.	.
3 Segundo ciclo de enseñanza secundaria	688.7	45.6	.	.	.	.
5A Primer ciclo de la educación terciaria - teóricos [6]	328.1	40.5	.	.	.	.
6 Segundo ciclo de la enseñanza terciaria	19.7	40.2	.	.	.	.
Situación en el empleo (CISE-58)	\multicolumn{2}{c}{1994 [4,5] Censo de población}				
Total	2 462.5	19.0	.	.	.	.
1 Empleadores y trabajadores por cuenta propia	891.1	12.1	.	.	.	.
2 Asalariados	1 228.2	25.7	.	.	.	.
3 Trabajadores familiares no remunerados	343.2	13.0	.	.	.	.

Guatemala

Situación en el empleo (CISE-1993)	2002 [1,2] Encuesta de la fuerza de trabajo	
Total	4 769.4	35.7
1 Asalariados	1 377.2	31.7
2 Empleadores	254.1	16.0
3 Trabajadores por cuenta propia	1 554.5	40.6
5 Trabajadores familiares auxiliares	1 069.9	39.1
6 Inclasificables según la situación	513.7	34.7

2. Población ('000), Tasa de actividad y Tasa de desempleo

Grupo de edad	Población 2006 Encuesta de la fuerza de trabajo			Tasa de actividad 2006 Encuesta de la fuerza de trabajo			Tasa de desempleo 2006 [1] Encuesta de la fuerza de trabajo		
	Total	Hombres	Mujeres	Total	Hombres	Mujeres	Total	Hombres	Mujeres
Total	12 987.8	6 220.8	6 767.0	42.8	55.3	31.4	1.8	1.5	2.4
15+	7 607.6	3 483.4	4 124.2	66.2	88.3	47.4	.	.	.
15-24	2 531.3	1 174.6	1 356.7	59.1	79.6	41.4	.	.	.
25-54	3 869.5	1 723.8	2 145.8	74.1	97.4	55.3	.	.	.
55+	1 206.7	585.0	621.8	55.5	79.1	33.3	.	.	.

3. Empleo remunerado ('000), Horas de trabajo (por semana) y Salarios

Actividad económica (CIIU-Rev.2)	Empleo remunerado 2003 [7] Registros de seguros			Horas de trabajo 1985 [8] Encuesta industrial/comercial Horas efectivamente trabajadas / Obreros			Salarios 2006 Registros de seguros Ganancias por mes / Asalariados / Quetzal		
	Total	Hombres	Mujeres	Total	Hombres	Mujeres	Total	Hombres	Mujeres
Total	957.9	.	.	.	.	.	2 098.50	.	.
2-9	.	.	.	.	.	.	3 036.30	.	.
1	145.7	.	.	.	.	.	.	.	.
2	2.3	.	.	.	.	.	2 272.30	.	.
3	196.3	.	.	48.60	.	.	1 581.00	.	.
4	9.9 [9]	.	.	.	.	.	2 854.90	.	.
5	22.7	.	.	.	.	.	1 436.80	.	.
6	161.4 [10]	.	.	.	.	.	1 932.50	.	.
7	31.0	.	.	.	.	.	1 908.30	.	.
9	388.6 [11]	.	.	.	.	.	3 306.70 [12]	.	.

4. Lesiones profesionales y Huelgas y cierres patronales

Actividad económica (CIIU-Rev.2)	Tasas de lesiones mortales 1990 Registros de seguros Por 1 000 trabajadores asegurados Lesiones indemnizadas			Tasas de lesiones no mortales 1999 Registros de seguros Por 100 000 trabajadores asegurados Lesiones indemnizadas			Huelgas y cierres patronales 1997 Registros de inspección del trabajo		
	Total	Hombres	Mujeres	Total	Hombres	Mujeres	Huelgas y cierres patronales	Trabajadores implicados	Días no trabajados
Total	0.25	.	.	14 271	.	.	0	.	.
1	0.23	.	.	.	.	.	.	.	.
2	0.31	.	.	.	.	.	.	.	.
3	0.18	.	.	.	.	.	.	.	.
4	0.79	.	.	.	.	.	.	.	.
5	0.49	.	.	.	.	.	.	.	.
6	0.13 [13]	.	.	.	.	.	.	.	.
7	1.02	.	.	.	.	.	.	.	.
9	0.22 [14]	.	.	.	.	.	.	.	.

5. Índices de precios al consumidor (periodo de base: 2000=100)

Guatemala	2002	2003	2004	2005	2006	2007
Índices generales	116.0	122.5	131.8	143.8	153.2	163.7
Índices de la alimentación incluyendo las bebidas no alcohólicas [15]	121.5	128.5	141.7	160.5	171.9	188.9
Índices de la electricidad, gas y otros combustibles [16]	103.6	109.4	118.5	126.3	134.9	140.8
Índices del vestido, incl. calzado [16]	106.7	111.8	115.9	119.9	123.5	127.1
Índices del aquiler [16,17]	105.3	108.7	112.9	118.8	125.9	131.6

[1] Persons aged 10 years and over. [2] Excl. armed forces. [3] Guatemala City. [4] Persons aged 7 years and over. [5] April. [6] Levels 5. [7] Civilian employees. [8] Establishments with 5 or more persons employed. [9] Incl. sanitary services. [10] Incl. financing and insurance. [11] Excl. sanitary services. [12] Public sector. [13] Incl. financing, insurance and real estate. [14] Incl. business services. [15] Incl. meals outside home. [16] Index base 2001=100. [17] Incl. water, electricity, gas and other fuels.

[1] Personnes âgées de 10 ans et plus. [2] Non compris les forces armées. [3] Ville de Guatemala. [4] Personnes âgées de 7 ans et plus. [5] Avril. [6] Niveaux 5. [7] Salariés civils. [8] Etablissements occupant 5 personnes et plus. [9] Y compris les services sanitaires. [10] Y compris les banques et les assurances. [11] Non compris les services sanitaires. [12] Secteur public. [13] Y compris les banques, les assurances et les affaires immobilières. [14] Y compris les services aux entreprises. [15] Y compris les repas en dehors du foyer. [16] Indice base 2001=100. [17] Y compris l'eau, l'électricité, le gaz et autres combustibles.

[1] Personas de 10 años y más. [2] Excl. las fuerzas armadas. [3] Ciudad de Guatemala. [4] Personas de 7 años y más. [5] Abril. [6] Niveles 5. [7] Asalariados civiles. [8] Establecimientos con 5 y más trabajadores. [9] Incl. los servicios de saneamiento. [10] Incl. bancos y seguros. [11] Excl. los servicios de saneamiento. [12] Sector público. [13] Incl. bancos, seguros y bienes inmuebles. [14] Incl. los servicios para las empresas. [15] Incl. las comidas fuera del hogar. [16] Indice base 2001=100. [17] Incl. el agua, la electricidad, el gas y otros combustibles.

Guernsey

1. Economically active population, Employment and Unemployment ('000)

	Economically active population		Employment		Unemployment	
	Total	Women (%)	Total	Women (%)	Total	Women (%)
Age group	1996 [1,2] Population census					
Total	31.335	44.5	.	.	.	.
15-19	1.388	47.2	.	.	.	.
20-24	3.354	50.5	.	.	.	.
25-29	4.159	48.6	.	.	.	.
30-34	4.005	43.7	.	.	.	.
35-39	3.726	44.7	.	.	.	.
40-44	3.537	43.7	.	.	.	.
45-49	3.964	45.3	.	.	.	.
50-54	2.672	42.3	.	.	.	.
55-59	2.299	38.8	.	.	.	.
60-64	1.411	33.8	.	.	.	.
65-69	0.500	38.8	.	.	.	.
70-74	0.202	30.2	.	.	.	.
75+	0.118	48.3	.	.	.	.
Economic activity (ISIC-Rev.2)	1996 [1,2] Population census					
Total	30.7	44.7	.	.	.	.
1 Agriculture, Hunting, Forestry and Fishing	1.9	40.5	.	.	.	.
2 Mining and Quarrying	-		.	.	.	.
3 Manufacturing	2.1	31.2	.	.	.	.
4 Electricity, Gas and Water	0.4	17.0	.	.	.	.
5 Construction	2.7	4.8	.	.	.	.
6 Wholesale and Retail Trade and Restaurants and Hotels	7.0	46.0	.	.	.	.
7 Transport, Storage and Communication	2.0	25.1	.	.	.	.
8 Financing, Insurance, Real Estate and Business Services	7.4	53.7	.	.	.	.
9 Community, Social and Personal Services	7.1	61.5	.	.	.	.
0 Activities not Adequately Defined	-		.	.	.	.
Occupation (ISCO-1968)	1996 [1,2] Population census					
Total	30.7	44.7	.	.	.	.
0/1 Professional, technical and related workers	2.7	41.9	.	.	.	.
2 Administrative and managerial workers	3.8	28.9	.	.	.	.
3 Clerical and related workers	6.8	66.2	.	.	.	.
4 Sales workers	1.6	69.3	.	.	.	.
5 Service workers	0.4	12.6	.	.	.	.
6 Agriculture, animal husbandry and forestry workers ...	1.7	33.8	.	.	.	.
7/8/9 Production and related workers, transport equipment ...	13.7	38.3	.	.	.	.
X Not classifiable by occupation	0.0	.	.	.	.	.
AF Armed forces	0.0	.	.	.	.	.
Status in employment (ICSE-1993)	1996 [1,2] Population census					
Total	30.7	44.7	.	.	.	.
1 Employees	26.7	48.0	.	.	.	.
3 Own-account workers	4.0	22.9	.	.	.	.

2. Population ('000), Activity rate and Unemployment rate

	Population 1996 [2,3] Population census			Activity rate 1996 [2,3] Population census			Unemployment rate		
Age group	Total	Men	Women	Total	Men	Women	Total	Men	Women
Total	58.681	28.244	30.437	53.4	61.6	45.8	.	.	.
15+	48.337	22.967	25.370	64.8	75.7	55.0	.	.	.
15-24	7.430	3.618	3.812	63.8	66.1	61.6	.	.	.
25-54	25.657	12.637	13.020	86.0	96.1	76.1	.	.	.
55+	15.250	6.712	8.538	29.7	42.5	19.7	.	.	.

3. Paid employment ('000), Hours of work (weekly) and Wages

Statistics not available.

4. Occupational injuries and Strikes and Lockouts

Statistics not available.

5. Consumer price indices (base period: 2000=100)

Statistics not available for the period 2002-2007.

---

[1] Persons aged 15 years and over. [2] March. [3] "De jure" population.

Guinea Ecuatorial

1. Población económicamente activa, Empleo y Desempleo ('000)

	Población económicamente activa		Empleo		Desempleo	
	Total	Mujeres (%)	Total	Mujeres (%)	Total	Mujeres (%)
Grupo de edad	1983 [1,2] Censo de población				1983 [1,2] Censo de población	
Total	102.565	35.7	.	.	24.825	27.3
0-9	0.381	48.8	.	.	.	.
10-14	2.864	50.3	.	.	.	.
15-19	17.675	40.5	.	.	.	.
20-24	13.332	32.9	.	.	.	.
25-29	10.498	32.2	.	.	.	.
30-34	9.758	34.0	.	.	.	.
35-39	8.852	37.2	.	.	.	.
40-44	9.491	36.5	.	.	.	.
45-49	8.299	31.8	.	.	.	.
50-54	7.496	34.8	.	.	.	.
55-59	4.202	30.3	.	.	.	.
60-64	4.929	40.8	.	.	.	.
65-69	1.739	33.3	.	.	.	.
70-74	1.642	34.1	.	.	.	.
75+	1.402	24.3	.	.	.	.
?	0.005	60.0	.	.	.	.
Actividad económica (CIIU-Rev.2)			1983 [1,2] Censo de población			
Total	.	.	77.8	38.3	.	.
1 Agricultura, caza, silvicultura y pesca	.	.	59.4	45.1	.	.
2 Explotación de minas y canteras	.	.	0.1	.	.	.
3 Industrias manufactureras	.	.	1.5	13.3	.	.
4 Electricidad, gas y agua	.	.	0.2	.	.	.
5 Construcción	.	.	1.9	.	.	.
6 Comercio al por mayor y al por menor y restaurantes y ...	.	.	3.1	32.3	.	.
7 Transportes, almacenamiento y comunicaciones	.	.	1.8	11.1	.	.
8 Establecimientos financieros, seguros, bienes inmuebles ...	.	.	0.4	25.0	.	.
9 Servicios comunales, sociales y personales	.	.	8.4	14.3	.	.
0 Actividades no bien especificadas	.	.	1.0	20.0	.	.
Ocupación (CIUO-1968)			1983 [1,2] Censo de población			
Total	.	.	77.8	38.3	.	.
0/1 Profesionales, técnicos y trabajadores asimilados	.	.	2.4	25.0	.	.
2 Directores y funcionarios públicos superiores	.	.	0.2	.	.	.
3 Personal administrativo y trabajadores asimilados	.	.	3.0	16.7	.	.
4 Comerciantes y vendedores	.	.	2.3	34.8	.	.
5 Trabajadores de los servicios	.	.	3.8	15.8	.	.
6 Trabajadores agrícolas y forestales, pescadores y cazadores	.	.	59.1	45.3	.	.
7/8/9 Obreros no agrícolas, conductores de máquinas y ...	.	.	6.9	5.8	.	.
X No pueden clasificarse según la ocupación	.	.	0.1	100.0	.	.
Situación en el empleo (CISE-1993)			1983 [1,2] Censo de población			
Total	.	.	77.8	38.3	.	.
1 Asalariados	.	.	16.4	11.0	.	.
2, 3	.	.	29.8	16.8	.	.
5 Trabajadores familiares auxiliares	.	.	30.7	74.3	.	.
6 Inclasificables según la situación	.	.	0.9	.	.	.

2. Población ('000), Tasa de actividad y Tasa de desempleo

	Población			Tasa de actividad			Tasa de desempleo		
Grupo de edad	1983 [2] Censo de población			1983 [2] Censo de población			1983 [1,2] Censo de población		
	Total	Hombres	Mujeres	Total	Hombres	Mujeres	Total	Hombres	Mujeres
Total	261.8	125.7	136.1	39.2	52.5	26.9	24.2	27.4	18.5
15+	154.7	72.2	82.6	64.2	89.1	42.4	.	.	.
15-24	49.2	22.8	26.3	63.0	85.2	43.8	.	.	.
25-54	79.7	36.8	42.8	68.3	96.9	43.7	.	.	.
55+	25.9	12.5	13.4	53.8	73.2	35.6	.	.	.

3. Empleo remunerado ('000), Horas de trabajo (por semana) y Salarios

Datos no disponibles.

4. Lesiones profesionales y Huelgas y cierres patronales

Datos no disponibles.

Guinea Ecuatorial

5. Índices de precios al consumidor (periodo de base: 2000=100)

Malabo	2002	2003	2004	2005	2006	2007
Índices generales	117.0	125.5	130.9	.	144.5	.
Índices de la alimentación incluyendo las bebidas no alcohólicas	122.2	130.0	135.7	.	153.6	.
Índices del vestido, incl. calzado	110.3	122.7	128.4	.	.	.
Índices del aquiler [3]	103.4	104.4	107.3	.	.	.

[1] Persons aged 6 years and over. [2] July. [3] Incl. water, electricity, gas and other fuels.

[1] Personnes âgées de 6 ans et plus. [2] Juillet. [3] Y compris l'eau, l'électricité, le gaz et autres combustibles.

[1] Personas de 6 años y más. [2] Julio. [3] Incl. el agua, la electricidad, el gas y otros combustibles.

Guinée

1. Population active, Emploi et Chômage ('000)

	Population active		Emploi		Chômage	
	Total	Femmes (%)	Total	Femmes (%)	Total	Femmes (%)
Groupe d'âge	1983 [1,2] Recensement de la population				1992 Fichiers des bureaux de placement	
Total	1 823.067	39.4	.	.	2.729	11.5
10-14	156.654	40.1	.	.	.	.
15-19	213.969	44.0	.	.	.	.
20-24	192.036	46.6	.	.	.	.
25-29	240.248	45.7	.	.	.	.
30-34	200.354	43.4	.	.	.	.
35-39	180.019	39.3	.	.	.	.
40-44	156.509	38.6	.	.	.	.
45-49	132.363	33.8	.	.	.	.
50-54	115.351	33.5	.	.	.	.
55-59	78.470	26.8	.	.	.	.
60-64	66.376	29.9	.	.	.	.
65-69	39.460	22.6	.	.	.	.
70-74	21.132	23.6	.	.	.	.
75+	29.002	20.2	.	.	.	.
?	1.124	20.1	.	.	.	.
Activité économique (CITI-Rév.3)	1996 [3] Recensement de la population					
Total	3 278.8	47.9	.	.	.	.
A Agriculture, chasse et sylviculture	2 422.6	52.9	.	.	.	.
B Pêche	10.9	8.2	.	.	.	.
C Activités extractives	35.0	23.9	.	.	.	.
D Activités de fabrication	90.9	6.5	.	.	.	.
E Production et distribution d'électricité, de gaz et d'eau	4.7	6.9	.	.	.	.
F Construction	60.5	1.2	.	.	.	.
G Commerce de gros et de détail; réparation de véhicules ...	367.8	52.0	.	.	.	.
H Hôtels et restaurants	6.0	46.9	.	.	.	.
I Transports, entreposage et communications	77.1	2.2	.	.	.	.
J Intermédiation financière	2.4	26.6	.	.	.	.
K Immobilier, locations et activités de services aux entreprises	1.1	19.2	.	.	.	.
L Administration publique et défense; sécurité sociale obligatoire	63.2	20.2	.	.	.	.
M Education	18.8	20.1	.	.	.	.
N Santé et action sociale	8.3	42.5	.	.	.	.
O Autres activités de services collectifs, sociaux et personnels	93.2	51.8	.	.	.	.
P Ménages privés employant du personnel domestique	11.8	52.8	.	.	.	.
Q Organisations et organismes extraterritoriaux	4.8	22.8	.	.	.	.
Profession (CITP-1968)	1983 [1,2] Recensement de la population					
Total	1 823.0	.	.	.	.	.
0/1 Personnel des professions scientifiques, techniques ...	45.3	.	.	.	.	.
2-3	14.4	.	.	.	.	.
4 Personnel commercial et vendeurs	28.9	.	.	.	.	.
5 Travailleurs spécialisés dans les services	23.7	.	.	.	.	.
6 Agriculteurs, éleveurs, forestiers, pêcheurs et chasseurs	1 508.3	.	.	.	.	.
7/8/9 Ouvriers et manoeuvres non agricoles et conducteurs ...	139.1	.	.	.	.	.
X Ne pouvant être classés selon la profession	32.1	.	.	.	.	.
AF Forces armées	13.0	.	.	.	.	.
Chômeurs n'ayant jamais travaillé	18.2	.	.	.	.	.
Situation dans la profession (CISP-58)	1983 [1,2] Recensement de la population					
Total	1 823.1	.	.	.	.	.
1 Employeurs et personnes travaillant à leur propre compte	659.8	.	.	.	.	.
2 Salariés	284.7	.	.	.	.	.
3 Travailleurs familiaux non rémunérés	684.8	.	.	.	.	.
4 Inclassables d'après la situation	193.9	.	.	.	.	.

2. Population ('000), Taux d'activité et Taux de chômage

	Population			Taux d'activité			Taux de chômage		
Groupe d'âge	1983 [2] Recensement de la population			1983 [2] Recensement de la population					
	Total	Hommes	Femmes	Total	Hommes	Femmes	Total	Hommes	Femmes
Total	4 660.6	2 270.1	2 390.5	39.1	48.7	30.1	.	.	.
15+	2 719.8	1 262.6	1 457.2	61.2	80.0	45.0	.	.	.
15-24	791.3	363.0	428.3	51.3	61.2	42.9	.	.	.
25-54	1 466.8	658.6	808.2	69.9	93.2	50.9	.	.	.
55+	461.6	240.9	220.7	50.8	72.1	27.5	.	.	.

Guinée

3. Emploi rémunéré ('000), Durée du travail (hebdomadaire) et Salaires

Activité économique (CITI-Rév.2)	Emploi rémunéré Total	Hommes	Femmes	Durée du travail Total	Hommes	Femmes	Salaires 1996 Fichiers administratifs et sources connexes Taux de salaire par mois / Salariés / Franc Total	Hommes	Femmes
3	.	.	.	.	.	.	153 000	.	.
4	.	.	.	.	.	.	165 000	.	.
5	.	.	.	.	.	.	175 000	.	.
6	.	.	.	.	.	.	88 000	.	.
7	.	.	.	.	.	.	125 000	.	.
8	.	.	.	.	.	.	245 000	.	.

4. Lésions professionnelles et Grèves et lock-out

Activité économique (CITI-Rév.3)	Taux de lésions mortelles 1996 Fichiers des assurances Pour 100 000 travailleurs assurés Lésions indemnisées Total	Hommes	Femmes	Taux de lésions non mortelles Total	Hommes	Femmes	Grèves et lock-out 1996 [4] Fichiers d'inspection du travail Grèves et lock-out	Travailleurs impliqués [5]	Journées non effectuées
Total	11	.	.	.	.	.	3	1 622	.
A-B	10	.	.	.	.	.	.	.	.
A	.	.	.	.	.	.	0	0	.
B	.	.	.	.	.	.	0	0	.
C	-	.	.	.	.	.	1	962	.
D	140	.	.	.	.	.	1	187	.
E	120	.	.	.	.	.	0	0	.
F	30	.	.	.	.	.	0	0	.
G	0	.	.	.	.	.	0	0	.
H	.	.	.	.	.	.	0	0	.
I	60	.	.	.	.	.	1	473	.
J	.	.	.	.	.	.	0	0	.
K	.	.	.	.	.	.	0	0	.
L	.	.	.	.	.	.	0	0	.
M	.	.	.	.	.	.	0	0	.
N	.	.	.	.	.	.	0	0	.
O	.	.	.	.	.	.	0	0	.

5. Indices des prix à la consommation (période de base: 2000=100)

Conakry	2002	2003	2004	2005	2006	2007
Indices généraux	108.4	122.4	141.1	185.3	249.6	306.6
Indices de l'alimentation, y compris les boissons non alcoolisées	114.4 [6]	138.8	168.3	230.6	328.6	.
Indices de l'habillement, y compris les chaussures [7]	100.0	.	109.8	121.9	.	.
Indices du loyer [7][8]	100.0	.	114.0	142.7	.	.

[1] Persons aged 10 years and over. [2] Feb. [3] Dec. [4] Strikes only. [5] Excl. workers indirectly involved. [6] July-Dec. [7] Index base 2002=100. [8] Incl. water, electricity, gas and other fuels.

[1] Personnes âgées de 10 ans et plus. [2] Fév. [3] Déc. [4] Grèves seulement. [5] Non compris les travailleurs indirectement impliqués. [6] Juillet-déc. [7] Indice base 2002=100. [8] Y compris l'eau, l'électricité, le gaz et autres combustibles.

[1] Personas de 10 años y más. [2] Feb. [3] Dic. [4] Huelgas solamente. [5] Excl. los trabajadores indirectamente implicados. [6] Julio-dic. [7] Indice base 2002=100. [8] Incl. el agua, la electricidad, el gas y otros combustibles.

Guinée-Bissau

1. Population active, Emploi et Chômage ('000)

	Population active		Emploi		Chômage	
	Total	Femmes (%)	Total	Femmes (%)	Total	Femmes (%)
Groupe d'âge	1988 [1][2] Estimations officielles				1983 Estimations officielles	
Total	279.1	3.3	.	.	1.1	9.9
Activité économique (CNTI)					1982 Fichiers des bureaux de placement	
Total	.	.	.	.	0.312	.
4	.	.	.	.	-	.
5	.	.	.	.	0.019	.
6	.	.	.	.	0.009	.
7	.	.	.	.	0.022	.
8	.	.	.	.	-	.
9	.	.	.	.	0.025	.
0	.	.	.	.	0.087	.
					0.150	

2. Population ('000), Taux d'activité et Taux de chômage

	Population			Taux d'activité			Taux de chômage		
Groupe d'âge	1988 [2] Estimations officielles			1988 [2] Estimations officielles					
	Total	Hommes	Femmes	Total	Hommes	Femmes	Total	Hommes	Femmes
Total	930.3	448.6	481.7	30.0	60.1	1.9	.	.	.

3. Emploi rémunéré ('000), Durée du travail (hebdomadaire) et Salaires

Activité économique (CITI-Rév.2)	Emploi rémunéré 1983 Enquête auprès des établissements, relative au travail			Durée du travail			Salaires		
	Total	Hommes	Femmes	Total	Hommes	Femmes	Total	Hommes	Femmes
Total	16 380	11 530	4 850	.	.	.	.	.	.

4. Lésions professionnelles et Grèves et lock-out

Activité économique (CITI-Rév.2)	Taux de lésions mortelles 1991 Fichiers des assurances Pour 100 000 travailleurs exposés au risque Lésions déclarées			Taux de lésions non mortelles			Grèves et lock-out		
	Total	Hommes	Femmes	Total	Hommes	Femmes	Grèves et lock-out	Travailleurs impliqués	Journées non effectuées
Total	0	.	.	.	.	.	.	.	.

5. Indices des prix à la consommation (période de base: 2000=100)

Bissau [3]	2002	2003	2004	2005	2006	2007
Indices généraux	.	100.0	100.9	104.3	106.4	111.2
Indices de l'alimentation, y compris les boissons non alcoolisées [4]	.	100.0	101.1	104.7	105.2	111.3
Indices de l'habillement, y compris les chaussures	.	100.0	98.9	99.0	108.0	112.0
Indices du loyer [5]	.	100.0	101.7	101.9	105.8	111.6

[1] Persons aged 10 years and over. [2] Jan. [3] Index base 2003=100. [4] Incl. alcoholic beverages and tobacco. [5] Incl. water, electricity, gas and other fuels.

[1] Personnes âgées de 10 ans et plus. [2] Janv. [3] Indice base 2003=100. [4] Y compris les boissons alcoolisées et le tabac. [5] Y compris l'eau, l'électricité, le gaz et autres combustibles.

[1] Personas de 10 años y más. [2] Enero. [3] Indice base 2003=100. [4] Incl. las bebidas alcohólicas y el tabaco. [5] Incl. el agua, la electricidad, el gas y otros combustibles.

Guyana

1. Economically active population, Employment and Unemployment ('000)

	Economically active population		Employment		Unemployment	
	Total	Women (%)	Total	Women (%)	Total	Women (%)
Age group	2002 [1] Population census		2002 ★ Population census		2002 [1] Population census	
Total	271.728	30.6	239.610	29.4	32.118	39.3
15-19	23.358	32.6	14.853	27.5	8.505	41.4
20-24	40.758	32.5	33.825	30.3	6.933	43.0
25-29	39.760	30.2	35.472	28.7	4.288	42.8
30-34	38.156	29.4	34.928	28.2	3.228	41.5
35-39	35.259	30.6	32.551	29.9	2.708	39.0
40-44	31.403	31.2	29.205	31.0	2.198	34.0
45-49	23.776	31.3	22.190	31.5	1.586	29.4
50-54	17.657	29.9	16.521	30.1	1.136	27.5
55-59	9.405	27.0	8.789	27.3	0.616	23.2
60-64	5.084	26.7	4.769	26.8	0.315	25.1
65-69	2.481	25.6	2.341	25.6	0.140	26.4
70-74	1.017	24.8	0.966	24.6	0.051	27.5
75+	0.659	21.1	0.610	20.2	0.049	32.7
?	2.956	26.9	2.590	27.7	0.366	21.0

Economic activity (ISIC-Rev.3)			2002 [1] Population census			
Total	.	.	239.6	29.4	.	.
A Agriculture, Hunting and Forestry	.	.	45.6	10.5	.	.
B Fishing	.	.	5.6	4.7	.	.
C Mining and Quarrying	.	.	9.5	7.3	.	.
D Manufacturing	.	.	30.6	23.3	.	.
E Electricity, Gas and Water Supply	.	.	2.3	22.1	.	.
F Construction	.	.	16.2	1.9	.	.
G Wholesale and Retail Trade; Repair of Motor Vehicles ...	.	.	37.9	41.1	.	.
H Hotels and Restaurants	.	.	5.6	64.5	.	.
I Transport, Storage and Communications	.	.	17.0	11.5	.	.
J Financial Intermediation	.	.	3.1	56.2	.	.
K Real Estate, Renting and Business Activities	.	.	7.4	38.3	.	.
L Public Administration and Defence; Compulsory Social ...	.	.	15.1	42.4	.	.
M Education	.	.	13.1	76.2	.	.
N Health and Social Work	.	.	5.6	76.8	.	.
O Other Community, Social and Personal Service Activities	.	.	9.7	32.9	.	.
P Households with Employed Persons	.	.	6.2	78.4	.	.
Q Extra-Territorial Organizations and Bodies	.	.	0.5	54.8	.	.
X Not classifiable by economic activity	.	.	8.7	24.1	.	.

Occupation (ISCO-88)			2002 [1] Population census			
Total	.	.	239.6	29.4	.	.
1 Legislators, senior officials and managers	.	.	6.5	25.4	.	.
2 Professionals	.	.	5.7	51.1	.	.
3 Technicians and associate professionals	.	.	18.2	61.0	.	.
4 Clerks	.	.	16.4	66.8	.	.
5 Service workers and shop and market sales workers	.	.	34.4	43.0	.	.
6 Skilled agricultural and fishery workers	.	.	25.8	13.0	.	.
7 Craft and related trade workers	.	.	37.8	10.1	.	.
8 Plant and machine operators and assemblers	.	.	20.9	4.5	.	.
9 Elementary occupations	.	.	66.0	28.7	.	.
0 Armed forces	.	.	0.8	28.3	.	.

2. Population ('000), Activity rate and Unemployment rate

	Population 2002 Population census			Activity rate 2002 Population census			Unemployment rate 2002 [1] Population census		
Age group	Total	Men	Women	Total	Men	Women	Total	Men	Women
Total	751.2	376.0	375.2	36.2	50.2	22.1	11.8	10.3	15.2
15+	478.7	237.5	241.1	56.2	78.5	34.1	11.8	10.3	15.3
15-24	131.3	65.4	65.9	48.8	66.2	31.6	24.1	20.6	31.2
25-54	282.2	141.2	141.0	65.9	91.7	40.1	8.1	7.2	10.2
55+	65.2	30.9	34.2	28.6	44.4	14.4	6.3	6.4	5.9

3. Paid employment ('000), Hours of work (weekly) and Wages

Economic activity (ISIC-Rev.2)	Paid employment			Hours of work			Wages 1994 Insurance records Earnings per month / Employees / Dollar		
	Total	Men	Women	Total	Men	Women	Total	Men	Women
1	.	.	.	.	.	.	430.06	.	.
4	.	.	.	.	.	.	1 246.94	.	.
6	.	.	.	.	.	.	1 135.45	.	.
8 [2]	.	.	.	.	.	.	845.63	.	.
9 [3]	.	.	.	.	.	.	707.92	.	.

Guyana

4. Occupational injuries and Strikes and Lockouts

Economic activity (ISIC-Rev.2)	Rates of fatal injuries 1999 Labour inspectorate records Per 100,000 employees Reported injuries			Rates of non-fatal injuries 1999 Labour inspectorate records Per 100,000 employees Reported injuries			Strikes and lockouts 2001 Labour relations records		
	Total	Men	Women	Total	Men	Women	Strikes and lockouts	Workers involved	Days not worked
Total	9.98	.	.	2 093	.	.	235	.	60 755
1	.	.	.	.	.	.	232	.	54 890
4	.	.	.	.	.	.	1	.	1 818
9	.	.	.	.	.	.	2	.	2 430

5. Consumer price indices (base period: 2000=100)

Georgetown	2002	2003	2004	2005	2006	2007
General indices	108.2	114.6	120.0	128.3	136.9	153.6
Food index, including non-alcoholic beverages [4]	104.4	108.5	113.3	121.7	130.0	150.3
Clothing indices, including footwear [5]	101.8 [6]	102.6 [6]	102.6	102.6	102.9	117.4
Rent indices [6,7]	111.3	118.9	122.9	140.6	144.5	154.8

[1] Persons aged 15 years and over. [2] Private sector. [3] Public sector. [4] Incl. tobacco. [5] Excl. footwear. [6] Dec. [7] Incl. water, electricity, gas and other fuels.

[1] Personnes âgées de 15 ans et plus. [2] Secteur privé. [3] Secteur public. [4] Y compris le tabac. [5] Non compris la chaussure. [6] Déc. [7] Y compris l'eau, l'électricité, le gaz et autres combustibles.

[1] Personas de 15 años y más. [2] Sector privado. [3] Sector público. [4] Incl. el tabaco. [5] Excl. el calzado. [6] Dic. [7] Incl. el agua, la electricidad, el gas y otros combustibles.

Guyane française

1. Population active, Emploi et Chômage ('000)

	Population active		Emploi		Chômage	
	Total	Femmes (%)	Total	Femmes (%)	Total	Femmes (%)
Groupe d'âge	1999 [1,2] Recensement de la population		1999 ★ Recensement de la population		2007 [1,3] Enquête sur la main-d'oeuvre	
Total	62.634	43.8	43.851	40.5	12.819	54.1
15-19	1.328	47.7	0.377	40.1	.	.
15-24	.	.	.	.	2.346	52.3
20-24	5.947	42.2	3.015	34.1	.	.
25-29	9.476	48.6	6.130	44.0	.	.
25-49	.	.	.	.	9.064	56.3
30-34	10.434	45.9	7.398	42.6	.	.
35-39	10.243	44.5	7.437	40.8	.	.
40-44	8.767	43.9	6.534	41.5	.	.
45-49	7.077	41.5	5.395	39.7	.	.
50+	.	.	.	.	1.409	43.2
50-54	5.071	39.0	4.034	37.6	.	.
55-59	2.860	37.7	2.272	37.8	.	.
60-64	1.067	37.2	0.895	37.8	.	.
65-69	0.214	34.1	0.214	34.1	.	.
70-74	0.072	23.6	.	.	.	.
75+	0.078	41.0	.	.	.	.

Activité économique (CNTI)					1983 [4,5] Fichiers des bureaux de placement	
Total	.	.	.	.	2.412	48.5
1	.	.	.	.	0.084	2.4
2	.	.	.	.	0.001	.
3	.	.	.	.	0.112	21.4
4	.	.	.	.	0.051	3.9
5	.	.	.	.	0.574	0.5
6	.	.	.	.	0.257	82.9
7	.	.	.	.	0.149	0.7
8	.	.	.	.	0.104	27.9
9	.	.	.	.	1.080	82.9
	.	.	.	.	0.497 [6]	57.9

Niveau d'instruction (CITE-97)	1999 [1,2] Recensement de la population					
Total	62.634	43.8	.	.	.	.
1 Enseignement primaire ou premier cycle de l'éducation ...	14.457	41.8	.	.	.	.
2 Premier cycle de l'enseignement secondaire ou deuxième ...	24.992	41.6	.	.	.	.
3 Enseignement secondaire (deuxième cycle)	11.733	48.4	.	.	.	.
5A Premier cycle de l'enseignement supérieur - théorie [7]	11.452	46.5	.	.	.	.

2. Population ('000), Taux d'activité et Taux de chômage

	Population			Taux d'activité			Taux de chômage		
Groupe d'âge	1999 [2] Recensement de la population			1999 [2] Recensement de la population			1999 [1,2] Recensement de la population		
	Total	Hommes	Femmes	Total	Hommes	Femmes	Total	Hommes	Femmes
Total	156.790	78.963	77.827	39.9	44.6	35.3	30.0	25.8	35.3
15+	103.517	51.841	51.676	60.5	67.9	53.1	30.0	25.8	35.3
15-24	25.449	12.982	12.467	28.6	31.8	25.2	53.4	46.4	62.5
25-54	64.328	31.951	32.377	79.4	88.8	70.1	27.7	23.6	32.8
55+	13.740	6.908	6.832	31.2	39.0	23.4	17.7	17.9	17.5

3. Emploi rémunéré ('000), Durée du travail (hebdomadaire) et Salaires

Activité économique (CITI-Rév.3)	Emploi rémunéré 2007 Estimations officielles			Durée du travail			Salaires 2001 Enquête auprès des établissements, relative au travail Gains par heure / Salariés / Euro		
	Total	Hommes	Femmes	Total	Hommes	Femmes	Total	Hommes	Femmes
Total	46.997	.	.	.	.	.	11.81	12.51	.
A-B	.	.	.	.	.	.	10.13 [8]	9.82 [8]	.
E	.	.	.	.	.	.	16.07	16.75	.
F	.	.	.	.	.	.	9.96	10.05	.
50	.	.	.	.	.	.	9.43	9.62	.
51	.	.	.	.	.	.	10.20	10.83	.
52	.	.	.	.	.	.	7.72	8.33	.
H	.	.	.	.	.	.	7.15	7.43	.
I	.	.	.	.	.	.	12.57 [9]	13.00 [9]	.
64	.	.	.	.	.	.	13.18	14.54	.
J	.	.	.	.	.	.	15.15	18.55	.
K	.	.	.	.	.	.	12.11	13.62	.
73	.	.	.	.	.	.	22.61	26.30	.
L	.	.	.	.	.	.	12.98	15.08	.
M	.	.	.	.	.	.	10.38	11.08	.
N	.	.	.	.	.	.	13.77	16.03	.
O	.	.	.	.	.	.	9.67	9.99	.
92	.	.	.	.	.	.	12.76	13.91	.
P	.	.	.	.	.	.	5.86	6.39	.

Guyane française

4. Lésions professionnelles et Grèves et lock-out

Activité économique (CITI-Rév.2)	Taux de lésions mortelles			Taux de lésions non mortelles			Grèves et lock-out 1991 Source inconnue		
	Total	Hommes	Femmes	Total	Hommes	Femmes	Grèves et lock-out	Travailleurs impliqués	Journées non effectuées
Total	.	.	.	.	.	.	19	1 511	13 576
1	.	.	.	.	.	.	2	183	4 790
2	.	.	.	.	.	.	0	0	0
3	.	.	.	.	.	.	0	0	0
4	.	.	.	.	.	.	0	0	0
5	.	.	.	.	.	.	8	732	6 455
6	.	.	.	.	.	.	4	242	1 243
7	.	.	.	.	.	.	2	128	624
8	.	.	.	.	.	.	0	0	0
9	.	.	.	.	.	.	0	0	0
0	.	.	.	.	.	.	3	126	464

5. Indices des prix à la consommation (période de base: 2000=100)

	2002	2003	2004	2005	2006	2007
Indices généraux	103.1	105.2	106.4	108.2	110.4	114.2
Indices de l'alimentation, y compris les boissons non alcoolisées	105.3	109.3	109.8	110.5	111.4	113.6
Indices de l'électricité, gaz et autres combustibles	99.6	100.2	102.1	110.2	115.6	121.6
Indices de l'habillement, y compris les chaussures	95.7	93.3	90.2	89.4	85.8	81.0
Indices du loyer	102.3	103.7	104.9	107.0	111.5	120.3

[1] Persons aged 15 years and over. [2] March. [3] June. [4] Cayenne and Kourou. [5] Persons aged 16 years and over. [6] Persons seeking their first job are distributed among major divisions of economic activity. [7] Levels 5-6. [8] Excl. hunting. [9] Excl. storage and communications.

[1] Personnes âgées de 15 ans et plus. [2] Mars. [3] Juin. [4] Cayenne et Kourou. [5] Personnes âgées de 16 ans et plus. [6] Personnes en quête d'un premier emploi réparties dans les différentes branches d'activité économique. [7] Niveaux 5-6. [8] Non compris la chasse. [9] N.c. l'entreposage et les communications.

[1] Personas de 15 años y más. [2] Marzo. [3] Junio. [4] Cayena y Kourou. [5] Personas de 16 años y más. [6] Personas en busca de su primer empleo distribuidas en las grandes divisiones de actividad económica. [7] Niveles 5-6. [8] Excl. la caza. [9] Excl. el almacenamiento y las comunicaciones.

Haïti

1. Population active, Emploi et Chômage ('000)

	Population active Total	Population active Femmes (%)	Emploi Total	Emploi Femmes (%)	Chômage Total	Chômage Femmes (%)
Groupe d'âge		1990 [1 2] Estimations officielles				1990 [1 2] Estimations officielles
Total	2 679.14	40.0	.	.	339.68	43.7
10-14	182.86	45.6	.	.	36.23	39.6
15-19	274.42	44.1	.	.	67.78	44.1
20-24	390.60	41.5	.	.	88.88	43.9
25-29	380.51	39.4	.	.	55.00	40.9
30-34	311.68	39.5	.	.	32.50	45.5
35-39	222.29	28.3	.	.	14.80	36.4
40-44	217.92	40.9	.	.	13.75	53.1
45-49	186.27	41.9	.	.	9.79	55.7
50-54	152.08	41.9	.	.	7.13	49.2
55-59	124.81	39.6	.	.	4.46	54.4
60-64	90.66	37.9	.	.	3.93	38.4
65-69	66.62	38.7	.	.	2.25	31.0
70-74	42.38	35.5	.	.	1.33	48.6
75+	36.06	39.0	.	.	1.91	47.8
Activité économique (CITI-Rév.2)				1990 [1 2] Estimations officielles		
Total	.	.	2 339.46	39.5		
1 Agriculture, chasse, sylviculture et pêche	.	.	1 535.44	29.8		
2 Industries extractives	.	.	24.01	50.2		
3 Industries manufacturières	.	.	151.39	45.1		
4 Electricité, gaz et eau	.	.	2.58	36.0		
5 Bâtiment et travaux publics	.	.	28.00	15.8		
6 Commerce de gros et de détail; restaurants et hôtels	.	.	352.97	76.9		
7 Transports, entrepôts et communications	.	.	20.69	13.7		
8 Banques, assurances, affaires immobilières et services ...	.	.	5.06	31.4		
9 Services fournis à la collectivité, services sociaux ...	.	.	155.35	47.3		
0 Activités mal désignées	.	.	63.97	47.3		
Profession (CITP-1968)				1990 [1 2] Estimations officielles		
Total	.	.	2 339.46	45.8		
0/1 Personnel des professions scientifiques, techniques ...	.	.	54.07	39.3		
2 Directeurs et cadres administratifs supérieurs	.	.	14.31	32.6		
3 Personnel administratif et travailleurs assimilés	.	.	9.89	59.4		
4 Personnel commercial et vendeurs	.	.	244.81	89.4		
5 Travailleurs spécialisés dans les services	.	.	58.31	65.2		
6 Agriculteurs, éleveurs, forestiers, pêcheurs et chasseurs	.	.	1 336.58	24.8		
7/8/9 Ouvriers et manoeuvres non agricoles et conducteurs ...	.	.	179.86	30.7		
X Ne pouvant être classés selon la profession	.	.	441.64	56.2		
Situation dans la profession (CISP-1993)				1990 [1 2] Estimations officielles		
Total	.	.	2 339.46	39.5		
1 Salariés	.	.	442.50	44.2		
2, 3	.	.	1 582.89	38.4		
5 Travailleurs familiaux collaborant à l'entreprise familiale	.	.	278.10	37.3		
6 Inclassables d'après la situation	.	.	35.97	46.4		

2. Population ('000), Taux d'activité et Taux de chômage

Groupe d'âge	Population 1990 [2] Estimations officielles Total	Hommes	Femmes	Taux d'activité 1990 [2] Estimations officielles Total	Hommes	Femmes	Taux de chômage 1990 [1 2] Estimations officielles Total	Hommes	Femmes
Total	6 512.0	3 195.9	3 316.1	41.1	50.3	32.3	12.7	11.9	13.8
15+	3 894.9	1 877.0	2 017.9	64.1	80.3	49.0	12.2	11.2	13.6
15-24	1 291.4	645.2	646.1	51.5	59.2	43.8	23.6	23.0	24.4
25-54	2 028.2	965.4	1 062.7	72.5	93.7	53.3	9.0	8.2	10.4
55+	575.3	266.3	309.0	62.7	83.3	44.9	3.9	3.5	4.5

3. Emploi rémunéré ('000), Durée du travail (hebdomadaire) et Salaires

Activité économique (CITI-Rév.2)	Emploi rémunéré 1988 [1] Estimations officielles Total	Hommes	Femmes	Durée du travail Total	Hommes	Femmes	Salaires Total	Hommes	Femmes
2	85.160	47.810	3.735	.	.	.	.	.	.
3	59.329	337.360	25.593	.	.	.	.	.	.
5	14.411	124.130	1.998	.	.	.	.	.	.
7	10.133	87.920	1.341	.	.	.	.	.	.

Haïti

4. Lésions professionnelles et Grèves et lock-out

Activité économique (CITI-Rév.2)	Taux de lésions mortelles 1985 [3]			Taux de lésions non mortelles			Grèves et lock-out 1988 Source inconnue		
	Total	Hommes	Femmes	Total	Hommes	Femmes	Grèves et lock-out	Travailleurs impliqués	Journées non effectuées
	Pour 1 000 années de 300 journées de travail								
Total	.	.	.	.	.	.	1 564	2 126	409 564
1	0.000	.	.	.	.	.	26	26	232
2	0.000	.	.	.	.	.	0	1	27
3	0.050	.	.	.	.	.	800	1 186	369 689
4	0.010	.	.	.	.	.	12	13	340
5	0.070	.	.	.	.	.	70	103	19 059
6	0.000	.	.	.	.	.	125	145	4 922
7	0.010	.	.	.	.	.	8	10	505
8	0.000	.	.	.	.	.	4	4	104
9	0.000	.	.	.	.	.	255	276	5 547
0	.	.	.	.	.	.	264	362	9 139

5. Indices des prix à la consommation (période de base: 2000=100)

[4]	2002	2003	2004	2005	2006	2007
Indices généraux	125.3	174.5	214.3	255.4	286.9	311.3
Indices de l'alimentation, y compris les boissons non alcoolisées [5]	127.4	174.2	223.2	263.2	300.1	324.5
Indices de l'habillement, y compris les chaussures	123.4	155.1	179.4	203.4	225.9	250.0
Indices du loyer [6]	121.9	170.1	198.8	226.3	272.7	309.6

[1] Persons aged 10 years and over. [2] July. [3] Year ending in Sep. of the year indicated. [4] Metropolitan areas. [5] Incl. alcoholic beverages and tobacco. [6] Incl. water, electricity, gas and other fuels.

[1] Personnes âgées de 10 ans et plus. [2] Juillet. [3] Année se terminant en sept. de l'année indiquée. [4] Régions métropolitaines. [5] Y compris les boissons alcoolisées et le tabac. [6] Y compris l'eau, l'électricité, le gaz et autres combustibles.

[1] Personas de 10 años y más. [2] Julio. [3] Año que termina en sept. del año indicado. [4] Areas metropolitanas. [5] Incl. las bebidas alcohólicas y el tabaco. [6] Incl. el agua, la electricidad, el gas y otros combustibles.

Honduras

1. Población económicamente activa, Empleo y Desempleo ('000)

	Población económicamente activa		Empleo		Desempleo	
	Total	Mujeres (%)	Total	Mujeres (%)	Total	Mujeres (%)
Grupo de edad	2005 [1,2,3]		2005 ★		2005 [2,3]	
	Encuesta de la fuerza de trabajo		Encuesta de la fuerza de trabajo		Encuesta de la fuerza de trabajo	
Total	2 651.3	32.4	2 543.5	31.7	107.8	48.8
10-14	109.6	19.8	107.7	19.5	1.8	34.8
15-19	272.3	23.4	.	.	.	.
15-24	.	.	.	.	53.2	48.1
20-24	484.6	33.9	.	.	.	.
25-29	343.9	35.2	323.9	33.7	20.1	59.4
30-34	285.1	38.2	.	.	.	.
30-44	.	.	.	.	23.9	52.6
35-39	252.9	39.6	.	.	.	.
40-44	233.2	36.2	.	.	.	.
45-49	192.9	35.2	.	.	.	.
45-59	.	.	.	.	7.1	26.1
50-54	164.9	30.8	.	.	.	.
55-59	111.2	27.5	.	.	.	.
60+	200.7	23.3	199.1	23.5	1.6	0.0
Actividad económica (CIIU-Rev.2)	2005 [1,2,3]		2005 [1,2,3]		2005 [2,3]	
	Encuesta de la fuerza de trabajo		Encuesta de la fuerza de trabajo		Encuesta de la fuerza de trabajo	
Total	2 651.3	32.4	2 543.5	31.7	107.8	48.8
1 Agricultura, caza, silvicultura y pesca	1 005.4	10.8	997.3	10.6	8.1	29.4
2 Explotación de minas y canteras	6.9	6.8	6.2	7.5	0.7	.
3 Industrias manufactureras	397.1	49.0	378.1	48.6	19.0	57.0
4 Electricidad, gas y agua	11.8	13.8	11.0	14.8	0.8	.
5 Construcción	147.1	1.8	135.5	1.5	11.6	5.2
6 Comercio al por mayor y al por menor y restaurantes y ...	522.3	50.2	503.8	50.0	18.5	55.7
7 Transportes, almacenamiento y comunicaciones	90.4	12.4	87.4	12.2	3.0	17.3
8 Establecimientos financieros, seguros, bienes inmuebles ...	83.8	34.3	81.7	34.1	2.1	40.9
9 Servicios comunales, sociales y personales	352.0	65.9	337.8	65.6	14.2	73.9
0 Actividades no bien especificadas	4.7	21.5	4.7	21.2	-	.
Desempleados sin empleo anterior	29.6	56.1	.	.	29.6	56.1
Ocupación (CIUO-1968)	2005 [1,2,3]		2005 [1,2,3]		2005 [2,3]	
	Encuesta de la fuerza de trabajo		Encuesta de la fuerza de trabajo		Encuesta de la fuerza de trabajo	
Total	2 651.3	32.4	2 543.5	31.7	107.8	48.8
0/1 Profesionales, técnicos y trabajadores asimilados	171.3	51.8	171.3	51.8	.	.
2 Directores y funcionarios públicos superiores	71.5	40.7	68.8	40.5	2.7	45.4
3 Personal administrativo y trabajadores asimilados	92.9	55.7	86.3	56.0	6.6	51.0
4 Comerciantes y vendedores	353.5	56.7	342.5	56.5	11.0	63.1
5 Trabajadores de los servicios	274.5	66.9	261.9	66.3	12.6	79.5
6 Trabajadores agrícolas y forestales, pescadores y cazadores	989.2	10.1	983.1	10.1	6.1	18.1
7/8/9 Obreros no agrícolas, conductores de máquinas y ...	662.3	28.2	627.3	27.9	35.0	33.3
X No pueden clasificarse según la ocupación	6.3	38.1	2.3	28.3	3.9	42.0
Desempleados sin empleo anterior	29.6	56.1	.	.	29.6	56.1
Nivel de educación (CINE-76)					1998 [2]	
					Encuesta de la fuerza de trabajo	
Total	.	.	.	.	87.67	36.7
0 Enseñanza anterior al primer grado	.	.	.	.	7.44	23.8
1 Enseñanza de primer grado	.	.	.	.	48.65	29.7
2 Enseñanza de segundo grado, ciclo inferior	.	.	.	.	6.71	38.2
3 Enseñanza de segundo grado, ciclo superior	.	.	.	.	19.60	49.2
5 Enseñanza de tercer grado que no permite obtener un ...	.	.	.	.	0.21	52.4
6 Enseñanza de tercer grado que permite obtener un primer ...	.	.	.	.	4.88	54.5
9 Enseñanza que no puede definirse por grados	.	.	.	.	0.17	.
Situación en el empleo (CISE-1993)			2005 [1,2,3]			
			Encuesta de la fuerza de trabajo			
Total	.	.	2 543.5	31.7	.	.
1 Asalariados	.	.	1 269.5	33.4	.	.
2, 3	.	.	996.1	31.7	.	.
5 Trabajadores familiares auxiliares	.	.	277.5	24.0	.	.

2. Población ('000), Tasa de actividad y Tasa de desempleo

	Población 2006			Tasa de actividad 2006			Tasa de desempleo 2005 [2,3]		
Grupo de edad	Encuesta de la fuerza de trabajo			Encuesta de la fuerza de trabajo			Encuesta de la fuerza de trabajo		
	Total	Hombres	Mujeres	Total	Hombres	Mujeres	Total	Hombres	Mujeres
Total	7 416.0	3 594.4	3 821.6	37.9	51.1	25.5	4.1	3.1	6.1
15+	4 495.6	2 118.9	2 376.7	60.0	82.6	39.9	4.2	3.2	6.2
15-24	1 570.3	754.8	815.5	49.4	69.1	31.1	7.0	5.2	11.2
25-54	2 180.2	1 004.8	1 175.5	71.4	95.8	50.5	.	.	.
55+	745.0	359.3	385.7	49.3	73.7	26.5	.	.	.

Honduras

3. Empleo remunerado ('000), Horas de trabajo (por semana) y Salarios

Actividad económica (CIIU-Rev.2)	Empleo remunerado 2005 [1,2,3] Encuesta de la fuerza de trabajo			Horas de trabajo			Salarios		
	Total	Hombres	Mujeres	Total	Hombres	Mujeres	Total	Hombres	Mujeres
Total	1 266.1	842.3	423.8	.	.	.	.	.	.
1	319.7	289.1	30.7	.	.	.	.	.	.
2	4.8	4.3	0.5	.	.	.	.	.	.
3	242.5	149.4	93.1	.	.	.	.	.	.
4	10.2	8.8	1.4	.	.	.	.	.	.
5	89.8	88.1	1.7	.	.	.	.	.	.
6	197.3	124.3	73.0	.	.	.	.	.	.
7	48.5	40.1	8.4	.	.	.	.	.	.
8	64.2	39.3	24.9	.	.	.	.	.	.
9	289.0	98.9	190.1	.	.	.	.	.	.

Actividad económica (CIIU-Rev.3)	Empleo remunerado			Horas de trabajo			Salarios 2006 [4] Encuesta de la fuerza de trabajo Tasas de salarios por día / Asalariados / Lempira		
	Total	Hombres	Mujeres	Total	Hombres	Mujeres	Total	Hombres	Mujeres
Total	.	.	.	.	.	.	16.79	.	.
C	.	.	.	.	.	.	9.05	.	.
D	.	.	.	.	.	.	21.74	.	.
E	.	.	.	.	.	.	19.39	.	.
F	.	.	.	.	.	.	19.89	.	.
G	.	.	.	.	.	.	24.27	.	.
H	.	.	.	.	.	.	24.27	.	.
I	.	.	.	.	.	.	24.35	.	.
J	.	.	.	.	.	.	23.39	.	.
K	.	.	.	.	.	.	23.39	.	.
L	.	.	.	.	.	.	19.54	.	.
M	.	.	.	.	.	.	19.54	.	.
N	.	.	.	.	.	.	19.54	.	.

4. Lesiones profesionales y Huelgas y cierres patronales

Actividad económica (CIIU-Rev.2)	Tasas de lesiones mortales 1998 [5] Registros de inspección del trabajo Por 100 000 trabajadores empleados Lesiones declaradas			Tasas de lesiones no mortales			Huelgas y cierres patronales 2000 Recolección especial de datos		
	Total	Hombres	Mujeres	Total	Hombres	Mujeres	Huelgas y cierres patronales	Trabajadores implicados	Días no trabajados
Total	114	.	.	.	.	.	63	.	.
1	4	.	.	.	.	.	5	.	.
2	.	.	.	.	.	.	1	.	.
3	720	.	.	.	.	.	4	.	.
4	.	.	.	.	.	.	1	.	.
5	4 620	.	.	.	.	.	0	.	.
6	1 820	.	.	.	.	.	0	.	.
7	.	.	.	.	.	.	9	.	.
8	.	.	.	.	.	.	0	.	.
9	1 530	.	.	.	.	.	42	.	.
0	.	.	.	.	.	.	1	.	.

5. Índices de precios al consumidor (periodo de base: 2000=100)

	2002	2003	2004	2005	2006	2007
Índices generales	118.0	127.1	137.5	149.5	157.9	168.9
Índices de la alimentación incluyendo las bebidas no alcohólicas	112.8	117.0	124.9	137.5	143.7	159.2
Índices de la electricidad, gas y otros combustibles [6]	124.8	140.8	154.8	167.3	178.3	188.8
Índices del vestido, incl. calzado	119.7	128.6	137.0	144.6	153.6	163.7
Índices del aquiler [7]	131.6	142.7	154.3	170.6	179.2	

[1] Excl. armed forces. [2] Persons aged 10 years and over. [3] March. [4] Private sector. [5] Private sector; establishments with 10 or more persons employed. [6] Incl. dwelling. [7] Dec.

[1] Non compris les forces armées. [2] Personnes âgées de 10 ans et plus. [3] Mars. [4] Secteur privé. [5] Secteur privé; établissements employant 10 personnes ou plus. [6] Y compris le logement. [7] Déc.

[1] Excl. las fuerzas armadas. [2] Personas de 10 años y más. [3] Marzo. [4] Sector privado. [5] Sector privado; establecimientos con 10 y más trabajadores. [6] Incl. el alojamiento. [7] Dic.

Hong Kong, China

1. Economically active population, Employment and Unemployment ('000)

Age group	Economically active population Total	Women (%)	Employment Total	Women (%)	Unemployment Total	Women (%)
	2007 [1,2] Labour force survey		2007 ★ Labour force survey		2007 [1,2] Labour force survey	
Total	3 640.5	46.1	3 494.9	46.3	145.6	38.9
15-19	62.6	46.6	50.2	47.2	12.4	44.4
20-24	323.1	54.1	300.9	55.1	22.2	41.4
25-29	462.7	54.0	448.2	54.6	14.5	37.2
30-34	476.8	52.2	461.6	52.4	15.2	44.7
35-39	480.3	51.0	468.0	51.2	12.3	42.3
40-44	530.6	46.8	513.6	47.0	17.0	41.8
45-49	522.8	41.7	503.6	41.8	19.2	40.1
50-54	396.4	37.8	378.7	38.0	17.7	33.3
55-59	252.9	33.1	241.1	33.2	11.8	30.5
60-64	88.6	23.6	85.8	23.9	2.8	14.3
65-69	27.3	18.3	27.3	18.3	-	.
70-74	12.1	18.2	12.1	18.2	-	.
75+	4.3	18.6	4.3	18.6	-	.

Economic activity (ISIC-Rev.2)

2007 [1,2] Labour force survey

	Total	Women (%)	Total	Women (%)	Total	Women (%)
Total	3 640.5	46.1	3 495.0	46.3	145.6	38.9
1 Agriculture, Hunting, Forestry and Fishing	6.8	38.2	6.4	37.5	-	.
2 Mining and Quarrying	.	.	.	.	-	.
3 Manufacturing	213.8	35.6	204.1	35.4	9.7	38.1
4 Electricity, Gas and Water	15.5	16.8	15.4	16.9	-	.
5 Construction	302.7	7.0	277.6	7.3	25.1	3.6
6 Wholesale and Retail Trade and Restaurants and Hotels	1 196.4	50.9	1 147.3	50.9	49.1	50.9
7 Transport, Storage and Communication	386.3	22.7	373.4	22.9	12.9	17.8
8 Financing, Insurance, Real Estate and Business Services	561.2	41.7	547.5	41.8	13.7	38.0
9 Community, Social and Personal Services	940.6	67.4	923.2	67.6	17.5	57.1
Unemployed seeking their first job	17.1	55.0	.	.	17.1	55.0

Occupation (ISCO-88)

2007 ★ / 2007 [1,2] Labour force survey

	Total	Women (%)	Total	Women (%)	Total	Women (%)
Total	3 640.6	46.0	3 495.0	46.3	145.6	38.9
1 Legislators, senior officials and managers	355.1	29.6	350.8	29.6	4.3	30.2
2 Professionals	242.2	36.4	238.8	36.6	3.4	26.5
3 Technicians and associate professionals	686.0	43.3	670.2	43.5	15.8	36.1
4 Clerks	565.5	72.6	547.5	72.9	18.0	64.4
5 Service workers and shop and market sales workers	565.4	52.8	537.4	52.7	28.0	55.0
6 Skilled agricultural and fishery workers	5.3	32.1	5.3	32.1	-	.
7 Craft and related trade workers	285.1	3.8	265.6	3.9	19.5	2.6
8 Plant and machine operators and assemblers	225.8	9.8	218.7	9.5	7.1	21.1
9 Elementary occupations	692.8	62.4	660.7	63.9	32.1	32.4
Unemployed seeking their first job	.	.	.	.	17.1	55.0

Education level (ISCED-97)

2007 [1,2] / 2007 ★ Labour force survey

	Total	Women (%)	Total	Women (%)	Total	Women (%)
Total	3 640.5	46.1	3 494.9	46.3	145.6	38.9
X No schooling	30.6	57.8	28.9	58.8	1.7	41.2
1 Primary education or first stage of basic education	444.1	46.1	419.3	46.9	24.8	33.9
2 Lower secondary or second stage of basic education	614.3	37.8	579.7	38.1	34.6	33.8
3 Upper secondary education	1 422.5	48.3	1 368.1	48.5	54.4	41.7
4 Post-secondary non-tertiary education	195.4	50.9	189.5	51.1	5.9	42.4
5A First stage of tertiary education - theoretically based	181.6	49.3	166.2	50.0	15.4	42.2
5B First stage of tertiary education - practically oriented	591.6	47.9	585.6	47.9	6.0	48.3
6 Second stage of tertiary education	160.3	39.2	157.6	39.0	2.7	48.1

Status in employment (ICSE-1993)

2007 [1,2] Labour force survey

	Total	Women (%)
Total	3 495.0	46.3
1 Employees	3 101.1	49.1
2 Employers	144.6	19.4
3 Own-account workers	229.5	22.7
5 Contributing family workers	19.8	89.4

2. Population ('000), Activity rate and Unemployment rate

Age group	Population 2007 [1] Total	Men	Women	Activity rate 2007 [1] Total	Men	Women	Unemployment rate 2007 [1,2] Total	Men	Women
Total	6 848.6	3 255.1	3 593.5	53.2	60.3	46.7	4.0	4.5	3.4
15+	5 930.1	2 781.3	3 148.7	61.4	70.6	53.2	.	.	.
15-24	898.6	442.4	456.2	42.9	41.1	44.7	9.0	11.0	7.2
25-54	3 504.5	1 591.9	1 912.8	81.9	94.8	71.1	3.3	3.8	2.8
55+	1 527.0	747.0	779.7	25.2	36.5	14.4	.	.	.

Hong Kong, China

3. Paid employment ('000), Hours of work (weekly) and Wages

Economic activity (ISIC-Rev.2)	Paid employment 2007 Labour-related establishment survey			Hours of work 2007 [1 2] Labour force survey Hours actually worked / Employees			Wages 2007 Labour-related establishment survey Wage rates per day / Wage earners / Dollar		
	Total	Men	Women	Total	Men	Women	Total	Men	Women
Total	2 586.07	1 338.39	1 247.68	46.6	47.2	46.0	.	.	.
2-9	.	.	.	46.6	47.2	46.0	440.8 [3]	491.7 [3]	283.0 [3]
1	.	.	.	43.5	44.0	42.9	.	.	.
2	0.11	0.11	-	.	.	.	.	.	.
3	157.00	90.21	66.79	45.8	47.8	42.4	342.8	436.4	259.6
4	7.91 [4]	6.70 [4]	1.21 [4]	42.5	43.0	40.4	.	.	.
5	50.19 [5]	46.58 [5]	3.60 [5]	43.1	43.1	42.7	.	.	.
6	1 055.57 [6]	517.50 [6]	538.07 [6]	47.2	49.3	45.3	.	.	.
7	189.43 [7]	119.40 [7]	70.03 [7]	46.7	48.5	41.8	511.2 [8]	510.9 [8]	.
8	505.44 [9]	285.87 [9]	219.57 [9]	46.5	48.5	43.8	447.4	447.4	.
9	466.63 [10]	170.28 [10]	296.35 [10]	47.3	44.6	48.5	548.0 [11]	548.0 [11]	.
0	153.80 [12]	101.74 [12]	52.06 [12]	.	.	.	.	.	.

4. Occupational injuries and Strikes and Lockouts

Economic activity (ISIC-Rev.2)	Rates of fatal injuries 2006 Labour inspectorate records Per 100,000 employees Reported injuries			Rates of non-fatal injuries 2006 [13] Labour inspectorate records Per 100,000 employees Reported injuries			Strikes and lockouts		
	Total	Men	Women	Total	Men	Women	Strikes and lockouts	Workers involved	Days not worked
Total	7.3	.	.	1 833	.	.	.	.	.
1	0.0	.	.	.	.	.	.	.	.
2	.	.	.	0	.	.	.	.	.
3	13.1	.	.	2 621	.	.	.	.	.
4	0.0 [4]	.	.	627	.	.	.	.	.
5	37.8 [14]	.	.	6 581	.	.	.	.	.
6	2.5	.	.	1 410	.	.	.	.	.
7	15.7	.	.	2 948	.	.	.	.	.
8	11.5	.	.	1 222	.	.	.	.	.
9	5.7 [15]	.	.	2 056	.	.	.	.	.

Economic activity (ISIC-Rev.3)	Rates of fatal injuries			Rates of non-fatal injuries			Strikes and lockouts 2007 [16] Labour relations records		
	Total	Men	Women	Total	Men	Women	Strikes and lockouts [16]	Workers involved [17]	Days not worked
Total [18]	.	.	.	.	.	.	3	849	8 027
A	.	.	.	.	.	.	0	0	0
B	.	.	.	.	.	.	0	0	0
C	.	.	.	.	.	.	0	0	0
D	.	.	.	.	.	.	0	0	0
E	.	.	.	.	.	.	0	0	0
F	.	.	.	.	.	.	1	800	8 010
G	.	.	.	.	.	.	0	0	0
H	.	.	.	.	.	.	0	0	0
I	.	.	.	.	.	.	2	49	17
J	.	.	.	.	.	.	0	0	0
K	.	.	.	.	.	.	0	0	0
M	.	.	.	.	.	.	0	0	0
N	.	.	.	.	.	.	0	0	0
O	.	.	.	.	.	.	0	0	0

5. Consumer price indices (base period: 2000=100)

	2002	2003	2004	2005	2006	2007
General indices	95.4	93.0	92.6	93.6	95.5	97.4
Food index, including non-alcoholic beverages	97.1	95.7	96.7	98.4	100.1	104.4
Electricity, gas and other fuel indices [19]	91.3	92.5	103.1	107.3	109.6	108.8
Clothing indices, including footwear	96.1	93.6	99.6	101.5	102.5	106.8
Rent indices	91.4	87.0	82.5	82.5	86.4	88.1
General index, excluding housing	97.1	95.5	96.8	98.0	98.8	100.9

Hong Kong, China

[1] Excl. marine, military and institutional populations. [2] Persons aged 15 years and over. [3] Excl. major divisions 2, 5 and 6. [4] Excl. water. [5] Manual workers at construction sites only. [6] Hawkers and retail pitches are excluded. [7] Taxis, public light buses, goods vehicles, barges, lighters and stevedoring services are excluded [8] Excl. storage and communication. [9] Excl. self-employed insurance with no business registration. [10] Public admin., religious org., indep. artists, domestic helpers, miscellaneous recreational and personal services are excluded. [11] Excl. community and social services. [12] Civil servants. Incl. water. [13] Incapacity of 4 days or more. [14] Manual workers. [15] Incl. water. [16] Incl. stoppages involving fewer than 10 workers or lasting less than one day. [17] Excl. workers indirectly involved. [18] Excl. government sector. [19] Incl. water and sewerage.

[1] Non compris le personnel militaire, de la marine et la population institutionnelle. [2] Personnes âgées de 15 ans et plus. [3] Non compris les branches 2, 5 et 6. [4] Non compris l'eau. [5] Seulement travailleurs manuels sur les chantiers. [6] Les colporteurs et vendeurs au détail sont exclus. [7] Les taxis, les autobus publiques, les véhicules de marchandises, les chalends, les allumeurs et les services d'arrimage sont exclus. [8] Non compris les entrepôts et communications. [9] Non compris les travailleurs indépendants des assurances qui ne sont pas inscrits au registre du commerce. [10] L'admin. publique, les org. religieux, les artistes indép., les aides ménagères, les centres de loisirs et pers. divers sont exclus. [11] Non compris les services fournis à la collectivité et services sociaux. [12] Fonctionnaires. Y compris l'eau. [13] Incapacité de 4 jours et plus. [14] Travailleurs manuels. [15] Y compris l'eau. [16] Y compris les arrêts impliquant moins de 10 travailleurs ou de moins d'un jour. [17] Non compris les travailleurs indirectement impliqués. [18] Non compris le secteur gouvernemental. [19] Y compris l'eau et le traitement des eaux résiduaires.

[1] Excl. el personal militar y de la marina, y la población institucional. [2] Personas de 15 años y más. [3] Excl. las grandes divisiones 2, 5 y 6. [4] Excl. el agua. [5] Unicamente trabajadores manuales de la construcción. [6] Excluyen a los vendedores ambulantes y los vendedores al detalle. [7] Los taxis, autobuses públicos pequeños, bienes vehículos, barcazas, y servicios de trasbordo son excluidos. [8] Excl. almacenaje y comunicaciones. [9] Excl. los trabajadores independientes de los seguros que no estan registrados en el registro del comercio. [10] La admin. pública, org. religiosas, artistas ind. ayudantes domésticos, y servicios mixtos vacacionales son excluidos. [11] Excl. los servicios comunales y sociales. [12] Funcionarios. Incl. el agua. [13] Incapacidad de 4 días y más. [14] Trabajadores manuales. [15] Incl. el agua. [16] Incl. las interrupciones con menos de 10 trabajadores o de menos de un día. [17] Excl. los trabajadores indirectamente implicados. [18] Excl. el sector gubernamental. [19] Incl. el agua y el tratamiento de aguas residuales.

Hungary

1. Economically active population, Employment and Unemployment ('000)

	Economically active population		Employment		Unemployment	
	Total	Women (%)	Total	Women (%)	Total	Women (%)
Age group	2007 [1][2] Labour force survey		2007 ★ Labour force survey		2007 [2] Labour force survey	
Total	4 238.1	45.6	3 926.2	45.4	311.9	47.4
15-19	27.4	34.7	17.6	35.2	9.8	33.7
20-24	291.8	43.1	244.0	42.6	47.8	45.6
25-29	597.2	42.1	546.9	42.0	50.3	42.5
30-34	638.5	41.7	592.5	41.1	46.0	49.3
35-39	619.2	44.4	578.4	43.8	40.8	52.5
40-44	499.3	47.9	465.7	47.5	33.6	53.9
45-49	516.2	51.6	485.0	51.6	31.2	50.6
50-54	598.4	50.4	564.0	50.7	34.4	46.5
55-59	346.8	44.5	330.2	44.7	16.6	41.0
60-64	73.9	40.9	72.7	41.0	1.2	33.3
65-69	24.9	41.0	24.7	41.3	0.2	0.0
70-74	4.5	33.3	4.5	33.3	0.0	.

Economic activity (ISIC-Rev.3)	2007 [1][2] Labour force survey		2007 [1][2] Labour force survey		2007 [2] Labour force survey	
Total	4 238.1	45.6	3 926.2	45.4	311.9	47.4
A-B	193.2	23.2	182.9	23.0	10.3	27.2
C Mining and Quarrying	15.1	13.2	14.6	13.0	0.5	20.0
D Manufacturing	935.2	39.7	872.0	38.8	63.2	50.9
E Electricity, Gas and Water Supply	67.2	25.4	64.2	25.2	3.0	30.0
F Construction	355.7	6.9	330.5	7.0	25.2	5.6
G Wholesale and Retail Trade; Repair of Motor Vehicles ...	626.2	53.4	591.5	53.2	34.7	57.6
H Hotels and Restaurants	170.1	57.8	156.1	56.6	14.0	70.7
I Transport, Storage and Communications	311.4	25.8	301.7	25.8	9.7	27.8
J Financial Intermediation	86.4	67.6	83.8	67.9	2.6	57.7
K Real Estate, Renting and Business Activities	295.2	46.1	282.9	45.9	12.3	50.4
L Public Administration and Defence; Compulsory Social ...	318.4	49.4	285.3	51.3	33.1	33.5
M Education	325.2	77.0	316.3	77.1	8.9	73.0
N Health and Social Work	269.9	78.1	260.4	78.1	9.5	77.9
O Other Community, Social and Personal Service Activities	192.0	54.2	180.3	54.2	11.8	52.5
P Households with Employed Persons	2.7	77.8	2.5	80.0	0.1	100.0
Q Extra-Territorial Organizations and Bodies	1.2	25.0	1.2	25.0	0.0	.
X Not classifiable by economic activity	26.1	57.7	-	.	26.1	57.9
Unemployed seeking their first job	46.9	50.4	.	.	46.9	50.3

Occupation (ISCO-88)	2007 [1][2] Labour force survey		2007 [1][2] Labour force survey		2007 [2] Labour force survey	
Total	4 238.1	45.6	3 926.2	45.4	311.9	47.4
1 Legislators, senior officials and managers	288.6	35.4	283.1	35.2	5.5	43.6
2 Professionals	539.2	56.3	530.2	56.2	9.0	61.1
3 Technicians and associate professionals	586.6	64.4	566.6	64.3	20.0	67.0
4 Clerks	268.8	91.9	256.1	92.1	12.7	87.4
5 Service workers and shop and market sales workers	681.4	56.9	639.0	56.5	42.4	63.4
6 Skilled agricultural and fishery workers	111.0	26.8	102.4	27.0	8.6	25.6
7 Craft and related trade workers	804.3	14.4	755.2	13.9	49.1	23.0
8 Plant and machine operators and assemblers	510.2	27.7	475.4	26.9	34.8	39.7
9 Elementary occupations	338.0	53.4	282.1	56.1	55.9	39.9
0 Armed forces	37.0	16.2	36.1	16.3	0.9	11.1
X Not classifiable by occupation	26.1	57.7	-	.	26.1	57.9
Unemployed seeking their first job	46.9	50.4	.	.	46.9	50.3

Education level (ISCED-97)	2007 [1][2] Labour force survey		2007 ★ Labour force survey		2007 [2] Labour force survey	
Total	4 238.1	45.6	3 926.2	45.4	311.9	47.4
1 Primary education or first stage of basic education	20.1	34.3	10.8	27.8	9.3	41.9
2 Lower secondary or second stage of basic education	578.3	48.5	484.3	49.3	94.0	44.8
3 Upper secondary education	2 670.6	42.6	2 494.8	42.3	175.8	46.6
4 Post-secondary non-tertiary education	94.4	44.9	87.0	43.8	7.4	58.1
5A First stage of tertiary education - theoretically based	834.7	53.0	811.5	52.8	23.2	61.2
5B First stage of tertiary education - practically oriented	24.6	66.3	22.4	67.0	2.2	59.1
6 Second stage of tertiary education	15.4	30.5	15.4	30.5	0.0	.

Status in employment (ICSE-1993)	2007 [1][2] Labour force survey		2007 [1][2] Labour force survey		2007 ★ Labour force survey	
Total	4 238.1	45.6	3 926.2	45.4	311.9	47.4
1 Employees	3 667.8	47.0	3 439.7	47.1	228.1	45.8
2 Employers	209.0	27.7	205.5	27.6	3.5	28.6
3 Own-account workers	265.5	36.2	258.9	36.0	6.6	43.9
4 Members of producers' cooperatives	4.5	31.1	4.4	31.8	0.1	.
5 Contributing family workers	18.3	69.9	17.7	68.9	0.6	100.0
6 Not classifiable by status	73.0	53.0	-	.	73.0	53.0

2. Population ('000), Activity rate and Unemployment rate

	Population			Activity rate			Unemployment rate		
Age group	2007 [1][3] Labour force survey			2007 [1][3] Labour force survey			2007 [2] Labour force survey		
	Total	Men	Women	Total	Men	Women	Total	Men	Women
Total	.	.	.	.	.	.	7.4	7.1	7.6
15+	7 719.4	3 693.2	4 026.2	54.9	62.5	48.0	7.4	7.1	7.6
15-24	1 246.2	626.9	619.3	25.6	29.3	21.8	18.0	17.7	18.6
25-54	4 335.4	2 151.0	2 184.4	80.0	86.9	73.2	6.8	6.5	7.2

Hungary

3. Paid employment ('000), Hours of work (weekly) and Wages

Economic activity (ISIC-Rev.3)	Paid employment 2007 [4] Labour-related establishment survey			Hours of work 2007 [5,6,7] Labour-related establishment survey Hours actually worked / Wage earners			Wages 2007 [5,8] Labour-related establishment survey Earnings per month / Employees / Forint		
	Total	Men	Women	Total	Men	Women	Total	Men	Women
Total	2 760.0	.	.	.	.	.	185 004	.	.
C-Q	.	.	.	.	.	.	187 115	.	.
A	88.8	.	.	.	.	.	122 298	.	.
B	1.1	.	.	.	.	.	104 756	.	.
C	4.7	.	.	147.7	.	.	200 921	.	.
D	692.3	.	.	148.2	.	.	172 942	.	.
E	48.4	.	.	145.9	.	.	250 432	.	.
F	129.5	.	.	.	.	.	135 937	.	.
G	355.0	.	.	.	.	.	157 963	.	.
H	86.3	.	.	.	.	.	112 039	.	.
I	214.6	.	.	.	.	.	194 127	.	.
J	67.0	.	.	.	.	.	390 350	.	.
K	234.7	.	.	.	.	.	191 712	.	.
L	267.8	.	.	.	.	.	253 509	.	.
M	273.3	.	.	.	.	.	193 196	.	.
N	209.9	.	.	.	.	.	159 787	.	.
O	86.7	.	.	.	.	.	181 062	.	.

4. Occupational injuries and Strikes and Lockouts

Economic activity (ISIC-Rev.3)	Rates of fatal injuries 2007 Labour inspectorate records Per 100,000 employees Reported injuries			Rates of non-fatal injuries 2007 [9] Labour inspectorate records Per 100,000 employees Reported injuries			Strikes and lockouts 2007 [10] Special data collection		
	Total	Men	Women	Total	Men	Women	Strikes and lockouts	Workers involved	Days not worked [11]
Total	3.01	5.41	0.11	530	673	358	23	64 612	28 324
A-B	7.65	9.94	0.00	488	534	335	.	.	.
A	.	.	.	.	.	.	0	0	0
B	.	.	.	.	.	.	0	0	0
C	0.00	0.00	0.00	62	63	53	0	0	0
D	2.06	3.19	0.30	1 012	1 256	627	4	1 281	675
E	3.12	4.17	0.00	402	452	253	2	4 817	1 202
F	13.62	14.64	0.00	379	399	116	1	723	181
G	0.68	1.44	0.00	442	542	354	1	35	31
H	0.64	1.48	0.00	304	287	318	0	0	0
I	5.97	7.59	1.29	795	821	722	8	17 406	5 357
J	1.19	3.72	0.00	126	100	139	0	0	0
K	2.49	4.58	0.00	294	371	205	1	229	57
L	1.40	2.88	0.00	183	153	211	0	0	0
M	0.00	0.00	0.00	257	309	241	2	31 200	18 600
N	0.77	3.51	0.00	454	811	353	2	8 801	2 200
O	1.09	2.38	0.00	340	580	138	2	120	21
Q	0.00	0.00	0.00	0	0	0	.	.	.

5. Consumer price indices (base period: 2000=100)

	2002	2003	2004	2005	2006	2007
General indices	115.0	120.3	128.5	133.1	138.3	149.3
Food index, including non-alcoholic beverages	119.9	123.2	131.2	134.5	144.8	161.5
Electricity, gas and other fuel indices	116.4	124.8	142.4	151.3	160.9	200.6
Clothing indices, including footwear	109.5	112.8	116.6	116.9	116.1	117.2
Rent indices	131.2	141.0	154.8	161.6	168.4	181.2
General index, excluding housing [12]	114.9	120.2	128.4	133.0	138.1	157.3

[1] Excl. conscripts. [2] Persons aged 15 to 74 years. [3] "De facto" population. [4] Establishments with 5 or more persons employed. [5] Enterprises with 5 or more employees. [6] Per month. [7] Full-time workers. [8] Full-time employees. [9] Incapacity of 4 workdays or more. [10] Excl. work stoppages involving fewer than 10 workers. [11] Computed on the basis of an eight-hour working day. [12] Excl. rental value of owner occupied dwellings.

[1] Non compris les conscrits. [2] Personnes âgées de 15 à 74 ans. [3] Population "de facto". [4] Etablissements occupant 5 personnes et plus. [5] Entreprises occupant 5 salariés et plus. [6] Par mois. [7] Travailleurs à plein temps. [8] Salariés à plein temps. [9] Incapacité de 4 journées de travail et plus. [10] Non compris les arrêts du travail impliquant moins de 10 travailleurs. [11] Calculées sur la base de journées de travail de huit heures. [12] Non compris la valeur locative des logements occupés par leurs propriétaires.

[1] Excl. los conscriptos. [2] Personas de 15 a 74 años. [3] Población "de facto". [4] Establecimientos con 5 y más trabajadores. [5] Empresas con 5 y más asalariados. [6] Por mes. [7] Trabajadores a tiempo completo. [8] Asalariados a tiempo completo. [9] Incapacidad de 4 días de trabajo y más. [10] Excl. las interrupciones del trabajo que implican menos de 10 trabajadores. [11] Calculados en base a días de trabajo de ocho horas. [12] Excl. el valor locativo de la vivienda ocupada por su propietario.

Iceland

1. Economically active population, Employment and Unemployment ('000)

	Economically active population		Employment		Unemployment	
	Total	Women (%)	Total	Women (%)	Total	Women (%)
Age group	2007 [1,2] Labour force survey		2007 ★ Labour force survey		2007 [2,3] Labour force survey	
Total	181.5	45.5	177.3	45.5	4.2	45.2
16-19	14.3	50.3	12.8	51.6	1.5	40.0
20-24	17.0	46.0	16.2	45.8	0.8	50.0
25-29	19.6	44.1	19.3	44.2	0.3	33.3
30-34	19.1	43.7	18.8	43.8	0.3	33.3
35-39	19.4	44.7	19.1	44.3	0.3	66.7
40-44	20.9	46.8	20.7	46.2	0.2	100.0
45-49	20.4	45.7	20.2	45.6	0.2	50.0
50-54	18.4	44.4	18.1	44.6	0.3	33.3
55-59	15.4	47.0	15.3	47.3	0.1	0.0
60-64	10.8	44.6	10.7	44.1	0.1	100.0
65-69	4.8	47.1	4.7	48.1	0.1	0.0
70-74	1.3	26.9	1.3	26.9	-	

Economic activity (ISIC-Rev.3)	2002 [1,2,3] Labour force survey		2007 [1,2] Labour force survey		2002 [2,3] Labour force survey	
Total	159.8	47.4	177.3	45.5	5.3	41.5
A Agriculture, Hunting and Forestry	6.1	36.1	6.0	30.0	0.1	.
B Fishing	5.4	9.3	.	.	0.3	.
C Mining and Quarrying	0.3	33.3	0.1	.	-	.
D Manufacturing	22.6	31.9	19.0	30.0	0.9	11.1
E Electricity, Gas and Water Supply	1.5	33.3	1.7	23.5	-	.
F Construction	12.3	4.9	15.7	3.8	0.2	.
G Wholesale and Retail Trade; Repair of Motor Vehicles ...	21.6	47.7	25.4	43.7	0.9	33.3
H Hotels and Restaurants	5.6	51.8	6.2	59.7	0.3	66.7
I Transport, Storage and Communications	9.7	37.1	11.2	33.9	0.3	33.3
J Financial Intermediation	6.1	65.6	8.7	58.6	0.1	100.0
K Real Estate, Renting and Business Activities	13.4	42.5	17.2	33.7	0.4	50.0
L Public Administration and Defence; Compulsory Social ...	7.8	46.2	8.9	49.4	0.2	50.0
M Education	12.7	70.9	13.5	65.9	-	.
N Health and Social Work	21.8	84.4	26.0	85.0	0.2	100.0
O Other Community, Social and Personal Service Activities	10.2	52.9	12.1	54.5	0.3	33.3
P Households with Employed Persons	0.0	.	-	.	-	.
Q Extra-Territorial Organizations and Bodies	0.8	37.5	0.5	60.0	-	.
X Not classifiable by economic activity	1.6	62.5	0.3	33.3	0.4	50.0
Unemployed seeking their first job	0.7	71.4	.	.	0.7	57.1

Occupation (ISCO-88)	2002 [1,2,3] Labour force survey		2007 [1,2] Labour force survey		2002 [2,3] Labour force survey	
Total	162.0	46.9	176.9	45.5	5.3	41.5
1 Legislators, senior officials and managers	12.8	28.9	16.1	29.8	0.1	.
2 Professionals	25.3	54.5	31.1	51.1	0.2	50.0
3 Technicians and associate professionals	22.1	56.1	27.8	60.4	0.3	33.3
4 Clerks	12.9	86.0	12.5	84.0	0.3	33.3
5 Service workers and shop and market sales workers	32.0	65.0	36.8	62.0	1.2	66.7
6 Skilled agricultural and fishery workers	9.2	20.7	7.2	18.1	0.2	.
7 Craft and related trade workers	22.8	13.6	21.4	10.3	0.3	.
8 Plant and machine operators and assemblers	10.3	10.7	10.1	5.9	0.5	.
9 Elementary occupations	12.6	54.8	13.9	41.0	0.3	33.3
X Not classifiable by occupation	1.4	35.7	.	.	1.2	33.3
Unemployed seeking their first job	0.7	57.1	.	.	0.7	57.1

Education level (ISCED-97)	2002 [2,4,5] Labour force survey		2002 ★ Labour force survey		2002 [2,3] Labour force survey	
Total	162.0	46.9	156.7	47.1	5.3	41.5
1 Primary education or first stage of basic education	2.7	70.4	2.6	69.2	0.1	100.0
2 Lower secondary or second stage of basic education	60.5	53.6	57.4	54.2	3.1	41.9
3 Upper secondary education	46.9	45.8	45.7	45.7	1.2	50.0
5A First stage of tertiary education - theoretically based	26.9	48.0	26.6	47.7	0.3	66.7
5B First stage of tertiary education - practically oriented	23.3	27.9	22.8	28.1	0.5	20.0
6 Second stage of tertiary education	1.4	28.6	1.4	28.6	-	.
? Level not stated	0.2	50.0	0.2	50.0	-	.

Status in employment (ICSE-1993)			2007 [1,2] Labour force survey			
Total	.	.	177.3	45.5	.	.
1 Employees	.	.	152.5	48.7	.	.
2 Employers	.	.	8.6	25.6	.	.
3 Own-account workers	.	.	15.4	24.7	.	.
5 Contributing family workers	.	.	0.1	.	.	.
6 Not classifiable by status	.	.	0.6	66.7	.	.

2. Population ('000), Activity rate and Unemployment rate

	Population 2007 [1] Labour force survey			Activity rate 2007 [1] Labour force survey			Unemployment rate 2007 [2,3] Labour force survey		
Age group	Total	Men	Women	Total	Men	Women	Total	Men	Women
Total	.	.	.	.	.	.	2.3	2.3	2.3
15+	218.0	112.9	105.1	83.2	87.5	78.6			
15-24	39.1	20.4	18.7	80.1	80.0	80.1	7.4	8.0	6.7
25-54	130.1	68.1	62.0	90.6	95.3	85.4	1.4	1.2	1.5

Iceland

3. Paid employment ('000), Hours of work (weekly) and Wages

Economic activity (ISIC-Rev.3)	Paid employment 2007[2] Labour force survey			Hours of work 2007 Labour force survey Hours actually worked / Employees			Wages 2007[6,7] Labour-related establishment survey Earnings per month / Employees / Krona		
	Total	Men	Women	Total	Men	Women	Total	Men	Women
Total	152.7	78.3	74.4	39.6	44.7	33.9	.	.	.
C-Q	.	.	.	.	.	.	447 000 [8]	496 000 [8]	343 000 [8]
A	2.0	1.3	0.7	.	.	.	.	.	.
B	3.8	3.6	0.2	.	.	.	.	.	.
C	0.1	0.1	-	61.3	61.3	.	.	.	.
D	17.4	12.0	5.4	42.2	45.1	35.3	390 000	426 000	303 000
E	1.7	1.3	0.4	42.1	44.2	35.9	.	.	.
F	10.8	10.4	0.4	47.1	47.8	26.2	457 000	461 000	.
G	22.7	12.6	10.1	38.9	43.8	32.6	377 000	411 000	285 000
H	5.6	2.2	3.5	36.6	39.6	34.6	.	.	.
I	9.6	5.9	3.7	41.6	45.8	34.4	402 000	465 000	305 000
J	8.4	3.3	5.1	40.1	44.0	37.6	704 000	1 145 000	435 000
K	13.4	8.5	4.9	40.3	43.5	34.2	.	.	.
L	8.8	4.5	4.4	42.4	46.9	37.8	.	.	.
M	13.3	4.4	8.9	34.7	36.1	34.0	.	.	.
N	24.6	3.5	21.1	33.8	38.8	33.0	.	.	.
O	9.7	4.4	5.3	35.7	41.5	30.7	.	.	.
P	-	-	-	.	.	.	.	.	.
Q	0.5	0.3	0.3	34.2	39.6	28.5	.	.	.
X	0.2	0.2	0.1	42.1	44.0	37.8	.	.	.

Share of women in wage employment in the non-agricultural sector [2] (2007 - Labour force survey): **50.0%**

4. Occupational injuries and Strikes and Lockouts

Economic activity (ISIC-Rev.3)	Rates of fatal injuries			Rates of non-fatal injuries			Strikes and lockouts 2004 Special data collection		
	Total	Men	Women	Total	Men	Women	Strikes and lockouts	Workers involved	Days not worked
Total	.	.	.	.	.	.	1	4 256	140 448

5. Consumer price indices (base period: 2000=100)

[9]	2002	2003	2004	2005	2006	2007
General indices	111.8	114.2	117.8	122.6	130.9	137.5
Food index, including non-alcoholic beverages	111.1	108.4	109.7	106.7	115.7	113.8
Electricity, gas and other fuel indices	104.8	109.1	114.3	120.2	119.2	121.2
Clothing indices, including footwear	100.2	98.6	98.4	97.3	97.3	98.6
Rent indices [10]	111.8	122.0	131.9	153.6	173.8	196.1
General index, excluding housing	111.7	112.5	114.9	116.0	121.6	124.6

[1] Excl. armed forces and conscripts. [2] Persons aged 16 to 74 years. [3] April and Nov. of each year. [4] April and Nov. [5] Excl. armed forces. [6] Methodology revised. [7] Full-time adult employees; excl. overtime payments and payments in kind. [8] Manufacturing, construction, trade and transport. [9] Annual averages are based on the months Feb.-Dec. and of January of the following year. [10] Housing.

[1] Non compris les forces armées et les conscrits. [2] Personnes âgées de 16 à 74 ans. [3] Avril et nov. de chaque année. [4] Avril et novembre. [5] Non compris les forces armées. [6] Méthodologie révisée. [7] Salariés adultes à plein temps; n.c. la rémunération des heures supplémentaires et la valeur des paiments en nature. [8] Industries manufacturières, construction, commerce et transport. [9] Les moyennes annuelles sont basées sur les mois de fév.-déc. et de janvier de l'année suivante. [10] Logement.

[1] Excl. las fuerzas armadas y los conscriptos. [2] Personas de 16 a 74 años. [3] Abril y nov. de cada año. [4] Abril y nov. [5] Excl. las fuerzas armadas. [6] Metodología revisada. [7] Asalariados adultos a tiempo completo; excl. los pagos por horas extraordinarias y el valor de los pagos en especie. [8] Industrías manufactureras, construcción, comercio y transporte. [9] Le media anual esta basada sobre Feb.-Dic. y de enero del año siguiente. [10] Vivienda.

India

1. Economically active population, Employment and Unemployment ('000)

	Economically active population		Employment		Unemployment	
	Total	Women (%)	Total	Women (%)	Total	Women (%)
Age group	2001 [1] Population census		2000 Labour force survey		2006 [2,3] Employment office records	
Total	402 234.7	31.6	368 966.1 [4]	28.9	41 466.0	28.4
0-19					9 097.0	29.9
5-9	1 849.7	45.8				
10-14	10 816.7	46.4				
15-19	32 389.6	35.2				
20-24	48 211.4	32.1				
20-29					19 955.0	27.4
25-29	54 170.7	32.0				
30-34	52 313.3	32.2				
30-39					10 114.0	28.3
35-39	51 349.9	32.0				
40-49	76 021.7	30.1			2 003.0	31.4
50-59	43 374.2	29.1			275.0	33.5
60+					22.0	31.8
60-69	22 461.4	28.4				
70-79	6 714.6	20.8				
80+	1 710.2	20.7				
?	851.4	31.9				

Occupation (ISCO-1968)					2006 [2,3] Employment office records	
Total					41 466	28.4
0/1 Professional, technical and related workers					3 594	39.7
2 Administrative and managerial workers					33	48.5
3 Clerical and related workers					2 685	30.3
4 Sales workers					96	11.5
5 Service workers					472	30.7
6 Agriculture, animal husbandry and forestry workers ...					103	29.1
7/8/9 Production and related workers, transport equipment ...					4 443	15.5
X Not classifiable by occupation [5]					30 040	28.8

Education level (ISCED-76)					2005 [2,3] Employment office records	
Total					39 348	27.0
X-2					11 402	26.9
3 Second level, second stage					14 833	26.0
5 Third level, first stage, leading to an award not equivalent ...					7 727	25.6
6 Third level, first stage, leading to a first university degree ...					4 422	30.0
7 Third level, second stage					964	39.0

2. Population ('000), Activity rate and Unemployment rate

	Population			Activity rate			Unemployment rate		
Age group	2001 [1] Population census			2001 [1] Population census			2000 Labour force survey		
	Total	Men	Women	Total	Men	Women	Total	Men	Women
Total	1 028 610.3	532 156.8	496 453.6	39.1	51.7	25.6	4.3	4.3	4.3
15+	662 261.0	341 168.9	321 092.2	58.7	78.4	37.7	.	.	.
15-24	189 980.0	100 261.1	89 718.9	42.4	53.6	29.9	.	.	.

3. Paid employment ('000), Hours of work (weekly) and Wages

Economic activity (ISIC-Rev.2)	Paid employment			Hours of work			Wages		
	2005 [1,6,7] Labour-related establishment survey			2007 [3] Labour-related establishment survey Hours actually worked / Employees			2005 [8] Labour-related establishment survey Earnings per month / Wage earners / Rupee		
	Total	Men	Women	Total	Men	Women	Total	Men	Women
Total	26 458	21 442	5 016						
1	1 479	995	484						
2	1 093	1 015	77						
3	5 619	4 780	939	47.2			1 234.4		
4	910	857	53						
5	960	893	67						
6	559	510	50						
7	2 837	2 645	192						
8	1 931	1 628	302						
9	11 072	8 220	2 852						

India

4. Occupational injuries and Strikes and Lockouts

Economic activity (ISIC-Rev.3)	Rates of fatal injuries 2007 Labour inspectorate records Per 100,000 employees			Rates of non-fatal injuries 2007 Labour inspectorate records Per 100,000 employees			Strikes and lockouts 2007 [9][10] Special data collection		
	Total	Men	Women	Total	Men	Women	Strikes and lockouts	Workers involved	Days not worked
Total	.	.	.	.	.	.	367	648 659	19 192 871
A	.	.	.	.	.	.	17	12 662	865 043
B	.	.	.	.	.	.	0	0	0
C	27	.	.	166	.	.	8	11 434	69 803
D	.	.	.	.	.	.	213	340 480	17 809 077
E	.	.	.	.	.	.	6	46 783	67 697
F	.	.	.	.	.	.	1	.	.
G	.	.	.	.	.	.	1	50	2 050
H	.	.	.	.	.	.	7	316	16 771
I	.	.	.	.	.	.	31	118 872	142 315
J	.	.	.	.	.	.	57	116 873	119 620
K	.	.	.	.	.	.	0	0	0
L	.	.	.	.	.	.	0	0	0
M	.	.	.	.	.	.	0	0	0
N	.	.	.	.	.	.	1	170	1 020
O	.	.	.	.	.	.	24	985	96 075
P	.	.	.	.	.	.	1	34	3 400

5. Consumer price indices (base period: 2000=100)

Agricultural workers	2002	2003	2004	2005	2006	2007
General indices [11]	102.6	106.8	109.8	113.4	121.2	130.9
Food index, including non-alcoholic beverages	100.3	104.9	107.8	111.1	119.2	130.3
Electricity, gas and other fuel indices	113.1	117.0	120.1	123.3	130.7	139.9
Clothing indices, including footwear	108.1	111.4	115.6	118.5	121.8	124.7

Industrial workers	2002	2003	2004	2005	2006	2007
General indices	108.2	112.5	116.6	121.5	127.7	136.0
Food index, including non-alcoholic beverages	104.9	108.4	111.5	115.0	124.7	137.0
Electricity, gas and other fuel indices	120.5	128.3	138.6	136.1	139.8	144.1
Clothing indices, including footwear	104.7	106.6	108.9	111.4	114.4	118.5
Rent indices	120.4	126.5	136.4	157.9	136.5	142.0
General index, excluding housing	107.0	110.9	114.5	118.0	125.9	135.2

Urban non-manual employees	2002	2003	2004	2005	2006	2007
General indices	109.8	113.7	118.0	123.2	130.6	139.1
Food index, including non-alcoholic beverages [12]	105.3	107.7	111.2	114.9	123.4	134.0
Electricity, gas and other fuel indices	125.1	131.0	137.2	146.4	151.4	161.5
Clothing indices, including footwear	105.8	108.8	111.3	113.5	117.0	121.4
Rent indices	117.9	125.0	131.8	141.5	149.4	157.1

Delhi, Industrial workers	2002	2003	2004	2005	2006	2007
General indices	107.0	110.9	116.3	126.1	125.6	131.7
Food index, including non-alcoholic beverages	102.6	107.8	112.3	114.5	118.4	130.5
Electricity, gas and other fuel indices	129.6	129.6	139.9	158.0	171.5	171.5
Clothing indices, including footwear	100.5	100.0	102.1	106.3	109.1	111.1
Rent indices	107.1	110.5	122.6	164.4	124.7	126.8
General index, excluding housing	106.9	110.9	115.0	118.0	125.5	134.7

[1] March. [2] Persons aged 14 years and over. [3] Dec. [4] Jan. [5] Incl. persons seeking their first job. [6] Public sector and establishments of non-agricultural private sector with 10 or more persons employed. [7] Incl. working proprietors. [8] Fluctuations due to various changes in workers' coverage. [9] Excl. political and sympathetic strikes. [10] Excl. work stoppages involving fewer than 10 workers. [11] Excl. "Rent". [12] Incl. tobacco.

[1] Mars. [2] Personnes âgées de 14 ans et plus. [3] Déc. [4] Janv. [5] Y compris les personnes en quête de leur premier emploi. [6] Secteur public et établissements du secteur privé non agricole occupant 10 personnes et plus. [7] Y compris les propriétaires-exploitants. [8] Fluctuations dues aux divers changements de couverture des travailleurs. [9] Non compris les grèves politiques et les grèves de solidarité. [10] Non compris les arrêts du travail impliquant moins de 10 travailleurs. [11] Non compris le groupe "Loyer". [12] Y compris le tabac.

[1] Marzo. [2] Personas de 14 años y más. [3] Dic. [4] Enero. [5] Incl. las personas en busca de su primer empleo. [6] Sector público y establecimientos del sector no agrícola con 10 y más trabajadores. [7] Incl. los empresarios propietarios. [8] Fluctuaciones debidas a varios cambios de lacobertura de los trabajadores. [9] Excl. huelgas políticas y huelgas de solidaridad. [10] Excl. las interrupciones del trabajo que implican menos de 10 trabajadores. [11] Excl. el grupo "Alquiler". [12] Incl. el tabaco.

Indonesia

1. Economically active population, Employment and Unemployment ('000)

	Economically active population		Employment		Unemployment	
	Total	Women (%)	Total	Women (%)	Total	Women (%)
Age group	2007 [1] Labour force survey		2007 ★ Labour force survey		2007 [1,2] Labour force survey	
Total	109 941.4	37.5	99 930.2	36.8	10 011.1	44.3
15-19	8 072.5	39.2	5 649.2	37.6	2 423.3	42.9
20-24	14 440.1	38.5	11 203.3	37.6	3 236.8	41.5
25-29	14 651.3	38.3	12 830.7	37.0	1 820.6	47.8
30-34	14 080.5	37.1	13 035.2	35.9	1 045.4	51.9
35-39	13 586.1	37.8	12 929.2	37.1	656.9	51.3
40-44	12 434.9	38.0	12 146.0	37.8	288.9	43.9
45-49	10 573.9	37.6	10 393.1	37.7	180.8	35.0
50-54	8 089.9	36.2	7 962.5	36.3	127.4	31.0
55-59	5 635.3	35.2	5 522.3	35.2	113.0	37.9
60-64	3 694.0	36.2	3 638.1	36.2	55.9	37.1
65-69	2 432.3	35.3	2 375.6	35.7	56.7	21.7
70-74	1 368.7	32.8	1 365.4	32.8	3.3	35.8
75+	881.9	30.2	879.7	30.1	2.3	66.3

Economic activity (ISIC-Rev.3)			2007 [1,2] Labour force survey			
Total	.	.	99 930	36.8	.	.
A Agriculture, Hunting and Forestry	.	.	39 371	38.3	.	.
B Fishing	.	.	1 836	7.8	.	.
C Mining and Quarrying	.	.	995	12.1	.	.
D Manufacturing	.	.	12 369	42.4	.	.
E Electricity, Gas and Water Supply	.	.	175	12.1	.	.
F Construction	.	.	5 253	2.5	.	.
G Wholesale and Retail Trade; Repair of Motor Vehicles ...	.	.	16 531	48.5	.	.
H Hotels and Restaurants	.	.	4 023	53.7	.	.
I Transport, Storage and Communications	.	.	5 959	6.2	.	.
J Financial Intermediation	.	.	740	36.2	.	.
K Real Estate, Renting and Business Activities	.	.	660	20.7	.	.
L Public Administration and Defence; Compulsory Social ...	.	.	2 679	20.2	.	.
M Education	.	.	3 460	53.2	.	.
N Health and Social Work	.	.	683	60.1	.	.
O Other Community, Social and Personal Service Activities	.	.	3 246	25.9	.	.
P Households with Employed Persons	.	.	1 885	75.6	.	.
Q Extra-Territorial Organizations and Bodies	.	.	4	38.6	.	.
X Not classifiable by economic activity	.	.	63	29.7	.	.

Occupation (ISCO-1968)			2007 [1,2] Labour force survey		1989 [3] Employment office records	
Total	.	.	99 930.2	36.8	1 518.5	34.7
0/1 Professional, technical and related workers	.	.	4 720.7	47.7	185.6	42.8
2 Administrative and managerial workers	.	.	518.6	13.8	29.8	41.5
3 Clerical and related workers	.	.	4 027.8	38.4	718.1	36.7
4 Sales workers	.	.	18 114.0	50.7	88.8	42.1
5 Service workers	.	.	5 527.6	43.4	96.9	41.2
6 Agriculture, animal husbandry and forestry workers ...	.	.	40 689.3	37.1	67.4	34.7
7/8/9 Production and related workers, transport equipment ...	.	.	25 840.2	24.0	331.9	21.2
X Not classifiable by occupation	.	.	492.0 [4]	4.7	.	.

Education level (ISCED-76)	2007 [1,2] Labour force survey		2007 ★ Labour force survey		2007 [1,2] Labour force survey	
Total	109 941.4	37.5	99 930.2	36.8	10 011.1	44.3
X No schooling	5 489.0	55.3	5 394.7	55.3	94.3	55.2
0 Education preceding the first level	13 451.6	42.1	13 013.1	42.1	438.5	44.2
1 First level	40 140.9	36.9	37 961.2	36.6	2 179.8	43.7
2 Second level, first stage	21 094.4	34.0	18 830.2	32.9	2 264.2	42.9
3 Second level, second stage	22 606.2	32.3	18 535.7	30.1	4 070.6	42.1
5 Third level, first stage, leading to an award not equivalent ...	1 488.8	55.8	1 312.8	54.2	176.0	67.7
6 Third level, first stage, leading to a first university degree ...	1 506.0	46.6	1 284.8	44.6	221.2	58.3
7 Third level, second stage	4 164.4	40.4	3 597.8	38.2	566.6	54.6

Status in employment (ICSE-1993)			2007 [1,2] Labour force survey			
Total	.	.	99 930	36.8	.	.
1 Employees	.	.	33 960	33.2	.	.
2 Employers	.	.	2 884	17.6	.	.
3 Own-account workers	.	.	45 808	27.6	.	.
5 Contributing family workers	.	.	17 279	71.5	.	.

2. Population ('000), Activity rate and Unemployment rate

	Population 2006 [5] Labour force survey			Activity rate 2006 [5] Labour force survey			Unemployment rate 2007 [1] Labour force survey		
Age group	Total	Men	Women	Total	Men	Women	Total	Men	Women
Total	219 204.6	109 801.7	109 402.9	48.5	61.6	35.3	9.1	8.1	10.8
15+	157 223.2	78 277.2	78 946.0	67.6	86.5	48.9	9.1	8.1	10.8
15-24	42 106.2	21 251.6	20 854.6	53.3	62.7	43.8	25.1	23.8	27.3
25-54	91 615.7	45 619.3	45 996.4	77.1	100.0	54.4	5.6	4.7	7.2
55+	23 501.3	11 406.3	12 095.0	56.3	76.6	37.1	1.7	1.7	1.6

Indonesia

3. Paid employment ('000), Hours of work (weekly) and Wages

Economic activity (ISIC-Rev.2)	Paid employment 2002 [1 6] Labour force survey			Hours of work			Wages 2001 [7 8 9] Labour-related establishment survey Wage rates per week / Wage earners / Rupiah		
	Total	Men	Women	Total	Men	Women	Total	Men	Women
2-9	26 280.8	18 471.8	7 809.0	.	.	.	.	.	.
2	.	.	.	.	.	.	282.8	.	.
3	.	.	.	.	.	.	129.2	.	.
6	.	.	.	.	.	.	126.7 [10]	.	.

Economic activity (ISIC-Rev.3)	Paid employment			Hours of work 2007 [1 2] Labour force survey Hours actually worked / Total employment			Wages		
	Total	Men	Women	Total	Men	Women	Total	Men	Women
Total	.	.	.	40.0	42.0	37.0	.	.	.
A	.	.	.	31.0	34.0	27.0	.	.	.
B	.	.	.	43.0	45.0	29.0	.	.	.
C	.	.	.	44.0	45.0	35.0	.	.	.
D	.	.	.	43.0	46.0	40.0	.	.	.
E	.	.	.	43.0	43.0	37.0	.	.	.
F	.	.	.	46.0	46.0	43.0	.	.	.
G	.	.	.	49.0	49.0	48.0	.	.	.
H	.	.	.	50.0	52.0	48.0	.	.	.
I	.	.	.	49.0	49.0	43.0	.	.	.
J	.	.	.	43.0	45.0	41.0	.	.	.
K	.	.	.	44.0	45.0	40.0	.	.	.
L	.	.	.	41.0	42.0	39.0	.	.	.
M	.	.	.	34.0	36.0	32.0	.	.	.
N	.	.	.	40.0	41.0	39.0	.	.	.
O	.	.	.	43.0	46.0	37.0	.	.	.
P	.	.	.	51.0	48.0	51.0	.	.	.
Q	.	.	.	40.0	40.0	40.0	.	.	.
X	.	.	.	42.0	45.0	34.0	.	.	.

4. Occupational injuries and Strikes and Lockouts

Economic activity (ISIC-Rev.3)	Rates of fatal injuries 1992 Labour inspectorate records Per 1,000 workers employed Reported injuries			Rates of non-fatal injuries			Strikes and lockouts 1997 Special data collection		
	Total	Men	Women	Total	Men	Women	Strikes and lockouts	Workers involved	Days not worked
Total	0.437	.	.	.	.	.	234	145 559	1 250 403

5. Consumer price indices (base period: 2000=100)

	2002	2003	2004	2005	2006	2007
General indices	124.7	133.0	141.3	156.0	176.5	187.8
Food index, including non-alcoholic beverages	120.2	121.2	128.3	140.3	161.9	180.4
Electricity, gas and other fuel indices [11]	166.8	207.7	.	.	.	.
Clothing indices, including footwear	114.3	119.2	125.9	.	.	.
Rent indices	128.3	142.3	.	.	.	.

[1] Persons aged 15 years and over. [2] Aug. [3] Persons aged 10 to 56 years. [4] Incl. the armed forces. [5] Feb. [6] May. [7] Production workers. [8] Figures in thousands. [9] Dec. [10] Hotels. [11] Incl. water.

[1] Personnes âgées de 15 ans et plus. [2] Août. [3] Personnes âgées de 10 à 56 ans. [4] Y compris les forces armées. [5] Fév. [6] Mai. [7] Travailleurs à la production. [8] Données en milliers. [9] Déc. [10] Hôtels. [11] Y compris l'eau.

[1] Personas de 15 años y más. [2] Agosto. [3] Personas de 10 a 56 años. [4] Incl. las fuerzas armadas. [5] Feb. [6] Mayo. [7] Trabajadores participando en el proceso de producción. [8] Cifras en millares. [9] Dic. [10] Hoteles. [11] Incl. el agua.

Iran, Islamic Rep. of

1. Economically active population, Employment and Unemployment ('000)

	Economically active population		Employment		Unemployment	
	Total	Women (%)	Total	Women (%)	Total	Women (%)
Age group	2007 [1] Labour force survey		2007 ★ Labour force survey		2007 [1] Labour force survey	
Total	23 578.7	19.4	21 092.7	18.3	2 486.0	29.0
10-14	204.1	29.8	195.1	30.7	9.0	11.1
15-19	1 620.3	20.6	1 356.3	19.8	264.0	25.0
20-24	3 643.3	22.8	2 733.3	19.9	910.0	31.4
25-29	3 752.7	22.5	3 122.7	19.3	630.0	38.3
30-34	2 993.7	21.4	2 748.7	20.5	245.0	31.4
35-39	2 849.3	19.0	2 709.3	19.1	140.0	18.6
40-44	2 492.8	17.8	2 399.8	18.0	93.0	12.9
45-49	2 215.8	16.8	2 136.8	17.0	79.0	8.9
50-54	1 573.2	14.9	1 514.2	15.3	59.0	5.1
55-59	922.9	14.8	889.9	15.1	33.0	6.1
60-64	573.3	14.3	557.3	14.7	16.0	0.0
65+	737.3	9.1	729.3	9.2	8.0	0.0

Economic activity (ISIC-Rev.3)

			2007 [1] Labour force survey		2007 [1] Labour force survey	
Total	.	.	21 092	18.3	2 486	29.0
A Agriculture, Hunting and Forestry	.	.	4 730	27.0	107	8.5
B Fishing	.	.	79	1.9	4	3.0
C Mining and Quarrying	.	.	128	3.4	8	0.5
D Manufacturing	.	.	3 834	28.4	251	16.8
E Electricity, Gas and Water Supply	.	.	196	4.3	8	6.6
F Construction	.	.	2 601	0.9	317	0.9
G Wholesale and Retail Trade; Repair of Motor Vehicles ...	.	.	3 017	5.5	160	9.6
H Hotels and Restaurants	.	.	193	6.6	21	7.5
I Transport, Storage and Communications	.	.	1 976	1.9	124	4.9
J Financial Intermediation	.	.	282	13.5	7	30.7
K Real Estate, Renting and Business Activities	.	.	438	16.0	36	32.6
L Public Administration and Defence; Compulsory Social ...	.	.	1 353	7.7	354	3.7
M Education	.	.	1 321	49.7	35	64.1
N Health and Social Work	.	.	461	43.7	22	61.1
O Other Community, Social and Personal Service Activities	.	.	442	34.0	29	35.3
P Households with Employed Persons	.	.	28	76.3	2	75.4
Q Extra-Territorial Organizations and Bodies	.	.	1	4.6	0	100.0
X Not classifiable by economic activity	.	.	12	7.7	1	33.0
Unemployed seeking their first job	.	.	.	.	999	56.9

Occupation (ISCO-88)

			2007 [1] Labour force survey		2007 [1] Labour force survey	
Total	.	.	21 092	18.3	2 486	29.0
1 Legislators, senior officials and managers	.	.	593	13.3	19	15.8
2 Professionals	.	.	1 657	43.6	63	54.0
3 Technicians and associate professionals	.	.	978	17.0	66	25.8
4 Clerks	.	.	1 009	24.2	70	45.7
5 Service workers and shop and market sales workers	.	.	2 689	10.7	141	14.9
6 Skilled agricultural and fishery workers	.	.	3 995	27.0	57	7.0
7 Craft and related trade workers	.	.	4 165	23.4	292	9.2
8 Plant and machine operators and assemblers	.	.	2 382	1.0	157	1.9
9 Elementary occupations	.	.	3 133	9.0	315	3.2
X Not classifiable by occupation	.	.	491	0.9	307	0.3
Unemployed seeking their first job	.	.	.	.	999	56.9

Education level (ISCED-76)

	2005 [1] Labour force survey		2005 ★ Labour force survey		2005 [1] Labour force survey	
Total	22 317	20.5	19 761	19.2	2 556	30.4
X No schooling	2 797	31.6	2 705	32.3	92	9.8
1 First level	6 774	17.3	6 266	17.7	508	12.6
2 Second level, first stage	4 432	9.8	3 871	9.3	561	13.2
3 Second level, second stage	5 048	19.5	4 160	15.3	888	39.1
5 Third level, first stage, leading to an award not equivalent ...	1 004	32.6	828	29.0	176	49.4
6 Third level, first stage, leading to a first university degree ... [2]	2 203	35.0	1 877	.	326	.
? Level not stated	5	20.0	.	.	.	.

Status in employment (ICSE-1993)

			2007 [1] Labour force survey			
Total	.	.	21 092	18.3	.	.
1 Employees	.	.	10 834	15.1	.	.
2 Employers	.	.	1 145	3.2	.	.
3 Own-account workers	.	.	6 825	13.2	.	.
5 Contributing family workers	.	.	2 186	57.7	.	.
6 Not classifiable by status	.	.	101	30.3	.	.

2. Population ('000), Activity rate and Unemployment rate

	Population 2007 Labour force survey			Activity rate 2007 Labour force survey			Unemployment rate 2007 [1] Labour force survey		
Age group	Total	Men	Women	Total	Men	Women	Total	Men	Women
Total	70 202.4	35 499.1	34 703.4	33.6	53.5	13.2	10.5	9.3	15.8
15+	52 681.5	26 470.1	26 211.3	44.4	71.2	17.3	10.6	12.0	15.9
15-24	16 670.9	8 466.0	8 204.9	31.6	48.4	14.2	22.3	20.0	30.2
25-54	28 233.4	14 054.7	14 178.7	56.2	91.1	21.7	7.8	10.8	11.9
55+	7 777.2	3 949.4	3 827.8	28.7	49.3	7.5	2.6	2.8	0.7

Iran, Islamic Rep. of

3. Paid employment ('000), Hours of work (weekly) and Wages

Economic activity (ISIC-Rev.3)	Paid employment 1996 Population census			Hours of work			Wages 2001 Labour-related establishment survey Earnings per month / Employees / Rial		
	Total	Men	Women	Total	Men	Women	Total	Men	Women
Total	7 585	6 629	957	.	.	.	.	.	.
A	453	409	44	.	.	.	.	.	.
B	22	22	0	.	.	.	.	.	.
C	111	106	4	.	.	.	.	.	.
D	1 458	1 306	152	.	.	.	1 014 285	1 029 232	828 265
E	141	136	5	.	.	.	.	.	.
F	1 035	1 024	11	.	.	.	.	.	.
G	518	501	17	.	.	.	.	.	.
H	41	39	2	.	.	.	.	.	.
I	419	407	13	.	.	.	.	.	.
J	146	133	13	.	.	.	.	.	.
K	85	76	10	.	.	.	.	.	.
L	1 565	1 472	93	.	.	.	.	.	.
M	990	556	434	.	.	.	.	.	.
N	272	164	108	.	.	.	.	.	.
O	113	97	16	.	.	.	.	.	.
P	22	20	2	.	.	.	.	.	.
Q	1	1	0	.	.	.	.	.	.
X	194	161	33	.	.	.	.	.	.

Share of women in wage employment in the non-agricultural sector (1996 - Population census): **12.7%**

4. Occupational injuries and Strikes and Lockouts

Statistics not available.

5. Consumer price indices (base period: 2000=100)

	2002	2003	2004	2005	2006	2007
General indices	127.3	148.2	170.1	192.9	215.9	246.1
Food index, including non-alcoholic beverages [3]	124.0	145.9	164.8	186.3	205.5	.
Electricity, gas and other fuel indices [4]	129.7	149.6	166.4	176.4	179.5	.
Clothing indices, including footwear	109.2	116.9	127.3	140.0	151.8	168.6
Rent indices	143.1	172.0	204.2	236.0	271.1	.
General index, excluding housing	121.8	139.9	158.3	178.1	.	.

[1] Persons aged 10 years and over. [2] Levels 6-9. [3] Incl. tobacco. [4] Incl. water.

[1] Personnes âgées de 10 ans et plus. [2] Niveaux 6-9. [3] Y compris le tabac. [4] Y compris l'eau.

[1] Personas de 10 años y más. [2] Niveles 6-9. [3] Incl. el tabaco. [4] Incl. el agua.

Iraq

1. Economically active population, Employment and Unemployment ('000)

	Economically active population		Employment		Unemployment	
	Total	Women (%)	Total	Women (%)	Total	Women (%)
Age group	1997 [1 2] Population census					
Total	4 862.1	10.4	.	.	.	.
6-9	48.7	10.9	.	.	.	.
10-14	286.7	7.2	.	.	.	.
15-19	667.3	4.5	.	.	.	.
20-24	780.6	8.4	.	.	.	.
25-29	853.9	11.4	.	.	.	.
30-34	653.5	13.7	.	.	.	.
35-39	396.8	16.8	.	.	.	.
40-44	392.9	13.5	.	.	.	.
45-49	257.8	12.5	.	.	.	.
50-54	184.9	10.9	.	.	.	.
55-59	121.1	8.3	.	.	.	.
60-64	68.7	7.9	.	.	.	.
65+	144.2	5.8	.	.	.	.
?	4.9	11.3	.	.	.	.
Economic activity (ISIC-Rev.3)	1997 [1 2] Population census					
Total	4 862.1	10.4	.	.	.	.
A Agriculture, Hunting and Forestry	925.4	13.4	.	.	.	.
B Fishing	24.9	2.3	.	.	.	.
C Mining and Quarrying	30.8	11.5	.	.	.	.
D Manufacturing	219.5	14.6	.	.	.	.
E Electricity, Gas and Water Supply	28.3	14.1	.	.	.	.
F Construction	218.4	1.3	.	.	.	.
G Wholesale and Retail Trade; Repair of Motor Vehicles ...	862.5	2.6	.	.	.	.
H Hotels and Restaurants	41.8	2.4	.	.	.	.
I Transport, Storage and Communications	273.2	3.1	.	.	.	.
J Financial Intermediation	16.2	70.7	.	.	.	.
K Real Estate, Renting and Business Activities	24.0	10.9	.	.	.	.
L Public Administration and Defence; Compulsory Social ...	909.5	4.7	.	.	.	.
M Education	297.8	62.8	.	.	.	.
N Health and Social Work	80.8	38.4	.	.	.	.
O Other Community, Social and Personal Service Activities	74.0	14.0	.	.	.	.
P Households with Employed Persons	9.3	10.1	.	.	.	.
Q Extra-Territorial Organizations and Bodies	1.4	20.4	.	.	.	.
X Not classifiable by economic activity	12.3	46.2	.	.	.	.
Unemployed seeking their first job	812.0	1.6	.	.	.	.
Occupation (ISCO-1968)	1997 [1 2] Population census		1985 [3] Labour-related establishment survey			
Total	4 862.09	10.4	212.98	2.8	.	.
0/1 Professional, technical and related workers	447.41	48.8	7.43	5.1	.	.
2 Administrative and managerial workers	11.76	14.8	1.46	2.9	.	.
3 Clerical and related workers	932.33	8.1	6.19	11.3	.	.
4 Sales workers	710.24	2.6	25.85	3.7	.	.
5 Service workers	148.07	15.4	25.12	2.4	.	.
6 Agriculture, animal husbandry and forestry workers ...	941.46	13.1	0.43	1.4	.	.
7/8/9 Production and related workers, transport equipment ...	851.34	3.1	146.50	2.3	.	.
X Not classifiable by occupation	7.44	65.9	.	.	.	.
Status in employment (ICSE-1993)	1997 [1 2] Population census					
Total	4 862.1	10.4	.	.	.	.

2. Population ('000), Activity rate and Unemployment rate

Age group	Population 1997 [2 4] Population census			Activity rate 1997 [2 4] Population census			Unemployment rate 2004 [5] Labour force survey		
	Total	Men	Women	Total	Men	Women	Total	Men	Women
Total	.	.	.	.	.	.	26.8	29.4	15.0
15+	10 698.7	5 232.0	5 466.7	42.3	77.3	8.7	.	.	.
15-24	4 018.1	2 016.9	2 001.2	36.0	67.1	4.8	.	.	.
25-54	5 431.7	2 641.6	2 790.1	50.4	90.1	12.9	.	.	.
55+	1 248.9	573.5	675.4	26.7	54.1	3.5	.	.	.

3. Paid employment ('000), Hours of work (weekly) and Wages

Economic activity (ISIC-Rev.2)	Paid employment 2001 [3] Labour-related establishment survey			Hours of work			Wages		
	Total	Men	Women	Total	Men	Women	Total	Men	Women
3	109.345	.	.	.	.	.	.	.	.

Iraq

4. Occupational injuries and Strikes and Lockouts

Economic activity (ISIC-Rev.2)	Rates of fatal injuries 1992 Per 1,000 workers exposed to risk Compensated injuries			Rates of non-fatal injuries			Strikes and lockouts		
	Total	Men	Women	Total	Men	Women	Strikes and lockouts	Workers involved	Days not worked
Total	0.245	.	.	.	.	.	.	.	.

5. Consumer price indices (base period: 2000=100)

	2002	2003	2004	2005	2006	2007
General indices	138.9	185.5	235.6	322.6	494.3	646.8
Food index, including non-alcoholic beverages	118.0	137.5	149.5	182.9	237.4	270.4
Electricity, gas and other fuel indices	97.9	516.9	339.9	676.7	1 935.5	3 320.9
Clothing indices, including footwear	108.0	112.8	108.7	118.9	144.5	156.6
Rent indices	268.2	380.0	644.9	918.6	1 240.9	1 538.1

[1] Persons aged 6 years and over. [2] Oct. [3] Private sector. [4] "De facto" population. [5] Persons aged 15 years and over.

[1] Personnes âgées de 6 ans et plus. [2] Oct. [3] Secteur privé. [4] Population "de facto". [5] Personnes âgées de 15 ans et plus.

[1] Personas de 6 años y más. [2] Oct. [3] Sector privado. [4] Población "de facto". [5] Personas de 15 años y más.

Ireland

1. Economically active population, Employment and Unemployment ('000)

	Economically active population		Employment		Unemployment	
	Total	Women (%)	Total	Women (%)	Total	Women (%)
Age group	2007 [1,2] Labour force survey		2007 ★ Labour force survey		2007 [1,2] Labour force survey	
Total	2 201.9	42.7	2 101.6	42.8	100.3	40.2
15-19	77.4	46.0	66.7	46.8	10.7	41.1
20-24	261.4	46.2	242.7	46.5	18.7	42.2
25-29	353.1	46.6	336.8	46.9	16.3	41.1
30-34	300.0	43.6	286.7	43.8	13.3	37.6
35-39	272.5	41.7	262.0	41.8	10.5	39.0
40-44	245.6	41.9	236.3	41.8	9.3	45.2
45-49	226.6	43.2	219.1	43.4	7.5	37.3
50-54	189.5	42.1	182.0	42.3	7.5	38.7
55-59	144.4	38.0	139.8	38.0	4.6	37.0
60-64	87.7	33.9	86.2	34.0	1.5	26.7
65-69	26.6	27.4	26.2	27.5	0.4	25.0
70-74	10.3	18.4	10.3	18.4	0.0	.
75+	7.0	14.3	7.0	14.3	0.0	.
Economic activity (ISIC-Rev.3)	1997 ★ Labour force survey		2007 [1,2] Labour force survey		1997 [1,2] Labour force survey	
Total	1 539.0	39.1	2 101.6	42.8	159.0	39.0
A Agriculture, Hunting and Forestry	142.3	11.6	111.3	10.5	3.1	16.1
B Fishing	2.8	.	2.4	12.5	0.6	.
C Mining and Quarrying	6.9	5.8	10.8	9.3	0.5	.
D Manufacturing	294.2	32.1	270.8	29.5	24.3	34.6
E Electricity, Gas and Water Supply	12.5	13.6	13.6	19.1	0.3	.
F Construction	128.3	5.1	281.8	4.9	17.9	2.8
G Wholesale and Retail Trade; Repair of Motor Vehicles ...	207.9	43.6	294.5	48.9	14.6	42.5
H Hotels and Restaurants	87.3	57.3	132.3	58.1	10.9	57.8
I Transport, Storage and Communications	68.7	20.7	122.2	22.0	3.7	16.2
J Financial Intermediation	52.1	55.5	91.1	59.5	1.8	72.2
K Real Estate, Renting and Business Activities	88.1	42.3	194.8	47.4	3.8	44.7
L Public Administration and Defence; Compulsory Social ...	74.5	37.6	101.6	51.5	2.3	34.8
M Education	97.6	64.3	139.7	73.4	4.4	68.2
N Health and Social Work	124.0	76.9	213.2	81.8	4.3	65.1
O Other Community, Social and Personal Service Activities	81.2	50.4	103.2	53.5	7.8	47.4
P Households with Employed Persons	7.7	77.9	9.7	92.8	1.1	72.7
Q Extra-Territorial Organizations and Bodies	1.2	50.0	1.2	50.0	0.0	.
X Not classifiable by economic activity	34.0	42.6	7.6	30.3	30.2	42.4
Unemployed seeking their first job	.	.	.	.	27.4	44.2
Occupation (ISCO-88)	1997 ★ Labour force survey		2007 [1,2] Labour force survey		1997 [1,2] Labour force survey	
Total	1 538.9	39.1	2 101.6	42.8	159.0	39.0
1 Legislators, senior officials and managers	65.2	26.1	310.4	31.2	1.4	21.4
2 Professionals	215.3	52.6	353.1	54.8	5.6	55.4
3 Technicians and associate professionals	150.6	37.5	130.7	48.7	7.0	44.3
4 Clerks	189.5	72.6	265.1	73.2	9.8	72.4
5 Service workers and shop and market sales workers	261.8	51.7	367.8	67.2	21.9	56.6
6 Skilled agricultural and fishery workers	132.4	7.9	14.7	8.8	3.3	9.1
7 Craft and related trade workers	177.2	10.2	303.0	4.0	18.6	10.2
8 Plant and machine operators and assemblers	143.9	22.8	155.9	14.3	13.6	30.9
9 Elementary occupations	135.6	40.6	194.4	35.4	21.4	24.8
0 Armed forces	8.7	3.4	6.5	4.6	0.4	.
X Not classifiable by occupation	31.3	42.5	-		28.7	42.5
Unemployed seeking their first job	.	.			27.4	44.2
Education level (ISCED-97)	2006 [1,2] Labour force survey		2006 ★ Labour force survey		2006 [1,2] Labour force survey	
Total	2 108.3	42.3	2 015.5	42.4	92.8	39.7
X No schooling	2.9	34.5	2.6	34.6	0.3	33.3
1 Primary education or first stage of basic education	193.1	28.5	177.1	28.9	16.0	23.8
2 Lower secondary or second stage of basic education	327.3	31.8	306.7	31.6	20.6	35.0
3 Upper secondary education	10.6	40.6	9.9	40.4	0.7	42.9
4 Post-secondary non-tertiary education	576.4	43.5	551.9	43.4	24.5	44.5
5A First stage of tertiary education - theoretically based	603.6	52.1	587.9	52.2	15.7	48.4
5B First stage of tertiary education - practically oriented	229.2	43.5	219.5	43.0	9.7	54.6
6 Second stage of tertiary education	55.1	49.5	53.9	49.5	1.2	50.0
? Level not stated	110.0	31.4	105.7	31.6	4.3	25.6
Status in employment (ICSE-1993)	2002 [1,3] Population census		2007 [1,2] Labour force survey			
Total	1 800.9	40.9	2 101.6	42.8	.	.
1 Employees	1 359.2	46.5	1 749.2	47.8	.	.
2 Employers	109.2	18.5	122.7	18.4	.	.
3 Own-account workers	167.8	14.4	216.6	15.4	.	.
5 Contributing family workers	5.4	42.1	13.1	61.1	.	.
6 Not classifiable by status	.	.	-		.	.

Ireland

2. Population ('000), Activity rate and Unemployment rate

Age group	Population 2007 [2] Labour force survey			Activity rate 2007 [2] Labour force survey			Unemployment rate 2007 [1,2] Labour force survey		
	Total	Men	Women	Total	Men	Women	Total	Men	Women
Total	4 339.0	2 171.1	2 167.9	50.7	58.1	43.4	4.6	4.8	4.3
15+	3 455.3	1 718.0	1 737.2	63.7	73.4	54.1	4.6	4.8	4.3
15-24	633.8	320.4	313.4	53.5	57.0	49.9	8.7	9.3	7.9
25-54	1 933.0	977.7	955.2	82.1	91.8	72.2	4.1	4.3	3.7
55+	888.5	419.9	468.6	31.1	43.2	20.2	2.4	2.4	2.3

3. Paid employment ('000), Hours of work (weekly) and Wages

Economic activity (ISIC-Rev.3)	Paid employment 2007 [1,2] Labour force survey			Hours of work 2007 [2] Labour force survey Hours usually worked / Total employment			Wages 2006 [4,4,5] Labour-related establishment survey Earnings per week / Employees / Euro		
	Total	Men	Women	Total	Men	Women	Total	Men	Women
Total	1 749.2	913.0	836.2	36.4	40.6	31.4	.	.	.
A-B	.	.	.	51.6	53.5	37.3	.	.	.
C-Q	.	.	.	35.9	36.9	31.4	.	.	.
A	23.8	18.7	5.1	51.7	53.5	37.3	.	.	.
B	1.4	1.1	0.3	49.3	51.6	38.1	.	.	.
C	9.8	8.9	1.0	40.8	41.5	34.7	781.53	.	.
D	246.6	170.7	75.9	39.1	40.5	35.9	678.26	.	.
E	12.8	10.3	2.4	38.5	39.6	34.7	1 179.31	.	.
F	208.5	196.2	12.2	40.9	41.4	33.0	.	.	.
G	254.4	120.0	134.4	34.1	38.7	29.5	.	.	.
H	116.5	46.5	69.9	33.4	37.4	30.5	.	.	.
I	96.5	71.8	24.7	38.9	40.4	34.0	.	.	.
J	87.1	33.5	53.5	37.4	41.2	35.0	.	.	.
K	156.9	74.7	82.2	37.0	40.8	33.1	.	.	.
L	101.0	49.0	52.0	35.6	38.7	32.9	.	.	.
M	134.6	36.1	98.5	28.0	32.0	26.6	.	.	.
N	201.1	33.8	167.3	32.6	39.4	31.1	.	.	.
O	81.9	35.7	46.2	34.0	38.5	30.4	.	.	.
P	8.2	0.6	7.6	30.9	42.0	30.1	.	.	.
Q	1.2	0.5	0.6	34.4	34.7	34.2	.	.	.
X	7.1	4.9	2.3	31.1	32.2	28.4	.	.	.

Share of women in wage employment in the non-agricultural sector [1,2] (2007 - Labour force survey): **48.3%**

4. Occupational injuries and Strikes and Lockouts

Economic activity (ISIC-Rev.3)	Rates of fatal injuries 2002 Labour inspectorate records Per 100,000 workers employed Reported injuries			Rates of non-fatal injuries			Strikes and lockouts 2007 [6] Special data collection		
	Total	Men	Women	Total	Men	Women	Strikes and lockouts	Workers involved	Days not worked
Total	3.5	5.9	0.1	.	.	.	6	1 436	6 038
A-B	.	.	.	.	.	.	0	0	0
C	.	.	.	.	.	.	0	0	0
D	.	.	.	.	.	.	2	400	2 700
E	.	.	.	.	.	.	0	0	0
F	11.4	.	.	.	.	.	0	0	0
G	0.4	.	.	.	.	.	1	450	186
H	0.0	.	.	.	.	.	0	0	0
I	6.4	.	.	.	.	.	2	479	2 315
J-K	.	.	.	.	.	.	0	0	0
L	3.6	.	.	.	.	.	1	107	837
M	.	.	.	.	.	.	0	0	0
N	.	.	.	.	.	.	0	0	0
O	1.0	.	.	.	.	.	0	0	0
O-Q	.	.	.	.	.	.	0	0	0
P	.	.	.	.	.	.	0	0	0
Q	.	.	.	.	.	.	0	0	0

5. Consumer price indices (base period: 2000=100)

	2002	2003	2004	2005	2006	2007
General indices	109.7	113.5	116.0	118.8	123.5	129.5
Food index, including non-alcoholic beverages	110.7	112.3	111.9	111.2	112.7	116.0
Electricity, gas and other fuel indices	105.4	112.7	120.7	139.7	153.2	164.7
Clothing indices, including footwear	92.4	88.6	85.5	83.1	81.5	78.8
Rent indices [7]	117.0	114.0	117.1	125.7	147.3	182.0
General index, excluding housing	109.1	113.7	116.1	118.3	121.3	124.2

[1] Persons aged 15 years and over. [2] Second quarter. [3] April. [4] Adult and non-adult rates of pay. [5] Establishments with 10 or more persons employed. [6] Work stoppages lasting at least one day or with at least 10 days not worked. [7] Housing.

[1] Personnes âgées de 15 ans et plus. [2] Deuxième trimestre. [3] Avril. [4] Salariés rémunérés sur la base de taux de salaires pour adultes et non-adultes. [5] Etablissements occupant 10 personnes et plus. [6] Arrêts de travail d'un jour au moins ou avec un minimum de 10 jours de travail non effectués. [7] Logement.

[1] Personas de 15 años y más. [2] Segundo trimestre. [3] Abril. [4] Asalariados pagados sobre la base de tasas de salarios para adultos y no adultos. [5] Establecimientos con 10 y más trabajadores. [6] Interrupciones del trabajo de un día por lo menos o de un mínimo de 10 días no trabajados. [7] Vivienda.

Isle of Man

1. Economically active population, Employment and Unemployment ('000)

	Economically active population		Employment		Unemployment	
	Total	Women (%)	Total	Women (%)	Total	Women (%)
Age group	2006 [1,2] Population census		2006 ★ Population census		2006 [1,2] Population census	
Total	41.793	45.8	40.783	46.0	1.010	37.2
15-19	1.554	45.4	1.376	47.1	0.178	32.0
20-24	3.304	47.4	3.128	48.2	0.176	34.1
25-29	4.049	48.5	3.933	48.9	0.116	32.8
30-34	4.625	48.2	4.543	48.4	0.082	36.6
35-39	5.391	46.3	5.298	46.4	0.093	38.7
40-44	5.759	46.5	5.674	46.5	0.085	45.9
45-49	5.215	48.1	5.136	48.2	0.079	48.1
50-54	4.448	45.0	4.355	44.9	0.093	48.4
55-59	4.209	43.8	4.139	43.8	0.070	42.9
60-64	2.158	35.4	2.121	35.9	0.037	5.4
65-69	0.680	35.4	0.679	35.3	0.001	100.0
70-74	0.252	33.7	0.252	33.7	-	.
75+	0.149	39.6	0.149	39.6	-	.
Economic activity (ISIC-Rev.3)			2006 [1,2] Population census			
Total	.	.	40.783	46.0	.	.
A Agriculture, Hunting and Forestry	.	.	0.669	17.3	.	.
B Fishing	.	.	0.111	15.3	.	.
C Mining and Quarrying	.	.	0.082	17.1	.	.
D Manufacturing	.	.	2.096	22.0	.	.
E Electricity, Gas and Water Supply	.	.	0.605	16.9	.	.
F Construction	.	.	3.239	4.8	.	.
G Wholesale and Retail Trade; Repair of Motor Vehicles ...	.	.	5.103	45.2	.	.
H Hotels and Restaurants	.	.	1.538	50.6	.	.
I Transport, Storage and Communications	.	.	3.208	27.3	.	.
J Financial Intermediation	.	.	6.824	56.6	.	.
K Real Estate, Renting and Business Activities	.	.	4.706	43.6	.	.
L Public Administration and Defence; Compulsory Social ...	.	.	2.706	41.2	.	.
M Education	.	.	2.794	74.1	.	.
N Health and Social Work	.	.	4.250	78.4	.	.
O Other Community, Social and Personal Service Activities	.	.	2.680	51.6	.	.
P Households with Employed Persons	.	.	0.153	77.1	.	.
X Not classifiable by economic activity	.	.	0.019	21.1	.	.
Status in employment (ICSE-1993)			2001 [1] Population census			
Total	.	.	39.050	45.5	.	.
1 Employees	.	.	33.347	49.1	.	.
2 Employers	.	.	1.740	24.9	.	.
3 Own-account workers	.	.	3.963	23.7	.	.

2. Population ('000), Activity rate and Unemployment rate

	Population			Activity rate			Unemployment rate		
Age group	2006 [2] Population census			2006 [2] Population census			2006 [1] Population census		
	Total	Men	Women	Total	Men	Women	Total	Men	Women
Total	80.1	39.5	40.5	52.2	57.3	47.2	2.4	2.8	2.0
15+	66.5	32.5	34.0	62.8	69.8	56.2	.	.	.
15-24	9.3	4.8	4.5	52.2	54.3	50.0	7.3	9.2	5.1
25-54	33.2	16.5	16.6	88.9	94.5	83.4	1.9	2.1	1.6
55+	24.1	11.2	12.9	31.0	39.8	23.2	.	.	.

3. Paid employment ('000), Hours of work (weekly) and Wages

Economic activity (ISIC-Rev.3)	Paid employment 2001 [1] Population census			Hours of work 2007 [3] Labour-related establishment survey Hours paid for / Employees			Wages 2007 [3] Labour-related establishment survey Earnings per hour / Employees / Pound		
	Total	Men	Women	Total	Men	Women	Total	Men	Women
Total	33.347	16.968	16.379	34.3	34.3	30.8	13.50	14.30	12.80
C-Q	.	.	.	34.4	34.4	30.9	13.70	14.50	12.90
A	0.194	0.161	0.033	.	.	.	.	.	.
B	0.014	0.012	0.002	.	.	.	.	.	.
C	0.104	0.097	0.007	.	.	.	.	.	.
D	2.682	2.024	0.658	38.6	39.4	34.8	12.00	12.70	9.00
E	0.492	0.400	0.092	39.0	39.1	.	17.10	17.30	.
F	1.380	1.239	0.141	44.0	44.0	.	10.00	10.20	.
G	4.019	1.962	2.057	31.6	38.0	25.8	8.60	9.10	8.10
H	1.501	0.687	0.814	30.4	33.0	28.2	8.50	9.30	7.80
I	2.677	1.832	0.845	41.3	43.1	38.3	12.40	12.80	11.80
J	7.066	3.024	4.042	34.1	35.7	32.7	17.40	18.60	16.50
K	2.261	1.099	1.162	35.0	36.8	33.4	14.00	15.70	12.50
L	2.849	1.728	1.121	37.7	39.4	35.0	15.70	17.60	12.70
M	2.633	0.846	1.787	27.2	31.0	25.0	17.40	20.00	16.00
N	2.993	0.576	2.417	34.4	38.2	33.4	12.90	14.50	12.50
O	2.419	1.269	1.150	27.4	34.5	20.3	8.60	9.10	8.00
P	0.063	0.012	0.051	.	.	.	.	.	.

Share of women in wage employment in the non-agricultural sector [1] (2001 - Population census): 49.3%

Isle of Man

4. Occupational injuries and Strikes and Lockouts

Economic activity (ISIC-Rev.3)	Rates of fatal injuries 2007 Labour inspectorate records Per 100,000 workers employed Reported injuries			Rates of non-fatal injuries 2007[4] Labour inspectorate records Per 100,000 workers employed Reported injuries			Strikes and lockouts 2007 Labour relations records		
	Total	Men	Women	Total	Men	Women	Strikes and lockouts	Workers involved	Days not worked
Total	0	.	.	441	.	.	0	0	0

5. Consumer price indices (base period: 2000=100)

	2002	2003	2004	2005	2006	2007
General indices	104.1	107.3	112.8	117.5	121.0	125.8
Food index, including non-alcoholic beverages	113.0	119.6	126.3	131.0	135.1	141.2
Electricity, gas and other fuel indices	92.1	100.3	114.5	139.4	151.4	159.1
Clothing indices, including footwear	111.6	111.3	111.6	113.5	117.6	115.5
Rent indices	120.9	136.1	144.2	150.0	153.4	157.8
General index, excluding housing	105.2	108.3	113.5	118.3	122.0	125.9

[1] Persons aged 15 years and over. [2] April. [3] June. [4] Incapacity of 4 days or more.

[1] Personnes âgées de 15 ans et plus. [2] Avril. [3] Juin. [4] Incapacité de 4 jours et plus.

[1] Personas de 15 años y más. [2] Abril. [3] Junio. [4] Incapacidad de 4 días y más.

Israel

1. Economically active population, Employment and Unemployment ('000)

	Economically active population		Employment		Unemployment	
	Total	Women (%)	Total	Women (%)	Total	Women (%)
Age group	2007 [1,2] Labour force survey		2007 ★ Labour force survey		2007 [2] Labour force survey	
Total	2 893.8	46.6	2 682.0	46.2	211.8	50.5
15-17	32.7	43.7	24.1	43.2	8.6	45.3
18-24	340.5	52.4	289.2	51.7	51.3	56.1
25-34	820.8	46.6	762.2	46.0	58.6	54.1
35-44	680.3	46.3	642.7	46.3	37.6	47.3
45-54	586.8	47.5	553.2	47.4	33.6	50.0
55-59	237.5	45.8	224.9	46.1	12.6	40.5
60-64	125.7	39.3	119.1	39.7	6.6	31.8
65-69	42.7	30.7	40.7	32.2	2.0	.
70+	27.0	27.0	27.0	27.0	-	.
Economic activity (ISIC-Rev.3)	2007 [1,2] Labour force survey		2007 [1,2] Labour force survey		2007 [2] Labour force survey	
Total	2 893.8	46.6	2 682.0	46.2	211.8	50.5
A-B	44.6	17.5	43.3	16.9	1.2	.
C-D	434.0	28.6	421.6	28.5	12.4	33.1
E Electricity, Gas and Water Supply	17.4	20.7	16.8	21.4	-	.
F Construction	155.9	6.1	150.2	6.0	5.6	.
G Wholesale and Retail Trade; Repair of Motor Vehicles ...	375.3	41.5	358.2	41.2	17.0	50.0
H Hotels and Restaurants	132.2	41.1	122.1	40.5	10.1	48.5
I Transport, Storage and Communications	178.5	30.5	171.2	29.8	7.5	46.7
J Financial Intermediation	96.8	60.8	95.0	60.6	1.7	76.5
K Real Estate, Renting and Business Activities	390.2	42.8	375.3	42.4	14.9	53.0
L Public Administration and Defence; Compulsory Social ...	121.9	44.1	120.3	43.9	1.6	62.5
M Education	351.6	76.8	344.4	76.6	7.3	87.7
N Health and Social Work	272.4	76.7	267.0	76.6	5.5	80.0
O Other Community, Social and Personal Service Activities	128.2	48.7	124.2	49.0	4.0	37.5
P Households with Employed Persons	50.9	91.7	49.0	91.4	1.9	100.0
Q Extra-Territorial Organizations and Bodies	1.3	.	1.3	.	0.0	.
X Not classifiable by economic activity	24.1	36.5	22.1	36.2	1.9	.
Unemployed seeking their first job	118.6	50.7	.	.	118.6	50.7
Occupation (ISCO-88)	2007 [1,2] Labour force survey		2007 [1,2] Labour force survey		2007 [2] Labour force survey	
Total	2 893.8	46.6	2 682.0	46.2	211.8	50.5
1 Legislators, senior officials and managers	206.6	30.1	201.3	29.7	5.3	44.8
2 Professionals	429.3	51.0	423.3	51.0	5.9	57.0
3 Technicians and associate professionals	497.4	53.8	484.4	53.8	13.0	53.1
4 Clerks	420.5	73.8	402.8	73.8	17.7	75.2
5 Service workers and shop and market sales workers	446.6	60.7	424.8	60.5	21.8	64.3
6 Skilled agricultural and fishery workers	32.1	10.5	31.6	10.4	0.5	.
7 Craft and related trade workers	275.2	5.0	266.7	5.1	8.5	.
8 Plant and machine operators and assemblers	225.3	16.9	217.4	16.7	7.9	20.7
9 Elementary occupations	210.3	43.7	199.6	43.9	10.7	39.4
X Not classifiable by occupation	31.9	30.5	30.1	30.2	1.8	.
Unemployed seeking their first job	93.3	50.4	.	.	118.6	50.7
Education level (ISCED-97)	2007 [1,2] Labour force survey		2007 ★ Labour force survey		2007 [2] Labour force survey	
Total	2 893.8	46.6	2 682.0	46.2	211.8	50.5
X No schooling	13.6	45.2	12.1	43.6	1.5	58.3
0 Pre-primary education	30.8	49.8	28.2	49.9	2.5	48.5
1 Primary education or first stage of basic education	-		-		-	
2 Lower secondary or second stage of basic education	169.3	25.2	143.3	24.3	25.9	29.9
3 Upper secondary education	211.7	30.7	184.6	29.3	27.1	40.6
5A First stage of tertiary education - theoretically based	1 173.9	45.2	1 070.8	44.3	103.1	53.6
5B First stage of tertiary education - practically oriented	809.4	54.3	781.6	54.2	27.8	57.2
6 Second stage of tertiary education	446.6	52.5	423.9	51.9	22.7	62.9
? Level not stated	37.3	36.9	36.2	.	1.2	.
Status in employment (ICSE-1993)	2007 [1,2] Labour force survey		2007 [1,2] Labour force survey		2007 ★ Labour force survey	
Total	2 893.8	46.6	2 682.0	46.2	211.8	50.5
1 Employees	2 431.1	48.7	2 341.7	48.6	89.4	51.5
2 Employers	113.3	18.5	112.3	18.5	1.0	20.0
3 Own-account workers	194.9	32.5	192.2	32.6	2.7	22.2
4 Members of producers' cooperatives	30.1	45.8	30.0	45.7	0.1	100.0
5 Contributing family workers	5.8	81.0	5.7	82.5	0.1	.
6 Not classifiable by status	118.6	50.7	-	.	118.6	50.7

2. Population ('000), Activity rate and Unemployment rate

	Population			Activity rate			Unemployment rate		
Age group	2007 [1] Labour force survey			2007 [1] Labour force survey			2007 [2] Labour force survey		
	Total	Men	Women	Total	Men	Women	Total	Men	Women
Total	.	.	.	.	.	.	7.3	6.8	7.9
15+	5 142.3	2 504.2	2 638.1	56.3	61.8	51.1	.	.	.
15-24	1 151.8	587.8	564.0	32.4	30.7	34.1	16.1	15.1	17.0
25-54	2 683.3	1 327.8	1 355.5	77.8	83.7	72.0	6.2	5.7	6.8
55+	1 307.2	588.6	718.6	33.1	43.2	24.8	.	.	.

Israel

3. Paid employment ('000), Hours of work (weekly) and Wages

Economic activity (ISIC-Rev.3)	Paid employment 2007 [1,2] Labour force survey Total	Men	Women	Hours of work 2007 [1,2] Labour force survey Hours actually worked / Total employment Total	Men	Women	Wages 2006 [3,4] Insurance records Earnings per month / Employees / New shekel Total	Men	Women
Total	2 341.7	1 203.5	1 138.2	39.3	44.0	33.6	7 466	.	.
A-B	28.4	23.0	5.4	44.1	45.7	34.9	4 585	.	.
C-Q	.	.	.	39.2	43.9	33.6	7 551	.	.
C-D	391.7	278.2	113.5	.	.	.	10 370	.	.
D	.	.	.	44.0 [5]	45.9 [5]	39.1 [5]	.	.	.
E	16.6	13.0	3.6	43.2	43.9	40.5	18 305	.	.
F	122.5	114.0	8.5	43.9	44.4	37.4	6 163	.	.
G	292.7	162.4	130.3	41.6	45.9	35.3	6 613	.	.
H	107.6	62.6	46.0	38.2	41.3	33.6	3 621	.	.
I	143.8	94.1	49.7	43.3	45.3	38.3	3 883	.	.
J	87.0	30.8	56.2	39.8	43.4	37.5	14 989	.	.
K	307.4	170.3	137.1	40.3	43.7	35.5	7 639	.	.
L	119.9	67.3	52.6	42.0	45.3	37.8	11 835	.	.
M	327.8	74.8	253.0	30.5	34.6	29.2	5 867	.	.
N	243.0	53.3	189.7	33.6	41.5	31.2	6 042	.	.
O	86.2	43.9	42.3	35.3	40.9	29.4	5 146	.	.
P	45.4	3.7	41.7	30.8	39.7	30.0	.	.	.
Q	1.3	-	-	40.1	.	.	.	.	.
X	20.6	12.7	7.9	.	.	.	.	.	.

Share of women in wage employment in the non-agricultural sector [1,2] (2007 - Labour force survey): **49.1%**

4. Occupational injuries and Strikes and Lockouts

Economic activity (ISIC-Rev.3)	Rates of fatal injuries 2007 [6] Insurance records Per 100,000 workers employed Compensated injuries Total	Men	Women	Rates of non-fatal injuries 2007 [7] Insurance records Per 100,000 workers employed Compensated injuries Total	Men	Women	Strikes and lockouts 2007 [8] Labour relations records Strikes and lockouts	Workers involved	Days not worked
Total	2.6	.	.	2 313	.	.	30	386 075	2 548 627
A	.	.	.	.	.	.	0	0	0
B	.	.	.	.	.	.	0	0	0
C-D	.	.	.	.	.	.	4	2 490	7 237
E	.	.	.	.	.	.	0	0	0
F	.	.	.	.	.	.	0	0	0
G	.	.	.	.	.	.	0	0	0
H	.	.	.	.	.	.	1	45	585
I	.	.	.	.	.	.	7	8 245	14 460
J	.	.	.	.	.	.	2	6 500	6 500
K	.	.	.	.	.	.	0	0	0
L	.	.	.	.	.	.	8	308 300	319 500
M	.	.	.	.	.	.	5	59 800	2 199 200
N	.	.	.	.	.	.	1	450	900
O	.	.	.	.	.	.	1	50	50
P	.	.	.	.	.	.	0	0	0
Q	.	.	.	.	.	.	0	0	0
X	.	.	.	.	.	.	1	195	195

5. Consumer price indices (base period: 2000=100)

	2002	2003	2004	2005	2006	2007
General indices	106.9	107.6	107.2	108.6	111.0	111.5
Food index, including non-alcoholic beverages	105.4	108.4	108.0	109.9	115.1	119.5
Electricity, gas and other fuel indices	115.0	127.9	134.4	146.7	145.9	147.7
Clothing indices, including footwear	91.4	86.3	83.0	78.0	77.1	74.8
Rent indices	115.8	110.2	107.2	106.1	107.3	105.0
General index, excluding housing	104.5	107.0	107.2	109.1	111.6	112.9

[1] Excl. armed forces. [2] Persons aged 15 years and over. [3] Incl. payments subject to income tax. [4] Incl. workers from the Judea, Samaria and Gaza areas. [5] Incl. mining and quarrying. [6] Only deaths resulting from accidents occurring during the same year. [7] Incapacity of 3 days or more. [8] Excl. work stoppages in which less than 10 workdays not worked.

[1] Non compris les forces armées. [2] Personnes âgées de 15 ans et plus. [3] Y compris les versements soumis à l'impôt sur le revenu. [4] Y compris les travailleurs des régions de Judée, Samarie et Gaza. [5] Y compris les industries extractives. [6] Seulement les décès dus à des accidents survenus pendant la même année. [7] Incapacité de 3 jours et plus. [8] Non compris les arrêts de travail de moins de 10 journées de travail non effectuées.

[1] Excl. las fuerzas armadas. [2] Personas de 15 años y más. [3] Incl. los pagos sometidos al impuesto sobre la renta. [4] Incl. los trabajadores de las regiones de Judea, Samaria y Gaza. [5] Incl. las minas y canteras. [6] Solamente los fallecimientos resultados a accidentes ocurridos en el mismo año. [7] Incapacidad de 3 días y más. [8] Excl. las interrupciones de trabajo de menos de 10 días de trabajo no trabajados.

Italy

1. Economically active population, Employment and Unemployment ('000)

	Economically active population		Employment		Unemployment	
	Total	Women (%)	Total	Women (%)	Total	Women (%)
Age group	2007 [1] Labour force survey		2007 ★ Labour force survey		2007 [1] Labour force survey	
Total	24 727.9	40.2	23 221.8	39.5	1 506.0	52.0
15-19	324.2	36.9	222.1	33.4	102.0	44.3
20-24	1 547.4	41.1	1 269.6	39.7	277.7	47.2
25-29	2 636.8	43.6	2 362.3	42.5	274.5	53.1
30-34	3 629.0	42.1	3 382.8	41.2	246.1	54.8
35-39	3 889.8	41.4	3 695.5	40.5	194.3	58.4
40-44	3 845.8	40.9	3 682.6	40.1	163.2	58.7
45-49	3 288.7	40.5	3 170.5	40.0	118.2	54.9
50-54	2 738.4	38.9	2 669.9	38.6	68.6	49.4
55-59	1 795.2	37.4	1 752.9	37.5	42.4	33.7
60-64	654.5	28.0	637.9	28.1	16.6	21.9
65-69	242.4	22.9	240.2	22.7	2.1	40.4
70-74	87.9	18.6	87.5	18.7	0.4	8.2
75+	48.0	21.2	.	.	.	.
Economic activity (ISIC-Rev.3)	2007 ★ Labour force survey		2007 [1] Labour force survey		2007 [1] Labour force survey	
Total	24 728	40.2	23 222	39.5	1 506	52.0
A Agriculture, Hunting and Forestry	941	32.0	888	31.3	52	44.9
B Fishing	36	9.4	35	9.5	1	0.0
C Mining and Quarrying	40	14.8	39	13.9	1	45.5
D Manufacturing	5 034	28.7	4 870	28.3	164	42.3
E Electricity, Gas and Water Supply	141	18.2	139	17.7	2	53.3
F Construction	2 072	5.2	1 955	5.3	116	4.5
G Wholesale and Retail Trade; Repair of Motor Vehicles ...	3 691	41.5	3 541	41.1	150	52.6
H Hotels and Restaurants	1 256	49.2	1 154	48.7	102	54.9
I Transport, Storage and Communications	1 297	23.3	1 257	23.2	40	27.8
J Financial Intermediation	674	41.0	664	40.5	9	75.2
K Real Estate, Renting and Business Activities	2 629	44.7	2 542	44.1	87	61.3
L Public Administration and Defence; Compulsory Social ...	1 440	33.2	1 418	33.0	22	44.0
M Education	1 639	74.7	1 606	74.6	34	76.2
N Health and Social Work	1 604	67.7	1 575	67.5	29	79.8
O Other Community, Social and Personal Service Activities	1 239	54.1	1 167	53.6	72	62.1
P Households with Employed Persons	376	89.2	349	89.0	27	93.0
Q Extra-Territorial Organizations and Bodies	23	42.7	22	43.9	1	9.1
X Not classifiable by economic activity	126	65.0	-	.	126	65.0
Unemployed seeking their first job	.	.	.	.	471	56.8
Occupation (ISCO-88)	2007 ★ Labour force survey		2007 [1] Labour force survey		2007 [1] Labour force survey	
Total	24 728	40.2	23 222	39.5	1 506	52.0
1 Legislators, senior officials and managers	1 952	33.6	1 923	33.5	29	39.5
2 Professionals	2 348	45.4	2 317	45.2	30	60.3
3 Technicians and associate professionals	5 210	47.8	5 104	47.5	106	58.3
4 Clerks	2 613	59.7	2 513	59.5	100	67.0
5 Service workers and shop and market sales workers	2 885	58.0	2 685	57.5	200	64.6
6 Skilled agricultural and fishery workers	482	23.9	470	23.7	13	34.3
7 Craft and related trade workers	3 970	14.8	3 792	14.5	178	21.9
8 Plant and machine operators and assemblers	2 133	18.4	2 058	18.0	75	29.2
9 Elementary occupations	2 281	46.2	2 108	46.2	173	46.5
0 Armed forces	256	2.4	252	2.3	4	13.2
X Not classifiable by occupation	.	.	.	.	126	65.0
Unemployed seeking their first job	.	.	.	.	471	56.8
Education level (ISCED-97)	2007 [1] Labour force survey		2007 ★ Labour force survey		2007 [1] Labour force survey	
Total	24 727.9	40.2	23 221.8	39.5	1 506.0	52.0
X No schooling	240.6	33.9	218.3	32.5	22.4	48.2
1 Primary education or first stage of basic education	1 569.8	31.2	1 458.3	30.5	111.5	39.8
2 Lower secondary or second stage of basic education	8 071.9	32.7	7 482.5	31.6	589.4	46.9
3 Upper secondary education	10 622.6	43.0	10 044.3	42.3	578.2	55.4
4 Post-secondary non-tertiary education	330.9	57.2	297.1	56.7	33.8	62.4
5A First stage of tertiary education - theoretically based	3 702.6	50.7	3 541.3	50.1	161.3	65.1
5B First stage of tertiary education - practically oriented	142.9	52.4	134.5	52.1	8.3	57.4
6 Second stage of tertiary education	46.6	49.0	45.6	48.6	1.0	70.7
Status in employment (ICSE-1993)	2006 [1] Labour force survey		2006 [1] Labour force survey		2006 ★ Labour force survey	
Total	24 661.6	40.2	22 988.0	39.4	1 673.6	52.1
1 Employees	17 718.1	42.9	16 915.0	42.6	803.1	49.3
2 Employers	347.9	19.3	346.0	19.4	1.9	11.0
3 Own-account workers	4 840.6	26.0	4 767.0	25.9	73.6	30.2
4 Members of producers' cooperatives	45.9	41.2	39.0	41.0	6.9	42.1
5 Contributing family workers	430.1	58.3	425.0	58.4	5.1	52.9
6 Not classifiable by status	12 783.7	5.7	497.0	57.3	12 286.7	3.6

Italy

2. Population ('000), Activity rate and Unemployment rate

Age group	Population 2007 [2] Labour force survey			Activity rate 2007 [2] Labour force survey			Unemployment rate 2007 [1] Labour force survey		
	Total	Men	Women	Total	Men	Women	Total	Men	Women
Total	58 880.0	28 628.8	30 251.2	42.0	51.6	32.9	6.1	4.9	7.9
15+	50 552.8	24 349.9	26 202.9	48.9	60.7	38.0	6.1	4.9	7.9
15-24	6 049.6	3 088.7	2 960.8	30.9	36.1	25.5	20.3	18.2	23.3
25-54	25 812.5	12 934.5	12 878.0	77.6	91.0	64.1	5.3	4.0	7.1
55+	18 690.7	8 326.6	10 364.0	15.1	22.7	9.0	.	.	.

3. Paid employment ('000), Hours of work (weekly) and Wages

Economic activity (ISIC-Rev.3)	Paid employment 2007 [1] Labour force survey			Hours of work 2007 [1] Labour force survey Hours actually worked / Total employment			Wages		
	Total	Men	Women	Total	Men	Women	Total	Men	Women
Total	17 167	9 834	7 333	34.8	38.2	29.8	.	.	.
A-B	.	.	.	40.2	43.1	34.0	.	.	.
C-Q	.	.	.	34.5	37.9	29.7	.	.	.
A	428	290	138	40.2	43.1	34.0	.	.	.
B	14	14	1	40.3	42.1	22.5	.	.	.
C	36	32	5	37.1	37.8	31.1	.	.	.
D	4 114	2 910	1 204	36.3	38.1	32.1	.	.	.
E	135	111	24	36.4	36.9	33.5	.	.	.
F	1 229	1 149	80	37.2	37.6	29.2	.	.	.
G	2 042	1 085	957	38.2	41.4	33.6	.	.	.
H	757	360	398	38.8	44.1	33.9	.	.	.
I	1 051	789	262	37.5	39.1	32.0	.	.	.
J	556	316	240	35.1	37.6	31.6	.	.	.
K	1 448	668	780	34.4	38.6	29.4	.	.	.
L	1 390	938	452	32.7	34.0	30.2	.	.	.
M	1 522	376	1 146	22.4	25.5	21.3	.	.	.
N	1 347	398	949	31.2	34.6	29.6	.	.	.
O	728	348	380	32.4	35.7	29.5	.	.	.
P	349	39	310	25.5	31.3	24.9	.	.	.
Q	21	12	9	31.7	34.1	29.3	.	.	.

Share of women in wage employment in the non-agricultural sector [1] (2007 - Labour force survey): **43.0%**

4. Occupational injuries and Strikes and Lockouts

Economic activity (ISIC-Rev.3)	Rates of fatal injuries 2006 Insurance records Per 100,000 workers insured Compensated injuries			Rates of non-fatal injuries 2006 Insurance records Per 100,000 workers insured Compensated injuries			Strikes and lockouts 2007 [4] Special data collection		
	Total	Men	Women	Total	Men	Women	Strikes and lockouts	Workers involved	Days not worked [5]
Total	5	.	.	2 744	.	.	654	882 097	903 286
A-B							18	22 301	27 571
A	11	.	.	4 755	.	.			
B	11	.	.	1 259	.	.			
C	22	.	.	2 327	.	.	0	0	0
D	4	.	.	3 420	.	.	315	554 560	485 143
E	3	.	.	1 647	.	.	4	405	429
F	15	.	.	4 656	.	.	13	5 523	5 714
G	3	.	.	2 076	.	.	23	68 793	95 286
H	3	.	.	3 224	.	.	3	556	857
I	9	.	.	3 830	.	.	109	75 457	131 429
J	0	.	.	285	.	.	12	994	1 286
K	2	.	.	1 671	.	.			
K,O							62	23 685	36 857
L	1	.	.	1 558	.	.	57	86 690	72 857
M	1	.	.	1 016	.	.	11	23 660	21 000
N	2	.	.	2 352	.	.	27	19 473	24 857
O	3	.	.	2 334	.	.			
P	0	.	.	326	.	.			
X	.	.	.	.	.	.	0	0	0

Italy

5. Consumer price indices (base period: 2000=100)

	2002	2003	2004	2005	2006	2007
General indices [6]	105.4	108.2	110.5	112.4	114.7	116.9
Food index, including non-alcoholic beverages	107.9	111.3	113.7	113.7	115.6	119.0
Electricity, gas and other fuel indices	101.1	104.9	105.1	113.7	124.8	126.5
Clothing indices, including footwear	105.9	109.0	111.5	113.2	114.7	116.3
Rent indices	104.6	107.5	110.5	113.2	116.0	119.0
General index, excluding housing	105.4	108.2	110.3	112.4	114.7	116.8

[1] Persons aged 15 years and over. [2] "De facto" population. [3] Incl. the value of payments in kind. [4] Figures rounded to nearest 100. [5] Computed on the basis of a seven-hour working day. [6] Excl. tobacco.

[1] Personnes âgées de 15 ans et plus. [2] Population "de facto". [3] Y compris la valeur des paiements en nature. [4] Chiffres arrondis au 100 le plus proche. [5] Calculées sur la base de journées de travail de sept heures. [6] Non compris le tabac.

[1] Personas de 15 años y más. [2] Población "de facto". [3] Incl. el valor de los pagos en especie. [4] Cifras redondeadas al 100 más próximo. [5] Calculados en base a días de trabajo de siete horas. [6] Excl. el tabaco.

Jamaica

1. Economically active population, Employment and Unemployment ('000)

	Economically active population		Employment		Unemployment	
	Total	Women (%)	Total	Women (%)	Total	Women (%)
Age group	2004 [1][2] Labour force survey		2004 ★ Labour force survey		2004 [2] Labour force survey	
Total	1 195.5	44.1	1 058.7	42.0	136.8	60.5
14-19	50.2	38.6	31.1	28.9	19.1	54.5
20-24	158.8	43.8	119.2	39.9	39.6	55.3
25-34	340.2	45.9	302.3	43.2	37.9	67.3
35-44	308.2	47.9	282.6	46.1	25.6	67.2
45-54	184.6	43.2	174.7	42.5	9.9	56.6
55-64	96.4	37.6	93.0	37.1	3.4	50.0
65+	57.2	33.2	55.9	33.1	1.3	38.5
Economic activity (ISIC-Rev.2)	2006 [1][2] Labour force survey		2006 [2] Labour force survey		2006 [2] Labour force survey	
Total	1 249.1	44.1	1 129.5	42.5	119.6	59.9
1 Agriculture, Hunting, Forestry and Fishing	211.2	20.2	206.1	19.4	5.1	52.9
2 Mining and Quarrying	7.1	9.9	6.4	9.4	0.7	14.3
3 Manufacturing	82.0	25.0	73.6	21.9	8.4	52.4
4 Electricity, Gas and Water	8.3	30.1	7.1	32.4	1.2	16.7
5 Construction	128.6	3.8	113.1	2.8	15.5	11.0
6 Wholesale and Retail Trade and Restaurants and Hotels	302.7	65.7	272.4	64.2	30.3	78.9
7 Transport, Storage and Communication	84.7	20.1	79.3	20.2	5.4	18.5
8 Financing, Insurance, Real Estate and Business Services	63.1	56.4	59.3	56.0	3.8	63.2
9 Community, Social and Personal Services	332.4	62.8	310.4	61.9	22.0	75.9
0 Activities not Adequately Defined	3.1	67.7	1.8	66.7	1.3	69.2
Unemployed seeking their first job	25.9	68.0	.	.	25.9	68.0
Occupation (ISCO-88)	2006 [1][2] Labour force survey		2006 [2] Labour force survey		2006 [2] Labour force survey	
Total	1 249.1	44.1	1 129.5	42.5	119.6	59.9
1-3	221.8	59.4	214.8	59.1	7.0	68.6
4 Clerks	110.0	78.3	96.7	77.6	13.3	83.5
5 Service workers and shop and market sales workers	231.4	65.3	206.5	63.2	24.9	81.9
6 Skilled agricultural and fishery workers	196.5	17.5	193.5	17.0	3.0	50.0
7 Craft and related trade workers	194.4	11.7	178.7	11.9	15.7	8.9
8 Plant and machine operators and assemblers	73.9	10.6	67.2	7.7	6.7	38.8
9 Elementary occupations	193.9	51.1	171.6	50.9	22.3	52.5
X Not classifiable by occupation	1.3	76.9	0.5	100.0	0.8	62.5
Unemployed seeking their first job	25.9	68.0	.	.	25.9	68.0
Education level (ISCED-97)					2006 [2] Labour force survey	
Total	.	.	.	.	119.6	59.9
X No schooling	.	.	.	.	88.2	56.2
0 Pre-primary education	.	.	.	.	4.4	86.4
1 Primary education or first stage of basic education	.	.	.	.	4.1	73.2
2 Lower secondary or second stage of basic education	.	.	.	.	7.5	69.3
3 Upper secondary education	.	.	.	.	4.8	66.7
4 Post-secondary non-tertiary education	.	.	.	.	0.3	0.0
5A First stage of tertiary education - theoretically based	.	.	.	.	3.1	71.0
5B First stage of tertiary education - practically oriented	.	.	.	.	1.2	83.3
6 Second stage of tertiary education	.	.	.	.	5.7	63.2
Status in employment (ICSE-1993)			2006 [2] Labour force survey			
Total	.	.	1 129.5	42.5	.	.
1 Employees	.	.	691.7	45.8	.	.
2 Employers	.	.	35.0	28.6	.	.
3 Own-account workers	.	.	386.2	36.3	.	.
5 Contributing family workers	.	.	13.6	76.5	.	.
6 Not classifiable by status	.	.	3.0	70.0	.	.

2. Population ('000), Activity rate and Unemployment rate

	Population 2004 [1] Labour force survey			Activity rate 2004 [1] Labour force survey			Unemployment rate 2004 [2] Labour force survey		
Age group	Total	Men	Women	Total	Men	Women	Total	Men	Women
Total	2 650.1	1 305.4	1 344.7	45.1	51.2	39.2	11.4	8.1	15.7
15+	1 860.6	906.3	954.3	64.3	73.7	55.3	11.4	8.1	15.7
15-24	529.9	263.1	266.8	39.4	45.6	33.3	28.1	22.0	36.3
25-54	982.5	477.4	505.1	84.8	94.1	75.9	8.8	5.6	12.6
55+	348.2	165.8	182.4	44.1	59.3	30.3	3.1	2.5	4.0

Jamaica

3. Paid employment ('000), Hours of work (weekly) and Wages

Economic activity (ISIC-Rev.2)	Paid employment 2002 [3,4] Labour-related establishment survey			Hours of work 2002 [5] Labour-related establishment survey Hours paid for / Wage earners			Wages 2002 Labour-related establishment survey / Employees / Dollar		
	Total	Men	Women	Total	Men	Women	Total	Men	Women
Total	131.963	.	.	.	.	.	.	.	.
2	3.602	.	.	39.99	.	.	9 979.06	.	.
3	43.351	.	.	39.14	.	.	6 092.94	.	.
4	4.318	.	.	40.00	.	.	14 258.30	.	.
5	5.684	.	.	40.11	.	.	4 804.99	.	.
6	32.856	.	.	40.31	.	.	6 431.29	.	.
7	11.966	.	.	39.45	.	.	19 773.70	.	.
8	24.491	.	.	55.54	.	.	11 245.63	.	.
9	5.695	.	.	44.99	.	.	7 589.43	.	.

4. Occupational injuries and Strikes and Lockouts

Economic activity (ISIC-Rev.2)	Rates of fatal injuries 1990 Labour inspectorate records Per 1,000 workers exposed to risk Reported injuries			Rates of non-fatal injuries			Strikes and lockouts 2005 Labour relations records		
	Total	Men	Women	Total	Men	Women	Strikes and lockouts	Workers involved	Days not worked
Total	0.038	.	.	.	.	.	7	680	1 340
1	.	.	.	.	.	.	0	0	0
2	.	.	.	.	.	.	0	0	0
3	0.019	.	.	.	.	.	2	300	500
4	0.848	.	.	.	.	.	1	40	40
5	0.000	.	.	.	.	.	0	0	0
6	0.000	.	.	.	.	.	0	0	0
7	0.000	.	.	.	.	.	3	320	780
8	.	.	.	.	.	.	0	0	0
9	.	.	.	.	.	.	1	20	20

5. Consumer price indices (base period: 2000=100)

	2002	2003	2004	2005	2006	2007
General indices	114.6	126.4	143.6	165.5	179.8	196.8
Food index, including non-alcoholic beverages	109.7	120.2	136.5	161.4	172.0	194.8 [6]
Electricity, gas and other fuel indices [7]	114.9	129.9	151.1	177.7	198.1	.
Clothing indices, including footwear	107.2	112.9	118.3	124.3	133.8	144.7
Rent indices	145.5	157.1	246.4	289.8	327.5	.

[1] Excl. armed forces. [2] Persons aged 14 years and over. [3] Non-agricultural activities. [4] Establishments with 10 or more persons employed. [5] Jan.-Sep. [6] Series replacing former series; prior to 2007: incl. alcoholic beverages. [7] Fuel only.

[1] Non compris les forces armées. [2] Personnes âgées de 14 ans et plus. [3] Activités non agricoles. [4] Etablissements occupant 10 personnes et plus. [5] Janv.-sept. [6] Série remplaçant la précédente; avant 2007: y compris les boissons alcoolisées. [7] Combustible seulement.

[1] Excl. las fuerzas armadas. [2] Personas de 14 años y más. [3] Actividades no agrícolas. [4] Establecimientos con 10 y más trabajadores. [5] Enero-sept. [6] Serie que substituye a la anterior; antes de 2007: incl. las bebidas alcohólicas. [7] Combustible solamente.

Japan

1. Economically active population, Employment and Unemployment ('000)

	Economically active population		Employment		Unemployment	
	Total	Women (%)	Total	Women (%)	Total	Women (%)
Age group	2007 [1] Labour force survey		2007 ★ Labour force survey		2007 [1] Labour force survey	
Total	66 690	41.4	64 120	41.5	2 570	40.1
15-19	1 030	48.5	940	48.9	90	44.4
20-24	5 070	48.5	4 690	48.8	380	44.7
25-29	6 670	43.8	6 290	43.9	380	42.1
30-34	7 590	39.1	7 270	38.9	320	43.8
35-39	7 590	39.4	7 310	39.1	280	46.4
40-44	6 890	42.2	6 680	42.1	210	47.6
45-49	6 670	43.6	6 490	43.6	180	44.4
50-54	6 760	42.6	6 570	42.8	190	36.8
55-59	8 100	40.0	7 860	40.3	240	29.2
60-64	4 830	37.5	4 640	37.9	190	26.3
65-69	2 860	36.7	2 780	37.1	80	25.0
70+	2 630	37.3	2 600	37.3	30	33.3

Economic activity (ISIC-Rev.3)			2007 [1] Labour force survey		2007 [1 2] Labour force survey	
Total			64 120	41.5	1 830	43.2
A Agriculture, Hunting and Forestry			2 510	43.0	10	0.0
B Fishing			210	28.6	0	.
C Mining and Quarrying			40	25.0	0	.
D Manufacturing			11 980	31.5	270 [3]	33.3
E Electricity, Gas and Water Supply			330	9.1	0	.
F Construction			5 520	14.7	150	13.3
G Wholesale and Retail Trade; Repair of Motor Vehicles ...			11 780	48.9	320 [4]	53.1
H Hotels and Restaurants			3 420	59.6	130	61.5
I Transport, Storage and Communications			3 970	19.6	.	.
I,K,O			.	.	510	37.3
J Financial Intermediation			1 550	50.3	40	75.0
K Real Estate, Renting and Business Activities			7 610	38.6	.	.
L Public Administration and Defence; Compulsory Social ...			2 260 [5]	22.6	20	50.0
M Education			2 840	53.9	40	75.0
N Health and Social Work			5 790	76.0	110	81.8
O Other Community, Social and Personal Service Activities			3 540	49.7	.	.
X Not classifiable by economic activity			770	42.9	30 [6]	33.3
Unemployed seeking their first job			.	.	200	35.0

Occupation (ISCO-1968)			2007 [1] Labour force survey		2007 [1 2] Labour force survey	
Total			64 120	41.5	1 820	42.9
0/1 Professional, technical and related workers			9 380	46.2	130	53.8
2 Administrative and managerial workers			1 730	9.2	10	0.0
3 Clerical and related workers			12 620	61.3	350	71.4
4 Sales workers			8 880	38.0	280	42.9
5 Service workers			7 870 [7]	56.8	240	58.3
6 Agriculture, animal husbandry and forestry workers ...			2 690	40.5	20	0.0
7/8/9 Production and related workers, transport equipment ... [8]			20 250	25.4	590	22.0
X Not classifiable by occupation			700	41.4	.	.
Unemployed seeking their first job			.	.	200	35.0

Education level (ISCED-76)	2007 [1 9] Labour force survey				2007 [1 9] Labour force survey	
Total	63 940	41.4			2 500	40.0
X No schooling	40	25.0			.	.
1 First level	38 440 [10]	41.7			.	.
1-3	.	.			1 680	38.1
5 Third level, first stage, leading to an award not equivalent ...	10 420	64.9			390	64.1
6 Third level, first stage, leading to a first university degree ...	15 070 [11]	24.2			.	.
6-7	.	.			430	25.6

Status in employment (ICSE-1993)			2007 [1] Labour force survey			
Total			64 120	41.5		
1 Employees			55 230	41.6		
2 Employers			1 640	17.7		
3 Own-account workers			4 580	27.5		
5 Contributing family workers			2 360	82.2		
6 Not classifiable by status			300	43.3		

2. Population ('000), Activity rate and Unemployment rate

	Population 2007 [12] Labour force survey			Activity rate 2007 [12] Labour force survey			Unemployment rate 2007 [1] Labour force survey		
Age group	Total	Men	Women	Total	Men	Women	Total	Men	Women
Total	127 770	62 310	65 460	52.2	62.7	42.2	3.9	3.9	3.7
15+	110 440	53 430	57 010	60.4	73.1	48.4	3.9	4.0	3.8
15-24	13 580	6 970	6 620	44.9	45.1	44.7	7.7	8.3	7.1
25-54	50 650	25 530	25 100	83.3	96.2	70.0	3.7	3.6	3.9
55+	46 210	20 930	25 290	39.9	54.2	28.0	2.9	3.5	2.1

Japan

3. Paid employment ('000), Hours of work (weekly) and Wages

Economic activity (ISIC-Rev.3)	Paid employment 2007 [1] Labour force survey			Hours of work 2007 Labour-related establishment survey Hours actually worked / Employees			Wages 2007 [13][14] Labour-related establishment survey Earnings per month / Employees / Yen		
	Total	Men	Women	Total	Men	Women	Total	Men	Women
Total	55 230	32 260	22 970	.	.	.	.	.	.
C-Q	.	.	.	35.6	38.5	31.2	.	.	.
A	450	240	210	.	.	.	.	.	.
B	70	60	20	.	.	.	.	.	.
C	40	30	10	38.2	38.6	35.6	301 900	314 300	206 000
D	11 220	7 800	3 420	38.7	40.2	34.6	296 800	328 500	197 700
E	330	290	30	36.7	37.2	33.5	405 700	418 000	296 000
F	4 490	3 800	690	40.2	40.8	36.0	321 100	336 100	211 800
G	10 320	5 200	5 120	32.7	37.2	28.8	295 500 [4]	336 300 [4]	215 600 [4]
H	2 660	1 050	1 610	28.3	32.9	24.6	239 500	274 300	184 500
I	3 780	3 040	760	.	.	.	.	.	.
J	1 490	730	770	35.2	36.8	33.3	377 300	477 400	257 900
K	6 660	4 030	2 620	.	.	.	.	.	.
L	2 260 [5]	1 760 [5]	510 [5]	.	.	.	.	.	.
M	2 590	1 250	1 340	31.8	33.3	29.6	382 900	441 900	299 800
N	5 470	1 180	4 290	33.7	34.7	33.4	269 800	355 000	242 100
O	2 930	1 540	1 390	.	.	.	.	.	.
X	480	280	210	.	.	.	.	.	.

Share of women in wage employment in the non-agricultural sector [1] (2007 - Labour force survey): **41.5%**

4. Occupational injuries and Strikes and Lockouts

Economic activity (ISIC-Rev.3)	Rates of fatal injuries 2007 [15] Labour inspectorate records Per 1,000,000 hours worked Reported injuries			Rates of non-fatal injuries			Strikes and lockouts 2006 [16] Labour relations records		
	Total	Men	Women	Total	Men	Women	Strikes and lockouts	Workers involved [17]	Days not worked
Total	0.01 [18]	.	.	.	.	.	18	1 820	1 831
A	.	.	.	.	.	.	0	0	0
B	.	.	.	.	.	.	0	0	0
C	0.00	.	.	.	.	.	2	4	10
D	0.01	.	.	.	.	.	9	667	667
E	0.00	.	.	.	.	.	1	15	0
F	0.04 [19]	.	.	.	.	.	0	0	0
G [4]	0.00	.	.	.	.	.	1	54	54
H	.	.	.	.	.	.	0	0	0
I	.	.	.	.	.	.	0	0	0
J	.	.	.	.	.	.	0	0	0
K	.	.	.	.	.	.	0	0	0
L	.	.	.	.	.	.	0	0	0
M	.	.	.	.	.	.	2	9	23
N	.	.	.	.	.	.	3	1 071	1 077
O	.	.	.	.	.	.	0	0	0

5. Consumer price indices (base period: 2000=100)

	2002	2003	2004	2005	2006	2007
General indices	98.4	98.1	98.1	97.8	98.1	98.1
Food index, including non-alcoholic beverages	98.6	98.4	99.3	98.4	98.9	99.2
Electricity, gas and other fuel indices [20]	99.4	98.9	99.0	99.8	103.4	104.2
Clothing indices, including footwear	95.6	93.8	93.6	94.3	95.1	95.6
Rent indices	100.4	100.5	100.3	100.3	100.3	100.1
General index, excluding housing [21]	98.0	97.7	97.7	97.3	97.6	97.7

[1] Persons aged 15 years and over. [2] Refer only to unemployed who left the previous job in the past 3 years. [3] Excl. publishing. [4] Excl. repair of motor vehicles, motor cycles and personal and household goods. [5] Incl. self-defence forces. [6] Incl. repair of motor vehicles, motor cycles and personal and household goods, divisions 71, 73 and 74. [7] Incl. self-defence forces. Excl. cleaners. [8] Incl. cleaners. [9] Refer only to persons graduated from school. [10] Levels 1-3. [11] Levels 6-7. [12] "De facto" population. [13] Private sector; establishments with 10 or more regular employees; June of each year. [14] Regular scheduled cash earnings. [15] Establishments with 100 or more regular employees. [16] Excl. work stoppages lasting less than half a day. [17] Excl. workers indirectly involved. [18] Excl. general construction. [19] General construction only. [20] Incl. water and sewerage. [21] Excl. imputed rent only.

[1] Personnes âgées de 15 ans et plus. [2] Se rapportent seulement aux chômeurs dont le dernier travail date de moins de 3 ans. [3] Non compris l'édition. [4] Non compris réparation de véhicules automobiles, de motocycles et de biens personnels et domestiques. [5] Y compris les forces d'autodéfense. [6] Non compris la réparation de véhicules automobiles, de motocycles et de biens personnels et domestiques, divisions 71, 73 et 74. [7] Y compris les forces d'autodéfense. Non compris les nettoyeurs. [8] Y compris les nettoyeurs. [9] Se rapportent seulement aux personnes diplômées de l'école. [10] Niveaux 1-3. [11] Niveaux 6-7. [12] Population "de facto". [13] Secteur privé; établissements occupant 10 salariés stables ou plus; juin de chaque années. [14] Gains en espèce tarifés réguliers. [15] Etablissements de 100 salariés stables et plus. [16] Non compris les arrêts du travail de durée inférieure à une demi-journée. [17] Non compris les travailleurs indirectement impliqués. [18] Non compris la construction générale. [19] Construction générale seulement. [20] Y compris l'eau et le traitement des eaux résiduaires. [21] Non compris le loyer imputé seulement.

[1] Personas de 15 años y más. [2] Se refieren solamente de las desempleados cuyo último trabajo fue hace menos de 3 años. [3] Excl. las editoriales. [4] Excl. reparación de vehículos automotores, motocicletas, efectos personals y enseres domesticos. [5] Incl. a las fuerzas de autodefensa. [6] Excl. la reparación de vehículos automotores, motocicletas, efectos personales y enseresdomesticos, divisiones 71, 73 y 74. [7] Incl. a las fuerzas de autodefensa. Excl. los limpiadores. [8] Incl. los limpiadores. [9] Se refieren solamente de las personas con diploma. [10] Niveles 1-3. [11] Niveles 6-7. [12] Población "de facto". [13] Sector privado; establecimientos con 10 y mas asalariados estables; junio de cada año. [14] Ganancias en especie tarifadas regulares. [15] Establecimientos de 100 y más asalariados estables. [16] Excl. las interrupciones del trabajo de duración inferior a medio día. [17] Excl. los trabajadores indirectamente implicados. [18] Excl. construcción general. [19] Construcción general solamente. [20] Incl. el agua y el tratamiento de aguas residuales. [21] Excl. el alquiler imputado solamente.

Jersey

1. Economically active population, Employment and Unemployment ('000)

	Economically active population		Employment		Unemployment	
	Total	Women (%)	Total	Women (%)	Total	Women (%)
Age group	1996 [1,2] Population census		2007 [3] Official estimates		2007 [3] Employment office records	
Total	46.992	44.6	53.000	.	0.320	.
15-19	1.428	44.0	.	.	.	.
20-24	4.516	50.6	.	.	.	.
25-29	7.063	48.4	.	.	.	.
30-34	7.000	45.1	.	.	.	.
35-39	6.160	44.5	.	.	.	.
40-44	5.495	45.4	.	.	.	.
45-49	5.499	45.1	.	.	.	.
50-54	3.905	43.4	.	.	.	.
55-59	3.201	38.1	.	.	.	.
60-64	1.849	28.9	.	.	.	.
65-69	0.509	36.1	.	.	.	.
70-74	0.246	37.4	.	.	.	.
75+	0.121	36.4	.	.	.	.

Economic activity (ISIC-Rev.2)	1996 [1,2] Population census					
Total	45.4	45.0	.	.	.	.
1 Agriculture, Hunting, Forestry and Fishing	2.2	25.6	.	.	.	.
2 Mining and Quarrying	0.2	5.2	.	.	.	.
3 Manufacturing	1.7	22.9	.	.	.	.
4 Electricity, Gas and Water	0.6	15.2	.	.	.	.
5 Construction	4.2	3.7	.	.	.	.
6 Wholesale and Retail Trade and Restaurants and Hotels	11.0	44.4	.	.	.	.
7 Transport, Storage and Communication	2.6	25.0	.	.	.	.
8 Financing, Insurance, Real Estate and Business Services	11.6	56.4	.	.	.	.
9 Community, Social and Personal Services	10.2	62.0	.	.	.	.
0 Activities not Adequately Defined	1.2	73.0	.	.	.	.

Economic activity (ISIC-Rev.3)			2007 [3] Administrative reports			
Total	.	.	44.1	.	.	.
A-B	.	.	1.5	.	.	.
C,F	.	.	4.7	.	.	.
D Manufacturing	.	.	1.4	.	.	.
E Electricity, Gas and Water Supply	.	.	0.5	.	.	.
G Wholesale and Retail Trade; Repair of Motor Vehicles ...	.	.	8.2	.	.	.
H Hotels and Restaurants	.	.	4.5	.	.	.
I Transport, Storage and Communications	.	.	2.5	.	.	.
J Financial Intermediation	.	.	13.0	.	.	.
K Real Estate, Renting and Business Activities	.	.	3.0	.	.	.
L-O	.	.	4.5	.	.	.

Occupation (ISCO-88)			2001 [4] Population census			
Total	.	.	45.6	45.5	.	.
1 Legislators, senior officials and managers	.	.	7.1	29.5	.	.
2 Professionals	.	.	3.3	43.1	.	.
3 Technicians and associate professionals	.	.	6.2	53.3	.	.
4 Clerks	.	.	8.6	80.0	.	.
5 Service workers and shop and market sales workers	.	.	6.7	5.5	.	.
6 Skilled agricultural and fishery workers	.	.	2.9	84.7	.	.
7 Craft and related trade workers	.	.	2.8	64.1	.	.
8 Plant and machine operators and assemblers	.	.	2.1	6.0	.	.
9 Elementary occupations	.	.	5.8	39.1	.	.

Status in employment (ICSE-1993)	1996 [1,2] Population census					
Total	45.4	45.0	.	.	.	.

2. Population ('000), Activity rate and Unemployment rate

	Population 2001 Population census			Activity rate 1996 [2,5] Population census			Unemployment rate 2007 [3] Employment office records		
Age group	Total	Men	Women	Total	Men	Women	Total	Men	Women
Total	87.2	42.5	44.7	.	.	.	0.6	.	.
15+	72.4	34.9	37.5	66.2	76.2	56.8	.	.	.
15-24	9.9	4.8	5.0	59.9	62.6	57.4	.	.	.
25-54	41.2	20.3	20.9	86.7	95.6	78.0	.	.	.
55+	21.3	9.7	11.6	28.8	41.5	18.3	.	.	.

Jersey

3. Paid employment ('000), Hours of work (weekly) and Wages

Economic activity (ISIC-Rev.3)	Paid employment Total	Men	Women	Hours of work 2001 [6,7] Population census Hours actually worked / Total employment Total	Men	Women	Wages 2007 [8,9,10] Labour-related establishment survey Earnings per week / Employees / Pound Total	Men	Women
Total	.	.	.	.	.	.	580	.	.
A-B	.	.	.	45 [11]	.	.	.	.	.
A	.	.	.	.	.	.	340 [11]	.	.
C,F	.	.	.	42	.	.	.	.	.
D	.	.	.	41	.	.	550	.	.
E	.	.	.	40	.	.	650	.	.
F	.	.	.	.	.	.	550	.	.
G	.	.	.	41	.	.	410	.	.
H	.	.	.	45	.	.	320	.	.
I	.	.	.	41	.	.	690	.	.
J	.	.	.	38	.	.	770	.	.
K	.	.	.	39 [12]	.	.	.	.	.
72	.	.	.	39 [13]	.	.	.	.	.
74	.	.	.	.	.	.	520	.	.
L	.	.	.	.	.	.	760	.	.
M-O	.	.	.	39	.	.	.	.	.

4. Occupational injuries and Strikes and Lockouts

Statistics not available.

5. Consumer price indices (base period: 2000=100)

[14,15]	2002	2003	2004	2005	2006	2007
General indices	108.3	112.9	118.3	122.6	126.2	131.6
Food index, including non-alcoholic beverages	107.3	109.6	114.0	114.4	117.0	122.1
Electricity, gas and other fuel indices	99.4	102.0	108.6	124.9	142.4	157.0
Clothing indices, including footwear	96.1	94.5	92.4	90.3	90.0	87.0
Rent indices	109.5	114.3	125.9	136.9	140.0	156.0

[1] Persons aged 15 years and over. [2] March. [3] December. [4] Persons aged 16 years and over. [5] "De facto" population. [6] Full-time employees and self-employed persons. [7] Main occupation; excl. overtime. [8] Approximate levels since survey aims at measuring changes; excl. bonuses. [9] Full-time equivalent employees. [10] June. [11] Excl. hunting and forestry. [12] Business services. [13] Computer and related activities. [14] Index base June 2000=100. [15] June of each year.

[1] Personnes âgées de 15 ans et plus. [2] Mars. [3] Décembre. [4] Personnes âgées de 16 ans et plus. [5] Population "de facto". [6] Salariés à temps complet et travailleurs indépendants. [7] Profession principale; non compris les heures supplémentaires. [8] Niveaux approximatifs étant donné que l'enquête vise à mesurer l'évolution; non compris les primes. [9] Salariés en équivalents à plein temps. [10] Juin. [11] Non compris la chasse et la sylviculture. [12] Services aux entreprises. [13] Activités informatiques et activités rattachées. [14] Indice base juin 2000=100. [15] Juin de chaque année.

[1] Personas de 15 años y más. [2] Marzo. [3] Diciembre. [4] Personas de 16 años y más. [5] Población "de facto". [6] Asalariados a tiempo completeo y trabajadores independientes. [7] Ocupación principal; excl. las horas extraordinarias. [8] Niveles aproximativos ya que la encuesta tiene por objetivo medir cambios; excl. las primas. [9] Asalariados en equivalentes a tiempo completo. [10] Junio. [11] Excl. caza y silvicultura. [12] Servicios para empresas. [13] Informática y actividades conexas. [14] Indice base junio 2000=100. [15] Junio de cada año.

Jordan

1. Economically active population, Employment and Unemployment ('000)

Statistics not available.

2. Population ('000), Activity rate and Unemployment rate

Statistics not available.

3. Paid employment ('000), Hours of work (weekly) and Wages

Economic activity (ISIC-Rev.3)	Paid employment Total	Men	Women	Hours of work 2005 [1,2] Labour-related establishment survey Hours paid for / Employees Total	Men	Women	Wages 2005 [1] Labour-related establishment survey Earnings per month / Employees / Dinar Total	Men	Women
C	.	.	.	249.0	249.0	246.0	440.0	439.0	471.0
C-O	.	.	.	.	.	.	262.0	273.0	231.0
D	.	.	.	259.0	261.0	254.0	203.0	222.0	136.0
E	.	.	.	224.0	224.0	225.0	337.0	339.0	301.0
F	.	.	.	250.0	250.0	249.0	284.0	283.0	341.0
G	.	.	.	284.0	286.0	261.0	202.0	187.0	204.0
H	.	.	.	268.0	269.0	252.0	201.0	199.0	427.0
I	.	.	.	253.0	254.0	248.0	419.0	418.0	473.0
J	.	.	.	245.0	245.0	246.0	594.0	644.0	258.0
K	.	.	.	251.0	252.0	247.0	274.0	277.0	256.0
L	.	.	.	214.0	213.0	219.0	247.0	246.0	256.0
M	.	.	.	205.0	212.0	199.0	308.0	371.0	255.0
N	.	.	.	227.0	226.0	228.0	276.0	328.0	225.0
O	.	.	.	.	255.0	257.0	190.0	208.0	160.0

4. Occupational injuries and Strikes and Lockouts

Economic activity (ISIC-Rev.3)	Rates of fatal injuries 2006 Insurance records Per 1,000,000 hours worked Reported injuries Total	Men	Women	Rates of non-fatal injuries 2006 Insurance records Per 1,000,000 hours worked Reported injuries Total	Men	Women	Strikes and lockouts 2005 Labour relations records Strikes and lockouts	Workers involved	Days not worked
Total	0.055	.	.	9.640	.	.	0	0	0

5. Consumer price indices (base period: 2000=100)

	2002	2003	2004	2005	2006	2007
General indices	103.6	105.3	108.9	112.7	119.7	126.2
Food index, including non-alcoholic beverages [3]	100.5	103.1	107.8	113.4	121.8	133.1
Electricity, gas and other fuel indices	112.3	117.3	123.3	134.4	167.0	173.3
Clothing indices, including footwear	100.5	97.2	94.9	94.5	97.1	103.3
Rent indices	104.0	106.3	107.8	109.1	110.8	111.8
General index, excluding housing	103.6	106.0				

[1] Oct. [2] Per month. [3] Incl. tobacco.   [1] Oct. [2] Par mois. [3] Y compris le tabac.   [1] Oct. [2] Por mes. [3] Incl. el tabaco.

Kazakhstan

1. Economically active population, Employment and Unemployment ('000)

	Economically active population		Employment		Unemployment	
	Total	Women (%)	Total	Women (%)	Total	Women (%)
Age group	2004 [1] Labour force survey		2004 ★ Labour force survey		2004 [1] Labour force survey	
Total	7 840.6	49.0	7 181.8	48.2	658.8	57.3
15-19	410.1	44.1	336.7	42.9	73.4	49.5
20-24	932.4	45.6	814.2	45.0	118.2	50.0
25-29	1 118.3	47.7	1 012.5	46.9	105.8	55.7
30-34	1 167.7	49.7	1 078.8	48.3	88.9	65.7
35-39	941.2	49.6	873.9	48.9	67.3	59.0
40-44	1 068.2	51.8	1 003.4	51.2	64.8	62.2
45-49	891.7	51.0	830.5	50.3	61.2	60.8
50-54	699.2	51.4	650.9	50.3	48.3	66.9
55-59	353.7	48.5	329.1	47.8	24.6	57.7
60-64	150.6	40.8	.	.	.	.
65-69	81.3	49.0	81.3	49.0	.	.
70+	26.3	55.1	26.3	55.1	.	.

Economic activity (ISIC-Rev.3)

2004 [1] Labour force survey

	Total	Women (%)
Total	7 181.8	48.2
A Agriculture, Hunting and Forestry	2 387.9	46.3
B Fishing	18.1	12.7
C Mining and Quarrying	186.0	21.5
D Manufacturing	519.8	36.4
E Electricity, Gas and Water Supply	163.8	32.8
F Construction	380.7	20.5
G Wholesale and Retail Trade; Repair of Motor Vehicles ...	1 058.7	60.1
H Hotels and Restaurants	82.0	72.9
I Transport, Storage and Communications	519.7	25.0
J Financial Intermediation	60.7	60.5
K Real Estate, Renting and Business Activities	233.6	48.5
L Public Administration and Defence; Compulsory Social ...	334.7	42.6
M Education	666.2	73.1
N Health and Social Work	318.7	79.6
O Other Community, Social and Personal Service Activities	201.3	53.1
P Households with Employed Persons	49.4	58.7
Q Extra-Territorial Organizations and Bodies	0.5	100.0

Occupation (ISCO-88)

2004 [1] Labour force survey

	Total	Women (%)
Total	7 181.8	48.2
1 Legislators, senior officials and managers	374.1	38.0
2 Professionals	828.7	67.9
3 Technicians and associate professionals	575.8	64.5
4 Clerks	170.7	75.6
5 Service workers and shop and market sales workers	995.0	66.3
6 Skilled agricultural and fishery workers	1 276.7	45.5
7 Craft and related trade workers	699.5	21.4
8 Plant and machine operators and assemblers	622.4	9.5
9 Elementary occupations	1 604.7	49.9
X Not classifiable by occupation	34.2	23.7

Education level (ISCED-97)

	Economically active population 2004 [1] Labour force survey		Employment 2004 ★ Labour force survey		Unemployment 2004 [1] Labour force survey	
	Total	Women (%)	Total	Women (%)	Total	Women (%)
Total	7 840.6	49.0	7 181.8	48.2	658.8	57.3
1 Primary education or first stage of basic education	101.0	48.5	93.8	48.8	7.2	44.4
2 Lower secondary or second stage of basic education	368.3	45.0	327.1	44.4	41.2	50.0
3 Upper secondary education	2 460.0	46.2	2 197.6	45.2	262.4	55.0
4 Post-secondary non-tertiary education	987.7	40.1	900.5	38.9	87.2	52.9
5A First stage of tertiary education - theoretically based	2 155.5	53.1	1 991.3	52.2	164.2	64.2
5B First stage of tertiary education - practically oriented	246.8	50.4	219.5	50.5	27.3	50.2
6 Second stage of tertiary education	1 521.3	54.2	1 452.0	53.7	69.3	64.1

Status in employment (ICSE-1993)

2004 [1] Labour force survey

	Total	Women (%)
Total	7 181.8	48.2
1 Employees	4 469.9	46.7
2 Employers	82.3	27.0
3 Own-account workers	2 487.4	51.8
4 Members of producers' cooperatives	58.2	36.3
5 Contributing family workers	84.0	54.3

2. Population ('000), Activity rate and Unemployment rate

	Population 2004 Labour force survey			Activity rate 2004 Labour force survey			Unemployment rate 2004 [1] Labour force survey		
Age group	Total	Men	Women	Total	Men	Women	Total	Men	Women
Total	.	.	.	.	.	.	8.4	7.0	9.8
15+	11 224.0	5 292.0	5 932.0	69.9	75.6	64.8	.	.	.
15-24	2 712.7	1 394.2	1 318.5	49.5	52.8	46.0	14.3	13.1	15.7
25-54	6 448.3	3 097.2	3 351.1	91.3	94.9	88.0	7.4	5.8	9.1
55+	2 063.0	800.6	1 262.4	29.7	40.5	22.8	.	.	.

Kazakhstan

3. Paid employment ('000), Hours of work (weekly) and Wages

Economic activity (ISIC-Rev.2)	Paid employment			Hours of work 1993[2] Labour-related establishment census Hours actually worked / Wage earners			Wages		
	Total	Men	Women	Total	Men	Women	Total	Men	Women
2	.	.	.	128.47	.	.	.	.	.
3	.	.	.	136.91	.	.	.	.	.
4	.	.	.	157.36	.	.	.	.	.
5	.	.	.	147.06	.	.	.	.	.

Economic activity (ISIC-Rev.3)	Paid employment 2004[1] Labour force survey			Hours of work			Wages 2004 Labour-related establishment census Earnings per month / Employees / Tenge		
	Total	Men	Women	Total	Men	Women	Total	Men	Women
Total	4 469.9	2 383.7	2 086.2	.	.	.	28 329	34 648	21 445
A	605.8	426.4	179.4	.	.	.	11 978	12 978	9 869
B	7.8	6.6	1.2	.	.	.	10 999	11 528	9 504
C	186.0	146.1	39.9	.	.	.	54 305	58 548	40 459
D	495.8	318.9	176.9	.	.	.	30 234	33 542	23 433
E	163.8	110.1	53.7	.	.	.	26 899	28 977	22 052
F	332.9	263.6	69.3	.	.	.	38 622	39 569	33 133
G	457.3	175.6	281.7	.	.	.	27 595	31 131	22 749
H	71.8	18.4	53.4	.	.	.	44 925	65 740	33 800
I	396.0	273.3	122.7	.	.	.	41 637	45 409	34 431
J	60.7	24.0	36.7	.	.	.	64 532	87 571	52 541
K	220.3	112.8	107.5	.	.	.	40 628	45 349	32 372
L	334.7	192.2	142.5	.	.	.	26 031	28 390	22 227
M	657.2	176.4	480.8	.	.	.	17 964	21 000	16 916
N	311.1	63.2	247.9	.	.	.	15 195	17 427	14 739
O	153.8	71.6	82.2	.	.	.	29 510	37 054	22 371
P	14.5	4.6	9.9	.	.	.	.	.	.
Q	0.5	-	0.5	.	.	.	139 888	153 226	122 739

Share of women in wage employment in the non-agricultural sector [1] (2004 - Labour force survey): **49.4%**

4. Occupational injuries and Strikes and Lockouts

Economic activity (ISIC-Rev.3)	Rates of fatal injuries 1999 Labour inspectorate records Per 100,000 workers employed Reported injuries			Rates of non-fatal injuries 1999 Labour inspectorate records Per 100,000 workers employed Reported injuries			Strikes and lockouts 1993 Source unknown		
	Total	Men	Women	Total	Men	Women	Strikes and lockouts	Workers involved	Days not worked
Total	9.7	16.4	1.8	122	184	49	0	0	0
A	9.4	12.4	0.0	100	106	81	.	.	.
B	13.9	19.2	0.0	347	462	50	.	.	.
C	17.7	23.9	0.0	250	309	86	.	.	.
D	16.9	23.9	4.7	298	413	101	.	.	.
E	17.7	24.9	0.0	158	181	101	.	.	.
F	24.4	28.1	10.5	199	235	67	.	.	.
G	6.2	10.8	0.0	35	50	15	.	.	.
H	0.0	0.0	0.0	24	21	26	.	.	.
I	9.7	14.2	1.1	120	152	57	.	.	.
J	12.3	16.6	9.8	40	41	39	.	.	.
K	6.0	9.0	1.8	58	77	32	.	.	.
L	6.0	10.6	1.6	54	72	35	.	.	.
M	2.0	3.3	1.4	25	34	23	.	.	.
N	2.3	7.7	1.0	48	77	41	.	.	.
O	11.6	21.7	0.0	93	149	28	.	.	.
Q	0.0	0.0	0.0	0	0	0	.	.	.

5. Consumer price indices (base period: 2000=100)

	2002	2003	2004	2005	2006	2007
General indices	114.7	122.1	130.5	140.3	.	.
Food index, including non-alcoholic beverages [3]	119.0	127.3	137.1	148.2	.	.
Electricity, gas and other fuel indices	110.4	115.7	121.0	.	.	.
Clothing indices, including footwear	114.8	124.1	132.2	.	.	.
Rent indices	102.7	104.7	108.9	.	.	.

[1] Persons aged 15 years and over. [2] Per month. [3] Incl. alcoholic beverages and tobacco.

[1] Personnes âgées de 15 ans et plus. [2] Par mois. [3] Y compris les boissons alcoolisées et le tabac.

[1] Personas de 15 años y más. [2] Por mes. [3] Incl. las bebidas alcohólicas y el tabaco.

Kenya

1. Economically active population, Employment and Unemployment ('000)

Age group	Economically active population Total	Women (%)	Employment Total	Women (%)	Unemployment Total	Women (%)
	1999 [1,2] Population census		1999 [1,2] Population census		1999 [1,2] Population census	
Total	15 750.1	.	14 474.2	.	1 275.8	.
0-14	2 678.3	.				
15-19	2 110.6	.				
20-24	2 350.4	.				
25-29	2 053.0	.				
30-34	1 513.7	.				
35-39	1 284.6	.				
40-44	937.1	.				
45-49	767.3	.				
50-54	622.3	.				
55-59	406.9	.				
60-64	354.5	.				
65+	676.1	.				

2. Population ('000), Activity rate and Unemployment rate

Age group	Population 1999 [1,2] Population census Total	Men	Women	Activity rate 1999 [1,2] Population census Total	Men	Women	Unemployment rate 1999 [1,2] Population census Total	Men	Women
Total	23 837.6	.	.	66.1	.	.	8.1	.	.
15+	15 936.2	.	.	82.1	.	.	.	.	.
15-24	6 178.1	.	.	72.2	.	.	.	.	.
25-54	7 951.4	.	.	90.3	.	.	.	.	.
55+	1 806.7	.	.	79.6	.	.	.	.	.

3. Paid employment ('000), Hours of work (weekly) and Wages

Economic activity (ISIC-Rev.2)	Paid employment 2000 [3,4] Labour-related establishment survey Total	Men	Women	Hours of work 1997 [4] Labour-related establishment census Hours paid for / Employees Total	Men	Women	Wages 1997 [4,5] Labour-related establishment census Earnings per month / Employees / Shilling Total	Men	Women
Total	1 677.4	.	.	.	.	.	.	.	.
2-9	.	.	.	40	.	.	5 608.3	5 495.7	5 846.1
1	311.6	.	.	43	.	.	2 311.0	1 700.5	.
2	5.2	.	.	36	.	.	5 617.9	3 231.6	5 660.1
3	217.9	.	.	44	.	.	5 510.8	5 294.3	6 509.5
4	22.3	.	.	40	.	.	.	3 373.5	2 159.5
5	78.0	.	.	41	.	.	4 667.2	4 696.8	4 372.6
6	155.5	.	.	41	.	.	7 600.7	8 596.8	6 044.6
7	83.4	.	.	38	.	.	7 711.8	8 718.7	5 003.5
8	84.7	.	.	41	.	.	11 063.0	9 547.5	15 463.0
9	718.9	.	.	40	.	.	4 409.0	4 117.7	4 846.3

4. Occupational injuries and Strikes and Lockouts

Economic activity (ISIC-Rev.2)	Rates of fatal injuries Total	Men	Women	Rates of non-fatal injuries Total	Men	Women	Strikes and lockouts 1997 Labour inspectorate records Strikes and lockouts	Workers involved	Days not worked [6]
Total	.	.	.	.	.	.	44	16 029	217 012
1	.	.	.	.	.	.	12	8 170	133 766
2	.	.	.	.	.	.	3	532	1 775
3	.	.	.	.	.	.	15	5 587	79 615
4	.	.	.	.	.	.	0	0	0
5	.	.	.	.	.	.	1	45	28
6	.	.	.	.	.	.	2	38	45
7	.	.	.	.	.	.	0	0	0
8	.	.	.	.	.	.	0	0	0
9	.	.	.	.	.	.	7	1 340	1 301
0	.	.	.	.	.	.	4	317	482

5. Consumer price indices (base period: 2000=100)

Nairobi [7]	2002	2003	2004	2005	2006	2007
General indices	105.3	116.7	133.5	149.1	178.3	195.1
Food index, including non-alcoholic beverages	103.9	120.9	143.8	164.8	210.8	233.8
Electricity, gas and other fuel indices	114.9	121.4	142.6	176.4	197.0	.
Clothing indices, including footwear	99.9	100.8	105.6	111.7	116.0	118.7
Rent indices	109.4	111.6	114.5	118.6	122.1	130.4

[1] Persons aged 15 years and over. [2] Aug. [3] Excl. small establishments in rural areas. [4] June. [5] Incl. the value of payments in kind. [6] Computed on the basis of an eight-hour working day. [7] Low income group.

[1] Personnes âgées de 15 ans et plus. [2] Août. [3] Non compris les petites entreprises des zones rurales. [4] Juin. [5] Y compris la valeur des paiements en nature. [6] Calculées sur la base de journées de travail de huit heures. [7] Familles à revenu modique.

[1] Personas de 15 años y más. [2] Agosto. [3] Excl. las pequeñas empresas de las zonas rurales. [4] Junio. [5] Incl. el valor de los pagos en especie. [6] Calculados en base a días de trabajo de ocho horas. [7] Familias de ingresos módicos.

Kiribati

1. Economically active population, Employment and Unemployment ('000)

Age group	Economically active population Total	Women (%)	Employment Total	Women (%)	Unemployment Total	Women (%)
	1995 [1,2] Population census		2000 [1] Population census			
Total	38.179	47.8	9.200	36.8	.	.

Economic activity (ISIC-Rev.2)			2000 [1] Population census			
Total	.	.	9.200	36.8	.	.
1 Agriculture, Hunting, Forestry and Fishing	.	.	0.254	14.6	.	.
2 Mining and Quarrying	.	.	0.000	.	.	.
3 Manufacturing	.	.	0.150	37.3	.	.
4 Electricity, Gas and Water	.	.	0.187	14.4	.	.
5 Construction	.	.	0.346	6.1	.	.
6 Wholesale and Retail Trade and Restaurants and Hotels	.	.	1.181	41.0	.	.
7 Transport, Storage and Communication	.	.	0.944	23.9	.	.
8 Financing, Insurance, Real Estate and Business Services	.	.	0.317	46.7	.	.
9 Community, Social and Personal Services	.	.	5.821	41.1	.	.

Occupation (ISCO-1968)			2000 [1] Population census			
Total	.	.	9.200	36.8	.	.
0/1 Professional, technical and related workers	.	.	3.493	44.4	.	.
2 Administrative and managerial workers	.	.	0.622	26.5	.	.
3 Clerical and related workers	.	.	1.143	67.5	.	.
4 Sales workers	.	.	0.812	26.0	.	.
5 Service workers	.	.	1.718	33.8	.	.
6 Agriculture, animal husbandry and forestry workers ...	.	.	0.201	10.0	.	.
7/8/9 Production and related workers, transport equipment ...	.	.	1.211	7.5	.	.

2. Population ('000), Activity rate and Unemployment rate

Age group	Population 1995 [2,3] Population census			Activity rate 1995 [2,3] Population census			Unemployment rate		
	Total	Men	Women	Total	Men	Women	Total	Men	Women
Total	45.446	21.910	23.536	84.0	91.0	77.5	.	.	.

3. Paid employment ('000), Hours of work (weekly) and Wages

Statistics not available.

4. Occupational injuries and Strikes and Lockouts

Statistics not available.

5. Consumer price indices (base period: 2000=100)

Tarawa	2002	2003	2004	2005	2006	2007
General indices	109.4	111.4	110.3	110.0	108.3	.
Food index, including non-alcoholic beverages	109.7	112.8	112.8	112.7	108.3	.
Clothing indices, including footwear	93.3	94.7	90.2	94.5	87.3	.
Rent indices	102.2	102.7	102.4	102.5	102.4	.

[1] Persons aged 15 years and over. [2] Nov. [3] "De facto" population.

[1] Personnes âgées de 15 ans et plus. [2] Nov. [3] Population "de facto".

[1] Personas de 15 años y más. [2] Nov. [3] Población "de facto".

Korea, Republic of

1. Economically active population, Employment and Unemployment ('000)

	Economically active population		Employment		Unemployment	
	Total	Women (%)	Total	Women (%)	Total	Women (%)
Age group	2007 [1,2] Labour force survey		2007 ★ Labour force survey		2007 [2] Labour force survey	
Total	24 215.7	41.7	23 432.7	41.9	783.0	34.0
15-19	232.2	53.4	210.2	53.7	22.0	50.0
20-24	1 438.9	62.3	1 312.9	63.6	126.0	49.2
25-29	2 858.8	46.0	2 678.8	47.1	180.0	30.0
30-34	2 885.6	35.9	2 778.6	36.1	107.0	30.8
35-39	3 347.3	37.5	3 257.3	37.7	90.0	30.0
40-44	3 313.5	40.7	3 237.5	40.7	76.0	36.8
45-49	3 305.2	41.0	3 246.2	41.1	59.0	30.5
50-54	2 535.4	39.7	2 482.4	39.9	53.0	30.2
55-59	1 645.1	38.2	1 611.1	38.5	34.0	23.5
60-64	1 130.1	40.0	1 104.1	40.4	26.0	26.9
65-69	806.4	41.9	799.4	42.1	7.0	14.3
70-74	470.4	45.6	467.4	45.7	3.0	33.3
75+	246.8	49.3	245.8	49.5	1.0	0.0
Economic activity (ISIC-Rev.3)	2007 ★ Labour force survey		2007 [2,3] Labour force survey		2007 [2] Labour force survey	
Total	24 216	41.7	23 433	41.9	783	34.0
A Agriculture, Hunting and Forestry	1 674	47.4	1 670	47.4	4	50.0
B Fishing	57	36.8	56	37.5	1	0.0
C Mining and Quarrying	18	5.6	18	5.6	0	.
D Manufacturing	4 232	32.5	4 119	32.6	113	29.2
E Electricity, Gas and Water Supply	87	23.0	86	22.1	1	100.0
F Construction	1 942	9.2	1 850	9.3	92	6.5
G Wholesale and Retail Trade; Repair of Motor Vehicles ...	3 774	45.4	3 677	45.6	97	36.1
H Hotels and Restaurants	2 114	68.6	2 049	69.1	65	53.8
I Transport, Storage and Communications	1 521	12.1	1 498	12.1	23	8.7
J Financial Intermediation	821	51.7	809	51.8	12	50.0
K Real Estate, Renting and Business Activities	2 422	35.2	2 350	35.2	72	33.3
L Public Administration and Defence; Compulsory Social ...	807	32.1	797	31.9	10	50.0
M Education	1 708	67.7	1 687	67.8	21	66.7
N Health and Social Work	758	73.5	745	73.3	13	84.6
O Other Community, Social and Personal Service Activities	1 898	45.8	1 845	46.1	53	34.0
P Households with Employed Persons	164	97.7	161	97.7	3	100.0
Q Extra-Territorial Organizations and Bodies	15	19.6	15	19.6	0	.
X Not classifiable by economic activity	.	.	.	.	159	34.6
Unemployed seeking their first job					41	39.0
Occupation (ISCO-88)	2007 ★ Labour force survey		2007 [2,3] Labour force survey		2007 [2] Labour force survey	
Total	24 216	41.7	23 433	41.9	783	34.0
1 Legislators, senior officials and managers	562	8.9	556	8.8	6	16.7
2 Professionals	2 056	46.1	2 032	46.1	24	50.0
3 Technicians and associate professionals	2 668	35.0	2 609	35.1	59	32.2
4 Clerks	3 396	52.2	3 309	52.1	87	56.3
5 Service workers and shop and market sales workers	5 709	62.3	5 567	62.6	142	49.3
6 Skilled agricultural and fishery workers	1 627	45.2	1 624	45.3	3	33.3
7 Craft and related trade workers	2 505	14.9	2 423	15.1	82	7.3
8 Plant and machine operators and assemblers	2 657	12.4	2 588	12.4	69	11.6
9 Elementary occupations	2 836	46.6	2 725	47.4	111	27.0
X Not classifiable by occupation	.	.	.	.	159	34.6
Unemployed seeking their first job					41	39.0
Education level (ISCED-97)	2007 [1,2] Labour force survey		2007 ★ Labour force survey		2007 [2] Labour force survey	
Total	24 215.7	41.7	23 432.7	41.9	783.0	34.0
0 Pre-primary education	2 978.7 [4]	59.1	2 931.7	59.5	47.0	36.2
2 Lower secondary or second stage of basic education	2 582.6	45.2	2 510.6	45.5	72.0	33.3
3 Upper secondary education	10 167.1	39.9	9 778.1	40.2	389.0	32.1
5A First stage of tertiary education - theoretically based [5]	5 782.2	32.6	5 629.2	32.6	153.0	34.0
5B First stage of tertiary education - practically oriented	2 705.1	45.3	2 582.1	45.6	123.0	37.4
Status in employment (ICSE-1993)			2007 [2,3] Labour force survey			
Total	.	.	23 433	41.9	.	.
1 Employees	.	.	15 970	42.3	.	.
2 Employers	.	.	1 562	22.3	.	.
3 Own-account workers	.	.	4 487	32.8	.	.
5 Contributing family workers	.	.	1 413	88.4	.	.

2. Population ('000), Activity rate and Unemployment rate

	Population			Activity rate			Unemployment rate		
Age group	2007 [1,6] Labour force survey			2007 [1,8] Labour force survey			2007 [2] Labour force survey		
	Total	Men	Women	Total	Men	Women	Total	Men	Women
Total							3.2	3.7	2.8
15+	39 170.0	19 083.6	20 086.3	61.8	74.0	50.2	3.2	3.7	2.6
15-24	5 937.3	2 817.5	3 119.7	28.1	23.1	32.7	8.9	11.4	7.2
25-54	23 882.6	12 078.6	11 804.0	76.4	90.5	62.0	3.1	3.6	2.4
55+	9 350.1	4 187.5	5 162.6	46.0	60.7	34.0	1.7	2.1	1.0

Korea, Republic of

3. Paid employment ('000), Hours of work (weekly) and Wages

Economic activity (ISIC-Rev.3)	Paid employment 2007 [2][3] Labour force survey			Hours of work 2007 [7] Labour-related establishment survey Hours actually worked / Employees			Wages 2007 [8][9][10] Labour-related establishment survey Earnings per month / Employees / Won		
	Total	Men	Women	Total	Men	Women	Total	Men	Women
Total	15 970	9 214	6 756	.	.	.	.	.	.
A	151	52	99	.	.	.	.	.	.
B	23	12	10	.	.	.	.	.	.
C	18	16	1	43.4	43.4	42.6	2 767.0	2 865.0	1 596.0
C-X	.	.	.	43.4	43.9	42.4	2 683.0	3 039.0	1 908.0
D	3 520	2 354	1 165	45.5	45.5	45.3	2 688.0	3 025.0	1 742.0
E	85	66	19	41.6	41.7	41.1	4 648.0	4 895.0	2 723.0
F	1 423	1 277	146	41.2	41.2	40.6	2 436.0	2 587.0	1 535.0
G	1 968	996	972	41.3	41.6	41.0	2 693.0	3 088.0	1 893.0
H	1 133	286	847	46.3	45.4	47.2	1 622.0	1 992.0	1 350.0
I	901	745	156	44.6	45.1	39.2	2 297.0	2 352.0	1 942.0
J	758	359	399	39.6	39.7	39.3	4 070.0	4 313.0	3 361.0
K	1 979	1 245	733	38.5	38.6	38.5	4 403.0	5 251.0	3 103.0
L	797	543	254	.	.	.	.	.	.
M	1 339	459	879	41.0	41.4	40.4	2 590.0	3 013.0	1 679.0
N	683	162	521	41.2	41.5	42.1	2 544.0	3 730.0	2 113.0
O	1 024	626	397	39.2	39.5	38.9	2 892.0	3 659.0	2 126.0
P	156	4	153	.	.	.	.	.	.
Q	15	12	3	.	.	.	.	.	.

Share of women in wage employment in the non-agricultural sector [2][3] (2007 - Labour force survey): **42.1%**

4. Occupational injuries and Strikes and Lockouts

Economic activity (ISIC-Rev.3)	Rates of fatal injuries 2007 Insurance records Per 1,000,000 hours worked Compensated injuries			Rates of non-fatal injuries			Strikes and lockouts 2007 Labour relations records		
	Total	Men	Women	Total	Men	Women	Strikes and lockouts	Workers involved [11]	Days not worked
Total	0.04	.	.	.	.	.	115	93 385	536 285
A	0.08 [12]	.	.	.	.	.	.	.	.
B	0.16	.	.	.	.	.	.	.	.
C	0.41	.	.	.	.	.	.	.	.
D	0.05	.	.	.	.	.	.	.	.
E	0.03	.	.	.	.	.	.	.	.
F	0.08	.	.	.	.	.	.	.	.
G-H,K,M-P,X	0.02 [13]	.	.	.	.	.	.	.	.
I	0.06	.	.	.	.	.	.	.	.
J	0.01	.	.	.	.	.	.	.	.

5. Consumer price indices (base period: 2000=100)

	2002	2003	2004	2005	2006	2007
General indices	106.9	110.7	114.7	117.8	120.4	123.5
Food index, including non-alcoholic beverages	107.7	112.4	119.5	128.6 [14]	129.2	132.4
Electricity, gas and other fuel indices	107.1	113.1	119.4	122.5 [15]	132.0	135.3
Clothing indices, including footwear	106.3	110.1	110.5	111.6	114.6	117.6
Rent indices	110.1	114.0	115.8	115.6	116.1	118.1
General index, excluding housing	106.5	110.2	114.5	118.1 [16]	121.1	124.1

[1] Excl. armed forces and conscripts. [2] Persons aged 15 years and over. [3] Excl. armed forces. [4] Levels 0-1. [5] Levels 5A and 6. [6] "De facto" population. [7] Establishments with 10 or more regular employees. [8] Incl. family allowances and the value of payments in kind. [9] Establishments with 5 or more regular employees. [10] Figures in thousands. [11] Excl. workers indirectly involved. [12] Excl. hunting. [13] Incl. hunting. [14] Series replacing former series; prior to 2005: incl. alcoholic beverages. [15] Series replacing former series; prior to 2005: incl. water. [16] Series replacing former series; prior to 2005: Excl. Rent.

[1] Non compris les forces armées et les conscrits. [2] Personnes âgées de 15 ans et plus. [3] Non compris les forces armées. [4] Niveaux 0-1. [5] Niveaux 5A et 6. [6] Population "de facto". [7] Etablissements occupant 10 salariés stables ou plus. [8] Y compris les allocations familiales et la valeur des paiements en nature. [9] Etablissements occupant 5 salariés stables et plus. [10] Données en milliers. [11] Non compris les travailleurs indirectement impliqués. [12] Non compris la chasse. [13] Y compris la chasse. [14] Série remplaçant la précédente; avant 2005: y compris les boissons alcoolisées. [15] Série remplaçant la précédente; avant 2005: y compris l'eau. [16] Série remplaçant la précédente; avant 2005: non compris le loyer.

[1] Excl. las fuerzas armadas y los conscriptos. [2] Personas de 15 años y más. [3] Excl. las fuerzas armadas. [4] Niveles 0-1. [5] Niveles 5A y 6. [6] Población "de facto". [7] Establecimientos con 10 y más asalariados estables. [8] Incl. las asignaciones familiares y el valor de los pagos en especie. [9] Establecimientos con 5 y más asalariados estables. [10] Cifras en millares. [11] Excl. los trabajadores indirectamente implicados. [12] Excl. la caza. [13] Incl. caza. [14] Serie base que substituye a la anterior; antes de 2005: incl. las bebidas alcohólicas. [15] Serie base que substituye a la anterior; antes de 2005: incl. el agua. [16] Serie base que substituye a la anterior; antes de 2005: excl. el alquiler.

Kosovo (Serbia)

1. Economically active population, Employment and Unemployment ('000)

Statistics not available.

2. Population ('000), Activity rate and Unemployment rate

Age group	Population			Activity rate			Unemployment rate 2006 Labour force survey		
	Total	Men	Women	Total	Men	Women	Total	Men	Women
Total	.	.	.	.	.	.	41.3	32.7	60.2

3. Paid employment ('000), Hours of work (weekly) and Wages

Statistics not available.

4. Occupational injuries and Strikes and Lockouts

Statistics not available.

5. Consumer price indices (base period: 2000=100)

[1]	2002	2003	2004	2005	2006	2007
General indices	98.8 [2]	100.0	98.9	97.6	98.2	102.6
Food index, including non-alcoholic beverages	97.6 [2]	100.0	98.9	96.5	99.7	100.7
Clothing indices, including footwear	101.2 [2]	100.0	93.7	87.3	84.6	87.1
Rent indices [3]	99.3 [2]	100.0	100.3	96.9	95.3	96.1

[1] Index base 2003=100. [2] May-Dec. [3] Incl. water, electricity, gas and other fuels.

[1] Indice base 2003=100. [2] Mai-déc. [3] Y compris l'eau, l'électricité, le gaz et autres combustibles.

[1] Indice base 2003=100. [2] Mayo-dic. [3] Incl. el agua, la electricidad, el gas y otros combustibles.

Kuwait

1. Economically active population, Employment and Unemployment ('000)

	Economically active population		Employment		Unemployment	
	Total	Women (%)	Total	Women (%)	Total	Women (%)
Age group	2003 [1] Labour force survey		1995 ★ Population census		1995 [1,2] Population census	
Total	1 172.666	30.9	731.615	25.2	15.919	17.2
15-19	12.224	28.8	0.891	33.7	4.620	13.9
20-24	116.543	41.8	68.607	32.3	5.927	20.4
25-29	208.910	40.3	165.768	29.0	2.705	18.9
30-34	258.267	35.3	167.906	27.6	0.944	15.6
35-39	224.137	28.9	138.085	25.8	0.530	19.4
40-44	164.205	24.2	91.048	20.9	0.449	22.9
45-49	97.950	19.6	51.852	16.1	0.197	9.1
50-54	52.833	13.8	25.744	11.2	0.227	2.2
55-59	23.157	10.2	14.006	7.8	0.189	2.6
60-64	10.258	6.2	5.225	7.8	0.131	.
65-69	3.339	7.6	1.644	6.1	-	.
70-74	0.717	5.9	0.522	11.9	-	.
75+	0.126	66.7	0.317	8.2	-	.
Economic activity (ISIC-Rev.2)	1996 [1] Official estimates		1988 [3,4] Labour force survey			
Total	1 140.085	23.2	718.848	24.1		
1 Agriculture, Hunting, Forestry and Fishing	21.470	.	9.524	1.4		
2 Mining and Quarrying	7.939	.	6.530	3.1		
3 Manufacturing	77.332	.	54.664	2.6		
4 Electricity, Gas and Water	7.684	.	7.613	1.1		
5 Construction	126.787	.	114.534	1.4		
6 Wholesale and Retail Trade and Restaurants and Hotels	192.056	.	83.335	4.9		
7 Transport, Storage and Communication	40.703	.	37.772	7.0		
8 Financing, Insurance, Real Estate and Business Services	39.433	.	21.562	17.5		
9 Community, Social and Personal Services	554.296	.	383.584	41.5		
0 Activities not Adequately Defined	72.385	.	.	.		
Occupation (ISCO-1968)	1995 [1,2] Population census		1988 [3,4] Labour force survey			
Total	747.534	25.0	718.848 [4]	24.1		
0/1 Professional, technical and related workers	143.628	28.3	122.512 [4]	36.8		
2 Administrative and managerial workers	39.493	9.9	11.697 [4]	5.2		
3 Clerical and related workers	74.507	31.0	88.063 [4]	25.9		
4 Sales workers	37.321	5.6	39.376 [4]	3.2		
5 Service workers	252.367	45.0	223.370 [4]	46.0		
6 Agriculture, animal husbandry and forestry workers	13.878	0.1	8.410 [4]	0.5		
7/8/9 Production and related workers, transport equipment ...	160.270	1.1	225.420 [4]	0.3		
X Not classifiable by occupation	9.428	20.0	.	.		
AF Armed forces	16.647	0.0	.	.		
Education level (ISCED-97)	2003 [1] Labour force survey				2006 [5] Administrative reports	
Total	1 172.659	30.9	.	.	24.921	52.4
X No schooling	372.781	42.4	.	.	7.323	47.3
1 Primary education or first stage of basic education	89.836	31.7	.	.	1.699	24.7
2 Lower secondary or second stage of basic education	205.972	19.2	.	.	3.146	21.4
3 Upper secondary education	245.007	21.3	.	.	5.080	54.1
4 Post-secondary non-tertiary education	63.425	37.6	.	.	5.230	75.5
5A First stage of tertiary education - theoretically based [6]	183.810	31.2	.	.	2.385	73.8
6 Second stage of tertiary education	11.828	20.6	.	.	0.013	23.1
? Level not stated	.	.	.	.	0.045	.
Status in employment (ICSE-1993)	1995 [1,2] Population census					
Total	747.534	25.0				
1 Employees	729.081	25.5				
2 Employers	5.717	4.7				
3 Own-account workers	10.586	2.3				
5 Contributing family workers	0.317	19.6				
6 Not classifiable by status	1.833	14.3				

2. Population ('000), Activity rate and Unemployment rate

	Population 2003 Labour force survey			Activity rate 2003 Labour force survey			Unemployment rate 1995 [1,2] Population census		
Age group	Total	Men	Women	Total	Men	Women	Total	Men	Women
Total	2 419.9	1 332.8	1 087.2	48.5	60.8	33.3	2.1	2.3	1.4
15+	1 767.8	994.3	773.5	66.3	81.5	46.8	.	.	.
15-24	398.6	197.7	200.9	32.3	38.7	26.0	13.2	15.6	7.6
25-54	1 248.7	724.9	523.8	80.6	96.5	58.5	0.8	0.9	0.5
55+	120.4	71.7	48.7	31.2	47.7	7.0	.	.	.

Kuwait

3. Paid employment ('000), Hours of work (weekly) and Wages

Economic activity (ISIC-Rev.2)	Paid employment 1999 Labour-related establishment survey			Hours of work 1999 Labour-related establishment survey / Employees			Wages 1999 Labour-related establishment survey / Employees / Dinar		
	Total	Men	Women	Total	Men	Women	Total	Men	Women
Total	294.018	.	.	.	.	.	.	.	.
2	6.427 [7]	.	.	42.6	.	.	6.015	.	.
3	69.022	.	.	47.3	.	.	1.231	.	.
5	67.684	.	.	48.0	.	.	0.828	.	.
6	108.857	.	.	48.0	.	.	0.913	.	.
7	32.924	.	.	48.0	.	.	1.609	.	.
8	9.104	.	.	47.0	.	.	1.647	.	.
9	70.606	.	.	47.9	.	.	0.612	.	.

4. Occupational injuries and Strikes and Lockouts

Statistics not available.

5. Consumer price indices (base period: 2000=100)

	2002	2003	2004	2005	2006	2007
General indices	102.3	103.2	104.5	108.8	112.1	.
Food index, including non-alcoholic beverages	101.1	106.6	110.0	119.4	124.0	.
Electricity, gas and other fuel indices	100.5	.	.	.	.	.
Clothing indices, including footwear	105.6	108.0	111.0	118.1	122.8	.
Rent indices	102.9	.	.	.	.	.

[1] Persons aged 15 years and over. [2] April. [3] Civilian labour force employed. [4] March. [5] June. [6] Levels 5. [7] Excl. quarrying.

[1] Personnes âgées de 15 ans et plus. [2] Avril. [3] Main-d'oeuvre civile occupée. [4] Mars. [5] Juin. [6] Niveaux 5. [7] Non compris les carrières.

[1] Personas de 15 años y más. [2] Abril. [3] Fuerza de trabajo civil ocupada. [4] Marzo. [5] Junio. [6] Niveles 5. [7] Excl. las canteras.

Kyrgyzstan

1. Economically active population, Employment and Unemployment ('000)

	Economically active population		Employment		Unemployment	
	Total	Women (%)	Total	Women (%)	Total	Women (%)
Age group	2006 [1,2] Labour force survey		2006 ★ Labour force survey		2006 [1,2] Labour force survey	
Total	2 285.0	42.4	2 096.1	42.1	188.9	46.3
15-19	173.0	38.4	146.3	37.7	26.7	42.3
20-24	326.8	38.4	280.7	37.7	46.1	43.2
25-29	351.7	41.2	323.9	40.6	27.8	47.8
30-34	318.7	42.2	295.1	41.1	23.6	55.9
35-39	295.9	44.5	278.7	44.1	17.2	51.2
40-44	290.4	46.9	273.2	46.9	17.2	48.3
45-49	236.6	46.4	221.0	46.7	15.6	42.3
50-54	143.9	46.2	135.5	46.2	8.4	46.4
55-59	84.5	38.0	79.6	38.3	4.9	32.7
60-64	25.5	29.4	24.5	29.4	1.0	30.0
65+	38.1	36.7	37.6	36.4	0.5	60.0
Economic activity (ISIC-Rev.3)	2006 ★ Labour force survey		2006 [1,2] Labour force survey		2006 [1,2] Labour force survey	
Total	2 285.0	42.4	2 096.1	42.1	188.9	46.3
A Agriculture, Hunting and Forestry	784.1	41.0	760.0	41.0	24.1	41.5
B Fishing	0.2	50.0	0.2	50.0	-	.
C Mining and Quarrying	13.0	4.6	11.8	5.1	1.2	0.0
D Manufacturing	194.5	45.7	177.9	45.4	16.6	48.8
E Electricity, Gas and Water Supply	38.8	16.5	35.6	17.7	3.2	3.1
F Construction	196.8	3.8	181.4	3.9	15.4	1.9
G Wholesale and Retail Trade; Repair of Motor Vehicles ...	333.7	50.0	308.4	49.2	25.3	60.5
H Hotels and Restaurants	58.2	70.1	49.0	69.6	9.2	72.8
I Transport, Storage and Communications	125.1	15.8	120.2	16.3	4.9	4.1
J Financial Intermediation	9.8	57.1	9.5	56.8	0.3	66.7
K Real Estate, Renting and Business Activities	37.6	46.0	36.5	45.8	1.1	54.5
L Public Administration and Defence; Compulsory Social ...	106.7	36.2	101.0	36.3	5.7	33.3
M Education	158.7	73.8	152.9	73.8	5.8	72.4
N Health and Social Work	89.6	77.1	87.0	77.2	2.6	73.1
O Other Community, Social and Personal Service Activities	53.1	49.3	48.8	49.2	4.3	51.2
P Households with Employed Persons	15.7	41.4	15.3	41.2	0.4	50.0
Q Extra-Territorial Organizations and Bodies	0.5	100.0	0.5	100.0	0.0	.
Unemployed seeking their first job	.	.	.	.	68.7	51.8
Occupation (ISCO-88)	2006 ★ Labour force survey		2006 [1,2] Labour force survey		2006 [1,2] Labour force survey	
Total	2 285.0	42.4	2 096.1	42.1	188.9	46.3
1 Legislators, senior officials and managers	50.5	34.9	49.2	35.2	1.3	23.1
2 Professionals	203.7	61.7	197.2	62.1	6.5	49.2
3 Technicians and associate professionals	144.4	63.2	137.4	63.1	7.0	64.3
4 Clerks	47.3	74.6	45.8	74.5	1.5	80.0
5 Service workers and shop and market sales workers	373.3	58.1	342.7	56.9	30.6	70.9
6 Skilled agricultural and fishery workers	740.7	40.9	718.0	40.8	22.7	44.1
7 Craft and related trade workers	349.6	18.9	319.9	18.6	29.7	21.9
8 Plant and machine operators and assemblers	145.5	3.6	135.2	3.3	10.3	7.8
9 Elementary occupations	161.3	45.0	150.7	45.7	10.6	34.9
Unemployed seeking their first job	.	.	.	.	68.7	51.8
Education level (ISCED-97)	2006 [1,2] Labour force survey		2006 ★ Labour force survey		2006 [1,2] Labour force survey	
Total	2 285.0	42.4	2 096.1	42.1	188.9	46.3
X No schooling	371.9	50.5	371.9	50.5	-	.
0 Pre-primary education	53.6	42.6	53.6	42.6	.	.
1 Primary education or first stage of basic education	308.8	57.5	303.3	57.9	5.5	32.7
2 Lower secondary or second stage of basic education	233.2	26.9	213.5	25.5	19.7	41.6
3 Upper secondary education	1 103.9	40.1	986.6	39.5	117.3	45.9
4 Post-secondary non-tertiary education	155.7	34.1	127.4	30.2	28.3	51.6
5A First stage of tertiary education - theoretically based	50.7	36.4	32.5	29.5	18.2	48.9
5B First stage of tertiary education - practically oriented	4.6	48.1	4.6	48.1	-	.
6 Second stage of tertiary education	2.5	52.2	2.5	52.2	-	.
Status in employment (ICSE-1993)			2006 [1,2] Labour force survey			
Total	.	.	2 096.1	42.1	.	.
1 Employees	.	.	1 065.6	42.8	.	.
2 Employers	.	.	23.6	24.2	.	.
3 Own-account workers	.	.	714.1	34.3	.	.
4 Members of producers' cooperatives	.	.	16.3	30.7	.	.
5 Contributing family workers	.	.	276.4	61.5	.	.

2. Population ('000), Activity rate and Unemployment rate

	Population 2006 [2] Labour force survey			Activity rate 2006 [2] Labour force survey			Unemployment rate 2006 [1,2] Labour force survey		
Age group	Total	Men	Women	Total	Men	Women	Total	Men	Women
Total	.	.	.	.	.	.	8.3	7.7	9.0
15+	3 489.3	1 702.2	1 787.1	65.5	77.3	54.2	8.3	7.7	9.0
15-24	1 074.6	540.5	534.2	46.5	56.9	36.0	14.6	13.6	16.2
25-54	1 921.1	950.9	970.2	85.2	96.1	74.6	6.7	6.1	7.5
55+	493.6	210.8	282.8	30.0	44.9	19.0	4.3	4.4	4.1

Kyrgyzstan

3. Paid employment ('000), Hours of work (weekly) and Wages

Economic activity (ISIC-Rev.3)	Paid employment 2007 Official estimates			Hours of work 2005 Labour-related establishment census Hours actually worked / Employees			Wages 2007 Labour-related establishment census Earnings per month / Employees / Som		
	Total	Men	Women	Total	Men	Women	Total	Men	Women
Total	559.740	280.820	278.920	35.7	.	.	3 970.00	.	.
A-B	.	.	.	37.4	.	.	1 788.20 3	.	.
C-Q	.	.	.	35.7	.	.	4 039.00	.	.
A	22.060	16.280	5.780	37.4	.	.	1 733.20 3	.	.
B	0.092	0.072	0.020	36.1	.	.	1 471.30 3	.	.
C	5.749	4.793	0.956	34.5	.	.	4 609.00	.	.
D	67.805	42.415	25.390	34.5	.	.	6 254.00	.	.
E	25.150	18.830	6.320	35.3	.	.	6 315.00	.	.
F	23.390	19.311	4.079	35.2	.	.	3 613.00	.	.
G	23.230	13.110	10.120	36.3	.	.	3 142.00	.	.
H	4.065	1.845	2.220	39.1	.	.	4 191.00	.	.
I	33.240	20.900	12.340	33.7	.	.	6 497.00	.	.
J	12.240	6.620	5.620	35.5	.	.	10 791.00	.	.
K	34.140	21.700	12.440	35.5	.	.	4 576.00	.	.
L	50.760	31.690	19.070	36.5	.	.	4 469.00	.	.
M	153.920	42.520	111.400	35.6	.	.	2 676.00	.	.
N	66.160	14.690	51.470	37.2	.	.	2 541.00	.	.
O	37.740	26.040	11.700	35.6	.	.	2 536.00	.	.

Share of women in wage employment in the non-agricultural sector (2007 - Official estimates): **50.8%**

4. Occupational injuries and Strikes and Lockouts

Economic activity (ISIC-Rev.3)	Rates of fatal injuries 2006 Labour inspectorate records Per 100,000 workers employed Reported injuries			Rates of non-fatal injuries 2006 Labour inspectorate records Per 100,000 workers employed Reported injuries			Strikes and lockouts		
	Total	Men	Women	Total	Men	Women	Strikes and lockouts	Workers involved	Days not worked
Total	5	.	.	32	.	.	.	.	.
A	0	.	.	30	.	.	.	.	.
B	0	.	.	0	.	.	.	.	.
C	157	.	.	315	.	.	.	.	.
D	12	.	.	110	.	.	.	.	.
E	14	.	.	101	.	.	.	.	.
F	10	.	.	55	.	.	.	.	.
G	0	.	.	9	.	.	.	.	.
H	0	.	.	0	.	.	.	.	.
I	3	.	.	49	.	.	.	.	.
J	0	.	.	0	.	.	.	.	.
K	4	.	.	17	.	.	.	.	.
L	2	.	.	7	.	.	.	.	.
M	0	.	.	2	.	.	.	.	.
N	0	.	.	5	.	.	.	.	.
O	0	.	.	11	.	.	.	.	.
P	0	.	.	.	.	.	.	.	.

5. Consumer price indices (base period: 2000=100)

	2002	2003	2004	2005	2006	2007
General indices	109.1	112.5	117.1	122.2	129.0	.
Food index, including non-alcoholic beverages	105.9	108.9	112.4	118.3	128.7	.
Electricity, gas and other fuel indices	149.8	153.1	160.1	177.8	188.5	.
Clothing indices, including footwear	105.2	106.6	107.0	108.1	109.4	.
Rent indices [4]	168.3	175.0	201.2	214.2	235.4	.

[1] Persons aged 15 years and over. [2] Nov. [3] Incl. the value of housing. [4] Housing; incl. water.

[1] Personnes âgées de 15 ans et plus. [2] Nov. [3] Y compris la valeur du logement. [4] Logement; y compris l'eau.

[1] Personas de 15 años y más. [2] Nov. [3] Incl. el valor de vivienda. [4] Vivienda; incl. el agua.

Latvia

1. Economically active population, Employment and Unemployment ('000)

	Economically active population		Employment		Unemployment	
	Total	Women (%)	Total	Women (%)	Total	Women (%)
Age group	2007 [1,2] Labour force survey		2007 ★ Labour force survey		2007 [2] Labour force survey	
Total	1 191.1	48.5	1 119.0	48.8	72.1	45.4
15-19	28.8	41.2	23.3	42.3	5.5	36.4
20-24	126.1	42.5	114.7	42.7	11.4	40.4
25-29	134.6	44.8	125.2	44.4	9.4	48.9
30-34	138.5	45.9	131.5	45.7	7.0	50.0
35-39	143.1	48.7	135.1	49.1	8.0	42.5
40-44	141.3	49.7	134.1	50.1	7.2	41.7
45-49	153.2	51.9	144.9	52.2	8.3	45.8
50-54	129.1	52.9	121.5	52.9	7.6	52.6
55-59	104.1	53.9	97.4	54.9	6.7	38.8
60-64	47.8	46.7	47.8	46.7	-	.
65-69	31.5	51.7	31.5	51.7	-	.
70-74	13.0	51.1	13.0	51.1	-	.
Economic activity (ISIC-Rev.3)	2007 [1,2] Labour force survey		2007 [1,2] Labour force survey		2007 [2] Labour force survey	
Total	1 191.1	48.5	1 119.0	48.7	72.1	45.4
A-B	.	.	.	.	4.3	27.9
A Agriculture, Hunting and Forestry	111.7	36.6	107.5	37.0		
B Fishing	2.9	.	2.8	.		
C Mining and Quarrying	6.7	.	6.6	.		
C-F					20.7	30.4
D Manufacturing	177.5	43.3	164.8	43.1		
E Electricity, Gas and Water Supply	21.6	22.7	20.7	22.2		
F Construction	132.8	7.9	125.6	8.2		
G Wholesale and Retail Trade; Repair of Motor Vehicles ...	194.5	62.3	184.6	61.9		
G-Q					26.3	37.6
H Hotels and Restaurants	34.4	82.8	31.2	82.1		
I Transport, Storage and Communications	107.3	31.1	104.0	31.1		
J Financial Intermediation	22.4	72.9	22.0	73.6		
K Real Estate, Renting and Business Activities	77.0	50.8	74.0	51.1		
L Public Administration and Defence; Compulsory Social ...	85.9	53.3	83.9	53.3		
M Education	83.8	82.4	81.8	82.4		
N Health and Social Work	50.9	85.5	50.1	85.4		
O Other Community, Social and Personal Service Activities	55.2	62.4	53.7	62.2		
P Households with Employed Persons	3.5	.	3.3	.		
Q Extra-Territorial Organizations and Bodies	-	.				
X Not classifiable by economic activity	-	.				
Unemployed seeking their first job	20.6	41.2			20.6 [3]	41.3
Occupation (ISCO-88)	2007 [1,2] Labour force survey		2007 [1,2] Labour force survey		2007 [2] Labour force survey	
Total	1 191.1	48.5	1 119.0	48.7	72.1	.
1 Legislators, senior officials and managers	95.9	41.3	94.0	41.3	-	.
2 Professionals	154.4	66.5	151.7	66.6	2.6	.
3 Technicians and associate professionals	188.5	65.1	181.4	64.9	7.2	.
4 Clerks	55.8	77.4	53.2	77.4	2.6	.
5 Service workers and shop and market sales workers	148.3	75.7	140.9	75.7	7.4	.
6 Skilled agricultural and fishery workers	58.4	44.5	56.5	44.8		.
7 Craft and related trade workers	200.5	17.9	189.9	17.6	10.7	.
8 Plant and machine operators and assemblers	116.5	13.9	111.2	13.7	5.3	.
9 Elementary occupations	148.9	47.1	137.1	47.3	11.9	.
X Not classifiable by occupation	2.2	.	-	.		
Unemployed seeking their first job	20.6	41.2			20.6 [3]	.
Education level (ISCED-97)	2007 [1,2] Labour force survey		2007 ★ Labour force survey		2007 [2] Labour force survey	
Total	1 191.1	48.5	1 119.0	48.8	72.1	45.4
X No schooling	-	.	-	.	-	.
0 Pre-primary education						
1 Primary education or first stage of basic education	7.8	34.0	6.1	43.4	1.7	.
2 Lower secondary or second stage of basic education	161.8	31.7	146.0	31.6	15.8	32.9
3 Upper secondary education	660.6	46.5	621.3	46.4	39.3	47.3
4 Post-secondary non-tertiary education	75.1	57.9	71.2	58.6	3.9	46.2
5A First stage of tertiary education - theoretically based [4]	278.1	61.4	267.6	61.3	10.5	61.9
6 Second stage of tertiary education	3.1	.	3.1	.	-	.
? Level not stated	3.6	38.4				
Status in employment (ICSE-1993)	2007 [1,2] Labour force survey		2007 [1,2] Labour force survey		2007 ★ Labour force survey	
Total	1 191.1	48.5	1 119.0	48.7	72.1	45.4
1 Employees	1 050.9	49.9	1 000.1	50.0	50.8	47.5
2 Employers	36.2	29.4	36.0	29.4	0.2	27.0
3 Own-account workers	65.5	38.8	65.3	38.9	0.2	24.8
5 Contributing family workers	17.7	50.4	17.6	50.6	0.1	25.6
6 Not classifiable by status	20.6	41.2	-	.	20.6	41.2

Latvia

2. Population ('000), Activity rate and Unemployment rate

Age group	Population 2007 [1,5] Labour force survey			Activity rate 2007 [1,5] Labour force survey			Unemployment rate 2007 [2] Labour force survey		
	Total	Men	Women	Total	Men	Women	Total	Men	Women
Total	2 281.3	1 051.5	1 229.8	52.2	58.3	47.0	6.0	6.4	5.7
15+	1 963.4	888.8	1 074.6	.	.	.	.	.	.
15-24	358.6	182.8	175.9	43.2	49.0	37.2	10.9	11.5	10.1
25-54	962.6	470.2	492.3	87.2	91.1	83.6	5.7	5.9	5.4
55+	642.2	235.8	406.4	.	.	.	.	.	.

3. Paid employment ('000), Hours of work (weekly) and Wages

Economic activity (ISIC-Rev.3)	Paid employment 2007 [6] Labour-related establishment survey			Hours of work 2007 [7] Labour force survey Hours actually worked / Employees			Wages 2007 [6] Labour-related establishment survey Earnings per month / Employees / Lat		
	Total	Men	Women	Total	Men	Women	Total	Men	Women
Total	1 005.5	486.1	519.4	39.1	40.8	37.4	353.83	385.41	323.48
A-B	.	.	.	40.8	41.8	38.2	311.77	326.97	282.40
C-Q	.	.	.	39.0	40.8	37.4	354.75	387.15	324.08
A	20.6	13.1	7.5	40.6	41.6	38.2	315.03	332.78	282.19
B	1.5	1.2	0.3	45.2	.	.	267.62	262.58	285.77
C	2.3	1.8	0.5	41.2	.	.	392.17	415.08	295.88
D	159.9	89.3	70.6	38.8	39.6	37.9	315.03	350.27	269.73
E	14.4	10.3	4.1	38.3	38.9	36.5	537.71	566.68	468.15
F	83.9	71.0	13.0	41.4	41.9	36.6	323.32	326.93	301.48
G	193.7	83.7	110.0	39.2	40.7	38.4	296.65	350.52	254.60
H	32.1	9.6	22.4	40.2	41.7	39.9	223.55	262.33	207.34
I	87.5	56.8	30.7	40.7	42.2	37.5	371.59	384.89	345.74
J	21.4	7.0	14.4	36.7	39.4	35.8	860.95	1 240.98	680.47
K	99.8	53.2	46.6	39.3	41.4	37.5	377.72	408.18	342.47
L	76.5	37.2	39.4	38.8	40.9	36.9	490.45	488.87	491.91
M	102.5	21.4	81.1	34.9	35.3	34.8	327.14	351.39	321.13
N	55.3	9.8	45.4	38.7	41.9	38.2	365.60	418.83	354.58
O	54.1	21.1	33.0	37.4	39.0	36.4	318.98	379.24	277.89
P	.	.	.	35.4	.	.	.	.	.

Share of women in wage employment in the non-agricultural sector [1,2] (2007 - Labour force survey): **51.3%**

4. Occupational injuries and Strikes and Lockouts

Economic activity (ISIC-Rev.3)	Rates of fatal injuries 2005 Labour-related establishment survey Per 100,000 employees Reported injuries			Rates of non-fatal injuries 2005 Labour-related establishment survey Per 100,000 employees Reported injuries			Strikes and lockouts 2007 Establishment survey		
	Total	Men	Women	Total	Men	Women	Strikes and lockouts	Workers involved [8]	Days not worked
Total	6.0	.	.	163	.	.	0	0	0
A	14.4	.	.	379	.	.	.	.	.
B	61.2	.	.	184	.	.	.	.	.
C	0.0	.	.	347	.	.	.	.	.
D	5.5	.	.	321	.	.	0	0	0
E	33.2	.	.	188	.	.	.	.	.
F	24.6	.	.	257	.	.	.	.	.
G	1.1	.	.	59	.	.	.	.	.
H	0.0	.	.	72	.	.	.	.	.
I	12.4	.	.	311	.	.	0	0	0
J	4.7	.	.	38	.	.	.	.	.
L	1.3	.	.	77	.	.	0	0	0
M	1.0	.	.	87	.	.	0	0	0
N	0.0	.	.	203	.	.	0	0	0
O	11.9	.	.	109	.	.	0	0	0
X	0.0	.	.	.	.	.	.	.	.

5. Consumer price indices (base period: 2000=100)

	2002	2003	2004	2005	2006	2007
General indices	104.5	107.5	114.2	121.9	129.9	143.0
Food index, including non-alcoholic beverages	108.4	111.2	119.5	130.5 [9]	141.1	160.1
Electricity, gas and other fuel indices	101.8	104.7	114.0	121.0	139.6	158.4
Clothing indices, including footwear	100.1	103.7	106.4	106.2	106.2	108.7
Rent indices	103.2	104.9	112.3	126.5	141.0	167.3
General index, excluding housing	104.5	107.6	114.2	121.9	129.8	142.7

[1] Excl. conscripts. [2] Persons aged 15 to 74 years. [3] Incl. the unemployed whose last job was 8 years ago or over. [4] Levels 5. [5] "De jure" population. [6] First quarter. [7] On the main job. [8] Excl. workers indirectly involved. [9] Series replacing former series; prior to 2005: incl. alcoholic beverages and tobacco.

[1] Non compris les conscrits. [2] Personnes âgées de 15 à 74 ans. [3] Y compris les chômeurs dont le dernier emploi date de 8 ans ou plus. [4] Niveaux 5. [5] Population "de jure". [6] Premier trimestre. [7] Emploi principal. [8] Non compris les travailleurs indirectement impliqués. [9] Série remplaçant la précédente; avant 2005: y compris les boissons alcoolisées et le tabac.

[1] Excl. los conscriptos. [2] Personas de 15 a 74 años. [3] Incl. los desempleados cuyo último trabajo fue hace 8 años o más. [4] Niveles 5. [5] Población "de jure". [6] Primer trimestre. [7] Empleo principal. [8] Excl. los trabajadores indirectamente implicados. [9] Serie que substituye a la anterior: antes de 2005: incl. las bebidas acohólicas y el tabaco.

Lesotho

1. Economically active population, Employment and Unemployment ('000)

	Economically active population		Employment		Unemployment	
	Total	Women (%)	Total	Women (%)	Total	Women (%)
Age group	1999[1] Household survey		1999 ★ Household survey		1999[1] Household survey	
Total	849.308	48.5	617.566	43.9	231.742	60.7
10-14	91.976	35.3	67.055	25.8	24.921	60.8
15-19	130.191	42.8	89.759	36.3	40.432	57.3
20-24	124.475	45.0	79.494	38.6	44.981	56.5
25-29	80.671	48.4	54.798	46.0	25.873	53.4
30-34	69.251	55.4	51.970	52.9	17.281	62.7
35-39	65.123	58.5	49.301	54.6	15.822	70.5
40-44	56.044	54.9	44.213	51.2	11.831	68.6
45-49	50.010	55.7	40.713	52.4	9.297	70.1
50-54	44.766	51.6	37.362	49.6	7.404	62.0
55-59	40.226	47.0	31.349	42.3	8.877	63.6
60-64	27.218	49.2	22.216	46.4	5.002	61.6
65-69	34.268	51.9	26.077	46.8	8.191	68.0
70-74	15.035	55.3	10.558	50.5	4.477	66.7
75+	20.304	56.1	13.201	52.0	7.103	63.5

Economic activity (ISIC-Rev.3)

1999[1] Household survey

	Total	Women (%)
Total	617.566	43.9
A Agriculture, Hunting and Forestry	446.679	39.3
B Fishing	0.125	0.0
C Mining and Quarrying	3.003	20.3
D Manufacturing	21.795	63.5
E Electricity, Gas and Water Supply	3.263	47.2
F Construction	29.495	35.8
G Wholesale and Retail Trade; Repair of Motor Vehicles ...	29.014	61.7
H Hotels and Restaurants	4.447	79.4
I Transport, Storage and Communications	10.670	12.8
J Financial Intermediation	1.851	43.8
K Real Estate, Renting and Business Activities	5.437	37.4
L Public Administration and Defence; Compulsory Social ...	7.576	31.6
M Education	13.224	61.2
N Health and Social Work	4.965	58.3
O Other Community, Social and Personal Service Activities	9.451	81.3
P Households with Employed Persons	26.444	83.1
Q Extra-Territorial Organizations and Bodies	0.126	0.0

Occupation (ISCO-88)

1999[1] Household survey

	Total	Women (%)
Total	617.566	43.9
1 Legislators, senior officials and managers	11.235	51.7
2 Professionals	14.151	57.6
3 Technicians and associate professionals	11.674	58.1
4 Clerks	11.004	73.7
5 Service workers and shop and market sales workers	25.482	51.1
6 Skilled agricultural and fishery workers	442.873	39.2
7 Craft and related trade workers	30.578	44.0
8 Plant and machine operators and assemblers	13.422	21.0
9 Elementary occupations	56.816	69.1
X Not classifiable by occupation	0.331	31.1

Status in employment (ICSE-1993)

1999[1] Household survey

	Total	Women (%)
Total	617.566	43.9
1 Employees	158.800	51.0
2 Employers	4.689	45.3
3 Own-account workers	29.467	54.9
6 Not classifiable by status	424.610	40.4

2. Population ('000), Activity rate and Unemployment rate

	Population 1999[2] Household survey			Activity rate 1999[2] Household survey			Unemployment rate 1999[1] Household survey		
Age group	Total	Men	Women	Total	Men	Women	Total	Men	Women
Total	.	.	.	.	.	.	27.3	20.8	34.2
15+	1 038.9	478.0	560.9	72.9	79.2	67.5	27.3	21.5	33.1
15-24	393.3	202.2	191.1	64.7	70.6	58.5	33.5	25.8	43.4
25-54	437.6	188.3	249.3	83.6	89.4	79.1	23.9	19.3	27.9
55+	208.0	87.5	120.5	65.9	76.9	57.9	24.6	17.6	31.2

3. Paid employment ('000), Hours of work (weekly) and Wages

Statistics not available.

4. Occupational injuries and Strikes and Lockouts

Statistics not available.

Lesotho

5. Consumer price indices (base period: 2000=100)

	2002	2003	2004	2005	2006	2007
General indices [3]	120.1	129.0	135.5	140.1	148.4	160.6
Food index, including non-alcoholic beverages	134.8	142.4	148.1	152.0	165.9	189.9
Electricity, gas and other fuel indices	124.8	135.0	142.4	153.2	166.0	179.4
Clothing indices, including footwear	110.2	114.6	117.9	121.5	124.5	128.1
General index, excluding housing	120.1	129.0	135.5	140.1	148.4	160.6

[1] Persons aged 10 years and over. [2] "De jure" population. [3] Excl. "Rent".

[1] Personnes âgées de 10 ans et plus. [2] Population "de jure". [3] Non compris le groupe "Loyer".

[1] Personas de 10 años y más. [2] Población "de jure". [3] Excl. el grupo "Alquiler".

Liban

1. Population active, Emploi et Chômage ('000)

Groupe d'âge	Population active Total	Population active Femmes (%)	Emploi Total	Emploi Femmes (%)	Chômage Total	Chômage Femmes (%)
	2004 Enquête auprès des ménages		2004 ★ Enquête auprès des ménages		2004 Enquête auprès des ménages	
Total	1 170.759	21.2	1 074.406	.	96.353	.
5-9	0.225	.		.	0.225	.
10-14	7.874	.	5.739	.	2.135	.
15-19	59.395	.	43.098	.	16.297	.
20-24	156.608	.	127.686	.	28.922	.
25-29	167.146	.	151.281	.	15.865	.
30-34	161.519	.	152.183	.	9.336	.
35-39	141.754	.	135.578	.	6.176	.
40-44	134.132	.	128.377	.	5.755	.
45-49	105.068	.	101.729	.	3.339	.
50-54	85.119	.	82.500	.	2.619	.
55-59	59.156	.	57.733	.	1.423	.
60-64	44.291	.	42.472	.	1.819	.
65-69	25.925	.	24.380	.	1.545	.
70-74	14.668	.	14.020	.	0.648	.
75-79	6.668	.	6.419	.	0.249	.
80+	1.443	.	1.443	.	-	.

2. Population ('000), Taux d'activité et Taux de chômage

Groupe d'âge	Population 1997 Estimations officielles Total	Hommes	Femmes	Taux d'activité 1997 Estimations officielles Total	Hommes	Femmes	Taux de chômage 2004 Enquête auprès des ménages Total	Hommes	Femmes
Total	4 005.0	.	.	34.0	.	.	8.2	.	.
15+	2 877.6	.	.	46.8	.	.	.	.	.
15-24	836.9	.	.	32.2	.	.	20.9	.	.
25-54	1 503.1	.	.	59.5	.	.	5.4	.	.
55+	537.6	.	.	34.0	.	.	.	.	.

3. Emploi rémunéré ('000), Durée du travail (hebdomadaire) et Salaires

Données non disponibles.

4. Lésions professionnelles et Grèves et lock-out

Données non disponibles.

5. Indices des prix à la consommation (période de base: 2000=100)

Beyrouth	2002	2003	2004	2005	2006	2007
Indices généraux	95.3	.	.	.	.	.

Liberia

1. Economically active population, Employment and Unemployment ('000)

Age group	Economically active population Total	Economically active population Women (%)	Employment Total	Employment Women (%)	Unemployment Total	Unemployment Women (%)
	1984 [1][2][3] Population census					
Total	704.3	41.0	.	.	.	.
10-14	34.1	47.0	.	.	.	.
15-19	54.2	55.4	.	.	.	.
20-24	79.7	48.9	.	.	.	.
25-29	102.3	41.3	.	.	.	.
30-34	87.1	40.4	.	.	.	.
35-39	80.1	41.6	.	.	.	.
40-44	62.7	38.8	.	.	.	.
45-49	54.3	37.5	.	.	.	.
50-54	43.2	38.1	.	.	.	.
55-59	29.6	34.3	.	.	.	.
60-64	30.2	31.8	.	.	.	.
65-69	19.2	29.4	.	.	.	.
70-74	10.8	23.3	.	.	.	.
75+	16.9	22.8	.	.	.	.

2. Population ('000), Activity rate and Unemployment rate

Age group	Population 1984 [1][3] Population census Total	Men	Women	Activity rate 1984 [1][3] Population census Total	Men	Women	Unemployment rate 1983 Employment office records Total	Men	Women
Total	2 101.6	1 063.1	1 038.5	33.5	39.1	27.8	15.9	.	.
15+	1 194.8	598.1	596.7	56.1	66.5	45.7	.	.	.
15-24	424.3	202.8	221.5	31.6	32.0	31.2	.	.	.
25-54	601.3	299.8	301.5	71.4	86.0	57.0	.	.	.
55+	169.2	95.5	73.6	63.1	78.4	43.2	.	.	.

3. Paid employment ('000), Hours of work (weekly) and Wages

Economic activity (ISIC-Rev.2)	Paid employment 1985 [4] Labour-related establishment survey Total	Men	Women	Hours of work Total	Men	Women	Wages Total	Men	Women
Total	101.343	.	.	.	.	.	.	.	.
1	28.837	.	.	.	.	.	.	.	.
2	5.546	.	.	.	.	.	.	.	.
3	6.671	.	.	.	.	.	.	.	.
4	2.464	.	.	.	.	.	.	.	.
5	4.109	.	.	.	.	.	.	.	.
6	7.879	.	.	.	.	.	.	.	.
7	5.476	.	.	.	.	.	.	.	.
8	1.806	.	.	.	.	.	.	.	.
9	38.555	.	.	.	.	.	.	.	.

4. Occupational injuries and Strikes and Lockouts

Statistics not available.

5. Consumer price indices (base period: 2000=100)

Statistics not available for the period 2002-2007.

[1] Excluding armed forces [2] Persons aged 10 years and over. [3] Feb. [4] Establishments with 5 or more persons employed.

[1] Non compris les forces armées [2] Personnes âgées de 10 ans et plus. [3] Fév. [4] Etablissements occupant 5 personnes et plus.

[1] Excluidas las fuerzas armadas [2] Personas de 10 años y más. [3] Feb. [4] Establecimientos con 5 y más trabajadores.

Libyan Arab Jamahiriya

1. Economically active population, Employment and Unemployment ('000)

	Economically active population		Employment		Unemployment	
	Total	Women (%)	Total	Women (%)	Total	Women (%)
Age group			2001 Labour force survey			
Total	.	.	805.9	32.2	.	.
Economic activity (ISIC-Rev.2)			1986 [1] Official estimates			
Total	.	.	904.7	.	.	.
1 Agriculture, Hunting, Forestry and Fishing	.	.	178.5	.	.	.
2 Mining and Quarrying	.	.	20.6	.	.	.
3 Manufacturing	.	.	77.0	.	.	.
4 Electricity, Gas and Water	.	.	24.4	.	.	.
5 Construction	.	.	149.7	.	.	.
6 Wholesale and Retail Trade and Restaurants and Hotels	.	.	46.0	.	.	.
7 Transport, Storage and Communication	.	.	74.0	.	.	.
8 Financing, Insurance, Real Estate and Business Services	.	.	13.5	.	.	.
9 Community, Social and Personal Services	.	.	321.0	.	.	.

2. Population ('000), Activity rate and Unemployment rate

Statistics not available.

3. Paid employment ('000), Hours of work (weekly) and Wages

Statistics not available.

4. Occupational injuries and Strikes and Lockouts

Statistics not available.

5. Consumer price indices (base period: 2000=100)

Statistics not available for the period 2002-2007.

[1] Excl. armed forces. [1] Non compris les forces armées. [1] Excl. las fuerzas armadas.

Liechtenstein

1. Economically active population, Employment and Unemployment ('000)

Age group	Economically active population Total	Economically active population Women (%)	Employment Total	Employment Women (%)	Unemployment Total	Unemployment Women (%)
	1980 [1,2] Population census		2005 Official estimates		2004 Official estimates	
Total	13.000	35.5	30.757	39.2	0.725	.
15-19	1.275	47.5	.	.	.	.
20-24	2.008	49.1	.	.	.	.
25-29	1.883	36.4	.	.	.	.
30-34	1.838	28.7	.	.	.	.
35-39	1.585	29.8	.	.	.	.
40-44	1.142	29.6	.	.	.	.
45-49	0.897	32.3	.	.	.	.
50-54	0.799	33.7	.	.	.	.
55-59	0.758	31.3	.	.	.	.
60-64	0.483	24.6	.	.	.	.
65-69	0.202	30.2	.	.	.	.
70-74	0.086	27.9	.	.	.	.
75+	0.044	15.9	.	.	.	.

2. Population ('000), Activity rate and Unemployment rate

Age group	Population 1980[2] Total	Men	Women	Activity rate 1980[2] Total	Men	Women	Unemployment rate Total	Men	Women
	Population census			Population census					
Total	25.2	12.5	12.7	51.6	66.9	36.4	.	.	.
15+	19.4	9.6	9.8	66.9	87.1	47.1	.	.	.
15-24	4.3	2.1	2.2	76.4	80.3	72.7	.	.	.
25-54	10.8	5.6	5.2	75.2	98.9	49.7	.	.	.
55+	4.3	1.9	2.4	36.5	59.7	18.5	.	.	.

3. Paid employment ('000), Hours of work (weekly) and Wages

Statistics not available.

4. Occupational injuries and Strikes and Lockouts

Economic activity (ISIC-Rev.3)	Rates of fatal injuries Total	Men	Women	Rates of non-fatal injuries Total	Men	Women	Strikes and lockouts 2006 Special data collection Strikes and lockouts	Workers involved	Days not worked
Total	.	.	.	.	.	.	0	0	0

5. Consumer price indices (base period: 2000=100)

Statistics not available for the period 2002-2007.

[1] Persons aged 15 years and over. [2] Dec.   [1] Personnes âgées de 15 ans et plus. [2] Déc.   [1] Personas de 15 años y más. [2] Dic.

Lithuania

1. Economically active population, Employment and Unemployment ('000)

	Economically active population		Employment		Unemployment	
	Total	Women (%)	Total	Women (%)	Total	Women (%)
Age group	2007 [1,2] Labour force survey		2007 ★ Labour force survey		2007 [2] Labour force survey	
Total	1 603.1	49.3	1 534.1	49.3	69.0	49.7
15-19	12.2	29.8	9.7	30.3	2.5	28.0
20-24	133.9	41.8	124.4	40.8	9.5	55.8
25-29	184.6	46.2	175.4	46.3	9.2	43.5
30-34	205.1	49.0	197.6	49.4	7.5	38.7
35-39	216.7	50.8	206.8	50.6	9.9	53.5
40-44	227.0	50.2	218.3	50.2	8.7	49.4
45-49	227.4	52.0	220.4	51.8	7.0	57.1
50-54	172.4	53.3	165.2	53.0	7.2	61.1
55-59	134.6	53.4	128.1	53.6	6.5	49.2
60-64	60.9	45.8	59.9	46.1	1.0	30.0
65-69	20.3	43.1	20.3	43.1	-	.
70-74	5.9	37.7	5.9	37.7	-	.
75+	2.3	32.1	2.3	32.1	-	.
Economic activity (ISIC-Rev.3)	2007 [1,2] Labour force survey		2007 [1,2] Labour force survey		2007 [2] Labour force survey	
Total	1 603.1	49.3	1 534.2	49.3	69.0	49.7
A Agriculture, Hunting and Forestry	160.5	37.7	156.9	37.8	3.6	36.1
B Fishing	2.7	3.7	2.6	3.8	0.1	.
C Mining and Quarrying	5.9	22.0	5.3	17.0	0.6	66.7
D Manufacturing	281.8	48.2	267.9	48.3	13.9	46.0
E Electricity, Gas and Water Supply	26.8	25.7	26.2	26.0	0.6	16.7
F Construction	178.8	7.1	170.9	7.3	7.9	5.1
G Wholesale and Retail Trade; Repair of Motor Vehicles ...	273.0	55.6	262.4	55.3	10.6	64.2
H Hotels and Restaurants	36.5	80.8	33.5	81.2	2.9	79.3
I Transport, Storage and Communications	114.7	28.6	111.4	28.1	3.3	45.5
J Financial Intermediation	22.5	69.3	22.3	69.5	0.2	50.0
K Real Estate, Renting and Business Activities	78.5	49.9	75.4	49.7	3.1	54.8
L Public Administration and Defence; Compulsory Social ...	85.2	48.8	83.5	48.5	1.7	64.7
M Education	146.4	81.6	144.3	81.9	2.1	61.9
N Health and Social Work	102.1	85.6	100.7	85.5	1.4	92.9
O Other Community, Social and Personal Service Activities	69.2	66.8	67.1	66.6	2.1	71.4
P Households with Employed Persons	4.0	42.5	3.9	38.5	0.2	100.0
Q Extra-Territorial Organizations and Bodies	-	.	.	.	.	.
Unemployed seeking their first job	14.5	54.2	.	.	14.5 [3]	54.5
Occupation (ISCO-88)	2007 [1,2] Labour force survey		2007 [1,2] Labour force survey		2007 [2] Labour force survey	
Total	1 603.1	49.3	1 534.2	49.3	69.0	49.7
1 Legislators, senior officials and managers	150.7	38.2	148.1	38.4	2.6	30.8
2 Professionals	283.6	68.0	279.1	68.2	4.5	60.0
3 Technicians and associate professionals	137.1	73.4	133.9	73.0	3.2	87.5
4 Clerks	69.8	77.1	67.6	76.8	2.1	90.5
5 Service workers and shop and market sales workers	196.2	75.3	188.4	74.8	7.9	87.3
6 Skilled agricultural and fishery workers	111.5	42.2	110.7	42.1	0.8	62.5
7 Craft and related trade workers	303.8	24.3	290.2	24.4	13.6	22.8
8 Plant and machine operators and assemblers	156.3	13.3	151.8	13.2	4.5	17.8
9 Elementary occupations	175.3	50.3	160.0	50.8	15.3	45.8
0 Armed forces	4.3	6.1	4.3	7.0	-	.
Unemployed seeking their first job	14.5	54.2	.	.	14.5 [3]	54.5
Education level (ISCED-97)	2007 [1,2] Labour force survey		2007 ★ Labour force survey		2007 [2] Labour force survey	
Total	1 603.1	49.3	1 534.1	49.3	69.0	49.7
1 Primary education or first stage of basic education	13.5	31.5	12.8	30.9	0.7	42.9
2 Lower secondary or second stage of basic education	121.2	36.0	112.1	35.9	9.1	37.4
3 Upper secondary education	569.9	39.8	535.5	39.4	34.4	45.6
4 Post-secondary non-tertiary education	384.7	56.0	370.5	55.9	14.2	59.2
5A First stage of tertiary education - theoretically based	371.4	58.4	365.5	58.5	5.9	55.9
5B First stage of tertiary education - practically oriented	138.2	59.6	133.5	59.3	4.7	68.1
6 Second stage of tertiary education	4.3	33.0	4.3	33.0	.	.
Status in employment (ICSE-1993)	2007 [1,2] Labour force survey		2007 [1,2] Labour force survey			
Total	1 603.1	49.3	1 534.2	49.3	.	.
1 Employees	1 377.1	50.8	1 324.4	50.8	.	.
2 Employers	32.4	25.9	.	.	.	.
2, 3	.	.	183.2	35.6	.	.
3 Own-account workers	152.0	37.6	.	.	.	.
5 Contributing family workers	27.1	66.6	26.7	67.4	.	.
6 Not classifiable by status	14.5	54.2	-	.	.	.

2. Population ('000), Activity rate and Unemployment rate

	Population			Activity rate			Unemployment rate		
Age group	2007 [1,4] Labour force survey			2007 [1,4] Labour force survey			2007 [2] Labour force survey		
	Total	Men	Women	Total	Men	Women	Total	Men	Women
Total	3 384.9	1 577.0	1 807.9	47.4	51.5	43.7	4.3	4.3	4.3
15+	2 846.8	1 301.2	1 545.6	56.3	62.4	51.2	.	.	.
15-24	533.1	271.6	261.5	27.4	31.8	22.8	8.2	6.9	10.1
25-54	1 434.3	698.2	736.1	86.0	87.9	84.2	4.0	4.0	4.0
55+	879.4	331.3	548.1	25.5	33.9	20.3	.	.	.

Lithuania

3. Paid employment ('000), Hours of work (weekly) and Wages

Economic activity (ISIC-Rev.3)	Paid employment 2007[1,2] Labour force survey			Hours of work 2007[1,2,5] Labour force survey Hours paid for / Employees			Wages 2007[6,7] Labour-related establishment survey Earnings per hour / Employees / Litas		
	Total	Men	Women	Total	Men	Women	Total	Men	Women
Total	1 324.4	651.1	673.3	38.4	39.4	37.4	11.60	12.85	10.37
A-B	.	.	.	35.4	36.6	33.6	.	.	.
C-Q	.	.	.	38.8	39.8	37.9	11.67	12.96	10.41
A	54.8	40.3	14.6	35.3	36.6	33.6	.	.	.
B	2.4	2.3	0.1	39.6	39.6	40.0	.	.	.
C	5.3	4.4	0.9	40.7	40.5	41.2	14.46	14.77	12.90
D	255.3	129.9	125.4	39.2	39.5	38.9	11.01	12.70	9.01
E	26.0	19.1	6.8	39.1	39.4	38.2	14.41	14.99	12.76
F	150.0	138.3	11.7	40.0	40.1	38.3	13.38	13.65	11.34
G	222.7	94.6	128.1	39.7	40.1	39.4	11.05	12.70	9.50
H	30.8	4.7	26.1	40.0	39.3	40.2	6.81	7.75	6.56
I	107.2	76.3	30.8	40.2	41.6	37.0	11.43	11.57	11.12
J	21.7	6.4	15.3	38.8	39.2	38.6	22.25	32.15	18.44
K	64.7	31.6	33.1	38.6	39.8	37.3	12.07	12.47	11.64
L	83.5	43.0	40.5	39.4	40.2	38.5	15.11	15.50	14.68
M	143.5	26.1	117.4	34.6	35.3	34.4	10.24	10.17	10.26
N	96.8	12.6	84.2	38.0	38.3	38.0	11.05	13.66	10.57
O	56.9	19.7	37.2	37.5	38.2	37.2	9.44	10.75	8.37
P	2.9	1.7	1.1	39.3	38.2	40.4	.	.	.
Q	.	.	.	.	.	.	.	.	.

Share of women in wage employment in the non-agricultural sector [1,2] (2007 - Labour force survey): **52.0%**

4. Occupational injuries and Strikes and Lockouts

Economic activity (ISIC-Rev.3)	Rates of fatal injuries 2006 Labour inspectorate records Per 100,000 employees Reported injuries			Rates of non-fatal injuries 2006 Labour inspectorate records Per 100,000 employees Reported injuries			Strikes and lockouts 2007 Establishment survey		
	Total	Men	Women	Total	Men	Women	Strikes and lockouts	Workers involved	Days not worked
Total	9.6	19.0	1.0	295	437	166	161	7 033	9 559
A	30.3	10.6	0.0	364	365	362	.	.	.
B	114.5	141.5	0.0	172	212	0	.	.	.
C	0.0	0.0	0.0	816	878	529	.	.	.
D	6.0	11.5	0.0	547	761	327	0	0	0
E	16.3	22.0	0.0	232	264	142	.	.	.
F	30.7	34.1	8.2	641	702	230	.	.	.
G	4.5	8.9	0.9	166	249	97	.	.	.
H	3.4	16.7	0.0	142	134	144	.	.	.
I	33.8	49.2	0.0	430	496	286	0	0	0
J	0.0	0.0	0.0	86	96	82	.	.	.
K	5.6	11.6	0.0	124	154	96	.	.	.
L	1.3	2.4	0.0	112	123	99	.	.	.
M	2.8	8.8	0.9	86	103	81	161	7 033	9 559
N	0.0	0.0	0.0	171	241	157	.	.	.
O	4.6	0.0	8.0	247	379	149	0	0	0

5. Consumer price indices (base period: 2000=100)

	2002	2003	2004	2005	2006	2007
General indices	101.6	100.4	101.6	104.3	108.2	114.4
Food index, including non-alcoholic beverages	102.8	99.0	101.2	105.3	111.7	124.3
Electricity, gas and other fuel indices	105.2	105.4	104.9	109.7	117.1	130.0
Clothing indices, including footwear	92.4	89.9	89.1	87.5	83.7	81.2
Rent indices	104.3	105.2	108.6	115.0	123.1	138.8
General index, excluding housing	101.1	99.7	100.7	103.1	106.8	112.8

[1] Excl. conscripts. [2] Persons aged 15 years and over. [3] Incl. the unemployed whose last job was 8 years ago or over. [4] "De facto" population. [5] On the main job. [6] Excl. individual unincorporated enterprises. [7] All employees converted into full-time units.

[1] Non compris les conscrits. [2] Personnes âgées de 15 ans et plus. [3] Y compris les chômeurs dont le dernier emploi date de 8 ans ou plus. [4] Population "de facto". [5] Emploi principal. [6] Non compris les entreprises individuelles non constituées en société. [7] Ensemble des salariés convertis en unités à plein temps.

[1] Excl. los conscriptos. [2] Personas de 15 años y más. [3] Incl. los desempleados cuyo último trabajo fue hace 8 años o más. [4] Población "de facto". [5] Empleo principal. [6] Excl. las empresas individuales no constituidas en sociedad. [7] Todos los asalariados convertidos en unidades a tiempo completo.

Luxembourg

1. Population active, Emploi et Chômage ('000)

Groupe d'âge	Population active Total	Population active Femmes (%)	Emploi Total	Emploi Femmes (%)	Chômage Total	Chômage Femmes (%)
	2007[1] Enquête sur la main-d'oeuvre		2007 ★ Enquête sur la main-d'oeuvre		2007 Enquête sur la main-d'oeuvre	
Total	213.2	44.5	204.3	44.2	8.9	51.7
15-19	2.5	44.0	1.8	38.9	0.7	57.1
20-24	12.8	46.1	11.2	45.5	1.6	50.0
25-29	26.6	48.1	25.1	48.6	1.5	40.0
30-34	32.0	46.3	30.4	45.7	1.6	56.3
35-39	34.9	44.4	34.2	44.2	0.7	57.1
40-44	34.4	43.9	33.4	43.7	1.0	50.0
45-49	29.9	42.5	29.1	41.9	0.8	62.5
50-54	24.1	40.7	23.3	40.3	0.8	50.0
55-59	13.2	44.7	12.9	45.0	0.3	33.3
60-64	2.6	42.3	2.6	42.3	0.0	.
65+	0.4	25.0	0.4	25.0	0.0	.

Activité économique (CITI-Rév.3)						
	2001[1,2] Recensement de la population		2007[3] Estimations officielles			
Total	191.2	41.0	332.5	.	.	.
A-B	.	.	4.7	.	.	.
A Agriculture, chasse et sylviculture	3.2	31.7	.	.	.	.
B Pêche	0.0	50.0	.	.	.	.
C Activités extractives	0.2	13.2	.	.	.	.
C-E	.	.	35.7	.	.	.
D Activités de fabrication	18.3	19.9	.	.	.	.
E Production et distribution d'électricité, de gaz et d'eau	0.9	12.4	.	.	.	.
F Construction	16.0	9.1	35.3	.	.	.
G Commerce de gros et de détail; réparation de véhicules ...	22.2	46.2	.	.	.	.
G-I	.	.	85.2	.	.	.
H Hôtels et restaurants	8.5	51.3	.	.	.	.
I Transports, entreposage et communications	12.8	21.6	.	.	.	.
J Intermédiation financière	19.3	44.1	.	.	.	.
J-K	.	.	97.6	.	.	.
K Immobilier, locations et activités de services aux entreprises	14.7	48.6	.	.	.	.
L Administration publique et défense; sécurité sociale obligatoire	20.2	35.9	.	.	.	.
L-P	.	.	74.0	.	.	.
M Education	7.2	57.1	.	.	.	.
N Santé et action sociale	14.0	75.9	.	.	.	.
O Autres activités de services collectifs, sociaux et personnels	5.9	53.8	.	.	.	.
P Ménages privés employant du personnel domestique	2.2	96.7	.	.	.	.
Q Organisations et organismes extraterritoriaux	8.3	46.6	.	.	.	.
X Ne pouvant être classés selon l'activité économique	11.3	45.9	.	.	.	.
Chômeurs n'ayant jamais travaillé	5.8	47.5	.	.	.	.

Profession (CITP-88)						
	2001[1,2] Recensement de la population					
Total	191.2	41.0	.	.	.	.
1 Membres de l'exécutif et des corps législatifs, cadres ...	11.7	31.2	.	.	.	.
2 Professions intellectuelles et scientifiques	24.5	39.6	.	.	.	.
3 Professions intermédiaires	31.4	46.5	.	.	.	.
4 Employés de type administratif	28.3	54.4	.	.	.	.
5 Personnel des services et vendeurs de magasin et de marché	15.6	60.7	.	.	.	.
6 Agriculteurs et ouvriers qualifiés de l'agriculture ...	4.5	26.9	.	.	.	.
7 Artisans et ouvriers des métiers de type artisanal	22.7	5.1	.	.	.	.
8 Conducteurs d'installations et de machines ...	9.6	4.6	.	.	.	.
9 Ouvriers et employés non qualifiés	18.9	67.8	.	.	.	.
0 Forces armées	0.7	4.1	.	.	.	.
X Ne pouvant être classés selon la profession	17.2	41.7	.	.	.	.
Chômeurs n'ayant jamais travaillé	5.8	47.5	.	.	.	.

Niveau d'instruction (CITE-76)						
					2007[4] Fichiers des bureaux de placement	
Total	.	.	.	.	9.623	48.7
0-2	.	.	.	.	4.989	46.8
3 Second degré, deuxième cycle	.	.	.	.	3.371	50.0
5-7	.	.	.	.	1.110	49.6
? Niveau inconnu	.	.	.	.	0.153	76.5

Niveau d'instruction (CITE-97)						
	2007[1] Enquête sur la main-d'oeuvre					
Total	213.2	44.5	.	.	.	.
0 Education préprimaire	10.2	46.5	.	.	.	.
1 Enseignement primaire ou premier cycle de l'éducation ...	20.7	41.9	.	.	.	.
2 Premier cycle de l'enseignement secondaire ou deuxième ...	34.6	47.1	.	.	.	.
3 Enseignement secondaire (deuxième cycle)	77.6	43.2	.	.	.	.
4 Enseignement postsecondaire qui n'est pas du supérieur	7.9	36.5	.	.	.	.
5A Premier cycle de l'enseignement supérieur - théorie	39.5	43.5	.	.	.	.
5B Premier cycle de l'enseignement supérieur - pratique	20.2	53.2	.	.	.	.
6 Deuxième cycle de l'enseignement supérieur	2.5	27.9	.	.	.	.

Situation dans la profession (CISP-1993)						
	2001[1,2] Recensement de la population					
Total	191.2	41.0	.	.	.	.
1 Salariés	158.7	40.6	.	.	.	.
2 Employeurs	6.3	25.2	.	.	.	.
3 Personnes travaillant pour leur propre compte	9.7	37.9	.	.	.	.
5 Travailleurs familiaux collaborant à l'entreprise familiale	3.2	79.4	.	.	.	.
6 Inclassables d'après la situation	7.5	47.0	.	.	.	.

Luxembourg

2. Population ('000), Taux d'activité et Taux de chômage

Groupe d'âge	Population 2007[5] Enquête sur la main-d'oeuvre			Taux d'activité 2007[5] Enquête sur la main-d'oeuvre			Taux de chômage 2007 Enquête sur la main-d'oeuvre		
	Total	Hommes	Femmes	Total	Hommes	Femmes	Total	Hommes	Femmes
Total	476.2	235.8	240.4	44.8	50.2	39.4	4.2	3.6	4.9
15+	388.9	190.8	198.0	54.9	62.1	47.9	4.2	3.6	4.9
15-24	56.1	28.7	27.4	27.3	28.9	25.5	15.0	13.3	17.1
25-54	216.5	109.2	107.3	84.0	92.5	75.2	3.5	3.0	4.1
55+	116.3	52.9	63.3	13.9	17.2	11.2	1.9	2.2	1.4

3. Emploi rémunéré ('000), Durée du travail (hebdomadaire) et Salaires

Activité économique (CITI-Rév.2)	Emploi rémunéré			Durée du travail 1993[6] Recensement des établissements, relatif au travail Heures rémunérées / Ouvriers			Salaires		
	Total	Hommes	Femmes	Total	Hommes	Femmes	Total	Hommes	Femmes
2-9 [7]	.	.	.	41.1	41.2	39.4	.	.	.
2	.	.	.	45.1	45.2	.	.	.	.
3	.	.	.	40.6	40.8	39.4	.	.	.
5	.	.	.	41.6	41.6	39.2	.	.	.

Activité économique (CITI-Rév.3)	Emploi rémunéré 2007[3] Estimations officielles			Durée du travail			Salaires 2007[6] Recensement des établissements, relatif au travail Gains par heure / Ouvriers / Euro		
	Total	Hommes	Femmes	Total	Hommes	Femmes	Total	Hommes	Femmes
Total	312.2	.	.	.	.	.	.	.	.
A-B	1.4	.	.	.	.	.	.	.	.
C	.	.	.	.	.	.	14.90	14.94	12.58
C-E	35.2	.	.	.	.	.	.	.	.
D	.	.	.	.	.	.	14.82	15.31	11.12
E	.	.	.	.	.	.	20.21	20.48	15.04
F	34.2	.	.	.	.	.	13.48	13.51	11.23
G	.	.	.	.	.	.	12.21	12.89	10.48
G-I	78.2	.	.	.	.	.	.	.	.
H	.	.	.	.	.	.	11.27	12.33	10.17
J	.	.	.	.	.	.	15.88	16.21	13.90
J-K	92.8	.	.	.	.	.	.	.	.
L-P	70.4	.	.	.	.	.	.	.	.

Pourcentage de salariées dans le secteur non agricole qui sont femmes (1998 - Fichiers des assurances): **36.5%**

4. Lésions professionnelles et Grèves et lock-out

Activité économique (CITI-Rév.3)	Taux de lésions mortelles 2004 Fichiers des assurances Pour 100 000 travailleurs assurés Lésions indemnisées			Taux de lésions non mortelles 2004 Fichiers des assurances Pour 100 000 travailleurs assurés Lésions indemnisées			Grèves et lock-out 2006 Source inconnue		
	Total	Hommes	Femmes	Total	Hommes	Femmes	Grèves et lock-out	Travailleurs impliqués	Journées non effectuées
Total	1.9	3.1	0.0	6 563	8 696	3 202	0	0	0
A	0.0	0.0	0.0	17 207	20 950	8 953	.	.	.
B	0.0	0.0	0.0	0	0	0	.	.	.
C	0.0	0.0	0.0	10 638	10 638	0	.	.	.
D	2.9	3.6	0.0	8 429	9 734	3 104	.	.	.
E	0.0	0.0	0.0	5 158	5 876	0	.	.	.
F	6.4	7.0	0.0	17 871	19 435	1 128	.	.	.
G	0.0	0.0	0.0	5 953	8 316	3 213	.	.	.
H	0.0	0.0	0.0	7 564	7 700	7 428	.	.	.
I	11.7	14.4	0.0	6 984	7 970	2 683	.	.	.
J	0.0	0.0	0.0	617	531	740	.	.	.
K	0.0	0.0	0.0	5 826	8 345	3 058	.	.	.
L	0.0	0.0	0.0	3 947	4 674	2 674	.	.	.
M	0.0	0.0	0.0	1 737	1 064	2 150	.	.	.
N	0.0	0.0	0.0	6 885	8 791	6 313	.	.	.
O	0.0	0.0	0.0	3 520	4 382	2 551	.	.	.
P	0.0	0.0	0.0	906	0	801	.	.	.
Q	0.0	0.0	0.0	2 437	0	2 532	.	.	.
X	0.0	0.0	0.0	1 790	2 305	924	.	.	.

5. Indices des prix à la consommation (période de base: 2000=100)

	2002	2003	2004	2005	2006	2007
Indices généraux	104.8	106.9	109.3	112.0	115.0	117.7
Indices de l'alimentation, y compris les boissons non alcoolisées	108.9	111.0	113.0	114.8	117.6	121.5
Indices de l'électricité, gaz et autres combustibles	95.0	98.0	104.1	120.9	135.0	137.5
Indices de l'habillement, y compris les chaussures	103.8	105.3	105.8	106.5	106.6	107.1
Indices du loyer	105.8	107.7	109.4	112.6	115.2	117.3
Indices généraux, non compris le logement [8]	104.7	106.9	109.4	112.1	.	.

Luxembourg

[1] Persons aged 15 years and over. [2] Feb. [3] Incl. the armed forces. [4] Persons aged 16 to 64 years. [5] "De jure" population. [6] Oct. [7] Excl. major divisions 6, 7, 8 and 9. [8] Excl. Water, Electricity, Gas and Other Fuels.

[1] Personnes âgées de 15 ans et plus. [2] Fév. [3] Y compris les forces armées. [4] Personnes âgées de 16 à 64 ans. [5] Population "de jure". [6] Oct. [7] Non compris les branches 6, 7, 8 et 9. [8] Non compris l'eau, l'électricité, le gaz et autres combustibles.

[1] Personas de 15 años y más. [2] Feb. [3] Incl. las fuerzas armadas. [4] Personas de 16 a 64 años. [5] Población "de jure". [6] Oct. [7] Excl. las grandes divisiones 6, 7, 8 y 9. [8] Excl. el agua, la electricidad, el gas y otros combustibles.

Macau, China

1. Economically active population, Employment and Unemployment ('000)

	Economically active population		Employment		Unemployment	
	Total	Women (%)	Total	Women (%)	Total	Women (%)
Age group	2007 [1][2] Labour force survey		2007 ★ Labour force survey		2007 [2] Labour force survey	
Total	309.8	46.4	300.3	46.5	9.5	41.1
14-19	8.4	47.6	7.4	50.0	1.0	30.0
20-24	35.5	52.2	33.8	53.1	1.7	35.3
25-29	35.4	50.0	34.7	49.8	0.7	57.1
30-34	38.2	49.6	37.3	49.7	0.9	44.4
35-39	40.4	51.1	39.6	50.9	0.8	62.5
40-44	43.4	48.8	42.4	48.8	1.0	50.0
45-49	44.5	44.0	43.3	44.1	1.2	41.7
50-54	33.8	39.0	32.6	39.2	1.2	33.3
55-59	19.2	35.7	18.5	35.5	0.7	42.9
60-64	7.4	29.3	7.2	30.1	0.2	0.0
65-69	2.1	25.0	2.1	25.0	0.0	.
70-74	0.9	22.2	0.9	22.2	0.0	.
75+	0.7	22.8	0.7	22.8	0.0	.
Economic activity (ISIC-Rev.3)	2007 ★ Labour force survey		2007 [1][2] Labour force survey		2007 [2] Labour force survey	
Total	309.9	46.4	300.4	46.5	9.5	41.1
A Agriculture, Hunting and Forestry	0.2	50.0	0.1	100.0	0.1	.
B Fishing	0.1	.	0.1	.	-	.
C Mining and Quarrying	.	.	-	.	0.0	.
D Manufacturing	25.1	64.1	24.0	64.2	1.1	63.6
E Electricity, Gas and Water Supply	1.2	16.7	1.2	16.7	0.0	.
F Construction	40.3	12.2	38.6	12.2	1.7	11.8
G Wholesale and Retail Trade; Repair of Motor Vehicles ...	39.9	49.9	38.4	49.7	1.5	53.3
H Hotels and Restaurants	36.1	51.8	34.7	52.2	1.4	42.9
I Transport, Storage and Communications	16.7	27.5	16.4	27.4	0.3	33.3
J Financial Intermediation	8.0	61.3	7.9	60.8	0.1	100.0
K Real Estate, Renting and Business Activities	20.6	42.2	20.1	42.3	0.5	40.0
L Public Administration and Defence; Compulsory Social ...	22.0	35.5	22.0	35.5	-	.
M Education	12.0	68.3	11.9	68.1	0.1	100.0
N Health and Social Work	6.1	72.1	6.0	71.7	0.1	100.0
O Other Community, Social and Personal Service Activities	70.2	50.9	69.1	50.9	1.1	45.5
P Households with Employed Persons	9.7	94.8	9.6	94.8	0.1	100.0
Q Extra-Territorial Organizations and Bodies	0.1	100.0	0.1	100.0	0.0	.
X Not classifiable by economic activity	-	.	-	.		
Unemployed seeking their first job	.	.	.	.	1.3	38.5
Occupation (ISCO-88)	2007 ★ Labour force survey		2007 [1][2] Labour force survey		2007 [2] Labour force survey	
Total	309.9	46.4	300.4	46.5	9.5	41.1
1 Legislators, senior officials and managers	14.7	25.9	14.6	26.0	0.1	.
2 Professionals	10.4	42.3	10.3	41.7	0.1	100.0
3 Technicians and associate professionals	28.5	46.3	28.2	46.5	0.3	33.3
4 Clerks	80.7	61.7	79.4	61.7	1.3	61.5
5 Service workers and shop and market sales workers	63.1	46.6	60.7	46.3	2.4	54.2
6 Skilled agricultural and fishery workers	1.0	20.0	0.9	22.2	0.1	.
7 Craft and related trade workers	33.1	4.5	31.8	4.4	1.3	7.7
8 Plant and machine operators and assemblers	22.7	37.4	21.9	37.0	0.8	50.0
9 Elementary occupations	54.1	60.1	52.5	60.8	1.6	37.5
X Not classifiable by occupation	.	.	0.0	.	0.0	.
Unemployed seeking their first job	.	.	.	.	1.3	38.5
Education level (ISCED-97)	2007 [1][2] Labour force survey		2007 ★ Labour force survey		2007 [2] Labour force survey	
Total	309.8	46.4	300.3	46.5	9.5	41.1
X No schooling	4.0	66.0	3.8	66.8	0.2	50.0
0 Pre-primary education	14.8	46.2	14.2	46.0	0.6	50.0
1 Primary education or first stage of basic education	63.1	42.8	60.5	43.3	2.6	30.8
2 Lower secondary or second stage of basic education	93.9	46.2	90.9	46.4	3.0	40.0
3 Upper secondary education	75.3	46.7	73.2	46.8	2.1	42.9
5A First stage of tertiary education - theoretically based [3]	47.5	47.6	46.7	47.5	0.8	50.0
5B First stage of tertiary education - practically oriented	11.0	53.9	10.9	53.5	0.1	100.0
? Level not stated	0.1	52.4	0.1	52.4	0.0	.
Status in employment (ICSE-1993)	2006 [1][2] Labour force survey		2007 [1][2] Labour force survey		2006 ★ Labour force survey	
Total	275.5	46.6	300.4	46.5	10.4	46.2
1 Employees	240.4	48.2	274.4	48.2	.	.
2 Employers	10.0	20.0	10.4	20.2	.	.
3 Own-account workers	12.2	28.7	13.4	26.1	.	.
5 Contributing family workers	2.5	88.0	2.1	90.5	.	.
6 Not classifiable by status	10.4	46.2	.	.	.	.

Macau, China

2. Population ('000), Activity rate and Unemployment rate

Age group	Population 2007 [1,4] Labour force survey			Activity rate 2007 [1,4] Labour force survey			Unemployment rate 2007 [2] Labour force survey		
	Total	Men	Women	Total	Men	Women	Total	Men	Women
Total	513.7	252.8	260.9	60.3	65.7	55.1	3.1	3.4	2.7
15+	447.8	218.6	229.2	69.2	76.0	62.7	3.0	3.4	2.7
15-24	99.1	49.1	50.1	44.3	43.5	45.0	6.1	8.9	4.0
25-54	269.2	130.7	138.5	87.5	95.2	80.3	2.5	2.5	2.4
55+	79.5	38.9	40.6	38.1	52.4	24.4	3.0	3.4	3.0

3. Paid employment ('000), Hours of work (weekly) and Wages

Economic activity (ISIC-Rev.3)	Paid employment 2007 [5] Labour-related establishment survey			Hours of work 2007 [6] Labour force survey Hours actually worked / Total employment			Wages 2007 Labour-related establishment survey Earnings per month / Employees / Pataca		
	Total	Men	Women	Total	Men	Women	Total	Men	Women
Total	.	.	.	46.9	47.1	46.6	.	.	.
C-Q	.	.	.	46.9	47.1	46.6	.	.	.
C	.	.	.	52.8	52.8	.	.	.	.
D	28.0	8.3	19.7	47.3	47.5	47.2	4 990 [5]	6 716 [5]	4 272 [5]
E	1.1	0.8	0.2	41.8	42.1	40.6	20 790 [5]	21 483 [5]	18 097 [5]
F	.	.	.	47.1	47.4	45.4	.	.	.
G	24.1	11.3	12.8	48.8	49.3	48.2	9 294 [7]	10 019 [7]	8 610 [7]
H	42.6	20.1	22.4	48.7	48.9	48.6	9 127 [5]	11 116 [5]	7 269 [5]
I	7.3 [8]	4.8 [8]	2.6 [8]	47.1	48.5	44.3	18 575 [7]	20 269 [7]	15 428 [7]
J	5.1	2.1	3.1	43.2	43.6	42.9	15 539 [5]	19 756 [5]	12 684 [5]
K	.	.	.	48.0	50.6	46.1	7 244 [7]	7 030 [7]	8 313 [7]
L	.	.	.	38.9	39.4	38.2	.	.	.
M	.	.	.	41.9	41.2	42.2	.	.	.
N	.	.	.	43.3	42.7	43.6	.	.	.
O	44.7 [9]	21.7 [9]	0.6 [9]	47.0	47.0	46.9	15 060 [7]	15 814 [7]	14 349 [7]
P	.	.	.	48.7	48.4	48.7	.	.	.

Share of women in wage employment in the non-agricultural sector [1,2] (2007 - Labour force survey): **48.2%**

4. Occupational injuries and Strikes and Lockouts

Economic activity (ISIC-Rev.3)	Rates of fatal injuries 2007 [10] Labour inspectorate records Per 100,000 workers employed Reported injuries			Rates of non-fatal injuries 2007 [10] Labour inspectorate records Per 100,000 workers employed Reported injuries			Strikes and lockouts		
	Total	Men	Women	Total	Men	Women	Strikes and lockouts	Workers involved	Days not worked
Total	5	8	1	757	780	731	.	.	.
A	0	0	0	2 000	5 556	0	.	.	.
B	0	0	0	0	0	0	.	.	.
C	0	0	0	0	0	0	.	.	.
D	0	0	0	992	1 310	805	.	.	.
E	0	0	0	417	500	0	.	.	.
F	18	0	21	798	755	1 106	.	.	.
G	0	0	0	753	917	586	.	.	.
H	0	0	0	1 614	1 575	1 641	.	.	.
I	6	8	0	854	983	533	.	.	.
J	0	0	0	114	129	104	.	.	.
K	0	0	0	677	598	776	.	.	.
L	0	0	0	114	106	128	.	.	.
M	0	0	0	294	342	272	.	.	.
N	0	0	0	650	529	698	.	.	.
O	9	18	0	687	614	759	.	.	.
P	0	0	0	135	0	143	.	.	.
Q	0	0	0	0	0	0	.	.	.

5. Consumer price indices (base period: 2000=100)

	2002	2003	2004	2005	2006	2007
General indices	95.4	93.9	94.9	99.0	104.1	109.9
Food index, including non-alcoholic beverages	96.5	95.2	97.4	101.3	105.0	113.6
Electricity, gas and other fuel indices	95.0	98.5	99.9	110.9	119.9	114.6
Clothing indices, including footwear	85.5	74.9	77.4	76.7	73.1	74.0
Rent indices	94.8	92.7	92.1	98.1	112.0	128.3
General index, excluding housing	95.6	94.2	95.5	99.2	102.7	106.8

[1] Excl. armed forces and conscripts. [2] Persons aged 14 years and over. [3] Levels 5A and 6. [4] "De jure" population. [5] Third quarter. [6] Median. [7] Fourth quarter. [8] Excluding travel agencies. [9] Including Gaming industry. [10] Private sector.

[1] Non compris les forces armées et les conscrits. [2] Personnes âgées de 14 ans et plus. [3] Niveaux 5A et 6. [4] Population "de jure". [5] Troisième trimestre. [6] Médiane. [7] Quatrième trimestre. [8] Non compris les agences de voyages. [9] Inclus les industries du jeux. [10] Secteur privé.

[1] Excl. las fuerzas armadas y los conscriptos. [2] Personas de 14 años y más. [3] Niveles 5A y 6. [4] Población "de jure". [5] Tercer trimestre. [6] Mediana. [7] Cuarto trimestre. [8] Excl. Las agencias de viajes. [9] Incl. las industrias de juegos de azar. [10] Sector privado.

Macedonia, The Former Yugoslav Rep. of

1. Economically active population, Employment and Unemployment ('000)

	Economically active population		Employment		Unemployment	
	Total	Women (%)	Total	Women (%)	Total	Women (%)
Age group	2007 [1] Labour force survey		2007 ★ Labour force survey		2007 [1] Labour force survey	
Total	907.000	39.6	590.095	39.2	316.905	40.3
15-19	28.937	33.1	10.823	33.4	18.114	32.9
20-24	88.111	38.6	38.669	37.7	49.442	39.3
25-29	120.806	41.1	69.495	40.3	51.311	42.2
30-34	124.921	41.4	79.746	39.4	45.175	45.0
35-39	117.847	40.8	81.557	40.4	36.290	41.9
40-44	118.379	41.2	84.392	39.5	33.987	45.4
45-49	114.341	41.3	85.013	40.7	29.328	42.8
50-54	101.507	39.8	72.168	40.0	29.339	39.3
55-59	62.249	33.8	44.715	36.8	17.534	26.1
60-64	22.159	26.3	16.029	30.7	6.130	14.8
65-69	4.765	33.3	4.512	34.5	0.253	11.5
70-74	2.159	36.7	2.159	36.7	-	-
75+	0.958	36.6	0.958	36.6	-	-
Economic activity (ISIC-Rev.2)	1991 [2,3] Population census						
Total	697.44	39.7	.	.	.	.
1 Agriculture, Hunting, Forestry and Fishing	115.36	35.6	.	.	.	.
2-4	205.42	39.0	.	.	.	.
5 Construction	43.98	10.3	.	.	.	.
6 Wholesale and Retail Trade and Restaurants and Hotels	69.96	45.8	.	.	.	.
7 Transport, Storage and Communication	27.80	14.0	.	.	.	.
8 Financing, Insurance, Real Estate and Business Services	12.83	49.4	.	.	.	.
9 Community, Social and Personal Services	105.77	50.2	.	.	.	.
0 Activities not Adequately Defined	23.79	36.4	.	.	.	.
Unemployed seeking their first job	92.53	50.7	.	.	.	.
Economic activity (ISIC-Rev.3)			2007 [1] Labour force survey			
Total	.	.	590.234	39.2	.	.
A Agriculture, Hunting and Forestry	.	.	107.433	37.2	.	.
B Fishing	.	.	0.284	.	.	.
C Mining and Quarrying	.	.	5.093	5.0	.	.
D Manufacturing	.	.	126.193	48.3	.	.
E Electricity, Gas and Water Supply	.	.	15.636	15.5	.	.
F Construction	.	.	38.006	7.0	.	.
G Wholesale and Retail Trade; Repair of Motor Vehicles ...	.	.	82.971	41.7	.	.
H Hotels and Restaurants	.	.	17.486	32.5	.	.
I Transport, Storage and Communications	.	.	35.461	16.6	.	.
J Financial Intermediation	.	.	9.041	49.8	.	.
K Real Estate, Renting and Business Activities	.	.	15.909	47.6	.	.
L Public Administration and Defence; Compulsory Social ...	.	.	41.409	28.9	.	.
M Education	.	.	34.367	61.5	.	.
N Health and Social Work	.	.	32.947	70.9	.	.
O Other Community, Social and Personal Service Activities	.	.	24.714	35.0	.	.
P Households with Employed Persons	.	.	1.415	39.3	.	.
Q Extra-Territorial Organizations and Bodies	.	.	1.869	58.2	.	.
Occupation (ISCO-1968)	1991 [2,3] Population census					
Total	697.44	39.7	.	.	.	.
0/1 Professional, technical and related workers	79.67	51.3	.	.	.	.
2 Administrative and managerial workers	16.54	16.2	.	.	.	.
3 Clerical and related workers	64.11	59.9	.	.	.	.
4 Sales workers	53.62	42.0	.	.	.	.
5 Service workers	36.72	62.6	.	.	.	.
6 Agriculture, animal husbandry and forestry workers ...	94.01	37.7	.	.	.	.
7/8/9 Production and related workers, transport equipment ...	214.96	26.6	.	.	.	.
X Not classifiable by occupation	27.40	34.9	.	.	.	.
AF Armed forces	17.86	0.7	.	.	.	.
Unemployed seeking their first job	92.53	50.7	.	.	.	.
Occupation (ISCO-88)			2007 [1] Labour force survey			
Total	.	.	590.234	39.2	.	.
1 Legislators, senior officials and managers	.	.	34.225	29.3	.	.
2 Professionals	.	.	58.720	52.9	.	.
3 Technicians and associate professionals	.	.	63.424	52.4	.	.
4 Clerks	.	.	40.629	49.5	.	.
5 Service workers and shop and market sales workers	.	.	83.634	39.7	.	.
6 Skilled agricultural and fishery workers	.	.	7.670	22.8	.	.
7 Craft and related trade workers	.	.	80.113	18.0	.	.
8 Plant and machine operators and assemblers	.	.	76.334	41.7	.	.
9 Elementary occupations	.	.	138.739	40.0	.	.
0 Armed forces	.	.	6.748	4.5	.	.
Status in employment (ICSE-58)	1991 [2,3] Population census					
Total	697.44	39.7	.	.	.	.
1 Employers and own-account workers	62.91	29.3	.	.	.	.
2 Employees	500.67	37.9	.	.	.	.
3 Unpaid family workers	21.11	67.8	.	.	.	.
4 Not classifiable by status	112.76	48.3	.	.	.	.

Macedonia, The Former Yugoslav Rep. of

Status in employment (ICSE-1993)	2007 [1] Labour force survey	
Total	590.234	39.2
1 Employees	426.662	41.7
2 Employers	32.655	23.5
3 Own-account workers	71.245	15.7
5 Contributing family workers	59.672	57.8

2. Population ('000), Activity rate and Unemployment rate

Age group	Population 2007 Labour force survey			Activity rate 2007 Labour force survey			Unemployment rate 2007 [1] Labour force survey		
	Total	Men	Women	Total	Men	Women	Total	Men	Women
Total	.	.	.	.	.	.	34.9	34.5	35.5
15+	1 628.6	814.6	814.0	55.7	67.3	44.1	.	.	.
15-24	326.4	167.8	158.6	35.9	43.8	27.5	57.7	57.4	58.2
25-54	895.5	455.9	439.6	77.9	90.4	65.0	32.3	31.2	33.8
55+	406.8	191.0	215.8	22.7	32.8	13.7	.	.	.

3. Paid employment ('000), Hours of work (weekly) and Wages

Economic activity (ISIC-Rev.3)	Paid employment 2007 [1] Labour force survey			Hours of work			Wages 2007 [4] Labour-related establishment survey Earnings per month / Employees / Denar		
	Total	Men	Women	Total	Men	Women	Total	Men	Women
Total	426.662	248.649	178.013	.	.	.	14 584	.	.
A	12.388	10.069	2.318	.	.	.	10 740	.	.
B	0.209	0.209	0.000	.	.	.	10 565	.	.
C	5.027	4.772	0.256	.	.	.	16 327	.	.
D	116.820	57.847	58.973	.	.	.	11 653	.	.
E	15.636	13.205	2.431	.	.	.	19 626	.	.
F	28.826	26.394	2.432	.	.	.	10 564	.	.
G	54.372	27.891	26.481	.	.	.	13 951	.	.
H	14.512	9.256	5.256	.	.	.	11 639	.	.
I	28.086	22.574	5.511	.	.	.	17 779	.	.
J	8.821	4.316	4.506	.	.	.	28 419	.	.
K	11.788	5.973	5.816	.	.	.	14 906	.	.
L	41.409	29.424	11.986	.	.	.	17 160	.	.
M	33.873	13.177	20.696	.	.	.	13 957	.	.
N	30.701	8.448	22.253	.	.	.	13 320	.	.
O	21.711	14.068	7.643	.	.	.	13 553	.	.
P	0.613	0.244	0.369	.	.	.	.	.	.
Q	1.869	0.782	1.087	.	.	.	.	.	.

Share of women in wage employment in the non-agricultural sector [1] (2007 - Labour force survey): **42.4%**

4. Occupational injuries and Strikes and Lockouts

Statistics not available.

5. Consumer price indices (base period: 2000=100)

	2002	2003	2004	2005	2006	2007
General indices	107.4	108.7	108.2	108.8	112.3	114.8
Food index, including non-alcoholic beverages	108.8	107.3	104.0	102.7	105.0	109.1
Electricity, gas and other fuel indices	104.9	109.6	112.8	114.0	118.2	125.0
Clothing indices, including footwear	108.2	110.5	111.6	114.0	114.2	116.3
Rent indices [5]	115.9	120.4	120.0	120.4	119.5	127.1
General index, excluding housing	107.1	108.3	107.9	108.4	112.0	114.3

[1] Persons aged 15 years and over. [2] Persons aged 10 years and over. [3] June. [4] Net earnings. [5] Housing.

[1] Personnes âgées de 15 ans et plus. [2] Personnes âgées de 10 ans et plus. [3] Juin. [4] Gains nets. [5] Logement.

[1] Personas de 15 años y más. [2] Personas de 10 años y más. [3] Junio. [4] Ganancias netas. [5] Vivienda.

Madagascar

1. Population active, Emploi et Chômage ('000)

Groupe d'âge	Population active Total	Femmes (%)	Emploi Total	Femmes (%)	Chômage Total	Femmes (%)
	2005[1,2] Enquête sur la main-d'oeuvre		2005[1,2] Enquête auprès des ménages		2005[2] Enquête auprès des ménages	
Total	9 844.1	49.6	9 570.4	49.4	274.3	63.4
6-9	335.0	48.8	.	.	24.6	55.8
10-14	655.2	48.0	.	.	17.9	34.1
15-19	1 228.3	51.0	.	.	20.3	50.2
20-24	1 233.9	51.7	.	.	35.5	69.9
25-29	1 250.1	52.4	.	.	37.4	48.3
30-34	1 094.9	50.9	.	.	12.4	72.4
35-39	952.1	50.1	.	.	9.4	70.0
40-44	831.6	47.5	.	.	8.4	80.8
45-49	729.2	48.1	.	.	10.6	80.8
50-54	612.4	47.4	.	.	27.5	84.5
55-59	353.9	49.6	.	.	29.3	76.9
60-64	231.9	49.6	.	.	32.8	56.7
65-69	156.5	36.9	.	.	2.3	96.2
70-74	95.0	43.3	.	.	2.0	34.9
75+	84.1	32.2	.	.	3.9	71.8

Activité économique (CITI-Rév.3)

2005[1,2] Enquête auprès des ménages

	Total	Femmes (%)
Total	9 570.4	49.4
A Agriculture, chasse et sylviculture	7 745.3	50.0
B Pêche	99.0	31.2
C Activités extractives	18.8	45.0
D Activités de fabrication	267.5	23.3
E Production et distribution d'électricité, de gaz et d'eau	27.5	22.3
F Construction	13.0	7.1
G Commerce de gros et de détail; réparation de véhicules ...	470.5	63.0
H Hôtels et restaurants	63.9	52.4
I Transports, entreposage et communications	86.3	6.3
J Intermédiation financière	4.1	34.1
K Immobilier, locations et activités de services aux entreprises	-	
L Administration publique et défense; sécurité sociale obligatoire	202.4	34.0
M Education	44.5	58.3
N Santé et action sociale	9.9	48.5
O Autres activités de services collectifs, sociaux et personnels	517.7	60.6

Profession (CITP-88)

2005[1,2] Enquête auprès des ménages

	Total	Femmes (%)
Total	9 570.4	49.4
1 Membres de l'exécutif et des corps législatifs, cadres ...	21.2	22.1
2 Professions intellectuelles et scientifiques	146.5	48.9
3 Professions intermédiaires	57.8	28.7
4 Employés de type administratif	70.7	42.6
5 Personnel des services et vendeurs de magasin et de marché	442.6	62.7
6 Agriculteurs et ouvriers qualifiés de l'agriculture ...	7 575.4	49.8
7 Artisans et ouvriers des métiers de type artisanal	491.5	43.9
8 Conducteurs d'installations et de machines ...	98.8	19.3
9 Ouvriers et employés non qualifiés	628.3	49.8
0 Forces armées	37.7	22.3

Niveau d'instruction (CITE-76)

	2005[1,2] Enquête sur la main-d'oeuvre Total	Femmes (%)	2005[2] Enquête auprès des ménages Total	Femmes (%)
Total	9 844.1	49.6	274.3	63.4
X Non scolarisé	2 766.0	54.5	63.1	72.5
0 Enseignement précédant le premier degré [3]	5 448.8	48.5	120.3	64.2
2 Second degré, premier cycle [4]	1 324.6	47.1	65.3	60.3
5 Troisième degré, premier niveau, conduisant à un titre ... [5]	304.6	35.6	25.6	45.0

Situation dans la profession (CISP-1993)

2005[1,2] Enquête auprès des ménages

	Total	Femmes (%)
Total	9 570.4	49.4
1 Salariés	1 285.8	39.7
3 Personnes travaillant pour leur propre compte	3 268.2	23.3
5 Travailleurs familiaux collaborant à l'entreprise familiale	5 004.8	69.0
6 Inclassables d'après la situation	11.5	44.1

2. Population ('000), Taux d'activité et Taux de chômage

Groupe d'âge	Population 2005[1] Enquête sur la main-d'oeuvre			Taux d'activité 2005[1] Enquête sur la main-d'oeuvre			Taux de chômage 2005[2] Enquête auprès des ménages		
	Total	Hommes	Femmes	Total	Hommes	Femmes	Total	Hommes	Femmes
Total	.	.	.	.	.	.	2.8	2.0	3.6
15+	10 184.2	4 974.8	5 209.4	86.9	89.4	84.6	.	.	.
15-24	3 357.2	1 626.3	1 731.0	73.3	73.6	73.1	.	.	.
25-54	5 710.5	2 770.5	2 940.0	95.8	99.1	92.7	.	.	.
55+	1 116.5	578.0	538.5	82.5	87.4	77.3	.	.	.

Madagascar

3. Emploi rémunéré ('000), Durée du travail (hebdomadaire) et Salaires

Activité économique (CITI-Rév.3)	Emploi rémunéré 2005 [2] Enquête auprès des ménages Total	Hommes	Femmes	Durée du travail 2005 Enquête auprès des ménages Heures réellement effectuées / Salariés Total	Hommes	Femmes	Salaires 2005 Enquête auprès des ménages Gains par heure / Salariés / Franc Total	Hommes	Femmes
Total	1 285.8	775.1	510.7	36	38	33	2 173	2 421	1 790
A-B	.	.	.	34	36	31	979	1 025	924
C-Q	.	.	.	45	47	42	2 536	2 796	2 106
A	300.8	159.2	141.6	34	36	31	971	1 014	920
B	7.4	6.5	0.9	41	44	34	1 320	1 291	1 533
C	11.1	6.1	5.0	38	42	34	2 632	3 799	1 224
D	222.9	171.1	51.8	49	49	49	2 033	2 106	1 794
E	18.1	12.6	5.5	41	41	42	2 676	2 581	2 952
F	10.4	9.9	0.5	51	53	33	3 000	3 021	1 839
G	56.1	29.8	26.3	47	48	47	1 933	1 689	2 216
H	27.6	14.4	13.2	50	47	53	2 201	1 882	2 550
I	73.7	68.5	5.1	54	55	51	2 233	2 178	2 971
J	4.1	2.7	1.4	44	45	44	6 211	7 404	3 913
L	195.4	129.5	65.9	40	42	36	4 733	5 245	3 738
M	42.3	17.2	25.0	36	39	33	2 350	2 225	2 438
N	8.1	3.7	4.3	45	44	47	3 989	6 058	2 201
O	307.9	143.8	164.2	41	47	38	1 584	1 819	1 380

Pourcentage de salariées dans le secteur non agricole qui sont femmes [2] (2005 - Enquête auprès des ménages): **37.7%**

4. Lésions professionnelles et Grèves et lock-out

Activité économique (CITI-Rév.2)	Taux de lésions mortelles Total	Hommes	Femmes	Taux de lésions non mortelles Total	Hommes	Femmes	Grèves et lock-out 1983 Source inconnue Grèves et lock-out	Travailleurs impliqués	Journées non effectuées
Total	.	.	.	.	.	.	18	324	2 642
1	.	.	.	.	.	.	7	44	2 082
3	.	.	.	.	.	.	5	280	560
6	.	.	.	.	.	.	6	0	0
0	.	.	.	.	.	.	0	0	0

5. Indices des prix à la consommation (période de base: 2000=100)

Cinq régions	2002	2003	2004	2005	2006	2007
Indices généraux	125.1	123.0	139.9	165.9	183.7	202.6
Indices de l'alimentation, y compris les boissons non alcoolisées [6]	117.2	112.9	134.7	170.2	180.8	202.1
Indices de l'électricité, gaz et autres combustibles	122.8	117.6	134.7	156.5	207.3	214.9
Indices de l'habillement, y compris les chaussures [7]	111.3	115.4	118.8	122.0	149.6	144.4
Indices du loyer [8]	160.7	186.0	212.7	233.7	268.7	289.2
Indices généraux, non compris le logement [9]	123.4	119.6	136.7	164.1	179.3	198.1

[1] Excl. armed forces and conscripts. [2] Persons aged 6 years and over. [3] Levels 0-1. [4] Levels 2-3. [5] Levels 5-7. [6] Incl. beverages and tobacco. [7] Incl. household linen. [8] Incl. housing, water, electriciy and other fuels. [9] Excl. housing, water, electriciy and other fuels.

[1] Non compris les forces armées et les conscrits. [2] Personnes âgées de 6 ans et plus. [3] Niveaux 0-1. [4] Niveaux 2-3. [5] Niveaux 5-7. [6] Y compris les boissons et le tabac. [7] Y compris le linge de maison. [8] Y compris le logement, l'eau, l'électricité et autres combustibles. [9] Non compris le logement, l'eau, l'électricité autres combustibles.

[1] Excl. las fuerzas armadas y los conscriptos. [2] Personas de 6 años y más. [3] Niveles 0-1. [4] Niveles 2-3. [5] Niveles 5-7. [6] Incl. las bebidas y el tabaco. [7] Incl. la ropa de casa. [8] Incl. la vivienda, el agua, la electricidad y otros combustibles. [9] Excl. la vivienda, el agua, la electricidad y otros combustibles.

Malawi

1. Economically active population, Employment and Unemployment ('000)

	Economically active population		Employment		Unemployment	
	Total	Women (%)	Total	Women (%)	Total	Women (%)
Age group	1998 [1,2] Population census				1983 [3] Labour force survey	
Total	4 509.3	50.2	.	.	179.3	56.2
10-14	177.2	48.5	.	.	.	.
10-19	.	.	.	.	72.5	51.9
15-19	400.0	60.9	.	.	.	.
20-24	712.9	56.6	.	.	33.9	65.8
25-29	693.1	46.9	.	.	.	.
25-44	.	.	.	.	51.3	61.8
30-34	546.4	46.1	.	.	.	.
35-39	447.0	47.6	.	.	.	.
40-44	336.3	47.5	.	.	.	.
45-49	313.2	47.8	.	.	.	.
45-54	.	.	.	.	9.6	54.2
50-54	225.2	47.7	.	.	.	.
55-59	165.6	46.8	.	.	4.6	28.3
60+	.	.	.	.	4.3	39.5
60-64	143.0	50.9	.	.	.	.
65-69	129.5	50.8	.	.	.	.
70-74	87.8	51.0	.	.	.	.
75+	132.2	49.5	.	.	.	.
?	.	.	.	.	3.6	25.0
Economic activity (ISIC-Rev.2)	1998 [1,2] Population census					
Total	4 509.3	50.2	.	.	.	.
1 Agriculture, Hunting, Forestry and Fishing	3 765.8	55.3	.	.	.	.
2 Mining and Quarrying	2.5	11.7	.	.	.	.
3 Manufacturing	118.5	20.2	.	.	.	.
4 Electricity, Gas and Water	7.3	9.1	.	.	.	.
5 Construction	73.4	4.4	.	.	.	.
6 Wholesale and Retail Trade and Restaurants and Hotels	257.4	31.4	.	.	.	.
7 Transport, Storage and Communication	32.6	9.8	.	.	.	.
8 Financing, Insurance, Real Estate and Business Services	14.0	25.0	.	.	.	.
9 Community, Social and Personal Services	237.8	28.2	.	.	.	.
Occupation (ISCO-1968)	1998 [1,2] Population census		1983 [3] Labour force survey			
Total	4 509.3	50.2	3 120.9	51.3	.	.
0/1 Professional, technical and related workers	124.4	35.9	30.4	34.5	.	.
2 Administrative and managerial workers	7.3	15.0	3.5	2.9	.	.
3 Clerical and related workers	57.8	30.0	41.9	19.8	.	.
4 Sales workers	236.8	32.6	95.4	39.3	.	.
5 Service workers	126.1	17.6	83.4	27.8	.	.
6 Agriculture, animal husbandry and forestry workers ...	3 720.3	55.8	2 679.0	55.6	.	.
7/8/9 Production and related workers, transport equipment ...	236.7	12.0	186.8	15.7	.	.
X Not classifiable by occupation	.	.	0.5	100.0	.	.
Status in employment (ICSE-58)	1998 [1,2] Population census					
Total	4 509.3	50.2	.	.	.	.
1 Employers and own-account workers	266.3	23.9	.	.	.	.
2 Employees	687.2	22.7	.	.	.	.
3 Unpaid family workers	3 505.5	57.9	.	.	.	.
4 Not classifiable by status	50.4	31.1	.	.	.	.

2. Population ('000), Activity rate and Unemployment rate

	Population			Activity rate			Unemployment rate		
Age group	1998 [2] Population census			1998 [2] Population census			1983 [3,3] Labour force survey		
	Total	Men	Women	Total	Men	Women	Total	Men	Women
Total	9 933.9	4 867.6	5 066.3	45.4	46.1	44.7	5.4	4.9	5.9
15+	5 600.6	2 712.7	2 887.9	77.4	79.3	75.5	6.0	5.4	6.5
15-24	2 067.0	963.0	1 104.0	53.8	48.4	58.6	12.7	12.4	13.0
25-54	2 810.8	1 402.7	1 408.2	91.1	96.6	85.7	3.6	2.9	4.2
55+	722.8	347.0	375.8	91.0	95.6	86.8	2.2	2.7	1.6

Malawi

3. Paid employment ('000), Hours of work (weekly) and Wages

Economic activity (ISIC-Rev.2)	Paid employment 1995 Labour-related establishment survey			Hours of work			Wages 1995 Labour-related establishment census Earnings per month / Employees / Kwacha		
	Total	Men	Women	Total	Men	Women	Total	Men	Women
Total	700.56	554.52	146.03	.	.	.	187.96	.	.
2-9	.	.	.	.	.	.	.	.	.
1	375.94	266.51	109.44	.	.	.	65.25 4	.	.
2	0.83	0.82	0.02	.	.	.	270.79	.	.
3	101.72	97.51	4.21	.	.	.	195.79	.	.
4	6.35	5.83	0.52	.	.	.	217.99	.	.
5	46.77	44.78	1.99	.	.	.	260.95	.	.
6	29.82	26.31	3.51	.	.	.	387.12	.	.
7	22.54	20.73	1.81	.	.	.	386.32	.	.
8	33.83	27.72	6.11	.	.	.	1 160.37	.	.
9	82.75 5	64.33 5	18.42 5	.	.	.	185.66	.	.

4. Occupational injuries and Strikes and Lockouts

Economic activity (ISIC-Rev.2)	Rates of fatal injuries 1984 Insurance records Per 100,000 workers exposed to risk			Rates of non-fatal injuries			Strikes and lockouts 1987 Source unknown		
	Total	Men	Women	Total	Men	Women	Strikes and lockouts	Workers involved	Days not worked
Total	.	.	.	.	.	.	0	0	0
1	.	.	.	.	.	.	0	0	0
2	.	.	.	.	.	.	0	0	0
3	16	.	.	.	.	.	0	0	0
4	.	.	.	.	.	.	0	0	0
5	42	.	.	.	.	.	0	0	0
6	.	.	.	.	.	.	0	0	0
7	55	.	.	.	.	.	0	0	0
8	.	.	.	.	.	.	0	0	0
9	.	.	.	.	.	.	0	0	0

5. Consumer price indices (base period: 2000=100)

	2002	2003	2004	2005	2006	2007
General indices	140.8	154.3	172.0	198.5	226.1	244.1
Food index, including non-alcoholic beverages	136.4	143.6	154.4	181.0	209.1	224.7
Clothing indices, including footwear	152.7	166.8	179.5	192.8	208.8	.
Rent indices	156.6	180.0	211.7	236.9	266.9	.

[1] Persons aged 10 years and over. [2] Sep. [3] Nov. [4] Incl. forestry and fishing. [5] Excl. domestic services.

[1] Personnes âgées de 10 ans et plus. [2] Sept. [3] Nov. [4] Y compris la sylviculture et la pêche. [5] Non compris les services domestiques.

[1] Personas de 10 años y más. [2] Sept. [3] Nov. [4] Incl. la silvicultura y la pesca. [5] Excl. los servicios domésticos.

Malaysia

1. Economically active population, Employment and Unemployment ('000)

	Economically active population		Employment		Unemployment	
	Total	Women (%)	Total	Women (%)	Total	Women (%)
Age group	2007 [1,2] Labour force survey		2007 ★ Labour force survey		2007 [2] Labour force survey	
Total	10 889.5	36.1	10 538.1	36.0	351.4	38.4
15-19	476.4	36.9	397.7	36.5	78.7	38.8
20-24	1 615.8	40.9	1 466.6	40.5	149.2	44.2
25-29	1 793.4	40.3	1 736.6	40.4	56.8	39.1
30-34	1 552.5	37.1	1 532.6	37.2	19.9	35.2
35-39	1 434.0	35.3	1 421.0	35.4	13.0	23.8
40-44	1 307.9	34.3	1 297.3	34.4	10.6	16.0
45-49	1 117.0	33.1	1 107.7	33.2	9.3	9.7
50-54	869.9	31.3	860.7	31.4	9.2	19.6
55-59	473.5	27.3	471.1	27.3	2.4	25.0
60-64	249.1	26.0	246.9	25.8	2.2	54.5

Economic activity (ISIC-Rev.3)			2007 [1,2] Labour force survey			
Total	.	.	10 538.1	36.0	.	.
A Agriculture, Hunting and Forestry	.	.	1 437.3	25.9	.	.
B Fishing	.	.	120.9	4.5	.	.
C Mining and Quarrying	.	.	39.4	14.5	.	.
D Manufacturing	.	.	1 977.3	39.5	.	.
E Electricity, Gas and Water Supply	.	.	60.8	14.5	.	.
F Construction	.	.	922.5	7.4	.	.
G Wholesale and Retail Trade; Repair of Motor Vehicles ...	.	.	1 712.1	34.6	.	.
H Hotels and Restaurants	.	.	760.7	47.7	.	.
I Transport, Storage and Communications	.	.	538.2	16.4	.	.
J Financial Intermediation	.	.	282.2	49.6	.	.
K Real Estate, Renting and Business Activities	.	.	558.1	38.5	.	.
L Public Administration and Defence; Compulsory Social ...	.	.	716.1	28.1	.	.
M Education	.	.	632.7	65.0	.	.
N Health and Social Work	.	.	238.9	68.6	.	.
O Other Community, Social and Personal Service Activities	.	.	266.5	45.7	.	.
P Households with Employed Persons	.	.	272.7	92.8	.	.
Q Extra-Territorial Organizations and Bodies	.	.	1.7	41.2	.	.

Occupation (ISCO-88)			2007 [1,2] Labour force survey			
Total	.	.	10 538.1	36.0	.	.
1 Legislators, senior officials and managers	.	.	770.4	23.0	.	.
2 Professionals	.	.	596.8	45.3	.	.
3 Technicians and associate professionals	.	.	1 400.5	39.1	.	.
4 Clerks	.	.	1 029.5	68.9	.	.
5 Service workers and shop and market sales workers	.	.	1 705.6	44.2	.	.
6 Skilled agricultural and fishery workers	.	.	1 355.3	26.0	.	.
7 Craft and related trade workers	.	.	1 133.2	14.1	.	.
8 Plant and machine operators and assemblers	.	.	1 347.4	28.3	.	.
9 Elementary occupations	.	.	1 199.3	36.6	.	.

Education level (ISCED-97)	2007 [1,2] Labour force survey		2007 ★ Labour force survey		2007 [2] Labour force survey	
Total	10 889.5	36.1	10 538.1	36.0	351.4	38.4
X No schooling	432.5	48.7	.	.	.	.
1 Primary education or first stage of basic education	2 103.9	32.1	2 096.2	32.1	7.7	33.8
2 Lower secondary or second stage of basic education [3]	6 133.9	32.9	5 878.4	32.9	255.5	33.5
5A First stage of tertiary education - theoretically based [4]	2 210.1	46.0	2 121.9	45.7	88.2	53.3

Status in employment (ICSE-1993)			2007 [1,2] Labour force survey			
Total	.	.	10 538.1	36.0	.	.
1 Employees	.	.	7 824.0	37.5	.	.
2 Employers	.	.	362.5	14.0	.	.
3 Own-account workers	.	.	1 831.5	25.9	.	.
5 Contributing family workers	.	.	520.1	64.4	.	.

2. Population ('000), Activity rate and Unemployment rate

	Population			Activity rate			Unemployment rate		
Age group	2000 [1] Labour force survey			2000 [1] Labour force survey			2007 [2] Labour force survey		
	Total	Men	Women	Total	Men	Women	Total	Men	Women
Total	23 263.5	11 911.6	11 351.9	41.3	52.7	29.4	3.2	3.1	3.4
15+	15 579.2	7 941.7	7 637.5	.	.	.	3.2	3.1	3.4
15-24	4 525.0	2 311.2	2 213.8	49.5	57.8	40.9	10.9	10.5	11.5
25-54	8 986.0	4 635.0	4 351.0	75.9	97.8	52.5	1.5	1.6	1.3
55+	2 068.2	995.5	1 072.7	.	.	.	.	.	.

Malaysia

3. Paid employment ('000), Hours of work (weekly) and Wages

Economic activity (ISIC-Rev.3)	Paid employment 2007 [1,2] Labour force survey			Hours of work 2007 Labour force survey Hours actually worked / Total employment			Wages 2001 Labour-related establishment survey Earnings per month / Employees / Ringgit		
	Total	Men	Women	Total	Men	Women	Total	Men	Women
Total	7 824.0	4 893.4	2 930.7	47.30	47.80	46.50	.	.	.
A	565.0	452.5	112.5	39.10	42.00	35.70			
B	28.6	27.5	1.1	47.00	47.30	40.10			
C	37.9	32.2	5.7	51.00	51.70	47.40			
D	1 789.8	1 109.6	680.2	49.10	50.20	47.30	1 531		
E	60.2	51.4	8.8	46.20	46.50	44.70			
F	688.8	625.9	62.9	48.50	48.60	46.40			
G	1 103.1	692.3	410.8	50.50	50.60	50.10			
H	435.3	228.7	206.6	51.00	52.50	49.30			
I	436.0	355.4	80.7	50.90	51.80	46.50			
J	262.0	127.5	134.4	45.80	46.30	45.20			
K	484.7	286.2	198.5	49.00	50.90	46.00			
L	709.7	509.6	200.1	44.80	45.70	42.40			
M	614.6	213.5	401.2	36.60	38.30	35.60			
N	218.8	65.6	153.3	45.70	46.70	45.20			
O	202.0	105.3	96.7	47.50	47.10	47.90			
P	185.9	9.4	176.5	67.20	49.60	68.60			
Q	1.7	1.0	0.7	.	.	.			

Share of women in wage employment in the non-agricultural sector [1,2] (2007 - Labour force survey): **39.0%**

4. Occupational injuries and Strikes and Lockouts

Economic activity (ISIC-Rev.3)	Rates of fatal injuries 2002 Insurance records Per 100,000 workers insured Compensated injuries			Rates of non-fatal injuries 2002 Insurance records Per 100,000 workers insured Compensated injuries			Strikes and lockouts 2003 [5] Labour relations records		
	Total	Men	Women	Total	Men	Women	Strikes and lockouts	Workers involved	Days not worked
Total	10.8	.	.	1 023	.	.	2	.	.

5. Consumer price indices (base period: 2000=100)

	2002	2003	2004	2005	2006	2007
General indices	103.2	104.4	105.9	109.1	113.0	115.3
Food index, including non-alcoholic beverages	101.4	102.7	105.0	108.8	112.5	115.9
Electricity, gas and other fuel indices [6]	101.3	100.0	100.5	101.9	105.7	.
Clothing indices, including footwear	95.2	93.3	91.6	90.7	89.5	88.2
Rent indices [7]	102.0	103.0	104.0	105.3	106.8	108.2
General index, excluding housing [6]	.	100.0	101.6	105.0	109.3	.

[1] Excl. armed forces. [2] Persons aged 15 to 64 years. [3] Levels 2-3. [4] Levels 5-6. [5] Strikes only. [6] Index base 2003=100. [7] Incl. "Fuel and light".

[1] Non compris les forces armées. [2] Personnes âgées de 15 à 64 ans. [3] Niveaux 2-3. [4] Niveaux 5-6. [5] Grèves seulement. [6] Indice base 2003=100. [7] Y compris le groupe "Combustible et éclairage".

[1] Excl. las fuerzas armadas. [2] Personas de 15 a 64 años. [3] Niveles 2-3. [4] Niveles 5-6. [5] Huelgas solamente. [6] Indice base 2003=100. [7] Incl. el grupo "Combustible y alumbrado".

Maldives

1. Economically active population, Employment and Unemployment ('000)

Age group	Economically active population Total	Women (%)	Employment Total	Women (%)	Unemployment Total	Women (%)
	2006 [1,2] Population census		2006 ★ Population census		2006 [2] Population census	
Total	128.836	41.3	110.231	36.8	18.605	67.9
15-19	14.055	45.0	9.913	41.3	4.142	53.9
20-24	25.420	44.8	20.802	39.5	4.618	68.8
25-29	18.379	42.5	16.056	38.1	2.323	72.9
30-34	15.559	41.5	13.896	37.2	1.663	77.6
35-39	13.697	41.0	12.193	36.3	1.504	79.3
40-44	11.944	39.9	10.608	34.9	1.336	79.6
45-49	10.346	39.3	9.132	34.3	1.214	76.7
50-54	5.892	37.3	5.267	33.3	0.625	71.5
55-59	4.192	37.5	3.795	34.7	0.397	65.0
60-64	3.500	36.0	3.171	33.9	0.329	56.2
65+	5.847	28.6	5.393	28.1	0.454	34.6

Economic activity (ISIC-Rev.3)

2006 [1,2] Population census

	Total	Women (%)
Total	110.231	36.8
A Agriculture, Hunting and Forestry	4.236	64.3
B Fishing	8.388	1.8
C Mining and Quarrying	0.339	8.3
D Manufacturing	19.259	65.0
E Electricity, Gas and Water Supply	1.229	12.6
F Construction	5.930	3.3
G Wholesale and Retail Trade; Repair of Motor Vehicles ...	11.711	36.6
H Hotels and Restaurants	12.090	12.5
I Transport, Storage and Communications	7.098	12.9
J Financial Intermediation	0.582	56.4
K Real Estate, Renting and Business Activities	1.156	24.5
L Public Administration and Defence; Compulsory Social ...	15.949	26.7
M Education	9.872	72.2
N Health and Social Work	4.182	67.9
O Other Community, Social and Personal Service Activities	3.248	34.1
Q Extra-Territorial Organizations and Bodies	0.216	35.6
X Not classifiable by economic activity	4.746	42.8

Occupation (ISCO-88)

2006 [1,2] Population census

	Total	Women (%)
Total	110.231	36.8
1 Legislators, senior officials and managers	6.528	14.3
2 Professionals	9.603	59.2
3 Technicians and associate professionals	11.431	39.7
4 Clerks	8.905	53.3
5 Service workers and shop and market sales workers	13.207	32.0
6 Skilled agricultural and fishery workers	12.302	23.1
7 Craft and related trade workers	25.329	49.6
8 Plant and machine operators and assemblers	5.921	3.4
9 Elementary occupations	10.129	26.7
0 Armed forces	2.337	6.0
X Not classifiable by occupation	4.539	43.4

Status in employment (ICSE-1993)

2006 [1,2] Population census

	Total	Women (%)
Total	110.231	36.8
1 Employees	60.837	30.0
2 Employers	3.829	12.2
3 Own-account workers	17.856	54.6
5 Contributing family workers	14.825	62.7
6 Not classifiable by status	7.124	4.9

2. Population ('000), Activity rate and Unemployment rate

Age group	Population 2006 [1] Total	Men	Women	Activity rate 2006 [1] Total	Men	Women	Unemployment rate 2006 [2] Total	Men	Women
Total	299.0	151.5	147.5	43.1	50.0	36.0	14.4	7.9	23.7
15+	200.8	100.3	100.5	64.1	75.4	52.9	14.4	7.9	23.8
15-24	74.7	37.1	37.6	52.8	58.6	47.1	22.2	15.4	30.5
25-54	100.8	49.6	51.2	75.2	90.6	60.4	11.4	4.6	21.4
55+	25.4	13.7	11.7	53.4	66.0	38.6	8.7	6.4	13.3

3. Paid employment ('000), Hours of work (weekly) and Wages

Statistics not available.

4. Occupational injuries and Strikes and Lockouts

Statistics not available.

Maldives

5. Consumer price indices (base period: 2000=100)

Male	2002	2003	2004	2005	2006	2007
General indices	101.6	98.7	105.0	108.5	110.0	117.5
Food index, including non-alcoholic beverages	105.7	99.3	115.2	117.6	104.0 [3]	120.8
Electricity, gas and other fuel indices	100.3	99.3	97.3	103.3	112.5	.
Clothing indices, including footwear	95.2	95.0	93.0	93.1	93.7	.

[1] Excl. conscripts. [2] Persons aged 15 years and over. [3] Series (base 2005=100) replacing former series; prior to 2005 incl. alcoholic beverages and tobacco.

[1] Non compris les conscrits. [2] Personnes âgées de 15 ans et plus. [3] Série (base 2005=100) remplaçant la précédente; avant 2005 y compris les boissons alcoolisées et le tabac.

[1] Excl. los conscriptos. [2] Personas de 15 años y más. [3] Serie (base 2005=100) que substituye a la anterior; antes de 2005 incl. las bebidas alcohólicas y el tabaco.

Mali

1. Population active, Emploi et Chômage ('000)

Groupe d'âge	Population active Total	Femmes (%) 2004[1] Enquête sur la main-d'oeuvre	Emploi Total	Femmes (%) 2004[1] Enquête sur la main-d'oeuvre	Chômage Total	Femmes (%) 2004[1] Enquête sur la main-d'oeuvre
Total	2 598.2	42.5	2 370.8	41.4	227.5	53.0
15-19	331.5	43.0	.	.	.	.
20-24	347.9	50.0	.	.	.	.
25-29	341.5	50.8	.	.	.	.
30-34	326.5	47.5	.	.	.	.
35-39	293.4	45.7	.	.	.	.
40-44	269.6	38.0	.	.	.	.
45-49	215.0	42.6	.	.	.	.
50-54	182.9	32.3	.	.	.	.
55-59	119.6	27.5	.	.	.	.
60-64	80.1	22.6	.	.	.	.
65+	90.2	21.6	.	.	.	.

Activité économique (CITI-Rév.3)			Total	Femmes (%) 2004[1] Enquête sur la main-d'oeuvre		
Total	.	.	2 370.8	41.4	.	.
A Agriculture, chasse et sylviculture	.	.	949.4	30.7	.	.
B Pêche	.	.	35.2	5.6	.	.
C Activités extractives	.	.	11.4	26.1	.	.
D Activités de fabrication	.	.	272.5	50.1	.	.
E Production et distribution d'électricité, de gaz et d'eau	.	.	5.1	0.0	.	.
F Construction	.	.	102.1	4.6	.	.
G Commerce de gros et de détail; réparation de véhicules ...	.	.	668.1	60.2	.	.
H Hôtels et restaurants	.	.	7.6	82.0	.	.
I Transports, entreposage et communications	.	.	55.3	6.3	.	.
J Intermédiation financière	.	.	4.4	0.0	.	.
K Immobilier, locations et activités de services aux entreprises	.	.	4.0	14.0	.	.
L Administration publique et défense; sécurité sociale obligatoire	.	.	39.9	16.4	.	.
M Education	.	.	53.9	33.9	.	.
N Santé et action sociale	.	.	20.9	45.4	.	.
O Autres activités de services collectifs, sociaux et personnels	.	.	35.3	32.5	.	.
P Ménages privés employant du personnel domestique	.	.	103.9	81.9	.	.
Q Organisations et organismes extraterritoriaux	.	.	0.9	100.0	.	.

Situation dans la profession (CISP-1993)			Total	Femmes (%) 2004[1] Enquête sur la main-d'oeuvre		
Total	.	.	2 370.8	41.4	.	.
1 Salariés	.	.	322.8	34.6	.	.
2,3	.	.	1 692.0	45.5	.	.
5 Travailleurs familiaux collaborant à l'entreprise familiale [2]	.	.	355.3	28.2	.	.

2. Population ('000), Taux d'activité et Taux de chômage

Groupe d'âge	Population 2004 Enquête sur la main-d'oeuvre Total	Hommes	Femmes	Taux d'activité 2004 Enquête sur la main-d'oeuvre Total	Hommes	Femmes	Taux de chômage 2004[1] Enquête sur la main-d'oeuvre Total	Hommes	Femmes
Total	.	.	.	.	.	.	8.8	7.2	10.9
15+	5 256.3	2 259.3	2 997.0	49.4	66.2	36.8	.	.	.
15-24	1 772.8	755.3	1 017.5	38.3	48.0	31.1	.	.	.
25-54	2 733.6	1 084.4	1 649.3	59.6	84.2	43.4	.	.	.
55+	749.9	419.6	330.3	38.7	52.3	21.3	.	.	.

3. Emploi rémunéré ('000), Durée du travail (hebdomadaire) et Salaires

Activité économique (CITI-Rév.3)	Emploi rémunéré 2000[3] Enquête auprès des établissements, relative au travail Total	Hommes	Femmes	Durée du travail Total	Hommes	Femmes	Salaires Total	Hommes	Femmes
Total	61.7	.	.	.	.	.	.	.	.

4. Lésions professionnelles et Grèves et lock-out

Activité économique (CITI-Rév.2)	Taux de lésions mortelles Total	Hommes	Femmes	Taux de lésions non mortelles Total	Hommes	Femmes	Grèves et lock-out 1989 Source inconnue Grèves et lock-out	Travailleurs impliqués	Journées non effectuées [4]
Total	.	.	.	.	.	.	3	270	2 308
1	.	.	.	.	.	.	0	0	0
2	.	.	.	.	.	.	0	0	0
3	.	.	.	.	.	.	1	18	432
4	.	.	.	.	.	.	0	0	0
5	.	.	.	.	.	.	1	217	1 736
6	.	.	.	.	.	.	0	0	0
7	.	.	.	.	.	.	1	35	140
8	.	.	.	.	.	.	0	0	0
9	.	.	.	.	.	.	0	0	0

Mali

5. Indices des prix à la consommation (période de base: 2000=100)

Bamako	2002	2003	2004	2005	2006	2007
Indices généraux	110.4	109.1	105.6	112.3	114.1	115.7
Indices de l'alimentation, y compris les boissons non alcoolisées [5]	115.8	111.1	103.3	115.1	114.6	117.3
Indices de l'habillement, y compris les chaussures	104.7	106.9	99.5	96.3	98.2	97.3
Indices du loyer [6]	112.1	111.9	110.1	107.5	110.1	112.3

[1] Persons aged 15 years and over. [2] Incl. apprentices. [3] Modern sector. [4] Workhours not worked. [5] Incl. beverages and tobacco. [6] Incl. water, electricity, gas and other fuels.

[1] Personnes âgées de 15 ans et plus. [2] Y compris les apprentis. [3] Secteur moderne. [4] Heures de travail non effectuées. [5] Y compris les boissons et le tabac. [6] Y compris l'eau, l'électricité, le gaz et autres combustibles.

[1] Personas de 15 años y más. [2] Incl. los aprendices. [3] Sector moderno. [4] Horas de trabajo no trabajadas. [5] Incl. las bebidas y el tabaco. [6] Incl. el agua, la electricidad, el gas y otros combustibles.

Malta

1. Economically active population, Employment and Unemployment ('000)

	Economically active population Total	Women (%)	Employment Total	Women (%)	Unemployment Total	Women (%)
Age group		2007 [1] Labour force survey		2007 ★ Labour force survey		2007 [1] Labour force survey
Total	166.244	33.3	155.515	32.9	10.729	39.7
15-19	10.104	45.5	7.574	46.8	2.530	41.7
20-24	23.346	45.8	21.421	46.9	1.925	33.7
25-29	22.350	41.6	21.230	42.3	1.120	28.9
30-34	20.084	35.3	19.125	35.2	0.959	37.9
35-39	17.675	34.1	16.822	33.0	0.853	55.8
40-44	19.532	26.3	18.500	25.3	1.032	43.6
45-49	20.719	25.8	19.644	24.2	1.075	54.4
50-54	19.498	22.6	18.705	23.6	0.793	.
55-59	9.682	23.8	9.682	23.8	-	.
60-64	2.508	15.2	2.508	15.2	-	.
65-69	-	.	-	.	-	.
70-74	-	.	-	.	-	.
75+	-	.	-	.	-	.
Economic activity (ISIC-Rev.3)		2007 ★ Labour force survey		2007 [1] Labour force survey		2007 [1] Labour force survey
Total	166.244	33.3	155.515	32.9	10.729	39.7
A Agriculture, Hunting and Forestry	2.537	7.8	2.537	7.8	-	.
B Fishing	-	.	-	.	-	.
C Mining and Quarrying	.	.	.	.	-	.
D Manufacturing	28.184	26.5	25.651	24.3	2.533	48.9
E Electricity, Gas and Water Supply	3.058	6.9	3.058	6.9	-	.
F Construction	12.249	2.9	11.454	3.1	0.795	0.0
G Wholesale and Retail Trade; Repair of Motor Vehicles ...	25.854	34.1	24.581	32.9	1.273	56.1
H Hotels and Restaurants	14.351	36.3	12.913	36.6	1.438	34.1
I Transport, Storage and Communications	12.457	21.2	12.030	21.9	0.427	.
J Financial Intermediation	6.425	53.1	6.425	53.1	-	.
K Real Estate, Renting and Business Activities	11.453	37.8	11.453	37.8	-	.
L Public Administration and Defence; Compulsory Social ...	13.854	27.8	13.854	27.8	-	.
M Education	12.711	63.2	12.711	63.2	-	.
N Health and Social Work	11.200	54.3	11.200	54.3	-	.
O Other Community, Social and Personal Service Activities	6.448	42.0	6.448	42.0	-	.
P Households with Employed Persons	-	.	-	.	-	.
Q Extra-Territorial Organizations and Bodies	-	.	-	.	-	.
Unemployed seeking their first job	.	.	.	.	2.857	38.9
Occupation (ISCO-88)		2007 ★ Labour force survey		2007 [1] Labour force survey		2007 [1] Labour force survey
Total	166.244	33.3	155.515	32.9	10.729	39.7
1 Legislators, senior officials and managers	12.086	18.5	12.086	18.5	-	.
2 Professionals	17.990	47.0	17.990	47.0	-	.
3 Technicians and associate professionals	23.542	35.9	23.542	35.9	.	.
4 Clerks	19.613	58.3	18.928	60.4	0.685	.
5 Service workers and shop and market sales workers	27.065	43.7	25.010	43.3	2.055	48.9
6 Skilled agricultural and fishery workers	2.231	4.9	2.231	4.9	-	.
7 Craft and related trade workers	21.534	3.3	20.569	3.0	0.965	8.2
8 Plant and machine operators and assemblers	15.366	31.7	13.713	29.3	1.653	51.7
9 Elementary occupations	21.356	25.4	19.707	25.1	1.649	29.9
0 Armed forces	1.739	.	1.739	0.0	-	.
Unemployed seeking their first job	.	.	.	.	2.857	38.9
Education level (ISCED-97)		2007 [1] Labour force survey		2007 ★ Labour force survey		2007 [1] Labour force survey
Total	166.244	33.3	155.515	32.9	10.729	39.7
1 Primary education or first stage of basic education	20.218	19.4	18.418	18.6	1.800	27.4
2 Lower secondary or second stage of basic education	81.672	32.1	74.847	31.4	6.825	40.5
3 Upper secondary education	17.589	47.0	16.642	46.8	0.947	51.1
4 Post-secondary non-tertiary education	18.061	22.1	18.061	22.1	-	.
5A First stage of tertiary education - theoretically based	5.351	40.1	5.351	40.1	-	.
5B First stage of tertiary education - practically oriented	22.427	47.6	22.427	47.6	-	.
6 Second stage of tertiary education	0.663	16.9	0.663	16.9	-	.
Status in employment (ICSE-1993)				2007 [1] Labour force survey		
Total	.	.	155.5	32.9	.	.
1 Employees	.	.	134.0	35.4	.	.
2 Employers	.	.	7.1	11.0	.	.
3 Own-account workers	.	.	14.3	19.5	.	.
5 Contributing family workers	.	.	.	.	.	.
6 Not classifiable by status	.	.	-	.	.	.

2. Population ('000), Activity rate and Unemployment rate

	Population 2007 Labour force survey			Activity rate 2007 Labour force survey			Unemployment rate 2007 [1] Labour force survey		
Age group	Total	Men	Women	Total	Men	Women	Total	Men	Women
Total	406.8	201.8	205.0	40.9	54.9	27.0	6.5	5.8	7.7
15+	328.1	160.8	167.4	.	.	.	.	.	.
15-24	62.9	32.1	30.8	53.1	56.5	49.6	13.3	15.1	11.1
25-54	173.7	87.7	86.0	69.0	94.1	43.4	4.9	.	.
55+	91.5	40.9	50.6	.	.	.	.	.	.

Malta

3. Paid employment ('000), Hours of work (weekly) and Wages

Economic activity (ISIC-Rev.3)	Paid employment 2007[1] Labour force survey			Hours of work 2007[1,2] Labour force survey Hours actually worked / Total employment			Wages 2007[1,2] Labour force survey Earnings per hour / Total employment / Lira		
	Total	Men	Women	Total	Men	Women	Total	Men	Women
Total	134.048	86.547	47.501	38.9	41.1	34.2	2.8	2.9	2.7
A-B	.	.	.	47.7	48.8	.	2.5	2.4	.
C-Q	.	.	.	38.7	40.9	34.2	.	2.9	2.7
A	1.213	1.125	0.088	48.1	49.4	.	2.5	2.4	.
B	-	-	-	.	.	.	.	.	.
C	-	-	-	.	.	.	.	.	.
D	23.612	17.467	6.145	40.3	41.1	37.9	2.6	2.7	2.3
E	3.058	2.847	0.211	39.5	39.8	35.0	2.9	2.9	.
F	7.740	7.400	0.340	40.1	40.1	38.3	2.4	2.4	2.3
G	17.564	10.796	6.768	39.0	41.1	34.4	2.5	2.6	2.2
H	11.838	7.258	4.580	37.9	40.6	32.9	2.4	2.5	2.3
I	10.325	7.944	2.381	40.5	41.9	35.6	3.1	3.2	2.7
J	6.288	2.888	3.400	37.6	40.4	35.2	3.7	4.4	3.2
K	8.992	5.188	3.804	39.1	42.5	33.7	3.1	3.1	3.1
L	13.798	9.953	3.845	40.0	41.7	35.7	2.7	2.7	2.8
M	12.569	4.616	7.953	31.2	34.0	29.4	3.6	3.8	3.6
N	10.864	4.960	5.904	38.1	42.5	34.2	2.7	2.9	2.6
O	5.213	3.335	1.878	37.0	39.9	32.9	2.7	3.0	2.3
P	-	-	-	.	.	.	.	.	.
Q	-	-	-	.	.	.	.	.	.

Share of women in wage employment in the non-agricultural sector [1] (2007 - Labour force survey): **35.7%**

4. Occupational injuries and Strikes and Lockouts

Economic activity (ISIC-Rev.3)	Rates of fatal injuries 2007 Insurance records Per 100,000 workers employed Compensated injuries			Rates of non-fatal injuries 2007[3] Insurance records Per 100,000 workers employed Compensated injuries			Strikes and lockouts 2007 Special data collection		
	Total	Men	Women	Total	Men	Women	Strikes and lockouts	Workers involved	Days not worked
Total	4.5	6.8	0.0	2 777	3 696	4	5	1 106	721
A	0.0	0.0	0.0	1 952	1 896	5 714	0	0	0
B	0.0	0.0	0.0	3 526	3 526	0	0	0	0
C	0.0	0.0	0.0	6 273	7 637	0	0	0	0
D	3.9	5.2	0.0	5 525	6 890	1 506	0	0	0
E	31.5	33.3	0.0	4 561	4 802	1 506	0	0	0
F	33.7	34.6	0.0	5 808	5 925	1 329	0	0	0
G	4.1	6.2	0.0	1 647	2 290	418	0	0	0
H	0.0	0.0	0.0	2 368	3 086	1 290	0	0	0
I	0.0	0.0	0.0	4 504	5 503	1 254	3	679	614
J	0.0	0.0	0.0	164	170	158	0	0	0
K	0.0	0.0	0.0	1 742	2 525	754	0	0	0
L	0.0	0.0	0.0	1 165	1 397	483	0	0	0
M	0.0	0.0	0.0	456	372	513	2	427	107
N	0.0	0.0	0.0	2 210	1 913	2 448	0	0	0
O	0.0	0.0	0.0	838	1 312	224	0	0	0
P	0.0	0.0	0.0	0	0	0	.	.	.
Q	0.0	0.0	0.0	2 551	2 098	3 774	.	.	.
X	0.0	0.0	0.0	0	0	0	.	.	.

5. Consumer price indices (base period: 2000=100)

	2002	2003	2004	2005	2006	2007
General indices	105.1	105.8	108.7	112.0	115.0	116.5
Food index, including non-alcoholic beverages	107.4	109.2	109.5	111.4	113.6	118.5
Electricity, gas and other fuel indices [4]	104.8	114.4	115.9	142.6	179.7	167.7
Clothing indices, including footwear	96.5	87.7	85.6	85.1	83.6	83.9
Rent indices [5]	107.6	110.8	115.0	120.7	126.5	130.1
General index, excluding housing [6]	.	.	100.0	102.8	105.5	106.7

[1] Persons aged 15 years and over. [2] Dec. [3] Incapacity of 4 days or more. [4] Incl. water. [5] Housing. [6] Index base: 2004=100.

[1] Personnes âgées de 15 ans et plus. [2] Déc. [3] Incapacité de 4 jours et plus. [4] Y compris l'eau. [5] Logement. [6] Base de l'indice: 2004=100.

[1] Personas de 15 años y más. [2] Dic. [3] Incapacidad de 4 días y más. [4] Incl. el agua. [5] Vivienda. [6] Base del indice: 2004=100.

Maroc

1. Population active, Emploi et Chômage ('000)

	Population active Total	Femmes (%)	Emploi Total	Femmes (%)	Chômage Total	Femmes (%)
Groupe d'âge	2006[1] Enquête sur la main-d'oeuvre		2007[1] Enquête sur la main-d'oeuvre		2006[1] Enquête sur la main-d'oeuvre	
Total	10 990.2	27.1	10 332.5	27.7	1 062.5	27.1
15-24	2 505.4	28.4	.	.	414.9	24.2
25-34	3 103.2	26.9	.	.	433.4	30.8
35-44	2 460.3	27.1	.	.	146.7	29.8
45-59	2 277.3	26.8	.	.	64.3	15.6
60+	644.1	24.9	.	.	3.1	25.5
Activité économique (CITI-Rév.3)	2005 ★ Enquête sur la main-d'oeuvre		2005[1] Enquête sur la main-d'oeuvre		2005[1] Enquête sur la main-d'oeuvre	
Total	11 139.7	27.1	9 913.3	27.0	1 226.4	28.4
A-B	4 581.5	36.1	4 505.2	36.4	76.3	15.5
C Activités extractives	43.1	1.6	41.8	1.6	1.3	0.0
D Activités de fabrication	1 320.3	36.0	1 153.9	35.9	166.4	36.5
E Production et distribution d'électricité, de gaz et d'eau	34.2	9.1	31.7	8.7	2.5	13.6
F Construction	813.7	0.9	705.4	0.9	108.2	0.9
G-H	1 805.3	8.6	1 656.9	8.2	148.4	13.1
I Transports, entreposage et communications	406.9	8.1	380.3	7.9	26.6	10.9
J-K	147.9	30.8	130.2	30.0	17.7	36.4
L-Q	1 379.2	31.3	1 301.4	30.7	77.8	41.7
X Ne pouvant être classés selon l'activité économique	7.6	28.8	6.5	29.6	1.1	24.1
Chômeurs n'ayant jamais travaillé					600.1	35.6
Profession (CITP-88)	2005 ★ Enquête sur la main-d'oeuvre		2005[1] Enquête sur la main-d'oeuvre		2005[1] Enquête sur la main-d'oeuvre	
Total	11 139.7	27.1	9 913.3	27.0	1 226.4	28.4
1 Membres de l'exécutif et des corps législatifs, cadres ...	80.9	12.3	79.1	12.4	1.8	6.7
2 Professions intellectuelles et scientifiques	121.7	27.7	114.3	27.1	7.4	37.2
3 Professions intermédiaires	432.0	40.2	351.8	38.2	80.3	48.7
4 Employés de type administratif	891.2	26.5	780.5	24.7	110.7	39.3
5 Personnel des services et vendeurs de magasin et de marché	772.4	4.6	747.6	4.7	24.8	3.6
6 Agriculteurs et ouvriers qualifiés de l'agriculture ...	4 531.3	36.3	4 461.9	36.6	69.4	13.1
7 Artisans et ouvriers des métiers de type artisanal	1 860.0	20.8	1 614.5	20.0	245.5	25.5
8 Conducteurs d'installations et de machines ...	326.6	4.8	298.6	4.4	28.0	8.7
9 Ouvriers et employés non qualifiés	1 664.9	20.3	1 464.2	20.4	200.7	19.9
X Ne pouvant être classés selon la profession	458.8	32.4	1.0	14.5	457.8	32.4
Chômeurs n'ayant jamais travaillé					600.1	35.6
Niveau d'instruction (CITE-97)	2006[1] Enquête sur la main-d'oeuvre				2005[1,2] Enquête sur la main-d'oeuvre	
Total	10 990.2	27.1	.	.	1 028.7	31.6
X Non scolarisé	3 988.2	43.0	.	.	44.0	41.3
0 Education préprimaire	.	.	.	.	.	.
1 Enseignement primaire ou premier cycle de l'éducation ...	2 783.1	14.5	.	.	232.0	18.5
2 Premier cycle de l'enseignement secondaire ou deuxième ...	1 552.6	15.9	.	.	293.2	26.0
3 Enseignement secondaire (deuxième cycle)[3]	1 083.5	23.3	.	.	230.7	33.7
5A Premier cycle de l'enseignement supérieur - théorie[4]	952.2	33.4	.	.	222.4	48.9
? Niveau inconnu	630.7	7.3	.	.	6.4	23.2
Situation dans la profession (CISP-1993)	2006[1] Enquête sur la main-d'oeuvre		2006[1] Enquête sur la main-d'oeuvre			
Total	10 990.2	27.1	9 927.7	27.1		
1 Salariés	4 734.4	21.2	4 286.2	21.0		
2 Employeurs	257.5	6.3	252.0	6.2		
3 Personnes travaillant pour leur propre compte	2 492.4	10.9	2 427.5	10.8		
4 Membres de coopératives de producteurs	232.6	8.8	227.3	8.8		
5 Travailleurs familiaux collaborant à l'entreprise familiale	2 737.2	54.5	2 721.8	54.8		
6 Inclassables d'après la situation	15.8	44.9	12.9	47.7		

2. Population ('000), Taux d'activité et Taux de chômage

Groupe d'âge	Population 2005 Enquête sur la main-d'oeuvre			Taux d'activité 2005 Enquête sur la main-d'oeuvre			Taux de chômage 2007[1] Enquête sur la main-d'oeuvre		
	Total	Hommes	Femmes	Total	Hommes	Femmes	Total	Hommes	Femmes
Total	30 189.1	15 052.2	15 136.9	38.0	55.2	20.9	9.5	9.6	9.4
15+	21 380.6	10 559.7	10 820.9	52.1	76.9	27.9	.	.	.
15-24	6 300.0	3 205.0	3 095.0	42.6	61.1	23.3	.	.	.

3. Emploi rémunéré ('000), Durée du travail (hebdomadaire) et Salaires

Activité économique (CITI-Rév.3)	Emploi rémunéré 2002[1,2] Enquête sur la main-d'oeuvre			Durée du travail			Salaires		
	Total	Hommes	Femmes	Total	Hommes	Femmes	Total	Hommes	Femmes
Total	2 755.4	2 035.8	719.6	.	.	.	.	.	.

Pourcentage de salariées dans le secteur non agricole qui sont femmes[1,2] (2002 - Enquête sur la main-d'oeuvre): .%

Maroc

4. Lésions professionnelles et Grèves et lock-out

Activité économique (CITI-Rév.3)	Taux de lésions mortelles 1998 Fichiers des assurances Pour 100 000 salariés			Taux de lésions non mortelles			Grèves et lock-out 2002 [5] Fichiers des relations du travail		
	Total	Hommes	Femmes	Total	Hommes	Femmes	Grèves et lock-out	Travailleurs impliqués	Journées non effectuées
Total	.	.	.	.	.	.	267	21 238	141 083
A	.	.	.	.	.	.	30	3 669	5 625
C	22.5	.	.	.	.	.	5	82	9 275
D	.	.	.	.	.	.	148	14 004	105 643
E	.	.	.	.	.	.	0	0	0
F	.	.	.	.	.	.	17	620	4 959
G	.	.	.	.	.	.	13	272	4 140
H	.	.	.	.	.	.	16	842	1 750
I	.	.	.	.	.	.	18	944	6 645
J	.	.	.	.	.	.	3	144	110
K	.	.	.	.	.	.	6	258	365
L	.	.	.	.	.	.	0	0	0
M	.	.	.	.	.	.	3	22	23
N	.	.	.	.	.	.	1	34	17
O	.	.	.	.	.	.	7	347	2 531

5. Indices des prix à la consommation (période de base: 2000=100)

	2002	2003	2004	2005	2006	2007
Indices généraux	103.4	104.6	106.2	107.2	110.8	113.0
Indices de l'alimentation, y compris les boissons non alcoolisées [6]	103.2	104.6	106.2	106.5	110.7	114.3
Indices de l'électricité, gaz et autres combustibles [7]	.	105.0	107.4	108.5	111.7	.
Indices de l'habillement, y compris les chaussures	103.0	103.9	104.9	105.6	106.8	.
Indices du loyer	101.6	102.8	105.6	107.1	108.2	.

[1] Persons aged 15 years and over. [2] Urban areas. [3] Levels 3-4. [4] Levels 5-6. [5] Strikes only. [6] Incl. tobacco. [7] Incl. water.

[1] Personnes âgées de 15 ans et plus. [2] Régions urbaines. [3] Niveaux 3-4. [4] Niveaux 5-6. [5] Grèves seulement. [6] Y compris le tabac. [7] Y compris l'eau.

[1] Personas de 15 años y más. [2] Areas urbanas. [3] Niveles 3-4. [4] Niveles 5-6. [5] Huelgas solamente. [6] Incl. el tabaco. [7] Incl. el agua.

Marshall Islands

1. Economically active population, Employment and Unemployment ('000)

	Economically active population		Employment		Unemployment	
	Total	Women (%)	Total	Women (%)	Total	Women (%)
Age group	1999 [1] Population census		1999 ★ Population census		1999 [1] Population census	
Total	14.677	34.1	10.141	.	4.536	.
15-19	1.249	.	0.335	.	0.914	.
20-24	2.193	.	0.951	.	1.242	.
25-29	2.324	.	1.482	.	0.842	.
30-34	2.139	.	1.642	.	0.497	.
35-39	1.928	.	1.548	.	0.380	.
40-44	1.665	.	1.405	.	0.260	.
45-49	1.414	.	1.231	.	0.183	.
50-54	0.898	.	0.784	.	0.114	.
55-59	0.454	.	0.401	.	0.053	.
60-64	0.236	.	0.188	.	0.048	.
65-69	0.105	.	0.103	.	0.002	.
70-74	0.044	.	0.044	.	0.000	.
75+	0.028	.	0.027	.	0.001	.

Economic activity (ISIC-Rev.2)

1999 [1,2] Population census

			Total	Women (%)		
Total	.	.	10.1	30.9	.	.
1 Agriculture, Hunting, Forestry and Fishing	.	.	2.1	11.7	.	.
2 Mining and Quarrying	.	.	-	.	.	.
3 Manufacturing	.	.	0.8	89.4	.	.
4 Electricity, Gas and Water	.	.	0.3	6.2	.	.
5 Construction	.	.	0.8	1.7	.	.
6 Wholesale and Retail Trade and Restaurants and Hotels	.	.	0.8	53.8	.	.
7 Transport, Storage and Communication	.	.	0.8	13.6	.	.
8 Financing, Insurance, Real Estate and Business Services	.	.	0.6	45.4	.	.
9 Community, Social and Personal Services	.	.	3.8	34.4	.	.
0 Activities not Adequately Defined	.	.	0.2	34.0	.	.

Occupation (ISCO-1968)

1999 [1] Population census

			Total	Women (%)		
Total	.	.	10.141	30.9	.	.
0/1 Professional, technical and related workers	.	.	1.546	35.9	.	.
2 Administrative and managerial workers	.	.	0.436	19.3	.	.
3 Clerical and related workers	.	.	1.365	60.9	.	.
4 Sales workers	.	.	0.344	38.4	.	.
5 Service workers	.	.	1.687	31.5	.	.
6 Agriculture, animal husbandry and forestry workers ...	.	.	2.079	11.6	.	.
7/8/9 Production and related workers, transport equipment ...	.	.	2.471	28.0	.	.
X Not classifiable by occupation	.	.	0.213	31.5	.	.

Status in employment (ICSE-1993)

1999 [1,2] Population census

			Total	Women (%)		
Total	.	.	10.1	30.9	.	.
1 Employees	.	.	7.2	29.3	.	.
2 Employers	.	.	0.1	39.1	.	.
3 Own-account workers	.	.	2.6	33.9	.	.
5 Contributing family workers	.	.	0.1	34.5	.	.
6 Not classifiable by status	.	.	0.1	53.1	.	.

2. Population ('000), Activity rate and Unemployment rate

	Population			Activity rate			Unemployment rate 1999 [1] Population census		
Age group	Total	Men	Women	Total	Men	Women	Total	Men	Women
Total	.	.	.	.	.	.	30.9	27.6	37.3
15+	.	.	.	.	.	.	30.9	.	.
15-24	.	.	.	.	.	.	62.6	.	.
25-54	.	.	.	.	.	.	22.0	.	.
55+	.	.	.	.	.	.	12.0	.	.

3. Paid employment ('000), Hours of work (weekly) and Wages

Statistics not available.

4. Occupational injuries and Strikes and Lockouts

Statistics not available.

5. Consumer price indices (base period: 2000=100)

Majuro	2002	2003	2004	2005	2006	2007
General indices	103.0	100.1	102.3	106.9	111.5	115.1
Food index, including non-alcoholic beverages	102.7	102.5	106.0	106.3	109.4	111.0
Electricity, gas and other fuel indices	98.3	.	.	.	.	.
Clothing indices, including footwear	115.5	94.1	96.7	96.0	98.7	97.1
Rent indices	106.0	.	.	.	.	.

Marshall Islands

[1] Persons aged 15 years and over. [2] June.   [1] Personnes âgées de 15 ans et plus. [2] Juin.   [1] Personas de 15 años y más. [2] Junio.

Martinique

1. Population active, Emploi et Chômage ('000)

Groupe d'âge	Population active Total	Population active Femmes (%)	Emploi Total	Emploi Femmes (%)	Chômage Total	Chômage Femmes (%)
		1999 [1][2] Recensement de la population		1999 ★ Recensement de la population		2007 [1][3] Enquête sur la main-d'oeuvre
Total	173.930	50.3	116.957	47.7	42.155	54.7
15-19	1.205	35.4	0.321	31.8	.	.
15-24	.	.	.	.	8.236	49.4
20-24	11.989	44.8	4.779	39.2	.	.
25-29	24.794	51.8	13.554	48.2	.	.
25-49	.	.	.	.	28.246	57.7
30-34	28.636	52.2	17.452	47.2	.	.
35-39	29.629	51.3	19.898	47.2	.	.
40-44	24.737	50.6	17.875	48.3	.	.
45-49	20.814	51.5	16.381	50.4	.	.
50+	.	.	.	.	5.673	47.6
50-54	16.574	50.0	13.469	49.5	.	.
55-59	10.248	47.5	8.403	48.4	.	.
60-64	4.153	44.8	3.674	44.2	.	.
65-69	0.697	37.4	.	.	.	.
70-74	0.207	37.2	0.207	37.2	.	.
75+	0.247	45.3	0.247	45.3	.	.

Activité économique (CITI-Rév.2)				1990 [1][2] Recensement de la population		
Total	.	.	110.1	45.4	.	.
1 Agriculture, chasse, sylviculture et pêche	.	.	8.4	27.4	.	.
4 Electricité, gaz et eau	.	.	9.7	25.2	.	.
5 Bâtiment et travaux publics	.	.	9.3	7.5	.	.
6-8	.	.	47.1	49.3	.	.
9 Services fournis à la collectivité, services sociaux ...	.	.	35.5	59.9	.	.
0 Activités mal désignées	.	.	.	.	.	.

Niveau d'instruction (CITE-97)		1999 [1][2] Recensement de la population				
Total	174.0	50.3	.	.	.	.
1 Enseignement primaire ou premier cycle de l'éducation ...	26.9	42.6	.	.	.	.
2 Premier cycle de l'enseignement secondaire ou deuxième ...	80.4	47.6	.	.	.	.
3 Enseignement secondaire (deuxième cycle)	36.6	57.1	.	.	.	.
5A Premier cycle de l'enseignement supérieur - théorie [4]	30.0	56.3	.	.	.	.

2. Population ('000), Taux d'activité et Taux de chômage

Groupe d'âge	Population Total	Hommes	Femmes	Taux d'activité Total	Hommes	Femmes	Taux de chômage Total	Hommes	Femmes
	1999 [2] Recensement de la population			1999 [2] Recensement de la population			1999 [1] Recensement de la population		
Total	381.325	180.910	200.415	45.6	47.8	43.7	32.8	29.3	36.2
15+	297.424	138.632	158.792	58.5	62.3	55.1	.	.	.
15-24	51.764	26.195	25.569	25.5	28.3	22.7	61.3	57.7	65.9
25-54	166.028	77.348	88.680	87.4	91.3	84.0	32.1	27.9	36.0
55+	79.632	35.089	44.543	19.5	23.9	16.1	.	.	.

3. Emploi rémunéré ('000), Durée du travail (hebdomadaire) et Salaires

Activité économique (CITI-Rév.3)	Emploi rémunéré 2005 Estimations officielles Total	Hommes	Femmes	Durée du travail Total	Hommes	Femmes	Salaires 2001 Enquête auprès des établissements, relative au travail Gains par heure / Salariés / Euro Total	Hommes	Femmes
Total	113.1	.	.	.	.	.	10.37	10.80	9.86
A-B	5.9	.	.	.	.	.	6.50 [5]	6.72 [5]	6.06 [5]
D	7.8	.	.	.	.	.	.	.	.
E	1.2	.	.	.	.	.	14.43	14.79	12.73
F	6.0	.	.	.	.	.	8.83	8.90	8.24
G	15.0	.	.	.	.	.	.	.	.
50	.	.	.	.	.	.	8.42	.	.
51	.	.	.	.	.	.	10.34	.	.
52	.	.	.	.	.	.	7.92	.	.
H	4.7	.	.	.	.	.	7.58	.	.
I	5.9	.	.	.	.	.	10.74 [6]	11.40 [6]	9.32 [6]
64	.	.	.	.	.	.	14.00	14.96	12.61
J	2.3	.	.	.	.	.	13.84	16.89	12.03
K	8.7	.	.	.	.	.	8.68	10.05	7.07
73	.	.	.	.	.	.	12.29	13.88	9.05
L	19.5	.	.	.	.	.	13.02	.	12.32
M	13.9	.	.	.	.	.	8.17	8.88	7.72
N	12.3	.	.	.	.	.	12.73	13.47	12.40
O	4.6	.	.	.	.	.	8.60	9.31	8.14
92	.	.	.	.	.	.	9.77	10.28	9.07
P	5.4	.	.	.	.	.	6.05	6.59	5.83
X	.	.	.	.	.	.	7.12	5.62	7.40

Martinique

4. Lésions professionnelles et Grèves et lock-out

Activité économique (CITI-Rév.2)	Taux de lésions mortelles			Taux de lésions non mortelles			Grèves et lock-out 1980 Source inconnue		
	Total	Hommes	Femmes	Total	Hommes	Femmes	Grèves et lock-out	Travailleurs impliqués	Journées non effectuées
Total	.	.	.	.	.	.	23	1 862	6 388

5. Indices des prix à la consommation (période de base: 2000=100)

	2002	2003	2004	2005	2006	2007
Indices généraux	104.2	106.4	108.6	111.2	113.9	116.7
Indices de l'alimentation, y compris les boissons non alcoolisées	108.8	112.5	114.6	118.3	120.5	124.5
Indices de l'électricité, gaz et autres combustibles	105.3	105.5	108.6	117.8	127.6	131.1
Indices de l'habillement, y compris les chaussures	100.0	98.3	98.2	97.8	97.2	98.1
Indices du loyer	101.9	105.9	109.1	114.4	119.3	123.3

[1] Persons aged 15 years and over. [2] March. [3] June. [4] Levels 5-6. [5] Excl. hunting. [6] Excl. storage and communications.

[1] Personnes âgées de 15 ans et plus. [2] Mars. [3] Juin. [4] Niveaux 5-6. [5] Non compris la chasse. [6] N.c. l'entreposage et les communications.

[1] Personas de 15 años y más. [2] Marzo. [3] Junio. [4] Niveles 5-6. [5] Excl. la caza. [6] Excl. el almacenamiento y las comunicaciones.

Mauritanie

1. Population active, Emploi et Chômage ('000)

Groupe d'âge	Population active Total	Population active Femmes (%)	Emploi Total	Emploi Femmes (%)	Chômage Total	Chômage Femmes (%)
	2001 [1] Estimations officielles		2000 [1] Estimations officielles		2000 [1] Estimations officielles	
Total	788.4	37.1	609.3	28.3	158.2	72.7

2. Population ('000), Taux d'activité et Taux de chômage

Groupe d'âge	Population 1988 Recensement de la population			Taux d'activité 1988 Recensement de la population			Taux de chômage 2000 [1] Estimations officielles		
	Total	Hommes	Femmes	Total	Hommes	Femmes	Total	Hommes	Femmes
Total	1 260.3	613.8	646.5	46.5	68.8	25.3	20.6	8.9	41.2

3. Emploi rémunéré ('000), Durée du travail (hebdomadaire) et Salaires

Données non disponibles.

4. Lésions professionnelles et Grèves et lock-out

Données non disponibles.

5. Indices des prix à la consommation (période de base: 2000=100)

	2002	2003	2004	2005	2006	2007
Indices généraux	108.9	114.4	124.2	139.3	147.9	158.7
Indices de l'alimentation, y compris les boissons non alcoolisées	111.3	117.9 [2]	131.2	149.3	157.3	173.9
Indices de l'habillement, y compris les chaussures	102.9	105.4 [2]	121.2	131.1	143.5	149.7
Indices du loyer [3]	108.6	114.1 [2]	123.3	134.7	145.1	157.3

[1] Persons aged 10 years and over. [2] Jan.-Nov. [3] Incl. water, electricity, gas and other fuels.

[1] Personnes âgées de 10 ans et plus. [2] janv.-nov. [3] Y compris l'eau, l'électricité, le gaz et autres combustibles.

[1] Personas de 10 años y más. [2] enero-nov. [3] Incl. el agua, la electricidad, el gas y otros combustibles.

Mauritius

1. Economically active population, Employment and Unemployment ('000)

	Economically active population		Employment		Unemployment	
	Total	Women (%)	Total	Women (%)	Total	Women (%)
Age group	2007 [1 2] Labour force survey		2007 ★ Labour force survey		2007 [2] Labour force survey	
Total	548.9	35.6	502.1	33.3	46.8 [3]	60.3
16-19	19.4	37.1	12.0	32.5	7.4	44.6
20-24	59.6	41.6	47.6	38.0	12.0 [3]	55.8
25-29	81.4	37.3	73.0	34.5	8.4 [3]	61.9
30-34	73.3	37.4	67.1	33.8	6.2 [3]	75.8
35-39	68.9	37.3	64.7	35.2	4.2 [3]	69.0
40-44	75.3	35.1	72.0	33.2	3.3 [3]	75.8
45-49	65.3	33.8	62.8	32.6	2.5 [3]	64.0
50-54	53.4	30.7	52.0	30.0	1.4 [3]	57.1
55-59	37.5	29.3	36.7	29.2	0.8 [3]	37.5
60-64	8.5	25.9	7.9	25.3	0.6 [3]	33.3
65-69	3.6	33.3	3.6	33.3	0.0 [3]	.
70-74	1.8	22.2	1.8	22.2	0.0 [3]	.
75+	0.9	11.1	0.9	11.1	0.0 [3]	.
Economic activity (ISIC-Rev.3)	2007 ★ Labour force survey		2007 [1 2 3] Labour force survey		2007 [2] Labour force survey	
Total	548.9	35.6	502.1	33.3	46.8 [3]	60.3
A-B	.	.	.	.	1.1	.
A Agriculture, Hunting and Forestry	40.1	30.9	40.0	30.0	0.1 [3]	400.0
B Fishing	5.8	12.1	5.7	12.3	0.1 [3]	0.0
C Mining and Quarrying	0.4	25.0	0.3	33.3	0.1 [3]	0.0
D Manufacturing	113.2	43.8	102.2	40.7	11.0 [3]	72.7
E Electricity, Gas and Water Supply	4.1	14.6	4.1	14.6	0.0 [3]	.
F Construction	60.0	1.5	55.5	1.4	4.5 [3]	2.2
G Wholesale and Retail Trade; Repair of Motor Vehicles ...	75.0	39.5	71.3	38.4	3.7 [3]	59.5
H Hotels and Restaurants	36.8	33.7	34.8	33.3	2.0 [3]	40.0
I Transport, Storage and Communications	37.1	15.1	35.9	14.2	1.2 [3]	41.7
J Financial Intermediation	10.6	44.3	10.3	43.7	0.3 [3]	66.7
K Real Estate, Renting and Business Activities	22.8	33.3	21.5	32.6	1.3 [3]	46.2
L Public Administration and Defence; Compulsory Social ...	34.9	21.2	34.7	21.3	0.2 [3]	0.0
M Education	29.8	56.4	28.9	55.7	0.9 [3]	77.8
N Health and Social Work	18.5	52.4	18.1	51.9	0.4 [3]	75.0
O Other Community, Social and Personal Service Activities	17.4	36.2	16.5	35.2	0.9 [3]	55.6
P Households with Employed Persons	21.0	85.7	18.8	85.6	2.2 [3]	86.4
Q Extra-Territorial Organizations and Bodies	.	.	0.5	20.0	.	.
X Not classifiable by economic activity	3.0	26.7	3.0	26.7	0.0 [3]	.
Unemployed seeking their first job	.	.	.	.	16.9 [3]	71.0
Occupation (ISCO-88)	1995 ★ Labour force survey		2007 [1 2 3] Labour force survey		2005 [4 5] Employment office records	
Total	484.0	32.9	502.1	33.3	33.6	54.3
1 Legislators, senior officials and managers	11.7	22.7	14.8	20.3	0.1	32.4
2 Professionals	13.4	33.8	17.7	35.0	0.3	54.1
3 Technicians and associate professionals	32.3	41.1	45.6	48.9	1.0	67.5
4 Clerks	38.4	50.5	46.0	59.1	5.3	80.9
5 Service workers and shop and market sales workers	56.4	29.0	93.4	37.8	2.9	58.0
6 Skilled agricultural and fishery workers	20.2	18.0	18.5	21.6	0.3	5.8
7 Craft and related trade workers	91.3	8.1	96.6	12.9	7.3	42.1
8 Plant and machine operators and assemblers	82.9	46.5	64.7	26.6	4.1	42.7
9 Elementary occupations	114.1	35.7	101.8	37.9	6.0	32.6
X Not classifiable by occupation	.	.	3.0	26.7	.	.
Unemployed seeking their first job	.	.	.	.	6.4	72.5
Education level (ISCED-97)	2007 [1 2] Labour force survey		2007 ★ Labour force survey		2007 [2 3] Labour force survey	
Total	548.9	35.6	502.1	33.3	46.8	60.3
X No schooling [6]	12.2	59.0	11.5	58.3	0.7	71.4
1 Primary education or first stage of basic education	191.6	32.4	176.9	30.6	14.7	53.7
2 Lower secondary or second stage of basic education	63.1	26.5	57.1	23.5	6.0	55.0
3 Upper secondary education	223.2	38.5	200.5	35.4	22.7	66.1
5A First stage of tertiary education - theoretically based [7]	58.8	40.0	55.8	40.3	3.0	33.3
Status in employment (ICSE-1993)			2007 [1 2 3] Labour force survey			
Total	.	.	502.1	33.3	.	.
1 Employees	.	.	397.7	35.0	.	.
2 Employers	.	.	16.1	14.3	.	.
3 Own-account workers	.	.	73.6	22.8	.	.
4 Members of producers' cooperatives	.	.	0.8	37.5	.	.
5 Contributing family workers	.	.	10.9	71.6	.	.
6 Not classifiable by status	.	.	3.0	26.7	.	.

Mauritius

2. Population ('000), Activity rate and Unemployment rate

Age group	Population 2007[18] Labour force survey			Activity rate 2007[18] Labour force survey			Unemployment rate 2007[2] Labour force survey		
	Total	Men	Women	Total	Men	Women	Total	Men	Women
Total							8.5	5.3	14.4
15+	932.1	458.2	473.9	58.9	77.2	41.2	8.5	5.3	14.4
15-24	173.7	88.9	84.8	45.5	52.9	37.7	24.6	20.0	31.3
25-54	567.8	284.0	283.8	73.5	94.8	52.3	6.2	3.1	11.9
55+	190.6	85.3	105.3	27.4	43.8	14.2	2.7	2.4	3.4

3. Paid employment ('000), Hours of work (weekly) and Wages

Economic activity (ISIC-Rev.3)	Paid employment 2007[9 10] Labour-related establishment survey			Hours of work 2007 Labour force survey Hours actually worked / Total employment			Wages 2007[9 10] Labour-related establishment census Earnings per month / Employees / Rupee		
	Total	Men	Women	Total	Men	Women	Total	Men	Women
Total	299.666	192.716	106.950	.	.	.	13 378	.	.
A-B	21.684	18.047	3.637	45	45	45	10 410	.	.
C-Q	.	.	.	.	.	.	13 626	.	.
A	.	.	.	45	45	45	10 290	.	.
B	.	.	.	45	45	45	13 839	.	.
C	0.140	0.075	0.065	.	.	.	6 340	.	.
D	92.261	45.004	47.257	45	.	.	8 626	.	.
E	2.999	2.821	0.178	45	.	.	24 125	.	.
F	13.629	13.070	0.559	45	.	.	14 143	.	.
G	18.835	12.860	5.975	45	.	.	14 387	.	.
H	22.026	16.746	5.280	48	.	.	11 326	.	.
I	18.513	15.049	3.464	45	.	.	17 554	.	.
J	9.293	5.031	4.262	45	.	.	24 117	.	.
K	17.196	10.884	6.312	45	.	.	13 657	.	.
L	39.887	30.529	9.358	.	.	.	15 497	.	.
M	24.040	11.337	12.703	.	.	.	16 682	.	.
N	12.984	6.619	6.365	.	.	.	18 866	.	.
O	6.179	4.644	1.535	.	.	.	12 555	.	.
P	.	.	.	48	.	.	.	.	.

Share of women in wage employment in the non-agricultural sector[9 10] (2007 - Labour-related establishment survey): **37.2%**

4. Occupational injuries and Strikes and Lockouts

Economic activity (ISIC-Rev.3)	Rates of fatal injuries 2002[11 12 13] Insurance records Per 100,000 workers insured Reported injuries			Rates of non-fatal injuries 2007[11 14] Insurance records Per 100,000 workers insured Reported injuries			Strikes and lockouts 2007 Labour relations records		
	Total	Men	Women	Total	Men	Women	Strikes and lockouts	Workers involved[15]	Days not worked
Total	7	.	.	845	1 240	213	29	4 687	15 214
A	.	.	.	4 584	5 198	2 747	0	0	0
B	.	.	.	93	124	62	0	0	0
C	.	.	.	0	0	0	0	0	0
D	.	.	.	434	747	99	29	4 687	15 214
E	.	.	.	374	511	0	0	0	0
F	.	.	.	3 524	388	0	0	0	0
G	.	.	.	448	605	220	0	0	0
H	.	.	.	160	182	109	0	0	0
I	.	.	.	1 192	1 444	367	0	0	0
J	.	.	.	9	17	0	0	0	0
K	.	.	.	172	255	19	0	0	0
L	.	.	.	0	0	0	0	0	0
M	.	.	.	63	46	74	0	0	0
N	.	.	.	613	1 925	40	0	0	0
O	.	.	.	148	182	96	0	0	0
P	.	.	.	5 419	5 085	5 882	.	.	.
X	.	.	.	.	.	.	0	0	0

5. Consumer price indices (base period: 2000=100)

	2002	2003	2004	2005	2006	2007
General indices	112.2	116.5	122.1	128.1	139.5	154.9[16]
Food index, including non-alcoholic beverages	112.2	115.4	122.3	129.5	142.4	168.9[16]
Electricity, gas and other fuel indices[17]	100.0[16]	100.0	100.2	102.8	124.0	133.3[16]
Clothing indices, including footwear[17]	98.9[16]	100.0	101.6	102.9	109.7	118.1[16]
Rent indices[17 18]	99.8[16]	100.0	100.5	101.3	123.2	128.1[16]
General index, excluding housing[17]	97.4[16]	100.0	104.8	110.0	119.9	.

Mauritius

[1] Excl. armed forces. [2] Persons aged 16 years and over. [3] Prior to 2007: persons aged 15 years and over. [4] Excl. Rodrigues. [5] Persons aged 15 years and over. [6] Levels X-0. [7] Levels 5-6. [8] "De jure" population. [9] Establishments with 10 or more persons employed. [10] March. [11] Excl. public sector and parastatal bodies. [12] Not strictly comparable. [13] Up to 2002: deaths occurring within 30 days of accident. [14] Up to 2002: incapacity of 3 days or more. [15] Excl. workers indirectly involved. [16] July-Dec. [17] Index base 2003=100. [18] Incl. housing, water, electriciy and other fuels.

[1] Non compris les forces armées. [2] Personnes âgées de 16 ans et plus. [3] Avant 2006: personnes âgées de 15 ans et plus. [4] Non compris Rodriguez. [5] Personnes âgées de 15 ans et plus. [6] Niveaux X-0. [7] Niveaux 5-6. [8] Population "de jure". [9] Etablissements occupant 10 personnes et plus. [10] Mars. [11] Non compris le secteur public et les organismes paraétatiques. [12] Non strictement comparable. [13] Jusqu'à 2002: les décès survenant pendant les 30 jours qui suivent l'accident. [14] Jusqu'à 2002: incapacité de 3 jours et plus. [15] Non compris les travailleurs indirectement impliqués. [16] Juillet-déc. [17] Indice base 2003=100. [18] Y compris le logement, l'eau, l'électricité et autres combustibles.

[1] Excl. las fuerzas armadas. [2] Personas de 16 años y más. [3] Antes de 2006: personas de 15 años y más. [4] Excl. Rodríguez. [5] Personas de 15 años y más. [6] Niveles X-0. [7] Niveles 5-6. [8] Población "de jure". [9] Establecimientos con 10 y más trabajadores. [10] Marzo. [11] Excl. el sector público y los organismos paraestatales. [12] No estrictamente comparable. [13] Hasta 2002: los fallecimientos que se produzcan durante los 30 días posteriores al accidente. [14] Hasta 2002: incapacidad de 3 días y más. [15] Excl. los trabajadores indirectamente implicados. [16] Julio-dic. [17] Indice base 2003=100. [18] Incl. la vivienda, el agua, la electricidad y otros combustibles.

México

1. Población económicamente activa, Empleo y Desempleo ('000)

	Población económicamente activa		Empleo		Desempleo	
	Total	Mujeres (%)	Total	Mujeres (%)	Total	Mujeres (%)
Grupo de edad	2007 [1,2] Encuesta de la fuerza de trabajo		2007 ★ Encuesta de la fuerza de trabajo		2007 [1,2] Encuesta de la fuerza de trabajo	
Total	44 411.9	37.6	42 906.7	37.4	1 505.2	41.2
12-14	348.7	26.2	339.4	26.3	9.3	25.2
15-19	3 827.5	33.6	3 553.7	33.4	273.8	36.1
20-24	5 411.3	39.7	5 067.0	39.3	344.3	46.1
25-29	5 514.0	39.9	5 249.3	39.7	264.8	43.0
30-34	5 611.3	39.8	5 447.2	39.4	164.1	52.2
35-39	5 500.4	39.1	5 365.1	38.9	135.3	47.5
40-44	5 058.6	40.1	4 958.6	40.2	100.0	33.6
45-49	4 154.3	39.9	4 076.9	39.8	77.3	46.8
50-54	3 270.0	35.9	3 211.8	36.0	58.2	28.8
55-59	2 289.6	31.7	2 251.2	32.0	38.4	14.9
60-64	1 503.2	30.4	1 481.0	30.7	22.1	8.9
65-69	892.2	28.8	883.6	28.9	8.6	15.6
70-74	552.8	28.5	548.3	28.8	4.5	2.6
75+	462.5	24.4	458.8	24.6	3.7	0.0
?	15.6	29.7	14.9	31.1	0.7	0.0
Actividad económica (CIIU-Rev.3)	2006 ★ Encuesta de la fuerza de trabajo		2006 [1,2] Encuesta de la fuerza de trabajo		2006 [1,2] Encuesta de la fuerza de trabajo	
Total	43 575.5	37.1	42 197.8	37.0	1 377.7	41.1
A Agricultura, ganadería, caza y silvicultura	5 910.1	12.3	5 865.7	12.3	44.4	10.1
B Pesca	169.1	6.3	167.3	6.0	1.8	27.8
C Explotación de minas y canteras	167.1	9.8	164.1	9.9	3.0	3.3
D Industrias manufactureras	7 262.3	38.5	7 078.7	38.4	183.6	39.1
E Suministro de electricidad, gas y agua	188.8	19.7	186.3	19.4	2.5	40.0
F Construcción	3 605.8	3.0	3 452.5	2.9	153.3	3.9
G Comercio al por mayor y al por menor; reparación ...	9 800.7	43.9	9 594.9	43.9	205.8	40.5
H Hoteles y restaurantes	2 593.2	58.4	2 514.9	58.6	78.3	51.3
I Transporte, almacenamiento y comunicaciones	2 046.1	10.0	2 001.4	9.9	44.7	12.3
J Intermediación financiera	370.5	47.5	362.6	47.4	7.9	53.2
K Actividades inmobiliarias, empresariales y de alquiler	1 995.9	35.6	1 925.3	35.3	70.6	41.6
L Administración pública y defensa; planes de seguridad ...	2 071.9	34.7	2 032.1	34.6	39.8	43.0
M Enseñanza	2 275.5	62.4	2 252.4	62.4	23.1	63.2
N Servicios sociales y de salud	1 172.2	68.6	1 161.3	68.4	10.9	87.2
O Otras actividades de servicios comunitarios ...	1 401.1	46.1	1 369.4	46.2	31.7	42.6
P Hogares privados con servicio doméstico	1 793.0	91.8	1 756.4	91.9	36.6	90.2
Q Organizaciones y órganos extraterritoriales	8.5	22.4	2.8	67.9	5.7	0.0
X No pueden clasificarse según la actividad económica	566.3	41.5	309.7	32.8	256.6	52.1
Desempleados sin empleo anterior	.	.	.	.	177.4	55.5
Ocupación (CIUO-88)	2006 [1,2] Encuesta de la fuerza de trabajo		2006 [1,2] Encuesta de la fuerza de trabajo		2006 [1,2] Encuesta de la fuerza de trabajo	
Total	43 575.5	37.1	42 197.8	37.0	1 377.7	41.1
1 Miembros del poder ejecutivo y de los cuerpos legislativos ...	908.9	27.5	898.7	27.3	10.2	40.2
2 Profesionales científicos e intelectuales	2 837.7	44.2	2 803.5	44.2	34.2	44.7
3 Técnicos y profesionales de nivel medio	4 253.9	39.8	4 154.5	39.9	99.4	36.6
4 Empleados de oficina	2 942.0	61.1	2 830.8	61.1	111.2	61.3
5 Trabajadores de los servicios y vendedores de comercios ...	7 715.5	54.2	7 537.4	54.4	178.1	46.7
6 Agricultores y trabajadores calificados agropecuarios ...	5 847.2	11.9	5 802.6	12.0	44.6	7.6
7 Oficiales, operarios y artesanos de artes mecánicas ...	6 759.7	22.8	6 605.6	22.9	154.2	18.5
8 Operadores de instalaciones y máquinas y montadores	3 915.0	21.3	3 806.8	21.3	108.2	23.4
9 Trabajadores no calificados	7 913.1	46.6	7 684.4	47.0	228.7	31.8
0 Fuerzas armadas	70.9	1.4	69.9	1.4	1.0	0.0
X No pueden clasificarse según la ocupación	234.0	56.5	3.6	41.7	230.4	56.7
Desempleados sin empleo anterior	177.4	55.5	.	.	177.4	55.5
Nivel de educación (CINE-97)	2007 [1,2] Encuesta de la fuerza de trabajo		2007 ★ Encuesta de la fuerza de trabajo		2007 [1,2] Encuesta de la fuerza de trabajo	
Total	44 411.9	37.6	42 906.7	37.4	1 505.2	41.2
X Sin escolaridad	2 498.4	38.2	2 471.2	38.4	27.1	19.4
1 Enseñanza primaria o primer ciclo de la educación básica	13 484.8	34.0	13 179.1	34.1	305.7	30.5
2 Primer ciclo de enseñanza secundaria o segundo ciclo de ...	11 968.4	34.8	11 510.5	34.7	457.8	38.1
3 Segundo ciclo de enseñanza secundaria	6 442.1	34.9	6 161.6	34.6	280.6	42.3
4 Enseñanza postsecundaria, no terciaria	2 351.8	65.7	2 263.0	65.6	88.9	67.4
5A Primer ciclo de la educación terciaria - teóricos	6 917.4	41.5	6 584.8	41.2	332.6	48.7
5B Primer ciclo de la educación terciaria - práctica	192.3	51.4	186.2	52.0	6.1	35.0
6 Segundo ciclo de la enseñanza terciaria	527.4	37.3	521.1	37.0	6.2	61.8
? Nivel desconocido	29.2	47.7	29.1	47.6	0.2	63.6
Situación en el empleo (CISE-1993)			2007 [1,2] Encuesta de la fuerza de trabajo			
Total	.	.	42 906.7	37.4	.	.
1 Asalariados	.	.	28 104.0	37.2	.	.
2 Empleadores	.	.	2 161.9	18.9	.	.
3 Trabajadores por cuenta propia	.	.	9 704.3	36.9	.	.
5 Trabajadores familiares auxiliares	.	.	2 936.4	55.0	.	.
6 Inclasificables según la situación	.	.	0.0	.	.	.

México

2. Población ('000), Tasa de actividad y Tasa de desempleo

Grupo de edad	Población 2007 [2,3] Encuesta de la fuerza de trabajo			Tasa de actividad 2007 [2,3] Encuesta de la fuerza de trabajo			Tasa de desempleo 2007 [1,2] Encuesta de la fuerza de trabajo		
	Total	Hombres	Mujeres	Total	Hombres	Mujeres	Total	Hombres	Mujeres
Total	105 677.4	50 624.4	55 053.0	42.0	54.8	30.3	3.4	3.2	3.7
15+	73 383.0	34 232.7	39 150.4	60.0	80.2	42.4	3.4	3.2	3.7
15-24	19 484.6	9 410.8	10 073.8	47.4	61.7	34.1	6.7	6.2	7.5
25-54	40 288.5	18 533.9	21 754.6	72.3	95.3	52.6	2.7	2.5	3.1
55+	13 609.9	6 287.9	7 322.0	41.9	63.4	23.4	1.4	1.7	0.5

3. Empleo remunerado ('000), Horas de trabajo (por semana) y Salarios

Actividad económica (CIIU-Rev.3)	Empleo remunerado 2007 [1,2] Encuesta de la fuerza de trabajo			Horas de trabajo 2007 [1,2] Encuesta de la fuerza de trabajo Horas efectivamente trabajadas / Asalariados			Salarios 2007 [1,2] Encuesta de la fuerza de trabajo Ganancias por mes / Asalariados / Nuevo peso		
	Total	Hombres	Mujeres	Total	Hombres	Mujeres	Total	Hombres	Mujeres
Total	28 104.0	17 638.2	10 465.8	43.9	46.6	39.3	4 716.3	5 043.6	4 157.1
A-B	.	.	.	38.9	40.3	29.0	2 522.9	2 551.8	2 252.8
C-Q	.	.	.	44.1	47.2	39.4	4 898.3	5 350.5	4 196.0
A	2 001.5	2 022.5	194.5	39.0	40.3	29.1	2 494.1	2 522.3	2 232.1
B	37.4	34.9	2.5	37.5	38.5	22.8	4 157.0	4 187.5	3 778.6
C	177.3	157.2	20.1	50.9	51.8	39.4	10 010.3	9 799.7	11 684.4
D	5 449.3	3 577.8	1 871.5	45.5	46.6	43.4	4 689.2	5 242.5	3 651.1
E	219.7	182.2	37.5	42.3	43.2	38.0	7 391.0	7 651.4	6 141.9
F	2 580.1	2 479.2	101.0	46.3	46.3	45.5	4 476.8	4 431.4	5 657.0
G	4 622.0	2 982.0	1 640.0	47.2	48.6	44.5	4 154.0	4 514.5	3 491.1
H	1 481.8	737.8	744.0	46.2	47.7	44.7	3 760.6	4 170.0	3 346.2
I	1 503.5	1 324.3	179.2	54.4	56.0	43.1	5 647.3	5 694.0	5 292.5
J	389.9	206.5	183.4	43.2	45.1	41.0	8 876.9	10 239.8	7 293.1
K	1 411.6	851.9	559.8	45.7	48.6	41.4	5 155.0	5 410.4	4 763.9
L	2 029.0	1 311.7	717.3	45.1	48.5	38.8	6 498.4	6 551.1	6 399.6
M	2 248.3	887.8	1 360.5	31.3	33.4	30.0	6 549.6	7 315.3	6 045.4
N	1 016.5	282.8	733.7	39.0	40.2	38.5	6 620.5	8 391.3	5 941.4
O	790.9	480.0	310.8	41.9	42.8	40.6	4 622.8	5 031.3	3 991.6
P	1 858.3	144.6	1 713.7	34.1	46.2	33.0	2 340.7	3 555.5	2 247.2
Q	6.3	3.1	3.2	44.6	48.6	40.8	.	.	.
X	280.7	187.4	93.2	.	.	.	.	.	.

Proporción de mujeres entre los empleados remunerados en el sector no agrícola [1,2] (2007 - Encuesta de la fuerza de trabajo): **39.5%**

4. Lesiones profesionales y Huelgas y cierres patronales

Actividad económica (CIIU-Rev.3)	Tasas de lesiones mortales 2007 [4] Registros de seguros Por 100 000 trabajadores asegurados Lesiones declaradas			Tasas de lesiones no mortales 2007 [4] Registros de seguros Por 100 000 trabajadores asegurados Lesiones declaradas			Huelgas y cierres patronales 2007 [5,6] Registros de relaciones laborales		
	Total	Hombres	Mujeres	Total	Hombres	Mujeres	Huelgas y cierres patronales	Trabajadores implicados [7]	Días no trabajados
Total	9	19	1	3 120	4 094	1 484	28	10 601	200 856
A	.	.	.	.	.	.	0	0	0
B	.	.	.	.	.	.	0	0	0
C	.	.	.	.	.	.	3	2 205	3 308
D	.	.	.	.	.	.	13	1 864	27 582
E	.	.	.	.	.	.	0	0	0
F	.	.	.	.	.	.	4	150	1 313
G	.	.	.	.	.	.	0	0	0
H	.	.	.	.	.	.	0	0	0
I	.	.	.	.	.	.	4	962	22 658
J	.	.	.	.	.	.	1	41	1 087
K	.	.	.	.	.	.	0	0	0
M	.	.	.	.	.	.	1	5 364	144 828
N	.	.	.	.	.	.	0	0	0
O	.	.	.	.	.	.	2	15	80

5. Índices de precios al consumidor (periodo de base: 2000=100)

	2002	2003	2004	2005	2006	2007
Índices generales	111.7	116.8	122.3	127.2	131.8	137.0
Índices de la alimentación incluyendo las bebidas no alcohólicas [8]	109.6	115.1	122.9	129.4	134.1	142.6
Índices de la electricidad, gas y otros combustibles	117.2	135.8	149.1	160.6	173.1	.
Índices del vestido, incl. calzado	108.9	109.8	110.9	112.1	113.5	115.0
Índices del aquiler [9]	114.3	120.6	125.2	129.1	133.2	.

[1] Persons aged 14 years and over. [2] Second quarter. [3] "De jure" population. [4] Data for IMSS only. [5] Strikes only, beginning in the year indicated. [6] Excl. enterprises covered by local jurisdiction. [7] Excl. workers indirectly involved and workers in positions of trust; union members only. [8] Incl. alcoholic beverages and tobacco. [9] Incl. "Fuel and light".

[1] Personnes âgées de 14 ans et plus. [2] Deuxième trimestre. [3] Population "de jure". [4] Données relatives à l'IMSS seulement. [5] Grèves seulement, commençant pendant l'année indiquée. [6] Non compris les entreprises sous juridiction locale. [7] Non compris les travailleurs indirectement impliqués et les travailleurs de confiance; travailleurs syndiqués seulement. [8] Y compris les boissons alcoolisées et le tabac. [9] Y compris le groupe "Combustible et éclairage".

[1] Personas de 14 años y más. [2] Segundo trimestre. [3] Población "de jure". [4] Datos relativos al IMSS solamente. [5] Huelgas solamente, que empiezan en el año indicado. [6] Excl. las empresas de jurisdicción local. [7] Excl. trabajadores indirectamente implicados y trabajadores de confianza; trabajadores sindicados solamente. [8] Incl. las bebidas alcohólicas y el tabaco. [9] Incl. el grupo "Combustible y alumbrado".

Moldova, Republic of

1. Economically active population, Employment and Unemployment ('000)

	Economically active population		Employment		Unemployment	
	Total	Women (%)	Total	Women (%)	Total	Women (%)
Age group	2007 [1] Labour force survey		2007 ★ Labour force survey		2007 [1] Labour force survey	
Total	1 313.9	49.5	1 247.2	50.2	66.7	37.8
15-19	34.5	34.5	28.3	35.3	6.2	30.6
20-24	105.9	44.7	91.8	44.7	14.1	44.7
25-29	126.0	47.0	118.5	47.8	7.5	34.7
30-34	137.0	48.8	129.2	49.3	7.8	41.0
35-39	148.2	51.8	141.6	52.6	6.6	34.8
40-44	175.9	53.8	168.8	54.3	7.1	40.8
45-49	217.6	53.6	209.9	54.1	7.7	41.6
50-54	154.8	51.4	149.9	51.9	4.9	36.7
55-59	127.5	46.0	123.3	46.9	4.2	21.4
60-64	40.8	44.1	40.4	44.6	0.4	0.0
65+	45.5	46.4	45.4	46.3	0.1	100.0
Economic activity (ISIC-Rev.3)	2007 [1] Labour force survey		2007 [1] Labour force survey		2007 [1] Labour force survey	
Total	1 313.9	49.5	1 247.2	50.2	66.7	37.8
A Agriculture, Hunting and Forestry	412.3	45.9	407.8	46.1	4.5	26.7
B Fishing	0.8	.	0.8	0.0	0.0	.
C Mining and Quarrying	3.9	13.4	3.7	13.5	0.2	0.0
D Manufacturing	136.5	49.0	128.5	49.1	8.0	47.5
E Electricity, Gas and Water Supply	26.6	25.4	25.9	25.9	0.7	14.3
F Construction	81.2	9.5	75.7	9.4	5.5	10.9
G Wholesale and Retail Trade; Repair of Motor Vehicles ...	182.7	56.8	176.4	57.1	6.3	47.6
H Hotels and Restaurants	22.3	74.9	21.5	75.3	0.8	50.0
I Transport, Storage and Communications	71.1	28.2	68.7	28.7	2.4	12.5
J Financial Intermediation	15.7	66.1	15.5	67.1	0.3	0.0
K Real Estate, Renting and Business Activities	29.8	37.8	28.9	38.8	0.8	0.0
L Public Administration and Defence; Compulsory Social ...	68.5	43.0	66.3	43.1	2.2	36.4
M Education	118.1	79.6	116.8	79.8	1.3	69.2
N Health and Social Work	67.9	80.5	67.4	80.6	0.5	60.0
O Other Community, Social and Personal Service Activities	38.2	54.5	37.1	55.5	1.1	18.2
P Households with Employed Persons	5.6	84.7	5.3	84.9	0.3	66.7
Q Extra-Territorial Organizations and Bodies	0.9	53.1	0.9	55.6	-	.
X Not classifiable by economic activity	11.6	47.4	-	.	11.6	47.4
Unemployed seeking their first job	20.2	38.6	.	.	20.2	38.6
Occupation (ISCO-88)	2007 [1] Labour force survey		2007 [1] Labour force survey		2007 [1] Labour force survey	
Total	1 357.2	49.1	1 247.2	50.2	66.7	37.8
1 Legislators, senior officials and managers	90.3	38.8	82.6	40.2	1.6	18.8
2 Professionals	176.0	61.9	161.3	64.4	2.5	44.0
3 Technicians and associate professionals	101.2	67.8	97.4	73.8	2.3	43.5
4 Clerks	26.6	82.1	22.5	82.2	0.6	83.3
5 Service workers and shop and market sales workers	166.5	70.7	163.6	74.1	5.5	58.2
6 Skilled agricultural and fishery workers	229.9	52.2	185.0	49.9	1.7	41.2
7 Craft and related trade workers	130.6	27.7	123.8	26.8	8.4	29.8
8 Plant and machine operators and assemblers	95.3	6.4	92.3	7.0	3.6	8.3
9 Elementary occupations	287.5	46.3	311.6	46.4	8.1	27.2
0 Armed forces	7.7	1.3	7.1	1.4	0.6	50.0
X Not classifiable by occupation	25.3	45.5	-	.	11.6	47.4
Unemployed seeking their first job	20.2	38.6	.	.	20.2	38.6
Status in employment (ICSE-1993)	2007 [1] Labour force survey		2007 [1] Labour force survey		2007 ★ Labour force survey	
Total	1 313.9	49.5	1 247.2	50.2	66.7	37.7
1 Employees	860.5	51.9	831.7	52.4	28.8	36.7
2 Employers	11.7	38.2	11.2	39.3	0.5	11.9
3 Own-account workers	380.6	43.5	375.2	43.8	5.4	20.4
4 Members of producers' cooperatives	0.1	.	0.1	.	0.0	.
5 Contributing family workers	29.2	72.8	29.0	72.8	0.2	82.5
6 Not classifiable by status	31.8	41.8	-	.	31.8	41.8

2. Population ('000), Activity rate and Unemployment rate

	Population			Activity rate			Unemployment rate		
Age group	2005 [2] Labour force survey			2005 [2] Labour force survey			2007 [1] Labour force survey		
	Total	Men	Women	Total	Men	Women	Total	Men	Women
Total	3 600.4	1 724.8	1 875.6	39.5	40.0	39.1	5.1	6.3	3.9
15+	2 916.6	1 373.8	1 542.7	48.8	50.2	47.5	5.1	6.2	3.9
15-24	701.1	354.8	346.3	21.7	22.9	20.5	14.5	14.9	13.9
25-54	1 569.0	758.4	810.6	66.7	65.0	68.2	4.3	5.5	3.2
55+	646.5	260.6	385.8	34.7	44.1	28.3	2.2	3.1	1.0

Moldova, Republic of

3. Paid employment ('000), Hours of work (weekly) and Wages

Economic activity (ISIC-Rev.3)	Paid employment 2007 Labour force survey			Hours of work 2007[3] Labour-related establishment census Hours actually worked / Employees			Wages 2007[3] Labour-related establishment census Earnings per month / Employees / Leu		
	Total	Men	Women	Total	Men	Women	Total	Men	Women
Total	831.7	395.8	435.9	31.0	.	.	2 065.0	.	.
A-B	.	.	.	23.5	.	.	1 099.7	.	.
C-Q	.	.	.	32.2	.	.	2 175.6	.	.
A	90.2	58.6	31.6	23.4	.	.	1 098.6	.	.
B	0.6	0.5	0.0	35.2	.	.	1 281.0	.	.
C	3.7	3.2	0.5	32.4	.	.	3 098.3	.	.
D	122.8	61.7	61.1	31.3	.	.	2 314.1	.	.
E	25.8	19.1	6.7	34.3	.	.	3 595.8	.	.
F	45.7	40.3	5.4	32.2	.	.	2 967.6	.	.
G	130.2	55.0	75.3	34.3	.	.	2 088.7	.	.
H	20.8	5.0	15.8	32.6	.	.	1 759.5	.	.
I	62.1	42.6	19.5	32.1	.	.	3 039.5	.	.
J	15.5	5.1	10.4	34.8	.	.	4 648.3	.	.
K	25.4	15.5	9.9	34.2	.	.	2 583.6	.	.
L	66.3	37.6	28.6	32.6	.	.	2 389.0	.	.
M	116.7	23.5	93.2	28.5	.	.	1 351.2	.	.
N	66.4	12.5	53.9	36.4	.	.	1 703.2	.	.
O	33.3	14.3	19.0	34.7	.	.	1 600.3	.	.
P	5.3	0.8	4.5	.	.	.	.	.	.
Q	0.9	0.4	0.5	.	.	.	.	.	.

Share of women in wage employment in the non-agricultural sector (2007 - Labour force survey): **54.6%**

4. Occupational injuries and Strikes and Lockouts

Economic activity (ISIC-Rev.3)	Rates of fatal injuries 2007[4] Labour-related establishment census Per 100,000 employees Reported injuries			Rates of non-fatal injuries 2007[4] Labour-related establishment census Per 100,000 employees Reported injuries			Strikes and lockouts 1997 Source unknown		
	Total	Men	Women	Total	Men	Women	Strikes and lockouts[5]	Workers involved[6]	Days not worked
Total	7.1	.	.	71	.	.	0	0	0
A	2.3	.	.	50	.	.	.	.	.
B	138.0	.	.	.	.	.	.	.	.
C	60.0	.	.	481	.	.	.	.	.
D	8.9	.	.	147	.	.	.	.	.
E	26.7	.	.	182	.	.	.	.	.
F	42.0	.	.	132	.	.	.	.	.
G	0.0	.	.	19	.	.	.	.	.
H	.	.	.	18	.	.	.	.	.
I	17.0	.	.	72	.	.	.	.	.
J	.	.	.	94	.	.	.	.	.
K	4.5	.	.	54	.	.	.	.	.
L	3.7	.	.	96	.	.	.	.	.
M	1.6	.	.	9	.	.	.	.	.
N	4.7	.	.	81	.	.	.	.	.
O	3.5	.	.	28	.	.	.	.	.

5. Consumer price indices (base period: 2000=100)

	2002	2003	2004	2005	2006	2007
General indices	115.6	129.2	145.3	162.7	183.5	206.2
Food index, including non-alcoholic beverages	115.5	131.2	147.9	168.0	183.4	203.4

[1] Persons aged 15 years and over. [2] "De facto" population. [3] Enterprises with 20 or more employees. [4] Enterprises with 20 or more employees, state-owned and municipal enterprises, institutions and organisations. [5] One strike represents one establishment on strike. [6] Excl. workers indirectly involved.

[1] Personnes âgées de 15 ans et plus. [2] Population "de facto". [3] Entreprises occupant 20 salariés et plus. [4] Entreprises occupant 20 salariés et plus, entreprises d'Etat et municipales, institutions et organisations. [5] Une grève représente un établissement en grève. [6] Non compris les travailleurs indirectement impliqués.

[1] Personas de 15 años y más. [2] Población "de facto". [3] Empresas con 20 y más asalariados. [4] Empresas con 20 y más asalariados, empresas estatales y municipales, instituciones y organisaciones. [5] Una huelga representa un establecimiento en huelga. [6] Excl. los trabajadores indirectamente implicados.

Monaco

1. Population active, Emploi et Chômage ('000)

Groupe d'âge	Population active Total	Femmes (%) 2000 Recensement de la population	Emploi Total	Femmes (%) 2000 ★ Recensement de la population	Chômage Total	Femmes (%) 2000 [1] Recensement de la population
Total	12.696	39.8	12.239	39.2	0.457	58.0
17-19	0.046	23.9	0.041	22.0	0.005	40.0
20-24	0.417	46.3	0.390	46.2	0.027	48.1
25-29	1.220	43.8	1.162	43.5	0.058	50.0
30-34	1.834	41.3	1.760	40.7	0.074	56.8
35-39	1.823	41.7	1.772	41.2	0.051	60.8
40-44	1.736	42.3	1.689	41.6	0.047	66.0
45-49	1.582	39.1	1.531	38.4	0.051	60.8
50-54	1.681	38.8	1.619	38.0	0.062	59.7
55-59	1.314	37.1	1.257	36.4	0.057	52.6
60-64	0.618	31.2	0.593	29.3	0.025	76.0
65-69	0.218	25.2	0.218	25.2	0.000	.
70-74	0.097	34.0	0.097	34.0	0.000	.
75+	0.110	32.7	0.110	32.7	0.000	.

2. Population ('000), Taux d'activité et Taux de chômage

Groupe d'âge	Population 2000 Recensement de la population Total	Hommes	Femmes	Taux d'activité 2000 Recensement de la population Total	Hommes	Femmes	Taux de chômage 2000 [1] Recensement de la population Total	Hommes	Femmes
Total	32.020	15.543	16.474	39.7	49.1	30.7	3.6	2.5	5.2
25-54	13.460	6.740	6.718	73.4	86.3	60.4	3.5	2.4	5.0
55+	11.672	5.223	6.449	20.2	29.9	12.5	3.5	2.1	6.1

3. Emploi rémunéré ('000), Durée du travail (hebdomadaire) et Salaires

Données non disponibles.

4. Lésions professionnelles et Grèves et lock-out

Données non disponibles.

5. Indices des prix à la consommation (période de base: 2000=100)

Données non disponibles pour la période de 2002 à 2007.

---

[1] Persons aged 17 years and over.   [1] Personnes âgées de 17 ans et plus.   [1] Personas de 17 años y más.

Mongolia

1. Economically active population, Employment and Unemployment ('000)

	Economically active population		Employment		Unemployment	
	Total	Women (%)	Total	Women (%)	Total	Women (%)
Age group	2005 [1][2] Official estimates		2005 ★ Official estimates		2005 [1][2] Official estimates	
Total	1 001.2	50.7	968.3	50.5	32.9	55.7
0-15	0.4	27.6	.	.	.	.
16-19	84.2	47.8	81.5	47.5	2.7	56.6
20-24	139.9	49.8	135.1	49.5	4.8	56.2
25-29	156.8	50.6	151.4	50.2	5.4	61.9
30-34	157.5	51.6	151.9	51.4	5.6	57.9
35-39	141.8	52.8	136.6	52.6	5.2	58.0
40-44	121.5	53.8	117.2	53.7	4.3	55.1
45-49	97.6	49.9	94.5	50.0	3.1	48.6
50-54	60.5	48.8	59.0	49.1	1.6	36.9
55-59	34.0	44.7	33.8	44.9	0.2	23.9
60+	7.1	42.6	7.1	42.6	-	.

Economic activity (ISIC-Rev.3)	1998 [1][2] Official estimates		2007 [1][2] Official estimates		1998 [1][2] Official estimates	
Total	840.9	48.0	1 024.1	50.8	48.3	52.9
A-B	398.8	46.8	385.6	46.9	5.8	49.0
C Mining and Quarrying	21.8	33.0	44.1	33.0	3.2	53.3
D Manufacturing	62.2	43.1	47.9	54.3	5.1	59.3
E Electricity, Gas and Water Supply	23.6	34.5	31.1	41.6	1.4	46.6
F Construction	31.7	40.3	60.0	43.1	4.2	49.5
G Wholesale and Retail Trade; Repair of Motor Vehicles ...	76.8	49.7	162.2	59.5	2.3	62.7
H Hotels and Restaurants	16.2	69.4	32.4	66.6	0.9	60.9
I Transport, Storage and Communications	35.7	37.2	44.1	34.8	2.3	38.1
J Financial Intermediation	8.1	61.6	17.4	59.1	0.7	56.4
K Real Estate, Renting and Business Activities	5.3	47.2	14.5	53.4	0.2	50.2
L Public Administration and Defence; Compulsory Social ...	31.6	42.8	48.5	43.7	0.7	45.1
M Education	43.7	66.6	64.8	67.7	1.2	59.2
N Health and Social Work	36.8	68.9	40.2	68.3	1.2	64.1
O Other Community, Social and Personal Service Activities	26.8	48.8	19.7	47.8	1.7	58.0
P Households with Employed Persons	3.9	47.6	11.6	53.4	0.7	51.4
X Not classifiable by economic activity	2.9	46.6	.	.	1.6	47.5
Unemployed seeking their first job	15.1	53.0	.	.	15.1	52.9

Occupation (ISCO-88)			2007 [1][2] Official estimates		1998 [1][2] Official estimates	
Total	.	.	1 024.1	50.8	48.3	52.9
1 Legislators, senior officials and managers	.	.	43.1	48.1	1.4	36.1
2 Professionals	.	.	113.2	58.6	4.1	55.1
3 Technicians and associate professionals	.	.	45.1	42.7	3.2	54.7
4 Clerks	.	.	24.4	59.6	1.3	63.2
5 Service workers and shop and market sales workers	.	.	174.3	59.0	3.7	61.3
6 Skilled agricultural and fishery workers	.	.	302.6	47.1	3.6	48.3
7 Craft and related trade workers	.	.	74.2	45.3	5.5	57.7
8 Plant and machine operators and assemblers	.	.	32.2	34.1	4.1	44.7
9 Elementary occupations	.	.	214.9	50.7	6.0	52.3
0 Armed forces	.	.	.	.	0.2	12.4
X Not classifiable by occupation	.	.	.	.	0.1	68.3
Unemployed seeking their first job	.	.	.	.	15.1	52.9

Education level (ISCED-97)					2004 [1][2] Official estimates	
Total	.	.	.	.	35.6	.
X No schooling	.	.	.	.	0.3	.
1 Primary education or first stage of basic education	.	.	.	.	1.8	.
2 Lower secondary or second stage of basic education	.	.	.	.	10.7	.
3 Upper secondary education	.	.	.	.	12.6	.
4 Post-secondary non-tertiary education	.	.	.	.	3.7	.
5A First stage of tertiary education - theoretically based	.	.	.	.	3.1	.
5B First stage of tertiary education - practically oriented	.	.	.	.	3.5	.

Status in employment (ICSE-1993)			2000 [3] Population census			
Total	.	.	779.2	46.0	.	.
1 Employees	.	.	321.4	48.6	.	.
2 Employers	.	.	10.0	28.0	.	.
3 Own-account workers	.	.	243.2	24.1	.	.
4 Members of producers' cooperatives	.	.	3.7	45.9	.	.
5 Contributing family workers	.	.	197.5	70.1	.	.
6 Not classifiable by status	.	.	3.4	23.5	.	.

2. Population ('000), Activity rate and Unemployment rate

	Population 2005 [2][4] Official estimates			Activity rate 2005 [2][4] Official estimates			Unemployment rate 2005 [1][2] Official estimates		
Age group	Total	Men	Women	Total	Men	Women	Total	Men	Women
Total	2 533.4	1 234.9	1 298.6	39.5	40.0	39.1	3.3	3.0	3.6
15+	1 729.8	829.4	900.4	57.9	59.5	56.3	.	.	.
15-24	492.0	239.8	252.2	45.5	47.6	43.6	3.3	2.9	3.8
25-54	1 020.0	491.1	528.9	72.1	72.6	71.7	3.4	3.1	3.7
55+	217.8	98.5	119.3	18.9	23.2	15.3	.	.	.

Mongolia

3. Paid employment ('000), Hours of work (weekly) and Wages

Economic activity (ISIC-Rev.3)	Paid employment			Hours of work			Wages 2005 [5] Labour-related establishment survey Earnings per month / Employees / Tughriks		
	Total	Men	Women	Total	Men	Women	Total	Men	Women
Total	.	.	.	.	.	.	101.2	110.0	92.3
C-Q	.	.	.	.	.	.	103.3	108.7	97.8
A	.	.	.	.	.	.	52.8	57.7	46.1
C	.	.	.	.	.	.	122.8	127.3	105.7
D	.	.	.	.	.	.	100.5	114.9	88.9
E	.	.	.	.	.	.	119.6	121.4	116.8
F	.	.	.	.	.	.	110.9	113.2	102.5
G	.	.	.	.	.	.	73.0	81.7	67.0
H	.	.	.	.	.	.	116.1	122.1	113.7
I	.	.	.	.	.	.	112.4	113.5	111.2
J	.	.	.	.	.	.	163.9	176.5	155.5
K	.	.	.	.	.	.	68.3	67.3	68.9
L	.	.	.	.	.	.	106.2	108.7	100.4
M	.	.	.	.	.	.	92.8	100.6	90.5
N	.	.	.	.	.	.	84.6	97.7	82.0
O	.	.	.	.	.	.	68.4	68.1	68.7

4. Occupational injuries and Strikes and Lockouts

Statistics not available.

5. Consumer price indices (base period: 2000=100)

Ulan Bator	2002	2003	2004	2005	2006	2007
General indices	107.3	112.8	122.1	137.6	.	157.7
Food index, including non-alcoholic beverages [6]	98.5	105.5	118.5	139.4	.	.
Electricity, gas and other fuel indices [7]	148.8	149.4	152.1	165.2	.	.
Clothing indices, including footwear	105.5	108.8	109.9	111.9	.	.

[1] Persons aged 16 years and over. [2] Dec. [3] Persons aged 15 years and over. [4] "De jure" population. [5] Figures in thousands. [6] Incl. alcoholic beverages and tobacco. [7] Incl. "Rent".

[1] Personnes âgées de 16 ans et plus. [2] Déc. [3] Personnes âgées de 15 ans et plus. [4] Population "de jure". [5] Données en milliers. [6] Y compris les boissons alcoolisées et le tabac. [7] Y compris le groupe "loyer".

[1] Personas de 16 años y más. [2] Dic. [3] Personas de 15 años y más. [4] Población "de jure". [5] Cifras en millares. [6] Incl. las bebidas alcohólicas y el tabaco. [7] Incl. el grupo "alquiler".

Montenegro

1. Economically active population, Employment and Unemployment ('000)

Age group	Economically active population Total	Women (%)	Employment Total	Women (%)	Unemployment Total	Women (%)
	2005 [1 2] Labour force survey		2005 [1 2] Labour force survey		2005 [1 2] Labour force survey	
Total	256.6	44.2	178.8	40.9	77.8	51.9
15-19	7.1	27.3	.	.	.	.
20-24	26.7	38.6	.	.	.	.
25-29	30.9	48.2	.	.	.	.
30-34	33.6	46.0	.	.	.	.
35-39	34.2	42.2	.	.	.	.
40-44	36.7	46.3	.	.	.	.
45-49	32.6	50.4	.	.	.	.
50-54	32.3	47.3	.	.	.	.
55-59	15.4	29.1	.	.	.	.
60-64	4.8	45.1	.	.	.	.
65-69	1.6	72.8	.	.	.	.
70-74	0.2	0.0	.	.	.	.
75+	0.5	0.0	.	.	.	.

Economic activity (ISIC-Rev.3)

2005 [1 2] Labour force survey

	Total	Women (%)
Total	178.8	40.9
A Agriculture, Hunting and Forestry	15.2	42.4
B Fishing	0.2	0.0
C Mining and Quarrying	1.7	52.1
D Manufacturing	21.9	22.1
E Electricity, Gas and Water Supply	5.6	17.4
F Construction	5.2	0.0
G Wholesale and Retail Trade; Repair of Motor Vehicles ...	29.9	54.1
H Hotels and Restaurants	11.0	36.8
I Transport, Storage and Communications	14.6	21.9
J Financial Intermediation	2.2	54.7
K Real Estate, Renting and Business Activities	4.5	35.5
L Public Administration and Defence; Compulsory Social ...	22.8	36.7
M Education	13.5	67.6
N Health and Social Work	12.2	67.7
O Other Community, Social and Personal Service Activities	17.8	44.9
P Households with Employed Persons	-	.
Q Extra-Territorial Organizations and Bodies	0.4	0.0

Occupation (ISCO-88)

2005 [1 2] Labour force survey

	Total	Women (%)
Total	178.8	40.9
1 Legislators, senior officials and managers	12.9	19.7
2 Professionals	16.4	50.7
3 Technicians and associate professionals	35.0	63.8
4 Clerks	16.4	43.1
5 Service workers and shop and market sales workers	32.7	58.2
6 Skilled agricultural and fishery workers	14.2	42.8
7 Craft and related trade workers	19.5	3.5
8 Plant and machine operators and assemblers	14.8	1.2
9 Elementary occupations	14.7	46.4
0 Armed forces	2.3	8.4

Education level (ISCED-97)

	Econ. active 2005 [1 2] Total	Women (%)	Employment 2005 ★ Total	Women (%)	Unemployment 2005 [1 2] Total	Women (%)
Total	256.6	44.2	178.8	40.9	77.8	51.9
X No schooling	1.8	48.3	1.4	33.2	0.4	100.0
0 Pre-primary education	5.2	60.5	4.5	66.1	0.8	28.2
1 Primary education or first stage of basic education	29.3	40.7	17.3	36.2	12.0	47.1
2 Lower secondary or second stage of basic education [3]	171.4	43.7	114.2	39.1	57.3	52.8
4 Post-secondary non-tertiary education	18.4	38.3	15.8	35.6	2.5	54.7
5A First stage of tertiary education - theoretically based [4]	30.4	51.4	25.7	51.4	4.8	51.2

Status in employment (ICSE-1993)

2005 [1 2] Labour force survey

	Total	Women (%)
Total	178.8	40.9
1 Employees	143.9	43.4
2, 3	31.0	28.2
5 Contributing family workers	3.9	48.8

2. Population ('000), Activity rate and Unemployment rate

Age group	Population 2005 [2] Labour force survey			Activity rate 2005 [2] Labour force survey			Unemployment rate 2005 [1 2] Labour force survey		
	Total	Men	Women	Total	Men	Women	Total	Men	Women
Total	.	.	.	.	.	.	30.3	26.2	35.5
15+	514	249	265	49.9	57.4	42.9	.	.	.
15-24	104	57	47	32.6	37.8	26.3	.	.	.
25-54	263	125	138	76.0	85.5	67.6	.	.	.
55+	147	67	80	15.3	21.8	9.8	.	.	.

Montenegro

3. Paid employment ('000), Hours of work (weekly) and Wages

Statistics not available.

4. Occupational injuries and Strikes and Lockouts

Statistics not available.

5. Consumer price indices (base period: 2000=100)

Statistics not available for the period 2002-2007.

[1] Persons aged 15 to 64 years. [2] Oct. [3] Levels 2-3. [4] Levels 5-6.   [1] Personnes âgées de 15 à 64 ans. [2] Oct. [3] Niveaux 2-3. [4] Niveaux 5-6.   [1] Personas de 15 a 64 años. [2] Oct. [3] Niveles 2-3. [4] Niveles 5-6.

Montserrat

1. Economically active population, Employment and Unemployment ('000)

	Economically active population		Employment		Unemployment	
	Total	Women (%)	Total	Women (%)	Total	Women (%)
Age group	1980 [1,2] Population census		1987 [3] Official estimates		1987 Official estimates	
Total	5.107	41.6	5.209	.	0.106	.
15-19	0.827	43.8	.	.	.	.
20-24	0.889	45.4	.	.	.	.
25-29	0.766	44.5	.	.	.	.
30-34	0.623	40.6	.	.	.	.
35-39	0.434	42.6	.	.	.	.
40-44	0.305	44.3	.	.	.	.
45-49	0.245	43.7	.	.	.	.
50-54	0.277	37.9	.	.	.	.
55-59	0.226	33.6	.	.	.	.
60-64	0.188	35.6	.	.	.	.
65+	0.327	27.2	.	.	.	.
Economic activity (ISIC-Rev.2)			1991 [1] Population census			
Total	.	.	4.520	42.0	.	.
1 Agriculture, Hunting, Forestry and Fishing	.	.	0.300	23.3	.	.
2 Mining and Quarrying	.	.	0.020	50.0	.	.
3 Manufacturing	.	.	0.240	54.2	.	.
4 Electricity, Gas and Water	.	.	0.110	27.3	.	.
5 Construction	.	.	0.990	2.0	.	.
6 Wholesale and Retail Trade and Restaurants and Hotels	.	.	0.870	58.6	.	.
7 Transport, Storage and Communication	.	.	0.420	28.6	.	.
8 Financing, Insurance, Real Estate and Business Services	.	.	0.240	62.5	.	.
9 Community, Social and Personal Services	.	.	1.310	65.6	.	.
0 Activities not Adequately Defined	.	.	0.040	25.0	.	.

2. Population ('000), Activity rate and Unemployment rate

	Population			Activity rate			Unemployment rate		
Age group	1980 [2] Population census			1980 [2] Population census			1987 Official estimates		
	Total	Men	Women	Total	Men	Women	Total	Men	Women
Total	11.597	5.581	6.016	44.0	53.4	35.3	2.0	.	.
15+	7.945	3.781	4.164	64.3	78.9	51.0	.	.	.
15-24	2.279	1.152	1.127	75.3	82.5	68.0	.	.	.
25-54	3.257	1.642	1.615	81.4	92.8	69.7	.	.	.
55+	2.409	0.987	1.422	30.8	51.6	16.3	.	.	.

3. Paid employment ('000), Hours of work (weekly) and Wages

Statistics not available.

4. Occupational injuries and Strikes and Lockouts

Statistics not available.

5. Consumer price indices (base period: 2000=100)

Statistics not available for the period 2002-2007.

---

[1] Persons aged 15 years and over. [2] May. [3] Excl. armed forces.

[1] Personnes âgées de 15 ans et plus. [2] Mai. [3] Non compris les forces armées.

[1] Personas de 15 años y más. [2] Mayo. [3] Excl. las fuerzas armadas.

Mozambique

1. Population active, Emploi et Chômage ('000)

	Population active		Emploi		Chômage	
	Total	Femmes (%)	Total	Femmes (%)	Total	Femmes (%)
Groupe d'âge	1997 [1,2] Recensement de la population		1997 [1,2] Recensement de la population		1997 [1,2] Recensement de la population	
Total	8 539.9	55.2	8 347.9	55.7	192.0	32.4
7-14	1 417.5	51.6	.	.	.	.
15-19	1 097.3	58.4	.	.	.	.
20-24	1 225.1	59.6	.	.	.	.
25-29	1 032.1	57.9	.	.	.	.
30-34	799.8	55.0	.	.	.	.
35-39	727.9	54.4	.	.	.	.
40-44	521.2	53.7	.	.	.	.
45-49	490.5	52.9	.	.	.	.
50-54	351.4	54.3	.	.	.	.
55-59	300.9	51.5	.	.	.	.
60-64	207.9	51.4	.	.	.	.
65-69	178.3	50.9	.	.	.	.
70-74	78.4	49.5	.	.	.	.
75+	111.6	48.3	.	.	.	.

2. Population ('000), Taux d'activité et Taux de chômage

	Population			Taux d'activité			Taux de chômage		
Groupe d'âge	1997 [2] Recensement de la population			1997 [2] Recensement de la population			1997 [1,2] Recensement de la population		
	Total	Hommes	Femmes	Total	Hommes	Femmes	Total	Hommes	Femmes
Total	.	.	.	.	.	.	2.2	3.4	1.3
15+	8 485.1	3 908.2	4 576.9	83.9	80.4	87.0	.	.	.
15-24	3 093.1	1 411.4	1 681.7	75.1	67.4	81.5	.	.	.
25-54	4 356.8	1 999.1	2 357.7	90.0	88.0	91.8	.	.	.
55+	1 035.2	497.7	537.5	84.7	86.8	82.8	.	.	.

3. Emploi rémunéré ('000), Durée du travail (hebdomadaire) et Salaires

Activité économique (CITI-Rév.2)	Emploi rémunéré 1988 Enquête auprès des établissements, relative au travail			Durée du travail			Salaires		
	Total	Hommes	Femmes	Total	Hommes	Femmes	Total	Hommes	Femmes
Total	201.61	.	.	.	.	.	.	.	.
1	16.94	.	.	.	.	.	.	.	.
2	4.91	.	.	.	.	.	.	.	.
3	116.99	.	.	.	.	.	.	.	.
4	2.91	.	.	.	.	.	.	.	.
5	21.48	.	.	.	.	.	.	.	.
6	6.43	.	.	.	.	.	.	.	.
7	29.25	.	.	.	.	.	.	.	.
9	2.71	.	.	.	.	.	.	.	.

4. Lésions professionnelles et Grèves et lock-out

Données non disponibles.

5. Indices des prix à la consommation (période de base: 2000=100)

	2002	2003	2004	2005	2006	2007
Indices généraux	130.4	145.4	162.0	173.3	196.9	214.9
Indices de l'alimentation, y compris les boissons non alcoolisées	132.3	148.8	164.9	173.9	203.6	224.6
Indices de l'électricité, gaz et autres combustibles	107.7	121.1	.	.	.	.
Indices de l'habillement, y compris les chaussures	119.5	120.7	123.1	124.9	128.7	.
Indices du loyer	136.0	149.1	.	.	.	.
Maputo	2002	2003	2004	2005	2006	2007
Indices généraux	127.4	144.5	162.7	173.2	196.1	212.1
Indices de l'alimentation, y compris les boissons non alcoolisées	126.4	147.9	169.9	175.7	205.6	224.0
Indices de l'électricité, gaz et autres combustibles	110.3	124.5	.	.	.	.
Indices de l'habillement, y compris les chaussures	123.5	122.3	.	.	.	.
Indices du loyer	134.0	142.4	.	.	.	.

[1] Persons aged 7 years and over. [2] Aug.   [1] Personnes âgées de 7 ans et plus. [2] Août.   [1] Personas de 7 años y más. [2] Agosto.

Myanmar

1. Economically active population, Employment and Unemployment ('000)

Age group	Economically active population Total	Women (%)	Employment Total	Women (%)	Unemployment Total	Women (%)
	1983 [1 2 3] Population census		1998 [1] Official estimates		2007 [4] Employment office records	
Total	12 200.0	36.0	18 335.0	.	118.7	.
10-14	462.9	51.8	.	.	.	.
15-19	1 568.0	43.2	.	.	.	.
20-24	1 878.9	35.8	.	.	.	.
25-29	1 703.2	33.4	.	.	.	.
30-34	1 357.1	32.7	.	.	.	.
35-39	1 060.7	32.7	.	.	.	.
40-44	930.5	34.6	.	.	.	.
45-49	886.8	34.3	.	.	.	.
50-54	799.2	35.0	.	.	.	.
55-59	597.7	34.5	.	.	.	.
60-64	440.4	35.9	.	.	.	.
65+	514.6	34.4	.	.	.	.

Economic activity (ISIC-Rev.2)			1998 [1] Official estimates			
Total	.	.	18 359	.	.	.
1 Agriculture, Hunting, Forestry and Fishing	.	.	11 507	.	.	.
2 Mining and Quarrying	.	.	121	.	.	.
3 Manufacturing	.	.	1 666	.	.	.
4 Electricity, Gas and Water	.	.	24	.	.	.
5 Construction	.	.	400	.	.	.
6 Wholesale and Retail Trade and Restaurants and Hotels	.	.	1 781	.	.	.
7 Transport, Storage and Communication	.	.	495	.	.	.
8 Financing, Insurance, Real Estate and Business Services	.	.	597	.	.	.
9-0	.	.	1 744	.	.	.

2. Population ('000), Activity rate and Unemployment rate

Age group	Population 1983 [1 3] Population census			Activity rate 1983 [1 3] Population census			Unemployment rate		
	Total	Men	Women	Total	Men	Women	Total	Men	Women
15+	20 965.3	10 276.5	10 688.8	56.0	73.8	38.9	.	.	.
15-24	7 021.8	3 454.6	3 567.2	49.1	60.7	37.8	.	.	.
25-54	10 777.6	5 312.9	5 464.7	62.5	84.2	41.5	.	.	.
55+	3 165.9	1 509.1	1 656.9	49.0	67.0	32.7	.	.	.

3. Paid employment ('000), Hours of work (weekly) and Wages

Economic activity (ISIC-Rev.2)	Paid employment			Hours of work 2007 [5 6] Labour-related establishment survey Hours actually worked / Employees			Wages 2005 [6 7] Labour-related establishment survey / Employees / Kyat		
	Total	Men	Women	Total	Men	Women	Total	Men	Women
2-9	.	.	.	8.0	.	.	.	.	.
2 [8]	.	.	.	8.0	.	.	.	36.89	36.09
3	.	.	.	8.0	.	.	.	31.89	28.36
5	.	.	.	8.0	.	.	.	41.08	42.66
7 [9]	.	.	.	8.0	.	.	.	32.40	32.26

4. Occupational injuries and Strikes and Lockouts

Economic activity (ISIC-Rev.3)	Rates of fatal injuries 2007 [10] Labour inspectorate records Per 100,000 employees Reported injuries			Rates of non-fatal injuries 2007 [10 11] Labour inspectorate records Per 100,000 employees Reported injuries			Strikes and lockouts 2007 Administrative records and related sources		
	Total	Men	Women	Total	Men	Women	Strikes and lockouts	Workers involved	Days not worked
Total	7	12	1	33	49	11	7	1 019	1 019
C	36	36	0	117	117	0	.	.	.
D	6	7	1	26	24	31	7	1 019	1 019
E	0	0	0	108	109	109	.	.	.
G	12	12	0	62	62	0	.	.	.

5. Consumer price indices (base period: 2000=100)

	2002	2003	2004	2005	2006	2007
General indices	190.2	259.8	271.6	297.1	356.5	481.3
Food index, including non-alcoholic beverages	201.2	274.3	277.5	303.2	365.7	493.9
Electricity, gas and other fuel indices	163.3	219.3	258.1	281.6	370.0	491.7
Clothing indices, including footwear	195.8	272.8	300.5	299.6	337.6	462.9
Rent indices	175.3	245.4	272.2	333.0	388.8	518.7

Myanmar

[1] Excl. armed forces. [2] Persons aged 10 years and over. [3] March. [4] Persons aged 18 years and over. [5] Per day. [6] Regular employees. [7] March and Sept. [8] Metal mining. [9] Excl. storage and communication; incl. sea transport. [10] Year ending in March of the year indicated. [11] Incapacity of 2 days or more.

[1] Non compris les forces armées. [2] Personnes âgées de 10 ans et plus. [3] Mars. [4] Personnes âgées de 18 ans et plus. [5] Par jour. [6] Salariés stables. [7] mars et sept. [8] Extraction de minerais métalliques. [9] Non compris les entrepôts et communications; y compris les transports maritimes. [10] Année se terminant en mars de l'année indiquée. [11] Incapacité de 2 jours et plus.

[1] Excl. las fuerzas armadas. [2] Personas de 10 años y más. [3] Marzo. [4] Personas de 18 años y más. [5] Por día. [6] Asalariados estables. [7] marzo y sept. [8] Extracción de minerales metálicos. [9] Excl. almacenaje y comunicaciones; incl. los transportes marítimos. [10] Año que termina en marzo del año indicado. [11] Incapacidad de 2 días y más.

Namibia

1. Economically active population, Employment and Unemployment ('000)

	Economically active population		Employment		Unemployment	
	Total	Women (%)	Total	Women (%)	Total	Women (%)
Age group	2004 [1] Labour force survey		2004 ★ Labour force survey		2004 [2] Labour force survey	
Total	493.448	45.6	385.329	43.8	108.119	51.9
15-19	25.173	47.7	14.289	44.6	10.884	51.8
20-24	80.830	48.1	47.516	43.2	33.314	55.0
25-29	89.983	45.2	64.671	41.8	25.312	54.0
30-34	80.384	46.2	63.997	45.7	16.387	48.0
35-39	67.263	47.2	56.837	46.0	10.426	54.0
40-44	52.866	46.9	46.320	46.3	6.546	51.7
45-49	36.235	44.4	33.821	44.8	2.414	38.4
50-54	27.016	41.8	25.810	42.2	1.206	33.5
55-59	18.509	37.5	17.408	39.0	1.101	14.3
60-64	7.750	30.4	6.900	34.1	0.850	0.0
65+	5.956	44.1	5.700	43.9	0.256	49.2
?	1.483	15.5	1.483	15.5	0.000	.
Economic activity (ISIC-Rev.2)	1991 [3][4] Population census					
Total	493.580	43.6	.	.	.	.
1 Agriculture, Hunting, Forestry and Fishing	189.929	47.4	.	.	.	.
2 Mining and Quarrying	14.686	5.8	.	.	.	.
3 Manufacturing	22.884	52.9	.	.	.	.
4 Electricity, Gas and Water	2.974	5.0	.	.	.	.
5 Construction	18.638	2.7	.	.	.	.
6 Wholesale and Retail Trade and Restaurants and Hotels	37.820	48.0	.	.	.	.
7 Transport, Storage and Communication	9.322	14.1	.	.	.	.
8 Financing, Insurance, Real Estate and Business Services	8.547	39.4	.	.	.	.
9 Community, Social and Personal Services	5.827	37.1	.	.	.	.
0 Activities not Adequately Defined	110.574	47.5	.	.	.	.
Unemployed seeking their first job	73.379	46.2	.	.	.	.
Economic activity (ISIC-Rev.3)			2004 [2] Labour force survey			
Total	.	.	385.329	43.8	.	.
A Agriculture, Hunting and Forestry	.	.	102.636	36.7	.	.
B Fishing	.	.	12.720	37.6	.	.
C Mining and Quarrying	.	.	7.562	21.9	.	.
D Manufacturing	.	.	23.755	49.1	.	.
E Electricity, Gas and Water Supply	.	.	6.151	18.2	.	.
F Construction	.	.	19.605	6.7	.	.
G Wholesale and Retail Trade; Repair of Motor Vehicles ...	.	.	53.895	49.9	.	.
H Hotels and Restaurants	.	.	13.132	55.2	.	.
I Transport, Storage and Communications	.	.	15.861	19.7	.	.
J Financial Intermediation	.	.	7.582	53.8	.	.
K Real Estate, Renting and Business Activities	.	.	9.375	43.7	.	.
L Public Administration and Defence; Compulsory Social ...	.	.	30.685	34.1	.	.
M Education	.	.	31.168	60.5	.	.
N Health and Social Work	.	.	14.010	74.8	.	.
O Other Community, Social and Personal Service Activities	.	.	12.632	40.8	.	.
P Households with Employed Persons	.	.	24.081	83.1	.	.
Q Extra-Territorial Organizations and Bodies	.	.	0.072	0.0	.	.
X Not classifiable by economic activity	.	.	0.407	25.1	.	.
Occupation (ISCO-1968)	1991 [3][4] Population census					
Total	493.580	43.6	.	.	.	.
0/1 Professional, technical and related workers	41.643	40.9	.	.	.	.
2 Administrative and managerial workers	9.452	20.8	.	.	.	.
3 Clerical and related workers	18.574	63.8	.	.	.	.
4 Sales workers	18.325	63.8	.	.	.	.
5 Service workers	19.521	37.6	.	.	.	.
6 Agriculture, animal husbandry and forestry workers ...	152.562	57.4	.	.	.	.
7/8/9 Production and related workers, transport equipment ...	65.918	17.5	.	.	.	.
X Not classifiable by occupation	94.206	34.0	.	.	.	.
Unemployed seeking their first job	73.379	46.2	.	.	.	.
Occupation (ISCO-88)			2004 [2] Labour force survey			
Total	.	.	385.329	43.8	.	.
1 Legislators, senior officials and managers	.	.	10.754	36.0	.	.
2 Professionals	.	.	34.258	55.6	.	.
3 Technicians and associate professionals	.	.	20.154	47.0	.	.
4 Clerks	.	.	25.565	72.7	.	.
5 Service workers and shop and market sales workers	.	.	52.671	52.5	.	.
6 Skilled agricultural and fishery workers	.	.	52.285	45.4	.	.
7 Craft and related trade workers	.	.	56.203	24.4	.	.
8 Plant and machine operators and assemblers	.	.	17.452	6.5	.	.
9 Elementary occupations	.	.	112.216	45.3	.	.
0 Armed forces	.	.	3.262	18.6	.	.
X Not classifiable by occupation	.	.	0.509	20.2	.	.

Namibia

Education level (ISCED-97)	2004 [1] Labour force survey						
Total	493.4	45.6	.	.	.	.	.
X No schooling	58.1	33.4					
0 Pre-primary education	0.3	32.6					
1 Primary education or first stage of basic education	139.1	41.8					
2 Lower secondary or second stage of basic education	158.8	49.6					
3 Upper secondary education	96.4	50.3					
4 Post-secondary non-tertiary education	1.7	53.8					
5A First stage of tertiary education - theoretically based	25.7	50.3					
5B First stage of tertiary education - practically oriented	8.0	49.8					
6 Second stage of tertiary education	5.5	39.0					

Status in employment (ICSE-58)	1991 [3 4] Population census						
Total	493.580	43.6					
1 Employers and own-account workers	87.953	49.3					
2 Employees	242.328	31.5					
3 Unpaid family workers	88.150	68.6					
4 Not classifiable by status	75.149	46.2					

Status in employment (ICSE-1993)			2004 [2] Labour force survey				
Total	.	.	385.329	43.8	.	.	.
1 Employees			280.329	41.4			
2 Employers			21.686	33.7			
3 Own-account workers			64.404	58.4			
5 Contributing family workers			16.867	58.5			
6 Not classifiable by status			1.696	44.8			

2. Population ('000), Activity rate and Unemployment rate

Age group	Population 2004 [6] Labour force survey			Activity rate 2004 [5] Labour force survey			Unemployment rate 2004 [2] Labour force survey		
	Total	Men	Women	Total	Men	Women	Total	Men	Women
Total	1 727.7	824.7	903.0	28.6	32.6	24.9	21.9	19.4	25.0
15+	1 024.1	473.7	550.4	48.0	56.5	40.8	22.1	19.3	25.0
15-24	345.7	165.2	180.4	30.7	33.4	28.2	41.7	36.7	47.1
25-54	523.6	241.2	282.5	67.6	79.6	57.3	17.6	15.4	19.7
55+	154.8	67.3	87.5	20.8	30.2	13.6	6.9	9.5	2.4

3. Paid employment ('000), Hours of work (weekly) and Wages

Economic activity (ISIC-Rev.2)	Paid employment			Hours of work			Wages 1992 Labour-related establishment census Earnings per month / Employees / Dollar		
	Total	Men	Women	Total	Men	Women	Total	Men	Women
Total	.	.	.	.	.	.	1 761	.	.
1							586		
2							3 001		
3							1 201		
4							2 138		
5							1 043		
6							1 166		
7							1 588		
8							2 677		
9							1 956		

Economic activity (ISIC-Rev.3)	Paid employment			Hours of work 2004 Labour force survey Hours actually worked / Total employment			Wages		
	Total	Men	Women	Total	Men	Women	Total	Men	Women
Total	.	.	.	63	64	63	.	.	.
A-B				74	72	76			
C-Q				60	60	60			
A				76	75	79			
B				57	57	58			
C				61	60	61			
D				65	63	67			
E				57	57	59			
F				61	62	57			
G				58	57	58			
H				68	75	64			
I				59	57	65			
J				59	60	58			
K				63	66	59			
L				58	59	58			
M				60	63	58			
N				60	61	60			
O				58	58	59			
P				62	63	62			
Q				35	72	.			

Namibia

4. Occupational injuries and Strikes and Lockouts

Economic activity (ISIC-Rev.2)	Rates of fatal injuries 2001 Insurance records Per 100,000 workers employed Compensated injuries			Rates of non-fatal injuries			Strikes and lockouts 1994 [6] Source unknown		
	Total	Men	Women	Total	Men	Women	Strikes and lockouts	Workers involved	Days not worked
Total	5	.	.	.	.	.	7	.	.
1	.	.	.	.	.	.	0	.	.
2	.	.	.	.	.	.	0	.	.
3	.	.	.	.	.	.	4	.	.
4	.	.	.	.	.	.	0	.	.
5	.	.	.	.	.	.	1	.	.
6	.	.	.	.	.	.	0	.	.
7	.	.	.	.	.	.	2	.	.
8	.	.	.	.	.	.	0	.	.
9	.	.	.	.	.	.	0	.	.
0	.	.	.	.	.	.	0	.	.

5. Consumer price indices (base period: 2000=100)

[7]	2002	2003	2004	2005	2006	2007
General indices	100.0	107.1	111.6	114.1	119.9	127.9
Food index, including non-alcoholic beverages	100.0	109.5	110.4	112.0	119.3	133.8
Clothing indices, including footwear	100.0	104.1	104.6	103.5	100.5	103.8
Rent indices [8][9]	100.0	107.3	114.6	116.4	120.1	124.3

[1] Persons aged 15 years and over. [2] Persons aged 15 to 69 years. [3] Persons aged 10 years and over. [4] Nov. [5] "De jure" population. [6] Strikes only. [7] Index base 2002=100. [8] Housing. [9] Incl. water, electricity, gas and other fuels.

[1] Personnes âgées de 15 ans et plus. [2] Personnes âgées de 15 à 69 ans. [3] Personnes âgées de 10 ans et plus. [4] Nov. [5] Population "de jure". [6] Grèves seulement. [7] Indice base 2002=100. [8] Logement. [9] Y compris l'eau, l'électricité, le gaz et autres combustibles.

[1] Personas de 15 años y más. [2] Personas de 15 a 69 años. [3] Personas de 10 años y más. [4] Nov. [5] Población "de jure". [6] Huelgas solamente. [7] Indice base 2002=100. [8] Vivienda. [9] Incl. el agua, la electricidad, el gas y otros combustibles.

Nepal

1. Economically active population, Employment and Unemployment ('000)

	Economically active population		Employment		Unemployment	
	Total	Women (%)	Total	Women (%)	Total	Women (%)
Age group	1999 Labour force survey		1999 ★ Labour force survey		1999 [1] Labour force survey	
Total	11 628	50.6	11 450	50.7	178	44.9
5-9	510	55.9	510	55.9	-	.
10-14	1 476	53.4	1 476	53.4	-	.
15-19	1 486	51.9	1 451	52.3	35	34.3
20-24	1 332	53.3	1 283	53.8	49	40.8
25-29	1 254	51.7	1 222	51.7	32	50.0
30-44	2 961	50.9	2 915	50.8	46	54.3
45-59	1 779	47.0	1 767	47.1	12	41.7
60+	831	40.3	827	40.1	4	75.0

Economic activity (ISIC-Rev.3)			2001 [2,3] Population census			
Total	.	.	9 900.2	43.4	.	.
A Agriculture, Hunting and Forestry	.	.	6 496.2	48.1	.	.
B Fishing	.	.	8.5	14.6	.	.
C Mining and Quarrying	.	.	16.0	35.6	.	.
D Manufacturing	.	.	872.3	47.6	.	.
E Electricity, Gas and Water Supply	.	.	148.2	77.6	.	.
F Construction	.	.	286.4	17.8	.	.
G Wholesale and Retail Trade; Repair of Motor Vehicles ...	.	.	863.8	39.6	.	.
H Hotels and Restaurants	.	.	120.9	34.5	.	.
I Transport, Storage and Communications	.	.	161.6	3.6	.	.
J Financial Intermediation	.	.	46.8	14.6	.	.
K Real Estate, Renting and Business Activities	.	.	29.9	13.6	.	.
L Public Administration and Defence; Compulsory Social ...	.	.	301.0	11.8	.	.
M Education	.	.	228.4	26.0	.	.
N Health and Social Work	.	.	61.8	29.4	.	.
O Other Community, Social and Personal Service Activities	.	.	72.6	14.6	.	.
P Households with Employed Persons	.	.	105.1	40.2	.	.
Q Extra-Territorial Organizations and Bodies	.	.	58.3	6.3	.	.
X Not classifiable by economic activity	.	.	22.4	41.3	.	.

Occupation (ISCO-88)			2001 [2,3] Population census			
Total	.	.	9 900.2	43.4	.	.
1 Legislators, senior officials and managers	.	.	56.5	13.8	.	.
2 Professionals	.	.	243.7	23.3	.	.
3 Technicians and associate professionals	.	.	170.2	14.4	.	.
4 Clerks	.	.	201.1	12.8	.	.
5 Service workers and shop and market sales workers	.	.	781.0	24.7	.	.
6 Skilled agricultural and fishery workers	.	.	5 901.4	49.3	.	.
7 Craft and related trade workers	.	.	916.8	44.6	.	.
8 Plant and machine operators and assemblers	.	.	141.4	13.0	.	.
9 Elementary occupations	.	.	1 479.8	43.6	.	.
X Not classifiable by occupation	.	.	8.4	50.9	.	.

Education level (ISCED-76)	1995 [4] Labour force survey					
Total	139.9	50.2	.	.	.	.
X No schooling	29.3	51.8	.	.	.	.
1 First level	40.0	52.8	.	.	.	.
2 Second level, first stage	42.4	50.6	.	.	.	.
3 Second level, second stage	11.3	48.4	.	.	.	.
5 Third level, first stage, leading to an award not equivalent ...	5.6	42.2	.	.	.	.
6 Third level, first stage, leading to a first university degree ...	5.2	35.5	.	.	.	.
7 Third level, second stage	1.0	39.3	.	.	.	.
9 Education not definable by level	0.0	36.4	.	.	.	.
? Level not stated	5.1	48.1	.	.	.	.

Status in employment (ICSE-1993)			2001 [2,3] Population census			
Total	.	.	9 900.2	43.4	.	.
1 Employees	.	.	2 438.3	22.5	.	.
2 Employers	.	.	376.3	42.5	.	.
3 Own-account workers	.	.	6 210.8	48.8	.	.
5 Contributing family workers	.	.	874.7	63.2	.	.

2. Population ('000), Activity rate and Unemployment rate

	Population			Activity rate			Unemployment rate		
Age group	2001 [3,5] Population census			2001 [3,5] Population census			1999 [1] Labour force survey		
	Total	Men	Women	Total	Men	Women	Total	Men	Women
Total	.	.	.	.	.	.	1.8	2.0	1.7
15+	13 788.347	6 796.770	6 991.577	70.9	81.7	60.4	1.8	2.0	1.7
15-24	4 405.770	2 132.568	2 273.202	58.0	61.8	54.4	3.0	4.0	2.2
25-54	7 303.105	3 600.752	3 702.353	81.5	95.5	67.9	.	.	.
55+	2 079.472	1 063.450	1 016.022	61.0	74.7	46.6	.	.	.

Nepal

3. Paid employment ('000), Hours of work (weekly) and Wages

Economic activity (ISIC-Rev.3)	Paid employment 1999 [1] Labour force survey			Hours of work 1999 [1,6] Labour force survey Hours actually worked / Employees			Wages 1999 [1,6,7] Labour force survey Earnings per month / Employees / Rupee		
	Total	Men	Women	Total	Men	Women	Total	Men	Women
Total	1 473	1 118	356	46	47	41	2 143	2 389	1 368
A	546	330	216	44	46	40	1 246	1 419	981
B	0	0	0	47	47	.	2 827	2 827	.
C	3	3	0	41	39	60	2 073	1 949	3 543
D	224	181	43	50	51	45	2 567	2 867	1 292
E	24	22	1	44	45	30	3 373	3 370	3 427
F	207	184	23	47	47	42	2 298	2 408	1 408
G	35	33	2	57	57	56	2 331	2 333	2 310
H	13	12	1	57	58	56	2 988	3 014	2 754
I	83	80	3	54	54	44	2 950	2 922	3 722
J	19	16	2	42	42	41	4 468	4 557	3 866
K	10	8	2	48	48	47	3 399	3 420	3 310
L	67	62	5	43	43	41	3 078	3 092	2 921
M	157	121	36	38	38	38	2 844	2 944	2 505
N	28	22	6	44	45	39	2 948	2 941	2 971
O	21	18	3	45	46	43	2 561	2 578	2 459
P	31	20	11	46	47	43	1 519	1 688	1 213
Q	6	5	1	46	46	44	3 425	3 576	2 842

Share of women in wage employment in the non-agricultural sector [1] (1999 - Labour force survey): **15.1%**

4. Occupational injuries and Strikes and Lockouts

Economic activity (ISIC-Rev.3)	Rates of fatal injuries			Rates of non-fatal injuries			Strikes and lockouts 2002 [8] Labour relations records		
	Total	Men	Women	Total	Men	Women	Strikes and lockouts	Workers involved	Days not worked
Total	.	.	.	.	.	.	22	.	12 355

5. Consumer price indices (base period: 2000=100)

	2002	2003	2004	2005	2006	2007
General indices	105.9	112.0	115.2	123.2	132.6	140.5
Food index, including non-alcoholic beverages	104.4	110.1	112.9	120.3	129.1	139.6
Electricity, gas and other fuel indices [9]	106.3	122.8	130.0	157.4	185.4	191.4
Clothing indices, including footwear [10]	104.4	106.3	108.4	111.5	114.1	116.6
Rent indices	110.9	116.4	120.9	126.2	131.9	179.0

[1] Persons aged 15 years and over. [2] Persons aged 10 years and over. [3] June. [4] Persons aged 6 years and over. [5] "De jure" population. [6] 12 months ending in May of year indicated; main occupation. [7] Fluctuations in wages due to small sample size. [8] Financial year ending in year indicated. [9] Incl. water. [10] Excl. footwear.

[1] Personnes âgées de 15 ans et plus. [2] Personnes âgées de 10 ans et plus. [3] Juin. [4] Personnes âgées de 6 ans et plus. [5] Population "de jure". [6] 12 mois se terminant en mai de l'année indiquée; occupation principale. [7] Fluctuations des salaires dues à la faible taille de l'échantillon. [8] Année fiscale se terminant en l'année indiquée. [9] Y compris l'eau. [10] Non compris la chaussure.

[1] Personas de 15 años y más. [2] Personas de 10 años y más. [3] Junio. [4] Personas de 6 años y más. [5] Población "de jure". [6] 12 meses que terminan en mayo del año indicado; ocupación principal. [7] Fluctuaciones de los salarios debidas al pequeño tamaño muestral. [8] Año fiscal que se termina en el año indicado. [9] Incl. el agua. [10] Excl. el calzado.

Netherlands

1. Economically active population, Employment and Unemployment ('000)

	Economically active population		Employment		Unemployment	
	Total	Women (%)	Total	Women (%)	Total	Women (%)
Age group	2007 [1] Labour force survey		2007 ★ Labour force survey		2007 [2] Labour force survey	
Total	8 611.0	45.5	8 311.0	45.3	300.0	52.3
15-19	631.0	49.8	575.0	49.4	56.0	53.6
20-24	794.0	48.4	759.0	48.4	35.0	48.6
25-29	878.0	47.7	854.0	47.4	24.0	58.3
30-34	931.0	46.6	907.0	46.4	24.0	54.2
35-39	1 126.0	46.0	1 099.0	45.7	27.0	59.3
40-44	1 136.0	46.0	1 104.0	45.5	32.0	62.5
45-49	1 063.0	45.8	1 034.0	45.6	29.0	55.2
50-54	910.0	44.2	882.0	43.9	28.0	53.6
55-59	744.0	40.3	714.0	40.5	30.0	36.7
60-64	290.0	36.6	275.0	37.1	15.0	26.7
65-69	68.0	32.4	.	.	.	.
70-74	28.0	21.4	.	.	.	.
75+	13.0	38.5	.	.	.	.
Economic activity (ISIC-Rev.3)			2005 [1] Labour force survey			
Total	.	.	7 959	44.4	.	.
A-B	.	.	273	29.3	.	.
C Mining and Quarrying	.	.	7	28.6	.	.
D Manufacturing	.	.	1 033	22.3	.	.
E Electricity, Gas and Water Supply	.	.	43	23.3	.	.
F Construction	.	.	488	8.8	.	.
G Wholesale and Retail Trade; Repair of Motor Vehicles ...	.	.	1 153	47.7	.	.
H Hotels and Restaurants	.	.	319	53.0	.	.
I Transport, Storage and Communications	.	.	489	25.6	.	.
J Financial Intermediation	.	.	258	44.6	.	.
K Real Estate, Renting and Business Activities	.	.	945	39.6	.	.
L Public Administration and Defence; Compulsory Social ...	.	.	529	37.1	.	.
M Education	.	.	508	59.6	.	.
N Health and Social Work	.	.	1 204	81.2	.	.
O Other Community, Social and Personal Service Activities	.	.	316	55.7	.	.
P Households with Employed Persons	.	.	4	100.0	.	.
Q Extra-Territorial Organizations and Bodies	.	.	-	.	.	.
X Not classifiable by economic activity	.	.	390	46.7	.	.
Occupation (ISCO-88)			2005 [1] Labour force survey			
Total	.	.	7 959	44.4	.	.
1 Legislators, senior officials and managers	.	.	785	25.2	.	.
2 Professionals	.	.	1 438	45.6	.	.
3 Technicians and associate professionals	.	.	1 426	51.3	.	.
4 Clerks	.	.	1 001	68.5	.	.
5 Service workers and shop and market sales workers	.	.	1 110	69.7	.	.
6 Skilled agricultural and fishery workers	.	.	126	27.0	.	.
7 Craft and related trade workers	.	.	757	5.0	.	.
8 Plant and machine operators and assemblers	.	.	471	10.6	.	.
9 Elementary occupations	.	.	737	46.8	.	.
0 Armed forces	.	.	35	8.6	.	.
X Not classifiable by occupation	.	.	71	31.0	.	.
Education level (ISCED-97)	2007 [1] Labour force survey		2007 ★ Labour force survey		2007 [2] Labour force survey	
Total	8 310.0	45.3	8 010.0	45.0	300.0	52.3
X No schooling	32.0	31.3	28.0	28.6	4.0	50.0
0 Pre-primary education	408.0	38.7	406.0	38.9	2.0	.
1 Primary education or first stage of basic education	1 709.0	45.1	1 672.0	45.0	37.0	45.9
2 Lower secondary or second stage of basic education	3 350.0	46.3	3 263.0	46.1	87.0	56.3
3 Upper secondary education	284.0	47.2	172.0	43.0	112.0	53.6
4 Post-secondary non-tertiary education	2 252.0	45.8	2 245.0	45.7	7.0	57.1
5A First stage of tertiary education - theoretically based	132.0	41.7	84.0	36.9	48.0	50.0
5B First stage of tertiary education - practically oriented	59.0	30.5	56.0	32.1	3.0	.
6 Second stage of tertiary education	84.0	39.3	84.0	39.3	-	.
Status in employment (ICSE-1993)	2005 [1] Labour force survey		2005 [1] Labour force survey			
Total	8 308.0	45.1	7 959.0	44.4	.	.
1 Employees	6 897.0	46.4	.	.	.	.
1,4	.	.	6 868.0	45.9	.	.
2 Employers	936.0	32.5	.	.	.	.
2,3	.	.	1 041.0	32.9	.	.
5 Contributing family workers	44.0	79.5	50.0	80.0	.	.
6 Not classifiable by status	432.0	48.6	.	.	.	.

Netherlands

2. Population ('000), Activity rate and Unemployment rate

Age group	Population 2007 Labour force survey			Activity rate 2007 Labour force survey			Unemployment rate 2007 [2] Labour force survey		
	Total	Men	Women	Total	Men	Women	Total	Men	Women
Total							3.5	3.1	4.0
15+	13 222.0	6 511.0	6 712.0	65.1	72.1	58.4	3.5	3.0	4.0
15-24	1 957.0	994.0	963.0	72.8	73.1	72.5	6.4	5.9	6.7
25-54	6 958.0	3 495.0	3 465.0	86.9	93.3	80.3	2.7	2.1	3.4
55+	4 307.0	2 022.0	2 284.0	26.5	34.9	19.2	.	.	.

3. Paid employment ('000), Hours of work (weekly) and Wages

Economic activity (ISIC-Rev.3)	Paid employment 2007 [1] Labour force survey			Hours of work 2005 [3 4 5] Labour-related establishment survey Hours usually worked / Employees			Wages 2005 [5 6 7] Labour-related establishment survey Earnings per month / Employees / Euro		
	Total	Men	Women	Total	Men	Women	Total	Men	Women
Total	7 171	3 802	3 370	29.7	34.1	24.3	2 836	2 944	2 429
A-B	130	92	38	29.4	32.3	21.8	2 197	2 248	1 726
C-Q	.	.	.	29.7	34.1	24.4	2 846	2 956	2 434
C	9	7	2	38.0	38.7	33.5	4 413	4 508	.
D	972	752	220	35.2	37.0	28.5	2 689	2 740	2 282
E	42	31	11	36.3	37.7	31.4	3 530	3 620	2 862
F	392	358	35	37.3	38.4	25.9	2 627	2 637	2 322
G	1 035	526	509	27.7	32.1	22.4	2 523	2 676	1 994
H	303	137	166	21.0	23.6	18.8	2 018	2 118	1 799
I	470	345	125	32.6	34.7	26.8	2 575	2 630	2 237
J	247	130	118	33.0	36.0	29.3	3 613	3 955	2 737
K	788	447	341	29.7	33.2	24.8	3 164	3 352	2 536
L	537	325	212	33.1	35.5	29.1	3 058	3 145	2 738
M	509	196	312	29.0	33.2	26.1	3 221	3 444	2 824
N	1 216	197	1 018	24.2	30.9	22.8	2 972	3 471	2 519
O	255	116	140	27.2	30.7	23.9	2 773	2 913	2 440
P	3	0	3	.	.	.	.	.	.
Q	-	-	-	.	.	.	.	.	.
X	264	143	121	.	.	.	.	.	.

Share of women in wage employment in the non-agricultural sector [1] (2007 - Labour force survey): **47.4%**

4. Occupational injuries and Strikes and Lockouts

Economic activity (ISIC-Rev.2)	Rates of fatal injuries 1989 [8] Insurance records Per 1,000 workers insured Reported injuries			Rates of non-fatal injuries			Strikes and lockouts		
	Total	Men	Women	Total	Men	Women	Strikes and lockouts	Workers involved	Days not worked
Total	0.017	.	.	.	.	.	.	.	.
1	0.037	.	.	.	.	.	.	.	.
2	0.000	.	.	.	.	.	.	.	.
3	0.015	.	.	.	.	.	.	.	.
5	0.041	.	.	.	.	.	.	.	.
6	0.016	.	.	.	.	.	.	.	.
7	0.047	.	.	.	.	.	.	.	.
8	0.000	.	.	.	.	.	.	.	.
9 [9]	0.004	.	.	.	.	.	.	.	.

Economic activity (ISIC-Rev.3)	Rates of fatal injuries			Rates of non-fatal injuries			Strikes and lockouts 2007 Special data collection		
	Total	Men	Women	Total	Men	Women	Strikes and lockouts	Workers involved	Days not worked
Total	.	.	.	.	.	.	20	20 700	26 400
A	.	.	.	.	.	.	0	0	0
B	.	.	.	.	.	.	0	0	0
C	.	.	.	.	.	.	0	0	0
D	.	.	.	.	.	.	4	2 800	4 100
E	.	.	.	.	.	.	0	0	0
F	.	.	.	.	.	.	0	0	0
G	.	.	.	.	.	.	0	0	0
H	.	.	.	.	.	.	0	0	0
I	.	.	.	.	.	.	7	2 600	7 200
J	.	.	.	.	.	.	0	0	0
K	.	.	.	.	.	.	4	1 200	1 000
L	.	.	.	.	.	.	5	14 100	14 200
O	.	.	.	.	.	.	0	0	0

5. Consumer price indices (base period: 2000=100)

	2002	2003	2004	2005	2006	2007
General indices	107.6	109.9	111.2	113.1	114.4	116.2
Food index, including non-alcoholic beverages	110.5	111.7	107.8	106.5	108.3	109.4
Electricity, gas and other fuel indices	121.2	130.0	134.6	153.5	168.2	175.1
Clothing indices, including footwear	105.0	101.8	99.9	97.3	97.8	99.0
Rent indices	105.5	108.8	112.2	115.0	117.7	120.1
General index, excluding housing	107.9	110.0	110.9	112.6	113.6	115.3

Netherlands

[1] Persons aged 15 years and over. [2] Persons aged 15 to 64 years. [3] Excl. overtime. [4] Full and part-time employees. [5] Dec. [6] Excl. overtime payments. [7] Full-time employees only. [8] Per 1,000 full-time equivalent years of persons insured. [9] Excl. government, state hospitals, state and subsidized education.

[1] Personnes âgées de 15 ans et plus. [2] Personnes âgées de 15 à 64 ans. [3] Non compris les heures supplémentaires. [4] Salariés à temps complet et à temps partiel. [5] Déc. [6] Non compris la rémunération des heures supplémentaires. [7] Salariés à plein temps seulement. [8] Pour 1 000 années équivalentes à plein temps des personnes assurées. [9] Non compris le gouvernement, les hôpitaux d'Etat et l'éducation publique et subsidiée.

[1] Personas de 15 años y más. [2] Personas de 15 a 64 años. [3] Excl. las horas extraordinarias. [4] Asalariados a tiempo completo y a tiempo parcial. [5] Dic. [6] Excl. los pagos por horas extraordinarias. [7] Asalariados a tiempo completo solamente. [8] Por 1 000 años equivalentes a tiempo completo de las personas aseguradas. [9] Excl. gobierno, hospitales estatales, educación pública y subsidiada.

Netherlands Antilles

1. Economically active population, Employment and Unemployment ('000)

	Economically active population		Employment		Unemployment	
	Total	Women (%)	Total	Women (%)	Total	Women (%)
Age group	2007 [1][2][3] Labour force survey		2007 ★ Labour force survey		2007 [1][2][3] Labour force survey	
Total	61.123	51.9	53.778	50.8	7.345	60.3
15-19	1.092	32.5	0.737	29.9	0.355	38.0
20-24	4.098	43.9	3.197	42.4	0.901	49.2
25-29	5.323	56.3	4.314	54.6	1.009	63.7
30-34	6.869	53.6	5.954	52.9	0.915	58.0
35-39	8.933	54.9	7.831	52.9	1.102	69.4
40-44	9.611	53.5	8.655	51.8	0.956	68.6
45-49	9.359	53.3	8.354	52.2	1.005	62.7
50-54	7.210	52.6	6.617	51.9	0.593	60.7
55-59	5.701	48.8	5.410	49.6	0.291	33.3
60-64	2.008	46.3	1.837	43.0	0.171	81.3
65+	1.100	45.5	1.053	44.4	0.047	68.1
Economic activity (ISIC-Rev.3)			2007 [1][2][3] Labour force survey			
Total	.	.	53.8	.	.	.
A-B	.	.	0.7	.	.	.
C Mining and Quarrying	.	.	0.1	.	.	.
D Manufacturing	.	.	3.6	.	.	.
E Electricity, Gas and Water Supply	.	.	0.8	.	.	.
F Construction	.	.	4.2	.	.	.
G Wholesale and Retail Trade; Repair of Motor Vehicles ...	.	.	9.6	.	.	.
H Hotels and Restaurants	.	.	4.4	.	.	.
I Transport, Storage and Communications	.	.	3.2	.	.	.
J Financial Intermediation	.	.	4.0	.	.	.
K Real Estate, Renting and Business Activities	.	.	5.5	.	.	.
L Public Administration and Defence; Compulsory Social ...	.	.	5.2	.	.	.
M Education	.	.	2.7	.	.	.
N Health and Social Work	.	.	4.6	.	.	.
O Other Community, Social and Personal Service Activities	.	.	3.4	.	.	.
P Households with Employed Persons	.	.	2.0	.	.	.
Q Extra-Territorial Organizations and Bodies	.	.	0.1	.	.	.
Occupation (ISCO-88)	2007 [1][2][3][3] Labour force survey		2007 [1][2][3] Labour force survey			
Total	61.1	51.9	53.8	50.8	.	.
1 Legislators, senior officials and managers	7.3	36.8	7.0	34.2	.	.
2 Professionals	5.1	60.5	4.9	58.8	.	.
3 Technicians and associate professionals	8.7	56.4	8.1	55.5	.	.
4 Clerks	9.7	76.7	8.7	77.8	.	.
5 Service workers and shop and market sales workers	10.4	63.6	8.4	60.5	.	.
6 Skilled agricultural and fishery workers	0.3	19.0	0.4	24.8	.	.
7 Craft and related trade workers	7.3	7.5	6.1	8.6	.	.
8 Plant and machine operators and assemblers	2.9	15.1	2.6	18.6	.	.
9 Elementary occupations	9.1	65.2	6.9	63.1	.	.
0 Armed forces	0.4	13.6	0.4	.	.	.
Education level (ISCED-76)					2007 [1][2][3] Labour force survey	
Total	.	.	.	.	7.346	60.4
X-1	.	.	.	.	0.980	68.2
2 Second level, first stage	.	.	.	.	4.066	56.0
3 Second level, second stage	.	.	.	.	1.957	66.2
5 Third level, first stage, leading to an award not equivalent ...	.	.	.	.	0.342	57.3
6 Third level, first stage, leading to a first university degree ...	.	.	.	.	0.000	.
Education level (ISCED-97)	2007 [1][2][3] Labour force survey					
Total	61.1	51.9	.	.	.	.
1 Primary education or first stage of basic education	5.6	53.0	.	.	.	.
2 Lower secondary or second stage of basic education [4]	43.2	51.1	.	.	.	.
5A First stage of tertiary education - theoretically based [5]	10.8	53.9	.	.	.	.
? Level not stated	1.5	55.9	.	.	.	.
Status in employment (ICSE-1993)			2007 [1][2][3] Labour force survey			
Total	.	.	53.8	.	.	.
1 Employees	.	.	41.3	.	.	.
2 Employers	.	.	6.2	.	.	.
3 Own-account workers	.	.	5.9	.	.	.
5 Contributing family workers	.	.	0.1	.	.	.
6 Not classifiable by status	.	.	0.2	.	.	.

Netherlands Antilles

2. Population ('000), Activity rate and Unemployment rate

Age group	Population 2007 [1,6] Labour force survey			Activity rate 2007 [1,6] Labour force survey			Unemployment rate 2007 [1,2,3] Labour force survey		
	Total	Men	Women	Total	Men	Women	Total	Men	Women
Total	135.5	61.7	73.8	45.1	47.6	43.0	12.0	9.9	14.0
15+	105.5	46.5	59.1	58.1	63.4	53.9	12.0	9.9	13.9
15-24	17.7	8.7	9.0	29.3	35.0	23.8	24.2	22.3	26.8
25-54	57.0	24.8	32.2	83.0	87.8	79.3	11.8	9.2	14.1
55+	30.8	13.0	17.9	28.6	35.4	23.5	5.8	5.3	6.4

3. Paid employment ('000), Hours of work (weekly) and Wages

Economic activity (ISIC-Rev.3)	Paid employment			Hours of work 2000 [1] Labour force survey Hours actually worked / Employees			Wages 2000 [1] Labour force survey / Employees / Guilder		
	Total	Men	Women	Total	Men	Women	Total	Men	Women
Total	.	.	.	38.5	40.1	36.8	.	.	.
D	.	.	.	39.9	40.1	38.8	2 565	.	.
E	.	.	.	40.3	40.3	40.0	3 450	.	.
F	.	.	.	37.8	37.7	39.3	1 967	.	.
G	.	.	.	39.7	41.0	38.5	1 781	.	.
H	.	.	.	40.0	39.3	40.6	1 525	.	.
I	.	.	.	39.7	41.1	37.9	2 860	.	.
J	.	.	.	39.4	41.3	38.4	3 479	.	.
K	.	.	.	39.4	42.5	34.7	3 012	.	.
L	.	.	.	40.1	40.5	39.4	3 816	.	.
M	.	.	.	36.0	38.7	34.6	3 713	.	.
N	.	.	.	37.5	41.1	36.7	2 354	.	.
O	.	.	.	35.6	38.6	33.5	1 729	.	.
P	.	.	.	28.3	29.6	28.3	.	.	.
Q	.	.	.	40.0	40.0	.	.	.	.

4. Occupational injuries and Strikes and Lockouts

Economic activity (ISIC-Rev.3)	Rates of fatal injuries 1999 Insurance records Per 100,000 workers insured Reported injuries			Rates of non-fatal injuries 1999 Insurance records Per 100,000 workers insured Reported injuries			Strikes and lockouts 2000 [1] Labour relations records		
	Total	Men	Women	Total	Men	Women	Strikes and lockouts	Workers involved	Days not worked
Total	0	0	0	2 569	3 628	1 180	24	3 877	5 446
A	.	.	.	.	.	.	0	0	0
B	.	.	.	.	.	.	0	0	0
C	.	.	.	.	.	.	0	0	0
D	.	.	.	.	.	.	0	0	0
E	.	.	.	.	.	.	3	1 350	3 025
F	.	.	.	.	.	.	0	0	0
G	.	.	.	.	.	.	0	0	0
H	.	.	.	.	.	.	0	0	0
I	.	.	.	.	.	.	4	725	725
J	.	.	.	.	.	.	0	0	0
K	.	.	.	.	.	.	0	0	0
L	.	.	.	.	.	.	11	1 430	1 440
M	.	.	.	.	.	.	0	0	0
N	.	.	.	.	.	.	5	360	250
O	.	.	.	.	.	.	1	12	6
Q	.	.	.	.	.	.	0	0	0
X	.	.	.	.	.	.	.	0	.

5. Consumer price indices (base period: 2000=100)

Curaçao	2002	2003	2004	2005	2006	2007
General indices	102.1	103.8	105.2	109.4	113.0	116.4
Food index, including non-alcoholic beverages	107.3	109.5	114.7	123.3	133.0	145.0
Electricity, gas and other fuel indices	105.5	120.6	121.2	141.6	147.1	151.1
Clothing indices, including footwear	96.9	97.2	97.0	96.4	96.8	97.8
Rent indices	104.3	106.4	108.6	110.8	113.0	115.8
General index, excluding housing	101.8	103.8	105.1	109.0	.	.

[1] Curaçao. [2] Oct. [3] Persons aged 15 years and over. [4] Levels 2-3. [5] Levels 5-6. [6] "De facto" population.

[1] Curaçao. [2] Oct. [3] Personnes âgées de 15 ans et plus. [4] Niveaux 2-3. [5] Niveaux 5-6. [6] Population "de facto".

[1] Curaçao. [2] Oct. [3] Personas de 15 años y más. [4] Niveles 2-3. [5] Niveles 5-6. [6] Población "de facto".

New Zealand

1. Economically active population, Employment and Unemployment ('000)

	Economically active population		Employment		Unemployment	
	Total	Women (%)	Total	Women (%)	Total	Women (%)
Age group	2007 [1][2] Labour force survey		2007 ★ Labour force survey		2007 [2] Labour force survey	
Total	2 235.4	46.3	2 155.6	46.1	79.8	50.0
15-19	177.8	49.8	153.0	50.2	24.8	47.2
20-24	216.2	45.2	202.7	44.9	13.5	48.9
25-29	217.9	44.9	209.5	44.8	8.4	47.6
30-34	221.6	46.5	215.8	46.3	5.8	51.7
35-39	251.6	46.1	245.7	45.8	5.9	59.3
40-44	267.5	47.8	261.3	47.5	6.2	62.9
45-49	267.9	48.0	261.7	47.9	6.2	53.2
50-54	227.1	47.6	223.4	47.6	3.7	48.6
55-59	191.8	46.0	188.7	46.1	3.1	41.9
60-64	125.7	41.8	124.2	41.8	1.5	40.0
65-69	48.0	38.5	47.5	38.5	0.5	40.0
70-74	16.1	34.8	16.1	34.8	-	.
75+	6.2	27.4	6.2	27.4	-	.
Economic activity (ISIC-Rev.3)	2007 [1][2] Labour force survey		2007 [1][2] Labour force survey		2007 [2] Labour force survey	
Total	2 235.3	46.3	2 155.5	46.1	79.7	50.1
A Agriculture, Hunting and Forestry	158.0	32.8	152.2	32.4	5.7	43.9
B Fishing	2.3	17.4	2.2	18.2	0.1	.
C Mining and Quarrying	5.2	15.4	5.1	15.7	0.0	.
D Manufacturing	282.2	27.7	274.4	27.5	7.8	34.6
E Electricity, Gas and Water Supply	8.9	20.2	8.8	20.5	0.1	0.0
F Construction	187.1	11.3	183.1	11.3	4.0	12.5
G Wholesale and Retail Trade; Repair of Motor Vehicles ...	390.7	47.4	377.9	47.2	12.7	55.1
H Hotels and Restaurants	114.3	62.5	107.8	62.3	6.5	64.6
I Transport, Storage and Communications	117.8	28.2	115.4	28.0	2.4	37.5
J Financial Intermediation	72.1	53.5	71.4	53.5	0.7	57.1
K Real Estate, Renting and Business Activities	255.7	47.2	249.0	47.4	6.7	41.8
L Public Administration and Defence; Compulsory Social ...	138.5	51.0	136.1	51.0	2.4	54.2
M Education	170.3	69.9	167.2	70.0	3.1	67.7
N Health and Social Work	203.5	84.1	200.1	84.0	3.4	91.2
O Other Community, Social and Personal Service Activities	93.8	54.6	90.7	54.8	3.2	46.9
P Households with Employed Persons	3.9	92.3	3.7	91.9	0.3	66.7
Q Extra-Territorial Organizations and Bodies	-		-		-	
X Not classifiable by economic activity	17.2	47.4	10.5	41.0	6.7	56.7
Unemployed seeking their first job	13.9	49.3	.	.	13.9	48.9
Occupation (ISCO-88)	2007 [1][2] Labour force survey		2007 [1][2] Labour force survey		2007 [2] Labour force survey	
Total	2 235.3	46.3	2 155.5	46.1	79.7	50.1
1 Legislators, senior officials and managers	286.9	39.6	282.9	39.6	3.9	46.2
2 Professionals	361.8	53.6	357.2	53.6	4.6	56.5
3 Technicians and associate professionals	260.4	55.2	256.2	55.1	4.2	61.9
4 Clerks	271.6	77.1	263.8	77.4	7.8	62.8
5 Service workers and shop and market sales workers	340.6	66.1	326.1	66.0	14.5	69.0
6 Skilled agricultural and fishery workers	155.4	28.7	149.6	28.4	5.8	36.2
7 Craft and related trade workers	227.3	4.4	222.7	4.4	4.6	4.3
8 Plant and machine operators and assemblers	180.0	17.4	175.1	17.1	4.9	28.6
9 Elementary occupations	124.8	39.3	115.7	39.1	9.2	41.3
X Not classifiable by occupation	12.7	52.0	6.3	46.0	6.4	57.8
Unemployed seeking their first job	13.9	48.9	.	.	13.9	48.9
Education level (ISCED-97)	2007 [1][2] Labour force survey		2007 ★ Labour force survey		2007 [2] Labour force survey	
Total	2 235.4	46.3	2 155.6	46.1	79.8	50.0
0 Pre-primary education [3]	399.9	44.1	375.5	44.0	24.4	45.1
1 Primary education or first stage of basic education	0.1	100.0	0.1	100.0	0.0	.
3 Upper secondary education	679.8	51.4	653.0	51.3	26.8	52.6
4 Post-secondary non-tertiary education	238.6	12.5	234.4	12.2	4.2	31.0
5A First stage of tertiary education - theoretically based	365.0	47.5	356.0	47.4	9.0	48.9
5B First stage of tertiary education - practically oriented	322.2	60.2	312.8	60.1	9.4	63.8
6 Second stage of tertiary education	146.9	49.5	143.8	49.4	3.1	51.6
? Level not stated	82.8	47.2	79.9	47.1	2.9 [4]	51.7
Status in employment (ICSE-1993)	2007 [1][2] Labour force survey		2007 [1][2] Labour force survey		2007 ★ Labour force survey	
Total	2 235.3	46.3	2 155.5	46.1	79.8	50.0
1 Employees	1 837.3	48.7	1 781.0	48.7	56.3	50.3
2 Employers	115.6	28.0	115.1	28.0	0.5	40.0
3 Own-account workers	235.5	33.9	233.1	33.9	2.4	33.3
5 Contributing family workers	24.3	63.4	24.1	63.5	0.2	50.0
6 Not classifiable by status	22.6	50.9	2.3	39.1	20.3	52.2

New Zealand

2. Population ('000), Activity rate and Unemployment rate

Age group	Population 2007[1,5] Labour force survey			Activity rate 2007[1,5] Labour force survey			Unemployment rate 2007[2] Labour force survey		
	Total	Men	Women	Total	Men	Women	Total	Men	Women
Total	4 230.7	2 072.0	2 158.8	52.8	58.0	47.9	3.6	3.3	3.9
15+	3 342.6	1 617.2	1 725.3	66.9	74.3	60.0	.	.	.
15-24	613.6	310.6	303.1	64.2	66.9	61.4	9.7	9.6	9.8
25-54	1 761.3	852.2	908.9	82.5	90.6	75.0	2.5	2.2	2.9
55+	967.7	454.4	513.3	40.1	48.7	32.5	.	.	.

3. Paid employment ('000), Hours of work (weekly) and Wages

Economic activity (ISIC-Rev.3)	Paid employment 2007[1,2] Labour force survey			Hours of work 2007[1,2] Labour force survey Hours actually worked / Employees			Wages 2006[6,7,8] Labour-related establishment survey Earnings per hour / Employees / Dollar		
	Total	Men	Women	Total	Men	Women	Total	Men	Women
Total	1 781.0	914.1	866.9	33.9	38.4	28.6	.	.	.
A-B	.	.	.	39.2	44.1	28.8	.	.	.
C-Q	.	.	.	33.5	37.9	28.6	.	.	.
A	82.3	58.1	24.2	39.3	44.3	28.8	.	.	.
B	1.3	1.0	0.3	35.9	37.7	29.9	.	.	.
C	4.7	4.0	0.7	44.2	46.6	32.6	29.19	29.66	24.47
D	245.1	178.0	67.1	37.6	39.3	32.8	20.51	21.52	17.62
E	8.6	6.9	1.7	37.7	39.4	31.3	32.13	34.77	25.56
F	124.1	110.8	13.3	37.9	39.4	25.5	19.12	19.23	17.90
G	324.5	165.1	159.4	33.3	38.1	28.0	17.90	19.59	15.63
H	93.6	33.5	60.1	28.6	34.0	25.3	13.46	14.35	12.84
I	99.5	70.7	28.8	38.1	40.7	31.5	21.68	22.57	19.74
J	65.2	28.6	36.6	35.2	38.9	32.1	29.27	37.26	23.67
K	179.3	86.9	92.4	33.6	36.8	29.9	25.01	28.42	21.54
L	131.6	64.0	67.7	34.6	37.3	32.0	26.79	29.28	24.30
M	160.5	48.2	112.3	28.3	33.4	26.2	28.90	29.66	28.48
N	184.4	26.8	157.6	29.4	35.3	28.3	22.60	31.95	20.70
O	65.4	26.8	38.6	28.3	32.2	25.2	20.10	22.37	18.23
P	3.2	0.2	3.0	21.4	7.5	22.6	.	.	.
Q	-	-	-	.	.	.	.	.	.
X	7.7	4.7	3.0	32.6	34.8	29.1	.	.	.

Share of women in wage employment in the non-agricultural sector [12] (2007 - Labour force survey): **49.7%**

4. Occupational injuries and Strikes and Lockouts

Economic activity (ISIC-Rev.2)	Rates of fatal injuries 1993[9] Insurance records Per 1,000 workers employed Compensated injuries			Rates of non-fatal injuries			Strikes and lockouts		
	Total	Men	Women	Total	Men	Women	Strikes and lockouts	Workers involved	Days not worked
Total	0.053	.	.	.	.	.	.	.	.
1	0.092	.	.	.	.	.	.	.	.
2	1.341	.	.	.	.	.	.	.	.
3	0.039	.	.	.	.	.	.	.	.
4	0.000	.	.	.	.	.	.	.	.
5	0.033	.	.	.	.	.	.	.	.
6	0.016	.	.	.	.	.	.	.	.
7	0.043	.	.	.	.	.	.	.	.
8	0.006	.	.	.	.	.	.	.	.
9	0.016	.	.	.	.	.	.	.	.

Economic activity (ISIC-Rev.3)	Rates of fatal injuries			Rates of non-fatal injuries			Strikes and lockouts 2006[10] Labour relations records		
	Total	Men	Women	Total	Men	Women	Strikes and lockouts[11]	Workers involved	Days not worked[12]
Total	.	.	.	.	.	.	42	10 079	27 983
A	.	.	.	.	.	.	0	0	0
B	.	.	.	.	.	.	0	0	0
C	.	.	.	.	.	.	0	0	0
D	.	.	.	.	.	.	13	1 706	3 056
E	.	.	.	.	.	.	2	.	.
F	.	.	.	.	.	.	4	754	9
G	.	.	.	.	.	.	2	.	.
H	.	.	.	.	.	.	1	.	.
I	.	.	.	.	.	.	3	274	197
J	.	.	.	.	.	.	0	0	0
K	.	.	.	.	.	.	1	.	.
L	.	.	.	.	.	.	5	2 343	1 042
M	.	.	.	.	.	.	1	.	.
N	.	.	.	.	.	.	7	3 579	11 873
O	.	.	.	.	.	.	3	505	470

New Zealand

5. Consumer price indices (base period: 2000=100)

	2002	2003	2004	2005	2006	2007
General indices	105.4	107.2	109.7	113.0	116.8	119.6
Food index, including non-alcoholic beverages	109.4	109.4	110.3	113.1	116.2	120.6
Electricity, gas and other fuel indices	105.6	112.3	122.7	131.8	140.2	149.5
Clothing indices, including footwear	102.9	102.4	101.8	101.6	101.6	101.6
Rent indices [13]	91.8	94.7	97.6	100.0	102.3	105.2
General index, excluding housing	106.3	107.2	108.5	111.1	114.2	116.2

[1] Excl. armed forces. [2] Persons aged 15 years and over. [3] Levels X,0,2. [4] Incl. overseas qualifications. [5] "De jure" population. [6] Establishments with the equivalent of more than 0.5 full-time paid employees. [7] Full-time equivalent employees. [8] Feb. [9] Year beginning in July of year indicated. [10] Excl. work stoppages in which less than 5 workdays not worked. [11] Incl. partial strikes and lockouts. [12] Computed on the basis of an eight-hour working day. [13] Excl. rental value of owner occupied dwellings.

[1] Non compris les forces armées. [2] Personnes âgées de 15 ans et plus. [3] Niveaux X,0,2. [4] Y compris les qualifications étrangères. [5] Population "de jure". [6] Etablissements occupant plus de l'équivalent de 0.5 salarié à plein temps. [7] Salariés en équivalents à plein temps. [8] Fév. [9] Année commençant en juillet de l'année indiquée. [10] Non compris les arrêts de travail de moins de 5 journées de travail non effectuées. [11] Y compris les grèves et lock-out partiels. [12] Calculées sur la base de journées de travail de huit heures. [13] Non compris la valeur locative des logements occupés par leurs propriétaires.

[1] Excl. las fuerzas armadas. [2] Personas de 15 años y más. [3] Niveles X,0,2. [4] Incl. las calificaciones extranjeras. [5] Población "de jure". [6] Establecimientos con más del equivalente de 0.5 asalariado a tiempo completo. [7] Asalariados en equivalentes a tiempo completo. [8] Feb. [9] Año que comienza en julio del año indicado. [10] Excl. las interrupciones de trabajo de menosde 5 días de trabajo no trabajados. [11] Incl. huelgas y cierres patronales parciales. [12] Calculados en base a días de trabajo de ocho horas. [13] Excl. el valor locativo de la vivienda ocupada por su propietario.

# Nicaragua

1. Población económicamente activa, Empleo y Desempleo ('000)

	Población económicamente activa		Empleo		Desempleo	
	Total	Mujeres (%)	Total	Mujeres (%)	Total	Mujeres (%)
Grupo de edad	2006 [1] Encuesta de la fuerza de trabajo		2006 ★ Encuesta de la fuerza de trabajo		2006 [1] Encuesta de la fuerza de trabajo	
Total	2 204.3	37.5	2 089.8	37.6	114.5	35.2
10-14	74.3	25.8	73.0	26.1	1.3	7.9
15-19	236.1	27.0	216.4	26.0	19.7	37.2
20-24	354.6	35.2	323.5	35.2	31.1	35.1
25-29	289.4	37.9	268.6	37.3	20.8	45.2
30-34	229.9	44.1	218.8	44.4	11.1	39.6
35-39	224.6	44.1	217.0	44.3	7.6	37.0
40-44	216.7	43.2	208.9	43.8	7.7	29.4
45-49	177.9	42.8	172.3	43.3	5.6	29.9
50-54	134.9	39.0	130.9	39.5	4.0	23.5
55-59	98.6	37.7	95.7	38.5	2.9	10.9
60-64	65.6	32.7	64.7	33.1	0.8	0.0
65-69	42.7	28.0	41.7	28.5	1.0	10.1
70-74	30.7	24.5	30.2	24.5	0.5	19.9
75+	28.4	29.7	28.1	30.1	0.3	0.0
Actividad económica (CIIU-Rev.3)	2006 [1] Encuesta de la fuerza de trabajo		2006 [1] Encuesta de la fuerza de trabajo		2006 ★ Encuesta de la fuerza de trabajo	
Total	2 204.3	37.5	2 089.8	37.6	114.5	35.2
A Agricultura, ganadería, caza y silvicultura	602.2	10.9	593.6	10.9	8.5	6.0
B Pesca	16.3	7.6	15.5	6.7	0.8	25.0
C Explotación de minas y canteras	7.1	11.2	6.7	11.8	0.4	0.3
D Industrias manufactureras	302.6	46.3	289.2	47.1	13.4	30.9
E Suministro de electricidad, gas y agua	6.8	17.1	6.5	18.0	0.3	.
F Construcción	118.3	1.7	100.8	1.7	17.5	1.8
G Comercio al por mayor y al por menor; reparación ...	426.3	51.6	409.1	52.2	17.2	37.0
H Hoteles y restaurantes	76.4	73.5	72.0	74.8	4.4	52.4
I Transporte, almacenamiento y comunicaciones	94.2	7.9	89.0	7.5	5.3	14.0
J Intermediación financiera	16.9	51.7	15.9	52.9	1.0	32.3
K Actividades inmobiliarias, empresariales y de alquiler	57.5	23.1	54.0	22.1	3.5	39.1
L Administración pública y defensa; planes de seguridad ...	78.1	38.8	73.7	39.5	4.4	26.5
M Enseñanza	97.6	69.9	94.5	69.8	3.1	73.0
N Servicios sociales y de salud	55.9	64.1	54.5	63.6	1.4	81.2
O Otras actividades de servicios comunitarios ...	93.8	62.9	89.2	63.0	4.6	61.3
P Hogares privados con servicio doméstico	125.0	80.8	117.4	80.8	7.6	80.8
Q Organizaciones y órganos extraterritoriales	8.6	59.9	8.1	61.7	0.4	25.1
Desempleados sin empleo anterior	19.7	53.4	.	.	.	.
Ocupación (CIUO-88)	2006 [1] Encuesta de la fuerza de trabajo		2006 [1] Encuesta de la fuerza de trabajo		2006 ★ Encuesta de la fuerza de trabajo	
Total	2 204.3	37.5	2 089.8	37.6	114.5	35.2
1 Miembros del poder ejecutivo y de los cuerpos legislativos ...	55.2	40.9	53.4	41.0	1.9	39.2
2 Profesionales científicos e intelectuales	74.6	44.5	72.1	44.7	2.5	41.3
3 Técnicos y profesionales de nivel medio	194.0	53.6	184.3	53.9	9.6	48.8
4 Empleados de oficina	52.8	61.5	46.7	60.5	6.2	69.4
5 Trabajadores de los servicios y vendedores de comercios ...	471.2	63.3	455.8	63.8	15.4	46.4
6 Agricultores y trabajadores calificados agropecuarios ...	245.7	6.8	244.3	6.8	1.4	.
7 Oficiales, operarios y artesanos de artes mecánicas ...	264.1	25.4	247.5	26.6	16.6	7.6
8 Operadores de instalaciones y máquinas y montadores	137.8	18.9	130.5	19.4	7.3	10.2
9 Trabajadores no calificados	684.6	31.3	651.8	31.4	32.8	30.0
0 Fuerzas armadas	3.0	17.5	2.8	18.8	0.2	0.5
X No pueden clasificarse según la ocupación	0.6	100.0	0.6	100.0	.	.
Desempleados sin empleo anterior	19.7	53.4	.	.	.	.
Nivel de educación (CINE-76)	1995 [2] Encuesta de la fuerza de trabajo		1995 ★ Encuesta de la fuerza de trabajo			
Total	1 445.1	29.5	1 352.3	28.8	.	.
X Sin escolaridad	380.1	22.2	375.5	22.0	.	.
0 Enseñanza anterior al primer grado	3.5	25.5	3.5	25.5	.	.
1 Enseñanza de primer grado	645.7	27.2	610.5	26.6	.	.
2 Enseñanza de segundo grado, ciclo inferior	201.3	36.2	174.0	35.2	.	.
3 Enseñanza de segundo grado, ciclo superior	127.5	45.0	110.3	45.4	.	.
5 Enseñanza de tercer grado que no permite obtener un ...	12.4	47.6	12.4	47.6	.	.
6 Enseñanza de tercer grado que permite obtener un primer ... [3]	74.7	40.0	71.5	39.8	.	.
Nivel de educación (CINE-97)					2006 [1] Encuesta de la fuerza de trabajo	
Total	.	.	.	.	114.5	35.2
0 Enseñanza preescolar	.	.	.	.	8.1	24.0
1 Enseñanza primaria o primer ciclo de la educación básica	.	.	.	.	33.1	23.6
2-3	.	.	.	.	50.3	41.1
4 Enseñanza postsecundaria, no terciaria	.	.	.	.	2.4	47.8
5	.	.	.	.	20.6	42.3
Situación en el empleo (CISE-1993)	2006 [1] Encuesta de la fuerza de trabajo		2006 [1] Encuesta de la fuerza de trabajo		2006 ★ Encuesta de la fuerza de trabajo	
Total	2 204.3	37.5	2 089.8	37.6	114.5	35.2
1 Asalariados	1 133.5	38.2	1 054.8	38.6	78.7	33.1
2 Empleadores	90.1	21.5	88.8	21.8	1.4	0.3
3 Trabajadores por cuenta propia	721.1	40.1	708.3	40.4	12.9	26.8
4 Miembros de cooperativas de productores	2.7	33.5	2.6	30.8	0.1	101.0
5 Trabajadores familiares auxiliares	231.2	30.9	230.6	31.0	0.6	.
6 Inclasificables según la situación	20.7	51.7	4.7	41.7	16.0	54.6

Nicaragua

2. Población ('000), Tasa de actividad y Tasa de desempleo

Grupo de edad	Población 2006 Encuesta de la fuerza de trabajo			Tasa de actividad 2006 Encuesta de la fuerza de trabajo			Tasa de desempleo 2006 [1] Encuesta de la fuerza de trabajo		
	Total	Hombres	Mujeres	Total	Hombres	Mujeres	Total	Hombres	Mujeres
Total	5 559.2	2 726.9	2 832.2	39.7	50.5	29.2	5.2	5.4	4.9
15+	3 549.0	1 691.8	1 857.2	60.0	78.2	43.5	5.3	5.5	5.0
15-24	1 237.5	634.1	603.4	47.7	63.5	31.2	8.6	8.1	9.7
25-54	1 716.9	790.0	926.8	74.2	93.7	57.5	4.5	4.8	4.0
55+	594.6	267.6	327.0	44.7	67.0	26.4	2.1	2.9	0.6

3. Empleo remunerado ('000), Horas de trabajo (por semana) y Salarios

Actividad económica (CIIU-Rev.2)	Empleo remunerado 2002 Registros de seguros			Horas de trabajo 2002 [4] Encuesta de la fuerza de trabajo Horas efectivamente trabajadas / Asalariados			Salarios 2006 Encuesta de establecimientos relacionada con el trabajo Ganancias por mes / Asalariados / Córdoba		
	Total	Hombres	Mujeres	Total	Hombres	Mujeres	Total	Hombres	Mujeres
Total	311.50	.	.	.	.	.	4 926.0	.	.
2-9							4 853.0		
1	14.69	.	.	48.39	48.89	44.93	.	.	.
2	1.80	.	.	58.86	58.86	.	5 800.0	.	.
3	73.16	.	.	50.77	50.12	52.14	3 393.0	.	.
4	6.25	.	.	50.20	50.84	48.33	5 994.0 [5]	.	.
5	9.86	.	.	49.31	49.46	46.46	3 901.0	.	.
6	39.44	.	.	50.78	50.66	50.95	5 580.0	.	.
7	9.05	.	.	52.46	53.38	47.27	4 758.0	.	.
8	23.46	.	.	51.39	52.25	50.63	10 925.0	.	.
9	133.50	.	.	49.49	50.31	49.01	5 438.0	.	.
0	0.29	.	.	.	.	.	.	.	.

4. Lesiones profesionales y Huelgas y cierres patronales

Actividad económica (CIIU-Rev.3)	Tasas de lesiones mortales 2003 [6] Registros de seguros Por 100 000 trabajadores asegurados Lesiones indemnizadas			Tasas de lesiones no mortales 2003 Registros de seguros Por 100 000 trabajadores asegurados Lesiones indemnizadas			Huelgas y cierres patronales 2004 [7] Registros de relaciones laborales		
	Total	Hombres	Mujeres	Total	Hombres	Mujeres	Huelgas y cierres patronales	Trabajadores implicados	Días no trabajados
Total	6	11	1	3 483	4 341	2 500	1	51	51
A	7	8	0	2 071	2 310	950	.	.	.
B	0	0	0	911	1 241	351	.	.	.
C	0	0	0	2 538	2 608	1 786	.	.	.
D	8	16	0	6 514	8 456	4 454	.	.	.
E	0	0	0	4 250	4 786	2 587	.	.	.
F	39	44	0	5 111	5 600	1 441	.	.	.
G	3	5	0	2 711	3 269	1 769	.	.	.
H	16	31	0	4 108	5 214	2 919	.	.	.
I	10	0	34	2 135	2 668	938	.	.	.
J	0	0	0	1 432	1 597	1 282	.	.	.
K	0	0	0	1 538	1 956	373	.	.	.
L	0	0	0	191	245	148	.	.	.
M	10	22	2	4 435	5 713	3 579	.	.	.
N	0	0	0	0	0	0	.	.	.
O	0	0	0	0	0	0	.	.	.
P	0	0	0	0	0	0	.	.	.
Q	0	0	0	0	0	0	.	.	.

5. Índices de precios al consumidor (periodo de base: 2000=100)

[8]	2002	2003	2004	2005	2006	2007
Índices generales	117.7	124.0	134.5	147.4	160.9	178.8
Índices de la alimentación incluyendo las bebidas no alcohólicas	115.7	120.7	133.6	149.0	162.5	188.9
Índices del vestido, incl. calzado	109.5	112.0	114.6	117.8	122.3	129.5
Índices del aquiler [9]	125.6	133.5	144.8	156.0	175.0	189.7

[1] Persons aged 10 years and over. [2] April. [3] Levels 6-7. [4] 17 main cities and 40 municipalities; August. [5] Excl. gas. [6] Deaths occurring within 15 days of accident. [7] Strikes only. [8] Index base 1999=100. [9] Incl. water, electricity, gas and other fuels.

[1] Personnes âgées de 10 ans et plus. [2] Avril. [3] Niveaux 6-7. [4] 17 villes principales et 40 municipalités; août. [5] Non compris le gaz. [6] Décès survenant pendant les 15 jours qui suivent l'accident. [7] Grèves seulement. [8] Indices base 1999=100. [9] Y compris l'eau, l'électricité, le gaz et autres combustibles.

[1] Personas de 10 años y más. [2] Abril. [3] Niveles 6-7. [4] 17 ciudades principales y 40 municipios; agosto. [5] Excl. gas. [6] Fallecimientos que se produzcan durante los 15 días posteriores al accidente. [7] Huelgas solamente. [8] Indice base 1999=100. [9] Incl. el agua, la electricidad, el gas y otros combustibles.

Niger

1. Population active, Emploi et Chômage ('000)

	Population active		Emploi		Chômage	
	Total	Femmes (%)	Total	Femmes (%)	Total	Femmes (%)
Groupe d'âge	2001 [1,2] Recensement de la population		2001 ★ Recensement de la population		2001 [1] Recensement de la population	
Total	4 073.298	32.4	4 015.728	32.6	57.570	22.0
10-14	437.510	33.9	433.266	33.8	4.244	40.5
15-19	565.420	35.9	552.005	36.1	13.415	27.1
20-24	510.929	33.2	490.319	34.1	20.610	12.5
25-29	493.464	33.3	486.411	33.5	7.053	23.1
30-34	419.004	33.9	415.104	34.0	3.900	21.3
35-39	453.409	29.2	450.938	29.3	2.471	23.1
40-44	400.278	29.6	398.524	29.7	1.754	19.5
45-49	159.913	37.7	159.306	37.7	0.607	27.5
50-54	224.951	31.5	224.083	31.5	0.868	19.7
55-59	124.623	26.6	123.810	26.5	0.813	51.8
60-64	117.066	30.9	116.420	30.9	0.646	23.4
65-69	37.194	33.3	36.961	33.3	0.233	18.9
70-74	69.666	24.9	69.322	24.8	0.344	44.8
75+	59.845	21.3	59.238	21.1	0.607	43.5
?	0.026	3.8	0.021	4.8	0.005	.

Activité économique (CITI-Rév.2)					1986 [3] Fichiers des bureaux de placement	
Total	.	.	.	.	27.747	3.8
1 Agriculture, chasse, sylviculture et pêche	.	.	.	.	2.058	2.2
2 Industries extractives	.	.	.	.	2.805	3.3
3 Industries manufacturières	.	.	.	.	1.510	5.0
4 Electricité, gaz et eau	.	.	.	.	1.207	4.8
5 Bâtiment et travaux publics	.	.	.	.	12.611	1.8
6 Commerce de gros et de détail; restaurants et hôtels	.	.	.	.	1.039	12.6
7 Transports, entrepôts et communications	.	.	.	.	1.260	8.1
8 Banques, assurances, affaires immobilières et services ...	.	.	.	.	1.830	6.7
9 Services fournis à la collectivité, services sociaux ...	.	.	.	.	3.427	5.5

Profession (CITP-1968)					1991 Fichiers des bureaux de placement	
Total	.	.	.	.	20.926	4.7
0/1 Personnel des professions scientifiques, techniques ...	.	.	.	.	0.196	9.2
2 Directeurs et cadres administratifs supérieurs	.	.	.	.	0.122	7.4
3 Personnel administratif et travailleurs assimilés	.	.	.	.	3.539	23.1
7/8/9 Ouvriers et manoeuvres non agricoles et conducteurs ...	.	.	.	.	16.919	0.8

Niveau d'instruction (CITE-76)	2001 [1,2] Recensement de la population					
Total	4 073.3	32.4	.	.	.	.
X Non scolarisé	2 904.9	37.8	.	.	.	.
1 Premier degré	301.9	21.4	.	.	.	.
2 Second degré, premier cycle	105.2	21.0	.	.	.	.
3 Second degré, deuxième cycle	17.6	22.0	.	.	.	.
5 Troisième degré, premier niveau, conduisant à un titre ... [4]	16.1	22.0	.	.	.	.
9 Enseignement impossible à définir selon le degré	722.5	17.9	.	.	.	.

2. Population ('000), Taux d'activité et Taux de chômage

	Population			Taux d'activité			Taux de chômage		
Groupe d'âge	2001 [2] Recensement de la population			2001 [2] Recensement de la population			2001 [1] Recensement de la population		
	Total	Hommes	Femmes	Total	Hommes	Femmes	Total	Hommes	Femmes
Total	11 060.3	5 516.6	5 543.7	36.8	49.9	23.8	1.4	1.6	1.0
15+	5 801.2	2 819.1	2 982.2	62.7	87.4	39.3	1.5	1.7	0.9
15-24	1 998.2	925.8	1 072.4	53.9	76.0	34.7	3.2	4.0	1.7
25-54	3 108.3	1 538.8	1 569.5	69.2	95.0	43.9	0.8	0.9	0.5
55+	694.7	354.5	340.2	58.8	83.7	32.9	0.6	0.5	0.9

3. Emploi rémunéré ('000), Durée du travail (hebdomadaire) et Salaires

Activité économique (CITI-Rév.2)	Emploi rémunéré 1991 Fichiers des assurances			Durée du travail			Salaires		
	Total	Hommes	Femmes	Total	Hommes	Femmes	Total	Hommes	Femmes
Total	24.131	22.111	2.020	.	.	.	.	.	.
1	1.935	1.829	0.106	.	.	.	.	.	.
2	3.085	3.010	0.075	.	.	.	.	.	.
3	1.746	1.664	0.082	.	.	.	.	.	.
4	4.461	4.188	0.273	.	.	.	.	.	.
5	2.341	2.294	0.047	.	.	.	.	.	.
6	2.370	2.079	0.291	.	.	.	.	.	.
7	3.391	2.928	0.463	.	.	.	.	.	.
8	0.804	0.589	0.215	.	.	.	.	.	.
9	3.998	3.530	0.468	.	.	.	.	.	.

Niger

4. Lésions professionnelles et Grèves et lock-out

Activité économique (CITI-Rév.3)	Taux de lésions mortelles			Taux de lésions non mortelles			Grèves et lock-out 1991 [5] Fichiers des relations du travail		
	Total	Hommes	Femmes	Total	Hommes	Femmes	Grèves et lock-out [5]	Travailleurs impliqués	Journées non effectuées
Total	.	.	.	.	.	.	3	2 272	.
A	.	.	.	.	.	.	0	0	.
B	.	.	.	.	.	.	0	0	.
C	.	.	.	.	.	.	3	2 265	.
D	.	.	.	.	.	.	0	0	.
E	.	.	.	.	.	.	0	0	.
F	.	.	.	.	.	.	0	0	.
G	.	.	.	.	.	.	0	0	.
H	.	.	.	.	.	.	0	0	.
I	.	.	.	.	.	.	0	0	.
J	.	.	.	.	.	.	0	0	.
K	.	.	.	.	.	.	0	7	.
L	.	.	.	.	.	.	0	0	.
M	.	.	.	.	.	.	0	0	.
N	.	.	.	.	.	.	0	0	.

5. Indices des prix à la consommation (période de base: 2000=100)

Niamey, Afric.	2002	2003	2004	2005	2006	2007
Indices généraux [6]	106.7	105.1	105.2	113.5	113.6	113.6
Indices de l'alimentation, y compris les boissons non alcoolisées [7]	111.9	106.7	105.1	120.7	118.4	117.6
Indices de l'habillement, y compris les chaussures	101.3	101.1	99.4	102.6	100.0	99.8
Indices du loyer [8]	101.5	103.9	105.3	106.2	107.5	108.1

[1] Persons aged 10 years and over. [2] May. [3] Persons aged 18 to 60 years. [4] Levels 5-7. [5] Strikes only. [6] Excl. "Rent". [7] Incl. tobacco. [8] Incl. water, electricity, gas and other fuels.

[1] Personnes âgées de 10 ans et plus. [2] Mai. [3] Personnes âgées de 18 à 60 ans. [4] Niveaux 5-7. [5] Grèves seulement. [6] Non compris le groupe "Loyer". [7] Y compris le tabac. [8] Y compris l'eau, l'électricité, le gaz et autres combustibles.

[1] Personas de 10 años y más. [2] Mayo. [3] Personas de 18 a 60 años. [4] Niveles 5-7. [5] Huelgas solamente. [6] Excl. el grupo "Alquiler". [7] Incl. el tabaco. [8] Incl. el agua, la electricidad, el gas y otros combustibles.

Nigeria

1. Economically active population, Employment and Unemployment ('000)

	Economically active population		Employment		Unemployment	
	Total	Women (%)	Total	Women (%)	Total	Women (%)
Age group	1986 [1][2] Labour force survey		1986 [3] Labour force survey		1986 Labour force survey	
Total	30 765.5	33.3	28 535.0	32.0	1 263.6	35.9
10-14	379.6	27.8	.	.	64.9	11.4
15-19	2 035.8	28.9	.	.	205.6	85.8
20-24	2 599.6	40.9	.	.	506.0	37.8
25-29	4 330.6	33.0	.	.	269.3	18.1
30-34	4 078.7	32.4	.	.	66.3	15.1
35-39	3 910.9	36.7	.	.	37.1	13.2
40-44	3 582.4	34.5	.	.	22.8	3.1
45-49	3 352.8	34.1	.	.	29.1	19.9
50-54	2 660.4	32.8	.	.	15.0	4.7
55-59	1 516.5	26.8	.	.	11.4	39.5
60-64	1 137.2	26.0	.	.	15.7	14.6
65+	1 181.0	29.9	.	.	20.4	4.9
Economic activity (ISIC-Rev.2)	1986 [1][2] Labour force survey		1986 [3] Labour force survey		1986 ★ Labour force survey	
Total	30 765.50	33.3	28 535.00	32.0	2 230.50	50.4
1 Agriculture, Hunting, Forestry and Fishing	13 259.00	26.1	13 369.00	25.7	-110.00	.
2 Mining and Quarrying	6.80	.	3.08	2 662	3.72	.
3 Manufacturing	1 263.70	36.2	1 234.00	24.8	29.70	509.4
4 Electricity, Gas and Water	130.40	2.6	97.00	13.4	33.40	-28.7
5 Construction	545.60	.	495.00	8.7	50.60	.
6 Wholesale and Retail Trade and Restaurants and Hotels	7 417.40	63.9	6 994.00	61.3	423.40	107.9
7 Transport, Storage and Communication	1 111.90	1.5	1 089.00	1.7	22.90	-7.9
8 Financing, Insurance, Real Estate and Business Services	120.10	8.6	105.00	2.9	15.10	48.3
9 Community, Social and Personal Services	4 902.10	19.6	4 295.00	20.5	607.10	13.6
0 Activities not Adequately Defined	789.40	20.5	624.00	28.5	165.40	-10.0
Unemployed seeking their first job	1 219.10	36.1	.	.	.	.
Occupation (ISCO-1968)	1991 [4][5] Population census		1986 [3] Labour force survey		1991 [6] Employment office records	
Total	26 624.9	36.9	28 535.0	32.0	60.2	.
0/1 Professional, technical and related workers	1 806.3	33.2	1 681.5	23.7	0.0	.
2 Administrative and managerial workers	654.1	22.3	110.7	6.8	0.0	.
3 Clerical and related workers	831.8	32.7	1 143.7	22.4	3.9	.
4 Sales workers	5 934.5	65.2	6 954.6	60.8	0.4	.
5 Service workers	857.8	37.6	973.1	15.9	1.7	.
6 Agriculture, animal husbandry and forestry workers ...	11 976.5	29.2	13 235.5	25.7	0.0	.
7/8/9 Production and related workers, transport equipment ...	3 687.6	24.0	3 797.9	13.4	11.3	.
X Not classifiable by occupation	876.3	27.4	638.0	27.0	42.9 [7]	.
Status in employment (ICSE-58)	1986 [1][2] Labour force survey					
Total	30 765.5	33.3	.	.	.	.
1 Employers and own-account workers	19 868.3	36.4	.	.	.	.
2 Employees	5 783.5	15.2	.	.	.	.
3 Unpaid family workers	3 293.7	46.2	.	.	.	.
4 Not classifiable by status	1 820.0	34.0	.	.	.	.

2. Population ('000), Activity rate and Unemployment rate

Age group	Population 1986 [2] Labour force survey			Activity rate 1986 [2] Labour force survey			Unemployment rate 1986 Labour force survey		
	Total	Men	Women	Total	Men	Women	Total	Men	Women
Total	98 936.8	49 960.3	48 976.5	31.1	41.1	20.9	4.1	3.9	4.4
15+	53 104.6	25 834.4	27 270.2	57.2	78.3	37.2	3.9	3.7	4.4
15-24	15 273.0	7 074.3	8 198.7	30.4	42.2	20.1	15.4	11.5	22.3
25-54	31 427.9	14 913.1	16 514.8	69.7	97.1	45.0	2.0	2.5	1.0
55+	6 403.7	3 847.0	2 556.7	59.9	72.2	41.3	1.2	1.4	0.7

3. Paid employment ('000), Hours of work (weekly) and Wages

Economic activity (NSIC)	Paid employment 1980 [8] Labour-related establishment survey			Hours of work			Wages		
	Total	Men	Women	Total	Men	Women	Total	Men	Women
3	294.981	.	.	.	.	.	.	.	.

Nigeria

4. Occupational injuries and Strikes and Lockouts

Economic activity (ISIC-Rev.2)	Rates of fatal injuries Total	Men	Women	Rates of non-fatal injuries Total	Men	Women	Strikes and lockouts 2004[9] Strikes and lockouts	Workers involved[10]	Days not worked
Total	.	.	.	.	.	.	26	127 377	2 737 399
1	.	.	.	.	.	.	0	0	.
2	.	.	.	.	.	.	0	0	.
3	.	.	.	.	.	.	10	8 483	.
4	.	.	.	.	.	.	0	0	.
5	.	.	.	.	.	.	2	516	.
6	.	.	.	.	.	.	0	0	.
7	.	.	.	.	.	.	1	120	.
8	.	.	.	.	.	.	2	18 805	.
9	.	.	.	.	.	.	4	36 263	.
0	.	.	.	.	.	.	7	63 190	.

5. Consumer price indices (base period: 2000=100)

	2002	2003	2004	2005	2006	2007
General indices	134.2	153.1	176.0	207.4	224.5	236.6
Food index, including non-alcoholic beverages	144.8	153.8	175.8	216.3	228.3	232.6
Clothing indices, including footwear	97.6	117.8	126.2	126.9	137.9	149.8
Rent indices [11]	116.1	155.4	187.5	210.1	245.5	270.1

[1] Persons aged 14 years and over. [2] Sep. [3] Civilian labour force employed. [4] Persons aged 10 years and over. [5] Nov. [6] Persons aged 15 years and over. [7] Incl. persons seeking their first job. [8] Establishments with 10 or more persons employed. [9] Year beginning in April of year indicated. [10] Excl. workers indirectly involved. [11] Incl. water, electricity, gas and other fuels.

[1] Personnes âgées de 14 ans et plus. [2] Sept. [3] Main-d'oeuvre civile occupée. [4] Personnes âgées de 10 ans et plus. [5] Nov. [6] Personnes âgées de 15 ans et plus. [7] Y compris les personnes en quête de leur premier emploi. [8] Etablissements occupant 10 personnes et plus. [9] Année commençant en avril de l'année indiquée. [10] Non compris les travailleurs indirectement impliqués. [11] Y compris l'eau, l'électricité, le gaz et autres combustibles.

[1] Personas de 14 años y más. [2] Sept. [3] Fuerza de trabajo civil ocupada. [4] Personas de 10 años y más. [5] Nov. [6] Personas de 15 años y más. [7] Incl. las personas en busca de su primer empleo. [8] Establecimientos con 10 y más trabajadores. [9] Año que comienza en abril del año indicado. [10] Excl. los trabajadores indirectamente implicados. [11] Incl. el agua, la electricidad, el gas y otros combustibles.

Niue

1. Economically active population, Employment and Unemployment ('000)

	Economically active population		Employment		Unemployment	
	Total	Women (%)	Total	Women (%)	Total	Women (%)
Age group	2001 [1] Population census		2001 ★ Population census		2001 [1] Population census	
Total	0.951	49.5	0.930	49.6	0.021	47.6
15-19	0.047	46.8	0.040	47.5	0.007	42.9
20-24	0.097	45.4	0.091	46.2	0.006	33.3
25-29	0.103	45.6	0.101	45.5	0.002	50.0
30-34	0.097	51.5	0.097	51.5	0.000	.
35-39	0.097	49.5	0.095	49.5	0.002	50.0
40-44	0.107	45.8	0.105	44.8	0.002	100.0
45-49	0.112	55.4	0.110	55.5	0.002	50.0
50-54	0.073	56.2	0.073	56.2	0.000	.
55-59	0.070	45.7	0.070	45.7	0.000	.
60-64	0.069	56.5	0.069	56.5	0.000	.
65+	0.079	46.8	0.079	46.8	0.000	.

Economic activity (ISIC-Rev.3) — 2001 [1] Population census

	Total	Women (%)
Total	0.663	41.6
A Agriculture, Hunting and Forestry	0.055	29.1
B Fishing	0.005	0.0
C Mining and Quarrying	0.017	.
D Manufacturing	0.019	73.7
E Electricity, Gas and Water Supply	0.027	14.8
F Construction	0.072	6.9
G Wholesale and Retail Trade; Repair of Motor Vehicles ...	0.048	50.0
H Hotels and Restaurants	0.029	72.4
I Transport, Storage and Communications	0.064	39.1
J Financial Intermediation	0.035	57.1
K Real Estate, Renting and Business Activities	0.003	33.3
L Public Administration and Defence; Compulsory Social ...	0.096	43.8
M Education	0.063	69.8
N Health and Social Work	0.072	48.6
O Other Community, Social and Personal Service Activities	0.051	41.2
Q Extra-Territorial Organizations and Bodies	0.004	50.0
X Not classifiable by economic activity	0.003	33.3

Occupation (ISCO-88) — 2001 [1] Population census

	Total	Women (%)
Total	0.663	41.6
1 Legislators, senior officials and managers	0.047	31.9
2 Professionals	0.063	46.0
3 Technicians and associate professionals	0.062	40.3
4 Clerks	0.091	53.8
5 Service workers and shop and market sales workers	0.087	52.9
6 Skilled agricultural and fishery workers	0.011	27.3
7 Craft and related trade workers	0.043	25.6
8 Plant and machine operators and assemblers	0.020	25.0
9 Elementary occupations	0.231	39.4
0 Armed forces	0.008	25.0

2. Population ('000), Activity rate and Unemployment rate

	Population 2001 Population census			Activity rate 2001 Population census			Unemployment rate 2001 [1] Population census		
Age group	Total	Men	Women	Total	Men	Women	Total	Men	Women
Total	1.788	0.897	0.891	53.2	53.5	52.9	2.2	2.3	2.1
15+	1.259	0.626	0.630	75.5	76.7	74.8	2.2	2.3	2.1
15-24	0.269	0.130	0.137	53.5	60.0	48.2	9.0	10.3	7.6
25-54	0.648	0.331	0.316	90.9	88.2	94.0	1.4	1.0	1.7
55+	0.342	0.165	0.177	63.7	66.7	61.0	0.0	0.0	0.0

3. Paid employment ('000), Hours of work (weekly) and Wages

Statistics not available.

4. Occupational injuries and Strikes and Lockouts

Statistics not available.

5. Consumer price indices (base period: 2000=100)

	2002	2003	2004	2005	2006	2007
General indices	109.7	112.3	116.6 [2]	117.0	119.7	127.8
Food index, including non-alcoholic beverages	115.1	118.3	121.2 [2]	122.0	127.2	134.9
Clothing indices, including footwear	108.4	109.8	115.4 [2]	132.2	131.9	144.6
Rent indices	96.8	96.8	97.5 [2]	98.7	100.5	107.0

[1] Persons aged 15 years and over. [2] Average of the last three quarters.

Norfolk Island

1. Economically active population, Employment and Unemployment ('000)

	Economically active population		Employment		Unemployment	
	Total	Women (%)	Total	Women (%)	Total	Women (%)
Age group		2006 Population census				
Total	1.1	47.5	.	.	.	.
Occupation (ISCO-1968)		1996 [1] Population census				
Total	1.1	48.1	.	.	.	.
0/1 Professional, technical and related workers	0.1	49.1	.	.	.	.
2 Administrative and managerial workers	0.1	28.2	.	.	.	.
3 Clerical and related workers	0.1	84.6	.	.	.	.
4 Sales workers	0.2	85.9	.	.	.	.
5 Service workers	0.2	64.8	.	.	.	.
6 Agriculture, animal husbandry and forestry workers ...	0.0	7.1	.	.	.	.
7/8/9 Production and related workers, transport equipment ...	0.3	6.7	.	.	.	.
X Not classifiable by occupation	0.0	60.0	.	.	.	.
Status in employment (ICSE-1993)		1996 [1] Population census				
Total	1.1	48.1	.	.	.	.

2. Population ('000), Activity rate and Unemployment rate

	Population			Activity rate			Unemployment rate		
Age group		2006 [2] Population census			2006 [2] Population census				
	Total	Men	Women	Total	Men	Women	Total	Men	Women
Total	1.9	0.9	0.9	60.1	64.1	56.2	.	.	.

3. Paid employment ('000), Hours of work (weekly) and Wages

Statistics not available.

4. Occupational injuries and Strikes and Lockouts

Statistics not available.

5. Consumer price indices (base period: 2000=100)

	2002	2003	2004	2005	2006	2007
General indices	105.9	109.1	118.6	125.2	134.4	.
Food index, including non-alcoholic beverages	112.4	118.4	123.4	129.9	137.3	.
Clothing indices, including footwear	101.2	103.7	105.4	106.3	106.4	.

[1] Aug. [2] "De jure" population.   [1] Août. [2] Population "de jure".   [1] Agosto. [2] Población "de jure".

Northern Mariana Islands

1. Economically active population, Employment and Unemployment ('000)

	Economically active population		Employment		Unemployment	
	Total	Women (%)	Total	Women (%)	Total	Women (%)
Age group	2003 [1] Labour force survey		2003 ★ Labour force survey		2003 [1] Labour force survey	
Total	39.179	59.1	37.388	59.2	1.791	55.4
16-19	0.892	57.3	0.705	56.2	0.187	61.5
20-24	6.234	81.1	6.004	82.1	0.230	55.2
25-29	7.739	71.1	7.548	71.4	0.191	58.1
30-34	7.264	62.5	7.034	62.5	0.230	63.0
35-39	5.732	48.5	5.520	47.6	0.212	70.3
40-44	4.165	42.5	4.002	42.7	0.163	36.2
45-49	3.543	43.7	3.342	43.4	0.201	49.8
50-54	1.778	42.1	1.616	42.8	0.162	35.2
55-59	0.990	46.7	0.874	43.9	0.116	67.2
60-64	0.531	32.6	0.498	29.9	0.033	72.7
65-69	0.209	21.1	0.161	20.5	0.048	22.9
70-74	0.044	38.6	0.027	.	0.017	100.0
75+	0.057	0.0	0.057	.	0.000	.

Economic activity (ISIC-Rev.2)			1995 [1,2] Population census			
Total	.	.	24.5	43.4	.	.
1 Agriculture, Hunting, Forestry and Fishing	.	.	0.3	6.1	.	.
2 Mining and Quarrying	.	.	0.1	115.9	.	.
3 Manufacturing	.	.	1.8	53.7	.	.
5 Construction	.	.	1.9	6.3	.	.
6 Wholesale and Retail Trade and Restaurants and Hotels	.	.	5.4	53.1	.	.
7 Transport, Storage and Communication	.	.	2.4	27.7	.	.
8 Financing, Insurance, Real Estate and Business Services	.	.	2.3	34.3	.	.
9 Community, Social and Personal Services	.	.	10.4	50.4	.	.

Occupation (ISCO-1968)			1995 [1,2] Population census			
Total	.	.	24.5	43.5	.	.
0/1 Professional, technical and related workers	.	.	2.7	42.0	.	.
2 Administrative and managerial workers	.	.	4.2	45.0	.	.
3 Clerical and related workers	.	.	2.5	56.8	.	.
4 Sales workers	.	.	2.5	62.3	.	.
5 Service workers	.	.	5.5	63.2	.	.
6 Agriculture, animal husbandry and forestry workers ...	.	.	0.8	2.9	.	.
7/8/9 Production and related workers, transport equipment ...	.	.	6.3	18.8	.	.

2. Population ('000), Activity rate and Unemployment rate

Age group	Population 2003 Labour force survey			Activity rate 2003 Labour force survey			Unemployment rate 2003 [1] Labour force survey		
	Total	Men	Women	Total	Men	Women	Total	Men	Women
Total	.	.	.	.	.	.	4.6	5.0	4.3
15+	47.883	19.423	28.457	81.8	82.5	81.3	4.6	5.0	4.3
15-24	10.217	3.153	7.064	69.7	49.4	78.8	5.9	11.2	4.3
25-54	34.349	14.461	19.886	88.0	92.2	84.9	3.8	4.0	3.7
55+	3.317	1.809	1.507	55.2	62.7	46.2	11.7	7.3	18.7

3. Paid employment ('000), Hours of work (weekly) and Wages

Statistics not available.

4. Occupational injuries and Strikes and Lockouts

Statistics not available.

5. Consumer price indices (base period: 2000=100)

Saipan	2002	2003	2004	2005	2006	2007
General indices	99.4	98.4	99.3	99.8	104.7	111.9
Food index, including non-alcoholic beverages	93.0	90.7	94.9	93.9	91.4	96.0
Clothing indices, including footwear	98.3	93.0	90.0	91.3	96.2	94.6
Rent indices [3]	.	97.8	94.9	.	.	.

[1] Persons aged 16 years and over. [2] April. [3] Housing.   [1] Personnes âgées de 16 ans et plus. [2] Avril. [3] Logement.   [1] Personas de 16 años y más. [2] Abril. [3] Vivienda.

Norway

1. Economically active population, Employment and Unemployment ('000)

	Economically active population		Employment		Unemployment	
	Total	Women (%)	Total	Women (%)	Total	Women (%)
Age group	2007 [1] Labour force survey		2007 ★ Labour force survey		2007 [1] Labour force survey	
Total	2 507.0	47.2	2 444.0	47.2	63.0	46.0
15-19	139.0	51.1	124.0	51.6	15.0	46.7
20-24	213.0	48.4	202.0	48.5	11.0	45.5
25-29	249.0	47.0	241.0	46.9	8.0	50.0
30-34	283.0	47.0	277.0	46.9	6.0	50.0
35-39	324.0	47.2	318.0	47.2	6.0	50.0
40-44	310.0	47.1	304.0	47.4	6.0	33.3
45-49	282.0	47.5	278.0	47.5	4.0	50.0
50-54	262.0	47.3	259.0	47.5	3.0	33.3
55-59	232.0	46.6	230.0	46.5	2.0	50.0
60-64	161.0	44.7	159.0	44.7	2.0	50.0
65-69	41.0	43.9	41.0	43.9	0.0	.
70-74	10.0	30.0	10.0	30.0	0.0	.
Economic activity (ISIC-Rev.2)	1995 ★ Labour force survey				1995 [2] Labour force survey	
Total	2 186	45.7	.	.	107	43.0
1 Agriculture, Hunting, Forestry and Fishing	109	26.6	.	.	3	33.3
3 Manufacturing [3]	318	25.8	.	.	10	30.0
5 Construction	131	6.1	.	.	5	.
6 Wholesale and Retail Trade and Restaurants and Hotels	369	52.3	.	.	12	58.3
7 Transport, Storage and Communication	174	29.9	.	.	4	25.0
8 Financing, Insurance, Real Estate and Business Services	164	42.7	.	.	4	50.0
9 Community, Social and Personal Services	821	64.8	.	.	18	61.1
0 Activities not Adequately Defined	11	27.3	.	.	6	33.3
Unemployed seeking their first job	.	.	.	.	45	42.2
Economic activity (ISIC-Rev.3)			2007 [1] Labour force survey			
Total	.	.	2 443	47.2	.	.
A Agriculture, Hunting and Forestry	.	.	56	25.0	.	.
B Fishing	.	.	13	7.7	.	.
C Mining and Quarrying	.	.	39	20.5	.	.
D Manufacturing	.	.	277	24.2	.	.
E Electricity, Gas and Water Supply	.	.	17	23.5	.	.
F Construction	.	.	180	7.2	.	.
G Wholesale and Retail Trade; Repair of Motor Vehicles ...	.	.	358	47.5	.	.
H Hotels and Restaurants	.	.	67	67.2	.	.
I Transport, Storage and Communications	.	.	158	25.3	.	.
J Financial Intermediation	.	.	55	47.3	.	.
K Real Estate, Renting and Business Activities	.	.	269	37.5	.	.
L Public Administration and Defence; Compulsory Social ...	.	.	154	47.4	.	.
M Education	.	.	215	64.2	.	.
N Health and Social Work	.	.	476	82.4	.	.
O Other Community, Social and Personal Service Activities	.	.	105	55.2	.	.
P Households with Employed Persons	.	.	3	100.0	.	.
X Not classifiable by economic activity	.	.	1	100.0	.	.
Occupation (ISCO-88)			2007 [1] Labour force survey		2007 [1] Employment office records	
Total	.	.	2 443	47.2	46	47.8
1 Legislators, senior officials and managers	.	.	141	31.2	3	33.3
2 Professionals	.	.	277	44.8	3	33.3
3 Technicians and associate professionals	.	.	616	53.7	5	60.0
4 Clerks	.	.	169	62.1	5	60.0
5 Service workers and shop and market sales workers	.	.	591	69.2	13	69.2
6 Skilled agricultural and fishery workers	.	.	61	21.3	1	0.0
7 Craft and related trade workers	.	.	275	7.3	4	0.0
8 Plant and machine operators and assemblers	.	.	178	15.7	4	25.0
9 Elementary occupations	.	.	117	65.8	6	50.0
0 Armed forces	.	.	19	10.5	1	0.0
X Not classifiable by occupation	.	.	.	.	3	33.3
Education level (ISCED-97)	2007 [1] Labour force survey		2007 ★ Labour force survey		2007 [1] Labour force survey	
Total	2 507.0	47.2	2 444.0	47.2	63.0	46.0
X No schooling	-	.	-	.	-	.
0 Pre-primary education	14.0	50.0	12.0	50.0	2.0	50.0
1 Primary education or first stage of basic education	1.0	100.0	1.0	100.0	-	.
2 Lower secondary or second stage of basic education	284.0	45.8	268.0	45.9	16.0	43.8
3 Upper secondary education	1 292.0	44.6	1 262.0	44.6	30.0	43.3
4 Post-secondary non-tertiary education	77.0	33.8	76.0	34.2	1.0	0.0
5A First stage of tertiary education - theoretically based	824.0 [4]	53.0	.	.	.	.
5					10.0	50.0
6 Second stage of tertiary education	15.0	33.3	12.0	25.0	3.0	66.7
Status in employment (ICSE-1993)			2007 [1] Labour force survey			
Total	.	.	2 443	47.2	.	.
1 Employees	.	.	2 248	48.9	.	.
2 Employers	.	.	52	28.8	.	.
3 Own-account workers	.	.	136	25.7	.	.
5 Contributing family workers	.	.	6	66.7	.	.
6 Not classifiable by status	.	.	0	.	.	.

Norway

2. Population ('000), Activity rate and Unemployment rate

Age group	Population 2007 [5] Labour force survey			Activity rate 2007 [5] Labour force survey			Unemployment rate 2007 [1] Labour force survey		
	Total	Men	Women	Total	Men	Women	Total	Men	Women
Total							2.5	2.6	2.5
15+	3 447.0	1 742.0	1 704.0	72.7	75.9	69.4	2.5	2.6	2.5
15-24	593.0	304.0	290.0	59.4	58.6	60.0	7.4	7.9	6.9
25-54	1 956.0	994.0	962.0	87.4	90.8	83.9	1.9	2.0	1.9

3. Paid employment ('000), Hours of work (weekly) and Wages

Economic activity (ISIC-Rev.3)	Paid employment 2007 [1] Labour force survey			Hours of work 2007 [6] Labour force survey Hours actually worked / Employees			Wages 2007 [7,8,9] Labour-related establishment survey Earnings per month / Employees / Krone		
	Total	Men	Women	Total	Men	Women	Total	Men	Women
Total	2 248	1 148	1 100	34.4	37.7	30.4	.	.	.
A-B	.	.	.	41.8	45.0	30.5	.	.	.
C-Q	.	.	.	34.1	37.4	30.4	33 387	35 024	30 303
A	17	12	6	40.4	43.7	30.5	.	.	.
B	9	8	1	49.3	50.8	30.2	31 439	31 700	29 655
C	39	31	8	45.0	46.9	36.7	50 076	50 920	46 303
D	268	203	65	36.7	38.1	32.1	31 983	32 710	29 124
E	17	13	4	35.6	35.9	34.7	38 222	38 890	35 461
F	153	141	12	38.1	38.7	30.3	30 957	30 986	30 419
G	335	173	162	31.8	35.6	27.5	32 351	34 097	28 319
H	63	21	42	29.4	31.7	28.2	24 811	26 344	23 525
I	145	106	39	38.5	40.6	32.2	32 755	33 592	30 090
J	54	28	26	35.8	37.1	34.3	44 013	51 456	35 291
K	236	143	94	35.8	38.2	31.7	37 718	40 333	32 628
L	154	81	73	33.1	33.9	32.2	31 764	33 820	30 282
M	212	75	137	33.7	36.5	32.1	32 297 [10]	33 820 [10]	30 178 [10]
N	456	75	381	30.9	35.1	29.9	28 148	34 599	26 672
O	86	38	48	32.7	36.3	29.7	34 254	36 465	31 505
P	3	0	3	14.0	21.4	13.3	.	.	.
Q	.	.	.	30.0	30.0	.	.	.	.
X	1	1	1	.	.	.	.	.	.

Share of women in wage employment in the non-agricultural sector [1] (2007 - Labour force survey): **49.2%**

4. Occupational injuries and Strikes and Lockouts

Economic activity (ISIC-Rev.3)	Rates of fatal injuries 2007 [11] Labour inspectorate records Per 100,000 workers employed Reported injuries			Rates of non-fatal injuries 2007 [11] Labour inspectorate records Per 100,000 workers employed Reported injuries			Strikes and lockouts 2007 [12] Records of employers'/workers' organizations		
	Total	Men	Women	Total	Men	Women	Strikes and lockouts	Workers involved [13]	Days not worked
Total	1.6	.	.	781	.	.	4	519	3 954
A	7.1	.	.	336	.	.	0	0	0
B	7.7 [14]	.	.	469 [14]	.	.	0	0	0
C	5.1 [15]	.	.	418 [15]	.	.	0	0	0
D	2.9	.	.	1 451	.	.	0	0	0
E	0.0	.	.	1 059	.	.	0	0	0
F	2.8	.	.	1 263	.	.	0	0	0
G	0.3	.	.	313	.	.	0	0	0
H	0.0	.	.	427	.	.	0	0	0
I	5.7 [16]	.	.	983 [16]	.	.	0	0	0
J	0.0	.	.	66	.	.	0	0	0
K	1.1	.	.	299	.	.	1	9	56
L	2.6	.	.	949	.	.	0	0	0
M	0.0	.	.	1 063	.	.	1	12	180
N	0.2	.	.	865	.	.	1	496	3 704
O	0.0	.	.	351	.	.	1	2	14
P	0.0	.	.	133	.	.	.	.	.

5. Consumer price indices (base period: 2000=100)

	2002	2003	2004	2005	2006	2007
General indices	104.4	106.9	107.4	109.1	111.6	112.4
Food index, including non-alcoholic beverages	96.5	99.7	101.5	103.1	104.6	107.3
Electricity, gas and other fuel indices	122.7	161.5	149.7	147.2	183.5	150.8
Clothing indices, including footwear	93.7	83.8	78.0	74.4	71.8	68.1
Rent indices [17]	109.4	113.9	116.0	118.2	120.9	122.7

Norway

[1] Persons aged 15 to 74 years. [2] Persons aged 16 to 74 years. [3] Incl. major divisions 2 and 4. [4] Levels 5. [5] "De jure" population. [6] Persons aged 15 to 74 years; prior to 2006: 16 to 74 years. [7] Only remuneration in cash; excl. overtime payments. [8] Full-time employees. [9] Oct. [10] Private education. [11] Cases reported during the year indicated. [12] Excl. work stoppages lasting less than one day. [13] Excl. workers indirectly involved. [14] Excl. sea fishing. [15] Excl. offshore oil extraction. [16] Excl. maritime transport. [17] Housing.

[1] Personnes âgées de 15 à 74 ans. [2] Personnes âgées de 16 à 74 ans. [3] Y compris les branches 2 et 4. [4] Niveaux 5. [5] Population "de jure". [6] Personnes âgées de 15 à 74 ans; avant 2006: 16 à 74 ans. [7] Seulement rémunération en espèces; non compris les paiements pour heures supplémentaires. [8] Salariés à plein temps. [9] Oct. [10] Enseignement privé. [11] Cas déclarés pendant l'année indiquée. [12] Non compris les arrêts du travail dont la durée est inférieure à une journée. [13] Non compris les travailleurs indirectement impliqués. [14] Non compris la pêche en mer. [15] Non compris l'extraction du pétrole en mer. [16] Non compris les transports maritimes. [17] Logement.

[1] Personas de 15 a 74 años. [2] Personas de 16 a 74 años. [3] Incl. las grandes divisiones 2 y 4. [4] Niveles 5. [5] Población "de jure". [6] Personas de 15 a 74 años; antes de 2006: 16 a 74 años. [7] Sólo remuneración en efectivo; excl. los pagos por horas extraordinarias. [8] Asalariados a tiempo completo. [9] Oct. [10] Enseñanza privada. [11] Casos declarados en el año indicado. [12] Excl. las interrupciones del trabajo de menos de un día de duración. [13] Excl. los trabajadores indirectamente implicados. [14] Excl. la pesca de altura y costera. [15] Excl. la extracción del petróleo en el mar. [16] Excl. el transporte marítimo. [17] Vivienda.

Nouvelle-Calédonie

1. Population active, Emploi et Chômage ('000)

	Population active		Emploi		Chômage	
	Total	Femmes (%)	Total	Femmes (%)	Total	Femmes (%)
Groupe d'âge	1996 [1] Recensement de la population		1996 ★ Recensement de la population		1996 [1] Recensement de la population	
Total	80.589	39.7	65.571	37.8	15.018	47.9
14-19	3.205	42.5	1.379	36.3	1.826	47.1
20-29	26.330	42.8	18.248	39.6	8.082	49.9
30-39	23.777	41.0	20.563	40.1	3.214	46.9
40-49	16.989	37.1	15.578	36.9	1.411	39.1
50-59	8.703	32.1	8.248	32.3	0.455	29.0
60-69	1.319	30.9	1.289	31.0	0.030	26.7
70+	0.266	34.2	0.266	34.2	-	.
Activité économique (CITI-Rév.2)	1989 [1,2] Recensement de la population					
Total	65.95	37.5	.	.	.	.
1 Agriculture, chasse, sylviculture et pêche	7.76	37.5	.	.	.	.
2 Industries extractives	0.91	4.6	.	.	.	.
3 Industries manufacturières	4.67	20.8	.	.	.	.
4 Electricité, gaz et eau	0.58	14.8	.	.	.	.
5 Bâtiment et travaux publics	4.48	4.2	.	.	.	.
6 Commerce de gros et de détail; restaurants et hôtels	9.45	42.4	.	.	.	.
7 Transports, entrepôts et communications	3.09	22.4	.	.	.	.
8 Banques, assurances, affaires immobilières et services ...	2.48	51.5	.	.	.	.
9 Services fournis à la collectivité, services sociaux ...	22.02	47.0	.	.	.	.
0 Activités mal désignées	5.23	36.8	.	.	.	.
Chômeurs n'ayant jamais travaillé	5.29	43.3	.	.	.	.
Activité économique (CITI-Rév.3)			1996 [1] Recensement de la population			
Total	.	.	64.377	38.5	.	.
A-B	.	.	4.663	22.0	.	.
C Activités extractives	.	.	1.948	6.1	.	.
D Activités de fabrication	.	.	5.532	25.0	.	.
E Production et distribution d'électricité, de gaz et d'eau	.	.	0.697	19.2	.	.
F Construction	.	.	6.890	6.7	.	.
G Commerce de gros et de détail; réparation de véhicules ...	.	.	8.375	40.9	.	.
H Hôtels et restaurants	.	.	2.875	59.8	.	.
I Transports, entreposage et communications	.	.	3.679	26.6	.	.
J Intermédiation financière	.	.	1.495	59.7	.	.
K Immobilier, locations et activités de services aux entreprises	.	.	3.344	37.2	.	.
L Administration publique et défense; sécurité sociale obligatoire	.	.	9.646	34.4	.	.
M Education	.	.	6.580	58.0	.	.
N Santé et action sociale	.	.	3.416	67.8	.	.
O Autres activités de services collectifs, sociaux et personnels	.	.	0.952	44.7	.	.
P Ménages privés employant du personnel domestique	.	.	3.395	91.3	.	.
Q Organisations et organismes extraterritoriaux	.	.	0.890	48.3	.	.
Profession (CITP-1968)	1989 [1,2] Recensement de la population					
Total	65.95	37.5	.	.	.	.
0/1 Personnel des professions scientifiques, techniques ...	7.69	46.2	.	.	.	.
2 Directeurs et cadres administratifs supérieurs	0.91	14.3	.	.	.	.
3 Personnel administratif et travailleurs assimilés	10.78	65.0	.	.	.	.
4 Personnel commercial et vendeurs	4.99	50.9	.	.	.	.
5 Travailleurs spécialisés dans les services	5.32	73.3	.	.	.	.
6 Agriculteurs, éleveurs, forestiers, pêcheurs et chasseurs	7.91	36.7	.	.	.	.
7/8/9 Ouvriers et manoeuvres non agricoles et conducteurs ...	20.56	11.6	.	.	.	.
AF Forces armées	2.50	1.4	.	.	.	.
Chômeurs n'ayant jamais travaillé	5.29	43.3	.	.	.	.
Niveau d'instruction (CITE-97)	2004 [1] Recensement de la population				1996 [1] Recensement de la population	
Total	169.056	.	.	.	15.018	47.9
X Non scolarisé	10.960	.	.	.	0.302	41.7
0 Education préprimaire	9.297	.	.	.	.	.
0-1	.	.	.	.	4.333	40.5
1 Enseignement primaire ou premier cycle de l'éducation ...	20.866	.	.	.	.	.
2 Premier cycle de l'enseignement secondaire ou deuxième ...	32.654	.	.	.	6.298	47.5
3 Enseignement secondaire (deuxième cycle)	17.261	.	.	.	3.557	57.0
4 Enseignement postsecondaire qui n'est pas du supérieur	12.426	.	.	.	.	.
5A Premier cycle de l'enseignement supérieur - théorie	65.592	.	.	.	.	.
5-6	.	.	.	.	0.528	55.3
Situation dans la profession (CISP-58)	1989 [1,2] Recensement de la population					
Total	65.95	37.5	.	.	.	.
1 Employeurs et personnes travaillant à leur propre compte	10.77	30.8	.	.	.	.
2 Salariés	42.43	38.7	.	.	.	.
3 Travailleurs familiaux non rémunérés	1.03	75.1	.	.	.	.
4 Inclassables d'après la situation	11.72	36.0	.	.	.	.
Situation dans la profession (CISP-1993)			1996 [1] Recensement de la population			
Total	.	.	64.377	38.5	.	.
1 Salariés	.	.	53.944	40.9	.	.
2,3	.	.	10.214	25.3	.	.
5 Travailleurs familiaux collaborant à l'entreprise familiale	.	.	0.219	53.0	.	.

Nouvelle-Calédonie

2. Population ('000), Taux d'activité et Taux de chômage

Groupe d'âge	Population 2004 Recensement de la population			Taux d'activité 1996 [3] Recensement de la population			Taux de chômage 1996 [1] Recensement de la population		
	Total	Hommes	Femmes	Total	Hommes	Femmes	Total	Hommes	Femmes
Total	230.8	116.5	114.3	40.9	48.2	33.3	18.6	16.5	22.5
15+	166.3	83.3	83.0	51.9	61.3	42.1	.	.	.
15-24	38.6	19.6	19.1	.	.	.	.	.	.
25-54	95.9	47.9	48.0	.	.	.	.	.	.
55+	31.7	15.8	15.9	.	.	.	.	.	.

3. Emploi rémunéré ('000), Durée du travail (hebdomadaire) et Salaires

Activité économique (CITI-Rév.3)	Emploi rémunéré 2002 Fichiers des assurances			Durée du travail			Salaires 2001 [4] Enquête auprès des établissements, relative au travail Gains par mois / Salariés / Franc CFP		
	Total	Hommes	Femmes	Total	Hommes	Femmes	Total	Hommes	Femmes
Total	62.243	.	.	.	.	.	.	.	.
C-K	.	.	.	.	.	.	285 302 [5]	.	.
D-E	.	.	.	.	.	.	310 151	.	.
G	.	.	.	.	.	.	253 493 [6]	.	.
J	.	.	.	.	.	.	397 812 [7]	.	.

4. Lésions professionnelles et Grèves et lock-out

Activité économique (CITI-Rév.2)	Taux de lésions mortelles			Taux de lésions non mortelles			Grèves et lock-out 1999 Source inconnue		
	Total	Hommes	Femmes	Total	Hommes	Femmes	Grèves et lock-out	Travailleurs impliqués	Journées non effectuées
Total	.	.	.	.	.	.	33	1 880	19 802
3-4	.	.	.	.	.	.	5	.	.
5	.	.	.	.	.	.	7	.	.
6	.	.	.	.	.	.	3	.	.
7	.	.	.	.	.	.	3	.	.
8-9	.	.	.	.	.	.	15	.	.

5. Indices des prix à la consommation (période de base: 2000=100)

Nouméa	2002	2003	2004	2005	2006	2007
Indices généraux	104.1	105.4	106.2	107.6	110.7	111.8
Indices de l'alimentation, y compris les boissons non alcoolisées	105.0	107.0	108.2	109.7	113.0	114.5
Indices de l'électricité, gaz et autres combustibles	105.6	107.0	107.4	108.0	113.1	114.7
Indices de l'habillement, y compris les chaussures	100.6	99.3	98.4	95.2	92.9	89.0
Indices du loyer	100.7	101.8	102.9	104.1	109.1	112.1

[1] Persons aged 14 years and over. [2] April. [3] "De facto" population. [4] Excl. overtime. [5] Private sector. [6] Incl. insurance. [7] Financial intermediation only.

[1] Personnes âgées de 14 ans et plus. [2] Avril. [3] Population "de facto". [4] Non compris les heures supplémentaires. [5] Secteur privé. [6] Y compris les assurances. [7] Intermédiation financière seulement.

[1] Personas de 14 años y más. [2] Abril. [3] Población "de facto". [4] Excl. las horas extraordinarias. [5] Sector privado. [6] Incl. seguros. [7] Sólo intermediación financiera.

Oman

1. Economically active population, Employment and Unemployment ('000)

	Economically active population		Employment		Unemployment	
	Total	Women (%)	Total	Women (%)	Total	Women (%)
Age group	2003 [1 2 3] Population census		2000 [1 4 5] Labour force survey		1996 [4] Labour force survey	
Total	856.947	18.4	281.645	13.7	52.640	28.3
15-19	36.778	34.2	.	.	.	.
20-24	149.180	30.7	.	.	.	.
25-29	173.820	22.6	.	.	.	.
30-34	146.074	16.5	.	.	.	.
35-39	117.615	13.4	.	.	.	.
40-44	95.108	10.5	.	.	.	.
45-49	65.565	8.1	.	.	.	.
50-54	38.259	6.6	.	.	.	.
55-59	17.520	6.1	.	.	.	.
60-64	9.166	4.8	.	.	.	.
65-69	3.640	5.7	.	.	.	.
70-74	2.121	5.4	.	.	.	.
75+	1.517	7.8	.	.	.	.
?	0.584	18.0	.	.	.	.

Economic activity (ISIC-Rev.3)

2000 [1 4 5] Labour force survey

	Total	Women (%)
Total	281.645	13.7
A Agriculture, Hunting and Forestry	10.702	19.1
B Fishing	7.246	0.6
C Mining and Quarrying	8.468	7.8
D Manufacturing	13.887	32.3
E Electricity, Gas and Water Supply	1.097	3.9
F Construction	7.956	2.6
G Wholesale and Retail Trade; Repair of Motor Vehicles ...	16.557	14.5
H Hotels and Restaurants	2.509	8.5
I Transport, Storage and Communications	20.366	4.2
J Financial Intermediation	6.073	23.2
K Real Estate, Renting and Business Activities	3.032	36.5
L Public Administration and Defence; Compulsory Social ...	136.909	2.4
M Education	33.785	47.3
N Health and Social Work	10.609	51.1
O Other Community, Social and Personal Service Activities	1.413	14.4
P Households with Employed Persons	0.022	.
Q Extra-Territorial Organizations and Bodies	0.114	57.9
X Not classifiable by economic activity	0.895	11.6

Occupation (ISCO-88)

2000 [1 4 5] Labour force survey

	Total	Women (%)
Total	281.644	13.7
1 Legislators, senior officials and managers	8.887	9.3
2 Professionals	30.543	46.6
3 Technicians and associate professionals	28.875	18.1
4 Clerks	38.523	14.5
5 Service workers and shop and market sales workers	65.287	6.4
6 Skilled agricultural and fishery workers	19.291	9.7
7 Craft and related trade workers	13.298	7.4
8 Plant and machine operators and assemblers	36.167	7.9
9 Elementary occupations	39.591	6.9
X Not classifiable by occupation	1.182	7.0

Education level (ISCED-76)

	2000 [1 4 5] Labour force survey		1996 ★ Labour force survey		1996 [4] Labour force survey	
	Total	Women (%)	Total	Women (%)	Total	Women (%)
Total	365.889	17.6	595.329	12.3	52.640	28.3
X No schooling	96.564	7.2	199.141	10.4	8.751	8.2
1 First level	71.542	7.4	97.877	6.6	14.439	7.0
2 Second level, first stage	55.927	7.0	107.021	6.9	8.558	22.7
3 Second level, second stage	91.221	30.1	81.345	14.4	18.570	56.2
5 Third level, first stage, leading to an award not equivalent ...	28.226	42.2	34.829	31.1	1.627	34.5
6 Third level, first stage, leading to a first university degree ...	20.588	39.6	68.178	21.4	0.695	35.3
7 Third level, second stage	1.675	36.2	6.336	15.7	-	.
? Level not stated	0.146	.	0.602	49.2	.	.

Status in employment (ICSE-1993)

2000 [1 4 5] Labour force survey

	Total	Women (%)
Total	281.645	13.7
1 Employees	247.371	13.7
2 Employers	5.047	4.7
3 Own-account workers	27.002	13.2
6 Not classifiable by status	2.225	40.0

2. Population ('000), Activity rate and Unemployment rate

	Population 2003 [1 3] Population census			Activity rate 2003 [1 3] Population census			Unemployment rate		
Age group	Total	Men	Women	Total	Men	Women	Total	Men	Women
Total	2 340.8	1 313.2	1 027.6	36.6	53.3	15.3	.	.	.
15+	1 547.9	908.6	639.3	55.3	76.9	24.6	.	.	.
15-24	519.6	267.6	252.0	35.8	47.7	23.1	.	.	.
25-54	889.6	563.5	326.1	71.5	95.7	29.7	.	.	.
55+	138.7	77.5	61.2	24.5	41.3	3.2	.	.	.

Oman

3. Paid employment ('000), Hours of work (weekly) and Wages

Economic activity (ISIC-Rev.3)	Paid employment 2002 [6][7] Labour-related establishment survey			Hours of work			Wages		
	Total	Men	Women	Total	Men	Women	Total	Men	Women
Total	547.477	.	.	.	.	.	.	.	.
A-B	65.900	.	.	.	.	.	.	.	.
C	5.975	.	.	.	.	.	.	.	.
D	70.627	.	.	.	.	.	.	.	.
E	1.365	.	.	.	.	.	.	.	.
F	134.179	.	.	.	.	.	.	.	.
G	148.350	.	.	.	.	.	.	.	.
H	22.710	.	.	.	.	.	.	.	.
I	4.660	.	.	.	.	.	.	.	.
J	1.374	.	.	.	.	.	.	.	.
K	4.909	.	.	.	.	.	.	.	.
M	4.970	.	.	.	.	.	.	.	.
N	8.932	.	.	.	.	.	.	.	.
O	5.127	.	.	.	.	.	.	.	.
P	67.487	.	.	.	.	.	.	.	.
Q	0.912	.	.	.	.	.	.	.	.

Share of women in wage employment in the non-agricultural sector [5] (2001 - Labour-related establishment survey): **25.3%**

4. Occupational injuries and Strikes and Lockouts

Statistics not available.

5. Consumer price indices (base period: 2000=100)

Muscat	2002	2003	2004	2005	2006	2007
General indices	98.3	97.9	98.3	100.2	103.3	108.5
Food index, including non-alcoholic beverages [8]	98.3	98.2	98.5	102.7	108.3	118.9
Electricity, gas and other fuel indices [9]	100.0	100.1	100.4	100.1	100.1	100.2
Clothing indices, including footwear	99.6	97.5	95.6	99.2	98.8	99.1
Rent indices	99.2	99.2	99.0	96.5	98.7	106.1
General index, excluding housing [10]	97.9	97.3	97.8	101.2	104.9	110.0

[1] Excl. armed forces. [2] Persons aged 15 years and over. [3] Dec. [4] Persons aged 12 years and over. [5] Omanis. [6] Private sector. [7] Expatriates. [8] Incl. tobacco. [9] Incl. water. [10] Excl. Water, Electricity, Gas and Other Fuels.

[1] Non compris les forces armées. [2] Personnes âgées de 15 ans et plus. [3] Déc. [4] Personnes âgées de 12 ans et plus. [5] Omanais. [6] Secteur privé. [7] Expatriés. [8] Y compris le tabac. [9] Y compris l'eau. [10] Non compris l'eau, l'électricité, le gaz et autres combustibles.

[1] Excl. las fuerzas armadas. [2] Personas de 15 años y más. [3] Dic. [4] Personas de 12 años y más. [5] Omanís. [6] Sector privado. [7] Expatriados. [8] Incl. el tabaco. [9] Incl. el agua. [10] Excl. el agua, la electricidad, el gas y otros combustibles.

Pakistan

1. Economically active population, Employment and Unemployment ('000)

	Economically active population		Employment		Unemployment	
	Total	Women (%)	Total	Women (%)	Total	Women (%)
Age group	2007 [1 2 3] Labour force survey		2007 ★ Labour force survey		2007 [2 3] Labour force survey	
Total	50 331	20.7	47 651	20.0	2 680	32.6
10-14	2 777	32.1	2 524	33.3	253	20.2
15-19	6 699	21.2	6 138	21.2	561	21.2
20-24	7 440	19.9	6 944	19.3	496	27.8
25-29	6 137	19.1	5 887	18.5	250	32.0
30-34	5 033	21.6	4 933	21.3	100	36.0
35-39	5 310	21.4	5 231	21.1	79	35.4
40-44	4 528	20.7	4 448	20.1	80	53.8
45-49	3 985	19.9	3 882	19.3	103	39.8
50-54	2 871	18.8	2 733	17.3	138	48.6
55-59	2 225	18.3	2 060	15.9	165	48.5
60-64	1 614	16.7	1 458	13.7	156	44.2
65+	1 712	16.4	1 413	11.3	299	40.5
Economic activity (ISIC-Rev.2)	2007 ★ Labour force survey		2007 [1 2 3] Labour force survey		2007 [2 3] Labour force survey	
Total	50 331	20.7	47 651	20.0	2 680	32.6
1 Agriculture, Hunting, Forestry and Fishing	20 806	33.2	20 780	33.2	26	38.5
2 Mining and Quarrying	53	1.9	52	1.9	1	.
3 Manufacturing	6 519	17.7	6 454	17.7	65	10.8
4 Electricity, Gas and Water	363	1.7	360	1.7	3	.
5 Construction	3 164	1.7	3 127	1.7	37	2.7
6 Wholesale and Retail Trade and Restaurants and Hotels	6 912	3.1	6 872	3.1	40	.
7 Transport, Storage and Communication	2 589	0.7	2 569	0.7	20	.
8 Financing, Insurance, Real Estate and Business Services	553	2.4	544	2.4	9	.
9 Community, Social and Personal Services	6 919	17.3	6 868	17.3	51	19.6
0 Activities not Adequately Defined	26	3.8	25	4.0	1	.
Unemployed seeking their first job	.	.	.	.	2 427	34.8
Occupation (ISCO-1968)	1996 ★ Labour force survey		2000 [1 2 3] Labour force survey			
Total	34 318	13.3	36 847	14.0	.	.
0/1 Professional, technical and related workers	1 636	20.6	1 959	25.6	.	.
2 Administrative and managerial workers	304	3.9	242	8.7	.	.
3 Clerical and related workers	1 500	4.2	1 181	4.1	.	.
4 Sales workers	4 450	2.4	6 485	4.7	.	.
5 Service workers	1 457	14.8	1 842	10.6	.	.
6 Agriculture, animal husbandry and forestry workers ...	14 961	17.7	16 005	20.7	.	.
7/8/9 Production and related workers, transport equipment ...	8 327	6.9	9 133	8.4	.	.
X Not classifiable by occupation	-	.	-	.	.	.
Occupation (ISCO-88)					2007 [2 3] Labour force survey	
Total	.	.	.	.	2 680	32.6
1 Legislators, senior officials and managers	.	.	.	.	22	.
2 Professionals	.	.	.	.	6	16.7
3 Technicians and associate professionals	.	.	.	.	21	33.3
4 Clerks	.	.	.	.	7	.
5 Service workers and shop and market sales workers	.	.	.	.	44	.
6 Skilled agricultural and fishery workers	.	.	.	.	10	10.0
7 Craft and related trade workers	.	.	.	.	51	21.6
8 Plant and machine operators and assemblers	.	.	.	.	19	.
9 Elementary occupations	.	.	.	.	73	11.0
0 Armed forces	.	.	.	.	-	.
Unemployed seeking their first job	.	.	.	.	2 427	34.8
Education level (ISCED-76)	2007 [1 2 3] Labour force survey		2007 ★ Labour force survey		2007 [2 3] Labour force survey	
Total	50 331	20.7	47 651	20.0	2 680	32.6
X No schooling	23 311	32.8	22 108	32.0	1 203	47.3
0 Education preceding the first level	1 676	11.2	1 593	10.9	83	18.1
2 Second level, first stage	8 071	11.7	7 687	11.1	384	22.9
3 Second level, second stage	5 558	6.4	5 252	6.0	306	12.7
5 Third level, first stage, leading to an award not equivalent ...	6 310	8.3	5 921	7.5	389	20.6
6 Third level, first stage, leading to a first university degree ...	2 517	10.8	2 354	10.0	163	23.3
7 Third level, second stage	2 693	16.8	2 547	16.1	146	30.1
9 Education not definable by level	195	15.9	189	16.4	6	.
Status in employment (ICSE-1993)			2007 [1 2 3] Labour force survey			
Total	.	.	47 651	20.0	.	.
1 Employees	.	.	17 829	13.2	.	.
2 Employers	.	.	391	3.1	.	.
3 Own-account workers	.	.	16 449	7.7	.	.
5 Contributing family workers	.	.	12 982	45.5	.	.

Pakistan

2. Population ('000), Activity rate and Unemployment rate

Age group	Population 2007 [1,3,4] Labour force survey			Activity rate 2007 [1,3,4] Labour force survey			Unemployment rate 2007 [2,3] Labour force survey		
	Total	Men	Women	Total	Men	Women	Total	Men	Women
Total	158 170	81 252	76 918	31.8	49.1	13.5	5.3	4.5	8.4
15+	90 532	45 784	44 748	52.5	83.1	21.3	5.1	4.2	8.6
15-24	31 957	16 253	15 704	44.2	69.2	18.4	7.5	7.1	8.9
25-54	46 545	22 815	23 730	59.9	97.3	23.9	2.7	2.0	5.2
55+	12 030	6 716	5 314	46.1	68.4	18.0	11.2	7.6	28.2

3. Paid employment ('000), Hours of work (weekly) and Wages

Economic activity (ISIC-Rev.2)	Paid employment 2006 [1,2,5] Labour force survey			Hours of work			Wages 2002 Administrative reports Earnings per month / Employees / Rupee		
	Total	Men	Women	Total	Men	Women	Total	Men	Women
Total	17 490	15 142	2 348	.	.	.	.	.	.
1	1 854	1 246	609	.	.	.	.	.	.
2	40	39	1	.	.	.	.	.	.
3	4 331	3 715	617	.	.	.	4 113.74	.	.
4	306	304	2	.	.	.	.	.	.
5	2 643	2 611	32	.	.	.	.	.	.
6	1 430	1 400	30	.	.	.	.	.	.
7	1 627	1 605	22	.	.	.	.	.	.
8	293	280	14	.	.	.	.	.	.
9	4 946	3 924	1 022	.	.	.	.	.	.
0	18	18	-	.	.	.	.	.	.

4. Occupational injuries and Strikes and Lockouts

Economic activity (ISIC-Rev.3)	Rates of fatal injuries 2002 Labour inspectorate records Per 100,000 workers employed			Rates of non-fatal injuries 2002 Labour inspectorate records Per 100,000 workers employed			Strikes and lockouts 2003 Labour relations records		
	Total	Men	Women	Total	Men	Women	Strikes and lockouts	Workers involved	Days not worked
Total	.	.	.	.	.	.	17	1 263	7 183
B	.	.	.	.	.	.	0	0	0
C	77.7	.	.	53.5	.	.	0	0	0
D	27.6	.	.	48.1	.	.	17	1 263	7 183
E	.	.	.	.	.	.	0	0	0
F	.	.	.	.	.	.	0	0	0
G	.	.	.	.	.	.	0	0	0
H	.	.	.	.	.	.	0	0	0
I	.	.	.	.	.	.	0	0	0
J	.	.	.	.	.	.	0	0	0
K	.	.	.	.	.	.	0	0	0
N	.	.	.	.	.	.	0	0	0
O	.	.	.	.	.	.	0	0	0

5. Consumer price indices (base period: 2000=100)

	2002	2003	2004	2005	2006	2007
General indices	107.4	110.5	118.7	129.5	139.7	150.3
Food index, including non-alcoholic beverages	105.9	108.6	120.2	132.1	143.3	158.8
Electricity, gas and other fuel indices [6]	100.0	104.9	107.5	113.8	126.9	133.1
Clothing indices, including footwear [6]	100.0	104.1	105.9	110.3	114.6	122.9
Rent indices [6]	100.0	101.6	110.2	123.0	132.7	142.1

[1] Excl. armed forces. [2] Persons aged 10 years and over. [3] Jan. [4] "De jure" population. [5] July. [6] Index base 2002=100.

[1] Non compris les forces armées. [2] Personnes âgées de 10 ans et plus. [3] Janv. [4] Population "de jure". [5] Juillet. [6] Indice base 2002=100.

[1] Excl. las fuerzas armadas. [2] Personas de 10 años y más. [3] Enero. [4] Población "de jure". [5] Julio. [6] Indice base 2002=100.

Palau

1. Economically active population, Employment and Unemployment ('000)

	Economically active population		Employment		Unemployment	
	Total	Women (%)	Total	Women (%)	Total	Women (%)
Age group	1995 [1,2] Population census		1995 ★ Population census		1995 [1,2] Population census	
Total	8.368	39.6	7.780	39.1	0.588	45.4
16-19	0.260	40.8	0.166	41.0	0.094	40.4
20-24	1.018	48.3	0.870	48.0	0.148	50.0
25-29	1.431	43.5	1.343	43.2	0.088	47.7
30-34	1.427	38.3	1.342	37.8	0.085	47.1
35-39	1.325	37.2	1.270	37.2	0.055	36.4
40-44	1.067	38.0	1.036	37.7	0.031	45.2
45-49	0.780	35.3	0.758	35.4	0.022	31.8
50-54	0.472	37.7	0.458	37.1	0.014	57.1
55-59	0.301	31.6	0.291	31.3	0.010	40.0
60-64	0.124	33.9	0.106	31.1	0.018	50.0
65-74	0.126	34.1	0.112	33.9	0.014	35.7
75+	0.037	37.8	0.028	28.6	0.009	66.7

Economic activity (ISIC-Rev.2)			2000 [1,3] Population census			
Total	.	.	9.4	37.9	.	.
1 Agriculture, Hunting, Forestry and Fishing	.	.	0.7	16.3	.	.
3 Manufacturing	.	.	0.1	18.5	.	.
5 Construction	.	.	1.2	6.4	.	.
6 Wholesale and Retail Trade and Restaurants and Hotels	.	.	4.2	47.9	.	.
7 Transport, Storage and Communication	.	.	0.5	23.2	.	.
8 Financing, Insurance, Real Estate and Business Services	.	.	0.4	50.3	.	.
9 Community, Social and Personal Services	.	.	2.4	44.4	.	.

Occupation (ISCO-1968)			2000 [1,3] Population census			
Total	.	.	9.4	37.9	.	.
0/1 Professional, technical and related workers	.	.	1.3	43.8	.	.
2 Administrative and managerial workers	.	.	1.2	35.5	.	.
3 Clerical and related workers	.	.	1.1	61.6	.	.
4 Sales workers	.	.	0.6	76.6	.	.
5 Service workers	.	.	1.8	53.8	.	.
6 Agriculture, animal husbandry and forestry workers ...	.	.	0.7	12.0	.	.
7/8/9 Production and related workers, transport equipment ...	.	.	2.7	14.2	.	.

2. Population ('000), Activity rate and Unemployment rate

	Population			Activity rate			Unemployment rate		
Age group	1995 [2,4] Population census			1995 [2,4] Population census			1995 [1,2] Population census		
	Total	Men	Women	Total	Men	Women	Total	Men	Women
Total	.	.	.	.	.	.	7.0	6.3	8.1
15+	12.114	6.549	5.565	69.1	77.2	59.5	7.0	6.3	8.1
15-24	2.438	1.254	1.184	52.4	54.2	50.5	18.9	19.1	18.7
25-54	7.848	4.470	3.378	82.8	89.1	74.6	4.5	4.1	5.2
55+	1.828	0.825	1.003	32.2	47.8	19.3	8.7	6.9	12.4

3. Paid employment ('000), Hours of work (weekly) and Wages

Statistics not available.

4. Occupational injuries and Strikes and Lockouts

Statistics not available.

5. Consumer price indices (base period: 2000=100)

Statistics not available for the period 2002-2007.

---

[1] Persons aged 16 years and over. [2] Sep. [3] April. [4] "De facto" population.

[1] Personnes âgées de 16 ans et plus. [2] Sept. [3] Avril. [4] Population "de facto".

[1] Personas de 16 años y más. [2] Sept. [3] Abril. [4] Población "de facto".

Panamá

1. Población económicamente activa, Empleo y Desempleo ('000)

	Población económicamente activa		Empleo		Desempleo	
	Total	Mujeres (%)	Total	Mujeres (%)	Total	Mujeres (%)
Grupo de edad	2007 [1,2] Encuesta de la fuerza de trabajo		2007 ★ Encuesta de la fuerza de trabajo		2007 [1,2] Encuesta de la fuerza de trabajo	
Total	1 355.928	37.8	1 263.958	36.8	91.970	51.7
15-19	83.346	26.6	68.490	24.4	14.856	36.6
20-24	172.599	38.1	145.291	34.7	27.308	55.9
25-29	171.225	39.7	154.939	37.7	16.286	59.2
30-34	162.834	39.9	.	.	.	.
30-39	.	.	.	.	16.297	59.8
35-39	176.807	43.5	.	.	.	.
40-44	163.143	41.7	.	.	.	.
40-49	.	.	.	.	11.223	51.7
45-49	137.439	37.9	.	.	.	.
50-54	111.140	41.0	.	.	.	.
50-59	.	.	.	.	4.462	32.0
55-59	73.828	32.7	.	.	.	.
60-64	48.086	26.5	.	.	.	.
60-69	.	.	.	.	1.538	11.6
65-69	26.056	26.6	.	.	.	.
70+	.	.	.	.	.	.
70-74	16.219	20.8	.	.	.	.
75+	13.206	14.8	.	.	.	.
Actividad económica (CIIU-Rev.3)	2007 [1,2] Encuesta de la fuerza de trabajo		2007 [1,2] Encuesta de la fuerza de trabajo		2007 [1,2] Encuesta de la fuerza de trabajo	
Total	1 355.928	37.8	1 264.000	36.8	91.970	51.7
A Agricultura, ganadería, caza y silvicultura	178.733	8.6	176.500	8.6	2.239	6.8
B Pesca	9.812	4.0	9.800	4.1	0.056	.
C Explotación de minas y canteras	3.642	6.5	3.600	5.6	0.038	100.0
D Industrias manufactureras	115.907	34.6	109.600	34.8	6.300	32.1
E Suministro de electricidad, gas y agua	8.970	27.7	8.100	28.4	0.881	22.5
F Construcción	132.620	3.8	122.400	3.8	10.180	3.9
G Comercio al por mayor y al por menor; reparación ...	260.889	41.9	240.700	40.7	20.154	55.9
H Hoteles y restaurantes	74.899	61.6	69.500	60.9	5.378	71.0
I Transporte, almacenamiento y comunicaciones	96.097	14.2	91.900	13.5	4.179	30.9
J Intermediación financiera	30.488	59.7	28.800	60.8	1.672	42.6
K Actividades inmobiliarias, empresariales y de alquiler	71.538	39.5	67.000	38.4	4.575	56.3
L Administración pública y defensa; planes de seguridad ...	82.185	42.3	79.600	41.7	2.626	61.9
M Enseñanza	68.757	66.1	65.300	66.0	3.457	69.0
N Servicios sociales y de salud	51.925	68.9	50.600	68.4	1.342	88.2
O Otras actividades de servicios comunitarios ...	68.986	46.0	63.800	46.1	5.223	45.0
P Hogares privados con servicio doméstico	84.655	89.7	76.100	89.0	8.515	97.2
Q Organizaciones y órganos extraterritoriales	0.670	40.7	0.700	42.9	-	.
X No pueden clasificarse según la actividad económica	15.155	60.8	.	.	.	.
Desempleados sin empleo anterior	15.155	60.8	.	.	15.155	60.8
Ocupación (CIUO-88)	2007 [1,2] Encuesta de la fuerza de trabajo		2007 [1,2] Encuesta de la fuerza de trabajo		2007 [1,2] Encuesta de la fuerza de trabajo	
Total	1 355.928	37.8	1 264.000	36.8	91.970	51.7
1 Miembros del poder ejecutivo y de los cuerpos legislativos ...	37.879	43.6	37.200	43.5	0.640	45.2
2 Profesionales científicos e intelectuales	121.616	57.1	117.700	57.0	3.884	60.2
3 Técnicos y profesionales de nivel medio	64.726	41.8	61.700	41.7	3.052	43.2
4 Empleados de oficina	153.955	69.8	141.600	69.1	12.309	78.6
5 Trabajadores de los servicios y vendedores de comercios ...	226.741	50.4	210.400	48.9	16.329	69.9
6 Agricultores y trabajadores calificados agropecuarios ...	185.828	8.1	183.200	8.1	2.607	5.8
7 Oficiales, operarios y artesanos de artes mecánicas ...	189.404	14.4	180.700	14.4	8.717	12.5
8 Operadores de instalaciones y máquinas y montadores	87.876	3.9	84.600	3.5	3.264	12.7
9 Trabajadores no calificados	272.748	45.1	246.700	45.1	26.013	44.6
X No pueden clasificarse según la ocupación	15.155	60.8	.	.	-	.
Desempleados sin empleo anterior	15.155	60.8	.	.	15.155	60.8
Nivel de educación (CINE-97)	2007 [1,2] Encuesta de la fuerza de trabajo		2007 ★ Encuesta de la fuerza de trabajo		2007 [1,2] Encuesta de la fuerza de trabajo	
Total	1 355.928	37.8	1 263.958	36.8	91.970	51.7
X Sin escolaridad	33.789	26.9	33.451	27.0	0.338	17.2
1 Enseñanza primaria o primer ciclo de la educación básica	345.262	26.0	332.880	25.7	12.382	32.5
2 Primer ciclo de enseñanza secundaria o segundo ciclo de ...	244.534	31.4	223.797	30.5	20.737	40.4
3 Segundo ciclo de enseñanza secundaria	404.427	39.2	368.147	37.4	36.280	57.5
4 Enseñanza postsecundaria, no terciaria	2.254	58.3	2.072	54.6	0.182	100.0
5A Primer ciclo de la educación terciaria - teóricos [3]	325.662	54.3	303.611	53.7	22.051	63.4
Situación en el empleo (CISE-1993)	2007 [1,2] Encuesta de la fuerza de trabajo		2007 [1,2] Encuesta de la fuerza de trabajo		2007 ★ Encuesta de la fuerza de trabajo	
Total	1 355.928	37.8	1 264.000	36.8	91.928	51.6
1 Asalariados	942.087	40.7	873.300	39.7	68.787	53.0
2 Empleadores	40.924	21.2	40.600	20.9	0.324	49.4
3 Trabajadores por cuenta propia	320.430	29.0	312.900	29.1	7.530	23.5
4 Miembros de cooperativas de productores	0.133	.	0.100	.	0.033	.
5 Trabajadores familiares auxiliares	37.199	49.7	37.100	49.8	0.099	.
6 Inclasificables según la situación	15.155	60.8	.	.	.	.

Panamá

2. Población ('000), Tasa de actividad y Tasa de desempleo

Grupo de edad	Población 2007[2] Encuesta de la fuerza de trabajo			Tasa de actividad 2007[2] Encuesta de la fuerza de trabajo			Tasa de desempleo 2007[1,2] Encuesta de la fuerza de trabajo		
	Total	Hombres	Mujeres	Total	Hombres	Mujeres	Total	Hombres	Mujeres
Total	.	.	.	.	.	.	6.8	5.3	9.3
15+	2 180.870	1 071.211	1 109.659	62.2	78.7	46.2	.	.	.
15-24	543.079	275.451	267.628	47.1	61.0	32.8	16.5	12.8	23.6
25-54	1 166.962	569.618	597.344	79.1	96.1	62.8	.	.	.
55+	470.829	226.142	244.687	37.7	56.7	20.1	.	.	.

3. Empleo remunerado ('000), Horas de trabajo (por semana) y Salarios

Actividad económica (CIIU-Rev.3)	Empleo remunerado 2007[1,2] Encuesta de la fuerza de trabajo			Horas de trabajo 2007[1,2] Encuesta de la fuerza de trabajo Horas efectivamente trabajadas / Empleo total			Salarios 2007[1,2,4] Encuesta de la fuerza de trabajo Ganancias por hora / Empleo total / Balboa		
	Total	Hombres	Mujeres	Total	Hombres	Mujeres	Total	Hombres	Mujeres
Total	873.300	526.500	346.800	43.1	44.3	41.4	2.3	2.3	2.3
A-B	.	.	.	39.3	39.2	41.6	1.0	1.0	1.5
C-Q	.	.	.	43.5	45.1	41.4	2.4	2.4	2.3
A	70.600	68.200	2.400	38.6	38.5	40.7	1.0	1.0	1.5
B	4.000	3.800	0.200	51.8	51.8	51.9	1.3	1.3	1.2
C	3.600	3.400	0.200	47.7	47.8	46.1	1.6	1.6	2.0
D	72.000	54.900	17.100	45.6	46.3	43.4	2.2	2.2	2.1
E	8.100	5.800	2.300	44.0	44.0	44.2	3.3	2.6	4.9
F	90.300	86.300	4.000	45.3	45.5	40.8	2.0	2.0	2.9
G	148.600	89.000	59.600	45.8	46.3	45.0	1.9	1.8	2.0
H	46.000	21.800	24.200	44.7	46.8	42.7	1.4	1.5	1.3
I	53.000	42.200	10.800	44.1	44.7	41.8	3.7	3.8	3.2
J	27.300	10.700	16.600	43.8	43.8	43.9	4.2	4.4	4.0
K	53.800	31.700	22.100	46.1	48.1	43.2	2.5	2.4	2.8
L	79.600	46.400	33.200	42.3	43.6	40.4	3.0	3.1	2.9
M	64.200	21.800	42.400	38.5	39.2	38.2	3.3	3.4	3.2
N	43.300	15.400	27.800	41.9	42.6	41.5	4.0	4.6	3.6
O	32.300	16.200	16.100	42.4	41.8	43.0	1.9	2.0	1.8
P	76.100	8.500	67.700	38.4	41.7	38.0	0.8	0.9	0.8
Q	0.700	0.400	0.300	41.6	41.2	42.3	9.6	11.7	6.6

Proporción de mujeres entre los empleados remunerados en el sector no agrícola [1,2] (2007 - Encuesta de la fuerza de trabajo): **43.1%**

4. Lesiones profesionales y Huelgas y cierres patronales

Actividad económica (CIIU-Rev.3)	Tasas de lesiones mortales 1998 Registros de seguros Por 100 000 asalariados Lesiones indemnizadas			Tasas de lesiones no mortales			Huelgas y cierres patronales 2007 Registros de relaciones laborales		
	Total	Hombres	Mujeres	Total	Hombres	Mujeres	Huelgas y cierres patronales	Trabajadores implicados[5]	Días no trabajados[6]
Total	14	.	.	.	.	.	4	690	110 610
A	12	.	.	.	.	.	0	0	0
B	0	.	.	.	.	.	0	0	0
C	0	.	.	.	.	.	0	0	0
D	14	.	.	.	.	.	0	0	0
E	58	.	.	.	.	.	0	0	0
F	52	.	.	.	.	.	3	650	108 170
G	10	.	.	.	.	.	1	40	2 440
H	12	.	.	.	.	.	0	0	0
I	28	.	.	.	.	.	0	0	0
J	5	.	.	.	.	.	0	0	0
K	9	.	.	.	.	.	0	0	0
L	5	.	.	.	.	.	0	0	0
M	4	.	.	.	.	.	0	0	0
N	15	.	.	.	.	.	0	0	0
O	18	.	.	.	.	.	0	0	0
P	0	.	.	.	.	.	.	.	.

5. Índices de precios al consumidor (periodo de base: 2000=100)

[7,8]	2002	2003	2004	2005	2006	2007
Índices generales	.	100.0	100.4	103.3	105.9	110.3
Índices de la alimentación incluyendo las bebidas no alcohólicas	.	100.0	101.3	105.6	107.0	114.2
Índices del vestido, incl. calzado	.	100.0	97.1	97.1	96.3	94.9
Índices del aquiler [9]	.	100.0	99.8	104.0	109.3	114.3
Índices generales, excluyendo la vivienda	.	100.0	100.6	103.6	106.1	110.5

[1] Persons aged 15 years and over. [2] Aug. [3] Levels 5-6. [4] Median. [5] Excl. workers indirectly involved. [6] Computed on the basis of an eight-hour working day. [7] Urban areas. [8] Index base 2003=100. [9] Incl. water, electricity, gas and other fuels.

[1] Personnes âgées de 15 ans et plus. [2] Août. [3] Niveaux 5-6. [4] Médiane. [5] Non compris les travailleurs indirectement impliqués. [6] Calculées sur la base de journées de travail de huit heures. [7] Régions urbaines. [8] Indice base 2003=100. [9] Y compris l'eau, l'électricité, le gaz et autres combustibles.

[1] Personas de 15 años y más. [2] Agosto. [3] Niveles 5-6. [4] Mediana. [5] Excl. los trabajadores indirectamente implicados. [6] Calculados en base a días de trabajo de ocho horas. [7] Areas urbanas. [8] Indice base 2003=100. [9] Incl. el agua, la electricidad, el gas y otros combustibles.

Papua New Guinea

1. Economically active population, Employment and Unemployment ('000)

Age group	Economically active population Total	Women (%)	Employment Total	Women (%)	Unemployment Total	Women (%)
	2000 [1,2] Population census		2000 ★ Population census		2000 [1,2] Population census	
Total	2 413.357	47.9	2 344.734	.	68.623	.
10-14	155.413	48.5	152.754	.	2.659	.
15-19	275.696	49.2	262.696	.	13.000	.
20-24	333.585	49.7	314.468	.	19.117	.
25-29	350.978	49.9	337.675	.	13.303	.
30-34	312.896	48.4	305.095	.	7.801	.
35-39	274.533	47.8	269.312	.	5.221	.
40-44	210.235	47.4	207.118	.	3.117	.
45-49	165.629	45.9	163.584	.	2.045	.
50-54	120.964	45.8	119.854	.	1.110	.
55-59	83.980	43.8	83.374	.	0.606	.
60-64	62.300	43.5	61.954	.	0.346	.
65-69	36.361	41.7	36.195	.	0.166	.
70-74	18.292	39.3	18.226	.	0.066	.
75+	12.495	36.1	12.429	.	0.066	.

Economic activity (ISIC-Rev.3)

2000 [1,2] Population census

			Total			
Total	.	.	2 344.734	.	.	.
A Agriculture, Hunting and Forestry	.	.	1 666.247	.	.	.
B Fishing	.	.	30.024	.	.	.
C Mining and Quarrying	.	.	9.282	.	.	.
D Manufacturing	.	.	25.557	.	.	.
E Electricity, Gas and Water Supply	.	.	2.208	.	.	.
F Construction	.	.	48.312	.	.	.
G Wholesale and Retail Trade; Repair of Motor Vehicles ...	.	.	353.186	.	.	.
H Hotels and Restaurants	.	.	4.395	.	.	.
I Transport, Storage and Communications	.	.	24.513	.	.	.
J Financial Intermediation	.	.	3.670	.	.	.
K Real Estate, Renting and Business Activities	.	.	27.459	.	.	.
L Public Administration and Defence; Compulsory Social ...	.	.	32.043	.	.	.
M Education	.	.	27.118	.	.	.
N Health and Social Work	.	.	12.341	.	.	.
O Other Community, Social and Personal Service Activities	.	.	31.409	.	.	.
P Households with Employed Persons	.	.	15.523	.	.	.
Q Extra-Territorial Organizations and Bodies	.	.	0.163	.	.	.
X Not classifiable by economic activity	.	.	31.284	.	.	.

Occupation (ISCO-88)

2000 [1,2] Population census

			Total			
Total	.	.	2 344.734	.	.	.
1 Legislators, senior officials and managers	.	.	16.687	.	.	.
2 Professionals	.	.	24.175	.	.	.
3 Technicians and associate professionals	.	.	46.323	.	.	.
4 Clerks	.	.	27.260	.	.	.
5 Service workers and shop and market sales workers	.	.	46.188	.	.	.
6 Skilled agricultural and fishery workers	.	.	1 928.836	.	.	.
7 Craft and related trade workers	.	.	72.115	.	.	.
8 Plant and machine operators and assemblers	.	.	26.789	.	.	.
9 Elementary occupations	.	.	143.775	.	.	.
0 Armed forces	.	.	12.586	.	.	.

2. Population ('000), Activity rate and Unemployment rate

Age group	Population 2000 [2,3] Population census Total	Men	Women	Activity rate 2000 [2,3] Population census Total	Men	Women	Unemployment rate 2000 [1,2] Population census Total	Men	Women
Total	5 190.8	2 690.5	2 500.2	46.5	46.7	46.3	2.8	4.3	1.3
15+	3 115.9	1 600.5	1 515.4	72.5	73.5	71.3	2.9	.	.
15-24	1 029.3	533.1	496.1	59.2	57.7	60.8	5.3	.	.
25-54	1 765.1	891.7	873.5	81.3	83.7	78.9	2.3	.	.
55+	321.4	175.7	145.8	66.4	69.9	62.2	0.6	.	.

3. Paid employment ('000), Hours of work (weekly) and Wages

Economic activity (ISIC-Rev.2)	Paid employment 2000 [1,2] Population census Total	Men	Women	Hours of work Total	Men	Women	Wages Total	Men	Women
2-9	415.898	282.532	133.366	.	.	.	.	.	.

Papua New Guinea

4. Occupational injuries and Strikes and Lockouts

Economic activity (ISIC-Rev.2)	Rates of fatal injuries Total	Men	Women	Rates of non-fatal injuries Total	Men	Women	Strikes and lockouts	Workers involved	Days not worked
Total	.	.	.	.	.	.	10	2 095	5 424
1	.	.	.	.	.	.	2	199	533
2	.	.	.	.	.	.	1	1 200	3 600
3	.	.	.	.	.	.	2	166	466
4 [4]	.	.	.	.	.	.	0	0	0
5	.	.	.	.	.	.	1	250	250
6	.	.	.	.	.	.	0	0	0
7	.	.	.	.	.	.	2	230	525
8	.	.	.	.	.	.	0	0	0
9 [5]	.	.	.	.	.	.	2	50	50
0	.	.	.	.	.	.	0	0	0

Strikes and lockouts: 1993 — Labour relations records

5. Consumer price indices (base period: 2000=100)

	2002	2003	2004	2005	2006	2007
General indices	122.2	140.2	143.2	145.6	149.8	.
Food index, including non-alcoholic beverages	128.3	145.3	146.1	151.2	157.7	.
Clothing indices, including footwear	121.6	127.2	130.5	127.9	131.4	.
Rent indices [6]	109.5	116.1	124.3	135.7	145.5	.

[1] Persons aged 10 years and over. [2] July. [3] "De facto" population. [4] Incl. sanitary and similar services. [5] Excl. sanitary and similar services. [6] Incl. water, electricity, gas and other fuels.

[1] Personnes âgées de 10 ans et plus. [2] Juillet. [3] Population "de facto". [4] Y compris les services sanitaires et connexes. [5] Non compris les services sanitaires et connexes. [6] Y compris l'eau, l'électricité, le gaz et autres combustibles.

[1] Personas de 10 años y más. [2] Julio. [3] Población "de facto". [4] Incl. los servicios de saneamiento y otros servicios conexos. [5] Excl. los servicios de saneamiento y otros servicios conexos. [6] Incl. el agua, la electricidad, el gas y otros combustibles.

Paraguay

1. Población económicamente activa, Empleo y Desempleo ('000)

Grupo de edad	Población económicamente activa Total	Mujeres (%)	Empleo Total	Mujeres (%)	Desempleo Total	Mujeres (%)
	2007 [1 2 3] Encuesta de la fuerza de trabajo		2007 ★ Encuesta de la fuerza de trabajo		2007 [2 3] Encuesta de la fuerza de trabajo	
Total	2 877.530	39.9	2 716.365	39.1	161.165	53.7
10-14	106.692	25.7	101.193	26.0	5.499	19.2
15-19	337.838	34.5	295.481	31.6	42.357	55.4
20-24	380.209	39.4	335.070	37.2	45.139	56.0
25-29	359.568	44.5	335.831	43.7	23.737	55.6
30-34	287.217	42.8	276.440	42.1	10.777	59.7
35-39	283.181	42.3	273.377	41.2	9.804	73.4
40-44	286.561	45.4	281.567	45.2	4.994	56.2
45-49	255.178	41.8	249.788	41.2	5.390	68.1
50-54	212.259	37.0	207.023	37.6	5.236	12.5
55-59	126.704	33.3	123.603	33.0	3.101	47.4
60-64	99.736	38.7	97.797	39.2	1.939	11.8
65+	.	.	.	.	3.192	34.8
65-69	63.411	41.3	.	.	.	.
70-74	44.445	33.6	.	.	.	.
75+	34.531	44.3	.	.	.	.

Actividad económica (CIIU-Rev.3)	2007 [1 2 3] Encuesta de la fuerza de trabajo		2007 ★ Encuesta de la fuerza de trabajo		2007 [2 3] Encuesta de la fuerza de trabajo	
Total	2 877.530	39.9	2 716.365	39.1	161.165	53.7
A-B	802.609	31.1	800.577	31.2	2.032	23.9
C Explotación de minas y canteras	8.873	.	8.617	.	0.256	.
D Industrias manufactureras	333.336	28.8	319.250	29.0	14.086	24.4
E Suministro de electricidad, gas y agua	9.391	9.9	8.799	8.6	0.592	29.2
F Construcción	169.740	0.8	154.915	0.6	14.825	2.5
G-H	666.080	44.7	639.523	44.4	26.557	51.9
I Transporte, almacenamiento y comunicaciones	107.830	16.7	101.453	15.5	6.377	36.0
J-K	109.023	37.8	104.225	37.0	4.798	56.2
L-Q	621.470	66.7	578.426	65.7	43.044	80.2
X No pueden clasificarse según la actividad económica	49.178	59.5	.	.	.	.
Desempleados sin empleo anterior	48.598	59.4	.	.	48.598	59.4

Ocupación (CIUO-88)	2007 [1 2 3] Encuesta de la fuerza de trabajo		2007 ★ Encuesta de la fuerza de trabajo		2007 [2 3] Encuesta de la fuerza de trabajo	
Total	2 877.530	39.9	2 716.365	39.1	161.165	53.7
1 Miembros del poder ejecutivo y de los cuerpos legislativos ...	95.153	35.3	91.147	34.6	4.006	50.9
2 Profesionales científicos e intelectuales	133.314	58.5	131.357	58.8	1.957	41.4
3 Técnicos y profesionales de nivel medio	120.138	40.5	115.226	40.5	4.912	40.7
4 Empleados de oficina	156.769	54.0	147.594	53.2	9.175	66.9
5 Trabajadores de los servicios y vendedores de comercios ...	446.461	59.8	425.591	59.0	20.870	74.6
6 Agricultores y trabajadores calificados agropecuarios ...	742.972	32.8	739.834	32.9	3.138	15.5
7 Oficiales, operarios y artesanos de artes mecánicas ...	440.674	16.7	422.994	16.8	17.680	13.1
8 Operadores de instalaciones y máquinas y montadores	116.828	3.5	109.764	3.8	7.064	.
9 Trabajadores no calificados	567.429	50.5	523.664	49.3	43.765	64.9
0 Fuerzas armadas	9.194	4.7	.	.	.	.
X No pueden clasificarse según la ocupación	48.598	59.4	.	.	.	.
Desempleados sin empleo anterior	48.598	59.4	.	.	48.598	59.4

Nivel de educación (CINE-97)	2007 [1 2 3] Encuesta de la fuerza de trabajo		2007 ★ Encuesta de la fuerza de trabajo		2007 [2 3] Encuesta de la fuerza de trabajo	
Total	2 877.530	39.9	2 716.365	39.1	161.165	53.7
X Sin escolaridad	74.329	49.4	70.717	48.5	3.612	66.4
0 Enseñanza preescolar	0.239	.	.	.	.	.
1 Enseñanza primaria o primer ciclo de la educación básica	1 331.464	39.0	1 279.335	38.5	52.129	51.4
2 Primer ciclo de enseñanza secundaria o segundo ciclo de ...	439.294	34.0	410.982	33.2	28.312	44.5
3 Segundo ciclo de enseñanza secundaria	642.305	37.5	581.113	35.2	61.192	60.2
5A Primer ciclo de la educación terciaria - teóricos	112.985	62.8	108.865	62.2	4.120	77.8
5B Primer ciclo de la educación terciaria - práctica	258.407	48.5	246.607	48.8	11.800	40.4
6 Segundo ciclo de la enseñanza terciaria	17.384	38.8	.	.	.	.
? Nivel desconocido	1.123	.	.	.	.	.

Situación en el empleo (CISE-1993)	2002 [2 4] Censo de población		2007 [2 3] Encuesta de la fuerza de trabajo			
Total	1 980.5	32.1	2 716.4	39.1	.	.
1 Asalariados	963.8	40.8	1 307.4	38.1	.	.
2 Empleadores	58.8	24.1	138.1	21.7	.	.
3 Trabajadores por cuenta propia	826.0	23.6	997.2	44.2	.	.
5 Trabajadores familiares auxiliares	99.5	17.3	273.1	34.6	.	.
6 Inclasificables según la situación	13.2	43.2	0.6	67.7	.	.

2. Población ('000), Tasa de actividad y Tasa de desempleo

Grupo de edad	Población 2007 [1 3] Encuesta de la fuerza de trabajo			Tasa de actividad 2007 [1 3] Encuesta de la fuerza de trabajo			Tasa de desempleo 2007 [2 3] Encuesta de la fuerza de trabajo		
	Total	Hombres	Mujeres	Total	Hombres	Mujeres	Total	Hombres	Mujeres
Total	6 054.976	3 019.745	3 035.231	47.5	57.2	37.9	5.6	4.3	7.5
15+	3 985.882	1 949.522	2 036.360	69.5	84.6	55.1	5.6	4.3	7.6
15-24	1 235.879	618.846	617.033	58.1	72.9	43.2	12.2	8.6	18.3
25-54	2 058.304	1 005.156	1 053.148	81.8	96.1	68.2	3.6	2.7	4.7
55+	691.699	325.520	366.179	53.3	71.1	37.5	2.2	2.3	2.0

Paraguay

3. Empleo remunerado ('000), Horas de trabajo (por semana) y Salarios

Actividad económica (CIIU-Rev.3)	Empleo remunerado 2007 [2,3] Encuesta de la fuerza de trabajo			Horas de trabajo 2007 [3] Encuesta de la fuerza de trabajo Horas usualmente trabajadas / Asalariados			Salarios 2007 [3] Encuesta de la fuerza de trabajo Ganancias por mes / Asalariados / Guarani		
	Total	Hombres	Mujeres	Total	Hombres	Mujeres	Total	Hombres	Mujeres
Total	1 307.4	809.9	497.5	49	52	44	6 415.5	6 392.9	6 452.3
A-B	86.1	80.6	5.9	52	53	37	3 782.8	3 838.7	2 970.0
C-Q	.	.	.	49	52	44	6 601.2	6 675.3	.
C	6.0	6.0	-	51	51	.	4 121.1	4 121.1	.
D	201.6	163.7	37.9	52	53	49	5 399.1	5 550.4	4 745.9
E	8.8	8.0	0.8	47	48	31	13 112.8	13 653.5	7 360.5
F	98.0	97.0	1.0	54	54	43	4 565.5	4 526.5	8 337.0
G-H	254.4	179.8	74.5	53	54	51	6 374.2	5 922.1	7 465.2
I	81.5	68.6	12.9	54	55	47	7 639.3	7 230.5	9 819.2
J-K	75.1	46.1	29.1	48	54	39	8 303.8	8 004.6	8 778.0
L-Q	495.7	159.9	335.8	43	45	42	7 095.5	9 109.7	6 139.7
X	0.2	0.2	-	.	.	.	.	.	.

Proporción de mujeres entre los empleados remunerados en el sector no agrícola [2,3] (2007 - Encuesta de la fuerza de trabajo): **40.3%**

4. Lesiones profesionales y Huelgas y cierres patronales

Datos no disponibles.

5. Índices de precios al consumidor (periodo de base: 2000=100)

Asunción	2002	2003	2004	2005	2006	2007
Índices generales	118.5	135.4	141.3	149.5	165.4	178.8
Índices de la alimentación incluyendo las bebidas no alcohólicas	114.4	139.3	149.7	156.2	182.5	213.2
Índices del vestido, incl. calzado	108.4	117.0	122.5	128.6	137.1	141.5
Índices del aquiler [5,6]	125.4	137.8	139.8	145.5	155.7	159.7

[1] Excl. armed forces and conscripts. [2] Persons aged 10 years and over. [3] Fourth quarter. [4] Aug. [5] Incl. housing, water, electriciy and other fuels. [6] Incl. certain household equipment and cleaning products.

[1] Non compris les forces armées et les conscrits. [2] Personnes âgées de 10 ans et plus. [3] Quatrième trimestre. [4] Août. [5] Y compris le logement, l'eau, l'électricité et autres combustibles. [6] Y compris certains biens d'équipement de ménage et les produits d'entretien.

[1] Excl. las fuerzas armadas y los conscriptos. [2] Personas de 10 años y más. [3] Cuarto trimestre. [4] Agosto. [5] Incl. la vivienda, el agua, la electricidad y otros combustibles. [6] Incl. ciertos enseres domésticos y los productos de limpieza.

Perú

1. Población económicamente activa, Empleo y Desempleo ('000)

	Población económicamente activa		Empleo		Desempleo	
	Total	Mujeres (%)	Total	Mujeres (%)	Total	Mujeres (%)
Grupo de edad	2007 [1][2][3]		2007 ★		2007 [1][3]	
	Encuesta de la fuerza de trabajo		Encuesta de la fuerza de trabajo		Encuesta de la fuerza de trabajo	
Total	4 474.0	46.1	4 162.5	45.5	311.5	54.2
10-14	33.4	37.4	19.9	37.6	13.5	37.0
15-19	337.5	50.5	257.1	50.2	80.4	51.6
20-24	552.7	49.4	506.2	49.1	46.5	53.3
25-29	608.4	47.1	563.4	46.9	45.0	50.4
30-34	577.1	47.0	551.9	46.5	25.2	56.0
35-39	536.0	45.8	518.8	45.1	17.2	66.9
40-44	473.2	45.9	458.1	45.1	15.1	71.5
45-49	402.5	46.3	388.0	45.6	14.5	64.8
50-54	361.4	49.4	342.8	48.2	18.6	71.5
55-59	237.8	39.9	221.9	38.3	15.9	62.3
60-64	180.7	37.2	167.7	38.0	13.0	26.2
65-69	96.2	39.5	93.9	39.7	2.3	30.4
70-74	49.7	28.3	47.2	26.2	2.5	68.0
75+	27.4	24.0	25.6	25.7	1.8	.
Actividad económica (CIIU-Rev.3)	2007 ★		2007 [1][3][4]		2007 [1][3]	
	Encuesta de la fuerza de trabajo		Encuesta de la fuerza de trabajo		Encuesta de la fuerza de trabajo	
Total	4 474.0	46.1	4 162.5	45.5	311.5	54.2
A Agricultura, ganadería, caza y silvicultura	49.9	16.2	48.5	16.7	1.4	.
B Pesca	24.9	16.5	22.3	15.2	2.6	26.9
C Explotación de minas y canteras	763.8	35.7	728.0	34.5	35.8	58.4
D Industrias manufactureras	9.0	10.0	9.0	10.0	-	.
E Suministro de electricidad, gas y agua	265.6	1.5	245.9	1.6	19.7	.
F Construcción	951.7	60.0	901.3	59.7	50.4	65.5
G Comercio al por mayor y al por menor; reparación ...	293.4	71.0	270.9	70.5	22.5	76.9
H Hoteles y restaurantes	422.6	16.5	404.1	15.7	18.5	35.1
I Transporte, almacenamiento y comunicaciones	44.7	45.4	40.1	41.9	4.6	76.1
J Intermediación financiera	320.8	35.7	306.3	36.1	14.5	26.9
K Actividades inmobiliarias, empresariales y de alquiler	221.2	29.9	205.7	27.9	15.5	56.8
L Administración pública y defensa; planes de seguridad ...	272.4	64.3	249.9	65.6	22.5	50.2
M Enseñanza	136.0	68.9	131.1	68.0	4.9	91.8
N Servicios sociales y de salud	328.2	40.2	309.1	39.3	19.1	56.0
O Otras actividades de servicios comunitarios ...	305.4	94.8	289.1	94.5	16.3	100.0
P Hogares privados con servicio doméstico			1.2	100.0		
Desempleados sin empleo anterior					63.2	49.8
Ocupación (CIUO-1968)	1993 [5]				1994 [3][6][7]	
	Censo de población				Encuesta de la fuerza de trabajo	
Total	7 305.78	30.0			262.97	
0/1 Profesionales, técnicos y trabajadores asimilados	946.00	40.8			36.64	
2 Directores y funcionarios públicos superiores	73.65	24.3			7.47	
3 Personal administrativo y trabajadores asimilados	366.66	51.4			39.12	
4 Comerciantes y vendedores	.	.			43.79	
5 Trabajadores de los servicios	2 335.46	33.8			34.23	
6 Trabajadores agrícolas y forestales, pescadores y cazadores	1 227.56	15.1			2.39	
7/8/9 Obreros no agrícolas, conductores de máquinas y ...	1 320.00	14.4			78.69	
X No pueden clasificarse según la ocupación	778.87	42.9				
Desempleados sin empleo anterior	257.58	39.2			20.65	
Ocupación (CIUO-88)			2007 [1][3][4]			
			Encuesta de la fuerza de trabajo			
Total			4 162.5			
1 Miembros del poder ejecutivo y de los cuerpos legislativos ...			16.3	27.6		
2 Profesionales científicos e intelectuales			390.0	55.5		
3 Técnicos y profesionales de nivel medio			503.6	40.6		
4 Empleados de oficina			315.9	53.9		
5 Trabajadores de los servicios y vendedores de comercios ...			645.6	65.7		
6 Agricultores y trabajadores calificados agropecuarios ...			21.7	13.4		
7 Oficiales, operarios y artesanos de artes mecánicas ...			519.7	26.7		
8 Operadores de instalaciones y máquinas y montadores			412.1	7.9		
9 Trabajadores no calificados			1 261.6	55.2		
0 Fuerzas armadas			76.0	4.5		
Nivel de educación (CINE-76)	2006 [4][8][9]					
	Encuesta de la fuerza de trabajo					
Total	4 007.6	43.1				
X Sin escolaridad	31.4	78.1				
1 Enseñanza de primer grado	401.7	50.2				
2 Enseñanza de segundo grado, ciclo inferior [10]	2 133.0	40.9				
5 Enseñanza de tercer grado que no permite obtener un ...	683.4	46.9				
6 Enseñanza de tercer grado que permite obtener un primer ... [11]	758.1	40.7				
Nivel de educación (CINE-97)					2007 [1][3]	
					Encuesta de la fuerza de trabajo	
Total					311.5	54.2
0 Enseñanza preescolar					1.4	100.0
1 Enseñanza primaria o primer ciclo de la educación básica					27.7	69.7
2 Primer ciclo de enseñanza secundaria o segundo ciclo de ...					65.9	39.3
3 Segundo ciclo de enseñanza secundaria					99.4	57.1
5A Primer ciclo de la educación terciaria - teóricos					53.0	59.1
5B Primer ciclo de la educación terciaria - práctica					60.3	54.7
6 Segundo ciclo de la enseñanza terciaria					3.9	25.6

Perú

Situación en el empleo (CISE-1993)	1993[5] Censo de población		2007[1 3 4] Encuesta de la fuerza de trabajo	
Total	7 305.8	30.0	4 162.5	45.5
1 Asalariados	3 411.1	29.7	2 624.2	43.1
2 Empleadores	169.1	24.1	234.0	29.2
3 Trabajadores por cuenta propia	2 382.4	22.6	1 119.0	51.8
5 Trabajadores familiares auxiliares	755.8	45.7	180.2	62.7
6 Inclasificables según la situación	587.4	43.1	5.2	42.0

2. Población ('000), Tasa de actividad y Tasa de desempleo

Grupo de edad	Población 2007[1 2] Encuesta de la fuerza de trabajo			Tasa de actividad 2007[1 2] Encuesta de la fuerza de trabajo			Tasa de desempleo 2007[1 3] Encuesta de la fuerza de trabajo		
	Total	Hombres	Mujeres	Total	Hombres	Mujeres	Total	Hombres	Mujeres
Total	.	.	.	.	.	.	7.0	5.9	8.2
15+	6 355.9	2 972.4	3 383.6	69.9	80.4	60.6	6.7	5.6	.
15-24	1 557.1	730.2	826.9	57.2	61.1	53.7	14.3	13.6	14.9
25-54	3 494.1	1 637.1	1 857.1	84.7	96.1	74.6	4.6	3.4	5.9
55+	1 304.7	605.1	699.6	45.4	61.3	31.6	6.0	5.3	.

3. Empleo remunerado ('000), Horas de trabajo (por semana) y Salarios

Actividad económica (CIIU-Rev.3)	Empleo remunerado 2007[1 3 4] Encuesta de la fuerza de trabajo			Horas de trabajo 2007[1 2] Encuesta de establecimientos relacionada con el trabajo Horas pagadas / Obreros			Salarios 2007[1 2 13] Encuesta de establecimientos relacionada con el trabajo / Obreros / Nuevo sol		
	Total	Hombres	Mujeres	Total	Hombres	Mujeres	Total	Hombres	Mujeres
Total	2 624.2	1 494.0	1 130.2	47.79	.	.	.	.	.
C-Q	.	.	.	48.02	.	.	29.16	.	.
A	25.3	20.8	4.5	.	.	.	.	.	.
B	21.7	18.2	3.4	.	.	.	.	.	.
C	536.4	367.9	168.4	47.31[13]	.	.	60.12	.	.
D	9.0	8.1	0.9	48.22[13]	.	.	27.77	.	.
E	155.6	153.3	2.2	44.68[13]	.	.	57.64	.	.
F	338.7	190.9	147.8	47.52[13]	.	.	38.22	.	.
G	103.2	45.6	57.6	47.99[13]	.	.	29.18	.	.
H	189.7	146.0	43.7	48.14[13]	.	.	20.79	.	.
I	37.3	21.5	15.8	47.31[13]	.	.	30.93	.	.
J	215.6	138.3	77.3	42.92[13]	.	.	39.30	.	.
K	205.7	148.2	57.4	50.03[13]	.	.	23.58	.	.
L	224.6	75.0	149.5	.	.	.	.	.	.
M	112.0	35.7	76.3	45.22[13]	.	.	42.85	.	.
N	170.5	108.8	61.7	47.76[13]	.	.	23.88	.	.
O	278.0	15.6	262.4	43.78[13]	.	.	27.18	.	.
P	1.2	-	1.2	.	.	.	.	.	.

Proporción de mujeres entre los empleados remunerados en el sector no agrícola[1 3 4] (2007 - Encuesta de la fuerza de trabajo): **43.5%**

4. Lesiones profesionales y Huelgas y cierres patronales

Actividad económica (CIIU-Rev.3)	Tasas de lesiones mortales 2007 Registros de seguros Por 1 000 trabajadores asegurados Lesiones indemnizadas			Tasas de lesiones no mortales			Huelgas y cierres patronales 2007[14] Registros de relaciones laborales		
	Total	Hombres	Mujeres	Total	Hombres	Mujeres	Huelgas y cierres patronales	Trabajadores implicados	Días no trabajados[15]
Total	304.000	.	.	.	.	.	73	48 096	2 216 520
A	.	.	.	.	.	.	2	800	6 400
B	.	.	.	.	.	.	0	0	0
C	.	.	.	.	.	.	29	41 676	2 057 232
D	.	.	.	.	.	.	8	1 089	24 368
E	.	.	.	.	.	.	3	518	9 776
F	.	.	.	.	.	.	9	790	25 792
G	.	.	.	.	.	.	0	0	0
H	.	.	.	.	.	.	0	0	0
I	.	.	.	.	.	.	13	2 736	87 632
J	.	.	.	.	.	.	1	8	64
K	.	.	.	.	.	.	2	100	800
L	.	.	.	.	.	.	4	386	4 032
M	.	.	.	.	.	.	2	53	424
N	.	.	.	.	.	.	0	0	0
O	.	.	.	.	.	.	0	0	0
P	.	.	.	.	.	.	0	0	0
X	.	.	.	.	.	.	0	0	0

5. Índices de precios al consumidor (periodo de base: 2000=100)

Lima[16]	2002	2003	2004	2005	2006	2007
Índices generales	102.2	104.5	108.3	110.1	112.3	114.3
Índices de la alimentación incluyendo las bebidas no alcohólicas	100.2	101.0	106.6	107.6	110.2	113.0
Índices de la electricidad, gas y otros combustibles	102.5	113.4	121.8	129.7	132.5	132.9
Índices del vestido, incl. calzado	103.9	104.6	105.9	107.5	109.1	111.9
Índices del aquiler[17]		104.0	110.5	115.5	120.3	123.3	124.5

Perú

[1] Metropolitan Lima. [2] Excl. armed forces and conscripts. [3] Persons aged 14 years and over. [4] Excl. conscripts. [5] July. [6] Lima. [7] Sep.-Oct. [8] Metropolitan Lima; persons aged 14 years and over. [9] October. [10] Levels 2-3. [11] Levels 6-7. [12] Figures at the desaggregated level are not representative because of the small sample size. [13] Second quarter. [14] Strikes only; private sector. [15] Computed on the basis of an eight-hour working day. [16] Metropolitan areas. [17] Incl. water, electricity, gas and other fuels.

[1] Lima métropolitaine. [2] Non compris les forces armées et les conscrits. [3] Personnes âgées de 14 ans et plus. [4] Non compris les conscrits. [5] Juillet. [6] Lima. [7] Sept.-oct. [8] Lima métropolitaine; personnes âgées de 14 ans et plus. [9] Octobre. [10] Niveaux 2-3. [11] Niveaux 6-7. [12] Chiffres non représentatifs au niveau désagrégé en raison de la faible taille de l'échantillonage. [13] Deuxième trimestre. [14] Grèves seulement; secteur privé. [15] Calculées sur la base de journées de travail de huit heures. [16] Régions métropolitaines. [17] Y compris l'eau, l'électricité, le gaz et autres combustibles.

[1] Lima metropolitana. [2] Excl. las fuerzas armadas y los conscriptos. [3] Personas de 14 años y más. [4] Excl. los conscriptos. [5] Julio. [6] Lima. [7] Sept.-oct. [8] Lima metropolitana; personas de 14 años y más. [9] Octubre. [10] Niveles 2-3. [11] Niveles 6-7. [12] Cifras no reprentativas al nivel de desagregación debidas al pequeño tamaño muestral. [13] Segundo trimestre. [14] Huelgas solamente; sector privado. [15] Calculados en base a días de trabajo de ocho horas. [16] Areas metropolitanas. [17] Incl. el agua, la electricidad, el gas y otros combustibles.

Philippines

1. Economically active population, Employment and Unemployment ('000)

	Economically active population		Employment		Unemployment	
	Total	Women (%)	Total	Women (%)	Total	Women (%)
Age group	2007 [1,2,3] Labour force survey		2007 ★ Labour force survey		2007 [2,3] Labour force survey	
Total	35 918	38.3	33 672	38.4	2 246	36.6
15-24	7 680	37.9	6 535	37.2	1 145	42.1
25-34	9 597	35.9	8 946	36.1	651	34.4
35-44	8 090	38.0	7 871	38.3	219	29.2
45-54	5 989	40.3	5 848	40.8	141	22.7
55-64	3 137	41.1	3 062	41.6	75	20.0
65+	1 423	41.5	1 409	41.7	14	28.6
?	1	100.0	1	100.0	-	.

Economic activity (ISIC-Rev.3)

2007 [1,2,3] Labour force survey

Total			33 672	38.4		
A Agriculture, Hunting and Forestry	.	.	10 768	27.5	.	.
B Fishing	.	.	1 393	8.2	.	.
C Mining and Quarrying	.	.	135	8.1	.	.
D Manufacturing	.	.	3 060	44.4	.	.
E Electricity, Gas and Water Supply	.	.	141	19.1	.	.
F Construction	.	.	1 740	2.4	.	.
G Wholesale and Retail Trade; Repair of Motor Vehicles ...	.	.	6 176	59.6	.	.
H Hotels and Restaurants	.	.	907	54.7	.	.
I Transport, Storage and Communications	.	.	2 600	6.3	.	.
J Financial Intermediation	.	.	384	58.9	.	.
K Real Estate, Renting and Business Activities	.	.	881	36.0	.	.
L Public Administration and Defence; Compulsory Social ...	.	.	1 569	38.4	.	.
M Education	.	.	1 043	76.2	.	.
N Health and Social Work	.	.	396	71.2	.	.
O Other Community, Social and Personal Service Activities	.	.	779	50.4	.	.
P Households with Employed Persons	.	.	1 699	84.8	.	.
Q Extra-Territorial Organizations and Bodies	.	.	3	33.3	.	.

Occupation (ISCO-88)

	2007 ★ Labour force survey		2007 [1,2,3] Labour force survey		2007 [2,3] Labour force survey	
Total	35 918	38.3	33 672	38.4	2 246	36.6
1 Legislators, senior officials and managers	3 857	57.0	3 817	57.1	40	40.0
2 Professionals	1 541	69.5	1 503	70.1	38	47.4
3 Technicians and associate professionals	958	50.0	887	51.0	71	38.0
4 Clerks	1 820	63.8	1 691	64.3	129	57.4
5 Service workers and shop and market sales workers	3 479	50.1	3 141	50.1	338	49.4
6 Skilled agricultural and fishery workers	6 377	14.0	6 314	14.0	63	11.1
7 Craft and related trade workers	3 039	23.7	2 812	24.3	227	16.3
8 Plant and machine operators and assemblers	2 742	10.4	2 603	10.0	139	18.0
9 Elementary occupations	11 330	43.1	10 768	43.9	562	29.5
0 Armed forces	142	16.9	134	17.2	8	12.5
Unemployed seeking their first job	.	.	.	.	632	44.8

Education level (ISCED-97)

	2007 [1,2,3] Labour force survey		2007 ★ Labour force survey		2007 [2,3] Labour force survey	
Total	35 918	38.3	33 672	38.4	2 246	36.6
X No schooling	673	36.7	658	36.6	15	40.0
0 Pre-primary education [4]	5 548	30.4	5 412	30.5	136	25.7
2 Lower secondary or second stage of basic education	5 824	35.7	5 654	36.0	170	27.6
3 Upper secondary education	4 716	33.1	4 424	33.4	292	29.5
4 Post-secondary non-tertiary education	9 191	37.4	8 445	37.4	746	37.7
5A First stage of tertiary education - theoretically based	4 814	38.3	4 328	38.4	486	37.4
5B First stage of tertiary education - practically oriented [5]	5 152	55.8	4 752	56.6	400	46.0

Status in employment (ICSE-1993)

2007 [1,2,3] Labour force survey

Total	.	.	33 672	38.4	.	.
1 Employees	.	.	17 198	38.3	.	.
2 Employers	.	.	1 419	22.0	.	.
3 Own-account workers	.	.	10 873	33.9	.	.
5 Contributing family workers	.	.	4 182	55.6	.	.

2. Population ('000), Activity rate and Unemployment rate

	Population 2007 [1,3] Labour force survey			Activity rate 2007 [1,3] Labour force survey			Unemployment rate 2007 [2,3,3] Labour force survey		
Age group	Total	Men	Women	Total	Men	Women	Total	Men	Women
Total	.	.	.	.	.	.	7.3	7.5	7.0
15+	56 839	28 328	28 511	63.2	78.3	48.2	6.3	6.4	6.0
15-24	17 366	8 807	8 559	44.2	54.1	34.0	14.9	13.9	16.5
25-54	31 092	15 579	15 513	76.1	94.6	57.7	4.3	4.7	3.6
55+	8 381	3 942	4 439	54.4	68.0	42.4	2.0	2.6	1.0

Philippines

3. Paid employment ('000), Hours of work (weekly) and Wages

Economic activity (ISIC-Rev.3)	Paid employment 2007 [1 2 3] Labour force survey			Hours of work 2007 [3] Labour force survey Hours actually worked / Total employment			Wages 2007 [3] Labour force survey Wage rates per day / Employees / Peso		
	Total	Men	Women	Total	Men	Women	Total	Men	Women
Total	17 198	10 608	6 590	41.7	41.4	42.1	274.52	274.91	273.92
A-B	.	.	.	32.2	34.5	25.4	138.17	142.70	119.60
C-Q	.	.	.	.	.	.	299.01	308.89	286.34
A	2 553	2 041	512	31.5	33.8	25.3	136.18	140.63	118.98
B	305	292	12	37.7	38.7	25.9	170.22	170.50	164.28
C	80	75	5	44.9	45.4	39.2	236.22	231.05	309.99
D	2 282	1 358	924	44.9	46.2	42.8	276.52	286.62	261.84
E	136	111	25	45.4	45.5	45.1	484.10	484.79	481.16
F	1 614	1 579	36	43.9	43.9	44.2	264.36	261.90	373.79
G	1 957	1 088	869	50.2	48.0	51.7	246.14	258.30	230.68
H	629	321	308	49.3	47.6	50.7	247.16	277.89	214.84
I	1 421	1 278	143	50.0	50.3	45.9	340.22	313.66	480.41
J	362	150	211	43.1	44.0	42.5	460.75	456.93	463.50
K	723	472	251	48.4	51.0	43.9	390.12	360.48	447.12
L	1 569	967	602	39.9	42.2	36.3	419.14	415.97	424.84
M	1 028	243	785	40.2	41.2	39.8	477.30	475.74	477.79
N	341	93	248	42.8	45.1	41.9	416.58	446.05	404.37
O	498	280	218	36.5	39.4	33.7	278.33	285.39	270.39
P	1 699	258	1 441	54.1	51.2	54.6	119.62	174.52	109.97
Q	3	2	1	44.5	43.0	48.0	1 491.57	1 791.47	794.54

Share of women in wage employment in the non-agricultural sector [1 2 3] (2007 - Labour force survey): **42.3%**

4. Occupational injuries and Strikes and Lockouts

Economic activity (ISIC-Rev.3)	Rates of fatal injuries 2003 [6] Labour-related establishment survey Per 1,000,000 hours worked Reported injuries			Rates of non-fatal injuries 2003 [6] Labour-related establishment survey Per 1,000,000 hours worked Reported injuries			Strikes and lockouts 2007 [7] Special data collection		
	Total	Men	Women	Total	Men	Women	Strikes and lockouts	Workers involved [8]	Days not worked
Total	0.03	.	.	4.04	.	.	6	915	12 112
A	.	.	.	.	.	.	0	0	0
B	.	.	.	.	.	.	0	0	0
C	0.21	.	.	2.20	.	.	1	200	600
D	0.01	.	.	6.45	.	.	3	405	5 832
E	0.19	.	.	5.78	.	.	0	0	0
F	0.02	.	.	5.85	.	.	0	0	0
G	0.06	.	.	3.05	.	.	0	0	0
H	0.03	.	.	4.21	.	.	0	0	0
I	0.08	.	.	3.59	.	.	1	180	5 420
J	0.01	.	.	0.46	.	.	0	0	0
K	0.02	.	.	0.81	.	.	0	0	0
L	.	.	.	.	.	.	0	0	0
M	0.01	.	.	0.33	.	.	0	0	0
N	0.00	.	.	0.71	.	.	1	130	260
O	0.00	.	.	4.37	.	.	0	0	0

5. Consumer price indices (base period: 2000=100)

	2002	2003	2004	2005	2006	2007
General indices	110.1	113.9	120.6	129.8	137.9	141.8
Food index, including non-alcoholic beverages [9]	107.1	109.4	116.3	123.8	130.6	134.9
Electricity, gas and other fuel indices [10]	115.9	123.2	132.3	156.2	176.4	182.1
Clothing indices, including footwear	107.7	111.4	114.4	118.4	122.0	124.8
Rent indices	112.2	117.0	121.4	126.9	131.9	133.9
General index, excluding housing	109.5	113.2	120.4	130.4	139.2	143.4

[1] Excl. regular military living in barracks. [2] Persons aged 15 years and over. [3] Oct. [4] Levels 0-1. [5] Levels 5B and 6. [6] Establishments with 20 or more persons employed. [7] Excl. work stoppages lasting less than a full day or shift. [8] Excl. workers indirectly involved. [9] Incl. alcoholic beverages and tobacco. [10] Incl. water.

[1] Non compris les militaires de carrière vivant dans des casernes. [2] Personnes âgées de 15 ans et plus. [3] Oct. [4] Niveaux 0-1. [5] Niveaux 5B et 6. [6] Etablissements occupant 20 personnes et plus. [7] Non compris les arrêts du travail dont la durée est inférieure à une journée ou à un poste de travail. [8] Non compris les travailleurs indirectement impliqués. [9] Y compris les boissons alcoolisées et le tabac. [10] Y compris l'eau.

[1] Excl. los militares profesionales que viven en casernas. [2] Personas de 15 años y más. [3] Oct. [4] Niveles 0-1. [5] Niveles 5B y 6. [6] Establecimientos con 20 y más trabajadores. [7] Excl. las interrupciones del trabajo de duración menor de un día o turno completo. [8] Excl. los trabajadores indirectamente implicados. [9] Incl. las bebidas alcohólicas y el tabaco. [10] Incl. el agua.

Poland

1. Economically active population, Employment and Unemployment ('000)

	Economically active population		Employment		Unemployment	
	Total	Women (%)	Total	Women (%)	Total	Women (%)
Age group	2007 [1,2] Labour force survey		2007 ★ Labour force survey		2007 [3] Labour force survey	
Total	16 859	45.2	15 240	44.9	1 619	48.7
15-19	210	39.5	163	36.8	47	48.9
20-24	1 647	44.6	1 291	43.7	356	48.0
25-29	2 485	44.9	2 222	44.7	263	46.8
30-34	2 437	45.8	2 238	45.3	199	51.8
35-39	2 096	46.4	1 956	45.6	140	57.9
40-44	2 051	47.5	1 894	47.1	157	51.6
45-49	2 267	48.8	2 072	48.6	195	51.3
50-54	2 051	46.3	1 887	46.3	164	47.0
55-59	1 045	34.8	968	35.1	77	31.2
60-64	321	33.6	305	35.4	16	.
65-69	133	40.6	133	40.6	-	.
70-74	77	40.3	77	40.3	-	.
75+	40	40.0	40	40.0	-	.
Economic activity (ISIC-Rev.3)	2007 [1,2] Labour force survey		2007 [1,2] Labour force survey		2007 [3] Labour force survey	
Total	16 859	45.2	15 241	44.9	1 619	48.7
A Agriculture, Hunting and Forestry	2 276	43.3	2 239	43.3	37	43.2
B Fishing	9	.	8	12.5	-	.
C Mining and Quarrying	255	13.3	248	13.3	6	.
D Manufacturing	3 427	34.3	3 162	34.1	265	37.4
E Electricity, Gas and Water Supply	225	21.8	218	22.0	8	.
F Construction	1 168	5.7	1 054	6.0	114	.
G Wholesale and Retail Trade; Repair of Motor Vehicles ...	2 468	54.7	2 264	54.2	205	61.0
H Hotels and Restaurants	335	69.0	291	69.4	43	67.4
I Transport, Storage and Communications	1 023	22.3	973	21.9	50	30.0
J Financial Intermediation	378	69.6	363	68.9	15	86.7
K Real Estate, Renting and Business Activities	1 012	44.7	953	44.3	58	51.7
L Public Administration and Defence; Compulsory Social ...	991	50.3	937	50.1	53	54.7
M Education	1 162	77.3	1 128	77.3	34	76.5
N Health and Social Work	904	80.9	871	80.7	33	84.8
O Other Community, Social and Personal Service Activities	551	52.8	511	53.2	40	47.5
P Households with Employed Persons	20	95.0	16	100.0	4	.
X Not classifiable by economic activity	655	54.0	.	.	288 [4]	59.7
Unemployed seeking their first job	.	.	.	.	361	49.9
Occupation (ISCO-88)	2007 [1,2] Labour force survey		2007 [1,2] Labour force survey		2007 [3] Labour force survey	
Total	16 859	45.2	15 241	44.9	1 619	48.7
1 Legislators, senior officials and managers	997	36.3	970	36.2	27	40.7
2 Professionals	2 380	64.2	2 337	64.2	43	67.4
3 Technicians and associate professionals	1 781	54.0	1 701	53.6	80	62.5
4 Clerks	1 195	65.7	1 114	65.4	80	70.0
5 Service workers and shop and market sales workers	1 964	66.5	1 783	66.1	182	70.3
6 Skilled agricultural and fishery workers	2 047	44.7	2 033	44.7	14	42.9
7 Craft and related trade workers	2 748	15.7	2 498	15.4	249	18.9
8 Plant and machine operators and assemblers	1 652	13.9	1 563	13.8	89	15.7
9 Elementary occupations	1 381	54.6	1 180	55.8	201	47.8
0 Armed forces	59	.	57	.	-	.
X Not classifiable by occupation	656	53.8	5	.	288 [5]	59.7
Unemployed seeking their first job	.	.	.	.	361	49.9
Education level (ISCED-97)	2007 [1,2] Labour force survey		2007 ★ Labour force survey		2007 [3] Labour force survey	
Total	16 859	45.2	15 240	44.9	1 619	48.7
1 Primary education or first stage of basic education [6]	1 715	40.1	1 449	39.9	266	41.0
3 Upper secondary education	10 878	40.9	9 747	40.2	1 131	47.1
4 Post-secondary non-tertiary education	636	68.4	582	68.0	54	72.2
5A First stage of tertiary education - theoretically based [7]	3 631	56.5	3 463	56.1	168	64.3
Status in employment (ICSE-1993)	2007 [1,2] Labour force survey		2007 [1,2] Labour force survey		2007 ★ Labour force survey	
Total	16 859	45.2	15 241	44.9	1 618	48.7
1 Employees	12 559	46.3	11 666	46.4	893	45.9
2 Employers	632	30.5	616	30.7	16	25.0
3 Own-account workers	2 372	35.9	2 317	36.0	55	34.5
5 Contributing family workers	647	63.7	643	63.5	4	100.0
6 Not classifiable by status	650	54.0	.	.	.	.

2. Population ('000), Activity rate and Unemployment rate

	Population			Activity rate			Unemployment rate		
Age group	2007 [1] Labour force survey			2007 [1] Labour force survey			2007 [3] Labour force survey		
	Total	Men	Women	Total	Men	Women	Total	Men	Women
Total	.	.	.	.	.	.	9.6	9.0	10.3
15+	31 393	14 909	16 485	53.7	61.9	46.3	.	.	.
15-24	5 633	2 846	2 788	33.0	36.5	29.3	21.7	20.0	23.7
25-54	16 378	8 133	8 246	81.7	88.0	75.6	8.4	7.8	9.1
55+	9 382	3 930	5 451	17.2	26.5	10.5	.	.	.

Poland

3. Paid employment ('000), Hours of work (weekly) and Wages

Economic activity (ISIC-Rev.3)	Paid employment 2007 Labour-related establishment survey			Hours of work 2007 Labour force survey Hours actually worked / Employees			Wages 2007 [8] Labour-related establishment survey Earnings per month / Employees / Zloty		
	Total	Men	Women	Total	Men	Women	Total	Men	Women
Total	9 272.0	.	.	39.9	42.1	37.2	2 691.03	.	.
A-B	.	.	.	37.5	40.5	33.7	.	.	.
C-Q	.	.	.	40.5	42.5	38.0	2 682.12	.	.
A	152.6	.	.	37.5	40.5	33.7	.	.	.
B	3.3	.	.	47.2	48.3	42.3	.	.	.
C	179.5	.	.	40.9	41.0	39.8	4 895.60	.	.
D	2 426.1	.	.	41.4	42.1	40.0	2 457.46	.	.
E	213.4	.	.	40.0	40.1	39.4	3 732.21	.	.
F	549.1	.	.	44.7	45.1	38.2	2 307.63	.	.
G	1 465.5	.	.	42.3	44.2	40.7	2 186.48	.	.
H	159.2	.	.	42.0	44.8	40.9	1 663.30	.	.
I	613.4	.	.	43.9	45.1	39.3	2 817.79	.	.
J	258.5	.	.	39.4	41.2	38.7	4 889.40	.	.
K	760.5	.	.	40.0	42.1	37.3	2 825.15	.	.
L	574.9	.	.	39.4	40.4	38.3	3 368.91	.	.
M	1 002.9	.	.	30.6	31.8	30.2	2 717.65	.	.
N	641.0	.	.	38.8	40.5	38.4	2 466.47	.	.
O	272.7	.	.	38.1	39.3	37.2	2 520.90	.	.
P	.	.	.	29.7	15.3	30.2	.	.	.
Q	.	.	.	40.0	40.0	.	.	.	.
X	.	.	.	39.4	43.1	19.0	.	.	.

Share of women in wage employment in the non-agricultural sector [1,2] (2007 - Labour force survey): **46.7%**

4. Occupational injuries and Strikes and Lockouts

Economic activity (ISIC-Rev.3)	Rates of fatal injuries 2007 [9] Labour inspectorate records Per 100,000 workers employed Reported injuries			Rates of non-fatal injuries			Strikes and lockouts 2007 Labour relations records		
	Total	Men	Women	Total	Men	Women	Strikes and lockouts	Workers involved	Days not worked
Total	4.3 [10]	.	.	.	.	.	1 736	59 909	186 213
A	17.4 [10]	.	.	.	.	.	0	0	0
B	0.0	.	.	.	.	.	0	0	0
C	14.8	.	.	.	.	.	0	0	0
D	4.6	.	.	.	.	.	26	23 616	25 343
E	10.4	.	.	.	.	.	0	0	0
F	12.8	.	.	.	.	.	0	0	0
G	2.5	.	.	.	.	.	0	0	0
H	0.4	.	.	.	.	.	0	0	0
I	8.2	.	.	.	.	.	53	1 779	11 821
J	1.3	.	.	.	.	.	0	0	0
K	3.0	.	.	.	.	.	1	55	10
L	1.5	.	.	.	.	.	0	0	0
M	1.1	.	.	.	.	.	1 543	26 419	11 396
N	0.6	.	.	.	.	.	113	8 040	137 643
O	5.0	.	.	.	.	.	0	0	0
P	0.0	.	.	.	.	.	.	.	.

5. Consumer price indices (base period: 2000=100)

	2002	2003	2004	2005	2006	2007
General indices	107.5	108.4	112.2	114.6	115.8	118.6
Food index, including non-alcoholic beverages [11]	104.6	103.0	108.6	110.6	110.6	115.9
Electricity, gas and other fuel indices	117.1	121.1	124.7	129.5	138.1	143.2
Clothing indices, including footwear	100.7	98.2	94.6	89.5	83.3	77.1
Rent indices [12]	122.8	128.8	133.4	138.2	142.0	147.6
General index, excluding housing [13]	106.8	107.5	111.3	113.5	114.5	117.2

[1] Excl. regular military living in barracks and conscripts. [2] Persons aged 15 years and over. [3] Persons aged 15 to 74 years. [4] Incl. the unemployed whose last job was 8 years ago or over, except for 1994-1996. [5] Incl. the unemployed whose last job was 8 years ago or over. [6] Levels 1-2. [7] Levels 5A, 5B and 6. [8] Incl. the value of payments in kind. [9] Deaths occurring within six months of accident. [10] Excl. private farms in agriculture. [11] Incl. alcoholic beverages. [12] Incl. water supply. [13] Excl. water supply.

Polynésie française

1. Population active, Emploi et Chômage ('000)

Groupe d'âge	Population active Total	Femmes (%) 2002 [1] Recensement de la population	Emploi Total	Femmes (%) 2002 ★ Recensement de la population	Chômage Total	Femmes (%) 2002 [1] Recensement de la population
Total	99.498	40.0	87.843	39.2	11.655	45.6
15-19	4.756	36.0	2.425	28.8	2.331	43.5
20-24	12.897	41.5	9.366	38.4	3.531	49.5
25-29	15.242	42.7	13.126	41.9	2.116	47.1
30-34	16.271	40.9	14.784	40.5	1.487	44.7
35-39	15.693	40.7	14.597	40.5	1.096	43.2
40-44	12.421	39.3	11.868	39.2	0.553	41.2
45-49	10.324	38.9	9.996	39.1	0.328	35.7
50-54	6.398	36.7	6.248	36.8	0.150	33.3
55-59	3.688	36.1	3.633	36.1	0.055	32.7
60-64	1.210	34.0	1.204	33.7	0.006	83.3
65-69	0.378	26.2	0.376	26.3	0.002	.
70-74	0.145	29.7	0.145	29.7	-	.
75+	0.075	29.3	0.075	29.3	-	.

Activité économique (CITI-Rév.3)			2002 [1] Recensement de la population			
Total	.	.	87.843	39.2	.	.
A Agriculture, chasse et sylviculture	.	.	4.398	23.8	.	.
B Pêche	.	.	3.850	20.1	.	.
C Activités extractives	.	.	0.300	6.7	.	.
D Activités de fabrication	.	.	7.134	33.1	.	.
E Production et distribution d'électricité, de gaz et d'eau	.	.	0.550	16.0	.	.
F Construction	.	.	7.773	4.9	.	.
G Commerce de gros et de détail; réparation de véhicules ...	.	.	11.471	41.1	.	.
H Hôtels et restaurants	.	.	7.643	57.3	.	.
I Transports, entreposage et communications	.	.	5.693	35.2	.	.
J Intermédiation financière	.	.	1.532	58.1	.	.
K Immobilier, locations et activités de services aux entreprises	.	.	3.679	39.7	.	.
L Administration publique et défense; sécurité sociale obligatoire	.	.	18.060	34.6	.	.
M Education	.	.	6.061	63.7	.	.
N Santé et action sociale	.	.	4.228	69.4	.	.
O Autres activités de services collectifs, sociaux et personnels	.	.	3.412	47.7	.	.
P Ménages privés employant du personnel domestique	.	.	2.059	80.7	.	.

Situation dans la profession (CISP-1993)			2002 [1] Recensement de la population			
Total	.	.	87.843	39.2	.	.
1 Salariés	.	.	70.829	40.7	.	.
2, 3	.	.	14.840	31.0	.	.
5 Travailleurs familiaux collaborant à l'entreprise familiale	.	.	2.174	48.3	.	.

2. Population ('000), Taux d'activité et Taux de chômage

Groupe d'âge	Population 2002 Recensement de la population Total	Hommes	Femmes	Taux d'activité 2002 Recensement de la population Total	Hommes	Femmes	Taux de chômage 2002 [1] Recensement de la population Total	Hommes	Femmes
Total	.	.	.	58.0	67.9	47.6	11.7	10.6	13.4
15+	171.581	88.017	83.564						
15-24	44.044	22.238	21.806	40.1	47.6	32.4	33.2	29.3	39.1
25-54	101.388	52.494	48.894	75.3	86.8	63.0	7.5	7.0	8.2
55+	26.149	13.285	12.864	21.0	27.0	14.8	.	.	.

Polynésie française

3. Emploi rémunéré ('000), Durée du travail (hebdomadaire) et Salaires

Activité économique (CITI-Rév.2)	Emploi rémunéré 2002 Fichiers des assurances			Durée du travail			Salaires		
	Total	Hommes	Femmes	Total	Hommes	Femmes	Total	Hommes	Femmes
Total	61.802	35.522	26.280	.	.	.	.	.	.

Activité économique (CITI-Rév.3)	Emploi rémunéré			Durée du travail 2003 [2] Rapports administratifs Heures rémunérées / Salariés			Salaires 2003 Rapports administratifs Gains par mois / Salariés / Franc CFP		
	Total	Hommes	Femmes	Total	Hommes	Femmes	Total	Hommes	Femmes
Total	.	.	.	.	153	139	.	225 524	201 481
A	.	.	.	.	137	127	.	109 815	100 531
B	.	.	.	.	147	146	.	141 163	130 219
C	.	.	.	.	153	135	.	168 017	172 005
D	.	.	.	.	158	146	.	213 876	186 653
E	.	.	.	.	170	163	.	403 711	340 367
F	.	.	.	.	146	128	.	153 384	163 953
G	.	.	.	.	159	148	.	217 981	175 530
H	.	.	.	.	144	135	.	171 493	132 624
I	.	.	.	.	152	145	.	282 738	243 776
J	.	.	.	.	166	160	.	410 961	323 686
K	.	.	.	.	139	121	.	196 866	154 274
L	.	.	.	.	161	151	.	268 890	273 428
M	.	.	.	.	149	139	.	244 272	234 100
N	.	.	.	.	156	148	.	345 288	256 980
O	.	.	.	.	138	130	.	232 758	170 340
P	.	.	.	.	117	58	.	107 958	42 781
Q	.	.	.	.	.	49	.	.	47 861

4. Lésions professionnelles et Grèves et lock-out

Activité économique (CITI-Rév.2)	Taux de lésions mortelles			Taux de lésions non mortelles			Grèves et lock-out 1989 Source inconnue		
	Total	Hommes	Femmes	Total	Hommes	Femmes	Grèves et lock-out	Travailleurs impliqués	Journées non effectuées
Total	.	.	.	.	.	.	0	0	0

5. Indices des prix à la consommation (période de base: 2000=100)

	2002	2003	2004	2005	2006	2007
Indices généraux	103.9	104.3	104.8	105.8	108.7	110.9
Indices de l'alimentation, y compris les boissons non alcoolisées	107.4	108.2	110.6	113.2	117.5	121.0
Indices de l'électricité, gaz et autres combustibles [3]	100.0	100.0	99.5	95.6	102.0	100.6
Indices de l'habillement, y compris les chaussures	98.3	98.1	94.5	93.2	90.2	86.7
Indices du loyer [3][4]	100.0	100.0	100.5	102.6	105.4	109.4

[1] Persons aged 15 years and over. [2] Per month. [3] Index base 2002=100. [4] Incl. water.

[1] Personnes âgées de 15 ans et plus. [2] Par mois. [3] Indice base 2002=100. [4] Y compris l'eau.

[1] Personas de 15 años y más. [2] Por mes. [3] Indice base 2002=100. [4] Incl. el agua.

Portugal

1. Population active, Emploi et Chômage ('000)

	Population active Total	Population active Femmes (%)	Emploi Total	Emploi Femmes (%)	Chômage Total	Chômage Femmes (%)
Groupe d'âge	2007 [1,2] Enquête sur la main-d'oeuvre		2007 ★ Enquête sur la main-d'oeuvre		2007 [2] Enquête sur la main-d'oeuvre	
Total	5 618.3	46.9	5 169.7	46.0	448.6	56.1
15-19	98.0	39.7	74.4	37.5	23.6	46.6
20-24	420.3	46.1	358.0	44.0	62.3	58.3
25-29	688.2	48.5	608.0	46.4	80.2	63.8
30-34	787.7	47.9	724.0	47.0	63.7	58.2
35-39	716.3	47.7	664.3	47.0	52.0	57.7
40-44	704.4	48.1	661.1	47.1	43.3	62.4
45-49	649.6	46.5	609.8	45.9	39.8	56.3
50-54	549.4	46.2	510.1	46.0	39.3	48.9
55-59	412.7	45.8	382.2	46.2	30.5	40.7
60-64	257.8	44.4	244.6	44.7	13.2	39.4
65-69	138.4	46.2	137.8	46.3	0.6	16.7
70-74	101.5	41.6	101.4	41.6	0.1	.
75+	93.9	45.2	93.9	45.2	-	.
Activité économique (CITI-Rév.3)	2007 [1,2] Enquête sur la main-d'oeuvre		2007 [2] Enquête sur la main-d'oeuvre		2007 [2] Enquête sur la main-d'oeuvre	
Total	5 618.3	46.9	5 169.7	46.0	448.6	56.1
A Agriculture, chasse et sylviculture	595.4	49.9	584.3	49.6	11.1 [3]	64.9
B Pêche	18.2	8.8	17.1 [3]	7.6	1.1 [3]	27.3
C Activités extractives	19.9	6.5	19.3 [3]	6.2	0.6 [3]	16.7
D Activités de fabrication	1 066.2	44.2	954.0	42.2	112.2	61.2
E Production et distribution d'électricité, de gaz et d'eau	34.5	22.0	33.7	22.0	0.8 [3]	25.0
F Construction	620.7	4.8	570.8	4.4	49.9 [3]	9.4
G Commerce de gros et de détail; réparation de véhicules ...	814.9	45.3	750.2	44.5	64.7	54.6
H Hôtels et restaurants	321.6	60.1	288.8	58.9	32.8	70.7
I Transports, entreposage et communications	239.2	21.8	223.7	21.8	15.5 [3]	21.9
J Intermédiation financière	98.7	46.5	95.7	46.4	3.0 [3]	50.0
K Immobilier, locations et activités de services aux entreprises	349.4	52.3	325.4	51.8	24.0	59.6
L Administration publique et défense; sécurité sociale obligatoire	338.5	38.2	327.0	37.5	11.5 [3]	58.3
M Education	325.3	75.3	306.7	75.1	18.6 [3]	79.6
N Santé et action sociale	357.5	82.2	340.2	82.0	17.3 [3]	86.7
O Autres activités de services collectifs, sociaux et personnels	176.7	55.6	162.4	54.9	14.3 [3]	63.6
P Ménages privés employant du personnel domestique	176.6	98.6	167.5	98.6	9.1 [3]	100.0
Q Organisations et organismes extraterritoriaux	3.1	48.4	2.8 [3]	46.4	0.3 [3]	66.7
X Ne pouvant être classés selon l'activité économique	61.5	62.1	.	.	-	.
Chômeurs n'ayant jamais travaillé	61.5	62.1	.	.	61.5	62.1
Profession (CITP-88)	2007 [1,2] Enquête sur la main-d'oeuvre		2007 [2] Enquête sur la main-d'oeuvre		2007 [2] Enquête sur la main-d'oeuvre	
Total	5 618.3	46.9	5 169.7	46.0	448.6	56.1
1 Membres de l'exécutif et des corps législatifs, cadres ...	356.3	32.1	344.5	31.5	11.8 [3]	49.2
2 Professions intellectuelles et scientifiques	463.8	56.6	442.6	56.4	21.2 [3]	60.4
3 Professions intermédiaires	481.1	45.3	453.0	45.2	28.1	47.7
4 Employés de type administratif	522.7	62.4	479.7	62.6	43.0	60.0
5 Personnel des services et vendeurs de magasin et de marché	844.8	68.7	767.1	68.3	77.7	73.0
6 Agriculteurs et ouvriers qualifiés de l'agriculture ...	569.0	49.0	562.2	48.8	6.8 [3]	64.7
7 Artisans et ouvriers des métiers de type artisanal	1 107.3	22.5	1 020.8	21.1	86.5	38.8
8 Conducteurs d'installations et de machines ...	444.5	19.4	402.8	16.9	41.7	43.9
9 Ouvriers et employés non qualifiés	731.3	64.7	662.1	65.0	69.2	61.8
0 Forces armées	36.2	14.1	35.0 [3]	14.6	1.2 [3]	.
X Ne pouvant être classés selon la profession	61.5	62.1	.	.	-	.
Chômeurs n'ayant jamais travaillé	61.5	62.1	.	.	61.5	62.1
Niveau d'instruction (CITE-97)	2007 [1,2] Enquête sur la main-d'oeuvre		2007 ★ Enquête sur la main-d'oeuvre		2007 [2] Enquête sur la main-d'oeuvre	
Total	5 618.3	46.9	5 169.7	46.0	448.6	56.1
X Non scolarisé [4]	288.0	55.6	273.4	56.0	14.6	47.9
1 Enseignement primaire ou premier cycle de l'éducation ...	2 648.5	42.7	2 441.0	41.8	207.5	52.7
2 Premier cycle de l'enseignement secondaire ou deuxième ...	1 043.9	42.8	945.7	41.5	98.2	54.5
3 Enseignement secondaire (deuxième cycle)	805.6	50.4	741.1	49.7	64.5	58.6
4 Enseignement postsecondaire qui n'est pas du supérieur	40.1	43.6	35.6	42.4	4.5	53.3
5A Premier cycle de l'enseignement supérieur - théorie	636.2	62.0	586.2	61.0	50.0	73.8
5B Premier cycle de l'enseignement supérieur - pratique	112.3	53.1	104.7	53.1	7.6	52.6
6 Deuxième cycle de l'enseignement supérieur	43.8	42.2	42.1	41.8	1.7	52.9
Situation dans la profession (CISP-1993)	2007 [1,2] Enquête sur la main-d'oeuvre		2007 [2] Enquête sur la main-d'oeuvre		2007 ★ Enquête sur la main-d'oeuvre	
Total	5 618.3	46.9	5 169.7	46.0	448.6	56.1
1 Salariés	4 268.5	47.9	3 902.2	47.2	366.3	55.6
2 Employeurs	289.9	28.6	286.7	28.5	3.2	37.5
3 Personnes travaillant pour leur propre compte	915.2	45.5	900.1	45.5	15.1	49.0
5 Travailleurs familiaux collaborant à l'entreprise familiale	55.6	63.7	55.1	63.7	0.5	60.0
6 Inclassables d'après la situation	89.2	59.1	25.6	52.3	63.6	61.8

Portugal

2. Population ('000), Taux d'activité et Taux de chômage

Groupe d'âge	Population 2007 [1,5] Enquête sur la main-d'oeuvre			Taux d'activité 2007 [1,5] Enquête sur la main-d'oeuvre			Taux de chômage 2007 [2] Enquête sur la main-d'oeuvre		
	Total	Hommes	Femmes	Total	Hommes	Femmes	Total	Hommes	Femmes
Total	10 604.4	5 133.1	5 471.3	53.0	58.2	48.1	8.0	6.6	9.6
15+	8 969.7	4 293.5	4 675.7	62.6	69.5	56.3	.	.	.
15-24	1 238.0	630.8	607.0	41.9	45.3	38.4	16.6	13.5	20.3
25-54	4 665.1	2 313.7	2 351.4	87.8	92.8	82.8	7.8	6.1	9.6
55+	3 066.6	1 349.0	1 717.3	32.7	41.0	26.3	.	.	.

3. Emploi rémunéré ('000), Durée du travail (hebdomadaire) et Salaires

Activité économique (CITI-Rév.3)	Emploi rémunéré 2007 [2] Enquête sur la main-d'oeuvre			Durée du travail 2007 Enquête auprès des établissements, relative au travail Heures rémunérées / Salariés			Salaires 2007 Enquête auprès des établissements, relative au travail Gains par mois / Salariés / Euro		
	Total	Hommes	Femmes	Total	Hommes	Femmes	Total	Hommes	Femmes
Total	3 902.2	2 061.1	1 841.1	.	.	.	.	.	.
A	88.0	59.8	28.3	.	.	.	.	.	.
B	9.9 [3]	9.7 [3]	0.3 [3]	.	.	.	.	.	.
C	18.4 [3]	17.3 [3]	1.1 [3]	40.67	40.78	39.83	975	975	973
D	841.6	473.8	367.8	40.12	40.20	40.00	893	1 026	696
E	31.5	24.8	6.7	38.36	38.55	37.40	1 603	1 616	1 542
F	439.3	419.4	19.9	40.30	40.39	39.60	879	874	928
G	534.5	286.5	248.0	39.88	39.90	39.85	949	1 051	810
H	199.5	70.9	128.7	40.05	40.17	39.97	666	795	583
I	199.2	152.6	46.6	40.51	41.17	38.56	1 539	1 554	1 494
J	89.1	46.4	42.7	35.80	35.72	35.90	2 088	2 342	1 792
K	254.8	112.4	142.4	39.65	40.15	39.00	1 305	1 503	1 047
L	324.0	202.6	121.3	.	.	.	.	.	.
M	298.2	71.9	226.3	34.64	34.84	34.57	1 157	1 382	1 077
N	319.1	53.4	265.7	38.21	38.37	38.18	866	1 243	804
O	119.3	56.2	63.0	37.83	37.75	38.20	1 233	1 608	952
P	133.2	1.9	131.3	.	.	.	.	.	.
Q	2.5 [3]	1.5 [3]	1.0 [3]	.	.	.	.	.	.

Pourcentage de salariées dans le secteur non agricole qui sont femmes [2] (2007 - Enquête sur la main-d'oeuvre): **47.6%**

4. Lésions professionnelles et Grèves et lock-out

Activité économique (CITI-Rév.3)	Taux de lésions mortelles 2005 Fichiers des assurances Pour 100 000 travailleurs assurés Lésions déclarées			Taux de lésions non mortelles 2005 Fichiers des assurances Pour 100 000 travailleurs assurés Lésions déclarées			Grèves et lock-out 2006 [6] Fichiers des relations du travail		
	Total	Hommes	Femmes	Total	Hommes	Femmes	Grèves et lock-out	Travailleurs impliqués [7]	Journées non effectuées
Total	7.0 [8]	11.7 [8]	0.7 [8]	3 867 [8]	5 354 [8]	1 885 [8]	174 [9]	33 493 [9]	44 732 [9]
A	3.6	7.0	0.3	838	1 352	379	0	0	0
B	37.5	42.5	0.0	7 043	7 556	3 216	0	0	0
C	31.4	33.5	0.0	8 299	8 644	2 997	1	28	4
D	5.8	9.3	1.0	5 547	7 664	2 627	79	12 275	18 830
E	4.0	4.9	0.0	3 584	3 813	2 528	2	106	69
F	20.0	21.0	0.0	7 022	7 251	2 257	2	39	12
G	3.1	5.1	0.6	3 217	4 280	1 848	6	172	157
H	0.7	0.9	0.6	2 616	2 798	2 498	9	375	621
I	14.5	18.9	1.8	3 233	3 807	1 577	47	16 087	19 900
J	0.0	0.0	0.0	424	423	426	1	2 271	2 771
K	7.1	13.3	0.0	3 353	4 402	2 168	21	1 881	1 937
M	.	.	.	.	.	.	3 [9]	79 [9]	116 [9]
N	.	.	.	.	.	.	0	0	0
O	0.6	1.5	2.0	2 138	2 982	1 501	3	180	315
P	2.0	0.0	2.0	440	2 364	418	.	.	.
Q	0.0	0.0	.	154	153	154	.	.	.

5. Indices des prix à la consommation (période de base: 2000=100)

	2002	2003	2004	2005	2006	2007
Indices généraux [10]	108.0	111.6	114.2	116.7	120.4	123.3
Indices de l'alimentation, y compris les boissons non alcoolisées	108.1	110.9	112.1	111.3	114.2	117.0
Indices de l'électricité, gaz et autres combustibles	105.3	109.9	112.6	119.4	124.3	128.7
Indices de l'habillement, y compris les chaussures	104.1	105.5	104.3	103.1	103.9	106.3
Indices du loyer	109.0	112.6	116.0	119.5	123.4	123.7

[1] Excl. conscripts. [2] Persons aged 15 years and over. [3] Data not reliable; coefficient of variation greater than 20%. [4] Levels X-0. [5] "De jure" population. [6] Strikes only. [7] Excl. workers indirectly involved. [8] Excl. public administration and services and defence. [9] Excl. public administration. [10] Excl. "Rent".

[1] Non compris les conscrits. [2] Personnes âgées de 15 ans et plus. [3] Données non fiables; coefficient de variation supérieur à 20%. [4] Niveaux X-0. [5] Population "de jure". [6] Grèves seulement. [7] Non compris les travailleurs indirectement impliqués. [8] Non compris l'administration publique, les services publics et la défense. [9] Non compris l'administration publique. [10] Non compris le groupe "Loyer".

[1] Excl. los conscriptos. [2] Personas de 15 años y más. [3] Datos no fiables; coeficiente de variación superior a 20%. [4] Niveles X-0. [5] Población "de jure". [6] Huelgas solamente. [7] Excl. los trabajadores indirectamente implicados. [8] Excl. la administración pública, los servicios públicos y defensa. [9] Excl. la administración pública. [10] Excl. el grupo "Alquiler".

Puerto Rico

1. Economically active population, Employment and Unemployment ('000)

	Economically active population		Employment		Unemployment	
	Total	Women (%)	Total	Women (%)	Total	Women (%)
Age group	2007 [1,2,3] Labour force survey		2007 ★ Labour force survey		2007 [3,4] Labour force survey	
Total	1 394	44.8	1 242	45.5	152	38.8
16-19	34	35.3	25	40.0	9	22.2
20-24	133	38.3	105	39.0	28	35.7
25-34	348	46.0	303	46.5	45	42.2
35-44	362	47.5	329	48.0	33	42.4
45-54	314	47.1	291	47.4	23	43.5
55-64	157	40.1	144	41.0	13	30.8
65+	43	30.2	42	31.0	1	.
Economic activity (ISIC-Rev.2)	2007 ★ Labour force survey		2007 [2,3] Labour force survey		2007 [3,4] Labour force survey	
Total	1 393	44.7	1 241	45.4	152	38.8
1 Agriculture, Hunting, Forestry and Fishing	18	11.1	14	14.3	4	.
3 Manufacturing	154	38.3	133	38.3	21	38.1
4 Electricity, Gas and Water	15	13.3	15	13.3	-	.
5 Construction	114	5.3	90	5.6	24	4.2
6 Wholesale and Retail Trade and Restaurants and Hotels [5]	290	46.2	256	45.7	34	50.0
7 Transport, Storage and Communication	43	25.6	39	25.6	4	25.0
8 Financing, Insurance, Real Estate and Business Services	44	63.6	42	64.3	2	50.0
9 Community, Social and Personal Services [6]	705	53.2	652	53.7	53	47.2
Unemployed seeking their first job	.	.	.	.	10	50.0
Occupation (ISCO-88)	2007 ★ Labour force survey		2007 [2,3] Labour force survey		2007 [3,4] Labour force survey	
Total	1 393	44.7	1 241	45.4	152	38.8
1 Legislators, senior officials and managers	160	41.3	151	41.1	9	44.4
2 Professionals	218	65.6	209	66.0	9	55.6
3 Technicians and associate professionals	51	58.8	48	58.3	3	66.7
4 Clerks	221	77.8	202	78.2	19	73.7
5 Service workers and shop and market sales workers [7]	336	45.2	298	44.3	38	52.6
6 Skilled agricultural and fishery workers	38	5.3	30	6.7	8	.
7 Craft and related trade workers	130	2.3	108	2.8	22	.
8 Plant and machine operators and assemblers	155	27.1	136	26.5	19	31.6
9 Elementary occupations [8]	74	10.8	59	11.9	15	6.7
Unemployed seeking their first job	.	.	.	.	10	50.0
Status in employment (ICSE-1993)			2007 [2,3] Labour force survey			
Total	.	.	1 241	45.4	.	.
1 Employees	.	.	1 050	48.8	.	.
2, 3	.	.	189	26.5	.	.
5 Contributing family workers	.	.	2	.	.	.

2. Population ('000), Activity rate and Unemployment rate

	Population 2007 [1,2] Labour force survey			Activity rate 2007 [1,2] Labour force survey			Unemployment rate 2007 [3,4] Labour force survey		
Age group	Total	Men	Women	Total	Men	Women	Total	Men	Women
Total	.	.	.	.	.	.	10.9	12.1	9.5
15+	3 022	1 353	1 669	46.0	56.8	37.1	10.9	.	.
15-24	525	252	272	31.8	40.9	23.2	22.2	24.3	19.0
25-54	1 501	664	838	68.2	81.6	57.3	9.9	10.7	9.0
55+	996	437	559	20.1	28.4	13.6	7.0	.	.

3. Paid employment ('000), Hours of work (weekly) and Wages

Economic activity (ISIC-Rev.2)	Paid employment 2003 Labour-related establishment survey			Hours of work 2007 [9] Labour-related establishment survey Hours paid for / Wage earners			Wages 2007 Labour-related establishment survey Earnings per hour / Wage earners / US dollar		
	Total	Men	Women	Total	Men	Women	Total	Men	Women
3	116.3	69.7	46.6	40.9	.	.	11.93	.	.

Puerto Rico

4. Occupational injuries and Strikes and Lockouts

Economic activity (ISIC-Rev.2)	Rates of fatal injuries 1994 Labour-related establishment survey Per 100,000 employees Reported injuries			Rates of non-fatal injuries			Strikes and lockouts		
	Total	Men	Women	Total	Men	Women	Strikes and lockouts	Workers involved	Days not worked
Total	4.9	.	.	.	.	.	.	.	.
1	0.0	.	.	.	.	.	.	.	.
2	0.0	.	.	.	.	.	.	.	.
3	1.9	.	.	.	.	.	.	.	.
5	15.1	.	.	.	.	.	.	.	.
6	1.7	.	.	.	.	.	.	.	.
7	17.2	.	.	.	.	.	.	.	.
8	0.0	.	.	.	.	.	.	.	.
9 [10]	6.8	.	.	.	.	.	.	.	.
0 [11]	6.1	.	.	.	.	.	.	.	.

Economic activity (ISIC-Rev.3)	Rates of fatal injuries			Rates of non-fatal injuries 2005 Labour-related establishment survey Per 100,000 full-time equivalent employees Reported injuries			Strikes and lockouts 2007 [12] Labour relations records		
	Total	Men	Women	Total	Men	Women	Strikes and lockouts	Workers involved	Days not worked
Total	.	.	.	4 300	.	.	1	44	88
A-B	.	.	.	3 300 [13]	.	.			
A	.	.	.	.	.	.	0	0	0
B	.	.	.	.	.	.	0	0	0
C	.	.	.	.	.	.	0	0	0
D	.	.	.	3 300	.	.	0	0	0
E	.	.	.	.	.	.	0	0	0
F	.	.	.	.	.	.	0	0	0
G	.	.	.	3 200 [14]	.	.	0	0	0
G,I	.	.	.	.	.	.	0	0	0
H	.	.	.	5 100	.	.	1	44	88
I	.	.	.	4 500 [15]	.	.	0	0	0
J	.	.	.	.	.	.	0	0	0
K	.	.	.	3 300	.	.	0	0	0
L	.	.	.	5 400	.	.	0	0	0
M	.	.	.	8 900 [16]	.	.	0	0	0
N	.	.	.	.	.	.	0	0	0
O	.	.	.	3 000 [15]	.	.	0	0	0

5. Consumer price indices (base period: 2000=100)

	2002	2003	2004	2005	2006	2007
General indices	81.3	87.6	98.1	111.7	128.0	136.7
Food index, including non-alcoholic beverages	127.8	145.8	176.3	212.1	257.1	281.0
Electricity, gas and other fuel indices	100.6	105.6	110.9	136.5	157.2	171.8
Clothing indices, including footwear	97.0	95.5	95.2	95.1	95.5	100.7
Rent indices	104.4	106.0	107.5	109.0	110.9	114.0
General index, excluding housing	113.6	122.6	137.3	156.3	.	.

[1] Totals do not include persons whose level of education is unknown. [2] Excl. armed forces. [3] Persons aged 16 years and over. [4] Excl. persons temporarily laid off. [5] Excl. hotels. [6] Incl. hotels. [7] Incl. sales and services elementary occupations. [8] Excl. sales and services elementary occupations. [9] Persons aged 15 years and over; prior to 1998: 14 years and over. [10] Excl. state and local government. [11] State and local government. [12] Strikes and lockouts ending during the 12 months beginning in July of the year indicated. [13] Excl. farms with fewer than 11 employees. [14] Retail trade. [15] Private sector. [16] Public sector.

[1] Les totaux n'incluent pas les personnes dont le niveau d'éducation est inconnu. [2] Non compris les forces armées. [3] Personnes âgées de 16 ans et plus. [4] Non compris les personnes temporairement mises à pied. [5] Non compris les hôtels. [6] Y compris les hôtels. [7] Y compris les employés non qualifiés des services et de la vente. [8] Non compris les employés non qualifiés des services et de la vente. [9] Personnes âgées de 15 ans et plus; avant 1998: 14 ans et plus. [10] Non compris l'Etat et gouvernement local. [11] L'Etat et gouvernement local. [12] Grèves et lock-out se terminant pendant les 12 mois commençant en juillet de l'année indiquée. [13] Non compris les fermes avec moins de 11 salariés. [14] Commerce de détail. [15] Secteur privé. [16] Secteur public.

[1] Los totales no incluyen a las personas cuyo nivel de educación se desconoce. [2] Excl. las fuerzas armadas. [3] Personas de 16 años y más. [4] Excl. las personas temporalmente despedidas. [5] Excl. hoteles. [6] Incl. hoteles. [7] Incl. los trabajadores no calificados de ventas y servicios. [8] Excl. los trabajadores no calificados de ventas y servicios. [9] Personas de 15 años y más; antes de 1998: 14 años y más. [10] Excl. el estado y gobierno local. [11] El estado y gobierno local. [12] Huelgas y cierres patronales que terminan dentro de los 12 meses que comienzan en julio del año indicado. [13] Excl. granjas con menos de 11 asalariados. [14] Comercio al por menor. [15] Sector privado. [16] Sector público.

Qatar

1. Economically active population, Employment and Unemployment ('000)

Age group	Economically active population Total	Women (%)	Employment Total	Women (%)	Unemployment Total	Women (%)
	2004 [1,2] Population census		2004 ★ Population census		2004 [1,2] Population census	
Total	444.133	15.1	437.561	14.7	6.572	39.7
15-19	3.316	17.1	2.304	13.2	1.012	26.0
20-24	39.648	13.8	36.035	10.9	3.613	42.3
25-29	71.358	18.2	69.757	17.7	1.601	43.2
30-34	82.142	19.2	81.836	19.2	0.306	39.2
35-39	74.521	18.0	74.483	18.0	0.038	5.3
40-44	65.486	14.4	65.486	14.4	-	.
45-49	51.353	11.0	51.351	11.0	0.002	.
50-54	31.556	8.2	31.556	8.2	-	.
55-59	15.720	5.2	15.720	5.2	-	.
60-64	5.967	4.2	5.967	4.2	-	.
65-69	1.818	3.3	1.818	3.3	-	.
70-74	0.880	2.3	0.880	2.3	-	.
75+	0.368	6.3	0.368	6.3	-	.

Economic activity (ISIC-Rev.3)

	2006 [1,3] Labour force survey		2006 [1,2] Labour force survey		2006 ★ Labour force survey	
Total	535.807	14.9	529.304	14.5	6.503	50.5
A Agriculture, Hunting and Forestry	12.463	0.0	12.463	.	.	.
B Fishing	3.247	0.0	3.247	.	.	.
C Mining and Quarrying	27.353	4.8	27.199	4.8	0.154	.
D Manufacturing	62.700	1.1	62.641	1.1	0.059	.
E Electricity, Gas and Water Supply	4.750	5.0	4.678	5.1	0.072	.
F Construction	125.663	0.6	125.510	0.6	0.153	28.1
G Wholesale and Retail Trade; Repair of Motor Vehicles ...	70.027	3.3	69.987	3.3	0.040	.
H Hotels and Restaurants	15.010	7.6	15.010	7.6	.	.
I Transport, Storage and Communications	23.888	11.7	23.784	11.6	0.104	27.9
J Financial Intermediation	6.240	26.4	6.190	26.6	0.050	.
K Real Estate, Renting and Business Activities	15.919	5.2	15.919	5.2	.	.
L Public Administration and Defence; Compulsory Social ...	47.750	13.4	46.982	13.5	0.768	6.5
M Education	23.292	66.8	22.791	66.5	0.501	82.6
N Health and Social Work	16.825	51.3	16.691	51.2	0.134	70.9
O Other Community, Social and Personal Service Activities	12.182	16.7	12.085	16.9	0.097	.
P Households with Employed Persons	62.510	52.4	62.497	52.4	0.013	100.0
Q Extra-Territorial Organizations and Bodies	1.630	9.9	1.630	9.9	.	.
X Not classifiable by economic activity	4.358	61.1	-	.	4.358	61.1

Occupation (ISCO-88)

	2006 [1,3] Labour force survey		2006 [1,2] Labour force survey		2006 ★ Labour force survey	
Total	535.807	14.9	529.304	14.5	6.503	50.5
1 Legislators, senior officials and managers	16.483	7.2	16.349	7.3	0.134	.
2 Professionals	72.689	28.2	72.053	27.9	0.636	67.9
3 Technicians and associate professionals	39.445	19.1	39.092	19.1	0.353	16.4
4 Clerks	41.051	22.7	40.585	22.7	0.466	26.0
5 Service workers and shop and market sales workers	48.615	12.7	48.528	12.7	0.087	.
6 Skilled agricultural and fishery workers	5.231	.	5.231	.	.	.
7 Craft and related trade workers	128.046	0.1	127.953	0.1	0.093	.
8 Plant and machine operators and assemblers	63.692	0.0	63.597	0.0	0.095	.
9 Elementary occupations	116.197	27.9	115.916	28.0	0.281	11.7
X Not classifiable by occupation	4.358	61.1	-	.	4.358	61.1

Education level (ISCED-97)

	2004 [1,2] Population census		1997 ★ Population census		1997 [1,2] Population census	
Total	444.133	15.1	273.558	13.0	6.564	31.6
X No schooling	47.762	12.9	46.311	15.2	0.589	13.2
0 Pre-primary education	116.340	18.8	83.379	13.8	1.052	10.8
1 Primary education or first stage of basic education	42.696	4.0	25.532	4.2	0.861	16.4
2 Lower secondary or second stage of basic education	64.475	3.7	30.677	4.7	0.735	26.1
3 Upper secondary education	63.046	10.6	35.985	8.6	1.636	37.2
4 Post-secondary non-tertiary education	20.721	19.6	12.024	14.6	0.256	43.4
5A First stage of tertiary education - theoretically based	75.883	26.7	35.129	25.5	1.362	59.7
5B First stage of tertiary education - practically oriented	1.982	26.8	1.042	15.7	0.015	33.3
6 Second stage of tertiary education	4.593	16.2	2.831	16.1	0.035	25.7
? Level not stated	6.572	39.7	0.648	33.5	0.023	26.1

Status in employment (ICSE-1993)

	2006 [1,3] Labour force survey					
Total	535.807	14.9	.	.	.	.
1 Employees	527.401	14.6	.	.	.	.
2 Employers	2.788	4.1	.	.	.	.
3 Own-account workers	1.260	.	.	.	.	.
6 Not classifiable by status	4.358	61.1	.	.	.	.

2. Population ('000), Activity rate and Unemployment rate

Age group	Population 2006 [3] Labour force survey Total	Men	Women	Activity rate 2006 [3] Labour force survey Total	Men	Women	Unemployment rate 2004 [1,2] Population census Total	Men	Women
Total	.	.	.	.	.	.	1.5	1.1	3.9
15+	666.509	.	.	80.4	.	.	.	.	.
15-24	126.899	.	.	54.8	.	.	10.8	7.7	29.8
25-54	501.222	.	.	88.3	.	.	.	.	.
55+	38.388	.	.	61.2	.	.	.	.	.

Qatar

3. Paid employment ('000), Hours of work (weekly) and Wages

Economic activity (ISIC-Rev.3)	Paid employment 2001 [1,4] Labour force survey			Hours of work 2006 [5] Labour force survey Hours actually worked / Employees			Wages 2006 [5] Labour force survey Wage rates per month / Employees / Riyal		
	Total	Men	Women	Total	Men	Women	Total	Men	Women
Total	.	.	.	50	50	52	5 206	5 611	4 131
C-Q	306.525	262.132	44.393	.	.	.	.	.	.
C	.	.	.	45	46	43	11 685	11 987	7 637
D	.	.	.	54	55	46	3 677	3 668	4 092
E	.	.	.	42	42	39	8 249	8 438	6 264
F	.	.	.	53	53	47	3 477	3 418	7 365
G	.	.	.	54	54	50	3 135	3 109	3 659
H	.	.	.	56	56	53	2 823	2 682	3 820
I	.	.	.	47	48	42	6 920	7 158	5 638
J	.	.	.	42	42	40	8 787	9 994	6 106
K	.	.	.	52	52	47	4 983	4 934	.
L	.	.	.	39	40	37	8 731	9 085	6 741
M	.	.	.	37	39	36	7 949	3 205	7 448
N	.	.	.	42	43	41	7 675	8 872	6 684
O	.	.	.	46	48	41	6 525	.	4 893
P	.	.	.	62	60	64	1 649	1 701	1 610
Q	.	.	.	43	44	39	14 775	16 281	8 750

Share of women in wage employment in the non-agricultural sector [1] (2001 - Labour force survey): **14.5%**

4. Occupational injuries and Strikes and Lockouts

Statistics not available.

5. Consumer price indices (base period: 2000=100)

	2002	2003	2004	2005	2006	2007
General indices	101.6	104.0	111.0	120.9	135.2	153.6
Food index, including non-alcoholic beverages [6]	101.1	100.7	104.4	107.7	115.1	123.6
Electricity, gas and other fuel indices [7]	100.0	100.4	99.0	106.5	121.6	.
Clothing indices, including footwear	103.8	103.5	106.9	104.4	117.4	.
Rent indices [8]	103.4	121.9	141.7	182.1	229.9	.

[1] Persons aged 15 years and over. [2] March. [3] Oct. [4] April. [5] October. [6] Incl. tobacco. [7] Index base 2002=100. [8] Incl. Fuel and Energy.

[1] Personnes âgées de 15 ans et plus. [2] Mars. [3] Oct. [4] Avril. [5] Octobre. [6] Y compris le tabac. [7] Indice base 2002=100. [8] Y compris le combustible et l'énergie.

[1] Personas de 15 años y más. [2] Marzo. [3] Oct. [4] Abril. [5] Octubre. [6] Incl. el tabaco. [7] Indice base 2002=100. [8] Incl. combustible y energía.

República Dominicana

1. Población económicamente activa, Empleo y Desempleo ('000)

	Población económicamente activa		Empleo		Desempleo	
	Total	Mujeres (%)	Total	Mujeres (%)	Total	Mujeres (%)
Grupo de edad	2007 [1]		2007 ★		2007 [1]	
	Encuesta de la fuerza de trabajo		Encuesta de la fuerza de trabajo		Encuesta de la fuerza de trabajo	
Total	4 204.8	38.7	3 550.9	34.2	654.0	63.2
10-14	50.8	20.7	47.1	20.3	3.7	25.9
15-19	346.7	31.4	230.1	21.1	116.6	51.9
20-24	606.1	43.2	434.0	36.2	172.1	60.8
25-29	580.0	42.1	477.1	36.7	103.0	67.5
30-34	542.4	43.0	465.6	38.3	76.8	71.4
35-39	506.0	45.1	442.9	40.8	63.1	75.5
40-44	473.8	41.8	424.4	38.1	49.5	73.3
45-49	357.2	40.4	326.1	38.1	31.1	63.8
50-54	287.6	32.2	266.6	30.4	21.0	55.2
55-59	173.2	28.1	163.8	26.9	9.5	48.9
60+	278.4	20.2	270.8	19.7	7.6	39.5
Actividad económica (CIIU-Rev.3)	2007 ★		2007 [1]		2007 [1]	
	Encuesta de la fuerza de trabajo		Encuesta de la fuerza de trabajo		Encuesta de la fuerza de trabajo	
Total	4 204.8	38.7	3 550.9	34.2	654.0	63.2
A Agricultura, ganadería, caza y silvicultura	512.7	5.4	502.3	5.0	10.5	23.1
B Pesca	13.1	1.1	12.8	1.2	0.3	.
C Explotación de minas y canteras	6.0	.	6.0	2.7	0.0	.
D Industrias manufactureras	565.0	33.4	494.5	30.2	70.5	55.6
E Suministro de electricidad, gas y agua	35.0	29.4	30.8	28.3	4.2	37.6
F Construcción	263.2	3.0	246.9	3.0	16.3	2.7
G Comercio al por mayor y al por menor; reparación ...	792.8	35.1	732.4	33.5	60.4	54.6
H Hoteles y restaurantes	256.4	54.1	222.3	53.0	34.0	61.7
I Transporte, almacenamiento y comunicaciones	270.6	10.2	257.5	9.0	13.1	34.3
J Intermediación financiera	80.3	55.8	73.5	55.0	6.8	64.1
K Actividades inmobiliarias, empresariales y de alquiler	103.8	35.9	94.0	33.4	9.8	59.9
L Administración pública y defensa; planes de seguridad ...	166.5	33.0	152.6	30.7	14.0	58.1
M Enseñanza	179.3	68.1	169.9	67.4	9.4	80.3
N Servicios sociales y de salud	107.7	71.8	96.4	70.8	11.3	80.3
O Otras actividades de servicios comunitarios ...	291.5	62.0	263.0	60.5	28.5	76.4
P Hogares privados con servicio doméstico	242.3	91.3	194.6	90.0	47.7	96.9
Q Organizaciones y órganos extraterritoriales	1.5	87.9	1.5	87.9	-	.
X No pueden clasificarse según la actividad económica	.	.	.	.	.	.
Desempleados sin empleo anterior	.	.	.	.	317.1	65.7
Ocupación (CIUO-88)	2007 ★		2007 [1]		2007 [1]	
	Encuesta de la fuerza de trabajo		Encuesta de la fuerza de trabajo		Encuesta de la fuerza de trabajo	
Total	4 204.8	38.7	3 550.9	34.2	654.0	63.2
1 Miembros del poder ejecutivo y de los cuerpos legislativos ...	112.0	31.2	107.4	30.6	4.6	45.8
2 Profesionales científicos e intelectuales	232.5	56.2	223.7	55.7	8.8	68.0
3 Técnicos y profesionales de nivel medio	253.6	48.2	230.6	46.3	23.0	67.1
4 Empleados de oficina	285.9	70.6	236.5	67.6	49.4	84.9
5 Trabajadores de los servicios y vendedores de comercios ...	757.7	53.2	691.0 [2]	52.1	66.7	64.8
6 Agricultores y trabajadores calificados agropecuarios ...	369.3	4.9	365.7	4.9	3.7	4.7
7 Oficiales, operarios y artesanos de artes mecánicas ...	571.9	9.1	536.8	8.9	35.1	12.2
8 Operadores de instalaciones y máquinas y montadores	443.9	19.0	392.4	14.8	51.4	51.2
9 Trabajadores no calificados	830.5	44.3	736.8	41.1	93.7	70.0
0 Fuerzas armadas	30.6	11.5	30.0	11.8	0.6	.
Desempleados sin empleo anterior	.	.	.	.	317.1	65.7
Nivel de educación (CINE-76)	2007 [1]		2007 ★		2007 [1]	
	Encuesta de la fuerza de trabajo		Encuesta de la fuerza de trabajo		Encuesta de la fuerza de trabajo	
Total	4 204.8	.	3 550.9	.	654.0	63.2
X Sin escolaridad	283.2	.	256.4	.	26.8	58.8
1 Enseñanza de primer grado	1 790.1	.	1 561.1	.	229.0	61.4
2 Enseñanza de segundo grado, ciclo inferior [3]	1 362.1	.	1 070.9	.	291.2	62.4
6 Enseñanza de tercer grado que permite obtener un primer ... [4]	769.5	.	.	.	.	.
Situación en el empleo (CISE-1993)			2007 [1]			
			Encuesta de la fuerza de trabajo			
Total	.	.	3 550.9	34.2	.	.
1 Asalariados	.	.	1 903.5	42.9	.	.
2 Empleadores	.	.	141.7	21.8	.	.
3 Trabajadores por cuenta propia	.	.	1 397.1	23.2	.	.
5 Trabajadores familiares auxiliares	.	.	108.5	38.4	.	.

2. Población ('000), Tasa de actividad y Tasa de desempleo

	Población 2007			Tasa de actividad 2007			Tasa de desempleo 2007 [1]		
Grupo de edad	Encuesta de la fuerza de trabajo			Encuesta de la fuerza de trabajo			Encuesta de la fuerza de trabajo		
	Total	Hombres	Mujeres	Total	Hombres	Mujeres	Total	Hombres	Mujeres
Total	9 304.4	4 663.2	4 641.2	45.2	55.3	35.1	10.0	6.0	16.0
15+	6 459.8	3 189.1	3 270.7	64.3	79.5	49.4	15.7	9.4	25.5
15-24	1 815.7	923.2	892.4	52.5	63.0	41.5	30.3	21.2	44.5
25-54	3 466.3	1 692.6	1 773.7	79.2	94.9	64.3	12.5	6.5	21.0
55+	1 177.8	573.2	604.5	38.3	60.5	17.4	3.8	2.7	7.3

República Dominicana

3. Empleo remunerado ('000), Horas de trabajo (por semana) y Salarios

Actividad económica (CIIU-Rev.3)	Empleo remunerado 2007 [1] Encuesta de la fuerza de trabajo			Horas de trabajo 2007 Encuesta de la fuerza de trabajo Horas usualmente trabajadas / Empleo total			Salarios 2004 Encuesta de la fuerza de trabajo Ganancias por hora / Asalariados / Peso		
	Total	Hombres	Mujeres	Total	Hombres	Mujeres	Total	Hombres	Mujeres
Total	3 442.8	2 270.1	1 172.8	39.6	.	37.5	41.7	.	.
A-B	.	.	.	38.4	38.4	.	.	.	.
C-Q	.	.	.	40.6	42.1	39.1	.	.	.
A	462.1	440.6	21.5	35.0	38.5	31.5	.	.	.
B	12.8	12.5	0.3	38.3	38.3	.	.	.	.
C	6.1	5.8	0.3	44.7	46.4	43.0	26.1	.	.
D	490.4	342.9	147.5	42.7	44.0	41.4	50.8	.	.
E	30.8	22.1	8.7	40.7	43.0	38.4	39.4	.	.
F	246.4	239.0	7.4	42.3	42.0	42.6	73.4	.	.
G	684.6	465.6	219.0	41.5	43.0	40.1	51.6	.	.
H	211.8	100.3	111.5	40.7	44.1	37.3	41.5	.	.
I	256.8	233.7	23.1	43.3	43.0	43.7	35.0 [5]	.	.
J	73.5	33.1	40.5	43.4	44.6	42.2	48.2	.	.
K	92.4	61.8	30.5	40.0	41.5	38.5	69.1	.	.
L	152.6	105.8	46.8	39.6	42.2	36.9	45.5	.	.
M	169.3	55.1	114.3	34.3	35.7	.	.	.	.
N	96.1	28.2	67.9	38.4	39.3	37.5	.	.	.
O	260.8	103.7	157.1	35.2	36.3	34.1	.	.	.
P	194.6	19.5	175.1	41.3	43.9	38.6	.	.	.
Q	1.7	0.4	1.3	40.9	43.0	38.8	.	.	.

Proporción de mujeres entre los empleados remunerados en el sector no agrícola [1] (2007 - Encuesta de la fuerza de trabajo): **38.8%**

4. Lesiones profesionales y Huelgas y cierres patronales

Actividad económica (CIIU-Rev.2)	Tasas de lesiones mortales			Tasas de lesiones no mortales			Huelgas y cierres patronales 1998 Registros administrativos y fuentes relacionadas		
	Total	Hombres	Mujeres	Total	Hombres	Mujeres	Huelgas y cierres patronales	Trabajadores implicados	Días no trabajados
Total	.	.	.	.	.	.	8	3 774	.
1	.	.	.	.	.	.	0	0	.
2	.	.	.	.	.	.	1	332	.
3	.	.	.	.	.	.	6	3 374	.
4	.	.	.	.	.	.	0	0	.
5	.	.	.	.	.	.	0	0	.
6	.	.	.	.	.	.	0	0	.
7	.	.	.	.	.	.	0	0	.
8	.	.	.	.	.	.	0	0	.
9	.	.	.	.	.	.	1	68	.

5. Índices de precios al consumidor (periodo de base: 2000=100)

	2002	2003	2004	2005	2006	2007
Índices generales	114.6	146.1	221.2	230.5	247.9	263.1
Índices de la alimentación incluyendo las bebidas no alcohólicas [6]	110.7	140.1	237.0	233.2	242.8	258.8
Índices del vestido, incl. calzado	108.4	117.1	163.5	178.9	192.9	205.2
Índices del aquiler [7]	120.6	165.0	206.6	227.0	253.7	262.9

[1] Persons aged 10 years and over. [2] Incl. the armed forces. [3] Levels 2-5. [4] Levels 6-7. [5] Excl. storage. [6] Incl. alcoholic beverages and tobacco. [7] Incl. "Fuel and light" and certain household equipment.

[1] Personnes âgées de 10 ans et plus. [2] Y compris les forces armées. [3] Niveaux 2-5. [4] Niveaux 6-7. [5] Non compris les entrepôts. [6] Y compris les boissons alcoolisées et le tabac. [7] Y compris le groupe "Combustible et éclairage" et certains biens d'équipement de ménage.

[1] Personas de 10 años y más. [2] Incl. las fuerzas armadas. [3] Niveles 2-5. [4] Niveles 6-7. [5] Excl. almacenaje. [6] Incl. las bebidas alcohólicas y el tabaco. [7] Incl. "Combustible y luz" y ciertos enseres domésticos.

République centrafricaine

1. Population active, Emploi et Chômage ('000)

	Population active		Emploi		Chômage	
	Total	Femmes (%)	Total	Femmes (%)	Total	Femmes (%)
Groupe d'âge	1988 [1,2] Recensement de la population		2003 [1] Recensement de la population		1994 [3] Fichiers des bureaux de placement	
Total	1 186.972	46.8	1 162.024	46.8	9.885	6.5
6-9	32.041	52.3	.	.	.	.
10-14	69.650	52.5	.	.	.	.
15-19	143.205	49.3	.	.	0.405	6.2
20-24	164.223	44.2	.	.	2.239	7.4
25-29	160.491	44.1	.	.	2.654	8.4
30-34	129.409	43.6	.	.	1.705	9.0
35-39	103.877	46.2	.	.	.	.
35-44	.	.	.	.	0.732	6.7
40-44	86.852	47.0	.	.	.	.
45-49	78.887	49.3	.	.	0.495	3.6
50-54	67.541	49.7	.	.	0.316	0.9
55-59	54.461	48.8	.	.	0.190	0.5
60+	.	.	.	.	.	.
60-64	42.358	47.3	.	.	.	.
65+	52.896	42.7	.	.	.	.
?	1.081	88.7	.	.	.	.

Niveau d'instruction (CITE-76)					1995 [3] Fichiers des bureaux de placement	
Total	.	.	.	.	7.561	11.4
X Non scolarisé	.	.	.	.	2.316	5.6
1 Premier degré	.	.	.	.	3.007	9.9
2 Second degré, premier cycle	.	.	.	.	1.334	14.9
3 Second degré, deuxième cycle	.	.	.	.	0.293	13.0
5 Troisième degré, premier niveau, conduisant à un titre ...	.	.	.	.	0.022	9.1
6-7	.	.	.	.	0.134	5.2
9 Enseignement impossible à définir selon le degré	.	.	.	.	0.449	40.3

2. Population ('000), Taux d'activité et Taux de chômage

	Population 1988 [2] Recensement de la population			Taux d'activité 1988 [2] Recensement de la population			Taux de chômage		
Groupe d'âge	Total	Hommes	Femmes	Total	Hommes	Femmes	Total	Hommes	Femmes
15+	1 395.0	669.6	725.4	77.7	87.1	69.0	.	.	.
15-24	478.4	230.5	247.9	64.3	71.2	57.8	.	.	.
25-54	733.0	348.6	384.4	85.5	97.1	75.0	.	.	.
55+	183.6	90.5	93.1	81.6	89.0	74.4	.	.	.

3. Emploi rémunéré ('000), Durée du travail (hebdomadaire) et Salaires

Activité économique (CITI-Rév.2)	Emploi rémunéré 1992 [4] Enquête auprès des établissements, relative au travail			Durée du travail			Salaires		
	Total	Hommes	Femmes	Total	Hommes	Femmes	Total	Hommes	Femmes
Total	14.045	.	.	.	.	.	.	.	.

4. Lésions professionnelles et Grèves et lock-out

Activité économique (CITI-Rév.2)	Taux de lésions mortelles			Taux de lésions non mortelles			Grèves et lock-out 1993 Fichiers des relations du travail		
	Total	Hommes	Femmes	Total	Hommes	Femmes	Grèves et lock-out	Travailleurs impliqués	Journées non effectuées
Total	.	.	.	.	.	.	2	.	.
1	.	.	.	.	.	.	0	.	.
2	.	.	.	.	.	.	0	.	.
3	.	.	.	.	.	.	1	.	.
4	.	.	.	.	.	.	0	.	.
5	.	.	.	.	.	.	0	.	.
6	.	.	.	.	.	.	0	.	.
7	.	.	.	.	.	.	0	.	.
8	.	.	.	.	.	.	1	.	.
9	.	.	.	.	.	.	0	.	.

5. Indices des prix à la consommation (période de base: 2000=100)

Bangui	2002	2003	2004	2005	2006	2007
Indices généraux [5]	105.2	110.9	108.6	111.7	119.1	120.3
Indices de l'alimentation, y compris les boissons non alcoolisées	106.8	112.4	107.2	110.9	.	.
Indices de l'électricité, gaz et autres combustibles	104.2	103.4	98.9	96.9	.	.
Indices de l'habillement, y compris les chaussures	104.9	109.8	123.8	122.5	.	.

[1] Persons aged 6 years and over. [2] Dec. [3] Bangui. [4] Private sector. [5] Excl. "Rent".

[1] Personnes âgées de 6 ans et plus. [2] Déc. [3] Bangui. [4] Secteur privé. [5] Non compris le groupe "Loyer".

[1] Personas de 6 años y más. [2] Dic. [3] Bangui. [4] Sector privado. [5] Excl. el grupo "Alquiler".

République dém. pop. lao

1. Economically active population, Employment and Unemployment ('000)

	Economically active population		Employment		Unemployment	
	Total	Women (%)	Total	Women (%)	Total	Women (%)
Age group	1995 [1,2] Population census		2005 [3,4] Population census		2005 [3,4] Population census	
Total	2 219.664	51.8	2 740.477	50.2	37.540	50.4
10-14	144.176	62.8	.	.	.	.
15-19	275.694	60.6	.	.	.	.
20-24	327.309	54.8	.	.	.	.
25-29	323.387	51.6	.	.	.	.
30-34	268.925	49.7	.	.	.	.
35-39	255.138	48.3	.	.	.	.
40-44	173.555	48.5	.	.	.	.
45-49	147.947	49.6	.	.	.	.
50-54	112.905	49.6	.	.	.	.
55-59	83.656	44.2	.	.	.	.
60-64	52.279	39.2	.	.	.	.
65-69	32.031	34.0	.	.	.	.
70+	22.662	31.5	.	.	.	.

Occupation (ISCO-88)			1995 [1,2] Population census			
Total	.	.	2 166.2	51.8	.	.
1 Legislators, senior officials and managers	.	.	9.5	6.1	.	.
2 Professionals	.	.	26.9	33.4	.	.
3 Technicians and associate professionals	.	.	62.6	38.4	.	.
4 Clerks	.	.	5.2	54.7	.	.
5 Service workers and shop and market sales workers	.	.	85.7	57.0	.	.
6 Skilled agricultural and fishery workers	.	.	1 852.7	54.2	.	.
7 Craft and related trade workers	.	.	55.9	40.8	.	.
8 Plant and machine operators and assemblers	.	.	21.2	3.6	.	.
9 Elementary occupations	.	.	25.3	27.5	.	.
X Not classifiable by occupation	.	.	21.2	7.5	.	.

2. Population ('000), Activity rate and Unemployment rate

	Population 1995 [2,5] Population census			Activity rate 1995 [2,5] Population census			Unemployment rate 2005 [3,4] Population census		
Age group	Total	Men	Women	Total	Men	Women	Total	Men	Women
Total							1.4	1.3	1.4
15+	2 551.195	1 231.425	1 319.770	81.4	82.6	80.3	.	.	.
15-24	819.833	393.175	426.658	73.6	65.3	81.2	.	.	.
25-54	1 360.724	660.181	700.543	94.2	97.5	91.0	.	.	.
55+	370.638	178.069	192.569	51.4	65.4	39.2	.	.	.

3. Paid employment ('000), Hours of work (weekly) and Wages

Statistics not available.

4. Occupational injuries and Strikes and Lockouts

Statistics not available.

5. Consumer price indices (base period: 2000=100)

	2002	2003	2004	2005	2006	2007
General indices	119.3	137.7	152.1	163.0	.	.
Food index, including non-alcoholic beverages	117.0	134.8	148.8	160.2	.	.

[1] Persons aged 10 years and over. [2] March. [3] Persons aged 15 years and over. [4] Jan. [5] "De facto" population.

[1] Personnes âgées de 10 ans et plus. [2] Mars. [3] Personnes âgées de 15 ans et plus. [4] Janv. [5] Population "de facto".

[1] Personas de 10 años y más. [2] Marzo. [3] Personas de 15 años y más. [4] Enero. [5] Población "de facto".

Réunion

1. Population active, Emploi et Chômage ('000)

Groupe d'âge	Population active Total	Femmes (%)	Emploi Total	Femmes (%)	Chômage Total	Femmes (%)
	1999 [1,2] Recensement de la population		1999 ★ Recensement de la population		2007 [1,3] Enquête sur la main-d'oeuvre	
Total	298.847	44.8	174.644	41.8	75.852	47.5
15-19	6.435	40.1	1.295	30.3	.	.
15-24	.	.	.	.	19.159	40.2
20-24	35.334	47.7	13.454	44.3	.	.
25-29	46.646	47.2	24.227	43.6	.	.
25-49	.	.	.	.	49.472	50.8
30-34	52.717	45.4	.	.	.	.
35-39	49.164	44.5	.	.	.	.
40-44	38.769	44.3	.	.	.	.
45-49	31.513	43.6	.	.	.	.
50+	.	.	.	.	7.221	43.6
50-54	21.016	40.8	.	.	.	.
55-59	12.490	40.7	.	.	.	.
60-64	3.707	41.9	.	.	.	.
65-69	0.592	35.0	.	.	.	.
70-74	0.166	34.9	.	.	.	.
75+	0.298	45.6	0.298	45.6	.	.

Niveau d'instruction (CITE-97)	1999 [1,2] Recensement de la population		1999 ★ Recensement de la population		1999 [1,2] Recensement de la population	
Total	298.847	44.8	174.644	41.8	124.203	48.9
1 Enseignement primaire ou premier cycle de l'éducation ...	57.477	36.5	28.526	33.7	28.951	39.3
2 Premier cycle de l'enseignement secondaire ou deuxième ...	141.233	42.8	69.377	36.2	71.856	49.2
3 Enseignement secondaire (deuxième cycle)	54.358	53.8	36.679	51.0	17.679	59.7
5A Premier cycle de l'enseignement supérieur - théorie [4]	45.779	50.2	40.062	48.9	5.717	59.4

2. Population ('000), Taux d'activité et Taux de chômage

Groupe d'âge	Population 1999 [2] Recensement de la population			Taux d'activité 1999 [2] Recensement de la population			Taux de chômage 1999 [1,2] Recensement de la population		
	Total	Hommes	Femmes	Total	Hommes	Femmes	Total	Hommes	Femmes
Total	706.2	347.1	359.1	42.3	47.6	37.2	41.6	38.5	45.4
15+	515.3	250.1	265.3	58.0	66.0	50.4	.	.	.
15-24	119.2	59.7	59.5	35.0	37.5	32.6	64.7	62.4	67.3
25-54	299.8	147.4	152.4	80.0	89.9	70.4	.	.	.
55+	96.3	43.0	53.3	17.9	23.8	13.2	.	.	.

3. Emploi rémunéré ('000), Durée du travail (hebdomadaire) et Salaires

Activité économique (CITI-Rév.3)	Emploi rémunéré 2006 Estimations officielles			Durée du travail			Salaires		
	Total	Hommes	Femmes	Total	Hommes	Femmes	Total	Hommes	Femmes
Total	196.600	.	.	.	.	.	.	.	.
A-B	3.192	.	.	.	.	.	.	.	.
D	12.480	.	.	.	.	.	.	.	.
E	1.806	.	.	.	.	.	.	.	.
F	16.940	.	.	.	.	.	.	.	.
G	26.770	.	.	.	.	.	.	.	.
H	4.683	.	.	.	.	.	.	.	.
I	10.230	.	.	.	.	.	.	.	.
J	3.736	.	.	.	.	.	.	.	.
K	15.800	.	.	.	.	.	.	.	.
L	39.660	.	.	.	.	.	.	.	.
M	24.730	.	.	.	.	.	.	.	.
N	16.900	.	.	.	.	.	.	.	.
O	8.961	.	.	.	.	.	.	.	.
P	10.680	.	.	.	.	.	.	.	.

4. Lésions professionnelles et Grèves et lock-out

Activité économique (CITI-Rév.2)	Taux de lésions mortelles			Taux de lésions non mortelles			Grèves et lock-out 1993 Source inconnue		
	Total	Hommes	Femmes	Total	Hommes	Femmes	Grèves et lock-out	Travailleurs impliqués	Journées non effectuées
Total	.	.	.	.	.	.	23	938	4 269
1	.	.	.	.	.	.	.	.	742
2	.	.	.	.	.	.	.	.	0
3	.	.	.	.	.	.	.	.	386
4	.	.	.	.	.	.	.	.	0
5	.	.	.	.	.	.	.	.	907
6	.	.	.	.	.	.	.	.	1 465
7	.	.	.	.	.	.	.	.	20
8	.	.	.	.	.	.	.	.	659
9	.	.	.	.	.	.	.	.	90
0	.	.	.	.	.	.	.	.	0

Réunion

5. Indices des prix à la consommation (période de base: 2000=100)

	2002	2003	2004	2005	2006	2007
Indices généraux	105.1	106.3	108.1	110.4	113.2	114.8
Indices de l'alimentation, y compris les boissons non alcoolisées	108.3	107.5	107.5	108.8	111.2	114.0
Indices de l'électricité, gaz et autres combustibles	102.3	103.0	104.6	111.9	121.1	119.7
Indices de l'habillement, y compris les chaussures	98.0	99.1	100.4	101.4	103.5	103.7
Indices du loyer	103.1	105.2	109.3	113.6	118.4	122.1

[1] Persons aged 15 years and over. [2] March. [3] Second quarter. [4] Levels 5A, 5B and 6.

[1] Personnes âgées de 15 ans et plus. [2] Mars. [3] Deuxième trimestre. [4] Niveaux 5A, 5B et 6.

[1] Personas de 15 años y más. [2] Marzo. [3] Segundo trimestre. [4] Niveles 5A, 5B y 6.

Roumanie

1. Population active, Emploi et Chômage ('000)

	Population active Total	Femmes (%)	Emploi Total	Femmes (%)	Chômage Total	Femmes (%)
Groupe d'âge	2007 [1] Enquête sur la main-d'oeuvre		2007 ★ Enquête sur la main-d'oeuvre		2007 [1] Enquête sur la main-d'oeuvre	
Total	9 994.3	44.8	9 353.3	45.3	641.0	37.8
15-19	215.1	34.8	156.3	33.6	58.8	37.9
20-24	761.3	41.3	623.4	42.4	137.9	36.7
25-29	1 328.5	45.5	1 227.2	46.0	101.3	39.3
30-34	1 379.7	44.4	1 305.9	45.0	73.8	33.7
35-39	1 602.1	45.3	1 522.8	45.4	79.3	43.0
40-44	996.8	46.2	943.7	46.3	53.1	44.6
45-49	1 154.3	46.5	1 090.1	46.9	64.2	40.3
50-54	1 059.2	44.5	1 010.1	44.9	49.1	36.3
55-59	682.1	40.9	662.1	41.8	20.0	13.0
60-64	303.6	46.2	303.6	46.2	-	.
65-69	292.5	49.4	292.5	49.4	-	.
70-74	219.0	51.3	.	.	-	.
75+	.	.	.	.	.	.
Activité économique (CITI-Rév.3)	2007 [1] Enquête sur la main-d'oeuvre		2007 [1] Enquête sur la main-d'oeuvre		2007 [1] Enquête sur la main-d'oeuvre	
Total	9 994.3	44.8	9 353.3	45.3	641.0	37.8
A Agriculture, chasse et sylviculture	2 791.2	47.4	2 756.7	47.6	34.5	28.7
C Activités extractives	117.1	13.8	109.2	13.0	7.9	.
D Activités de fabrication	2 094.2	46.4	1 973.8	46.7	120.5	41.5
E Production et distribution d'électricité, de gaz et d'eau	180.6	23.2	175.9	23.3	-	.
F Construction	709.3	9.9	678.6	10.1	30.7	5.9
G Commerce de gros et de détail; réparation de véhicules ...	1 188.6	53.8	1 151.4	53.9	37.1	52.3
H Hôtels et restaurants	147.8	65.7	136.6	65.9	11.3	62.8
I Transports, entreposage et communications	505.5	22.3	488.7	22.2	16.9	26.6
J Intermédiation financière	98.9	70.3	97.2	70.2	-	.
K Immobilier, locations et activités de services aux entreprises	290.1	37.6	282.0	37.7	8.1	.
L Administration publique et défense; sécurité sociale obligatoire	477.7	35.8	468.4	36.0	9.3	31.2
M Education	403.4	74.3	400.2	74.4	-	.
N Santé et action sociale	378.7	77.6	375.4	77.6	-	.
O Autres activités de services collectifs, sociaux et personnels	265.3	50.1	253.9	50.2	11.4	.
X Ne pouvant être classés selon l'activité économique	345.9	37.8	.	.	84.4 [2]	47.0
Chômeurs n'ayant jamais travaillé	.	.	.	.	268.9	39.8
Profession (CITP-88)	2007 [1] Enquête sur la main-d'oeuvre		2007 [1] Enquête sur la main-d'oeuvre		2007 [1] Enquête sur la main-d'oeuvre	
Total	9 994.3	44.8	9 353.3	45.3	641.0	37.8
1 Membres de l'exécutif et des corps législatifs, cadres ...	255.4	28.4	252.6	28.1	-	.
2 Professions intellectuelles et scientifiques	884.6	51.1	876.2	51.2	8.3	.
3 Professions intermédiaires	874.9	61.1	857.4	61.2	17.5	56.6
4 Employés de type administratif	422.6	71.8	410.8	71.9	11.9	67.2
5 Personnel des services et vendeurs de magasin et de marché	982.7	64.7	946.0	64.6	36.7	67.3
6 Agriculteurs et ouvriers qualifiés de l'agriculture ...	2 354.8	49.4	2 343.5	49.5	11.3	30.1
7-8	1 616.3	25.1	1 523.8	25.0	92.5	25.3
9 Ouvriers et employés non qualifiés	1 122.6	41.7	1 053.4	42.1	69.3	35.9
X Ne pouvant être classés selon la profession	1 480.4	30.1	1 089.6	27.8	124.6 [2]	32.9
Chômeurs n'ayant jamais travaillé	.	.	.	.	268.9	39.8
Niveau d'instruction (CITE-97)	2007 [1] Enquête sur la main-d'oeuvre		2007 ★ Enquête sur la main-d'oeuvre		2007 [1] Enquête sur la main-d'oeuvre	
Total	9 994.3	44.8	9 353.3	45.3	641.0	37.8
X Non scolarisé	82.1	49.6	69.9	54.1	12.2	23.8
1 Enseignement primaire ou premier cycle de l'éducation ...	583.3	51.9	549.6	53.5	33.7	26.1
2 Premier cycle de l'enseignement secondaire ou deuxième ...	1 837.2	48.1	1 705.8	49.1	131.4	35.8
3 Enseignement secondaire (deuxième cycle)	5 726.4	41.8	5 318.1	42.1	408.3	38.1
4 Enseignement postsecondaire qui n'est pas du supérieur	436.2	48.4	419.8	48.4	16.4	47.0
5A Premier cycle de l'enseignement supérieur - théorie	1 115.5	48.1	1 084.3	48.0	31.2	51.3
5B Premier cycle de l'enseignement supérieur - pratique	213.6	51.2	205.8	51.1	7.8	53.8
Situation dans la profession (CISP-1993)	2007 [1] Enquête sur la main-d'oeuvre		2007 [1] Enquête sur la main-d'oeuvre		2007 ★ Enquête sur la main-d'oeuvre	
Total	9 994.3	44.8	9 353.3	45.3	641.0	37.8
1 Salariés	6 458.0	45.3	6 197.2	45.5	260.8	38.9
2 Employeurs	138.7	21.9	136.7	21.4	2.0	60.5
3 Personnes travaillant pour leur propre compte	1 870.6	29.4	1 840.0	29.5	30.6	21.2
5 Travailleurs familiaux collaborant à l'entreprise familiale	1 181.8	71.7	1 175.3	71.8	6.5	49.6
6 Inclassables d'après la situation	345.9	37.8	.	.	.	.

2. Population ('000), Taux d'activité et Taux de chômage

Groupe d'âge	Population 2007 [3] Enquête sur la main-d'oeuvre			Taux d'activité 2007 [3] Enquête sur la main-d'oeuvre			Taux de chômage 2007 [1] Enquête sur la main-d'oeuvre		
	Total	Hommes	Femmes	Total	Hommes	Femmes	Total	Hommes	Femmes
Total	21 551.3	10 503.9	11 047.4	46.4	52.5	40.5	6.4	7.3	5.4
15+	18 247.9	8 809.4	9 438.6	.	.	.	.	.	.
15-24	3 198.8	1 635.1	1 563.7	30.5	35.9	24.9	20.1	21.1	18.7
25-54	9 522.5	4 780.0	4 742.5	79.0	85.9	72.0	5.6	6.2	4.9
55+	5 526.7	2 394.3	3 132.4	.	.	.	.	.	.

Roumanie

3. Emploi rémunéré ('000), Durée du travail (hebdomadaire) et Salaires

Activité économique (CITI-Rév.3)	Emploi rémunéré 2007[1] Enquête sur la main-d'oeuvre Total	Hommes	Femmes	Durée du travail 2007[1] Enquête sur la main-d'oeuvre Heures réellement effectuées / Emploi total Total	Hommes	Femmes	Salaires 2006 Enquête auprès des établissements, relative au travail Gains par mois / Salariés / Leu Total	Hommes	Femmes
Total	6 197.2	3 376.4	2 820.8	39.7	40.7	38.6	1 146	1 222	1 062
A-B	.	.	.	35.2	37.0	33.3	802	807	787
C-Q	.	.	.	.	.	.	1 156	1 240	1 066
A	142.5	111.3	31.2	35.2	37.0	33.3	805	811	788
B	-	-	-	42.2	42.6	40.0	647	635	705
C	107.8	93.9	13.9	40.1	40.1	40.1	2 024	2 045	1 904
D	1 924.0	1 010.7	913.3	41.6	41.7	41.5	950	1 087	807
E	175.8	134.8	41.0	40.8	40.9	40.5	1 801	1 832	1 711
F	527.9	461.4	66.5	43.2	43.4	41.4	936	931	966
G	951.9	401.4	550.5	42.3	42.7	42.0	862	1 002	737
H	128.2	40.5	87.7	43.5	44.6	42.9	693	767	649
I	452.3	344.7	107.6	42.8	43.3	40.7	1 420	1 464	1 312
J	95.5	28.3	67.2	41.1	41.5	40.9	3 078	3 581	2 846
K	261.5	163.2	98.3	41.2	41.7	40.5	1 102	1 060	1 177
L	468.4	299.6	168.8	41.1	41.2	40.8	2 112	2 125	2 103
M	398.8	101.9	296.9	38.7	39.1	38.5	1 443	1 616	1 363
N	363.4	79.1	284.3	41.2	41.3	41.2	1 085	1 264	1 036
O	196.1	103.3	92.8	39.8	39.6	40.0	985	1 043	920
Q							1 512	1 786	1 238

Pourcentage de salariées dans le secteur non agricole qui sont femmes [1] (2007 - Enquête sur la main-d'oeuvre): **46.1%**

4. Lésions professionnelles et Grèves et lock-out

Activité économique (CITI-Rév.3)	Taux de lésions mortelles 2007 Fichiers d'inspection du travail Pour 100 000 salariés Lésions déclarées Total	Hommes	Femmes	Taux de lésions non mortelles 2007 Fichiers d'inspection du travail Pour 100 000 salariés Lésions déclarées Total	Hommes	Femmes	Grèves et lock-out 2007[4] Fichiers des relations du travail Grèves et lock-out	Travailleurs impliqués	Journées non effectuées
Total	6	.	.	70	.	.	12	8 081	494 034
A	11	.	.	33	.	.	1	500	10 000
B	8	.	.	8	.	.	0	0	0
C	8	.	.	284	.	.	0	0	0
D	4	.	.	88	.	.	7	5 921	348 234
E	7	.	.	83	.	.	1	1 000	2 000
F	23	.	.	156	.	.	0	0	0
G	5	.	.	38	.	.	0	0	0
H	3	.	.	33	.	.	0	0	0
I	10	.	.	64	.	.	3	660	133 800
J	1	.	.	15	.	.	0	0	0
K	9	.	.	83	.	.	0	0	0
L	5	.	.	40	.	.	0	0	0
M	0	.	.	7	.	.	0	0	0
N	0	.	.	25	.	.	0	0	0
O	3	.	.	45	.	.	0	0	0
P	0	.	.	0	.	.	.	.	.
Q	0	.	.	0	.	.	.	.	.

5. Indices des prix à la consommation (période de base: 2000=100)

	2002	2003	2004	2005	2006	2007
Indices généraux	164.8	189.9	212.5	231.7	246.9	258.8
Indices de l'alimentation, y compris les boissons non alcoolisées	160.5	184.1	201.5	213.8	222.0	230.6
Indices de l'électricité, gaz et autres combustibles	200.9	244.9	297.8	350.9	388.2	417.1
Indices de l'habillement, y compris les chaussures	148.2	163.8	175.4	183.2	188.7	194.9
Indices du loyer	140.4	162.1	187.8	204.6	216.7	372.2
Indices généraux, non compris le logement	164.8	189.9	212.5	231.7	246.9	258.8

[1] Persons aged 15 years and over. [2] Incl. the unemployed whose last job was 8 years ago or over, except for 1994-1996. [3] "De jure" population. [4] Strikes only.

[1] Personnes âgées de 15 ans et plus. [2] Y compris les chômeurs dont le dernier emploi date de 8 ans ou plus, sauf pour 1994-1996. [3] Population "de jure". [4] Grèves seulement.

[1] Personas de 15 años y más. [2] Incl. los desempleados cuyo último trabajo fue hace 8 años o más, excepto por 1994-1996. [3] Población "de jure". [4] Huelgas solamente.

Russian Federation

1. Economically active population, Employment and Unemployment ('000)

	Economically active population		Employment		Unemployment	
	Total	Women (%)	Total	Women (%)	Total	Women (%)
Age group	2007 [1] Labour force survey		2007 ★ Labour force survey		2007 [1] Labour force survey	
Total	75 159	49.3	70 571	49.5	4 588	46.6
15-19	1 736	41.6	1 305	40.5	431	45.2
20-24	7 834	45.6	6 878	45.6	956	45.5
25-29	9 777	47.0	9 181	47.1	596	46.3
30-34	9 340	48.2	8 835	48.3	505	47.3
35-39	8 647	49.7	8 196	49.8	451	47.7
40-44	9 734	51.1	9 232	51.4	502	47.2
45-49	10 879	52.3	10 361	52.5	518	49.2
50-54	9 018	53.2	8 628	53.4	390	47.9
55-59	5 562	47.1	5 390	47.4	172	39.0
60-64	1 378	47.0	1 338	47.0	40	47.5
65-72	1 253	50.0	1 226	50.2	27	40.7
Economic activity (ISIC-Rev.3)	2007 ★ Labour force survey		2007 [1] Labour force survey		2007 [1] Labour force survey	
Total	75 158	49.3	70 570	49.5	4 588	46.6
A Agriculture, Hunting and Forestry	6 698	38.4	6 155	38.8	543	33.7
B Fishing	214	17.3	192	17.7	22	13.6
C Mining and Quarrying	1 378	21.4	1 324	21.1	54	27.8
D Manufacturing	12 903	42.8	12 324	42.6	579	46.6
E Electricity, Gas and Water Supply	2 085	30.8	2 017	31.1	68	23.5
F Construction	5 225	17.8	4 933	18.0	292	15.4
G Wholesale and Retail Trade; Repair of Motor Vehicles ...	11 593	61.1	11 096	61.1	497	61.0
H Hotels and Restaurants	1 435	79.4	1 344	79.0	91	85.7
I Transport, Storage and Communications	6 819	29.9	6 573	30.1	246	25.2
J Financial Intermediation	1 272	67.0	1 249	66.7	23	82.6
K Real Estate, Renting and Business Activities	4 556	43.5	4 410	43.4	146	45.2
L Public Administration and Defence; Compulsory Social ...	5 052	37.2	4 903	37.3	149	36.2
M Education	6 612	80.2	6 420	80.2	192	78.6
N Health and Social Work	5 285	81.3	5 177	81.4	108	78.7
O Other Community, Social and Personal Service Activities	2 550	68.4	2 439	68.8	111	60.4
P Households with Employed Persons	17	64.7	16	68.8	1	.
Q Extra-Territorial Organizations and Bodies	-	.	-	.	-	.
Unemployed seeking their first job	.	.	.	.	1 468	48.8
Occupation (ISCO-88)	2007 ★ Labour force survey		2007 [1] Labour force survey		2007 [1] Labour force survey	
Total	75 158	49.3	70 570	49.5	4 588	46.6
1 Legislators, senior officials and managers	4 948	38.8	4 868	38.7	80	47.5
2 Professionals	12 912	61.2	12 693	61.2	219	59.8
3 Technicians and associate professionals	10 846	67.2	10 532	67.3	314	63.7
4 Clerks	2 194	90.2	2 101	90.1	93	92.5
5 Service workers and shop and market sales workers	10 377	71.1	9 868	70.9	509	75.4
6 Skilled agricultural and fishery workers	3 301	50.8	3 147	51.0	154	48.1
7 Craft and related trade workers	11 269	23.9	10 666	23.7	603	27.5
8 Plant and machine operators and assemblers	9 072	12.5	8 650	12.6	422	10.4
9 Elementary occupations	8 771	49.7	8 045	50.5	726	40.9
X Not classifiable by occupation	.	.	.	.	1 468	48.8
Education level (ISCED-97)	2007 [1] Labour force survey		2007 ★ Labour force survey		2007 [1] Labour force survey	
Total	75 159	49.3	70 571	49.5	4 588	46.6
1 Primary education or first stage of basic education	438	42.2	374	44.1	64	31.3
2 Lower secondary or second stage of basic education	4 344	39.1	3 779	39.3	565	37.7
3 Upper secondary education	17 322	44.1	15 676	44.1	1 646	44.7
4 Post-secondary non-tertiary education	13 584	37.7	12 745	37.6	839	38.5
5A First stage of tertiary education - theoretically based	19 229	59.3	18 404	59.3	825	58.5
5B First stage of tertiary education - practically oriented	1 219	51.2	1 086	51.0	133	52.6
6 Second stage of tertiary education	19 023	54.6	18 506	54.5	517	56.3
Status in employment (ICSE-1993)			2007 [1] Labour force survey			
Total	.	.	70 570	49.1	.	.
1 Employees	.	.	65 384	49.8	.	.
2 Employers	.	.	980	39.0	.	.
3 Own-account workers	.	.	4 033	46.9	.	.
4 Members of producers' cooperatives	.	.	93	31.2	.	.
5 Contributing family workers	.	.	80	46.3	.	.

2. Population ('000), Activity rate and Unemployment rate

	Population 2007 [2] Labour force survey			Activity rate 2007 [2] Labour force survey			Unemployment rate 2007 [1] Labour force survey		
Age group	Total	Men	Women	Total	Men	Women	Total	Men	Women
Total	142 115	65 783	76 332	52.9	57.9	48.5	6.1	6.4	5.8
15+	121 263	55 105	66 158	.	.	.	.	.	.
15-24	23 365	11 862	11 503	41.0	44.5	37.3	14.5	14.4	14.7
25-54	64 341	31 017	33 324	89.2	92.0	86.6	5.2	5.4	4.9
55+	33 557	12 226	21 331	.	.	.	.	.	.

Russian Federation

3. Paid employment ('000), Hours of work (weekly) and Wages

Economic activity (ISIC-Rev.3)	Paid employment 2007 [1] Labour-related establishment survey Total	Men	Women	Hours of work 2007 [3,4] Labour-related establishment survey Hours actually worked / Employees Total	Men	Women	Wages 2007 Labour-related establishment survey Earnings per month / Employees / Rouble Total	Men	Women
Total	48 943.7	.	.	7.1	.	.	13 593	.	.
A-B	.	.	.	7.5	.	.	6 441	.	.
C-Q	.	.	.	7.1	.	.	13 997	.	.
A	2 524.0	.	.	7.5	.	.	6 144	.	.
B	89.7	.	.	7.4	.	.	14 797	.	.
C	974.5	.	.	6.9	.	.	28 108	.	.
D	9 258.9	.	.	7.0	.	.	12 879	.	.
E	1 845.3	.	.	7.1	.	.	15 587	.	.
F	3 163.3	.	.	7.2	.	.	14 333	.	.
G	5 259.3	.	.	7.4	.	.	11 476	.	.
H	792.1	.	.	7.2	.	.	9 339	.	.
I	4 166.5	.	.	7.0	.	.	16 452	.	.
J	977.0	.	.	7.3	.	.	34 880	.	.
K	4 319.8	.	.	7.2	.	.	16 642	.	.
L	3 542.5	.	.	7.3	.	.	16 896	.	.
M	5 767.7	.	.	6.7	.	.	8 778	.	.
N	4 450.9	.	.	7.2	.	.	10 037	.	.
O	1 811.3	.	.	7.1	.	.	10 392	.	.
Q	0.7	.	.	7.2	.	.	30 339	.	.

Share of women in wage employment in the non-agricultural sector [1] (2007 - Labour force survey): **51.0%**

4. Occupational injuries and Strikes and Lockouts

Economic activity (ISIC-Rev.3)	Rates of fatal injuries 2007 [5] Labour-related establishment survey Per 100,000 employees Reported injuries Total	Men	Women	Rates of non-fatal injuries 2007 [5] Labour-related establishment survey Per 100,000 employees Reported injuries Total	Men	Women	Strikes and lockouts 2007 [6] Labour relations records Strikes and lockouts	Workers involved	Days not worked
Total	12.4	21.2	1.6	262	361	168	7	2 894	20 457
A	.	.	.	.	.	.	0	0	0
D	.	.	.	.	.	.	3	1 684	15 963
E	.	.	.	.	.	.	0	0	0
F	.	.	.	.	.	.	0	0	0
I	.	.	.	.	.	.	4	1 210	4 494
K	.	.	.	.	.	.	0	0	0
M	.	.	.	.	.	.	0	0	0
N	.	.	.	.	.	.	0	0	0
O	.	.	.	.	.	.	0	0	0
X	.	.	.	.	.	.	0	0	0

5. Consumer price indices (base period: 2000=100)

	2002	2003	2004	2005	2006	2007
General indices	140.6	159.9	177.3	199.7	219.1	238.8
Food index, including non-alcoholic beverages	136.5	151.8	167.4	190.3	208.4	227.2
Clothing indices, including footwear [7,8]	131.1	145.2	156.8	168.5	181.7	196.5
Rent indices [7,9]	251.9	330.8	427.2	581.5	684.3	769.0

[7,10]	2002	2003	2004	2005	2006	2007
Electricity, gas and other fuel indices	181.2	209.0	239.1	282.0	329.2	367.2

[1] Persons aged 15 to 72 years. [2] "De jure" population. [3] Large and middle size enterprises. [4] Per day. [5] Excl. activities with low injury rates. [6] Excl. work stoppages lasting less than one day. [7] Dec. of each year; Index base Dec. 2000=100. [8] Excl. footwear. [9] Rent for municipal housing. [10] Electricity only.

[1] Personnes âgées de 15 à 72 ans. [2] Population "de jure". [3] Entreprises grandes et moyennes. [4] Par jour. [5] Non compris les activités avec les taux de lésion bas. [6] Non compris les arrêts du travail dont la durée est inférieure à une journée. [7] Déc. de chaque année; base des indices déc. 2000=100. [8] Non compris la chaussure. [9] Loyer d'un logement municipal. [10] Electricité seulement.

[1] Personas de 15 a 72 años. [2] Población "de jure". [3] Empresas grandes y medias. [4] Por día. [5] Excl. las actividades con tasas de lesion bajas. [6] Excl. las interrupciones del trabajo de menos de un día de duración. [7] Dic. de cada año; base de los índices dic. 2000=100. [8] Excl. el calzado. [9] Alquiler de una vivienda municipal. [10] Electricidad solamente.

Rwanda

1. Population active, Emploi et Chômage ('000)

	Population active		Emploi		Chômage	
	Total	Femmes (%)	Total	Femmes (%)	Total	Femmes (%)
Groupe d'âge	1996 [1,2] Enquête sur la main-d'oeuvre		1996 ★ Enquête sur la main-d'oeuvre		1996 [2,3] Enquête sur la main-d'oeuvre	
Total	2 941.710	55.3	2 925.425	55.4	16.285	34.0
10-14	240.923	51.9	239.847	52.0	1.076	25.4
15-19	511.663	52.4	508.630	52.5	3.033	31.6
20-24	405.795	57.9	402.027	58.1	3.768	41.8
25-29	326.771	58.7	323.875	58.9	2.896	39.4
30-34	332.624	56.1	330.827	56.2	1.797	39.4
35-39	288.989	54.3	287.947	54.3	1.042	37.4
40-44	239.977	56.0	239.127	56.2	0.850	5.4
45-49	160.779	56.2	160.146	56.4	0.633	14.1
50-54	128.239	59.1	127.675	59.1	0.564	42.6
55-59	92.779	56.6	92.617	56.6	0.162	43.2
60-64	83.156	55.6	82.888	55.8	0.268	.
65-69	59.957	50.3	.	.	.	.
70-74	37.992	50.7	.	.	.	.
75+	27.792	45.2	.	.	.	.
?	4.274	56.7	4.078	58.4	0.196	23.0

Activité économique (CITI-Rév.2)	1996 [1,2] Enquête sur la main-d'oeuvre					
Total	2 941.710	55.3				
1 Agriculture, chasse, sylviculture et pêche	2 672.540	57.4				
2 Industries extractives	1.058	6.4				
3 Industries manufacturières	15.775	24.7				
4 Electricité, gaz et eau	1.531	6.0				
5 Bâtiment et travaux publics	26.816	1.6				
6 Commerce de gros et de détail; restaurants et hôtels	39.366	44.7				
7 Transports, entrepôts et communications	6.878	8.7				
8 Banques, assurances, affaires immobilières et services ...	2.215	28.7				
9 Services fournis à la collectivité, services sociaux ...	124.865	40.3				
0 Activités mal désignées	50.666	36.2				

Profession (CITP-1968)	1996 [1,2] Enquête sur la main-d'oeuvre					
Total	2 941.710	55.3				
0/1 Personnel des professions scientifiques, techniques ...	9.870	41.4				
2 Directeurs et cadres administratifs supérieurs	33.376	45.8				
3 Personnel administratif et travailleurs assimilés	15.781	38.4				
4 Personnel commercial et vendeurs	36.534	46.7				
5 Travailleurs spécialisés dans les services	41.054	44.9				
6 Agriculteurs, éleveurs, forestiers, pêcheurs et chasseurs	2 673.646	57.5				
7/8/9 Ouvriers et manoeuvres non agricoles et conducteurs ...	86.467	14.8				
X Ne pouvant être classés selon la profession	44.982	37.8				

Niveau d'instruction (CITE-76)	1996 [1,2] Estimations officielles				2000 Estimations officielles	
Total	2 956.883	55.3			53.338	60.4
X Non scolarisé	1 234.993	62.5			4.928	41.1
0 Enseignement précédant le premier degré	1 521.812 [4]	50.5				
1 Premier degré	.	.			29.112	58.6
2 Second degré, premier cycle	75.232	54.5			3.278	62.4
3 Second degré, deuxième cycle	93.133	42.3			12.879	62.3
5 Troisième degré, premier niveau, conduisant à un titre ...	7.374 [5]	17.5				
5-7					3.141	96.5
? Niveau inconnu	24.339	59.0			-	

Situation dans la profession (CISP-58)	1996 [1,2] Enquête sur la main-d'oeuvre					
Total	2 941.710	55.3				
1 Employeurs et personnes travaillant à leur propre compte	1 811.749	59.0				
2 Salariés	173.453	30.5				
3 Travailleurs familiaux non rémunérés	923.006	53.4				
4 Inclassables d'après la situation	33.502	35.6				

2. Population ('000), Taux d'activité et Taux de chômage

	Population 1996 [2] Enquête sur la main-d'oeuvre			Taux d'activité 1996 [2] Enquête sur la main-d'oeuvre			Taux de chômage 1996 [2,3] Enquête sur la main-d'oeuvre		
Groupe d'âge	Total	Hommes	Femmes	Total	Hommes	Femmes	Total	Hommes	Femmes
Total							0.6	0.8	0.3
15+	3 136.3	1 374.2	1 762.2	86.0	87.1	85.1	0.6	0.8	.
15-24	1 161.5	526.9	634.7	79.0	78.7	79.3	0.7	1.0	0.5
25-54	1 554.2	662.9	891.3	95.1	96.8	93.8	0.5	0.8	0.3
55+	420.6	184.4	236.1	71.7	76.4	68.1	.	.	.

Rwanda

3. Emploi rémunéré ('000), Durée du travail (hebdomadaire) et Salaires

Activité économique (CITI-Rév.2)	Emploi rémunéré Total	Hommes	Femmes	Durée du travail Total	Hommes	Femmes	Salaires 1997[6] Rapports administratifs Gains par mois / Salariés / Franc Total	Hommes	Femmes
1	.	.	.	.	.	.	11 628	.	.
3	.	.	.	.	.	.	27 659	.	.
4	.	.	.	.	.	.	18 711	.	.
5	.	.	.	.	.	.	20 789	.	.
6	.	.	.	.	.	.	28 763	.	.
7	.	.	.	.	.	.	34 538	.	.
8	.	.	.	.	.	.	52 053	.	.
9	.	.	.	.	.	.	34 367	.	.

4. Lésions professionnelles et Grèves et lock-out

Activité économique (CITI-Rév.3)	Taux de lésions mortelles Total	Hommes	Femmes	Taux de lésions non mortelles Total	Hommes	Femmes	Grèves et lock-out 1999 Fichiers d'inspection du travail Grèves et lock-out	Travailleurs impliqués	Journées non effectuées
Total	.	.	.	.	.	.	49	2 545	.

5. Indices des prix à la consommation (période de base: 2000=100)

Kigali	2002	2003	2004	2005	2006	2007
Indices généraux	105.4	113.2	126.7	138.3	150.6	164.2
Indices de l'alimentation, y compris les boissons non alcoolisées	104.7	119.2	141.7	156.1	171.5	185.0
Indices de l'habillement, y compris les chaussures	109.7	111.7	.	119.0	118.2	119.2
Indices du loyer [7]	104.2	106.9	.	145.3	171.0	200.6

[1] Persons aged 10 years and over. [2] Nov. [3] Persons aged 10 to 65 years. [4] Levels 0-1. [5] Levels 5-7. [6] June. [7] Incl. water, electricity, gas and other fuels.

[1] Personnes âgées de 10 ans et plus. [2] Nov. [3] Personnes âgées de 10 à 65 ans. [4] Niveaux 0-1. [5] Niveaux 5-7. [6] Juin. [7] Y compris l'eau, l'électricité, le gaz et autres combustibles.

[1] Personas de 10 años y más. [2] Nov. [3] Personas de 10 a 65 años de edad. [4] Niveles 0-1. [5] Niveles 5-7. [6] Junio. [7] Incl. el agua, la electricidad, el gas y otros combustibles.

Saint Helena

1. Economically active population, Employment and Unemployment ('000)

Age group	Economically active population Total	Women (%)	Employment Total	Women (%)	Unemployment Total	Women (%)
	1998 [1 2] Population census		1998 ★ Population census		1998 [2 3] Population census	
Total	2.486	42.2	2.037	43.7	0.449	35.4
15-19	0.243	49.8	0.181	49.7	0.062	50.0
20-24	0.286	48.6	0.222	49.1	0.064	46.9
25-29	.	.	.	.	0.080	36.3
25-39	0.971	47.3	.	.	.	.
30-34	.	.	.	.	0.049	44.9
35-39	.	.	.	.	0.056	39.3
40-44	0.274	35.8	0.238	37.4	0.036	25.0
45-49	0.264	37.1	0.228	39.5	0.036	22.2
50-54	0.266	30.1	0.225	33.8	0.041	9.8
55-59	0.128	25.0	0.109	27.5	0.019	10.5
60-64	0.023	43.5	0.022	45.5	0.001	0.0
65-69	0.015	46.7	0.013	46.2	0.002	50.0
70-74	0.005	40.0	.	.	.	.
75+	0.007	42.9	.	.	.	.
?	0.004	25.0	.	.	.	.

Economic activity (ISIC-Rev.3)

1998 [2 3] Population census

	Total	Women (%)
Total	2.037	43.7
A Agriculture, Hunting and Forestry	0.187	18.7
B Fishing	0.020	.
D Manufacturing	0.087	16.1
E Electricity, Gas and Water Supply	0.048	4.2
F Construction	0.267	1.5
G Wholesale and Retail Trade; Repair of Motor Vehicles ...	0.344	58.4
H Hotels and Restaurants	0.024	66.7
I Transport, Storage and Communications	0.181	37.0
J Financial Intermediation	0.017	41.2
K Real Estate, Renting and Business Activities	0.007	57.1
L Public Administration and Defence; Compulsory Social ...	0.293	56.0
M Education	0.187	77.5
N Health and Social Work	0.196	75.0
O Other Community, Social and Personal Service Activities	0.087	60.9
P Households with Employed Persons	0.074	36.5
Q Extra-Territorial Organizations and Bodies	0.011	18.2
X Not classifiable by economic activity	0.007	42.9

Occupation (ISCO-88)

1998 [2 3] Population census

	Total	Women (%)
Total	2.037	43.7
1 Legislators, senior officials and managers	0.108	43.5
2 Professionals	0.094	64.9
3 Technicians and associate professionals	0.238	70.2
4 Clerks	0.274	74.8
5 Service workers and shop and market sales workers	0.382	72.5
6 Skilled agricultural and fishery workers	0.090	3.3
7 Craft and related trade workers	0.245	5.7
8 Plant and machine operators and assemblers	0.108	4.6
9 Elementary occupations	0.566	20.7
X Not classifiable by occupation	0.007	42.9

2. Population ('000), Activity rate and Unemployment rate

Age group	Population Total	Men	Women	Activity rate Total	Men	Women	Unemployment rate Total	Men	Women
	1998 [2] Population census			1998 [2] Population census			1998 [2 3] Population census		
Total	4.913	2.499	2.414	50.6	57.5	43.5	18.1	20.2	15.1
15+	3.854	1.922	1.932	64.4	74.6	54.3	18.0	20.1	15.1
15-24	0.752	0.371	0.381	70.3	72.5	68.2	23.8	24.2	23.5
25-54	2.112	1.070	1.042	84.0	97.2	70.5	16.8	19.6	12.8
55+	0.990	0.481	0.509	18.0	25.8	10.6	.	.	.

Saint Helena

3. Paid employment ('000), Hours of work (weekly) and Wages

Economic activity (ISIC-Rev.3)	Paid employment			Hours of work			Wages 2002 [4] Tax records Earnings per month / Employees / Pound		
	Total	Men	Women	Total	Men	Women	Total	Men	Women
Total	.	.	.	.	.	.	265.6	281.0	245.7
C-Q	.	.	.	.	.	.	286.7	301.0	233.1
D	.	.	.	.	.	.	296.8	317.1	229.5
E	.	.	.	.	.	.	286.7	298.5	130.2
F	.	.	.	.	.	.	238.0	238.0	.
G	.	.	.	.	.	.	240.5	265.8	219.4
H	.	.	.	.	.	.	292.2	326.3	196.7
I	.	.	.	.	.	.	534.0	540.3	510.7
K	.	.	.	.	.	.	383.0	302.9	407.1
L	.	.	.	.	.	.	328.9	322.3	333.3
M	.	.	.	.	.	.	292.3	274.8	307.4
N	.	.	.	.	.	.	203.7	296.7	182.0
O	.	.	.	.	.	.	155.8	165.1	141.3
P	.	.	.	.	.	.	259.7	347.9	171.3
Q	.	.	.	.	.	.	295.6	302.9	251.3
X	.	.	.	.	.	.	206.4	212.5	183.1

4. Occupational injuries and Strikes and Lockouts

Economic activity (ISIC-Rev.3)	Rates of fatal injuries			Rates of non-fatal injuries			Strikes and lockouts 2005 Labour relations records		
	Total	Men	Women	Total	Men	Women	Strikes and lockouts	Workers involved	Days not worked
Total	.	.	.	.	.	.	0	0	0

5. Consumer price indices (base period: 2000=100)

[5]	2002	2003	2004	2005	2006	2007
General indices	100.0	100.0	108.8	112.9	116.5	123.1
Food index, including non-alcoholic beverages	100.0	103.8	112.9	116.1	117.4	121.7
Electricity, gas and other fuel indices	100.0	107.8	121.8	131.7	137.6	139.2
Clothing indices, including footwear	100.0	102.4	110.4	119.0	121.6	107.2
Rent indices	100.0	100.8	102.8	103.4	104.3	104.6

[1] Persons aged 15 years and over. [2] March. [3] Persons aged 15 to 69 years. [4] Year ending in March of the year indicated. [5] Index base 2002=100.

[1] Personnes âgées de 15 ans et plus. [2] Mars. [3] Personnes âgées de 15 à 69 ans. [4] Année se terminant en mars de l'année indiquée. [5] Indice base 2002=100.

[1] Personas de 15 años y más. [2] Marzo. [3] Personas de 15 a 69 años. [4] Año que termina en marzo del año indicado. [5] Indice base 2002=100.

Saint Kitts and Nevis

1. Economically active population, Employment and Unemployment ('000)

	Economically active population		Employment		Unemployment	
	Total	Women (%)	Total	Women (%)	Total	Women (%)
Age group	1991 [1,2] Population census		1984 Official estimates			
Total	17.794	44.3	14.803	39.7	.	.
15-19	1.548	40.7	.	.	.	.
20-24	2.988	45.1	.	.	.	.
25-29	3.006	46.4	.	.	.	.
30-34	2.838	47.6	.	.	.	.
35-39	2.202	45.1	.	.	.	.
40-44	1.308	42.7	.	.	.	.
45-49	0.957	44.3	.	.	.	.
50-54	0.765	44.4	.	.	.	.
55-59	0.689	42.5	.	.	.	.
60-64	0.593	37.8	.	.	.	.
65+	0.900	36.6	.	.	.	.
Economic activity (ISIC-Rev.2)			1984 Official estimates			
Total	.	.	14.80	39.7	.	.
1 Agriculture, Hunting, Forestry and Fishing	.	.	4.38	18.6	.	.
2 Mining and Quarrying	.	.	0.00	.	.	.
3 Manufacturing	.	.	2.17	44.3	.	.
4 Electricity, Gas and Water	.	.	1.03	2.2	.	.
5 Construction	.	.	0.40	9.5	.	.
6 Wholesale and Retail Trade and Restaurants and Hotels	.	.	0.94	74.8	.	.
7 Transport, Storage and Communication	.	.	0.45	55.6	.	.
8 Financing, Insurance, Real Estate and Business Services	.	.	0.28	28.7	.	.
9 Community, Social and Personal Services	.	.	4.70	60.4	.	.
0 Activities not Adequately Defined	.	.	0.46	38.0	.	.

2. Population ('000), Activity rate and Unemployment rate

	Population			Activity rate			Unemployment rate		
Age group	1991 [2] Population census			1991 [2] Population census					
	Total	Men	Women	Total	Men	Women	Total	Men	Women
Total	40.618	19.933	20.685	43.8	49.7	38.1	.	.	.
15+	26.698	12.896	13.802	66.6	76.9	57.1	.	.	.
15-24	7.449	3.739	3.710	60.9	68.4	53.3	.	.	.
25-54	13.068	6.430	6.638	84.8	93.6	76.2	.	.	.
55+	6.181	2.727	3.454	35.3	49.0	24.5	.	.	.

3. Paid employment ('000), Hours of work (weekly) and Wages

Statistics not available.

4. Occupational injuries and Strikes and Lockouts

Economic activity (ISIC-Rev.2)	Rates of fatal injuries			Rates of non-fatal injuries			Strikes and lockouts 1991 Source unknown		
	Total	Men	Women	Total	Men	Women	Strikes and lockouts	Workers involved	Days not worked
Total	.	.	.	.	.	.	0	0	0

5. Consumer price indices (base period: 2000=100)

Statistics not available for the period 2002-2007.

[1] Persons aged 15 years and over. [2] May.

[1] Personnes âgées de 15 ans et plus. [2] Mai.

[1] Personas de 15 años y más. [2] Mayo.

Saint Lucia

1. Economically active population, Employment and Unemployment ('000)

	Economically active population		Employment		Unemployment	
	Total	Women (%)	Total	Women (%)	Total	Women (%)
Age group	2004 [1] Labour force survey		2004 ★ Labour force survey		2004 [1] Labour force survey	
Total	78.792	46.4	62.265	44.0	16.527	55.3
15-19	5.420	41.5	2.273	36.2	3.147	45.3
20-24	10.820	44.5	7.348	41.2	3.472	51.6
25-34	19.935	49.2	15.540	46.1	4.395	60.4
35-44	20.155	50.7	17.648	48.2	2.507	68.0
45-54	12.285	42.5	10.760	40.4	1.525	57.4
55-64	5.840	44.4	5.020	43.1	0.820	52.4
65+	4.337	38.3	3.677	38.1	0.660	39.7
Economic activity (ISIC-Rev.3)	2000 ★ Labour force survey		2004 [1] Labour force survey		2000 [1] Labour force survey	
Total	76.005	47.2	62.265	44.1	12.535	59.6
A Agriculture, Hunting and Forestry	17.940	40.7	8.490	30.7	5.590	58.6
B Fishing	0.845	2.4	0.753	12.4	-	
D Manufacturing	7.390	61.1	4.668	51.0	1.190	73.5
E Electricity, Gas and Water Supply	0.795	21.4	0.428	14.0	0.110	40.9
F Construction	6.840	7.3	4.928	3.4	0.845	8.9
G Wholesale and Retail Trade; Repair of Motor Vehicles ...	12.790	62.3	9.778	55.3	1.445	63.7
H Hotels and Restaurants	7.800	56.1	6.760	55.3	1.215	68.3
I Transport, Storage and Communications	4.390	19.6	3.325	25.2	0.295	23.7
J Financial Intermediation	1.065	66.7	1.153	62.7	0.080	50.0
K Real Estate, Renting and Business Activities	1.625	45.8	2.535	42.0	0.320	78.1
L Public Administration and Defence; Compulsory Social ...	8.140	57.6	8.180	54.6	0.610	56.6
M Education	1.195	68.6	1.058	80.6	0.055	63.6
N Health and Social Work	0.620	61.3	0.385	87.0	0.020	100.0
O Other Community, Social and Personal Service Activities	1.580	54.7	1.953	45.6	0.075	53.3
P Households with Employed Persons	2.120	80.9	1.850	89.5	0.665	97.0
X Not classifiable by economic activity	0.870	31.0	6.025	35.9	0.020	.
Occupation (ISCO-88)	2004 ★ Labour force survey		2004 [1] Labour force survey		2004 [1] Labour force survey	
Total	78.792	46.9	62.265	44.0	16.527	57.9
1 Legislators, senior officials and managers	4.062	52.5	3.895	52.3	0.167	58.1
2 Professionals	5.617	63.1	5.405	61.9	0.212	92.0
3 Technicians and associate professionals	2.807	43.2	2.582	43.8	0.225	36.4
4 Clerks	5.050	81.1	4.380	81.1	0.670	80.9
5 Service workers and shop and market sales workers	9.772	52.4	7.980	49.7	1.792	64.3
6 Skilled agricultural and fishery workers	8.675	30.2	8.450	30.4	0.225	20.9
7 Craft and related trade workers	9.127	15.9	7.502	14.1	1.625	24.3
8 Plant and machine operators and assemblers	3.512	31.5	3.042	24.2	0.470	78.7
9 Elementary occupations	10.827	52.6	8.385	53.0	2.442	51.2
X Not classifiable by occupation	19.339	51.9	10.642	43.1	8.697	62.6
Education level (ISCED-76)					2000 [1] Labour force survey	
Total	.	.	.	.	12.535	59.6
X No schooling	.	.	.	.	0.340	54.4
0 Education preceding the first level	.	.	.	.	1.000	51.0
1 First level	.	.	.	.	5.490	60.7
2 Second level, first stage	.	.	.	.	1.215	52.7
3 Second level, second stage	.	.	.	.	3.570	62.0
5 Third level, first stage, leading to an award not equivalent ...	.	.	.	.	0.415	57.8
6 Third level, first stage, leading to a first university degree ...	.	.	.	.	0.145	72.4
9 Education not definable by level	.	.	.	.	0.360	66.7
Status in employment (ICSE-1993)			2000 [1] Labour force survey			
Total	.	.	63.470	44.8		
1 Employees	.	.	40.670	49.4		
2 Employers	.	.	3.440	25.3		
3 Own-account workers	.	.	17.615	38.5		
5 Contributing family workers	.	.	0.600	68.3		
6 Not classifiable by status	.	.	1.245	24.1		

2. Population ('000), Activity rate and Unemployment rate

	Population 2003 [2] Labour force survey			Activity rate 2003 [2] Labour force survey			Unemployment rate 2004 [1] Labour force survey		
Age group	Total	Men	Women	Total	Men	Women	Total	Men	Women
Total	160.5	80.0	80.5	51.1	55.0	47.3	21.0	17.5	25.0
15+	119.5	58.6	61.0	68.7	75.2	62.3	21.0	17.5	25.0
15-24	27.7	14.4	13.3	59.4	62.6	55.3	40.8	37.1	45.5
25-54	64.6	31.4	33.2	86.2	92.3	80.5	16.1	11.8	20.7
55+	27.3	12.8	14.5	36.4	47.3	26.8	14.5	13.3	16.3

Saint Lucia

3. Paid employment ('000), Hours of work (weekly) and Wages

Economic activity (ISIC-Rev.2)	Paid employment 1986 Labour-related establishment survey			Hours of work			Wages		
	Total	Men	Women	Total	Men	Women	Total	Men	Women
Total	47.6	21.6	26.0	.	.	.	.	.	.
1	10.5	7.9	2.6	.	.	.	.	.	.
2	0.1	0.1	0.0	.	.	.	.	.	.
3	2.6	0.6	2.0	.	.	.	.	.	.
4	3.6	1.7	1.9	.	.	.	.	.	.
5	4.5	4.3	0.3	.	.	.	.	.	.
6	5.7	2.3	3.4	.	.	.	.	.	.
7	1.1	1.0	0.1	.	.	.	.	.	.
8	0.1	0.1	0.1	.	.	.	.	.	.
9	0.2	0.1	0.2	.	.	.	.	.	.
0	19.1	3.6	15.5	.	.	.	.	.	.

Economic activity (ISIC-Rev.3)	Paid employment			Hours of work 2003[3] Labour-related establishment survey Hours actually worked / Wage earners			Wages 2003[3] Labour-related establishment survey Earnings per hour / Wage earners / EC dollar		
	Total	Men	Women	Total	Men	Women	Total	Men	Women
A	.	.	.	17	.	.	.	3.67 [4]	3.32 [4]
D	.	.	.	42	.	.	.	7.01 [4]	4.96 [4]
E	.	.	.	40	.	.	.	13.34 [4]	13.34 [4]
F	.	.	.	39	.	.	.	13.67 [4]	8.22 [4]
G	.	.	.	38	.	.	.	5.87 [4]	4.51 [4]
H	.	.	.	40	.	.	.	6.71 [4]	6.85 [4]
I	.	.	.	41	.	.	.	10.65 [4]	9.00 [4]
K	.	.	.	39	.	.	.	7.17 [4]	10.25 [4]
M	.	.	.	28	.	.	.	8.83 [4]	5.49 [4]
N	.	.	.	35	.	.	.	6.87 [4]	3.83 [4]
O	.	.	.	37	.	.	.	7.67 [4]	7.04 [4]

4. Occupational injuries and Strikes and Lockouts

Economic activity (ISIC-Rev.2)	Rates of fatal injuries			Rates of non-fatal injuries			Strikes and lockouts 1987 Source unknown		
	Total	Men	Women	Total	Men	Women	Strikes and lockouts	Workers involved	Days not worked
Total	.	.	.	.	.	.	0	0	0

5. Consumer price indices (base period: 2000=100)

	2002	2003	2004	2005	2006	2007
General indices	105.0	106.0	107.6	111.8	114.4	.
Food index, including non-alcoholic beverages	101.9	104.1	104.9	112.3	116.0	.
Electricity, gas and other fuel indices	97.1	100.0	103.5	111.5	117.2	.
Clothing indices, including footwear	100.3	100.3	105.3	105.3	105.3	.
Rent indices	123.8	123.8	123.8	123.8	124.0	.

[1] Persons aged 15 years and over. [2] May. [3] Unweighted survey results. [4] Minimum rates.

[1] Personnes âgées de 15 ans et plus. [2] Mai. [3] Résultats d'enquête non pondérés. [4] Taux minima.

[1] Personas de 15 años y más. [2] Mayo. [3] Resultados de la encuesta no ponderados. [4] Tasas mínimas.

Saint Vincent and the Grenadines

1. Economically active population, Employment and Unemployment ('000)

Age group	Economically active population Total	Women (%) 1991 [1,2] Population census	Employment Total	Women (%) 1991 ★ Population census	Unemployment Total	Women (%) 1991 [1,2] Population census
Total	41.682	35.9	33.444	34.8	8.238	40.1
15-19	5.039	30.7	2.581	24.6	2.458	37.1
20-24	7.509	38.0	5.409	34.7	2.100	46.6
25-29	7.409	37.4	6.043	35.4	1.366	46.2
30-34	6.084	37.3	5.264	36.6	0.820	42.0
35-39	4.348	39.9	3.896	40.1	0.452	38.1
40-44	3.112	36.0	2.754	36.3	0.358	33.5
45-49	2.329	35.2	2.083	36.2	0.246	26.4
50-54	1.966	33.6	1.799	34.8	0.167	20.4
55-59	1.531	33.5	1.405	34.2	0.126	25.4
60-64	1.144	29.3	1.058	30.3	0.086	16.3
65+	1.204	26.8	1.145	27.9	0.059	5.1
?	0.007	14.3	.	.	.	.

2. Population ('000), Activity rate and Unemployment rate

Age group	Population 1991[2] Pop. census Total	Men	Women	Activity rate 1991[2] Pop. census Total	Men	Women	Unemployment rate 1991[1,2] Pop. census Total	Men	Women
Total	106.499	53.165	53.334	39.1	50.3	28.0	19.8	18.4	22.1
15+	66.856	33.092	33.764	62.3	80.8	44.3	19.8	18.4	22.1
15-24	21.958	11.146	10.812	57.1	73.1	40.7	36.3	32.7	43.0
25-54	32.792	16.599	16.193	77.0	95.6	57.9	13.5	12.9	14.6
55+	12.106	5.347	6.759	32.0	50.6	17.3	7.0	8.2	4.2

3. Paid employment ('000), Hours of work (weekly) and Wages

Economic activity (ISIC-Rev.3)	Paid employment Total	Men	Women	Hours of work Total	Men	Women	Wages 2002 Labour-related establishment survey Wage rates per day / Employees / EC dollar Total	Men	Women
A	.	.	.	.	.	.	29.70	.	.
C	.	.	.	.	.	.	50.92	.	.
D	.	.	.	.	.	.	26.52	.	.
E	.	.	.	.	.	.	50.92	.	.
F	.	.	.	.	.	.	47.74	.	.
G	.	.	.	.	.	.	26.52	.	.
H	.	.	.	.	.	.	26.52	.	.
I	.	.	.	.	.	.	53.04	.	.
J	.	.	.	.	.	.	.	.	.
K	.	.	.	.	.	.	60.25	.	.
L-N [3]	.	.	.	.	.	.	.	.	.
O	.	.	.	.	.	.	31.82	.	.
P	.	.	.	.	.	.	16.48	.	.

4. Occupational injuries and Strikes and Lockouts

Economic activity (ISIC-Rev.3)	Rates of fatal injuries Total	Men	Women	Rates of non-fatal injuries Total	Men	Women	Strikes and lockouts 2000[4] Labour relations records Strikes and lockouts	Workers involved	Days not worked[5]
Total	.	.	.	.	.	.	3	1 634	11
A	.	.	.	.	.	.	0	0	0
B	.	.	.	.	.	.	0	0	0
C	.	.	.	.	.	.	0	0	0
D	.	.	.	.	.	.	1	15	2
E	.	.	.	.	.	.	0	0	0
F	.	.	.	.	.	.	0	0	0
G	.	.	.	.	.	.	0	0	0
H	.	.	.	.	.	.	0	0	0
I	.	.	.	.	.	.	0	0	0
J	.	.	.	.	.	.	1	119	2
K	.	.	.	.	.	.	0	0	0
L	.	.	.	.	.	.	1	1 500	7
M	.	.	.	.	.	.	0	0	0
N	.	.	.	.	.	.	0	0	0
O	.	.	.	.	.	.	0	0	0
X	.	.	.	.	.	.	0	0	0

5. Consumer price indices (base period: 2000=100)

St. Vincent	2002	2003	2004	2005	2006	2007
General indices	101.5	101.8	104.8	108.7	112.0	119.8
Food index, including non-alcoholic beverages	101.6	100.9	105.6	111.3	115.3	123.9
Electricity, gas and other fuel indices	104.0	106.0	108.1	128.5	142.0	.
Clothing indices, including footwear	97.7	97.1	97.2	97.0	97.4	.
Rent indices	102.8	103.4	102.6	103.4	103.9	.

Saint Vincent and the Grenadines

[1] Persons aged 15 years and over. [2] May. [3] Mid-point of a wage rate range. [4] Strikes only. [5] Computed on the basis of an eight-hour working day.

[1] Personnes âgées de 15 ans et plus. [2] Mai. [3] Milieu d'une fourchete de taux de salaire. [4] Grèves seulement. [5] Calculées sur la base de journées de travail de huit heures.

[1] Personas de 15 años y más. [2] Mayo. [3] Punto medio de un rango de tasa de salario. [4] Huelgas solamente. [5] Calculados en base a días de trabajo de ocho horas.

Saint-Pierre-et-Miquelon

1. Population active, Emploi et Chômage ('000)

	Population active Total	Population active Femmes (%)	Emploi Total	Emploi Femmes (%)	Chômage Total	Chômage Femmes (%)
Groupe d'âge	1982 [1,2] Recensement de la population		1989 [3,4] Estimations officielles		1993 [5] Fichiers des bureaux de placement	
Total	2.380	31.8	2.501	28.9	0.393	.
15-19	0.127	42.5	.	.	.	.
20-24	0.389	41.1	.	.	.	.
25-29	0.390	33.8	.	.	.	.
30-34	0.370	31.6	.	.	.	.
35-39	0.285	27.0	.	.	.	.
40-44	0.241	21.2	.	.	.	.
45-49	0.210	30.0	.	.	.	.
50-54	0.164	25.6	.	.	.	.
55-59	0.129	24.0	.	.	.	.
60-64	0.045	35.6	.	.	.	.
65+	0.030	43.3	.	.	.	.

Activité économique (CITI-Rév.2)			1989 [3,4] Estimations officielles			
Total	.	.	2.501	.	.	.
1 Agriculture, chasse, sylviculture et pêche	.	.	0.052	.	.	.
3 Industries manufacturières	.	.	0.432	.	.	.
4 Electricité, gaz et eau	.	.	0.058	.	.	.
5 Bâtiment et travaux publics	.	.	0.175	.	.	.
6 Commerce de gros et de détail; restaurants et hôtels	.	.	0.475	.	.	.
7 Transports, entrepôts et communications	.	.	0.119	.	.	.
8 Banques, assurances, affaires immobilières et services ...	.	.	0.090	.	.	.
9 Services fournis à la collectivité, services sociaux ...	.	.	0.992	.	.	.
0 Activités mal désignées	.	.	0.067	.	.	.

2. Population ('000), Taux d'activité et Taux de chômage

	Population 1982 [2] Recensement de la population			Taux d'activité 1982 [2] Recensement de la population			Taux de chômage 1989 [5] Fichiers des bureaux de placement		
Groupe d'âge	Total	Hommes	Femmes	Total	Hommes	Femmes	Total	Hommes	Femmes
Total	6.037	2.981	3.056	39.4	54.5	24.7	11.3	9.9	18.1
15+	4.409	2.180	2.229	54.0	74.5	33.9	.	.	.
15-24	1.101	0.567	0.534	46.9	53.3	40.1	.	.	.
25-54	2.322	1.218	1.104	71.5	96.7	43.7	.	.	.
55+	0.986	0.395	0.591	20.7	36.5	10.2	.	.	.

3. Emploi rémunéré ('000), Durée du travail (hebdomadaire) et Salaires

Activité économique (CITI-Rév.2)	Emploi rémunéré 1984 Estimations officielles			Durée du travail 1989 [6] / Salariés			Salaires		
	Total	Hommes	Femmes	Total	Hommes	Femmes	Total	Hommes	Femmes
2-9	.	.	.	46	.	.	.	.	.
3	0.211	0.142	0.069	.	.	.	.	.	.
5	0.076	0.073	0.003	.	.	.	.	.	.
7	0.099	0.092	0.007	.	.	.	.	.	.

4. Lésions professionnelles et Grèves et lock-out

Activité économique (CITI-Rév.2)	Taux de lésions mortelles			Taux de lésions non mortelles			Grèves et lock-out 1987 Source inconnue		
	Total	Hommes	Femmes	Total	Hommes	Femmes	Grèves et lock-out	Travailleurs impliqués	Journées non effectuées
Total	.	.	.	.	.	.	0	0	0

5. Indices des prix à la consommation (période de base: 2000=100)

	2002	2003	2004	2005	2006	2007
Indices généraux	102.5	104.8	106.9	114.0	.	.
Indices de l'alimentation, y compris les boissons non alcoolisées	106.1	106.7	104.9	109.7	.	.

[1] Persons aged 15 years and over. [2] March. [3] Excl. unpaid family workers. [4] 31st Dec. of each year. [5] Persons aged 16 to 60 years. [6] Employees.

[1] Personnes âgées de 15 ans et plus. [2] Mars. [3] Non compris les travailleurs familiaux non rémunérés. [4] 31 déc. de chaque année. [5] Personnes âgées de 16 à 60 ans. [6] Salariés.

[1] Personas de 15 años y más. [2] Marzo. [3] Excl. los trabajadores familiares no remunerados. [4] 31 dic. de cada año. [5] Personas de 16 a 60 años de edad. [6] Asalariados.

Samoa

1. Economically active population, Employment and Unemployment ('000)

Age group	Economically active population Total	Economically active population Women (%)	Employment Total	Employment Women (%)	Unemployment Total	Unemployment Women (%)
	1991 [1,2] Population census					
Total	57.142	32.0	.	.	.	.
15-19	5.001	26.2	.	.	.	.
20-24	11.689	32.7	.	.	.	.
25-29	9.776	33.6	.	.	.	.
30-34	7.745	34.2	.	.	.	.
35-39	5.848	34.5	.	.	.	.
40-44	4.526	34.2	.	.	.	.
45-49	3.894	34.6	.	.	.	.
50-54	3.510	35.3	.	.	.	.
55-59	2.799	33.2	.	.	.	.
60-64	1.431	7.6	.	.	.	.
65-69	0.887	4.8	.	.	.	.
70-74	0.025	4.0	.	.	.	.
75+	0.011	9.1	.	.	.	.

2. Population ('000), Activity rate and Unemployment rate

Age group	Population Total	Population Men	Population Women	Activity rate Total	Activity rate Men	Activity rate Women	Unemployment rate Total	Unemployment rate Men	Unemployment rate Women
	1991 [2] Population census			1991 [2] Population census					
Total	161.298	84.601	76.697	35.4	45.9	23.9	.	.	.
15+	95.829	50.270	45.559	59.6	77.3	40.2	.	.	.
15-24	35.927	19.706	16.221	46.5	58.6	31.6	.	.	.
25-54	46.013	23.652	22.361	76.7	98.1	54.1	.	.	.
55+	13.889	6.912	6.977	37.1	58.9	15.5	.	.	.

3. Paid employment ('000), Hours of work (weekly) and Wages

Statistics not available.

4. Occupational injuries and Strikes and Lockouts

Statistics not available.

5. Consumer price indices (base period: 2000=100)

	2002	2003	2004	2005	2006	2007
General indices [3]	112.2	112.3	130.5	133.0	138.1	.
Food index, including non-alcoholic beverages	117.3	115.1	146.2	146.7	152.5	.
Clothing indices, including footwear	98.3	96.2	93.4	85.0	81.4	.
Rent indices	103.1	104.9				.

[1] Persons aged 15 years and over. [2] Nov. [3] Excl. "Rent".   [1] Personnes âgées de 15 ans et plus. [2] Nov. [3] Non compris le groupe "Loyer".   [1] Personas de 15 años y más. [2] Nov. [3] Excl. el grupo "Alquiler".

San Marino

1. Economically active population, Employment and Unemployment ('000)

	Economically active population		Employment		Unemployment	
	Total	Women (%)	Total	Women (%)	Total	Women (%)
Age group	2007 [1,2] Official estimates		2007 ★ Official estimates		2007 [1,2] Official estimates	
Total	22.056	41.9	21.483	41.0	0.573	73.3
15-19	0.173	26.0	0.146	26.7	0.027	22.2
20-24	1.095	40.9	1.016	39.8	0.079	55.7
25-29	2.275	43.7	2.142	41.9	0.133	73.7
30-34	3.449	43.8	3.347	42.7	0.102	81.4
35-39	4.014	41.3	3.937	40.4	0.077	85.7
40-44	3.862	41.6	3.799	40.9	0.063	84.1
45-49	3.064	40.8	3.015	40.2	0.049	77.6
50-54	2.212	43.0	2.185	42.6	0.027	77.8
55-59	1.570	40.3	1.560	40.1	0.010	60.0
60-64	0.287	43.2	0.282	42.2	0.005	100.0
65-69	0.036	36.1	0.035	37.1	0.001	.
70-74	0.014	7.1	0.014	7.1	-	.
75+	0.005	60.0	0.005	60.0	-	.
Economic activity (ISIC-Rev.3)			2007 [1,2] Official estimates			
Total	.	.	21.483	41.0	.	.
A Agriculture, Hunting and Forestry	.	.	0.082	29.3	.	.
D Manufacturing	.	.	6.422	28.1	.	.
F Construction	.	.	1.687	7.9	.	.
G Wholesale and Retail Trade; Repair of Motor Vehicles ...	.	.	3.358	47.6	.	.
H Hotels and Restaurants	.	.	0.188	67.0	.	.
I Transport, Storage and Communications	.	.	0.560	38.0	.	.
J Financial Intermediation	.	.	0.959	46.4	.	.
K Real Estate, Renting and Business Activities	.	.	2.926	42.6	.	.
L Public Administration and Defence; Compulsory Social ...	.	.	4.020	57.7	.	.
M Education	.	.	0.045	48.9	.	.
N Health and Social Work	.	.	0.174	74.1	.	.
O Other Community, Social and Personal Service Activities	.	.	1.047	71.6	.	.
X Not classifiable by economic activity	.	.	0.015	33.3	.	.
Occupation (ISCO-1968)	1993 ★ Official estimates				1993 [1,2] Official estimates	
Total	14.874	40.8	.	.	0.616	71.3
0/1 Professional, technical and related workers	1.728	45.3	.	.	0.205	73.7
2 Administrative and managerial workers	0.515	17.3	.	.	-	.
3 Clerical and related workers	3.241	57.1	.	.	0.236	78.0
4 Sales workers	1.518	53.9	.	.	0.021	95.2
5 Service workers	1.260	63.3	.	.	0.013	69.2
6 Agriculture, animal husbandry and forestry workers ...	0.294	43.5	.	.	-	.
7/8/9 Production and related workers, transport equipment ...	6.318	25.3	.	.	0.141	53.2
Occupation (ISCO-88)			2007 [1,2] Official estimates			
Total	.	.	21.483	41.0	.	.
1 Legislators, senior officials and managers	.	.	0.332	19.0	.	.
2 Professionals	.	.	1.950	44.1	.	.
3 Technicians and associate professionals	.	.	4.440	54.8	.	.
4 Clerks	.	.	2.910	61.5	.	.
5 Service workers and shop and market sales workers	.	.	0.120	6.7	.	.
7 Craft and related trade workers	.	.	3.951	14.8	.	.
8 Plant and machine operators and assemblers	.	.	2.979	35.1	.	.
9 Elementary occupations	.	.	2.654	51.4	.	.
X Not classifiable by occupation	.	.	2.147	31.0	.	.
Education level (ISCED-97)	2002 [1,2] Population census				2007 [1,2] Official estimates	
Total	19.959	41.5	.	.	0.573	73.3
X No schooling	0.079	38.0	.	.	.	.
1 Primary education or first stage of basic education	2.453	31.7	.	.	0.010	70.0
2 Lower secondary or second stage of basic education	7.454	35.3	.	.	0.154	74.0
3 Upper secondary education	7.825	49.0	.	.	0.233	68.2
5A First stage of tertiary education - theoretically based	0.303	64.7	.	.	.	.
5A, 6	.	.	.	.	0.133	82.0
5B First stage of tertiary education - practically oriented	1.594	46.0	.	.	0.041	70.7
? Level not stated	0.251	35.5	.	.	0.002	100.0
Status in employment (ICSE-1993)			2007 [1,2] Official estimates			
Total	.	.	21.483	41.0	.	.
1 Employees	.	.	19.427	42.1	.	.
2-4	.	.	2.056	30.6	.	.
5 Contributing family workers	.	.	-	.	.	.
6 Not classifiable by status	.	.	-	.	.	.

San Marino

2. Population ('000), Activity rate and Unemployment rate

Age group	Population 1999 [2] Population census Total	Men	Women	Activity rate 1999 [2] Population census Total	Men	Women	Unemployment rate 2007 [1,2] Official estimates Total	Men	Women
Total	32.5	17.2	15.3	58.8	66.6	50.0	2.6	1.2	4.5
15+	28.4	15.1	13.3	67.2	76.0	57.3	.	.	.
15-24	3.6	1.8	1.7	49.6	52.6	46.4	8.4	7.2	10.1
25-54	17.4	9.7	7.6	89.4	95.4	81.8	2.4	0.8	4.5
55+	7.5	3.5	4.0	24.1	33.9	15.6	.	.	.

3. Paid employment ('000), Hours of work (weekly) and Wages

Economic activity (ISIC-Rev.3)	Paid employment 2004 [1,2] Official estimates Total	Men	Women	Hours of work 2004 Official estimates Hours actually worked / Employees Total	Men	Women	Wages 2004 Official estimates Earnings per month / Employees / Euro Total	Men	Women
Total	17.686	10.226	7.460	39.1 [3]	.	.	1 967	.	.
A-B	.	.	.	39.1	.	.	.	.	.
C-Q	.	.	.	.	.	.	1 968	.	.
A	0.024	0.021	0.003	.	.	.	1 620	.	.
D	6.132	4.646	1.786	36.9	.	.	1 900	.	.
F	1.436	1.308	0.128	38.8	.	.	1 868	.	.
G	2.559	1.200	1.359	44.5	.	.	1 676	.	.
H	-	-	-	.	.	.	1 867	.	.
I	0.405	0.237	0.168	37.5	.	.	1 838	.	.
J	0.739	0.395	0.344	29.1	.	.	3 358	.	.
K	-	-	-	.	.	.	.	.	.
L	2.180	0.746	1.434	.	.	.	2 219	.	.
M	0.040	0.010	0.030	.	.	.	2 009	.	.
M-O	.	.	.	36.6	.	.	.	.	.
N	1.054	0.326	0.728	.	.	.	2 533	.	.
O	3.117	1.637	1.480	.	.	.	1 526	.	.
P	-	-	-	.	.	.	.	.	.
Q	-	-	-	.	.	.	.	.	.
X	0.003	.	.	.	.	.	.	.	.

Share of women in wage employment in the non-agricultural sector [1,2] (2007 - Official estimates): .%

4. Occupational injuries and Strikes and Lockouts

Economic activity (ISIC-Rev.3)	Rates of fatal injuries 2005 Labour inspectorate records Per 100,000 employees Reported injuries Total	Men	Women	Rates of non-fatal injuries 2006 Labour inspectorate records Per 100,000 employees Reported injuries Total	Men	Women	Strikes and lockouts 2006 Special data collection Strikes and lockouts	Workers involved	Days not worked
Total	0	.	.	4 652	.	.	0	.	.
A	.	.	.	7 895	.	.	.	.	.
D	.	.	.	6 128	.	.	.	.	.
F	.	.	.	9 414	.	.	.	.	.
G	.	.	.	5 917	.	.	.	.	.
H	.	.	.	1 342	.	.	.	.	.
I	.	.	.	2 581	.	.	.	.	.
J	.	.	.	589	.	.	.	.	.
K	.	.	.	2 327	.	.	.	.	.
L	.	.	.	2 939	.	.	.	.	.
O	.	.	.	2 450	.	.	.	.	.

5. Consumer price indices (base period: 2000=100)

[4]	2002	2003	2004	2005	2006	2007
General indices	.	100.0	101.4	103.1	105.3	107.9
Food index, including non-alcoholic beverages	.	100.0	103.3	108.9	115.0	120.7
Clothing indices, including footwear	.	100.0	99.7	100.1	100.2	100.7
Rent indices [5]	.	100.0	99.9	100.2	100.3	104.6

[1] Persons aged 15 years and over. [2] Dec. [3] Excl. mining and quarrying. [4] Index base 2003=100. [5] Incl. water, electricity, gas and other fuels.

[1] Personnes âgées de 15 ans et plus. [2] Déc. [3] Non compris les industries extractives. [4] Indice base 2003=100. [5] Y compris l'eau, l'électricité, le gaz et autres combustibles.

[1] Personas de 15 años y más. [2] Dic. [3] Excl. las minas y canteras. [4] Indice base 2003=100. [5] Incl. el agua, la electricidad, el gas y otros combustibles.

Sao Tomé-et-Principe

1. Población económicamente activa, Empleo y Desempleo ('000)

	Población económicamente activa		Empleo		Desempleo	
	Total	Mujeres (%)	Total	Mujeres (%)	Total	Mujeres (%)
Grupo de edad	1991 [1,2] Censo de población		1991 ★ Censo de población		1991 [1,2] Censo de población	
Total	35.382	33.6	34.068	33.2	1.314	44.9
10-14	0.334	29.0	0.302	28.1	0.032	37.5
15-19	3.741	29.4	3.373	27.6	0.368	46.2
20-24	6.071	30.6	5.678	29.8	0.393	42.5
25-29	5.830	36.3	5.631	36.0	0.199	46.2
30-34	4.467	38.5	4.330	38.2	0.137	46.7
35-39	3.524	40.7	3.453	40.5	0.071	49.3
40-44	2.491	37.0	2.451	36.8	0.040	52.5
45-49	2.090	36.2	2.062	36.2	0.028	35.7
50-54	2.336	32.3	2.315	32.1	0.021	52.4
55-59	1.970	27.5	1.950	27.4	0.020	30.0
60-64	1.300	23.9	1.298	24.0	0.002	.
65-69	0.768	25.0	0.767	24.9	0.001	100.0
70+	0.460	20.7	0.458	20.5	0.002	50.0

Actividad económica (CIIU-Rev.2)

			1991 [1,2] Censo de población			
Total	.	.	34.068	33.2	.	.
1 Agricultura, caza, silvicultura y pesca	.	.	13.592	29.1	.	.
3 Industrias manufactureras	.	.	1.510	13.3	.	.
4 Electricidad, gas y agua	.	.	0.269	4.5	.	.
5 Construcción	.	.	2.866	2.5	.	.
6 Comercio al por mayor y al por menor y restaurantes y ...	.	.	4.451	74.2	.	.
7 Transportes, almacenamiento y comunicaciones	.	.	2.186	6.0	.	.
8 Establecimientos financieros, seguros, bienes inmuebles ...	.	.	0.176	43.2	.	.
9 Servicios comunales, sociales y personales	.	.	7.961	39.7	.	.
0 Actividades no bien especificadas	.	.	1.057	37.6	.	.

Ocupación (CIUO-1968)

			1991 [1,2] Censo de población			
Total	.	.	34.068	33.2	.	.
0/1 Profesionales, técnicos y trabajadores asimilados	.	.	3.775	29.8	.	.
2 Directores y funcionarios públicos superiores	.	.	2.529	32.8	.	.
5 Trabajadores de los servicios	.	.	2.906	36.6	.	.
6 Trabajadores agrícolas y forestales, pescadores y cazadores	.	.	1.504	16.5	.	.
7/8/9 Obreros no agrícolas, conductores de máquinas y ...	.	.	6.740	1.5	.	.
X No pueden clasificarse según la ocupación	.	.	16.614	47.8	.	.

Situación en el empleo (CISE-1993)

			1991 [1,2] Censo de población			
Total	.	.	34.068	33.2	.	.
1 Asalariados	.	.	24.256	32.1	.	.
2 Empleadores	.	.	0.123	10.6	.	.
3 Trabajadores por cuenta propia	.	.	8.991	36.6	.	.
5 Trabajadores familiares auxiliares	.	.	0.265	29.4	.	.
6 Inclasificables según la situación	.	.	0.433	30.9	.	.

2. Población ('000), Tasa de actividad y Tasa de desempleo

	Población 1991 [2] Censo de población			Tasa de actividad 1991 [2] Censo de población			Tasa de desempleo 1991 [1,2] Censo de población		
Grupo de edad	Total	Hombres	Mujeres	Total	Hombres	Mujeres	Total	Hombres	Mujeres
Total	.	.	.	.	.	.	3.7	3.1	5.0
15+	62.401	30.284	32.117	56.2	76.8	36.8	3.7	.	.
15-24	22.634	11.428	11.206	43.4	60.0	26.4	7.8	6.2	11.4
25-54	28.863	13.638	15.225	71.8	95.6	50.6	2.4	2.0	3.0
55+	10.904	5.218	5.686	41.3	64.4	20.0	0.6	.	.

3. Empleo remunerado ('000), Horas de trabajo (por semana) y Salarios

Datos no disponibles.

4. Lesiones profesionales y Huelgas y cierres patronales

Datos no disponibles.

5. Índices de precios al consumidor (periodo de base: 2000=100)

Datos no disponibles para el periodo de 2002 a 2007.

[1] Personas de 10 años y más. [2] Agosto.

Saudi Arabia

1. Economically active population, Employment and Unemployment ('000)

	Economically active population		Employment		Unemployment	
	Total	Women (%)	Total	Women (%)	Total	Women (%)
Age group		1992 [1] Population census		2007 ★ Labour force survey		2007 [2] Labour force survey
Total	5 310.550	10.9	7 766.345	14.2	463.313	36.2
10-14	22.049	15.3	.	.	.	.
15-19	175.198	9.0	.	.	28.546	8.6
20-24	666.513	11.3	.	.	207.383	33.8
25-29	1 105.938	10.8	.	.	160.010	45.9
30-34	1 122.785	16.0	.	.	47.912	42.5
35-39	852.375	12.0	.	.	6.093	12.4
40-44	532.047	8.5	.	.	8.256	7.6
45-49	323.062	6.0	.	.	3.113	6.4
50-54	211.880	4.9	.	.	1.053	.
55-59	128.311	3.1	.	.	0.947	.
60-64	87.007	2.9	.	.	-	.
65+	83.385	1.9	.	.	-	.

Economic activity (ISIC-Rev.3)

2007 [2] Labour force survey

	Total	Women (%)
Total	7 766.350	14.2
A Agriculture, Hunting and Forestry	364.184	1.2
C Mining and Quarrying	102.807	1.2
D Manufacturing	565.774	1.5
E Electricity, Gas and Water Supply	74.381	.
F Construction	793.586	0.4
G Wholesale and Retail Trade; Repair of Motor Vehicles ...	1 250.270	0.6
H Hotels and Restaurants	248.697	1.1
I Transport, Storage and Communications	343.552	3.4
J Financial Intermediation	83.787	5.3
K Real Estate, Renting and Business Activities	250.247	1.8
L Public Administration and Defence; Compulsory Social ...	1 400.092	2.3
M Education	929.199	44.8
N Health and Social Work	335.921	25.9
O Other Community, Social and Personal Service Activities	175.877	4.4
P Households with Employed Persons	838.126	61.0
Q Extra-Territorial Organizations and Bodies	9.850	.

Occupation (ISCO-88)

2007 [2] Labour force survey

	Total	Women (%)
Total	7 766.347	14.2
1 Legislators, senior officials and managers	335.550	10.0
2 Professionals	613.942	18.7
3 Technicians and associate professionals	884.370	35.6
4 Clerks	578.278	8.9
5 Service workers and shop and market sales workers	713.794	1.1
6 Skilled agricultural and fishery workers	2 407.490	23.3
7 Craft and related trade workers	393.076	1.1
8 Plant and machine operators and assemblers	203.626	2.1
9 Elementary occupations	1 636.221	0.6

Education level (ISCED-97)

2007 [2] Labour force survey

	Total	Women (%)
Total	463.313	36.2
X No schooling	2.423	.
1 Primary education or first stage of basic education	58.233	3.9
2 Lower secondary or second stage of basic education	63.098	5.6
3 Upper secondary education	159.152	22.6
4 Post-secondary non-tertiary education	47.648	36.9
5	131.129	82.1
6 Second stage of tertiary education	1.630	49.0

2. Population ('000), Activity rate and Unemployment rate

	Population			Activity rate			Unemployment rate		
Age group		1992 [3] Population census			1992 [3] Population census			2007 [2] Labour force survey	
	Total	Men	Women	Total	Men	Women	Total	Men	Women
Total	16 948.4	9 480.0	7 468.4	31.3	49.9	7.8	5.6	4.2	13.2
15+	9 872.3	5 892.6	3 979.6	53.6	80.0	14.5	.	.	.
15-24	2 898.9	1 525.2	1 373.6	29.0	49.2	6.6	.	.	.
25-54	6 028.3	3 815.4	2 212.9	68.8	96.2	21.6	.	.	.
55+	945.1	552.0	393.1	31.6	52.6	2.1	.	.	.

Saudi Arabia

3. Paid employment ('000), Hours of work (weekly) and Wages

Economic activity (ISIC-Rev.3)	Paid employment 2002² Labour force survey			Hours of work			Wages 1997 Labour-related establishment census Earnings per week / Employees / Riyal		
	Total	Men	Women	Total	Men	Women	Total	Men	Women
C-Q	5 649.279	4 857.271	792.308	.	.	.	.	.	.
C	.	.	.	.	.	.	1 080	.	.
D	.	.	.	.	.	.	657	.	.
E	.	.	.	.	.	.	1 915	.	.
F	.	.	.	.	.	.	588	.	.
G	.	.	.	.	.	.	557	.	.
H	.	.	.	.	.	.	384	.	.
I	.	.	.	.	.	.	1 206	.	.
J	.	.	.	.	.	.	2 400	.	.
K	.	.	.	.	.	.	683	.	.
M	.	.	.	.	.	.	623	.	.
N	.	.	.	.	.	.	815	.	.
O	.	.	.	.	.	.	398	.	.

Share of women in wage employment in the non-agricultural sector ² (2002 - Labour force survey): **14.0%**

4. Occupational injuries and Strikes and Lockouts

Statistics not available.

5. Consumer price indices (base period: 2000=100)

[4]	2002	2003	2004	2005	2006	2007
General indices	98.6	97.2	99.5	100.2	102.4	106.7
Food index, including non-alcoholic beverages [5]	100.0	96.9	104.4	107.5	113.3	121.2
Electricity, gas and other fuel indices	100.0	100.1	.	99.5	99.5	.
Clothing indices, including footwear	95.8	95.3	104.2	93.2	92.6	90.4
Rent indices	100.0	100.0	100.2	99.7	100.9	111.2
General index, excluding housing	98.4	98.4	.	.	.	.

[1] Persons aged 10 years and over. [2] Persons aged 15 years and over. [3] "De facto" population. [4] All cities. [5] Incl. tobacco.

[1] Personnes âgées de 10 ans et plus. [2] Personnes âgées de 15 ans et plus. [3] Population "de facto". [4] Ensemble des villes. [5] Y compris le tabac.

[1] Personas de 10 años y más. [2] Personas de 15 años y más. [3] Población "de facto". [4] Todas las ciudades. [5] Incl. el tabaco.

Sénégal

1. Population active, Emploi et Chômage ('000)

	Population active		Emploi		Chômage	
	Total	Femmes (%)	Total	Femmes (%)	Total	Femmes (%)
Groupe d'âge		1990 [1][2] Estimations officielles		2006 Enquête auprès des ménages		2006 Enquête auprès des ménages
Total	2 433.148	26.0	3 152.937	35.0	351.370	49.7
0-9	269.634	34.3	.	.	.	.
10-19	523.227	28.0	.	.	.	.
15-19	.	.	.	.	71.074	47.2
20-24	.	.	.	.	76.472	48.4
20-29	577.771	24.8	.	.	.	.
25-29	.	.	.	.	66.358	46.8
30-34	.	.	.	.	45.887	54.4
30-39	439.803	23.9	.	.	.	.
35-39	.	.	.	.	31.661	64.3
40-44	.	.	.	.	20.651	47.5
40-49	270.530	24.4	.	.	.	.
45-49	.	.	.	.	13.706	55.7
50-54	.	.	.	.	10.118	48.2
50-59	190.826	23.4	.	.	.	.
55-59	.	.	.	.	6.553	25.4
60+	161.357	21.4	.	.	.	.
60-64	.	.	.	.	3.142	40.8
65-69	.	.	.	.	2.833	58.0
70-74	.	.	.	.	0.909	1.1
75+	.	.	.	.	2.006	34.4

Activité économique (CITI-Rév.3)			2006 Enquête auprès des ménages			
Total	.	.	3 152.9	35.0	.	.
A Agriculture, chasse et sylviculture	.	.	986.5	35.9	.	.
B Pêche	.	.	76.9	13.5	.	.
C Activités extractives	.	.	14.1	18.5	.	.
D Activités de fabrication	.	.	245.4	17.0	.	.
E Production et distribution d'électricité, de gaz et d'eau	.	.	21.8	15.1	.	.
F Construction	.	.	186.6	3.7	.	.
G Commerce de gros et de détail; réparation de véhicules ...	.	.	785.9	50.6	.	.
H Hôtels et restaurants	.	.	28.6	57.5	.	.
I Transports, entreposage et communications	.	.	141.7	4.1	.	.
J Intermédiation financière	.	.	16.7	29.4	.	.
L-N	.	.	157.7	24.7	.	.
Q Organisations et organismes extraterritoriaux	.	.	7.0	53.0	.	.
X Ne pouvant être classés selon l'activité économique	.	.	484.0	44.9	.	.

Niveau d'instruction (CITE-97)					2006 Enquête auprès des ménages	
Total	.	.	.	.	350.3	49.8
X-0	.	.	.	.	176.6	52.6
1 Enseignement primaire ou premier cycle de l'éducation ...	.	.	.	.	91.6	50.3
2 Premier cycle de l'enseignement secondaire ou deuxième ...	.	.	.	.	49.1	40.8
3 Enseignement secondaire (deuxième cycle)	.	.	.	.	24.1	44.9
5-6	.	.	.	.	8.6	41.8
? Niveau inconnu	.	.	.	.	1.4	73.3

2. Population ('000), Taux d'activité et Taux de chômage

	Population			Taux d'activité			Taux de chômage		
Groupe d'âge		1990 [2] Estimations officielles			1990 [2] Estimations officielles			2006 Enquête auprès des ménages	
	Total	Hommes	Femmes	Total	Hommes	Femmes	Total	Hommes	Femmes
Total	7 264.918	3 534.577	3 730.341	33.5	50.9	17.0	11.1	7.9	13.6
15+	4 681.583	2 246.737	2 434.846	46.2	72.3	22.2	.	.	.

3. Emploi rémunéré ('000), Durée du travail (hebdomadaire) et Salaires

Activité économique (CITI-Rév.2)	Emploi rémunéré 1991 Enquête auprès des établissements, relative au travail			Durée du travail			Salaires		
	Total	Hommes	Femmes	Total	Hommes	Femmes	Total	Hommes	Femmes
Total	97.85	.	.	.	.	.	.	.	.
2-9	88.29	.	.	.	.	.	.	.	.

Sénégal

4. Lésions professionnelles et Grèves et lock-out

Activité économique (CITI-Rév.2)	Taux de lésions mortelles Total	Hommes	Femmes	Taux de lésions non mortelles Total	Hommes	Femmes	Grèves et lock-out 1992[3] Fichiers des relations du travail Grèves et lock-out	Travailleurs impliqués	Journées non effectuées
Total	.	.	.	.	.	.	19	3 954	.
1	.	.	.	.	.	.	2	400	.
2	.	.	.	.	.	.	0	0	.
3	.	.	.	.	.	.	4	325	.
4	.	.	.	.	.	.	1	63	.
5	.	.	.	.	.	.	0	218	.
6	.	.	.	.	.	.	5	807	.
7	.	.	.	.	.	.	0	0	.
8	.	.	.	.	.	.	0	0	.
9	.	.	.	.	.	.	7	2 141	.

5. Indices des prix à la consommation (période de base: 2000=100)

Dakar	2002	2003	2004	2005	2006	2007
Indices généraux	105.4	105.3	105.9	107.7	110.0	116.4
Indices de l'alimentation, y compris les boissons non alcoolisées [4]	110.1	109.4	110.3	114.5	116.0	124.4
Indices de l'électricité, gaz et autres combustibles	108.0	112.7	114.9	113.7	112.0	123.2
Indices de l'habillement, y compris les chaussures	95.2	93.4	90.3	87.3	85.9	88.4
Indices du loyer	102.9	103.0	103.4	104.6	108.2	119.1
Indices généraux, non compris le logement	105.6	105.5	106.6	107.9	110.5	117.1

[1] Persons aged 6 years and over. [2] Dec. [3] Strikes only. [4] Incl. tobacco.

[1] Personnes âgées de 6 ans et plus. [2] Déc. [3] Grèves seulement. [4] Y compris le tabac.

[1] Personas de 6 años y más. [2] Dic. [3] Huelgas solamente. [4] Incl. el tabaco.

Serbia

1. Economically active population, Employment and Unemployment ('000)

	Economically active population		Employment		Unemployment	
	Total	Women (%)	Total	Women (%)	Total	Women (%)
Age group	2007 [1][2] Labour force survey		2007 ★ Labour force survey		2007 [1][2] Labour force survey	
Total	3 241.2	43.4	2 655.7	41.8	585.5	50.5
15-19	65.6	32.6	30.8	31.1	34.8	33.9
20-24	226.5	41.7	133.6	37.6	92.9	47.4
25-29	316.1	42.6	226.8	40.2	89.4	48.7
30-34	404.6	48.1	327.2	45.5	77.4	59.1
35-39	408.5	46.4	342.8	43.4	65.8	61.9
40-44	414.2	47.2	353.9	45.8	60.3	55.3
45-49	433.9	45.4	371.3	43.5	62.6	57.2
50-54	436.6	44.9	377.8	44.3	58.8	48.5
55-59	305.9	35.1	267.2	36.1	38.7	28.1
60-64	97.9	29.4	94.2	29.6	3.6	24.1
65-69	54.5	35.4	53.2	35.4	1.3	34.6
70-74	40.9	36.3	40.9	36.3	-	.
75+	36.0	34.0	36.0	34.0	-	.
Economic activity (ISIC-Rev.3)	2007 [1][2] Labour force survey		2007 [1][2] Labour force survey		2007 [1][2] Labour force survey	
Total	3 241.2	43.4	2 655.7	41.8	585.5	50.5
A Agriculture, Hunting and Forestry	571.5	38.9	551.7	39.2	19.8	30.7
B Fishing	2.1	19.0	0.9	.	1.2	32.6
C Mining and Quarrying	43.1	22.5	41.3	23.5	1.9	.
D Manufacturing	661.0	36.6	521.7	33.5	139.2	48.4
E Electricity, Gas and Water Supply	60.4	27.7	58.0	28.0	2.5	20.1
F Construction	183.0	11.2	161.3	10.4	21.7	16.4
G Wholesale and Retail Trade; Repair of Motor Vehicles ...	475.9	55.6	398.5	53.2	77.5	67.8
H Hotels and Restaurants	91.9	51.7	72.3	51.8	19.6	51.2
I Transport, Storage and Communications	183.0	20.1	169.8	20.1	13.2	19.4
J Financial Intermediation	48.9	61.2	43.0	59.7	5.8	72.1
K Real Estate, Renting and Business Activities	99.8	44.1	88.9	41.8	10.9	63.0
L Public Administration and Defence; Compulsory Social ...	154.8	42.1	141.9	43.4	12.8	27.7
M Education	123.0	67.0	118.1	67.5	4.9	54.4
N Health and Social Work	177.4	77.2	166.4	77.0	11.0	79.2
O Other Community, Social and Personal Service Activities	123.2	47.1	114.1	46.4	9.1	56.1
P Households with Employed Persons	7.6	94.9	6.4	94.0	1.2	100.0
Q Extra-Territorial Organizations and Bodies	1.5	68.0	1.5	68.0	-	.
X Not classifiable by economic activity	233.1	51.7	-	.	.	.
Unemployed seeking their first job	233.1	51.7	.	.	233.1	51.7
Occupation (ISCO-88)	2007 [1][2] Labour force survey		2007 [1][2] Labour force survey		2007 [1][2] Labour force survey	
Total	3 241.2	43.4	2 655.7	41.8	585.5	50.5
1 Legislators, senior officials and managers	98.8	35.2	93.9	35.4	4.8	30.6
2 Professionals	276.9	52.0	264.5	50.8	12.4	77.0
3 Technicians and associate professionals	470.0	57.7	412.6	57.3	57.3	60.5
4 Clerks	178.2	50.8	150.9	49.7	27.3	56.7
5 Service workers and shop and market sales workers	466.0	61.1	384.4	59.3	81.6	69.6
6 Skilled agricultural and fishery workers	468.9	38.8	463.7	39.0	5.2	22.9
7 Craft and related trade workers	436.3	20.2	361.8	16.8	74.5	36.8
8 Plant and machine operators and assemblers	263.7	12.8	226.9	10.5	36.8	27.1
9 Elementary occupations	334.4	46.6	285.8	48.0	48.1	37.8
0 Armed forces	14.9	.	11.0	.	4.3	10.5
X Not classifiable by occupation	233.1	51.7	.	.	.	.
Unemployed seeking their first job	233.1	51.7	.	.	233.1	51.7
Status in employment (ICSE-1993)	2007 [1][2] Labour force survey		2007 [1][2] Labour force survey		2007 ★ Labour force survey	
Total	3 241.2	43.4	2 655.7	41.8	585.5	50.5
1 Employees	2 510.5	45.5	1 940.8	43.9	569.7	51.1
2 Employers	114.1	28.5	111.1	29.3	3.0	.
3 Own-account workers	434.2	22.0	423.7	21.8	10.4	29.2
5 Contributing family workers	182.4	73.5	180.1	73.6	2.4	63.4

2. Population ('000), Activity rate and Unemployment rate

	Population			Activity rate			Unemployment rate		
Age group	2007 [2] Labour force survey			2007 [2] Labour force survey			2007 [1][2] Labour force survey		
	Total	Men	Women	Total	Men	Women	Total	Men	Women
Total	7 558.6	3 670.2	3 888.4	42.9	50.0	36.2	18.1	15.1	21.0
15+	6 356.6	3 073.8	3 282.9	51.0	59.7	42.8	.	.	.
15-24	877.6	463.3	414.3	33.3	38.1	27.9	43.7	40.7	48.3
25-54	2 952.4	1 458.0	1 494.4	81.8	89.6	74.1	17.2	14.3	20.6
55+	2 526.6	1 152.5	1 374.1	21.2	30.6	13.3	.	.	.

Serbia

3. Paid employment ('000), Hours of work (weekly) and Wages

Economic activity (ISIC-Rev.3)	Paid employment			Hours of work			Wages 2007 [3] Labour-related establishment survey Earnings per month / Employees / New Dinar		
	Total	Men	Women	Total	Men	Women	Total	Men	Women
Total	.	.	.	.	.	.	38 744	.	.
A	.	.	.	.	.	.	29 680	.	.
B	.	.	.	.	.	.	21 699	.	.
C	.	.	.	.	.	.	48 978	.	.
D	.	.	.	.	.	.	30 620	.	.
E	.	.	.	.	.	.	53 128	.	.
F	.	.	.	.	.	.	34 944	.	.
G	.	.	.	.	.	.	34 685	.	.
H	.	.	.	.	.	.	25 844	.	.
I	.	.	.	.	.	.	41 568	.	.
J	.	.	.	.	.	.	82 041	.	.
K	.	.	.	.	.	.	47 154	.	.
L	.	.	.	.	.	.	47 728	.	.
M	.	.	.	.	.	.	40 286	.	.
N	.	.	.	.	.	.	42 900	.	.
O	.	.	.	.	.	.	38 641	.	.

4. Occupational injuries and Strikes and Lockouts

Statistics not available.

5. Consumer price indices (base period: 2000=100)

	2002	2003	2004	2005	2006	2007
General indices	233.0	256.1	284.2	330.0	368.6	392.4
Food index, including non-alcoholic beverages	209.8	211.5	235.1	280.9	310.1	328.7
Clothing indices, including footwear	217.6	235.2	252.3	271.0	301.9	316.0
Rent indices	356.1	494.7	615.9	757.6	858.3	928.0

[1] Persons aged 15 years and over. [2] Oct. [3] Excl. province of Kosovo.

[1] Personnes âgées de 15 ans et plus. [2] Oct. [3] Non compris la province de Kosovo.

[1] Personas de 15 años y más. [2] Oct. [3] Excl. provincia de Kosovo.

Seychelles

1. Economically active population, Employment and Unemployment ('000)

Age group	Economically active population Total	Women (%)	Employment Total	Women (%)	Unemployment Total	Women (%)
	2002 [1,2] Population census		2002 ★ Population census		2002 [1,2] Population census	
Total	43.859	.	39.558	.	4.301	.
15-19	2.630	.	1.753	.	0.877	.
20-24	6.386	.	5.430	.	0.956	.
25-29	6.571	.	5.967	.	0.604	.
30-34	6.783	.	6.282	.	0.501	.
35-39	6.546	.	6.125	.	0.421	.
40-44	5.573	.	5.220	.	0.353	.
45-49	3.824	.	3.586	.	0.238	.
50-54	2.541	.	2.380	.	0.161	.
55-59	1.718	.	1.598	.	0.120	.
60-64	0.974	.	0.914	.	0.060	.
65+	0.313	.	0.303	.	0.010	.

Occupation (ISCO-1968)					1985 [3] Employment office records	
Total	.	.	.	.	5.713	.
0/1 Professional, technical and related workers	.	.	.	.	0.143	.
2 Administrative and managerial workers	.	.	.	.	0.036	.
3 Clerical and related workers	.	.	.	.	0.250	.
4 Sales workers	.	.	.	.	0.107	.
5 Service workers	.	.	.	.	1.176	.
6 Agriculture, animal husbandry and forestry workers ...	.	.	.	.	0.214	.
7/8/9 Production and related workers, transport equipment ...	.	.	.	.	1.604	.
X Not classifiable by occupation	.	.	.	.	0.035	.
Unemployed seeking their first job	.	.	.	.	2.148	.

2. Population ('000), Activity rate and Unemployment rate

Age group	Population 2002 [2] Population census			Activity rate 2002 [2] Population census			Unemployment rate 2002 [2] Population census		
	Total	Men	Women	Total	Men	Women	Total	Men	Women
Total	.	.	.	.	.	.	9.8	.	.
15+	60.675	.	.	72.3	.	.	9.8	.	.
15-24	14.564	.	.	61.9	.	.	20.3	.	.
25-54	35.326	.	.	90.1	.	.	7.2	.	.
55+	10.785	.	.	27.9	.	.	6.3	.	.

3. Paid employment ('000), Hours of work (weekly) and Wages

Economic activity (ISIC-Rev.3)	Paid employment 2004 Insurance records			Hours of work			Wages 2006 Insurance records Earnings per month / Employees / Rupee		
	Total	Men	Women	Total	Men	Women	Total	Men	Women
Total	32.78	.	.	.	.	.	3 817	.	.
A-B	.	.	.	.	.	.	3 276 [4]	.	.
A	0.61	.	.	.	.	.	.	.	.
B	0.43	.	.	.	.	.	3 104	.	.
C	0.02	.	.	.	.	.	5 475	.	.
D	4.21	.	.	.	.	.	3 350	.	.
E	1.05	.	.	.	.	.	4 582	.	.
F	2.12	.	.	.	.	.	2 949	.	.
G	2.48	.	.	.	.	.	2 963	.	.
H	4.54	.	.	.	.	.	3 672	.	.
I	3.09	.	.	.	.	.	5 370	.	.
J	0.63	.	.	.	.	.	5 713	.	.
K	1.41	.	.	.	.	.	3 613	.	.
L	5.71	.	.	.	.	.	4 224	.	.
M	2.61	.	.	.	.	.	4 315	.	.
N	1.72	.	.	.	.	.	4 740	.	.
O	2.13	.	.	.	.	.	3 019	.	.

4. Occupational injuries and Strikes and Lockouts

Statistics not available.

5. Consumer price indices (base period: 2000=100)

	2002	2003	2004	2005	2006	2007
General indices	106.2	109.7	114.0	115.0	114.6	122.1
Food index, including non-alcoholic beverages	105.6	108.2	109.2	110.3	114.3	125.6
Clothing indices, including footwear [5]	100.0	105.7	118.0	121.2	117.9	130.5
Rent indices [5,6]	100.2	101.8	103.1	103.8	103.1	103.4

Seychelles

[1] Persons aged 15 years and over. [2] Aug. [3] Persons aged 15 to 63 years. [4] Excl. hunting. [5] Index base 2001=100. [6] Incl. water, electricity, gas and other fuels.

[1] Personnes âgées de 15 ans et plus. [2] Août. [3] Personnes âgées de 15 à 63 ans. [4] Non compris la chasse. [5] Indice base 2001=100. [6] Y compris l'eau, l'électricité, le gaz et autres combustibles.

[1] Personas de 15 años y más. [2] Agosto. [3] Personas de 15 a 63 años de edad. [4] Excl. la caza. [5] Indice base 2001=100. [6] Incl. el agua, la electricidad, el gas y otros combustibles.

Sierra Leone

1. Economically active population, Employment and Unemployment ('000)

	Economically active population		Employment		Unemployment	
	Total	Women (%)	Total	Women (%)	Total	Women (%)
Age group	2004 [1,2,3] Population census		2004 ★ Population census		2004 [1,2,3] Population census	
Total	2 021.075	48.4	1 952.823	48.9	68.252	32.7
10-14	152.097	50.2	147.822	50.4	4.275	45.3
15-19	144.769	59.0	138.613	59.8	6.156	42.1
20-24	244.703	54.5	230.801	55.6	13.902	36.4
25-29	298.657	50.4	284.868	51.3	13.789	32.2
30-34	246.232	49.2	237.474	49.9	8.758	31.1
35-39	242.719	47.6	236.052	48.1	6.667	27.6
40-44	175.062	44.8	170.383	45.3	4.679	24.7
45-49	147.292	40.6	143.890	41.0	3.402	21.6
50-54	103.712	43.0	101.498	43.5	2.214	22.6
55-59	67.505	40.8	66.078	41.2	1.427	22.1
60-64	63.869	47.1	62.892	47.4	0.977	27.4
65+	134.458	40.5	132.452	40.6	2.006	36.7
Economic activity (ISIC-Rev.3)	2004 [2,3] Population census		2004 [2,3] Population census		2004 [2,3] Population census	
Total	1 934.723	48.9	1 933.009	48.9	1.714	32.8
A Agriculture, Hunting and Forestry	1 272.842	51.4	1 272.234	51.4	0.608	33.1
B Fishing	51.165	34.8	51.139	34.9	0.026	23.1
C Mining and Quarrying	69.077	14.0	68.974	14.0	0.103	10.7
D Manufacturing	9.427	21.4	9.412	21.4	0.015	6.7
E Electricity, Gas and Water Supply	8.375	14.9	8.347	14.9	0.028	14.3
F Construction	39.132	27.7	39.068	27.7	0.064	10.9
G Wholesale and Retail Trade; Repair of Motor Vehicles ...	269.888	62.0	269.495	62.1	0.393	45.8
H Hotels and Restaurants	4.944	46.9	4.931	46.9	0.013	46.2
I Transport, Storage and Communications	15.738	8.0	15.682	8.0	0.056	8.9
J Financial Intermediation	6.949	42.4	6.934	42.4	0.015	46.7
K Real Estate, Renting and Business Activities	10.791	49.2	10.785	49.2	0.006	33.3
L Public Administration and Defence; Compulsory Social ...	26.010	18.7	25.979	18.7	0.031	35.5
M Education	34.663	32.7	34.580	32.8	0.083	22.9
N Health and Social Work	19.875	50.3	19.828	50.3	0.047	44.7
O Other Community, Social and Personal Service Activities	83.671	46.8	83.486	46.8	0.185	36.2
P Households with Employed Persons	8.319	51.9	8.289	51.9	0.030	40.0
Q Extra-Territorial Organizations and Bodies	3.857	34.8	3.846	34.8	0.011	27.3
Status in employment (ICSE-1993)			2004 [2,3] Population census			
Total	.	.	1 933.009	48.9	.	.
1 Employees	.	.	146.062	23.7	.	.
2 Employers	.	.	1 436.141	49.2	.	.
5 Contributing family workers	.	.	350.806	58.3	.	.

2. Population ('000), Activity rate and Unemployment rate

	Population 2004 [1,3] Population census			Activity rate 2004 [1,3] Population census			Unemployment rate 2004 [1,2,3] Population census		
Age group	Total	Men	Women	Total	Men	Women	Total	Men	Women
Total	.	.	.	.	.	.	2.8	3.1	2.5
15+	2 747.069	1 293.678	1 453.394	68.0	74.8	62.0	3.4	4.5	2.3
15-24	794.245	369.136	425.110	49.0	46.2	51.5	5.2	7.3	3.5
25-54	1 556.781	733.811	822.971	78.0	87.7	69.3	3.3	4.4	2.0
55+	396.043	190.731	205.313	67.1	80.6	54.6	1.7	2.0	1.2

Sierra Leone

3. Paid employment ('000), Hours of work (weekly) and Wages

Economic activity (ISIC-Rev.2)	Paid employment Total	Men	Women	Hours of work 1987 [4][5] Hours actually worked / Employees Total	Men	Women	Wages 1987 [4][5] Earnings per week / Employees / Leone Total	Men	Women
2-9 [6]	.	.	.	43.0	.	.	99.26	.	.
2	.	.	.	45.0	.	.	151.14	.	.
3	.	.	.	42.0	.	.	80.52	.	.
5	.	.	.	44.0	.	.	102.36	.	.
7	.	.	.	44.0 [7]	.	.	128.93	.	.

Economic activity (ISIC-Rev.3)	Paid employment 2004 [2][3] Population census Total	Men	Women	Hours of work Total	Men	Women	Wages Total	Men	Women
Total	146.062	111.440	34.622	.	.	.	.	.	.
A	17.613	12.475	5.138	.	.	.	.	.	.
B	2.981	2.561	0.420	.	.	.	.	.	.
C	4.574	4.265	0.309	.	.	.	.	.	.
D	2.606	2.298	0.308	.	.	.	.	.	.
E	3.320	3.078	0.242	.	.	.	.	.	.
F	7.566	7.060	0.506	.	.	.	.	.	.
G	11.960	9.117	2.843	.	.	.	.	.	.
H	2.900	1.676	1.224	.	.	.	.	.	.
I	8.273	7.624	0.649	.	.	.	.	.	.
J	3.422	2.384	1.038	.	.	.	.	.	.
K	2.697	2.147	0.550	.	.	.	.	.	.
L	23.487	19.504	3.983	.	.	.	.	.	.
M	28.152	19.344	8.808	.	.	.	.	.	.
N	9.832	5.304	4.528	.	.	.	.	.	.
O	12.202	9.337	2.865	.	.	.	.	.	.
P	2.329	1.604	0.725	.	.	.	.	.	.
Q	2.148	1.662	0.486	.	.	.	.	.	.

Share of women in wage employment in the non-agricultural sector [2][3] (2004 - Population census): **23.2%**

4. Occupational injuries and Strikes and Lockouts

Economic activity (ISIC-Rev.2)	Rates of fatal injuries Total	Men	Women	Rates of non-fatal injuries Total	Men	Women	Strikes and lockouts 1981 Source unknown Strikes and lockouts	Workers involved	Days not worked
Total	.	.	.	.	.	.	.	.	8 597
1	.	.	.	.	.	.	.	.	810
2	.	.	.	.	.	.	.	.	3 800
3	.	.	.	.	.	.	.	.	1 260
4	.	.	.	.	.	.	.	.	1 214
5	.	.	.	.	.	.	.	.	1 300
6	.	.	.	.	.	.	.	.	200
7	.	.	.	.	.	.	.	.	10
8	.	.	.	.	.	.	.	.	0
9	.	.	.	.	.	.	.	.	3
0	.	.	.	.	.	.	.	.	0

5. Consumer price indices (base period: 2000=100)

[8]	2002	2003	2004	2005	2006	2007
General indices	.	100.0	114.9	131.8	142.5	160.8
Food index, including non-alcoholic beverages	.	100.0	120.1	137.6	141.0	159.3
Clothing indices, including footwear	.	100.0	113.2	128.6	125.2	120.5
Rent indices	.	100.0	116.2	140.3	182.7	178.3

[1] The data refer to the usually active population. [2] Persons aged 10 years and over. [3] Dec. [4] ø: May and Nov. of each year. [5] Adults. [6] Excl. major divisions 4, 7, 8 and 9. [7] Incl. sea transport. [8] Index base 2003=100.

[1] Les données se réfèrent à la population habituellement active. [2] Personnes âgées de 10 ans et plus. [3] Déc. [4] ø: mai et nov. de chaque année. [5] Adultes. [6] Non compris les branches 4, 7, 8 et 9. [7] Y compris les transports par mer. [8] Indice base 2003=100.

[1] Los datos se refieren a la población habitualmente activa. [2] Personas de 10 años y más. [3] Dic. [4] ø: mayo y nov. de cada año. [5] Adultos. [6] Excl. las grandes divisiones 4, 7, 8 y 9. [7] Incl. el transporte marítimo. [8] Indice base 2003=100.

Singapore

1. Economically active population, Employment and Unemployment ('000)

	Economically active population		Employment		Unemployment	
	Total	Women (%)	Total	Women (%)	Total	Women (%)
Age group	2007 [1,2] Labour force survey		2007 ★ Labour force survey		2007 [1,2] Labour force survey	
Total	1 918.1	42.7	1 842.0	42.5	76.1	46.6
15-19	36.9	41.2	33.7	38.9	3.2	65.6
20-24	142.6	48.0	129.9	47.1	12.7	56.7
25-29	214.8	50.7	204.6	51.1	10.2	43.1
30-34	253.5	47.1	246.1	46.9	7.4	55.4
35-39	257.6	43.2	249.5	42.9	8.1	54.3
40-44	263.4	42.3	255.3	42.0	8.1	50.6
45-49	262.2	41.2	253.6	41.2	8.6	40.7
50-54	220.1	39.1	212.6	39.1	7.5	38.7
55-59	151.7	34.9	145.5	35.1	6.2	30.6
60-64	67.4	32.2	64.8	32.7	2.6	19.2
65+	48.0	30.4	46.7	30.4	1.3	30.8
Economic activity (ISIC-Rev.3)	2007 ★ Labour force survey		2007 [1,2] Labour force survey		2007 [1,2] Labour force survey	
Total	1 918.2	42.6	1 842.1	42.5	76.1	46.6
A-C, E, X	21.8	20.2	21.0	19.5	0.8	37.5
D Manufacturing	325.9	38.2	313.4	37.8	12.5	48.8
F Construction	107.3	18.5	103.4	18.6	3.9	15.4
G Wholesale and Retail Trade; Repair of Motor Vehicles ...	292.9	47.1	282.3	47.1	10.6	49.1
H Hotels and Restaurants	133.8	51.6	125.4	51.7	8.4	51.2
I Transport, Storage and Communications	282.9	28.6	273.1	28.5	9.8	31.6
J Financial Intermediation	115.2	57.3	112.4	57.4	2.8	53.6
K Real Estate, Renting and Business Activities	238.6	46.4	228.7	46.3	9.9	48.5
L, M	229.1	43.6	223.6	43.3	5.5	58.2
N Health and Social Work	73.0	75.8	71.6	75.6	1.4	85.7
O-Q	90.8	50.4	87.2	50.5	3.6	50.0
Unemployed seeking their first job	.	.	.	.	6.8	51.5
Occupation (ISCO-88)	2007 ★ Labour force survey		2007 [1,2] Labour force survey		2007 [1,2] Labour force survey	
Total	1 918.2	42.6	1 842.1	42.5	76.1	46.6
1 Legislators, senior officials and managers	276.3	30.4	270.0	30.5	6.3	25.4
2 Professionals	286.8	41.2	280.4	41.0	6.4	53.1
3 Technicians and associate professionals	361.2	48.6	350.3	48.6	10.9	48.6
4 Clerks	265.1	77.5	251.9	77.6	13.2	75.0
5 Service workers and shop and market sales workers	225.1	45.6	212.9	45.6	12.2	46.7
6 Skilled agricultural and fishery workers	1.2	16.7	1.2	16.7	-	.
7 Craft and related trade workers	100.1	10.3	96.0	10.2	4.1	12.2
8 Plant and machine operators and assemblers	176.8	21.6	169.5	21.1	7.3	34.2
9 Elementary occupations	155.6	50.5	147.3	51.3	8.3	37.3
0-X	63.0	2.1	62.4	2.1	0.6	.
Unemployed seeking their first job	.	.	.	.	6.8	51.5
Education level (ISCED-97)	2007 [1,2] Labour force survey		2007 ★ Labour force survey		2007 [1,2] Labour force survey	
Total	1 918.1	42.7	1 842.0	42.5	76.1	46.6
X No schooling [3]	288.4	39.4	276.8	39.5	11.6	37.1
2 Lower secondary or second stage of basic education	242.9	34.3	230.9	34.0	12.0	39.2
3 Upper secondary education	457.9	47.6	438.4	47.5	19.5	49.2
4 Post-secondary non-tertiary education [4]	475.0	43.5	458.1	43.3	16.9	47.9
6 Second stage of tertiary education	454.0	43.4	438.0	42.9	16.0	55.6
Status in employment (ICSE-1993)			2007 [1,2] Labour force survey			
Total	.	.	1 842.1	42.5	.	.
1 Employees	.	.	1 560.0	45.1	.	.
2 Employers	.	.	94.1	23.1	.	.
3 Own-account workers	.	.	173.4	27.2	.	.
5 Contributing family workers	.	.	14.6	67.8	.	.

2. Population ('000), Activity rate and Unemployment rate

	Population			Activity rate			Unemployment rate		
Age group	2007 [1,2] Labour force survey			2007 [1,2] Labour force survey			2007 [1,2] Labour force survey		
	Total	Men	Women	Total	Men	Women	Total	Men	Women
Total	.	.	.	.	.	.	4.0	3.7	4.3
15+	2 944.7	1 438.3	1 506.4	65.1	76.5	54.3	4.0	3.7	4.3
15-24	486.9	253.2	233.7	36.9	37.9	35.8	8.9	6.9	11.1
25-54	1 760.4	856.9	903.3	83.6	96.4	71.4	3.4	3.2	3.6
55+	697.4	328.2	369.4	38.3	54.1	24.1	3.8	4.2	3.1

Singapore

3. Paid employment ('000), Hours of work (weekly) and Wages

Economic activity (ISIC-Rev.3)	Paid employment 2007 [1,2] Labour force survey Total	Men	Women	Hours of work 2007 Labour-related establishment census Hours paid for / Employees Total	Men	Women	Wages 2007 Insurance records Earnings per month / Employees / Dollar Total	Men	Women
Total	1 560.0	856.1	703.8	46.3	.	.	3 773	4 335	3 148
A-C,E,X	19.4	15.5	3.9	.	.	.	.	.	.
A-B,D-E,X	.	.	.	45.2	.	.	.	.	.
D	295.5	181.1	114.4	50.6	.	.	3 764	4 359	2 815
F	82.1	64.7	17.4	52.2	.	.	2 646	2 929	2 010
G	224.3	107.4	116.9	43.5	.	.	3 262	3 885	2 616
H	99.7	45.5	54.1	39.8	.	.	1 442	1 618	1 288
I	213.3	139.1	74.2	45.6 [5]	.	.	4 222	4 566	3 649
64	.	.	.	41.9	.	.	.	.	.
J	96.5	37.8	58.8	42.0	.	.	6 768	8 367	5 468
K	191.4	97.9	93.5	44.4	.	.	3 518	3 928	3 089
74	.	.	.	49.5	.	.	.	.	.
73	.	.	.	44.0	.	.	.	.	.
L-Q	.	.	.	.	.	.	4 074	5 000	3 391
L,M	210.4	122.7	87.7	41.5	.	.	.	.	.
N	65.6	13.8	51.8	42.1	.	.	.	.	.
O	.	.	.	42.7	.	.	.	.	.
O-Q	61.8	30.6	31.2	.	.	.	.	.	.

Share of women in wage employment in the non-agricultural sector [1,2] (2007 - Labour force survey): **45.1%**

4. Occupational injuries and Strikes and Lockouts

Economic activity (ISIC-Rev.3)	Rates of fatal injuries 2007 Labour inspectorate records Per 100,000 workers employed Reported injuries Total	Men	Women	Rates of non-fatal injuries 2007 [6] Labour inspectorate records Per 100,000 employees Reported injuries Total	Men	Women	Strikes and lockouts 2006 Labour relations records Strikes and lockouts	Workers involved	Days not worked
Total	2.9	.	.	460.0	.	.	0	0	0
D	5.3	.	.	520.0	.	.	.	.	.
F	8.1	.	.	831.0	.	.	.	.	.
G	0.3	.	.	111.0	.	.	.	.	.
H	3.8	.	.	326.0	.	.	.	.	.
J	0.0	.	.	429.0	.	.	.	.	.
K	0.0	.	.	30.0	.	.	.	.	.
L	0.0	.	.	63.0	.	.	.	.	.
M	0.0	.	.	243.0	.	.	.	.	.
N	0.0	.	.	113.0	.	.	.	.	.
O	2.4	.	.	139.0	.	.	.	.	.
P	0.2	.	.	132.0	.	.	.	.	.
X	0.0	.	.	.	.	.	.	.	.

5. Consumer price indices (base period: 2000=100)

	2002	2003	2004	2005	2006	2007
General indices	100.6	101.1	102.8	103.2	104.2	106.4
Food index, including non-alcoholic beverages	100.5	101.1	103.2	104.6	106.2	109.4
Electricity, gas and other fuel indices	95.7	98.8	100.7	109.4	128.3	125.8
Clothing indices, including footwear	100.7	101.1	101.2	101.2	101.9	102.7
Rent indices	99.8	98.7	98.2	98.1	98.8	100.3
General index, excluding housing	100.7	101.5	103.5	104.1	105.1	107.4

[1] The data refer to the residents (Singapore citizens and permanent residents) aged 15 years and over. [2] June. [3] Levels X-1. [4] Levels 4-5. [5] Excl. communications. [6] Incapacity of 4 days or more.

[1] Les données se réfèrent aux résidents (citoyens de Singapour et résidents permanents) âgés de 15 ans et plus. [2] Juin. [3] Niveaux X-1. [4] Niveaux 4-5. [5] Non compris les communications. [6] Incapacité de 4 jours et plus.

[1] Los datos se refieren a los residentes (ciudadanos de Singapur y residentes permanentes) de 15 años y más. [2] Junio. [3] Niveles X-1. [4] Niveles 4-5. [5] Excl. las comunicaciones. [6] Incapacidad de 4 días y más.

Slovakia

1. Economically active population, Employment and Unemployment ('000)

	Economically active population		Employment		Unemployment	
	Total	Women (%)	Total	Women (%)	Total	Women (%)
Age group	2007 [1] Labour force survey		2007 ★ Labour force survey		2007 [1,2] Labour force survey	
Total	2 649.2	44.7	2 357.3	43.9	291.9	50.8
15-19	32.8	42.1	17.7	38.4	15.1	46.4
20-24	260.1	42.8	216.2	43.2	43.9	40.8
25-29	381.1	41.1	338.5	39.9	42.6	50.9
30-34	373.6	43.1	335.3	42.0	38.3	52.2
35-39	328.4	46.5	298.4	45.6	30.0	55.7
40-44	351.4	49.0	315.4	48.8	36.0	50.8
45-49	352.6	48.6	319.3	47.7	33.3	57.1
50-54	339.3	50.0	304.8	48.7	34.5	61.2
55-59	183.0	33.6	167.4	33.5	15.6	35.3
60-64	39.4	26.6	37.0	25.7	2.4	41.7
65-69	4.8	56.3	4.6	56.5	0.2	50.0
70-74	2.0	50.0	2.0	50.0	-	.
75+	0.7	28.6	0.7	28.6	-	.
Economic activity (ISIC-Rev.3)	2007 [1,3] Labour force survey		2007 [1,2,4] Labour force survey		2007 [1,2] Labour force survey	
Total	2 673.6	44.7	2 357.3	43.9	291.9	50.8
A-B		.	99.3	23.5	13.7	34.3
A Agriculture, Hunting and Forestry	110.4	25.2	.	.	.	.
B Fishing	0.7	.	.	.	.	.
C Mining and Quarrying	18.6	9.1	16.4	5.5	1.8	5.6
D Manufacturing	692.1	37.4	634.2	36.4	52.9	56.7
E Electricity, Gas and Water Supply	43.1	16.5	40.3	17.1	0.5	60.0
F Construction	257.7	5.4	237.1	5.4	15.0	0.7
G Wholesale and Retail Trade; Repair of Motor Vehicles ...	328.1	57.8	300.0	56.9	22.6	69.9
H Hotels and Restaurants	115.1	63.3	102.0	63.2	8.7	71.3
I Transport, Storage and Communications	177.0	25.8	165.3	25.4	6.6	31.8
J Financial Intermediation	47.1	66.2	47.6	64.1	1.0	70.0
K Real Estate, Renting and Business Activities	156.2	44.2	145.7	42.8	3.4	29.4
L Public Administration and Defence; Compulsory Social ...	171.4	50.1	159.8	50.6	8.5	54.1
M Education	168.6	79.9	163.4	78.9	6.9	82.6
N Health and Social Work	159.5	83.3	154.7	82.2	7.2	84.7
O Other Community, Social and Personal Service Activities	92.1	54.8	82.1	54.9	9.4	45.7
P Households with Employed Persons	8.2	96.3	8.2	98.8	1.1	81.8
Q Extra-Territorial Organizations and Bodies	1.2	58.3	0.8	75.0	-	.
X Not classifiable by economic activity	126.7	51.1	0.5	20.0	62.8	51.3
Unemployed seeking their first job	.	.	.	.	70.1	47.9
Occupation (ISCO-88)	2007 [1,3] Labour force survey		2007 [1,2,4] Labour force survey		2007 [1,2] Labour force survey	
Total	2 673.6	44.7	2 357.3	43.9	291.9	50.8
1 Legislators, senior officials and managers	137.2	30.4	128.5	30.9	2.6	34.6
2 Professionals	249.8	58.0	246.9	58.3	4.7	63.8
3 Technicians and associate professionals	464.8	58.5	443.1	58.3	13.3	69.2
4 Clerks	155.4	69.7	150.0	67.9	8.4	71.4
5 Service workers and shop and market sales workers	377.9	71.2	332.5	70.1	30.0	81.0
6 Skilled agricultural and fishery workers	26.2	35.1	23.1	26.4	3.5	51.4
7 Craft and related trade workers	474.3	14.8	434.4	13.9	32.3	30.3
8 Plant and machine operators and assemblers	386.4	22.7	359.3	22.2	26.5	38.1
9 Elementary occupations	262.6	48.4	227.6	49.4	37.0	47.6
0 Armed forces	12.7	3.1	12.1	4.1	1.0	40.0
X Not classifiable by occupation	126.2	51.1	-	.	62.4	51.3
Unemployed seeking their first job	.	.	.	.	70.1	47.9
Education level (ISCED-97)	2007 [1,3] Labour force survey				2007 [1,2] Labour force survey	
Total	2 673.6	44.7	.	.	291.9	50.8
0 Pre-primary education	0.3	100.0	.	.	0.2	100.0
1 Primary education or first stage of basic education	4.6	36.6	.	.	5.2	42.3
2 Lower secondary or second stage of basic education	178.7	51.7	.	.	80.0	49.3
3 Upper secondary education	2 085.1	43.2	.	.	190.5	50.7
5A First stage of tertiary education - theoretically based	380.1	48.5	.	.	14.1	62.4
5B First stage of tertiary education - practically oriented	19.2	72.9	.	.	1.5	73.3
6 Second stage of tertiary education	5.5	30.9	.	.	-	.
Status in employment (ICSE-1993)	2007 [1,3] Labour force survey		2007 [1,2,4] Labour force survey			
Total	2 673.6	44.7	2 357.3	43.9	.	.
1 Employees	2 219.3	47.1	.	.	.	.
1,4	.	.	2 043.6	46.6	.	.
2 Employers	78.9	25.5	73.5	27.8	.	.
3 Own-account workers	237.5	23.4	227.9	23.7	.	.
4 Members of producers' cooperatives	6.2	45.2	.	.	.	.
5 Contributing family workers	2.9	62.1	2.2	63.6	.	.
6 Not classifiable by status	135.0	52.9	9.6	72.9	.	.

Slovakia

2. Population ('000), Activity rate and Unemployment rate

Age group	Population 2007 Labour force survey			Activity rate 2007 Labour force survey			Unemployment rate 2007 [1,2] Labour force survey		
	Total	Men	Women	Total	Men	Women	Total	Men	Women
Total	5 391.4	2 617.1	2 774.3	49.1	56.0	42.7	11.0	9.8	12.5
15+	4 508.9	2 165.0	2 343.9	58.8	67.7	50.5	.	.	.
15-24	849.1	433.5	415.6	34.5	38.7	30.1	20.1	20.3	19.9
25-54	2 450.7	1 229.8	1 220.9	86.8	93.0	80.5	10.1	8.6	11.9
55+	1 209.2	501.7	707.4	19.0	30.7	10.7	.	.	.

3. Paid employment ('000), Hours of work (weekly) and Wages

Economic activity (ISIC-Rev.3)	Paid employment 2007 [5,6] Labour-related establishment survey			Hours of work 2007 [5,7] Labour-related establishment census Hours actually worked / Employees			Wages 2007 [5] Labour-related establishment census Earnings per month / Employees / Koruna		
	Total	Men	Women	Total	Men	Women	Total	Men	Women
Total	1 295	653	642	140	.	.	20 146	.	.
A-B	.	.	.	.	.	.	15 766	.	.
A	46	33	13	152	.	.	15 763	.	.
B	-	-	-	.	.	.	.	.	.
C	9	8	1	139	.	.	22 219	.	.
D	378	220	158	142	.	.	20 024	.	.
E	35	27	8	138	.	.	29 769	.	.
F	46	40	6	147	.	.	15 561	.	.
G	99	40	59	146	.	.	20 035	.	.
H	13	5	8	147	.	.	15 045	.	.
I	101	67	34	141	.	.	21 270	.	.
J	33	10	23	142	.	.	40 871	.	.
K	78	47	31	145	.	.	25 129	.	.
L	145	75	70	141	.	.	25 372	.	.
M	160	36	124	125	.	.	16 632	.	.
N	106	20	86	131	.	.	17 540	.	.
O	46	25	21	140	.	.	15 442	.	.

Share of women in wage employment in the non-agricultural sector [2,4,8] (2007 - Labour force survey): **47.4%**

4. Occupational injuries and Strikes and Lockouts

Economic activity (ISIC-Rev.3)	Rates of fatal injuries 2007 Labour-related establishment census Per 100,000 workers insured Reported injuries			Rates of non-fatal injuries 2007 Labour-related establishment census Per 100,000 workers insured Reported injuries			Strikes and lockouts 2007 Labour relations records		
	Total	Men	Women	Total	Men	Women	Strikes and lockouts	Workers involved	Days not worked
Total	4	6	1	648	849	363	1	72	6
A	2	12	0	1 415	728	712	0	0	0
B	0	0	0	1 219	1 219	0	0	0	0
C	0	0	0	4 254	2 645	777	0	0	0
D	5	4	4	1 279	1 122	631	0	0	0
E	0	0	0	366	290	115	0	0	0
F	23	11	0	1 073	509	248	0	0	0
G	8	12	2	523	623	289	0	0	0
H	0	0	0	419	242	204	0	0	0
I	9	10	2	595	544	392	1	72	6
J	0	0	0	155	140	137	0	0	0
K	3	6	0	384	495	247	0	0	0
L	0	0	0	325	460	187	0	0	0
M	0	0	0	183	203	180	0	0	0
N	0	0	0	240	275	194	0	0	0
O	2	3	0	446	654	146	0	0	0
P	0	0	0	0	0	0	.	.	.
Q	0	0	0	0	59	7	.	.	.
X	0	.	.	0	406	362	.	.	.

5. Consumer price indices (base period: 2000=100)

	2002	2003	2004	2005	2006	2007
General indices	110.7	120.2	129.2	132.8	138.7	142.5
Food index, including non-alcoholic beverages	107.3	111.0	116.4	114.7	116.4	121.0
Electricity, gas and other fuel indices [9]	122.9	153.2	176.3	190.6	217.5	222.3
Clothing indices, including footwear	105.6	108.4	108.9	107.9	107.7	108.5
Rent indices [10]	122.2	158.0	198.6	209.9	214.8	223.4

[1] Persons aged 15 years and over. [2] Excl. persons on child-care leave. [3] Fourth quarter. [4] Excl. conscripts. [5] Excl. enterprises with less than 20 employees. [6] 31st Dec. of each year. [7] Per month. [8] Employees and members of producers' cooperatives aged 15 years and over. [9] Fuel only. [10] Incl. water, electricity, gas and other fuels.

[1] Personnes âgées de 15 ans et plus. [2] Non compris les personnes en congé parental. [3] Quatrième trimestre. [4] Non compris les conscrits. [5] Non compris les entreprises occupant moins de 20 salariés. [6] 31 déc. de chaque année. [7] Par mois. [8] Salariés et membres de coopératives de producteurs âgés de 15 ans et plus. [9] Combustible seulement. [10] Y compris l'eau, l'électricité, le gaz et autres combustibles.

[1] Personas de 15 años y más. [2] Excl. las personas con licencia parental. [3] Cuarto trimestre. [4] Excl. los conscriptos. [5] Excl. las empresas con menos de 20 asalariados. [6] 31 dic. de cada año. [7] Por mes. [8] Asalariados y miembros de cooperativas de productores de 15 años y más. [9] Combustible solamente. [10] Incl. el agua, la electricidad, el gas y otros combustibles.

Slovenia

1. Economically active population, Employment and Unemployment ('000)

	Economically active population		Employment		Unemployment	
	Total	Women (%)	Total	Women (%)	Total	Women (%)
Age group	2007 [1 2 3] Labour force survey		2007 ★ Labour force survey		2007 [2 3] Labour force survey	
Total	1 041.6	46.0	993.6	45.4	48.0	58.3
15-19	21.7	37.5	19.7	36.2	2.0	50.0
20-24	81.4	40.6	74.4	40.3	7.0	42.9
25-29	138.6	48.2	128.6	45.8	10.0	80.0
30-34	137.8	47.1	131.8	46.2	6.0	66.7
35-39	141.6	49.0	136.6	47.9	5.0	80.0
40-44	133.5	48.3	129.5	48.3	4.0	50.0
45-49	150.8	48.6	145.8	48.2	5.0	60.0
50-54	118.6	46.5	112.6	46.3	6.0	50.0
55-59	67.1	32.5	64.1	32.5	3.0	33.3
60-64	20.3	40.9	20.3	40.9	-	.
65-69	13.2	41.8	13.2	41.8	-	.
70-74	8.9	49.1	8.9	49.1	-	.
75+	8.1	47.7	8.1	47.7	-	.
Economic activity (ISIC-Rev.3)	2007 ★ Labour force survey		2007 [2 3] Labour force survey		2007 [2 3] Labour force survey	
Total	1 042	46.0	994	45.4	48	58.3
A Agriculture, Hunting and Forestry	102	46.1	101	46.5	1	.
C Mining and Quarrying	4	25.0	4	25.0	-	.
D Manufacturing	278	36.7	266	36.1	12	50.0
E Electricity, Gas and Water Supply	9	22.2	9	22.2	-	.
F Construction	64	7.8	61	8.2	3	.
G Wholesale and Retail Trade; Repair of Motor Vehicles ...	124	52.4	119	51.3	5	80.0
H Hotels and Restaurants	40	65.0	37	64.9	3	66.7
I Transport, Storage and Communications	60	21.7	60	21.7	-	.
J Financial Intermediation	23	65.2	23	65.2	.	.
K Real Estate, Renting and Business Activities	69	43.5	66	42.4	3	66.7
L Public Administration and Defence; Compulsory Social ...	60	45.0	59	44.1	1	100.0
M Education	81	77.8	78	79.5	3	33.3
N Health and Social Work	58	79.3	57	78.9	1	100.0
O Other Community, Social and Personal Service Activities	46	45.7	44	45.5	2	50.0
P Households with Employed Persons	.	.	1	100.0	.	.
X Not classifiable by economic activity	11	54.5	10	50.0	1	100.0
Unemployed seeking their first job	.	.	.	.	13	61.5
Occupation (ISCO-88)	2007 ★ Labour force survey		2007 [2 3] Labour force survey		2007 [2 3] Labour force survey	
Total	1 042	46.0	994	45.4	48	58.3
1 Legislators, senior officials and managers	59	33.9	58	34.5	1	.
2 Professionals	150	59.3	147	59.2	3	66.7
3 Technicians and associate professionals	165	53.9	160	53.8	5	60.0
4 Clerks	86	60.5	84	59.5	2	100.0
5 Service workers and shop and market sales workers	121	63.6	115	62.6	6	83.3
6 Skilled agricultural and fishery workers	75	44.0	75	44.0	-	.
7 Craft and related trade workers	112	8.0	108	7.4	4	25.0
8 Plant and machine operators and assemblers	163	31.9	157	31.2	6	50.0
9 Elementary occupations	77	58.4	71	57.7	6	66.7
0 Armed forces	.	.	5	.	.	.
X Not classifiable by occupation	15	40.0	14	42.9	1	.
Unemployed seeking their first job	.	.	.	.	13	61.5
Education level (ISCED-97)	2006 [1 2 3] Labour force survey		2006 ★ Labour force survey		2006 [2 3] Labour force survey	
Total	1 030.1	46.7	969.1	46.2	61.0	54.1
0 Pre-primary education	2.1	46.6	2.1	46.6	-	.
1 Primary education or first stage of basic education	14.6	46.5	13.6	42.5	1.0	100.0
2 Lower secondary or second stage of basic education	147.0	49.1	135.0	49.7	12.0	41.7
3 Upper secondary education	636.1	43.0	595.1	42.1	41.0	56.1
5A First stage of tertiary education - theoretically based	101.5	55.8	99.5	55.9	2.0	50.0
5B First stage of tertiary education - practically oriented	109.0	57.2	104.0	57.1	5.0	60.0
6 Second stage of tertiary education	19.9	42.5	19.9	42.5	-	.
Status in employment (ICSE-1993)			2007 [2 3] Labour force survey			
Total	.	.	994	45.4	.	.
1 Employees	.	.	831	46.6	.	.
2 Employers	.	.	33	21.2	.	.
3 Own-account workers	.	.	81	30.9	.	.
5 Contributing family workers	.	.	48	66.7	.	.

2. Population ('000), Activity rate and Unemployment rate

	Population 2007 [1 3 4] Labour force survey			Activity rate 2007 [1 3 4] Labour force survey			Unemployment rate 2007 [2 3] Labour force survey		
Age group	Total	Men	Women	Total	Men	Women	Total	Men	Women
Total	2 010.4	987.0	1 023.4	51.8	57.0	46.8	4.6	3.6	5.8
15+	1 729.3	842.4	886.9	60.2	66.8	54.0	.	.	.
15-24	253.5	133.2	120.2	40.7	46.5	34.2	8.7	8.1	9.7
25-54	913.2	465.6	447.7	89.9	91.7	88.0	4.4	3.5	6.1
55+	562.6	243.6	319.0	20.9	30.3	13.8	.	.	.

Slovenia

3. Paid employment ('000), Hours of work (weekly) and Wages

Economic activity (ISIC-Rev.3)	Paid employment 2007 [2,3] Labour force survey			Hours of work 2007 [2,3] Labour force survey Hours actually worked / Employees			Wages 2007 [5] Labour-related establishment census Earnings per month / Employees / Euro		
	Total	Men	Women	Total	Men	Women	Total	Men	Women
Total	831	443	387	34.9	36.7	32.9	1 285	.	.
A-B	.	.	.	38.2	37.7	39.4	1 069	.	.
C-Q	.	.	.	34.9	36.6	32.8	1 287	.	.
A	12	8	4	.	.	.	1 069	.	.
B	.	.	.	.	.	.	1 063	.	.
C	4	3	1	36.4	38.2	27.3	1 608	.	.
D	251	159	92	35.1	35.9	33.9	1 124	.	.
E	9	7	2	37.5	37.2	38.9	1 657	.	.
F	48	44	4	38.3	39.2	29.4	1 061	.	.
G	107	48	59	34.4	37.1	32.2	1 161	.	.
H	32	11	21	33.8	35.5	33.0	937	.	.
I	52	40	12	37.1	38.3	33.5	1 368	.	.
J	23	7	15	36.2	36.7	35.9	1 986	.	.
K	55	31	24	33.6	35.3	31.6	1 361	.	.
L	59	32	26	34.8	36.8	32.4	1 507	.	.
M	77	15	62	33.8	35.7	33.3	1 550	.	.
N	53	11	43	33.3	38.6	32.0	1 400	.	.
O	38	22	17	32.5	34.9	29.5	1 440	.	.
P	-	-	-	34.3	.	34.3	.	.	.
X	9	4	5	28.6	32.8	24.4	.	.	.

Share of women in wage employment in the non-agricultural sector [2,3] (2007 - Labour force survey): .%

4. Occupational injuries and Strikes and Lockouts

Economic activity (ISIC-Rev.3)	Rates of fatal injuries 2006 Labour inspectorate records Per 100,000 workers insured Reported injuries			Rates of non-fatal injuries 2006 [6] Labour inspectorate records Per 100,000 workers insured Reported injuries			Strikes and lockouts		
	Total	Men	Women	Total	Men	Women	Strikes and lockouts	Workers involved	Days not worked
Total	3.8	.	.	4 437	.	.	.	.	.
A	10.2	.	.	4 289	.	.	.	.	.
B	0.0	.	.	2 966	.	.	.	.	.
C	26.0	.	.	8 566	.	.	.	.	.
D	4.4	.	.	5 929	.	.	.	.	.
E	0.0	.	.	5 791	.	.	.	.	.
F	14.1	.	.	6 560	.	.	.	.	.
G	0.0	.	.	3 149	.	.	.	.	.
H	0.0	.	.	3 861	.	.	.	.	.
I	9.4	.	.	4 733	.	.	.	.	.
J	4.5	.	.	1 990	.	.	.	.	.
K	2.7	.	.	2 725	.	.	.	.	.
L	1.9	.	.	4 952	.	.	.	.	.
M	0.0	.	.	2 164	.	.	.	.	.
N	0.0	.	.	3 550	.	.	.	.	.
O	0.0	.	.	2 690	.	.	.	.	.
P	0.0	.	.	0	.	.	.	.	.
Q	0.0	.	.	.	.	.	.	.	.

5. Consumer price indices (base period: 2000=100)

[7]	2002	2003	2004	2005	2006	2007
General indices	116.5	123.0	127.4	130.6	133.8	138.6
Food index, including non-alcoholic beverages	117.5	123.1	124.2	124.3	127.2	136.8
Electricity, gas and other fuel indices	112.2	116.7	123.8	139.0	150.4	155.5
Clothing indices, including footwear	105.9	112.4	114.4	113.2	112.4	114.9
Rent indices	124.5	152.9	177.8	187.7	195.9	201.6
General index, excluding housing	116.4	122.6	126.9	129.7	132.8	137.8

[1] Excl. conscripts. [2] Persons aged 15 years and over. [3] Second quarter. [4] "De jure" population. [5] Prior to 2007: SIT; 1 Euro = 239.64 SIT. [6] Incl. commuting accidents. [7] Urban areas.

[1] Non compris les conscrits. [2] Personnes âgées de 15 ans et plus. [3] Deuxième trimestre. [4] Population "de jure". [5] Avant 2007: SIT; 1 Euro = 239,64 SIT. [6] Y compris les accidents de trajet. [7] Régions urbaines.

[1] Excl. los conscriptos. [2] Personas de 15 años y más. [3] Segundo trimestre. [4] Población "de jure". [5] Antes de 2007: SIT; 1 Euro = 239,64 SIT. [6] Incl. accidentes del trayecto. [7] Areas urbanas.

Solomon Islands

1. Economically active population, Employment and Unemployment ('000)

Age group	Economically active population Total	Women (%)	Employment Total	Women (%)	Unemployment Total	Women (%)
	1999 [1] Population census		1999 ★ Population census		1999 [1] Population census	
Total	85.124	32.2	57.472	30.8	27.652	35.1
14-14	0.829	45.1	0.261	43.7	0.568	45.8
15-19	8.935	41.3	3.855	39.3	5.080	42.7
20-24	16.000	36.0	9.605	34.6	6.395	38.1
25-29	15.929	31.0	11.212	30.2	4.717	32.9
30-34	12.078	30.1	8.835	29.0	3.243	32.9
35-39	9.735	29.5	7.300	29.1	2.435	31.0
40-44	6.917	29.9	5.269	29.8	1.648	30.3
45-49	5.605	29.1	4.232	28.9	1.373	29.9
50-54	3.811	28.8	2.939	28.8	0.872	28.9
55-59	2.578	25.2	1.892	26.2	0.686	22.4
60-64	1.330	26.9	1.021	28.6	0.309	21.4
65+	1.377	23.9	1.051	24.5	0.326	22.1

2. Population ('000), Activity rate and Unemployment rate

Age group	Population 1999 Population census Total	Men	Women	Activity rate 1999 Population census Total	Men	Women	Unemployment rate 1999 [1] Population census Total	Men	Women
Total	.	.	.	.	.	.	32.5	31.1	35.4
15+	239	123	116	35.2	46.6	23.2	32.1	30.8	34.9
15-24	86	44	42	29.0	35.4	22.3	46.0	44.4	48.7
25-54	123	63	60	43.9	60.2	26.9	26.4	25.8	27.9
55+	30	16	14	17.7	24.3	9.8	25.0	26.1	21.8

3. Paid employment ('000), Hours of work (weekly) and Wages

Economic activity (ISIC-Rev.2)	Paid employment 1995 [2] Labour-related establishment survey Total	Men	Women	Hours of work Total	Men	Women	Wages 1996 [2,3] Labour-related establishment census Earnings per month / Employees / Dollar Total	Men	Women
Total	33.103	.	.	.	.	.	.	.	.
2-9	.	.	.	.	.	.	1 067	.	.
1	8.627	.	.	.	.	.	.	.	.
3	4.122 [3]	.	.	.	.	.	987	.	.
4	0.325 [4]	.	.	.	.	.	.	.	.
5	1.053	.	.	.	.	.	1 168	.	.
6	3.884	.	.	.	.	.	727	.	.
7	1.683	.	.	.	.	.	2 225	.	.
8	1.240	.	.	.	.	.	.	.	.
9	12.169	.	.	.	.	.	.	.	.

4. Occupational injuries and Strikes and Lockouts

Economic activity (ISIC-Rev.2)	Rates of fatal injuries Total	Men	Women	Rates of non-fatal injuries Total	Men	Women	Strikes and lockouts 1985 Source unknown Strikes and lockouts	Workers involved	Days not worked
Total	.	.	.	.	.	.	18	.	.
1	.	.	.	.	.	.	4	.	.
2	.	.	.	.	.	.	0	.	.
3	.	.	.	.	.	.	0	.	.
4	.	.	.	.	.	.	0	.	.
5	.	.	.	.	.	.	5	.	.
6	.	.	.	.	.	.	2	.	.
7	.	.	.	.	.	.	3	.	.
8	.	.	.	.	.	.	0	.	.
9	.	.	.	.	.	.	0	.	.
0	.	.	.	.	.	.	4	.	.

5. Consumer price indices (base period: 2000=100)

Honiara	2002	2003	2004	2005	2006	2007
General indices	119.5	129.4	138.7	149.3	161.2	178.1
Food index, including non-alcoholic beverages	122.1	125.0	136.8	145.1	156.7	168.1
Clothing indices, including footwear	100.6	101.2	101.6	101.7	105.0	121.4
Rent indices [5]	122.4	145.3	150.7	169.1	188.9	223.3

[1] Persons aged 14 years and over. [2] June. [3] Incl. mining and quarrying. [4] Excl. gas. [5] Incl. water, electricity, gas and other fuels.

[1] Personnes âgées de 14 ans et plus. [2] Juin. [3] Y compris les industries extractives. [4] Non compris le gaz. [5] Y compris l'eau, l'électricité, le gaz et autres combustibles.

[1] Personas de 14 años y más. [2] Junio. [3] Incl. las minas y canteras. [4] Excl. gas. [5] Incl. el agua, la electricidad, el gas y otros combustibles.

South Africa

1. Economically active population, Employment and Unemployment ('000)

	Economically active population		Employment		Unemployment	
	Total	Women (%)	Total	Women (%)	Total	Women (%)
Age group	2007 [1][2] Labour force survey		2007 ★ Labour force survey		2007 [1][2] Labour force survey	
Total	17 178.1	45.0	13 233.1	42.8	3 945.0	52.2
15-19	480.7	38.1	204.7	34.3	276.0	40.9
20-24	2 414.2	45.6	1 333.2	41.0	1 081.0	51.2
25-29	3 136.9	45.5	2 181.9	41.5	955.0	54.5
30-34	2 989.7	44.1	2 369.7	41.3	620.0	54.5
35-39	2 342.8	44.7	1 969.8	42.8	373.0	54.4
40-44	1 778.6	46.8	1 545.6	45.3	233.0	57.1
45-49	1 605.8	46.3	1 382.8	44.7	223.0	56.1
50-54	1 220.4	48.8	1 116.4	49.3	104.0	44.2
55-59	780.8	41.0	719.8	41.4	61.0	36.1
60-64	376.1	37.1	359.1	38.0	17.0	17.6
65+	52.1	40.2	49.1	38.6	3.0	66.7
Economic activity (ISIC-Rev.3)	2007 ★ Labour force survey		2007 [1][2] Labour force survey		2007 [2][3] Labour force survey	
Total	17 179	45.0	13 234	42.8	3 945	52.2
A-B	1 300	34.0	1 164	31.4	136	55.9
C Mining and Quarrying	493	8.1	455	7.9	38	10.5
D Manufacturing	2 084	31.7	1 799	31.5	285	32.6
E Electricity, Gas and Water Supply	128	40.6	116	41.4	12	33.3
F Construction	1 282	11.3	1 066	11.2	216	12.0
G-H	3 371	50.7	2 952	49.3	419	60.9
I Transport, Storage and Communications	667	22.6	596	22.7	71	22.5
J-K	1 481	42.6	1 340	41.6	141	51.8
L-O	2 614	58.5	2 452	58.0	162	65.4
P Households with Employed Persons	1 531	76.7	1 244	76.0	287	80.1
Q Extra-Territorial Organizations and Bodies	.	.	.	.	8	50.0
X Not classifiable by economic activity	.	.	51	43.1	.	.
Unemployed seeking their first job	.	.	.	.	2 170	54.1
Occupation (ISCO-88)	2007 ★ Labour force survey		2007 [1][2] Labour force survey		2007 [2][3] Labour force survey	
Total	17 179	45.0	13 234	42.8	3 945	52.2
1 Legislators, senior officials and managers	907	33.7	884	33.7	23	34.8
2 Professionals	873	52.5	853	52.2	20	65.0
3 Technicians and associate professionals	1 321	56.7	1 252	56.5	69	59.4
4 Clerks	1 361	69.1	1 206	67.6	155	81.3
5 Service workers and shop and market sales workers	1 849	43.4	1 595	42.4	254	49.2
6 Skilled agricultural and fishery workers	392	45.9	342	43.6	50	62.0
7 Craft and related trade workers	2 129	16.6	1 822	16.2	307	19.2
8 Plant and machine operators and assemblers	1 415	16.4	1 262	15.5	153	23.5
9 Elementary occupations	3 659	43.1	2 923	38.8	736	60.3
0 Armed forces	.	.	1 057	88.6	.	.
X Not classifiable by occupation	44	45.5	38	44.7	6	50.0
Unemployed seeking their first job	.	.	.	.	2 170	54.1
Education level (ISCED-97)	2007 [1][2] Labour force survey		2007 ★ Labour force survey		2007 [2][3] Labour force survey	
Total	17 178	45.0	13 233	42.8	3 945	52.2
X No schooling	787	41.9	681	41.9	106	42.5
1 Primary education or first stage of basic education	3 297	39.1	2 547	37.6	750	44.1
2 Lower secondary or second stage of basic education	2 480	43.8	1 802	41.1	678	51.2
3 Upper secondary education	7 893	46.9	5 714	43.6	2 179	55.6
4 Post-secondary non-tertiary education	329	37.7	285	36.8	44	43.2
5A First stage of tertiary education - theoretically based [4]	2 298	50.7	2 120	50.2	178	57.3
? Level not stated	95	31.6	86	30.2	9	44.4
Status in employment (ICSE-1993)			2007 [1][2] Labour force survey			
Total	.	.	13 234	42.8	.	.
1 Employees	.	.	10 902	42.0	.	.
2 Employers	.	.	1 946	45.4	.	.
3 Own-account workers	.	.	300	52.0	.	.
5 Contributing family workers	.	.	53	62.3	.	.
6 Not classifiable by status	.	.	33	42.4	.	.

2. Population ('000), Activity rate and Unemployment rate

	Population 2007 [2] Labour force survey			Activity rate 2007 [2] Labour force survey			Unemployment rate 2007 [1][2] Labour force survey		
Age group	Total	Men	Women	Total	Men	Women	Total	Men	Women
Total	47 937.8	23 588.1	24 310.0	35.8	40.0	31.8	23.0	20.0	26.7
15+	32 699.8	15 609.7	17 062.1	52.5	60.5	45.3	23.0	20.0	26.6
15-24	9 648.0	4 913.5	4 724.1	30.0	32.6	27.2	46.9	43.0	52.0
25-54	17 683.9	8 476.9	9 197.8	73.9	83.8	64.8	19.2	16.1	22.9
55+	5 367.8	2 219.3	3 140.2	22.5	32.7	15.3	6.7	7.3	5.6

South Africa

3. Paid employment ('000), Hours of work (weekly) and Wages

Economic activity (ISIC-Rev.2)	Paid employment 2007[5] Labour-related establishment survey			Hours of work 2002[6,7] Labour-related establishment survey Hours paid for / Employees			Wages 2006 Labour-related establishment survey Earnings per month / Employees / Rand		
	Total	Men	Women	Total	Men	Women	Total	Men	Women
Total	8 288.418	.	.	.	.	.	.	.	.
2-9	.	.	.	173.0	.	.	7 610	.	.
2	496.894	.	.	173.1	.	.	.	.	.
3	1 323.498	.	.	175.3	.	.	6 912	.	.
4	53.640	.	.	164.0	.	.	14 120	.	.
5	472.571	.	.	178.2	.	.	4 977	.	.
6	1 729.862	.	.	184.0	.	.	5 259	.	.
7	358.939	.	.	180.0	.	.	10 672	.	.
8	1 824.609	.	.	169.0	.	.	8 826	.	.
9	2 028.405	.	.	159.0	.	.	8 942	.	.

4. Occupational injuries and Strikes and Lockouts

Economic activity (ISIC-Rev.3)	Rates of fatal injuries 1989 Administrative records and related sources Per 1,000 workers insured Reported injuries			Rates of non-fatal injuries			Strikes and lockouts 2007 Labour relations records		
	Total	Men	Women	Total	Men	Women	Strikes and lockouts	Workers involved	Days not worked
Total	0.400	.	.	.	.	.	75	608 919	9 528 945
A	.	.	.	.	.	.	3	2 753	30 728
C	.	.	.	.	.	.	17	161 193	536 740
D	.	.	.	.	.	.	16	98 839	695 156
E	.	.	.	.	.	.	1	69	345
F	.	.	.	.	.	.	3	7 052	50 548
G	.	.	.	.	.	.	4	466	18 299
I	.	.	.	.	.	.	9	3 470	25 881
J	.	.	.	.	.	.	3	3 003	9 947
O	.	.	.	.	.	.	19	332 074	8 161 301

5. Consumer price indices (base period: 2000=100)

	2002	2003	2004	2005	2006	2007
General indices	115.4	122.1	123.8	128.0	134.0	143.5
Food index, including non-alcoholic beverages	122.0	131.9	134.9	137.9	147.8	163.1
Electricity, gas and other fuel indices	114.5	121.4	129.0	135.7	141.9	153.3
Clothing indices, including footwear	98.3	99.8	96.0	92.3	84.6	76.8
Rent indices [8]	114.0	120.9	111.2	113.4	118.2	129.7
General index, excluding housing	115.6	122.3	127.4	132.2	138.4	147.4

[1] Persons aged 15 years and over. [2] Sep. [3] Persons aged 15 to 65 years. [4] Levels 5-6. [5] Second quarter. [6] Per month. [7] Full-time employees. [8] Housing.

[1] Personnes âgées de 15 ans et plus. [2] Sept. [3] Personnes âgées de 15 à 65 ans. [4] Niveaux 5-6. [5] Deuxième trimestre. [6] Par mois. [7] Salariés à plein temps. [8] Logement.

[1] Personas de 15 años y más. [2] Sept. [3] Personas de 15 a 65 años. [4] Niveles 5-6. [5] Segundo trimestre. [6] Por mes. [7] Asalariados a tiempo completo. [8] Vivienda.

Sri Lanka

1. Economically active population, Employment and Unemployment ('000)

	Economically active population		Employment		Unemployment	
	Total	Women (%)	Total	Women (%)	Total	Women (%)
Age group	2007 [1,2] Labour force survey		2007 ★ Labour force survey		2007 [1,2] Labour force survey	
Total	7 488.9	35.1	7 041.9	33.9	447.0	53.1
15-19	322.9	33.9	253.0	32.2	69.9	40.2
20-24	871.6	39.0	688.0	35.1	183.6	53.5
25-29	934.7	33.2	846.7	30.3	88.0	61.8
30-39	1 741.4	35.4	1 683.1	34.4	58.3	63.3
40+	3 602.3	34.5	3 555.8	34.4	46.5	40.6
?	16.0	42.2	.	.	.	.
Economic activity (ISIC-Rev.3)			2007 [1,2] Labour force survey			
Total	.	.	7 041.9	33.9	.	.
A-B	.	.	2 202.1	40.0	.	.
C-E [3]	.	.	542.5	3.5	.	.
D Manufacturing	.	.	1 331.4	47.2	.	.
G Wholesale and Retail Trade; Repair of Motor Vehicles ...	.	.	932.0	26.1	.	.
H Hotels and Restaurants	.	.	118.5	28.2	.	.
I Transport, Storage and Communications	.	.	456.8	4.7	.	.
J-K	.	.	215.2	29.5	.	.
L Public Administration and Defence; Compulsory Social ...	.	.	433.0	28.8	.	.
M Education	.	.	259.5	69.5	.	.
N Health and Social Work	.	.	115.9	57.5	.	.
O-Q	.	.	104.6	25.6	.	.
P Households with Employed Persons	.	.	87.4	69.1	.	.
X Not classifiable by economic activity	.	.	242.9	13.6	.	.
Occupation (ISCO-88)			2007 [1,2] Labour force survey			
Total	.	.	7 041.9	33.9	.	.
1 Legislators, senior officials and managers	.	.	617.8	23.8	.	.
2 Professionals	.	.	366.7	59.7	.	.
3 Technicians and associate professionals	.	.	381.6	32.4	.	.
4 Clerks	.	.	283.7	51.2	.	.
5 Service workers and shop and market sales workers	.	.	508.5	37.3	.	.
6 Skilled agricultural and fishery workers	.	.	1 503.7	38.4	.	.
7 Craft and related trade workers	.	.	1 201.6	35.2	.	.
8 Plant and machine operators and assemblers	.	.	563.9	10.5	.	.
9 Elementary occupations	.	.	1 574.1	32.0	.	.
X Not classifiable by occupation	.	.	40.3	.	.	.
Education level (ISCED-97)	2007 [1,2] Labour force survey		2007 ★ Labour force survey		2007 [1,2] Labour force survey	
Total	7 488.9	35.1	7 041.9	33.9	447.0	53.1
X No schooling [4]	1 506.0	37.0	1 486.3	37.0	19.7	38.6
2 Lower secondary or second stage of basic education	3 551.4	29.9	3 368.1	29.2	183.3	43.4
3 Upper secondary education	1 194.3	34.9	1 095.8	33.7	98.5	47.7
5A First stage of tertiary education - theoretically based [5]	1 237.2	47.7	1 091.6	44.7	145.6	70.8
Status in employment (ICSE-1993)			2007 [1,2] Labour force survey			
Total	.	.	7 041.9	33.9	.	.
1 Employees	.	.	3 976.6	33.1	.	.
2 Employers	.	.	200.4	8.4	.	.
3 Own-account workers	.	.	2 140.1	25.1	.	.
5 Contributing family workers	.	.	724.7	71.6	.	.

2. Population ('000), Activity rate and Unemployment rate

	Population			Activity rate			Unemployment rate		
Age group	2005 [6,7] Labour force survey			2005 [6,7] Labour force survey			2007 [1,2] Labour force survey		
	Total	Men	Women	Total	Men	Women	Total	Men	Women
Total	20 032.3	9 717.5	10 314.8	40.6	55.8	26.2	6.0	4.3	9.0
15+	14 976.6	7 152.2	7 824.4	54.3	75.8	34.5	6.0	4.3	9.0
15-24	3 641.2	1 804.8	1 836.3	41.8	54.1	29.6	21.2	17.1	28.1

Sri Lanka

3. Paid employment ('000), Hours of work (weekly) and Wages

Economic activity (ISIC-Rev.2)	Paid employment			Hours of work 2007[8] Labour-related establishment survey Hours paid for / Wage earners			Wages 2007[8] Labour-related establishment survey Earnings per hour / Wage earners / Rupee		
	Total	Men	Women	Total	Men	Women	Total	Men	Women
Total [9]	.	.	.	49.9	49.3	50.5	38.75	39.28	37.51
2-9 [9]	.	.	.	54.2	54.1	54.3	45.70	46.26	44.70
1	.	.	.	42.5	40.7	44.2	.	.	.
3	.	.	.	53.0	53.1	52.9	45.36	46.09	42.95
5	.	.	.	63.3	63.3	.	40.71	40.70	.
6	.	.	.	55.8	55.8	55.8	42.47	42.47	42.47
7	.	.	.	48.4	48.4	.	44.19	44.19	.

Economic activity (ISIC-Rev.3)	Paid employment 2006[10,11] Labour-related establishment survey			Hours of work			Wages		
	Total	Men	Women	Total	Men	Women	Total	Men	Women
Total	787.1	442.6	344.5	.	.	.	.	.	.
A-B	220.1	102.6	117.5	.	.	.	.	.	.
C	4.6	3.8	0.8	.	.	.	.	.	.
D	243.9	105.9	138.0	.	.	.	.	.	.
E	16.3	14.8	1.5	.	.	.	.	.	.
F	23.8	19.9	3.9	.	.	.	.	.	.
G-H	74.1	49.7	24.4	.	.	.	.	.	.
I	53.9	47.9	6.0	.	.	.	.	.	.
J-K	56.7	37.8	18.9	.	.	.	.	.	.
N-O	93.7	60.2	33.5	.	.	.	.	.	.

Share of women in wage employment in the non-agricultural sector [10,11] (2006 - Labour-related establishment survey): **40.0%**

4. Occupational injuries and Strikes and Lockouts

Economic activity (ISIC-Rev.2)	Rates of fatal injuries			Rates of non-fatal injuries			Strikes and lockouts 2007[12,13] Administrative reports		
	Total	Men	Women	Total	Men	Women	Strikes and lockouts[14]	Workers involved[15]	Days not worked
Total	.	.	.	.	.	.	25	7 547	39 237
1 [16]	.	.	.	.	.	.	8	1 468	5 489
2	.	.	.	.	.	.	0	0	0
3	.	.	.	.	.	.	17	6 079	33 748
4	.	.	.	.	.	.	0	.	0
5	.	.	.	.	.	.	0	.	0
6	.	.	.	.	.	.	0	.	0
7	.	.	.	.	.	.	0	.	0
8	.	.	.	.	.	.	0	.	0
9	.	.	.	.	.	.	0	.	0
0	.	.	.	.	.	.	0	.	0

Economic activity (ISIC-Rev.3)	Rates of fatal injuries 2007 Labour inspectorate records Per 1,000,000 hours worked Reported injuries			Rates of non-fatal injuries 2007 Labour inspectorate records Per 1,000,000 hours worked Reported injuries			Strikes and lockouts		
	Total	Men	Women	Total	Men	Women	Strikes and lockouts	Workers involved	Days not worked
Total	0.012	.	.	0.274	.	.	.	.	.
C	0.036	.	.	0.988	.	.	.	.	.
D	0.030	.	.	1.342	.	.	.	.	.
E	0.157	.	.	0.236	.	.	.	.	.
F	0.032	.	.	0.050	.	.	.	.	.
G	0.000	.	.	0.000	.	.	.	.	.
H	0.000	.	.	0.062	.	.	.	.	.
I	0.033	.	.	1.366	.	.	.	.	.
O	0.000	.	.	0.000	.	.	.	.	.

5. Consumer price indices (base period: 2000=100)

Colombo	2002	2003	2004	2005	2006	2007
General indices	125.1	133.0	143.0	159.7	181.5	213.3
Food index, including non-alcoholic beverages	127.5	134.9	145.5	163.0	184.6	218.2
Electricity, gas and other fuel indices	124.3	143.2	157.0	178.1	228.3	286.2
Clothing indices, including footwear [17]	108.9	111.6	112.7	117.6	122.2	127.8
Rent indices	100.0	100.0	100.0	100.0	100.0	100.0
General index, excluding housing	125.1	133.0	143.1	159.8	.	.

Sri Lanka

[1] Excl. Northern and Eastern provinces. [2] Persons aged 15 years and over. [3] Incl. construction. [4] Levels X-1. [5] Levels 5-6. [6] Excl. Northern province. [7] Aug. [8] March and Sept. [9] Excl. major divisions 4, 8 and 9. [10] Establishments with 5 or more persons employed. [11] June. [12] Excl. work stoppages involving fewer than 5 workers. [13] Incl. work stoppages lasting less than one day only if more than 50 workdays not worked. [14] Number of strikes that ended during the year; excl. political strikes. [15] Excl. workers indirectly involved. [16] Plantations. [17] Excl. footwear.

[1] Non compris les provinces du Nord et de l'Est. [2] Personnes âgées de 15 ans et plus. [3] Y compris la construction. [4] Niveaux X-1. [5] Niveaux 5-6. [6] Non compris la province du Nord. [7] Août. [8] mars et sept. [9] Non compris les branches 4, 8 et 9. [10] Etablissements occupant 5 personnes et plus. [11] Juin. [12] Non compris les arrêts du travail impliquant moins de 5 travailleurs. [13] Y compris les arrêts du travail d'une durée inférieure à une journée si plus de 50 journées de travail non effectuées. [14] Nombre de grèves qui se sont terminées pendant l'année; non compris les grèves politiques. [15] Non compris les travailleurs indirectement impliqués. [16] Plantations. [17] Non compris la chaussure.

[1] Excl. las provincias del Norte y del Este. [2] Personas de 15 años y más. [3] Incl. construcción. [4] Niveles X-1. [5] Niveles 5-6. [6] Excl. la provincia del Norte. [7] Agosto. [8] marzo y sept. [9] Excl. las grandes divisiones 4, 8 y 9. [10] Establecimientos con 5 y más trabajadores. [11] Junio. [12] Excl. las interrupciones del trabajo que implican menos de 5 trabajadores. [13] Incl. las interrupciones del trabajo de menos de un día si no se han trabajado más de 50 días. [14] Número de huelgas que terminaron durante el año; excl. las huelgas políticas. [15] Excl. los trabajadores indirectamente implicados. [16] Plantaciones. [17] Excl. el calzado.

Sudan

1. Economically active population, Employment and Unemployment ('000)

Age group	Economically active population Total	Women (%)	Employment Total	Women (%)	Unemployment Total	Women (%)
	1996 Official estimates		2007 Official estimates		2007 Official estimates	
Total	7 983.0	30.6	9 300.0	.	2 300.0	.
0-9	103.7	52.1	.	.	.	.
10-14	464.1	48.2	.	.	.	.
15-19	780.3	40.3	.	.	.	.
20-24	1 044.0	38.0	.	.	.	.
25-29	1 225.6	37.1	.	.	.	.
30-34	945.2	31.1	.	.	.	.
35-39	851.0	25.8	.	.	.	.
40-44	582.8	24.5	.	.	.	.
45-49	524.0	21.2	.	.	.	.
50-54	469.8	21.3	.	.	.	.
55-59	285.4	14.9	.	.	.	.
60-64	273.0	18.1	.	.	.	.
65-69	172.4	6.9	.	.	.	.
70-74	137.6	8.8	.	.	.	.
75+	124.1	12.7	.	.	.	.

2. Population ('000), Activity rate and Unemployment rate

Age group	Population 1996 Official estimates Total	Men	Women	Activity rate 1996 Official estimates Total	Men	Women	Unemployment rate 2007 Official estimates Total	Men	Women
Total	23 680.8	11 732.1	11 948.7	33.7	47.2	20.4	19.8	.	.
15+	14 465.1	7 026.5	7 438.5	51.3	74.7	29.1	.	.	.
15-24	5 157.3	2 495.4	2 661.9	35.4	44.6	26.7	.	.	.
25-54	7 483.8	3 490.4	3 993.3	61.4	93.9	33.1	.	.	.
55+	1 824.0	1 040.7	783.3	54.4	82.7	16.8	.	.	.

3. Paid employment ('000), Hours of work (weekly) and Wages

Economic activity (ISIC-Rev.2)	Paid employment 1992[1] Labour-related establishment survey Total	Men	Women	Hours of work 1992[2][3] Labour-related establishment census Hours paid for / Wage earners Total	Men	Women	Wages 1992 Labour-related establishment census Earnings per month / Wage earners / Dinar Total	Men	Women
Total	243.95	196.89	47.06	.	.	.	.	.	.
2-9	.	.	.	224.50	.	.	1 055.0	.	.
1	11.83	11.31	0.52	.	.	.	.	.	.
2	0.05	0.05	.	196.30	.	.	.	.	.
3	10.94	80.93	7.46	243.50	.	.	1 210.3	.	.
4	34.08	32.34	1.75	.	.	.	.	.	.
5	2.65	2.43	0.22	235.10	.	.	1 250.5	.	.
6	3.46	3.28	0.19	.	.	.	.	.	.
7	40.75	35.97	4.48	214.50	.	.	1 340.2	.	.
8	23.27	17.75	5.52	.	.	.	.	.	.
9	116.91	85.67	31.25	.	.	.	.	.	.

4. Occupational injuries and Strikes and Lockouts

Economic activity (ISIC-Rev.2)	Rates of fatal injuries Total	Men	Women	Rates of non-fatal injuries Total	Men	Women	Strikes and lockouts 1989 Source unknown Strikes and lockouts	Workers involved	Days not worked
Total	.	.	.	.	.	.	3	.	.
1	.	.	.	.	.	.	0	.	.
2	.	.	.	.	.	.	1	.	.
3	.	.	.	.	.	.	0	.	.
4	.	.	.	.	.	.	0	.	.
5	.	.	.	.	.	.	1	.	.
6	.	.	.	.	.	.	0	.	.
7	.	.	.	.	.	.	0	.	.
8	.	.	.	.	.	.	1	.	.
9	.	.	.	.	.	.	0	.	.
0	.	.	.	.	.	.	0	.	.

5. Consumer price indices (base period: 2000=100)

Statistics not available for the period 2002-2007.

[1] Public sector. [2] Excl. overtime. [3] Per month.

[1] Secteur public. [2] Non compris les heures supplémentaires. [3] Par mois.

[1] Sector público. [2] Excl. las horas extraordinarias. [3] Por mes.

Suisse

1. Population active, Emploi et Chômage ('000)

	Population active Total	Femmes (%)	Emploi Total	Femmes (%)	Chômage Total	Femmes (%)
Groupe d'âge	2007 [1,2,3] Enquête sur la main-d'oeuvre		2007 ★ Enquête sur la main-d'oeuvre		2007 [2,3] Enquête sur la main-d'oeuvre	
Total	4 278	45.6	4 122	45.2	156	56.4
15-19	240	48.5	223	48.6	17	47.1
20-24	362	46.0	336	45.7	26	50.0
25-29	421	46.1	401	45.6	20	55.0
30-34	453	45.0	440	44.3	13	69.2
35-39	526	46.8	508	46.1	18	66.7
40-44	573	45.9	558	45.6	15	60.0
45-49	519	46.9	505	46.6	14	57.1
50-54	444	44.9	432	44.8	12	50.0
55-59	391	46.1	380	45.6	11	63.6
60-64	242	40.1	233	39.9	9	44.4
65-69	57	42.6	.	.	.	.
70-74	27	28.5	.	.	.	.
75+	22	36.2	.	.	.	.
Activité économique (CITI-Rév.3)	2007 [1,2,3] Enquête sur la main-d'oeuvre		2007 [1,2,3] Enquête sur la main-d'oeuvre		2007 [2,3] Enquête sur la main-d'oeuvre	
Total	4 278	45.6	4 122	45.2	156	.
A-B	165	31.6	164	31.7	.	.
C-E	689	26.7	668	25.9	22	.
F Construction	283	11.3	276	11.6	7	.
G Commerce de gros et de détail; réparation de véhicules ...	576	51.7	552	51.3	23	.
H Hôtels et restaurants	168	58.6	154	57.8	14	.
I Transports, entreposage et communications	224	28.5	218	28.4	7 [4]	.
J Intermédiation financière	241	42.0	238	41.6	3 [4]	.
K Immobilier, locations et activités de services aux entreprises	523	38.1	505	38.0	18	.
L, Q	220	44.9	216	44.9	4 [4]	.
M Education	330	63.2	326	62.9	4 [4]	.
N Santé et action sociale	527	77.2	515	77.1	12	.
O-P	295	63.3	284	62.7	12	.
X Ne pouvant être classés selon l'activité économique	36	58.7	7	57.1	28	.
Profession (CITP-88)	2007 [1,2,3] Enquête sur la main-d'oeuvre		2007 [1,2,3] Enquête sur la main-d'oeuvre		2007 [2,3] Enquête sur la main-d'oeuvre	
Total	4 278	45.6	4 122	45.2	156	56.4
1 Membres de l'exécutif et des corps législatifs, cadres ...	270	30.9	264	30.3	6	50.0
2 Professions intellectuelles et scientifiques	757	35.4	743	35.3	14	42.9
3 Professions intermédiaires	896	56.2	877	56.0	19	68.4
4 Employés de type administratif	494	70.9	474	70.9	20	70.0
5 Personnel des services et vendeurs de magasin et de marché	569	68.5	540	68.7	28	71.4
6 Agriculteurs et ouvriers qualifiés de l'agriculture ...	173	30.5	171	30.4	2 [4]	.
7 Artisans et ouvriers des métiers de type artisanal	630	14.3	611	13.9	19	26.3
8 Conducteurs d'installations et de machines ...	197	18.2	190	17.4	8	37.5
9 Ouvriers et employés non qualifiés	240	62.0	229	62.0	11	63.6
X Ne pouvant être classés selon la profession	52	54.3	21	52.4	28	60.7
Niveau d'instruction (CITE-97)	2007 [1,2,3] Enquête sur la main-d'oeuvre		2007 ★ Enquête sur la main-d'oeuvre		2007 [2,3] Enquête sur la main-d'oeuvre	
Total	4 278	45.6	4 122	45.2	156	56.4
1 Enseignement primaire ou premier cycle de l'éducation ... [5]	658	48.7	613	48.2	45	55.6
3 Enseignement secondaire (deuxième cycle) [6]	2 345	50.6	2 262	50.2	83	60.2
5A Premier cycle de l'enseignement supérieur - théorie [7]	1 271	34.8	1 243	34.5	28	46.4
? Niveau inconnu	3 [4]	61.8	.	.	.	.
Situation dans la profession (CISP-1993)	2007 [1,2,3] Enquête sur la main-d'oeuvre		2007 [1,2,3] Enquête sur la main-d'oeuvre		2007 ★ Enquête sur la main-d'oeuvre	
Total	4 278	45.6	4 122	45.2	156	56.3
1 Salariés	3 577	46.7	3 456	46.4	121	56.8
2 Employeurs	251	24.9	248	25.0	3	19.0
3 Personnes travaillant pour leur propre compte	324	43.2	320	43.1	4	52.4
5 Travailleurs familiaux collaborant à l'entreprise familiale	99	60.6	97	60.8	2	50.4
6 Inclassables d'après la situation	28	60.5	.	.	.	.

2. Population ('000), Taux d'activité et Taux de chômage

	Population 2007 [1,3] Enquête sur la main-d'oeuvre			Taux d'activité 2007 [1,3] Enquête sur la main-d'oeuvre			Taux de chômage 2007 [2,3] Enquête sur la main-d'oeuvre		
Groupe d'âge	Total	Hommes	Femmes	Total	Hommes	Femmes	Total	Hommes	Femmes
Total	.	.	.	.	.	.	3.6	2.9	4.5
15+	6 326	3 071	3 255	67.6	75.8	59.9	3.6	2.8	4.5
15-24	893	454	439	67.4	70.2	64.5	7.1	6.6	7.4
25-54	3 304	1 655	1 649	88.9	95.8	81.9	3.1	2.3	4.1
55+	2 130	962	1 168	34.7	43.9	27.2			

Suisse

3. Emploi rémunéré ('000), Durée du travail (hebdomadaire) et Salaires

Activité économique (CITI-Rév.3)	Emploi rémunéré 2007 [2,3,8] Enquête sur la main-d'oeuvre			Durée du travail 2007 Enquête sur la main-d'oeuvre Heures réellement effectuées / Salariés			Salaires 2006 [9] Enquête auprès des établissements, relative au travail Gains par mois / Salariés / Franc		
	Total	Hommes	Femmes	Total	Hommes	Femmes	Total	Hommes	Femmes
Total	3 240	1 728	1 512	36.1	41.9	29.4	.	.	.
A-B	29	20	9	39.7	43.7	30.3	.	.	.
C-Q	.	.	.	36.0	41.8	29.4	6 617	7 234	5 517
A	.	.	.	.	.	.	4 254	4 402	3 674
C	.	.	.	42.9	43.1	25.0	6 128	6 134	6 061
C-E	566	418	148	.	.	.	.	.	.
D	.	.	.	40.5	42.9	34.0	6 527	6 915	5 353
E	.	.	.	41.0	43.9	28.6	7 935	8 155	6 437
F	187	169	18	40.8	42.4	25.9	5 869	5 905	5 354
G	420	195	225	35.3	41.7	29.7	5 861	6 703	4 863
H	122	51	72	33.4	40.4	28.5	4 192	4 454	3 951
I	197	140	57	38.3	42.2	28.7	6 439	6 688	5 698
J	223	129	94	41.1	45.2	35.5	10 253	12 017	7 483
K	352	203	149	36.3	41.8	28.7	7 914	8 827	6 242
L	.	.	.	37.1	42.2	30.3	8 286	8 502	7 580
L,Q	208	117	91	.	.	.	.	.	.
M	296	107	189	31.4	37.8	27.8	7 525	8 252	6 765
N	423	94	329	32.1	39.3	30.0	6 112	7 210	5 755
O	.	.	.	30.8	38.3	24.9	6 337	7 288	5 397
O-P	211	80	131	.	.	.	.	.	.
P	.	.	.	17.6	31.6	15.3	.	.	.
Q	.	.	.	40.5	43.7	37.5	.	.	.
X	5 [4]	2 [4]	2 [4]	.	.	.	.	.	.

Pourcentage de salariées dans le secteur non agricole qui sont femmes [2,3,8] (2007 - Enquête sur la main-d'oeuvre): **46.8%**

4. Lésions professionnelles et Grèves et lock-out

Activité économique (CITI-Rév.3)	Taux de lésions mortelles 2006 [10] Fichiers des assurances Pour 100 000 travailleurs assurés Lésions indemnisées			Taux de lésions non mortelles 2006 [11] Fichiers des assurances Pour 100 000 travailleurs assurés Lésions indemnisées			Grèves et lock-out 2007 [12] Collecte spéciale de données		
	Total	Hommes	Femmes	Total	Hommes	Femmes	Grèves et lock-out	Travailleurs impliqués	Journées non effectuées
Total	1.4	.	.	2 349	.	.	2	5 083	7 083
A	6.9	.	.	6 501	.	.	0	0	0
B	0.0	.	.	2 151	.	.	0	0	0
C	.	.	.	.	.	.	0	0	0
C-D	1.7	.	.	.	.	.	.	.	.
D	.	.	.	2 538	.	.	0	0	0
E	0.0	.	.	1 772	.	.	0	0	0
F	4.5	.	.	7 028	.	.	2	5 083	7 083
G	0.6	.	.	1 824	.	.	0	0	0
H	0.0	.	.	3 289	.	.	0	0	0
I	5.9	.	.	3 517	.	.	0	0	0
J	0.0	.	.	145	.	.	0	0	0
K	0.9	.	.	2 172	.	.	0	0	0
L	0.0	.	.	515	.	.	0	0	0
M	0.0	.	.	1 049	.	.	0	0	0
N	0.0	.	.	963	.	.	0	0	0
O	0.0	.	.	2 285	.	.	0	0	0
P	0.0	.	.	759	.	.	.	.	.
Q	0.0	.	.	380	.	.	.	.	.
X	0.9	.	.	1 053	.	.	0	0	0

5. Indices des prix à la consommation (période de base: 2000=100)

	2002	2003	2004	2005	2006	2007
Indices généraux	101.7	102.3	103.1	104.4	105.4	106.1
Indices de l'alimentation, y compris les boissons non alcoolisées	104.4	105.7	106.3	105.5	105.4	106.0
Indices de l'électricité, gaz et autres combustibles	94.8	95.8	98.8	109.9	117.4	118.9
Indices de l'habillement, y compris les chaussures	92.7	92.4	89.8	89.7	91.5	91.7
Indices du loyer	103.9	104.2	105.5	106.9	109.1	111.6
Indices généraux, non compris le logement	101.0	101.8	102.5	103.6	104.5	104.9

[1] Excluding armed forces and seasonal/border workers. [2] Persons aged 15 years and over. [3] Second quarter. [4] Relative statistical reliability. [5] Levels 1-2. [6] Levels 3-4. [7] Levels 5A, 5B and 6. [8] Excl. apprentices. [9] Standardised monthly earnings (40 hours x 4,3 weeks). [10] Only deaths resulting from accidents occurring during the same year. [11] Incapacity of 3 days or more. [12] Excl. work stoppages lasting less than one day.

[1] Non compris les forces armées et les travailleurs saisonniers et frontaliers. [2] Personnes âgées de 15 ans et plus. [3] Deuxième trimestre. [4] Fiabilité statistique relative. [5] Niveaux 1-2. [6] Niveaux 3-4. [7] Niveaux 5A, 5B et 6. [8] Non compris les apprentis. [9] Gains mensuels standardisés (40 heures x 4,3 semaines). [10] Seulement les décès dus à des accidents survenus pendant la même année. [11] Incapacité de 3 jours et plus. [12] Non compris les arrêts du travail dont la durée est inférieure à une journée.

[1] Excluidas las fuerzas armadas y excl. a los trabajadores temporales y fronterizos. [2] Personas de 15 años y más. [3] Segundo trimestre. [4] Confiabilidad estadística relativa. [5] Niveles 1-2. [6] Niveles 3-4. [7] Niveles 5A, 5B y 6. [8] Excl. los aprendices. [9] Ganancias medias estandarizadas (40 horas x 4,3 semanas). [10] Solamente los fallecimientos resultados a accidentes ocurridos en el mismo año. [11] Incapacidad de 3 días y más. [12] Excl. las interrupciones del trabajo de menos de un día de duración.

Suriname

1. Economically active population, Employment and Unemployment ('000)

Age group	Economically active population Total	Economically active population Women (%)	Employment Total	Employment Women (%)	Unemployment Total	Unemployment Women (%)
	2004 [1,2] Population census		2004 ★ Population census		2004 [1,2] Population census	
Total	173.112	36.7	156.687	.	16.425	.
15-19	8.510	.	6.234	.	2.276	.
20-24	20.470	.	16.514	.	3.956	.
25-29	23.565	.	20.685	.	2.880	.
30-34	27.545	.	25.247	.	2.298	.
35-39	26.992	.	25.178	.	1.814	.
40-44	24.761	.	23.338	.	1.423	.
45-49	17.903	.	17.057	.	0.846	.
50-54	13.243	.	12.726	.	0.517	.
55-59	8.059	.	7.791	.	0.268	.
60-64	2.082	.	1.935	.	0.147	.

Economic activity (ISIC-Rev.3)

2004 [1,2] Population census

	Total	Women (%)
Total	156.705	34.9
A-B	12.593	19.6
C Mining and Quarrying	9.308	10.0
D Manufacturing	10.971	26.6
E Electricity, Gas and Water Supply	1.659	14.9
F Construction	14.031	3.6
G Wholesale and Retail Trade; Repair of Motor Vehicles ...	25.012	37.2
H Hotels and Restaurants	4.833	60.6
I Transport, Storage and Communications	8.711	12.8
J Financial Intermediation	2.723	49.2
K Real Estate, Renting and Business Activities	6.350	29.8
L Public Administration and Defence; Compulsory Social ...	27.995	41.9
M Education	8.355	78.6
N Health and Social Work	6.797	77.1
O Other Community, Social and Personal Service Activities	9.911	49.5
X Not classifiable by economic activity	7.456	36.0

Occupation (ISCO-88)

2004 [1,2] Population census

	Total
Total	156.705
1 Legislators, senior officials and managers	10.101
2 Professionals	11.769
3 Technicians and associate professionals	11.966
4 Clerks	16.047
5 Service workers and shop and market sales workers	23.931
6 Skilled agricultural and fishery workers	13.896
7 Craft and related trade workers	22.833
8 Plant and machine operators and assemblers	11.772
9 Elementary occupations	28.754
0 Armed forces	5.636

Status in employment (ICSE-1993)

1998 [3] Labour force survey

	Total	Women (%)
Total	88.244	32.3
1 Employees	71.228	34.7
2 Employers	0.569	10.5
3 Own-account workers	13.847	19.0
5 Contributing family workers	1.021	45.4
6 Not classifiable by status	1.579	38.6

2. Population ('000), Activity rate and Unemployment rate

Age group	Population 1999 [4] Labour force survey Total	Men	Women	Activity rate 1999 [4] Labour force survey Total	Men	Women	Unemployment rate 2004 [1,2] Population census Total	Men	Women
Total	248.4	123.5	124.9	34.6	43.9	25.3	9.5	.	.
15+	184.2	88.7	95.6	46.6	61.1	33.1	9.5	.	.
15-24	47.6	22.4	25.1	25.5	38.1	14.3	21.5	.	.
25-54	90.5	44.1	46.4	71.3	88.1	55.3	7.3	.	.
55+	46.2	22.2	24.0	20.0	30.7	10.0	.	.	.

3. Paid employment ('000), Hours of work (weekly) and Wages

Economic activity (NSIC)	Paid employment 1990 Official estimates Total	Men	Women	Hours of work Total	Men	Women	Wages Total	Men	Women
NSIC	67.4	.	.	.	.	.	.	.	.
2	2.7	.	.	.	.	.	.	.	.
3	4.9	.	.	.	.	.	.	.	.
5	2.4	.	.	.	.	.	.	.	.
7	3.4	.	.	.	.	.	.	.	.

Suriname

4. Occupational injuries and Strikes and Lockouts

Economic activity (ISIC-Rev.2)	Rates of fatal injuries 1988 Labour inspectorate records Per 1,000 workers employed			Rates of non-fatal injuries			Strikes and lockouts 1998 Special data collection		
	Total	Men	Women	Total	Men	Women	Strikes and lockouts	Workers involved	Days not worked
Total	.	.	.	.	.	.	17 [5]	2 600 [5]	44 829 [5]
1	.	.	.	.	.	.	0	0	0
2	0.33	.	.	.	.	.	2	521	14 067
3	0.00	.	.	.	.	.	5	448	3 764
4	0.00	.	.	.	.	.	0	0	0
5	0.00	.	.	.	.	.	0	0	0
6	0.00	.	.	.	.	.	0	0	0
7	0.33	.	.	.	.	.	3	107	267
8	0.00	.	.	.	.	.	5	650	14 976
9	0.00	.	.	.	.	.	2 [5]	874 [5]	11 755 [5]

5. Consumer price indices (base period: 2000=100)

Paramaribo [6]	2002	2003	2004	2005	2006	2007
General indices	115.9	.	156.9 [7]	171.4	.	.
Food index, including non-alcoholic beverages	118.1	.	157.8 [7]	174.2	.	.
Clothing indices, including footwear	96.3	.	.	128.2	.	.

[1] Persons aged 15 years and over. [2] Aug. [3] Persons aged 14 years and over. [4] First semester. [5] Excl. public administration and defence. [6] Index base 2001=100. [7] March-Dec.

[1] Personnes âgées de 15 ans et plus. [2] Août. [3] Personnes âgées de 14 ans et plus. [4] Premier semestre. [5] Non compris l'administration publique et la défense. [6] Indice base 2001=100. [7] Mars-déc.

[1] Personas de 15 años y más. [2] Agosto. [3] Personas de 14 años y más. [4] Primer semestre. [5] Excl. la administración pública y la defensa. [6] Indice base 2001=100. [7] Marzo-dic.

Swaziland

1. Economically active population, Employment and Unemployment ('000)

Age group	Economically active population Total	Women (%)	Employment Total	Women (%)	Unemployment Total	Women (%)
	1986 [1,2] Population census		1997 [3] Population census		1989 Labour force survey	
Total	160.355	34.4	239.568	42.8	50.351	41.6
10-14	2.349	45.9	.	.	.	.
15-24	48.679	43.5	.	.	.	.
25-29	26.895	38.3	.	.	.	.
30-34	20.558	33.4	.	.	.	.
35-39	17.315	30.2	.	.	.	.
40-44	13.178	28.2	.	.	.	.
45-49	11.916	23.0	.	.	.	.
50-54	7.611	21.3	.	.	.	.
55-69	9.286	19.6	.	.	.	.
70+	1.543	17.9	.	.	.	.
?	1.025	30.3	.	.	.	.

2. Population ('000), Activity rate and Unemployment rate

Age group	Population 1986 [2] Population census Total	Men	Women	Activity rate 1986 [2] Population census Total	Men	Women	Unemployment rate Total	Men	Women
Total	681.059	321.579	359.480	23.5	32.7	15.3	.	.	.
15+	355.058	160.624	194.434	44.2	64.3	27.7	.	.	.
15-24	134.060	60.808	73.252	36.3	45.2	28.9	.	.	.
25-54	177.304	80.247	97.057	55.0	83.5	31.4	.	.	.
55+	43.694	19.569	24.125	24.8	44.6	8.7	.	.	.

3. Paid employment ('000), Hours of work (weekly) and Wages

Economic activity (ISIC-Rev.2)	Paid employment 1996 [4] Labour-related establishment survey Total	Men	Women	Hours of work Total	Men	Women	Wages 1997 [4,5,6] Labour-related establishment census Earnings per month / Skilled / Lilangeni Total	Men	Women
Total	89.86	63.54	26.32	.	.	.	.	2 289	2 120
1	22.44	18.34	4.10	.	.	.	.	3 224 [7]	2 327 [7]
2	11.38	1.10	0.04	.	.	.	.	1 568	.
3	16.17	12.53	3.64	.	.	.	.	2 948	1 850
4	1.19	1.05	0.14	.	.	.	.	.	.
5	5.00	4.81	0.19	.	.	.	.	1 199	1 000
6	11.89	6.79	5.10	.	.	.	.	1 835	2 550
7	2.70	2.44	0.27	.	.	.	.	2 725	2 713
8	6.17	4.17	2.00	.	.	.	.	2 119	2 431
9	23.17	12.31	10.86	.	.	.	.	1 789	1 966

4. Occupational injuries and Strikes and Lockouts

Economic activity (ISIC-Rev.3)	Rates of fatal injuries Total	Men	Women	Rates of non-fatal injuries Total	Men	Women	Strikes and lockouts	Strikes and lockouts 1996 Labour relations records Workers involved	Days not worked [8]
Total	.	.	.	.	.	.	1	59	2 242
A	.	.	.	.	.	.	0	0	0
B	.	.	.	.	.	.	0	0	0
C	.	.	.	.	.	.	0	0	0
D	.	.	.	.	.	.	1	59	2 242
E	.	.	.	.	.	.	0	0	0
F	.	.	.	.	.	.	0	0	0
G	.	.	.	.	.	.	0	0	0
H	.	.	.	.	.	.	0	0	0
I	.	.	.	.	.	.	0	0	0
J	.	.	.	.	.	.	0	0	0
K	.	.	.	.	.	.	0	0	0
L	.	.	.	.	.	.	0	0	0
M	.	.	.	.	.	.	0	0	0
N	.	.	.	.	.	.	0	0	0
O	.	.	.	.	.	.	0	0	0

5. Consumer price indices (base period: 2000=100)

	2002	2003	2004	2005	2006	2007
General indices	120.2	129.0	133.5	139.9	.	.
Food index, including non-alcoholic beverages	129.8	145.7	155.7	169.2	.	.
Electricity, gas and other fuel indices	105.6	114.0	119.2	123.9	.	.
Clothing indices, including footwear	109.2	114.4	115.2	116.9	.	.
Rent indices	104.9	105.7	117.5	119.6	.	.

Swaziland

[1] Persons aged 12 years and over. [2] Aug. [3] May. [4] June. [5] Private sector. [6] Skilled wage earners. [7] Beginning 1989: excl. forestry. [8] Computed on the basis of an eight-hour working day.

[1] Personnes âgées de 12 ans et plus. [2] Août. [3] Mai. [4] Juin. [5] Secteur privé. [6] Ouvriers qualifiés. [7] A partir de 1989: non compris la sylviculture. [8] Calculées sur la base de journées de travail de huit heures.

[1] Personas de 12 años y más. [2] Agosto. [3] Mayo. [4] Junio. [5] Sector privado. [6] Obreros calificados. [7] Desde 1989: excl. silvicultura. [8] Calculados en base a días de trabajo de ocho horas.

Sweden

1. Economically active population, Employment and Unemployment ('000)

	Economically active population		Employment		Unemployment	
	Total	Women (%)	Total	Women (%)	Total	Women (%)
Age group	2007 [1] Labour force survey		2007 ★ Labour force survey		2007 [1] Labour force survey	
Total	4 838	47.5	4 540	47.4	298	49.7
15-19	210	53.8	147	54.4	63	52.4
20-24	400	47.3	345	47.2	55	47.3
25-29	472	46.8	439	46.5	33	51.5
30-34	543	47.1	517	46.8	26	53.8
35-39	577	47.3	553	47.0	24	54.2
40-44	612	47.2	587	47.0	25	52.0
45-49	529	48.4	511	48.5	18	44.4
50-54	512	48.2	495	48.3	17	47.1
55-59	500	48.2	483	48.2	17	47.1
60-64	393	46.3	375	46.7	18	38.9
65-69	67	37.3	67	37.3	-	.
70-74	23	30.4	23	30.4	-	.
Economic activity (ISIC-Rev.3)	2007 ★ Labour force survey		2007 [1] Labour force survey		2007 [1] Labour force survey	
Total	4 839	47.5	4 541	47.3	298	49.7
A-B	105	20.0	102	19.6	3	33.3
C Mining and Quarrying	9	11.1	9	11.1	-	.
D Manufacturing	687	25.5	658	25.2	29	31.0
E Electricity, Gas and Water Supply	26	26.9	25	28.0	1	.
F Construction	301	7.6	290	7.6	11	9.1
G Wholesale and Retail Trade; Repair of Motor Vehicles ...	587	43.6	557	43.1	30	53.3
H Hotels and Restaurants	162	53.7	143	53.8	19	52.6
I Transport, Storage and Communications	294	26.5	281	26.3	13	30.8
J Financial Intermediation	91	50.5	89	50.6	2	50.0
K Real Estate, Renting and Business Activities	700	39.0	664	38.9	36	41.7
L, Q	269	53.2	260	53.1	9	55.6
M Education	511	74.6	491	74.5	20	75.0
N Health and Social Work	749	82.9	724	83.0	25	80.0
O-P	255	54.9	240	55.0	15	53.3
X Not classifiable by economic activity	17	41.2	8	37.5	9	44.4
Unemployed seeking their first job	.	.	.	.	75	52.0
Occupation (ISCO-88)	2007 ★ Labour force survey		2007 [1] Labour force survey		2007 [1] Labour force survey	
Total	4 839	47.5	4 541	47.3	298	49.7
1 Legislators, senior officials and managers	240	32.1	236	31.8	4	50.0
2 Professionals	903	50.6	881	50.6	22	50.0
3 Technicians and associate professionals	913	50.5	889	50.6	24	45.8
4 Clerks	427	67.7	401	68.1	26	61.5
5 Service workers and shop and market sales workers	924	74.6	866	74.8	58	70.7
6 Skilled agricultural and fishery workers	97	21.6	92	21.7	5	20.0
7 Craft and related trade workers	506	6.1	482	6.0	24	8.3
8 Plant and machine operators and assemblers	469	15.8	446	15.5	23	21.7
9 Elementary occupations	258	60.1	230	60.0	28	60.7
0 Armed forces	.	.	10	.	.	.
X Not classifiable by occupation	15	46.7	7	42.9	8	50.0
Unemployed seeking their first job	.	.	.	.	75	52.0
Education level (ISCED-97)	2007 [1] Labour force survey		2007 ★ Labour force survey		2007 [1] Labour force survey	
Total	4 838	47.5	4 540	47.4	298	49.7
1 Primary education or first stage of basic education	184	37.0	170	35.9	14	50.0
2 Lower secondary or second stage of basic education	571	42.2	489	40.9	82	50.0
3 Upper secondary education	2 283	45.6	2 164	45.3	119	49.6
4 Post-secondary non-tertiary education	315	39.4	297	39.1	18	44.4
5A First stage of tertiary education - theoretically based	992	55.3	958	55.5	34	50.0
5B First stage of tertiary education - practically oriented	400	60.3	384	60.4	16	56.3
6 Second stage of tertiary education	51	31.4	50	32.0	1	.
? Level not stated	43	44.2	31	41.9	12	50.0
Status in employment (ICSE-1993)			2007 [1] Labour force survey			
Total			4 541	47.3		
1 Employees			4 060	49.9		
2 Employers			468	25.4		
5 Contributing family workers			13	46.2		

2. Population ('000), Activity rate and Unemployment rate

	Population 2007 Labour force survey			Activity rate 2007 Labour force survey			Unemployment rate 2007 [1] Labour force survey		
Age group	Total	Men	Women	Total	Men	Women	Total	Men	Women
Total	.	.	.	.	.	.	6.1	5.9	6.5
15+	6 804	3 437	3 366	71.1	73.9	68.3	.	.	.
15-24	1 177	603	573	51.8	51.2	52.7	19.3	18.8	19.5
25-54	3 606	1 835	1 771	90.0	92.9	87.1	4.4	4.2	4.7

Sweden

3. Paid employment ('000), Hours of work (weekly) and Wages

Economic activity (ISIC-Rev.3)	Paid employment 2007[1] Labour force survey			Hours of work 2007[2] Labour force survey Hours actually worked / Employees			Wages 2007[3,4,5] Labour-related establishment survey Earnings per hour / Wage earners / Krona		
	Total	Men	Women	Total	Men	Women	Total	Men	Women
Total	4 060	2 034	2 025	35.2	37.6	32.7	133.80	137.40	123.00
A-B	38	29	9	37.9	39.4	32.3	123.60	126.10	113.40
C-Q	.	.	.	35.2	37.6	32.7	.	.	.
A	.	.	.	37.7	39.2	32.3	.	.	.
B	.	.	.	46.6	48.5	.	.	.	.
C	8	7	1	44.3	44.7	41.3	169.10	169.50	164.80
D	618	460	158	37.2	37.9	34.9	139.50	142.10	128.60
E	25	18	7	37.3	38.0	35.3	154.20	154.90	135.20
F	233	212	20	38.0	38.6	32.7	147.30	147.80	125.10
G	474	257	218	34.3	37.3	30.7	129.50	131.30	127.10
H	118	48	70	30.7	33.7	28.5	112.50	114.70	110.80
I	256	184	72	37.0	38.2	33.7	131.90	132.60	125.50
J	86	41	45	35.3	37.2	33.4	.	.	.
K	556	325	231	35.8[6]	37.5[6]	33.3[6]	121.70	124.80	114.20
L	.	.	.	36.5	38.3	34.9	.	.	.
L,Q	260	122	138	.	.	.	.	.	.
M	484	121	363	34.8[7]	37.3[7]	33.9[7]	116.50	119.60	115.10
N	706	117	589	32.9	35.8	32.3	123.10	124.10	122.80
O	.	.	.	33.2	36.8	30.0	121.30	123.60	118.10
O-P	190	87	102	.	.	.	.	.	.
P	.	.	.	31.5	.	30.9	.	.	.
Q	.	.	.	30.5	31.2	29.2	.	.	.
X	7	4	3	35.8	36.7	34.4	.	.	.

Share of women in wage employment in the non-agricultural sector [1] (2007 - Labour force survey): **50.1%**

4. Occupational injuries and Strikes and Lockouts

Economic activity (ISIC-Rev.3)	Rates of fatal injuries 2006 Insurance records Per 100,000 workers employed Reported injuries			Rates of non-fatal injuries 2006 Insurance records Per 100,000 workers employed Reported injuries			Strikes and lockouts 2007[8] Special data collection		
	Total	Men	Women	Total	Men	Women	Strikes and lockouts	Workers involved[9]	Days not worked
Total	1.6	3.0	0.1	751	848	645	14	3 635	13 666
A	11.7	14.7	0.0	587	592	568	0	0	0
B	71.0	77.5	0.0	426	387	0	0	0	0
C	13.3	15.1	0.0	2 003	2 059	0	0	0	0
D	1.7	2.1	0.6	1 277	1 380	962	5	1 151	1 920
E	0.0	0.0	0.0	554	635	317	0	0	0
F	4.1	4.4	0.0	1 208	1 274	421	2	1 022	4 138
G	1.3	2.4	0.0	391	458	306	0	0	0
H	0.9	1.9	0.0	403	362	437	0	0	0
I	4.9	6.6	0.0	1 192	1 264	984	2	1 450	7 201
J	0.0	0.0	0.0	270	172	350	0	0	0
K	1.0	1.3	0.4	353	399	283	1	6	306
L	2.0	4.5	0.0	656	860	486	0	0	0
M	0.0	0.0	0.0	592	393	658	2	2	15
N	0.1	0.9	0.0	937	705	982	1	1	85
O	1.0	2.1	0.0	432	580	306	1	3	1
P	0.0	0.0	0.0	0	0	0	.	.	.
Q	0.0	0.0	0.0	0	0	0	.	.	.

5. Consumer price indices (base period: 2000=100)

	2002	2003	2004	2005	2006	2007
General indices	104.6	106.6	107.0	107.5	109.0	111.4
Food index, including non-alcoholic beverages	106.2	106.6	106.1	105.4	106.2	108.3
Electricity, gas and other fuel indices	119.9	146.3	147.8	149.9	167.7	166.4
Clothing indices, including footwear	103.6	103.6	101.6	100.5	103.7	106.2
Rent indices[10]	106.8	111.5	111.7	112.1	116.0	120.6
General index, excluding housing	103.7	104.7	105.2	105.8	106.2	108.7

[1] Persons aged 15 to 74 years. [2] Persons in main job and at work. [3] Private sector; Sep. of each year. [4] Excl. holidays, sick-leave and overtime payments. [5] Adults; prior to 1998: 2nd quarter of each year; 1998-2000: Sept-Oct. of each year. [6] Excl. research and development. [7] Incl. research and development. [8] Work stoppages in which at least 8 hours not worked. [9] Excl. workers indirectly involved. [10] Incl. water, electricity, gas and other fuels.

[1] Personnes âgées de 15 à 74 ans. [2] Personnes dans l'emploi principal et au travail. [3] Secteur privé; sept. de chaque année. [4] Non compris les versements pour les vacances, congés maladie ainsi que la rémunération des heures supplémentaires. [5] Adultes; avant 1998: 2ème trimestre de chaque année; 1998-2000: sept.-oct. de chaque année. [6] Non compris recherche-développement. [7] Y compris recherche-développement. [8] Arrêts de travail avec un minimum de 8 heures de travail non effectuées. [9] Non compris les travailleurs indirectement impliqués. [10] Y compris l'eau, l'électricité, le gaz et autres combustibles.

[1] Personas de 15 a 74 años. [2] Personas en el empleo principal y trabajando. [3] Sector privado; sept. de cada ano. [4] Excl. los pagos por vacancias, licencias de enfermedad, y pagos por horas extraordinarias. [5] Adultos; antes de 1998: segundo trimestre de cada año; 1998-2000:sept-oct. de cada año. [6] Excl. investigación y desarrollo. [7] Incl. investigación y desarrollo. [8] Interrupciones del trabajo de un mínimo de 8 horas no trabajadas. [9] Excl. los trabajadores indirectamente implicados. [10] Incl. el agua, la electricidad, el gas y otros combustibles.

Syrian Arab Republic

1. Economically active population, Employment and Unemployment ('000)

	Economically active population		Employment		Unemployment	
	Total	Women (%)	Total	Women (%)	Total	Women (%)
Age group	2003 [1] Labour force survey		2003 ★ Labour force survey		2003 [1] Labour force survey	
Total	4 981.870	19.3	4 468.870	17.0	513.000	39.2
15-19	648.556	21.4	532.556	19.4	116.000	30.4
20-24	850.308	23.2	674.508	18.0	175.800	43.3
25-29	691.475	22.2	590.575	18.9	100.900	41.2
30-34	616.382	21.7	565.682	19.3	50.700	48.1
35-39	577.134	20.1	547.834	18.9	29.300	42.7
40-44	478.892	17.5	463.792	17.0	15.100	35.8
45-49	367.289	15.9	359.889	15.8	7.400	17.6
50-54	309.183	12.8	302.983	12.6	6.200	25.8
55-59	175.471	10.7	171.771	10.2	3.700	35.1
60-64	115.232	10.5	112.632	10.1	2.600	26.9
65-69	72.440	8.2	70.540	7.2	1.900	47.4
70-74	50.835	5.4	49.235	5.2	1.600	12.5
75+	28.673	3.9	27.773	3.3	0.900	22.2
Economic activity (ISIC-Rev.2)	1991 ★ Labour force survey		2002 [1] Labour force survey		1991 [2 3 4] Labour force survey	
Total	3 485.37	18.0	4 821.76	18.4	235.43	37.4
1 Agriculture, Hunting, Forestry and Fishing	924.27	31.8	1 461.86	35.3	7.32	28.7
2 Mining and Quarrying	6.85	.	.	.	0.20	.
2-4	.	.	661.45	7.8	.	.
3 Manufacturing	466.26	7.7	.	.	10.10	12.5
4 Electricity, Gas and Water	8.83	8.7	.	.	0.41	51.1
5 Construction	350.62	1.8	634.27	1.4	9.84	.
6 Wholesale and Retail Trade and Restaurants and Hotels	384.72	2.6	724.42	3.0	6.47	13.0
7 Transport, Storage and Communication	170.18	5.1	264.88	2.3	3.21	.
8 Financing, Insurance, Real Estate and Business Services	25.05	17.9	61.14	14.1	0.40	.
9 Community, Social and Personal Services	963.92	19.4	1 013.74	27.2	12.82	29.5
0 Activities not Adequately Defined	.	.	.	.	.	.
Unemployed seeking their first job	.	.	.	.	184.66	43.3
Occupation (ISCO-1968)	1991 ★ Labour force survey		2001 [1] Labour force survey		1991 [2 3 4] Labour force survey	
Total	3 485.37	18.0	4 730.00	17.0	235.43	37.4
0/1 Professional, technical and related workers	407.40	37.3	558.00	40.0	6.17	58.2
2 Administrative and managerial workers	7.05	2.6	.	.	0.19	.
2-3	.	.	474.00	14.6	.	.
3 Clerical and related workers	317.07	16.3	.	.	3.32	16.8
4 Sales workers	343.86	1.3	.	.	4.33	.
4-5	.	.	695.00	4.3	.	.
5 Service workers	163.23	5.5	.	.	3.17	12.5
6 Agriculture, animal husbandry and forestry workers ...	909.93	32.2	1 386.00	31.0	7.33	31.1
7/8/9 Production and related workers, transport equipment ...	1 152.17	3.3	1 610.00	3.2	26.26	5.2
X Not classifiable by occupation	.	.	7.00	.	.	.
Unemployed seeking their first job	.	.	.	.	184.66	43.3
Education level (ISCED-97)	2003 [1] Labour force survey				2002 [1] Labour force survey	
Total	4 981.872	19.3	.	.	637.805	.
X No schooling	587.889	32.7	.	.	33.367	.
1 Primary education or first stage of basic education	2 660.160	11.6	.	.	396.044	.
2 Lower secondary or second stage of basic education	624.812	14.9	.	.	83.591	.
3 Upper secondary education	430.647	27.7	.	.	65.425	.
4 Post-secondary non-tertiary education	363.958	45.2	.	.	.	.
5A First stage of tertiary education - theoretically based	314.406 [5]	26.8	.	.	.	.
5A, 6	.	.	.	.	20.013	.
5B First stage of tertiary education - practically oriented	.	.	.	.	42.233	.
? Level not stated	.	.	.	.	0.132	.
Status in employment (ICSE-1993)			2001 [1] Labour force survey			
Total	.	.	4 730	17.0	.	.
1 Employees	.	.	2 329	16.1	.	.
2 Employers	.	.	394	2.8	.	.
3 Own-account workers	.	.	1 228	5.1	.	.
5 Contributing family workers	.	.	779	45.6	.	.

2. Population ('000), Activity rate and Unemployment rate

	Population 2003 Labour force survey			Activity rate 2003 Labour force survey			Unemployment rate 2003 [1 4] Labour force survey		
Age group	Total	Men	Women	Total	Men	Women	Total	Men	Women
Total	.	.	.	.	.	.	10.3	7.6	20.9
15+	10 359.7	5 254.1	5 105.5	48.1	76.5	18.8	10.3	7.8	20.9
15-24	3 690.9	1 900.0	1 790.9	40.6	61.2	18.8	19.5	15.6	33.1
25-54	5 261.3	2 574.7	2 686.6	57.8	95.4	21.8	6.9	5.0	14.8
55+	1 407.5	779.4	628.1	31.4	51.6	6.5	2.4	1.8	8.1

Syrian Arab Republic

3. Paid employment ('000), Hours of work (weekly) and Wages

Economic activity (ISIC-Rev.2)	Paid employment 2000 Labour-related establishment survey			Hours of work 2003 Labour force survey Hours paid for / Salaried employees			Wages		
	Total	Men	Women	Total	Men	Women	Total	Men	Women
Total	.	.	.	44	.	.	.	.	.
2	23.360 [6]	.	.	.	.	.	.	.	.
3	377.033	.	.	47	.	.	.	.	.
4	52.366	.	.	.	.	.	.	.	.
5	.	.	.	41	.	.	.	.	.
6	.	.	.	51	.	.	.	.	.
7	.	.	.	49	.	.	.	.	.
8	.	.	.	46	.	.	.	.	.
9	.	.	.	41	.	.	.	.	.

4. Occupational injuries and Strikes and Lockouts

Economic activity (ISIC-Rev.2)	Rates of fatal injuries			Rates of non-fatal injuries			Strikes and lockouts 1984 Source unknown		
	Total	Men	Women	Total	Men	Women	Strikes and lockouts	Workers involved	Days not worked
Total	.	.	.	.	.	.	2 993	.	.

5. Consumer price indices (base period: 2000=100)

	2002	2003	2004	2005	2006	2007
General indices	101.4	108.8	113.5	121.9	134.1	.
Food index, including non-alcoholic beverages	99.6	107.2	112.8	122.5	138.0	.
Electricity, gas and other fuel indices [7]	111.2	119.5	120.0	122.0	.	.
Clothing indices, including footwear	96.5	102.9	104.0	109.0	.	.
Rent indices	102.9	124.0	134.0	162.0	.	.

[1] Persons aged 15 years and over. [2] Persons aged 10 years and over. [3] April. [4] Sep. [5] Levels 5A, 5B and 6. [6] Excl. quarrying. [7] Incl. water.

[1] Personnes âgées de 15 ans et plus. [2] Personnes âgées de 10 ans et plus. [3] Avril. [4] Sept. [5] Niveaux 5A, 5B et 6. [6] Non compris les carrières. [7] Y compris l'eau.

[1] Personas de 15 años y más. [2] Personas de 10 años y más. [3] Abril. [4] Sept. [5] Niveles 5A, 5B y 6. [6] Excl. las canteras. [7] Incl. el agua.

Taiwan, China

1. Economically active population, Employment and Unemployment ('000)

	Economically active population		Employment		Unemployment	
	Total	Women (%)	Total	Women (%)	Total	Women (%)
Age group	2007 [1,2] Labour force survey		2007 ★ Labour force survey		2007 [2] Labour force survey	
Total	10 713	42.9	10 294	.	419	.
15-19	155	.	138	.	17	.
20-24	818	.	732	.	86	.
25-29	1 640	.	1 544	.	96	.
30-34	1 528	.	1 469	.	59	.
35-39	1 511	.	1 469	.	42	.
40-44	1 533	.	1 490	.	43	.
45-49	1 383	.	1 349	.	34	.
50-54	1 079	.	1 054	.	25	.
55-59	629	.	617	.	12	.
60-64	246	.	243	.	3	.
65+	187	.	187	.	-	.

Economic activity (ISIC-Rev.3)

2007 [1,2] Labour force survey

	Total	Women (%)
Total	10 294	.
A-B	543	.
C Mining and Quarrying	6	.
D Manufacturing	2 842	.
E Electricity, Gas and Water Supply	93	.
F Construction	846	.
G Wholesale and Retail Trade; Repair of Motor Vehicles ...	1 782	.
H Hotels and Restaurants	681	.
I Transport, Storage and Communications [3]	621	.
J Financial Intermediation	404	.
K Real Estate, Renting and Business Activities	589	.
L Public Administration and Defence; Compulsory Social ...	332	.
M Education	588	.
N Health and Social Work	340	.
O Other Community, Social and Personal Service Activities	523	.
X Not classifiable by economic activity	101	.

Occupation (ISCO-88)

2007 [1,2] Labour force survey

	Total
Total	10 294
1 Legislators, senior officials and managers	462
2 Professionals	866
3 Technicians and associate professionals	2 020
4 Clerks	1 133
5 Service workers and shop and market sales workers	1 964
6 Skilled agricultural and fishery workers	531
8, 9	3 319

Education level (ISCED-76)

	2007 [1,2] Labour force survey		2007 ★ Labour force survey		2007 [2] Labour force survey	
	Total	Women (%)	Total	Women (%)	Total	Women (%)
Total	10 713	.	10 294	.	419	.
1 First level	1 163	.	1 137	.	26	.
2 Second level, first stage	1 616	.	1 553	.	63	.
3 Second level, second stage	923	.	886	.	37	.
5 Third level, first stage, leading to an award not equivalent ...	2 923	.	2 794	.	129	.
6 Third level, first stage, leading to a first university degree ...	1 825	.	1 764	.	61	.
7 Third level, second stage	2 263	.	2 161	.	102	.

Status in employment (ICSE-1993)

2007 [1,2] Labour force survey

	Total
Total	10 294
1 Employees	7 735
2 Employers	523
3 Own-account workers	1 396
5 Contributing family workers	641

2. Population ('000), Activity rate and Unemployment rate

	Population 2007 [1] Labour force survey			Activity rate 2007 [1] Labour force survey			Unemployment rate 2007 [2] Labour force survey		
Age group	Total	Men	Women	Total	Men	Women	Total	Men	Women
Total	.	.	.	.	.	.	5.1	.	.
15+	18 388	.	.	58.2	.	.	.	.	.
15-24	3 129	.	.	31.1	.	.	10.6	.	.
25-54	10 924	.	.	79.4	.	.	3.4	.	.
55+	4 335	.	.	24.5	.	.	.	.	.

Taiwan, China

3. Paid employment ('000), Hours of work (weekly) and Wages

Economic activity (ISIC-Rev.3)	Paid employment 2006 Labour-related establishment survey			Hours of work 2006 [4] Labour-related establishment survey / Employees			Wages 2006 Labour-related establishment survey / Employees / New dollar		
	Total	Men	Women	Total	Men	Women	Total	Men	Women
Total	6 037.923	.	.	.	.	.	.	.	.
C	5.946	.	.	184.1	184.7	182.2	49 574	54 571	32 063
D	2 457.691	.	.	187.3	189.3	184.6	42 293	48 567	33 386
E	33.716	.	.	170.5	170.9	168.0	95 664	98 326	80 821
F	396.526	.	.	178.0	179.0	173.6	39 175	41 030	30 643
G	1 479.000	.	.	175.3	175.1	175.4	40 028	43 412	36 813
H	163.423	.	.	174.4	174.4	174.3	25 482	28 011	23 723
I	320.601	.	.	177.9	181.3	170.2	53 313	56 717	46 017
J	368.905	.	.	168.6	169.8	167.8	69 132	75 306	65 342
K	82.380	.	.	181.9 [5]	186.0 [5]	176.4 [5]	38 213 [5]	40 784 [5]	34 659 [5]
74	.	.	.	171.5	172.5	170.3	55 579	60 902	50 365
M	218.681	.	.	.	.	.	.	.	.
N	210.689	.	.	175.3	175.7	175.1	55 735	93 066	45 854
O	81.496	.	.	.	.	.	.	.	.
92	.	.	.	173.1	172.4	174.0	42 108	45 367	37 341
93	.	.	.	198.1	202.5	192.7	31 447	32 782	29 823
X	218.869	.	.	.	.	.	.	.	.

4. Occupational injuries and Strikes and Lockouts

Economic activity (ISIC-Rev.2)	Rates of fatal injuries 2005 Labour inspectorate records Per 100,000 workers insured Reported injuries			Rates of non-fatal injuries 2005 Labour inspectorate records Per 100,000 workers insured Reported injuries			Strikes and lockouts		
	Total	Men	Women	Total	Men	Women	Strikes and lockouts	Workers involved	Days not worked
Total	4.5	.	.	433	.	.	.	.	.
1	10.7	.	.	99	.	.	.	.	.
2	19.0	.	.	739	.	.	.	.	.
3	3.8	.	.	625	.	.	.	.	.
4	14.2	.	.	14	.	.	.	.	.
5	17.2	.	.	1 262	.	.	.	.	.
6	2.1	.	.	315	.	.	.	.	.
7	7.9	.	.	343	.	.	.	.	.
8	4.9	.	.	74	.	.	.	.	.
9	1.3	.	.	155	.	.	.	.	.

5. Consumer price indices (base period: 2000=100)

	2002	2003	2004	2005	2006	2007
General indices	99.8	99.5	101.1	103.5	104.1	105.9
Food index, including non-alcoholic beverages	98.8	98.7	103.1	110.7	110.0	113.1
Electricity, gas and other fuel indices [6]	99.3	100.2	101.5	103.3	107.3	111.0
Clothing indices, including footwear	98.9	100.3	103.4	103.3	100.8	103.9
Rent indices	99.0	98.0	97.3	97.3	97.5	97.7

[1] Excl. armed forces. [2] Persons aged 15 years and over. [3] Incl. information service activities. [4] Per month. [5] Excl. business services. [6] Incl. water.

[1] Non compris les forces armées. [2] Personnes âgées de 15 ans et plus. [3] Y compris les activités de service d'information. [4] Par mois. [5] Non compris les services aux entreprises. [6] Y compris l'eau.

[1] Excl. las fuerzas armadas. [2] Personas de 15 años y más. [3] Incl. actividad de servicio de información. [4] Por mes. [5] Excl. servicios para las empresas. [6] Incl. el agua.

Tajikistan

1. Economically active population, Employment and Unemployment ('000)

	Economically active population		Employment		Unemployment	
	Total	Women (%)	Total	Women (%)	Total	Women (%)
Age group	2004 [1,2] Labour force survey		2006 Labour force survey		2007 Employment office records	
Total	2 648.5	41.7	2 137.0	.	51.7	54.7
15-17	.	.	.	.	2.1	57.1
15-19	491.0	46.9	.	.	.	.
18-24	.	.	.	.	10.0	57.0
20-24	336.9	40.4	.	.	.	.
25-29	362.3	37.6	.	.	15.3	57.5
30-34	350.4	41.2	.	.	0.6	66.7
35+	.	.	.	.	23.7	51.1
35-39	320.3	42.7	.	.	.	.
40-44	309.6	43.8	.	.	.	.
45-49	204.4	42.8	.	.	.	.
50-54	136.1	43.3	.	.	.	.
55-59	53.5	30.6	.	.	.	.
60-64	41.6	28.3	.	.	.	.
65-69	24.3	23.5	.	.	.	.
70-74	18.1	28.4	.	.	.	.
75+	.	.	.	.	.	.

Economic activity (ISIC-Rev.3)			2004 Labour force survey		1997 Employment office records	
Total	.	.	2 452.6	41.2	51.1	.
A Agriculture, Hunting and Forestry	.	.	1 361.0	55.7	14.0	.
C Mining and Quarrying	.	.	11.7	12.8	.	.
D Manufacturing	.	.	114.5	30.0	.	.
E Electricity, Gas and Water Supply	.	.	17.3	8.1	-	.
F Construction	.	.	296.0	3.7	4.0	.
G Wholesale and Retail Trade; Repair of Motor Vehicles ...	.	.	202.1	23.9	.	.
H Hotels and Restaurants	.	.	23.8	48.7	.	.
I Transport, Storage and Communications	.	.	64.4	7.5	-	.
J Financial Intermediation	.	.	18.9	22.2	.	.
K Real Estate, Renting and Business Activities	.	.	16.6	12.7	.	.
L Public Administration and Defence; Compulsory Social ...	.	.	70.6	16.3	.	.
M Education	.	.	122.8	52.0	4.0	.
N Health and Social Work	.	.	62.8	66.2	2.0	.
O Other Community, Social and Personal Service Activities	.	.	57.2	18.2	.	.
P Households with Employed Persons	.	.	3.4	29.4	6.0	.
X Not classifiable by economic activity	.	.	9.5	48.4	.	.
Unemployed seeking their first job	.	.	.	.	21.1	.

Occupation (ISCO-88)					1997 Employment office records	
Total	.	.	.	.	51.1	.
1 Legislators, senior officials and managers	.	.	.	.	0.4	.
2 Professionals	.	.	.	.	-	.
3 Technicians and associate professionals	.	.	.	.	1.0	.
4 Clerks	.	.	.	.	-	.
5 Service workers and shop and market sales workers	.	.	.	.	0.6	.
6 Skilled agricultural and fishery workers	.	.	.	.	13.2	.
7 Craft and related trade workers	.	.	.	.	-	.
8 Plant and machine operators and assemblers	.	.	.	.	3.8	.
X Not classifiable by occupation	.	.	.	.	11.0	.
Unemployed seeking their first job	.	.	.	.	21.1	.

Education level (ISCED-97)	2004 [1,2] Labour force survey				2007 Employment office records	
Total	2 648.5	41.7	.	.	51.7	54.7
0 Pre-primary education	19.7	64.5	.	.	.	.
1 Primary education or first stage of basic education	114.8	57.1	.	.	.	.
2 Lower secondary or second stage of basic education	448.4	52.9	.	.	34.4	55.2
3 Upper secondary education	1 533.2	41.7	.	.	7.9	57.0
4 Post-secondary non-tertiary education	210.9	38.1	.	.	7.0	51.4
5A First stage of tertiary education - theoretically based [3]	289.1	22.8	.	.	2.4	45.8
? Level not stated	32.5	13.7	.	.	.	.

2. Population ('000), Activity rate and Unemployment rate

	Population			Activity rate			Unemployment rate		
Age group	2004 [1] Labour force survey			2004 [1] Labour force survey			2007 Employment office records		
	Total	Men	Women	Total	Men	Women	Total	Men	Women
Total	6 780.4	3 401.4	3 379.0	39.1	45.4	32.7	2.5	.	.
15+	4 200.9	2 085.8	2 115.1	.	.	.	.	.	.
15-24	1 507.4	761.4	746.0	54.9	60.6	49.1	.	.	.
25-54	2 219.1	1 095.4	1 123.7	75.8	89.8	62.3	.	.	.
55+	474.4	229.0	245.4	.	.	.	.	.	.

Tajikistan

3. Paid employment ('000), Hours of work (weekly) and Wages

Economic activity (ISIC-Rev.2)	Paid employment			Hours of work			Wages 1997 Labour-related establishment census Earnings per month / Employees / Somoni		
	Total	Men	Women	Total	Men	Women	Total	Men	Women
Total	.	.	.	.	.	.	4 975.0	.	.
1	.	.	.	.	.	.	2 837.0	.	.
3 [4]	.	.	.	.	.	.	14 977.0	.	.
5	.	.	.	.	.	.	9 201.0	.	.
6	.	.	.	.	.	.	4 169.0	.	.
7	.	.	.	.	.	.	6 098.0	.	.
8	.	.	.	.	.	.	16 944.0	.	.

4. Occupational injuries and Strikes and Lockouts

Statistics not available.

5. Consumer price indices (base period: 2000=100)

Statistics not available for the period 2002-2007.

[1] Excl. armed forces and conscripts. [2] Persons aged 15 years and over. [3] Levels 5-6. [4] Incl. major divisions 2 and 4.

[1] Non compris les forces armées et les conscrits. [2] Personnes âgées de 15 ans et plus. [3] Niveaux 5-6. [4] Y compris les branches 2 et 4.

[1] Excl. las fuerzas armadas y los conscriptos. [2] Personas de 15 años y más. [3] Niveles 5-6. [4] Incl. las grandes divisiones 2 y 4.

Tanzania (Tanganyika)

1. Economically active population, Employment and Unemployment ('000)

	Economically active population		Employment		Unemployment	
	Total	Women (%)	Total	Women (%)	Total	Women (%)
Age group	2001 [12] Labour force survey		2001 ★ Labour force survey		2001 [12] Labour force survey	
Total	17 827.6	51.0	16 914.8	.	912.8	.
10-14	2 336.8	48.5	2 204.7	.	132.2	.
15-19	2 699.2	48.9	2 452.7	.	246.5	.
20-24	2 291.3	54.5	2 091.4	.	199.9	.
25-29	2 041.1	57.3	1 912.1	.	129.0	.
30-34	1 709.9	56.0	1 639.4	.	70.5	.
35-39	1 675.4	56.1	1 637.6	.	37.8	.
40-44	1 225.7	53.7	1 204.2	.	21.5	.
45-49	1 155.5	46.9	1 128.2	.	27.3	.
50-54	833.9	47.5	820.4	.	13.6	.
55-59	583.2	42.2	569.1	.	14.1	.
60-64	480.4	38.4	473.0	.	7.4	.
65-69	371.4	40.7	366.6	.	4.8	.
70+	423.5	33.6	415.4	.	8.1	.

Economic activity (ISIC-Rev.2)			2001 [12] Labour force survey			
Total	.	.	16 914.8	50.6	.	.
1 Agriculture, Hunting, Forestry and Fishing	.	.	13 890.1	51.8	.	.
2 Mining and Quarrying	.	.	29.2	47.1	.	.
3 Manufacturing	.	.	245.4	34.1	.	.
4 Electricity, Gas and Water	.	.	14.7	8.4	.	.
5 Construction	.	.	151.7	2.8	.	.
6 Wholesale and Retail Trade and Restaurants and Hotels	.	.	1 263.0	55.2	.	.
7 Transport, Storage and Communication	.	.	111.6	6.9	.	.
8 Financing, Insurance, Real Estate and Business Services	.	.	26.5	16.4	.	.
9 Community, Social and Personal Services	.	.	1 182.7	47.3	.	.

Occupation (ISCO-88)			2001 [12] Labour force survey			
Total	.	.	16 914.8	50.6	.	.
1 Legislators, senior officials and managers	.	.	377.1	49.1	.	.
2 Professionals	.	.	51.1	26.4	.	.
3 Technicians and associate professionals	.	.	346.1	32.4	.	.
4 Clerks	.	.	59.6	53.0	.	.
5 Service workers and shop and market sales workers	.	.	732.8	51.7	.	.
6 Skilled agricultural and fishery workers	.	.	13 363.8	52.8	.	.
7 Craft and related trade workers	.	.	403.6	18.9	.	.
8 Plant and machine operators and assemblers	.	.	123.0	9.4	.	.
9 Elementary occupations	.	.	1 457.7	47.5	.	.

Status in employment (ICSE-1993)			2001 [12] Labour force survey			
Total	.	.	16 914.8	50.6	.	.
1 Employees	.	.	1 159.5	29.3	.	.
2 Employers	.	.	160.3	29.8	.	.
3 Own-account workers	.	.	14 947.6	52.0	.	.
5 Contributing family workers	.	.	647.4	61.5	.	.

2. Population ('000), Activity rate and Unemployment rate

	Population			Activity rate			Unemployment rate		
Age group	2001 [13] Labour force survey			2001 [13] Labour force survey			2001 [12] Labour force survey		
	Total	Men	Women	Total	Men	Women	Total	Men	Women
Total	.	.	.	.	.	.	5.1	4.4	5.8
15+	17 543.4	8 392.4	9 151.0	88.3	89.8	86.9	5.0	.	.
15-24	6 166.0	3 019.5	3 146.5	80.9	80.3	81.6	8.9	.	.
25-54	9 007.8	4 074.8	4 933.0	95.9	97.6	94.6	3.5	.	.
55+	2 369.5	1 298.1	1 071.4	78.4	87.4	67.6	1.9	.	.

3. Paid employment ('000), Hours of work (weekly) and Wages

Economic activity (ISIC-Rev.2)	Paid employment			Hours of work			Wages		
	2001 [12] Labour force survey								
	Total	Men	Women	Total	Men	Women	Total	Men	Women
Total	1 159.5	.	.	.	.	.	.	.	.
1	176.6	.	.	.	.	.	.	.	.
2	6.0	.	.	.	.	.	.	.	.
3	94.8	.	.	.	.	.	.	.	.
4	14.5	.	.	.	.	.	.	.	.
5	55.4	.	.	.	.	.	.	.	.
6	152.2	.	.	.	.	.	.	.	.
7	92.0	.	.	.	.	.	.	.	.
8	23.7	.	.	.	.	.	.	.	.
9	544.2	.	.	.	.	.	.	.	.

Tanzania (Tanganyika)

4. Occupational injuries and Strikes and Lockouts

Economic activity (ISIC-Rev.2)	Rates of fatal injuries 1989 Insurance records Per 100,000 workers employed Compensated injuries			Rates of non-fatal injuries			Strikes and lockouts		
	Total	Men	Women	Total	Men	Women	Strikes and lockouts	Workers involved	Days not worked
Total	13.8	.	.	.	.	.	.	.	.
1	14.4	.	.	.	.	.	.	.	.
2	70.2	.	.	.	.	.	.	.	.
3	10.9	.	.	.	.	.	.	.	.
4	10.3	.	.	.	.	.	.	.	.
5	74.4	.	.	.	.	.	.	.	.
6	8.0	.	.	.	.	.	.	.	.
7	25.0	.	.	.	.	.	.	.	.
8	0.0	.	.	.	.	.	.	.	.
9	6.7	.	.	.	.	.	.	.	.

5. Consumer price indices (base period: 2000=100)

	2002	2003	2004	2005	2006	2007
General indices	106.2	109.8	114.5	119.4	130.3	.
Food index, including non-alcoholic beverages	107.1	112.0	118.6	125.6	140.5	.
Electricity, gas and other fuel indices [4]	105.1	107.7	112.9	107.6		.
Clothing indices, including footwear	104.5	106.6	109.0	113.2		.
Rent indices	105.0	111.2	113.8	122.4		.
General index, excluding housing	110.1	114.9				.

[1] March. [2] Persons aged 10 years and over. [3] "De jure" population. [4] Incl. water.

[1] Mars. [2] Personnes âgées de 10 ans et plus. [3] Population "de jure". [4] Y compris l'eau.

[1] Marzo. [2] Personas de 10 años y más. [3] Población "de jure". [4] Incl. el agua.

Tanzania (Zanzibar)

1. Economically active population, Employment and Unemployment ('000)

Statistics not available.

2. Population ('000), Activity rate and Unemployment rate

Statistics not available.

3. Paid employment ('000), Hours of work (weekly) and Wages

Economic activity (ISIC-Rev.2)	Paid employment 1986 Labour-related establishment survey			Hours of work			Wages		
	Total	Men	Women	Total	Men	Women	Total	Men	Women
Total	35.802	.	.	.	.	.	.	.	.
2-9	.	22.534	7.371	.	.	.	.	.	.
1	5.897	.	.	.	.	.	.	.	.
2	0.862	.	.	.	.	.	.	.	.
3	3.308	.	.	.	.	.	.	.	.
4	1.034	.	.	.	.	.	.	.	.
5	1.966	.	.	.	.	.	.	.	.
6	2.437	.	.	.	.	.	.	.	.
7	3.759	.	.	.	.	.	.	.	.
8	0.438	.	.	.	.	.	.	.	.
9	16.101	.	.	.	.	.	.	.	.

4. Occupational injuries and Strikes and Lockouts

Statistics not available.

5. Consumer price indices (base period: 2000=100)

[1]	2002	2003	2004	2005	2006	2007
General indices	105.2	114.7	124.0	136.1	.	.
Food index, including non-alcoholic beverages	106.9	116.7	128.6	143.7	.	.
Electricity, gas and other fuel indices	100.0	106.0	.	.	.	.
Clothing indices, including footwear	106.7	128.3	.	.	.	.
Rent indices	104.9	118.0	.	.	.	.

[1] Index base 2001=100.   [1] Indice base 2001=100.   [1] Indice base 2001=100.

Tchad

1. Population active, Emploi et Chômage ('000)

	Population active		Emploi		Chômage	
Groupe d'âge	Total	Femmes (%)	Total	Femmes (%)	Total	Femmes (%)
	1993 [1,2]				1986	
	Recensement de la population				Fichiers des bureaux de placement	
Total	2 719.443	47.9	.	.	4.544	0.8
0-9	145.443	45.7	.	.		
0-19					0.191	0.5
10-14	250.763	49.3	.	.	.	.
15-19	306.087	55.4	.	.		
20-24	295.558	52.0	.	.	0.586	1.5
25-29	342.277	49.2	.	.		
25-44					2.920	0.9
30-34	284.890	45.2	.	.		
35-39	245.749	45.7	.	.		
40-44	214.920	46.7	.	.		
45-49	149.636	45.8	.	.		
45-54					0.847	0.0
50-54	148.894	47.1	.	.		
55-59	77.330	44.1	.	.		
60-64	102.263	45.0	.	.		
65+	148.705	38.6	.	.		
?	6.928	53.5	.	.	.	.

Activité économique (CITI-Rév.2)					1990	
					Fichiers des bureaux de placement	
Total	.	.	.	.	2.392	3.0
1 Agriculture, chasse, sylviculture et pêche	.	.	.	.	0.026	3.8
2 Industries extractives	.	.	.	.	-	-
3 Industries manufacturières	.	.	.	.	0.043	0.0
4 Electricité, gaz et eau	.	.	.	.	0.053	0.0
5 Bâtiment et travaux publics	.	.	.	.	0.526	0.0
6 Commerce de gros et de détail; restaurants et hôtels	.	.	.	.	0.083	20.5
7 Transports, entrepôts et communications	.	.	.	.	0.809	0.0
8 Banques, assurances, affaires immobilières et services ...	.	.	.	.	0.043	2.3
9 Services fournis à la collectivité, services sociaux ...	.	.	.	.	0.595	8.9
0 Activités mal désignées	.	.	.	.	0.213	0.0

Niveau d'instruction (CITE-76)					1993 [3]	
					Recensement de la population	
Total	.	.	.	.	16.293	.
X Non scolarisé	.	.	.	.	6.921	.
1 Premier degré	.	.	.	.	3.753	.
2-3	.	.	.	.	3.669	.
5 Troisième degré, premier niveau, conduisant à un titre ...	.	.	.	.	0.985	.
6-7	.	.	.	.	0.955	.
? Niveau inconnu	.	.	.	.	0.010	.

2. Population ('000), Taux d'activité et Taux de chômage

	Population			Taux d'activité			Taux de chômage		
Groupe d'âge	1993 [2]			1993 [2]			1993 [3]		
	Recensement de la population			Recensement de la population			Recensement de la population		
	Total	Hommes	Femmes	Total	Hommes	Femmes	Total	Hommes	Femmes
Total	6 193.5	3 001.4	3 192.2	43.9	47.2	40.8	0.6	.	.
15+	3 203.9	1 490.5	1 713.4	72.3	81.0	64.7	.	.	.
15-24	1 064.6	497.1	567.5	56.5	56.0	56.9	.	.	.
25-54	1 712.0	781.4	930.6	81.0	94.4	69.7	.	.	.
55+	427.3	212.0	215.3	76.8	89.9	63.9	.	.	.

3. Emploi rémunéré ('000), Durée du travail (hebdomadaire) et Salaires

Activité économique (CITI-Rév.2)	Emploi rémunéré			Durée du travail			Salaires		
	1997 [4]								
	Enquête auprès des établissements, relative au travail								
	Total	Hommes	Femmes	Total	Hommes	Femmes	Total	Hommes	Femmes
Total	13.522	.	.	.	.	.	.	.	.
1	0.240	.	.	.	.	.	.	.	.
2	0.208	.	.	.	.	.	.	.	.
3	5.359	.	.	.	.	.	.	.	.
4	0.476	.	.	.	.	.	.	.	.
5	1.815	.	.	.	.	.	.	.	.
6	0.616	.	.	.	.	.	.	.	.
7	1.130	.	.	.	.	.	.	.	.
8	0.615	.	.	.	.	.	.	.	.
9	2.981	.	.	.	.	.	.	.	.
0	0.082	.	.	.	.	.	.	.	.

4. Lésions professionnelles et Grèves et lock-out

Données non disponibles.

Tchad

5. Indices des prix à la consommation (période de base: 2000=100)

N'Djamena	2002	2003	2004	2005	2006	2007
Indices généraux	117.5	115.4	109.3	117.8	127.5	115.9
Indices de l'alimentation, y compris les boissons non alcoolisées	125.8	122.6	116.0	129.2	144.0	.
Indices de l'électricité, gaz et autres combustibles	119.6	126.8	115.4	130.6	149.0	.
Indices de l'habillement, y compris les chaussures	112.3	107.1	87.2	78.6	75.2	.
Indices du loyer	96.7	96.9	107.1	127.3	133.6	.

[1] Persons aged 6 years and over. [2] April. [3] Persons aged 15 years and over. [4] Excl. unpaid family workers.

[1] Personnes âgées de 6 ans et plus. [2] Avril. [3] Personnes âgées de 15 ans et plus. [4] Non compris les travailleurs familiaux non rémunérés.

[1] Personas de 6 años y más. [2] Abril. [3] Personas de 15 años y más. [4] Excl. los trabajadores familiares no remunerados.

Thailand

1. Economically active population, Employment and Unemployment ('000)

	Economically active population		Employment		Unemployment	
	Total	Women (%)	Total	Women (%)	Total	Women (%)
Age group	2007 [1,2] Labour force survey		2007 ★ Labour force survey		2007 [1,2] Labour force survey	
Total	37 611.7	46.2	37 169.4	46.2	442.3	41.6
15-19	1 498.4	37.8	1 424.5	37.4	73.9	45.9
20-24	3 715.7	43.1	3 556.7	43.4	159.0	37.6
25-29	4 663.4	45.5	4 595.6	45.4	67.8	49.9
30-34	4 890.6	47.2	4 849.9	47.4	40.7	30.7
35-39	5 031.9	48.9	5 003.8	49.0	28.1	42.7
40-49	9 195.9	48.4	9 152.7	48.4	43.2	43.8
50-59	5 828.7	46.1	5 805.9	46.2	22.8	38.6
60+	2 787.1	41.7	2 780.3	41.6	6.8	66.2

Economic activity (ISIC-Rev.3)			2007 [1,2,3] Labour force survey			
Total	.	.	37 122.2	46.2	.	.
A Agriculture, Hunting and Forestry	.	.	15 081.8	44.8	.	.
B Fishing	.	.	410.0	22.5	.	.
C Mining and Quarrying	.	.	53.9	21.3	.	.
D Manufacturing	.	.	5 593.0	52.8	.	.
E Electricity, Gas and Water Supply	.	.	104.9	14.4	.	.
F Construction	.	.	1 938.7	16.5	.	.
G Wholesale and Retail Trade; Repair of Motor Vehicles ...	.	.	5 525.4	48.3	.	.
H Hotels and Restaurants	.	.	2 302.5	66.9	.	.
I Transport, Storage and Communications	.	.	1 026.5	14.9	.	.
J Financial Intermediation	.	.	350.2	56.5	.	.
K Real Estate, Renting and Business Activities	.	.	717.4	41.9	.	.
L Public Administration and Defence; Compulsory Social ...	.	.	1 286.9	30.8	.	.
M Education	.	.	1 085.0	56.4	.	.
N Health and Social Work	.	.	647.2	76.1	.	.
O Other Community, Social and Personal Service Activities	.	.	718.0	57.5	.	.
P Households with Employed Persons	.	.	229.1	86.1	.	.
Q Extra-Territorial Organizations and Bodies	.	.	1.1	18.2	.	.
X Not classifiable by economic activity	.	.	50.6	45.1	.	.

Occupation (ISCO-88)	2007 ★ Labour force survey		2007 [1,2,3] Labour force survey		2007 [1,2] Labour force survey	
Total	37 566.3	46.1	37 124.0	46.2	442.3	41.6
1 Legislators, senior officials and managers	2 486.4	29.8	2 480.0	29.7	6.4	43.8
2 Professionals	1 481.1	56.8	1 478.0	56.8	3.1	51.6
3 Technicians and associate professionals	1 577.9	50.2	1 569.0	50.2	8.9	56.2
4 Clerks	1 384.5	67.7	1 361.0	67.8	23.5	59.1
5 Service workers and shop and market sales workers	5 233.5	64.7	5 186.0	64.8	47.5	56.6
6 Skilled agricultural and fishery workers	14 247.4	44.8	14 219.0	44.7	28.4	59.9
7 Craft and related trade workers	3 912.3	32.5	3 856.0	32.6	56.3	23.8
8 Plant and machine operators and assemblers	3 008.5	31.1	2 966.0	31.0	42.5	38.4
9 Elementary occupations	4 015.1	49.7	3 956.0	49.9	59.1	37.2
X Not classifiable by occupation	53.7	42.3	53.0	41.5	0.7	100.0
Unemployed seeking their first job	.	.	.	.	165.9	38.9

Education level (ISCED-97)					2007 [1,2] Labour force survey	
Total	.	.	.	.	442.3	41.6
X No schooling	.	.	.	.	61.5	52.8
1 Primary education or first stage of basic education	.	.	.	.	76.2	30.3
2 Lower secondary or second stage of basic education	.	.	.	.	103.1	38.9
3 Upper secondary education	.	.	.	.	76.8	37.5
4 Post-secondary non-tertiary education	.	.	.	.	124.3	48.0
6 Second stage of tertiary education	.	.	.	.	0.4	.

Status in employment (ICSE-1993)			2007 [1,2,3] Labour force survey			
Total	.	.	37 122.0	46.2	.	.
1 Employees	.	.	16 175.0	45.0	.	.
2 Employers	.	.	1 101.3	23.7	.	.
3 Own-account workers	.	.	11 866.5	37.6	.	.
4 Members of producers' cooperatives	.	.	51.6	58.5	.	.
5 Contributing family workers	.	.	7 927.6	64.6	.	.

2. Population ('000), Activity rate and Unemployment rate

	Population 2007 [2] Labour force survey			Activity rate 2007 [2] Labour force survey			Unemployment rate 2007 [1,2] Labour force survey		
Age group	Total	Men	Women	Total	Men	Women	Total	Men	Women
Total	65 800.1	32 286.1	33 514.0	57.2	62.7	51.8	1.2	1.3	1.1
15+	51 118.8	24 789.8	26 329.0	73.6	81.7	66.0	1.2	1.3	1.1
15-24	10 539.6	5 368.1	5 171.5	49.5	56.7	41.9	4.5	4.6	4.3

Thailand

3. Paid employment ('000), Hours of work (weekly) and Wages

Economic activity (ISIC-Rev.2)	Paid employment 1993 Labour-related establishment survey			Hours of work			Wages		
	Total	Men	Women	Total	Men	Women	Total	Men	Women
Total	4 911.787	.	.	.	.	.	.	.	.
2	24.580	.	.	.	.	.	.	.	.
3	2 576.777	.	.	.	.	.	.	.	.
4	109.657	.	.	.	.	.	.	.	.
5	377.014	.	.	.	.	.	.	.	.
6	917.509	.	.	.	.	.	.	.	.
7	256.308	.	.	.	.	.	.	.	.
8	356.567	.	.	.	.	.	.	.	.
9	293.375	.	.	.	.	.	.	.	.

Economic activity (ISIC-Rev.3)	Paid employment			Hours of work 2003 Labour force survey Hours actually worked / Employees			Wages 2007 Labour force survey Wage rates per month / Employees / Baht		
	Total	Men	Women	Total	Men	Women	Total	Men	Women
Total	.	.	.	48.9	.	.	7 357.4	.	.
A	.	.	.	41.6	.	.	3 284.3	.	.
B	.	.	.	61.7	.	.	5 258.0	.	.
C	.	.	.	50.4	.	.	9 325.0	.	.
D	.	.	.	50.5	.	.	6 999.2	.	.
E	.	.	.	45.5	.	.	14 613.9	.	.
F	.	.	.	49.7	.	.	5 477.8	.	.
G	.	.	.	50.4	.	.	7 455.6	.	.
H	.	.	.	51.9	.	.	6 011.1	.	.
I	.	.	.	49.1	.	.	11 745.9	.	.
J	.	.	.	49.5	.	.	18 364.0	.	.
K	.	.	.	52.2	.	.	10 792.6	.	.
L	.	.	.	.	.	.	11 924.5	.	.
M	.	.	.	39.3	.	.	13 531.8	.	.
N	.	.	.	49.9	.	.	10 177.9	.	.
O	.	.	.	46.4	.	.	6 825.6	.	.
P	.	.	.	58.3	.	.	4 903.1	.	.
Q	.	.	.	.	.	.	33 664.2	.	.
X	.	.	.	.	.	.	11 087.3	.	.

4. Occupational injuries and Strikes and Lockouts

Economic activity (ISIC-Rev.3)	Rates of fatal injuries 2007 Insurance records Per 100,000 workers insured Compensated injuries			Rates of non-fatal injuries 2007 [4] Insurance records Per 100,000 workers insured Compensated injuries			Strikes and lockouts 2007 Special data collection		
	Total	Men	Women	Total	Men	Women	Strikes and lockouts	Workers involved	Days not worked
Total	9.1	.	.	658	.	.	5	620	11 601
A	.	.	.	.	.	.	0	0	0
B	.	.	.	.	.	.	0	0	0
C	.	.	.	.	.	.	0	0	0
D	.	.	.	.	.	.	5	620	11 601
E	.	.	.	.	.	.	0	0	0
F	.	.	.	.	.	.	0	0	0
G-H	.	.	.	.	.	.	0	0	0
I	.	.	.	.	.	.	0	0	0
J-K	.	.	.	.	.	.	0	0	0
L-O	.	.	.	.	.	.	0	0	0

5. Consumer price indices (base period: 2000=100)

	2002	2003	2004	2005	2006	2007
General indices	102.3	104.1	107.0	111.8	117.0	119.6
Food index, including non-alcoholic beverages	101.0	104.7	109.4	114.9	120.1	125.0
Electricity, gas and other fuel indices	109.3	111.1	116.0	119.0	127.1	126.4
Clothing indices, including footwear	101.4	101.5	101.7	102.1	102.3	102.5
Rent indices	99.1	97.8	97.2	97.5	97.7	97.9

[1] Persons aged 15 years and over. [2] Third quarter. [3] Excl. armed forces. [4] Incapacity of 3 days or more.

[1] Personnes âgées de 15 ans et plus. [2] Troisième trimestre. [3] Non compris les forces armées. [4] Incapacité de 3 jours et plus.

[1] Personas de 15 años y más. [2] Tercer trimestre. [3] Excl. las fuerzas armadas. [4] Incapacidad de 3 días y más.

Togo

1. Population active, Emploi et Chômage ('000)

	Population active		Emploi		Chômage	
	Total	Femmes (%)	Total	Femmes (%)	Total	Femmes (%)
Groupe d'âge	1981 [1,2] Recensement de la population		1987 Enquête sur la main-d'oeuvre			
Total	901.5	43.8	4 137.7	.	.	.
10-14	39.7	45.4	.	.	.	.
15-19	97.4	48.4	.	.	.	.
20-24	115.2	48.8	.	.	.	.
25-29	143.4	46.6	.	.	.	.
30-39	200.6	45.2	.	.	.	.
40-49	137.7	40.9	.	.	.	.
50-59	75.0	38.6	.	.	.	.
60+	90.4	33.3	.	.	.	.
?	2.2	41.0	.	.	.	.

2. Population ('000), Taux d'activité et Taux de chômage

	Population			Taux d'activité			Taux de chômage		
Groupe d'âge	1981 [2] Recensement de la population			1981 [2] Recensement de la population					
	Total	Hommes	Femmes	Total	Hommes	Femmes	Total	Hommes	Femmes
Total	2 722.6	1 327.6	1 394.9	33.1	38.1	28.3	.	.	.
15+	1 367.8	625.6	742.2	62.9	77.3	50.7	.	.	.
15-24	471.0	221.4	249.6	45.1	49.3	41.4	.	.	.

3. Emploi rémunéré ('000), Durée du travail (hebdomadaire) et Salaires

Activité économique (CITI-Rév.2)	Emploi rémunéré 1997 Fichiers des assurances			Durée du travail			Salaires		
	Total	Hommes	Femmes	Total	Hommes	Femmes	Total	Hommes	Femmes
Total	49.136	.	.	.	.	.	.	.	.
1	4.013	.	.	.	.	.	.	.	.
2	2.726	.	.	.	.	.	.	.	.
3	3.200	.	.	.	.	.	.	.	.
4	2.145	.	.	.	.	.	.	.	.
5	2.640	.	.	.	.	.	.	.	.
6 [3]	5.194	.	.	.	.	.	.	.	.
7	3.748	.	.	.	.	.	.	.	.
9	33.309	.	.	.	.	.	.	.	.

4. Lésions professionnelles et Grèves et lock-out

Activité économique (CITI-Rév.2)	Taux de lésions mortelles 2004 Fichiers des assurances Pour 100 000 salariés Lésions déclarées			Taux de lésions non mortelles 2004 Fichiers des assurances Pour 100 000 salariés Lésions déclarées			Grèves et lock-out 1983 Source inconnue		
	Total	Hommes	Femmes	Total	Hommes	Femmes	Grèves et lock-out	Travailleurs impliqués	Journées non effectuées
Total	16.3	.	.	484	.	.	205	.	.
2	0.0	.	.	1 333	.	.	.	.	.
3	57.8	.	.	1 878	.	.	.	.	.
4	54.7	.	.	1 284	.	.	.	.	.
5	0.0	.	.	172	.	.	.	.	.
6,8	10.7	.	.	171	.	.	.	.	.
7	22.9	.	.	1 029	.	.	.	.	.
9	6.7	.	.	157	.	.	.	.	.

5. Indices des prix à la consommation (période de base: 2000=100)

Lomé	2002	2003	2004	2005	2006	2007
Indices généraux	107.1	106.0	106.5	113.7	116.3	117.3
Indices de l'alimentation, y compris les boissons non alcoolisées [4]	109.3	103.1	101.9	113.0	111.7	114.9
Indices de l'habillement, y compris les chaussures	98.9	103.8	110.4	111.5	110.8	108.8
Indices du loyer [5]	103.7	104.8	104.9	108.1	115.8	118.1

[1] Persons aged 10 years and over. [2] Nov. [3] Incl. major division 8. [4] Incl. alcoholic beverages and tobacco. [5] Incl. water, electricity, gas and other fuels.

[1] Personnes âgées de 10 ans et plus. [2] Nov. [3] Y compris la branche 8. [4] Y compris les boissons alcoolisées et le tabac. [5] Y compris l'eau, l'électricité, le gaz et autres combustibles.

[1] Personas de 10 años y más. [2] Nov. [3] Incl. la gran división 8. [4] Incl. las bebidas alcohólicas y el tabaco. [5] Incl. el agua, la electricidad, el gas y otros combustibles.

Tonga

1. Economically active population, Employment and Unemployment ('000)

	Economically active population		Employment		Unemployment	
	Total	Women (%)	Total	Women (%)	Total	Women (%)
Age group	1996 [1,2] Population census		1996 ★ Population census		2003 [1] Labour force survey	
Total	33.908	36.0	29.406	37.4	1.889	59.9
15-19	2.528	28.9	1.444	28.8	0.281	39.5
20-24	5.627	36.7	4.242	38.3	0.532	55.1
25-29	5.604	36.0	.	.	0.295	57.3
30-34	4.215	35.5	.	.	0.313	73.8
35-39	3.249	38.1	.	.	0.201	57.7
40-44	2.874	40.4	.	.	0.093	94.6
45-49	2.432	41.1	.	.	0.020	100.0
50-54	2.137	37.6	.	.	0.027	100.0
55-59	1.923	32.7	.	.	0.039	48.7
60-64	1.500	32.2	.	.	0.040	47.5
65+	.	.	.	.	0.048	79.2
65-69	1.012	33.1	.	.	.	.
70-74	0.507	32.1	.	.	.	.
75+	0.300	30.7	.	.	.	.

Economic activity (ISIC-Rev.3)			2003 [1] Labour force survey			
Total	.	.	34.56	40.9	.	.
A Agriculture, Hunting and Forestry	.	.	9.95	4.7	.	.
B Fishing	.	.	1.05	17.1	.	.
C Mining and Quarrying	.	.	0.06	0.0	.	.
D Manufacturing	.	.	8.53	89.4	.	.
E Electricity, Gas and Water Supply	.	.	0.53	30.2	.	.
F Construction	.	.	1.44	2.1	.	.
G Wholesale and Retail Trade; Repair of Motor Vehicles ...	.	.	2.93	54.3	.	.
H Hotels and Restaurants	.	.	0.63	63.5	.	.
I Transport, Storage and Communications	.	.	1.58	27.2	.	.
J Financial Intermediation	.	.	0.51	56.9	.	.
K Real Estate, Renting and Business Activities	.	.	0.26	34.6	.	.
L Public Administration and Defence; Compulsory Social ...	.	.	2.59	26.6	.	.
M Education	.	.	1.78	59.6	.	.
N Health and Social Work	.	.	0.66	57.6	.	.
O Other Community, Social and Personal Service Activities	.	.	1.33	25.6	.	.
P Households with Employed Persons	.	.	0.61	57.4	.	.
Q Extra-Territorial Organizations and Bodies	.	.	0.09	33.3	.	.

Occupation (ISCO-88)			2003 [1] Labour force survey			
Total	.	.	34.56	40.9	.	.
1 Legislators, senior officials and managers	.	.	0.94	26.6	.	.
2 Professionals	.	.	1.96	48.5	.	.
3 Technicians and associate professionals	.	.	2.11	37.4	.	.
4 Clerks	.	.	1.93	70.5	.	.
5 Service workers and shop and market sales workers	.	.	4.35	56.3	.	.
6 Skilled agricultural and fishery workers	.	.	10.40	4.5	.	.
7 Craft and related trade workers	.	.	10.12	74.0	.	.
8 Plant and machine operators and assemblers	.	.	1.00	2.0	.	.
9 Elementary occupations	.	.	1.54	21.4	.	.
0 Armed forces	.	.	0.22	18.2	.	.

Status in employment (ICSE-1993)			1996 [1,2] Population census			
Total	.	.	29.406	37.4	.	.
1 Employees	.	.	12.424	35.6	.	.
2 Employers	.	.	0.149	21.5	.	.
3 Own-account workers	.	.	7.603	36.9	.	.
5 Contributing family workers	.	.	9.159	40.4	.	.
6 Not classifiable by status	.	.	0.071	59.2	.	.

2. Population ('000), Activity rate and Unemployment rate

	Population			Activity rate			Unemployment rate		
Age group	1996 [2] Population census			1996 [2] Population census			1996 [1,2] Population census		
	Total	Men	Women	Total	Men	Women	Total	Men	Women
Total	96.020	48.663	47.357	35.3	44.6	25.8	13.3	15.2	9.9
15+	58.106	28.822	29.284	58.4	75.3	41.7	13.3	15.2	9.9
15-24	19.388	9.938	9.450	42.1	53.9	29.6	30.3	32.0	27.0
25-54	28.353	13.788	14.565	72.3	92.8	53.0	.	.	.
55+	10.365	5.096	5.269	50.6	69.5	32.3	.	.	.

Tonga

3. Paid employment ('000), Hours of work (weekly) and Wages

Economic activity (ISIC-Rev.2)	Paid employment 1980 Labour-related establishment survey			Hours of work 1994[3] Labour force survey Hours paid for / Employees			Wages 1994[3] Labour force survey Earnings per week / Employees / Pa'anga		
	Total	Men	Women	Total	Men	Women	Total	Men	Women
Total	.	.	.	39.9	.	.	96.4	.	.
1	.	.	.	43.5	.	.	80.6	.	.
2	.	.	.	34.5	.	.	64.0	.	.
3	1.116	0.747	0.369	38.5	.	.	66.6	.	.
4	.	.	.	39.0	.	.	76.0	.	.
5	.	.	.	42.9	.	.	91.4	.	.
6	.	.	.	44.6	.	.	71.0	.	.
7	.	.	.	45.0	.	.	85.4	.	.
8	.	.	.	39.2	.	.	88.7	.	.
9	.	.	.	38.3	.	.	106.6	.	.

4. Occupational injuries and Strikes and Lockouts

Statistics not available.

5. Consumer price indices (base period: 2000=100)

	2002	2003	2004	2005	2006	2007
General indices [4]	119.5	133.5	148.1	160.4	172.0	180.8
Food index, including non-alcoholic beverages	130.6	143.1	156.1	165.5	170.4	182.9
Clothing indices, including footwear [5]	100.0	111.5	118.2	131.2	144.7	153.2
Rent indices [5]	100.0	102.1	109.1	121.8	138.2	144.1

[1] Persons aged 15 years and over. [2] Nov. [3] 1993/1994 survey. [4] Excl. "Rent". [5] Index base 2002=100.

[1] Personnes âgées de 15 ans et plus. [2] Nov. [3] Enquête 1993/1994. [4] Non compris le groupe "Loyer". [5] Indice base 2002=100.

[1] Personas de 15 años y más. [2] Nov. [3] Encuesta 1993/1994. [4] Excl. el grupo "Alquiler". [5] Indice base 2002=100.

Trinidad and Tobago

1. Economically active population, Employment and Unemployment ('000)

	Economically active population		Employment		Unemployment	
	Total	Women (%)	Total	Women (%)	Total	Women (%)
Age group	2005 [1] Labour force survey		2005 ★ Labour force survey		2005 [1] Labour force survey	
Total	623.7	41.5	574.0	40.1	49.7	57.1
15-19	34.4	38.1	26.6	34.2	7.8	51.3
20-24	97.3	42.2	83.4	40.0	13.9	55.4
25-29	89.8	42.5	83.4	41.4	6.4	57.8
30-34	71.7	43.0	67.1	41.9	4.6	58.7
35-39	71.0	43.2	66.9	42.0	4.1	63.4
40-44	75.1	40.9	70.9	39.6	4.2	61.9
45-49	67.5	40.7	64.3	39.7	3.2	62.5
50-54	56.1	42.1	53.8	41.4	2.3	56.5
55-59	36.0	40.3	34.2	39.2	1.8	61.1
60-64	14.8	39.2	13.7	38.0	1.1	54.5
65+	10.1	27.7	9.9	27.3	0.2	50.0
Economic activity (ISIC-Rev.2)	2005 ★ Labour force survey		2005 [1] Labour force survey		2005 [1] Labour force survey	
Total	623.7	41.5	574.0	40.1	49.7	57.1
1 Agriculture, Hunting, Forestry and Fishing	26.5	15.5	24.8	15.7	1.7	11.8
2 Mining and Quarrying	22.2	19.4	20.4 [2]	17.6	1.8 [2]	38.9
3 Manufacturing	59.0	30.8	55.6	30.4	3.4	38.2
4 Electricity, Gas and Water	7.1	22.5	6.9 [3]	20.3	0.2 [3]	100.0
5 Construction	112.2	20.1	94.8	15.4	17.4	46.0
6 Wholesale and Retail Trade and Restaurants and Hotels	112.9	58.9	103.5	57.1	9.4	78.7
7 Transport, Storage and Communication	43.5	20.7	41.8	19.9	1.7	41.2
8 Financing, Insurance, Real Estate and Business Services	47.1	52.2	45.0	51.6	2.1	66.7
9 Community, Social and Personal Services	190.0	56.1	178.5	55.1	11.5	71.3
0 Activities not Adequately Defined	3.0	43.3	2.5	40.0	0.5	60.0
Occupation (ISCO-88)	2005 ★ Labour force survey		2005 [1] Labour force survey		2005 [1] Labour force survey	
Total	623.7	41.5	574.0	40.1	49.7	57.1
1 Legislators, senior officials and managers	46.7	43.5	46.0	43.5	0.7	42.9
2 Professionals	19.7	46.7	19.1	46.6	0.6	50.0
3 Technicians and associate professionals	67.5	55.3	65.5	55.3	2.0	55.0
4 Clerks	79.6	77.0	71.7	76.3	7.9	83.5
5, 0	90.8	58.9	82.5	56.4	8.3	84.3
6 Skilled agricultural and fishery workers	15.0	11.3	14.8	11.5	0.2	.
7 Craft and related trade workers	96.3	10.9	90.5	10.9	5.8	10.3
8 Plant and machine operators and assemblers	53.5	8.8	51.5	8.5	2.0	15.0
9 Elementary occupations	152.1	39.2	130.1	36.5	22.0	55.0
X Not classifiable by occupation	2.4	33.3	2.1	28.6	0.3	66.7
Education level (ISCED-76)					2002 [1] Labour force survey	
Total	.	.	.	.	61.1	54.5
X No schooling	.	.	.	.	0.1	.
0 Education preceding the first level	.	.	.	.	1.2	58.3
1 First level	.	.	.	.	19.7	48.2
2 Second level, first stage	.	.	.	.	14.3	59.4
3 Second level, second stage	.	.	.	.	24.8	55.6
5 Third level, first stage, leading to an award not equivalent ...	.	.	.	.	0.3	66.7
6-7	.	.	.	.	0.8	62.5
9 Education not definable by level	.	.	.	.	0.1	100.0
Status in employment (ICSE-1993)			2005 [1] Labour force survey			
Total	.	.	574.0	40.1	.	.
1 Employees	.	.	453.7	42.2	.	.
2 Employers	.	.	25.3	25.3	.	.
3 Own-account workers	.	.	84.8	31.0	.	.
5 Contributing family workers	.	.	5.0	80.0	.	.
6 Not classifiable by status	.	.	5.2	48.1	.	.

2. Population ('000), Activity rate and Unemployment rate

	Population 2005 Labour force survey			Activity rate 2005 Labour force survey			Unemployment rate 2005 [1] Labour force survey		
Age group	Total	Men	Women	Total	Men	Women	Total	Men	Women
Total	978.9	485.0	493.9	.	.	.	8.0	5.8	11.0
15+	.	.	.	63.7	75.3	52.4	8.0	5.8	11.0
15-24	244.7	124.6	120.1	53.8	62.2	45.1	16.5	12.9	21.6
25-54	527.1	265.3	261.8	81.8	94.1	69.3	5.8	4.0	8.2
55+	207.1	95.1	112.0	29.4	39.7	20.6	5.1	3.4	7.8

Trinidad and Tobago

3. Paid employment ('000), Hours of work (weekly) and Wages

Economic activity (ISIC-Rev.2)	Paid employment 2002[1] Labour force survey			Hours of work			Wages		
	Total	Men	Women	Total	Men	Women	Total	Men	Women
Total	405.7	244.2	161.5	.	.	.	.	.	.
1	20.1	18.3	1.8	.	.	.	.	.	.
2	17.5	14.7	2.8	.	.	.	.	.	.
3	48.2	33.7	14.5	.	.	.	.	.	.
4	6.5	5.6	0.9	.	.	.	.	.	.
5	56.7	48.9	7.8	.	.	.	.	.	.
6	61.8	27.6	34.2	.	.	.	.	.	.
7	25.3	17.7	7.6	.	.	.	.	.	.
8	39.8	18.9	20.9	.	.	.	.	.	.
9	125.8	56.1	69.7	.	.	.	.	.	.
0	4.0	2.4	1.6	.	.	.	.	.	.

Economic activity (ISIC-Rev.3)	Paid employment			Hours of work			Wages 2002 Labour-related establishment survey Earnings per week / Employees / Dollar		
	Total	Men	Women	Total	Men	Women	Total	Men	Women
D	.	.	.	.	.	.	1 161.63	.	.
E	.	.	.	.	.	.	2 564.24	.	.

4. Occupational injuries and Strikes and Lockouts

Economic activity (ISIC-Rev.2)	Rates of fatal injuries 2006 Labour inspectorate records Per 100,000 workers employed Reported injuries			Rates of non-fatal injuries 2006 Labour inspectorate records Per 100,000 workers employed Reported injuries			Strikes and lockouts 2004 Labour relations records		
	Total	Men	Women	Total	Men	Women	Strikes and lockouts	Workers involved	Days not worked
Total	1.9	.	.	64	.	.	22	7 469	1 583 373
1	0.0	.	.	0	.	.	0	0	0
2	4.9	.	.	161	.	.	15	3 420	7 064
3	1.8	.	.	463	.	.	3	1 404	292 667
4	39.0	.	.	26	.	.	0	0	0
5	2.1	.	.	10	.	.	1	2 500	1 275 000
6	0.0	.	.	103	.	.	1	0	0
7	2.3	.	.	37	.	.	2	145	8 642
8	0.0	.	.	37	.	.	0	0	0
9	1.1	.	.	1	.	.	0	0	0
0	.	.	.	0	.	.	0	0	0

5. Consumer price indices (base period: 2000=100)

	2002	2003	2004	2005	2006	2007
General indices	109.9	114.2	118.3	126.5	137.0	147.9
Food index, including non-alcoholic beverages	125.6	142.9	161.1	198.1	244.1	286.6
Electricity, gas and other fuel indices [4]	101.2	101.8	103.2	103.9	105.3	107.1
Clothing indices, including footwear	96.4	95.3	90.1	88.6	88.1	90.0
Rent indices	102.5	105.9	110.8	117.1	121.4	126.4

[1] Persons aged 15 years and over. [2] Incl. petroleum and gas extraction. [3] Excl. gas. [4] Incl. water.

[1] Personnes âgées de 15 ans et plus. [2] Y compris l'extraction du pétrole et du gaz. [3] Non compris le gaz. [4] Y compris l'eau.

[1] Personas de 15 años y más. [2] Incl. extracción de petróleo y gas. [3] Excl. gas. [4] Incl. el agua.

Tunisie

1. Population active, Emploi et Chômage ('000)

	Population active		Emploi		Chômage	
	Total	Femmes (%)	Total	Femmes (%)	Total	Femmes (%)
Groupe d'âge	2005 [1]		2005 ★		2005 [1]	
	Enquête sur la main-d'oeuvre		Enquête sur la main-d'oeuvre		Enquête sur la main-d'oeuvre	
Total	3 415.0	26.6	2 928.6	25.7	486.4	32.4
15-19	218.4	31.4	150.7	33.2	67.7	27.3
20-24	452.7	33.5	314.5	33.6	138.2	33.4
25-29	565.2	34.3	433.2	33.1	132.0	38.3
30-34	494.1	30.0	429.7	29.0	64.4	37.3
35-39	445.6	25.3	413.6	24.9	32.0	30.6
40-44	396.6	22.0	374.6	22.0	22.0	21.8
45+	842.3	17.4	.	.	.	.
45-54	.	.	.	.	23.3	13.7
55+	.	.	.	.	6.7	7.5

Activité économique (CITI-Rév.3)			1989 [1]			
			Enquête sur la main-d'oeuvre			
Total	.	.	1 978.8	19.5	.	.
A-B	.	.	509.7	17.2	.	.
C,E	.	.	35.2	4.8	.	.
D Activités de fabrication	.	.	382.7	43.3	.	.
F Construction	.	.	247.6	1.1	.	.
G Commerce de gros et de détail; réparation de véhicules ...	.	.	213.8	6.0	.	.
H Hôtels et restaurants	.	.	49.1	9.4	.	.
I Transports, entreposage et communications	.	.	95.8	5.5	.	.
J Intermédiation financière	.	.	15.4	29.9	.	.
K Immobilier, locations et activités de services aux entreprises	.	.	51.7	42.0	.	.
L Administration publique et défense; sécurité sociale obligatoire	.	.	177.9	8.5	.	.
M Education	.	.	104.8	33.1	.	.
N Santé et action sociale	.	.	42.2	43.6	.	.
O Autres activités de services collectifs, sociaux et personnels	.	.	22.2	29.3	.	.
X Ne pouvant être classés selon l'activité économique	.	.	30.7	14.7	.	.

Profession (CITP-1968)					1989 [2][3]	
					Fichiers des bureaux de placement	
Total	.	.	.	.	111.78	
0/1 Personnel des professions scientifiques, techniques ...	.	.	.	.	0.69	
2 Directeurs et cadres administratifs supérieurs	.	.	.	.	-	
3 Personnel administratif et travailleurs assimilés	.	.	.	.	1.33	
4 Personnel commercial et vendeurs	.	.	.	.	0.09	
5 Travailleurs spécialisés dans les services	.	.	.	.	1.93	
6 Agriculteurs, éleveurs, forestiers, pêcheurs et chasseurs	.	.	.	.	0.45	
7/8/9 Ouvriers et manoeuvres non agricoles et conducteurs ...	.	.	.	.	59.11	
Chômeurs n'ayant jamais travaillé [4]	.	.	.	.	48.18	

Niveau d'instruction (CITE-76)	1997		1997 ★		2005 [1]	
	Enquête sur la main-d'oeuvre		Enquête sur la main-d'oeuvre		Enquête sur la main-d'oeuvre	
Total	2 978.3	24.3	2 503.5	23.9	486.4	32.4
X Non scolarisé	565.0	31.0	507.4	30.9	35.3	27.8
0 Enseignement précédant le premier degré [5]	1 316.6	19.8	1 062.9	18.9	201.5	25.0
2 Second degré, premier cycle [6]	885.8	25.1	739.5	24.6	183.2	33.1
5 Troisième degré, premier niveau, conduisant à un titre ... [7]	210.9	30.4	193.8	29.8	66.2	55.4
? Niveau inconnu	.	.	.	.	0.2	50.0

Situation dans la profession (CISP-1993)			2003 [1]			
			Enquête sur la main-d'oeuvre			
Total	.	.	2 951.2	.	.	.
1 Salariés	.	.	1 896.5	.	.	.
2, 3	.	.	791.9	.	.	.
5 Travailleurs familiaux collaborant à l'entreprise familiale	.	.	257.4	.	.	.
6 Inclassables d'après la situation	.	.	5.4	.	.	.

2. Population ('000), Taux d'activité et Taux de chômage

	Population			Taux d'activité			Taux de chômage		
Groupe d'âge	2005			2005			2005 [1]		
	Enquête sur la main-d'oeuvre			Enquête sur la main-d'oeuvre			Enquête sur la main-d'oeuvre		
	Total	Hommes	Femmes	Total	Hommes	Femmes	Total	Hommes	Femmes
Total	.	.	.	.	.	.	14.2	13.1	17.3
15+	7 382.8	3 652.1	3 730.8	46.3	68.6	24.4	14.2	13.1	17.3
15-24	2 043.1	1 027.7	1 015.4	32.8	43.9	21.7	30.7	31.4	29.3

3. Emploi rémunéré ('000), Durée du travail (hebdomadaire) et Salaires

Activité économique (CITI-Rév.2)	Emploi rémunéré			Durée du travail			Salaires		
	2000						1994		
	Rapports administratifs						Législation		
							Taux de salaire par jour / Ouvriers / Dinar		
	Total	Hommes	Femmes	Total	Hommes	Femmes	Total	Hommes	Femmes
1	.	.	.	.	.	.	4.46	.	.
2	2.663 [8]	.	.	.	.	.	.	.	.
3	294.224	.	.	.	.	.	.	.	.
4	17.885	.	.	.	.	.	.	.	.

Tunisie

4. Lésions professionnelles et Grèves et lock-out

Activité économique (CITI-Rév.3)	Taux de lésions mortelles 2004 Fichiers des assurances Pour 100 000 travailleurs assurés Lésions indemnisées			Taux de lésions non mortelles 2004 [9] Fichiers des assurances Pour 100 000 travailleurs assurés Lésions indemnisées			Grèves et lock-out 2007 Fichiers des relations du travail		
	Total	Hommes	Femmes	Total	Hommes	Femmes	Grèves et lock-out	Travailleurs impliqués [10]	Journées non effectuées
Total	13.1	.	.	3 639	.	.	382	98 210	107 515
A	28.7	.	.	1 958	.	.	14	1 907	2 789
B	28.3	.	.	1 335	.	.	4	639	318
C	22.0	.	.	3 184	.	.	13	1 797	2 979
D	5.2	.	.	4 445	.	.	201	43 757	53 524
E	.	.	.	.	.	.	3	703	699
E-F	46.5	.	.	5 399	.	.	.	.	.
F	.	.	.	.	.	.	26	2 805	3 791
G	.	.	.	.	.	.	12	8 168	11 063
G,J	10.0	.	.	1 820	.	.	.	.	.
H	4.3	.	.	2 826	.	.	23	1 228	1 617
I	19.2	.	.	2 910	.	.	7	1 572	1 529
J	.	.	.	.	.	.	6	1 892	4 021
K-Q	9.1	.	.	2 969	.	.	.	.	.
L	.	.	.	.	.	.	11 [11]	1 011 [11]	2 005 [11]
M	.	.	.	.	.	.	10	14 772	9 157
N	.	.	.	.	.	.	9	10 440	7 630
O	.	.	.	.	.	.	43	7 519	6 420

5. Indices des prix à la consommation (période de base: 2000=100)

	2002	2003	2004	2005	2006	2007
Indices généraux	104.8	107.6	111.5	113.8	118.9	122.6
Indices de l'alimentation, y compris les boissons non alcoolisées	106.1	109.7	115.1	115.2	121.4	124.8
Indices de l'électricité, gaz et autres combustibles	105.0	109.5	115.0	125.3	134.4	139.7
Indices de l'habillement, y compris les chaussures	103.2	104.1	105.8	108.9	111.9	115.6
Indices du loyer	106.6	109.6	114.7	118.3	121.8	.
Indices généraux, non compris le logement	104.7	107.5	111.4	113.6	118.7	122.5

[1] Persons aged 15 years and over. [2] Persons aged 18 years and over. [3] Dec. [4] Incl. workers not classifiable by occupation. [5] Levels 0-1. [6] Levels 2-3. [7] Levels 5-7. [8] Excl. quarrying. [9] Incapacity of 4 days or more. [10] Excl. workers indirectly involved. [11] Incl. category N and state education.

[1] Personnes âgées de 15 ans et plus. [2] Personnes âgées de 18 ans et plus. [3] Déc. [4] Y compris les travailleurs ne pouvant être classés selon la profession. [5] Niveaux 0-1. [6] Niveaux 2-3. [7] Niveaux 5-7. [8] Non compris les carrières. [9] Incapacité de 4 jours et plus. [10] Non compris les travailleurs indirectement impliqués. [11] Y compris la catégorie N et l'éducation publique.

[1] Personas de 15 años y más. [2] Personas de 18 años y más. [3] Dic. [4] Incl. los trabajadores que no pueden ser clasificados según la ocupación. [5] Niveles 0-1. [6] Niveles 2-3. [7] Niveles 5-7. [8] Excl. las canteras. [9] Incapacidad de 4 días y más. [10] Excl. los trabajadores indirectamente implicados. [11] Incl. la categoría N y la educación pública.

Turkey

1. Economically active population, Employment and Unemployment ('000)

	Economically active population		Employment		Unemployment	
	Total	Women (%)	Total	Women (%)	Total	Women (%)
Age group	2007 [1,2] Labour force survey		2007 ★ Labour force survey		2007 [2] Labour force survey	
Total	23 523	26.2	21 190	26.1	2 333	27.0
15-19	1 603	30.7	1 295	31.1	308	28.9
20-24	2 658	35.1	2 130	34.6	528	37.1
25-29	3 908	25.1	3 430	24.7	478	28.0
30-34	3 869	23.9	3 541	23.6	328	26.8
35-39	3 319	24.7	3 082	24.7	237	25.7
40-44	2 739	23.9	2 562	24.2	177	19.2
45-49	2 099	22.9	1 960	23.6	139	12.9
50-54	1 440	24.3	1 358	25.3	82	7.3
55-59	852	26.6	814	27.5	38	7.9
60-64	511	29.0	497	29.6	14	7.1
65+	525	28.0	521	28.2	4	.
Economic activity (ISIC-Rev.3)	2007 ★ Labour force survey		2007 [2,3] Labour force survey		2007 [2] Labour force survey	
Total	23 522	26.2	21 189	26.1	2 333	27.0
A-B	5 787	45.9	5 601	46.7	186	20.4
C Mining and Quarrying	146	2.1	135	1.5	11	9.1
D Manufacturing	4 393	20.3	3 949	19.7	444	25.7
E Electricity, Gas and Water Supply	102	3.9	100	4.0	2	.
F Construction	1 578	2.6	1 224	2.7	354	2.3
G Wholesale and Retail Trade; Repair of Motor Vehicles ...	3 820	16.4	3 500	15.3	320	29.1
H Hotels and Restaurants	1 152	13.7	989	13.5	163	14.7
I Transport, Storage and Communications	1 236	7.0	1 123	6.6	113	11.5
J Financial Intermediation	252	38.1	235	37.4	17	47.1
K Real Estate, Renting and Business Activities	861	25.3	773	24.2	88	35.2
L Public Administration and Defence; Compulsory Social ...	1 320	13.6	1 283	13.3	37	21.6
M Education	901	44.2	856	42.6	45	73.3
N Health and Social Work	580	53.4	546	52.7	34	64.7
O-Q	973	29.4	875	28.7	98	35.7
Unemployed seeking their first job					422	48.1
Occupation (ISCO-88)	2007 ★ Labour force survey		2007 [2,3] Labour force survey		2007 [2] Labour force survey	
Total	23 522	26.2	21 189	26.1	2 333	27.0
1 Legislators, senior officials and managers	1 890	8.2	1 816	8.1	74	10.8
2 Professionals	1 374	39.0	1 294	37.9	80	57.5
3 Technicians and associate professionals	1 471	29.6	1 358	28.9	113	38.1
4 Clerks	1 429	43.1	1 265	41.0	164	59.1
5 Service workers and shop and market sales workers	2 825	20.7	2 524	19.7	301	28.6
6 Skilled agricultural and fishery workers	4 698	43.1	4 641	43.3	57	22.8
7 Craft and related trade workers	3 410	8.9	2 992	9.1	418	7.7
8 Plant and machine operators and assemblers	2 508	9.8	2 286	9.5	222	13.1
9 Elementary occupations	3 496	30.2	3 013	32.6	483	15.3
Unemployed seeking their first job					422	48.1
Education level (ISCED-97)	2007 [1,2] Labour force survey		2007 ★ Labour force survey		2007 [2] Labour force survey	
Total	23 523	26.2	21 190	26.1	2 333	27.0
X No schooling	1 082	67.6	1 028	69.9	54	22.2
0 Pre-primary education	1 044	37.8	938	40.4	106	15.1
1 Primary education or first stage of basic education	9 672	22.9	8 866	23.5	806	16.0
2 Lower secondary or second stage of basic education	3 495	16.9	3 081	16.6	414	18.8
3 Upper secondary education	5 152	22.4	4 495	20.2	657	37.6
5A First stage of tertiary education - theoretically based [4]	3 078	35.0	2 782	33.3	296	50.3
Status in employment (ICSE-1993)			2007 [2,3] Labour force survey			
Total			21 189	26.1		
1 Employees			12 316	21.8		
2 Employers			1 159	6.1		
3 Own-account workers			4 728	14.1		
5 Contributing family workers			2 986	70.7		

2. Population ('000), Activity rate and Unemployment rate

	Population			Activity rate			Unemployment rate		
Age group	2007 [1] Labour force survey			2007 [1] Labour force survey			2007 [2] Labour force survey		
	Total	Men	Women	Total	Men	Women	Total	Men	Women
Total							9.9	9.8	10.3
15+	49 214	24 352	24 860	47.8	71.3	24.8	9.9	9.8	.
15-24	11 271	5 440	5 830	37.8	52.1	24.4	19.6	19.4	20.0
25-54	29 403	14 877	14 525	59.1	88.5	29.0	8.3	8.3	8.1
55+	8 540	4 035	4 505	22.1	33.9	11.6	3.0	3.8	.

Turkey

3. Paid employment ('000), Hours of work (weekly) and Wages

Economic activity (ISIC-Rev.3)	Paid employment 2007[2] Labour force survey			Hours of work 2007[2] Labour force survey Hours actually worked / Total employment			Wages 2001[5 6 7] Labour-related establishment survey Earnings per month / Employees / Lira		
	Total	Men	Women	Total	Men	Women	Total	Men	Women
Total	12 316	9 636	2 681	49.0	51.9	41.1	.	.	.
A-B	458	298	160	41.0	45.0	36.8	.	.	.
C-Q	.	.	.	51.8	53.3	45.0	.	.	.
A	.	.	.	40.9	44.9	36.8	491 792.0	.	.
B	.	.	.	38.9	.	.	.	.	.
C	130	128	2	51.3	51.5	39.5	722 863.0	.	.
D	3 344	2 670	674	51.8	53.1	46.7	525 175.7 [8]	.	.
E	100	96	4	43.5	43.7	38.0	879 048.0	.	.
F	986	956	30	51.9	52.0	46.5	.	.	.
G	1 813	1 449	365	57.1	58.2	51.1	.	.	.
H	670	568	102	62.2	63.7	52.6	.	.	.
I	699	628	71	53.9	54.4	45.4	.	.	.
J	219	133	86	43.4	44.1	42.2	.	.	.
K	601	439	162	48.9	50.1	45.3	.	.	.
L	1 283	1 112	171	43.8	44.4	39.4	.	.	.
M	846	483	363	36.9	38.1	35.3	.	.	.
N	523	241	282	44.7	45.3	44.3	.	.	.
O-Q	644	435	209	51.1	55.2	40.9	.	.	.

Share of women in wage employment in the non-agricultural sector [2] (2007 - Labour force survey): **21.3%**

4. Occupational injuries and Strikes and Lockouts

Economic activity (ISIC-Rev.2)	Rates of fatal injuries 2006 Insurance records Per 100,000 workers insured Reported injuries			Rates of non-fatal injuries 2006 Insurance records Per 100,000 workers insured Reported injuries			Strikes and lockouts		
	Total	Men	Women	Total	Men	Women	Strikes and lockouts	Workers involved	Days not worked
Total	20.5	25.6	0.9	29	36	4	.	.	.
1	20.1	23.3	0.0	26	29	9	.	.	.
2	74.2	75.7	0.0	416	424	0	.	.	.
3	9.2	11.2	1.1	35	42	6	.	.	.
4	17.7	19.2	0.0	24	26	0	.	.	.
5	33.5	34.9	0.0	36	37	2	.	.	.
6	6.9	9.3	0.4	8	10	3	.	.	.
7	29.9	34.0	0.0	24	27	9	.	.	.
8	1.7	3.0	0.0	1	2	0	.	.	.
9	4.0	5.9	0.3	6	9	1	.	.	.

Economic activity (ISIC-Rev.3)	Rates of fatal injuries			Rates of non-fatal injuries			Strikes and lockouts 2007[9] Labour relations records		
	Total	Men	Women	Total	Men	Women	Strikes and lockouts	Workers involved	Days not worked
Total	.	.	.	.	.	.	15	25 920	1 353 558
A	.	.	.	.	.	.	0	0	0
B	.	.	.	.	.	.	0	0	0
C	.	.	.	.	.	.	0	0	0
D	.	.	.	.	.	.	10	1 636	196 680
E	.	.	.	.	.	.	0	0	0
F	.	.	.	.	.	.	0	0	0
G	.	.	.	.	.	.	0	0	0
H	.	.	.	.	.	.	1	19	760
I	.	.	.	.	.	.	3	24 016	1 152 632
J	.	.	.	.	.	.	0	0	0
K	.	.	.	.	.	.	0	0	0
L	.	.	.	.	.	.	0	0	0
M	.	.	.	.	.	.	0	0	0
N	.	.	.	.	.	.	0	0	0
O	.	.	.	.	.	.	1	249	3 486

5. Consumer price indices (base period: 2000=100)

	2002	2003	2004	2005	2006	2007
General indices	223.8	280.4	310.1	329.5	361.1	392.7
Food index, including non-alcoholic beverages	225.3	290.0	316.1	112.1 [10]	123.0	138.2
Electricity, gas and other fuel indices	291.6	349.3	371.0	400.0	446.0	479.1
Clothing indices, including footwear	231.3	293.9	305.3	324.6	324.3	339.0
Rent indices [11]	217.4	268.9	310.1	388.1	466.2	552.1

Turkey

[1] Excl. regular military living in barracks and conscripts. [2] Persons aged 15 years and over. [3] Excl. armed forces. [4] Levels 5A, 5B and 6. [5] Incl. overtime payments and irregular bonuses and allowances. [6] Public sector and establishments of non-agricultural private sector with 10 or more persons employed. [7] Figures in thousands; Jan - June. [8] Establishments with 10 or more persons employed. [9] Strikes only. [10] Series (base 2003=100) replacing former series; prior to 2005 incl. alcoholic beverages and tobacco. [11] Incl. water, electricity, gas and other fuels.

[1] Non compris les militaires de carrière vivant dans des casernes et les conscrits. [2] Personnes âgées de 15 ans et plus. [3] Non compris les forces armées. [4] Niveaux 5A, 5B et 6. [5] Y compris la rémunération des heures suppl émentaires et les prestations versées irrégulièrement. [6] Secteur public et établissements du secteur privé non agricole occupant 10 personnes et plus. [7] Chiffres en milliers; jan - juin. [8] Etablissements occupant 10 personnes et plus. [9] Grèves seulement. [10] Série (base 2003=100) remplaçant la précédente; avant 2005 y compris les boissons alcoolisées et le tabac. [11] Y compris l'eau, l'électricité, le gaz et autres combustibles.

[1] Excl. los militares profesionales que viven en casernas y los conscriptos. [2] Personas de 15 años y más. [3] Excl. las fuerzas armadas. [4] Niveles 5A, 5B y 6. [5] Incl. los pagos por horas extraordinarias y las prestaciones pagadas irregularmente. [6] Sector público y establecimientos del sector no agrícola con 10 y más trabajadores. [7] Cifras en milares; enero - junio. [8] Establecimientos con 10 y más trabajadores. [9] Huelgas solamente. [10] Serie (base 2003=100) que substituye a la anterior; antes de 2005 incl. las bebidas alcohólicas y el tabaco. [11] Incl. el agua, la electricidad, el gas y otros combustibles.

Turkmenistan

1. Economically active population, Employment and Unemployment ('000)

Age group	Economically active population Total	Women (%)	Employment Total	Women (%)	Unemployment Total	Women (%)
	1999 Official estimates		1999 Official estimates			
Total	2 551	.	1 908	.	.	.

2. Population ('000), Activity rate and Unemployment rate

Age group	Population 1999 Official estimates			Activity rate 1999 Official estimates			Unemployment rate		
	Total	Men	Women	Total	Men	Women	Total	Men	Women
Total	4 738	2 353	2 385	53.8	.	.	.	.	.

3. Paid employment ('000), Hours of work (weekly) and Wages

Statistics not available.

4. Occupational injuries and Strikes and Lockouts

Statistics not available.

5. Consumer price indices (base period: 2000=100)

Statistics not available for the period 2002-2007.

Turks and Caicos Islands

1. Economically active population, Employment and Unemployment ('000)

	Economically active population		Employment		Unemployment	
	Total	Women (%)	Total	Women (%)	Total	Women (%)
Age group	1980 [1,2] Population census		2005 [1] Official estimates		2005 [1] Official estimates	
Total	2.909	42.8	17.442	40.7	1.524	.
15-19	0.373	38.1	.	.	.	.
20-24	0.454	46.9	.	.	.	.
25-29	0.397	43.1	.	.	.	.
30-34	0.253	38.3	.	.	.	.
35-39	0.249	43.8	.	.	.	.
40-44	0.209	44.5	.	.	.	.
45-49	0.214	49.5	.	.	.	.
50-54	0.214	51.9	.	.	.	.
55-59	0.185	41.1	.	.	.	.
60-64	0.139	28.1	.	.	.	.
65+	0.221	39.8	.	.	.	.
?	0.001	0.0	.	.	.	.

Economic activity (ISIC-Rev.3)

2005 [1] Official estimates

Total	.	.	17.4	.	.	.
A Agriculture, Hunting and Forestry	.	.	0.1	.	.	.
B Fishing	.	.	0.2	.	.	.
C Mining and Quarrying	.	.	0.1	.	.	.
D Manufacturing	.	.	0.2	.	.	.
E Electricity, Gas and Water Supply	.	.	0.3	.	.	.
F Construction	.	.	2.4	.	.	.
G Wholesale and Retail Trade; Repair of Motor Vehicles ...	.	.	1.3	.	.	.
H Hotels and Restaurants	.	.	2.9	.	.	.
I Transport, Storage and Communications	.	.	0.7	.	.	.
J Financial Intermediation	.	.	0.5	.	.	.
K Real Estate, Renting and Business Activities	.	.	1.6	.	.	.
L Public Administration and Defence; Compulsory Social ...	.	.	2.3	.	.	.
M-N	.	.	0.5	.	.	.
O Other Community, Social and Personal Service Activities	.	.	1.0	.	.	.
P Households with Employed Persons	.	.	1.6	.	.	.
X Not classifiable by economic activity	.	.	1.9	.	.	.

Occupation (ISCO-88)

2005 [1] Official estimates

Total	.	.	17.4	.	.	.
1 Legislators, senior officials and managers	.	.	0.8	.	.	.
2 Professionals	.	.	1.1	.	.	.
3 Technicians and associate professionals	.	.	0.9	.	.	.
4 Clerks	.	.	1.2	.	.	.
5 Service workers and shop and market sales workers	.	.	2.3	.	.	.
6 Skilled agricultural and fishery workers	.	.	0.3	.	.	.
7 Craft and related trade workers	.	.	1.4	.	.	.
8 Plant and machine operators and assemblers	.	.	0.4	.	.	.
9 Elementary occupations	.	.	5.9	.	.	.
0 Armed forces	.	.	3.1	.	.	.

2. Population ('000), Activity rate and Unemployment rate

	Population 1980 [2] Population census			Activity rate 1980 [2] Population census			Unemployment rate		
Age group	Total	Men	Women	Total	Men	Women	Total	Men	Women
Total	7.413	3.580	3.833	39.2	46.5	32.5	.	.	.
15+	4.345	2.058	2.287	66.9	80.8	54.4	.	.	.
15-24	1.477	0.740	0.737	56.0	63.8	48.2	.	.	.
25-54	1.930	0.908	1.022	79.6	93.5	67.2	.	.	.
55+	0.938	0.410	0.528	58.1	83.4	38.4	.	.	.

3. Paid employment ('000), Hours of work (weekly) and Wages

Statistics not available.

4. Occupational injuries and Strikes and Lockouts

Statistics not available.

5. Consumer price indices (base period: 2000=100)

Statistics not available for the period 2002-2007.

---

[1] Persons aged 15 years and over. [2] May.   [1] Personnes âgées de 15 ans et plus. [2] Mai.   [1] Personas de 15 años y más. [2] Mayo.

Tuvalu

1. Economically active population, Employment and Unemployment ('000)

	Economically active population		Employment		Unemployment	
	Total	Women (%)	Total	Women (%)	Total	Women (%)
Age group	2002 [1] Population census		2002 [1,2] Population census		2002 [1] Population census	
Total	3.463	43.4	2.043	35.4	0.226	57.1

Occupation (ISCO-88)			2002 [1,2] Population census			
Total	.	.	2.043	35.4	.	.
1 Legislators, senior officials and managers	.	.	0.179	24.6	.	.
2 Professionals	.	.	0.549	50.5	.	.
4 Clerks	.	.	0.229	81.7	.	.
5 Service workers and shop and market sales workers	.	.	0.345	51.3	.	.
6 Skilled agricultural and fishery workers	.	.	0.014	.	.	.
9 Elementary occupations	.	.	0.727	5.4	.	.

Status in employment (ICSE-1993)			2002 [1,2] Population census			
Total	.	.	2.043	35.4	.	.
1 Employees	.	.	1.965	35.9	.	.
2 Employers	.	.	0.035	17.1	.	.
3 Own-account workers	.	.	0.037	29.7	.	.
5 Contributing family workers	.	.	0.003	33.3	.	.
6 Not classifiable by status	.	.	0.003	.	.	.

2. Population ('000), Activity rate and Unemployment rate

	Population 2002 Population census			Activity rate 2002 Population census			Unemployment rate 2002 [1] Population census		
Age group	Total	Men	Women	Total	Men	Women	Total	Men	Women
Total	9.6	4.7	4.8	36.2	41.4	31.1	6.5	4.9	8.6
15+	6.1	2.9	3.2	.	.	.	.	.	.
15-24	1.5	0.8	0.7	.	.	.	.	.	.
25-54	3.5	1.6	1.9	.	.	.	.	.	.
55+	1.1	0.5	0.6	.	.	.	.	.	.

3. Paid employment ('000), Hours of work (weekly) and Wages

Statistics not available.

4. Occupational injuries and Strikes and Lockouts

Statistics not available.

5. Consumer price indices (base period: 2000=100)

Funafuti	2002	2003	2004	2005	2006	2007
General indices	106.7	110.2	113.3	117.0	119.0	121.6
Food index, including non-alcoholic beverages	109.4	117.4	120.8	127.4	129.2	128.6
Electricity, gas and other fuel indices	106.7	106.9	.	.	.	.
Clothing indices, including footwear	108.3	111.8	113.8	115.5	129.8	163.3
Rent indices	120.0	134.3	135.1	139.3	143.8	141.7

[1] Persons aged 15 years and over. [2] November.   [1] Personnes âgées de 15 ans et plus. [2] Novembre.   [1] Personas de 15 años y más. [2] Noviembre.

Uganda

1. Economically active population, Employment and Unemployment ('000)

Age group	Economically active population Total	Women (%)	Employment Total	Women (%)	Unemployment Total	Women (%)
	1991 [1,2] Population census		1991 ★ Population census		1991 [1,3] Population census	
Total	6 348.379	46.9	6 286.262	47.0	62.117	29.3
10-14	355.579	52.8	350.046	53.0	5.533	39.3
15-19	783.601	54.6	765.288	55.2	18.313	31.1
20-24	1 023.747	48.9	1 007.816	49.2	15.931	32.4
25-29	986.841	45.6	977.749	45.8	9.092	27.0
30-34	762.765	44.1	758.169	44.2	4.596	22.5
35-39	562.836	44.7	560.165	44.8	2.671	17.8
40-44	442.037	46.0	440.076	46.1	1.961	19.2
45-49	372.578	45.0	371.278	45.1	1.300	21.6
50-54	345.755	45.4	344.639	45.5	1.116	21.3
55-59	211.659	42.3	211.112	42.3	0.547	17.7
60-64	208.007	44.9	207.614	44.9	0.393	30.0
65-69	119.769	40.4	119.532	40.4	0.237	15.6
70-74	91.613	39.1	91.412	39.1	0.201	13.9
75+	81.592	32.6	81.366	32.6	0.226	23.9

Economic activity (ISIC-Rev.3)

2003 [1] Labour force survey

	Total	Women (%)
Total	9 260.0	50.1
A Agriculture, Hunting and Forestry	6 278.3	55.9
B Fishing	83.3	5.5
C Mining and Quarrying	27.8	33.5
D Manufacturing	564.9	40.3
E Electricity, Gas and Water Supply	9.3	50.5
F Construction	120.4	4.1
G Wholesale and Retail Trade; Repair of Motor Vehicles ...	1 074.2	40.6
H Hotels and Restaurants	240.8	73.3
I Transport, Storage and Communications	175.9	2.6
J Financial Intermediation	0.0	.
K Real Estate, Renting and Business Activities	37.0	25.1
L Public Administration and Defence; Compulsory Social ...	74.1	12.6
M Education	240.8	34.7
N Health and Social Work	74.1	50.1
O Other Community, Social and Personal Service Activities	148.2	37.6
P Households with Employed Persons	111.1	71.0

Occupation (ISCO-88)

2003 [1] Labour force survey

	Total	Women (%)
Total	9 260.0	50.1
1 Legislators, senior officials and managers	13.8	33.3
2 Professionals	124.9	33.4
3 Technicians and associate professionals	259.1	35.8
4 Clerks	41.7	55.6
5 Service workers and shop and market sales workers	1 351.9	49.4
6 Skilled agricultural and fishery workers	6 117.4	56.2
7 Craft and related trade workers	462.8	31.1
8 Plant and machine operators and assemblers	64.7	7.1
9 Elementary occupations	823.5	27.0

2. Population ('000), Activity rate and Unemployment rate

Age group	Population 1991 [2,4] Population census Total	Men	Women	Activity rate 1991 [2,4] Population census Total	Men	Women	Unemployment rate 1991 [1,3] Population census Total	Men	Women
Total	.	.	.	.	.	.	1.0	1.3	0.6
15+	8 643.655	4 149.037	4 494.618	69.3	77.3	62.0	0.9	1.3	0.6
15-24	3 266.286	1 539.297	1 726.989	55.3	57.1	53.8	1.9	2.7	1.2
25-54	4 276.875	2 058.656	2 218.219	81.2	92.6	70.6	0.6	0.8	0.3
55+	1 100.494	551.084	549.410	64.8	76.1	53.4	0.2	0.3	0.1

3. Paid employment ('000), Hours of work (weekly) and Wages

Statistics not available.

4. Occupational injuries and Strikes and Lockouts

Economic activity (ISIC-Rev.3)	Rates of fatal injuries Total	Men	Women	Rates of non-fatal injuries Total	Men	Women	Strikes and lockouts 2004 Administrative records and related sources Strikes and lockouts	Workers involved	Days not worked
Total	.	.	.	.	.	.	3	1 412	3 936

Uganda

5. Consumer price indices (base period: 2000=100)

	2002	2003	2004	2005	2006	2007
General indices	101.6	110.5	114.5	124.1	133.3	141.5
Food index, including non-alcoholic beverages	92.5	106.7	111.4	126.1	139.1	142.8
Clothing indices, including footwear	100.5	102.7	100.5	102.3	106.8	111.9
Rent indices [5]	110.7	116.5	121.0	130.1	139.1	164.9

[1] Persons aged 10 years and over. [2] Jan. [3] January. [4] "De facto" population. [5] Incl. water, electricity, gas and other fuels.

[1] Personnes âgées de 10 ans et plus. [2] Janv. [3] Janvier. [4] Population "de facto". [5] Y compris l'eau, l'électricité, le gaz et autres combustibles.

[1] Personas de 10 años y más. [2] Enero. [3] Enero. [4] Población "de facto". [5] Incl. el agua, la electricidad, el gas y otros combustibles.

Ukraine

1. Economically active population, Employment and Unemployment ('000)

	Economically active population		Employment		Unemployment	
	Total	Women (%)	Total	Women (%)	Total	Women (%)
Age group	2005 [1] Labour force survey		2005 ★ Labour force survey		2005 [1] Labour force survey	
Total	22 280.8	48.5	20 680.0	48.7	1 600.8	46.1
15-19	614.0	43.9	478.5	44.2	135.5	42.5
20-24	2 397.7	43.0	2 084.9	43.2	312.8	41.7
25-29	2 775.2	45.1	2 563.4	45.0	211.8	45.7
30-34	2 740.7	47.0	2 553.4	46.8	187.3	50.1
35-39	2 657.0	49.3	2 485.2	49.5	171.8	46.7
40-44	3 110.1	51.4	2 915.8	51.6	194.3	48.2
45-49	2 961.5	52.4	2 760.2	52.2	201.3	55.5
50-54	2 479.3	52.5	2 336.9	52.6	142.4	49.5
55-59	1 283.6	41.9	1 243.4	43.0	40.2	5.5
60-64	630.0	52.7	627.3	52.7	2.7	37.0
65-70	631.7	54.3	631.0	54.3	0.7	57.1
Economic activity (ISIC-Rev.3)	2007 ★ Labour force survey		2007 Labour force survey		2007 [1] Labour force survey	
Total	22 322.3	.	20 904.7	.	1 417.6	45.6
A-B	.	.	3 484.5	.	.	.
A Agriculture, Hunting and Forestry	.	.	.	.	194.7	37.1
B Fishing	.	.	.	.	3.1	6.5
C Mining and Quarrying	.	.	.	.	29.8	23.5
C-E	.	.	3 973.0	.	.	.
D Manufacturing	.	.	.	.	234.1	50.8
E Electricity, Gas and Water Supply	.	.	.	.	26.7	22.8
F Construction	1 138.1	.	1 030.2	.	107.9	8.0
G Wholesale and Retail Trade; Repair of Motor Vehicles ...	.	.	.	.	178.9	57.2
G-H	.	.	4 564.4	.	.	.
H Hotels and Restaurants	.	.	.	.	45.1	79.6
I Transport, Storage and Communications	1 502.1	.	1 451.9	.	50.2	29.7
J Financial Intermediation	358.2	.	344.4	.	13.8	56.5
K Real Estate, Renting and Business Activities	1 153.9	.	1 134.7	.	19.2	53.1
L Public Administration and Defence; Compulsory Social ...	1 097.5	.	1 036.4	.	61.1	40.9
M Education	1 750.9	.	1 693.7	.	57.2	71.3
N Health and Social Work	1 396.6	.	1 359.0	.	37.6	69.9
O Other Community, Social and Personal Service Activities	.	.	.	.	28.1	61.6
O-Q	.	.	832.5	.	.	.
P Households with Employed Persons	.	.	.	.	2.3	56.5
Unemployed seeking their first job	.	.	.	.	327.8	46.4
Occupation (ISCO-88)	2007 ★ Labour force survey		2007 [1] Labour force survey		2007 [1] Labour force survey	
Total	22 322.3	48.3	20 904.7	48.5	1 417.6	45.6
1 Legislators, senior officials and managers	1 628.5	39.5	1 589.8	39.4	38.7	43.9
2 Professionals	2 710.1	63.5	2 634.3	63.9	75.8	50.5
3 Technicians and associate professionals	2 505.0	64.2	2 390.7	64.7	114.3	55.6
4 Clerks	811.1	82.9	759.7	83.0	51.4	81.7
5 Service workers and shop and market sales workers	3 050.8	68.4	2 846.8	68.5	204.0	66.8
6 Skilled agricultural and fishery workers	296.9	44.6	270.4	42.6	26.5	64.9
7 Craft and related trade workers	2 790.0	14.2	2 624.3	14.2	165.7	14.3
8 Plant and machine operators and assemblers	2 793.8	21.7	2 624.3	21.2	169.5	29.2
9 Elementary occupations	5 408.3	51.2	5 164.4	51.5	243.9	44.0
Unemployed seeking their first job	.	.	.	.	327.8	46.4
Education level (ISCED-76)	2005 [1] Labour force survey		2005 ★ Labour force survey		2005 [1] Labour force survey	
Total	22 280.8	48.5	20 680.0	48.7	1 600.8	46.1
1 First level	237.3	58.8	232.1	58.9	5.2	51.9
2 Second level, first stage	2 374.0	44.2	2 204.3	44.9	169.7	34.4
3 Second level, second stage	9 600.3	42.1	8 748.0	42.0	852.3	42.5
5 Third level, first stage, leading to an award not equivalent ...	5 382.0	57.8	5 006.2	57.8	375.8	57.3
6 Third level, first stage, leading to a first university degree ...	4 687.2 [2]	52.9	4 489.4	53.0	197.8	50.5
Status in employment (ICSE-1993)			2007 [1] Labour force survey			
Total	.	.	20 904.7	48.5	.	.
1 Employees	.	.	16 868.2	47.8	.	.
2, 3	.	.	3 957.9	51.7	.	.
5 Contributing family workers	.	.	78.6	40.1	.	.

2. Population ('000), Activity rate and Unemployment rate

	Population 2007 [3] Official estimates			Activity rate 2005 Labour force survey			Unemployment rate 2005 [1] Labour force survey		
Age group	Total	Men	Women	Total	Men	Women	Total	Men	Women
Total	46 192.3	21 297.7	24 894.6	.	.	.	7.2	7.5	6.8
15+	39 691.2	17 961.5	21 729.7	62.2	67.9	57.0	7.2	7.5	6.8
15-24	7 103.0	3 631.0	3 472.0	40.2	44.7	35.5	14.9	15.2	14.4
25-54	20 150.5	9 701.5	10 449.0	82.4	86.4	78.7	6.6	6.7	6.6
55+	12 437.7	4 629.0	7 808.7	.	.	.	.	.	.

Ukraine

3. Paid employment ('000), Hours of work (weekly) and Wages

Economic activity (ISIC-Rev.3)	Paid employment 2007 Labour-related establishment survey			Hours of work 2007 [4] Labour-related establishment census Hours actually worked / Employees			Wages 2007 Labour-related establishment census Earnings per month / Employees / Hryvnia		
	Total	Men	Women	Total	Men	Women	Total	Men	Women
Total	11 413	5 358	6 055	141	142	140	1 351.1	1 578.1	1 150.3
A-B	.	.	.	143	142	145	769.9	801.6	707.8
C-Q	.	.	.	141	142	139	1 400.0	1 672.9	1 173.2
A	868	573	295	143	142	145	770.6	803.0	707.7
B	12	10	2	140	139	143	721.3	720.0	726.5
C	501	368	133	126	122	140	1 970.5	2 252.6	1 914.0
D	2 268	1 297	971	143	144	142	1 456.4	1 667.0	1 175.3
E	518	322	196	147	147	146	1 576.8	1 724.3	1 334.5
F	500	400	100	147	147	145	1 486.0	1 535.2	1 289.3
G	874	435	439	151	152	150	1 144.5	1 284.2	1 005.6
H	88	25	63	144	144	144	943.9	1 116.0	874.6
I	977	573	404	143	145	140	1 669.7	1 886.7	1 361.8
J	298	92	206	151	150	152	2 770.1	3 635.7	2 386.1
K	615	314	301	148	149	147	1 594.8	1 673.5	1 512.6
L	599	198	401	142	142	143	1 851.9	2 130.0	1 714.2
M	1 641	383	1 258	122	124	122	1 059.6	1 206.9	1 014.6
N	1 274	221	1 050	145	142	145	870.5	991.6	845.1
O	383	147	236	138	140	137	1 090.3	1 347.0	930.9

Share of women in wage employment in the non-agricultural sector (2007 - Labour-related establishment survey): **54.7%**

4. Occupational injuries and Strikes and Lockouts

Economic activity (ISIC-Rev.3)	Rates of fatal injuries 2007 Labour inspectorate records Per 100,000 workers employed Reported injuries			Rates of non-fatal injuries 2007 Labour inspectorate records Per 100,000 workers employed Reported injuries			Strikes and lockouts 2007 Labour relations records		
	Total	Men	Women	Total	Men	Women	Strikes and lockouts [5]	Workers involved	Days not worked
Total	9.3	17.8	1.5	155	257	60	5	849	31 953
A	.	.	.	.	.	.	0	0	0
B	.	.	.	.	.	.	0	0	0
C	.	.	.	.	.	.	1	25	8 000
D	.	.	.	.	.	.	1	277	9 481
E	.	.	.	.	.	.	1	310	11 480
F	.	.	.	.	.	.	0	0	0
G	.	.	.	.	.	.	0	0	0
H	.	.	.	.	.	.	0	0	0
I	.	.	.	.	.	.	1	210	2 776
J	.	.	.	.	.	.	0	0	0
K	.	.	.	.	.	.	0	0	0
L	.	.	.	.	.	.	0	0	0
M	.	.	.	.	.	.	0	0	0
N	.	.	.	.	.	.	0	0	0
O	.	.	.	.	.	.	1	27	216

5. Consumer price indices (base period: 2000=100)

	2002	2003	2004	2005	2006	2007
General indices	112.8	118.7	129.4	146.9	160.2	180.8
Food index, including non-alcoholic beverages [6]	114.4	121.5	135.1	157.5	166.5	182.4

[1] Persons aged 15-70 years. [2] Levels 6-7. [3] "De facto" population. [4] Per month. [5] One strike represents one establishment on strike. [6] Incl. alcoholic beverages and tobacco.

[1] Personnes âgées de 15 à 70 ans. [2] Niveaux 6-7. [3] Population "de facto". [4] Par mois. [5] Une grève représente un établissement en grève. [6] Y compris les boissons alcoolisées et le tabac.

[1] Personas de 15 á 70 años. [2] Niveles 6-7. [3] Población "de facto". [4] Por mes. [5] Una huelga representa un establecimiento en huelga. [6] Incl. las bebidas alcohólicas y el tabaco.

United Arab Emirates

1. Economically active population, Employment and Unemployment ('000)

	Economically active population		Employment		Unemployment	
	Total	Women (%)	Total	Women (%)	Total	Women (%)
Age group	2005 [1,2] Population census		2005 ★ Population census		2005 [1] Population census	
Total	2 559.668	13.5	2 479.880	13.0	79.788	30.5
15-19	24.116	26.7	17.840	25.9	6.276	28.9
20-24	307.419	23.1	287.060	21.9	20.359	40.2
25-29	569.921	16.2	553.842	15.5	16.079	39.3
30-34	559.151	12.8	549.522	12.5	9.629	31.5
35-39	432.668	11.0	426.169	10.6	6.499	30.9
40-44	289.956	9.9	284.702	9.6	5.254	24.4
45-49	188.392	8.3	183.719	8.1	4.673	16.2
50-54	113.249	7.3	108.718	7.1	4.531	10.9
55-59	51.979	5.8	48.349	5.6	3.630	8.2
60-64	16.581	5.2	13.723	5.0	2.858	6.1
65+	5.800	6.6	.	.	.	.
?	0.436	63.8	0.436	63.8	-	.
Economic activity (ISIC-Rev.3)	2005 [1,2] Population census		2005 [1] Population census		2005 [1] Population census	
Total	2 559.668	13.5	2 479.880	13.0	79.788	30.5
A Agriculture, Hunting and Forestry	116.653	0.3	116.105	0.3	0.548	2.0
B Fishing	5.500	0.2	5.438	0.2	0.062	.
C Mining and Quarrying	45.382	3.9	45.030	3.8	0.352	10.5
D Manufacturing	200.495	5.6	199.572	5.5	0.923	10.2
E Electricity, Gas and Water Supply	25.108	4.7	24.489	4.7	0.619	3.4
F Construction	720.096	0.8	718.354	0.8	1.742	6.5
G Wholesale and Retail Trade; Repair of Motor Vehicles ...	336.502	8.8	334.193	8.7	2.309	17.8
H Hotels and Restaurants	100.757	12.3	100.400	12.3	0.357	19.9
I Transport, Storage and Communications	168.706	9.6	167.420	9.6	1.287	10.7
J Financial Intermediation	37.029	26.1	36.647	26.0	0.382	36.9
K Real Estate, Renting and Business Activities	128.626	9.9	127.739	9.8	0.887	22.8
L Public Administration and Defence; Compulsory Social ...	231.567	7.7	218.545	8.0	13.022	3.9
M Education	71.663	53.3	69.982	53.0	1.681	64.7
N Health and Social Work	45.466	47.4	44.492	47.3	0.974	50.4
O Other Community, Social and Personal Service Activities	57.334	13.0	56.533	12.9	0.800	19.1
P Households with Employed Persons	194.516	68.8	194.252	68.9	0.263	24.7
Q Extra-Territorial Organizations and Bodies	2.249	24.9	2.226	24.5	0.024	66.7
X Not classifiable by economic activity	19.860	24.4	18.463	22.1	1.397	54.8
Unemployed seeking their first job	.	.	.	.	52.159	38.4
Occupation (ISCO-88)	2005 [1,2] Population census		2005 [1] Population census		2005 ★ Population census	
Total	2 559.668	13.5	2 479.880	13.0	79.788	30.3
1 Legislators, senior officials and managers	96.534	10.2	95.485	10.2	1.049	15.7
2 Professionals	249.569	24.6	246.786	24.4	2.783	47.7
3 Technicians and associate professionals	206.959	17.3	203.867	17.2	3.092	23.7
4 Clerks	99.019	28.8	97.491	28.9	1.528	25.1
5 Service workers and shop and market sales workers	408.650	38.1	404.490	38.4	4.160	15.0
6 Skilled agricultural and fishery workers	46.262	0.2	45.917	0.2	0.345	.
7 Craft and related trade workers	686.946	1.0	685.259	1.0	1.687	2.2
8 Plant and machine operators and assemblers	230.953	2.5	228.949	2.5	2.004	1.2
9 Elementary occupations	402.922	4.0	400.457	4.0	2.465	4.9
0 Armed forces	59.651	2.6	52.903	2.7	6.748	1.8
X Not classifiable by occupation	20.044	19.4	18.276	17.0	1.768	44.3
Education level (ISCED-97)	2005 [1,3] Population census		2005 ★ Population census		2005 [1] Population census	
Total	2 559.668	13.5	2 479.880	13.0	79.788	30.5
X No schooling	259.388	8.5	252.512	8.6	6.876	7.8
0 Pre-primary education	387.374	12.3	379.750	12.4	7.624	9.2
1 Primary education or first stage of basic education	324.839	8.5	316.714	8.5	8.125	9.7
2 Lower secondary or second stage of basic education	425.595	8.3	414.367	8.1	11.228	15.5
3 Upper secondary education	618.308	13.4	593.790	12.5	24.518	35.2
4 Post-secondary non-tertiary education	118.660	22.9	114.460	21.7	4.200	53.7
5A First stage of tertiary education - theoretically based [4]	425.504	24.0	408.287	22.7	17.217	56.4
Status in employment (ICSE-1993)	2005 [1,2] Population census		2005 [1] Population census		2005 ★ Population census	
Total	2 559.668	13.5	2 479.880	13.0	79.788	30.3
1 Employees	2 429.517	13.2	2 403.201	13.2	26.316	15.6
2 Employers	37.448	6.4	37.085	6.4	0.363	11.3
3 Own-account workers	39.670	4.6	38.985	4.4	0.685	13.1
5 Contributing family workers	0.144	13.2	0.004	50.0	0.140	12.1
6 Not classifiable by status	52.889	37.9	0.605	17.9	52.284	38.2

2. Population ('000), Activity rate and Unemployment rate

	Population			Activity rate			Unemployment rate		
Age group	2005 [2] Population census			2005 [2] Population census			2005 [1] Population census		
	Total	Men	Women	Total	Men	Women	Total	Men	Women
Total	4 106.427	2 806.141	1 300.286	62.3	78.9	26.6	3.1	2.5	7.1
15+	3 302.445	2 388.151	914.294	77.5	92.7	37.8	3.1	2.5	7.1
15-24	665.792	393.424	272.368	49.8	64.6	28.4	8.0	6.5	12.9
25-54	2 508.670	1 904.814	603.856	85.8	99.2	43.7	2.2	1.7	5.3
55+	127.983	89.913	38.070	58.1	78.0	11.2	.	.	.

United Arab Emirates

3. Paid employment ('000), Hours of work (weekly) and Wages

Economic activity (ISIC-Rev.3)	Paid employment 2005 Population census Total	Men	Women	Hours of work Total	Men	Women	Wages Total	Men	Women
Total	2 403.201	2 086.183	317.018	.	.	.	.	.	.
A	115.507	115.205	0.302	.	.	.	.	.	.
B	5.008	4.998	0.010	.	.	.	.	.	.
C	44.779	43.064	1.715	.	.	.	.	.	.
D	193.324	182.534	10.790	.	.	.	.	.	.
E	24.203	23.061	1.142	.	.	.	.	.	.
F	711.120	705.285	5.835	.	.	.	.	.	.
G	299.703	272.285	27.418	.	.	.	.	.	.
H	98.322	86.174	12.148	.	.	.	.	.	.
I	155.480	139.532	15.948	.	.	.	.	.	.
J	35.763	26.289	9.474	.	.	.	.	.	.
K	121.567	109.552	12.015	.	.	.	.	.	.
L	218.545	201.103	17.442	.	.	.	.	.	.
M	69.466	32.550	36.916	.	.	.	.	.	.
N	43.057	22.230	20.827	.	.	.	.	.	.
O	52.917	46.218	6.699	.	.	.	.	.	.
P	194.252	60.438	133.814	.	.	.	.	.	.
Q	2.226	1.681	0.545	.	.	.	.	.	.
X	17.962	13.984	3.978	.	.	.	.	.	.

Share of women in wage employment in the non-agricultural sector (2005 - Population census): **13.8%**

4. Occupational injuries and Strikes and Lockouts

Statistics not available.

5. Consumer price indices (base period: 2000=100)

	2002	2003	2004	2005	2006	2007
General indices	105.8	109.1	114.6	121.7	133.0	.
Food index, including non-alcoholic beverages [5]	102.4	104.7	112.0	117.0	123.5	.
Electricity, gas and other fuel indices	104.4	104.8	.	.	.	.
Clothing indices, including footwear	104.9	106.6	112.0	114.8	119.2	.
Rent indices	107.1	112.7	119.0	130.1	150.1	.

[1] Persons aged 15 years and over. [2] Dec. [3] December. [4] Levels 5-6. [5] Incl. beverages and tobacco.

[1] Personnes âgées de 15 ans et plus. [2] Déc. [3] Décembre. [4] Niveaux 5-6. [5] Y compris les boissons et le tabac.

[1] Personas de 15 años y más. [2] Dic. [3] Diciembre. [4] Niveles 5-6. [5] Incl. las bebidas y el tabaco.

United Kingdom

1. Economically active population, Employment and Unemployment ('000)

	Economically active population		Employment		Unemployment	
	Total	Women (%)	Total	Women (%)	Total	Women (%)
Age group	2007 [1,2] Labour force survey		2007 ★ Labour force survey		2007 [1,3] Labour force survey	
Total	30 720.7	45.7	29 099.9	45.9	1 620.8	42.6
16-19	1 694.0	48.4	1 343.0	50.1	351.1	41.7
20-24	3 057.6	45.8	2 733.3	46.4	324.3	40.6
25-34	6 569.3	45.0	6 268.7	45.0	300.6	46.5
35-49	11 430.8	46.7	11 031.5	46.7	399.3	47.5
50+	7 968.9	44.2	7 723.4	44.5	245.5	34.1
Economic activity (ISIC-Rev.3)	2007 ★ Labour force survey		2007 [1,3] Labour force survey		2007 [1,3] Labour force survey	
Total	30 720.7	45.7	29 099.9	45.9	1 620.8	42.6
A Agriculture, Hunting and Forestry	396.3	25.7	388.2	25.7	8.0	27.7
B Fishing	10.1	8.4	10.1	8.4	-	.
C Mining and Quarrying	136.6	20.8	133.2	21.0	3.4	15.5
D Manufacturing	3 917.9	24.9	3 744.9	25.0	173.0	23.0
E Electricity, Gas and Water Supply	219.4	28.9	212.6	28.3	6.7	48.1
F Construction	2 484.3	9.3	2 387.5	9.5	96.8	3.7
G Wholesale and Retail Trade; Repair of Motor Vehicles ...	4 408.8	48.3	4 160.2	48.5	248.6	45.8
H Hotels and Restaurants	1 421.8	55.1	1 298.5	55.2	123.3	53.0
I Transport, Storage and Communications	2 029.3	24.4	1 956.1	24.3	73.2	26.1
J Financial Intermediation	1 289.7	48.6	1 263.1	48.6	26.6	46.4
K Real Estate, Renting and Business Activities	3 605.7	42.1	3 484.4	42.2	121.3	38.3
L Public Administration and Defence; Compulsory Social ...	2 074.9	50.5	2 037.8	50.7	37.1	38.5
M Education	2 691.3	72.5	2 644.7	72.6	46.6	64.0
N Health and Social Work	3 556.2	79.9	3 462.2	79.9	94.0	78.8
O Other Community, Social and Personal Service Activities	1 746.6	51.1	1 681.5	51.3	65.1	44.2
P Households with Employed Persons	124.1	58.0	119.7	57.8	4.4	63.8
Q Extra-Territorial Organizations and Bodies	10.6	42.0	10.6	42.0	-	.
X Not classifiable by economic activity	212.2	49.4	104.6	45.4	107.6	53.2
Unemployed seeking their first job					385.0	46.1
Occupation (ISCO-88)	2007 ★ Labour force survey		2007 [1,3] Labour force survey		2007 [1,3] Labour force survey	
Total	30 720.7	45.7	29 099.9	45.9	1 620.8	42.6
1 Legislators, senior officials and managers	4 445.5	34.1	4 355.9	34.0	89.6	38.7
2 Professionals	3 823.2	42.8	3 769.3	42.8	54.0	41.9
3 Technicians and associate professionals	4 138.3	51.2	4 055.8	51.4	82.5	41.4
4 Clerks	3 539.1	78.2	3 434.2	78.5	104.9	67.8
5 Service workers and shop and market sales workers	4 750.5	75.4	4 514.7	75.7	235.7	68.6
6,9	3 631.0	43.4	3 304.7	44.4	326.3	33.5
7 Craft and related trade workers	3 402.8	7.8	3 277.2	7.8	125.7	6.7
8 Plant and machine operators and assemblers	2 280.7	13.1	2 166.6	13.0	114.1	15.7
0 Armed forces	.	.	135.1	15.8	.	.
X Not classifiable by occupation	189.4	47.9	86.4	42.8	103.0	52.2
Unemployed seeking their first job					385.0	46.1
Education level (ISCED-76)	2007 [2,4] Labour force survey		2007 ★ Labour force survey		2007 [3,4] Labour force survey	
Total	29 488.0	44.8	27 894.7	45.0	1 593.4	42.5
X No schooling [5]	2 651.6	40.2	2 336.8	40.6	314.8	37.5
2 Second level, first stage	3 684.8	39.3	3 404.7	39.2	280.1	41.2
3 Second level, second stage	13 523.3	45.1	12 763.2	45.2	760.1	43.9
5 Third level, first stage, leading to an award not equivalent ...	2 789.1	52.5	2 724.6	52.5	64.4	51.3
6 Third level, first stage, leading to a first university degree ... [6]	6 604.3	46.2	6 441.0	46.3	163.3	44.4
9 Education not definable by level	235.0	37.1	224.3	37.5	10.7	30.0
Status in employment (ICSE-1993)			2007 [1,3] Labour force survey			
Total	.	.	29 099.9	45.9	.	.
1 Employees	.	.	25 237.3	48.6	.	.
2,3	.	.	3 763.1	27.2	.	.
5 Contributing family workers	.	.	99.5	63.4	.	.

2. Population ('000), Activity rate and Unemployment rate

	Population			Activity rate			Unemployment rate		
Age group	2007 [2] Labour force survey			2007 [2] Labour force survey			2007 [1,3] Labour force survey		
	Total	Men	Women	Total	Men	Women	Total	Men	Women
Total	60 114.0	29 519.1	30 594.9	51.1	56.5	45.9	5.3	5.6	4.9
15+	48 623.5	23 637.2	24 986.3	63.2	70.6	56.2	5.3	5.6	4.9
15-24	7 216.4	3 678.9	3 537.5	65.8	68.8	62.8	14.2	15.7	12.5

United Kingdom

3. Paid employment ('000), Hours of work (weekly) and Wages

Economic activity (ISIC-Rev.3)	Paid employment 2005 [7] Official estimates			Hours of work 2007 [8,9] Labour-related establishment survey Hours paid for / Employees			Wages 2007 [8,10,11] Labour-related establishment survey Earnings per hour / Employees / Pound		
	Total	Men	Women	Total	Men	Women	Total	Men	Women
Total	26 608	13 341	13 267	39.4	40.7	37.4	13.96	14.90	12.38
A-B	.	.	.	43.9	44.6	40.8	9.01	9.12	8.45
C-Q	.	.	.	39.4	40.6	37.4	13.99	14.95	12.39
A	235	156	79	43.9	44.6	40.8	9.04	9.18	8.26
B	5	5	1	43.6	44.2	.	8.25	7.10	.
C	57	49	8	44.1	45.0	38.0	17.20	17.17	17.42
D	3 131	2 326	805	40.9	41.5	38.6	13.20	13.71	10.99
E	102	71	31	39.7	40.3	37.9	15.90	16.86	12.53
F	1 193	1 010	183	43.0	43.6	38.2	13.20	13.38	11.47
G	4 602	2 251	2 352	40.3	41.2	38.4	11.40	12.24	9.77
H	1 843	786	1 057	41.0	42.0	39.8	8.51	9.09	7.77
I	1 582	1 150	432	42.2	43.2	38.6	13.00	13.11	12.34
J	1 078	498	581	36.2	36.3	36.0	20.90	25.56	15.30
K	4 210	2 319	1 892	39.2	40.1	37.6	16.10	17.53	13.36
L	1 542	723	818	39.0	39.8	37.8	14.10	15.30	12.42
M	2 327	664	1 662	35.7	36.7	35.0	15.30	16.47	14.46
N	3 292	627	2 665	38.4	39.4	38.0	13.80	17.75	12.18
O	.	.	.	39.6	40.5	38.2	13.00	14.09	11.13
O-Q	1 409	707	702	.	.	.	.	.	.
P	.	.	.	40.8	43.8	40.2	9.06	12.20	8.47
Q	.	.	.	38.4	39.0	38.0	17.30	19.69	15.51

Share of women in wage employment in the non-agricultural sector [7] (2005 - Official estimates): **50.0%**

4. Occupational injuries and Strikes and Lockouts

Economic activity (ISIC-Rev.3)	Rates of fatal injuries 2006 [12] Labour inspectorate records Per 100,000 employees Reported injuries			Rates of non-fatal injuries 2006 [12] Labour inspectorate records Per 100,000 employees Reported injuries			Strikes and lockouts 2007 [13,14] Special data collection		
	Total	Men	Women	Total	Men	Women	Strikes and lockouts	Workers involved [15]	Days not worked [15]
Total	1.0	1.4	0.1	1 113	745	651	152	744 800	1 041 100
A-B	.	.	.	.	.	.	1	0	0
A	6.4	8.5	1.4	545	673	245	.	.	.
B	14.9	17.1	0.0	461	461	463	.	.	.
C	15.4	17.9	0.0	1 400	1 593	209	0	0	0
D	1.3	1.8	0.0	942	1 104	460	22	13 500	15 600
E	1.0	1.4	0.0	925	1 263	217	0	0	0
F	4.5	5.3	0.0	868	1 006	25	4	800	2 300
G	0.1	0.3	0.0	389	483	289	0	0	0
H	0.2	0.4	0.1	284	326	251	0	0	0
I	2.1	2.9	0.0	1 541	1 857	647	55	399 300	657 500
J	0.0	0.0	0.0	96	59	129	0	0	0
K	0.2	0.3	0.0	207	281	117	6	1 500	2 200
L	0.4	0.7	0.1	1 352	1 806	945	20	317 400	324 700
M	1.0	0.8	0.1	2 382	391	1 082	21	8 700	30 500
N	1.6	0.9	0.2	3 981	1 059	1 679	12	2 100	4 700
O	1.2	2.4	0.0	296	432	165	11	1 600	3 500
O-Q	1.2	2.4	0.0	298	435	166	.	.	.

5. Consumer price indices (base period: 2000=100)

	2002	2003	2004	2005	2006	2007
General indices	103.5	106.5	109.6	112.7	116.3	121.3
Food index, including non-alcoholic beverages	104.0	105.4	106.0	107.3	109.6	114.6
Electricity, gas and other fuel indices	104.0	106.1	113.6	129.0	160.7	172.1
Clothing indices, including footwear	91.2	89.8	87.3	85.2	84.1	83.4
Rent indices	106.1	107.7	110.1	113.9	117.2	121.1
General index, excluding housing	102.9	104.7	106.0	107.7	110.5	113.6

[1] Persons aged 16 years and over. [2] Second quarter. [3] March-May. [4] Men aged 16 to 64 years; women aged 16-59 years. [5] Levels X-1. [6] Levels 6-7. [7] June. [8] April; full-time employees on adult rates. [9] Incl. overtime. [10] Results with imputation and weighting. [11] Incl. overtime payments. [12] Year beginning in April of year indicated. [13] Incl. stoppages involving fewer than 10 workers or lasting less than one day if 100 or more workdays not worked. [14] Excl. political strikes. [15] Figures rounded to nearest 100.

[1] Personnes âgées de 16 ans et plus. [2] Deuxième trimestre. [3] Mars-mai. [4] Hommes âgés de 16 à 64 ans; femmes âgées de 16 à 59 ans. [5] Niveaux X-1. [6] Niveaux 6-7. [7] Juin. [8] Avril; salariés à plein temps rémunérés sur la base de taux de salaires pour adultes. [9] Y compris les heures supplémentaires. [10] Résultats après imputation et pondération. [11] Y compris la rémunération des heures supplémentaires. [12] Année commençant en avril de l'année indiquée. [13] Y compris les arrêts impliquant moins de 10 travailleurs ou de moins d'un jour si plus de 100 journées de travail non effectuées. [14] Non compris les grèves politiques. [15] Chiffres arrondis au 100 le plus proche.

[1] Personas de 16 años y más. [2] Segundo trimestre. [3] Marzo-mayo. [4] Hombres de 16 a 64 años; mujeres de 16 a 59 años. [5] Niveles X-1. [6] Niveles 6-7. [7] Junio. [8] Abril; asalariados a tiempo completo pagados sobre la base de tasas de salarios para adultos. [9] Incl. las horas extraordinarias. [10] Resultados después imputación y ponderación. [11] Incl. los pagos por horas extraordinarias. [12] Año que comienza en abril del año indicado. [13] Incl. las interrupciones con menos de 10 trabajadores o de menos de un día si hubo más de 100 días de trabajo no trabajados. [14] Excl. las huelgas políticas. [15] Cifras redondeadas al 100 más próximo.

United States

1. Economically active population, Employment and Unemployment ('000)

	Economically active population		Employment		Unemployment	
	Total	Women (%)	Total	Women (%)	Total	Women (%)
Age group	2007 [1,2] Labour force survey		2007 ★ Labour force survey		2007 [2] Labour force survey	
Total	153 124	46.4	146 046	46.4	7 078	45.2
16-19	7 012	49.5	5 911	50.6	1 101	43.4
20-24	15 205	46.8	13 964	47.2	1 241	41.9
25-29	17 130	44.9	16 247	45.0	883	43.6
30-34	16 000	44.6	15 339	44.5	661	45.8
35-39	17 292	44.9	16 677	44.7	615	49.4
40-44	18 235	46.4	17 625	46.4	610	47.0
45-49	18 903	47.1	18 285	47.1	618	48.5
50-54	16 795	47.6	16 278	47.6	517	47.2
55-59	13 104	47.7	12 691	47.8	413	46.7
60-64	7 646	46.9	7 417	47.0	229	43.7
65-69	3 179	46.2	3 074	46.3	105	43.8
70-74	1 457	44.4	1 407	44.5	50	42.0
75+	1 167	42.8	1 132	42.8	35	42.9
Economic activity (ISIC-Rev.3)	2007 [1,2] Labour force survey		2007 [1,2] Labour force survey		2007 [2] Labour force survey	
Total	153 124	46.4	146 047	46.4	7 078	45.2
A-B	2 186	23.7	2 095	23.4	91	29.7
C Mining and Quarrying	762	13.9	736	13.7	26	15.4
D Manufacturing	17 017	30.3	16 302	30.0	715	37.9
E Electricity, Gas and Water Supply	1 210	21.7	1 193	21.5	17	29.4
F Construction	12 714	9.4	11 856	9.4	858	8.6
G Wholesale and Retail Trade; Repair of Motor Vehicles ...	21 953	45.2	20 937	45.0	1 016	50.8
H Hotels and Restaurants	10 340	53.0	9 582	52.8	758	55.7
I Transport, Storage and Communications	6 709	25.2	6 457	25.1	252	27.0
J Financial Intermediation	7 504	58.6	7 306	58.5	198	61.6
K Real Estate, Renting and Business Activities	19 726	43.6	18 802	43.6	924	44.4
L Public Administration and Defence; Compulsory Social ...	6 879	45.0	6 746	44.9	133	50.4
M Education	13 157	69.1	12 828	69.1	329	66.6
N Health and Social Work	18 345	78.8	17 834	78.7	511	81.4
O-X	14 622	48.0	13 371	48.2	623	46.5
Unemployed seeking their first job	627	45.5	.	.	627	45.5
Occupation (ISCO-88)	2007 [1,2] Labour force survey		2007 [1,2] Labour force survey		2007 [2] Labour force survey	
Total	153 124	46.4	146 047	46.4	7 078	45.2
1 Legislators, senior officials and managers	22 006	42.8	21 577	42.7	429	48.7
2-3	30 872	56.2	30 210	56.2	662	56.3
4 Clerks	20 317	75.0	19 513	75.2	804	69.2
5 Service workers and shop and market sales workers	43 191	54.3	40 835	54.1	2 356	58.6
6 Skilled agricultural and fishery workers	1 049	22.2	960	20.9	89	36.0
7-8	35 041	14.3	32 951	14.1	2 091	18.0
X Not classifiable by occupation	.	.	.	.	20	20.0
Unemployed seeking their first job	627	45.5	.	.	627	45.5
Education level (ISCED-76)	2007 [1,3] Labour force survey		2007 ★ Labour force survey		2007 [3,4] Labour force survey	
Total	130 907	46.1	126 172	46.1	4 735	46.4
X No schooling [5]	12 408	35.7	11 522	35.3	886	41.0
3 Second level, second stage	38 539	44.5	36 857	44.6	1 682	43.5
5 Third level, first stage, leading to an award not equivalent ...	35 887	50.3	34 612	50.2	1 275	52.2
6 Third level, first stage, leading to a first university degree ...	28 688	47.7	28 055	47.7	633	49.0
7 Third level, second stage	15 386	46.1	15 128	46.1	258	49.6
Status in employment (ICSE-58)	2007 [1,2] Labour force survey					
Total	153 124	46.4				
1 Employers and own-account workers	10 718	37.0				
2 Employees	141 644	47.1				
3 Unpaid family workers	135	68.9				
4 Not classifiable by status	627	45.5				
Status in employment (ICSE-1993)			2007 [1,2] Labour force survey			
Total	.	.	146 047	46.4		
1 Employees	.	.	135 502	47.1		
2,3	.	.	10 413	37.2		
5 Contributing family workers	.	.	131	68.7		

2. Population ('000), Activity rate and Unemployment rate

	Population			Activity rate			Unemployment rate		
Age group	2007 [1] Labour force survey			2007 [1] Labour force survey			2007 [2] Labour force survey		
	Total	Men	Women	Total	Men	Women	Total	Men	Women
Total	.	.	.	.	.	.	4.6	4.7	4.5
15+	231 866	112 173	119 695	66.0	73.2	59.3	4.6	4.7	4.5
15-24	37 409	18 909	18 501	59.4	61.5	57.2	10.5	11.6	9.4
25-54	125 696	62 081	63 615	83.0	90.9	75.4	3.7	3.7	3.8
55+	68 761	31 183	37 579	38.6	45.2	33.2	3.1	3.2	3.0

United States

3. Paid employment ('000), Hours of work (weekly) and Wages

Economic activity (ISIC-Rev.3)	Paid employment 2007 [6] Labour-related establishment survey			Hours of work 2007 [7,8] Labour-related establishment survey Hours paid for / Wage earners			Wages 2007 [7,8] Labour-related establishment survey Earnings per hour / Wage earners / Dollar		
	Total	Men	Women	Total	Men	Women	Total	Men	Women
Total	137 562.2	70 751.8	66 810.4	.	.	.	.	.	.
C	662.1	576.0	86.1	46.2	.	.	21.43	.	.
D	14 804.9	10 379.8	4 425.1	41.2 [9]	.	.	.	.	.
E	553.4 [10]	403.2 [10]	150.2 [10]	42.4	.	.	27.87	.	.
F	7 614.0	6 667.0	947.0	39.0	.	.	20.95	.	.
G	22 734.5	12 955.9	9 778.6	.	.	.	.	.	.
H	11 496.3	5 358.2	6 138.1	25.6	.	.	.	.	.
I	6 597.1	4 638.1	1 959.0	.	.	.	.	.	.
J	6 146.3	2 236.1	3 910.2	.	.	.	.	.	.
K	19 881.1	10 827.8	9 053.3	.	.	.	.	.	.
L	11 145.7	5 816.8	5 328.9	.	.	.	.	.	.
M	13 244.1	4 536.9	8 707.2	.	.	.	.	.	.
N	15 377.6	2 988.2	12 389.4	32.8	.	.	18.48	.	.
O	7 304.6 [11]	3 367.9 [11]	3 936.7 [11]	.	.	.	.	.	.

Share of women in wage employment in the non-agricultural sector [6] (2007 - Labour-related establishment survey): **48.6%**

4. Occupational injuries and Strikes and Lockouts

Economic activity (ISIC-Rev.3)	Rates of fatal injuries 2006 [12] Labour-related establishment census Per 100,000 workers employed Reported injuries			Rates of non-fatal injuries 2006 [13] Labour-related establishment survey Per 20,000,000 hours worked Reported injuries			Strikes and lockouts 2007 [14] Special data collection		
	Total	Men	Women	Total	Men	Women	Strikes and lockouts [15]	Workers involved [15]	Days not worked [16]
Total	4	7	1	1.3 [17]	.	.	23	192 900	1 264 800
A-B	30	.	.	1.9 [17]	.	.	0	0	0
A	.	.	.	.	.	.	0	0	0
B	.	.	.	.	.	.	1	1 200	9 600
C	28	.	.	1.4	.	.	6	90 700	561 400
D	3	.	.	1.4	.	.	0	0	0
E	6	.	.	1.2	.	.	2	4 000	18 400
F	11	.	.	2.2	.	.	0	0	0
G	.	.	.	.	.	.	0	0	0
H	2	.	.	1.1	.	.	5	62 800	104 800
I	.	.	.	.	.	.	0	0	0
J	1	.	.	0.2	.	.	1	10 500	409 500
K	.	.	.	.	.	.	0	0	0
L	2	.	.	.	.	.	4	6 700	83 100
M	1	.	.	0.7	.	.	2	10 000	25 000
N	1	.	.	1.5	.	.	2	7 000	53 000
O	.	.	.	.	.	.	.	.	.

5. Consumer price indices (base period: 2000=100)

[18]	2002	2003	2004	2005	2006	2007
General indices	104.5	106.9	109.7	113.4	117.1	120.4
Food index, including non-alcoholic beverages	105.0	107.3	111.0	113.6	116.3	120.9
Electricity, gas and other fuel indices	103.6	112.5	117.6	131.6	144.2	148.0
Clothing indices, including footwear	95.7	93.3	92.9	92.2	92.2	91.8
Rent indices	108.6	111.7	114.7	118.2	122.4	127.6
General index, excluding housing [19]	103.1	105.4	108.2	112.3	115.8	118.7

[1] Excl. armed forces. [2] Persons aged 16 years and over. [3] Persons aged 25 years and over. [4] Persons with diploma only. [5] Levels X-2. [6] Due to rounding, total may not equal sum of components. [7] National classification not strictly compatible with ISIC. [8] Private sector: production and construction workers and non-supervisory employees. [9] Private sector; production workers. [10] Incl. sewage and refuse disposal, sanitation and similar activities. [11] Excl. sewage and refuse disposal, sanitation and similar activities. [12] Total and category L also include government sector excluded from the other categories. [13] Private sector. [14] Excl. work stoppages involving fewer than 1,000 workers and lasting less than a full day or shift. [15] Work stoppages beginning in the year indicated. [16] Figures rounded to nearest 100. [17] Excl. farms with fewer than 11 employees. [18] All Urban Consumers. [19] Excl. also expenditure on insurance, maintenance and repairs.

Uruguay

1. Población económicamente activa, Empleo y Desempleo ('000)

	Población económicamente activa		Empleo		Desempleo	
	Total	Mujeres (%)	Total	Mujeres (%)	Total	Mujeres (%)
Grupo de edad	2007 [1] Encuesta de la fuerza de trabajo		1996 ★ Censo de población		2007 [1] Encuesta de la fuerza de trabajo	
Total	1 631.353	44.0	1 283.295	39.7	149.300	59.8
12-14	.	.	9.107	33.3	.	.
14-19	101.526	36.0	.	.	33.600	45.2
15-19	.	.	80.678	34.0	.	.
20-24	171.348	43.8	149.986	39.7	32.700	56.9
25-29	183.330	46.0	153.657	40.5	19.000	66.3
30-34	193.948	45.8	160.180	40.9	13.900	72.7
35-39	177.437	45.5	158.309	42.1	11.400	72.8
40-44	177.988	46.6	142.941	42.4	9.700	76.3
45-49	176.850	45.1	125.180	42.0	8.500	71.8
50-54	162.764	45.0	108.017	40.6	7.900	67.1
55-59	124.726	42.3	86.251	35.7	5.600	46.4
60-64	85.308	42.5	54.762	33.0	3.700	51.4
65-69	44.991	37.3	30.707	33.4	2.000	35.0
70-74	19.902	36.9	13.240	36.0	1.000	40.0
75+	11.236	32.4	10.280	42.2	0.300	33.3
?	.	.	.	.	.	.
Actividad económica (CIIU-Rev.3)	2007 [1] Encuesta de la fuerza de trabajo		2007 [1 2] Encuesta de la fuerza de trabajo		2007 ★ Encuesta de la fuerza de trabajo	
Total	1 631.353	44.0	1 482.100	42.4	149.253	59.9
A-C	173.507	19.3	163.300	18.6	10.207	30.9
D-E	236.675	36.3	219.900	34.7	16.775	56.4
F Construcción	113.143	3.2	102.100	2.8	11.043	6.9
G-H	345.878	43.9	319.200	42.5	26.678	60.6
I Transporte, almacenamiento y comunicaciones	88.555	19.2	83.900	18.4	4.655	33.8
J-K	123.924	41.7	114.400	41.1	9.524	48.9
L Administración pública y defensa; planes de seguridad ...	96.795	34.2	94.400	33.7	2.395	54.9
M Enseñanza	87.275	76.7	84.200	76.5	3.075	82.2
N Servicios sociales y de salud	101.852	74.9	97.200	74.1	4.652	91.8
O-Q	81.458	50.0	.	.	.	.
O,Q	.	.	75.200	47.9	.	.
P Hogares privados con servicio doméstico	.	.	128.200	91.0	.	.
Q Organizaciones y órganos extraterritoriales	154.026	91.8	.	.	.	.
X No pueden clasificarse según la actividad económica	28.265	57.8	1.900	.	26.365	61.9
Desempleados sin empleo anterior	28.265	57.8	.	.	.	.
Ocupación (CIUO-88)	2007 [1] Encuesta de la fuerza de trabajo		2007 [1 2] Encuesta de la fuerza de trabajo		2007 ★ Encuesta de la fuerza de trabajo	
Total	1 631.353	44.0	1 482.100	42.4	149.253	59.8
1 Miembros del poder ejecutivo y de los cuerpos legislativos ...	89.987	40.5	87.400	40.3	2.587	48.8
2 Profesionales científicos e intelectuales	142.302	63.4	139.100	63.3	3.202	70.7
3 Técnicos y profesionales de nivel medio	94.826	38.1	90.600	37.5	4.226	50.8
4 Empleados de oficina	191.546	61.4	180.700	60.5	10.846	75.2
5 Trabajadores de los servicios y vendedores de comercios ...	232.690	68.0	204.100	65.5	28.590	85.6
6 Agricultores y trabajadores calificados agropecuarios ...	84.346	14.7	82.200	14.7	2.146	15.8
7 Oficiales, operarios y artesanos de artes mecánicas ...	230.113	17.0	216.400	16.5	13.713	23.9
8 Operadores de instalaciones y máquinas y montadores	111.610	13.8	105.800	12.7	5.810	35.4
9 Trabajadores no calificados	413.320	47.5	363.900	45.9	49.420	58.5
0 Fuerzas armadas	12.347	2.9	11.900	2.5	0.447	13.9
X No pueden clasificarse según la ocupación	28.265	57.8	-	.	28.265	57.8
Desempleados sin empleo anterior	28.265	57.8	.	.	.	.
Nivel de educación (CINE-76)	2007 [1] Encuesta de la fuerza de trabajo				2007 [1] Encuesta de la fuerza de trabajo	
Total	1 631.353	44.0	.	.	149.000	59.9
X Sin escolaridad	7.945	35.5	.	.	0.400	50.0
1 Enseñanza de primer grado	470.626	37.4	.	.	42.600	60.1
2 Enseñanza de segundo grado, ciclo inferior	407.677	37.6	.	.	45.500	55.8
3 Enseñanza de segundo grado, ciclo superior	440.501	47.1	.	.	40.200	62.7
5 Enseñanza de tercer grado que no permite obtener un ...	93.344	73.8	.	.	4.000	77.5
6 Enseñanza de tercer grado que permite obtener un primer ...	211.259	51.9	.	.	16.600	59.6
Situación en el empleo (CISE-1993)	2007 [1] Encuesta de la fuerza de trabajo		2007 [1 2] Encuesta de la fuerza de trabajo		2007 ★ Encuesta de la fuerza de trabajo	
Total	1 631.353	44.0	1 482.100	42.4	149.253	59.9
1 Asalariados	1 137.703	45.9	1 035.700	44.1	102.003	63.7
2 Empleadores	73.078	26.0	71.100	26.0	1.978	27.1
3 Trabajadores por cuenta propia	362.465	38.5	345.300	38.3	17.165	42.6
5 Trabajadores familiares auxiliares	26.798	70.6	26.400	70.8	0.398	55.3
6 Inclasificables según la situación	31.310	59.3	3.100	74.2	28.210	57.7

Uruguay

2. Población ('000), Tasa de actividad y Tasa de desempleo

Grupo de edad	Población 2007 Encuesta de la fuerza de trabajo			Tasa de actividad 2007 Encuesta de la fuerza de trabajo			Tasa de desempleo 1996 [3][4] Censo de población		
	Total	Hombres	Mujeres	Total	Hombres	Mujeres	Total	Hombres	Mujeres
Total	3 323.906	1 605.466	1 718.440	49.1	56.9	41.8	10.9	9.2	13.4
15+	2 599.239	1 235.148	1 364.092	62.8	73.9	52.7	10.8	9.1	13.3
15-24	546.290	276.761	269.529	50.0	58.3	41.4	20.6	17.8	24.8
25-54	1 255.091	607.715	647.377	85.4	95.8	75.7	8.5	6.9	10.6
55+	797.858	350.672	447.186	35.9	48.3	26.1	7.8	6.8	9.6

3. Empleo remunerado ('000), Horas de trabajo (por semana) y Salarios

Actividad económica (CIIU-Rev.3)	Empleo remunerado 2007 [1][2] Encuesta de la fuerza de trabajo			Horas de trabajo 2007 Encuesta de la fuerza de trabajo Horas efectivamente trabajadas / Asalariados			Salarios 2001 [5] Encuesta industrial/comercial Ganancias por mes / Asalariados / Peso		
	Total	Hombres	Mujeres	Total	Hombres	Mujeres	Total	Hombres	Mujeres
Total	1 034.5	577.4	457.2	39.3	45.1	35.0	.	.	.
A-B	.	.	.	47.2	48.5	39.8	.	.	.
C-Q	.	.	.	39.9	44.6	34.9	.	.	.
A-C	93.4	80.6	12.8	.	.	.	.	.	.
D	.	.	.	.	.	.	6 856	.	.
D-E	156.6	110.5	46.1	45.0	46.2	42.4	.	.	.
F	58.7	56.8	1.9	44.9	45.2	35.1	.	.	.
G-H	181.3	105.4	75.9	43.6	45.0	41.9	.	.	.
I	64.8	51.8	13.0	47.6	49.6	40.5	.	.	.
J-K	64.2	32.9	31.2	38.7	40.7	36.8	.	.	.
L	94.2	62.6	31.7	43.7	47.5	36.7	.	.	.
M	76.8	17.9	58.9	29.2	32.5	28.2	.	.	.
N	81.1	20.7	60.4	36.4	37.8	36.0	.	.	.
O,Q	47.8	27.7	20.1	35.6	37.5	33.3	.	.	.
P	115.6	10.4	105.1	29.5	44.6	28.1	.	.	.
X	-	-	-	.	.	.	.	.	.

Proporción de mujeres entre los empleados remunerados en el sector no agrícola [1][2] (2007 - Encuesta de la fuerza de trabajo): **44.2%**

4. Lesiones profesionales y Huelgas y cierres patronales

Datos no disponibles.

5. Índices de precios al consumidor (periodo de base: 2000=100)

Montevideo	2002	2003	2004	2005	2006	2007
Índices generales	118.9	142.0	155.0	162.3	172.7	186.7
Índices de la alimentación incluyendo las bebidas no alcohólicas	117.2	142.5	159.2	165.7	176.0	202.5
Índices de la electricidad, gas y otros combustibles	125.4	175.4	199.8	209.6	226.1	.
Índices del vestido, incl. calzado	108.0	127.5	138.5	145.2	148.9	.
Índices del aquiler	103.0	100.8	101.7	107.4	116.5	.
Índices generales, excluyendo la vivienda	119.4	142.3	155.2	162.2	172.1	.

[1] Persons aged 14 years and over. [2] Excl. conscripts. [3] Persons aged 12 years and over. [4] May. [5] Establishments with 5 or more persons employed.

[1] Personnes âgées de 14 ans et plus. [2] Non compris les conscrits. [3] Personnes âgées de 12 ans et plus. [4] Mai. [5] Etablissements occupant 5 personnes et plus.

[1] Personas de 14 años y más. [2] Excl. los conscriptos. [3] Personas de 12 años y más. [4] Mayo. [5] Establecimientos con 5 y más trabajadores.

Uzbekistan

1. Economically active population, Employment and Unemployment ('000)

	Economically active population		Employment		Unemployment	
	Total	Women (%)	Total	Women (%)	Total	Women (%)
Age group			2005 Official estimates		2005 Employment office records	
Total	.	.	10 200.0	.	27.7	.
Economic activity (ISIC-Rev.2)			1999 Official estimates			
Total	.	.	8 885	.	.	.
1 Agriculture, Hunting, Forestry and Fishing	.	.	3 421	.	.	.
2-4	.	.	1 142	.	.	.
5 Construction	.	.	583	.	.	.
6 Wholesale and Retail Trade and Restaurants and Hotels	.	.	734	.	.	.
7 Transport, Storage and Communication	.	.	372	.	.	.
8 Financing, Insurance, Real Estate and Business Services	.	.	50	.	.	.
9 Community, Social and Personal Services	.	.	1 968	.	.	.
0 Activities not Adequately Defined	.	.	616	.	.	.

2. Population ('000), Activity rate and Unemployment rate

	Population			Activity rate			Unemployment rate 2005 Employment office records		
Age group	Total	Men	Women	Total	Men	Women	Total	Men	Women
Total	.	.	.	.	.	.	0.3	.	.

3. Paid employment ('000), Hours of work (weekly) and Wages

Economic activity (ISIC-Rev.3)	Paid employment			Hours of work			Wages 1999 Labour-related establishment survey Earnings per month / Employees / Sum		
	Total	Men	Women	Total	Men	Women	Total	Men	Women
Total	.	.	.	.	.	.	8 823	.	.
A	.	.	.	.	.	.	4 106	.	.
C-E	.	.	.	.	.	.	14 068	.	.
F	.	.	.	.	.	.	12 843	.	.
G	.	.	.	.	.	.	6 476	.	.
I	.	.	.	.	.	.	11 667	.	.
J [1]	.	.	.	.	.	.	16 213	.	.
K [2]	.	.	.	.	.	.	19 595	.	.
M	.	.	.	.	.	.	6 163	.	.
N	.	.	.	.	.	.	5 500	.	.

4. Occupational injuries and Strikes and Lockouts

Statistics not available.

5. Consumer price indices (base period: 2000=100)

Statistics not available for the period 2002-2007.

[1] Financial institutions [2] Computer services   [1] Etablissements financiers [2] Services informatiques   [1] Establecimientos financieros [2] Servicios informáticos

Vanuatu

1. Economically active population, Employment and Unemployment ('000)

	Economically active population		Employment		Unemployment	
	Total	Women (%)	Total	Women (%)	Total	Women (%)
Age group	1989 [1,2] Population census					
Total	66.957	46.3	.	.	.	.
15-19	9.936	48.3	.	.	.	.
20-24	10.705	48.2	.	.	.	.
25-29	10.045	48.0	.	.	.	.
30-34	7.830	48.2	.	.	.	.
35-39	7.015	45.8	.	.	.	.
40-44	5.226	45.8	.	.	.	.
45-49	4.791	42.3	.	.	.	.
50-54	3.054	44.5	.	.	.	.
55-59	2.615	42.6	.	.	.	.
60-64	2.143	42.1	.	.	.	.
65-69	1.613	40.1	.	.	.	.
70-74	0.884	42.4	.	.	.	.
75+	1.100	37.8	.	.	.	.
Occupation (ISCO-1968)			1983 [3,4] Labour-related establishment survey			
Total	.	.	6.19	.	.	.
0/1 Professional, technical and related workers	.	.	0.30	.	.	.
2 Administrative and managerial workers	.	.	0.12	.	.	.
3 Clerical and related workers	.	.	0.85	.	.	.
4 Sales workers	.	.	0.79	.	.	.
5 Service workers	.	.	1.50	.	.	.
6 Agriculture, animal husbandry and forestry workers ...	.	.	0.20	.	.	.
7/8/9 Production and related workers, transport equipment ...	.	.	2.24	.	.	.
X Not classifiable by occupation	.	.	0.18	.	.	.

2. Population ('000), Activity rate and Unemployment rate

	Population			Activity rate			Unemployment rate		
Age group	1989 [2] Population census			1989 [2] Population census					
	Total	Men	Women	Total	Men	Women	Total	Men	Women
Total	142.419	73.384	69.035	47.0	49.0	44.9	.	.	.
15+	79.669	40.589	39.080	84.0	88.6	79.3	.	.	.
15-24	26.311	13.098	13.213	78.5	81.5	75.4	.	.	.
25-54	42.768	21.597	21.171	88.8	94.3	83.1	.	.	.
55+	10.590	5.894	4.696	78.9	83.1	73.6	.	.	.

3. Paid employment ('000), Hours of work (weekly) and Wages

Economic activity (ISIC-Rev.2)	Paid employment 1983 [3,4] Labour-related establishment survey			Hours of work			Wages		
	Total	Men	Women	Total	Men	Women	Total	Men	Women
Total	6.19	.	.	.	.	.	.	.	.
1 [5]	0.28	.	.	.	.	.	.	.	.
3 [6]	0.73	.	.	.	.	.	.	.	.
5	0.46	.	.	.	.	.	.	.	.
6	2.29	.	.	.	.	.	.	.	.
7	0.63	.	.	.	.	.	.	.	.
8	0.47	.	.	.	.	.	.	.	.
9	1.33	.	.	.	.	.	.	.	.

4. Occupational injuries and Strikes and Lockouts

Statistics not available.

5. Consumer price indices (base period: 2000=100)

	2002	2003	2004	2005	2006	2007
General indices	105.7	108.8	110.4	111.7	114.0	118.5
Food index, including non-alcoholic beverages	102.7	105.0	108.5	108.1	111.8	116.1
Clothing indices, including footwear	100.5	101.8	101.6	101.5	101.4	101.3
Rent indices [7]	100.5	103.6	112.0	115.9	118.7	123.9

[1] Persons aged 15 years and over. [2] May. [3] Private sector. [4] Urban areas. [5] Incl. mining and quarrying. [6] Incl. electricity, gas and water. [7] Incl. water, electricity, gas and other fuels.

[1] Personnes âgées de 15 ans et plus. [2] Mai. [3] Secteur privé. [4] Régions urbaines. [5] Y compris les industries extractives. [6] Y compris l'électricité, le gaz et l'eau. [7] Y compris l'eau, l'électricité, le gaz et autres combustibles.

[1] Personas de 15 años y más. [2] Mayo. [3] Sector privado. [4] Areas urbanas. [5] Incl. las minas y canteras. [6] Incl. electricidad, gas y agua. [7] Incl. el agua, la electricidad, el gas y otros combustibles.

Venezuela, Rep. Bolivariana de

1. Población económicamente activa, Empleo y Desempleo ('000)

	Población económicamente activa		Empleo		Desempleo	
	Total	Mujeres (%)	Total	Mujeres (%)	Total	Mujeres (%)
Grupo de edad	2007 [1 2 3]		2007 ★		2007 [2 3]	
	Encuesta de la fuerza de trabajo		Encuesta de la fuerza de trabajo		Encuesta de la fuerza de trabajo	
Total	12 531.9	38.6	11 590.0	38.4	941.8	42.1
10-14	111.7	27.5	98.1	26.7	13.6	33.6
15-19	739.8	29.9	621.9	28.7	117.9	36.4
20-24	1 623.3	37.0	1 402.5	35.7	220.8	45.3
25-29	1 800.2	39.5	1 643.5	38.2	156.7	52.5
30-34	1 670.9	40.9	1 559.0	40.2	111.9	51.0
35-39	1 535.4	41.8	1 450.3	41.7	85.1	43.5
40-44	1 433.0	42.0	1 363.6	42.2	69.4	38.1
45-49	1 201.2	41.1	1 144.6	41.4	56.7	34.0
50-54	946.7	39.5	904.6	39.8	42.1	32.1
55-59	676.0	35.8	644.8	36.5	31.2	21.5
60-64	393.6	31.7	375.9	32.4	17.8	18.6
65-69	203.0	31.1	194.4	32.0	8.6	9.9
70-74	104.2	26.6	98.0	26.4	6.2	28.2
75+	92.8	27.4	88.8	28.3	3.9	8.5
Actividad económica (CIIU-Rev.2)	1997 ★		2007 [1 4]		1997 [4]	
	Encuesta de la fuerza de trabajo		Encuesta de la fuerza de trabajo		Encuesta de la fuerza de trabajo	
Total	9 347.5	35.3	11 491.9	38.5	1 060.7	44.1
1 Agricultura, caza, silvicultura y pesca	939.6	5.1	1 001.9	7.8	45.6	14.3
2 Explotación de minas y canteras	105.7	10.7	102.7	16.1	15.2	6.2
3 Industrias manufactureras	1 250.9	30.6	1 418.4	31.9	128.4	38.7
4 Electricidad, gas y agua	73.4	17.4	51.5	23.9	7.2	26.8
5 Construcción	841.4	3.7	1 109.7	4.6	147.0	3.3
6 Comercio al por mayor y al por menor y restaurantes y ...	2 169.1	44.3	2 703.8	51.6	183.6	57.5
7 Transportes, almacenamiento y comunicaciones	577.7	9.2	994.4	9.7	43.3	15.6
8 Establecimientos financieros, seguros, bienes inmuebles ...	523.3	40.8	589.6	37.9	57.0	49.7
9 Servicios comunales, sociales y personales	2 616.3	55.4	3 494.8	59.7	204.6	63.5
0 Actividades no bien especificadas	27.7	31.0	25.2	35.1	6.4	18.6
Desempleados sin empleo anterior	.	.	.	.	222.4	59.6
Ocupación (CIUO-1968)	2002 ★		2002 [1 4]		2002 [4]	
	Encuesta de la fuerza de trabajo		Encuesta de la fuerza de trabajo		Encuesta de la fuerza de trabajo	
Total	11 521.5	39.5	9 698.9	38.4	1 822.6	45.2
0/1 Profesionales, técnicos y trabajadores asimilados	1 178.2	61.5	1 059.4	61.3	118.8	63.3
2 Directores y funcionarios públicos superiores	285.1	28.1	256.1	27.4	29.0	34.5
3 Personal administrativo y trabajadores asimilados	879.1	66.9	718.9	65.5	160.2	73.2
4 Comerciantes y vendedores	2 279.9	53.4	1 982.5	51.9	297.4	63.8
5 Trabajadores de los servicios	2 229.9	60.7	1 875.1	59.4	354.8	67.4
6 Trabajadores agrícolas y forestales, pescadores y cazadores	1 080.2	6.2	978.2	6.2	102.0	5.6
7/8/9 Obreros no agrícolas, conductores de máquinas y ...	3 340.7	11.5	2 779.9	11.7	560.8	10.9
X No pueden clasificarse según la ocupación	105.2	41.3	48.7	16.6	56.5	62.5
Desempleados sin empleo anterior	.	.	.	.	143.0	63.1
Nivel de educación (CINE-76)					1999 [4]	
					Encuesta de la fuerza de trabajo	
Total	.	.	.	.	1 483.4	40.5
X Sin escolaridad	.	.	.	.	54.5	25.5
1-2	.	.	.	.	858.2	33.1
3-5	.	.	.	.	356.2	50.9
6-7	.	.	.	.	214.1	56.8
? Nivel desconocido	.	.	.	.	0.4	100.0
Situación en el empleo (CISE-1993)	2001 [2 5]		2007 [1 4]			
	Censo de población		Encuesta de la fuerza de trabajo			
Total	8 507.2	34.9	11 491.9	38.5	.	.
1 Asalariados	5 369.1	34.7	6 814.7	39.3	.	.
2 Empleadores	482.7	21.6	479.2	17.5	.	.
3 Trabajadores por cuenta propia	1 824.8	28.0	3 315.7	41.7	.	.
4 Miembros de cooperativas de productores	38.6	12.9	769.7	26.4	.	.
5 Trabajadores familiares auxiliares	48.1	27.7	112.7	63.0	.	.
6 Inclasificables según la situación	496.1	79.9	-		.	.

2. Población ('000), Tasa de actividad y Tasa de desempleo

	Población 2007 [1 3 6]			Tasa de actividad 2007 [1 3 6]			Tasa de desempleo 2007 [2 3]		
	Encuesta de la fuerza de trabajo			Encuesta de la fuerza de trabajo			Encuesta de la fuerza de trabajo		
Grupo de edad	Total	Hombres	Mujeres	Total	Hombres	Mujeres	Total	Hombres	Mujeres
Total	27 404.7	13 747.1	13 657.6	45.7	55.9	35.4	7.5	7.1	8.1
15+	19 112.2	9 511.8	9 600.4	65.0	80.0	50.1	7.5	7.1	8.1
15-24	5 220.6	2 649.5	2 571.1	45.3	58.2	32.0	14.3	12.7	17.4
25-54	10 645.4	5 310.7	5 334.7	80.7	95.7	65.7	6.1	5.6	6.7
55+	3 246.2	1 551.6	1 694.6	45.3	63.6	28.5	4.6	5.6	2.7

Venezuela, Rep. Bolivariana de

3. Empleo remunerado ('000), Horas de trabajo (por semana) y Salarios

Actividad económica (CIIU-Rev.2)	Empleo remunerado 1990 [7] Encuesta de establecimientos relacionada con el trabajo			Horas de trabajo 2007 Encuesta de la fuerza de trabajo Horas efectivamente trabajadas / Empleo total			Salarios 1997 [8] Estimaciones oficiales Ganancias por mes / Asalariados / Bolívar		
	Total	Hombres	Mujeres	Total	Hombres	Mujeres	Total	Hombres	Mujeres
Total	.	.	.	41	43	37	174 424	.	.
2-9	.	.	.	42	43	39	.	.	.
1	.	.	.	41	42	35	100 386	.	.
2	.	.	.	43	44	40	107 019	.	.
3	465.4	.	.	40	42	36	141 122	.	.
4	.	.	.	42	42	41	141 003	.	.
5	.	.	.	41	41	41	158 942	.	.
6	.	.	.	40	44	37	263 500	.	.
7	.	.	.	45	46	41	137 729	.	.
8	.	.	.	43	45	39	156 988	.	.
9	.	.	.	39	41	37	104 504	.	.
0	.	.	.	41	42	40	.	.	.

4. Lesiones profesionales y Huelgas y cierres patronales

Actividad económica (CIIU-Rev.3)	Tasas de lesiones mortales 1997 Registros de seguros Por 1 000 000 trabajadores empleados Lesiones declaradas			Tasas de lesiones no mortales			Huelgas y cierres patronales 2002 Registros administrativos y fuentes relacionadas		
	Total	Hombres	Mujeres	Total	Hombres	Mujeres	Huelgas y cierres patronales [9]	Trabajadores implicados	Días no trabajados
Total	5.75	.	.	.	.	.	35	.	.

5. Índices de precios al consumidor (periodo de base: 2000=100)

Caracas	2002	2003	2004	2005	2006	2007
Índices generales	137.8	180.6	219.9	255.0	289.8	343.9
Índices de la alimentación incluyendo las bebidas no alcohólicas	149.0	205.2	274.6	332.5	399.3	506.3
Índices del vestido, incl. calzado	114.9	142.9	168.6	187.2	203.3	232.5
Índices del aquiler	135.9	153.4	168.1	180.3	192.5	205.1

[1] Excl. armed forces. [2] Persons aged 10 years and over. [3] Second semester. [4] Persons aged 15 years and over. [5] Oct. [6] "De jure" population. [7] Establishments with 5 or more persons employed. [8] Sep. [9] Strikes only.

[1] Non compris les forces armées. [2] Personnes âgées de 10 ans et plus. [3] Second semestre. [4] Personnes âgées de 15 ans et plus. [5] Oct. [6] Population "de jure". [7] Etablissements occupant 5 personnes et plus. [8] Sept. [9] Grèves seulement.

[1] Excl. las fuerzas armadas. [2] Personas de 10 años y más. [3] Segundo semestre. [4] Personas de 15 años y más. [5] Oct. [6] Población "de jure". [7] Establecimientos con 5 y más trabajadores. [8] Sept. [9] Huelgas solamente.

Viet Nam

1. Economically active population, Employment and Unemployment ('000)

	Economically active population		Employment		Unemployment	
	Total	Women (%)	Total	Women (%)	Total	Women (%)
Age group	2004 [1][2]		2004 ★		2004 [1][2]	
	Labour force survey		Labour force survey		Labour force survey	
Total	43 242.0	49.0	42 315.6	48.8	926.4	55.8
15-19	3 864.0	48.3	3 711.4	48.3	152.6	48.4
20-24	5 412.3	46.7	5 136.7	46.4	275.7	51.0
25-29	5 151.6	49.1	5 005.1	48.8	146.4	58.2
30-34	5 789.5	49.4	5 689.1	49.1	100.4	68.8
35-39	5 835.2	49.7	5 753.6	49.4	81.6	70.9
40-44	5 883.5	49.9	5 814.9	49.8	68.6	56.4
45-49	4 750.8	50.3	4 695.6	50.3	55.2	53.2
50-54	3 208.2	49.7	3 180.1	49.8	28.1	49.3
55-59	1 653.9	45.8	1 640.8	45.8	13.2	46.3
60-64	873.6	48.4	871.4	48.4	2.3	37.4
65+	819.4	48.8	817.0	48.8	2.3	38.7

Economic activity (ISIC-Rev.3)			2004 [1][2]			
			Labour force survey			
Total	.	.	42 315.6	48.8	.	.
A Agriculture, Hunting and Forestry	.	.	23 068.6	52.1	.	.
B Fishing	.	.	1 429.2	25.9	.	.
C Mining and Quarrying	.	.	294.9	38.0	.	.
D Manufacturing	.	.	4 949.8	50.9	.	.
E Electricity, Gas and Water Supply	.	.	141.8	17.0	.	.
F Construction	.	.	1 956.6	9.3	.	.
G Wholesale and Retail Trade; Repair of Motor Vehicles ...	.	.	4 696.0	62.1	.	.
H Hotels and Restaurants	.	.	595.0	70.4	.	.
I Transport, Storage and Communications	.	.	1 292.9	12.7	.	.
J Financial Intermediation	.	.	159.0	49.2	.	.
K Real Estate, Renting and Business Activities	.	.	219.2	35.0	.	.
L Public Administration and Defence; Compulsory Social ...	.	.	698.9	26.2	.	.
M Education	.	.	1 185.0	69.7	.	.
N Health and Social Work	.	.	328.0	57.3	.	.
O Other Community, Social and Personal Service Activities	.	.	1 056.4	40.9	.	.
P Households with Employed Persons	.	.	241.1	59.6	.	.
Q Extra-Territorial Organizations and Bodies	.	.	3.3	43.5	.	.

Occupation (ISCO-88)	2003 ★		2003 [1][2]		2003 [1][2]	
	Labour force survey		Labour force survey		Labour force survey	
Total	42 124.7	49.3	41 175.7	49.1	949.0	57.6
1 Legislators, senior officials and managers	212.4	19.7	209.5	19.9	3.0	10.3
2 Professionals	1 326.9	48.6	1 323.2	48.6	3.7	46.0
3 Technicians and associate professionals	1 226.8	55.0	1 221.6	55.0	5.2	54.1
4 Clerks	412.1	53.3	406.4	53.2	5.6	65.4
5 Service workers and shop and market sales workers	3 699.4	66.9	3 661.7	66.9	37.7	70.9
6 Skilled agricultural and fishery workers	3 488.3	41.6	3 467.1	41.5	21.1	45.0
7 Craft and related trade workers	4 949.4	36.0	4 886.7	35.9	62.8	42.2
8 Plant and machine operators and assemblers	1 500.7	20.6	1 478.0	20.3	22.7	39.6
9 Elementary occupations	24 430.3	51.7	24 261.6	51.7	168.7	54.9
X Not classifiable by occupation	878.5	59.6	260.0	57.6	618.5	60.4

Status in employment (ICSE-1993)			2004 [1][2]			
			Labour force survey			
Total	.	.	42 315.6	48.8	.	.
1 Employees	.	.	10 818.7	40.4	.	.
2 Employers	.	.	215.3	29.1	.	.
3 Own-account workers	.	.	17 437.4	37.1	.	.
5 Contributing family workers	.	.	13 842.9	70.5	.	.
6 Not classifiable by status	.	.	1.3	49.9	.	.

2. Population ('000), Activity rate and Unemployment rate

	Population			Activity rate			Unemployment rate		
Age group	2004 [2]			2004 [2]			2004 [1][2]		
	Labour force survey			Labour force survey			Labour force survey		
	Total	Men	Women	Total	Men	Women	Total	Men	Women
Total	.	.	.	.	.	.	2.1	1.9	2.4
15+	60 556.7	29 221.8	31 334.9	71.4	75.5	67.6	2.1	1.9	2.4
15-24	16 523.7	8 593.9	7 929.7	56.1	56.8	55.4	4.6	4.4	4.9
25-54	33 520.8	16 123.5	17 397.4	91.3	95.6	87.4	1.6	1.2	1.9
55+	10 512.2	4 504.4	6 007.8	31.8	39.2	26.3	0.5	0.6	0.5

Viet Nam

3. Paid employment ('000), Hours of work (weekly) and Wages

Economic activity (ISIC-Rev.2)	Paid employment 1998 [3] Labour-related establishment survey			Hours of work			Wages		
	Total	Men	Women	Total	Men	Women	Total	Men	Women
Total	3 339	.	.	.	.	.	.	.	.
2-9	3 085	.	.	.	.	.	.	.	.
3 [4]	665	.	.	.	.	.	.	.	.
5	350	.	.	.	.	.	.	.	.
7	195	.	.	.	.	.	.	.	.

Economic activity (ISIC-Rev.3)	Paid employment			Hours of work 1999 Labour force survey Hours actually worked / Total employment			Wages		
	Total	Men	Women	Total	Men	Women	Total	Men	Women
Total	.	.	.	46.19	46.40	45.97	.	.	.
A	.	.	.	44.59	44.65	44.54	.	.	.
B	.	.	.	43.86	45.23	38.89	.	.	.
C	.	.	.	44.46	45.00	43.07	.	.	.
D	.	.	.	50.40	51.18	49.64	.	.	.
E	.	.	.	46.75	46.98	45.85	.	.	.
F	.	.	.	48.29	48.53	46.16	.	.	.
G	.	.	.	50.22	50.48	50.08	.	.	.
H	.	.	.	50.55	50.36	50.63	.	.	.
I	.	.	.	50.74	51.07	47.90	.	.	.
J	.	.	.	47.20	47.62	46.80	.	.	.
K	.	.	.	46.72	46.82	46.53	.	.	.
L	.	.	.	45.38	45.72	44.34	.	.	.
M	.	.	.	44.59	44.91	44.47	.	.	.
N	.	.	.	46.33	46.33	46.33	.	.	.
O	.	.	.	46.84	46.92	46.74	.	.	.
P	.	.	.	49.08	48.56	49.38	.	.	.
Q	.	.	.	48.03	48.90	45.99	.	.	.

4. Occupational injuries and Strikes and Lockouts

Statistics not available.

5. Consumer price indices (base period: 2000=100)

	2002	2003	2004	2005	2006	2007
General indices	103.7	107.0	115.0	.	.	.
Food index, including non-alcoholic beverages [5]	106.1	108.7	119.8	.	.	.

[1] Persons aged 15 years and over. [2] July. [3] State sector. [4] Incl. mining and quarrying, electricity, gas and water. [5] Incl. alcoholic beverages and tobacco.

[1] Personnes âgées de 15 ans et plus. [2] Juillet. [3] Secteur d'Etat. [4] Y compris les industries extractives, l'électricité, le gaz et l'eau. [5] Y compris les boissons alcoolisées et le tabac.

[1] Personas de 15 años y más. [2] Julio. [3] Sector de Estado. [4] Incl. minas y canteras, electricidad, gas y agua. [5] Incl. las bebidas alcohólicas y el tabaco.

Virgin Islands (British)

1. Economically active population, Employment and Unemployment ('000)

Age group	Economically active population Total	Women (%)	Employment Total	Women (%)	Unemployment Total	Women (%)
	1991 [1,2] Population census		1991 ★ Population census		1991 [1,2] Population census	
Total	8.996	43.4	8.700	43.5	0.296	40.5
15-19	0.453	46.1	0.408	47.1	0.045	37.8
20-24	1.307	47.4	1.231	47.4	0.076	47.4
25-29	1.673	44.8	1.616	45.0	0.057	40.4
30-34	1.527	44.9	1.488	45.1	0.039	38.5
35-39	1.246	45.1	1.210	45.1	0.036	44.4
40-44	0.983	42.4	0.958	42.6	0.025	36.0
45-49	0.698	42.4	0.692	42.8	0.006	.
50-54	0.426	39.4	0.424	39.6	0.002	.
55-59	0.247	33.2	0.244	32.8	0.003	66.7
60-64	0.204	30.9	0.198	30.8	0.006	33.3
65+	0.231	21.2	0.230	21.3	0.001	.
?	0.001	.	.	.	.	.

Status in employment (ICSE-1993)			1991 [1,2] Population census			
Total	.	.	8.700	43.5	.	.
1 Employees	.	.	7.532	45.7	.	.
2 Employers	.	.	0.507	29.0	.	.
3 Own-account workers	.	.	0.581	26.5	.	.
5 Contributing family workers	.	.	0.029	55.2	.	.
6 Not classifiable by status	.	.	0.051	39.2	.	.

2. Population ('000), Activity rate and Unemployment rate

Age group	Population 1991 [2,3] Population census			Activity rate 1991 [2,3] Population census			Unemployment rate 1991 [1,2] Population census		
	Total	Men	Women	Total	Men	Women	Total	Men	Women
Total	.	.	.	.	.	.	3.3	3.5	3.1
15+	11.728	6.044	5.684	76.7	84.3	68.6	3.3	3.5	.
15-24	2.728	1.345	1.383	64.5	69.3	59.9	6.9	7.3	6.4
25-54	7.382	3.838	3.544	88.8	95.7	81.2	2.5	2.8	.
55+	1.618	0.861	0.757	42.2	56.7	25.6	1.5	1.2	.

3. Paid employment ('000), Hours of work (weekly) and Wages

Economic activity (ISIC-Rev.3)	Paid employment 2005 Labour-related establishment survey			Hours of work			Wages 1994 Labour-related establishment survey Earnings per hour / Employees / US dollar		
	Total	Men	Women	Total	Men	Women	Total	Men	Women
Total	16.232	.	.	.	.	.	6.61	6.61	5.61
A-B	.	.	.	.	.	.	10.40	.	.
A	0.078	.	.	.	.	.	.	.	.
B	0.014	.	.	.	.	.	.	.	.
C	0.037	.	.	.	.	.	11.54	11.54	.
D	0.404	.	.	.	.	.	6.09	7.15	4.40
E	0.145	.	.	.	.	.	8.55	8.77	7.37
F	1.260	.	.	.	.	.	7.01	7.38	5.23
G	1.624	.	.	.	.	.	5.36	6.34	4.40
H	2.573	.	.	.	.	.	5.52	6.94	4.33
I	0.454	.	.	.	.	.	8.03	8.63	6.86
J	0.797	.	.	.	.	.	11.47	14.78	10.11
K	1.307	.	.	.	.	.	6.72	7.42	5.81
L	5.142	.	.	.	.	.	7.37	7.96	6.86
M	1.119	.	.	.	.	.	6.01	8.10	5.50
N	0.141	.	.	.	.	.	5.07	9.74	4.44
O	0.724	.	.	.	.	.	5.48	6.69	4.65
P	0.404	.	.	.	.	.	2.51	4.49	2.18
Q	-	.	.	.	.	.	.	.	.
X	0.009	.	.	.	.	.	4.85	4.38	4.99

Share of women in wage employment in the non-agricultural sector (1994 - Labour-related establishment survey): **48.3%**

4. Occupational injuries and Strikes and Lockouts

Statistics not available.

5. Consumer price indices (base period: 2000=100)

	2002	2003	2004	2005	2006	2007
General indices	103.5	107.2	108.3	110.4	.	.
Food index, including non-alcoholic beverages	105.3	107.1	108.4	112.1	.	.

[1] Persons aged 15 years and over. [2] May. [3] "De facto" population.

[1] Personnes âgées de 15 ans et plus. [2] Mai. [3] Population "de facto".

[1] Personas de 15 años y más. [2] Mayo. [3] Población "de facto".

Virgin Islands (US)

1. Economically active population, Employment and Unemployment ('000)

	Economically active population		Employment		Unemployment	
	Total	Women (%)	Total	Women (%)	Total	Women (%)
Age group		1990 [1,2]				1997 [3]
		Population census				Employment office records
Total	47.443	47.6	.	.	2.700	.
15-19	2.974	46.7	.	.	.	.
20-24	4.906	47.7	.	.	.	.
25-54	33.958	48.9	.	.	.	.
55-64	4.373	41.4	.	.	.	.
65+	1.232	36.9	.	.	.	.

2. Population ('000), Activity rate and Unemployment rate

	Population			Activity rate			Unemployment rate		
Age group		1990 [2]			1990 [2]			1997 [3]	
		Population census			Population census			Employment office records	
	Total	Men	Women	Total	Men	Women	Total	Men	Women
Total	101.809	49.210	52.599	46.6	50.5	42.9	5.9	.	.
15+	72.365	34.377	37.988	65.6	72.3	59.5	.	.	.
15-24	16.726	8.282	8.444	47.1	50.1	44.1	.	.	.
25-54	42.000	19.743	22.257	80.9	87.9	74.6	.	.	.
55+	13.639	6.352	7.287	41.1	52.6	31.1	.	.	.

3. Paid employment ('000), Hours of work (weekly) and Wages

Economic activity (ISIC-Rev.3)	Paid employment 2002 [4] Official estimates			Hours of work 2007 Labour-related establishment survey Hours paid for / Wage earners			Wages 2007 Labour-related establishment survey Earnings per hour / Wage earners / US dollar		
	Total	Men	Women	Total	Men	Women	Total	Men	Women
Total	43.20	.	.	.	.	.	.	.	.
D				42.2	.	.	26.35	.	.

4. Occupational injuries and Strikes and Lockouts

Economic activity (ISIC-Rev.3)	Rates of fatal injuries 1995 Labour-related establishment survey Per 100,000 workers employed Reported injuries			Rates of non-fatal injuries			Strikes and lockouts		
	Total	Men	Women	Total	Men	Women	Strikes and lockouts	Workers involved	Days not worked
Total	14.1	.	.	.	.	.	.	.	.
D	0.0	.	.	.	.	.	.	.	.
F	0.0	.	.	.	.	.	.	.	.
G [5]	10.1	.	.	.	.	.	.	.	.
I	78.3	.	.	.	.	.	.	.	.
J-K	0.0	.	.	.	.	.	.	.	.
L-O [6]	97.5	.	.	.	.	.	.	.	.

5. Consumer price indices (base period: 2000=100)

Statistics not available for the period 2002-2007.

---

[1] Persons aged 16 years and over. [2] April. [3] Persons aged 16 to 65 years. [4] Based on an establishment survey plus an estimation for agriculture. [5] Excl. restaurants and hotels. [6] Incl. restaurants and hotels.

[1] Personnes âgées de 16 ans et plus. [2] Avril. [3] Personnes âgées de 16 à 65 ans. [4] Basée sur une enquête auprès des établissements plus une estimation pour l'agriculture. [5] Non compris les restaurants et hôtels. [6] Y compris les restaurants et hôtels.

[1] Personas de 16 años y más. [2] Abril. [3] Personas de 16 a 65 años. [4] Basada en una encuesta de establecimientos más una estimación para la agricultura. [5] Excl. restaurantes y hoteles. [6] Incl. restaurantes y hoteles.

West Bank and Gaza Strip

1. Economically active population, Employment and Unemployment ('000)

	Economically active population		Employment		Unemployment	
	Total	Women (%)	Total	Women (%)	Total	Women (%)
Age group	2007[1] Labour force survey		2007 ★ Labour force survey		2007[1] Labour force survey	
Total	863.837	18.5	680.148	19.1	183.689	16.3
10-14	15.241	16.2	14.527	17.0	0.714	.
15-19	60.142	6.8	39.860	9.5	20.282	1.5
20-24	133.915	18.9	85.699	15.3	48.216	25.4
25-29	149.927	20.1	114.212	18.9	35.715	24.1
30-34	132.454	18.8	110.912	19.3	21.542	16.7
35-39	113.449	19.0	95.188	19.8	18.261	14.6
40-44	94.649	19.5	79.541	21.4	15.108	9.7
45-49	70.049	19.1	58.597	21.7	11.452	5.9
50-54	42.998	17.5	36.059	20.1	6.939	3.9
55-59	27.483	22.6	23.664	25.9	3.819	2.5
60-64	11.465	26.5	10.216	28.7	1.249	9.0
65-69	6.436	24.5	6.144	25.6	0.292	.
70-74	3.511	18.6	3.436	19.0	0.075	.
75+	2.117	31.4	2.092	31.7	0.025	.

Economic activity (ISIC-Rev.3)			2007[2] Labour force survey			
Total	.	.	665.620	19.2	.	.
A Agriculture, Hunting and Forestry	.	.	102.205	45.0	.	.
B Fishing	.	.	1.516	.	.	.
C Mining and Quarrying	.	.	1.542	.	.	.
D Manufacturing	.	.	81.964	14.7	.	.
E Electricity, Gas and Water Supply	.	.	2.230	.	.	.
F Construction	.	.	72.722	0.4	.	.
G Wholesale and Retail Trade; Repair of Motor Vehicles ...	.	.	116.408	8.0	.	.
H Hotels and Restaurants	.	.	13.407	4.0	.	.
I Transport, Storage and Communications	.	.	37.404	1.5	.	.
J Financial Intermediation	.	.	4.214	23.2	.	.
K Real Estate, Renting and Business Activities	.	.	11.380	15.9	.	.
L Public Administration and Defence; Compulsory Social ...	.	.	99.584	7.0	.	.
M Education	.	.	68.034	49.4	.	.
N Health and Social Work	.	.	24.525	35.2	.	.
O Other Community, Social and Personal Service Activities	.	.	20.594	21.6	.	.
P Households with Employed Persons	.	.	0.182	79.7	.	.
Q Extra-Territorial Organizations and Bodies	.	.	7.411	30.9	.	.

Occupation (ISCO-88)			2007[2] Labour force survey			
Total	.	.	665.620	19.2	.	.
1 Legislators, senior officials and managers	.	.	25.777	10.4	.	.
2 Professionals	.	.	79.131	37.9	.	.
3 Technicians and associate professionals	.	.	55.592	29.5	.	.
4 Clerks	.	.	14.889	33.0	.	.
5 Service workers and shop and market sales workers	.	.	136.404	9.3	.	.
6 Skilled agricultural and fishery workers	.	.	90.053	50.4	.	.
7 Craft and related trade workers	.	.	106.863	6.3	.	.
8 Plant and machine operators and assemblers	.	.	63.775	6.7	.	.
9 Elementary occupations	.	.	93.066	4.9	.	.
X Not classifiable by occupation	.	.	0.070	.	.	.

Education level (ISCED-97)	2006[1] Labour force survey		2006 ★ Labour force survey		2006[1] Labour force survey	
Total	886.951	17.4	680.801	18.1	206.150	15.0
X No schooling	85.033	25.3	65.797	30.8	19.236	6.4
1 Primary education or first stage of basic education	186.117	11.0	139.249	13.5	46.868	3.6
2 Lower secondary or second stage of basic education	273.396	9.6	205.086	11.4	68.310	4.1
3 Upper secondary education	133.558	9.6	105.785	10.2	27.773	7.2
5A First stage of tertiary education - theoretically based	125.058	37.2	110.735	36.0	14.323	46.8
5B First stage of tertiary education - practically oriented	72.502	34.5	43.733	19.8	28.769	56.9
6 Second stage of tertiary education	11.287	15.7	10.416	15.0	0.871	23.9

Status in employment (ICSE-1993)			2007[2] Labour force survey			
Total	.	.	665.620	19.2	.	.
1 Employees	.	.	397.915	16.7	.	.
2 Employers	.	.	26.975	2.9	.	.
3 Own-account workers	.	.	160.705	10.1	.	.
5 Contributing family workers	.	.	80.025	55.0	.	.

2. Population ('000), Activity rate and Unemployment rate

	Population			Activity rate			Unemployment rate		
Age group	2006[3] Labour force survey			2006[3] Labour force survey			2007[1] Labour force survey		
	Total	Men	Women	Total	Men	Women	Total	Men	Women
Total	3 888.3	1 970.3	1 918.0	22.8	37.2	8.1	21.3	21.8	18.7
15+	2 110.8	1 064.5	1 046.3	41.3	67.7	14.5	21.6	22.1	.
15-24	759.7	387.7	371.9	26.1	43.6	7.9	35.3	34.0	42.6
25-54	1 115.2	570.8	544.4	55.9	89.3	20.7	18.1	18.8	14.9
55+	235.9	105.9	130.0	21.5	39.1	7.1	10.7	13.5	.

West Bank and Gaza Strip

3. Paid employment ('000), Hours of work (weekly) and Wages

Economic activity (ISIC-Rev.3)	Paid employment 2007[2] Labour force survey			Hours of work 2007[2] Labour force survey Hours actually worked / Employees			Wages 2007[2,4] Labour force survey Earnings per day / Employees / New shekel		
	Total	Men	Women	Total	Men	Women	Total	Men	Women
Total	397.915	331.360	66.555	41.30	42.40	35.70	83.9	86.2	72.6
A-B	.	.	.	34.90	34.80	37.60	.	.	.
C-Q	.	.	.	41.60	42.70	35.70	.	.	.
A	13.353	12.704	0.649	.	.	.	.	.	.
B	0.187	0.187	-	.	.	.	.	.	.
C	1.092	1.092	-	47.60	47.60	.	94.9	94.9	.
D	49.867	42.643	7.224	43.80	44.30	41.30	71.1	76.4	40.4
E	2.178	2.178	-	45.80	45.80	38.10	105.4	105.4	.
F	53.562	53.313	0.248	38.70	38.70	44.70	102.1	102.2	85.0
G	35.620	33.290	2.330	48.70	49.00	31.20	72.3	73.7	51.3
H	9.860	9.564	0.295	46.00	46.50	37.40	100.7	100.9	89.9
I	12.325	11.896	0.429	46.10	46.40	39.50	73.6	73.4	79.4
J	3.811	2.905	0.906	41.60	42.20	38.90	111.1	101.2	144.6
K	5.798	4.490	1.308	44.40	46.10	36.00	87.8	90.5	78.4
L	99.416	92.451	6.965	43.20	43.80	32.20	78.7	79.7	78.1
M	65.939	33.107	32.832	33.40	34.50	32.20	87.0	96.7	77.2
N	22.453	14.406	8.047	41.00	43.10	36.70	89.7	99.8	71.7
O	14.874	11.975	2.899	41.10	42.20	31.10	80.3	84.8	61.4
P	0.170	0.036	0.134	32.70	38.40	31.10	82.9	183.2	55.9
Q	7.411	5.122	2.289	40.10	40.60	.	102.1	100.6	106.1

Share of women in wage employment in the non-agricultural sector[2] (2007 - Labour force survey): **17.1%**

4. Occupational injuries and Strikes and Lockouts

Statistics not available.

5. Consumer price indices (base period: 2000=100)

	2002	2003	2004	2005	2006	2007
General indices	107.0	111.7	115.1	119.1	123.5	126.9
Food index, including non-alcoholic beverages	102.1	106.8	109.1	113.3	118.8	124.4
Electricity, gas and other fuel indices	112.4	116.8	122.3	129.8	135.8	.
Clothing indices, including footwear	101.9	102.1	101.2	102.8	103.5	102.7
Rent indices	115.6	111.6	109.7	109.9	109.0	.

[1] Persons aged 10 years and over. [2] Persons aged 15 years and over. [3] "De jure" population. [4] Net earnings.

[1] Personnes âgées de 10 ans et plus. [2] Personnes âgées de 15 ans et plus. [3] Population "de jure". [4] Gains nets.

[1] Personas de 10 años y más. [2] Personas de 15 años y más. [3] Población "de jure". [4] Ganancias netas.

Yemen, Republic of

1. Economically active population, Employment and Unemployment ('000)

	Economically active population		Employment		Unemployment	
	Total	Women (%)	Total	Women (%)	Total	Women (%)
Age group	1994 [1] Population census		1994 ★ Population census		1999 [2] Labour force survey	
Total	3 553.400	20.2	3 228.886	21.0	469.001	16.9
0-14	232.398	48.2	184.776	52.3	.	.
15-19	364.182	28.2	286.567	31.6	111.566	20.5
20-24	445.196	17.7	378.046	19.4	115.568	18.5
25-29	481.399	18.2	441.942	19.3	79.527	19.9
30-34	436.569	18.1	414.048	18.9	41.996	18.6
35-39	424.956	18.1	406.826	18.8	35.879	10.6
40-44	313.694	17.8	301.113	18.4	30.730	10.7
45-49	243.583	16.5	233.558	17.1	20.646	8.8
50-54	212.053	16.3	202.871	16.9	15.003	10.5
55-59	111.656	14.2	106.088	14.8	9.856	4.1
60-64	134.117	12.8	127.830	13.3	5.087	10.5
65+	153.597	10.6	145.221	10.9	3.143	2.9
Economic activity (ISIC-Rev.3)	1999 ★ Labour force survey		1999 [2] Labour force survey		1999 [2] Labour force survey	
Total	4 090.680	23.7	3 621.679	24.6	469.001	16.9
A Agriculture, Hunting and Forestry	2 062.686	38.9	1 927.748	40.5	134.938	15.1
B Fishing	35.281	.	31.389	.	3.892	.
C Mining and Quarrying	19.152	5.4	17.699	5.6	1.453	3.7
D Manufacturing	148.938	16.6	135.503	17.0	13.435	12.8
E Electricity, Gas and Water Supply	12.844	5.8	11.731	6.4	1.113	.
F Construction	298.044	0.7	238.246	0.6	59.798	1.0
G Wholesale and Retail Trade; Repair of Motor Vehicles ...	429.789	2.8	394.144	3.0	35.645	0.5
H Hotels and Restaurants	47.432	2.3	42.857	2.1	4.575	4.2
I Transport, Storage and Communications	135.452	1.2	122.465	1.2	12.987	0.9
J Financial Intermediation	11.826	16.1	11.050	15.7	0.776	21.9
K Real Estate, Renting and Business Activities	20.440	4.6	18.912	4.6	1.528	3.7
L Public Administration and Defence; Compulsory Social ...	368.726	2.9	357.907	2.9	10.819	5.4
M Education	213.774	18.9	209.195	18.3	4.579	50.0
N Health and Social Work	44.814	26.0	42.350	25.0	2.464	43.4
O Other Community, Social and Personal Service Activities	58.371	7.2	53.104	7.6	5.267	3.6
P Households with Employed Persons	6.608	43.8	5.618	40.0	0.990	65.7
Q Extra-Territorial Organizations and Bodies	.	.	0.534	47.2	.	.
X Not classifiable by economic activity	1.321	25.3	1.221	27.4	0.100	.
Unemployed seeking their first job	.	.	.	.	174.642	29.2
Occupation (ISCO-88)	1999 ★ Labour force survey		1999 [2] Labour force survey		1999 [2] Labour force survey	
Total	4 090.680	23.7	3 621.679	24.6	469.001	16.9
1 Legislators, senior officials and managers	41.259	4.4	40.965	4.4	0.294	.
2 Professionals	112.675	15.4	109.470	15.3	3.205	17.6
3 Technicians and associate professionals	223.717	15.6	215.340	15.0	8.377	33.0
4 Clerks	62.719	15.1	58.813	14.5	3.906	24.1
5 Service workers and shop and market sales workers	411.863	3.7	376.943	3.7	34.920	3.5
6 Skilled agricultural and fishery workers	1 835.327	41.4	1 720.901	43.2	114.426	15.5
7 Craft and related trade workers	279.188	8.2	242.306	8.9	36.882	3.7
8 Plant and machine operators and assemblers	167.504	1.8	150.145	1.8	17.359	2.6
9 Elementary occupations	531.257	9.7	463.261	10.4	67.996	4.9
0 Armed forces	248.990	0.6	242.010	0.6	6.980	.
X Not classifiable by occupation	1.539	18.1	1.525	18.2	0.014	.
Unemployed seeking their first job	.	.	.	.	174.642	29.2
Education level (ISCED-97)	1999 [2] Labour force survey					
Total	4 090.7	23.7	.	.	.	.
X No schooling	1 891.8	41.0	.	.	.	.
0 Pre-primary education	1 014.3	8.3	.	.	.	.
1 Primary education or first stage of basic education	183.0	5.0	.	.	.	.
2 Lower secondary or second stage of basic education	329.3	5.7	.	.	.	.
3 Upper secondary education	41.7	10.3	.	.	.	.
4 Post-secondary non-tertiary education	40.4	12.5	.	.	.	.
5A First stage of tertiary education - theoretically based	338.5	10.0	.	.	.	.
5B First stage of tertiary education - practically oriented	80.4	13.3	.	.	.	.
6 Second stage of tertiary education	171.3	15.8	.	.	.	.
Status in employment (ICSE-1993)			1999 [2] Labour force survey			
Total	.	.	3 621.679	24.6	.	.
1 Employees	.	.	1 507.457	8.2	.	.
2 Employers	.	.	78.323	4.6	.	.
3 Own-account workers	.	.	1 122.623	18.7	.	.
4 Members of producers' cooperatives	.	.	901.303	61.1	.	.
5 Contributing family workers	.	.	11.973	26.0	.	.

Yemen, Republic of

2. Population ('000), Activity rate and Unemployment rate

Age group	Population 1994 [1,3] Population census			Activity rate 1994 [1,3] Population census			Unemployment rate 1994 [4] Population census		
	Total	Men	Women	Total	Men	Women	Total	Men	Women
Total	9 456.985	4 853.314	4 603.671	37.6	58.4	15.6	9.1	10.1	5.4
15+	7 253.052	3 666.295	3 586.757	45.8	74.1	16.9	8.3	9.3	3.9
15-24	2 476.761	1 299.284	1 177.477	32.7	48.3	15.4	17.9	20.2	9.8
25-54	3 767.011	1 835.277	1 931.734	56.1	94.7	19.4	5.3	6.2	1.3
55+	1 009.280	531.734	477.546	39.6	65.8	10.3	5.1	5.6	1.4

3. Paid employment ('000), Hours of work (weekly) and Wages

Economic activity (ISIC-Rev.3)	Paid employment 1999 [2] Labour force survey			Hours of work			Wages		
	Total	Men	Women	Total	Men	Women	Total	Men	Women
Total	1 507.457	1 384.464	122.993	.	.	.	.	.	.
A	292.576	248.124	44.452	.	.	.	.	.	.
B	17.152	17.152	-	.	.	.	.	.	.
C	16.164	15.267	0.897	.	.	.	.	.	.
D	78.739	73.845	4.894	.	.	.	.	.	.
E	11.044	10.293	0.751	.	.	.	.	.	.
F	213.961	213.030	0.931	.	.	.	.	.	.
G	119.529	117.537	1.992	.	.	.	.	.	.
H	31.433	30.928	0.505	.	.	.	.	.	.
I	52.248	50.931	1.317	.	.	.	.	.	.
J	10.635	8.900	1.735	.	.	.	.	.	.
K	12.288	11.497	0.791	.	.	.	.	.	.
L	357.907	347.655	10.252	.	.	.	.	.	.
M	208.175	170.452	37.723	.	.	.	.	.	.
N	38.061	27.795	10.263	.	.	.	.	.	.
O	40.654	36.860	3.794	.	.	.	.	.	.
P	5.542	3.295	2.247	.	.	.	.	.	.
Q	0.534	0.282	0.252	.	.	.	.	.	.
X	0.815	0.618	0.197	.	.	.	.	.	.

Share of women in wage employment in the non-agricultural sector [2] (1999 - Labour force survey): **6.5%**

4. Occupational injuries and Strikes and Lockouts

Statistics not available.

5. Consumer price indices (base period: 2000=100)

	2002	2003	2004	2005	2006	2007
General indices	125.6	139.2	156.6	174.5	211.6	232.8
Food index, including non-alcoholic beverages	121.2	141.4	168.3	199.9	269.5	317.9
Clothing indices, including footwear	112.1	115.8	118.8	121.9	120.0	.
Rent indices	116.8	129.4	132.3	139.7	146.8	.

[1] Dec. [2] Persons aged 15 years and over. [3] "De facto" population. [4] December.

[1] Déc. [2] Personnes âgées de 15 ans et plus. [3] Population "de facto". [4] Décembre.

[1] Dic. [2] Personas de 15 años y más. [3] Población "de facto". [4] Diciembre.

Zambia

1. Economically active population, Employment and Unemployment ('000)

	Economically active population		Employment		Unemployment	
	Total	Women (%)	Total	Women (%)	Total	Women (%)
Age group		2000 [1][2]		2000 ★		2000 [1][2]
		Population census		Population census		Population census
Total	3 165.2	41.3	2 755.4	42.1	409.8	36.0
12-19	500.1	51.5	390.3	52.3	109.8	48.5
20-24	557.1	43.6	441.1	45.1	116.0	38.1
25-29	515.9	38.0	444.2	39.2	71.7	30.7
30-34	402.0	36.4	363.1	37.4	38.9	27.0
35-54	867.3	39.2	807.1	40.2	60.2	24.8
55-64	183.6	42.0	175.4	42.9	8.2	23.2
65+	139.3	33.8	134.8	34.2	4.5	22.2

Economic activity (ISIC-Rev.2)

2000 [1][2][3] Population census

	Total	Women (%)
Total	2 812.428	44.7
1 Agriculture, Hunting, Forestry and Fishing	2 014.028	49.0
2 Mining and Quarrying	36.463	5.0
3 Manufacturing	77.515	27.0
4 Electricity, Gas and Water	11.016	10.0
5 Construction	36.790	4.0
6 Wholesale and Retail Trade and Restaurants and Hotels	190.354	44.0
7 Transport, Storage and Communication	53.736	7.0
8 Financing, Insurance, Real Estate and Business Services	29.151	32.0
9 Community, Social and Personal Services	363.375	37.0

Occupation (ISCO-1968)

2000 [1][2][3] Population census

	Total	Women (%)
Total	2 812.428	44.7
0/1 Professional, technical and related workers	126.456	31.3
2 Administrative and managerial workers	8.185	18.8
3 Clerical and related workers	34.702	36.0
4 Sales workers	205.991	43.9
5 Service workers	107.089	32.7
6 Agriculture, animal husbandry and forestry workers ...	2 010.404	49.3
7/8/9 Production and related workers, transport equipment ...	199.549	16.4
X Not classifiable by occupation	120.052	43.4

Status in employment (ICSE-1993)

2000 [1][2][3] Population census

	Total	Women (%)
Total	2 812.428	44.7
1 Employees	514.674	22.0
2 Employers	11.250	22.3
3 Own-account workers	1 116.534	32.6
5 Contributing family workers	1 169.970	66.3

2. Population ('000), Activity rate and Unemployment rate

Age group	Population 2000 [2] Population census			Activity rate 2000 [2] Population census			Unemployment rate 2000 [1] Population census		
	Total	Men	Women	Total	Men	Women	Total	Men	Women
Total	.	.	.	.	.	.	12.9	14.1	11.3
15+	5 682.5	2 770.9	2 908.4	55.7	67.1	44.9	12.9	14.1	11.3
15-24	2 646.5	1 261.2	1 382.3	39.9	44.1	36.2	21.4	23.1	19.5
25-54	2 501.9	1 237.0	1 267.3	71.4	89.2	53.8	9.6	11.2	6.9
55+	534.1	272.7	258.8	60.4	72.9	48.0	3.9	5.0	2.3

3. Paid employment ('000), Hours of work (weekly) and Wages

Economic activity (ISIC-Rev.2)	Paid employment 2005 Administrative reports			Hours of work			Wages 1983 [4][5][6] Earnings per month / Employees / Kwacha		
	Total	Men	Women	Total	Men	Women	Total	Men	Women
Total	436.07	.	.	.	.	.	.	.	.
2-9							237		
1	65.50						102		
2	32.10						307		
3	40.15						196		
4	6.31								
5	7.95						164		
6	67.25								
7	20.68						261		
8	22.31								
9	173.99								

Zambia

4. Occupational injuries and Strikes and Lockouts

Economic activity (ISIC-Rev.2)	Rates of fatal injuries 1987 Administrative records and related sources Per 1,000 workers exposed to risk Reported injuries			Rates of non-fatal injuries			Strikes and lockouts		
	Total	Men	Women	Total	Men	Women	Strikes and lockouts	Workers involved	Days not worked
3	0.005	.	.	.	.	.	.	.	.
4	0.001	.	.	.	.	.	.	.	.
5	0.000	.	.	.	.	.	.	.	.
8	0.000	.	.	.	.	.	.	.	.
0	0.000	.	.	.	.	.	.	.	.

Economic activity (ISIC-Rev.3)	Rates of fatal injuries			Rates of non-fatal injuries			Strikes and lockouts 1997 Special data collection		
	Total	Men	Women	Total	Men	Women	Strikes and lockouts	Workers involved	Days not worked
Total	.	.	.	.	.	.	60	20 513	81 707
A	.	.	.	.	.	.	6	1 454	6 411
B	.	.	.	.	.	.	5	383	1 169
C	.	.	.	.	.	.	35	16 033	69 924
D	.	.	.	.	.	.	5	383	1 169
F	.	.	.	.	.	.	2	76	33
G	.	.	.	.	.	.	3	820	1 360
I	.	.	.	.	.	.	2	1 093	1 099
J	.	.	.	.	.	.	2	271	542

5. Consumer price indices (base period: 2000=100)

	2002	2003	2004	2005	2006	2007
General indices	148.4	180.1	212.5	251.4	274.1	303.3
Food index, including non-alcoholic beverages [7]	151.1	184.5	214.7	254.5	267.1	281.1
Electricity, gas and other fuel indices [8]	139.4	168.8	.	.	.	.
Clothing indices, including footwear	145.1	176.5	.	.	.	.

[1] Persons aged 12 years and over. [2] Oct. [3] The data refer to the usually active population. [4] Zambians. [5] Second quarter. [6] Fourth quarter. [7] Incl. alcoholic beverages and tobacco. [8] Incl. "Rent".

[1] Personnes âgées de 12 ans et plus. [2] Oct. [3] Les données se réfèrent à la population habituellement active. [4] Zambiens. [5] Deuxième trimestre. [6] Quatrième trimestre. [7] Y compris les boissons alcoolisées et le tabac. [8] Y compris le groupe "loyer".

[1] Personas de 12 años y más. [2] Oct. [3] Los datos se refieren a la población habitualmente activa. [4] Zambianos. [5] Segundo trimestre. [6] Cuarto trimestre. [7] Incl. las bebidas alcohólicas y el tabaco. [8] Incl. el grupo "alquiler".

Zimbabwe

1. Economically active population, Employment and Unemployment ('000)

	Economically active population		Employment		Unemployment	
	Total	Women (%)	Total	Women (%)	Total	Women (%)
Age group		1999 [1]		1999 ★		1999 [1]
		Labour force survey		Labour force survey		Labour force survey
Total	4 963.3	48.2	4 665.5	48.9	297.8	37.2
15-19	568.0	51.2	487.5	52.3	80.5	44.5
20-24	813.1	47.2	699.8	49.4	113.3	33.4
25-29	791.6	44.3	737.8	45.2	53.8	31.6
30-34	573.9	44.7	555.4	44.8	18.5	41.0
35-39	486.5	50.1	472.7	50.6	13.8	32.2
40-44	412.7	52.2	406.1	52.5	6.7	32.4
45-49	369.6	51.2	366.2	51.2	3.4	48.5
50-54	277.7	50.6	274.9	50.5	2.9	61.1
55-59	214.5	46.9	212.5	47.1	2.0	28.6
60-64	169.9	47.5	169.7	47.5	0.2	44.1
65+	285.6	48.6	282.9	48.5	2.7	61.4
Occupation (ISCO-1968)				1992 [2,3]		1987 [1]
				Population census		Labour force survey
Total			2 776.159	39.7	234.000	52.6
0/1 Professional, technical and related workers			331.043	28.3	7.000	57.1
2 Administrative and managerial workers			55.758	21.9	-	
3 Clerical and related workers			97.231	36.8	9.000	44.4
4 Sales workers			-		9.000	66.7
5 Service workers			389.871	59.7	24.000	58.3
6 Agriculture, animal husbandry and forestry workers ...			1 196.126	51.3	55.000	56.4
7/8/9 Production and related workers, transport equipment ...			661.450	16.7	22.000	
X Not classifiable by occupation			44.680	7.3	5.000	100.0
Unemployed seeking their first job					102.000	55.9
Education level (ISCED-76)						1999 [1]
						Labour force survey
Total					297.8	37.2
X No schooling					2.8	83.0
1 First level					49.0	45.1
2-5					243.7	34.9
6-7					2.3	54.3
9 Education not definable by level					-	
Status in employment (ICSE-1993)		1992 [2,3]				
		Population census				
Total	3 600.5	39.6				
1 Employees	1 581.5	23.8				
2 Employers	13.6	21.1				
3 Own-account workers	852.6	57.1				
5 Contributing family workers	331.5	72.1				

2. Population ('000), Activity rate and Unemployment rate

Age group	Population 1999 Labour force survey			Activity rate 1999 Labour force survey			Unemployment rate 1999 [1] Labour force survey		
	Total	Men	Women	Total	Men	Women	Total	Men	Women
Total	11 960.2	5 772.1	6 188.1	41.5	44.6	38.6	6.0	7.3	4.6
15+	6 980.0	3 273.9	3 706.1	71.1	78.6	64.5	6.0	7.3	4.6
15-24	2 648.2	1 245.7	1 402.6	52.2	56.7	48.1	14.0	17.0	10.9
25-54	3 437.6	1 594.3	1 843.4	84.7	95.1	75.7	3.4	4.2	2.5
55+	894.2	433.9	460.2	74.9	80.6	69.6	0.7	0.7	0.7

3. Paid employment ('000), Hours of work (weekly) and Wages

Economic activity (ISIC-Rev.2)	Paid employment 2002 [4] Labour-related establishment survey			Hours of work			Wages 2002 Labour-related establishment survey / Employees / Dollar		
	Total	Men	Women	Total	Men	Women	Total	Men	Women
Total	1 071.1	815.1	256.1				201.00		
2-9									
1	220.9	150.8	70.1				26.00 [5]		
2	42.7	40.9	1.8				150.00		
3	172.8	154.7	18.1				144.00		
4	10.0	9.3	0.7				448.00		
5	42.1	39.6	2.5				81.00		
6	104.8	84.3	20.5				119.00		
7	40.8	36.9	3.9				173.00		
8	28.2 [6]	20.1 [6]	8.2 [6]				329.00		
9	408.8 [7]	278.5 [7]	130.3 [7]				167.00		

Zimbabwe

4. Occupational injuries and Strikes and Lockouts

Economic activity (ISIC-Rev.2)	Rates of fatal injuries Total	Men	Women	Rates of non-fatal injuries Total	Men	Women	Strikes and lockouts 1983 Source unknown Strikes and lockouts	Workers involved	Days not worked
Total	.	.	.	.	.	.	32	744	379
1	.	.	.	.	.	.	0	0	0
2	.	.	.	.	.	.	2	30	0
3	.	.	.	.	.	.	2	212	58
4	.	.	.	.	.	.	1	26	0
5	.	.	.	.	.	.	0	0	0
6	.	.	.	.	.	.	0	0	0
7	.	.	.	.	.	.	0	0	0
8	.	.	.	.	.	.	1	450	50
9	.	.	.	.	.	.	0	0	0
0	.	.	.	.	.	.	26	26	271

Economic activity (ISIC-Rev.3)	Rates of fatal injuries 2007[8] Insurance records Per 100,000 workers insured Reported injuries Total	Men	Women	Rates of non-fatal injuries 2007[8,9] Insurance records Per 100,000 workers insured Reported injuries Total	Men	Women	Strikes and lockouts Strikes and lockouts	Workers involved	Days not worked
Total	6.3	7.4	1.7	556	631	222	.	.	.
A	2.6	3.3	0.0	234	238	221	.	.	.
C	28.1	29.8	0.0	1 078	1 115	440	.	.	.
D	5.7	5.9	4.1	1 137	1 219	504	.	.	.
E	57.1	61.7	.	1 215	1 279	403	.	.	.
F	8.1	8.4	.	446	460	57	.	.	.
G	1.6	2.2	0.0	273	325	120	.	.	.
I	13.4	12.9	18.2	691	745	164	.	.	.
J-K	0.0	0.0	.	84	121	18	.	.	.
L	2.7	0.0	10.9	671	739	459	.	.	.
O	6.0	7.5	0.0	350	394	180	.	.	.

5. Consumer price indices (base period: 2000=100)

	2005	2006	2007
General indices [10]	28.3	316.6	21 602.0
Food index, including non-alcoholic beverages [10]	27.9	316.0	23 620.2
Clothing indices, including footwear [10]	37.8	350.2	14 789.5

[1] Persons aged 15 years and over. [2] Persons aged 10 years and over. [3] Aug. [4] Excl. small establishments in rural areas. [5] Agriculture and forestry. [6] Excl. business services. [7] Incl. business services. [8] Year ending in March of the year indicated. [9] Incl. non-fatal cases without lost workdays. [10] Due to lack of space, multiply each figure by 1000.

[1] Personnes âgées de 15 ans et plus. [2] Personnes âgées de 10 ans et plus. [3] Août. [4] Non compris les petites entreprises des zones rurales. [5] Agriculture et sylviculture. [6] Non compris les services aux entreprises. [7] Y compris les services aux entreprises. [8] Année se terminant en mars de l'année indiquée. [9] Y compris les cas non mortels sans perte de journées de travail. [10] En raison du manque de place, multiplier chaque chiffre par 1000.

[1] Personas de 15 años y más. [2] Personas de 10 años y más. [3] Agosto. [4] Excl. las pequeñas empresas de las zonas rurales. [5] Agricultura y silvicultura. [6] Excl. servicios para las empresas. [7] Incl. los servicios para las empresas. [8] Año que termina en marzo del año indicado. [9] Incl. los casos no mortales sin pérdida de días de trabajo. [10] Por falta de espacio, multiplicar cada indice por 1000.

Supplement

Supplément

Suplemento

Global and regional estimates of labour market indicators

The following world and regional estimates on labour market indicators have been produced by the ILO Employment Trends Unit. For further technical information on the world and regional estimation processes, see: www.ilo.org/trends

Labour force participation rates (%)

Region	1997	2000	2004	2005	2006	2007*
Total - World	66.8	66.3	65.8	65.7	65.6	65.6
Youth - World	57.2	56.1	54.8	54.5	54.6	54.6
Total						
World	66.8	66.3	65.8	65.7	65.6	65.6
Developed Economies and European Union	60.8	60.8	60.4	60.3	60.3	60.2
Central and Eastern Europe (non-EU) and CIS	60.2	58.4	59.0	58.9	58.9	59.1
East Asia	77.8	77.2	75.2	75.1	74.5	74.5
South-East Asia and the Pacific	69.9	70.2	70.3	70.6	70.7	70.8
South Asia	61.0	60.5	59.9	60.1	59.6	59.8
Latin America and the Caribbean	64.3	64.9	65.4	65.5	65.6	65.7
North Africa	50.5	50.8	51.2	51.4	51.6	51.9
Sub-Saharan Africa	75.5	75.0	74.3	74.3	74.2	74.0
Middle East	52.8	53.8	55.4	56.2	56.4	57.0
Male						
World	80.2	80.2	79.2	78.9	79.1	78.9
Developed Economies and European Union	70.8	70.4	68.9	68.9	68.3	68.2
Central and Eastern Europe (non-EU) and CIS	70.9	69.1	69.5	69.5	69.5	69.6
East Asia	84.5	83.6	82.0	81.7	81.6	81.4
South-East Asia and the Pacific	82.7	82.4	82.7	82.9	83.1	82.9
South Asia	83.9	83.2	82.4	82.5	82.2	82.0
Latin America and the Caribbean	81.9	81.4	80.1	80.1	79.2	78.8
North Africa	76.1	76.0	76.3	76.4	76.5	76.6
Sub-Saharan Africa	87.2	86.9	86.2	86.3	86.3	85.9
Middle East	77.5	77.5	78.0	78.1	78.2	78.3
Female						
World	53.0	52.6	52.4	52.4	52.5	52.5
Developed Economies and European Union	51.3	52.0	52.3	52.4	52.6	52.8
Central and Eastern Europe (non-EU) and CIS	50.8	49.0	49.4	49.4	49.6	49.7
East Asia	71.0	69.8	68.0	67.7	67.5	67.2
South-East Asia and the Pacific	57.4	57.8	58.2	58.6	58.8	59.3
South Asia	36.7	36.0	36.2	36.0	36.2	36.3
Latin America and the Caribbean	47.1	48.9	51.3	51.7	52.4	52.8
North Africa	25.0	25.6	26.5	26.7	27.0	27.3
Sub-Saharan Africa	64.2	63.6	62.9	62.7	62.8	62.7
Middle East	25.6	27.5	30.9	31.7	32.5	33.3

* 2007 preliminary estimates.
Source : ILO, Trends Econometric Models, October 2007; for further information see http://www.ilo.org/trends. Differences from earlier estimates are due to revisions of World Bank and IMF estimates of GDP and its components that are used in the models, as well as updates of the labour market information used.

Unemployment rates (%)

Region	1997	2000	2004	2005	2006	2007*
Total						
World	6.1	6.1	6.3	6.2	6.0	6.0
Developed Economies and European Union	7.4	6.7	7.2	6.9	6.3	6.4
Central and Eastern Europe (non-EU) and CIS	10.7	10.2	9.3	9.0	8.5	8.5
East Asia	3.7	3.9	3.5	3.5	3.4	3.3
South-East Asia and the Pacific	4.0	4.9	6.4	6.1	6.2	6.2
South Asia	4.7	4.6	5.4	5.3	5.1	5.1
Latin America and the Caribbean	8.0	8.5	8.4	8.4	8.5	8.5
North Africa	11.5	13.1	12.4	11.4	10.8	10.7
Sub-Saharan Africa	8.5	8.7	8.3	8.3	8.2	8.2
Middle East	13.0	11.7	11.4	11.9	11.8	11.8
Male						
World	5.8	5.9	6.1	5.9	5.7	5.7
Developed Economies and European Union	6.9	6.2	6.9	6.6	6.1	6.2
Central and Eastern Europe (non-EU) and CIS	10.6	10.1	9.6	9.2	8.7	8.7
East Asia	4.2	4.4	4.0	4.0	3.8	3.8
South-East Asia and the Pacific	3.9	4.9	6.3	5.6	5.7	5.6
South Asia	4.4	4.4	5.0	5.0	4.8	4.8
Latin America and the Caribbean	6.3	6.9	6.6	6.8	6.9	6.9
North Africa	10.0	11.5	10.5	9.6	9.0	8.9
Sub-Saharan Africa	7.7	8.0	7.6	7.6	7.5	7.5
Middle East	11.3	10.3	10.0	10.4	10.4	10.3
Female						
World	6.5	6.5	6.7	6.6	6.4	6.4
Developed Economies and European Union	8.1	7.3	7.5	7.2	6.7	6.7
Central and Eastern Europe (non-EU) and CIS	10.9	10.3	9.0	8.7	8.3	8.3
East Asia	3.1	3.2	2.9	2.9	2.8	2.7
South-East Asia and the Pacific	4.2	5.0	6.6	6.7	6.9	6.9
South Asia	5.3	5.1	6.2	6.0	5.7	5.8
Latin America and the Caribbean	10.7	11.1	11.2	10.8	10.9	10.9
North Africa	15.9	18.0	17.7	16.6	15.8	15.7
Sub-Saharan Africa	9.6	9.7	9.3	9.3	9.2	9.1
Middle East	18.6	16.3	15.2	15.9	15.8	15.6

* 2007 preliminary estimates.
Source : ILO, Trends Econometric Models, October 2007; for further information see http://www.ilo.org/trends. Differences from earlier estimates are due to revisions of World Bank and IMF estimates of GDP and its components that are used in the models, as well as updates of the labour market information used.

Sectoral shares in employment (%)

Region	Employment in sector as share of total employment				Female employment as share of total employment in sector
	1997	2005	2006	2007*	2007*
Agriculture					
World	41.4	37.1	36.0	34.9	41.3
Developed Economies and European Union	6.1	4.2	4.2	3.9	36.2
Central and Eastern Europe (non-EU) and CIS	27.0	21.1	20.4	19.5	44.0
East Asia	47.9	42.9	40.9	38.4	47.4
South-East Asia and the Pacific	48.8	45.5	45.2	43.9	41.4
South Asia	59.4	50.9	49.4	48.0	36.6
Latin America and the Caribbean	23.5	19.6	19.7	19.1	22.7
North Africa	38.5	36.8	36.9	35.9	25.9
Sub-Saharan Africa	71.9	66.8	64.9	64.4	44.5
Middle East	21.4	18.7	18.1	17.5	47.7
Industry					
World	21.1	21.4	21.9	22.4	31.2
Developed Economies and European Union	28.3	25.0	24.7	24.5	22.9
Central and Eastern Europe (non-EU) and CIS	28.3	25.6	25.8	26.1	30.8
East Asia	24.3	24.3	25.6	26.9	42.0
South-East Asia and the Pacific	17.1	18.2	18.5	19.0	35.9
South Asia	15.3	20.2	21.0	21.7	24.7
Latin America and the Caribbean	20.7	21.7	21.8	22.0	26.5
North Africa	18.9	19.0	19.3	19.7	17.8
Sub-Saharan Africa	8.5	9.1	9.5	9.7	25.5
Middle East	25.6	25.5	25.4	25.5	19.8
Services					
World	37.5	41.5	42.1	42.7	43.2
Developed Economies and European Union	65.6	70.8	71.2	71.5	52.9
Central and Eastern Europe (non-EU) and CIS	44.7	53.3	53.8	54.4	51.6
East Asia	27.8	32.7	33.5	34.7	42.8
South-East Asia and the Pacific	34.1	36.3	36.3	37.0	45.6
South Asia	25.2	28.9	29.6	30.3	20.2
Latin America and the Caribbean	55.8	58.7	58.5	58.9	51.1
North Africa	42.6	44.2	43.8	44.4	27.1
Sub-Saharan Africa	19.6	24.1	25.6	25.9	43.4
Middle East	52.9	55.9	56.5	57.0	23.7*

* 2007 preliminary estimates
Source : ILO, Trends Econometric Models, October 2007; for further information see http://www.ilo.org/trends. Differences from earlier estimates are due to revisions of World Bank and IMF estimates of GDP and its components that are used in the models, as well as updates of the labour market information used.

Other selected labour market indicators

Region	Employment-to-population ratio (%) 1997	2006	2007*	Annual GDP growth rate (%) 1997-2007	Annual labour force growth rate (%) 1997-2007*	Change in unemployment rate (percentage point) 2000-2007*
World	62.7	61.7	61.6	3.9	1.7	-0.1
Developed Economies and European Union	56.2	56.5	56.4	2.6	0.7	-0.3
Central and Eastern Europe (non-EU) and CIS	53.8	53.9	54.1	5.6	0.6	-1.7
East Asia	74.9	72.0	72.0	8.1	1.0	-0.6
South-East Asia and the Pacific	67.1	66.3	66.4	4.0	2.5	1.2
South Asia	58.1	56.6	56.8	6.6	2.4	0.5
Latin America and the Caribbean	59.1	60.0	60.1	3.2	2.4	0.1
North Africa	44.7	46.1	46.3	4.9	4.9	-2.4
Sub-Saharan Africa	69.0	68.1	68.0	5.1	4.1	-0.5
Middle East	46.0	49.7	50.3	4.7	4.9	0.1

* 2007 preliminary estimates.

Source : ILO, Trends Econometric Models, October 2007; for further information see http://www.ilo.org/trends. Differences from earlier estimates are due to revisions of World Bank and IMF estimates of GDP and its components that are used in the models, as well as updates of the labour market information used.

Estimations mondiales et régionales des indicateurs du marché du travail

Les estimations mondiales et régionales suivantes sur les indicateurs du marché du travail ont été réalisées par l'unité Tendance de l'Emploi du BIT. Pour plus d'informations techniques sur les processus d'estimations, suivez le lien suivant: www.ilo.org/trends (en anglais).

Taux d'activité (%)

Région	1997	2000	2004	2005	2006	2007*
Total - Monde	66.8	66.3	65.8	65.7	65.6	65.6
Jeunes - Monde	57.2	56.1	54.8	54.5	54.6	54.6
Total						
Monde	66.8	66.3	65.8	65.7	65.6	65.6
Economies développées et Union européenne	60.8	60.8	60.4	60.3	60.3	60.2
Europe centrale et orientale (hors UE) et CEI	60.2	58.4	59.0	58.9	58.9	59.1
Asie-Orient	77.8	77.2	75.2	75.1	74.5	74.5
Asie du Sud-Est et Pacifique	69.9	70.2	70.3	70.6	70.7	70.8
Asie du Sud	61.0	60.5	59.9	60.1	59.6	59.8
Amérique latine et Caraïbes	64.3	64.9	65.4	65.5	65.6	65.7
Afrique du Nord	50.5	50.8	51.2	51.4	51.6	51.9
Afrique subsaharienne	75.5	75.0	74.3	74.3	74.2	74.0
Moyen-Orient	52.8	53.8	55.4	56.2	56.4	57.0
Hommes						
Monde	80.2	80.2	79.2	78.9	79.1	78.9
Economies développées et Union européenne	70.8	70.4	68.9	68.9	68.3	68.2
Europe centrale et orientale (hors UE) et CEI	70.9	69.1	69.5	69.5	69.5	69.6
Asie-Orient	84.5	83.6	82.0	81.7	81.6	81.4
Asie du Sud-Est et Pacifique	82.7	82.4	82.7	82.9	83.1	82.9
Asie du Sud	83.9	83.2	82.4	82.5	82.2	82.0
Amérique latine et Caraïbes	81.9	81.4	80.1	80.1	79.2	78.8
Afrique du Nord	76.1	76.0	76.3	76.4	76.5	76.6
Afrique subsaharienne	87.2	86.9	86.2	86.3	86.3	85.9
Moyen-Orient	77.5	77.5	78.0	78.1	78.2	78.3
Femmes						
Monde	53.0	52.6	52.4	52.4	52.5	52.5
Economies développées et Union européenne	51.3	52.0	52.3	52.4	52.6	52.8
Europe centrale et orientale (hors UE) et CEI	50.8	49.0	49.4	49.4	49.6	49.7
Asie-Orient	71.0	69.8	68.0	67.7	67.5	67.2
Asie du Sud-Est et Pacifique	57.4	57.8	58.2	58.6	58.8	59.3
Asie du Sud	36.7	36.0	36.2	36.0	36.2	36.3
Amérique latine et Caraïbes	47.1	48.9	51.3	51.7	52.4	52.8
Afrique du Nord	25.0	25.6	26.5	26.7	27.0	27.3
Afrique subsaharienne	64.2	63.6	62.9	62.7	62.8	62.7
Moyen-Orient	25.6	27.5	30.9	31.7	32.5	33.3

* 2007 estimations préliminaires.
Source : BIT, Modèles Econométriques des Tendances, Octobre 2007. Pour plus d'informations suivez le lien http://www.ilo.org/trends. Les différences par rapport aux estimations précédentes sont dues aux révisions des estimations de la Banque Mondiale et du FMI sur le PIB et ses composants qui sont utilisées dans les modèles, tout comme des actualisations sur les informations des marchés du travail utilisées..

Taux de chômage (%)

Région	1997	2000	2004	2005	2006	2007*
	\multicolumn{6}{c}{Total}					
Monde	6.1	6.1	6.3	6.2	6.0	6.0
Economies développées et Union européenne	7.4	6.7	7.2	6.9	6.3	6.4
Europe centrale et orientale (hors UE) et CEI	10.7	10.2	9.3	9.0	8.5	8.5
Asie-Orient	3.7	3.9	3.5	3.5	3.4	3.3
Asie du Sud-Est et Pacifique	4.0	4.9	6.4	6.1	6.2	6.2
Asie du Sud	4.7	4.6	5.4	5.3	5.1	5.1
Amérique latine et Caraïbes	8.0	8.5	8.4	8.4	8.5	8.5
Afrique du Nord	11.5	13.1	12.4	11.4	10.8	10.7
Afrique subsaharienne	8.5	8.7	8.3	8.3	8.2	8.2
Moyen-Orient	13.0	11.7	11.4	11.9	11.8	11.8
			Hommes			
Monde	5.8	5.9	6.1	5.9	5.7	5.7
Economies développées et Union européenne	6.9	6.2	6.9	6.6	6.1	6.2
Europe centrale et orientale (hors UE) et CEI	10.6	10.1	9.6	9.2	8.7	8.7
Asie-Orient	4.2	4.4	4.0	4.0	3.8	3.8
Asie du Sud-Est et Pacifique	3.9	4.9	6.3	5.6	5.7	5.6
Asie du Sud	4.4	4.4	5.0	5.0	4.8	4.8
Amérique latine et Caraïbes	6.3	6.9	6.6	6.8	6.9	6.9
Afrique du Nord	10.0	11.5	10.5	9.6	9.0	8.9
Afrique subsaharienne	7.7	8.0	7.6	7.6	7.5	7.5
Moyen-Orient	11.3	10.3	10.0	10.4	10.4	10.3
			Femmes			
Monde	6.5	6.5	6.7	6.6	6.4	6.4
Economies développées et Union européenne	8.1	7.3	7.5	7.2	6.7	6.7
Europe centrale et orientale (hors UE) et CEI	10.9	10.3	9.0	8.7	8.3	8.3
Asie-Orient	3.1	3.2	2.9	2.9	2.8	2.7
Asie du Sud-Est et Pacifique	4.2	5.0	6.6	6.7	6.9	6.9
Asie du Sud	5.3	5.1	6.2	6.0	5.7	5.8
Amérique latine et Caraïbes	10.7	11.1	11.2	10.8	10.9	10.9
Afrique du Nord	15.9	18.0	17.7	16.6	15.8	15.7
Afrique subsaharienne	9.6	9.7	9.3	9.3	9.2	9.1
Moyen-Orient	18.6	16.3	15.2	15.9	15.8	15.6

* 2007 estimations préliminaires.
Source : BIT, Modèles Econométriques des Tendances, Octobre 2007. Pour plus d'informations suivez le lien http://www.ilo.org/trends. Les différences par rapport aux estimations précédentes sont dues aux révisions des estimations de la Banque Mondiale et du FMI sur le PIB et ses composants qui sont utilisées dans les modèles, tout comme des actualisations sur les informations des marchés du travail utilisées.

Taux de répartition sectorielle de l'emploi (%)

Région	Emploi dans le secteur comme quote-part de l'emploi total 1997	2005	2006	2007*	Emploi féminin comme quote-part de l'emploi total dans le secteur 2007*
			Agriculture		
Monde	41.4	37.1	36.0	34.9	41.3
Economies développées et Union européenne	6.1	4.2	4.2	3.9	36.2
Europe centrale et orientale (hors UE) et CEI	27.0	21.1	20.4	19.5	44.0
Asie-Orient	47.9	42.9	40.9	38.4	47.4
Asie du Sud-Est et Pacifique	48.8	45.5	45.2	43.9	41.4
Asie du Sud	59.4	50.9	49.4	48.0	36.6
Amérique latine et Caraïbes	23.5	19.6	19.7	19.1	22.7
Afrique du Nord	38.5	36.8	36.9	35.9	25.9
Afrique subsaharienne	71.9	66.8	64.9	64.4	44.5
Moyen-Orient	21.4	18.7	18.1	17.5	47.7
			Industrie		
Monde	21.1	21.4	21.9	22.4	31.2
Economies développées et Union européenne	28.3	25.0	24.7	24.5	22.9
Europe centrale et orientale (hors UE) et CEI	28.3	25.6	25.8	26.1	30.8
Asie-Orient	24.3	24.3	25.6	26.9	42.0
Asie du Sud-Est et Pacifique	17.1	18.2	18.5	19.0	35.9
Asie du Sud	15.3	20.2	21.0	21.7	24.7
Amérique latine et Caraïbes	20.7	21.7	21.8	22.0	26.5
Afrique du Nord	18.9	19.0	19.3	19.7	17.8
Afrique subsaharienne	8.5	9.1	9.5	9.7	25.5
Moyen-Orient	25.6	25.5	25.4	25.5	19.8
			Services		
Monde	37.5	41.5	42.1	42.7	43.2
Economies développées et Union européenne	65.6	70.8	71.2	71.5	52.9
Europe centrale et orientale (hors UE) et CEI	44.7	53.3	53.8	54.4	51.6
Asie-Orient	27.8	32.7	33.5	34.7	42.8
Asie du Sud-Est et Pacifique	34.1	36.3	36.3	37.0	45.6
Asie du Sud	25.2	28.9	29.6	30.3	20.2
Amérique latine et Caraïbes	55.8	58.7	58.5	58.9	51.1
Afrique du Nord	42.6	44.2	43.8	44.4	27.1
Afrique subsaharienne	19.6	24.1	25.6	25.9	43.4
Moyen-Orient	52.9	55.9	56.5	57.0	23.7

* 2007 estimations préliminaires.
Source : BIT, Modèles Econométriques des Tendances, Octobre 2007. Pour plus d'informations suivez le lien http://www.ilo.org/trends. Les différences par rapport aux estimations précédentes sont dues aux révisions des estimations de la Banque Mondiale et du FMI sur le PIB et ses composants qui sont utilisées dans les modèles, tout comme des actualisations sur les informations des marchés du travail utilisées.

Sélection des autres indicateurs du marché du travail

Région	Rapport emploi-population (%) 1997	2006	2007*	Taux annuel de croissance du PIB (%) 1997-2007	Taux annuel de croissance de la population active (%) 1997-2007*	Variation du taux de chômage (en points de pourcentage) 2000-2007*
Monde	62.7	61.7	61.6	3.9	1.7	-0.1
Economies développées et Union européenne	56.2	56.5	56.4	2.6	0.7	-0.3
Europe centrale et orientale (hors UE) et CEI	53.8	53.9	54.1	5.6	0.6	-1.7
Asie-Orient	74.9	72.0	72.0	8.1	1.0	-0.6
Asie du Sud-Est et Pacifique	67.1	66.3	66.4	4.0	2.5	1.2
Asie du Sud	58.1	56.6	56.8	6.6	2.4	0.5
Amérique latine et Caraïbes	59.1	60.0	60.1	3.2	2.4	0.1
Afrique du Nord	44.7	46.1	46.3	4.9	4.9	-2.4
Afrique subsaharienne	69.0	68.1	68.0	5.1	4.1	-0.5
Moyen-Orient	46.0	49.7	50.3	4.7	4.9	0.1

* 2007 estimations préliminaires.

Source : BIT, Modèles Econométriques des Tendances, Octobre 2007. Pour plus d'informations suivez le lien http://www.ilo.org/trends. Les différences par rapport aux estimations précédentes sont dues aux révisions des estimations de la Banque Mondiale et du FMI sur le PIB et ses composants qui sont utilisées dans les modèles, tout comme des actualisations sur les informations des marchés du travail utilisées.

Estimaciones mundiales y regionales de los indicadores del mercado de trabajo

Las estimaciones mundiales et regionales siguientes de los indicadores del mercado del trabajo fueron hechas por la Unidad de Tendencias del Empleo de la OIT. Para obtener más información técnica sobre los métodos de las estimaciones mundiales y regionales, por favor consulte: www.ilo.org/trends.

Tasa de participación de la fuerza de trabajo (porcentaje)

Región	1997	2000	2004	2005	2006	2007*
Total - Mundo	66.8	66.3	65.8	65.7	65.6	65.6
Jóvenes - Mundo	57.2	56.1	54.8	54.5	54.6	54.6
Total						
Mundo	66.8	66.3	65.8	65.7	65.6	65.6
Economías desarrolladas y Unión Europea	60.8	60.8	60.4	60.3	60.3	60.2
Europa Central y Oriental (no Unión Europea) y CEI	60.2	58.4	59.0	58.9	58.9	59.1
Asia Oriental	77.8	77.2	75.2	75.1	74.5	74.5
Sudeste de Asia y el Pacífico	69.9	70.2	70.3	70.6	70.7	70.8
Asia meridional	61.0	60.5	59.9	60.1	59.6	59.8
América Latina y el Caribe	64.3	64.9	65.4	65.5	65.6	65.7
Africa del Norte	50.5	50.8	51.2	51.4	51.6	51.9
Africa subsahariana	75.5	75.0	74.3	74.3	74.2	74.0
Oriente Medio	52.8	53.8	55.4	56.2	56.4	57.0
Hombres						
Mundo	80.2	80.2	79.2	78.9	79.1	78.9
Economías desarrolladas y Unión Europea	70.8	70.4	68.9	68.9	68.3	68.2
Europa Central y Oriental (no Unión Europea) y CEI	70.9	69.1	69.5	69.5	69.5	69.6
Asia Oriental	84.5	83.6	82.0	81.7	81.6	81.4
Sudeste de Asia y el Pacífico	82.7	82.4	82.7	82.9	83.1	82.9
Asia meridional	83.9	83.2	82.4	82.5	82.2	82.0
América Latina y el Caribe	81.9	81.4	80.1	80.1	79.2	78.8
Africa del Norte	76.1	76.0	76.3	76.4	76.5	76.6
Africa subsahariana	87.2	86.9	86.2	86.3	86.3	85.9
Oriente Medio	77.5	77.5	78.0	78.1	78.2	78.3
Mujeres						
Mundo	53.0	52.6	52.4	52.4	52.5	52.5
Economías desarrolladas y Unión Europea	51.3	52.0	52.3	52.4	52.6	52.8
Europa Central y Oriental (no Unión Europea) y CEI	50.8	49.0	49.4	49.4	49.6	49.7
Asia Oriental	71.0	69.8	68.0	67.7	67.5	67.2
Sudeste de Asia y el Pacífico	57.4	57.8	58.2	58.6	58.8	59.3
Asia meridional	36.7	36.0	36.2	36.0	36.2	36.3
América Latina y el Caribe	47.1	48.9	51.3	51.7	52.4	52.8
Africa del Norte	25.0	25.6	26.5	26.7	27.0	27.3
Africa subsahariana	64.2	63.6	62.9	62.7	62.8	62.7
Oriente Medio	25.6	27.5	30.9	31.7	32.5	33.3

* 2006 estimaciones preliminares.
Fuente : OIT, Modelos Econométricos de Tendencias, Octubre 2007. Para más información consulte http://www.ilo.org/trends. Las diferencias en comparación con las estimaciones anteriores son debidas a las revisiones de las estimaciones del Banco Mundial y del FMI sobre el PIB y sus componentes que son utilizadas en los modelos, así como las actualizaciones de las informaciones de los mercados del trabajo utilizadas.

Tasa de desempleo (porcentaje)

Región	1997	2000	2004	2005	2006	2007*
	\multicolumn{6}{c}{Total}					
Mundo	6.1	6.1	6.3	6.2	6.0	6.0
Economías desarrolladas y Unión Europea	7.4	6.7	7.2	6.9	6.3	6.4
Europa Central y Oriental (no Unión Europea) y CEI	10.7	10.2	9.3	9.0	8.5	8.5
Asia Oriental	3.7	3.9	3.5	3.5	3.4	3.3
Sudeste de Asia y el Pacífico	4.0	4.9	6.4	6.1	6.2	6.2
Asia meridional	4.7	4.6	5.4	5.3	5.1	5.1
América Latina y el Caribe	8.0	8.5	8.4	8.4	8.5	8.5
Africa del Norte	11.5	13.1	12.4	11.4	10.8	10.7
Africa subsahariana	8.5	8.7	8.3	8.3	8.2	8.2
Oriente Medio	13.0	11.7	11.4	11.9	11.8	11.8
	\multicolumn{6}{c}{Hombres}					
Mundo	5.8	5.9	6.1	5.9	5.7	5.7
Economías desarrolladas y Unión Europea	6.9	6.2	6.9	6.6	6.1	6.2
Europa Central y Oriental (no Unión Europea) y CEI	10.6	10.1	9.6	9.2	8.7	8.7
Asia Oriental	4.2	4.4	4.0	4.0	3.8	3.8
Sudeste de Asia y el Pacífico	3.9	4.9	6.3	5.6	5.7	5.6
Asia meridional	4.4	4.4	5.0	5.0	4.8	4.8
América Latina y el Caribe	6.3	6.9	6.6	6.8	6.9	6.9
Africa del Norte	10.0	11.5	10.5	9.6	9.0	8.9
Africa subsahariana	7.7	8.0	7.6	7.6	7.5	7.5
Oriente Medio	11.3	10.3	10.0	10.4	10.4	10.3
	\multicolumn{6}{c}{Mujeres}					
Mundo	6.5	6.5	6.7	6.6	6.4	6.4
Economías desarrolladas y Unión Europea	8.1	7.3	7.5	7.2	6.7	6.7
Europa Central y Oriental (no Unión Europea) y CEI	10.9	10.3	9.0	8.7	8.3	8.3
Asia Oriental	3.1	3.2	2.9	2.9	2.8	2.7
Sudeste de Asia y el Pacífico	4.2	5.0	6.6	6.7	6.9	6.9
Asia meridional	5.3	5.1	6.2	6.0	5.7	5.8
América Latina y el Caribe	10.7	11.1	11.2	10.8	10.9	10.9
Africa del Norte	15.9	18.0	17.7	16.6	15.8	15.7
Africa subsahariana	9.6	9.7	9.3	9.3	9.2	9.1
Oriente Medio	18.6	16.3	15.2	15.9	15.8	15.6

* 2007 estimaciones preliminares.

Fuente : OIT, Modelos Econométricos de Tendencias, Octubre 2007. Para más información consulte http://www.ilo.org/trends. Las diferencias en comparación con las estimaciones anteriores son debidas a las revisiones de las estimaciones del Banco Mundial y del FMI sobre el PIB y sus componentes que son utilizadas en los modelos, así como las actualizaciones de las informaciones de los mercados del trabajo utilizadas.

Tasa de repartición sectorial en el empleo (porcentaje)

Región	Empleo por sector en proporción al empleo total 1997	2005	2006	2007*	Empleo de mujeres en proporción al empleo total por sector 2007*
Agricultura					
Mundo	41.4	37.1	36.0	34.9	41.3
Economías desarrolladas y Unión Europea	6.1	4.2	4.2	3.9	36.2
Europa Central y Oriental (no Unión Europea) y CEI	27.0	21.1	20.4	19.5	44.0
Asia Oriental	47.9	42.9	40.9	38.4	47.4
Sudeste de Asia y el Pacífico	48.8	45.5	45.2	43.9	41.4
Asia meridional	59.4	50.9	49.4	48.0	36.6
América Latina y el Caribe	23.5	19.6	19.7	19.1	22.7
Africa del Norte	38.5	36.8	36.9	35.9	25.9
Africa subsahariana	71.9	66.8	64.9	64.4	44.5
Oriente Medio	21.4	18.7	18.1	17.5	47.7
Industria					
Mundo	21.1	21.4	21.9	22.4	31.2
Economías desarrolladas y Unión Europea	28.3	25.0	24.7	24.5	22.9
Europa Central y Oriental (no Unión Europea) y CEI	28.3	25.6	25.8	26.1	30.8
Asia Oriental	24.3	24.3	25.6	26.9	42.0
Sudeste de Asia y el Pacífico	17.1	18.2	18.5	19.0	35.9
Asia meridional	15.3	20.2	21.0	21.7	24.7
América Latina y el Caribe	20.7	21.7	21.8	22.0	26.5
Africa del Norte	18.9	19.0	19.3	19.7	17.8
Africa subsahariana	8.5	9.1	9.5	9.7	25.5
Oriente Medio	25.6	25.5	25.4	25.5	19.8
Servicios					
Mundo	37.5	41.5	42.1	42.7	43.2
Economías desarrolladas y Unión Europea	65.6	70.8	71.2	71.5	52.9
Europa Central y Oriental (no Unión Europea) y CEI	44.7	53.3	53.8	54.4	51.6
Asia Oriental	27.8	32.7	33.5	34.7	42.8
Sudeste de Asia y el Pacífico	34.1	36.3	36.3	37.0	45.6
Asia meridional	25.2	28.9	29.6	30.3	20.2
América Latina y el Caribe	55.8	58.7	58.5	58.9	51.1
Africa del Norte	42.6	44.2	43.8	44.4	27.1
Africa subsahariana	19.6	24.1	25.6	25.9	43.4
Oriente Medio	52.9	55.9	56.5	57.0	23.7

* 2007 estimaciones preliminares.
Fuente : OIT, Modelos Econométricos de Tendencias, Octubre 2007. Para más información consulte http://www.ilo.org/trends. Las diferencias en comparación con las estimaciones anteriores son debidas a las revisiones de las estimaciones del Banco Mundial y del FMI sobre el PIB y sus componentes que son utilizadas en los modelos, así como las actualizaciones de las informaciones de los mercados del trabajo utilizadas.

Otros indicadores del mercado laboral

Región	Relación empleo-población (porcentaje) 1997	2006	2007*	Tasa anual de crecimiento del PIB (porcentaje) 1997-2007	Tasa anual de crecimiento de la población activa (porcentaje) 1997-2007*	Cambio de la tasa de desempleo (en puntos porcentuales) 2000-2007*
Mundo	62.7	61.7	61.6	3.9	1.7	-0.1
Economías desarrolladas y Unión Europea	56.2	56.5	56.4	2.6	0.7	-0.3
Europa Central y Oriental (no Unión Europea) y CEI	53.8	53.9	54.1	5.6	0.6	-1.7
Asia Oriental	74.9	72.0	72.0	8.1	1.0	-0.6
Sudeste de Asia y el Pacífico	67.1	66.3	66.4	4.0	2.5	1.2
Asia meridional	58.1	56.6	56.8	6.6	2.4	0.5
América Latina y el Caribe	59.1	60.0	60.1	3.2	2.4	0.1
Africa del Norte	44.7	46.1	46.3	4.9	4.9	-2.4
Africa subsahariana	69.0	68.1	68.0	5.1	4.1	-0.5
Oriente Medio	46.0	49.7	50.3	4.7	4.9	0.1

* 2007 estimaciones preliminares.

Fuente : OIT, Modelos Econométricos de Tendencias, Octubre 2007. Para más información consulte http://www.ilo.org/trends. Las diferencias en comparación con las estimaciones anteriores son debidas a las revisiones de las estimaciones del Banco Mundial y del FMI sobre el PIB y sus componentes que son utilizadas en los modelos, así como las actualizaciones de las informaciones de los mercados del trabajo utilizadas.

Global and Regional Estimates of Consumer Price Inflation

Global and regional estimates of consumer price inflation are produced by ILO Bureau of Statistics in collaboration with the Federal Reserve Bank of Cleveland. The national CPI figures, both annual and monthly, including the CPI by expenditure groups, are collected by the ILO Bureau of Statistics and disseminated on its website http://laborsta.ilo.org/.

Global and regional price indices are calculated as a weighted geometric average of national price indices, with the weights being each respective country's 2007 GDP estimates in current dollars based on purchasing power parity (PPP)[1]. The weight of a country is its share in the total GDP for the world or region.

More information on the methodology used to estimate the global and regional consumer price inflation is presented in the *Bulletin of Labour Statistics 2006-2* (available at http://www.ilo.org/public/english/bureau/stat/papers/listart.htm).

---

[1] World Bank estimates of PPP are available at http://siteresources.worldbank.org/DATASTATISTICS/Resources/GDP_PPP.pdf

Global and regional CPI inflation estimates: Year-over-year percentage changes for the period 1998-2007

	1998	1999	2000	2001	2002	2003	2004	2005	2006	2007
World	6.1	6.2	5.0	4.6	3.9	4.1	3.9	3.9	3.8	4.1
Developed	2.0	1.9	3.1	2.6	1.8	2.0	2.2	2.4	2.5	2.3
Sub-Saharan Africa	11.9	13.8	15.9	14.4	12.7	12.5	8.2	9.4	7.8	7.2
North Africa	4.2	3.4	1.6	2.3	2.6	3.4	9.3	3.2	4.9	6.1
South Asia	12.0	7.8	5.3	4.6	5.5	5.9	5.8	6.2	7.3	8.5
South-East Asia	21.9	8.8	2.3	5.4	5.7	4.1	4.4	6.3	7.5	4.6
East Asia	0.5	-1.3	0.3	1.1	-0.4	1.4	3.7	1.9	1.6	4.4
West Asia	28.6	22.5	19.3	19.2	16.7	10.1	5.9	4.4	6.8	6.9
Latin America and the Caribbean	10.0	9.2	8.4	6.5	9.2	10.9	6.8	6.4	5.4	5.4
CIS	25.9	71.7	24.1	20.0	13.6	12.3	10.5	12.1	9.4	9.7
Oceania	10.5	10.9	11.2	7.9	9.1	11.4	3.0	2.1	3.1	4.5

Estimations mondiales et régionales de l'inflation des prix à la consommation

Estimations mondiales et régionales de l'inflation des prix à la consommation

Les estimations mondiales et régionales de l'inflation des prix à la consommation sont produites par le Bureau de Statistique du BIT en collaboration avec la Banque Fédérale de réserve de Cleveland. Les chiffres des IPC nationaux, annuels et mensuels, y compris les IPC par groupes de dépenses, sont collectés par le Bureau de Statistique et disséminés sur son site: http://laborsta.ilo.org/.

Les indices des prix mondiaux et régionaux sont calculés comme des moyennes géométriques pondérées des indices des prix nationaux, les pondérations correspondant aux évaluations 2007 du PIB de chaque pays respectif en dollars actuels basés sur la parité de pouvoir d'achat (PPA)[1]. La pondération de chaque pays est sa part dans le PIB total pour le monde ou la région.

Des informations supplémentaires sur la méthodologie utilisée pour estimer l'inflation mondiale et régionale des prix à la consommation sont présentées dans le Bulletin des statistiques du travail 2006-2 (disponible sur le site http://www.ilo.org/public/english/bureau/stat/papers/listart.htm).

[1] Les estimations de PPA de la Banque Mondiale sont disponibles sur le site: http://siteresources.worldbank.org/DATASTATISTICS/Resources/GDP_PPP.pdf

Estimations mondiales et régionales de l'inflation des prix à la consommation: Changements comparés par rapport à l'année précédente, exprimés en pourcentage, pour la période 1998-2007

	1998	1999	2000	2001	2002	2003	2004	2005	2006	2007
Monde	6.1	6.2	5.0	4.6	3.9	4.1	3.9	3.9	3.8	4.1
Pays développés	2.0	1.9	3.1	2.6	1.8	2.0	2.2	2.4	2.5	2.3
Afrique subsaharienne	11.9	13.8	15.9	14.4	12.7	12.5	8.2	9.4	7.8	7.2
Afrique du Nord	4.2	3.4	1.6	2.3	2.6	3.4	9.3	3.2	4.9	6.1
Asie du Sud	12.0	7.8	5.3	4.6	5.5	5.9	5.8	6.2	7.3	8.5
Asie du Sud-Est	21.9	8.8	2.3	5.4	5.7	4.1	4.4	6.3	7.5	4.6
Asie orientale	0.5	-1.3	0.3	1.1	-0.4	1.4	3.7	1.9	1.6	4.4
Asie occidentale	28.6	22.5	19.3	19.2	16.7	10.1	5.9	4.4	6.8	6.9
Amérique latine et les Caraïbes	10.0	9.2	8.4	6.5	9.2	10.9	6.8	6.4	5.4	5.4
CEI	25.9	71.7	24.1	20.0	13.6	12.3	10.5	12.1	9.4	9.7
Pacifique	10.5	10.9	11.2	7.9	9.1	11.4	3.0	2.1	3.1	4.5

Estimaciones mundiales y regionales de la inflación en los precios al consumidor

La Oficina de Estadísticas de la OIT produce estimaciones mundiales y regionales de la inflación en los precios al consumidor en colaboración con el Banco de la Reserva Federal de Cleveland. La Oficina de Estadísticas de la OIT compila las cifras de los IPC nacionales, anuales y mensuales, incluyendo los IPC por grupos de gastos, y las divulga en su página Web http://laborsta.ilo.org/.

Los índices de precios mundiales y regionales se calculan como una media geométrica ponderada de los índices de precios nacionales. Las ponderaciones son las estimaciones para 2007 del PIB de cada país respectivo en dólares actuales basadas en la paridad del poder adquisitivo (PPA)[1]. La ponderación de cada país es su proporción en el PIB total para el mundo o la región.

El Boletín de Estadísticas del Trabajo 2006-2 presenta más información sobre la metodología utilizada para estimar la'inflation mundial y regional de los precios al consumidor (disponible en http://www.ilo.org/public/english/bureau/stat/papers/listart.htm).

[1] Las estimaciones del Banco Mundial están disponibles en http://siteresources.worldbank.org/DATASTATISTICS/Resources/GDP_PPP.pdf.

Estimaciones mundiales y regionales de la inflación de los precios al consumidor: cambios porcentuales de un año al otro para el período de 1997-2006

	1998	1999	2000	2001	2002	2003	2004	2005	2006	2007
Mundo	6.1	6.2	5.0	4.6	3.9	4.1	3.9	3.9	3.8	4.1
Países desarrollados	2.0	1.9	3.1	2.6	1.8	2.0	2.2	2.4	2.5	2.3
África subsahariana	11.9	13.8	15.9	14.4	12.7	12.5	8.2	9.4	7.8	7.2
África del Norte	4.2	3.4	1.6	2.3	2.6	3.4	9.3	3.2	4.9	6.1
Asia meridional	12.0	7.8	5.3	4.6	5.5	5.9	5.8	6.2	7.3	8.5
Sudeste de Asia	21.9	8.8	2.3	5.4	5.7	4.1	4.4	6.3	7.5	4.6
Asia Oriental	0.5	-1.3	0.3	1.1	-0.4	1.4	3.7	1.9	1.6	4.4
Asia Occidental	28.6	22.5	19.3	19.2	16.7	10.1	5.9	4.4	6.8	6.9
América Latina y el Caribe	10.0	9.2	8.4	6.5	9.2	10.9	6.8	6.4	5.4	5.4
CEI	25.9	71.7	24.1	20.0	13.6	12.3	10.5	12.1	9.4	9.7
Pacífico	10.5	10.9	11.2	7.9	9.1	11.4	3.0	2.1	3.1	4.5

APPENDIX
ANNEXE
APENDICE

Explanatory notes
Notes explicatives
Notas explicativas

Classifications used in the *Yearbook*
Classifications utilisées dans l'*Annuaire*
Clasificaciones empleadas en el *Anuario*

References
Références
Referencias

Master table
Tableau principal
Cuadro maestro

Appendix

Explanatory notes

Full details, including methodological descriptions and time series, and additional statistics are shown in the on-line database LABORSTA at http://laborsta.ilo.org.

Classifications

International standard classifications by branch of economic activity (ISIC), occupation (ISCO), status in employment (ICSE) and education (ISCED) are listed separately in this publication.

A large and ever increasing number of countries can and do rearrange national classifications by branch of economic activity (industry), occupation and status in employment to the international standard classification schemes, including the most recent revisions.

The classification according to main economic activity carried out where work is performed (industry) is fundamentally different from that according to main type of duties performed (occupation). In the former, all persons working in a given establishment are classified under the same industry irrespective of their particular occupations. The latter, on the other hand, brings together individuals working in similar types of work, irrespective of where the work is performed.

Where the data are given according to national classifications, it should be borne in mind that the industrial and occupational classifications used by the different countries present many points of divergence. The actual content of industrial or occupational groups may differ from one country to another owing to variations in definitions and methods of tabulation. Classification into broad groups may also obscure fundamental differences in the industrial or occupational patterns of the various countries.

The International Classification of Status in Employment (ICSE) classifies jobs with respect to the type of explicit or implicit contract of employment the person has with other persons or organizations. The basic criteria to define groups of the classification are the type of economic risk and the type of authority over establishments and other workers which the job incumbent has or will have.

Up to 1993 the main ICSE groups were employers, own-account workers, employees, members of producers' cooperatives, and unpaid family workers. ICSE was revised and expanded in 1993, in a way which left the titles of these main groups basically unchanged, except for the last group now called *contributing family workers*. The content of the group *own-account workers* was enlarged, however, to include persons working in a family enterprise with the same degree of commitment as the head of enterprise. These people, usually women, were formerly considered unpaid family workers in the old ICSE. The revised ICSE also makes the distinctions between groups clearer.

Experience has shown that frequently, because of the way countries measure status in employment, the content of the groups is not easily comparable. For example, in most countries managers and directors of incorporated enterprises are classified as employees, while in some others they are classified as employers. Another example is that family members who regularly receive remuneration as wages, salary, commission, piece-rates or pay in kind, are mainly classified as employees, but some countries classify them as contributing family workers. Another important difference affecting the comparability of the number of contributing family workers arises from the fact that some countries are not able to measure such persons as in employment at all. Many countries cannot distinguish between own-account workers and employers in their basic observations, so only the sum of these two groups can be presented. Some countries which have few members of producers' cooperatives may group them with employees, while others group them with own-account workers.

It should be recalled that the purpose of international classification schemes is not to supersede national classifications but to provide a framework for the international comparison of national statistics. Many countries, particularly those developing classifications for the first time, or revising existing schemes, use international schemes as a central framework.

Economically active population

The *economically active population* comprises all persons of either sex who furnish the supply of labour for the production of goods and services during a specified time-reference period. According to the 1993 version of the System of National Accounts (SNA), production includes all individual or collective goods or services that are supplied to units other than their producers, or intended to be so supplied, including the production of goods or services used up in the process of producing such goods or services; the production of all goods that are retained by their producers for their own final use; the production of housing services by owner-occupiers and of domestic and personal services produced by employing paid domestic staff.

Two useful measures of the economically active population are the *usually active population* measured in relation to a long reference period such as a year, and the *currently active population*, or, equivalently, the *labour force* measured in relation to a short reference period such as one day or one week.

The data presented on the *total* and *economically active population*, have generally been drawn from the latest population census or labour force sample survey. These data include all persons who fulfil the requirements for inclusion among the *employed* or the *unemployed* (as defined below).

Two types of activity rates can be obtained from these statistics: *specific activity rates* i.e. ratios (expressed in per cent) of the economically active population aged 15 years and over to the total population of the corresponding age groups; and *crude activity rates*, i.e. ratios (expressed in per cent) of the total economically active population to the total population which includes persons who do not belong to the working-age population.

National practices (see also Sources and Methods descriptions available separately and also in the on-line database LABORSTA) vary between countries as regards the treatment of groups such as armed forces, members of religious orders, persons seeking their first job, seasonal workers or persons engaged in part-time economic activities. In certain countries, all or some of these groups are included among the economically active while in other countries they are treated as inactive. However, in general, the data on economically active population do not include students, persons occupied solely in domestic duties in their own households, members of collective households, inmates of institutions, retired persons, persons living entirely on their own means, and persons wholly dependent upon others.

The comparability of the data is hampered by the differences between countries and even within a country not only as regards details of the definitions used and groups covered, but also by differences in the methods of collection, classification and tabulation of the data. In particular, the extent to which contributing family workers, particularly women, who assist in family enterprises are included among the enumerated economically active population varies considerably from one country to another. There are also variations among countries in the treatment of unemployed persons not previously employed, and of students engaged in part-time economic activities, and these are particularly relevant in comparing statistics for young people.

The reference period is also an important factor of difference: in some countries data on the economically active population refer to the actual position of each individual on the day of the census or survey or during a brief specific period such as the week immediately prior to the census or survey date, while in others the data recorded refer to the usual position of each person, generally without reference to any given period of time.

Also, in most countries the statistics of the economically active population relate only to employed and unemployed persons above a specified age while in some there is no such age provision in the definition of the economically active population.

Coding systems used by countries present another factor of divergence in the data. In order that the groups of one classification be identical in content to those of another classification, the same coding criteria need to be used. In general, coding systems are more precise in labour force sample surveys than in population censuses.

Employment

Employment is defined as follows in the *Resolution concerning statistics of the economically active population, employment, unemployment and underemployment*, adopted by the Thirteenth International Conference of Labour Statisticians (Geneva, 1982):[1]

"(1) The employed comprise all persons above a specific age who during a specified brief period, either one week or one day, were in the following categories:

(a) paid employment:

(a1) at work: persons who during the reference period performed some work for wage or salary, in cash or in kind;

(a2) with a job but not at work: persons who, having already worked in their present job, were temporarily not at work during the reference period and had a formal attachment to their job.

This formal job attachment should be determined in the light of national circumstances, according to one or more of the following criteria:

(i) the continued receipt of wage or salary;

(ii) an assurance of return to work following the end of the contingency, or an agreement as to the date of return;

(iii) the elapsed duration of absence from the job which, wherever relevant, may be that duration for which workers can receive compensation benefits without obligations to accept other jobs.

(b) self-employment:

(b1) at work: persons who during the reference period performed some work for profit or family gain, in cash or in kind;

(b2) with an enterprise but not at work: persons with an enterprise, which may be a business enterprise, a farm or a service undertaking, who were temporarily not at work during the reference period for any specific reason.

(2) For operational purposes, the notion some work may be interpreted as work for at least one hour.

(3) Persons temporarily not at work because of illness or injury, holiday or vacation, strike or lockout, educational or training leave, maternity or parental leave, reduction in economic activity, temporary disorganization or suspension of work due to such reasons as bad weather, mechanical or electrical breakdown, or shortage of raw materials or fuels, or other temporary absence with or without leave should be considered as in paid employment provided they had a formal job attachment.

(4) Employers, own-account workers and members of producers' cooperatives should be considered as in self-employment and classified as at work or not at work, as the case may be.

(5) Unpaid family workers at work should be considered as in self-employment irrespective of the number of hours worked during the reference period. Countries which prefer for special reasons to set a minimum time criterion for the inclusion of unpaid family workers among the employed should identify and separately classify those who worked less than the prescribed time.

(6) Persons engaged in the production of economic goods and services for own and household consumption should be considered as in self-employment if such production comprises an important contribution to the total consumption of the household.

(7) Apprentices who received pay in cash or in kind should be considered in paid employment and classified as at work or not at work on the same basis as other persons in paid employment.

(8) Students, homemakers and others mainly engaged in non-economic activities during the reference period, who at the same time were in paid employment or self-employment as defined in subparagraph (1) above should be considered as employed on the same basis as other categories of employed persons and be identified separately, where possible.

(9) Members of the armed forces should be included among persons in paid employment. The armed forces should

---

[1] For the full text of the resolution, see ILO: Current international recommendations on labour statistics (Geneva, 2000) or the ILO Bureau of Statistics' web site: www.ilo.org/stat.

include both the regular and temporary members as specified in the most recent revision of the International Standard Classification of Occupations (ISCO)."

National definitions of employment may in a number of cases differ from the recommended international standard definition. (See also Sources and Methods descriptions available separately and also in the on-line database LABORSTA.)

In general, employment data are obtained from four main sources, namely, household sample surveys, establishment censuses or surveys, official national estimates, or administrative records of social insurance schemes. These four main sources of employment are identified in the tables; however statistics from only one source is generally used (additional statistics are shown in the on-line database LABORSTA), and priority is given to the use of household labour force surveys since these are more comprehensive.

For total employment, labour force sample surveys cover all status groups, that is, not only employees (wage earners and salaried employees), including paid family workers, but also employers, own-account workers, members of producers' cooperatives, contributing family workers and workers not classifiable by status. The data generally relate to employment during a specified brief period, either one week or one day. Usually, no distinction is made between persons employed full time and those working less than full time.

Establishment surveys provide data on the number of workers on establishment payrolls for a specified payroll period or working day in this period. In general, there are two types of establishment statistics:

The first type covers all establishments of a given importance, e.g. those fulfilling certain conditions, such as having more than a certain number of employees, having an annual output of more than a certain value, etc. The data thus obtained may be subject to some bias owing to the exclusion of establishments which are below the minimum size fixed for the statistics. Moreover, a shift of employment from small to large establishments will be reflected in a rising trend in the data. Provided that this minimum is small, the scope of these statistics is usually very wide and they can furnish a close approximation of the fluctuations in paid employment.

The second type of statistics relates to a sample of establishments. The chief difficulty with such statistics is to ensure that the sample of establishments remains representative of the whole. For example, changes in industrial structure, the growth and decline of individual establishments, general population movements and pronounced changes in the levels of activity in some sectors of the economy tend to introduce a cumulative bias in this sample which may become appreciable after several years.

In certain countries where statistics of the first type (all establishments of a given importance) are available only at annual or longer intervals, they may be combined either by linking or by interpolation with statistics of the second type (samples of establishments) which are available more frequently.

Some statistics are official estimates provided by national authorities. Such estimates are usually based on combined information drawn from sources such as social insurance records. This source covers the working population protected by sickness, accident or unemployment insurance schemes, or the like. The number of contributors or of contributions paid provides a measure of the number of insured persons in employment (unemployed persons being exempt from the obligation to pay contributions). Persons working a very short time, receiving very low pay or who are above a certain age, are sometimes excluded from these statistics. In addition to changes in the actual number of persons employed, employment statistics based on social insurance records may also reflect changes in coverage of particular industrial, occupational or status groups.

The "share of women in wage employment in the non-agricultural sector" is one of the indicators of the Millennium Development Goals.

Unemployment

Unemployment is defined as follows in the *Resolution concerning statistics of the economically active population, employment, unemployment and underemployment*, adopted by the Thirteenth International Conference of Labour Statisticians (Geneva, 1982):[2]

"(1) The unemployed comprise all persons above a specified age who during the reference period were:

(a) without work, i.e. were not in paid employment or self-employment, as defined in paragraph 9;

(b) currently available for work, i.e. were available for paid employment or self-employment during the reference period; and

(c) seeking work, i.e. had taken specific steps in a specified reference period to seek paid employment or self-employment. The specific steps may include registration at a public or private employment exchange; application to employers; checking at worksites, farms, factory gates, market or other assembly places; placing or answering newspaper advertisements; seeking assistance of friends or relatives; looking for land, building, machinery or equipment to establish own enterprise; arranging for financial resources; applying for permits and licences, etc.

(2) In situations where the conventional means of seeking work are of limited relevance, where the labour market is largely unorganized or of limited scope, where labour absorption is, at the time, inadequate, or where the labour force is largely self-employed, the standard definition of unemployment given in subparagraph (1) above may be applied by relaxing the criterion of seeking work.

(3) In the application of the criterion of current availability for work, especially in situations covered by subparagraph (2) above, appropriate tests should be developed to suit national circumstances. Such tests may be based on notions such as present desire for work and previous work experience, willingness to take up work for wage or salary on locally prevailing terms, or readiness to undertake self-employment activity given the necessary resources and facilities.

(4) Notwithstanding the criterion of seeking work embodied in the standard definition of unemployment, persons without work and currently available for work who had made arrangements to take up paid employment or undertake self-employment activity at a date subsequent to the reference period should be considered as unemployed.

(5) Persons temporarily absent from their jobs with no formal job attachment who were currently available for work and seeking work should also be regarded as unemployed in accordance with the standard definition of unemployment. Countries may, however, depending on national circumstances and policies, prefer to relax the seeking

---

[2] For the full text of the resolution, see ILO: *Current international recommendations on labour statistics* (Geneva, 2000) or the ILO Bureau of Statistics' web site: www.ilo.org/stat.

work criterion in the case of persons temporarily laid off. In such cases, persons temporarily laid off who were not seeking work but classified as unemployed should be identified as a separate subcategory.

(6) Students, homemakers and others mainly engaged in non-economic activities during the reference period who satisfy the criteria laid down in subparagraphs (1) and (2) above should be regarded as unemployed on the same basis as other categories of unemployed identified separately, where possible."

National definitions of unemployment may differ from the recommended international standard definition. The national definitions used may vary from one country to another as regards inter alia age limits, reference periods, criteria for seeking work, treatment of persons temporarily laid off and of persons seeking work for the first time. (See also Sources and Methods descriptions available separately and also in the on-line database LABORSTA.)

Differences between countries with regard to the treatment of unemployed persons with respect to classification by status in employment are particularly pronounced. In general, unemployed persons with previous job experience, classified according to their last job, are included with employees, but in some cases they and unemployed persons seeking their first job form the most important part of the group persons not classifiable by status.

Even when using international classification schemes (economic activity and occupation), national practices may also diverge concerning the classification of the unemployed with previous job experience, who are often included in the residual category of the international classification scheme, i.e. under activities not adequately defined (ISIC) or workers not classifiable by occupation (ISCO).

Inter-country comparisons are further hampered by the variety of types of source used to obtain information on unemployment and the differences in the scope and coverage of such sources. In general, four main sources of unemployment statistics may be distinguished. These sources are identified in the tables; however statistics from only one source is generally used here (additional statistics are shown in the on-line database LABORSTA), and priority is given to the use of household labour force surveys since these are more comprehensive.

Labour force sample surveys generally yield comprehensive statistics on unemployment since, in particular, they include groups of persons who are often not covered in unemployment statistics obtained by other methods, particularly persons seeking work for the first time and persons starting work without the assistance of public employment offices. Generally the definition of unemployment used for this type of statistics follows more closely the international recommendations and such statistics are more comparable internationally than those obtained from other sources. The percentages of unemployment are also generally more reliable since they are calculated by relating the estimated number of persons unemployed to the estimate of the total number of employed and unemployed persons (the labour force) derived from the same survey.

Some statistics are official estimates provided by national authorities and are usually based on combined information drawn from one or more of the other sources described below. However, the prevalence of this source is decreasing due to the increasing existence of labour force surveys in countries throughout the world.

Social insurance statistics: the statistics from this source are drawn from the records of compulsory unemployment insurance schemes which, where they exist, as a rule have a broad industrial coverage related to wage earners and salaried employees or to wage earners only. Unemployment rates are computed by comparing the number of recipients of insurance benefits to the total number of insured persons covered by the schemes. However, the extent to which the numbers and percentages of unemployed reported are representative of the general level of unemployment in the countries with this type of source is difficult if not impossible to ascertain.

Employment office statistics: these statistics generally refer to the number of persons looking for work who are entered on the registers at the end of each month. In addition to persons without a job, they may include persons on strike, or temporarily ill and unable to work and persons engaged on unemployment relief projects. In principle, these statistics do not include persons who are already in employment, which is identified in the tables as *registered unemployment*. However, some applicants are persons already in employment who are seeking a change of job or extra work who are also registered at employment offices. The coverage of these statistics is therefore identified in the tables as *work applicants*.

The value of the statistics from this source varies widely. In cases where the employment offices function in close connection with unemployment insurance, registration being a qualifying condition for the receipt of unemployment benefits, they are comparable in reliability to compulsory unemployment insurance statistics. Similarly, where employment offices operate in close connection with large unemployment relief schemes, they may also provide reasonably satisfactory figures during the currency of the schemes. However, where registration is entirely voluntary, and especially where the employment offices function only in the more populous, urban areas of a country or are not widely patronised by employees seeking work or by employers seeking workers, the data are generally very incomplete and do not give a reliable indication of the true extent of unemployment. The scope of the figures is determined partly by the manner in which the system of exchanges is organized and the advantages which registration brings, and partly by the extent to which workers are accustomed to register. In many cases persons engaged in agriculture and living in less populous areas are scarcely represented in the statistics, if at all. The scope of employment office statistics is therefore most difficult to ascertain, and in very few cases can satisfactory percentages of unemployment be calculated. In general, these statistics are not comparable from country to country. However, within a country, if there are no changes in legislation, administrative regulations and the like, fluctuations may reflect changes in the prevalence of registered unemployment over time.

Unless otherwise indicated, the data are generally annual averages of monthly, quarterly or semi-annual data. The numbers indicate the size of the problem and the percentages (unemployment rates) illustrate the relative severity of unemployment. These rates are calculated by relating the number of persons in the given group who are unemployed during the reference period (usually a particular day or a given week) to the total of employed and unemployed persons in the group at the same date. However, statistics by age are often only collected at a fixed calendar period or on a specific date of the year and are not therefore annual averages of monthly, quarterly or semi-annual data.

Unemployment rate by age group: the unemployment rate for the age group 15-24 is one of the indicators of the United Nations Millennium Development Goals.

When relating the data presented on unemployment classified by level of education with the data on economically active population by level of education, due note must be taken of differences in source, scope, coverage and reference periods.

In conformity with the international recommendations, unemployed persons with previous work experience are classified by industry or occupation on the basis of their last activity (under numerical codes according to the relevant category of the classification scheme presented). Unemployed persons without previous work experience are shown separately as far as possible, in order to distinguish them from unemployed persons with previous work experience classified under *activities not adequately defined in ISIC or workers not classifiable by occupation in ISCO*.

Hours of work

The hours of work relate to time spent by persons in the performance of activities which contribute to the production of goods and services as defined by the United Nations System of National Accounts. Since 1962, there are international statistical standards only for the *hours actually* worked and the *normal hours of work* concepts, adopted by the Tenth International Conference of Labour Statisticians.[3] These are confined to persons in paid employment and describe work situations that are more typical for production workers in manufacturing establishments. While they have served as a guide to countries when producing national estimates, many national definitions have now become more comprehensive. These international standards are currently being revised to improve the coverage of persons and work activities, and to better reflect diverse working time arrangements. New international standards are expected to be adopted by the forthcoming 18th International Conference of Labour Statisticians in 2008, that will include other concepts such as *hours usually worked* and *hours paid for*. The following are definitional elements for these concepts being measured by many countries.

The concept of *hours actually worked* relates to the time that persons in employment spend on work activities during a specified reference period, comprising:

(a) time spent directly on production (producing goods and services, including paid and unpaid overtime);

(b) time spent to facilitate production, necessary to work activities or to enhance the performance of persons (design, prepare, maintain the workplace, procedures, tools, including receipts, time sheets, reports), changing time (donning necessary work clothing), transporting activities (door to door, bringing agricultural produce to market) and training intended for the economic unit;

(c) time spent in-between main activities (awaiting customers, stand-by for reasons such as lack of supply of work or power, machinery breakdown, accident), travel time to meetings or work assignments, active on-call duty (as for health and technical service professional);

(d) resting time (short rest or refreshment including tea, coffee or prayer breaks).

Hours actually worked excludes time not worked, whether paid or unpaid, such as:

(a) annual leave, public holidays, sick leave, parental leave, etc.;

(b) meal breaks;

(c) time spent on travel from home to work and vice versa, also known as commuter travel, that is not actually time spent working.

Hours actually worked covers all types of workers, whether in self-employment jobs or in paid employment jobs; it may be paid or unpaid and carried out in any location, including the street, field, home, etc.

The concept of *hours paid for* would cover workers in paid employment and comprises all hours, whether worked or not, that have been paid by the employer. When compared to the *hours actually worked* of employees, it covers all paid hours, even those not worked, such as paid annual vacation, public holidays, paid sick leave, other paid leave, and excludes all unpaid time worked (for example, unpaid overtime).

The concept of *normal hours of work* covers a subset of persons in paid employment (e.g. those covered by labour laws and regulations) and relates to the number of hours fixed by laws and regulations, collective agreements or arbitral awards to be performed in paid employment jobs over a specified reference period, such as a day, week or year.

The *hours usually worked* would relate to the hours typically, or most commonly worked per week by persons in paid and self-employment during a long reference period such as a month, season, or other long period, i.e., the typical value of the weekly hours worked. As compared to the *normal hours of work*, all usual overtime would be included in *usual hours*. All time worked not on a usual basis is therefore excluded.

In general, hours of work data are obtained from two main sources, namely surveys or censuses of establishments and household sample surveys. Two other sources are official national estimates or administrative records of social insurance schemes. The first source relates to payroll data derived from establishment sample surveys or censuses that often furnish at the same time statistics on wages and on employment. These statistics often relate to *hours paid for* and, to a lesser extent, to *hours actually worked*. Statistics derived from establishment-based surveys tend to have limited worker coverage, as they cover employees or a subset of them (e.g., wage earners or salaried employees) or who work in establishments above a certain size or in certain industries only. The coverage of the statistics may therefore be importantly limited in countries where most workers are engaged, for example, in small-sized establishments or in self-employment jobs. These types of limitations are indicated in footnotes.

The second main source relates to labour force sample surveys or other household based surveys. Statistics derived from this source often relate to *hours actually worked*, and sometimes to the *usual hours*. In theory they cover the employed population as a whole, including the self-employed. Some statistics from labour force surveys relate to the hours of work in the main job only which is footnoted.

The statistics may relate to *employees*, as defined by the International Standard Classification of Status in Employment, ICSE-93. When statistics are derived from labour force surveys, they may refer to *total employment*. Establishment survey data may refer to a subgroup of employees, namely to *wage earners* or to *salaried employees*. Some countries further limit worker coverage to "adults", "skilled" or "unskilled" employees as indicated. There are no international definitions for *wage earners* or for *salaried employees*. The former are generally equated with "manual", "production" or "blue collar" workers, and the latter with "white collar workers".

The statistics are generally the average number of hours of work per week; in a few cases hours per day or per month.

---

[3] For the full text of the unrevised resolution, see ILO: *Current international recommendations on labour statistics* (Geneva, 2000) or the ILO Bureau of Statistics' web site (www.ilo.org/public/english/bureau/stat).

For statistics derived from establishment surveys, average hours actually worked or average hours paid for per week or per month are normally compiled by dividing the total number of hours actually worked or paid for during a week or a month by the average number of workers on the payrolls during the same period. Average hours actually worked or paid for per day are generally compiled by dividing the total number of hours actually worked or paid for during a week, fortnight or month by the total number of days actually worked or paid for during the same period.

In labour force surveys, average hours actually worked are normally derived by dividing the hours actually worked by all persons in employment (or all employees) by the number of persons in employment (or employees). In these calculations, persons absent from work during the whole survey reference week should be included in the calculation. Some statistics, however, exclude them to better reflect a "typical" work week, (which case is footnoted).

In deriving averages, statistics may be based on one single point in time (i.e., when the survey is carried out once in the year), on a set of points in time (i.e., monthly or quarterly surveys) or on continuous observations (i.e., surveys that cover all weeks in a year). The more points in time are involved in the calculation, the less the estimate will be affected by seasonal fluctuations, annual and sick leave actually taken during the year as well as by variations in strike activity.

In making comparisons of statistics on hours of work, it should be borne in mind that the data are influenced by the averaging method used, the number of data points used, and practices regarding the number of days normally worked per week, regulations and customs regarding weekend and overtime work, the extent of absence from work, etc. They will also be affected by industrial and job coverage. Statistics that exclude workers in agriculture, where hours worked follow different patterns than in other industries, will not be comparable with those that include them. Similarly, statistics that relate to the main job only will be lower than statistics that cover multiple jobs or jobs in all productive activities including unpaid services.[4]

Wages

The *Resolution concerning an integrated system of wages statistics* adopted by the Twelfth International Conference of Labour Statisticians (Geneva, 1973)[5] defines earnings and wage rates as follows:

"8. The concept of earnings, as applied in wages statistics, relates to remuneration in cash and in kind paid to employees, as a rule at regular intervals, for time worked or work done together with remuneration for time not worked, such as for annual vacation, other paid leave or holidays. Earnings exclude employers' contributions in respect of their employees paid to social security and pension schemes and also the benefits received by employees under these schemes. Earnings also exclude severance and termination pay.

9. Statistics of earnings should relate to employees' gross remuneration, i.e. the total before any deductions are made by the employer in respect of taxes, contributions of employees to social security and pension schemes, life insurance premiums, union dues and other obligations of employees.

10. (i) Earnings should include: direct wages and salaries, remuneration for time not worked (excluding severance and termination pay), bonuses and gratuities and housing and family allowances paid by the employer directly to this employee.

   (a) Direct wages and salaries for time worked, or work done, cover: (i) straight time pay of time-rated workers; (ii) incentive pay of time-rated workers; (iii) earnings of piece workers (excluding overtime premiums); (iv) premium pay for overtime, shift, night and holiday work; (v) commissions paid to sales and other personnel. Included are: premiums for seniority and special skills, geographical zone differentials, responsibility premiums, dirt, danger and discomfort allowances, payments under guaranteed wage systems, cost-of-living allowances and other regular allowances.

   (b) Remuneration for time not worked comprises direct payments to employees in respect of public holidays, annual vacations and other time off with pay granted by the employer.

   (c) Bonuses and gratuities cover seasonal and end-of-year bonuses, additional payments in respect of vacation period (supplementary to normal pay) and profit-sharing bonuses.

(ii) Statistics of earnings should distinguish cash earnings from payments in kind.

...

12. Wage rates should include basic wages, cost-of-living allowances and other guaranteed and regularly paid allowances, but exclude overtime payments, bonuses and gratuities, family allowances and other social security payments made by employers. Ex gratia payments in kind, supplementary to normal wage rates, are also excluded.

13. Statistics of wage rates fixed by or in pursuance of laws or regulations, collective agreements or arbitral awards (which are generally minimum or standard rates) should be clearly distinguished from statistics referring to wage rates actually paid to individual workers. Each of these types of wage rates is useful for particular purposes.

14. Time rates of wages for normal periods of work should be distinguished from special and other rates such as piece rates, overtime rates, premium rates for work on holidays and shift rates."

The statistics of wages are, in general, average earnings per worker or, in some cases, average wage rates. Occasionally wage indices are given in the absence of absolute wage data. Some of the statistics cover wage earners (i.e. manual or production workers) only, while others refer to salaried employees (i.e. non-manual workers), or all employees (i.e. wage earners and salaried employees). Where they refer to specific groups of workers (e.g. adults, skilled or unskilled workers), this is indicated in footnotes. Unless otherwise stated, the data cover workers of both sexes, irrespective of age. Data by sex are presented whenever possible.

---

[4] For information on the differences in scope, definitions and methods of calculation, etc., used for the various national series, see ILO: *Sources and Methods: Labour Statistics* (formerly *Statistical Sources and Methods*), Vol. 2: ~Employment, wages, hours of work and labour cost (establishment surveys)~, second edition (Geneva, 1995); Vol. 3: ~ Economically active population, employment, unemployment and hours of work (household surveys)~ , second edition (Geneva, 1990); Vol. 4: ~Employment, unemployment, wages and hours of work (administrative records and related sources)~ (Geneva, 1989). All these volumes can be consulted online at our statistical website http://laborsta.ilo.org.

[5] For the full text of the resolution, see ILO: *Current international recommendations on labour statistics* (Geneva, 2000) or the ILO Bureau of Statistics' web site: www.ilo.org/stat.

The data on average earnings are mostly obtained from payroll data and derived from establishment sample surveys or censuses often furnishing at the same time data on hours of work and on employment. In a few cases, average earnings are compiled on the basis of social insurance statistics, collective agreements or other sources. The types of sources used are shown in the tables. However where statistics are available from more than one source, only one source is used here – the most comprehensive – and statistics from the other sources are shown in the on-line database LABORSTA.

Earnings data from payrolls of establishments usually refer to cash payments received from employers (before deduction of taxes and social security contributions payable by workers) and include remuneration for normal working hours; overtime pay; remuneration for time not worked (public holidays, annual vacation, sick leave and other paid leave); bonuses and gratuities; cost-of-living allowances and special premiums (such as end-of-year bonuses). When earnings include the value of payments in kind and family allowances, this is indicated in a footnote. Statistics of earnings derived from social insurance records usually yield lower averages than payroll data because overtime pay, incentive pay and the like may be excluded as well as wages exceeding a certain upper limit.

Statistics of wage rates are in most cases based on collective agreements, arbitral awards or other wage fixing decisions, which generally specify minimum rates for particular occupations or groups of workers. In some countries rates actually paid correspond closely to these minima. In countries where the fixing of wage rates is widespread, statistics of average wage rates in particular industries or groups of industries are calculated, using as weights the numerical importance in a given year of the different occupations for which rates are available in the industries covered. Data on wage rates usually refer only to rates for adults working normal hours, and therefore payments for overtime and other supplementary wage elements are not taken into account; cost-of-living allowances, however, are often included, and other allowances fixed in the wage-setting process, such as housing allowances, are sometimes included. Some countries obtain average rates actually paid (straight-time earnings) from establishment payrolls in the same way as average earnings are obtained. Rates actually paid usually cover the remuneration on the basis of normal time worked, both for normal and overtime hours, but exclude incentive pay and other bonuses as well as the premium part of overtime pay. Rates actually paid are sometimes also gathered by labour inspectors.

The different types of wages statistics are indicated in the tables with footnotes.

All wages data are expressed in national currency.

Earnings data show fluctuations which reflect the influence both of changes in wage rates and supplementary wage payments. Weekly, daily and monthly earnings are in addition much dependent on variations in hours of work. Statistics of wage rates do not reflect the influence of changes in wage supplements nor the influence of variations in hours of work. The fluctuations of average earnings obtained from global payrolls are also influenced by changes in the employment structure, i.e. the relative importance of males, females, unskilled and skilled labour, full-time and part-time workers etc., while average wage rates are normally compiled using the employment structure of a given year as weights. Average hourly earnings are generally higher than hourly rates because the former include overtime payments, premiums, bonuses and allowances which do not enter into statistics of wage rates. Average weekly or monthly earnings should also be higher than the corresponding rates, but may sometimes fall short of wage rates because of loss of working time through sickness, other absences or part-time work. In making comparisons between wages statistics, account must be taken of differences in concepts, scope, methods of compilation and of presentation of the data.

It should be borne in mind that figures of wages do not reflect workers' disposable or net earnings, since they generally represent the gross wages, before deductions such as those for taxes or social security contributions.

In making comparisons of data on wages in agriculture and in other activities, it should be borne in mind that the methods of payment and the types of labour contracts and arrangements in agriculture are often quite different from those in other activities. Wherever possible, a distinction is made between permanent workers, seasonal workers and regular or casual day workers. In most cases, the statistics refer to total wages which are paid entirely in cash or to the money part of the wages only, although the workers receive payments in kind in addition. In a few cases, the value of meals and/or lodging furnished is included. Whenever possible, if earnings include the value of payments in kind, this is indicated in a footnote.

International comparisons of wages are subject to greater reservations with respect to agriculture than for other activities. The nature of the work carried out by the different categories of agricultural workers and the length of the working day and week also show considerable variation from one country to another. Seasonal fluctuations in agricultural wages are more important in some countries than in others. The methods followed in the different countries for estimating the money value of the payments in kind is not uniform.

International comparisons should also take into account differences between countries in the prices of consumer goods and services, as well as the need for a common currency and appropriate exchange rates, while analyses of wage changes over time should take into account changes in the relevant consumer prices during that time.

For further information, see ILO: *An integrated system of wages statistics: A manual on methods* (Geneva, 1979). For information on the differences in scope, definitions and methods of calculation, etc., used for the various national series, see the Sources and Methods component of the on-line database LABORSTA.

Occupational injuries

The *Resolution concerning statistics of occupational injuries (resulting from occupational accidents)* adopted by the Sixteenth International Conference of Labour Statisticians (ICLS) (Geneva, 1998)[6] contains the following definitions for statistical purposes:

"occupational accident: an unexpected and unplanned occurrence, including acts of violence, arising out of or in connection with work which results in one or more workers incurring a personal injury, disease or death;

as occupational accidents are to be considered travel, transport or road traffic accidents in which workers are injured and which arise out of or in the course of work, i.e. while engaged in an economic activity, or at work, or carrying on the business of the employer;

---

[6] For the full text of the resolution, see ILO: *Current international recommendations on labour statistics* (Geneva, 2000) or the ILO Bureau of Statistics' web site: www.ilo.org/stat.

occupational injury: any personal injury, disease or death resulting from an occupational accident; an occupational injury is therefore distinct from an occupational disease, which is a disease contracted as a result of an exposure over a period of time to risk factors arising from work activity;

case of occupational injury: the case of one worker incurring an occupational injury as a result of one occupational accident;

incapacity for work: inability of the victim, due to an occupational injury, to perform the normal duties of work in the job or post occupied at the time of the occupational accident."

The statistics of occupational injuries presented in this publication conform, as far as possible, to the guidelines contained in the Sixteenth ICLS Resolution. The data should cover all workers regardless of their status in employment (i.e. both employees and the self-employed, including employers and own-account workers), and the whole country, all branches of economic activity and all sectors of the economy.

The following are generally excluded: cases of occupational disease (an occupational disease is a disease contracted as a result of an exposure over a period of time to risk factors arising from work activity) and cases of injury due to commuting accidents (a commuting accident is an accident occurring on the habitual route, in either direction, between the place of work or work-related training and (i) the worker's principal or secondary residence; (ii) the place where the worker usually takes his or her meals; or (iii) the place where he or she usually receives his or her remuneration; which results in death or personal injury).

The type of statistics shown for a particular country depends on the source used. Data on occupational injuries are most frequently obtained from occupational accident reporting systems (e.g. to a labour inspectorate) or occupational injury compensation schemes, although surveys of establishments and of households are used in a few countries. The type of source determines the coverage of the statistics. In many countries, the coverage of reporting requirements or injury compensation, and thus the coverage of the statistics, is limited to certain types of workers (employees only in many cases), certain economic activities, cases of injury with more than a certain number of days of incapacity, etc. The type of source is shown in each table, and the type of injuries covered (reported or compensated) is also indicated.

The statistics presented relate to cases of occupational injury due to occupational accidents that occurred during the calendar year indicated. Total days lost as a result of a case of injury are included in the statistics for the calendar year in which the occupational accident took place.

Workers in the reference group are those workers in the particular group under consideration and covered by the source of the statistics of occupational injuries (e.g. those of a specific sex or in a specific economic activity, occupation, region, age group, or any combination of these, or those covered by a particular compensation scheme). The number of workers in the reference group varies between countries and economic activities and from one period to another, because of differences or changes in the size and composition of employment and other factors. The differences in numbers are taken into account by using comparative measures, such as frequency, incidence and severity rates.

A rise or fall in the number of cases of occupational injury over a period of time may reflect not only changes in conditions of work and the work environment, but also modifications in reporting procedures or data collection methods, or revisions to laws or regulations governing the reporting or compensation of occupational injuries in the country concerned.

Cases of temporary incapacity are the number of cases of occupational injury where the workers injured were unable to work from the day after the day of the accident, but were able to perform again the normal duties of work in the job or post occupied at the time of the occupational accident causing the injury within a period of one year from the day of the accident.

Frequency rates are generally calculated as the number of new cases of injury (fatal and non-fatal) during the calendar year divided by the total number of hours worked by workers in the reference group during the year, multiplied by 1,000,000. *Incidence* rates are calculated as the number of new cases of injury (fatal and non-fatal) during the calendar year divided by the number of workers in the reference group during the year, multiplied by 100,000.

The type of rate (per 1,000,000 hours worked, per 100,000 workers employed, per 100,000 employees, per 100,000 workers insured, etc.) is indicated at the beginning of the data for each country.

Days lost are the number of days lost by cases of occupational injury with temporary incapacity for work. In a few cases, they also include days lost by cases with permanent incapacity, which may include estimates. The days lost are generally the calendar days during which the injured worker was temporarily unable to work, excluding the day of the accident, up to a maximum of one year. In some countries, however, particularly those where the source of the statistics is an accident compensation scheme, days lost are expressed in workdays. Temporary absences from work of less than one day for medical treatment are not included.

Care should be taken when using the data on occupational injuries in this publication, particularly when making international comparisons. The sources, methods of data collection, coverage and classifications used differ between countries. For example, coverage may be limited to certain types of workers (employees, insured persons, full-time workers, etc.), certain economic activities, establishments employing more than a given number of workers, cases of injury losing more than a certain number of days of work, etc. Descriptions of the national sources, scope, definitions and methods used for compiling the statistics presented in this publication are given in the Sources and Methods component of the on-line database LABORSTA.

Strikes and lockouts

The *Resolution concerning statistics of strikes, lockouts and other action due to labour disputes*, adopted by the Fifteenth International Conference of Labour Statisticians (Geneva, 1993),[7] gives the following definitions for statistical purposes:

"A strike is a temporary work stoppage effected by one or more groups of workers with a view to enforcing or resisting demands or expressing grievances, or supporting other workers in their demands or grievances.

A lockout is a total or partial temporary closure of one or more places of employment, or the hindering of the normal work activities of employees, by one or more em-

---

[7] For the full text of the resolution, see ILO: *Current international recommendations on labour statistics* (Geneva, 2000) or the ILO Bureau of Statistics' web site: www.ilo.org/stat.

ployers with a view to enforcing or resisting demands or expressing grievances, or supporting other employers in their demands or grievances.

Workers involved in a strike: Workers directly involved in a strike are those who participated directly by stopping work. Workers indirectly involved in a strike are those employees of the establishments involved, or self-employed workers in the group involved, who did not participate directly by stopping work but who were prevented from working because of the strike.

Workers involved in a lockout: Workers directly involved in a lockout are those employees of the establishments involved who were directly concerned by the labour dispute and who were prevented from working by the lockout. Workers indirectly involved in a lockout are those employees of the establishments involved who were not directly concerned by the labour dispute but who were prevented from working by the lockout.

A labour dispute is a state of disagreement over a particular issue or group of issues over which there is conflict between workers and employers, or about which grievance is expressed by workers or employers, or about which workers or employers support other workers or employers in their demands or grievances."

The national definitions may differ from these, depending on the source of the statistics. In general, they are drawn from the administrative records of conciliation services, services concerned with labour relations, etc. The data may come from several sources, including strike notices, newspaper reports and direct enquiries addressed to employers or to workers' organizations. The type of source is shown in each table.

The data cover strikes and lockouts together, as most countries do not distinguish between these two types of action in their statistics. In general, the statistics cover all types of strikes and lockouts and all economic activities, and relate to action in progress during the calendar year, i.e. strikes and lockouts beginning during the year and those continuing from the previous year. Any differences from the above are indicated in footnotes. If the statistics cover only strikes and lockouts above a certain size (in terms of the number of workers involved, duration or the amount of time not worked, or a combination of two or more of these), the limit is also indicated in a footnote.

The international recommendations state that all work stoppages due to a single labour dispute should be counted as one strike or lockout, as long as the period between stoppages is not more than two months. Different criteria are used in some countries to identify a single strike or lockout; e.g. each stoppage in each establishment may be considered to be one strike or lockout. In these cases, the number of strikes and lockouts and the number of workers involved are often higher than they would have been if the international recommendations had been followed, and the total number of workers involved sometimes exceeds the total employment in the economic activity concerned.

When using these data, it should be borne in mind that the number of workers exposed to the risk of strikes and lockouts varies between economic activities and countries, and from one period to another. For this reason, it is useful to calculate relative measures such as the severity rate, in which the amount of time not worked because of strikes and lockouts is related to the total number of workers.

If a strike or lockout covers several economic activities, the information about it is usually given under each of the activities involved. As a result, the total number of strikes and lockouts shown for the total (all economic activities together) may be less that the sum for the component activities.

The number of days not worked as a result of strikes and lockouts in progress during the year indicated is usually measured in terms of the sum of the actual working days during which work would nor- mally have been carried out by each worker involved had there been no stoppage.

The statistics on severity rates of strikes and lockouts are generally calculated in terms of the number of days not worked per 1,000 workers. The type of rate is indicated by a footnote.

Descriptions of the national sources, scope, definitions and methods used for compiling the statistics presented in this publication are given in the Sources and Methods component of the on-line database LABORSTA.

Consumer prices

The *Resolution concerning consumer price indices*, adopted by the Seventeenth International Conference of Labour Statisticians (ICLS) (Geneva, 2003[8]) states the following:

1. The CPI is a current social and economic indicator that is constructed to measure changes over time in the general level of prices of consumer goods and services that households acquire, use or pay for consumption.

2. The index aims to measure the change in consumer prices over time. This may be done by measuring the cost of purchasing a fixed basket of consumer goods and services of constant quality and similar characteristics, with the products in the basket being selected to be representative of households' expenditure during a year or other specified period. Such an index is called a fixed-basket price index.

3. The index may also aim to measure the effects of price changes on the cost of achieving a constant standard of living (i.e. level of utility or welfare). This concept is called a cost-of-living index (COLI). A fixed-basket price index, or another appropriate design, may be employed as an approximation to a COLI."

A consumer price index is usually estimated as a series of summary measures of the period-to-period proportional change in the prices of a fixed set of consumer goods and services of constant quantity and characteristics, acquired, used or paid for by the reference population. Each summary measure is constructed as a weighted average of a large number of elementary aggregate indices. Each of the elementary aggregate indices is estimated using a sample of prices for a defined set of goods and services obtained in, or by residents of, a specific region from a given set of outlets or other sources of consumption goods and services.

Consumer price indices are used for a variety of purposes, including:

a) general economic and social analysis and policy determination;

b) negotiation or indexation, or both, by government (notably of taxes, social security benefits, civil service remuneration and pensions, licence fees, fines and public debt interest or principal) and in private contracts (e.g. wages, salaries, insurance premia and service charges) and in judicial decisions (e.g. alimony payments);

---

[8] For the full text of the resolution, see ILO: *Seventeenth International Conference of Labour Statisticians, Report of the Conference* (Geneva, 2004) or the ILO Bureau of Statistics' web site: http://www.ilo.org/stat.

c) establishing "real" changes, or the relationship between money and the goods or services for which it can be exchanged (e.g. for the deflation of current value aggregates in the national accounts and of retail sales); and

d) price movement comparisons done for business purposes, including inflation accounting.

Sub-indices rather than the all-items index may be suitable for some of the above uses.

Weights are the relative expenditure or consumption shares of the elementary aggregates estimated from available data. In this connection, the Seventeenth ICLS recommended the following:

"23. The two main sources for deriving the weights are the results from household expenditure surveys (HESs) and national accounts estimates on household consumption expenditure. The results from HES are appropriate for an index defined to cover the consumption expenditures of reference population groups resident within the country, while national account estimates are suitable for an index defined to cover consumption expenditures within the country. ..."

24. The information from the main source (HESs or national accounts) should be supplemented with all other available information on the expenditure pattern. Sources of such information that can be used for disaggregating the expenditures are surveys of sales in retail outlets, point-of-purchase surveys, surveys of production, export and import data and administrative sources. Based on these data the weights for certain products may be further disaggregated by region and type of outlet. ..."

The Seventeenth ICLS also recommended that the prices used for the computation of the indices should be the:

"54. ... actual transaction prices, including indirect taxes and nonconditional discounts, that would be paid, agreed or costed (accepted) by the reference population. ... Tips for services, where compulsory, should be treated as part of the price paid.

55. Exceptional prices charged for stale, shopsoiled, damaged, or otherwise imperfect goods sold at clearance prices should be excluded, unless the sale of such products is a permanent and widespread phenomenon. Sale prices, discounts, cut prices and special offers should be included when applicable to all customers without there being significant limits to the quantities that can be purchased by each customer.

52. Prices should be collected in all types of outlets that are important, including Internet sellers, open-air markets and informal markets, and in free markets as well as price-controlled markets. ..."

The scope of consumer price indices can vary between countries, in terms not only of the types of households or population groups covered, but also the geographic coverage.

National practices also differ as regards the treatment of certain issues relating to the computation of consumer price indices, including seasonal items, quality changes, new products, durable goods and owner-occupied housing. There are differences in the methods used for collecting prices and for compiling the indices. As a result, care should be taken when using the consumer price indices presented in these tables, particularly for the purposes of collective bargaining, indexation or deflation. The indices should only be used if the coverage of the consumer price index corresponds closely to that of the subject of negotiation, indexation or deflation.

Information on the scope, definitions and methods used for compiling the consumer price indices presented in this publication is given in the *Sources and Methods* component of the on-line database LABORSTA.

The general consumer price index is shown for all groups of consumption items combined. Also shown is an all-items index excluding housing. Housing has been excluded from the all-items index to make the rates of price change more comparable across countries, although it does not eliminate all the difficulties encountered when making such comparisons. This index is intended to mean primarily an index without rent (actual and/or imputed) and expenditure on maintenance and repairs of dwelling. However, if such an index is not available at the national level or if it is too difficult to compute one, then for practical purposes countries provide one that excludes the whole housing group, or only the rent. If this is the case, a footnote indicates the particular exclusions (for example, the whole housing group, rent, electricity, gas and other fuels, expenditure on maintenance and repairs of dwelling, etc.).

The CPI food index includes non-alcoholic beverages only. Where alcoholic beverages and/or tobacco are included, this is indicated in footnotes.

Three other major group indices, respectively for "Electricity, gas and other fuels", "Clothing (including footwear)" and "Rent" are also shown. These group indices, along with the food index, are components of the general index. For most countries, the general index and the general index excluding rent cover, in addition to these four group indices, all other main groups of expenditure, i.e. "alcoholic beverages and tobacco", "furniture, household equipment and routine household maintenance", "health", "transport", "communication", "recreation and culture", "education", "restaurants and hotels" and "miscellaneous goods and services". Indices relating to these latter groups are not shown separately in the *Yearbook*, because of the variations between countries in the composition of the groups.

The general and the group indices shown in the tables refer to annual averages, although these are compiled in most cases monthly and in a few cases quarterly or biannually. Annual averages are derived from the original series

As the original base periods of the national series vary, a uniform base period (2000) has been adopted for the presentation of the data. As many as possible of the series have been recalculated by dividing the index for each date shown by the index for the year 2000 and multiplying the quotient by 100. Where data are available only for periods subsequent to 2000, the indices are generally presented with the first available calendar year as base. This operation does not involve any change in the weighting systems, etc., used by the countries.

If a new series is sufficiently comparable with the former series, the two are linked to form a continuous historical time series. If a series has been discontinued and has been replaced by another which cannot be reconciled with the former by linking or some other estimation techniques, the break is indicated by a footnote.

Annexe

Notes explicatives

Pour de plus amples informations, y compris les descriptions méthodologiques, les séries chronologiques et des statistiques supplémentaires, consulter la base de données LABORSTA en ligne, sur le site: http://laborsta.ilo.org.

Classifications

Les Classifications internationales types, par industrie, de toutes les branches d'activité économique (CITI), des professions (CITP), de la situation dans la profession (CISP), et de l'éducation (CITE) sont présentées séparément dans cette publication.

Un nombre croissant de pays sont en mesure d'adapter les classifications nationales par branche d'activité économique (industrie), professions et situation dans la profession aux structures des classifications internationales, y compris aux révisions les plus récentes de ces classifications.

La classification selon l'activité économique principale (industrie) est fondamentalement différente de celle selon les principales tâches accomplies (profession). Dans la première, toutes les personnes travaillant dans un établissement donné sont classées dans la même industrie quelles que soient leurs professions. Par contre, dans la seconde, sont regroupées dans une même catégorie toutes les personnes accomplissant le même genre de travail quel que soit le lieu où ce travail est effectué.

Lorsque les données sont présentées selon les classifications nationales, il faut noter que les classifications industrielles ou professionnelles peuvent présenter de nombreuses divergences par rapport aux classifications internationales. La teneur des groupes d'industries ou de professions peut également varier d'un pays à un autre du fait des différentes définitions ou méthodes de classification. De plus, des classifications selon les groupes agrégés peuvent aussi cacher des différences fondamentales dans les systèmes industriels ou professionnels des différents pays.

La Classification internationale d'après la situation dans la profession (CISP) classe les emplois eu égard au type de contrat explicite ou implicite d'une personne avec d'autres personnes ou organisations. Les critères de base retenus pour définir les groupes sont la nature du risque économique encouru ou la nature du contrôle qu'exercent ou exerceront les titulaires sur les entreprises et sur d'autres salariés.

Jusqu'en 1993, les principaux groupes de la CISP étaient les suivants: employeur; personne travaillant pour son propre compte; salarié; membre de coopératives de producteurs et travailleur familial non rémunéré. En 1993, la CISP a été révisée et élargie, mais d'une manière telle que les titres de ces principaux groupes n'ont pas été modifiés à l'exception du dernier qui est devenu «travailleurs familiaux collaborant à l'entreprise familiale». Le contenu du groupe «personnes travaillant pour leur propre compte» a cependant été élargi pour inclure les personnes travaillant dans l'entreprise familiale avec les mêmes responsabilités que le chef de l'entreprise. Ces personnes, généralement des femmes, étaient classées en tant que «travailleurs familiaux non rémunérés» dans l'ancienne classification. La CISP révisée a également clarifié les distinctions entre les groupes.

L'expérience a montré que fréquemment, compte tenu de la manière dont les pays mesuraient la «situation dans la profession», la teneur des groupes n'était pas facilement comparable. Par exemple, dans la plupart des pays les propriétaires-gérants d'entreprises constituées en sociétés sont classés dans le groupe des salariés, alors qu'ils le seront dans celui des employeurs dans d'autres pays. Il en est de même pour les travailleurs familiaux qui, percevant régulièrement leur rémunération sous forme de salaire, traitement, primes, rémunération aux pièces ou paiements en nature, sont généralement classés comme salariés mais, dans d'autres pays, comme travailleurs familiaux collaborant à l'entreprise familiale. Une autre difficulté, quant à la comparabilité du nombre de ces travailleurs familiaux, vient du fait que certains pays ne sont pas en mesure de les dénombrer en tant que personnes ayant un emploi. Beaucoup de pays ne pouvant pas distinguer les personnes travaillant pour leur propre compte des employeurs dans leurs observations de base, seule la somme de ces deux catégories est disponible. Certains pays ayant peu de travailleurs membres de coopératives de producteurs peuvent les agréger au groupe des salariés, alors que d'autres le feront avec celui des personnes travaillant à leur propre compte.

Il faut toutefois rappeler que l'objectif des classifications internationales n'est pas de se substituer aux classifications nationales mais de donner un cadre général à la comparaison internationale de ces données. De plus, beaucoup de pays utilisent ces classifications internationales comme cadre lors de l'élaboration ou de la révision de leurs classifications.

Population active

La «*population active*» comprend toutes les personnes des deux sexes qui fournissent, durant une période de référence spécifiée, la main-d'œuvre disponible pour la production de biens et services. Selon la version de 1993 du Système de comptabilité nationale (SCN), la production comprend la production de tous les biens ou de tous les services individuels ou collectifs fournis ou destinés à être fournis à des unités autres que celles qui les produisent, y compris la production des biens et des services entièrement consommés dans le processus de production de ces biens ou de ces services; la production pour compte propre de tous les biens conservés par leurs producteurs pour leur propre consommation finale; la production des services des logements occupés par leurs propriétaires, et des services domestiques et personnels produits grâce à l'emploi de personnel domestique rémunéré.

Deux mesures utiles de la population active sont la *population habituellement active* mesurée en fonction d'une longue période de référence telle que l'année et la *population active du moment*, appelée encore *main-d'œuvre*, mesurée par rapport à une courte période de référence telle qu'une semaine ou un jour.

Les données présentées sur la *population totale* et la *population active* proviennent généralement du dernier recensement disponible sur la main-d'œuvre ou de la dernière enquête par sondage auprès de la main-d'œuvre. Ces données incluent toutes les personnes qui répondent aux critères nécessaires pour être considérées comme pourvues d'un emploi ou au chômage (selon les définitions ci-dessous).

Deux types de taux d'activité peuvent être calculés sur la base de ces statistiques: les *taux d'activité spécifiques*, c'est-à-dire les rapports (exprimés en pourcentage) de la population active âgée de 15 ans et plus à la population totale des groupes d'âge correspondants; et les *taux d'activité bruts*, c'est-à-dire les rapports (exprimés en pourcentage) de la population active totale à la population totale, y compris les personnes qui n'appartiennent pas à la population en âge de travailler.

Les pratiques nationales (voir également les descriptions des Sources et méthodes disponibles séparément ainsi que la base de données en ligne LABORSTA) varient selon les pays car certains groupes, tels que les membres des forces armées, les membres des institutions religieuses, les personnes en quête d'un premier emploi, les travailleurs saisonniers ou les personnes qui ont une activité à temps partiel, ne sont pas classés de la même manière dans tous les pays. Dans certains pays, tous ces groupes ou une partie seulement sont inclus dans la population active, alors que dans d'autres ils sont considérés comme inactifs. Cependant, en règle générale, les données sur la population active ne comprennent pas les étudiants, les personnes occupées exclusivement aux travaux ménagers de leur propre ménage, les membres de ménages collectifs, les pensionnaires d'institutions, les retraités, les rentiers et les personnes entièrement à la charge d'autrui.

La comparabilité des données entre pays et même pour un pays donné est donc affectée non seulement par les différences que présentent les définitions utilisées et les groupes de population couverts, mais aussi les méthodes de rassemblement, de classification et de tabulation des données de base. En particulier, il existe des variations considérables d'un pays à l'autre dans la mesure où les travailleurs familiaux contribuant à l'entreprise familiale, en particulier les femmes, sont considérés comme faisant, ou non, partie de la population active, ainsi que dans le traitement des chômeurs n'ayant jamais travaillé, et des étudiants ayant une activité à temps partiel – ces variations sont donc particulièrement importantes dans les comparaisons des statistiques se rapportant aux jeunes gens.

La période de référence constitue également un élément important de différence: dans certains pays, les données relatives à la population active se rapportent à la situation **effective** de chaque individu le jour du recensement ou de l'enquête, ou pendant une brève période déterminée, telle que la semaine précédant immédiatement la date du recensement ou de l'enquête; dans d'autres pays, les données recueillies ont trait à la situation **habituelle** de chaque individu et ne se rapportent pas à une période déterminée.

En outre, dans la plupart des pays, les statistiques de la population active incluent les personnes pourvues d'un emploi et les chômeurs au-delà d'un âge spécifique, alors que dans quelques autres la définition de la population active ne prévoit pas de limite d'âge.

Les systèmes de codification utilisés par les pays constituent un autre élément de différence entre les données. Pour que la teneur des groupes d'une classification soit identique à celle des groupes d'une autre classification, les mêmes critères de codification devraient être utilisés. En règle générale, les systèmes de codification utilisés dans les enquêtes auprès de la main-d'œuvre sont plus précis que ceux utilisés dans les recensements de population.

Emploi

L'emploi est défini de la manière suivante dans la *Résolution concernant les statistiques de la population active, de l'emploi, du chômage et du sous-emploi* adoptée par la treizième Conférence internationale des statisticiens du travail (Genève, 1982)[1]:

«1) Les 'personnes pourvues d'un emploi' comprennent toutes les personnes ayant dépassé un âge spécifié qui se trouvaient, durant une brève période de référence spécifiée telle qu'une semaine ou un jour, dans les catégories suivantes:

a) 'emploi salarié':

   a1) 'personnes au travail': personnes qui, durant la période de référence, ont effectué un travail moyennant un salaire ou un traitement en espèces ou en nature;

   a2) 'personnes qui ont un emploi mais qui ne sont pas au travail': personnes qui, ayant déjà travaillé dans leur emploi actuel, en étaient absentes durant la période de référence et avaient un lien formel avec leur emploi.

   Ce lien formel avec l'emploi devrait être déterminé à la lumière des circonstances nationales, par référence à l'un ou plusieurs des critères suivants:

   i) le service ininterrompu du salaire ou du traitement;

   ii) une assurance de retour au travail à la fin de la situation d'exception ou un accord sur la date de retour;

   iii) la durée de l'absence du travail qui, le cas échéant, peut être la durée pendant laquelle les travailleurs peuvent recevoir une indemnisation sans obligation d'accepter d'autres emplois qui leur seraient éventuellement proposés.

b) 'emploi non salarié':

   b1) 'personnes au travail': personnes qui, durant la période de référence, ont effectué un travail en vue d'un bénéfice ou d'un gain familial, en espèces ou en nature;

   b2) 'personnes ayant une entreprise mais n'étant pas au travail': personnes qui, durant la période de référence, avaient une entreprise qui peut être une entreprise industrielle, un commerce, une exploitation agricole ou une entreprise de prestations de services, mais n'étaient temporairement pas au travail pour toute raison spécifique.

2) Dans la pratique, on peut interpréter la notion de 'travail effectué au cours de la période de référence' comme étant un travail d'une durée d'une heure au moins.

3) Les personnes temporairement absentes de leur travail pour raison de maladie ou d'accident, de congé ou de vacances, de conflit du travail ou de grève, de congé-éducation ou formation, de congé-maternité ou parental, de mauvaise conjoncture économique ou de suspension temporaire du travail due à des causes telles que: conditions météorologiques défavorables, incidents mécaniques ou électriques, pénurie de matières premières ou de combustibles, ou toute autre cause d'absence temporaire avec ou sans autorisation, devraient être considérées

---

[1] Pour le texte intégral de la résolution, voir BIT: *Recommandations internationales en vigueur sur les statistiques du travail* (Genève, 2000) ou le site Web du Bureau de statistique du BIT: www.ilo.org/stat.

comme pourvues d'un emploi salarié, à condition qu'elles aient un lien formel avec leur emploi.

4) Les employeurs, les personnes travaillant à leur propre compte et les membres des coopératives de producteurs devraient être considérés comme travailleurs non salariés et classés comme 'étant au travail' ou 'n'étant pas au travail', selon les cas.

5) Les travailleurs familiaux non rémunérés devraient être considérés comme travailleurs non salariés indépendamment du nombre d'heures de travail effectué durant la période de référence. Les pays qui, pour des raisons particulières, préféraient choisir comme critère une durée minimale de temps de travail pour inclure les travailleurs familiaux non rémunérés parmi les personnes pourvues d'un emploi devraient identifier et classer séparément les personnes de cette catégorie qui ont travaillé moins que le temps prescrit.

6) Les personnes engagées dans la production de biens et services pour leur propre consommation ou celle du ménage devraient être considérées comme travailleurs non salariés si une telle production apporte une importante contribution à la consommation totale du ménage.

7) Les apprentis qui ont reçu une rétribution en espèces ou en nature devraient être considérés comme personnes pourvues d'un emploi salarié et classés comme 'étant au travail' ou 'n'étant pas au travail' sur la même base que les autres catégories de personnes pourvues d'un emploi salarié.

8) Les étudiants, les personnes s'occupant du foyer et autres personnes principalement engagées dans des activités non économiques durant la période de référence et qui étaient en même temps pourvues d'un emploi salarié ou non salarié comme défini au sous-paragraphe 1) ci-dessus devraient être considérées comme ayant un emploi, sur la même base que les autres catégories de personnes ayant un emploi, et être identifiés séparément lorsque cela est possible.

9) Les membres des forces armées devraient être inclus parmi les personnes pourvues d'un emploi salarié. Elles devraient comprendre aussi bien les membres permanents que les membres temporaires, comme spécifié dans la plus récente révision de la Classification internationale type des professions (CITP).»

Dans un certain nombre de cas, les définitions nationales de l'emploi peuvent s'écarter de la définition internationale type recommandée (voir également les descriptions des Sources et méthodes disponibles séparément ainsi que dans la base de données en ligne LABORSTA).

En général, les données sur l'emploi sont obtenues à partir de quatre sources principales, à savoir: les enquêtes par sondage auprès des ménages, les enquêtes ou les recensements auprès des établissements, les évaluations officielles et les registres administratifs provenant des régimes d'assurances sociales. Ces quatre sources principales des statistiques d'emploi sont identifiées dans les tableaux; cependant les statistiques dérivées d'une seule source sont en général utilisées ici, et la priorité a été donnée à l'utilisation des enquêtes auprès des ménages qui fournissent les statistiques les plus exhaustives (des statistiques supplémentaires sont disponibles dans la base de données en ligne LABORSTA).

Pour ce qui est de l'emploi total, les enquêtes par sondage auprès des ménages couvrent toutes les personnes occupées appartenant à toutes les catégories de situation dans la profession, c'est-à-dire non seulement les salariés (ouvriers et employés), y compris les travailleurs familiaux rémunérés, mais également les employeurs, les personnes travaillant pour leur propre compte, les membres de coopératives de producteurs, les travailleurs familiaux collaborant à l'entreprise familiale et les travailleurs inclassables selon la situation dans la profession. En général, les données se réfèrent à l'emploi au cours d'une brève période déterminée (une semaine ou un jour) et aucune distinction n'est faite entre les personnes pourvues d'un emploi à temps complet et celles travaillant à temps partiel.

Les enquêtes auprès des établissements couvrent les travailleurs inscrits sur les bordereaux de salaires au cours d'une période de paie déterminée ou d'un jour de travail de cette période. En général, on distingue deux types d'enquêtes auprès des établissements :

Le premier type de statistiques englobe tous les établissements d'une importance déterminée, c'est-à-dire ceux qui répondent à certains critères (par exemple les entreprises qui occupent plus d'un certain nombre de salariés; celles dont la production annuelle est supérieure à une certaine valeur, etc.). Les données ainsi rassemblées peuvent être sujettes à des écarts systématiques provenant de l'élimination d'établissements qui n'atteignent pas la limite minimale fixée pour ces statistiques; de plus, un déplacement de l'emploi des petits établissements vers les grands établissements se traduira par une tendance d'augmentation des données. Toutefois, lorsque la limite minimale est fixée assez bas, le champ de telles statistiques est généralement très étendu et elles reflètent assez fidèlement les fluctuations de l'emploi.

Les statistiques du second type reposent sur un échantillon d'établissements. Dans de telles séries, la difficulté principale consiste à conserver aux établissements sélectionnés un caractère représentatif. Par exemple, des variations de la structure industrielle, le développement ou le déclin d'établissements particuliers, le mouvement général de la population ou des changements marqués dans l'activité de certains secteurs économiques ont tendance à introduire un écart systématique cumulatif dans l'échantillon qui, au bout de quelques années, peut devenir sensible.

Dans certains pays où les statistiques du premier type (tous les établissements d'une importance déterminée) ne sont disponibles que tous les ans ou à des intervalles plus longs, elles peuvent être combinées, soit par enchaînement, soit par interpolation, avec les statistiques du second type (échantillon d'établissements) plus fréquemment disponibles.

Certaines statistiques sont des évaluations officielles fournies par les autorités nationales. De telles estimations sont généralement basées sur une combinaison d'informations tirées d'une ou de plusieurs sources telles que les registres d'assurances sociales. Cette source couvre les personnes occupées, protégées par l'assurance maladie, accident ou chômage, ou par un régime analogue. Le nombre de cotisants ou de cotisations versées fournit une mesure des effectifs assurés et occupés (les chômeurs étant dispensés du paiement de leur cotisation). Les personnes travaillant durant une très courte période, qui sont très peu rémunérées ou qui sont au-dessus d'un certain âge, sont quelquefois omises de ces statistiques. Outre les changements intervenant dans le nombre effectif de personnes occupées, les statistiques de l'emploi fondées sur les registres des assurances sociales peuvent également refléter des modifications de portée pour certains groupes classés selon la branche d'activité économique, la profession ou la situation dans la profession.

Le pourcentage de femmes salariées dans le secteur non agricole est l'un des indicateurs des objectifs du Millénaire pour le développement.

Chômage

Le chômage est défini de la manière suivante dans la *Résolution concernant les statistiques de la population active, de l'emploi, du chômage et du sous-emploi* adoptée par la treizième Conférence internationale des statisticiens du travail (Genève, 1982)[2]:

«1) Les 'chômeurs' comprennent toutes les personnes ayant dépassé un âge spécifié qui, au cours de la période de référence, étaient:

   a) 'sans travail', c'est-à-dire qui n'étaient pourvues ni d'un emploi salarié ni d'un emploi non salarié, comme défini au paragraphe 9;

   b) 'disponibles pour travailler' dans un emploi salarié ou non salarié durant la période de référence;

   c) 'à la recherche d'un travail', c'est-à-dire qui avaient pris des dispositions spécifiques au cours d'une période récente spécifiée pour chercher un emploi salarié ou un emploi non salarié. Ces dispositions spécifiques peuvent inclure: l'inscription à un bureau de placement public ou privé; la candidature auprès d'employeurs; les démarches sur les lieux de travail, dans les fermes ou à la porte des usines, sur les marchés ou dans les autres endroits où sont traditionnellement recrutés les travailleurs; l'insertion ou la réponse à des annonces dans les journaux; les recherches par relations personnelles; la recherche de terrain, d'immeubles, de machines ou d'équipement pour créer une entreprise personnelle; les démarches pour obtenir des ressources financières, des permis et licences, etc.

2) Dans les situations où les moyens conventionnels de recherche de travail sont peu appropriés, où le marché du travail est largement inorganisé ou d'une portée limitée, où l'absorption de l'offre de travail est, au moment considéré, insuffisante, où la proportion standard de main-d'œuvre non salariée est importante, la définition standard du chômage donnée au sous-paragraphe 1) ci-dessus peut être appliquée en renonçant au critère de la recherche de travail.

3) Pour appliquer le critère de la disponibilité pour le travail, spécialement dans les situations couvertes par le sous-paragraphe 2) ci-dessus, des méthodes appropriées devraient être mises au point pour tenir compte des circonstances nationales. De telles méthodes pourraient être fondées sur des notions comme l'actuelle envie de travailler et le fait d'avoir déjà travaillé, la volonté de prendre un emploi salarié sur la base des conditions locales ou le désir d'entreprendre une activité indépendante si les ressources et les facilités nécessaires sont accordées.

4) En dépit du critère de recherche de travail incorporé dans la définition standard du chômage, les personnes sans travail et disponibles pour travailler, qui ont pris des dispositions pour prendre un emploi salarié ou pour entreprendre une activité indépendante à une date ultérieure à la période de référence, devraient être considérées comme chômeurs.

5) Les personnes temporairement absentes de leur travail sans lien formel avec leur emploi, qui étaient disponibles pour travailler et à la recherche d'un travail, devraient être considérées comme chômeurs conformément à la définition standard du chômage. Les pays peuvent, cependant, en fonction des situations et politiques nationales, préférer renoncer au critère de la recherche d'un travail dans le cas des personnes temporairement mises à pied. Dans de tels cas, les personnes temporairement mises à pied qui n'étaient pas à la recherche d'un travail mais qui étaient néanmoins classées comme chômeurs devraient être identifiées et former une sous-catégorie à part.

6) Les étudiants, les personnes s'occupant du foyer et les autres personnes principalement engagées dans les activités non économiques durant la période de référence et qui satisfont aux critères exposés aux sous-paragraphes 1) et 2) ci-dessus devraient être considérés comme chômeurs au même titre que les autres catégories de chômeurs et être identifiés séparément lorsque cela est possible.»

Dans un certain nombre de cas, les définitions nationales du chômage peuvent s'écarter de la définition internationale type recommandée. Les définitions nationales peuvent varier d'un pays à un autre en ce qui concerne les limites d'âge, les périodes de référence, les critères retenus en matière de recherche d'emploi, le traitement des données concernant les personnes mises à pied temporairement et celles en quête d'emploi pour la première fois (voir également les descriptions des Sources et méthodes disponibles séparément ainsi que dans la base de données en ligne LABORSTA).

Selon les pays, les différences sont particulièrement marquées en ce qui concerne le traitement des chômeurs par rapport à leur classification d'après la situation dans la dernière profession exercée. En général, les chômeurs ayant déjà travaillé, classifiés selon leur dernier emploi, sont inclus dans le groupe des salariés; mais, dans quelques cas, ceux-ci et les chômeurs à la recherche d'un premier emploi constituent la majeure partie du groupe des travailleurs inclassables d'après la situation dans la profession.

En dépit de l'utilisation des classifications internationales (activités économiques et profession), les pratiques nationales peuvent également être différentes quant à la classification des chômeurs ayant déjà travaillé; très souvent, ceux-ci sont inclus dans la catégorie résiduelle de ces classifications, à savoir activités mal désignées (CITI) ou travailleurs ne pouvant être classés selon la profession (CITP).

Les comparaisons de pays à pays sont, de plus, affectées par la variété des sources utilisées pour rassembler les informations sur le chômage ainsi que par les différences dans le champ d'application et la portée propres à ces sources. On distingue, en général, quatre sources principales de statistiques, identifiées dans les tableaux; cependant les statistiques dérivées d'une seule source sont en général utilisées ici, et la priorité a été donnée à l'utilisation des enquêtes auprès des ménages qui fournissent les statistiques les plus exhaustives (des statistiques supplémentaires sont disponibles dans la base de données en ligne LABORSTA).

Les enquêtes par sondage sur la main-d'œuvre fournissent généralement les statistiques les plus complètes sur le chômage, car elles permettent en particulier de couvrir des groupes (tels que les personnes en quête d'emploi pour la première fois ou les personnes en quête d'emploi sans avoir recours aux services d'un bureau de placement) qui, souvent, ne sont pas compris dans les statistiques du chômage obtenues par d'autres méthodes. En général, la définition du chômage adoptée pour ce type de statistiques suit plus fidèlement les recommandations internationales et de telles statistiques sont plus comparables sur le plan international que celles obtenues d'autres sources. De même, les taux de chômage sont généralement plus fiables du fait qu'ils sont calculés en rapportant le nombre évalué de chômeurs au nombre total évalué de personnes occupées et de personnes en chômage (la main-d'œuvre) dérivé des mêmes enquêtes.

---

[2] Pour le texte intégral de la résolution, voir BIT: *Recommandations internationales en vigueur sur les statistiques du travail* (Genève, 2000) ou le site Web du Bureau de statistique du BIT: www.ilo.org/stat.

Certaines statistiques sont des évaluations officielles fournies par les autorités nationales et sont généralement basées sur une combinaison d'informations tirées d'une ou de plusieurs sources mentionnées ci-dessous. Toutefois, leur rôle a tendance à décroître du fait, corrélativement, de l'accroissement du nombre d'enquêtes sur la main-d'œuvre réalisées dans le monde.

Statistiques d'assurances sociales: les statistiques de cette source sont tirées de régimes d'assurance chômage obligatoire qui ont ordinairement une large portée industrielle et couvrent, en général, l'ensemble des ouvriers et des employés ou les ouvriers seulement. Les taux de chômage sont calculés en divisant le nombre de bénéficiaires d'allocations de chômage par le nombre total de travailleurs assurés couverts par les régimes. Toutefois il est difficile, sinon impossible, de déterminer jusqu'à quel point de telles statistiques indiquent le niveau général du chômage dans un pays donné.

Statistiques des bureaux de placement: ces statistiques donnent généralement le nombre de demandeurs d'emploi figurant sur les registres à la fin de chaque mois. Elles peuvent comprendre, outre les personnes sans travail, des personnes en grève ou dans l'incapacité temporaire de travailler par suite de maladie et des personnes occupées à des travaux entrepris pour secourir les chômeurs. En principe, lorsque les personnes déjà pourvues d'un emploi en sont exclues, ces statistiques sont présentées sous la rubrique «chômage enregistré». Cependant, si la série comprend également les personnes pourvues d'un emploi mais désireuses d'en changer ou d'effectuer, en plus, d'autres travaux, et inscrites dans les bureaux de placement, ces statistiques sont présentées sous la rubrique «demandeurs d'emploi».

La qualité de ces statistiques est très variable. Lorsque les bureaux de placement fonctionnent en rapport étroit avec une assurance chômage, l'inscription étant une des conditions mises à l'octroi des indemnités, les données sont aussi fiables que celles des statistiques d'assurance chômage obligatoire. Quand les bureaux sont en étroite relation avec des régimes d'assistance publique d'une large portée, les chiffres relevés peuvent également fournir des données satisfaisantes durant l'existence de tels régimes. Toutefois, lorsque les inscriptions sont purement volontaires et surtout lorsque les bureaux de placement ne fonctionnent que dans les zones urbaines à forte densité de population ou ne sont pas utilisés largement par les salariés en quête de travail ou par les employeurs qui cherchent des travailleurs, les statistiques sont en général très incomplètes et ne fournissent pas une indication sûre du niveau du chômage. La portée des données dépend donc, d'une part, de l'organisation du réseau des bureaux et, d'autre part, de l'habitude qu'ont les travailleurs de s'y inscrire et de l'intérêt qu'ils ont à le faire. Dans bien des cas, les personnes occupées dans l'agriculture et habitant des régions à population moins dense sont à peine couvertes par les statistiques, quand elles le sont. La portée des statistiques des bureaux de placement est de ce fait très difficile à préciser et il est très rare que les données permettent de calculer des pourcentages de chômage satisfaisants. En général, ces statistiques ne seront donc pas comparables d'un pays à un autre. Cependant, s'il n'y a pas de changements dans la législation ou dans les réglementations administratives et similaires, leurs fluctuations au sein d'un même pays peuvent indiquer les variations dans l'étendue du chômage dans le temps.

Sauf indication contraire, les données sont généralement des moyennes annuelles de données mensuelles, trimestrielles ou semestrielles. Le nombre de chômeurs indique l'étendue du problème et les taux de chômage font ressortir la gravité relative du chômage. Ces taux sont calculés en rapportant le nombre de travailleurs d'un certain groupe qui se trouvaient en chômage pendant la période de référence (en général, un jour donné ou une semaine donnée) au nombre total des personnes occupées et des chômeurs dans ce groupe à la même date. Toutefois, les statistiques du chômage par groupe d'âge se rapportent souvent à une période déterminée ou à une date en cours de l'année et non pas à des moyennes annuelles de données mensuelles, trimestrielles ou semestrielles.

Taux de chômage par groupe d'âge: le taux de chômage des jeunes âgés de 15 à 24 ans est l'un des indicateurs des objectifs du Millénaire pour le développement.

Si l'on veut rapprocher les données présentées sur le chômage par niveau d'instruction de celles sur la population active par niveau d'instruction, il faut veiller à la similitude des sources, champs d'application et périodes de référence.

En conformité avec les recommandations internationales, les personnes en chômage ayant précédemment travaillé sont classées par industrie ou par profession sur la base de leur dernier emploi (en utilisant les codes numériques spécifiques des classifications pertinentes). Les chômeurs n'ayant jamais travaillé sont présentés séparément, dans la mesure du possible, afin de les distinguer des chômeurs ayant précédemment travaillé mais classés sous *activités mal désignées de la CITI* ou sous *travailleurs ne pouvant être classés selon la profession de la CITP*.

Durée du travail

La durée du travail couvre les périodes que les personnes dédient à des activités qui contribuent à la production des biens et services définie par le Système de Comptes Nationaux des Nations Unies. Depuis 1962, les normes statistiques internationales existent uniquement pour les concepts des *heures réellement effectuées* et pour la *durée normale de travail*, adoptées par la dixième Conférence internationale des statisticiens du travail[3]. Elles sont confinées aux salariés et décrivent les situations de travail typiques des travailleurs de la production dans des établissements industriels. Bien qu'elles aient servi de guide pour les pays voulant produire des estimations nationales, beaucoup de définitions nationales sont maintenant devenues plus complètes. Les normes internationales sont en train d'être révisées pour améliorer leur couverture des travailleurs et des activités de travail, ainsi que pour mieux refléter les divers arrangements du travail. De nouvelles normes internationales pourront être adoptées par la 18e Conférence internationale des statisticiens du travail en 2008, qui inclura par exemple des concepts sur les *heures habituelles du travail* et les *heures rémunérées*. Les éléments de définition suivent pour chacun des concepts tels qu'ils sont mesurés par les pays.

Le concept des heures de *travail réellement effectuées* se réfère au temps que les personnes dédient à des activités de production pendant une période de référence spécifiée, et incluent:

a) le temps dédié directement à la production (consacré à produire des biens et des services, incluant le temps supplémentaire payé et non payé);

b) le temps dédié à faciliter la production, nécessaire aux activités de travail ou à améliorer la productivité des travailleurs (consacré aux conception, préparation, entretien du lieu de travail, procédures, outils, incluant

---

[3] Pour le texte intégral de la résolution, voir BIT: *Recommandations internationales en vigueur sur les statistiques du travail* (Genève, 2000) ou le site Web du Bureau de statistique du BIT: www.ilo.org/public/french/bureau/stat.

les reçus, fiches de durée d'opérations et rapports), activités de transport (pour le travail à domicile, transport des produits sur le marché) et la formation pour l'unité économique;

c) le temps entre les activités principales (temps morts, en raison, par exemple, du manque occasionnel de travail ou d'électricité, d'arrêts de machines, d'accidents), temps de voyage pour des réunions ou assignations de travail, temps de garde (pour le personnel de santé et les services techniques professionnels);

d) le temps de repos (courtes périodes de repos ou rafraîchissement, y compris les arrêts du travail pour collation ou prière).

Les *heures de travail réellement effectuées* excluent le temps non travaillé, payé ou non payé, tel que:

a) les congés annuels payés, congés parentaux, jours fériés payés, congés de maladie;

b) les pauses pour les repas;

c) le temps consacré aux trajets entre le domicile et le lieu de travail et vice versa, qui ne peut pas être considéré comme temps de travail.

Le concept révisé des *heures de travail réellement effectuées* couvrirait tous les types de travailleurs indépendants et salariés; elles peuvent être payées ou non et peuvent être faites dans n'importe quel endroit, y compris la rue, les champs, la maison, etc.

Le concept des *heures rémunérées* couvrirait les salariés et se référerait aux heures qui sont payées par l'employeur, effectuées ou non. Quand on les compare avec les *heures réellement effectuées* des salariés, elles incluent toutes les heures payées même si elles n'ont pas été effectuées, telles que les congés annuels, les jours fériés payés, les congés de maladie payés et autres congés payés, en excluant toutes les heures effectuées non payées (par exemple les heures supplémentaires non payées).

Le concept de la *durée normale du travail* couvre un sous-groupe de salariés (ceux qui sont couverts par la législation et la réglementation du travail), et se réfère aux heures travaillées par jour, semaine ou année selon ladite législation.

Le concept des *heures habituellement travaillées* serait lié avec les heures réellement effectuées hebdomadairement par les indépendants et les salariés, les plus communes pendant une période longue de référence telle que le mois, la saison ou autre longue période. Elles sont donc la valeur type des heures de travail hebdomadaires. Quand on les compare à la durée normale du travail, les heures habituellement travaillées incluent les heures supplémentaires habituelles et excluent les heures non travaillées habituellement.

En général, les statistiques de la durée du travail sont principalement tirées de deux types de sources: les enquêtes auprès des établissements et les enquêtes auprès des ménages. Deux autres sources sont les estimations officielles et les registres administratifs d'assurances sociales. La première source provient des bordereaux de salaire utilisés dans les enquêtes ou les recensements auprès des établissements qui fournissent fréquemment des données sur les salaires et sur l'emploi. Ces statistiques se réfèrent souvent aux *heures rémunérées* et dans une moindre mesure aux *heures réellement effectuées*. Les statistiques dérivées des enquêtes auprès des établissements ont souvent une couverture des travailleurs limitée, couvrant les salariés ou un sous-groupe de salariés, par exemple les ouvriers ou employés qui travaillent dans des établissements d'une certaine taille ou dans certaines industries. La couverture des statistiques peut être de ce fait considérablement limitée dans les pays où la plupart des travailleurs sont dans de petits établissements ou sont des indépendants. Ce type de limitation est indiqué par des notes. Le second type de source est les enquêtes par sondage auprès des ménages. Ces statistiques se réfèrent habituellement aux *heures réellement effectuées* et parfois aux *heures habituellement travaillées*. Ces enquêtes sont capables en théorie de couvrir toute la population occupée, incluant les travailleurs indépendants. Certaines statistiques se réfèrent seulement aux heures de travail dans l'emploi principal. Cela est aussi indiqué.

Les statistiques se réfèrent aux salariés, tels qu'ils sont définis par la Classification internationale de la situation dans l'emploi (CISE-93). Dans quelques cas, quand les statistiques sont tirées des enquêtes sur la main-d'œuvre elles peuvent se référer à l'emploi total, et quand elles sont tirées des enquêtes auprès des établissements, elles peuvent couvrir un sous-groupe de salariés, tel que les ouvriers ou les employés. Quelques pays limitent la couverture des travailleurs encore plus, en ne couvrant que les «adultes», les travailleurs «qualifiés» ou «non qualifiés». Il n'y a pas de définition internationale pour les ouvriers ni pour les employés. Le premier groupe est généralement identifié aux travailleurs manuels ou de la production, tandis que le second et identifié aux travailleurs de bureau.

Les statistiques sont généralement la moyenne du nombre d'heures de travail par semaine, mais dans quelques cas ce sont les heures par jour ou par mois (cela est indiqué dans les notes).

Pour les statistiques tirées des enquêtes auprès des établissements, le nombre moyen d'heures de travail (réellement effectuées ou rémunérées) par semaine ou par mois est généralement obtenu en divisant le nombre total d'heures (réellement effectuées ou rémunérées) pendant une semaine ou un mois par le nombre moyen de travailleurs figurant sur les bordereaux de salaires pendant la même période. La durée moyenne de la journée de travail effectuée ou rémunérée est généralement obtenue en divisant le nombre total d'heures (réellement effectuées ou rémunérées) pendant une semaine, une quinzaine ou un mois par le nombre total de journées réellement effectuées ou rémunérées pendant la même période. Pour les statistiques tirées des enquêtes auprès des ménages, le nombre moyen d'heures de travail réellement effectuées est généralement obtenu en divisant les heures de travail de toutes les personnes actives occupées (ou de tous les salariés) durant la période de référence par le nombre des personnes actives occupées (ou des salariés) dans la même période. Dans ces calculs, les personnes absentes du travail pendant toute la semaine de référence doivent être incluses; néanmoins, pour mieux refléter la semaine «typique» elles sont quelquefois exclues (cela est indiqué dans les notes).

Dans le calcul des moyennes, les statistiques peuvent être basées sur une seule observation (quand l'enquête se déroule une fois par année), sur un ensemble d'observations (quand l'enquête est mensuelle ou trimestrielle) ou par des observations continuelles (quand l'enquête couvre toutes les semaines de l'année). Plus il y a de points dans le calcul, moins grande sera l'influence des variations saisonnières et des conflits du travail, ainsi que des congés annuels et de maladie effectivement pris pendant l'année.

En comparant les statistiques relatives à la durée du travail, il ne faut pas perdre de vue que ces données sont influencées par la méthode utilisée pour calculer la moyenne, par le nombre d'observations utilisées, et par les différentes pratiques, en ce qui concerne le nombre de journées normalement effectuées par semaine, les règlements et les usages concernant le travail du week-end et les heures supplémentaires, les absence du travail, etc. Elles seront aussi affectées par la couverture industrielle et des emplois. Les statistiques qui excluent les travailleurs dans l'agriculture, où les heures de travail suivent des comportements différents des autres industries, ne seront pas comparables avec les statistiques qui les incluent. De façon similaire, les statistiques qui couvrent seulement l'emploi principal seront plus basses que les statistiques qui couvrent tous les emplois ou toutes les activités de production, y compris les services non payés[4].

Salaires

La *Résolution concernant un système intégré de statistiques des salaires*, adoptée par la douzième Conférence internationale des statisticiens du travail (Genève, 1973)[5], définit les gains et les *taux de salaire* de la manière suivante:

«8. Aux fins des statistiques des salaires, le concept de gains s'entend de la rémunération en espèces et en nature versée aux salariés, en règle générale à intervalles réguliers, au titre des heures de travail effectuées ou du travail accompli, ainsi que de la rémunération afférente aux heures non effectuées, par exemple pour le congé annuel, d'autres congés payés ou les jours fériés. Les gains ne comprennent pas les contributions que les employeurs versent pour leurs salariés aux régimes de sécurité sociale et de pensions, non plus que les prestations reçues par les salariés dans le cadre de ces régimes. Sont également exclues les indemnités de licenciement et de cessation de service.

9. Les statistiques des gains devraient être établies sur la base de la rémunération brute des salariés, c'est-à-dire le montant total avant toute déduction effectuée par l'employeur au titre des impôts, des cotisations des salariés aux régimes de sécurité sociale et de pensions, des primes d'assurance vie, des cotisations syndicales et d'autres obligations des salariés.

10. 1) Les gains devraient comprendre: les salaires et traitements directs, la rémunération des heures non effectuées (à l'exclusion des indemnités de licenciement et de cessation de service), les primes et gratifications, les allocations de logement et les allocations familiales payées directement par l'employeur à son salarié:

   a) les salaires et traitements directs pour les heures de travail effectuées ou pour le travail accompli couvrent: i) les paiements aux taux normaux des travailleurs rémunérés au temps; ii) les primes de stimulation pour les travailleurs rémunérés au temps; iii) les gains des travailleurs aux pièces (à l'exclusion des majorations pour heures supplémentaires); iv) les majorations pour heures supplémentaires, travail par équipes et de nuit et heures effectuées les jours fériés; v) les commissions payées au personnel de vente et à d'autres membres du personnel. Sont également compris: les primes pour ancienneté et qualifications spéciales, les primes compensatoires pour tenir compte de la zone géographique, les primes de responsabilité, les allocations pour un travail salissant, dangereux ou pénible, les versements effectués dans le cadre de systèmes de salaire garanti, les allocations de vie chère et d'autres allocations régulières;

   b) la rémunération des heures non effectuées comprend les paiements faits directement aux travailleurs au titre des jours fériés officiels, des congés annuels et d'autres congés payés accordés par l'employeur;

   c) les primes et gratifications couvrent les primes saisonnières et les primes de fin d'année, les primes de vacances (s'ajoutant à la rémunération normale) et les primes de participation aux bénéfices.

2) Les statistiques des gains devraient établir une distinction entre les gains en espèces et les paiements en nature.

...

12. Les taux de salaire devraient comprendre les salaires de base, les allocations de vie chère et les autres allocations garanties et versées régulièrement, mais exclure la rémunération des heures supplémentaires, les primes et gratifications, les allocations familiales et les autres versements de sécurité sociale effectués par les employeurs. Les avantages en nature accordés par l'employeur à titre gracieux et qui s'ajoutent aux taux normaux de salaire sont également exclus.

13. Les statistiques des taux de salaire fixés par les lois ou règlements, les conventions collectives ou les sentences arbitrales (qui sont en général des taux minima ou uniformes) devraient être nettement différenciées des statistiques des taux de salaire effectivement versés aux travailleurs pris individuellement. Chacun de ces types de taux de salaire est utile à certaines fins.

14. Il convient de distinguer les taux de salaire au temps correspondant aux périodes normales de travail des taux spéciaux et autres comme les taux aux pièces, les taux des heures supplémentaires, les taux majorés pour le travail effectué les jours fériés et les taux pour le travail posté.»

Les statistiques des salaires sont en général celles des gains moyens par travailleur ou, dans quelques cas, celles des taux de salaire moyens. Exceptionnellement, ce sont les indices des salaires qui sont reproduits, à défaut de données absolues sur les salaires. Certaines statistiques couvrent uniquement les ouvriers (travailleurs manuels ou travailleurs à la production) tandis que d'autres se rapportent aux employés (travailleurs non manuels) ou à l'ensemble des salariés (ouvriers et employés). Quand elles se réfèrent à des groupes spécifiques de travailleurs (adultes, travailleurs spécialisés ou travailleurs non spécialisés), ce fait est indiqué en notes de bas de page. Les données couvrent, sauf indication contraire, les travailleurs (hommes et femmes), sans distinction d'âge. Dans la mesure du possible, les données sont publiées par sexe.

Les données sur les gains moyens sont généralement tirées des bordereaux de salaires et proviennent d'enquêtes par sondage auprès des établissements ou de recensements qui, fréquemment, fournissent à la fois des données sur la durée du travail et sur l'emploi. Dans quelques cas, les gains moyens sont calculés à partir des statistiques d'assurances sociales, des conventions collectives et d'autres sources. Les types de sources utilisées sont indiqués dans chaque tableau. Lorsque plusieurs sources sont disponibles, une seule est utilisée ici, la plus exhaustive, et les statistiques dérivées d'autres sources sont disponibles dans la base de données en ligne LABORSTA.

---

[4] Pour des renseignements sur les différences de portée, définitions et méthodes de calcul, etc., utilisés pour les diverses séries nationales, voir BIT: *Sources et méthodes: statistiques du travail* (précédemment *Sources et méthodes statistiques*), vol. 2 «Emploi, salaires, durée du travail et coût de la main-d'œuvre (enquêtes auprès des établissements)», deuxième édition (Genève, 1995); vol. 3 «Population active, emploi, chômage et durée du travail (enquête auprès des ménages)», deuxième édition (Genève, 1991), publié sous forme de document de travail; vol. 4 «Emploi, chômage, salaires et durée du travail (documents administratifs et sources assimilées)» (Genève, 1989), publié sous forme de document de travail. Tous ces volumes peuvent être consultés sur LABORSTA.

[5] Pour le texte intégral de la résolution, voir BIT: *Recommandations internationales en vigueur sur les statistiques du travail* (Genève, 2000) ou le site Web du Bureau de statistique du BIT: www.ilo.org/public/french/bureau/stat.

Les données sur les gains, tirées des bordereaux de salaires des établissements, correspondent en général aux paiements en espèces de l'employeur (avant déduction des impôts et des cotisations de sécurité sociale à la charge des travailleurs) et comprennent la rémunération pour les heures normales de travail; le paiement des heures supplémentaires; la rémunération pour les heures de travail payées, mais non effectuées (jours fériés, congés annuels, congés de maladie et autres congés payés); les primes et gratifications, les allocations de cherté de vie et les versements spéciaux (par exemple les gratifications de fin d'année). Lorsque les gains comprennent également la valeur des paiements en nature et les allocations familiales, ce fait est indiqué en note de bas de page. Les statistiques des gains calculées à partir des registres d'assurances sociales fournissent généralement des moyennes inférieures à celles qui sont obtenues à partir des bordereaux de salaires, les heures supplémentaires, les primes de stimulation, etc. pouvant être exclues, de même que les salaires qui dépassent un certain niveau.

Les statistiques des taux de salaire se fondent le plus souvent sur les conventions collectives, les décisions d'arbitrage ou les décisions d'autorités réglementant les salaires, qui spécifient généralement des taux minima pour des professions particulières ou des catégories de travailleurs déterminées. Dans quelques pays, les taux effectivement payés sont très proches de ces minima. Dans d'autres, où il est d'usage de fixer des taux de salaire, on calcule des taux de salaire moyens dans des branches d'activité économique particulières ou dans des groupes de branches d'activité, en pondérant ces taux suivant l'importance numérique que revêtent, au cours d'une année donnée, les différentes professions pour lesquelles on connaît les taux appliqués dans les branches d'activité couvertes par ces statistiques. Les données relatives aux taux de salaire ne concernent généralement que les taux de rémunération des adultes travaillant pendant l'horaire normal. Par conséquent, il n'est pas tenu compte de la rémunération des heures supplémentaires et des autres éléments qui s'ajoutent au salaire; cependant, les allocations de cherté de vie sont souvent comprises dans les calculs, de même que d'autres allocations déterminées par la procédure de fixation des salaires, par exemple l'indemnité de logement. Dans quelques pays, on obtient les taux moyens effectivement payés (rémunération au temps exclusivement) en utilisant les bordereaux de salaires des établissements, de la même façon que pour les gains moyens. En général, les taux effectivement payés comprennent la rémunération calculée sur la base de la durée normale du travail, aussi bien pour les heures supplémentaires que pour la durée normale du travail, mais ils ne tiennent pas compte des primes de stimulation et d'autres versements spéciaux, pas plus que de la part de la rémunération des heures supplémentaires correspondant aux primes. Parfois, ce sont les inspecteurs du travail qui prennent note des taux effectivement payés.

Les différents types de statistiques des salaires sont indiqués dans les tableaux et des notes de bas de page.

Toutes les données sont exprimées en monnaie nationale.

Les données concernant les gains sont sujettes à des fluctuations qui traduisent des changements survenus aussi bien dans les taux de salaire que dans les paiements supplémentaires. En outre, les gains journaliers, hebdomadaires et mensuels dépendent très fortement des variations de la durée du travail. Par contre, les statistiques des taux de salaire ne subissent pas l'influence des changements affectant les suppléments de salaire, ni celle des variations de la durée du travail. Les fluctuations des gains moyens obtenus à partir de l'ensemble des bordereaux de salaires sont également influencées par les changements survenus dans la structure de l'emploi, c'est-à-dire par l'importance relative des travailleurs, des travailleuses, de la main-d'œuvre non qualifiée et de la main-d'œuvre qualifiée, des travailleurs à plein temps et à temps partiel, etc., tandis que les taux de salaire moyens sont calculés le plus souvent en prenant la structure de l'emploi d'une année donnée comme coefficient de pondération. Les gains horaires moyens sont généralement plus élevés que les taux de salaire horaires, les premiers comprenant la rémunération des heures supplémentaires, les gratifications, les primes et les allocations, qui n'entrent pas dans les statistiques des taux de salaire. Les gains hebdomadaires ou mensuels moyens devraient aussi être plus élevés que les taux de salaire correspondants, mais il arrive qu'ils leur soient inférieurs en raison des heures de travail perdues du fait de la maladie, des autres absences ou du travail à temps partiel. Lorsqu'on fait une comparaison entre des statistiques de salaires, il y a lieu de tenir compte des différences que peuvent présenter les notions, la portée économique, les méthodes d'établissement et la présentation des données.

Toutefois, il convient de garder présent à l'esprit que les données de salaires ne reflètent pas les gains nets ou disponibles des travailleurs et qu'elles se réfèrent généralement aux gains bruts, avant toute déduction telle qu'impôts ou cotisations de sécurité sociale.

Lorsque l'on fait une comparaison des données sur les salaires dans l'agriculture et dans d'autres secteurs d'activité, il convient de garder présent à l'esprit que les modes de rémunération, les types de contrat et les dispositions prises dans l'agriculture sont souvent très différents de ceux qui prévalent dans les autres branches d'activité économique. Lorsque c'est possible, on établit une distinction entre les travailleurs permanents, les travailleurs saisonniers et les travailleurs journaliers réguliers ou occasionnels. Dans la plupart des cas, les statistiques se réfèrent aux salaires totaux payés entièrement en espèces ou seulement à la partie du salaire payée en espèces bien que les travailleurs reçoivent en outre des prestations en nature. Parfois, la valeur des repas et du logement fournis par l'employeur est incluse. Si les gains incluent les paiements en nature, ce fait sera mentionné, lorsque c'est possible, en notes de bas de page.

Les comparaisons internationales des salaires sont sujettes à de plus grandes réserves pour l'agriculture que pour les autres branches d'activité. La nature du travail effectué par les différentes catégories de travailleurs agricoles et la durée de la journée de travail ou de la semaine de travail présentent également des différences considérables d'un pays à l'autre. Les fluctuations saisonnières des salaires agricoles sont plus accusées dans certains pays que dans d'autres. Les méthodes suivies dans les différents pays pour estimer la valeur nominale des paiements en nature accusent un manque d'uniformité.

Lors de comparaisons internationales, il convient également de tenir compte des différences, entre les pays, des prix à la consommation des biens et services et de la nécessité d'avoir une monnaie de référence et des taux de change appropriés; par contre, les analyses de l'évolution dans le temps des salaires devraient tenir compte des évolutions des prix à la consommation, pour les mêmes catégories de travailleurs, au cours de la même période.

Pour de plus amples informations, voir BIT: *Un système intégré de statistiques de salaires: manuel de méthodologie* (Genève, 1980). Pour des renseignements sur les différences de portée, définitions et méthodes de calcul, etc. utilisées pour les diverses séries nationales, voir les *Sources et méthodes* disponibles dans la base de données en ligne LABORSTA.

Lésions professionnelles

La *Résolution concernant les statistiques des lésions professionnelles (résultant des accidents du travail)* adoptée par la seizième Conférence internationale des statisticiens du travail (CIST) (Genève, 1998)[6] donne les définitions suivantes à des fins statistiques:

«accident du travail: tout événement inattendu et imprévu, y compris les actes de violence, survenant du fait du travail ou à l'occasion de celui-ci et qui entraîne, pour un ou plusieurs travailleurs, une lésion corporelle, une maladie ou la mort;

sont considérés comme des accidents du travail, les accidents de voyage, de transport ou de circulation dans lesquels les travailleurs sont blessés et qui surviennent à cause ou au cours du travail, c'est-à-dire lorsqu'ils exercent une activité économique, sont au travail ou s'occupent des affaires de l'employeur;

lésion professionnelle: lésion corporelle, maladie ou décès provoqués par un accident du travail; la lésion professionnelle est donc distincte de la maladie professionnelle, qui est une maladie contractée à la suite d'une exposition à des facteurs de risque découlant de l'activité professionnelle;

cas de lésion professionnelle: cas d'un seul travailleur victime d'une lésion professionnelle résultant d'un seul accident du travail;

incapacité de travail: incapacité de la personne blessée, due à la lésion professionnelle dont elle a été victime, d'exécuter les tâches normales correspondant à l'emploi ou au poste qu'elle occupait au moment où s'est produit l'accident du travail.»

Les statistiques des lésions professionnelles présentées dans cette publication sont conformes, dans la mesure du possible, aux recommandations de la seizième CIST. Les données devraient couvrir tous les travailleurs, quelle que soit leur situation dans la profession (c'est-à-dire les salariés et les travailleurs indépendants, y compris les employeurs et les travailleurs à leur propre compte), l'ensemble du pays, toutes les branches d'activité économique ainsi que tous les secteurs de l'économie.

En général, sont exclus: les cas de maladie professionnelle (une maladie professionnelle est une maladie contractée à la suite d'une exposition à des facteurs de risque découlant d'une activité professionnelle pendant une période de temps) et les cas de lésions résultant des accidents de trajet (un accident de trajet est un accident survenant sur le trajet habituellement emprunté par le travailleur, quelle que soit la direction dans laquelle il se déplace, entre son lieu de travail ou de formation liée à son activité professionnelle et: i) sa résidence principale ou secondaire, ii) le lieu où il prend normalement ses repas, ou iii) le lieu où il reçoit normalement son salaire, et qui entraîne la mort ou des lésions corporelles).

En principe, la source utilisée détermine le type de statistiques présentées pour chaque pays. Les sources les plus fréquentes de données dans ce domaine sont les systèmes de déclaration d'accident du travail (par exemple les services d'inspection du travail) ou les régimes d'indemnisation des lésions professionnelles, bien que les enquêtes auprès des établissements ou des ménages soient utilisées dans quelques pays. Le type de source détermine la portée des statistiques. Dans la plupart des pays, la portée des obligations de déclarer ou d'indemniser les lésions, et ainsi la portée des statistiques, est limitée à certains types de travailleurs (salariés, le plus souvent) ou certaines activités économiques ou à des cas de lésion avec incapacité pendant plus d'un nombre de jours précisé, etc. Le type de source apparaît dans chaque tableau, et le type de lésions couvertes (déclarées ou indemnisées) est également précisé.

Les statistiques présentées se réfèrent aux cas de lésion professionnelle résultant des accidents du travail survenant pendant l'année civile indiquée. Le total des journées perdues à cause d'un cas de lésion est compris dans les statistiques correspondant à l'année civile au cours de laquelle l'accident du travail a eu lieu.

Les travailleurs du groupe de référence sont les travailleurs du groupe particulier examiné qui sont couverts par la source des statistiques des lésions professionnelles (par exemple les hommes ou les femmes, les travailleurs d'une activité économique, d'une profession, d'une région, d'un groupe d'âge, etc., ou une combinaison de ceux-ci, ou les travailleurs couverts par un régime d'assurance particulier). Le nombre de travailleurs du groupe de référence varie d'un pays à l'autre, d'une activité économique à l'autre et à travers le temps, à cause de plusieurs facteurs dont les différences et les variations de taille et de structure de l'emploi. Ces différences sont prises en compte lors de l'utilisation des mesures comparatives telles que les taux de fréquence, d'incidence ou de gravité.

Les variations à la hausse ou à la baisse du nombre de cas de lésion professionnelle sur un certain laps de temps peuvent refléter non seulement une évolution des conditions du travail et de son environnement, mais aussi des modifications portant sur les méthodes de déclaration des accidents ou de collecte de données, ou encore des révisions de la législation relative à la déclaration et à l'indemnisation des lésions professionnelles dans le pays concerné.

Les cas d'incapacité temporaire correspondent au nombre de cas de lésion professionnelle où les travailleurs blessés n'ont pas pu travailler à partir du jour suivant le jour de l'accident, mais ont pu reprendre le travail et exécuter les tâches normales correspondant à l'emploi ou au poste occupé au moment où s'est produit l'accident du travail, dans un délai d'un an après le jour de l'accident.

Les *taux de fréquence* sont calculés en général comme le nombre de cas nouveaux de lésions (cas mortels ou cas non mortels) durant l'année divisé par le nombre total des heures effectuées par les travailleurs du groupe de référence durant l'année, et multiplié par 1 000 000. Les *taux d'incidence* sont calculés comme le nombre de cas nouveaux de lésions (cas mortels ou cas non mortels) durant l'année, divisé par le nombre de travailleurs du groupe de référence et multiplié par 100 000.

Le type de taux (par 1 000 000 heures effectuées, par 100 000 travailleurs occupés, par 100 000 salariés, par 100 000 travailleurs assurés, etc.) est indiqué au début de chaque série.

Les journées perdues correspondent au nombre total des journées perdues par les cas de lésion professionnelle avec incapacité temporaire de travailler. Les séries relatives à certains pays comprennent également des estimations des journées perdues par les cas d'incapacité permanente. En général, les journées perdues sont les jours civils pendant lesquels le travailleur blessé était temporairement dans l'incapacité de travailler, non compris le jour de l'accident, jusqu'à un maximum d'un an. Le nombre des journées perdues présenté pour quelques pays est exprimé en journées de travail, en particulier si la source des statistiques est un régime

---

[6] Pour le texte intégral de la résolution, voir BIT: *Recommandations internationales en vigueur sur les statistiques du travail* (Genève, 2000) ou le site Web du Bureau de statistique du BIT: www.ilo.org/stat.

d'indemnisation d'accidents. Les absences temporaires de travail de moins d'un jour pour traitement médical ne sont pas prises en compte.

Les données fournies dans cette publication doivent être utilisées avec précaution, en particulier s'il s'agit de procéder à des comparaisons internationales. Les sources, les méthodes de collecte de données, la portée et les classifications utilisées peuvent varier d'un pays à un autre. Par exemple, la portée pourrait ne concerner que certains types de travailleurs (salariés, personnes assurées, travailleurs à plein temps, etc.), certaines activités économiques, les établissements occupant plus d'un certain nombre de travailleurs, les cas de lésion ayant entraîné une incapacité de travail supérieure à un seuil minimal de jours, etc. Les descriptions des sources nationales, de la portée, des définitions, et des méthodes utilisées lors de la compilation des statistiques figurent dans *Sources et méthodes* et dans la base de données en ligne LABORSTA.

Grèves et lock-out

La *Résolution concernant les statistiques des conflits du travail: grèves, lock-out et autres actions de revendication*, adoptée par la quinzième Conférence internationale des statisticiens du travail (CIST) (Genève, 1993)[7] donne les définitions suivantes à des fins statistiques:

«Une grève est un arrêt temporaire de travail déclenché par un ou des groupes de travailleurs en vue d'imposer ou de s'opposer à une exigence ou de formuler des doléances, ou de soutenir d'autres travailleurs dans leurs revendications ou doléances.

Un lock-out est la fermeture temporaire totale ou partielle d'un ou plusieurs lieux de travail, ou les mesures prises par un ou plusieurs employeurs pour empêcher les travailleurs d'exécuter normalement leur travail, en vue d'imposer ou de s'opposer à une exigence ou de soutenir les revendications ou les doléances d'autres employeurs.

Travailleurs impliqués dans une grève: Les travailleurs directement impliqués dans une grève sont ceux qui y ont participé délibérément en cessant le travail. Les travailleurs indirectement impliqués dans une grève sont les salariés des établissements impliqués ou les travailleurs indépendants inclus dans le groupe impliqué, qui n'ont pas participé délibérément à la grève en cessant le travail mais qui ont été contraints de cesser le travail du fait de la grève.

Travailleurs impliqués dans un lock-out: Les travailleurs directement impliqués dans un lock-out sont ceux qui, dans les établissements impliqués, étaient directement concernés par le conflit du travail et ont été empêchés de travailler par le lock-out. Les travailleurs indirectement impliqués dans un lock-out sont ceux qui, dans les établissements impliqués, n'étaient pas directement concernés par le conflit du travail, mais qui ont été contraints de cesser le travail du fait du lock-out.

Un conflit du travail est un désaccord qui porte sur un problème ou un groupe de problèmes à propos duquel ou desquels il existe un différend entre des travailleurs et des employeurs, ou à propos duquel ou desquels une revendication a été formulée par des travailleurs ou des employeurs, ou à propos duquel ou desquels des travailleurs ou des employeurs soutiennent les revendications ou les doléances d'autres travailleurs ou employeurs.»

---

[7] Pour le texte intégral de la résolution, voir BIT: *Recommandations internationales en vigueur sur les statistiques du travail* (Genève, 2000) ou le site Web du Bureau de statistique du BIT: www.ilo.org/stat.

Les définitions nationales peuvent différer de ces définitions selon la source statistique utilisée. En général, les données statistiques proviennent de rapports administratifs des services d'arbitrage, des services impliqués dans les relations du travail, etc. Les données peuvent être extraites de diverses sources, dont des avis de grève, des articles de presse et des enquêtes directes auprès des employeurs et des organisations de travailleurs. Le type de source est indiqué dans chaque tableau.

Les données présentées dans cette publication englobent les grèves et les lock-out sans distinction, car la plupart des pays n'établissent pas de statistiques séparées pour ces deux types d'action. En général, les séries couvrent tous les types de grèves et lock-out ainsi que toutes les branches d'activité économique et se réfèrent aux actions en cours durant l'année civile en question, c'est-à-dire aux grèves et lock-out qui sont survenus au cours de l'année ou qui étaient déjà engagés avant l'année considérée. Toute divergence éventuelle (par rapport à cette façon de procéder) est indiquée en note de bas de page. Si les statistiques ne couvrent que les grèves et lock-out d'une certaine importance (en termes de nombre de travailleurs impliqués, de durée de l'action ou de temps de travail non effectué ou encore d'une combinaison de deux ou plus de ces caractéristiques), le seuil limite est également précisé en note de bas de page.

Les recommandations internationales précisent que tous les arrêts de travail dus à un même conflit du travail devraient être comptabilisés comme une grève ou un lock-out, tant que la période entre deux arrêts de travail n'excède pas deux mois. Certains pays utilisent différents critères pour identifier un même arrêt de travail; par exemple, chaque arrêt dans un établissement peut être considéré comme une grève ou un lock-out. De ce fait, le nombre de grèves ou de lock-out ainsi que le nombre de travailleurs impliqués sont souvent plus élevés qu'ils ne l'auraient été si on avait suivi les recommandations internationales, et le nombre total de travailleurs impliqués excède parfois l'emploi total dans l'activité économique concernée.

En utilisant ces données, il ne faut pas perdre de vue que le nombre de travailleurs exposés au risque de grèves ou de lock-out varie en fonction des différentes branches d'activité économique, des pays et d'une période à l'autre. Pour cette raison, il est utile d'adopter des mesures comparatives telles que le taux de gravité qui rapporte le temps non travaillé suite à une grève ou un lock-out au nombre total de travailleurs.

Si une grève ou un lock-out couvre plusieurs branches d'activité économique, l'information à ce sujet est généralement précisée pour chacune des branches concernées. Par conséquent le nombre total de grèves et de lock-out apparaissant pour l'ensemble (toutes branches d'activité économique confondues) peut être inférieur à la somme des chiffres pour chaque branche.

Le nombre de journées non effectuées à cause des grèves et des lock-out en cours pendant l'année indiquée se mesure généralement en termes de la somme des jours ouvrables qui auraient normalement été effectués par chaque travailleur impliqué si l'arrêt de travail n'était pas intervenu.

Les taux de gravité des grèves et des lock-out sont généralement calculés en termes de nombre de jours non travaillés pour 1 000 travailleurs. Le type de taux est indiqué dans chaque tableau.

Les descriptions des sources nationales, de la portée, des définitions et des méthodes utilisées lors de la compilation des statistiques sont publiées dans BIT: *Sources et méthodes* et disponibles dans la base de données en ligne LABORSTA.

Prix à la consommation

La *Résolution concernant les indices des prix à la consommation* adoptée par la dix-septième Conférence internationale des statisticiens du travail (CIST) (Genève, 2003)[8] stipule ce qui suit:

«1. L'IPC est un indicateur social et économique couramment utilisé pour mesurer les variations au cours du temps du niveau général des prix des biens et services acquis, utilisés ou payés par les ménages pour leur consommation.

2. L'indice vise à mesurer les variations dans le temps des prix à la consommation. Cela peut être réalisé en mesurant le coût d'achat d'un panier fixe de biens et de services dont la qualité est constante et les caractéristiques similaires aux produits du panier choisis pour être représentatifs des dépenses des ménages pendant une année ou une autre période spécifiée. Un tel indice s'appelle indice des prix d'un panier fixe.

3. L'indice peut également viser à mesurer les effets des variations de prix sur le coût que représente l'accès à un niveau de vie constant (niveau d'utilité ou de bien-être). Ce concept est dénommé indice du coût de la vie (ICV). Un indice des prix d'un panier fixe, ou une autre mesure appropriée, peut être utilisé en tant qu'approximation d'un ICV. »

Un indice est généralement estimé à partir d'une suite de mesures synthétiques des variations relatives, d'une période à l'autre, des prix d'un ensemble fixe de biens et de services de consommation constants en quantité et par leurs caractéristiques, acquis, utilisés ou payés par la population de référence. Chaque mesure synthétique est obtenue comme une moyenne pondérée d'un grand nombre d'indices de prix d'agrégats élémentaires. L'indice de chaque agrégat élémentaire est estimé au moyen d'un échantillon de prix pour un ensemble fixe de biens et de services que se procurent les individus de la population de référence dans une région donnée, ou qui habitent cette région, auprès d'un ensemble spécifié de points de vente ou auprès d'autres fournisseurs de biens et de services de consommation.

Les indices des prix à la consommation sont utilisés à diverses fins telles que:

a) l'analyse générale de la situation économique et sociale et la prise de décisions concernant les politiques correspondantes;

b) la négociation ou l'indexation, ou les deux, par les pouvoirs publics (en particulier des impôts, des prestations et cotisations sociales, des rémunérations et des pensions de la fonction publique, des patentes, des amendes et des emprunts publics (intérêts ou principal)), dans les contrats entre particuliers (par exemple des salaires et traitements, des primes d'assurance et du coût des services) et dans les décisions de justice (par exemple des pensions alimentaires);

c) la mesure des changements en termes réels ou des rapports entre l'argent et les biens ou les services contre lesquels il peut être échangé (par exemple la déflation de la valeur aux prix courants des agrégats de la comptabilité nationale et la déflation des ventes au détail);

d) les comparaisons des variations de prix à des fins commerciales, y compris la réévaluation comptable.

---

[8] Pour le texte intégral de la résolution, voir BIT: *Dix-septième Conférence internationale des statisticiens du travail, Rapport de la Conférence* (Genève, 2003) ou le site Web du Bureau de statistique du BIT: http://www.ilo.org/stat.

Des indices partiels peuvent être appropriés pour certaines des utilisations précédentes, en lieu et place de l'indice d'ensemble.

Les pondérations représentent les parts relatives des dépenses ou de la consommation des agrégats élémentaires, estimées sur la base des données disponibles. A cet égard, la dix-septième CIST a recommandé ce qui suit:

«23. Les deux principaux éléments permettant de dériver les pondérations sont les résultats obtenus à partir d'enquêtes sur les dépenses des ménages, ainsi que les estimations des dépenses de consommation des ménages de la comptabilité nationale. Les résultats d'une enquête sur les dépenses des ménages sont appropriés pour un indice que l'on a défini de manière à couvrir les dépenses de consommation des groupes de population de référence résidant dans le pays, alors que les estimations s'appuyant sur la comptabilité nationale conviennent à un indice défini pour couvrir les dépenses de consommation à l'intérieur du pays. ...

24. Les informations provenant de la source principale (enquêtes sur les dépenses des ménages ou comptabilité nationale) devraient être complétées par toute autre information disponible sur le schéma de dépenses. Les sources d'informations de ce type qui peuvent servir à désagréger les dépenses sont les enquêtes sur les points de vente au détail ou les points d'achat, les enquêtes sur la production, les données d'exportation et d'importation, et les sources administratives. Sur la base de ces données, les pondérations pour certains produits peuvent être encore ventilées par région et par type de point de vente...»

La dix-septième CIST a en outre recommandé que les prix servant au calcul des indices devraient être:

«54. ... les prix correspondant à des transactions effectives – y compris les impôts indirects et les rabais inconditionnels – qui seraient payées, convenues ou chiffrées (acceptées) par la population de référence. ... Les pourboires versés pour le service, lorsqu'ils sont obligatoires, doivent être traités comme faisant partie du prix payé.

55. Les prix exceptionnels payés pour des produits endommagés, défraîchis ou qui ont perdu de leur qualité pour d'autres raisons et qui sont vendus pour liquider les stocks devraient être exclus des relevés, à moins qu'il ne s'agisse d'un phénomène permanent et largement répandu pour la vente de ces produits. Les prix des produits soldés, au rabais ou faisant l'objet de campagnes spéciales de promotion devraient être inclus lorsqu'ils s'appliquent à tous les consommateurs et lorsqu'il n'y a pas de limite significative aux quantités que chaque client peut acheter.

52. Les prix doivent être collectés dans tous les types de points de vente qui sont importants, y compris les commerçants sur la toile (Internet), les marchés en plein air et les marchés informels, ainsi que sur les marchés libres et les marchés dont les prix sont contrôlés....»

Le champ d'application des indices des prix à la consommation peut varier d'un pays à un autre, non seulement quant aux types de ménages ou groupes de population couverts, mais aussi quant à sa portée géographique.

Les pratiques nationales varient également en ce qui concerne le traitement de certains éléments retenus dans le calcul des indices des prix à la consommation tels qu'articles saisonniers, changements de qualité, nouveaux articles, biens durables et logements occupés par leur propriétaire. Les méthodes de collecte des prix ou de calcul des indices sont également différentes. A ce titre, les indices des prix à la consommation publiés dans ces tableaux doivent être utilisés avec précaution, notamment en matière de négociations collectives et dans les calculs d'indexation ou de déflation. Ces indices ne peuvent être utilisés que si le champ d'application de l'indice des prix à la consommation correspond étroitement à celui du sujet de négociation, de l'indexation ou de la déflation.

Des informations sur le champ, les définitions et les méthodes utilisées dans le calcul des indices des prix à la consommation diffusés dans cette publication, sont publiées dans la série *Sources et Méthodes* et disponibles dans la base de données en ligne LABORSTA.

Les indices généraux des prix à la consommation sont présentés pour tous les groupes d'articles de consommation combinés. Un indice général excluant le logement est également présenté. Le logement a été exclu de l'indice général afin de rendre les taux de variation des prix plus comparables entre les pays, bien que cela n'élimine pas toutes les difficultés rencontrées en faisant de telles comparaisons. Cet indice s'entend principalement comme étant un indice sans loyer, qu'il soit réel et/ou imputé et les dépenses pour l'entretien et les réparations du logement.. Toutefois, si un tel indice n'est pas disponible au niveau national, ou s'il est trop difficile de le calculer, pour des raisons pratiques, les pays transmettent un indice qui exclut l'ensemble du groupe logement ou seulement le loyer. Dans un tel cas, une note de bas de page signale les exclusions spécifiques (par exemple l'ensemble du groupe logement, loyer, électricité, gaz et autres combustibles, dépenses pour l'entretien et les réparations du logement, etc.).

L'indice «Alimentation» inclut les boissons non alcoolisées seulement. Dans le cas où les boissons alcoolisées et/ou le tabac sont compris dans le groupe «alimentation», cela est signalé dans une note de bas de page.

Trois autres groupes principaux d'indices concernant respectivement: «Electricité, gaz et autres combustibles», «Habillement (y compris les chaussures)» et «Loyer» sont également présentés. Les indices de ces groupes, y compris celui de l'alimentation, sont des composantes de l'indice général. En plus de ces quatre groupes d'indices, dans la majorité des pays l'indice général et l'indice général non compris l'habitation comprennent tous les autres principaux groupes de dépenses tels que: «Boissons alcoolisées et tabac»; «Ameublement, équipement ménager et entretien courant du foyer»; «Santé»; «Transport»; «Communications»; «Loisirs et culture»; «Education»; «Restaurants et hôtels»; et «Autres biens et services». Les indices relatifs à ces derniers groupes ne sont pas présentés séparément dans l'*Annuaire*, en raison des variations dans la composition des groupes d'un pays à un autre.

Les indices généraux et les indices de groupes présentés dans les tableaux correspondent aux moyennes annuelles bien que, dans la plupart des cas, les indices soient calculés mensuellement et pour quelques cas trimestriellement ou semestriellement. Les données annuelles sont calculées à partir des séries originales.

Comme la période de base originale des séries nationales varie elle aussi, on a adopté une période de base uniforme (2000) pour la présentation des données. Le plus grand nombre possible des séries ont été recalculées en divisant l'indice se rapportant à chacune des dates indiquées par l'indice pour l'année 2000 et en multipliant le quotient par 100. Lorsqu'on ne dispose de données que pour des périodes postérieures à 2000, les indices sont généralement présentés en prenant pour période de base la première année civile pour laquelle existent des données. Ces opérations n'impliquent aucune modification des systèmes de pondération, etc., utilisés par les pays.

Lorsqu'une nouvelle série est suffisamment comparable avec la précédente, elle est enchaînée avec celle-ci pour obtenir une série temporelle continue. Lorsqu'une série est interrompue et remplacée par une autre série qui ne peut être liée à la précédente soit par enchaînement soit par d'autres techniques d'estimation, une note de bas de page indique la rupture.

Apéndice

Notas explicativas

Para más información, incluidas las descripciones metodológicas, las series cronológicas y estadísticas suplementarias, consultar la base de datos LABORSTA en línea, en el sitio: http://laborsta.ilo.org.

Clasificaciones

Las clasificaciones internacionales uniformes de todas las actividades económicas (CIIU), de ocupaciones (CIUO), de la situación en el empleo (CISE) y de la educación (CINE) figuran por separado en esta publicación.

Un número cada vez más elevado de países está en condiciones o en vías de adaptar sus clasificaciones nacionales de ramas de actividad, ocupaciones y situación en el empleo a las normas internacionales de clasificación, comprendidas las revisiones más recientes.

La clasificación de la principal actividad económica que se desarrolla en el lugar de trabajo (industria) difiere fundamentalmente de la que se refiere a la clase principal de tareas que se llevan a cabo (ocupación). En la primera, todas las personas que trabajan en el mismo establecimiento se clasifican en la misma industria, con independencia de sus ocupaciones. En la segunda, por el contrario, se reúnen los individuos que desempeñan el mismo tipo de trabajo, con independencia del lugar en que lo realizan.

Cuando los datos se dan según las clasificaciones nacionales, cabe tener presente que las clasificaciones industriales y de ocupaciones de los diversos países presentan varios puntos divergentes. En efecto, en cada país el contenido real de los grupos de industrias o de ocupaciones puede variar en función de las distintas definiciones y métodos de tabulación utilizados. La clasificación en grupos muy amplios puede también ocultar diferencias fundamentales de las características industriales o de ocupación propias de cada país.

La Clasificación Internacional de la Situación en el Empleo (CISE) clasifica los empleos en relación con el tipo de contrato de empleo, tácito o expreso, entre una persona y otras personas u organizaciones. El criterio básico para definir los grupos de clasificación son la clase de riesgo económico y el tipo de autoridad ejercida por los trabajadores sobre los establecimientos y otros trabajadores, en virtud del empleo que tienen o tendrán.

Hasta 1993, los principales grupos de la CISE eran «empleadores», «trabajadores por cuenta propia», «empleados», «miembros de cooperativas de productores» y «trabajadores familiares no remunerados». En 1993 se revisó y amplió la CISE sin modificar los títulos de estos grupos principales, salvo el último de los mencionados que ahora se llama «trabajadores familiares contribuyentes». Se amplió el contenido de los trabajadores por cuenta propia para que comprenda a las personas que trabajan en empresas familiares con la misma dedicación que el jefe de la empresa. Estas personas, generalmente mujeres, se consideraban antes como trabajadores familiares no remunerados. La CISE revisada también distingue los grupos con mayor claridad.

La experiencia demuestra que con frecuencia las distintas formas de medir la «situación en el empleo» de los países impide que el contenido de los grupos pueda compararse con facilidad. Por ejemplo, la mayoría de los países clasifican los gerentes y directores de empresas no personales como «empleados», mientras que algunos países los clasifican como «empleadores». Otro ejemplo son los trabajadores familiares que perciben periódicamente una remuneración, como sueldo o salario, comisión, pago a destajo o en especie, que la mayoría clasifica como «empleados» pero algunos países los incluyen entre los «trabajadores familiares contribuyentes». Otro importante factor que afecta la comparabilidad del número de estos trabajadores familiares es que algunos países no pueden medir a estas personas como personas con empleo. Muchos países no pueden distinguir entre «trabajadores por cuenta propia» y «empleadores» y por tal motivo presentan la suma de ambos. Entre los países donde el número de cooperativas de productores es muy escaso, algunos incluyen a sus miembros entre los «empleados», mientras que en otros países se incluyen entre los «trabajadores por cuenta propia».

Cabe recordar que el objetivo de los sistemas internacionales de clasificación no es sustituir las clasificaciones de cada país sino constituir un marco que facilite las comparaciones internacionales de las estadísticas nacionales. Muchos países, sobre todo los que elaboran clasificaciones por primera vez o las revisan, utilizan los sistemas internacionales como marco central.

Población económicamente activa

La «*población económicamente activa*» abarca todas las personas de uno u otro sexo que aportan su trabajo para producir bienes y servicios económicos, durante un período de referencia especificado. De acuerdo con la versión de 1993 del Sistema de Cuentas Nacionales (SCN), la «producción» incluye la producción de todos los bienes o servicios individuales o colectivos que se suministran, o que se piensa suministrar, a unidades distintas de aquellas que los producen, incluida la producción de los bienes o servicios utilizados completamente en el proceso de producción de dichos bienes o servicios; la producción por cuenta propia de todos los bienes que sus productores destinan a su autoconsumo final; la producción por cuenta propia de los servicios de las viviendas ocupadas por sus propietarios y de los servicios domésticos y personales producidos por personal de servicio doméstico remunerado.

Dos mediciones útiles de la población económicamente activa son la «*población habitualmente activa*», medida en relación a un largo período de referencia, tal como un año, y la «*población corrientemente activa*» o *fuerza de trabajo*, medida en relación con un corto período de referencia, tal como una semana o un día.

Las estadísticas que se presentan sobre la población total y la población económicamente activa son, en su mayoría, el resultado del último censo de población disponible, o de la última encuesta por muestra de la fuerza de trabajo.

Estos datos incluyen a todas las personas que responden a los criterios necesarios para ser consideradas como *personas con empleo* o como *personas desempleadas* (como definido más abajo).

Dos tipos de tasas de actividad se pueden obtener en base a estas estadísticas: *tasas de actividad específica*, es decir, razones (expresadas en porcentajes) entre la población económicamente activa de 15 años de edad y más y la población total del mismo grupo de edad; y *tasas brutas de actividad*, es decir, razones (expresadas en porcentajes) entre el total de la población económicamente activa y la población total de todos los grupos de edad, comprendidas las personas que no tienen la edad de trabajar.

Las prácticas nacionales (véase también las descripciones de *Fuentes y Métodos* disponibles por separado y en la base de datos en línea LABORSTA) difieren entre países debido al tratamiento de ciertos grupos, como las fuerzas armadas, hermandades religiosas, personas en busca de un primer empleo, trabajadores estacionales o personas ocupadas en actividades económicas a tiempo parcial. En ciertos países no se incluyen en la población económicamente activa a todos o a algunos de estos grupos. Cabe destacar que, en general, la población económicamente activa no abarca a estudiantes ni personas que sólo realizan labores domésticas en su propio hogar, personas que viven en colectividades, personas jubiladas que no trabajan ni buscan empleo, rentistas y a las totalmente dependientes de otras.

Así pues, la comparabilidad de las estadísticas de los distintos países se ve limitada por los detalles de las definiciones utilizadas y de los grupos que abarcan, así como por diferencias en los métodos de recolección, clasificación y tabulación de los datos básicos. En particular existen variaciones importantes entre los distintos países en los criterios utilizados para determinar hasta qué punto los trabajadores familiares contribuyentes en empresas familiares, en especial las mujeres, forman parte de la población económicamente activa, así como en el tratamiento de los desempleados sin empleo anterior, o los estudiantes con una actividad económica a tiempo parcial. Estas variaciones pueden afectar específicamente la comparabilidad de las estadísticas sobre los jóvenes.

El período de referencia también puede constituir un factor importante de disparidad: en algunos países, las estadísticas sobre la población económicamente activa se refieren a la situación real de cada individuo el día del censo o de la encuesta o durante un breve período específico, como la semana inmediatamente anterior a la fecha del censo o la encuesta; mientras que otras sólo registran la situación habitual de cada persona, generalmente sin ninguna referencia explícita a un período determinado.

En la mayoría de los países las estadísticas se refieren únicamente a las personas con empleo y personas desempleadas que tengan más de una cierta edad, mientras que en algunos países la definición de la población activa no hace ninguna referencia a un límite de edad.

Los sistemas de codificación utilizados por los países también pueden afectar la comparabilidad de las estadísticas. Para que el contenido de los grupos de una clasificación sea idéntico al de otra clasificación se deberían utilizar los mismos criterios de codificación. Por lo general, los sistemas de codificación utilizados en las encuestas sobre la fuerza de trabajo son más precisos que los utilizados en los censos de población.

Empleo

La *Resolución sobre estadísticas de la población económicamente activa, del empleo, del desempleo y del subempleo*, adoptada por la decimotercera Conferencia Internacional de Estadísticos del Trabajo (Ginebra, 1982)[1] define el empleo como sigue:

«1) Se considerará como «personas con empleo» a todas las personas que tengan más de cierta edad especificada y que durante un breve período de referencia, tal como una semana o un día, estuvieran en cualquiera de las siguientes categorías:

   a) Con 'empleo asalariado':

   a1) 'trabajando': personas que durante el período de referencia hayan realizado algún trabajo por un sueldo o salario en metálico o en especie;

   a2) 'con empleo pero sin trabajar': personas que, habiendo trabajado en su empleo actual, no estaban trabajando temporalmente durante el período de referencia y mantenían un vínculo formal con su empleo. Este vínculo formal al empleo debería determinarse en función de las circunstancias nacionales, de acuerdo con uno o más de los siguientes criterios:

   i) pago ininterrumpido de sueldos o salarios;

   ii) garantía de reintegración en el empleo al término de la contingencia o un acuerdo respecto de la fecha de reintegración;

   iii) duración de la ausencia del trabajo, la cual, cuando sea el caso, puede ser aquella por la que los trabajadores pueden percibir una compensación social sin obligación de aceptar otros trabajos.

   b) Con 'empleo independiente':

   b1) 'trabajando': las personas que durante el período de referencia hayan realizado algún trabajo para obtener beneficios o ganancia familiar, en metálico o en especie;

   b2) 'con una empresa pero sin trabajar': las personas que, teniendo una empresa – sea industrial, comercial, de explotación agrícola o de prestación de servicios –, estaban temporalmente ausentes del trabajo durante el período de referencia por cualquier razón específica.

2) Por razones prácticas, la noción 'algún trabajo' debe interpretarse como una hora de trabajo por lo menos.

3) Las personas ausentes de su trabajo temporalmente por causa de enfermedad o accidente, días festivos o vacaciones, huelga, paro de empleadores, licencia de estudios o de formación profesional, licencia de maternidad o paternidad, coyuntura económica difícil, desorganización o suspensión temporal del trabajo por razones tales como mal tiempo, averías mecánicas o eléctricas, escasez de materias primas o combustibles, u otras ausencias temporales con o sin licencia, deberían considerarse como personas con empleo asalariado, siempre que mantuvieran un vínculo formal con su empleo.

4) Debería considerarse como personas con empleo independiente a los empleadores, trabajadores por cuenta propia y miembros de cooperativas de producción, y

---

[1] Para el texto completo de la Resolución, véase OIT: *Recomendaciones internacionales de actualidad en estadísticas del trabajo* (Ginebra, 2000) o el sitio Web de la Oficina de Estadística de la OIT: www.ilo.org/stat.

clasificarse 'trabajando' o 'con empleo pero sin trabajar', según sea el caso.

5) Debería considerarse como personas con empleo independiente a los trabajadores familiares no remunerados que estén trabajando, sin consideración al número de horas trabajadas durante el período de referencia. Los países que, por razones particulares, prefieren introducir un criterio de tiempo mínimo de trabajo como condición para incluir a los trabajadores familiares no remunerados entre las personas con empleo deberían identificar y clasificar aparte a los que trabajan menos del tiempo prescrito.

6) Las personas ocupadas en la producción de bienes y servicios económicos para consumo propio o del hogar deberían considerarse como personas con empleo independiente si dicha producción constituye una aportación importante al consumo total del hogar.

7) Los aprendices que hayan recibido una retribución en metálico o en especie deberían considerarse como personas con empleo asalariado y clasificarse como 'trabajando' o 'con empleo pero sin trabajar', sobre las mismas bases que las demás personas con empleo asalariado.

8) Los estudiantes, trabajadores del hogar y otros dedicados principalmente a actividades no económicas durante el período de referencia y que al mismo tiempo tenían un empleo asalariado o un empleo independiente, según definiciones en el subpárrafo 1) anterior, deberían considerarse como personas con empleo, sobre las mismas bases que las otras categorías de personas con empleo y, si fuese posible, clasificarse aparte.

9) Los miembros de las fuerzas armadas deberían figurar entre las personas con empleo asalariado. Las fuerzas armadas incluirían los miembros permanentes y temporales, como se ha especificado en la última edición revisada de la Clasificación Internacional Uniforme de Ocupaciones (CIUO).»

Las definiciones nacionales de empleo pueden diferir en algunos casos de la definición internacional estándar recomendada (véase también las descripciones de *Fuentes y Métodos* disponibles por separado y en la base de datos en línea LABORSTA).

En general, las cuatro fuentes principales de los datos sobre el empleo son las encuestas por muestra a los hogares, los censos o encuestas de establecimientos, las estimaciones oficiales y los registros administrativos de los regímenes de seguridad social. Las cuatro fuentes mencionadas anteriormente están indicadas en los cuadros. Sin embargo, en general, las estadísticas que se presentan aquí provienen de únicamente una fuente con prioridad a las encuestas de hogares ya que suministran estadísticas más exhaustivas. (Estadísticas adicionales se encuentran en la base de datos en línea LABORSTA.)

Con respecto al empleo total, las encuestas de la fuerza de trabajo abarcan todos los grupos de situación, es decir, no sólo los asalariados (obreros y empleados), comprendidos los trabajadores familiares remunerados, sino también los empleadores, trabajadores por cuenta propia, miembros de cooperativas de productores, trabajadores familiares contribuyentes y otros no clasificables por su situación en el empleo. Los datos por lo general se refieren al empleo durante un breve período determinado (una semana o un día). Habitualmente no se distingue entre personas empleadas a tiempo completo y quienes trabajan menos horas.

Las encuestas de establecimientos permiten obtener datos sobre el número de trabajadores que figuran en las nóminas de salarios de los establecimientos en un período de pago determinado o un día de este último. Habitualmente se distinguen dos tipos de estadísticas de establecimientos.

El primero abarca todos los de una cierta importancia, como los que ocupan más de un cierto número de asalariados, o los que tienen una producción anual que supera un cierto valor, etc. Los datos así obtenidos pueden presentar un sesgo, o distorsión, debido a la exclusión de los establecimientos que no alcanzan los mínimos fijados. Más aún, con tendencia ascendente, las series reflejarán un desplazamiento del empleo de los pequeños establecimientos hacia los grandes. Cuando el mínimo es bajo, se supone que el ámbito de estas estadísticas será muy amplio y permitirá obtener una aproximación muy estrecha de la fluctuación del empleo remunerado.

El segundo tipo se relaciona con una muestra de establecimientos. Su principal dificultad es asegurar que la muestra siga siendo representativa del conjunto. Así, por ejemplo, la transformación de la estructura industrial, el auge y la decadencia de establecimientos individuales, la evolución demográfica y las considerables variaciones de los niveles de actividad de algunos sectores económicos contribuyen a una distorsión acumulativa de la muestra que puede llegar a ser importante al cabo de varios años.

Con respecto al primer tipo de estadísticas (todos los establecimientos de una cierta importancia), las de ciertos países, donde sólo se pueden obtener para períodos de un año o más, se las puede combinar con estadísticas del segundo tipo (muestras de establecimientos), que es posible obtener para períodos más breves, mediante enlaces (encadenamiento) o interpolaciones.

Algunas estadísticas se fundan en las estimaciones oficiales comunicadas por autoridades nacionales que, por lo general, se combinan con informaciones provenientes de una o más de otras fuentes, tales como los registros de seguros. Esta fuente abarca la población cubierta por regímenes de seguros de salud, accidente, paro y semejantes. El número de contribuyentes o de contribuciones pagadas da una medida del número de personas aseguradas con empleo (las personas sin empleo están exentas del pago de contribuciones). Con frecuencia se excluyen de estas estadísticas las personas que han trabajado muy poco tiempo, las que perciben pagos muy escasos y las mayores de una cierta edad. Además de la evolución del número de personas con empleo, las estadísticas basadas en datos de los registros de seguros también pueden reflejar modificaciones del alcance de la cobertura de ciertos grupos industriales, de ocupaciones o de situación en el empleo.

La proporción de mujeres entre los empleados asalariados en el sector no agrícola es uno de los indicadores de los Objetivos de Desarrollo del Milenio.

Desempleo

En la *Resolución sobre estadísticas de la población económicamente activa, del empleo, del desempleo y del subempleo*, adoptada por la decimotercera Conferencia Internacional de Estadísticos del Trabajo (Ginebra, 1982)[2], figura la siguiente definición del desempleo:

«1) 'Personas desempleadas' son todas aquellas personas que tengan más de cierta edad especificada y que durante el período de referencia se hallen:

---

[2] Para el texto completo de la resolución, véase OIT: *Recomendaciones internacionales de actualidad en estadísticas del trabajo* (Ginebra, 2000) o el sitio Web de la Oficina de Estadística de la OIT: www.ilo.org/stat.

a) 'sin empleo', es decir, que no tengan un empleo asalariado o un empleo independiente, tal como se les define en el párrafo 9;

b) 'corrientemente disponibles para trabajar', es decir, disponibles para trabajar en empleo asalariado o en empleo independiente durante el período de referencia; y

c) 'en busca de empleo', es decir, que habían tomado medidas concretas para buscar un empleo asalariado o un empleo independiente en un período reciente especificado. Las medidas concretas pueden incluir el registro en oficinas de colocación públicas o privadas, diligencias en los lugares de trabajo, explotaciones agrícolas, fábricas, mercados u otros lugares de concurrencia, avisos en los periódicos o respuestas a las ofertas que aparecen en ellos, solicitud de ayuda a amigos y familiares, búsqueda de terrenos, edificios, maquinaria o equipos para establecer su propia empresa, gestiones para conseguir recursos financieros, solicitudes para obtener permisos y licencias, etc.

2) En situaciones en que los medios convencionales de búsqueda de empleo son insuficientes, en que el mercado laboral está bastante desorganizado o es de alcance limitado, en que la absorción de la mano de obra es, en el momento considerado, inadecuada, o en que la fuerza de trabajo está compuesta principalmente por personas con empleo independiente, la definición estándar de desempleo dada en el subpárrafo 1) anterior puede aplicarse suprimiendo el criterio de búsqueda de empleo.

3) Al aplicarse el criterio de disponibilidad actual para trabajar, especialmente en las situaciones descritas en el subpárrafo 2) anterior, deberían considerarse métodos apropiados a fin de tener en cuenta las circunstancias nacionales. Estos métodos podrían basarse en nociones tales como el deseo actual de trabajar y que haya trabajado ya, la voluntad de aceptar un empleo remunerado con sueldo o salario en las condiciones prevalecientes en la localidad y la disposición para emprender una actividad independiente, de contar con los recursos financieros y las facilidades indispensables.

4) Aunque la definición estándar de desempleo implica el criterio de búsqueda de trabajo, las personas sin empleo y corrientemente disponibles para trabajar, que hayan tomado medidas para empezar a trabajar en un empleo asalariado o en un empleo independiente, en una fecha subsiguiente al período de referencia, deberían ser consideradas como desempleadas.

5) Se debería considerar como desempleadas a las personas ausentes temporalmente de su trabajo y sin un vínculo formal a su empleo, que se hallen actualmente disponibles para trabajar y buscando empleo, de conformidad con la definición estándar de desempleo. Sin embargo, y dependiendo de las circunstancias y políticas nacionales, los países podrían preferir suprimir el criterio de búsqueda de empleo en el caso de personas suspendidas de su trabajo. En tales casos, las personas suspendidas de su trabajo que no estaban en busca de empleo, pero se incluían en la categoría de desempleadas, deberían ser identificadas como una subcategoría aparte.

6) Los estudiantes, trabajadores del hogar y otras personas dedicadas a actividades no económicas durante el período de referencia, que satisfagan los criterios establecidos en los subpárrafos 1) y 2) anteriores, deberían considerarse como personas desempleadas y, si fuese posible, clasificarse aparte.»

Las definiciones nacionales de desempleo pueden diferir de la definición internacional estándar recomendada. Entre otros aspectos, las definiciones nacionales pueden variar de un país a otro respecto de los límites de edad, los períodos de referencia, los criterios para determinar que una persona está buscando trabajo, el tratamiento de las personas temporalmente suspendidas y de las que buscan empleo por primera vez (véase también las descripciones de *Fuentes y Métodos* disponibles por separado y en la base de datos en línea LABORSTA).

La forma de considerar a las personas desempleadas con respecto a la clasificación por situación en el empleo también presenta marcadas diferencias según los países. Por lo general, los desempleados con una experiencia de trabajo anterior se clasifican según su último empleo y se incluyen entre los asalariados, pero en ciertos casos, al igual que buscan un primer empleo, forman la parte más importante del grupo de personas no clasificables por su situación en el empleo.

Aún utilizando los sistemas internacionales de clasificación (de actividad económica y ocupación), las prácticas nacionales también pueden diferir en cuanto a la clasificación de los desempleados con experiencia de trabajo anterior, a menudo incluidos en la categoría residual de los sistemas internacionales, es decir, las actividades no definidas con precisión de la CIIU o los trabajadores no clasificables por ocupación de la CIUO.

La comparación entre países también se ve obstaculizada por la diversidad de fuentes utilizadas para obtener información sobre el desempleo y por las diferencias de ámbito y alcance de dichas fuentes.

En general, se pueden distinguir cuatro principales fuentes de estadísticas de desempleo, que se indican en los cuadros. Sin embargo, en general, las estadísticas que se presentan aquí provienen únicamente de una fuente con prioridad a las encuestas de hogares ya que proporcionan estadísticas más exhaustivas. (Estadísticas adicionales se encuentran en la base de datos en línea LABORSTA.)

Las encuestas de la fuerza de trabajo proporcionan generalmente estadísticas más completas sobre el desempleo pues incluyen, en particular, grupos de personas a menudo no abarcadas por las elaboradas a partir de otros métodos de recolección de datos, especialmente las personas que buscan un primer empleo o las personas buscando trabajo sin la ayuda de una oficina de colocación. Habitualmente la definición de desempleo se ajusta bastante a las recomendaciones internacionales y las estadísticas poseen un grado de comparabilidad internacional mayor que las obtenidas de otras fuentes. También son más fiables los porcentajes de desempleo pues se calculan relacionando el número estimado de personas desempleadas con el total estimado de empleados y desempleados (la fuerza de trabajo) derivados de las mismas encuestas.

Algunas de estas estadísticas son estimaciones oficiales comunicadas por autoridades nacionales que habitualmente se combinan con informaciones de una o más de las otras fuentes que aquí se describen. No obstante, como lo demuestran los cuadros, la importancia de esta fuente disminuye a medida que en todos los países aumentan las encuestas de la fuerza de trabajo.

Registros de seguros: las estadísticas de esta fuente se elaboran a partir de datos obtenidos de los registros de los regímenes obligatorios de seguro de paro, que, donde funcionan, suelen tener un vasto alcance de obreros y empleados, o sólo de obreros, del sector industrial. Las tasas de desempleo se calculan cotejando el número de quienes perciben las prestaciones del seguro con el número total de asegurados. Sin embargo, no es posible determinar en qué medida las cifras y los porcentajes de desempleo así obtenidos representan el nivel general del desempleo de los países donde se puede recurrir a esta fuente.

Registros de oficina de colocación: estas estadísticas se refieren por lo general al número de personas que buscan trabajo que figuran en los registros al final de cada mes. Además de las personas sin trabajo, también pueden incluir las que están en huelga, enfermas e incapacitadas temporalmente para trabajar y las que participan en programas de ayuda a los desempleados. En principio no comprenden a las personas que ya tienen un empleo, y su alcance se señala en los cuadros como «*desempleo registrado*». Sin embargo, algunos solicitantes son personas con empleo que buscan otro adicional o un cambio de empleo que también se inscriben en las oficinas de colocación. En consecuencia, el alcance de estas estadísticas se señala en los cuadros como «*solicitantes de empleo*».

El valor de las estadísticas de esta fuente es muy variable. En ciertos casos, cuando las oficinas de colocación funcionan en estrecha colaboración con el seguro de paro y la inscripción en las primeras es condición para recibir las prestaciones del segundo, su fiabilidad es semejante a las estadísticas de los seguros obligatorios de la fuente. En forma similar, cuando las oficinas de colocación funcionan en estrecha colaboración con otros grandes sistemas o programas de ayuda a los desempleados las cifras que de ellas pueden obtenerse son también relativamente satisfactorias durante el desarrollo de dichos programas o sistemas. Por el contrario, si el registro es totalmente voluntario, y especialmente cuando las oficinas sólo funcionan en las zonas urbanas más pobladas de un país, o no son respaldadas ampliamente por las personas que buscan empleo o los empleadores que buscan personal, los datos suelen ser muy incompletos y no constituyen una indicación fiable de la amplitud real del desempleo. El alcance de las cifras se determina en parte por la forma en que se organiza el sistema de colocación y por las ventajas que la inscripción trae consigo, y en parte por la medida en que los trabajadores están habituados a inscribirse. En muchos casos las personas que trabajan en la agricultura y viven en regiones poco pobladas resultan, en el mejor de los casos, poco representadas en las estadísticas. El alcance de las estadísticas de las oficinas de colocación es, pues, más difícil de determinar y sólo en un número muy limitado de casos permiten obtener porcentajes de desempleo satisfactorios. En términos generales, estas estadísticas no son comparables entre países pero, dentro de un mismo país, si no se modifican las leyes ni los reglamentos administrativos u otras disposiciones similares, sus fluctuaciones pueden reflejar cómo cambia la extensión del desempleo registrado con el correr del tiempo.

Salvo que se indique lo contrario, los datos suelen ser medias anuales de datos mensuales, trimestrales o semestrales. Los números indican el tamaño del problema y los porcentajes (tasas de desempleo) su relativa gravedad. Estas tasas se calculan relacionando el número de personas de un grupo dado que estaban desempleadas durante el período de referencia (generalmente un determinado día o semana) con el total de personas empleadas y desempleadas en las mismas fechas. Sin embargo, a menudo las estadísticas por grupo de edad sólo se reúnen en un período determinado o en una fecha específica del año civil y, por lo tanto, no son medias anuales de datos mensuales, trimestrales o semestrales.

Tasas de desempleo por grupo de edad: la tasa de desempleo de jóvenes comprendidos entre los 15 y los 24 años es uno de los indicadores de los Objetivos de Desarrollo del Milenio.

Al relacionar los datos sobre el desempleo por nivel de educación con los de la población económicamente activa por nivel de educación, cabe tener en cuenta las diferencias en materia de fuentes, ámbito, alcance y períodos de referencia.

De conformidad con las recomendaciones internacionales, las personas desempleadas con experiencia de trabajo anterior se clasifican por industria y ocupación en función del último empleo y con los códigos numéricos que corresponden a la categoría pertinente del correspondiente sistema de clasificación. Por otra parte, siempre que es posible se muestran por separado los desempleados sin experiencia de trabajo anterior con la finalidad de distinguirlos de los desempleados con experiencia de trabajo anterior clasificados en actividades no definidas adecuadamente de la CIIU o como trabajadores que no pueden ser clasificados según la ocupación de la CIUO.

Horas de trabajo

Las horas de trabajo se refieren al tiempo dedicado por las personas a actividades que contribuyen a la producción de bienes y servicios definidos por el Sistema de Cuentas Nacionales de las Naciones Unidas. Desde 1962 existen normas estadísticas internacionales únicamente para las horas efectivamente trabajadas y las horas normales de trabajo, adoptadas por la décima Conferencia Internacional de Estadísticos del Trabajo[3]. Están confinadas a los trabajadores asalariados y describen situaciones de trabajo que son típicas de los trabajadores de producción en establecimientos manufactureros. Estas normas sirven de guía para los países cuando producen sus estimaciones nacionales, pero ahora las definiciones nacionales son mucho más completas. Es por esta razón que se están revisando estas normas internacionales para mejorar la cobertura de trabajadores y de situaciones de trabajo, así como para reflejar mejor los diversos arreglos de trabajo. Se espera que la 18.ª Conferencia Internacional de Estadísticas del Trabajo adopte nuevas normas internacionales que incluirán también conceptos tales como las *horas habitualmente trabajadas* y las *horas pagadas*. Los siguientes párrafos proveen definiciones para cada uno de estos conceptos tal como se miden comúnmente en los países.

El concepto de las horas efectivamente trabajadas se refiere al tiempo que las personas ocupadas dedican a actividades laborales durante un período de referencia especificado, incluyendo:

a) tiempo dedicado directamente a la producción (produciendo bienes y servicios, incluyendo las horas extraordinarias pagadas y no pagadas);

b) tiempo dedicado a facilitar la producción, necesario para las actividades laborales o para mejorar la eficiencia de las personas (diseñando, preparando y manteniendo el lugar de trabajo, procedimientos, herramientas, incluyendo recibos, fichas de tiempos e informes), tiempo para cambiar de ropa, actividades de transporte (de puerta en puerta, trayendo productos agrícolas al mercado) y formación relacionada con el unidad económica;

---

[3] Para el texto completo de la resolución, véase OIT: *Recomendaciones internacionales de actualidad en estadísticas del trabajo* (Ginebra, 2000) o el sitio Web de la Oficina de Estadística de la OIT www.ilo.org/public/spanish/bureau/stat).

c) tiempo entre actividades principales (esperando clientes, tiempo muerto por razones tales como la falta ocasional de trabajo o electricidad, paro de máquinas, o accidentes), tiempo de viaje para atender reuniones o asignaciones de trabajo, tiempo de guardia (como para los trabajadores de la salud o de servicios técnicos);

d) tiempo de reposo (breves períodos de descanso o refrescamiento incluidas las interrupciones para tomar té, café o rezar.

Las horas efectivamente trabajadas excluyen el tiempo no trabajado, que sea pagado o no, tales como:

a) las vacaciones pagadas, días feriados pagados, ausencias por enfermedad o maternidad y paternidad;
b) las interrupciones para las comidas;
c) el tiempo dedicado a ir desde el domicilio del trabajador al lugar de trabajo y viceversa, que no es tiempo dedicado a trabajar.

Las horas efectivamente trabajadas cubrirían a todos los tipos de trabajadores, que sean independientes o asalariados; pueden ser pagadas o no y llevarse a cabo en cualquier lugar, incluyendo la calle, el campo, el domicilio, etc.

El concepto de las *horas pagadas* abarcaría a los trabajadores con un empleo asalariado y cubren todas las horas, trabajadas o no, que han sido pagadas por el empleador. Cuando se comparan con las horas efectivamente trabajadas por los asalariados, incluye todas las horas pagadas, aun las que no se trabajan, tales como las vacaciones anuales, los días feriados, ausencias por motivo de enfermedad y otros permisos pagados, y excluye todas las horas trabajadas pero no pagadas (por ejemplo, las horas extraordinarias no pagadas).

El concepto de *horas normales de trabajo* abarca a un subconjunto de los asalariados, esto es, los que están cubiertos por la legislación o reglamentos laborales, y se relaciona con las horas a ser trabajadas por día, semana o por año, de acuerdo con dicha legislación, acuerdo colectivo o laudos arbitrales.

Las *horas habitualmente trabajadas* se relacionan con las horas semanales más comúnmente trabajadas por personas con empleo asalariado o independiente durante un período de referencia largo, tal como un mes, una estación o cualquier otro período largo, esto es, es el valor típico de las horas de trabajo semanales. Cuando se comparan con las horas normales de trabajo, las horas habitualmente trabajadas incluyen todas las horas extraordinarias habituales. Todo el tiempo no trabajado de manera habitual queda por ende excluido.

En general, las estadísticas de horas de trabajo se obtienen principalmente de dos fuentes, las encuestas de establecimientos y las encuestas de hogares. Otras fuentes son las estimaciones oficiales o registros administrativos de la seguridad social. La primera fuente proviene de nóminas de salarios obtenidas por censos o encuestas por muestra a los establecimientos que, generalmente, también reúnen estadísticas de salarios y empleo. Estas estadísticas se refieren usualmente a las horas pagadas y en menor medida a las horas efectivamente trabajadas. Las estadísticas derivadas de estas encuestas o censos suelen tener una cobertura de trabajadores limitada a ciertos grupos de asalariados (por ejemplo, obreros y empleados) o que trabajan en establecimientos de cierto tamaño o sólo en ciertas industrias. La falta de cobertura de trabajadores puede ser un problema importante en los países en donde la mayoría de los trabajadores trabajan en establecimientos pequeños o son independientes. Las cuestiones de cobertura se indican. El segundo tipo de fuente se refiere a las encuestas de hogares. Las estadísticas derivadas de esta fuente se relacionan comúnmente a las horas efectivamente trabajadas y a veces a las horas habitualmente trabajadas. Pueden cubrir a toda la población ocupada, incluyendo a los trabajadores independientes. Algunas estadísticas de encuestas de la fuerza de trabajo se relacionan con las horas trabajadas en el empleo principal solamente (también indicado).

Las estadísticas se refieren a los asalariados en su conjunto, tal como se definen en la Clasificación Internacional de la Situación en el Empleo, CISE-93. Algunas estadísticas que se derivan de encuestas de hogares se refieren a todos los ocupados, y cuando se derivan de encuestas de establecimientos, a sólo un subconjunto de asalariados, por ejemplo, a los obreros o a los empleados. Algunos países limitan la cobertura de trabajadores aún más, incluyendo sólo a los «adultos», a los trabajadores «calificados» o a los «no calificados» (especificado). No existe una definición internacional de obrero ni de empleado. El primer grupo generalmente se refiere a los asalariados manuales o de la producción y el segundo a los trabajadores de oficina.

Las estadísticas generalmente muestran el número promedio de horas de trabajo por semana, pero en algunos casos se muestran las horas por día o por mes (indicado). Para las estadísticas derivadas de encuestas de establecimientos, las horas promedio efectivamente trabajadas o pagadas por semana o por mes se calculan generalmente dividiendo el total de las horas (pagadas o trabajadas) por el promedio de trabajadores en la nómina de salarios durante el mismo período. Las horas (pagadas o trabajadas) promedio por día se calculan generalmente dividiendo el total de las horas durante el mes o quincena por el total de días efectivamente trabajados o pagados durante el mismo período. En las encuestas de hogares el promedio de las horas efectivamente trabajadas se derivan generalmente dividiendo las horas efectivamente trabajadas por el número total de personas ocupadas (o asalariadas) durante el mismo período, usualmente una semana de referencia. En estos cálculos, las personas ausentes del trabajo durante toda la semana de referencia deberían incluirse. En algunas estadísticas las excluyen para reflejar mejor una semana «típica» de trabajo (indicado).

Estos cálculos pueden basarse en una sola observación en el año (cuando la encuesta se efectúa una vez por año), en un conjunto de observaciones (en encuestas mensuales o trimestrales) o en observaciones continuas (esto es, en encuestas que cubren todas las semanas del año). Cuantos más puntos en el tiempo incluya el cálculo del promedio, menor será el efecto de las fluctuaciones estacionales y las variaciones en los conflictos laborales, así como de las ausencias debidas a las vacaciones o la enfermedad.

Al comparar las estadísticas sobre horas de trabajo cabe tener presente que varían en función del método utilizado para calcular el promedio, el número de observaciones utilizadas para su cálculo, y las prácticas laborales relativas al número normal de días de trabajo por semana, de disposiciones reglamentarias y costumbres relativas al trabajo durante el fin de semana y de las horas extraordinarias, la amplitud de las ausencias del trabajo, etc. También estarán afectadas por la cobertura de industrias y empleos. Las estadísticas que excluyen trabajadores en la agricultura, donde las horas de trabajo varían según las estaciones, no serán comparables con las estadísticas que los incluyen. De igual manera, las estadísticas que se refieren al empleo principal solamente serán inferiores a las que cubren todos los empleos o todas las actividades de producción incluyendo a los servicios no pagados[4].

Salarios

La *Resolución sobre un sistema integrado de estadísticas de salarios* adoptada por la duodécima Conferencia Internacional de Estadísticos del Trabajo (Ginebra, 1973)[5] da las definiciones siguientes:

«8. El concepto de ganancias, aplicado a las estadísticas de salarios, se refiere a la remuneración en efectivo y en especie pagada a los trabajadores, en general a intervalos regulares, por el tiempo trabajado o el trabajo realizado, junto con la remuneración por períodos de tiempo no trabajados, tales como vacaciones anuales y otros permisos o días feriados. Las ganancias excluyen las contribuciones que el empleador paga respecto de sus trabajadores a los regímenes de seguridad social y de pensiones, así como las prestaciones recibidas de esos regímenes por los trabajadores. También excluyen las indemnizaciones por despido y por terminación del contrato de trabajo.

9. Las estadísticas de ganancias deberían referirse a la remuneración bruta, o sea al total pagado antes de todo descuento realizado por el empleador por concepto de impuestos, cotizaciones de los trabajadores a los regímenes de seguridad social y pensiones, primas del seguro de vida, cotizaciones sindicales y otras obligaciones del trabajador.

10. 1) Las ganancias incluirán: salarios y sueldos directos, remuneración por períodos de tiempo no trabajados (con exclusión de la indemnización por despido y terminación del contrato de trabajo), primas y gratificaciones, subsidios de vivienda y asignaciones familiares pagadas por el empleador directamente al trabajador.

   a) Los salarios y sueldos directos por el tiempo trabajado o el trabajo realizado incluyen: i) salario básico por tiempo normal trabajado; ii) incentivos pagados a los trabajadores remunerados por tiempo; iii) ganancias de los trabajadores a destajo (excluidos los suplementos por horas extraordinarias); iv) suplemento por cumplimiento de horas extraordinarias, trabajo por turnos, trabajo nocturno y en días feriados; v) comisiones pagadas al personal de ventas y otros empleados. Se incluyen: primas por antigüedad, por calificaciones especiales y por diferencias debidas a las zonas geográficas, primas de responsabilidad y por trabajos sucios, peligrosos y penosos; pagos efectuados de acuerdo con los sistemas de salario garantizado; asignaciones de costo de vida y otras asignaciones regulares;

   b) La remuneración por períodos de tiempo no trabajados comprenden los pagos directos a los trabajadores por días feriados públicos, vacaciones anuales y otros períodos no trabajados remunerados por el empleador;

   c) Las primas y gratificaciones abarcan las primas estacionales y de fin de año (aguinaldos), pagos adicionales por vacaciones como complemento de la paga normal de las mismas y primas de participación en los beneficios.

2) Las estadísticas de ganancias deberían distinguir entre los pagos en efectivo y los pagos en especie.

...

12. Las tasas de salarios deberían incluir los salarios básicos, el valor de las asignaciones por costo de vida y otros subsidios garantizados y pagados regularmente, pero deberían excluir los pagos por horas extraordinarias, primas y gratificaciones, asignaciones familiares y otros pagos de seguridad social a cargo de los empleadores. Las asignaciones concedidas graciosamente en especie, como complemento de las tasas normales de salarios, deben ser también excluidas.

13. Asimismo, deberían distinguirse claramente las estadísticas de tasas de salarios (generalmente tasas mínimas o corrientes) fijadas por la ley o los reglamentos, los contratos colectivos o laudos arbitrales, o en aplicación de los mismos, de las estadísticas que se refieren a las tasas de salarios efectivamente pagadas a los trabajadores en forma individual. Cada uno de estos tipos de tasas de salarios es útil y responde a propósitos particulares.

14. Las tasas de salario por tiempo durante los períodos normales de trabajo deberían distinguirse de las tasas especiales y de otro tipo, tales como las pagadas por trabajo a destajo, por horas extraordinarias y como suplemento por trabajo nocturno y en días feriados, y por trabajo por turnos.»

Las estadísticas de salarios son, generalmente, estadísticas de ganancias medias por trabajador y, en algunos casos, de tasas medias de salarios. Ocasionalmente, si faltan cifras absolutas, se reproducen índices de salarios. Algunas series sólo comprenden obreros (es decir, trabajadores manuales o de la producción), mientras que otras se refieren a los empleados (es decir, trabajadores no manuales) o a todos los asalariados (es decir, obreros y empleados). En las notas de pie de página se señala si se refieren a grupos específicos de trabajadores (como adultos, trabajadores calificados o no calificados). Salvo indicación expresa en contrario, las series se refieren tanto a trabajadores como a trabajadoras, con independencia de su edad. Siempre que es posible los datos se presentan desglosados por sexo.

Las estadísticas sobre ganancias medias se obtienen principalmente de los datos sobre nóminas reunidos por censos o encuestas por muestra a los establecimientos que, generalmente, también informan sobre horas de trabajo y empleo. En unos pocos casos las ganancias medias se fundan en estadísticas de la seguridad social, convenios colectivos u otras fuentes. Las distintas fuentes se indican en los cuadros. Cuando varias fuentes se encuentran disponibles, sólo una se utiliza aquí – la más exhaustiva –, y las estadísticas que provienen de otras fuentes se encuentran en la base de datos en línea LABORSTA.

Los datos sobre dichas ganancias, obtenidos de las nóminas de salarios, se refieren en general a los pagos en efectivo del empleador (antes de deducir los impuestos y las cotizaciones de la seguridad social a cargo de los trabajadores) y comprenden la remuneración de las horas normales de trabajo; el pago de las horas extraordinarias; la remuneración de las horas de trabajo pagadas pero no efectuadas (días feriados, vacaciones anuales, ausencias por motivo de

---

[4] Para más amplia información sobre las diferencias de alcance, definiciones y métodos de cálculo, etc., que utilizan las diversas series nacionales, véase OIT: *Fuentes y Métodos: Estadísticas del Trabajo* (anteriormente *Fuentes y Métodos Estadísticos*), Vol.2: «Empleo, salarios, horas de trabajo y costo de la mano de obra (encuestas de establecimientos)», segunda edición (Ginebra, 1995); Vol.3: «Población económicamente activa, empleo, desempleo y horas de trabajo (encuestas de hogares)», segunda edición (Ginebra, 1992), publicado como Documento de trabajo; Vol.4: «Empleo, desempleo, salarios y horas de trabajo (registros administrativos y fuentes conexas)» (Ginebra, 1989). Todas estas publicaciones se pueden consultar en nuestra base de datos en línea en http://laborsta.ilo.org.

[5] Para el texto completo de la resolución, véase OIT: *Recomendaciones internacionales de actualidad en estadísticas del trabajo* (Ginebra, 2000) o el sitio Web de la Oficina de Estadística de la OIT: www.ilo.org/stat.

enfermedad y otros permisos pagados); las primas y gratificaciones, las asignaciones por carestía de vida y pagos especiales (por ejemplo, las gratificaciones de fin de año). Cuando las ganancias comprenden también el valor de los pagos en especie y las asignaciones familiares, se indica el hecho en una nota a pie de página. Las estadísticas de las ganancias calculadas sobre la base de los registros del seguro social suelen arrojar promedios más bajos que los obtenidos basándose en las nóminas de salarios, ya que aquéllos pueden excluir los pagos por horas extraordinarias, primas de estímulo, etc., así como también los salarios que sobrepasan de determinado límite.

Las estadísticas de tasas de salarios se basan de ordinario en los contratos colectivos, en las decisiones arbitrales o en otros procedimientos de fijación de salarios, donde generalmente se especifican las tasas mínimas en determinadas ocupaciones o para grupos particulares de trabajadores. En algunos países las tasas realmente pagadas se aproximan mucho a esos mínimos. En países donde está muy generalizada la práctica de fijar las tasas de salarios, se calculan las tasas medias de salarios en determinadas industrias o grupos de industrias utilizando como ponderaciones las cifras correspondientes a la importancia numérica en un año dado de las diferentes ocupaciones sobre las cuales se dispone de tasas en las industrias comprendidas en las estadísticas. Las estadísticas de tasas de salarios se refieren generalmente sólo a las tasas para los adultos que trabajan las horas normales, y por lo mismo no se incluyen los pagos por horas extraordinarias y por suplementos de salarios. En cambio, con frecuencia se incluyen en las estadísticas tanto las asignaciones por carestía de vida como otras asignaciones determinadas por el sistema de fijación de salarios (por ejemplo, los subsidios de vivienda). Algunos países establecen promedios de tasas efectivamente pagadas (ganancias de tiempo seguido) sirviéndose de las nóminas de pagos de establecimientos y utilizando el mismo método que para las ganancias medias. Las tasas efectivamente pagadas comprenden en general la remuneración del tiempo normalmente trabajado, es decir, las horas ordinarias y las extraordinarias, pero excluyen las primas de estímulo y otras gratificaciones, como también la porción correspondiente a las primas en la remuneración por horas extraordinarias. Las tasas efectivamente pagadas son compiladas a veces por los inspectores del trabajo.

Los diferentes tipos de estadísticas de salarios se indican en los cuadros y en notas de pie de página.

Todos los datos se expresan en moneda nacional.

Los datos sobre las ganancias presentan fluctuaciones que reflejan la influencia tanto de los cambios en las tasas de salarios como en los demás suplementos de los salarios. Además, las ganancias diarias, semanales o mensuales dependen en gran parte de las variaciones en el promedio de horas de trabajo. Las estadísticas de las tasas de salarios no revelan la influencia de las modificaciones de los suplementos de los salarios ni la influencia de las variaciones de las horas de trabajo. Las fluctuaciones de las ganancias medias que se obtienen de las nóminas de salarios globales dependen también de los cambios en la estructura del empleo, es decir, la mayor o menor importancia relativa que tengan los hombres y las mujeres, los trabajadores no calificados y los trabajadores calificados, los trabajadores a tiempo completo y a tiempo parcial, etc.; las tasas medias de salarios se calculan ordinariamente utilizando como ponderación la estructura del empleo en un año determinado. Las ganancias medias por hora son ordinariamente mayores que las tasas por hora, ya que las primeras incluyen el pago de las horas extraordinarias, las primas, las bonificaciones y otras gratificaciones que no se incluyen en las estadísticas de tasas de salarios. Las ganancias medias por semana o por mes deberían ser más elevadas que sus correspondientes tasas, pero a veces pueden no superar dichas tasas de salarios por razón de la pérdida de tiempo laborable a causa de enfermedad, absentismo o trabajo a tiempo parcial. Al hacer comparaciones entre las estadísticas de salarios se deben tener presentes las diferencias de conceptos, alcance, métodos de compilación y de presentación de los datos.

Sin embargo, se debería tener presente que los datos sobre salarios no reflejan las ganancias netas o disponibles de los trabajadores y que se refieren más bien a las ganancias brutas, antes de cualquier deducción de los impuestos o de las cotizaciones de la seguridad social.

Al comparar datos sobre los salarios de la agricultura con los de otras actividades, se debería tener presente que los sistemas de pago, las clases de contratos y los acuerdos de trabajo del sector agrícola difieren con frecuencia de los que predominan en los demás. Siempre que es posible se distingue entre trabajadores permanentes y estacionales y entre jornaleros de plantilla y ocasionales. La mayoría de las estadísticas se refieren al salario total pagado íntegramente en metálico o a la parte del mismo pagada en efectivo, aun cuando los trabajadores reciban complementos en especie. En unos pocos casos se incluye el valor de los alimentos y/o del alojamiento que proporciona el empleador. Siempre que es posible se indica en notas de pie de página si las ganancias incluyen el valor de los pagos en especie.

Las comparaciones internacionales de salarios en la agricultura están sujetas a mayores reservas que en las demás actividades económicas. La naturaleza del trabajo realizado por las distintas clases de trabajadores agrícolas, así como el número de horas de trabajo por día y por semana, también presentan grandes variaciones según los países. Las fluctuaciones estacionales de los salarios agrícolas son más importantes en algunos países que en otros. Los métodos seguidos por los distintos países para estimar el valor monetario de las remuneraciones en especie no son uniformes.

En las comparaciones internacionales se deberían también tener en cuenta las diferencias existentes entre los países, los precios del consumo de los bienes y servicios y la necesidad de disponer de una moneda de referencia y de tasas de cambio adecuadas; en cambio, en los análisis sobre la evolución a través del tiempo de los salarios se debería tener en cuenta la evolución de los precios del consumo, para las mismas categorías de trabajadores, durante el mismo período.

Para más amplias informaciones, véase OIT: *Un sistema integrado de estadísticas de salarios: Manual metodológico* (Ginebra, 1992). Para información sobre las diferencias de alcance, definiciones y métodos de cálculo, etc. utilizados para las diversas series nacionales, véase OIT: *Fuentes y Métodos*, disponible en la base de datos en línea LABORSTA.

Lesiones profesionales

La *Resolución sobre estadísticas de lesiones profesionales (ocasionadas por accidentes del trabajo)* adoptada por la decimosexta Conferencia Internacional de Estadísticos del Trabajo (CIET) (Ginebra, 1998)[6] contiene las siguientes definiciones para los efectos de las estadísticas:

---

[6] Para el texto completo de la resolución, véase OIT: *Recomendaciones internacionales de actualidad en estadísticas del trabajo* (Ginebra, 2000) o el sitio Web de la Oficina de Estadística de la OIT: www.ilo.org/stat.

«accidente de trabajo: hecho imprevisto y no intencionado, incluidos los actos de violencia, que se deriva del trabajo o está en relación con el mismo y causa una lesión, una enfermedad o la muerte a uno o a más trabajadores;

se considerarán accidentes del trabajo los accidentes de viaje, de transporte o de tránsito por la vía pública en que los trabajadores resultan lesionados y que se originan con ocasión o en el curso del trabajo, es decir, que se producen mientras realizan alguna actividad económica, se encuentran en el lugar de trabajo o efectúan tareas encomendadas por el empleador;

lesión profesional: toda lesión corporal, enfermedad o muerte causadas por un accidente de trabajo; la lesión profesionales, por lo tanto, distinta de la enfermedad profesional, que es aquella contraída como resultado de la exposición a factores de riesgo inherentes a la actividad laboral;

caso de lesión profesional: el caso de un trabajador que sufre una lesión profesional causada por un accidente de trabajo;

incapacidad laboral: incapacidad de la víctima, a causa de una lesión profesional, para realizar las tareas habituales de su trabajo, correspondientes al empleo o puesto ocupado en el momento de sufrir el accidente.»

Las estadísticas de lesiones profesionales de esta publicación se conforman en la medida de lo posible a las recomendaciones de la decimosexta CIET. Los datos deberían abarcar a todos los trabajadores, independientemente de su situación en el empleo (por ejemplo, asalariados o trabajadores independientes, incluyendo empleadores y trabajadores por cuenta propia), todo el país, todas las ramas de actividad económica y todos los sectores de la economía.

En general, se excluyen los siguientes casos: casos de enfermedad profesional (una enfermedad profesional es aquella contraída como resultado de la exposición a factores de riesgo inherentes a la actividad laboral) y casos de lesión provocados por accidente de trayecto (un accidente de trayecto es un accidente que ocurre en el camino habitual, en cualquier dirección, que recorre el trabajador entre el lugar de trabajo o el lugar de formación relacionada con su trabajo y: i) su residencia principal o secundaria; ii) el lugar en que suele tomar sus comidas; o iii) el lugar en que suele cobrar su remuneración, y que le ocasiona la muerte o lesiones corporales).

Los tipos de estadísticas presentadas para los países se determinan por la fuente de los datos. Estos provienen en general de sistemas de declaración de accidentes del trabajo (por ejemplo, a la inspección del trabajo) o de los regímenes de indemnización de lesiones profesionales; no obstante las encuestas de establecimientos y de hogares se utilizan en ciertos países. El tipo de fuente define el alcance de las estadísticas. En muchos países, el alcance de las obligaciones de declarar un accidente del trabajo o de indemnizar las lesiones profesionales, así como el alcance de las estadísticas, puede limitarse a ciertos grupos de trabajadores (a los asalariados lo más frecuente), a ciertas actividades económicas, a los casos de lesión con un mínimo de días de incapacidad, etc. El tipo de fuente se indica en cada cuadro, y también se indica el tipo de lesiones abarcadas (declaradas o indemnizadas).

Las estadísticas se refieren a los casos de lesión profesional acaecidos durante el año indicado. El total de días perdidos como consecuencia de los mismos se incluye en las estadísticas relativas al año en que ocurre el accidente.

Los trabajadores en el grupo de referencia son aquellos trabajadores integrantes del grupo que se examina y que es abarcado por la fuente estadística de lesiones profesionales (como, por ejemplo, los hombres o las mujeres, una actividad económica, ocupación, región o grupo de edad específico, o en cualesquiera combinaciones de estas categorías, o los que están incluidos en un régimen de seguro específico). El número de trabajadores en el grupo de referencia varía según los países, la actividad económica y los períodos, debido a razones diferentes, incluyendo las diferencias de tamaño y composición del empleo. Estas diferencias se toman en cuenta utilizando medidas comparativas, como tasas de frecuencia, de incidencia o de gravedad.

Un aumento o una disminución del número de casos de lesión profesional ocurridos durante un período puede reflejar no sólo la modificación de las condiciones o del medio ambiente de trabajo, sino también la de los procedimientos de declaración o de recolección de datos, o de las leyes y reglamentos de declaración o indemnización de lesiones profesionales en el país de que se trata.

Los casos de incapacidad temporal corresponden al número de casos de lesión profesional en los cuales el trabajador lesionado no puede trabajar a partir del día siguiente a aquél del accidente, pero puede más tarde realizar las tareas habituales de su trabajo, correspondientes al empleo o puesto ocupado en el momento de sufrir el accidente, dentro de un período de un año a partir del día del accidente.

Las *tasas de frecuencia* se calculan en general como el número de nuevos casos de lesión (mortal y no mortal) durante el año dividido entre el total de horas trabajadas por los trabajadores del grupo de referencia durante el año, y multiplicado por 1.000.000. Las *tasas de incidencia* se calculan como el número de nuevos casos de lesión durante el año dividido entre el total de trabajadores del grupo de referencia durante el año, y multiplicado por 100.000.

El tipo de tasa (por 1.000.000 horas trabajadas, por 100.000 trabajadores empleados, por 100.000 asalariados, por 100.000 trabajadores asegurados, etc.) se indica al comienzo de cada cuadro.

Los días perdidos son el número total de días perdidos por casos de lesión profesional con incapacidad temporal. Para ciertos países se incluyen las estimaciones de días perdidos por casos de incapacidad permanente. Se miden en general en días civiles durante los cuales el trabajador lesionado fue incapaz temporalmente de trabajar, no incluido el día del accidente, hasta un año como máximo. Los datos para ciertos países, particularmente cuando la fuente es un régimen de indemnización de accidentes, se miden en días de trabajo. Las ausencias del trabajo de menos de un día para seguir un tratamiento médico no se incluyen.

La información que se presenta aquí ha de utilizarse cuidadosamente, sobre todo al efectuar comparaciones internacionales. Las fuentes, métodos de recolección y alcance de datos y clasificaciones utilizadas pueden variar de un país a otro. Así, por ejemplo, su alcance puede limitarse a ciertos grupos de trabajadores (asalariados, trabajadores asegurados, trabajadores a tiempo completo, etc.), a ciertas actividades económicas, a establecimientos que emplean más de un cierto número de trabajadores, a casos de lesión con incapacidad de más de un cierto número de días, etc. Las descripciones de las fuentes, ámbito, definiciones y métodos utilizados en cada país para elaborar las estadísticas figuran en *Fuentes y Métodos* y en la base de datos en línea LABORSTA.

Huelgas y cierres patronales

La *Resolución sobre las estadísticas de huelgas, cierres patronales y otras acciones causadas por conflictos laborales*, adoptada por la decimoquinta Conferencia Internacional de Estadísticos del Trabajo (Ginebra, 1993)[7], da, a efectos estadísticos, las definiciones siguientes:

«Se entiende por huelga una interrupción temporal del trabajo efectuada por uno o varios grupos de trabajadores con objeto de obtener reivindicaciones o rechazar exigencias o expresar quejas o de apoyar las reivindicaciones o las quejas de otros trabajadores.

Se entiende por cierre patronal el cierre temporal, ya sea parcial o total, de uno o varios centros de trabajo decidido por uno o varios empleadores o el impedimento por parte de éstos del desarrollo de la actividad laboral de sus trabajadores con objeto de lograr una reivindicación o rechazar exigencias o de apoyar las reivindicaciones o las quejas de otros empleadores.

Trabajadores implicados en una huelga: los trabajadores directamente implicados en una huelga son los que participaron directamente interrumpiendo el trabajo. Los trabajadores indirectamente implicados en una huelga son los asalariados de los establecimientos implicados o los trabajadores independientes que pertenecen al grupo implicado, que no participaron directamente interrumpiendo su trabajo, pero que no pudieron trabajar a causa de la huelga.

Trabajadores implicados en un cierre patronal: los trabajadores directamente implicados en un cierre patronal son los asalariados de los establecimientos implicados a los que el conflicto de trabajo afectó directamente y que no pudieron trabajar a causa del cierre patronal. Los trabajadores indirectamente implicados en un cierre patronal son los asalariados de los establecimientos implicados a los que el conflicto de trabajo no afectó directamente, pero que no pudieron trabajar a causa del cierre patronal.

Un conflicto de trabajo o conflicto laboral es una situación de desacuerdo referente a una cuestión o conjunto de cuestiones con relación a la cual o a las cuales existe una discrepancia entre trabajadores y empleadores, o acerca de la cual o las cuales los trabajadores o empleadores expresan una reivindicación o queja o dan su apoyo a las reivindicaciones o quejas de otros trabajadores o empleadores.»

Las definiciones que utilizan los países pueden variar de las anteriores según sea la fuente de las estadísticas. Estas provienen por lo general de registros administrativos de los servicios de conciliación u otros interesados en las relaciones laborales, etc. Los datos pueden provenir de diversas fuentes, comprendidos los avisos de huelgas, informes periodísticos y averiguación directa a empleadores o a organizaciones de trabajadores. El tipo de fuente se indica en cada cuadro.

Los datos abarcan indistintamente las huelgas y los conflictos laborales, pues las estadísticas de la mayoría de los países no hacen distinción entre estas dos clases de acción reivindicativa. En general, las series abarcan toda clase de huelgas y cierres patronales, así como toda actividad económica, y se refieren tanto a las acciones en curso durante el año como a las que continúan las iniciadas el año anterior. Toda diferencia con respecto a lo antes expresado se señala en notas de pie de página. Si las estadísticas sólo abarcan huelgas y cierres patronales de cierta entidad, es decir, que superan ciertos límites relativos al número de trabajadores implicados, duración, total del tiempo no trabajado o una combinación de dos o más de éstos, dichos límites también se indican en notas de pie de página.

Según las recomendaciones internacionales, todas las interrupciones del trabajo que se deban a un mismo conflicto laboral deben considerarse como una sola huelga o cierre patronal siempre que el lapso entre estas interrupciones no supere dos meses. En algunos países se utilizan criterios distintos para considerar como único un cierre patronal o una huelga; por ejemplo, cada interrupción del trabajo de cada establecimiento puede considerarse como un mismo y único cierre patronal o huelga. En tales casos, el número de huelgas y cierres patronales y el de trabajadores implicados suelen ser más elevados que los que se habrían podido obtener siguiendo las recomendaciones, al punto que algunas veces el número de trabajadores implicados supera el total del empleo de la rama de actividad económica interesada.

Al utilizar estos datos cabe tener presente que el número de trabajadores expuestos al riesgo de una huelga o un cierre patronal varía según la actividad económica o el país considerado y de un período a otro. Por tal motivo es útil calcular medidas relativas, como las tasas de gravedad, en las cuales el total del tiempo no trabajado como consecuencia de huelgas y cierres patronales se relaciona con el número total de trabajadores.

Si una huelga o un cierre patronal abarca varias actividades económicas, la información pertinente se da, habitualmente, para cada una de las actividades afectadas. En consecuencia, el número total de huelgas y cierres patronales que se presenta para la actividad económica en su conjunto puede ser inferior a la suma de los datos de cada actividad.

El número de días no trabajados como consecuencia de las huelgas y los cierres patronales que tuvieron lugar durante el año indicado se suele medir en términos de la suma de días laborables que hubieran sido normalmente trabajados por cada trabajador implicado de no haberse producido la interrupción de la actividad.

Las estadísticas de tasas de gravedad de huelgas y cierres patronales se calculan por lo general en términos de días no trabajados por 1.000 trabajadores. El tipo de tasa se indica en notas de pie de página.

Las descripciones de las fuentes, ámbito, definiciones y métodos utilizados en el plano nacional para elaborar las estadísticas figuran en *Fuentes y Métodos* y en la base de datos en línea LABORSTA.

Precios al consumidor

La *Resolución sobre índices de los precios al consumidor* adoptada por la decimoséptima Conferencia Internacional de Estadísticos del Trabajo (CIET) (Ginebra, 2003)[8] estipula lo siguiente:

«1. El IPC es un indicador social y económico de coyuntura, construido para medir los cambios experimentados a lo largo del tiempo en relación con el nivel general de precios de los bienes y servicios de consumo que los hogares pagan, adquieren o utilizan para ser consumidos.

2. El índice mide también los cambios experimentados a lo largo del tiempo de los precios de consumo. Esto se puede realizar midiendo el precio de una canasta fija de

---

[7] Para el texto completo de la resolución, véase OIT: *Recomendaciones internacionales de actualidad en estadísticas del trabajo* (Ginebra, 2000) o el sitio Web de la Oficina de Estadística de la OIT: www.ilo.org/stat.

[8] Para el texto completo de la resolución, véase OIT: *Decimoséptima Conferencia Internacional de Estadísticos del Trabajo, Informe de la Conferencia* (Ginebra, 2003) o el sitio Web de la Oficina de Estadística de la OIT, http://www.ilo.org/stat.

bienes y servicios de calidad y características semejantes a los artículos de la canasta seleccionados para ser representativos de los gastos de los hogares durante un año o durante otro período específico. Este índice se conoce con el nombre de índice de precios de una canasta fija.

3. El índice también puede apuntar a medir los efectos que la variación de los precios puede tener en el costo necesario para lograr un nivel de vida constante (es decir, nivel de utilidad o bienestar). Este concepto se denomina índice del costo de la vida (ICV). Un índice de precios de una canasta fija, u otra medida apropiada, puede ser utilizado como una aproximación de un ICV.»

Por lo general, la estimación de un índice de los precios al consumidor se lleva a cabo como una serie de mediciones de las variaciones relativas, de un período a otro, de los precios de un conjunto fijo, constante en cantidades y características, de bienes y servicios de consumo adquiridos, consumidos o pagados por la población de referencia. Cada medición es calculada como una media ponderada de un gran número de índices de agregados elementales. Los índices de cada agregado elemental son estimados utilizando una muestra de precios de un grupo determinado de bienes o servicios obtenidos en, o por residentes de, una región específica, a partir de un conjunto establecido de puntos de venta u otras fuentes de información.

Los índices de precios al consumidor se utilizan con diversos fines, tal como:

a) análisis generales de tipo económico y social y decisiones de políticas;

b) negociación, indización, o ambas cosas, por el gobierno (especialmente de impuestos, contribuciones y beneficios de la seguridad social, remuneraciones y pensiones de los funcionarios, tasa, multas, de la deuda pública y sus intereses), en los contratos privados (sueldos, salarios, primas de seguro y servicios) y en decisiones judiciales (pensiones alimentarias);

c) la medición de los cambios «reales», o las relaciones entre el dinero y los bienes o servicios por los cuales puede ser intercambiado (v.g. para la deflación del valor agregado actual en las cuentas nacionales y de las ventas al por menor); y

d) comparaciones en las variaciones de los precios realizadas con propósitos comerciales, incluida la revaluación contable.

Para algunas de las aplicaciones mencionadas anteriormente pueden ser más convenientes los índices parciales que el índice general de todos los bienes y servicios.

Las ponderaciones son las proporciones de los gastos o del consumo correspondientes a los agregados elementales estimadas sobre la base de la información disponible. A este respecto, la decimoséptima CIET ha recomendado lo siguiente:

«23. Las dos principales fuentes para deducir las ponderaciones son los resultados de las encuestas de gastos de los hogares y las estimaciones de las cuentas nacionales sobre el gasto en consumo de los hogares. Los resultados de las encuestas de gastos de los hogares son indicados para un índice concebido para abarcar los gastos de consumo de los grupos de población de referencia residentes dentro del país, mientras que las estimaciones de las cuentas nacionales son adecuadas para la elaboración de índices relativos a los gastos de consumo dentro del país. ...

24. La información procedente de la fuente principal (encuestas de gastos de los hogares o cuentas nacionales) debería complementarse con toda información disponible sobre las pautas de gasto. Las fuentes de tal información que pueden utilizarse para desglosar los gastos son las encuestas de ventas en establecimientos minoristas, las encuestas relativas a los lugares de compra, las encuestas de producción, los datos sobre exportaciones e importaciones y las fuentes administrativas. Tomando como base estos datos, es posible desglosar aún más las ponderaciones correspondientes a ciertos artículos, por región y tipo de punto de venta. ...»

La decimoséptima CIET ha recomendado además que los precios que sirven para el cálculo de los índices sean:

«54. ... los precios de las transacciones efectivas, incluidos los impuestos indirectos y los descuentos no condicionados, que la población de referencia pagaría, acordaría o calcularía (aceptaría). ... Las propinas pagadas por los servicios, cuando sean obligatorias, deberían considerarse como parte del precio pagado.

55. No deberían incluirse los precios cobrados excepcionalmente por ventas a precios de liquidación de mercancías viejas, echadas a perder durante el almacenamiento, averiadas o deterioradas por cualquier otro motivo, salvo que la venta de estos productos constituya un fenómeno permanente y generalizado. En cambio, deberían incluirse los precios de los saldos, los descuentos, los precios reducidos y las ofertas especiales cuando se apliquen a todos los consumidores sin que se limiten de manera importante las cantidades que cada cliente puede comprar.

52. Los precios deberían recolectarse en todos los tipos de puntos de venta importantes, incluidos los vendedores por Internet, los mercados al aire libre y los mercados informales, así como en los mercados libres y en los mercados de precio controlado. ...»

El campo de aplicación de los índices de los precios al consumidor puede variar de un país a otro, no sólo con respecto a los tipos de hogares o grupos de población cubiertos, sino también en cuanto a su alcance geográfico.

Las prácticas nacionales varían también en lo que se refiere al tratamiento de ciertos elementos que se tienen en cuenta en el cálculo de los índices de los precios al consumidor, tales como artículos estacionales, cambios de calidad, nuevos artículos, bienes duraderos y viviendas ocupadas por su propietario. Los métodos de recolección de los precios o de cálculo de los índices también son diferentes. Por esta razón, los índices de los precios al consumidor publicados en estos cuadros se deben utilizar con precaución, especialmente en materia de negociaciones colectivas y en los cálculos de indización o de deflación. Estos índices sólo pueden utilizarse si el campo de aplicación del índice de los precios al consumidor corresponde estrechamente al del tema de negociación, de indización o de deflación.

Se publican informaciones sobre el campo, las definiciones y los métodos utilizados en el cálculo de los índices de los precios al consumidor difundidos en estos cuadros en *Fuentes y Métodos* disponibles en la base de datos en línea LABORSTA.

Se presentan aquí los índices generales de los precios al consumidor de todos los grupos de artículos de consumo en su conjunto. También se presenta un índice general excluyendo la vivienda. La exclusión de la vivienda del índice general permite mejorar la comparabilidad de las tasas de cambio de los precios entre los países, si bien no elimina todas las dificultades que surgen cuando se hacen tales comparaciones. Este índice es primordialmente un índice que excluye el alquiler (real y/o asignado) y los gastos de conservación y reparaciones de la vivienda. Sin embargo, si tal índice no estuviera disponible a nivel nacional o si su cálculo fuera muy difícil, entonces, por razones prácticas, los países proveen un índice que excluye el componente de vivienda o solamente el alquiler. En tal caso, una nota a pie de página señala las exclusiones particulares (por ejemplo, todo el grupo de la vivienda, alquiler, electricidad, gas y otros combustibles, los gastos de conservación y reparaciones de la vivienda, etcétera).

El índice «Alimentación» incluye las bebidas no alcohólicas solamente. Si las bebidas alcohólicas y/o el tabaco son incluidas en el grupo «Alimentación», una nota a pie de página señala estos casos.

Otros tres grupos principales de índices correspondientes, respectivamente, a: «Electricidad, gas y otros combustibles», «Vestido (Incl. Calzado» y «Alquiler». Los índices de estos grupos, incluyendo el índice de la alimentación, constituyen componentes del índice general. Además de los cuatro grupos de índices, el índice general y el índice general excluyendo la habitación, en la mayoría de los casos, comprenden todos los otros grupos principales de gastos; es decir: «Bebidas alcohólicas y tabaco»; «Muebles, artículos para el hogar y para la conservación ordinaria del hogar»; «Sanidad»; «Transporte»; Comunicaciones»; «Ocio y cultura»; «Educación»; y «Restaurantes y hoteles», y «Otros bienes y servicios». Los índices relativos a estos últimos grupos no se presentan por separado en el Anuario por causa de las variaciones que existen de un país a otro en la composición de los mismos.

Los índices generales y los índices de grupos presentados en los cuadros corresponden a los promedios anuales, aunque en la mayor parte de los casos dichos índices se calculan mensualmente, y en algunos otros trimestral o semestralmente. Las cifras anuales se calculan tomando como base las series originales.

En vista de que también varía el período escogido como base en las diferentes series nacionales, se ha adoptado un período de base uniforme (2000) para la presentación de los datos. En la medida de lo posible, se han calculado nuevamente en su mayor parte estas series dividiendo el índice de cada fecha indicada por el índice del año 2000 y multiplicando el cociente por 100. Cuando se dispone de datos sólo para los años posteriores a 2000, generalmente se presentan los índices escogiendo como base el primer año civil accesible. Esta operación no implica ninguna modificación en el procedimiento de ponderación, etc., utilizado por los distintos países.

Cuando una nueva serie es suficientemente comparable con la anterior, se enlazan las dos series para formar una serie temporal continua. Cuando ha habido interrupción en una serie y ha sido reemplazada por otra serie que no se puede combinar con la anterior, sea por enlace sea por otras estimaciones técnicas, se indica la ruptura en una nota explicativa al pie de la página.

International Standard Industrial Classification of all Economic Activities (ISIC - Rev. 2, 1968) [1]

Major Division 1. Agriculture, Hunting, Forestry and Fishing
11   Agriculture and Hunting
   111   Agricultural and livestock production
   112   Agricultural services
   113   Hunting, trapping and game propagation
12   Forestry and Logging
   121   Forestry
   122   Logging
13   130   Fishing

Major Division 2. Mining and Quarrying
21   210   Coal Mining
22   220   Crude Petroleum and Natural Gas Production
23   230   Metal Ore Mining
29   290   Other Mining

Major Division 3. Manufacturing
31   Manufacture of Food, Beverages and Tobacco
   311-312   Food manufacturing
   313   Beverage industries
   314   Tobacco manufactures
32   Textile, Wearing Apparel and Leather Industries
   321   Manufacture of textiles
   322   Manufacture of wearing apparel, except footwear
   323   Manufacture of leather and products of leather, leather substitutes and fur, except footwear and wearing apparel
   324   Manufacture of footwear, except vulcanized or moulded rubber or plastic footwear
33   Manufacture of Wood and Wood Products, including Furniture
   331   Manufacture of wood and wood and cork products, except furniture
   332   Manufacture of furniture and fixtures, except primarily of metal
34   Manufacture of Paper and Paper Products, Printing and Publishing
   341   Manufacture of paper and paper products
   342   Printing, publishing and allied industries
35   Manufacture of Chemicals and Chemical, Petroleum, Coal, Rubber and Plastic Products
   351   Manufacture of industrial chemicals
   352   Manufacture of other chemical products
   353   Petroleum refineries
   354   Manufacture of miscellaneous products of petroleum and coal
   355   Manufacture of rubber products
   356   Manufacture of plastic products not elsewhere classified
36   Manufacture of Non-Metallic Mineral Products, except Products of Petroleum and Coal
   361   Manufacture of pottery, china and earthenware
   362   Manufacture of glass and glass products
   369   Manufacture of other non-metallic mineral products
37   Basic Metal Industries
   371   Iron and steel basic industries
   372   Non-ferrous metal basic industries
38   Manufacture of Fabricated Metal Products, Machinery and Equipment
   381   Manufacture of fabricated metal products, except machinery and equipment
   382   Manufacture of machinery except electrical
   383   Manufacture of electrical machinery apparatus, appliances and supplies
   384   Manufacture of transport equipment
   385   Manufacture of professional and scientific and measuring and controlling equipment not elsewhere classified, and of photographic and optical goods
39   390   Other Manufacturing Industries

Major Division 4. Electricity, Gas and Water
41   410   Electricity, Gas and Steam
42   420   Water Works and Supply

Major Division 5. Construction
50   500   Construction

Major Division 6. Wholesale and Retail Trade and Restaurants and Hotels
61   610   Wholesale Trade
62   620   Retail Trade
63   Restaurants and Hotels
   631   Restaurants, cafés and other eating and drinking places
   632   Hotels, rooming houses, camps and other lodging places

Major Division 7. Transport, Storage and Communication
71   Transport and Storage
   711   Land transport
   712   Water transport
   713   Air transport
   719   Services allied to transport
72   720   Communication

Major Division 8. Financing, Insurance, Real Estate and Business Services
81   810   Financial Institutions
82   820   Insurance
83   Real Estate and Business Services
   831   Real estate
   832   Business services except machinery and equipment rental and leasing
   833   Machinery and equipment rental and leasing

Major Division 9. Community, Social and Personal Services
91   910   Public Administration and Defence
92   920   Sanitary and Similar Services
93   Social and Related Community Services
   931   Education services
   932   Research and scientific institutes
   933   Medical, dental, other health and veterinary services
   934   Welfare institutions
   935   Business, professional and labour associations
   939   Other social and related community services
94   Recreational and Cultural Services
   941   Motion picture and other entertainment services
   942   Libraries, museums, botanical and zoological gardens, and other cultural services not elsewhere classified

	949	Amusement and recreational services not elsewhere classified
95		Personal and Household Services
	951	Repair services not elsewhere classified
	952	Laundries, laundry services, and cleaning and dyeing plants
	953	Domestic services
	959	Miscellaneous personal services
96	960	International and Other Extra-Territorial Bodies

Major Division 0. Activities not Adequately Defined

00   000   Activities not adequately defined

Note

[1] This Classification consists of Major Divisions (one-digit codes), Divisions (two-digit codes), Major Groups (three-digit codes) and Groups (four-digit codes); the last are not shown separately in this Annex.

For full details see United Nations: *Statistical Papers,* Series M, No. 4, rev. 2 (New York, 1968).

Classification internationale type, par industrie, de toutes les branches d'activité économique (CITI - Rév. 2, 1968) [1]

Branche 1.		**Agriculture, chasse, sylviculture et pêche**
11		Agriculture et chasse
	111	Production agricole et élevage
	112	Activités annexes de l'agriculture
	113	Chasse, piégeage et repeuplement en gibier
12		Sylviculture et exploitation forestière
	121	Sylviculture
	122	Exploitation forestière
13	130	Pêche
Branche 2.		**Industries extractives**
21	210	Extraction du charbon
22	220	Production de pétrole brut et de gaz naturel
23	230	Extraction des minerais métalliques
29	290	Extraction d'autres minéraux
Branche 3.		**Industries manufacturières**
31		Fabrication de produits alimentaires, boissons et tabacs
	311-312	Industries alimentaires
	313	Fabrication des boissons
	314	Industrie du tabac
32		Industries des textiles, de l'habillement et du cuir
	321	Industrie textile
	322	Fabrication d'articles d'habillement, à l'exclusion des chaussures
	323	Industrie du cuir, des articles en cuir et en succédanés du cuir, et de la fourrure, à l'exclusion des chaussures et des articles d'habillement
	324	Fabrication des chaussures, à l'exclusion des chaussures en caoutchouc vulcanisé ou moulé et des chaussures en matière plastique
33		Industrie du bois et fabrication d'ouvrages en bois, y compris les meubles
	331	Industrie du bois et fabrication d'ouvrages en bois et en liège, à l'exclusion des meubles
	332	Fabrication de meubles et d'accessoires, à l'exclusion des meubles et accessoires faits principalement en métal
34		Fabrication de papier et d'articles en papier; imprimerie et édition
	341	Fabrication de papier et d'articles en papier
	342	Imprimerie, édition et industries annexes
35		Industrie chimique et fabrication de produits chimiques, de dérivés du pétrole et du charbon, et d'ouvrages en caoutchouc et en matière plastique
	351	Industrie chimique
	352	Fabrication d'autres produits chimiques
	353	Raffineries de pétrole
	354	Fabrication de divers dérivés du pétrole et du charbon
	355	Industrie du caoutchouc
	356	Fabrication d'ouvrages en matière plastique non classés ailleurs
36		Fabrication de produits minéraux non métalliques, à l'exclusion des dérivés du pétrole et du charbon
	361	Fabrication des grès, porcelaines et faïences
	362	Industrie du verre
	369	Fabrication d'autres produits minéraux non métalliques
37		Industrie métallique de base
	371	Sidérurgie et première transformation de la fonte, du fer et de l'acier
	372	Production et première transformation des métaux non ferreux
38		Fabrication d'ouvrages en métaux, de machines et de matériel
	381	Fabrication d'ouvrages en métaux, à l'exclusion des machines et du matériel
	382	Construction de machines, à l'exclusion des machines électriques
	383	Fabrication de machines, appareils et fournitures électriques
	384	Construction de matériel de transport
	385	Fabrication de matériel médico-chirurgical, d'instruments de précision, d'appareils de mesure et de contrôle non classés ailleurs, de matériel photographique et d'instruments d'optique
39	390	Autres industries manufacturières
Branche 4.		**Electricité, gaz et eau**
41	410	Electricité, gaz et vapeur
42	420	Installations de distribution d'eau et distribution publique de l'eau
Branche 5.		**Bâtiment et travaux publics**
50	500	Bâtiment et travaux publics
Branche 6.		**Commerce de gros et de détail; restaurants et hôtels**
61	610	Commerce de gros
62	620	Commerce de détail
63		Restaurants et hôtels
	631	Restaurants et débits de boissons
	632	Hôtels, hôtels meublés et établissements analogues; terrains de camping
Branche 7.		**Transports, entrepôts et communications**
71		Transports et entrepôts
	711	Transports par la voie terrestre
	712	Transports par eau
	713	Transports aériens
	719	Services auxiliaires des transports
72	720	Communications
Branche 8.		**Banques, assurances, affaires immobilières et services fournis aux entreprises**
81	810	Etablissements financiers
82	820	Assurances
83		Affaires immobilières et services fournis aux entreprises
	831	Affaires immobilières
	832	Services fournis aux entreprises, à l'exclusion de la location de machines et de matériel
	833	Location de machines et de matériel
Branche 9.		**Services fournis à la collectivité, services sociaux et services personnels**
91	910	Administration publique et défense nationale
92	920	Services sanitaires et services analogues

93		Services sociaux et services connexes fournis à la collectivité
	931	Enseignement
	932	Institutions scientifiques et centres de recherche
	933	Services médicaux et dentaires et autres services sanitaires, et services vétérinaires
	934	Œuvres sociales
	935	Associations commerciales, professionnelles et syndicales
	939	Autres services sociaux et services connexes fournis à la collectivité
94		Services récréatifs et services culturels annexes
	941	Films cinématographiques et autres services récréatifs
	942	Bibliothèques, musées, jardins botaniques et zoologiques et autres services culturels non classés ailleurs
	949	Amusements et services récréatifs non classés ailleurs
95		Services fournis aux particuliers et aux ménages
	951	Services de réparation non classés ailleurs
	952	Blanchisserie, teinturerie
	953	Services domestiques
	959	Services personnels divers
96	960	Organisations internationales et autres organismes extra-territoriaux

Branche 0. Activités mal désignées

00	000	Activités mal désignées

Note

[1] Cette classification comprend des *branches* (codes à un chiffre), des *catégories* (codes à deux chiffres), des *classes* (codes à trois chiffres) et des *groupes* (codes à quatre chiffres); ces derniers ne sont pas présentés séparément dans cette annexe.

Pour de plus amples détails, voir Nations Unies: *Etudes statistiques,* série M, n° 4, rév. 2 (New York, 1969).

Clasificación Industrial Internacional Uniforme de Todas las Actividades Económicas (CIIU - Rev. 2, 1968) [1]

Gran división 1. Agricultura, caza, silvicultura y pesca
- 11   Agricultura y caza
  - 111   Producción agropecuaria
  - 112   Servicios agrícolas
  - 113   Caza ordinaria y mediante trampas, y repoblación de animales
- 12   Silvicultura y extracción de madera
  - 121   Silvicultura
  - 122   Extracción de madera
- 13   130   Pesca

Gran división 2. Explotación de minas y canteras
- 21   210   Explotación de minas de carbón
- 22   220   Producción de petróleo crudo y gas natural
- 23   230   Extracción de minerales metálicos
- 29   290   Extracción de otros minerales

Gran división 3. Industrias manufactureras
- 31   Productos alimenticios, bebidas y tabaco
  - 311-312   Fabricación de productos alimenticios
  - 313   Industrias de bebidas
  - 314   Industria del tabaco
- 32   Textiles, prendas de vestir e industrias del cuero
  - 321   Fabricación de textiles
  - 322   Fabricación de prendas de vestir, excepto calzado
  - 323   Industria del cuero y productos de cuero y sucedáneos de cuero y pieles, excepto el calzado y otras prendas de vestir
  - 324   Fabricación de calzado, excepto el de caucho vulcanizado o moldeado o de plástico
- 33   Industria de la madera y productos de la madera, incluidos muebles
  - 331   Industria de la madera y productos de madera y de corcho, excepto muebles
  - 332   Fabricación de muebles y accesorios, excepto los que son principalmente metálicos
- 34   Fabricación de papel y productos de papel; imprentas y editoriales
  - 341   Fabricación de papel y productos de papel
  - 342   Imprentas, editoriales e industrias conexas
- 35   Fabricación de sustancias químicas y de productos químicos, derivados del petróleo y del carbón, de caucho y plásticos
  - 351   Fabricación de sustancias químicas industriales
  - 352   Fabricación de otros productos químicos
  - 353   Refinerías de petróleo
  - 354   Fabricación de productos diversos derivados del petróleo y del carbón
  - 355   Fabricación de productos de caucho
  - 356   Fabricación de productos plásticos, n.e.p.
- 36   Fabricación de productos minerales no metálicos, exceptuando los derivados del petróleo y del carbón
  - 361   Fabricación de objetos de barro, loza y porcelana
  - 362   Fabricación de vidrio y productos de vidrio
  - 369   Fabricación de otros productos minerales no metálicos
- 37   Industrias metálicas básicas
  - 371   Industrias básicas de hierro y acero
  - 372   Industrias básicas de metales no ferrosos
- 38   Fabricación de productos metálicos, maquinaria y equipo
  - 381   Fabricación de productos metálicos, exceptuando maquinaria y equipo
  - 382   Construcción de maquinaria, exceptuando la eléctrica
  - 383   Construcción de maquinaria, aparatos, accesorios y suministros eléctricos
  - 384   Construcción de material de transporte
  - 385   Fabricación de equipo profesional y científico, instrumentos de medida y de control n.e.p., y de aparatos fotográficos e instrumentos de óptica
- 39   390   Otras industrias manufactureras

Gran división 4. Electricidad, gas y agua
- 41   410   Electricidad, gas y vapor
- 42   420   Obras hidráulicas y suministro de agua

Gran división 5. Construcción
- 50   500   Construcción

Gran división 6. Comercio al por mayor y al por menor y restaurantes y hoteles
- 61   610   Comercio al por mayor
- 62   620   Comercio al por menor
- 63   Restaurantes y hoteles
  - 631   Restaurantes, cafés y otros establecimientos que expenden comidas y bebidas
  - 632   Hoteles, casas de huéspedes, campamentos y otros lugares de alojamiento

Gran división 7. Transportes, almacenamiento y comunicaciones
- 71   Transporte y almacenamiento
  - 711   Transporte terrestre
  - 712   Transporte por agua
  - 713   Transporte aéreo
  - 719   Servicios conexos del transporte
- 72   720   Comunicaciones

Gran división 8. Establecimientos financieros, seguros, bienes inmuebles y servicios prestados a las empresas
- 81   810   Establecimientos financieros
- 82   820   Seguros
- 83   Bienes inmuebles y servicios prestados a las empresas
  - 831   Bienes inmuebles
  - 832   Servicios prestados a las empresas, exceptuando el alquiler y arrendamiento de maquinaria y equipo
  - 833   Alquiler y arrendamiento de maquinaria y equipo

Gran división 9. Servicios comunales, sociales y personales
- 91   910   Administración pública y defensa
- 92   920   Servicios de saneamiento y similares
- 93   Servicios sociales y otros servicios comunales conexos
  - 931   Instrucción pública
  - 932   Institutos de investigaciones y científicos
  - 933   Servicios médicos y odontológicos; otros servicios de sanidad y veterinaria
  - 934   Institutos de asistencia social

	935	Asociaciones comerciales, profesionales y laborales
	939	Otros servicios sociales y servicios comunales conexos
94		Servicios de diversión y esparcimiento y servicios
	941	Películas cinematográficas y otros servicios de esparcimiento
	942	Bibliotecas, museos, jardines botánicos y zoológicos y otros servicios culturales, n.e.p.
	949	Servicios de diversión y esparcimiento, n.e.p.
95		Servicios personales y de los hogares
	951	Servicios de reparación, n.e.p.
	952	Lavanderías y servicios de lavandería; establecimientos de limpieza y teñido
	953	Servicios domésticos
	959	Servicios personales diversos
96	960	Organizaciones internacionales y otros organismos extraterritoriales

Gran división 0. Actividades no bien especificadas

| 00 | 000 | Actividades no bien especificadas |

Nota

[1] Esta Clasificación se compone de *Grandes Divisiones* (clave de un dígito), *Divisiones* (clave de dos dígitos), *Agrupaciones* (clave de tres dígitos) y *Grupos* (clave de cuatro dígitos); estos últimos no están presentados separadamente en este anexo.

Para más amplios detalles, véanse Naciones Unidas: *Informes estadísticos,* serie M, núm. 4, rev. 2 (Nueva York, 1969).

International Standard Industrial Classification of all Economic Activities (ISIC - Rev. 3)[1]

Tabulation category A: Agriculture, Hunting and Forestry
01 Agriculture, Hunting and related service activities
02 Forestry, Logging and related service activities

Tabulation category B: Fishing
05 Fishing, Operation of Fish Hatcheries and Fish Farms; Service activities incidental to Fishing

Tabulation category C: Mining and Quarrying
10 Mining of Coal and Lignite; Extraction of Peat
11 Extraction of Crude Petroleum and Natural Gas; Service activities incidental to Oil and Gas extraction, excluding surveying
12 Mining of Uranium and Thorium Ores
13 Mining of Metal Ores
14 Other Mining and Quarrying

Tabulation category D: Manufacturing
15 Manufacture of Food Products and Beverages
16 Manufacture of Tobacco Products
17 Manufacture of Textiles
18 Manufacture of Wearing Apparel; Dressing and Dyeing of Fur
19 Tanning and Dressing of Leather; Manufacture of Luggage, Handbags, Saddlery, Harness and Footwear
20 Manufacture of Wood and of Products of Wood and Cork, except Furniture; Manufacture of articles of Straw and Plaiting Materials
21 Manufacture of Paper and Paper Products
22 Publishing, Printing and Reproduction of Recorded Media
23 Manufacture of Coke, Refined Petroleum Products and Nuclear Fuel
24 Manufacture of Chemicals and Chemical Products
25 Manufacture of Rubber and Plastics Products
26 Manufacture of Other Non-Metallic Mineral Products
27 Manufacture of Basic Metals
28 Manufacture of Fabricated Metal Products, except Machinery and Equipment
29 Manufacture of Machinery and Equipment NEC[2]
30 Manufacture of Office, Accounting and Computing Machinery
31 Manufacture of Electrical Machinery and Apparatus NEC[2]
32 Manufacture of Radio, Television and Communication Equipment and Apparatus
33 Manufacture of Medical, Precision and Optical Instruments, Watches and Clocks
34 Manufacture of Motor Vehicles, Trailers and Semi-Trailers
35 Manufacture of other Transport Equipment
36 Manufacture of Furniture; Manufacturing NEC[2]
37 Recycling

Tabulation category E: Electricity, Gas and Water Supply
40 Electricity, Gas, Steam and Hot Water Supply
41 Collection, Purification and Distribution of Water

Tabulation category F: Construction
45 Construction

Tabulation category G: Wholesale and Retail Trade; Repair of Motor Vehicles, Motorcycles and Personal and Household Goods
50 Sale, Maintenance and Repair of Motor Vehicles and Motorcycles; Retail Sale of Automotive Fuel
51 Wholesale Trade and Commission Trade, except of Motor Vehicles and Motorcycles
52 Retail Trade, except of Motor Vehicles and Motorcycles; Repair of Personal and Household Goods

Tabulation category H: Hotels and Restaurants
55 Hotels and Restaurants

Tabulation category I: Transport, Storage and Communications
60 Land Transport; Transport via Pipelines
61 Water Transport
62 Air Transport
63 Supporting and Auxiliary Transport Activities; Activities of Travel Agencies
64 Post and Telecommunications

Tabulation category J: Financial Intermediation
65 Financial Intermediation, except Insurance and Pension Funding
66 Insurance and Pension Funding, except Compulsory Social Security
67 Activities auxiliary to Financial Intermediation

Tabulation category K: Real Estate, Renting and Business Activities
70 Real Estate activities
71 Renting of Machinery and Equipment without Operator and of Personal and Household Goods
72 Computer and related activities
73 Research and Development
74 Other Business activities

Tabulation category L: Public Administration and Defence; Compulsory Social Security
75 Public Administration and Defence; Compulsory Social Security

Tabulation category M: Education
80 Education

Tabulation category N: Health and Social Work
85 Health and Social Work

Tabulation category O: Other Community, Social and Personal Service Activities
90 Sewage and Refuse Disposal, Sanitation and similar activities
91 Activities of Membership Organizations NEC**
92 Recreational, Cultural and Sporting activities
93 Other Service activities

Tabulation category P: Private Households with Employed Persons
95 Private Households with Employed Persons

Tabulation category Q: Extra-Territorial Organizations and Bodies
99 Extra-Territorial Organizations and Bodies

Additional category X: Not classifiable by economic activity

Notes
[1] For full details see United Nations: *Statistical Papers*, Series M, No. 4/ Rev. 3 (New York, 1990).
[2] Not elsewhere classified.

Classification internationale type, par industrie, de toutes les branches d'activité économique (CITI-Rév. 3)[1]

Catégorie de classement A: Agriculture, chasse et sylviculture

01	Agriculture, chasse et activités annexes
02	Sylviculture, exploitation forestière et activités annexes

Catégorie de classement B: Pêche

05	Pêche, pisciculture, aquaculture et activités annexes

Catégorie de classement C: Activités extractives

10	Extraction de charbon et de lignite; extraction de tourbe
11	Extraction de pétrole brut et de gaz naturel; activités annexes à l'extraction de pétrole et de gaz, sauf prospection
12	Extraction de minerais d'uranium et de thorium
13	Extraction de minerais métalliques
14	Autres activités extractives

Catégorie de classement D: Activités de fabrication

15	Fabrication de produits alimentaires et de boissons
16	Fabrication de produits à base de tabac
17	Fabrication des textiles
18	Fabrication d'articles d'habillement; préparation et teinture des fourrures
19	Apprêt et tannage des cuirs; fabrication d'articles de voyage et de maroquinerie, d'articles de sellerie et de bourrellerie; fabrication de chaussures
20	Production de bois et d'articles en bois et en liège (sauf fabrication de meubles); fabrication d'articles de vannerie et de sparterie
21	Fabrication de papier, de carton et d'articles en papier et en carton
22	Edition, imprimerie et reproduction de supports enregistrés
23	Fabrication de produits pétroliers raffinés; cokéfaction; traitement de combustibles nucléaires
24	Fabrication de produits chimiques
25	Fabrication d'articles en caoutchouc et en matières plastiques
26	Fabrication d'autres produits minéraux non métalliques
27	Fabrication de produits métallurgiques de base
28	Fabrication d'ouvrages en métaux (sauf machines et matériel)
29	Fabrication de machines et de matériel NCA[2]
30	Fabrication de machines de bureau, de machines comptables et de matériel de traitement de l'information
31	Fabrication de machines et d'appareils électriques NCA[2]
32	Fabrication d'équipements et appareils de radio, télévision et communication
33	Fabrication d'instruments médicaux, de précision et d'optique et d'horlogerie
34	Construction de véhicules automobiles, de remorques et de semi-remorques
35	Fabrication d'autres matériels de transport
36	Fabrication de meubles; activités de fabrication NCA[2]
37	Récupération

Catégorie de classement E: Production et distribution d'électricité, de gaz et d'eau

40	Production et distribution d'électricité, de gaz, de vapeur et d'eau chaude
41	Captage, épuration et distribution de l'eau

Catégorie de classement F: Construction

45	Construction

Catégorie de classement G: Commerce de gros et de détail; réparation de véhicules automobiles, de motocycles et de biens personnels et domestiques

50	Commerce, entretien et réparation de véhicules automobiles et de motocycles; commerce de détail de carburants automobiles
51	Commerce de gros et activités d'intermédiaires du commerce de gros (sauf de véhicules automobiles et de motocycles)
52	Commerce de détail; sauf de véhicules automobiles et de motocycles; réparation d'articles personnels et domestiques

Catégorie de classement H: Hôtels et restaurants

55	Hôtels et restaurants

Catégorie de classement I: Transports, entreposage et communications

60	Transports terrestres; transports par conduites
61	Transports par eau
62	Transports aériens
63	Activités annexes et auxiliaires des transports; activités d'agences de voyages
64	Postes et télécommunications

Catégorie de classement J: Intermédiation financière

65	Intermédiation financière (sauf activités d'assurance et de caisses de retraite)
66	Activités d'assurances et de caisses de retraite (sauf sécurité sociale obligatoire)
67	Activités auxiliaires de l'intermédiation financière

Catégorie de classement K: Immobilier, locations et activités de services aux entreprises

70	Activités immobilières
71	Location de machines et d'équipements sans opérateur et de biens personnels et domestiques
72	Activités informatiques et activités rattachées
73	Recherche-développement
74	Autres activités de services aux entreprises

Catégorie de classement L: Administration publique et défense; sécurité sociale obligatoire

75	Administration publique et défense; sécurité sociale obligatoire

Catégorie de classement M: Education

80	Education

Catégorie de classement N: Santé et action sociale

85	Santé et action sociale

Catégorie de classement O: Autres activités de services collectifs, sociaux et personnels

90	Assainissement et enlèvement des ordures; voirie et activités similaires
91	Activités associatives diverses
92	Activités récréatives, culturelles et sportives
93	Autres activités de services

Catégorie de classement P: Ménages privés employant du personnel domestique

95 Ménages privés employant du personnel domestique

Catégorie de classement Q: Organisations et organismes extraterritoriaux

99 Organisations et organismes extraterritoriaux

Catégorie supplémentaire X: Ne pouvant être classés selon l'activité économique

Notes

[1] Pour de plus amples détails, voir Nations Unies: *Etudes statistiques*, série M, n° 4, rév. 3 (New York, 1990).

[2] Non classés ailleurs.

Clasificación Industrial Internacional Uniforme de Todas las Actividades Económicas (CIIU - Rev. 3)[1]

Categoría de tabulación A: Agricultura, ganadería, caza y silvicultura

01   Agricultura, ganadería, caza y actividades de servicios conexas
02   Silvicultura, extracción de madera y actividades de servicios conexas

Categoría de tabulación B: Pesca

05   Pesca, explotación de criaderos de peces y granjas piscícolas; actividades de servicios relacionadas con la pesca

Categoría de tabulación C: Explotación de minas y canteras

10   Extracción de carbón y lignito; extracción de turba
11   Extracción de petróleo crudo y gas natural; actividades de tipo servicio relacionadas con la extracción de petróleo y gas, excepto las actividades de prospección
12   Extracción de minerales de uranio y torio
13   Extracción de minerales metalíferos
14   Explotación de otras minas y canteras

Categoría de tabulación D: Industrias manufactureras

15   Elaboración de productos alimenticios y bebidas
16   Elaboración de productos de tabaco
17   Fabricación de productos textiles
18   Fabricación de prendas de vestir; adobo y teñido de pieles
19   Curtido y adobo de cueros; fabricación de maletas, bolsos de mano, artículos de talabartería y guarnicionería, y calzado
20   Producción de madera y fabricación de productos de madera y corcho, excepto muebles; fabricación de artículos de paja y de materiales trenzables
21   Fabricación de papel y de productos de papel
22   Actividades de edición e impresión y de reproducción de grabaciones
23   Fabricación de coque, productos de la refinación del petróleo y combustible nuclear
24   Fabricación de sustancias y productos químicos
25   Fabricación de productos de caucho y plástico
26   Fabricación de otros productos minerales no metálicos
27   Fabricación de metales comunes
28   Fabricación de productos elaborados de metal, excepto maquinaria y equipo
29   Fabricación de maquinaria y equipo NCP[2]
30   Fabricación de maquinaria de oficina, contabilidad e informática
31   Fabricación de maquinaria y aparatos eléctricos NCP[2]
32   Fabricación de equipo y aparatos de radio, televisión y comunicaciones
33   Fabricación de instrumentos médicos, ópticos y de precisión y fabricación de relojes
34   Fabricación de vehículos automotores, remolques y semirremolques
35   Fabricación de otros tipos de equipo de transporte
36   Fabricación de muebles; industrias manufactureras NCP[2]
37   Reciclamiento

Categoría de tabulación E: Suministro de electricidad, gas y agua

40   Suministro de electricidad, gas, vapor y agua caliente
41   Captación, depuración y distribución de agua

Categoría de tabulación F: Construcción

45   Construcción

Categoría de tabulación G: Comercio al por mayor y al por menor; reparación de vehículos automotores, motocicletas, efectos personales y enseres domésticos

50   Venta, mantenimiento y reparación de vehículos automotores y motocicletas; venta al por menor de combustible para automotores
51   Comercio al por mayor y en comisión, excepto el comercio de vehículos automotores y motocicletas
52   Comercio al por menor, excepto el comercio de vehículos automotores y motocicletas; reparación de efectos personales y enseres domésticos

Categoría de tabulación H: Hoteles y restaurantes

55   Hoteles y restaurantes

Categoría de tabulación I: Transporte, almacenamiento y comunicaciones

60   Transporte por vía terrestre; transporte por tuberías
61   Transporte por vía acuática
62   Transporte por vía aérea
63   Actividades de transporte complementarias y auxiliares; actividades de agencias de viajes
64   Correo y telecomunicaciones

Categoría de tabulación J: Intermediación financiera

65   Intermediación financiera, excepto la financiación de planes de seguros y de pensiones
66   Financiación de planes de seguros y de pensiones, excepto los planes de seguridad social de afiliación obligatoria
67   Actividades auxiliares de la intermediación financiera

Categoría de tabulación K: Actividades inmobiliarias, empresariales y de alquiler

70   Actividades inmobiliarias
71   Alquiler de maquinaria y equipo sin operarios y de efectos personales y enseres domésticos
72   Informática y actividades conexas
73   Investigación y desarrollo
74   Otras actividades empresariales

Categoría de tabulación L: Administración pública y defensa; planes de seguridad social de afiliación obligatoria

75   Administración pública y defensa; planes de seguridad social de afiliación obligatoria

Categoría de tabulación M: Enseñanza

80   Enseñanza

Categoría de tabulación N: Servicios sociales y de salud

85   Servicios sociales y de salud

Categoría de tabulación O: Otras actividades de servicios comunitarios, sociales y personales

90   Eliminación de desperdicios y aguas residuales, saneamiento y actividades similares
91   Actividades de asociaciones NCP[2]

92	Actividades de esparcimiento y actividades culturales y deportivas
93	Otras actividades de servicios

Categoría de tabulación P: Hogares privados con servicio doméstico

95	Hogares privados con servicio doméstico

Categoría de tabulación Q: Organizaciones y órganos extraterritoriales

99	Organizaciones y órganos extraterritoriales

Categoría adicional X: No pueden clasificarse según la actividad económica

Notas

[1] Para más amplios detalles, véase Naciones Unidas: *Informes estadísticos*, serie M, núm. 4/Rev. 3 (Nueva York, 1990).

[2] No clasificados en otra parte.

International Classification by Status in Employment (ICSE)

ICSE - 1958

The United Nations Statistical Commission approved in 1958 the following classification: [1]

(a) *Employer:* a person who operates his or her own economic enterprise, or engages independently in a profession or trade, and hires one or more employees. Some countries may wish to distinguish among employers according to the number of persons they employ.

(b) *Own-account worker:* a person who operates his or her own economic enterprise, or engages independently in a profession or trade, and hires no employees.

(c) *Employee:* a person who works for a public or private employer and receives remuneration in wages, salary, commission, tips, piece-rates or pay in kind.

(d) *Unpaid family worker:* usually a person who works without pay in an economic enterprise operated by a related person living in the same household. Where it is customary for young persons, in particular, to work without pay in an economic enterprise operated by a related person who does not live in the same household, the requirement of "living in the same household" may be eliminated. If there are a significant number of unpaid family workers in enterprises of which the operators are members of a producers' cooperative who are classified in category (e), these unpaid family workers should be classified in a separate subgroup.

(e) *Member of producers' cooperative:* a person who is an active member of a producers' cooperative, regardless of the industry in which it is established. Where this group is not numerically important, it may be excluded from the classification, and members of producers' cooperatives should be classified under other headings, as appropriate.

(f) *Persons not classifiable by status:* experienced workers whose status is unknown or inadequately described and unemployed persons not previously employed (i.e. new entrants). A separate group for new entrants may be included if information for this group is not already available elsewhere.

ICSE - 1993

The 15th International Conference of Labour Statisticians adopted, in January 1993, a resolution concerning the ICSE which states [extract]: [2]

II. THE ISCE-93 GROUPS[3]

4. The ICSE-93 consists of the following groups, which are defined in section III:

1. employees;
   among whom countries may need and be able to distinguish "employees with stable contracts" (including "regular employees");
2. employers;
3. own-account workers;
4. members of producers' cooperatives;
5. contributing family workers;
6. workers not classifiable by status.

III. GROUP DEFINITIONS

5. The groups in the ICSE-93 are defined with reference to the distinction between "paid employment" jobs on the one side and self-employment jobs on the other. Groups are defined with reference to one or more aspects of the economic risk and/or the type of authority which the explicit or implicit employment contract gives the incumbents or to which it subjects them.

6. *Paid employment jobs* are those jobs where the incumbents hold explicit (written or oral) or implicit employment contracts which give them a basic remuneration which is not directly dependent upon the revenue of the unit for which they work (this unit can be a corporation, a non-profit institution, a government unit or a household). Some or all of the tools, capital equipment, information systems and/or premises used by the incumbents may be owned by others, and the incumbents may work under direct supervision of, or according to strict guidelines set by the owner(s) or persons in the owners' employment. (Persons in "paid employment jobs" are typically remunerated by wages and salaries, but, may be paid by commission from sales, by piece-rates, bonuses or in-kind payments such as food, housing or training.)

7. *Self-employment jobs* are those jobs where the remuneration is directly dependent upon the profits (or the potential for profits) derived from the goods and services produced (where own consumption is considered to be part of profits). The incumbents make the operational decisions affecting the enterprise, or delegate such decisions while retaining responsibility for the welfare of the enterprise. (In this context "enterprise" includes one-person operations.)

8. *Employees* are all those workers who hold the type of job defined as "paid employment jobs "(cf. paragraph 6). *Employees with stable contracts* are those "employees" who have had, and continue to have, an explicit (written or oral) or implicit contract of employment, or a succession of such contracts, with the same employer on a continuous basis. "On a continuous basis" implies a period of employment which is longer than a specified minimum determined according to national cirumstances. (If interruptions are allowed in this minimum period, their maximum duration should also be determined according to national circumstances.) *Regular employees* are those "employees with stable contracts" for whom the employing organization is responsible for payment of relevant taxes and social security

contributions and/or where the contractual relationship is subject to national labour legislation.

9. *Employers* are those workers who, working on their own account or with one or a few partners, hold the type of job defined as a "self-employment job" (cf. paragraph 7), and, in this capacity, on a continuous basis (including the reference period) have engaged one or more persons to work for them in their business as "employee(s)" (cf. paragraph 8). The meaning of "engage on a continuous basis" is to be determined by national circumstances, in a way which is consistent with the definition of "employees with stable contracts" (cf. paragraph 8). (The partners may or may not be members of the same family or household.)

10. *Own-account workers* are those workers who, working on their own account or with one or more partners, hold the type of job defined as "a self-employment job" (cf. paragraph 7), and have not engaged on a continuous basis any "employees" (cf. paragraph 8) to work for them during the reference period. It should be noted that during the reference period the members of this group may have engaged "employees", provided that this is on a non-continuous basis. (The partners may or may not be members of the same family or household.)

11. *Members of producers' cooperatives* are workers who hold a "self-employment" job (cf. paragraph 7) in a cooperative producing goods and services, in which each member takes part on an equal footing with other members in determining the organization of production, sales and/or other work of the establishment, the investments and the distribution of the proceeds of the establishment amongst their members. (It should be noted that "employees" (cf. paragraph 8) of producers' cooperatives are not to be classified to this group.)

12. *Contributing family workers* are those workers who hold a "self-employment" job (cf. paragraph 7) in a market-oriented establishment operated by a related person living in the same household, who cannot be regarded as a partner, because their degree of commitment to the operation of the establishment, in terms of working time or other factors to be determined by national circumstances, is not at a level comparable to that of the head of the establishment. (Where it is customary for young persons, in particular, to work without pay in an economic enterprise operated by a related person who does not live in the same household, the requirement of "living in the same household" may be eliminated.)

13. *Workers not classifiable by status* include those for whom insufficient relevant information is available, and/or who cannot be included in any of the preceding categories.

IV. STATISTICAL TREATMENT OF PARTICULAR GROUPS

14. This section outlines a possible statistical treatment of particular groups of workers. Some of the groups represent subcategories or disaggregations of one of the specific ICSE-93 categories. Others may cut across two or more of these categories. Countries may need and be able to distinguish one or more of the groups, in particular group (a), and may also create other groups according to national requirements:

(a) *Owner-managers of incorporated enterprises* are workers who hold a job in an incorporated enterprise, in which they: (a) alone, or together with other members of their families or one or a few partners, hold controlling ownership of the enterprise; and (b) have the authority to act on its behalf as regards contracts with other organizations and the hiring and dismissal of persons "in paid employment" with the same organization, subject only to national legislation regulating such matters and the rules established by the elected or appointed board of the organization. Different users of labour market, economic and social statistics may have different views on whether these workers are best classified as in "paid employment" (cf. paragraph 6) or as in "self-employment" (cf. paragraph 7), because these workers receive part of their remuneration in a way similar to persons in "paid employment" while their authority in and responsibility for the enterprise corresponds more to persons in "self-employment", and in particular to "employers". (Note, for example, that to classify them as "employees" will be consistent with their classification in the "System of National Accounts", while they may be best classified as "employers" or "own-account workers" for labour market analysis.) Countries should, therefore, according to the needs of users of their statistics and their data collection possibilities, endeavour to identify this group separately. This will also facilitate international comparisons.

Notes

[1] United Nations Statistical Office (1990): *Supplementary principles and recommendations for population and housing censuses.* Statistical Papers (doc. ST/ESA/STAT/SER./M/67/Add.1). United Nations, New York, 1990).

[2] ILO (1993): *Fifteenth International Conference of Labour Statisticians, Report of the Conference.* ICLS/15/D.6 (Rev. 1). International Labour Office, Geneva 1993.

[3] For linguistic convenience the group titles and definitions have been formulated in a way which corresponds to the situation where each person holds only one job during the reference period.

Classification internationale d'après la situation dans la profession (CISP)

CISP - 1958

La Commission de statistique des Nations Unies a approuvé en 1958 la classification suivante [1]:

a) *Employeur:* personne qui exploite sa propre entreprise économique ou qui exerce pour son propre compte une profession ou un métier, et qui emploie un ou plusieurs salariés. Certains pays classent aussi les employeurs selon le nombre de personnes qu'ils emploient.

b) *Personne travaillant pour son propre compte:* personne qui exploite sa propre entreprise économique ou qui exerce pour son propre compte une profession ou un métier, mais qui n'emploie aucun salarié.

c) *Salarié:* personne qui travaille pour un employeur public ou privé et qui reçoit une rémunération sous forme de traitement, salaire, commission, pourboires, salaire aux pièces ou paiement en nature.

d) *Travailleur familial non rémunéré:* personne qui travaille sans rémunération dans une entreprise exploitée par un parent vivant dans le même ménage. Lorsqu'il est fréquent que des jeunes, en particulier, accomplissent un travail non rémunéré dans une entreprise exploitée par un parent ne vivant pas dans le même ménage, on pourra supprimer le critère «vivant dans le même ménage». Si le nombre de travailleurs familiaux non rémunérés employés dans des entreprises gérées par les membres d'une coopérative de production appartenant à la catégorie qui fait l'objet de l'alinéa e) ci-dessous est important, ces travailleurs familiaux non rémunérés devront être classés dans un sous-groupe distinct.

e) *Membre d'une coopérative de producteurs:* personne qui est membre actif d'une coopérative de producteurs, quelle que soit la branche d'activité économique. Quand ce groupe n'est pas numériquement important, on peut ne pas le faire figurer dans la classification et répartir les membres des coopératives de producteurs entre les autres groupes, comme il convient.

f) *Personnes inclassables d'après la situation dans la profession:* travailleurs expérimentés dont la situation exacte n'est pas connue ou est mal définie, et chômeurs n'ayant jamais travaillé (nouveaux arrivants sur le marché du travail). On pourra classer les nouveaux arrivants sur le marché du travail dans un groupe distinct si des données concernant ce groupe n'existent pas déjà ailleurs.

CISP - 1993

La 15e Conférence internationale des statisticiens du travail a adopté, en janvier 1993, une résolution relative à la CISP qui dit *[extrait]* [2]:

II. GROUPES DÉFINIS DANS LA CISP-93 [3]

4. La CISP-93 comprend les groupes suivants, définis dans la section III:

1) salariés;
   parmi lesquels certains pays pourraient avoir le besoin et la capacité de distinguer les «salariés titulaires d'un contrat de travail stable» (y compris les «salariés réguliers»);
2) employeurs;
3) personnes travaillant pour leur propre compte;
4) membres de coopératives de producteurs;
5) travailleurs familiaux collaborant à l'entreprise familiale;
6) travailleurs inclassables d'après la situation dans la profession.

III. DÉFINITION DES GROUPES

5. Les groupes de la CISP sont définis conformément à la distinction faite entre l'«emploi rémunéré», d'une part, et l'«emploi à titre indépendant», d'autre part. Une fois opérée cette distinction élémentaire, des groupes sont définis en fonction d'un ou de plusieurs aspects du risque économique ou de la nature du contrôle que les contrats de travail explicites ou implicites octroient aux titulaires ou auquel ils les soumettent.

6. *Emplois rémunérés:* emplois pour lesquels les titulaires ont des contrats explicites ou implicites, écrits ou oraux, qui leur donnent droit à une rémunération de base qui n'est pas directement dépendante du revenu de l'unité pour laquelle ils travaillent (cette unité pouvant être une entreprise, une institution à but non lucratif, une administration publique ou un ménage). Les outils, les équipements lourds, les systèmes d'information et/ou les locaux utilisés par les titulaires peuvent appartenir pour partie ou en totalité à d'autres; et les titulaires peuvent être placés sous la supervision directe du (des) propriétaire(s) ou de personnes employées par lui (eux) ou devoir travailler selon de strictes directives établies par lui (eux). (De manière caractéristique, les personnes dans l'«emploi rémunéré» perçoivent des traitements et des salaires, mais peuvent aussi être payées à la commission sur ventes, à la pièce, à la prime ou en nature [par exemple nourriture, logement, formation].)

7. *Emplois à titre indépendant:* emplois dont la rémunération est directement dépendante des bénéfices (réalisés ou potentiels) provenant des biens ou services produits (lorsque la consommation propre est considérée comme faisant partie des bénéfices). Les titulaires prennent les décisions de gestion affectant l'entreprise ou délèguent cette compétence mais sont tenus pour responsables de la bonne santé de leur entreprise. (Dans ce contexte, l'«entreprise» inclut les entreprises unipersonnelles.)

8. *Salariés:* ensemble des travailleurs qui occupent un emploi défini comme «emploi rémunéré» (cf. paragraphe 6 ci-dessus). Les *salariés titulaires de contrats de travail stables* sont des salariés (cf. paragraphe 8) qui ont été et sont titulaires d'un contrat de travail explicite ou impli-

cite, écrit ou oral, ou d'une série de tels contrats, avec le même employeur continûment. «Continûment» implique une période d'emploi plus longue qu'un minimum spécifié et déterminé selon les conditions nationales. (Si des interruptions sont autorisées au cours de cette période minimum, leur durée maximum doit aussi être déterminée selon les conditions nationales.) Les *salariés réguliers* sont des «salariés titulaires de contrats de travail stables» pour lesquels l'organisation employeuse est responsable du paiement des impôts et contributions à la sécurité sociale appropriés et/ou la relation contractuelle est régie par la législation du travail normale.

9. *Employeurs:* personnes qui, travaillant pour leur propre compte ou avec un ou plusieurs associés (cf. paragraphe 11), occupent le type d'emploi défini comme «emploi indépendant» (cf. paragraphe 7 ci-dessus) et qui, à ce titre, engagent sur une période continue incluant la période de référence une ou plusieurs personnes pour travailler dans leur entreprise (cf. paragraphe 8 ci-dessus). La signification de «sur une période continue» doit être déterminée selon les conditions nationales, de façon à ce qu'il y ait correspondance avec la définition «salariés titulaires de contrats de travail stables» (cf. paragraphe 8 ci-dessus). (A noter que les associés peuvent être ou ne pas être membres de la même famille ou du même ménage.)

10. *Personnes travaillant pour leur propre compte:* personnes qui, travaillant pour leur propre compte ou avec un ou plusieurs associés, occupent un emploi défini comme «emploi à titre indépendant» (cf. paragraphe 7 ci-dessus) et qui, pendant la période de référence, n'ont engagé continûment aucun «salarié» pour travailler avec eux (cf. paragraphe 8). (Les partenaires peuvent être ou ne pas être membres de la même famille ou du même ménage.)

11. *Membres de coopératives de producteurs:* personnes qui occupent un «emploi indépendant» (cf. paragraphe 7) et, à ce titre, appartiennent à une coopérative produisant des biens et des services, dans laquelle chaque membre prend part sur un pied d'égalité à l'organisation de la production et des autres activités de l'établissement, décide des investissements ainsi que de la répartition des bénéfices de l'établissement entre les membres. (Il faut noter que les «salariés» des coopératives de producteurs ne doivent pas être classés dans ce groupe.)

12. *Travailleurs familiaux collaborant à l'entreprise familiale:* personnes qui occupent un «emploi indépendant» (cf. paragraphe 7) dans une entreprise orientée vers le marché et exploitée par un parent vivant dans le même ménage, mais qui ne peut pas être considéré comme associé, parce que leur degré d'engagement, en termes de temps de travail ou d'autres facteurs à déterminer selon les conditions nationales, n'est pas comparable à celui du dirigeant de l'établissement. (Lorsqu'il est fréquent que des jeunes, en particulier, accomplissent un travail non rémunéré dans une entreprise exploitée par un parent ne vivant pas dans le même ménage, on pourra supprimer le critère «vivant dans le même ménage».)

13. *Travailleurs inclassables d'après la situation dans la profession:* personnes pour lesquelles on ne dispose pas d'informations suffisantes. (Si l'on utilise la CISP-93 pour classer les personnes à la recherche d'un emploi, elles peuvent aussi être classées dans ce groupe: *a)* si elles ne rentrent pas dans la nouvelle classification des emplois d'après la situation dans la profession (classement sur la base de l'emploi recherché) ou *b)* si elles n'occupaient pas d'emploi auparavant [classement sur la base de l'emploi antérieurement occupé].)

IV. TRAITEMENT STATISTIQUE DES GROUPES PARTICULIERS

14. Cette section de la résolution montre une possibilité de traitement statistique de groupes particuliers de travailleurs. Certains de ces groupes représentent des sous-catégories ou distributions d'une des catégories spécifiques de la CISP-93. D'autres peuvent être trouvées dans deux ou plusieurs de ces catégories. Les pays peuvent avoir le besoin et la capacité de distinguer un ou plusieurs de ces groupes, en particulier le groupe a), ils peuvent aussi créer d'autres groupes selon les besoins nationaux:

a) Les propriétaires-gérants d'entreprises constituées en sociétés se définissent comme les personnes qui occupent un emploi dans une entreprise constituée en société dans laquelle *a)* seules, ou avec d'autres membres de leurs familles ou un ou plusieurs associés, elles possèdent une participation majoritaire dans cette société ou cette organisation; et *b)* elles sont habilitées à agir au nom de la société ou de l'organisation en ce qui concerne les contrats avec d'autres entreprises et l'embauche et le licenciement d'autres personnes occupant un «emploi rémunéré» au sein de la même société ou organisation, à la seule condition de se conformer à la législation nationale pertinente et aux règles établies par le conseil d'administration élu ou désigné de l'organisation. Différents utilisateurs des statistiques de l'emploi et des statistiques économiques et sociales peuvent avoir des vues divergentes sur le point de savoir s'il vaut mieux classer ces travailleurs dans l'«emploi rémunéré» (cf. paragraphe 6) ou dans l'«emploi indépendant» (cf. paragraphe 7), parce qu'ils reçoivent une partie de leur rémunération de la même manière que les personnes dans l'«emploi rémunéré», alors que leur autorité dans l'entreprise et leur responsabilité vis-à-vis d'elle correspondent aux personnes dans l'«emploi indépendant», en particulier les «employeurs». (Il faut noter, par exemple, que les classer dans les «salariés» serait cohérent avec leur classement dans le «système de comptabilité nationale», tandis qu'il vaudrait mieux les classer dans les «employeurs» ou les «personnes travaillant à leur propre compte» aux fins d'analyse du marché du travail.) Les pays devraient en conséquence, selon les besoins des utilisateurs de leurs statistiques et leurs possibilités de collecte de données, s'efforcer d'identifier ce groupe séparément. Cela facilitera aussi les comparaisons internationales.

Notes

[1] Bureau de statistique des Nations Unies (1990): *Principes et recommandations complémentaires concernant les recensements de la population et de l'habitation* (doc. ST/ESA/STAT/SER. M/67/Add. 1), Nations Unies, New York, 1990.

[2] BIT (1993): *Quinzième Conférence internationale des statisticiens du travail, Rapport de la Conférence.* ICLS/15/D.6 (Rev. 1), Bureau international du Travail, Genève, 1993.

[3] Pour des raisons d'ordre pratique, les définitions données dans cette section se réfèrent à la situation où chaque personne n'a occupé qu'un emploi pendant la période de référence. Les règles de classification des personnes ayant occupé plusieurs emplois sont données dans la section IV.

Clasificación Internacional de la Situación en el Empleo (CISE)

CISE - 1958

La Comisión de Estadística de las Naciones Unidas aprobó en 1958 la clasificación siguiente [1]:

a) *Empleador:* es la persona que dirige su propia empresa económica o que ejerce por cuenta propia una profesión u oficio, y que contrata a uno o más empleados. Algunos países tal vez encuentren conveniente dividir a los empleadores según el número de personas que emplean.

b) *Trabajador por cuenta propia:* es la persona que explota su propia empresa económica o que ejerce por cuenta propia una profesión u oficio, pero que no emplea asalariado alguno.

c) *Empleado:* es la persona que trabaja para un empleador público o privado y que percibe una remuneración en forma de salario, sueldo, comisión, propinas, pago a destajo o pago en especie.

d) *Trabajador familiar no remunerado:* es, por lo general, la persona que trabaja sin remuneración en una empresa económica explotada por una persona emparentada con él y que vive en el mismo hogar. Cuando sea costumbre que los jóvenes, en especial, trabajen sin remuneración en una empresa económica dirigida por un pariente que no vive en el mismo hogar, se puede suprimir el criterio «que vive en el mismo hogar». Cuando en empresas explotadas por miembros de una cooperativa de producción clasificada en la categoría e) infra haya un número importante de trabajadores familiares no remunerados, estos trabajadores deberán clasificarse en un subgrupo distinto.

e) *Miembro de una cooperativa de producción:* es la persona afiliada en forma activa a una cooperativa de esa clase, cualquiera que sea la rama de actividad económica en que se encuentre establecida. Cuando no tenga importancia numérica, este grupo podrá excluirse de la clasificación, y los miembros de las cooperativas de producción se incluirán en otras categorías, según convenga.

f) *Personas no clasificables por categoría en el empleo:* son los trabajadores con experiencia cuya categoría se desconoce, o está mal definida, y las personas desempleadas que nunca han trabajado (es decir, las personas que aspiran a ingresar por vez primera en la fuerza de trabajo). Estas últimas pueden ser incluidas en un grupo separado, si no hay información a su respecto en otra parte.

CISE - 1993

La decimoquinta Conferencia Internacional de Estadísticos del Trabajo adoptó, en enero de 1993, una resolución relativa a la CISE que dice *(extracto)* [2]:

II. LOS GRUPOS DE LA CISE-93 [3]

4. La CISE-93 se compone de los siguientes grupos, que se definen en la sección III:

1. Asalariados:
   los países quizás necesiten y puedan hacer una distinción suplementaria creando un grupo separado para los «empleados con contratos estables» (incluyendo a los «empleados regulares»).
2. Empleadores.
3. Trabajadores por cuenta propia.
4. Miembros de cooperativas de productores.
5. Trabajadores familiares auxiliares.
6. Trabajadores que no pueden clasificarse según la situación en el empleo.

III. DEFINICIONES DE LOS GRUPOS

5. Los grupos de la CISE-93 se definen haciendo referencia a la distinción entre los «empleos asalariados», por un lado, y los «empleos independientes», por el otro. Los grupos y subgrupos se definen haciendo referencia a uno o más aspectos del riesgo económico y/o del tipo de autoridad que el contrato de trabajo implícito o explícito confiere a los titulares o a que los somete.

6. *Empleos asalariados:* son aquellos empleos en los que los titulares tienen contratos de trabajo implícitos o explícitos (orales o escritos), por los que reciben una remuneración básica que no depende directamente de los ingresos de la unidad para la que trabajan (esta unidad puede ser una corporación, una institución sin fines de lucro, una unidad gubernamental o un hogar). Algunos o todos los instrumentos, bienes de capital, sistemas de información y/o locales utilizados por los titulares son la propiedad de terceras personas, y los titulares pueden trabajar bajo la supervisión directa de, o de acuerdo con directrices estrictas establecidas por el(los) propietario(s) o las personas empleadas por el (los) propietario(s). (Las personas con «empleos asalariados» se remuneran típicamente con sueldos y salarios, pero también pueden remunerarse por medio de comisiones de ventas, pagos a destajo, primas o pagos en especie tales como comida, habitación o formación.)

7. *Empleos independientes:* son aquellos empleos en los que la remuneración depende directamente de los beneficios (o del potencial para realizar beneficios) derivados de los bienes o servicios producidos (en estos empleos se considera que el consumo propio forma parte de los beneficios). Los titulares toman las decisiones operacionales que afectan a la empresa, o delegan tales decisiones, pero mantienen la responsabilidad por el bienestar de la empresa. (En este contexto, la «empresa» se define de manera suficientemente amplia para incluir a las operaciones de una sola persona.)

8. *Asalariados:* son todos aquellos trabajadores que tienen el tipo de empleo definido como «empleos asalariados» (véase el párrafo 6). *Empleados con contratos estables:* son aquellos «empleados» que han tenido, y continúan teniendo, un contrato de trabajo implícito o explícito (oral o escrito), o una serie de tales contratos,

con el mismo empleador de manera continua. El significado de «de manera continua» se refiere a un período de empleo que es más largo que una duración mínima especificada, la cual se determina de acuerdo con las circunstancias nacionales. (Si este período mínimo permite que haya interrupciones, la duración máxima también debe determinarse de acuerdo con las circunstancias nacionales.) Los *empleados regulares* son aquellos «empleados con contratos estables» ante quienes la organización empleadora es responsable por el pago de las cargas fiscales y de las contribuciones de la seguridad social y/o aquellos cuya relación contractual se rige por la legislación general del trabajo.

9. *Empleadores:* son aquellos trabajadores que, trabajando por su cuenta o con uno o más socios (véase el párrafo 11), tienen el tipo de empleo definido como «empleo independiente» (véase el párrafo 7) y que, en virtud de su condición de tales, han contratado a una o a varias personas para que trabajen para ellos en su empresa como «empleados» a lo largo de un período continuo que incluye el período de referencia (véase el párrafo 8). El significado de «a lo largo de un período continuo» se debe determinar de acuerdo con las circunstancias nacionales, de tal manera que corresponda con la definición de «empleados con contratos estables» (véase el párrafo 8). (Los socios no son necesariamente miembros de la misma familia u hogar.)

10. *Trabajadores por cuenta propia:* son aquellos trabajadores que, trabajando por su cuenta o con uno o más socios (véase el párrafo 11), tienen el tipo de empleo definido como «empleo independiente» (véase el párrafo 7) y no han contratado a ningún «empleado» de manera continua para que trabaje para ellos durante el período de referencia (véase el párrafo 8). Cabe notar que durante el período de referencia los miembros de este grupo pueden haber contratado «empleados», siempre y cuando lo hagan de manera no continua. (Los socios no son necesariamente miembros de la misma familia u hogar.)

11. *Miembros de cooperativas de productores:* son los trabajadores que tienen un «empleo independiente» (véase el párrafo 7) en una cooperativa que produce bienes y servicios, en la que cada miembro participa en pie de igualdad con los demás miembros en la determinación de la organización de la producción y en las demás actividades del establecimiento, en las inversiones y en la distribución de los beneficios del establecimiento entre los miembros. (Cabe precisar que los «empleados» de cooperativas de productores no deben clasificarse en este grupo.)

12. *Trabajadores familiares auxiliares:* son aquellos trabajadores que tienen un «empleo independiente» (véase el párrafo 7) en un establecimiento con orientación de mercado, dirigido por una persona de su familia que vive en el mismo hogar, pero a la que no puede considerarse como socia, debido a que el nivel de dedicación, en términos de tiempo de trabajo u otros factores que deben determinarse de acuerdo con circunstancias nacionales, no es comparable con aquel del jefe del establecimiento. (Cuando sea costumbre que los jóvenes, en especial, trabajen sin remuneración en una empresa económica dirigida por un pariente que no vive en el mismo hogar, se puede suprimir el criterio «que vive en el mismo hogar».)

13. *Trabajadores que no se pueden clasificar según la situación en el empleo:* en este grupo se incluye a los trabajadores sobre los que no se dispone de suficiente información pertinente, y/o que no pueden ser incluidos en ninguna de las categorías anteriores.

IV. TRATAMIENTO ESTADISTICO DE GRUPOS PARTICULARES

14. Esta sección presenta un posible tratamiento estadístico de grupos particulares de trabajadores. Algunos grupos representan subcategorías o divisiones de una categoría específica de la CISE-93. Otros grupos se encuentran en dos o más de estas categorías. Los países quizás necesiten y puedan distinguir uno o varios de estos grupos, en particular el grupo a), y pueden también crear otros grupos de acuerdo con las necesidades nacionales:

a) *Gerentes-propietarios de empresas constituidas en sociedad:* son trabajadores que tienen un empleo en una empresa constituida en sociedad, en la cual ellos: *a)* solos o junto con otros miembros de su familia, o con uno o varios socios, tienen una participación mayoritaria en la empresa u organización; y *b)* tienen la autoridad para actuar en su nombre en lo que se refiere a los contratos con otras organizaciones y a la contratación y el despido de personas con «empleos asalariados» de la misma organización, sujetos solamente a la legislación nacional sobre la materia y las normas establecidas por el consejo de administración de la organización elegido o designado. Los diferentes usuarios de las estadísticas del mercado de trabajo, económicas y sociales pueden tener diferentes opiniones acerca de si estos trabajadores se clasificarían mejor entre los «empleos asalariados» (véase el párrafo 6) o entre los «empleos independientes» (véase el párrafo 7), porque estos trabajadores reciben parte de su remuneración de manera similar a las personas con «empleos asalariados» mientras que su autoridad y responsabilidad sobre la empresa corresponde mejor a las personas con «empleos independientes», especialmente a los «empleadores». (Cabe notar, por ejemplo, que el clasificarlos como «empleados» será coherente con su clasificación en el «Sistema de Contabilidad Nacional», mientras que para el análisis del mercado de trabajo conviene mejor clasificarlos como «empleadores» o «trabajadores por cuenta propia».) Por lo tanto, los países deberán tratar de identificar a este grupo separadamente, de acuerdo con las necesidades de los usuarios de sus estadísticas y con las posibilidades de recolección de datos. Esto también facilitará las comparaciones internacionales.

Notas

[1] Oficina de Estadística de las Naciones Unidas (1990): *Principios y recomendaciones complementarios para los censos de poblaciones y habitación* (doc. ST/ESA/STAT/SER.M/67/Add.1), Naciones Unidas, Nueva York, 1990.

[2] OIT (1993): *Decimoquinta Conferencia Internacional de Estadísticos del Trabajo, Informe de la Conferencia.* ICLS/15/D.6 (Rev. 1). Oficina Internacional del Trabajo, Ginebra 1993.

[3] Por comodidad, los títulos de los grupos y las definiciones se refieren a la situación en que cada persona ocupa solamente un empleo durante el período de referencia. En la sección V se enuncian las reglas de clasificación de las personas que ocupan varios empleos en dicho período.

International Standard Classification of Occupations (ISCO-1968) [1,2]

Major Group 0/1	**Professional, technical and related workers**
0-1	Physical scientists and related technicians
0-2/3	Architects, engineers and related technicians
0-4	Aircraft and ships' officers
0-5	Life scientists and related technicians
0-6/7	Medical, dental, veterinary and related workers
0-8	Statisticians, mathematicians, systems analysts and related technicians
0-9	Economists
1-1	Accountants
1-2	Jurists
1-3	Teachers
1-4	Workers in religion
1-5	Authors, journalists and related writers
1-6	Sculptors, painters, photographers and related creative artists
1-7	Composers and performing artists
1-8	Athletes, sportsmen and related workers
1-9	Professional, technical and related workers not elsewhere classified
Major Group 2	**Administrative and managerial workers**
2-0	Legislative officials and government administrators
2-1	Managers
Major Group 3	**Clerical and related workers**
3-0	Clerical supervisors
3-1	Government executive officials
3-2	Stenographers, typists and card- and tape-punching machine operators
3-3	Bookkeepers, cashiers and related workers
3-4	Computing machine operators
3-5	Transport and communications supervisors
3-6	Transport conductors
3-7	Mail distribution clerks
3-8	Telephone and telegraph operators
3-9	Clerical related workers not elsewhere classified
Major Group 4	**Sales workers**
4-0	Managers (wholesale and retail trade)
4-1	Working proprietors (wholesale and retail trade)
4-2	Sales supervisors and buyers
4-3	Technical salesmen, commercial travellers and manufacturers' agents
4-4	Insurance, real estate, securities and business services salesmen and auctioneers
4-5	Salesmen, shop assistants and related workers
4-9	Sales workers not elsewhere classified
Major Group 5	**Service workers**
5-0	Managers (catering and lodging services)
5-1	Working proprietors (catering and lodging services)
5-2	Housekeeping and related service supervisors
5-3	Cooks, waiters, bartenders and related workers
5-4	Maids and related housekeeping service workers not elsewhere classified
5-5	Building caretakers, charworkers, cleaners and related workers
5-6	Launderers, dry-cleaners and pressers
5-7	Hairdressers, barbers, beauticians and related workers
5-8	Protective service workers
5-9	Service workers not elsewhere classified
Major Group 6	**Agriculture, animal husbandry and forestry workers, fishermen and hunters**
6-0	Farm managers and supervisors
6-1	Farmers
6-2	Agriculture and animal husbandry workers
6-3	Forestry workers
6-4	Fishermen, hunters and related workers
Major Group 7/8/9	**Production and related workers, transport equipment operators and labourers**
7-0	Production supervisors and general foremen
7-1	Miners, quarrymen, well drillers and related workers
7-2	Metal processers
7-3	Wood preparation workers and paper makers
7-4	Chemical processers and related workers
7-5	Spinners, weavers, knitters, dyers and related workers
7-6	Tanners, fellmongers and pelt dressers
7-7	Food and beverage processers
7-8	Tobacco preparers and tobacco product makers
7-9	Tailors, dressmakers, sewers, upholsterers and related workers
8-0	Shoemakers and leather goods makers
8-1	Cabinetmakers and related woodworkers
8-2	Stone cutters and carvers
8-3	Blacksmiths, toolmakers and machine-tool operators
8-4	Machinery fitters, machine assemblers and precision instrument makers (except electrical)
8-5	Electrical fitters and related electrical and electronics workers
8-6	Broadcasting station and sound equipment operators and cinema projectionists
8-7	Plumbers, welders, sheet metal and structural metal preparers and erectors
8-8	Jewellery and precious metal workers
8-9	Glass formers, potters and related workers
9-0	Rubber and plastics product makers
9-1	Paper and paper board products makers
9-2	Printers and related workers
9-3	Painters
9-4	Production and related workers not elsewhere classified
9-5	Bricklayers, carpenters and other construction workers
9-6	Stationary engine and related equipment operators
9-7	Material-handling and related equipment operators, dockers and freight handlers
9-8	Transport equipment operators
9-9	Labourers not elsewhere classified

Major Group X Workers not classifiable by occupation

X-1 New workers seeking employment
X-2 Workers reporting occupations unidentifiable or inadequately described
X-3 Workers not reporting any occupation

Armed Forces Members of the armed forces

Notes

[1] *Major* and *Minor groups* only. This Classification consists of *Major groups* (one-digit codes), *Minor groups* (two-digit codes), *Unit groups* (three-digit codes) and *Occupational categories* (five-digit codes).

For full details, see ILO: *International Standard Classification of Occupations, revised edition, 1968* (Geneva, 1969).

[2] The revised *International Standard Classification of Occupations* (ISCO-88), which was approved by the 14th International Conference of Labour Statisticians 1987, was published in 1990.

Classification internationale type des professions (CITP-1968) [1] [2]

Grand groupe 0/1   Personnel des professions scientifiques, techniques, libérales et assimilées

0-1	Spécialistes des sciences physico-chimiques et techniciens assimilés
0-2/3	Architectes, ingénieurs et techniciens assimilés
0-4	Pilotes, officiers de pont et officiers mécaniciens (marine et aviation)
0-5	Biologistes, agronomes et techniciens assimilés
0-6/7	Médecins, dentistes, vétérinaires et travailleurs assimilés
0-8	Statisticiens, mathématiciens, analystes de systèmes et techniciens assimilés
0-9	Economistes
1-1	Comptables
1-2	Juristes
1-3	Personnel enseignant
1-4	Membres du clergé et assimilés
1-5	Auteurs, journalistes et écrivains assimilés
1-6	Sculpteurs, peintres, photographes et artistes créateurs assimilés
1-7	Musiciens, acteurs, danseurs et artistes assimilés
1-8	Athlètes, sportifs et assimilés
1-9	Personnel des professions scientifiques, techniques, libérales et assimilées non classé ailleurs

Grand groupe 2   Directeurs et cadres administratifs supérieurs

2-0	Membres des corps législatifs et cadres supérieurs de l'administration publique
2-1	Directeurs et cadres dirigeants

Grand groupe 3   Personnel administratif et travailleurs assimilés

3-0	Chefs de groupe d'employés de bureau
3-1	Agents administratifs (administration publique)
3-2	Sténographes dactylographes et opérateurs sur machines perforatrices de cartes et de rubans
3-3	Employés de comptabilité, caissiers et travailleurs assimilés
3-4	Opérateurs sur machines à traiter l'information
3-5	Chefs de services de transports et de communications
3-6	Chefs de train et receveurs
3-7	Facteurs et messagers
3-8	Opérateurs des téléphones et télégraphes
3-9	Personnel administratif et travailleurs assimilés non classés ailleurs

Grand groupe 4   Personnel commercial et vendeurs

4-0	Directeurs (commerces de gros et de détail)
4-1	Propriétaires-gérants de commerces de gros et de détail
4-2	Chefs des ventes et acheteurs
4-3	Agents commerciaux techniciens et voyageurs de commerce
4-4	Agents d'assurances, agents immobiliers, courtiers en valeurs, agents de vente de services aux entreprises et vendeurs aux enchères.
4-5	Commis vendeurs, employés de commerce et travailleurs assimilés
4-9	Personnel commercial et vendeurs non classés ailleurs

Grand groupe 5   Travailleurs spécialisés dans les services

5-0	Directeurs d'hôtels, de cafés ou de restaurants
5-1	Propriétaires-gérants d'hôtel, de cafés ou de restaurants
5-2	Chefs de groupe d'employés de maison et travailleurs assimilés
5-3	Cuisiniers, serveurs, barmen et travailleurs assimilés
5-4	Employés de maison et travailleurs assimilés non classés ailleurs
5-5	Gardiens d'immeubles, nettoyeurs et travailleurs assimilés
5-6	Blanchisseurs, dégraisseurs et presseurs
5-7	Coiffeurs, spécialistes des soins de beauté et travailleurs assimilés
5-8	Personnel des services de protection et de sécurité
5-9	Travailleurs spécialisés dans les services non classés ailleurs

Grand groupe 6   Agriculteurs, éleveurs, forestiers, pêcheurs et chasseurs

6-0	Directeurs et chefs d'exploitation agricoles
6-1	Exploitants agricoles
6-2	Travailleurs agricoles
6-3	Travailleurs forestiers
6-4	Pêcheurs, chasseurs et travailleurs assimilés

Grand groupe 7/8/9   Ouvriers et manœuvres non agricoles et conducteurs d'engins de transport

7-0	Agents de maîtrise et assimilés
7-1	Mineurs, carriers, foreurs de puits et travailleurs assimilés
7-2	Ouvriers de la production et du traitement des métaux
7-3	Ouvriers de la première préparation des bois et de la fabrication du papier
7-4	Conducteurs de fours et d'appareils chimiques
7-5	Ouvriers du textile
7-6	Tanneurs, peaussiers, mégissiers et ouvriers de la pelleterie
7-7	Ouvriers de l'alimentation et des boissons
7-8	Ouvriers des tabacs
7-9	Tailleurs, couturiers, couseurs, tapissiers et ouvriers assimilés
8-0	Bottiers, ouvriers de la chaussure et du cuir
8-1	Ebénistes, menuisiers et travailleurs assimilés
8-2	Tailleurs et graveurs de pierres
8-3	Ouvriers du façonnage et de l'usinage des métaux
8-4	Ajusteurs-monteurs, installateurs de machines et mécaniciens de précision (électriciens exceptés)
8-5	Electriciens, électroniciens et travailleurs assimilés
8-6	Opérateurs de stations d'émissions de radio et de télévision, opérateurs d'appareils de sonorisation et projectionnistes de cinéma
8-7	Plombiers soudeurs, tôliers-chaudronniers, monteurs de charpentes et de structures métalliques
8-8	Joailliers et orfèvres
8-9	Verriers, potiers et travailleurs assimilés
9-0	Ouvriers de la fabrication d'articles en caoutchouc et en matières plastiques
9-1	Confectionneurs d'articles en papier et en carton
9-2	Compositeurs typographes et travailleurs assimilés

9-3	Peintres
9-4	Ouvriers à la production et assimilés non classés ailleurs
9-5	Maçons, charpentiers et autres travailleurs de la construction
9-6	Conducteurs de machines et d'installations fixes
9-7	Conducteurs d'engins de manutention et de terrassement, dockers et manutentionnaires
9-8	Conducteurs d'engins de transport
9-9	Manœuvres non classés ailleurs

Grand groupe X Travailleurs ne pouvant être classés selon la profession

X-1	Personnes en quête de leur premier emploi
X-2	Travailleurs ayant fait au sujet de leur profession une déclaration imprécise ou insuffisante
X-3	Travailleurs n'ayant déclaré aucune profession

Forces armées Membres des forces armées

Notes

[1] *Grands groupes* et *sous-groupes* seulement. Cette classification comprend des *grands groupes* (codes à un chiffre), des *sous-groupes* (codes à deux chiffres), des *groupes de base* (codes à trois chiffres) et des *catégories professionnelles* (codes à cinq chiffres).

Pour de plus amples détails, voir BIT: *Classification internationale type des professions, édition révisée, 1968* (Genève, 1969).

[2] La *Classification internationale type des professions*, révisée (CITP-88), qui a été approuvée par la 14ᵉ Conférence internationale des statisticiens du travail, 1987, a paru en 1991.

Clasificación Internacional Uniforme de Ocupaciones (CIUO - 1968) [1,2]

Gran grupo 0/1   Profesionales, técnicos y trabajadores asimilados

0-1	Especialistas en ciencias físico-químicas y técnicos asimilados
0-2/3	Arquitectos, ingenieros y técnicos asimilados
0-4	Pilotos y oficiales de cubierta y oficiales maquinistas (aviación y marina)
0-5	Biólogos, agrónomos y técnicos asimilados
0-6/7	Médicos, odontólogos, veterinarios y trabajadores asimilados
0-8	Estadígrafos, matemáticos, analistas de sistemas y técnicos asimilados
0-9	Economistas
1-1	Contadores
1-2	Juristas
1-3	Profesores
1-4	Miembros del clero y asimilados
1-5	Autores, periodistas y escritores asimilados
1-6	Escultores, pintores, fotógrafos y artistas asimilados
1-7	Músicos, artistas, empresarios y productores de espectáculos
1-8	Atletas, deportistas y trabajadores asimilados
1-9	Profesionales, técnicos y trabajadores asimilados no clasificados bajo otros epígrafes

Gran grupo 2   Directores y funcionarios públicos superiores

2-0	Miembros de los cuerpos legislativos y personal directivo de la administración pública
2-1	Directores y personal directivo

Gran grupo 3   Personal administrativo y trabajadores asimilados

3-0	Jefes de empleados de oficinas
3-1	Agentes administrativos (administración pública)
3-2	Taquígrafos, mecanógrafos y operadores de máquinas perforadoras de tarjetas y cintas
3-3	Empleados de contabilidad, cajeros y trabajadores asimilados
3-4	Operadores de máquinas para cálculos contables y estadísticos
3-5	Jefes de servicios de transportes y de comunicaciones
3-6	Jefes de tren, controladores de coches-cama y cobradores
3-7	Carteros y mensajeros
3-8	Telefonistas y telegrafistas
3-9	Personal administrativo y trabajadores asimilados no clasificados bajo otros epígrafes

Gran grupo 4   Comerciantes y vendedores

4-0	Directores (comercio al por mayor y al por menor)
4-1	Comerciantes propietarios (comercio al por mayor y al por menor)
4-2	Jefes de ventas y compradores
4-3	Agentes técnicos de ventas, viajantes de comercio y representantes de fábrica
4-4	Agentes de seguros, agentes inmobiliarios, agentes de cambio y bolsa, agentes de venta de servicios a las empresas y subastadores
4-5	Vendedores, empleados de comercio y trabajadores asimilados
4-9	Comerciantes y vendedores no clasificados bajo otros epígrafes

Gran grupo 5   Trabajadores de los servicios

5-0	Directores (servicios de hostelería, bares y similares)
5-1	Gerentes propietarios (servicios de hostelería, bares y similares)
5-2	Jefes de personal de servidumbre
5-3	Cocineros, camareros, bármanes y trabajadores asimilados
5-4	Personal de servidumbre no clasificado bajo otros epígrafes
5-5	Guardianes de edificios, personal de limpieza y trabajadores asimilados
5-6	Lavanderos, limpiadores en seco y planchadores
5-7	Peluqueros, especialistas en tratamientos de belleza y trabajadores asimilados
5-8	Personal de los servicios de protección y de seguridad
5-9	Trabajadores de los servicios no clasificados bajo otros epígrafes

Gran grupo 6   Trabajadores agrícolas y forestales, pescadores y cazadores

6-0	Directores y jefes de explotaciones agrícolas
6-1	Explotadores agrícolas
6-2	Obreros agrícolas
6-3	Trabajadores forestales
6-4	Pescadores, cazadores y trabajadores asimilados

Gran grupo 7/8/9   Obreros no agrícolas, conductores de máquinas y vehículos de transporte y trabajadores asimilados

7-0	Contramaestres y capataces mayores
7-1	Mineros, canteros, sondistas y trabajadores asimilados
7-2	Obreros metalúrgicos
7-3	Obreros del tratamiento de la madera y de la fabricación de papel
7-4	Obreros de los tratamientos químicos y trabajadores asimilados
7-5	Hilanderos, tejedores, tintoreros y trabajadores asimilados
7-6	Obreros de la preparación, curtido y tratamiento de pieles
7-7	Obreros de la preparación de alimentos y bebidas
7-8	Obreros del tabaco
7-9	Sastres, modistos, peleteros, tapiceros y trabajadores asimilados
8-0	Zapateros y guarnicioneros
8-1	Ebanistas, operadores de máquinas de labrar madera y trabajadores asimilados
8-2	Labrantes y adornistas
8-3	Obreros de la labra de metales
8-4	Ajustadores-montadores e instaladores de maquinaria e instrumentos de precisión, relojeros y mecánicos (excepto electricistas)
8-5	Electricistas, electronicistas y trabajadores asimilados
8-6	Operadores de estaciones emisoras de radio y televisión y de equipos de sonorización y de proyecciones cinematográficas

8-7	Fontaneros, soldadores, chapistas, caldereros y preparadores y montadores de estructuras metálicas
8-8	Joyeros y plateros
8-9	Vidrieros, ceramistas y trabajadores asimilados
9-0	Obreros de la fabricación de productos de caucho y plástico
9-1	Confeccionadores de productos de papel y cartón
9-2	Obreros de las artes gráficas
9-3	Pintores
9-4	Obreros manufactureros y trabajadores asimilados no clasificados bajo otros epígrafes
9-5	Obreros de la construcción
9-6	Operadores de máquinas fijas y de instalaciones similares
9-7	Obreros de la manipulación de mercancías y materiales y de movimiento de tierras
9-8	Conductores de vehículos de transporte
9-9	Peones no clasificados bajo otros epígrafes

Gran grupo X Trabajadores que no pueden ser clasificados según la ocupación

X-1	Personas en busca de su primer empleo
X-2	Trabajadores que han declarado ocupaciones no identificables o insuficientemente descritas
X-3	Trabajadores que no han declarado ninguna ocupación

Fuerzas armadas Miembros de las fuerzas armadas

Notas

[1] *Grandes grupos* y *Subgrupos* solamente. Esta Clasificación se compone de *Grandes grupos* (clave de un dígito), *Subgrupos* (clave de dos dígitos), *Grupos unitarios* (clave de tres dígitos) y *Categorías profesionales* (clave de cinco dígitos).

Para más amplios detalles, véase OIT: *Clasificación Internacional Uniforme de Ocupaciones, edición revisada, 1968* (Ginebra, 1970).

[2] La *Clasificación Internacional Uniforme de Ocupaciones* revisada (CIUO-88), que se aprobó por la 14.ª Conferencia Internacional de Estadísticos del Trabajo, 1987, apareció en 1991.

International Standard Classification of Occupations (ISCO-88) Major, Sub-Major and Minor Groups

Major Group 1 Legislators, senior officials and managers
11   Legislators and senior officials
     111   Legislators
     112   Senior government officials
     113   Traditional chiefs and heads of villages
     114   Senior officials of special-interest organisations
12   Corporate managers [1]
     121   Directors and chief executives
     122   Production and operations department managers
     123   Other department managers
13   General managers [2]
     131   General managers

Major Group 2 Professionals
21   Physical, mathematical and engineering science professionals
     211   Physicists, chemists and related professionals
     212   Mathematicians, statisticians and related professionals
     213   Computing professionals
     214   Architects, engineers and related professionals
22   Life science and health professional
     221   Life science professionals
     222   Health professionals (except nursing)
     223   Nursing and midwifery professionals
23   Teaching professionals
     231   College, university and higher education teaching professionals
     232   Secondary education teaching professionals
     233   Primary and pre-primary education teaching professionals
     234   Special education teaching professionals
     235   Other teaching professionals
24   Other professionals
     241   Business professionals
     242   Legal professionals
     243   Archivists, librarians and related information professionals
     244   Social science and related professionals
     245   Writers and creative or performing artists
     246   Religious professionals

Major Group 3 Technicians and associate professionals
31   Physical and engineering science associate professionals
     311   Physical and engineering science technicians
     312   Computer associate professionals
     313   Optical and electronic equipment operators
     314   Ship and aircraft controllers and technicians
     315   Safety and quality inspectors
32   Life science and health associate professionals
     321   Life science technicians and related associate professionals
     322   Modern health associate professionals (except nursing)
     323   Nursing and midwifery associate professionals
     324   Traditional medicine practitioners and faith healers
33   Teaching associate professionals
     331   Primary education teaching associate professionals
     332   Pre-primary education teaching associate professionals
     333   Special education teaching associate professionals
     334   Other teaching associate professionals
34   Other associate professionals
     341   Finance and sales associate professionals
     342   Business services agents and trade brokers
     343   Administrative associate professionals
     344   Customs, tax and related government associate professionals
     345   Police inspectors and detectives
     346   Social work associate professionals
     347   Artistic, entertainment and sports associate professionals
     348   Religious associate professionals

Major Group 4 Clerks
41   Office clerks
     411   Secretaries and keyboard-operating clerks
     412   Numerical clerks
     413   Material-recording and transport clerks
     414   Library, mail and related clerks
     419   Other office clerks
42   Customer service clerks
     421   Cashiers, tellers and related clerks
     422   Client information clerks

Major Group 5 Service workers and shop and market sales workers
51   Personal and protective services workers
     511   Travel attendants and related workers
     512   Housekeeping and restaurant services workers
     513   Personal care and related workers
     514   Other personal service workers
     515   Astrologers, fortune-tellers and related workers
     516   Protective services workers
52   Models, salespersons and demonstrators
     521   Fashion and other models
     522   Shop salespersons and demonstrators
     523   Stall and market salespersons

Major Group 6 Skilled agricultural and fishery workers
61   Market-oriented skilled agricultural and fishery workers
     611   Market-oriented gardeners and crop growers
     612   Market-oriented animal producers and related workers
     613   Market-oriented crop and animal producers
     614   Forestry and related workers
     615   Fishery workers, hunters and trappers
62   Subsistence agricultural and fishery workers
     621   Subsistence agricultural and fishery workers

Major Group 7 Craft and related trade workers
71   Extraction and building trade workers
     711   Miners, shotfirers, stone cutters and carvers
     712   Building frame and related trades workers
     713   Building finishers and related trades workers
     714   Painters, building structure cleaners and related trades workers
72   Metal, machinery and related trades workers
     721   Metal moulders, welders, sheet-metal workers, structural-metal preparers, and related trades workers

	722	Blacksmiths, tool-makers and related trades workers
	723	Machinery mechanics and fitters
	724	Electrical and electronic equipment mechanics and fitters
73		Precision, handicraft, printing and related trades workers
	731	Precision workers in metal and related materials
	732	Potters, glass-makers and related trades workers
	733	Handicraft workers in wood, textile, leather and related material
	734	Printing and related trades workers
74		Other craft and related trades workers
	741	Food processing and related trades workers
	742	Wood treaters, cabinet-makers and related trades workers
	743	Textile, garment and related trades workers
	744	Pelt, leather and shoemaking trades workers

Major Group 8 Plant and machine operators and assemblers

81		Stationary plant and related operators
	811	Mining and mineral-processing-plant operators
	812	Metal-processing-plant operators
	813	Glass, ceramics and related plant-operators
	814	Wood-processing-and papermaking-plant operators
	815	Chemical-processing-plant operators
	816	Power-production and related plant operators
	817	Automated-assembly-line and industrial-robot operators
82		Machine operators and assemblers
	821	Metal- and mineral-products machine operators
	822	Chemical-products machine operators
	823	Rubber- and plastic-products machine operators
	824	Wood-products machine operators
	825	Printing-, binding- and paper-products machine operators
	826	Textile-, fur- and leather-products machine operators
	827	Food and related products machine operators
	828	Assemblers
	829	Other machine operators and assemblers

83		Drivers and mobile plant operators
	831	Locomotive engine drivers and related workers
	832	Motor vehicle drivers
	833	Agricultural and other mobile plant operators
	834	Ships' deck crews and related workers

Major Group 9 Elementary occupations

91		Sales and services elementary occupations
	911	Street vendors and related workers
	912	Shoe cleaning and other street services elementary occupations
	913	Domestic and related helpers, cleaners and launderers
	914	Building caretakers, window and related cleaners
	915	Messengers, porters, doorkeepers and related workers
	916	Garbage collectors and related labourers
92		Agricultural, fishery and related labourers
	921	Agricultural, fishery and related labourers
93		Labourers in mining, construction, manufacturing and transport
	931	Mining and construction labourers
	932	Manufacturing labourers
	933	Transport labourers and freight handlers

Major Group 0 Armed forces

01		Armed forces
	011	Armed forces

Notes

[1] This sub-major group is intended to include persons who — as directors, chief executives or specialised managers — manage enterprises requiring a total of three or more managers.

[2] This sub-major group is intended to include persons who manage enterprises on their own behalf, or on behalf of the proprietor, with some non-managerial help and assistance of no more than one other manager.

Classification internationale type des professions (CITP-88) Grands groupes, sous-grands groupes et sous-groupes

Grand groupe 1   Membres de l'exécutif et des corps législatifs, cadres supérieurs de l'administration publique, dirigeants et cadres supérieurs d'entreprise

- 11   Membres de l'exécutif et des corps législatifs, et cadres supérieurs de l'administration publique
  - 111   Membres de l'exécutif et des corps législatifs
  - 112   Cadres supérieurs de l'administration publique
  - 113   Chefs traditionnels et chefs de village
  - 114   Dirigeants et cadres supérieurs d'organisations spécialisées
- 12   Directeurs de société [1]
  - 121   Directeurs
  - 122   Cadres de direction, production et opérations
  - 123   Autres cadres de direction
- 13   Dirigeants et gérants [2]
  - 131   Dirigeants et gérants

Grand groupe 2   Professions intellectuelles et scientifiques

- 21   Spécialistes des sciences physiques, mathématiques et techniques
  - 211   Physiciens, chimistes et assimilés
  - 212   Mathématiciens, statisticiens et assimilés
  - 213   Spécialistes de l'informatique
  - 214   Architectes, ingénieurs et assimilés
- 22   Spécialistes des sciences de la vie et de la santé
  - 221   Spécialistes des sciences de la vie
  - 222   Médecins et assimilés (à l'exception des cadres infirmiers)
  - 223   Cadres infirmiers et sages-femmes
- 23   Spécialistes de l'enseignement
  - 231   Professeurs d'université et d'établissements d'enseignement supérieur
  - 232   Professeurs de l'enseignement secondaire
  - 233   Instituteurs de l'enseignement primaire et préprimaire
  - 234   Enseignants spécialisés dans l'éducation des handicapés
  - 235   Autres spécialistes de l'enseignement
- 24   Autres spécialistes des professions intellectuelles et scientifiques
  - 241   Spécialistes des fonctions administratives et commerciales des entreprises
  - 242   Juristes
  - 243   Archivistes, bibliothécaires, documentalistes et assimilés
  - 244   Spécialistes des sciences sociales et humaines
  - 245   Ecrivains et artistes créateurs et exécutants
  - 246   Membres du clergé

Grand groupe 3   Professions intermédiaires

- 31   Professions intermédiaires des sciences physiques et techniques
  - 311   Techniciens des sciences physiques et techniques
  - 312   Pupitreurs et autres opérateurs de matériels informatiques
  - 313   Techniciens d'appareils optiques et électroniques
  - 314   Techniciens des moyens de transport maritime et aérien
  - 315   Inspecteurs d'immeubles, de sécurité, d'hygiène et de qualité
- 32   Professions intermédiaires des sciences de la vie et de la santé
  - 321   Techniciens et travailleurs assimilés des sciences de la vie de la santé
  - 322   Professions intermédiaires de la médecine moderne (à l'exception du personnel infirmier)
  - 323   Personnel infirmier et sages-femmes (niveau intermédiaire)
  - 324   Praticiens de la médecine traditionnelle et guérisseurs
- 33   Professions intermédiaires de l'enseignement
  - 331   Professions intermédiaires de l'enseignement primaire
  - 332   Professions intermédiaires de l'enseignement préprimaire
  - 333   Professions intermédiaires de l'éducation des handicapés
  - 334   Autres professions intermédiaires de l'enseignement
- 34   Autres professions intermédiaires
  - 341   Professions intermédiaires des finances et de la vente
  - 342   Agents commerciaux et courtiers
  - 343   Professions intermédiaires de la gestion administrative
  - 344   Professions intermédiaires de l'administration publique des douanes et des impôts, et assimilés
  - 345   Inspecteurs de police judiciaire et détectives
  - 346   Professions intermédiaires du travail social
  - 347   Professions intermédiaires de la création artistique, du spectacle et du sport
  - 348   Assistants laïcs des cultes

Grand groupe 4   Employés de type administratif

- 41   Employés de bureau
  - 411   Secrétaires et opérateurs sur claviers
  - 412   Employés des services comptables et financiers
  - 413   Employés d'approvisionnement, d'ordonnancement et des transports
  - 414   Employés de bibliothèque, de service du courrier et assimilés
  - 419   Autres employés de bureau
- 42   Employés de réception, caissiers, guichetiers et assimilés
  - 421   Caissiers, guichetiers et assimilés
  - 422   Employés de réception et d'information de la clientèle

Grand groupe 5   Personnel des services et vendeurs de magasin et de marché

- 51   Personnel des services directs aux particuliers et des services de protection et de sécurité
  - 511   Agents d'accompagnement et assimilés
  - 512   Intendants et personnel des services de restauration
  - 513   Personnel soignant et assimilé
  - 514   Autre personnel des services directs aux particuliers
  - 515   Astrologues, diseurs de bonne aventure et assimilés
  - 516   Personnel des services de protection et de sécurité
- 52   Modèles, vendeurs et démonstrateurs
  - 521   Mannequins et autres modèles
  - 522   Vendeurs et démonstrateurs en magasin
  - 523   Vendeurs à l'étal et sur les marchés

Grand groupe 6 Agriculteurs et ouvriers qualifiés de l'agriculture et de la pêche

61   Agriculteurs et ouvriers qualifiés de l'agriculture et de la pêche destinées aux marchés
   611   Agriculteurs et ouvriers qualifiés des cultures destinées aux marchés
   612   Eleveurs et ouvriers qualifiés de l'élevage destiné aux marchés et assimilés
   613   Agriculteurs et ouvriers qualifiés de polyculture et d'élevage destinés aux marchés
   614   Professions du forestage et assimilées
   615   Pêcheurs, chasseurs et trappeurs
62   Agriculteurs et ouvriers de l'agriculture et de la pêche de subsistance
   621   Agriculteurs et ouvriers de l'agriculture et de la pêche de subsistance

Grand groupe 7 Artisans et ouvriers des métiers de type artisanal

71   Artisans et ouvriers des métiers de l'extraction et du bâtiment
   711   Mineurs, carriers, boutefeux ettailleurs de pierre
   712   Ouvriers du bâtiment (gros œuvre) et assimilés
   713   Ouvriers du bâtiment (finitions) et assimilés
   714   Ouvriers peintres, ravaleurs de façades et assimilés
72   Artisans et ouvriers des métiers de la métallurgie, de la construction mécanique et assimilés
   721   Mouleurs de fonderie, soudeurs, tôliers-chaudronniers, monteurs de charpentes métalliques et assimilés
   722   Forgerons, outilleurs et assimilés
   723   Mécaniciens et ajusteurs de machines
   724   Mécaniciens et ajusteurs d'appareils électriques et électroniques
73   Artisans et ouvriers de la mécanique de précision, des métiers d'art, de l'imprimerie et assimilés
   731   Mécaniciens de précision sur métaux et matériaux similaires
   732   Potiers, souffleurs de verre et assimilés
   733   Ouvriers des métiers d'artisanat sur bois, sur textile, sur cuir et sur des matériaux similaires
   734   Artisans et ouvriers de l'imprimerie et assimilés
74   Autres artisans et ouvriers des métiers de type artisanal
   741   Artisans et ouvriers de l'alimentation et assimilés
   742   Artisans et ouvriers du traitement du bois, ébénistes et assimilés
   743   Artisans et ouvriers des métiers du textile et de l'habillement et assimilés
   744   Artisans et ouvriers du travail du cuir, des peaux et de la chaussure

Grand groupe 8 Conducteurs d'installations et de machines et ouvriers de l'assemblage

81   Conducteurs d'installations et de matériels fixes et assimilés
   811   Conducteurs d'installations d'exploitation minière et d'extraction des minéraux
   812   Conducteurs d'installations de transformation des métaux
   813   Conducteurs d'installations de verrerie et de céramique et assimilés
   814   Conducteurs d'installations pour le travail du bois et de la fabrication du papier
   815   Conducteurs d'installations de traitement chimique
   816   Conducteurs d'installations de production d'énergie et assimilés
   817   Conducteurs de chaînes de montage automatiques et de robots industriels
82   Conducteurs de machines et ouvriers de l'assemblage
   821   Conducteurs de machines à travailler les métaux et les produits minéraux
   822   Conducteurs de machines pour la fabrication des produits chimiques
   823   Conducteurs de machines pour la fabrication de produits en caoutchouc et en matières plastiques
   824   Conducteurs de machines à bois
   825   Conducteurs de machines d'imprimerie, de machines à relier et de machines de papeterie
   826   Conducteurs de machines pour la fabrication de produits textiles et d'articles en fourrure et en cuir
   827   Conducteurs de machines pour la fabrication de denrées alimentaires et de produits connexes
   828   Ouvriers de l'assemblage
   829   Autres conducteurs de machines et ouvriers de l'assemblage
83   Conducteurs de véhicules et d'engins lourds de levage et de manœuvre
   831   Conducteurs de locomotives et assimilés
   832   Conducteurs de véhicules à moteur
   833   Conducteurs de matériels mobiles agricoles et d'autres engins mobiles
   834   Matelots de pont et assimilés

Grand groupe 9 Ouvriers et employés non qualifiés

91   Employés non qualifiés des services et de la vente
   911   Vendeurs ambulants et assimilés
   912   Cireurs de chaussures et autres travailleurs des petits métiers des rues
   913   Aides de ménage et autres aides, nettoyeurs et blanchisseurs
   914   Personnel du service d'immeuble, laveurs de vitres et assimilés
   915   Messagers, porteurs, gardiens, portiers et assimilés
   916   Eboueurs et manœuvres assimilés
92   Manœuvres de l'agriculture, de la pêche et assimilés
   921   Manœuvres de l'agriculture, de la pêche et assimilés
93   Manœuvres des mines, du bâtiment et des travaux publics, des industries manufacturières et des transports
   931   Manœuvres des mines, du bâtiment et des travaux publics
   932   Manœuvres des industries manufacturières
   933   Manœuvres des transports et manutentionnaires

Grand groupe 0 Forces armées

01   Forces armées
   011   Forces armées

Notes

[1] Dans ce groupe doivent être classées les personnes qui — en tant que directeur ou cadre de direction — gèrent une entreprise ou un organisme comprenant en tout et nécessairement trois cadres de direction ou davantage.

[2] Dans ce groupe doivent être classées les personnes qui assument la gestion d'une entreprise ou, le cas échéant, d'un organisme, pour leur propre compte ou pour le compte de son propriétaire avec le concours d'un seul autre cadre de direction et d'assistants subalternes.

Clasificación Internacional Uniforme de Ocupaciones (CIUO - 88)
Grandes grupos, subgrupos principales y subgrupos

Gran grupo 1   **Miembros del poder ejecutivo y de los cuerpos legislativos y personal directivo de la administración pública y de empresas**

11   Miembros del poder ejecutivo y de los cuerpos legislativos y personal directivo de la administración pública
- 111   Miembros del poder ejecutivo y de los cuerpos legislativos
- 112   Personal directivo de la administración pública
- 113   Jefes de pequeñas poblaciones
- 114   Dirigentes y administradores de organizaciones especializadas

12   Directores de empresa [1]
- 121   Directores generales y gerentes generales de empresa
- 122   Directores de departamentos de producción y operaciones
- 123   Otros directores de departamentos

13   Gerentes de empresa [2]
- 131   Gerentes de empresa

Gran grupo 2   **Profesionales científicos e intelectuales**

21   Profesionales de las ciencias físicas, químicas y matemáticas y de la ingeniería
- 211   Físicos, químicos y afines
- 212   Matemáticos, estadísticos y afines
- 213   Profesionales de la informática
- 214   Arquitectos, ingenieros y afines

22   Profesionales de las ciencias biológicas, la medicina y la salud
- 221   Profesionales en ciencias biológicas y otras disciplinas relativas a los seres orgánicos
- 222   Médicos y profesionales afines (excepto el personal de enfermería y partería)
- 223   Personal de enfermería y partería de nivel superior

23   Profesionales de la enseñanza
- 231   Profesores de universidades y otros establecimientos de la enseñanza superior
- 232   Profesores de la enseñanza secundaria
- 233   Maestros de nivel superior de la enseñanza primaria y preescolar
- 234   Maestros e instructores de nivel superior de la enseñanza especial
- 235   Otros profesionales de la enseñanza

24   Otros profesionales científicos e intelectuales
- 241   Especialistas en organización y administración de empresas y afines
- 242   Profesionales del derecho
- 243   Archiveros, bibliotecarios, documentalistas y afines
- 244   Especialistas en ciencias sociales y humanas
- 245   Escritores, artistas creativos y ejecutantes
- 246   Sacerdotes de distintas religiones

Gran grupo 3   **Técnicos y profesionales de nivel medio**

31   Técnicos y profesionales de nivel medio de las ciencias físicas y químicas, la ingeniería y afines
- 311   Técnicos en ciencias físicas y químicas y en ingeniería
- 312   Técnicos en programación y control informáticos
- 313   Operadores de equipos ópticos y electrónicos
- 314   Técnicos en navegación marítima y aeronáutica
- 315   Inspectores de obras, seguridad y salud y control de calidad

32   Técnicos y profesionales de nivel medio de las ciencias biológicas, la medicina y la salud
- 321   Técnicos de nivel medio en ciencias biológicas, agronomía, zootecnia y afines
- 322   Profesionales de nivel medio de la medicina moderna y la salud (excepto el personal de enfermería y partería)
- 323   Personal de enfermería y partería de nivel medio
- 324   Practicantes de la medicina tradicional y curanderos

33   Maestros e instructores de nivel medio
- 331   Maestros de nivel medio de la enseñanza primaria
- 332   Maestros de nivel medio de la enseñanza preescolar
- 333   Maestros de nivel medio de la enseñanza especial
- 334   Otros maestros e instructores de nivel medio

34   Otros técnicos y profesionales de nivel medio
- 341   Profesionales de nivel medio en operaciones financieras y comerciales
- 342   Agentes comerciales y corredores
- 343   Profesionales de nivel medio de servicios de administración
- 344   Agentes de las administraciones públicas de aduanas, impuestos y afines
- 345   Inspectores de policía y detectives
- 346   Trabajadores y asistentes sociales de nivel medio
- 347   Profesionales de nivel medio de actividades artísticas, espectáculos y deportes
- 348   Auxiliares laicos de los cultos

Gran grupo 4   **Empleados de oficina**

41   Oficinistas
- 411   Secretarios y operadores de máquinas de oficina
- 412   Auxiliares contables y financieros
- 413   Empleados encargados del registro de materiales y de transportes
- 414   Empleados de bibliotecas y servicios de correos y afines
- 419   Otros oficinistas

42   Empleados en trato directo con el público
- 421   Cajeros, taquilleros y afines
- 422   Empleados de servicios de información a la clientela

Gran grupo 5   **Trabajadores de los servicios y vendedores de comercios y mercados**

51   Trabajadores de los servicios personales y de los servicios de protección y seguridad
- 511   Personal al servicio directo de los pasajeros
- 512   Personal de intendencia y de restauración
- 513   Trabajadores de los cuidados personales y afines
- 514   Otros trabajadores de servicios personales a particulares
- 515   Astrólogos, adivinadores y afines
- 516   Personal de los servicios de protección y seguridad

52   Modelos, vendedores y demostradores
- 521   Modelos de modas, arte y publicidad
- 522   Vendedores y demostradores de tiendas y almacenes
- 523   Vendedores de quioscos y de puestos de mercado

Gran grupo 6 Agricultores y trabajadores calificados agropecuarios y pesqueros

61 Agricultores y trabajadores calificados de explotaciones agropecuarias, forestales y pesqueras con destino al mercado
- 611 Agricultores y trabajadores calificados de cultivos para el mercado
- 612 Criadores y trabajadores pecuarios calificados de la cría de animales para el mercado y afines
- 613 Productores y trabajadores agropecuarios calificados cuya producción se destina al mercado
- 614 Trabajadores forestales calificados y afines
- 615 Pescadores, cazadores y tramperos

62 Trabajadores agropecuarios y pesqueros de subsistencia
- 621 Trabajadores agropecuarios y pesqueros de subsistencia

Gran grupo 7 Oficiales, operarios y artesanos de artes mecánicas y de otros oficios

71 Oficiales y operarios de las industrias extractivas y de la construcción
- 711 Mineros, canteros, pegadores y labrantes de piedra
- 712 Oficiales y operarios de la construcción (obra gruesa) y afines
- 713 Oficiales y operarios de la construcción (trabajos de acabado) y afines
- 714 Pintores, limpiadores de fachadas y afines

72 Oficiales y operarios de la metalurgia, la construcción mecánica y afines
- 721 Moldeadores, soldadores, chapistas, caldereros, montadores de estructuras metálicas y afines
- 722 Herreros, herramentistas y afines
- 723 Mecánicos y ajustadores de máquinas
- 724 Mecánicos y ajustadores de equipos eléctricos y electrónicos

73 Mecánicos de precisión, artesanos, operarios de las artes gráficas y afines
- 731 Mecánicos de precisión en metales y materiales similares
- 732 Alfareros, operarios de cristalerías y afines
- 733 Artesanos de la madera, tejidos, cuero y materiales similares
- 734 Oficiales y operarios de las artes gráficas y afines

74 Otros oficiales, operarios y artesanos de artes mecánicas y de otros oficios
- 741 Oficiales y operarios del procesamiento de alimentos y afines
- 742 Oficiales y operarios del tratamiento de la madera, ebanistas y afines
- 743 Oficiales y operarios de los textiles y de la confección y afines
- 744 Oficiales y operarios de las pieles, cuero y calzado

Gran grupo 8 Operadores de instalaciones y máquinas y montadores

81 Operadores de instalaciones fijas y afines
- 811 Operadores de instalaciones mineras y de extracción y procesamiento de minerales
- 812 Operadores de instalaciones de procesamiento de metales
- 813 Operadores de instalaciones de vidriería, cerámica y afines
- 814 Operadores de instalaciones de procesamiento de la madera y de la fabricación de papel
- 815 Operadores de instalaciones de tratamientos químicos
- 816 Operadores de instalaciones de producción de energía y afines
- 817 Operadores de cadenas de montaje automatizadas y de robots industriales

82 Operadores de máquinas y montadores
- 821 Operadores de máquinas para trabajar metales y produtos minerales
- 822 Operadores de máquinas para fabricar productos químicos
- 823 Operadores de máquinas para fabricar productos de caucho y de material plástico
- 824 Operadores de máquinas para fabricar productos de madera
- 825 Operadores de máquinas de imprenta, encuadernación y fabricación de productos de papel
- 826 Operadores de máquinas para fabricar productos textiles y artículos de piel y cuero
- 827 Operadores de máquinas para elaborar alimentos y productos afines
- 828 Montadores
- 829 Otros operadores de máquinas y montadores

83 Conductores de vehículos y operadores de equipos pesados móviles
- 831 Maquinistas de locomotoras y afines
- 832 Conductores de vehículos de motor
- 833 Operadores de maquinaria agrícola móvil y de otras máquinas móviles
- 834 Marineros de cubierta y afines

Gran grupo 9 Trabajadores no calificados

91 Trabajadores no calificados de ventas y servicios
- 911 Vendedores ambulantes y afines
- 912 Limpiabotas y otros trabajadores callejeros
- 913 Personal doméstico y afines, limpiadores, lavanderos y planchadores
- 914 Conserjes, lavadores de ventanas y afines
- 915 Mensajeros, porteadores, porteros y afines
- 916 Recolectores de basura y afines

92 Peones agropecuarios, forestales, pesqueros y afines
- 921 Peones agropecuarios, forestales, pesqueros y afines

93 Peones de la minería, la construcción, la industria manufacturera y el transporte
- 931 Peones de la minería y la construcción
- 932 Peones de la industria manufacturera
- 933 Peones del transporte

Gran grupo 0 Fuerzas armadas

01 Fuerzas armadas
- 011 Fuerzas armadas

Notas

[1] En este subgrupo principal se incluyen las personas que — en tanto que directores o personal directivo — dirigen una empresa u organismo que comprenda por lo menos tres o más directores.

[2] En este subgrupo principal se incluyen las personas que ejercen la dirección de una empresa o de un organismo, por cuenta propia o de su propietario con la ayuda de solo un director y de asistentes subalternos.

International Standard Classification of Education (ISCED-76)

X: No schooling

Less than one year of schooling.

Level 0: Education preceding the first level

Education delivered in kindergartens, nursery schools as well as in infant classes attached to primary schools.

Level 1: First level

Programmes are designed to give the students a sound basic education in reading, writing and arithmetic along with an elementary understanding of other subjects such as national history, geography, natural science, social science, art, music and religious instruction. Children enter these programmes when they are 5 to 7 years old. Literacy programmes for adults are also to be classified under Level 1.

Level 2: Second level, first stage

The basic programmes constituting the first level are continued, but usually on a more subject-oriented pattern. Some small beginnings of specialization may be seen at this level with some students having the opportunity to direct their attention more particularly to certain types of subjects, e.g. commercial or technical subjects. Vocational programmes designed to train for a specific occupation and often associated with relatively unskilled jobs, as well as apprenticeship programmes for skilled trades and crafts that provide further education as part of the programme, are also included.

Level 3: Second level, second stage

General education continues to be an important constituent of the programmes, but separate subject presentation and more specialization are found at this level. Also to be classified under Level 3 are programmes consisting of subject matter mainly with a specific vocational emphasis or apprenticeship programmes, with an entrance requirement of eight full years of education, or a combination of basic education and vocational experience that demonstrates the ability to handle the subject matter of that level.

Level 5: Third level, first stage, leading to an award not equivalent to a first university degree

Programmes of this type are usually "practical" in orientation in that they are designed to prepare students for particular vocational fields in which they can qualify as high level technicians, teachers, nurses, production supervisors, etc.

Level 6: Third level, first stage, leading to a first university degree or equivalent qualification

Programmes of this type comprise those leading to typical first university degrees such as a "Bachelor's degree", a "Licence", etc., as well as those which lead to first professional degrees such as "Doctorates" awarded after completion of studies in medicine, engineering, law, etc.

Level 7: Third level, second stage

Programmes leading to a post-graduate university degree or equivalent qualification. Programmes of this type generally require a first university degree or equivalent qualification for admission. They are intended to reflect specialization within a given subject area.

Level 9: Education not definable by level

Programmes for which there are no entrance requirements.

?: Level not stated

Classification internationale type de l'éducation (CITE-76)

X: Non scolarisé

Moins d'une année de scolarité.

Niveau 0: Enseignement précédant le premier degré

Il est dispensé dans les jardins d'enfants, les écoles maternelles et les classes enfantines des écoles primaires.

Niveau 1: Premier degré

Les programmes visent à donner aux élèves des bases solides en lecture, écriture et arithmétique tout en leur inculquant des connaissances élémentaires en histoire nationale, géographie, sciences naturelles, sciences sociales, beaux-arts, musique et éventuellement instruction religieuse. L'âge auquel les enfants accèdent à cet enseignement se situe entre 5 et 7 ans. Les programmes d'alphabétisation des adultes doivent aussi être classés dans le niveau 1.

Niveau 2: Second degré, premier cycle

Les programmes de base continuent ceux du premier niveau avec une subdivision plus nette par sujets. On constate à ce niveau un petit début de spécialisation, les élèves ayant la possibilité de s'intéresser plus particulièrement à certaines matières (commerciales, techniques, etc.). Les programmes professionnels visant à former du personnel peu qualifié pour une profession spécifique, ainsi que les programmes orientés vers la formation de personnels qualifiés (artisans ou techniciens) comprenant une part d'instruction générale, sont aussi inclus.

Niveau 3: Second degré, deuxième cycle

L'instruction générale continue à occuper une place importante dans les programmes mais les matières sont enseignées séparément et la tendance à la spécialisation est plus marquée qu'aux niveaux précédents. Doivent aussi être classés au niveau 3 les programmes à orientation professionnelle marquée ou les programmes d'apprentissage qui requièrent huit années d'études préalables à plein temps ou bien une instruction de base jointe à l'expérience professionnelle requise pour être apte à suivre un enseignement de ce niveau.

Niveau 5: Troisième degré, premier niveau, conduisant à un titre non équivalent au premier grade universitaire

Les programmes de ce type sont généralement de caractère «pratique» en ce sens qu'ils sont conçus pour former les étudiants à des domaines professionnels particuliers dans lesquels ils peuvent se qualifier comme techniciens de haut niveau, professeur, personnel infirmier, contremaître de production, etc.

Niveau 6: Troisième degré, premier niveau, conduisant au premier grade universitaire ou à un titre équivalent

Les programmes de ce type comprennent ceux qui conduisent à des premiers diplômes universitaires types tels qu'un «Bachelor's Degree», une «licence», etc., comme ceux qui conduisent à des premiers diplômes professionnels tels que les «doctorats» acquis après la fin d'études médicales, juridiques, d'ingénierie, etc.

Niveau 7: Troisième degré, deuxième niveau, conduisant à un grade universitaire supérieur ou à un titre équivalent

Les programmes de ce type sont généralement accessibles avec un premier diplôme universitaire ou un titre équivalent. Ils sont conçus pour refléter la spécialisation dans un domaine donné.

Niveau 9: Enseignement impossible à définir selon le degré

Programmes pour lesquels il n'existe pas de conditions d'entrée.

?: Niveau inconnu

Clasificación Internacional Normalizada de la Educación (CINE-76)

X: Sin escolaridad

Menos de un año de escolaridad.

Nivel 0: Enseñanza anterior al primer grado

Se da en las guarderías infantiles, las escuelas de párvulos y las clases infantiles de las escuelas primarias.

Nivel 1: Enseñanza de primer grado

Los programas están encaminados a dar a los alumnos sólidas bases en lectura, escritura y aritmética, junto con conocimientos elementales en historia nacional, geografía, ciencias naturales, ciencias sociales, bellas artes, música y eventualmente enseñanza religiosa. Los niños entran en esta enseñanza entre los 5 y los 7 años de edad. Hay que clasificar también los programas de alfabetización de los adultos en el nivel 1.

Nivel 2: Enseñanza de segundo grado, ciclo inferior

Los programas básicos continúan los del primer grado pero con una subdivisión más clara por temas. Se observa en este grado un pequeño comienzo de especialización; los alumnos tienen la posibilidad de interesarse más particularmente por ciertas asignaturas (comerciales, técnicas, etcétera). Los programas profesionales encaminados a formar a un personal poco calificado para una profesión específica, así como los programas de aprendizaje para personal calificado (artesano o técnico) que comprenden una parte de instrucción general, también están incluidos.

Nivel 3: Enseñanza de segundo grado, ciclo superior

La instrucción general sigue ocupando una parte importante en los programas pero las asignaturas se enseñan por separado y la tendencia a la especialización es más clara que en los niveles anteriores. Hay que clasificar en el nivel 3 también los programas con una orientación profesional acentuada o los programas de aprendizaje que necesitan el cumplimiento anterior de ocho años de estudios de dedicación exclusiva o bien una instrucción básica y la experiencia profesional requerida para tener la capacidad de seguir las clases a este nivel.

Nivel 5: Enseñanza de tercer grado que no permite obtener un primer título universitario o equivalente

Los programas de este tipo tienen por lo general un carácter «práctico» ya que están encaminados a formar los estudiantes en sectores profesionales especiales en que pueden calificarse como técnicos superiores, personal enfermero, encargado de producción, etcétera.

Nivel 6: Enseñanza de tercer grado que permite obtener un primer título universitario o equivalente

Los programas de este tipo comprenden los que conducen a un primer diploma universitario tal como una Licencia, etcétera, y también los que conducen a un primer diploma profesional tal como los Doctorados obtenidos después del cumplimiento de estudios de medicina, de derecho, de ingeniería, etcétera.

Nivel 7: Enseñanza de tercer grado que permite obtener un título o diploma universitario superior

Los programas de este tipo requieren por lo general un primer diploma universitario o un título equivalente. Están encaminados a reflejar la especialización en un sector particular.

Nivel 9: Enseñanza que no puede definirse por grados

Estos programas no necesitan el cumplimiento de estudios anteriores.

?: Nivel desconocido

International Standard Classification of Education (ISCED -97) [Summary]

X: No schooling

Less than one year of schooling

Level 0: Pre-primary education

Programmes are designed primarily to introduce children, aged at least three years, to a school type environment; they are school or centre-based.

Level 1: Primary education or first stage of basic education

Programmes are designed on a unit or project basis to give students a sound basic education in reading, writing and mathematics along with an elementary understanding of other subjects such as history, geography, natural science, social science, art and music; religious instruction may also be featured. The customary or legal age of entrance is between five and seven years. This level covers in principle six years of full-time schooling. Literacy programmes for adults are also included at this level.

Level 2: Lower secondary or second stage of basic education

Programmes are designed to complete the provision of basic education begun at Level 1. They are usually on a more subject-oriented pattern, often with teachers conducting classes in their field of specialization. The end of this level often coincides with the end of compulsory education where it exists.
Programmes can be sub-classified according to the subsequent education or destination for which they have been designed:
2A: direct access to Level 3 (3A or 3B) in a sequence leading ultimately to tertiary education;
2B: direct access to Level 3C;
2C: direct access to the labour market.
Programmes at Level 2 can also be sub-divided into three categories according to their orientation: those providing (i) General education, mainly designed to lead to a deeper understanding of a subject or group of subjects, especially (but not necessarily) in preparation for further education; (ii) Pre-vocational or pre-technical education, designed as a preparation for entry into vocational or technical education programmes; (iii) Vocational or technical education, mainly designed to lead to the acquisition of skills, necessary for employment in a particular occupation or trade, the successful completion of which leads to a labour-market relevant vocational qualification.

Level 3: Upper secondary education

Educational programmes typically require the completion of 9 years full-time education (since the beginning of Level 1) and the completion of Level 2 for admission; the entrance age is thus typically 15 or 16 years. More specialization may be observed and teachers more qualified or specialized.
As at Level 2, programmes can be sub-classified according to the subsequent education or destination for which they have been designed:
3A: direct access to Level 5A;
3B: direct access to Level 5B;
3C: not designed to lead directly to Levels 5A or 5B, but rather to the labour market or to Level 4 or other Level 3 programmes. The programme orientation categories are the same as for Level 2.

Level 4: Post-secondary non-tertiary education

Level 4 captures programmes that straddle the boundary between upper-secondary (Level 3) and post-secondary education. Due to their content they cannot be considered as tertiary programmes as they are often not significantly more advanced than Level 3 programmes but serve to broaden the knowledge of participants who have successfully completed Level 3 programmes. They have a typical full-time equivalent duration of between six months and two years. Programmes can be sub-classified into two categories according to the subsequent education or destination for which they have been designed:
4A: preparation for entry to Level 5;
4B: do not give access to Level 5 (primarily designed for labour market entry).
The programme orientation categories are the same as those for Levels 2 and 3.

Level 5: First stage of tertiary education (not leading directly to an advanced research qualification)

Entry to Level 5 programmes normally requires the successful completion of Level 3A or 3B or a similar qualification at Level 4A. Level 5 programmes are subdivided into two distinct categories:
5A: Programmes are largely theoretically based and are intended to provide sufficient qualifications for
gaining entry into advanced research programmes and professions with high skill requirements (e.g. medicine, dentistry, architecture, etc.) They have a minimum cumulative theoretical duration of three years full-time equivalent, although typically they are four or more years.
5B: Programmes are practically oriented/ occupationally specific and mainly designed to permit the acquisition of the practical skills and know-how necessary for employment in a particular occupation or trade; successful completion usually provides participants with a labour-market relevant qualification. Programmes are typically shorter than in 5A with a minimum duration of 2 years' full-time equivalent and they do not provide direct access to advanced research programmes.

Level 6: second stage of tertiary education (leading to an advanced research qualification)

Programmes are devoted to advanced study and original research and are not based on course-work only. They typically require the submission of a thesis or dissertation of publishable quality which is the product of original research and represents a significant contribution to knowledge.

?: Level not stated

Notes

[1] The full text of ISCED-97 is available in English, French, Spanish and Russian on UNESCO's website (www.uis.unesco.org).

[2] In order to maintain parallel structure to the educational and labour market destinations at Level 3, it has been proposed that Level 4 be split into 3 sub-categories, 4A, 4B and 4C. Although not formally part of ISCED-97 a sub-category 4C is used in the joint UNESCO/OECD/ EUROSTAT Data Collection on Education Systems.

Classification internationale type de l'éducation (CITE-97) [Résumé]

X: Non scolarisé

Moins d'une année de scolarité.

Niveau 0: Education préprimaire

Les programmes visent essentiellement à préparer les enfants, âgés de trois ans au moins, à un environnement scolaire; l'enseignement est dispensé dans une école ou dans un centre extérieur à la famille.

Niveau 1: Enseignement primaire ou premier cycle de l'éducation de base

S'articulant normalement autour d'une unité ou d'un projet les programmes visent à donner aux élèves un solide enseignement de base en lecture, en écriture et en mathématiques et des connaissances élémentaires dans d'autres matières telles que l'histoire, la géographie, les sciences naturelles, les sciences sociales, le dessin et la musique; une instruction religieuse peut éventuellement être prévue. L'âge habituel ou légal auquel les enfants accèdent à cet enseignement se situe entre 5 et 7 ans. La durée habituelle de scolarité est en principe de six ans à plein temps. Les programmes d'alphabétisation des adultes sont également inclus dans ce niveau.

Niveau 2: Premier cycle de l'enseignement secondaire ou deuxième cycle de l'éducation de base

Les programmes sont destinés à compléter l'éducation de base commencée au niveau 1. Ils ont généralement une structure davantage orientée vers les matières enseignées, et il est plus fréquent que plusieurs enseignants se chargent chacun d'une matière dans laquelle ils sont spécialisés. La fin de ce niveau coïncide souvent avec celle de la scolarité obligatoire dans les pays où celle-ci existe. Les programmes peuvent être classés en sous-catégories selon le type d'enseignement ou d'orientation ultérieurs pour lequel ils ont été conçus:
2A: accès direct au niveau 3 (3A ou 3B) dans une filière menant à terme à l'enseignement supérieur;
2B: accès direct au niveau 3C;
2C: accès direct au marché de travail.
Les programmes du niveau 2 peuvent aussi être répartis en trois catégories selon leur orientation, à savoir: (i) l'enseignement général, conçu principalement pour permettre aux participants de mieux comprendre une matière ou un groupe de matières afin, en particulier (mais non nécessairement), de les préparer à la poursuite d'autres études; (ii) Enseignement pré-professionel ou prétechnique, destiné à préparer les participants à recevoir un enseignement professionnel ou technique; (iii) Enseignement professionnel ou technique, destiné principalement à permettre aux participants d'acquérir les compétences qu'ils emploieront dans un métier ou une profession; ceux qui ont suivi avec succès un programme ayant cette orientation obtiennent un titre utilisable sur le marché du travail.

Niveau 3: Enseignement secondaire (deuxième cycle)

Les programmes exigent normalement l'accomplissement préalable de 9 ans d'études à plein temps (depuis le début du niveau 1) et, comme condition minimale d'admission, l'achèvement du niveau 2. L'âge d'admission est normalement de 15 ou 16 ans. On peut observer une plus grande spécialisation et les enseignants doivent souvent être plus qualifiés ou spécialisés qu'au niveau 2.
Comme pour le niveau 2, les programmes peuvent être classés en trois sous-catégories selon le type d'enseignement ou d'orientation ultérieurs pour lequel ils ont été conçus:
3A: accès direct au niveau 5A;
3B: accès direct au niveau 5B;
3C: ne sont pas conçus pour permettre d'accéder directement aux niveaux 5A ou 5B, mais mènent directement au marché du travail, à des programmes du niveau 4 ou à d'autres programmes du niveau 3.
Les programmes du niveau 3 peuvent être répartis selon les mêmes catégories d'orientation que ceux du niveau 2.

Niveau 4: Enseignement postsecondaire qui n'est pas du supérieur

Le niveau 4 regroupe des programme qui se situent à la limite entre le deuxième cycle du secondaire (niveau 3) et l'enseignement postsecondaire. Le contenu des programmes du niveau 4 ne peut être considéré comme relevant du supérieur. Souvent ces programmes ne sont pas d'un niveau sensiblement plus élevé que ceux du niveau 3, mais permettent d'élargir les connaissances des participants qui ont déjà terminé un programme au niveau 3. La durée normale des programmes est comprise entre six mois et deux ans en équivalent plein-temps. Les programmes peuvent être classés en deux sous-catégories selon le type d'enseignement ou d'orientation ultérieurs pour lequel ils ont été conçus:
4A: préparation à l'entrée au niveau 5A;
4B: ne donnent pas accès au niveau 5 (principalement conçus pour permettre un accès direct au marché du travail);
Les programmes du niveau 4 peuvent être répartis selon les mêmes catégories d'orientation que ceux des niveaux 2 et 3.

Niveau 5: premier cycle de l'enseignement supérieur (ne conduisant pas directement à un titre de chercheur de haut niveau)

L'admission aux programmes du niveau 5 exige normalement l'achèvement avec succès du niveau 3A ou 3B ou l'acquisition d'une qualification comparable au niveau 4A. Les programmes du niveau 5 sont subdivisés en deux catégories distinctes:
5A: Les programmes sont fondés principalement sur la théorie et destinés à offrir des qualifications suffisantes pour être admis à suivre des programmes de recherche de pointe ou à exercer une profession exigeant de hautes compétences (par exemple, médecine, dentisterie, architecture, etc.). Ils ont une durée cumulée minimale de trois ans en équivalent plein-temps, bien qu'ils durent habituellement quatre ans ou plus.
5B: Le contenu des programmes a une orientation pratique correspondant à une profession précise et est principalement destiné à permettre aux participants d'acquérir les compétences pratiques et le savoir-faire nécessaires pour occuper un emploi dans une profession ou un métier particulier. L'achèvement avec succès de ces programmes permet normalement aux participants d'obtenir un titre utilisable sur le marché du travail. Les qualifications correspondant aux programmes 5B sont normalement obtenues par des études plus courtes que celles de la catégorie 5A. Les programmes ont une durée minimale de deux ans en équivalent plein-temps et ne donnent pas directement accès à des programmes de formation à la recherche de pointe.

Niveau 6: Deuxième cycle de l'enseignement supérieur (conduisant à un titre de chercheur hautement qualifié)

Les programmes sont consacrés à des études approfondies et à des travaux de recherche originaux et ne sont pas fondés uniquement sur des cours. Ils exigent normalement que soit soutenue une thèse d'une qualité suffisante pour en permettre la publication, thèse qui doit être le produit d'un travail de recherche original et représenter une contribution appréciable à la connaissance.

?: Niveau inconnu

Notes

[1] Le texte intégral de la CITE-97 est disponible en français, anglais, espagnol et russe sur le site de l'UNESCO (www.uis.unesco.org).

[2] Afin de conserver une structure parallèle à celle du niveau 3 en ce qui concerne l'enseignement ultérieur et l'accès au marché du travail, il a été proposé que le niveau 4 soit classé en 3 sous-catégories, 4A, 4B et 4C. Bien que la sous-catégorie 4C ne fasse pas partie officiellement de la CITE-97 elle est utilisée par l'organisme conjoint de l'UNESCO/OCDE/ EUROSTAT pour la collecte de données sur les systèmes d'éducation.

Clasificación internacional Normalizada de la Educación (CINE-97) [Resumen]

X: Sin escolaridad

Menos de un año de escolaridad.

Nivel 0: Enseñanza preescolar

Los programas están destinados esencialmente a familiarizar a niños de por lo menos 3 años de edad con un entorno de tipo escolar; se organizan en una escuela o en un centro.

Nivel 1: Enseñanza primaria o primer ciclo de la educación básica

Basados en unidades o proyectos los programas están destinados a proporcionar una sólida educación básica en lectura, escritura y aritmética junto con conocimientos elementales en otras asignaturas como historia, geografía, ciencias naturales, ciencias sociales, arte y música; en algunos casos se imparte instrucción religiosa. La edad habitual o legal de ingreso es de 5 a 7 años. Este nivel comprende por lo general 6 años de escolarización de tiempo completo. También se incluyen en este nivel los programas de alfabetización de los adultos.

Nivel 2: Primer ciclo de enseñanza secundaria o segundo ciclo de educación básica

Los programas están destinados a completar la educación de base iniciada en el nivel 1. Suelen seguir un modelo más orientado por asignaturas: los profesores son más especializados y generalmente varios imparten enseñanza en su especialización. El final de este ciclo suele coincidir con el término de la escolarización obligatoria, donde existe. Los programas se pueden clasificar según el tipo de enseñanza ulterior o destino al que fueron asignados:

2A: acceso directo al nivel 3 (3A o 3B) en una secuencia que en último término llevaría a la educación terciaria;
2B: acceso directo al nivel 3C;
2C: acceso directo al mercado de trabajo.

Los programas de nivel 2 se subdividen también según su orientación, a saber: (i) enseñanza general, destinada principalmente a transmitir a los participantes un conocimiento más profundo de un tema o grupo de temas, en particular (pero no necesariamente), con miras a prepararlos a una educación ulterior; (ii) Educación preprofesional o pretécnica, destinada a preparar los participantes para que ingresen en la enseñanza profesional o técnica; (iii) Enseñanza profesional o técnica, destinada principalmente a que los participantes adquieran las competencias necesarias para que se les pueda emplear en una ocupación u oficio particular - los que terminan con éxito reciben la correspondiente calificación profesional para el mercado de trabajo.

Nivel 3: Segundo ciclo de enseñanza secundaria

Los programas exigen por lo general que se hayan cursado nueve años de enseñanza de tiempo completo (desde el nivel 1), siendo el requisito mínimo de ingreso la terminación de nivel 2; La edad normal de ingreso es de 15 o 16 años. Se puede observar una mayor especialización y con frecuencia es preciso que los profesores sean más calificados o especializados que en el nivel 2.
De la misma manera que el nivel 2, los programas se subdividen en tres grupos según el tipo de enseñanza ulterior o destino al que fueron asignados:

3A: acceso directo al nivel 5A;
3B: acceso directo al nivel 5B;
3C: no conducen directamente a los niveles 5A ni 5B, sino al mercado de trabajo, a los programas de nivel 4 o a otros programas de nivel 3.

Los programas de nivel 3 se subdividen también según las mismas categorías de orientación que los de nivel 2.

Nivel 4: Enseñanza postsecundaria, no terciaria

El nivel 4 comprende programas que unen el segundo ciclo de secundario (nivel 3) a la enseñanza postsecundaria. Habida cuenta de su contenido, los programas no pueden considerarse de nivel terciario. No suelen ser mucho más avanzados que los de nivel 3 pero sirven para ampliar los conocimientos de los participantes que ya han cursado un programa de nivel 3. La duración de programas, calculada en tiempo completo, suele oscilar entre 6 meses y 2 años. Se puede subdividir los programas en dos grupos según el tipo de enseñanza ulterior o destino al que fueron asignados:

4A: preparación para el ingreso al nivel 5A;
4B: no conducen al nivel 5 (destinados primariamente al ingreso directo en el mercado laboral).

Los programas de nivel 4 también se subdividen también según las mismas categorías de orientación que los de niveles 2 y 3.

Nivel 5: Primer ciclo de la educación terciaria (no conduce directamente a una calificación avanzada)

Para ingresar a programas de nivel 5 se suele exigir la aprobación del nivel 3A o 3B o una calificación similar de nivel 4A. Los programas de nivel 5 se subdividen en dos categorías distintas:
5A: Los programas son en gran parte teóricos, que están destinados a facilitar una calificación suficiente para ingresar en programas de investigación avanzada o que dan acceso al ejercicio de profesiones que requieren un alto nivel de capacitación (por ejemplo, medicina, odontología, arquitectura, etc.) Tienen una duración teórica total mínima de tres años, calculados en tiempo completo, aunque suelen durar cuatro años o más.
5B: El contenido de los programas está orientado a la práctica o es específico de una profesión y está concebido sobre todo para que los participantes adquieran las destrezas prácticas y los conocimientos necesarios para ejercer una profesión particular o un oficio. La aprobación de los correspondientes programas suele facilitar a los participantes la calificación adecuada para el mercado de trabajo. Las calificaciones del nivel 5B suelen exigir menos tiempo que las del 5A. Los programas tienen una duración mínima de 2 años calculados en tiempo completo y no facilita acceso directo a programas de investigación avanzada.

Nivel 6: Segundo ciclo de la enseñanza terciaria (conduce a una calificación de investigación avanzada)

Este nivel está reservado a los programas de enseñanza terciaria que conducen a una calificación de investigación avanzada; por consiguiente están dedicados a estudios avanzados e investigaciones originales, y no están basados únicamente en cursos. Por lo general se requiere presentar una tesis o disertación que se pueda publicar, sea fruto de una investigación original y represente una contribución significativa al conocimiento.

?: Nivel desconocido

Notes

[1] El texto completo de la CINE-97 está disponible en español, francés, inglés y ruso en el sitio de la UNESCO (www.uis.unesco.org).

[2] A fin de conservar una estructura paralela a la del nivel 3 en lo que concierne la enseñanza ulterior y el acceso al mercado de trabajo, se propone que el nivel 4 se subdivida en tres grupos, 4A, 4B y 4C. Aunque el grupo 4C oficialmente no forme parte de la CINE-97 está utilizado por el organismo conjunto de UNESCO/OCDE/EUROSTAT para la recopilación de datos sobre los Sistemas de Educación.

References – Références – Referencias

The references given below are a selected list of International Labour Office publications on methodology and practice in the field of labour statistics.

Les références présentées ci-dessous fournissent une liste sélectionnée de publications du Bureau international du Travail traitant des pratiques et des méthodes utilisées en matière de statistiques du travail.

Las referencias dadas abajo comprenden una selección de publicaciones de la Oficina Internacional del Trabajo sobre la metodología y la práctica en materia de estadísticas del trabajo.

General – Général – General

International Standard Classification of Occupations (Revised 1988) (Geneva, 1990)
Classification internationale type des professions (révisée, 1988) (Genève, 1991)
Clasificación internacional uniforme de ocupaciones (revisada, 1988) (Ginebra, 1991)

Current international recommendations on labour statistics (Geneva, 2000)
Recommandations internationales en vigueur sur les statistiques du travail (Genève, 2000)
Recomendaciones internacionales de actualidad en estadísticas del trabajo (Ginebra, 2000)

Fourteenth International Conference of Labour Statisticians, Reports I-IV; Report of the Conference (Geneva, 1987)
Quatorzième Conférence internationale des statisticiens du travail, rapports I-IV; rapport de la Conférence (Genève, 1987)
Decimocuarta Conferencia Internacional de Estadísticos del Trabajo, Informes I-IV; Informe de la Conferencia (Ginebra, 1987)

Fifteenth International Conference of Labour Statisticians, Reports I-IV; Report of the Conference (Geneva, 1993)
Quinzième Conférence internationale des statisticiens du travail, rapports I-IV; rapport de la Conférence (Genève, 1993)
Decimoquinta Conferencia Internacional de Estadísticos del Trabajo, Informes I-IV; Informe de la Conferencia (Ginebra, 1993)

Sixteenth International Conference of Labour Statisticans, Reports I-IV; Report of the Conference (Geneva, 1998)
Seizième Conférence internationale des statisticiens du travail, rapports I-IV; Rapport de la Conférence (Genève, 1998)
Decimosexta Conferencia Internacional de Estadísticos del Trabajo, In-formes I-IV; Informe de la Conferencia (Ginebra, 1998)

Seventeenth International Conference of Labour Statisticians, Reports I-III; Report of the Conference (Geneva, 2003)
Dix-septième Conférence internationale des statisticiens du travail, Rapports I-III ; Rapport de la Conférence (Genève, 2003)
Decimoséptima Conferencia Internacional de Estadísticos del Trabajo, Informes I-III, Informe de la Conferencia (Ginebra, 2003)

Revision of the International Standard Classification of Occupations, Fourteenth International Conference of Labour Statisticians, see Report of the Conference
Révision de la classification internationale type des professions, quatorzième Conférence internationale des statisticiens du travail, voir rapport de la conférence
Revisión de la Clasificación internacional uniforme de ocupaciones, Decimocuarta Conferencia Internacional de Estadísticos del Trabajo, ver Informe de la Conferencia

Revision of the International Classification of Status in Employment, Fifteenth International Conference of Labour Statisticians, see Report IV and Report of the Conference
Révision de la classification internationale d'après la situation dans la profession, quinzième Conférence internationale des statisticiens du travail, voir rapport IV et rapport de la Conférence
Revisión de la Clasificación internacional de la categoría en el empleo, Decimoquinta Conferencia Internacional de Estadísticos del Trabajo, ver Informe IV e Informe de la Conferencia

Sources and Methods: Labour Statistics, Vol. 6: Household income and expenditure surveys (Geneva, 1994)
Sources et méthodes: statistiques du travail, vol. 6: Enquêtes sur le revenu et les dépenses des ménages (Genève, 1994)
Fuentes y Métodos: Estadísticas del Trabajo, vol. 6: Encuestas sobre los ingresos de los hogares (Ginebra, 1994)

Sources and Methods: Labour Statistics, Vol. 9: Transition Countries (Geneva, 1999)
Sources et méthodes: statistiques du travail, vol. 9: Pays en transition (Genève, 1999)
Fuentes y Métodos: Estadísticas del Trabajo, vol. 9: Países en transición (Ginebra, 1999)

Total and economically active population, employment and unemployment – Population totale et population active, emploi et chômage – Población total y población económicamente activa, empleo y desempleo

Surveys on economically active population, employment, unemployment and underemployment – An ILO manual on concepts and methods (Geneva, 1990)
Enquêtes sur la population active, l'emploi, le chômage et le sous-emploi: Un manuel du BIT sur les concepts et méthodes (version française en préparation)
Encuestas de la población económicamente activa, empleo, desempleo y subempleo – Un manual de la OIT sobre conceptos y métodos (Madrid, 1993)

Labour Force, Employment, Unemployment and Underemployment, Thirteenth International Conference of Labour Statisticians, Report II (Geneva, 1982)
Main-d'œuvre, emploi, chômage et sous-emploi, treizième Conférence internationale des statisticiens du travail, rapport II (Genève, 1982)
Fuerza de trabajo, empleo, desempleo y subempleo, Decimotercera Conferencia Internacional de Estadísticos del Trabajo, Informe II (Ginebra, 1982)

Measurement of underemployment and inadequate employment situations, Sixteenth International Conference of La-

bour Statisticians, Report I and Report of the Conference (Geneva, 1998)
Mesure du sous-emploi et des situations d'emploi inadéquat, seizième Conférence internationale des statisticiens du travail, Rapport I et Rapport de la Conférence (Genève, 1998)
Medición del subempleo y las situaciones de empleo inadecuado, Decimosexta Conferencia Internacional de Estadísticos del Trabajo, Informe I e Informe de la Conferencia (Ginebra, 1998)

Economically Active Population, 1950-2010 (Geneva, 1996)
Vol. I: Asia – Vol. II: Africa – Vol. III: Latin America and the Caribbean – Vol. IV: Northern America, Europe and Oceania – Vol. V: World; Vol. VI: Methodological Supplement
Population active, 1950-2010 (Genève, 1996)
Vol. I: Asie – vol. II: Afrique – vol. III: Amérique latine et les Caraïbes – vol. IV: Amérique du Nord, Europe et Océanie – vol. V: Monde; vol. VI: Supplément méthodologique.
Población económicamente activa, 1950-2010 (Ginebra, 1996)
Vol. I: Asia – vol. II: Africa – vol. III: América Latina y las Antillas – vol. IV: América del Norte, Europa y Oceanía – vol. V: Mundo; vol. VI: Suplemento metodológico

Sources and Methods: Labour Statistics: Vol.10: Estimates and projections of the economically active population 1950-2010 (Geneva, 2000)
Sources et méthodes: statistique du travail: vol.10 : Evaluations et projections de la population active 1950-2010 (Genève, 2000)
Fuentes y Métodos: Estadísticas del Trabajo: vol. 10: Evaluaciones y proyecciones de la población económicamente activa 1950-2010 (Ginebra, 2000)

Economically Active Population Estimates and Projections, 1980-2020, updated version, see the following website: http://laborsta.ilo.org.
Population active, Evaluations et projections, 1980-2020, mise à jour; voir le site suivant: http://laborsta.ilo.org (en anglais seulement).
Población económicamente activa, Evaluaciones y proyecciones, 1980-2020, versión actualizada, véase el sitio Web: http://laborsta.ilo.org (sólo en inglés)

Sources and Methods: Labour Statistics (formerly *Statistical Sources and Methods*), Vol. 2: Employment, wages, hours of work and labour cost (establishment surveys), second edition (Geneva, 1995); Vol. 3: Economically active population, employment, unemployment and hours of work (Household surveys), third edition (Geneva, 2005); Vol. 4: Employment, unemployment, wages and hours of work (administrative records and related sources), second edition (Geneva, 2005); Vol. 5: Total and economically active population, employment and unemployment (population censuses), second edition (Geneva, 1996). A technical guide of series published in the *Yearbook of Labour Statistics* and the *Bulletin of Labour Statistics*
Sources et méthodes: statistique du travail (précédemment *Sources et méthodes statistiques*), vol. 2: Emploi, salaires, durée du travail et coût de la main-d'œuvre (enquêtes auprès des établissements), deuxième édition (Genève, 1995); vol. 3: Population active, emploi, chômage et durée du travail (enquête auprès des ménages), troisième édition (Genève, 2005); vol. 4: Emploi, chômage, salaires et durée du travail (documents administratifs et sources assimilées) deuxième édition (Genève, 2005); vol. 5: Population totale et population active, emploi et chômage (recensements de population), deuxième édition (Genève, 1996). Un guide technique des séries publiées dans l'*Annuaire des statistiques du travail* et le *Bulletin des statistiques du travail*
Fuentes y Métodos: Estadísticas del Trabajo (anteriormente *Fuentes y Métodos Estadísticos*), vol. 2: Empleo, salarios, horas de trabajo y costo de la mano de obra (encuestas de establecimientos), segunda edición (Ginebra, 1995); vol. 3: Población económicamente activa, empleo, desempleo y horas de trabajo (encuestas de hogares), tercera edición (Ginebra, 2005); vol. 4: Empleo, desempleo, salarios y horas de trabajo (registros administrativos y fuentes conexas) segunda edición (Ginebra, 2005); vol. 5: Población total y población económicamente activa, empleo y desempleo (censos de población), segunda edición (Ginebra, 1996). Una guía técnica de las series publicadas en el *Anuario de Estadísticas del Trabajo* y en el *Boletín de Estadísticas del Trabajo*

Yearbook of Labour Statistics: Retrospective edition on population censuses, 1945-89 (Geneva, 1990)
Annuaire des statistiques du travail: édition rétrospective sur les recensements de population, 1945-89 (Genève, 1990)
Anuario de Estadísticas del Trabajo: Edición retrospectiva sobre los censos de población, 1945-89 (Ginebra, 1990)

Statistics of employment in the informal sector, Fifteenth International Conference of Labour Statisticians, see Report III and Report of the Conference
Statistiques de l'emploi dans le secteur informel, quinzième Conférence internationale des statisticiens du travail, voir rapport III et rapport de la Conférence
Estadísticas del empleo en el sector informal, Decimoquinta Conferencia Internacional de Estadísticos del Trabajo, ver Informe III e Informe de la Conferencia

Hours of work – Durée du travail – Horas de trabajo

Statistics of Hours of Work, Tenth International Conference of Labour Statisticians, Report III (Geneva, 1962)
Statistiques de la durée du travail, dixième Conférence internationale des statisticiens du travail, rapport III (Genève, 1962)
Estadísticas de la duración del trabajo, Décima Conferencia Internacional de Estadísticos del Trabajo, Informe III (Ginebra, 1962)

Sources and Methods: Labour Statistics (formerly *Statistical Sources and Methods*), Vol. 2: Employment, wages, hours of work and labour cost (establishment surveys), second edition (Geneva, 1995); Vol. 3: Economically active population, employment, unemployment and hours of work (Household surveys), third edition (Geneva, 2005); Vol. 4: Employment, unemployment, wages and hours of work (administrative records and related sources) second edition (Geneva, 2005). A technical guide of series published in the *Yearbook of Labour Statistics* and the *Bulletin of Labour Statistics*
Sources et méthodes statistiques du travail (précédemment *Sources et méthodes statistiques*), vol. 2: Emploi, salaires, durée du travail et coût de la main-d'œuvre (enquêtes auprès des établissements), deuxième édition (Genève, 1995); vol. 3: Population active, emploi, chômage et durée du travail (enquêtes auprès des ménages), troisième édition (Genève, 2005); vol. 4: Emploi, chômage, salaires et durée du travail (documents administratifs et sources assimilées) deuxième édition (Genève, 2005). Un guide technique des séries publiées dans l'*Annuaire des statistiques du travail* et le *Bulletin des statistiques du travail*

Fuentes y Métodos: Estadísticas del Trabajo (anteriormente *Fuentes y Métodos Estadísticos*), vol. 2: Empleo, salarios, horas de trabajo y costo de la mano de obra (encuestas de establecimientos), segunda edición (Ginebra, 1995); vol. 3: Población económicamente activa, empleo, desempleo y horas de trabajo (encuestas de hogares), tercera edición (Ginebra, 2005); vol. 4: Empleo, desempleo, salarios y horas de trabajo (registros administrativos y fuentes conexas) segunda edición (Ginebra, 2005). Una guía técnica de las series pulicadas en el *Anuario de Estadísticas del Trabajo* y en el *Boletín de Estadísticas del Trabajo*

Wages – Salaires – Salarios

An integrated system of wages statistics: a manual on methods (Geneva, 1979)
Un système intégré des statistiques des salaires – Manuel de méthodologie (Genève, 1980)
Un Sistema integrado de estadísticas de salarios: manual metodológico (Ginebra, 1992)
Un sistema integrado de estadísticas de salarios: Manual de Metodología (Lisboa, 1992)

Sources and Methods: Labour Statistics (formerly *Statistical Sources and Methods*), Vol. 2: Employment, wages, hours of work and labour cost (establishment surveys), second edition (Geneva, 1995); Vol. 4: Employment, unemployment, wages and hours of work (administrative records and related sources) second edition (Geneva, 2005)
Sources et méthodes: statistiques du travail (précédemment *Sources et méthodes statistiques*), vol. 2: Emploi, salaires, durée du travail et coût de la main-d'œuvre (enquêtes auprès des établissements), deuxième édition (Genève, 1995); vol. 4: Emploi, chômage, salaires et durée du travail (documents administratifs et sources assimilées) deuxième édition (Genève, 2005)
Fuentes y Métodos: Estadísticas del Trabajo (anteriormente *Fuentes y Métodos Estadísticos*), vol. 2: Empleo, salarios, horas de trabajo y costo de la mano de obra (encuestas de establecimientos), segunda edición (Ginebra, 1995); vol. 4: Empleo, desempleo, salarios y horas de trabajo (registros administrativos y fuentes conexas), segunda edición (Ginebra, 2005)

Labour cost – Coût de la main-d'œuvre – Costo de la mano de obra

Statistics of Labour Cost, Eleventh International Conference of Labour Statisticians, Report II (Geneva, 1966)
Statistiques du coût de la main-d'œuvre, onzième Conférence internationale des statisticiens du travail, rapport II (Genève, 1966)
Estadísticas del costo de la mano de obra, Undécima Conferencia Internacional de Estadísticos del Trabajo, Informe II (Ginebra, 1966)

An integrated system of wages statistics: a manual on methods (Geneva, 1979)
Un système intégré des statistiques des salaires – Manuel de méthodologie (Genève, 1980)
Sistema integrado de estadísticas de salarios: manual metodológico (Ginebra, 1992)
Um sistema integrado de estadísticas de salários: Manual de Metodología (Lisboa, 1992)

Sources and Methods: Labour Statistics, Vol. 2: Employment, wages, hours of work and labour cost (establishment surveys), second edition (Geneva, 1995).

Sources et méthodes: statistiques du travail, vol. 2: Emploi, salaires, durée du travail et coût de la main-d'œuvre (enquêtes auprès des établissements), deuxième édition (Genève, 1995)
Fuentes y Métodos: Estadísticas del Trabajo, vol. 2: Empleo, salarios, horas de trabajo y costo de la mano de obra (encuestas de establecimientos), segunda edición (Ginebra, 1995)

The Cost of Social Security. Fourteenth international inquiry, 1987-1989 (Geneva, 1995)
Le coût de la sécurité sociale. Quatorzième enquête internationale, 1987-1989 (Genève, 1995)
El costo de la seguridad social. Decimocuarta encuesta internacional, 1987-1989 (Ginebra, 1995)

Consumer prices – Prix à la consommation – Precios al consumidor

Consumer price indices: An ILO manual (Geneva, 1989)

Consumer price index manual: Theory and practice (Geneva, 2004); joint publication of ILO/IMF/OECD/UN/Eurostat/World Bank
Manuel de l'indice des prix à la consommation: Théorie et pratique (Washington DC, 2006); joint publication of ILO/IMF/OECD/UN/Eurostat/World Bank
Manual del índice de precios al consumidor: Teoría y práctica (Washington DC, 2006); joint publication of ILO/IMF/OECD/UN/Eurostat/World Bank
Руководство по индексу потребительских цен: Теория и практика (Washington DC, 2006); joint publication of ILO/IMF/OECD/UN/Eurostat/World Bank

Sources and Methods: Labour Statistics, Vol. 1: Consumer price indices, third edition (Geneva, 1992)
Sources et méthodes: statistiques du travail, vol. 1: Indices des prix à la consommation, troisième édition (Genève, 1992)
Fuentes y Métodos: Estadísticas del Trabajo, vol. 1: Indices de los precios al consumidor, tercera edición (Ginebra, 1992)
Consumer price indices, Seventeenth International Conference of Labour Statisticians, Report III and Report of the Conference (Geneva, 2003)
Indices des prix à la consommation, dix-septième Conférence internationale des statisticiens du travail, rapport III et rapport de la Conférence (Genève, 2003)
Indices de precios al consumidor, Decimoséptima Conferencia Internacional de Estadísticos del Trabajo, Informe III e Informe de la Conferencia de la Conferencia (Ginebra, 2003)

Occupational injuries – Lésions professionnelles – Lesiones profesionales

Occupational injuries statistics from household surveys and establishment surveys, ILO manual on methods (Geneva, 2008 (in English only)
Occupational injuries, Thirteenth International Conference of Labour Statisticians, Report III (Geneva, 1982)
Lésions professionnelles, treizième Conférence internationale des statisticiens du travail, rapport III (Genève, 1982)
Lesiones profesionales, Decimotercera Conferencia Internacional de Estadísticos del Trabajo, Informe III (Ginebra, 1982)

Statistics of occupational injuries, Sixteenth International Conference of Labour Statisticians, Report III (Geneva, 1998)

Statistiques des lésions professionnelles, seizième Conférence internationale des statisticiens du travail, rapport III (Genève, 1998)
Estadísticas de lesiones profesionales, Decimosexta Conferencia Internacional de Estadísticos del Trabajo, Informe III (Ginebra, 1998)

Sources and Methods: Labour Statistics, Vol. 8: Occupational injuries (Geneva, 1999)
Sources et méthodes: statistiques du travail, vol. 8: Lésions professionnelles (Genève, 1999)
Fuentes y Métodos: Estadísticas del Trabajo, vol. 8: Lesiones profesionales (Ginebra, 1999)

Strikes and lockouts – Grèves et lock-out – Huelgas y cierres patronales

National methodologies for statistics of strikes and lockouts, Meeting of Experts on Statistics of Strikes and Lockouts, Geneva 1990; document MESS/D.2 (English only)

Statistics of strikes, lockouts and other forms of industrial action, Fifteenth International Conference of Labour Statisticians, Report II (Geneva, 1992) and Report of the Conference (Geneva, 1993)
Statistiques des grèves, des lock-out et d'autres actions de revendication, quinzième Conférence internationale des statisticiens du travail, rapport II (Genève, 1992) et rapport de la Conférence (Genève, 1993)
Estadísticas de huelgas, cierres patronales y otros tipos de acción laboral directa, Decimoquinta Conferencia Internacional de Estadísticos del Trabajo, Informe II (Ginebra, 1992) e Informe de la Conferencia (Ginebra, 1993)

Sources and Methods: Labour Statistics, Vol. 7: Strikes and lockouts (Geneva, 1993)
Sources et méthodes: statistiques du travail, vol. 7: Grèves et lock-out (Genève, 1993)
Fuentes y Métodos: Estadísticas del Trabajo, vol. 7: Huelgas y cierres patronales (Ginebra, 1993)

Master table — Tableau principal — Cuadro maestro

List of sources: shown on last page
Liste des sources : voir dernière page
Lista de fuentes: véase la última página

1. Economically active population, Employment and Unemployment ('000)
   Population active, Emploi et Chômage ('000)
   Población económicamente activa, Empleo y Desempleo ('000)

	Economically active population Population active Población económicamente activa		Employment Emploi Empleo		Unemployment Chômage Desempleo	
	Total	Women (%) Femmes (%) Mujeres (%)	Total	Women (%) Femmes (%) Mujeres (%)	Total	Women (%) Femmes (%) Mujeres (%)
Classification – see below **Classification – voir ci-dessous** **Clasificación – véase más abajo**	Year / Année / Año Source / Source / Fuente		Year / Année / Año Source / Source / Fuente		Year / Année / Año Source / Source / Fuente	

List of classifications (details of groups are given in separate Appendices):
Liste des classifications (les détails des groupes figurent en annexe):
Lista de clasificaciones (los detalles de los grupos figuran en el apéndice):

Age group	Groupe d'âge	Grupo de edad
Economic activity (ISIC)	Activité économique (CITI)	Actividad económica (CIIU)
Occupation (ISCO)	Profession (CITP)	Ocupación (CIUO)
Education level (ISCED)	Niveau d'éducation (CITE)	Nivel de educación (CINE)
Status in employment (ICSE)	Situation dans la profession (CISP)	Situación en el empleo (CISE)

2. Population, Activity rate and Unemployment rate
   Population, Taux d'activité et Taux de chômage
   Población, Tasa de actividad y Tasa de desempleo

Age group Groupe d'âge Grupo de edad	Population ('000) Population ('000) Población ('000) Year / Année / Año Source / Source / Fuente			Activity rate (%) Taux d'activité (%) Tasa de actividad (%) Year / Année / Año Source / Source / Fuente			Unemployment rate (%) Taux de chômage (%) Tasa de desempleo (%) Year / Année / Año Source / Source / Fuente		
	Total	Men Hommes Hombres	Women Femmes Mujeres	Total	Men Hommes Hombres	Women Femmes Mujeres	Total	Men Hommes Hombres	Women Femmes Mujeres

3. Paid employment, Hours of work (weekly) and Wages
   Emploi rémunéré, Durée du travail (hebdomadaire) et Salaires
   Empleo remunerado, Horas de trabajo (por semana) y Salarios

Economic activity (ISIC) Activité économique (CITI) Actividad económica (CIIU)	Paid employment ('000) Emploi rémunéré ('000) Empleo remunerado ('000) Year / Année / Año Source / Source / Fuente			Hours of work Durée du travail Horas de trabajo Year / Année / Año Source / Source / Fuente Coverage / Couverture / Cobertura			Wages Salaires Salarios Year / Année / Año Source / Source / Fuente Coverage / Couverture / Cobertura In national currency En monnaie nationale En moneda nacional		
	Total	Men Hommes Hombres	Women Femmes Mujeres	Total	Men Hommes Hombres	Women Femmes Mujeres	Total	Men Hommes Hombres	Women Femmes Mujeres

Coverage	**Couverture**	**Cobertura**
Wage rates	Taux de salaire	Tasas de salarios
Earnings	Gains	Ganancias
Per hour	Par heure	Por hora
Per day	Par jour	Por día
Per week	Par semaine	Por semana
Per month	Par mois	Por mes
Hours paid for	Heures rémunérées	Horas pagadas
Hours actually worked	Heures réellement effectuées	Horas efectivamente trabajadas
Total employment	Emploi total	Empleo total
Employees	Salariés	Asalariados
Wage earners	Ouvriers	Obreros
Salaried employees	Employés	Empleados

4. Occupational injuries, Strikes and lockouts
Lésions professionnelles, Grèves et lock-out
Lesiones profesionales, Huelgas y cierres patronales

Economic activity (ISIC) / Activité économique (CITI) / Actividad Económica (CIIU)	Rates of fatal occupational injury (%) / Taux de lésions professionnelles mortelles (%) / Tasas de lesiones profesionales mortales (%) — Year / Année / Año — Source / Source / Fuente			Rates of non-fatal occupational injury (%) / Taux de lésions professionnelles non mortelles (%) / Tasas de lesiones profesionales no mortales (%) — Year / Année / Año — Source / Source / Fuente			Strikes and lockouts ('000) / Grèves et lock-out ('000) / Huelgas y cierres patronales ('000) — Year / Année / Año — Source / Source / Fuente		
	Total	Men / Hommes / Hombres	Women / Femmes / Mujeres	Total	Men / Hommes / Hombres	Women / Femmes / Mujeres	Strikes and lockouts / Grèves et Lock-out / Huelgas y cierres patronales	Workers involved / Travailleurs impliqués / Trabajadores implicados	Days not worked / Journées non effectuées / Días no trabajados

Rates
Per 100,000 employees
Per 100,000 workers insured
Per 100,000 workers exposed to risk
Per 100,000 full-time equivalent workers
Per 100,000 full-time equivalent employees
Per 100,000 production and related workers
Per 200,000 hours worked
Per 1,000,000 hours worked
Per 20,000,000 hours worked
Per 1,000 years of 300 workdays
Per 100,000 workers employed

Taux
Pour 100 000 salariés
Pour 100 000 travailleurs assurés
Pour 100 000 travailleurs exposés au risque
Pour 100 000 travailleurs équivalents à plein temps
Pour 100 000 salariés équivalents à plein temps
Pour 100 000 travailleurs à la production et assimilés
Pour 200 000 heures effectuées
Pour 1 000 000 heures effectuées
Pour 20 000 000 heures effectuées
Pour 1 000 années de 300 journées de travail
Pour 100 000 travailleurs occupés

Tasas
Por 100 000 asalariados
Por 100 000 trabajadores asegurados
Por 100 000 trabajadores expuestos al riesgo
Por 100 000 trabajadores equivalentes a tiempo completo
Por 100 000 asalariados equivalentes a tiempo completo
Por 100 000 trabajadores manufactureros y asimilados
Por 200 000 horas trabajadas
Por 1 000 000 horas trabajadas
Por 20 000 000 horas trabajadas
Por 1 000 años de 300 días de trabajo
Por 100 000 trabajadores empleados

Type of statistics
Reported injuries
Compensated injuries

Type de statistiques
Lésions déclarées
Lésions indemnisées

Tipo de estadísticas
Lesiones notificadas
Lesiones indemnizadas

5. Consumer price indices (base period 2000 = 100)
Indices des prix à la consommation (période de base 2000 = 100)
Indices de precios al consumidor (período de base 2000 = 100)

Source / Source / Fuente	
General indices / Indices généraux / Indices generales	
General indices, excluding rent / Indices généraux, non compris le loyer / Indices generales, excl. el alquiler	
Food indices / Indices de l'alimentation / Indices de la alimentación	
Electricity, gas and other fuel indices / Indices de l'électricité, gaz et autres combustibles / Indices de la electricidad, gas y otros combustibles	
Clothing indices / Indices de l'habillement / Indices del vestido	
Rent indices / Indices du loyer / Indices del alquiler	

List of sources	**Liste des sources**	**Lista de fuentes**
Population census	Recensement de la population	Censo de población
Labour force survey	Enquête sur la main-d'œuvre	Encuesta de la fuerza de trabajo
Household income and/or expenditure survey	Enquête sur le revenu et/ou les dépenses des ménages	Encuesta sobre ingresos y/o de los hogares
Labour-related establishment census	Recensement des établissements relatif au travail	Censo de establecimientos relacionado con el trabajo
Industrial or commercial census	Recensement industriel ou commercial	Censo industrial o comercial
Labour-related establishment survey	Enquête auprès des établissements, relative au travail	Encuesta de establecimientos, relacionada con el trabajo
Industrial or commercial survey	Enquête industrielle ou commerciale	Encuesta industrial o comercial
Official estimate	Estimations officielles	Estimaciones oficiales
Insurance records	Fichiers des assurances	Registros de seguros
Employment office records	Fichiers des bureaux de placement	Registros de oficinas de colocación
Tax records	Fichiers fiscaux	Registros fiscales
Administrative reports	Rapports administratifs	Informes administrativos
Collective agreements	Conventions collectives	Convenios colectivos
Labour inspection records	Fichiers d'inspection du travail	Registros de inspección del trabajo
Labour relations records	Fichiers des relations du travail	Registros de relaciones laborales
Records of employers' or workers' organizations	Fichiers des organisations d'employeurs ou de travailleurs	Registros de organizaciones de empleadores o trabajadores
Regular collection of consumer prices	Collecte régulière des prix à la consommation	Recolección periódica de precios al consumidor
Special data collection	Collecte spéciale de données	Recolección especial de datos
Legislation	Législation	Legislación
Source unknown	Source inconnue	Fuente ignorada